Consumer Education and Economics

Fourth Edition

Teacher's Manual

Ross E. Lowe

Charles A. Malouf

Annette R. Jacobson

GLENCOE

McGraw-Hill

New York, New York Columbus, Ohio Mission Hills, California Peoria, Illinois

Glencoe/McGraw-Hill

A Division of The ***McGraw-Hill*** *Companies*

Copyright © 1997 by Glencoe/McGraw-Hill. All rights reserved. Except as permitted under the United States Copyright Act of 1976, no part of this publication may be reproduced or distributed in any form or by any means, or stored in a database or retrieval system, without prior written permission of the publisher.

Printed in the United States of America.

Send all inquiries to:
Glencoe/McGraw-Hill
15319 Chatsworth Street
P.O. Box 9609
Mission Hills, CA 91346-9609

ISBN 0-02-637223-1 (Student Edition)
ISBN 0-02-637224-X (Teacher's Annotated Edition)

2 3 4 5 6 7 8 9 QPH 04 03 02 01 00 99 98 97

Consumer Education and Economics

Fourth Edition

Teacher's Manual

Contents

Teaching with *Consumer Education and Economics*

Teaching with *Consumer Education and Economics,* Fourth Edition

Welcome to the Fourth Edition of *Consumer Education and Economics!* This new edition has been thoroughly updated to bring you the latest information in the Consumer and Family Sciences field. It combines the best of previous editions with exciting new material. Here's what you'll find in this edition:

- **New** chapter content on global economics, entrepreneurship, social responsibility, and the environment.
- **New** high-interest chapter and case-study features designed to pique student interest and involve students in higher-order thinking.
- An all-new, visually enticing, full-color design.
- Added emphasis on decision making, critical thinking, applied academics, and cooperative learning.
- A completely expanded teacher's resource package.
- Additional resources and activities emphasizing economic concepts and applications.

PROGRAM METHODOLOGY

In the past, most consumer skills were taught in the home. In recent years, however, home instruction has generally proved inadequate. Partly because of the diversity of the marketplace and the complex ways in which it is changing and partly because of alterations in family structure and lifestyle, the responsibility for providing consumer skills has shifted to the classroom.

In many schools, courses are now offered to teach students how to manage their personal resources by making informed choices in the marketplace. *Consumer Education and Economics*—the text and its ancillary materials—constitutes a complete instructional program for such a course. Here is what is included in the program:

- Student Text
- Teacher's Annotated Edition
- Student Activity Workbook
- Student Activity Workbook, Teacher's Annotated Edition
- **New**—Assessment Binder (including printed tests, a printed testbank, and test software for DOS and Macintosh platforms)
- **New**—Transparency Binder
- **New**—Lesson Plans
- **New**—Print, Media, and Internet Resource Handbook
- Hands-on Projects for *Consumer Education and Economics*
- **New**—Cooperative Learning Activities
- **New**—Math Practice for Economics
- **New**—Meeting the Special Needs of Students
- **New**—Leadership and Citizenship

Also available for use with this program

- **New**—Stocktracker software
- **New**—Level 1 Video: Economics in Action
- **New**—VHS Consumer Videos
- **New**—Economic Survival: A Financial Simulation

STUDENT TEXT

The student text contains 36 chapters divided into 12 units and is designed for use ideally over two semesters. Each unit brings together chapters with a common theme. Any combination of units, however, can be selected and used as the basis for a shorter course of study or for programs using block schedules.

Key Features

The text contains a number of special features intended to make its use easier for both students and teachers. These include the following:

- ***Attitude Inventory***
  Unique to *Consumer Education and Economics,* this survey of basic consumer beliefs is placed at the beginning of each unit. The students must decide whether they agree with, disagree with, or are undecided about the validity of each statement included. The purpose of doing this kind of survey *before* discussion of a topic is to expose any preconceptions or gaps in student knowledge. Later, after the unit content has been studied, the survey is repeated and any changes in attitude noted. This process provides students with tangible evidence of the difference education can make in their lives.

- ***Learning Objectives***
  Found at the beginning of each chapter, the *Learning Objectives* section summarizes key concepts. For students, the objectives serve a dual purpose. First, they are motivational. They tell students why material has been included in the text and thereby help them to establish study goals. Second, the objectives provide students with a convenient standard against which to measure their performance. By re-framing the statements as questions and trying to answer them, students can quickly assess their understanding of a topic. Then they can estimate the amount of review they will need before taking a test.

- ***Systematic Treatment of Vocabulary Development***
  Consumer Education and Economics employs a special three-step procedure in the area of vocabulary development, a procedure designed to get key consumer terms out of the text and into the students' composition and speech. First, key terms are previewed, that is, they are introduced in a special block, *Consumer Terms,* at the beginning of each chapter. The object at this point is recognition, building a basis for familiarity, rather than memorization. Second, the terms are presented in context. Attention is called to a term's first or principal use in the text through the use of boldface type. Third, the words are used in a vocabulary exercise at the end of each chapter. Thus, in their vocabulary study, students progress from introduction of a term to recognition in context to manipulation—first in an exercise situation, then on their own in composition and speech.

- ***Structured Format***
  Consumer Education and Economics is structured so that a listing of the headings in any chapter can be used as an outline. Teachers can use this outline, which appears as part of each unit lesson plan, as a framework for classroom discussion. Students can use it as a study aid by applying the procedure detailed under "Study Techniques" below.

- ***Chapter Features and Case Studies***
  Each chapter contains high-interest features that run throughout the text. *Real-World Journal* is a journal-writing exercise found on the chapter opening pages. This activity gives students an opportunity to investigate and record how consumer economics concepts relate to their lives. *People Making a Difference* focuses on people who have made a significant contribution to their community. The feature asks students to brainstorm ways that they can contribute to their community. *Dollars and Sense* gives short tips on how to budget and save. The Global Consumer tells facts that relate chapter content to consumers in the rest of the world.

Flashback—Flashforward provides "Did you know?"-type facts about what it was like to be a consumer 25 to 50 years ago compared with today. Each chapter also contains one of two case studies. *Consumer News Clips* are consumer news articles from newspapers and magazines such as the *Wall Street Journal* and *Time*. The articles conclude with two decision-making questions. *Careers in Focus* investigates consumer careers related to the unit. Each case study asks students two critical-thinking questions about the particular career.

- ***Functional Illustrations***
  Consumer Education and Economics contains an abundance of full-color photographs, forms, tables, charts, and diagrams. These have been selected to represent key content and placed so that they can serve as a review mechanism for either study or classroom discussion. Each illustration includes a teaching caption that concludes with a critical-thinking question. Also included in this edition are visual-verbals. These text features combine text and illustrations to help students focus on main ideas and simplify otherwise complicated concepts.

- ***Chapter Highlights***
  Placed at the end of each chapter is the full-page *Chapter Highlights*. This page concisely summarizes chapter content. The main points of the chapter appear in a bulleted list that is divided according to the major heads in the chapter. Also included are the boldfaced terms, listed under the major head in the chapter where they appear. Chapter Highlights can be used for review and reteaching.

- ***Chapter Reviews***
  The *Consumer Education and Economics* text itself provides a full range of classroom and homework activities for every chapter in the book. The chapter review includes:

  Reviewing Consumer Terms. A review of boldfaced terms in the text. Students are asked to use their communication skills in the individual exercises.

  Reviewing Facts and Ideas. Questions based on chapter objectives to check students' recall of basic knowledge.

  Problem Solving and Decision Making. Content-related activities that ask students to use their problem-solving and decision-making skills to answer questions.

  Building Academic Skills—Consumers Around the World. Applied math, communications, human relations, science, social studies, science, and technology activities that help students build cross-curricular skills and gain an international perspective on consumer issues.

  Beyond the Classroom—Consumer Projects. Real-life activities that encourage students to think and behave as consumers.

  Cooperative Learning—Family Economics. Simulations that show students how families in different financial circumstances react differently to various consumer purchases.

  Cooperative Learning—Debate the Issue. Debate activities. Given a consumer-related issue, students are asked to break into groups and debate, as a team, the pros and cons of the issue.

- ***Unit Labs.*** New to this edition are unit labs, **You and Your Community.** These hands-on labs provide an opportunity to transform the community into a classroom as students use the community as a resource for exploring consumer concepts learned in the unit. Student findings are summarized in a lab report.

Study Techniques

Ease of study—particularly for those students whose reading and retention levels are not high—was a key factor in structuring the content of *Consumer Education and Economics* and in planning its visual presentation. Taken together, the features listed above form the basis of a study technique that emphasizes repetition and paraphrasing rather than rote memorization.

To help students prepare for a Chapter Test, teachers may find the following techniques useful.

1. *Rereading the Chapter Highlights.* Ask students to reread the Chapter Highlights to focus on main points.
2. *Reviewing the Consumer Terms.* Ask students to define the terms in their own words. If they miss a definition, have students turn to the page on which that term appears in boldface type and reread the relevant paragraph.
3. *Checking the Reviewing Facts and Ideas.* If students cannot answer the questions satisfactorily, have them reread the relevant portions of the chapter and try again.
4. *Studying Each Illustration In the Chapter.* Review the illustrations with students and read the captions. Ask students to explain why they think these illustrations were included in the chapter. For forms and documents, have students point out the key features, especially those provisions that could create problems for consumers. For a diagram, table, or highlighted example, have students try to explain briefly the nature of the process or data depicted.
5. *Outlining the Chapter.* Have students write down all of the headings, indenting them by level and leaving a half-dozen lines between entries. Then ask students to write at least three amplifying points for each. If they cannot, have them set their outlines aside and reread the relevant portion of the text. They can then try outlining again. When students are finished, they should have a second version of the chapter, this one in their own words.

Students who complete this procedure will have reviewed a chapter's content in at least five different ways. They will have read a summary, defined the terms, verbalized key concepts, explained illustrations, and outlined the chapter. Throughout this process, they will have done little rote memorization, concentrating instead on developing their own understandings of concepts.

Family Economics

A challenging activity included at the end of each text chapter appears as the **Family Economics** feature. This family-centered project requires a minimum of 30 minutes of class time per chapter. The purpose of the project is twofold—first, to give students realistic, hands-on experience making consumer decisions in a family setting; and second, to make them aware of the constraints that income, family size, inflation, illness, and similar factors place on economic choices.

The Family Economics project consists of a series of problems that have several acceptable solutions. The project is built around eight model families of various sizes, ages, and economic circumstances.

Family 1—Christiann, Carolina, and Cassandra Three roommates, ages 19 to 21, sharing a two-bedroom apartment ($525 per month plus utilities). All have recently acquired minimum wage jobs (they earn about $8,840 each, working in the food-service industry). None has any savings. Christiann has an older-model car and drives Carolina to work; Cassandra takes the bus. All three are fitness-conscious and work out regularly.

Family 2—Nancy and Naboru Newpaint Husband, wife, and one preschool child living on $20,000. Only the husband works (he's been painting houses for the same company since he was in his late teens). The Newpaints live in a one-bedroom apartment ($425 per month plus utilities). They have savings of $1,500, which this year will earn $75 in interest. Naboru and Nancy are in their mid-twenties and in reasonably good health. Nancy, however, is seriously overweight and must watch her blood pressure. Naboru has sinus allergies, mostly to various kinds of pollen.

Family 3—Paula and Pedro Professional Husband, wife, and one preschool child living on $80,000. Pedro is a newly certified accountant who has just joined a large firm. Paula works for a publishing company as an editor. The Professionals live in a two-bedroom apartment in an upscale building ($600 per month plus utilities). They have two cars (3 and 6 years old) and savings of $20,000. (This year their savings will earn them $1,000 in interest.) Pedro and Paula are both in their late thirties and have no health problems. They cycle regularly, with the baby riding in a kiddie seat on the back of Pedro's bike.

Family 4—Alba and Antonio Auto Husband, wife, and two teenage children living on $30,000. Both husband and wife work (Alba has been with the same auto parts store for about ten years, and Antonio works for an answering service). The Autos live in a modest two-bedroom apartment ($500 per month plus utilities). They have savings of $3,000, which this year will earn them $155 in interest, and one car, now nearly 10 years old. Antonio and Alba are in their mid-thirties. Antonio smokes and has a history of respiratory problems, including bronchitis.

Family 5—Thea and Troy Teacher Husband, wife, and two teenage children living on $50,000. Thea is a college professor. Troy is an artist who works out of his home. The Teachers live in a spacious three-bedroom apartment in a luxury building ($900 per month plus utilities). They have two cars, one brand new and another 3 years old. They also have substantial savings—$45,000, which this year alone will earn them $3,000 in interest. Troy smokes. He has tried to quit but has not been successful. Troy's doctor says he should reconsider, as the smoking aggravates his already high blood pressure.

Family 6—Shashi and Sita Senior Retired couple in their late sixties living on a combination of social security ($13,000) and a modest pension (also $13,000). The Seniors have lived in the same one-bedroom apartment ($375 per month plus utilities) for the last 15 years. They have lifetime savings of $30,000, which this year will earn them $1,550 in interest. The Seniors drive a 20-year-old car that runs well enough for shopping and errands but not long-distance driving. Both Seniors have major health problems. Shashi has diabetes; Sita has arthritis and must use a walker.

Family 7—Sing-Chi Solo A widow with two children (8 and 10 years old). Sing-Chi is in her mid-thirties. She lost her husband four years ago to cancer and for the last three years has worked full-time as a physical therapist to support herself and her children. She earns $40,000 a year. She lives in a modest one-bedroom apartment ($400 per month plus utilities) and drives a 6-year-old car. She has minimal savings—$1,000, all that remains of the proceeds from her late husband's $10,000 life insurance policy. This year those savings will barely earn her $50 in interest. Sing-Chi and the children are all in good health. Sing-Chi underwent counseling for depression for some months following her husband's death but since then has had no major health problems. She tries to exercise regularly (mostly for its mood-lifting effects) but increasingly finds that the demands of working and raising a family leave her too little time.

Family 8—Leah and Larry Landscaper
Husband, wife, and two preschool children. To support the family for the last several years, Larry has worked at two jobs—full-time as a tree trimmer and part-time as a carpenter. His total annual income is $18,000, which places the family at the national poverty level. Leah is a graphic artist but is not able to find work at the moment. The Landscapers rent a small house (two bedrooms, one bath) for $500 per month plus utilities. They have no savings and no car. (Larry is picked up for his full-time job and uses public transportation for the part-time job.) Larry and Leah are in their early thirties.

Each family should be represented by a group of at least three or four students. The students may choose their family identities by lot at the beginning of the semester or school year and retain them throughout the course, or they may choose a different family for each chapter. Using their family identities, they will do budgets, fill out tax returns, plan menus, and apply for credit, life insurance, and even disability payments. With each successive step, their knowledge of their family's circumstances will grow until they are making decisions on something very much like a firsthand basis.

The process is one that should provide students with a great deal of reality training in economics. None of the families owns a home. Only a few have substantial savings. Many lack the funds to meet all of their basic needs. In the course of doing the Family Economics activities, then, most students will find themselves having to make hard choices, compromise often, and sometimes do without.

Use of the Family Economies project should follow a standard routine. The project should be the last activity done prior to testing; that is, the students should have read and reviewed the relevant chapter and done any other application and extension activities beforehand. At the beginning of the assigned period, the students should break into their family groups to discuss the problem posed and formulate an appropriate solution. While they are doing this, the teacher should circulate among the groups, suggesting approaches where a group seems to be stuck, pointing out omissions or oversimplifications where a group has jumped to a hasty conclusion, and in general pushing students to consider as many options as possible in their deliberations.

Once each family has decided what it is going to do, the small groups should reassemble as a class for a wider discussion in which they can compare and contrast their solutions. Students representing families with adequate incomes should realize the terrible constraints that poverty-level living places on people. Students struggling financially should appreciate how much less precarious life can be with an adequate income, savings, and an emergency fund. All students should be aware of the costs and sacrifices involved in raising a family.

The teacher has the option of making activities cumulative; that is, of holding students responsible in each problem for the spending decisions made as part of earlier problems in the text. Both teacher and students should be aware, however, that this is an extremely challenging way to proceed. To avoid being caught without resources for necessities at some unknown future point, the students will have to proceed cautiously and conservatively. They should, for example, be allowed to opt out of suggested purchases, particularly if the alternative is to save.

To help the teacher keep track of each family's finances, each group should be required to keep detailed records of all previous spending decisions, including revised budgets. Under these circumstances, it might be a good idea for family groups to appoint a "secretary," someone responsible for keeping all the family paperwork together and updated.

TEACHER'S ANNOTATED EDITION

The Teacher's Annotated Edition features a comprehensive program of marginal annotations as well as detailed lesson plans for each unit and chapter of the student text.

Annotations

The annotation program for *Consumer Education and Economics* uses a dozen different kinds of marginal notes. They include the following:

- *Unit Goal.* The overall objective of a unit featuring an enumerated breakdown of the unit by chapter.
- *Vocabulary.* Review of and supplement to the Consumer Terms; cross-references vocabulary activities in the lesson plans.
- *Student Motivator.* Ideas for sparking student interest in text content.
- *Discussion Starter.* Thought-provoking questions and situations to help initiate classroom discussions.
- *Learning Economics.* Questions that relate chapter content to basic economic concepts learned earlier in the text.
- *Math Application.* Simple computational problems designed to verify that students understand mathematical concepts included in the text.
- *Critical Thinking.* Questions with which teachers can verify that students have both read and understood text content; uses higher-level reading skills like drawing conclusions, making generalizations, and comparing and contrasting.
- *Reinforcement.* Activities or additional information that supports text content; includes cross-references to the Student Activity Workbook for relevant activities.
- *Extension.* Activities or additional information that takes text content one step further; includes cross-references to the Student Activity Workbook for relevant activities.
- *Research.* Topics for written or oral reports based on text content.
- *Answer.* Answers to in-text questions, including caption and case study questions.
- *Interesting Note.* Unusual or surprising facts that teachers can use to supplement text content.

The annotations are an especially effective adjunct to in-class reading. In many cases they provide the teacher with immediate feedback on the students' grasp of important content. They also allow the teacher to expand upon or highlight points for special emphasis. Most importantly, they enable students to review content in a variety of interesting ways, rather than by simply reading portions of the text back to the teacher.

Lesson Plans

Bound into the front of the new Teacher's Annotated Edition, along with this description of the program's methodology, is a comprehensive set of lesson plans. Unit lesson plans provide a general overview of content (in both prose and outline form) and suggestions for building student interest in the topic to be discussed. Each unit plan is followed by chapter plans for the chapters within the unit.

Chapter lesson plans begin with chapter objectives and teacher's resources. The Objectives section describes the competencies that students should have developed by the time they finish the chapter. Teacher's Classroom Resources lists the ancillary materials designed for use with the chapter. These sections are followed by the body of the lesson plans which are organized according to the four-step teaching plan.

Four-Step Teaching Plan The main activities in the chapter lesson plans are organized into four instructional sections according to a mastery approach designed to help the teacher develop the chapter concepts and materials in an organized, consistent manner. This widely accepted instructional method develops students' understanding of subject matter while providing a consistent framework that makes it easy to teach the material. The four steps in the plan are Focus, Teach, Assess, and Close.

Step 1—Focus The Focus section reinforces the Attitude Inventory. It also suggests devices for introducing the vocabulary words to the students.

Step 2—Teach The Teach section breaks the chapter into teaching segments that address the key concepts discussed in the chapter. Teaching suggestions employ a variety of approaches to support classroom instruction.

Step 3—Assess The Assess section provides evaluation and reteaching activities designed to accommodate a wide range of learning abilities. The activities specify in-class or homework assignments that can be used to review, apply, extend, and evaluate chapter content. The evaluation found in this section supplies you with a complete testing program which includes a testbank that allows you to individualize your tests to meet your curriculum needs.

Step 4—Close The final step in the teaching plan is to allow students to demonstrate to the teacher what they have learned. Through these activities, students review chapter material by preparing a report, poster, oral presentation, or other project.

STUDENT ACTIVITY WORKBOOK

The *Student Activity Workbook* was developed primarily as a source of homework assignments and discussion material. While the Student Text is primarily theoretical in orientation, the *Student Activity Workbook* is clearly hands on. It contains activities that provide a well-rounded review and application of chapter and unit content.

- *Attitude Inventories.* Gives students an opportunity to examine their basic consumer beliefs before and after studying each unit.

- *Reviewing Consumer Terms.* Reinforces students' understanding of vocabulary and chapter facts.
- *Reviewing Facts and Ideas.* Asks students comprehension questions on text content.
- *Application Activities.* Gives students direct experience with a variety of different consumer forms and documents. The students are also asked to comparison shop; to do extended computations; and to analyze everything from detailed hypotheticals to charts, graphs, floor plans, and articles reprinted from government and other publications.
- *Unit Labs.* Gives students an opportunity to explore consumer issues within their community.

The emphasis should be on getting students to think critically by drawing on their own experiences as well as the vocabulary and concepts of the text. Students should especially be encouraged to share their thoughts with the class. Workbook activities are ideally suited for classroom discussion.

Extensive answers are provided for workbook activities in the Teacher's Annotated Edition of the *Student Activity Workbook*. Teachers should make maximum use of these answers to acquaint students with possibilities they may not have considered and, especially, to teach them how to look at both sides of an issue.

ASSESSMENT BINDER

Each binder contains a booklet of reproducible printed tests, a printed testbank, and testbank software for both DOS and Macintosh platforms. Software user guides are also included in the binder.

Printed Tests

A printed test is provided for every chapter and unit of the text. Each test utilizes several question formats—matching, completion, multiple-choice, true/false, and essay. The combination of formats was selected instead of one in response to a basic difficulty: namely, those question forms that are easiest to grade (multiple-choice, completion, matching, and true/false), reveal the least about a student's understanding of material; those that are hardest to grade (essays), reveal the most. By combining question forms, the authors of *Consumer Education and Economics* have sought to find a middle ground: to develop tests that challenge students and at the same time limit additional demands on teachers.

Importance of Essay Questions The regular inclusion of essay questions is one of the most significant aspects of the testing program. It is not enough, the authors feel, for students to know or recognize key consumer concepts. Students must be able to apply those concepts in a variety of situations. Essay questions develop this ability, particularly those based on hypothetical situations.

There are other benefits as well. The regular use of essay questions throughout the program enables *Consumer Education and Economics* to meet a common demand in many school districts today, that all courses teach or reinforce writing skills. The printed tests alone offer students opportunities to use these skills. The essays also emphasize important writing skills—like analyzing situations, drawing conclusions, developing scenarios, and making or defending arguments.

Comprehensive answers to virtually all test essays are provided. Indeed, the answers probably offer far more detail and discussion than the average student will be able to supply. Teachers should use their knowledge of student abilities and limitations to determine what level of response is reasonable.

Final Examination. The tests conclude with a comprehensive final examination. The final is intended for use after students have completed all 12 units of the text.

The test is designed for maximum flexibility. It is divided into six parts, each comprehensive within itself. The parts can be used in various combinations, depending on the amount of time available for testing.

Printed Testbank and Testbank Software

In addition to the printed tests found in the Assessment Binder, the *Consumer Education and Economics* program also provides a printed testbank and testbank software.

The testbank provides an extensive bank of test questions in various formats—essay, multiple choice, completion, true/false, and matching. Using the testbank software, teachers can quickly and easily prepare computer-generated tests based on text content. The testbank software is extremely flexible. For example, teachers can choose and arrange items themselves or allow the program to do so. They can edit existing questions or create their own. They can print out one test or several versions of the same test. The software will also allow teachers to create their own unit and final examinations.

The testbank is available in both Macintosh and DOS versions. The program is user-friendly and comes with an easy-to-follow instruction booklet.

ADDITIONAL RESOURCES

The *Consumer Education and Economics* program contains a number of other resources. These components contribute to the creation of a well-rounded course curriculum.

Hands-on Projects for Consumer Education and Economics

Hands-on Projects are the logical continuation of the end-of-chapter activities in the student text. The text activities start with content review and proceed through application problems, research, and extended hypotheticals. What all of these activities have in common is that they are based on fictions. With Hands-on Projects, students have the opportunity to apply what they have learned to themselves and the community in which they live.

Each project consists of six or more detailed tasks requiring students, among other things, to observe, describe, and analyze local situations; to obtain, interpret, and fill out locally available consumer forms; and to explore local purchase, rental, and investment options in a given consumer area. The purpose of these kinds of activities is to help students make the transition from textbook to real world. By the time they go out on their own, students who have completed a number of the Hands-on Projects will have explored the local economy. They will have some idea of the problems they will have to confront and the resources available to solve them.

Hands-on Projects should be assigned only after a unit has been completed. Teachers using these projects should understand that the work involved is substantial and will take students some time. It should not be expected that students do all of the projects. Rather a certain number (perhaps two per semester) should be required, with the choice of units left up to the students. When complete, project activities should be bound together with their supporting documents into a single report folder and handed in for evaluation. In grading, the teacher should place primary emphasis on completion of all activities and quality of analysis.

Transparency Binder

The Transparency Binder contains transparencies of text illustrations with teaching suggestions. Building a class discussion around such materials can be very effective, especially in teaching students how to fill out consumer forms like check registers or budget records.

Print, Media, and Internet Resource Handbook

Teachers and students will both be able to enrich their knowledge of text content with the print, media, and Internet resources listed in this booklet. The booklet provides the titles of books, articles, government publications, and videos, as well as on-line addresses that can be used to supplement each chapter. It also gives the phone numbers and addresses of organizations and video distributors for added convenience.

Lesson Plans Booklet

This booklet provides a lesson plan for each chapter in the Student Text to help you organize and prepare each lesson. It includes chapter learning objectives, the four-step teaching plan, and the major features of each lesson.

Cooperative Learning Activities

This booklet teaches economic concepts through the collaborative group process. The activities reinforce learning and build interpersonal skills by requiring students to work together to complete projects.

Math Practice for Economics

Math Practice for Economics gives students additional practice in the math skills they need to succeed in consumer economics. The activities ask students to imagine themselves in a real-life situation in which they must use math skills to make a consumer decision or find a solution to a consumer problem.

Meeting the Special Needs of Students

This booklet provides methods for teaching students with special needs. It includes specific information on how to teach gifted students and students with disabilities and learning problems.

Leadership and Citizenship

This booklet provides information and resources on how to build leadership and citizenship skills. It includes information on how to develop young leaders through the Future Homemakers of America organization, parliamentary procedure, self-evaluation, the use of leadership skills at home and school, and skills for leaders. It also contains school and community citizenship projects and student handouts.

Meeting Individual and Special Needs

One of the greatest challenges a teacher faces is to provide a positive learning environment for *all* students in the classroom. Because each student has a unique set of abilities, perceptions, and needs, the learning styles and physical abilities of students may vary widely.

The chart shown here describes a few of the special needs that teachers encounter in students, and it identifies sources of information. Also included are tips for modifying teaching style to accommodate the special needs of these students.

Subject	Description	Sources of Information
English as a Second Language	Multicultural and/or bilingual students often speak English as a second language or not at all. Customs and behavior of people in the majority culture may be confusing for some of these students. Cultural values may inhibit some of these students from full participation.	*Teaching English as a Second Language Reporter* R.L. Jones (Ed.) *Mainstreaming and the Minority Child*
Behaviorally Disordered	Children with behavior disorders deviate from standards or expectations of behavior and impair the functioning of others and themselves. These children may also be gifted or learning disabled.	*Exceptional Children Journal of Special Education*
Visually Impaired	Children who are visually disabled have partial or total loss of sight. Individuals with visual impairments are not significantly different from their sighted peers in ability range or personality. However, blindness may affect cognitive, motor, or social development.	*Journal of Visual Impairment and Blindness* *Education of Visually Handicapped* *American Foundation for the Blind*
Hearing Impaired	Children who are hearing impaired have partial or total loss of hearing. Individuals with hearing impairments are not significantly different from their peers in ability range or personality. However, the chronic condition of deafness may affect cognitive, motor, social, and speech development.	*American Annals of the Deaf* *Journal of Speech and Hearing Research* *Sign Language Studies*
Physically Challenged	Children who are physically disabled fall into two categories—those with orthopedic impairments (use of one or more limbs severely restricted) and those with other health impairments (may require use of respirators or other medical equipment).	*The Source Book for the Disabled.* *Teaching Exceptional Children*
Gifted	Although no formal definition exists, these students can be described as having above average ability, task commitment, and creativity. They rank in the top 5 percent of their class. They usually finish work more quickly than other students and are capable of divergent thinking.	*Journal for the Education of the Gifted* *Gifted Child Quarterly* *Gifted Creative/Talented*
Learning Disabled	All learning disabled students have an academic problem in one or more areas, such as academic learning, language, perception, social-emotional adjustment, memory, or attention.	*Journal of Learning Disabilities* *Learning Disability Quarterly*

Tips for Instruction
■ Remember that students' ability to speak English does not reflect their academic ability. ■ Try to incorporate the student's cultural experience into your instruction. The help of a bilingual aide may be effective. ■ Include information about different cultures in your curriculum to help build students' self-image. Avoid cultural stereotypes. ■ Encourage students to share their cultures in the classroom.
■ Work for long-term improvement; do not expect immediate success. ■ Talk with students about their strengths and weaknesses; clearly outline objectives and how you will help them obtain their goals. ■ Structure schedules, rules, room arrangement, and safety for a positive environment. ■ Model appropriate behavior for students and reinforce proper behavior. ■ Adjust group requirements for individual needs.
■ Modify assignments as needed to help students become independent. ■ Teach classmates how to serve as guides; pair students so sighted peers can assist in cooperative learning work. ■ Tape lectures and reading assignments. ■ Encourage students to use their sense of touch; provide tactile models whenever possible. ■ Verbally describe people and events as they occur in the classroom. ■ Limit unnecessary noise in the classroom.
■ Provide favorable seating arrangements so students can see speakers and read their lips (or interpreters can assist); avoid visual distractions. ■ Write out all instructions on paper or on the board; overhead projectors enable you to maintain eye contact while writing. ■ Avoid standing with your back to the window or light source.
■ Determine with the student when you should offer aid. ■ Help other students and adults understand physically disabled students. ■ Learn about special devices or procedures and if any special safety precautions are needed. ■ Allow students to participate in all activities including field trips, special events, and projects.
■ Emphasize concepts, theories, relationships, ideas, and generalizations. ■ Let students express themselves in a variety of ways including drawing, creative writing, or acting. ■ Make arrangements for students to work on independent projects. ■ Utilize public services and resources, such as agencies providing free and inexpensive materials, community services and programs, and people in the community with specific expertise. ■ Make arrangements for students to take selected subjects early.
■ Establish conditions and create an environment that leads to success. ■ Provide assistance and direction; clearly define rules, assignments, and duties. ■ Allow for pair interaction during class time; use peer helpers. ■ Tape lecture material. ■ Practice skills frequently. ■ Distribute outlines of material presented in class. ■ Maintain student interest with games and drills. ■ Allow extra time to complete tests and assignments.

Lesson Plans

LESSON PLANS

UNIT 1 YOU IN THE ECONOMY

Overview

This unit introduces students to three economic roles they will play in their lives—citizen, worker, and consumer. An effort is made to take the mystery and complexity out of the modern marketplace and to encourage students to be responsible purchasers of goods and services.

In a brief, easy-to-follow manner, this unit provides students with background on our economic system and the role the government plays in it. Understanding this material is essential to being an informed consumer and playing an effective part in our market-based economy.

In Chapter 1, consumer rights and responsibilities are discussed along with the laws, government agencies, and community organizations that support consumerism.

The second chapter acquaints students with the four basic types of economic systems—traditional, command, market, and mixed. Consumer and producer decision making under free enterprise are explored as are important influences on them like production costs, competition, and supply and demand. The business cycle is also described with special emphasis on inflation and recession. Finally, the chapter explains commonly used economic statistics like GDP, GNP, CPI, and balance of trade.

Chapter 3 covers government's participation in the economy, which takes three principal forms—provision of public services, regulation of business activity, and transfer of income to the needy. The way government funds these activities is examined in some detail, starting with basic principles of taxation and extending through specific types of taxes and recent tax reforms.

Chapter 4 introduces students to the concept of international trade, including why nations trade and how nations create barriers to trade. Students also learn about international finance and the boom in telecommunications that fuels international trade.

Unit Outline

Chapter 1:
Consumers and the Economy

A. Our Economic Roles
- **1.** Economic Roles Defined

B. Consumer Rights and Responsibilities

C. Consumer Protection
- **1.** Federal Laws
- **2.** Government Agencies
  - **a.** Federal Agencies
  - **b.** State and Local Agencies
- **3.** Business-sponsored Organizations
  - **a.** Consumer Action Panels
  - **b.** Arbitration Services
  - **c.** Corporate Consumer Departments

D. The Consumer Movement
- **1.** Key Supporters
  - **a.** Publications and Testing Agencies
  - **b.** Popular Media

Chapter 2:
Our Market System

A. The Economy Is All Around Us

B. How Economic Systems Work

C. The Four Types of Economic Systems
- **1.** Traditional System
- **2.** Command, or Controlled, System
- **3.** Capitalist, or Market, System
- **4.** Mixed System

Introduction

1. *Attitude Inventory.* Before beginning the unit, have the class do the Unit 1 Attitude Inventory. Remind the students to retain their answers for periodic reevaluation.
2. *Motivation.* Consumerism—the determination of consumers to get a fair shake—has probably always existed, although methods have changed. In 1202, for example, bakers in England were notorious for short-weighting the bread they sold. A law was passed that year regulating the price and weight, and one baker was sentenced to be carried in a wagon "through the great streets that are most dirty, with the faulty loaf hanging from his neck." Ask students if they or someone they know has ever bought something that was not all it was claimed to be. Discuss with them how they felt and what they did about the problem. Then write the following time-honored slogans on the blackboard and discuss what they might mean in terms of today's marketplace.
   - **a.** *Caveat emptor.* (Let the buyer beware.)
   - **b.** The customer is always right.
3. *Motivation.* Government spending is always in the news and persists as a subject of discussion. Students will have heard their parents or television commentators talking about such topics as the national debt, the trade deficit, or the need to raise (or avoid raising) taxes. Obtain copies of news magazines featuring cover stories on the economy and display them. Ask students to explain what they understand to be the issues involved. Following this, invite someone who lived and worked during the Great Depression to come to class and reminisce about what life was like then, emphasizing the work situation, the bread lines, and the emotional pressures. (Many communities have senior citizens' groups that might suggest a volunteer speaker.) Afterwards, ask the students to think about economic conditions then and now. What similarities do they see? What differences?

Evaluation

Administer the Unit 1 Test in the Assessment Binder.

Unit Closure

Have students imagine that they have been asked by another person (student, parent or guardian, teacher, friend) to talk about what they are learning in this class. This person specifically wants to know what the students learned in this unit. Students should pretend they are talking to him or her and summarizing everything that they have learned.

Have students write an essay (300–500 words) explaining what was learned from their study of this unit. Be specific. This essay could be used as an article in your school or local newspaper, a script for a local radio station consumer broadcast, or as a handout given to other students as your students give a speech to them. It could also be used for recruiting students for next year's class.

CHAPTER 1: CONSUMERS AND THE ECONOMY

Objectives

1. Describe the three economic roles that most people play throughout their lives.
2. Name five consumer rights and the five consumer responsibilities that go with them.
3. List five federal agencies that are responsible for consumer protection and briefly describe their activities.

4. Identify at least a half dozen people who have been important in shaping the consumer movement.

Teacher's Classroom Resources

Student Activity Workbook
Transparency Binder
Assessment Binder
Lesson Plans
Print, Media, and Internet Resource Handbook
Hands-on Projects for Consumer Education and Economics
Cooperative Learning Activities
Math Practice for Economics
Meeting the Special Needs of Students
Leadership and Citizenship

Focus

1. *Attitude Inventory.* Have students consult their working copies of the Attitude Inventory. Call special attention to items related to Chapter 1. Have the students discuss their answers, encouraging individuals to qualify or rephrase those statements with which they disagree or about which they are undecided. Use this information to guide the choice of in-class reading, discussion topics, and follow-up assignments.
2. *Vocabulary.* Preview the Consumer Terms. Have students study the definitions given. In general, they fall into two categories—things related to laws and things related to business. Write the two categories on the chalkboard and ask students to place each term in the category to which it belongs.

Teach

For purposes of classroom presentation, this chapter may be broken into three parts: (1) economic roles and consumer rights and responsibilities, (2) federal statutes and government agencies, and (3) business-sponsored organizations and the consumer movement.

1. Discuss the list of consumer rights and responsibilities with students. Although the wording is concise, the items listed have many implications students should explore. Go over each of the items, asking students to give examples of what is meant and how they might exercise their right or responsibility. For example, what does the right to be "heard" mean? Do you have to make an appointment to speak to someone? Can you write a letter? Does voting count? Who will hear your complaint—a private organization or a government official?
2. Invite a member of a consumer action panel or an arbitration service to speak to the class about what the organization does and how consumers can make the best use of it. Ask students to have questions ready if time permits a question-and-answer session.
3. For extra credit, have students read one of the landmark books of the consumer movement mentioned in this chapter and make an oral report to the class.

Assess

Comprehension and Review
- Chapter Highlights
- Reviewing Consumer Terms *and* Reviewing Facts and Ideas

End-of-Chapter Applications
- Problem Solving and Decision Making
- Building Academic Skills—Consumers Around the World
- Student Activity Workbook activities for this chapter

Chapter Extension
- Beyond the Classroom—Consumer Project
- Cooperative Learning—Family Economics
- Cooperative Learning—Debate the Issue

Evaluation

- Administer the test for Chapter 1 in the Assessment Binder.

Close

Ask students to consider the question, "As a consumer, what are my rights and responsibilities, and where can I go for information and help?" Have students write a flyer, using the material in this chapter to answer the question. The flyer can be an 8½-by-11-inch sheet folded in thirds, with information printed and illustrated in an easy-to-read list format.

CHAPTER 2: OUR MARKET SYSTEM

Objectives

1. Explain what an economic system does and list the four questions it answers.
2. Describe the four types of economic systems, and name countries in which they are in practice.
3. List some types of resources that businesses use.
4. Chart the stages of a business cycle.
5. Define the economic indicators used to measure the American economy.

Teacher's Classroom Resources

Student Activity Workbook
Transparency Binder
Assessment Binder
Lesson Plans
Print, Media, and Internet Resource Handbook
Hands-on Projects for Consumer Education and Economics
Cooperative Learning Activities
Math Practice for Economics
Meeting the Special Needs of Students
Leadership and Citizenship

Focus

1. *Attitude Inventory.* Have students consult their working copies of the Attitude Inventory. Call special attention to items related to Chapter 2. Have the students discuss their answers, encouraging individuals to qualify or rephrase those statements with which they disagree or about which they are undecided. Use this information to guide the choice of in-class reading, discussion topics, and follow-up assignments.
2. *Vocabulary.* Preview the Consumer Terms. Have students study the definitions given. Then have them construct sentences that each use at least two terms. *Examples:*
   a. If a *recession* gets very severe, it can develop into a *depression.*
   b. In a *market* system, the use of *resources* like capital and land is determined by supply and demand.

Teach

For presentation purposes, this chapter may be broken into four parts: (1) the types of economic systems, (2) the workings of the U.S. economic system, (3) the business cycle, and (4) economic measurements of the U.S. system.

1. In 1991, the Soviet Union, the leading world proponent of the command system, collapsed. Various republics that made up the Soviet Union broke off to establish their own independent states. Ask students to speculate on why this collapse took place. In what way might the Soviet Union's economic system have contributed to its problems? What economic systems now exist in the former republics, including Russia and Ukraine? In what other countries is the command system still in practice? What kinds of abuses would a command system encourage? Why, for example, might

bribery and black market activities flourish?

2. Allow the class to break into their Family Economics groups or, if the class is not doing the Family Economics projects, divide students into small discussion groups. Ask them what they and their discussion group families might do in the event of another severe depression. (If a guest speaker has talked about the Great Depression, this should give them some ideas.) Ask them to take into consideration low employment, rent or house payments, food, etc. How would their lives change? What would they do to cope?

Assess

Comprehension and Review

- Chapter Highlights
- Reviewing Consumer Terms *and* Reviewing Facts and Ideas

End-of-Chapter Applications

- Problem Solving and Decision Making
- Building Academic Skills—Consumers Around the World
- Student Activity Workbook activities for this chapter

Chapter Extension

- Beyond the Classroom—Consumer Project
- Cooperative Learning—Family Economics
- Cooperative Learning—Debate the Issue

Evaluation

- Administer the test for Chapter 2 in the Assessment Binder.

Close

Ask students to imagine that students from several different foreign countries have just arrived in their school. The class is asked to acquaint the students with information that they need in order to understand how the U.S. economic system works. Have students create an outline of the chapter that gives the information clearly and succinctly.

CHAPTER 3: GOVERNMENT'S ROLE

Objectives

1. Name the three types of activities the government performs and give examples of each.
2. State why governments collect taxes and explain the basic principles of taxation.
3. Identify and describe the various kinds of taxes.
4. Describe how government spending at the national level differs from government spending at the state and local levels.
5. Summarize recent trends in tax reform at both the state and national levels.
6. Explain what income taxes mean to you and your first job.
7. Fill out and file your own income tax return.

Teacher's Classroom Resources

Student Activity Workbook
Transparency Binder
Assessment Binder
Lesson Plans
Print, Media, and Internet Resource Handbook
Hands-on Projects for Consumer Education and Economics
Cooperative Learning Activities
Math Practice for Economics
Meeting the Special Needs of Students
Leadership and Citizenship

Focus

1. *Attitude Inventory.* Have the students consult their working copies of the

Attitude Inventory. Call special attention to items related to Chapter 3. Have the students discuss their answers, encouraging individuals to qualify or rephrase those statements with which they disagree or about which they are undecided. Use this information to guide the choice of in-class reading, discussion topics, and any follow-up assignments.

2. *Vocabulary.* Preview the Consumer Terms. Have the students study the definitions. Then ask them to provide one or more illustrations of each, drawn from their own experiences. Where the students cannot think of an example, have them provide an opposite instead. Examples:
   a. *Monopoly*—Utility companies providing gas, electricity, and formerly telephone service; competition (opposite).
   b. *Progressive tax*—Income tax; regressive tax (opposite).

Teach

For presentation purposes, this chapter may be broken into four parts: (1) what government does, (2) where government gets its money, (3) how government spends, and (4) how to fill out and file your own income tax return.

1. Obtain from your local utility company information on how to make a consumer complaint regarding its services. Using photocopies or the overhead projector, distribute the information to the class. Create a hypothetical situation, such as poor service, and ask students to write letters to the proper agencies asking for a review.
2. Ask several students to research the following and report their findings to the class:
   a. Amusing or interesting stories from the history of taxation (for example, ancient Egyptian tax collectors, the Boston Tea Party).
   b. How taxation has changed in the United States since 1900.
   c. Taxation in other countries.
   d. U.S. tax court.
3. Ask students to use Figure 3–1 in the text to compare the spending patterns of government at the state or local and federal levels. Have the class speculate on why state and local taxes have been increasing based on what state and local tax dollars are used for. Ask questions such as the following:
   a. Why would utility costs be rising?
   b. Why would state and local education costs be so much larger than federal costs?

Assess

Comprehension and Review

- Chapter Highlights
- Reviewing Consumer Terms *and* Reviewing Facts and Ideas

End-of-Chapter Applications

- Problem Solving and Decision Making
- Building Academic Skills—Consumers Around the World
- Student Activity Workbook activities for this chapter

Chapter Extension

- Beyond the Classroom—Consumer Project
- Cooperative Learning—Family Economics
- Cooperative Learning—Debate the Issue

Evaluation

- Administer the test for Chapter 3 in the Assessment Binder.

Close

Using the information in this chapter, have students create a chart with the following headings: Type of Tax (for example, sales tax), Taxation Method (for example, regressive), Government (for example, local, state), and Use (for example, government services). Students should include the taxes deducted from their payroll checks.

CHAPTER 4: GLOBAL ECONOMICS

Objectives

1. Tell why countries trade with one another.
2. Describe how international trade affects the U.S. consumer.
3. Name three barriers to trade.
4. Explain the role of international finance.

Teacher's Classroom Resources

Student Activity Workbook
Transparency Binder
Assessment Binder
Lesson Plans
Print, Media, and Internet Resource Handbook
Hands-on Projects for Consumer Education and Economics
Cooperative Learning Activities
Math Practice for Economics
Meeting the Special Needs of Students
Leadership and Citizenship

Focus

1. *Attitude Inventory.* Have students consult their working copies of the Attitude Inventory. Call special attention to items related to Chapter 4. Have the students discuss their answers, encouraging individuals to qualify or rephrase those statements with which they disagree or about which they are undecided. Use this information to guide the choice of in-class reading, discussion topics, and follow-up assignments.
2. *Vocabulary.* Preview the Consumer Terms. Have the students study the definitions. Each of the terms can be used as a noun or noun phrase. Have students add an adjective or adjective phrase to modify each term. *Examples:*
   a. Inexpensive *import*
   b. *Currency* of foreign nations

Teach

For presentation purposes, this chapter may be broken into four parts: (1) the benefits to international trade, (2) the problems with international trade, (3) trade barriers, and (4) international finance.

1. Today we buy many products made in other countries. Ask students to play economic detectives and search their homes, making a list of at least ten different items manufactured in foreign countries. On their list they should indicate the country of origin. During class, compile the lists to get a general idea of which countries specialize in which items.
2. Individual attitudes multiplied by large numbers of people can create national attitudes that have an effect on the economy. Ask students how the way people think and live might influence such concerns as the national debt and the balance of trade. How do people today feel about "doing without" or living with hardship? How might such attitudes affect our purchase of items made in Japan or our tolerance of government spending?

Assess

Comprehension and Review
- Chapter Highlights
- Reviewing Consumer Terms *and* Reviewing Facts and Ideas
- Rechecking Your Attitude

End-of-Chapter Applications
- Problem Solving and Decision Making
- Building Academic Skills—Consumers Around the World
- Student Activity Workbook activities for this chapter

Chapter Extension

- Beyond the Classroom—Consumer Project
- Cooperative Learning—Family Economics
- Cooperative Learning—Debate the Issue
- Unit Lab: You and Your Community

Evaluation

- Administer the test for Chapter 4 in the Assessment Binder.

Close

Ask students to create a poster "International Trade and Finance," using the information in the chapter. The poster should have four sections: The Pros of International Trade, The Cons of International Trade, Barriers to Trade, and Foreign Exchange. Under foreign exchange, students can list the current exchange rates for eight or so foreign currencies. Display the posters at school.

Unit 2 Money Management: Earning and Spending

Overview

This unit considers the related tasks of obtaining and using personal income. The information discussed is basic not only to money management but also to the larger satisfactions of doing work that one enjoys.

The first chapter acquaints students with the issues involved in choosing a career. The roles that job trends, interests, and aptitudes play in making the right choice, as well as workplace and training requirements, are emphasized. This information is provided for those who want to work for others and those who want to work for themselves as entrepreneurs. Job search techniques and federal laws concerning employee rights are also covered.

The second chapter provides information on budgeting income. The forms presented in this chapter should be reviewed carefully to ensure a thorough understanding of the budgeting process.

In the third chapter, techniques for spending money wisely are explored. Factors that influence spending, steps in economic decision-making, and the importance of selecting the best time and place to buy are all discussed.

In the last chapter, common consumer problems are identified and solutions suggested to encourage students to use the public and private resources available to them.

Unit Outline

Chapter 5: Choosing a Career

A. Career Planning
- **1.** Know Yourself
  - **a.** Your Interests
  - **b.** Your Personality
  - **c.** Your Skills
- **2.** Consider Your Life Goals
- **3.** Consider Job Trends

B. Researching Careers
- **1.** Use a Variety of References
- **2.** Consider Consumer Careers
- **3.** Plan for Further Education or Training

C. Job Hunting
- **1.** Composing a Résumé
- **2.** Writing Letters
- **3.** Going on Interviews
  - **a.** Preparing Yourself
  - **b.** Making a Good Impression
  - **c.** Following Up

D. Employee Rights and Responsibilities
- **1.** Safe Working Conditions
- **2.** Equal Employment Opportunity Act
- **3.** Fair Labor Standards Act
  - **a.** Minimum Wage
  - **b.** Overtime

c. Equal Pay
d. Child Labor
4. Workplace Requirements
E. Entrepreneurship
1. Advantages and Disadvantages
2. Characteristics of Entrepreneurs
3. Necessary Skills

Chapter 6:
Budgeting Your Money

A. Developing a Budget
1. Consider Financial Goals
2. Estimate Income
3. Estimate Expenses
4. Plan for Savings
5. Develop a Trial Budget
B. Keeping Financial Records
1. Financial Records
2. Recordkeeping Systems
C. Revising a Budget
1. Immediate Adjustments
2. Adjustments Throughout Life
D. Budgeting Problems
E. Taking an Annual Inventory

Chapter 7:
Spending Money Wisely

A. Influences on Consumer Spending
1. Personal Factors
a. Values
b. Goals
c. Life Stage
d. Habit
e. Impulse
f. Resources
2. Social Factors
a. Popular Taste
b. Status
3. Business Factors
a. Sales Promotions
b. Shopping Environment
B. Deciding What to Buy
1. Define the Issue or Problem
2. Identify Relevant Values and Goals
3. List Possible Choices
4. Gather Information
5. Evaluate the Choices
6. Make a Decision and Evaluate the Results
C. Places to Shop
1. Retail Stores
a. Department Stores
b. Discount Department Stores and Variety Stores
c. Specialty Stores
d. Superstores
e. Outlet Stores
f. Warehouse Clubs
g. Secondhand Stores
2. Nonstore Retailers
a. Door-to-Door Selling
b. Mail-Order Retailers
c. Electronic Shopping
d. Vending Machines
e. Consumer Cooperatives
D. When to Buy
1. Sales
2. Seasonal Buying

Chapter 8:
Consumer Problems and Their Solutions

A. Defining Consumer Problems
1. Problems with Performance
B. Problems with Deception and Fraud
C. Deceptive Practices
1. Misleading Advertising
a. Free Gifts
b. Testimonials
c. Puffery
2. Trading Up
3. Sales Prices
4. Competitive Pricing
5. Manufacturer's Recommended Retail Price
6. Loss Leaders
D. Fraudulent Practices
1. Bait and Switch
2. Chain Letter and Pyramid Schemes
3. Other Fraudulent Schemes
E. Registering a Complaint
1. Telephone Complaints
2. Letter of Complaint
3. Dispute Resolution
F. Legal Action
1. Small-Claims Court
2. Class-Action Suit

Introduction

1. *Attitude Inventory.* Before beginning the unit, have the class do the Unit 2 Attitude Inventory. Remind the students to retain their answers for periodic reevaluation.
2. *Motivation.* Have students write a paragraph on how choosing a career might involve the same skills as making an important consumer purchase. When they have finished, discuss their responses, emphasizing such ideas as long-range planning, use of library and human resources, and comparison shopping.
3. *Motivation.* Ask the class to think about how people feel about money—earning it, spending it, and giving it away. Discuss terms like "big spender," "skinflint," "high roller," and "tightwad" as well as the aphorism "A fool and his money are soon parted." What attitudes toward money do these terms embody?

Evaluation

Administer the Unit 2 Test in the Assessment Binder.

Unit Closure

Have students write an essay of 350 to 500 words describing the connection between finding a job, budgeting income, planning for wise spending, and avoiding consumer problems.

CHAPTER 5: CHOOSING A CAREER

Objectives

1. Explain how personal qualifications, life goals, and job trends affect career decisions.
2. Describe how to use a variety of references to research careers, and explain the value of education and training.
3. Discuss effective job search techniques.
4. List employee rights and responsibilities.
5. Debate the advantages and disadvantages of being an entrepreneur.

Teacher's Classroom Resources

Student Activity Workbook
Transparency Binder
Assessment Binder
Lesson Plans
Print, Media, and Internet Resource Handbook
Hands-on Projects for Consumer Education and Economics
Cooperative Learning Activities
Math Practice for Economics
Meeting the Special Needs of Students
Leadership and Citizenship

Focus

1. *Attitude Inventory.* Have students consult their working copies of the Attitude Inventory. Call special attention to items related to Chapter 5. Have the students discuss their answers, encouraging individuals to qualify or rephrase those statements with which they disagree or about which they are undecided. Use this information to guide the choice of in-class reading, discussion topics, and follow-up assignments.
2. *Vocabulary.* Preview the Consumer Terms. Have students study the definitions given. Explain that all of the terms in the Consumer Terms have something to do with jobs. Then draw on the chalkboard the diagram shown on page T29, and have the students label each of the segments with a term from the Consumer Terms list.

Teach

For purposes of classroom presentation, this chapter may be broken into three parts: (1) planning for a career,

including entrepreneurial opportunities, (2) job hunting, and (3) employee rights and responsibilities.

1. Remind students that they will be at work eight hours each day and that most people work an average of 40 years. Their choice of career should satisfy them in as many ways as possible. As part of learning about themselves, they should explore just what they expect from their work life. Ask the class to make a list of goals they hope a career will help them achieve. These might include an improved standard of living, financial security, time for leisure activities, and an opportunity to make a better world. Ask them to be as specific as possible. For example, leisure activities could include sports such as skiing or sailing that would be expensive and require time for travel. Then have the students think about what kinds of careers would best meet their goals. Have students include working for themselves as an alternative to working for others.
2. Take a survey of class members who have a job. On the chalkboard, tally types of jobs. Categorize job search techniques that worked and those that did not. Use this activity as a springboard into a discussion of ways to find a job.
3. Present a history of child labor laws leading up to current laws. What recent abuses have been noted in the 1990s (for example, sweatshops in Los Angeles involving name-brand lines)? What other protection is provided by labor laws? Have students discuss why these laws are necessary.

Assess

Comprehension and Review
- Chapter Highlights
- Reviewing Consumer Terms *and* Reviewing Facts and Ideas

End-of-Chapter Applications
- Problem Solving and Decision Making
- Building Academic Skills—Consumers Around the World
- Student Activity Workbook activities for this chapter

Chapter Extension
- Beyond the Classroom—Consumer Project
- Cooperative Learning—Family Economics
- Cooperative Learning—Debate the Issue

Evaluation
- Administer the test for Chapter 5 in the Assessment Binder.

Close

Tell students that as career counselors, they must provide information to a student who wants to make an appropriate career choice and obtain a job in that area. In a 500-word report, students should summarize the steps they would take to help that student. Include basic information on career opportunities, job search techniques, and employee rights.

CHAPTER 6: BUDGETING YOUR MONEY

Objectives

1. Describe the five steps involved in developing a budget.

2. Explain four methods of keeping accurate financial records.
3. Discuss how to revise a budget.
4. Identify the three most common mistakes people make when budgeting.
5. Explain the value of doing an annual inventory.

Teacher's Classroom Resources

Student Activity Workbook
Transparency Binder
Assessment Binder
Lesson Plans
Print, Media, and Internet Resource Handbook
Hands-on Projects for Consumer Education and Economics
Cooperative Learning Activities
Math Practice for Economics
Meeting the Special Needs of Students
Leadership and Citizenship

Focus

1. *Attitude Inventory.* Have students consult their working copies of the Attitude Inventory. Call special attention to items related to Chapter 6. Have the students discuss their answers, encouraging individuals to qualify or rephrase those statements with which they disagree or about which they are undecided. Use this information to guide the choice of in-class reading, discussion topics, and follow-up assignments.
2. *Vocabulary.* Preview the Consumer Terms. Have students study the definitions given. Ask students to write a one-minute radio commercial using all the terms. The commercial should be for the firm of Scrimp & Skwander, Financial Managers.

Teach

For purposes of classroom presentation, this chapter may be broken into three parts: (1) developing a budget and keeping necessary records, (2) revising the budget based on records, and (3) taking a financial inventory. It should be noted that the budget forms used throughout the chapter illustrate a single family's finances. Both Dan and Lori work—Dan as a forms designer for a bank and Lori as a waitress. They rent a two-bedroom apartment and have a car on which they are still making payments.

1. Ask students to estimate how much they personally spend each week. Have them write down the estimate and save it for later reference. Then ask them to keep an accurate record of every penny they spend for one week. They should include expenditures for snacks, clothing, movies, gas for a car, school supplies, and so forth. When the week is done, have them compare the two amounts. How accurate was their estimate? How could they develop a budget from these figures?
2. Ask students to imagine that they are seriously in debt as the result of an unforeseen expense. Have them make a list of five ways they could cut back on previously budgeted expenses to get out of trouble. Methods might include reducing credit purchases; reducing impulse buying; shopping at sales; buying second-hand goods; and doing their own maintenance work on cars, clothing, and similar items.
3. Have students develop a simple balance sheet of their current assets and liabilities. Have them determine their net worth and develop short-term and long-term goals. What methods could they use to improve their financial position?

Assess

Comprehension and Review

- Chapter Highlights
- Reviewing Consumer Terms and Reviewing Facts and Ideas

End-of-Chapter Applications
- Problem Solving and Decision Making
- Building Academic Skills—Consumers Around the World
- Student Activity Workbook activities for this chapter

Chapter Extension
- Beyond the Classroom—Consumer Project
- Cooperative Learning—Family Economics
- Cooperative Learning—Debate the Issue

Evaluation
- Administer the test for Chapter 6 in the Assessment Binder.

Close

Tell students you work for the Consumer Credit Counseling Service, a nonprofit organization that helps consumers with too much debt develop (and stick to) a budget. Write down a checklist of procedures to help your clients plan a budget and keep track of their financial situation.

CHAPTER 7: SPENDING MONEY WISELY

Objectives

1. Identify the factors that influence consumer spending.
2. Describe how to apply the seven steps of economic decision making to a typical consumer purchase.
3. Show how to select the best place to purchase a given item.
4. Explain how timing can affect buying decisions.

Teacher's Classroom Resources

Student Activity Workbook
Transparency Binder
Assessment Binder
Lesson Plans
Print, Media, and Internet Resource Handbook
Hands-on Projects for Consumer Education and Economics
Cooperative Learning Activities
Math Practice for Economics
Meeting the Special Needs of Students
Leadership and Citizenship

Focus

1. *Attitude Inventory.* Have students consult their working copies of the Attitude Inventory. Call special attention to items related to Chapter 7. Have the students discuss their answers, encouraging individuals to qualify or rephrase those statements with which they disagree or about which they are undecided. Use this information to choose in-class reading, discussion topics, and follow-up assignments.
2. *Vocabulary.* Preview the Consumer Terms. Have students study the definitions given. The terms fall into two broad categories—those related to business and those related to individuals. Write these two categories on the chalkboard, and ask students to place each term in the proper category.

Teach

For purposes of classroom presentation, this chapter may be broken into three parts: (1) influences on consumer spending, (2) deciding what to buy, and (3) other key buying decisions such as where and when to buy.

1. Have students analyze the appeals made in ads drawn from newspapers, magazines, or junk mail. Which personal, social, or business factors are being played upon to get readers to buy? For example, an ad that emphasizes luxury is probably appealing to a person's need for status.

2. Have students use *Consumer Reports* to research potential purchases of their own choice. Suggest that they pay special attention to the tests administered and standards used so that they can report these to the class and discuss their validity. Are these standards ones that they would use, or at least agree with? Finally, ask the students, based on the magazine's evaluation, which product they would buy and why.
3. Invite an officer in a local consumer cooperative to talk to the class about how the organization works and its value to consumers. Inform students in advance that the speaker will be coming, and ask them to be ready with questions.

Assess

Comprehension and Review
- Chapter Highlights
- Reviewing Consumer Terms *and* Reviewing Facts and Ideas

End-of-Chapter Applications
- Problem Solving and Decision Making
- Building Academic Skills—Consumers Around the World
- Student Activity Workbook activities for this chapter

Chapter Extension
- Beyond the Classroom—Consumer Project
- Cooperative Learning—Family Economics
- Cooperative Learning—Debate the Issue

Evaluation
- Administer the test for Chapter 7 in the Assessment Binder.

Close

Tell your students to imagine they are employed as a personal shopper: That means they help people shop who cannot shop for themselves. To find out what they need to know about a particular client and begin their own planning process, develop a list of questions based on each major area of shopping (influences, making decisions on what to buy, deciding where and when to shop).

CHAPTER 8: CONSUMER PROBLEMS AND THEIR SOLUTIONS

Objectives

1. Distinguish between deception and fraud.
2. Identify some of the most common forms of deceptive advertising and sales practices.
3. Describe three fraudulent sales practices, and suggest a strategy for resisting them.
4. Explain how to make an effective consumer complaint.
5. Describe how a small-claims court works.

Teacher's Classroom Resources

Student Activity Workbook
Transparency Binder
Assessment Binder
Lesson Plans
Print, Media, and Internet Resource Handbook
Hands-on Projects for Consumer Education and Economics
Cooperative Learning Activities
Math Practice for Economics
Meeting the Special Needs of Students
Leadership and Citizenship

Focus

1. *Attitude Inventory.* Have the students consult their working copies of the Attitude Inventory. Call special attention to items related to Chapter 8.

Have the students discuss their answers, encouraging individuals to qualify or rephrase those statements with which they disagree or about which they are undecided. Use this information to guide the choice of in-class reading, discussion topics, and any follow-up assignments.

2. *Vocabulary.* Preview the Consumer Terms. Have students study the definitions given. Many of the terms have appeared in popular publications and on television. Ask students to suggest contexts in which they have heard the terms used.

Teach

For purposes of classroom presentation, this chapter may be broken into two parts: (1) defining consumer problems and (2) solving consumer problems.

1. Good advertising helps consumers by providing information they need to make a buying decision. Yet many ads "sell the sizzle, not the steak." Rather than give consumers useful information, they focus on intangibles meant to dazzle and inspire fantasies. Bring several common items such as toothpaste, breakfast cereal, or kitchen cleanser to class. Ask students to create two different ads—one filled with useful information about the product and the other filled with "sizzle." Display the results. Ask students to think about why the sizzle ads sometimes sell more products. Discuss the reasons.
2. Provide students with basic information about a service problem, and then have them dramatize a telephone complaint to remedy it. *Examples:*
   - **a.** The mail carrier drops all magazines and third-class mail for your building in one spot rather than sorting it into tenants' boxes.
   - **b.** The first bill for your newspaper subscription has a notation that this is the third request for payment.
   - **c.** The overnight package your uncle sent you is delivered a day late by a stranger who lives three blocks away.

Invite students to manufacture any additional details they need to make an effective complaint.

Assess

Comprehension and Review
- Chapter Highlights
- Reviewing Consumer Terms *and* Reviewing Facts and Ideas
- Rechecking Your Attitude

End-of-Chapter Applications
- Problem Solving and Decision Making
- Building Academic Skills—Consumers Around the World
- Student Activity Workbook activities for this chapter

Chapter Extension
- Beyond the Classroom—Consumer Project
- Cooperative Learning—Family Economics
- Cooperative Learning—Debate the Issue
- Unit Lab: You and Your Community

Evaluation
- Administer the test for Chapter 8 in the Assessment Binder.

Close

Have students write a 250-word essay, which summarizes some of the most common consumer complaints. Tell students to choose one and write an explanation of how to follow through from complaint to resolution.

UNIT 3 Money Management: Saving and Investing

Overview

After completing this unit, students should have some idea of what financial institutions are all about and how to use them. A savings plan is something students can begin at any time, the sooner the better, and this unit should answer many of the questions they may have.

The first chapter covers planning a savings program. It discusses reasons for saving, savings techniques, and different kinds of savings institutions.

The second chapter deals with financial services. In this chapter, savings and checking accounts, as well as electronic banking, are discussed. How to write checks is covered in detail.

The third chapter provides background on the more complex subject of investing. Stocks and bonds in particular are discussed.

Unit Outline

Chapter 9: Planning a Savings Program

A. Reasons for Saving
- **1.** Emergencies
- **2.** Expensive Purchases
- **3.** Recurring Expenses
- **4.** Retirement
- **5.** Special Goals

B. Savings as Investment
- **1.** Compounded Interest
- **2.** Rule of 72

C. Techniques for Building Savings
- **1.** Savings Plans
  - **a.** Self-discipline
  - **b.** Payroll Deductions
  - **c.** Automatic Deductions from Checking Accounts
- **2.** Guidelines for Saving Money

D. Savings Institutions
- **1.** Banks and Savings and Loan Associations
  - **a.** Commercial Banks
  - **b.** Mutual Savings Banks
  - **c.** Savings and Loan Associations
- **2.** Credit Unions

E. Alternative Forms of Saving
- **1.** Savings Bonds
  - **a.** Series EE Bonds
  - **b.** Series HH Bonds
- **2.** Insurance
- **3.** Employee Savings Plans

Chapter 10: Using Financial Services

A. Savings Accounts
- **1.** Passbook Accounts and Certificates of Deposits
- **2.** Money Market Accounts
- **3.** Retirement Accounts

B. Checking Accounts
- **1.** What Is a Check?
- **2.** Advantages of Checks
- **3.** Opening a Checking Account
- **4.** Checking Account Fees

C. Writing a Check
- **1.** How Checks Work
- **2.** Reconciling Your Bank Statement
  - **a.** Preparation
  - **b.** Procedure
- **3.** Endorsing a Check
  - **a.** What Is an Endorsement?
  - **b.** Kinds of Endorsements
- **4.** Check Deposits

D. Other Payment Methods
- **1.** Money Orders
- **2.** Telegraphic Money Order
- **3.** Traveler's Checks
- **4.** Certified Checks

E. Banking Electronically
- **1.** Electronic Fund Transfers
  - **a.** Automated Teller Machines
  - **b.** Automated Bill Payment
  - **c.** Debit and Check Cards
  - **d.** Banking from Home
- **2.** Electronic Banking Fees
- **3.** Consumer Protection

F. Additional Bank Services

Chapter 11:
Making Investments

A. Investment Strategy
- **1.** Investment Goals
- **2.** Knowledge of Investment Options
- **3.** Risk
- **4.** Professional Advice

B. Types of Securities
- **1.** Stocks
  - **a.** Preferred Stocks
  - **b.** Common Stock
  - **c.** Other Stock Categories
- **2.** Bonds
  - **a.** Municipal Bonds
  - **b.** Corportate Bonds
  - **c.** Federal Government Bonds

C. How to Invest
- **1.** Direct Sales of Stock
- **2.** Mutual Funds
- **3.** Stockbrokers
- **4.** Stock Exchanges
- **5.** Stock Market Quotations

Introduction

1. *Attitude Inventory.* Before beginning the unit, have the class do the Unit 3 Attitude Inventory. Remind the students to retain their answers for periodic reevaluation.

2. *Motivation.* Some people select a bank with the same amount of thought they apply to choosing a mailbox—the closest one will do. While convenience is certainly a consideration in choosing a bank or other financial institution, it is not the only or most important criterion. Today, because of government deregulation and increased competition, banking is in the grip of constant change. Free gifts to lure customers, automated teller machines, and the increased number of services available have turned money management into a rather bewildering affair. More than ever before, it pays to shop around. To make students aware of the kinds of choices they will have to make, obtain several ads from your local paper for banks and other financial institutions that compete. Post the ads in a prominent place and ask students if, from reading them, they can answer questions like these:
   - **a.** What is the cost to customers of the services mentioned in the ads?
   - **b.** How long do any advertised interest rates apply? How often can they be changed?
   - **c.** Which of the advertised services do you think you really need?

Evaluation

Administer the Unit 3 Test in the Assessment Binder.

Unit Closure

Have the class design and prepare a bulletin board on "Saving for College" or "Saving for a Bright Future." Ideally, the board should be posted in a well-traveled hallway where it will catch the attention of a maximum number of students from other classes.

CHAPTER 9: PLANNING A SAVINGS PROGRAM

Objectives

1. List five valid reasons for saving.

2. Explain how savings become investments.

3. List three savings plans and at least five guidelines for saving money.

4. Identify four kinds of financial institutions and describe three main factors in choosing a particular institution for saving.

5. Name at least two alternative forms of saving.

Teacher's Classroom Resources

Student Activity Workbook
Transparency Binder
Assessment Binder
Lesson Plans
Print, Media, and Internet Resource Handbook
Hands-on Projects for Consumer Education and Economics
Cooperative Learning Activities
Math Practice for Economics
Meeting the Special Needs of Students
Leadership and Citizenship

Focus

1. *Attitude Inventory.* Have students consult their working copies of the Attitude Inventory. Call special attention to items related to Chapter 9. Have the students discuss their answers, encouraging individuals to qualify or rephrase those statements with which they disagree or about which they are undecided. Use this information to choose in-class reading, discussion topics, and follow-up assignments.
2. *Vocabulary.* Preview the Consumer Terms. Have students study the definitions given. The terms fall into two categories—types of institutions and terms related to banking. Write the two categories on the chalkboard, and ask students to place each term in the appropriate category.

Teach

For purposes of classroom presentation, this chapter may be broken into two parts: (1) reasons for saving and savings techniques and (2) types of institutions and forms of saving.

1. Write this quotation on a blackboard: "A penny saved is a penny earned." Ask students to write a paragraph on whether they agree or disagree with the statement and why.
2. From at least two local savings institutions, obtain pamphlets that indicate current interest rates for various kinds of savings accounts. Create a fictional individual with a given amount of money to deposit and a set of specific needs, such as liquidity and highest possible interest rate. Using photocopies or an overhead projector, ask students to determine which institution they would recommend the person use.
3. As an extra credit assignment, ask that students research the FDIC. Why was it created? Can investors safely depend on it?

Assess

Comprehension and Review
- Chapter Highlights
- Reviewing Consumer Terms *and* Reviewing Facts and Ideas

End-of-Chapter Applications
- Problem Solving and Decision Making
- Building Academic Skills—Consumers Around the World
- Student Activity Workbook activities for this chapter

Chapter Extension
- Beyond the Classroom—Consumer Project
- Cooperative Learning—Family Economics
- Cooperative Learning—Debate the Issue

Evaluation
- Administer the test for Chapter 9 in the Assessment Binder.

Close

Ask students to choose one short-term and one long-term goal. Using the information in this chapter, ask them to make a list to show the steps they would take to save for these goals.

CHAPTER 10: USING FINANCIAL SERVICES

Objectives

1. Name two savings accounts that offer higher interest rates than a passbook account, and list three kinds of retirement accounts.
2. Describe the six elements filled in on a check, explain the purpose of and procedure for reconciling a bank statement, and name three kinds of endorsements.
3. Give an example of when each of the following methods of payment might be used: money orders, telegraphic money orders, traveler's checks, and certified checks.
4. Describe what electronic fund transfers are.

Teacher's Classroom Resources

Student Activity Workbook
Transparency Binder
Assessment Binder
Lesson Plans
Print, Media, and Internet Resource Handbook
Hands-on Projects for Consumer Education and Economics
Cooperative Learning Activities
Math Practice for Economics
Meeting the Special Needs of Students
Leadership and Citizenship

Focus

1. *Attitude Inventory.* Have students consult their working copies of the Attitude Inventory. Call special attention to items related to Chapter 10. Have the students discuss their answers, encouraging individuals to qualify or rephrase those statements with which they disagree or about which they are undecided. Use this information to choose in-class reading, discussion topics, and follow-up assignments.
2. *Vocabulary.* Preview the Consumer Terms. Have students study the definitions given. Ask students to write a short conversation between a banker and a customer. Have students use all the terms in the conversation.

Teach

For purposes of classroom presentation, this chapter may be broken into four parts: (1) using savings accounts, (2) writing checks and using checking accounts, (3) using other methods to make payments, and (4) using electronic banking and other services.

1. Obtain literature from a local bank that offers market rate options. Also obtain from the same bank literature on regular savings accounts. Using photocopies or an overhead projector, ask students to evaluate the two options. The money market account will probably pay higher interest, but other considerations may make it less satisfactory. Use questions such as these to guide the evaluation:
   a. Is the account insured?
   b. What is the minimum deposit required?
2. Some individuals' checking accounts seem to be chronically overdrawn. Discuss this problem with students, asking for reasons they think this might happen. What suggestions do they have for avoiding the problem?
3. Discuss with students the possible advantages and disadvantages of electronic fund transfer. Pose such questions as:
   a. Does EFT make recordkeeping more difficult?

   b. Some consumers find it difficult to control their spending. Would EFT make spending too easy for these people?
   c. Could having to manipulate a machine and keep track of secret "codes" seem too intimidating to some consumers?

Assess

Comprehension and Review

- Chapter Highlights
- Reviewing Consumer Terms *and* Reviewing Facts and Ideas

End-of-Chapter Applications

- Problem Solving and Decision Making
- Building Academic Skills—Consumers Around the World
- Student Activity Workbook activities for this chapter

Chapter Extension

- Beyond the Classroom—Consumer Project
- Cooperative Learning—Family Economics
- Cooperative Learning—Debate the Issue

Evaluation

- Administer the test for Chapter 10 in the Assessment Binder.

Close

Have students make a list of all the banking services they would like to use when they are working and on their own. Ask students to explain why each service seems attractive to them.

CHAPTER 11: MAKING INVESTMENTS

Objectives

1. Identify the four factors that should guide consumers in planning an investment strategy.
2. Explain the differences between stocks and bonds.
3. Describe ways to invest in stocks and bonds.

Teacher's Classroom Resources

Student Activity Workbook
Transparency Binder
Assessment Binder
Lesson Plans
Print, Media, and Internet Resource Handbook
Hands-on Projects for Consumer Education and Economics
Cooperative Learning Activities
Math Practice for Economics
Meeting the Special Needs of Students
Leadership and Citizenship

Focus

1. *Attitude Inventory.* Have students consult their working copies of the Attitude Inventory. Call special attention to items related to Chapter 11. Have the students discuss their answers, encouraging individuals to qualify or rephrase those statements with which they disagree or about which they are undecided. Use this information to choose in-class reading, discussion topics, and follow-up assignments.
2. *Vocabulary.* Preview the Consumer Terms. Have students study the definitions given. Most of the terms in this list can be paired for comparing and contrasting. Ask students to write questions that compare or contrast terms. Examples:
   a. How does a *stock* differ from a *bond?*
   b. How does *common stock* differ from *preferred stock?*
   c. How does a *stockbroker* differ from a *stock exchange?*

Teach

For purposes of classroom presentation, this chapter may be broken into three parts: (1) investment strategy and types of securities, (2) how to invest, and (3) reading stock quotations.

1. Post on a bulletin board articles clipped from *The Wall Street Journal, Barron's,* and other investment publications. Choose those that discuss stocks in industries that may be of interest to students, such as motion pictures, automobiles, and computers. Discuss with students why owning stock in an industry in which you are interested might have both advantages and disadvantages. For example, enthusiasm for a certain product might blind you to the reality that the stock is a poor investment. On the other hand, interest in the product might make you a more active and informed shareholder.
2. Invite a local stockbroker or financial manager to speak to the class. Give the person in advance a list of topics you would like covered such as how an investor should choose a broker, ways in which brokers anticipate movement in stocks, or what a leveraged buyout is and how it affects stock prices.

Assess

Comprehension and Review
- Chapter Highlights
- Reviewing Consumer Terms *and* Reviewing Facts and Ideas
- Rechecking Your Attitude

End-of-Chapter Applications
- Problem Solving and Decision Making
- Building Academic Skills—Consumers Around the World
- Student Activity Workbook activities for this chapter

Chapter Extension
- Beyond the Classroom—Consumer Project
- Cooperative Learning—Family Economics
- Cooperative Learning—Debate the Issue
- Unit Lab: You and Your Community

Evaluation
- Administer the test for Chapter 11 in the Assessment Binder.

Close

Ask students to create a wall chart to illustrate investment options. For each investment, have them give any significant characteristics and rate each investment option High or Low for risk and High or Low for income potential.

UNIT 4 TYPES OF CREDIT

Overview

Of all the units on handling money, those on credit are arguably the ones of greatest importance. Why? Because credit is so easy to abuse. Students should be made aware early of the consequences that can and will result if they do not learn to manage credit wisely.

The first chapter in Unit 4 is essentially historical. It acquaints students with the origins of credit, the history of its growth in the United States, and its importance to the consumer economy.

The second chapter discusses common credit problems. It also introduces students to the important concept of opportunity cost.

The third chapter begins a section-by-section focus on the types of consumer credit. Department store charge accounts are discussed first—their advantages, their costs, and the documents associated with them. Credit cards, a category that includes bank cards, travel and entertainment cards, and gasoline credit cards, are also discussed.

The final chapter explores installment credit. The chapter points out the distinguishing features and contract clauses that students should know.

Unit Outline

Chapter 12: Commercial and Consumer Credit

A. Meaning of Credit
- **1.** Good Feelings About Credit
- **2.** Bad Feelings About Credit

B. Beginnings of Credit
- **1.** Receipts as Money
- **2.** Credit Today

C. Commercial Credit

D. Consumer Credit
- **1.** Growth of Consumer Credit
- **2.** Extent of Consumer Credit
- **3.** Importance of Consumer Credit
- **4.** Types of Credit Cards
  - **a.** Retail Credit Cards
  - **b.** Bank Cards
  - **c.** Travel and Entertainment Cards
  - **d.** Gasoline Credit Cards

Chapter 13: Consumer Credit Problems

A. Credit and the Economy
- **1.** Inflation and Recession

B. Business Costs
- **1.** The Cost of Retail Credit Cards
- **2.** The Cost of Bank-Card Credit

C. Credit and the Consumer
- **1.** Overspending
- **2.** Reduced Purchasing Power
  - **a.** Temporary Expansion of Income
  - **b.** Opportunity Cost

D. Credit Illegalities
- **1.** Deceitful Practices by Creditors
- **2.** Discrimination
- **3.** Deceitful Practices by Customers
- **4.** Fraud
- **5.** Loss of Cards

Chapter 14: Charge Accounts

A. Advantages and Disadvantages of Charge Accounts
- **1.** Advantages of Charge Accounts
  - **a.** Temporary Expansion of Income
  - **b.** Reduced Need for Cash
  - **c.** Shopping Convenience
  - **d.** Establishment of Credit
  - **e.** Ease of Returns
  - **f.** Advance Notice of Sales
- **2.** Disadvantages of Charge Accounts

B. Types of Charge Accounts
- **1.** Regular Versus Revolving Credit
- **2.** Finance Charges

C. The Security Agreement
- **1.** Annual or Membership Fees
- **2.** Grace Period
- **3.** Payment Obligations
- **4.** Annual Percentage Rate
- **5.** Computation Method
- **6.** Minimum Finance Charge
- **7.** Other Fees
- **8.** Security Interest

D. The Monthly Statement

E. Fair Credit Billing Act

Chapter 15: Installment Credit

A. Installment Versus Open-End Credit

B. Installment Credit Characteristics
- **1.** Down Payment
- **2.** Security Interest
- **3.** Sales Finance Companies

C. Installment Credit Problems
- **1.** The Rule of 78s
- **2.** Balloon Payment Clause
- **3.** Acceleration Clause
- **4.** Add-On Clause
- **5.** Garnishment

D. Extent of Installment Debt

Introduction

1. *Attitude Inventory.* Before beginning the unit, have the class do the Unit 4 Attitude Inventory. Remind the students to retain their answers for periodic reevaluation.
2. *Motivation.* The seriousness of misusing credit cannot be stressed too much. If their families are not good money managers, students may have few role models to emulate in a society that seems determined to live beyond its means. As stated in the text, consumer credit outstanding in the United States amounted to more than $954 billion in 1995. All students will have seen some of the effects of using credit, both bad and good. Encourage them to think about what they have seen. Stimulate their thinking with questions like these:
   a. Do people who use credit buy more than those who use cash? (The answer is yes—from 25 to 35 percent more.)
   b. "Credit is easy to get but not always easy to pay for." What does this statement mean?

Evaluation

Administer the Unit 4 Test in the Assessment Binder.

Unit Closure

Have students write a paragraph on the topic, "Why Credit Is Important to Me."

CHAPTER 12: COMMERCIAL AND CONSUMER CREDIT

Objectives

1. Explain what credit is, and identify the essential element in credit.
2. Describe how credit was used in early business transactions.
3. Explain how commercial credit generates money that can be used to pay off a loan.
4. Explain how consumer credit differs from commercial credit, and name at least three types of credit cards.

Teacher's Classroom Resources

Student Activity Workbook
Transparency Binder
Assessment Binder
Lesson Plans
Print, Media, and Internet Resource Handbook
Hands-on Projects for Consumer Education and Economics
Cooperative Learning Activities
Math Practice for Economics
Meeting the Special Needs of Students
Leadership and Citizenship

Focus

1. *Attitude Inventory.* Have students consult their working copies of the Attitude Inventory. Call special attention to items related to Chapter 12. Have the students discuss their answers, encouraging individuals to qualify or rephrase those statements with which they disagree or about which they are undecided. Use this information to guide the choice of in-class reading, discussion topics, and follow-up assignments.
2. *Vocabulary.* Preview the Consumer Terms. Have students study the definitions given. Ask students to give three or more illustrations of these terms drawn from their own experiences. Examples:
   a. *Credit*—a car loan, a student loan, any purchase on a store charge.
   b. *Bank cards*—MasterCard, VISA.

Teach

For purposes of classroom presentation, this chapter may be broken into two parts: (1) the meaning, beginnings, and commercial forms of credit and (2) consumer credit.

1. Ask students to relate trust in business to trust in daily life. How do they determine whom to trust in everyday life? What character traits and behavior do they look for? How are their criteria similar to what a banker uses to evaluate someone for a loan? Ask students to make a checklist of criteria for trust.
2. Discuss changes that have occurred in our society over the past 100 years that have fostered the increased use of consumer credit. Ask students to compare and contrast the following factors:
   a. Standard of living
   b. Average family income
   c. Number and variety of goods and services available
   d. Number of people who own homes
   e. Types of credit available
3. Obtain brochures and application forms for three or four credit cards. Using an overhead projector or photocopies, ask students to evaluate the cards and choose the most economical. Determine the answers to questions such as these:
   a. What is the minimum monthly payment required?
   b. What is the annual fee?

Assess

Comprehension and Review

- Chapter Highlights
- Reviewing Consumer Terms *and* Reviewing Facts and Ideas

End-of-Chapter Applications

- Problem Solving and Decision Making
- Building Academic Skills—Consumers Around the World
- Student Activity Workbook activities for this chapter

Chapter Extension

- Beyond the Classroom—Consumer Project
- Cooperative Learning—Family Economics
- Cooperative Learning—Debate the Issue

Evaluation

- Administer the test for Chapter 12 in the Assessment Binder.

Close

Have students draw a poster illustrating the history of credit. Tell students to include captions for each picture.

CHAPTER 13: CONSUMER CREDIT PROBLEMS

Objectives

1. Describe how credit sometimes adds to the problems of recession and inflation, and to the cost of doing business.
2. Show how using credit in one year contributes to financial problems the following year.
3. Explain how bank-card credit can lead to increased prices for businesses and consumers.
4. Describe illegal discrimination against a credit applicant, and give three ways consumers can safeguard use of their credit cards.

Teacher's Classroom Resources

Student Activity Workbook
Transparency Binder
Assessment Binder
Lesson Plans
Print, Media, and Internet Resource Handbook
Hands-on Projects for Consumer Education and Economics
Cooperative Learning Activities
Math Practice for Economics
Meeting the Special Needs of Students
Leadership and Citizenship

Focus

1. *Attitude Inventory.* Have students consult their working copies of the Attitude Inventory. Call special attention to items related to Chapter 13. Have the students discuss their answers, encouraging individuals to qualify or rephrase those statements with which they disagree or about which they are undecided. Use this information to choose in-class reading, discussion topics, and follow-up assignments.
2. *Vocabulary.* Preview the Consumer Terms. Have students study the definitions given. Then have them use all the terms in no more than five sentences.
   Example: Consumers who spend more than their *disposable income* on purchases may end up in *bankruptcy* court as a result.

Teach

For purposes of classroom presentation, this chapter need not be divided.

1. Ask students to write a paragraph on the following statement: "When I use credit, it seems as though I'm not really spending money." Suggest they discuss the implications this statement has for the successful management of individual or family finances. Have volunteers read their paragraphs aloud and invite the class to agree or disagree with their conclusions. Afterwards, ask the class how common they think the attitude expressed in the statement is. Then discuss how current lifestyles may have contributed to its prevalence.
2. Ask students to make a list of at least ten behaviors they consider dishonest. You might get them started with a few examples like these:
   a. Stealing a sweater from a department store.
   b. Going out with someone behind your steady's back.
   c. Cheating on a test.
   If they do not do so, add to the list: "Borrowing money when you have no intention of paying it back." When the list is complete, ask students to rate the behaviors on a scale of one to three, with three being the worst. When they are finished, determine how not paying money back compares in seriousness to the rest. What conclusions do students draw from this? How do they think their attitude compares to that of the public at large? How do they think people feel who renege on debts?

Assess

Comprehension and Review
- Chapter Highlights
- Reviewing Consumer Terms *and* Reviewing Facts and Ideas

End-of-Chapter Applications
- Problem Solving and Decision Making
- Building Academic Skills—Consumers Around the World
- Student Activity Workbook activities for this chapter

Chapter Extension
- Beyond the Classroom—Consumer Project
- Cooperative Learning—Family Economics
- Cooperative Learning—Debate the Issue

Evaluation
- Administer the test for Chapter 13 in the Assessment Binder.

Close

Tell students to imagine a dialogue between two people. One person, Bill, contends that there is never any value to using credit; The other person, Jill, tries to convince Bill that credit is often useful. Have students write the dialogue to show how Jill responds to each of Bill's criticisms of credit.

CHAPTER 14: CHARGE ACCOUNTS

Objectives

1. List six advantages and three disadvantages of charge accounts.
2. Distinguish between regular and revolving charge accounts, and identify the balance computation method that is least costly to the consumer.
3. Explain the purpose of a security agreement, and list at least four items covered in one.
4. Identify information on a monthly statement that enables customers to manage their account.
5. Describe the first action consumers must take to secure their rights under the Fair Credit Billing Act.

Teacher's Classroom Resources

Student Activity Workbook
Transparency Binder
Assessment Binder
Lesson Plans
Print, Media, and Internet Resource Handbook
Hands-on Projects for Consumer Education and Economics
Cooperative Learning Activities
Math Practice for Economics
Meeting the Special Needs of Students
Leadership and Citizenship

Focus

1. *Attitude Inventory.* Have the students consult their working copies of the Attitude Inventory. Call special attention to items related to Chapter 14. Have the students discuss their answers, encouraging individuals to qualify or rephrase those statements with which they disagree or about which they are undecided. Use this information to guide the choice of in-class reading, discussion topics, and follow-up assignments.
2. *Vocabulary.* Preview the Consumer Terms. Have students study the definitions given. Tell the students to pretend that they are preparing clues for a crossword puzzle. Ask them to rewrite the definitions in the shortest possible form. *Examples:*
   a. *Finance charge*—cost of credit
   b. *Line of credit*—spending limit

For extra credit, have student volunteers use graph paper to prepare actual puzzles.

Teach

For purposes of classroom presentation, this chapter may be broken into two parts: (1) advantages of charge accounts and (2) types of accounts and account documents. The second part includes a typical charge account billing statement (Figure 14–2). This document should be read and reviewed thoroughly with the class.

1. Using the advantages listed in the text, ask students to list five items they would consider buying with a charge account and five they would not. In each case, have them explain why.
2. Ask students to write letters of complaint based on the facts below. Remind students to explain the problem completely and provide evidence that the earlier bill was paid.
   a. On March 1 you bought a shirt from Menswear Express for $18.95

and put the purchase on your charge account.

b. You paid the bill in full by check on March 30.

c. In early April you bought shoes for $52.56.

d. When your April billing statement arrived, it failed to show your $18.95 payment. Instead a $1.50 finance charge was levied against your account.

Assess

Comprehension and Review

- Chapter Highlights
- Reviewing Consumer Terms *and* Reviewing Facts and Ideas

End-of-Chapter Applications

- Problem Solving and Decision Making
- Building Academic Skills—Consumers Around the World
- Student Activity Workbook activities for this chapter

Chapter Extension

- Beyond the Classroom—Consumer Project
- Cooperative Learning—Family Economics
- Cooperative Learning—Debate the Issue

Evaluation

- Administer the test for Chapter 14 in the Assessment Binder.

Close

Have students imagine they are the owner of a retail store, and have decided that their consumers can use credit in your store. Have them draw a charge account plan that they will offer to their customers. Have students specify all the particulars that will be included in the security agreement and that will appear on the monthly statement.

CHAPTER 15: INSTALLMENT CREDIT

Objectives

1. Distinguish between open-end and closed-end credit.
2. List three installment credit features creditors use to guarantee receipt of payments.
3. Identify five installment credit problems.
4. Give the rule of thumb for how much debt a consumer can manage.

Teacher's Classroom Resources

Student Activity Workbook
Transparency Binder
Assessment Binder
Lesson Plans
Print, Media, and Internet Resource Handbook
Hands-on Projects for Consumer Education and Economics
Cooperative Learning Activities
Math Practice for Economics
Meeting the Special Needs of Students
Leadership and Citizenship

Focus

1. *Attitude Inventory.* Have students consult their working copies of the Attitude Inventory. Call special attention to items related to Chapter 15. Have the students discuss their answers, encouraging individuals to qualify or rephrase those statements with which they disagree or about which they are undecided. Use this information to choose in-class reading, discussion topics, and follow-up assignments.
2. *Vocabulary.* Preview the Consumer Terms. Have students study the definitions given. Explain that in many cases the terms themselves give clues

to their meanings. For example, *acceleration clause* contains the root word *accelerate* (to speed up). An acceleration clause allows the seller to "speed up" payments to the point that the whole amount owed is due at once. Have the students formulate similar memory aids for as many of the other terms as possible.

Teach

For purposes of classroom presentation, this chapter may be broken into two parts: (1) installment credit characteristics and (2) installment credit problems.

1. Invite the owner of a local business that carries its own credit contracts to speak to the class. Provide the person in advance with a list of topics you would like covered. These might include the following:
   - **a.** Why the store offers credit terms.
   - **b.** How the store decides to whom to extend credit.
   - **c.** How the store deals with any late payments.
   - **d.** How often the store must repossess merchandise.
   - **e.** How the store's credit policies in general have changed over the years.

2. Ask the students which of the problem clauses described in the chapter they would fight hardest to have removed from a credit contract and why. What arguments would they make? If alteration of the contract were refused, what alternatives would they have?

Assess

Comprehension and Review
- Chapter Highlights
- Reviewing Consumer Terms *and* Reviewing Facts and Ideas
- Rechecking Your Attitude

End-of-Chapter Applications
- Problem Solving and Decision Making
- Building Academic Skills—Consumers Around the World
- Student Activity Workbook activities for this chapter

Chapter Extension
- Beyond the Classroom—Consumer Project
- Cooperative Learning—Family Economics
- Cooperative Learning—Debate the Issue
- Unit Lab: You and Your Community

Evaluation
- Administer the test for Chapter 15 in the Assessment Binder.

Close

Tell students to write a fictional story about a family that uses the installment plan. In their stories, students should narrate the problems the family encounters with installment credit clauses. Stories should answer the question of whether or not the family resolves its problems, or goes deeper and deeper into debt.

UNIT 5 GETTING AND KEEPING CREDIT

Overview

This unit focuses on the practical aspects of credit—how to get it and how not to lose it. Using a step-by-step approach, the unit introduces students to the process in terms they can understand and relate to.

The first chapter deals with evaluating credit terms and includes some historical background on credit problems. Establishing credit is covered in this chapter. A credit application (Figure 16-2) is gone through in detail to familiarize the students with the information typically required. The credit bureau, credit reporting problems, and consumer credit rights are also discussed.

The second chapter concentrates on borrowing money. The various sources of cash loans are distinguished, and their relative advantages and disadvantages are pointed out.

Unit Outline

Chapter 16: Evaluating Credit Terms and Establishing Credit

A. Regulation of Lending
  1. Confusion in the Marketplace
  2. Truth-in-Lending Act
    a. Total Finance Charge
    b. Annual Percentage Rate
    c. Credit Disclosure Form
    d. Monthly Statement
    e. Right of Rescission
B. Getting Credit
  1. The Three C's of Credit
  2. The Credit Application
C. The Credit Bureau
D. Credit Reporting Problems
  1. Duration of Record
  2. Investigative Reporting
  3. Billing Disputes
E. Consumer Credit Rights

Chapter 17: Borrowing Money

A. When to Borrow Cash
B. Savings Institutions as Sources of Loans
  1. Commercial Banks
  2. Savings and Loan Associations
  3. Credit Unions
C. Other Sources of Loans
  1. Consumer Finance Companies
    a. Higher Charges
    b. Consolidation Loans
  2. Insurance Companies
  3. Private Loans

Introduction

1. *Attitude Inventory.* Before beginning the unit, have the class do the Unit 5 Attitude Inventory. Remind the students to retain their answers for periodic reevaluation.
2. *Motivation.* A bad credit rating can be hard to live with. Ask students to imagine they are married and have two small children. In what ways might their lives be affected if they could not obtain credit? How would they try to overcome these problems?

Evaluation

Administer the Unit 5 Test in the Assessment Binder.

Unit Closure

Divide the students into two groups. Have each group write a skit on one of the following topics:

"The Thompsons Apply for a Charge Account"

"Explaining a Credit Report to a Consumer With a Bad Credit Record."

Have the groups present the skit to the remainder of the class.

CHAPTER 16: EVALUATING CREDIT TERMS AND ESTABLISHING CREDIT

Objectives

1. Describe how lending is regulated, and tell how the right of rescission works.
2. Describe the facts credit managers consider when deciding whether to extend credit.
3. Describe what a credit bureau does and how creditors use credit bureaus.
4. Identifity common credit problems.
5. Identify the 15 important consumer rights related to credit reporting.

Teacher's Classroom Resources

Student Activity Workbook
Transparency Binder
Assessment Binder
Lesson Plans
Print, Media, and Internet Resource Handbook
Hands-on Projects for Consumer Education and Economics
Cooperative Learning Activities
Math Practice for Economics
Meeting the Special Needs of Students
Leadership and Citizenship

Focus

1. *Attitude Inventory.* Have students consult their working copies of the Attitude Inventory. Call special attention to items related to Chapter 16. Have the students discuss their answers, encouraging individuals to qualify or rephrase those statements with which they disagree or about which they are undecided. Use this information to choose in-class reading, discussion topics, and follow-up assignments.
2. *Vocabulary.* Preview the Consumer Terms. Have students study the definitions given. Ask a student volunteer to write a sentence on the chalkboard using one of the terms. Instead of inserting the term, however, the student should leave a blank that other students must try to fill. Whoever names the correct term gets to write the next sentence on the board using a different vocabulary term. Continue until all the terms have been covered.

Teach

For purposes of classroom presentation, this chapter may be broken into three parts: (1) credit terms, (2) the credit application process, and (3) credit reporting problems and consumer rights. A substantial amount of time should be spent reviewing the Truth-in-Lending credit disclosure form in Figure 16–1. It shows clearly how much buying on credit can add to the total cost of an item.

1. Many credit agreements are filled with legalese that consumers find hard to understand. Reproduce the following paragraph for students and ask them to attempt a translation:

   This note is secured by a security interest in all of the following described personal property and proceeds thereof: If checked at left, Consumer goods consisting of all household goods, furniture, appliances, and bric-a-brac now owned and hereafter acquired, including replacements, and located in or about the premises at the Debtor's residence (unless otherwise stated) or at any other location to which the goods may be moved. In addition, all other goods and chattels of like nature hereinafter acquired by the Debtor and kept or used in or about said premises and substituted for any property mentioned. Proceeds and Products of the collateral are also covered.
   Translation: If the debtor does not pay the loan on time, the creditor may seize all household goods.

   Explain that it was such difficult language, among other things, that led to the creation of simple, clear summarizing language such as that used in the Truth-in-Lending credit disclosure form.
2. According to bankers' estimates, only about 20 to 30 percent of credit applications are approved. Although each institution has its own methods (usually based on complex computer models and statistical graphs), in general, applicants are evaluated on the

basis of the three C's of credit. Ask students how they themselves plan to meet these criteria when the time comes, and why they think each is important.

3. Obtain enough copies of at least two different credit applications so that each student can have one to fill out. Provide generic income information and credit reference data for the class to use. After they have completed their applications and submitted them, tell the students that they have been turned down "because of an unfavorable credit history." Ask them how they would proceed, given what they know about their consumer credit rights.

Assess

Comprehension and Review

- Chapter Highlights
- Reviewing Consumer Terms *and* Reviewing Facts and Ideas

End-of-Chapter Applications

- Problem Solving and Decision Making
- Building Academic Skills—Consumers Around the World
- Student Activity Workbook activities for this chapter

Chapter Extension

- Beyond the Classroom—Consumer Project
- Cooperative Learning—Family Economics
- Cooperative Learning—Debate the Issue

Evaluation

- Administer the test for Chapter 16 in the Assessment Binder.

Close

Using the material in this chapter, have students write a short handbook on obtaining consumer credit. Tell them to focus on the issues faced by young people who are just starting to use credit.

CHAPTER 17: BORROWING MONEY

Objectives

1. Describe how borrowing cash can sometimes reduce financing costs.
2. Identify the usual sources of cash loans.
3. Explain the higher finance charges of consumer finance companies.

Teacher's Classroom Resources

Student Activity Workbook
Transparency Binder
Assessment Binder
Lesson Plans
Print, Media, and Internet Resource Handbook
Hands-on Projects for Consumer Education and Economics
Cooperative Learning Activities
Math Practice for Economics
Meeting the Special Needs of Students
Leadership and Citizenship

Focus

1. *Attitude Inventory.* Have students consult their working copies of the Attitude Inventory. Call special attention to items related to Chapter 17. Have the students discuss their answers, encouraging individuals to qualify or rephrase those statements with which they disagree or about which they are undecided. Use this information to choose in-class reading, discussion topics, and follow-up assignments.
2. *Vocabulary.* Preview the Consumer Terms. Have students study the definitions given. Place three headings on the chalkboard—Institutions, People, and Financial Devices. Have the stu-

dents list each vocabulary term in the proper column.

Teach

For purposes of classroom presentation, this chapter need not be divided. Collect brochures on one particular type of loan (auto, educational, consumer) from several different sources—commercial banks, S&Ls, finance companies, and credit unions. Divide the class into small groups, and distribute some of each type of literature to each group. Have each group compare the different sources and rank them according to which offers the best terms. Finally, have the different groups compare their rankings to see if they agree.

Assess

Comprehension and Review

- Chapter Highlights
- Reviewing Consumer Terms *and* Reviewing Facts and Ideas
- Rechecking Your Attitude

End-of-Chapter Applications

- Problem Solving and Decision Making
- Building Academic Skills—Consumers Around the World
- Student Activity Workbook activities for this chapter

Chapter Extension

- Beyond the Classroom—Consumer Project
- Cooperative Learning—Family Economics
- Cooperative Learning—Debate the Issue
- Unit Lab: You and Your Community

Evaluation

- Administer the test for Chapter 17 in the Assessment Binder.

Close

Tell students to imagine that a friend has asked for advice on borrowing money. Have students write a letter in which they explain the options open to the friend and make suggestions about how best to finance the loan.

UNIT 6 INSURANCE

Overview

This unit deals with one of the most important yet confusing areas of consumer spending, that of buying insurance. Since many students are unaware of the importance of insurance to their lives, this unit should be an eye-opener.

In the first chapter, the students learn what insurance is, how it works, and how to select an insurance agent or company. In addition, this chapter covers property and home insurance, discussing insurable interest, kinds of coverage, features of a homeowners policy, property insurance rates, and proof-of-loss considerations.

The second chapter deals with auto insurance. This material includes reasons for automobile insurance, kinds of auto insurance coverage, automobile insurance rates, alternative insurance systems, and the factors affecting auto insurance rates.

The third chapter deals with life insurance and health insurance. It details what these coverages are, why they are important, key features of policies, and factors to consider when purchasing.

In the last chapter, students learn about the social security system, how it works, and what other income insurance options are available through private companies.

Unit Outline

Chapter 18: Property and Home Insurance

A. How Insurance Works
- **1.** Principle of Indemnification
- **2.** Insurable Interest
- **3.** Use of Premiums
- **4.** Importance of Insurance
- **5.** Insurance and the Economy

B. Purchase Considerations
- **1.** Agent Qualifications
- **2.** Company Reputation
- **3.** Key Policy Elements
- **4.** Group Versus Individual Coverage

C. Types of Risk
- **1.** Property Risks
  - **a.** Fire Insurance
  - **b.** Theft Insurance
- **2.** Liability Risks
- **3.** Personal Risks

D. Property Insurance
- **1.** Liability Coverages
- **2.** Range of Coverage
- **3.** Additional Coverages
  - **a.** Flood Insurance
  - **b.** Earthquake Insurance
  - **c.** Crime Insurance
- **4.** Property Insurance Rates
- **5.** Proof of Loss

Chapter 19: Automobile Insurance

A. Reasons for Automobile Insurance
- **1.** Losses from Automobile Accidents
- **2.** Financial Responsibility Laws

B. Kinds of Coverage
- **1.** Bodily Injury Liability
- **2.** Medical Payments
- **3.** Uninsured Motorists
- **4.** Property Damage Liability
- **5.** Comprehensive Physical Damage
- **6.** Collision
  - **a.** How Collision Works
  - **b.** Deductibles
  - **c.** New Versus Old Cars

C. Other Types of Coverages
- **1.** Uninsured Motorists Property Damage
- **2.** Underinsured Motorists Coverage
- **3.** Towing and Labor
- **4.** Motorcycle Insurance

D. Automobile Insurance Rates
- **1.** Factors Affecting All Drivers
- **2.** Options for Problem Drivers

E. Alternative Insurance Systems
- **1.** Comparative Negligence System
- **2.** No-Fault System

Chapter 20: Life and Health Insurance

A. Life and Health Insurance

B. Kinds of Life Insurance
- **1.** Term Insurance
- **2.** Permanent Insurance
- **3.** Combination Insurance
  - **a.** Universal Life
  - **b.** Modified Life Policies

C. Policy Features and Provisions
- **1.** Beneficiaries
- **2.** Premiums
- **3.** Payments
  - **a.** Proceeds
  - **b.** Cash Value
  - **c.** Dividends
- **4.** Special Clauses

D. Purchase Considerations
- **1.** Term Versus Permanent Insurance
- **2.** How Much Insurance?
- **3.** Factors Affecting Cost

E. Medical Care Costs

F. Kinds of Health Insurance Coverage
- **1.** Hospital Expense
- **2.** Surgical Expense
- **3.** Physician's Expense
- **4.** Major Medical Expense
- **5.** Dental Expense Insurance

G. Government Health Insurance Programs
- **1.** Workers' Compensation
- **2.** Medicaid
- **3.** Medicare
  - **a.** Hospital Insurance (Part A)
  - **b.** Medical Insurance (Part B)
  - **c.** Medigap Coverage

H. Private Health Insurance Options
  1. Sources of Coverage
    a. Group Health Insurance
    b. Individual Health Insurance
    c. Hospital and Medical Organizations
  2. Sources of Managed Care Providers
    a. Managed Care Providers
    b. Health Maintenance Organizations
    c. Preferred Provider Organizations
    d. Exclusive Provider Organizations
    e. Point-of-Service Plans

Chapter 21: Income Insurance

A. Social Security Program
  1. History of the Program
  2. Current Benefits and Problems
B. How Social Security Works
  1. Social Security Number
  2. Contributions
  3. Eligibility
  4. Benefits
    a. Old-Age Benefits
    b. Survivors' Benefits
    c. Disability Benefits
    d. Hospital Insurance
    e. Payments to the Needy
C. Federal and State Unemployment Insurance
D. Private Income Insurance Programs
  1. Disability Income Insurance
    a. Benefit Period
    b. Extent of Disability
  2. Private Pension Plans
  3. Annuities

Introduction

1. *Attitude Inventory.* Before beginning the unit, have the class do the Unit 6 Attitude Inventory. Remind the students to retain their answers for periodic reevaluation.

2. *Motivation.* Many students will have begun driving a car and thinking about owning their own cars. Ask them to think of as many reasons as they can for buying car insurance. Then write the following three statements on the board and ask students if they are true or false and why.
  a. If you are careful, you don't need to buy insurance. (Anyone can be injured or can lose property.)
  b. If I have auto insurance, then I won't have to pay any money if I get into an accident. (Most people have to pay some money, even though they have full insurance coverage. Also, if limits of coverage are low, costs must be paid out of pocket.)
  c. If I don't have an accident or cause any injuries, I should get my insurance premium back at the end of the year. (Most, if not all, companies would go out of business if that were the policy.)

3. *Motivation.* The alarming cost of health care in this country makes health insurance almost mandatory. Obtain from your local hospital a list of estimated costs involved when someone is admitted with appendicitis and requires surgery. Review the figures with the students. Point out that they do not include doctor's fees, prescriptions, follow-up office visits, and similar items. Finally, remind the class that this is a fairly simple surgical procedure, unlike many today.

Evaluation

Administer the Unit 6 Test in the Assessment Binder.

Unit Closure

Tell students to write a consumer guide to help people who are thinking of purchasing insurance. Students should use a question format. First, they should list the general categories of insurance covered in the unit—homeowners, automobile, life, health, and income. Then, for each category, have them write down questions consumers should ask themselves to help determine the kinds of coverage they need in each category.

CHAPTER 18: PROPERTY AND HOME INSURANCE

Objectives

1. Explain what insurance is and how it works.
2. Tell how to select an insurance agent and an insurance company.
3. Identify the three types of insurance risk.
4. Describe what specific risks a homeowners policy covers.
5. List the factors that determine the cost of property insurance.
6. Illustrate how to prove property loss.

Teacher's Classroom Resources

Student Activity Workbook
Transparency Binder
Assessment Binder
Lesson Plans
Print, Media, and Internet Resource Handbook
Hands-on Projects for Consumer Education and Economics
Cooperative Learning Activities
Math Practice for Economics
Meeting the Special Needs of Students
Leadership and Citizenship

Focus

1. *Attitude Inventory.* Have students consult their working copies of the Attitude Inventory. Call special attention to items related to Chapter 18. Have the students discuss their answers, encouraging individuals to qualify or rephrase those statements with which they disagree or about which they are undecided. Use this information to guide the choice of in-class reading, discussion topics, and follow-up assignments.
2. *Vocabulary.* Preview the Consumer Terms. Have students study the definitions given. Divide the class into two teams. Scramble the letters of each term. Write one scrambled term on the chalkboard and give one team a clue to its identity—a sentence containing a blank where the term would go. The first team to identify the correct term gets one point. Keep score. Continue until all of the terms have been guessed and used properly.

Teach

For purposes of classroom presentation, this chapter may be broken into four parts: (1) how insurance works, (2) purchase considerations, (3) types of property coverages, and (4) property insurance rates.

1. Have the students bring in newspaper and magazine articles illustrating different kinds of economic losses. Have the students indicate the type of insurance needed for protection in each case. Ask what will happen to people who are not covered.
2. Invite an insurance agent to speak to the class about coverages included in property and homeowners insurance. Ask the person to relate anecdotes illustrating how insurance, or lack of it, affected different people.
3. Ask students to think about a particular home they know. Ask them to estimate costs—high, average, or low. They should consider such questions as the following:

a. Is a house made of stucco cheaper to insure than one made of wood? Why or why not?
b. Is the house located close to a fire station? Does this make the insurance cheaper?
c. Is there is a great deal of brush and vegetation around the house? Would the insurance company charge more or less? Why?

Assess

Comprehension and Review
- Chapter Highlights
- Reviewing Consumer Terms *and* Reviewing Facts and Ideas

End-of-Chapter Applications
- Problem Solving and Decision Making
- Building Academic Skills—Consumers Around the World
- Student Activity Workbook activities for this chapter

Chapter Extension
- Beyond the Classroom—Consumer Project
- Cooperative Learning—Family Economics
- Cooperative Learning—Debate the Issue

Evaluation
- Administer the test for Chapter 18 in the Assessment Binder.

Close

Tell students to write a short essay (350–500 words) on the topic "Insurance and How It Works." They should use homeowners insurance to illustrate different elements in their discussion.

CHAPTER 19: AUTOMOBILE INSURANCE

Objectives

1. Explain why automobile insurance is necessary.
2. Identify the six basic types of automobile insurance coverage.
3. State additional types of auto insurance coverage available to consumers.
4. List the factors that determine automobile insurance rates.
5. Identify two alternative auto insurance systems.

Teacher's Classroom Resources

Student Activity Workbook
Transparency Binder
Assessment Binder
Lesson Plans
Print, Media, and Internet Resource Handbook
Hands-on Projects for Consumer Education and Economics
Cooperative Learning Activities
Math Practice for Economics
Meeting the Special Needs of Students
Leadership and Citizenship

Focus

1. *Attitude Inventory.* Have students consult their working copies of the Attitude Inventory. Call special attention to items related to Chapter 19. Have the students discuss their answers, encouraging individuals to qualify or rephrase those statements with which they disagree or about which they are undecided. Use this information to choose in-class reading, discussion topics, and follow-up assignments.
2. *Vocabulary.* Preview the Consumer Terms. Have students study the definitions given. Many of these consumer terms are compound terms—made up of several words. Have students recast the terms, using the words involved, in another form that expresses the definition. *Examples:*
   a. *Financial responsibility laws—laws* that govern drivers' *responsibility* for *financial* obligations.

b. *Medical payments coverage—coverage* for your family for *payments* made for *medical* expenses resulting from an accident.

Teach

For purposes of classroom presentation, this chapter may be broken into two parts: (1) kinds of auto insurance coverage and (2) auto insurance rates and systems.

1. Many people think their auto insurance coverage will protect against all possible economic losses. Yet they may have only four or five of the six coverages and may be underinsured in some areas. To illustrate this point, make up sample policies for two drivers—one with your state's minimums and no collision or medical payments, the other with twice the state's minimums and all coverages (including $2,000 medical payments). Then hypothesize an accident with the following damages:
   a. Bodily injury liability—$260,000 (one person)
   b. Medical payments—$7,140 (three people)
   c. Property damage liability—$30,000 (two cars)
   What results? What amount of coverage should the drivers have had to be adequately covered?
2. As of 1995, thirteen states and Puerto Rico had some form of no-fault insurance. Whether they live in a no-fault state or not, it is important for students to understand the system. Have students form a panel to discuss the pros and cons of no-fault auto insurance. Give them some time to do research, and limit the presentation to 20 minutes.

Assess

Comprehension and Review
- Chapter Highlights
- Reviewing Consumer Terms and Reviewing Facts and Ideas

End-of-Chapter Applications
- Problem Solving and Decision Making
- Building Academic Skills—Consumers Around the World
- Student Activity Workbook activities for this chapter

Chapter Extension
- Beyond the Classroom—Consumer Project
- Cooperative Learning—Family Economics
- Cooperative Learning—Debate the Issue

Evaluation
- Administer the test for Chapter 19 in the Assessment Binder.

Close

Divide the class into groups. Each group should make a poster showing the different kinds of automobile insurance coverage available. Groups should define and explain each type of coverage. Posters should be illustrated.

CHAPTER 20: LIFE AND HEALTH INSURANCE

Objectives

1. Describe the various types of life insurance coverage.
2. List some of the key features and clauses commonly found in life insurance policies.
3. Identify the factors to consider when buying life insurance.
4. Explain what health insurance is and why it is important.
5. Describe the various kinds of health insurance coverage.
6. Identify some of the common government health insurance programs and tell how they work.

7. List and explain some of the basic private health insurance options.

Teacher's Classroom Resources

Student Activity Workbook
Transparency Binder
Assessment Binder
Lesson Plans
Print, Media, and Internet Resource Handbook
Hands-on Projects for Consumer Education and Economics
Cooperative Learning Activities
Math Practice for Economics
Meeting the Special Needs of Students
Leadership and Citizenship

Focus

1. *Attitude Inventory.* Have students consult their working copies of the Attitude Inventory. Call special attention to items related to Chapter 20. Have the students discuss their answers, encouraging individuals to qualify or rephrase those statements with which they disagree or about which they are undecided. Use this information to guide the choice of in-class reading, discussion topics, and follow-up assignments.
2. *Vocabulary.* Preview the Consumer Terms. Have students study the definitions given. Ask individual students to volunteer an advertising blurb for each item extolling its best feature. See if the rest of the class can identify the term from the blurb. Examples:
   a. *Cash Value*—Money that is always there when you need it!
   b. *Limited-payment life*—Pay a while. Be insured for life!
   c. *Managed care*—High-quality health care at reasonable cost!

Teach

For purposes of classroom presentation, this chapter may be broken into six parts: (1) kinds of life insurance, (2) life insurance policy features and provisions, (3) suggestions for buying life insurance, (4) kinds of health insurance coverage, (5) government health insurance programs, and (6) private health insurance options.

1. Ask students to determine the type of insurance appropriate to the lifestyle they plan to have after graduation. Advise them to consider such things as income, beneficiary, and type of occupation (hazardous, etc.).
2. Have students dramatize an exchange between a young consumer and a life insurance agent. Afterward, ask the class for suggestions.
   a. Did the agent give good reasons for buying?
   b. Did the customer ask the right questions?

Be sure to review the chart in Figure 20–4 as it clearly shows the benefits of carrying major medical coverage.

3. Have the students extend the table in Figure 20–3. Have them calculate costs for the next two 5-year periods, based on a continuation of the most recent percentage increases. Point out that the new figures represent projections of the prices they will be paying when they are out on their own.
4. Obtain brochures for several health insurance plans. Make photocopies or use an overhead projector. Ask the class to evaluate the plans. Point out that some people carry more than one policy. What would be the advantages and disadvantages of this? Is it possible to be overinsured, especially if you are insured by more than one company? Why could this be a problem?

Assess

Comprehension and Review
- Chapter Highlights
- Reviewing Consumer Terms and Reviewing Facts and Ideas

End-of-Chapter Applications

- Problem Solving and Decision Making
- Building Academic Skills—Consumers Around the World
- Student Activity Workbook activities for this chapter

Chapter Extension

- Beyond the Classroom—Consumer Project
- Cooperative Learning—Family Economics
- Cooperative Learning—Debate the Issue

Evaluation

- Administer the test for Chapter 20 in the Assessment Binder.

Close

Tell students to imagine they have just been hired by the state insurance commission. Their job is to explain life and health insurance to the press. Using the material in the chapter, ask student sto compose a short speech to be given at a press conference. Their speeches should explain the different life and health insurance options available to consumers.

CHAPTER 21: INCOME INSURANCE

Objectives

1. Summarize recent and past trends in the development of the social security system.
2. Identify the six programs that make up the social security system and explain how they work.
3. Explain the importance of federal and state unemployment insurance.
4. Describe the income insurance options available through private companies.

Teacher's Classroom Resources

Student Activity Workbook
Transparency Binder
Assessment Binder
Lesson Plans
Print, Media, and Internet Resource Handbook
Hands-on Projects for Consumer Education and Economics
Cooperative Learning Activities
Math Practice for Economics
Meeting the Special Needs of Students
Leadership and Citizenship

Focus

1. *Attitude Inventory.* Have students consult their working copies of the Attitude Inventory. Call special attention to items related to Chapter 21. Have the students discuss their answers, encouraging individuals to qualify or rephrase those statements with which they disagree or about which they are undecided. Use this information to guide the choice of in-class reading, discussion topics, and follow-up assignments.
2. *Vocabulary.* Preview the Consumer Terms. Have students study the definitions given. Where appropriate, ask the students to provide examples or suggest contexts in which they have heard the terms used. *Examples:*
   - **a.** No politician wants to suggest cutting the *social security program* as a way to reduce the federal debt.
   - **b.** You must put your *social security number* on your tax returns.
   - **c.** Many former asbestos workers now live on *disability benefits.*

Teach

For purposes of classroom presentation, this chapter may be broken into two parts: (1) the social security program and (2) private income insurance programs.

1. Most students will think social security is for old people and does not affect their age group. Many, however, are working and paying social security taxes. Ask a student volunteer to bring in one of his or her recent pay stubs. Call attention to the box labeled FICA and ask the students if they know what it stands for. Stress that if money is being taken out of their paycheck, they should know where it is going. Ask any working students to estimate what they pay in FICA contributions over a year's time.
2. Ask someone from the personnel department of a large local company with a pension plan to talk to the class about the types of plans available, why his or her company uses the one it does, and what the future holds for such plans.

Assess

Comprehension and Review

- Chapter Highlights
- Reviewing Consumer Terms *and* Reviewing Facts and Ideas
- Rechecking Your Attitude

End-of-Chapter Applications

- Problem Solving and Decision Making
- Building Academic Skills—Consumers Around the World
- Student Activity Workbook activities for this chapter

Chapter Extension

- Beyond the Classroom—Consumer Project
- Cooperative Learning—Family Economics
- Cooperative Learning—Debate the Issue
- Unit Lab: You and Your Community

Evaluation

- Administer the test for Chapter 21 in the Assessment Binder.

Close

Tell students to imagine that a visitor from another country has asked them what the social security program is. Tell students to write a brief description and list the different programs available under social security.

UNIT 7 TRANSPORTATION AND TRAVEL

Overview

This unit discusses what is for most people the second largest single expenditure of their lives—buying a car. New versus used cars are considered, as well as the option of leasing a car.

The first chapter spells out factors to consider when buying a new car and when negotiating a new-car deal. Similar points are covered for buying a used car and for leasing a car.

The responsibilities of owning a car are covered in the second chapter. Making payments and carrying out routine maintenance are especially discussed.

In the last chapter, public transportation is considered as an alternative to car ownership. Travel as recreation is also covered in this chapter, with emphasis on the type of transportation used.

Unit Outline

Chapter 22: Buying or Leasing a New or Used Car

A. Car Ownership
   1. Advantages and Disadvantages of Owning a Car
   2. Projected Use

3. Affordability
4. Car Size and Type
5. Options
6. Performance

B. Making the Best Deal on a New Car
1. Choosing a Dealer
2. Reading the Sticker
3. Test-Driving a Car
4. Settling Terms
5. Accepting Delivery

C. Buying a Used Car
1. Choosing Where to Buy a Used Car
2. Inspecting and and Accepting Delivery of a Used Car
3. On-Lot Inspection
4. Test-Driving

D. Leasing a Car

Chapter 23: Owning a Car

A. Ownership Means Responsibility

B. Financing Arrangements
1. Loan Sources
2. Down Payments
3. Monthly Payments

C. Maintaining Your Car
1. All About Warranties
   a. Federal Requirements
   b. New-Car Warranties
   c. Used-Car Buyers' Guide
2. Routine Maintenance

D. Smart Driving

Chapter 24: Choosing Other Forms of Transportation

A. Using Mass Transit to Get Around
1. The Benefits of Mass Transit
2. Overcoming Consumer Resistance
3. Paying for Modern Systems

B. Traveling for Pleasure
1. Choosing a Vacation Spot
2. Vacationing Near Home
3. Financing a Trip
   a. Saving Up
4. How to Get There
   a. Buses
   b. Trains
   c. Airlines
   d. Car or Motorcycle
5. Deciding on Lodging and Food
   a. Lodging
   b. Recreational Vehicles
6. Eating Out

Introduction

1. *Attitude Inventory.* Before beginning the unit, have the class do the Unit 7 Attitude Inventory. Remind the students to retain their answers for periodic reevaluation.
2. *Motivation.* For teens, driving (and perhaps owning) a car is an important step toward adult independence. It is also a step that involves many responsibilities, both personal and financial. Introduce the unit with a discussion of these responsibilities. Ask students to provide examples of car problems directly traceable to the actions or omissions of the driver or owner. Accidents caused by reckless behavior are the most obvious example. Lead the class, however, to focus on less sensational, everyday situations like running out of gas, neglecting basic maintenance until the result is a costly repair, or doing minor damage to the finish or interior of a borrowed vehicle. Also remind students of the need for insurance—why it is required and the often substantial costs that are involved, particularly for young drivers.

Evaluation

Administer the Unit 7 Test in the Assessment Binder.

Unit Closure

Divide the class into committees. Tell students to work with your committee to design and post a bulletin board on a topic related to transportation. Possible topics include "Buying a New Car," "Buying a Used Car," "Leasing a Car," or "Cost of Owning a Car."

CHAPTER 22: BUYING OR LEASING A NEW OR USED CAR

Objectives

1. List the advantages and disadvantages of owning a car.
2. Compare the different types of cars.
3. Compute how much you can afford to pay for a car.
4. Find and evaluate the performance records of older cars.
5. Make an on-lot inspection of a used car.
6. Weigh the relative merits of leasing a car.

Teacher's Classroom Resources

Student Activity Workbook
Transparency Binder
Assessment Binder
Lesson Plans
Print, Media, and Internet Resource Handbook
Hands-on Projects for Consumer Education and Economics
Cooperative Learning Activities
Math Practice for Economics
Meeting the Special Needs of Students
Leadership and Citizenship

Focus

1. *Attitude Inventory.* Have students consult their working copies of the Attitude Inventory. Call special attention to items related to Chapter 22. Have the students discuss their answers, encouraging individuals to qualify or rephrase those statements with which they disagree or about which they are undecided. Use this information to guide the choice of in-class reading, discussion topics, and follow-up assignments.
2. *Vocabulary.* Preview the Consumer Terms. Have students study the definitions given. Help the students to use them in a television or radio ad for a new car called the Road Master. In addition, point out that many terms have to do with used-car problems. Ask the students to see if they can identify the problems associated with the terms.
   Examples:
   a. An *odometer* can be turned back to hide the true mileage on a vehicle.
   b. Uneven *tire tread* can indicate a problem with wheel alignment or shock absorbers.

Teach

For purposes of classroom presentation, this chapter may be broken into three parts: (1) the factors involved in choosing a car, (2) buying a new car, and (3) buying a used car and leasing a car.

1. Give special attention to the window sticker. Typically, on the car lot, this complicated document must be read and absorbed under a great deal of pressure. In class it can be studied at leisure, without the distractions of salespeople and other customers.
2. Collect brochures, booklets, and other dealership literature on at least a half dozen car models. These should be of different sizes and price ranges. Divide the class into small groups and give each group the literature for one car. Have the students evaluate their car as either an individual or family purchase based on the factors described in the text. *Examples:*
   a. The group should figure an average number of miles the owner might travel in a week and multi-

ply this number by the miles-per-gallon rating on the car. How does the answer affect the car's affordability?

b. Which options would group members like on the car? Which options do they really need? Which could they do without?

When their analysis is complete, ask the students if, realistically, the car is one they would want to consider for purchase.

3. Using as a guide the list under "Choosing a Dealer," make up two descriptions of car dealers and ask the class to evaluate them. Slant the information in favor of one dealer, but do not be too obvious. Both dealers should have their good points. For example, the dealer who offers the better prices may have a poor service department. The dealer with the better service department may be located in an out-of-the-way neighborhood. During their discussion, encourage students to probe for information and give reasons for the questions they ask.

4. There are a number of guides to used-car prices, and several are available at public libraries, bookstores, and bank loan offices. Obtain a copy of one of these (such as the *NADA Official Used Car Guide*) and photocopy a few representative pages to show to the class. Most of the guides list almost all domestic and foreign cars, vans, and trucks sold in the United States, going back seven or eight years and giving original delivery price, current trade-in value, and current retail value. Also included are lists of options and mileage estimates. Use the guide to stimulate discussion on the kinds of features that affect prices most and the makes and models that seem to retain their value longest.

5. Obtain several copies of the annual *Consumer Reports* auto issue. From the magazine's repair history charts, select trios of different but comparable vehicles. Divide the class into small groups, and give each a copy of the magazine and a list of three cars to compare based on the magazine's survey data. Ask each group to decide which of the cars is, in the group's opinion, the best buy. Afterwards, the groups should share their decisions and the bases for them.

6. Have a committee of students interview the lease manager at a local dealership and share the results of that interview with the class. Perhaps the manager would prepare for them a tabulation comparing the cost of leasing versus the cost of buying a specific car under well-defined conditions.

Assess

Comprehension and Review

- Chapter Highlights
- Reviewing Consumer Terms *and* Reviewing Facts and Ideas

End-of-Chapter Applications

- Problem Solving and Decision Making
- Building Academic Skills—Consumers Around the World
- Student Activity Workbook activities for this chapter

Chapter Extension

- Beyond the Classroom—Consumer Project
- Cooperative Learning—Family Economics
- Cooperative Learning—Debate the Issue

Evaluation

- Administer the test for Chapter 22 in the Assessment Binder.

Close

Tell students to develop a chart that compares the advantages and disadvantages of buying a new car, buying a used car, and leasing a car. Students should give examples of when it might be better to choose one strategy over the other two.

CHAPTER 23: OWNING A CAR

Objectives

1. Identify possible sources of automobile loans.
2. Plan a maintenance schedule to preserve the value of a car.
3. Describe the difference between a full warranty and a limited warranty.
4. Explain how to exercise your basic rights under the lemon law.
5. List smart driving steps.

Teacher's Classroom Resources

Student Activity Workbook
Transparency Binder
Assessment Binder
Lesson Plans
Print, Media, and Internet Resource Handbook
Hands-on Projects for Consumer Education and Economics
Cooperative Learning Activities
Math Practice for Economics
Meeting the Special Needs of Students
Leadership and Citizenship

Focus

1. *Attitude Inventory.* Have students consult their working copies of the Attitude Inventory. Call special attention to items related to Chapter 23. Have the students discuss their answers, encouraging individuals to qualify or rephrase those statements with which they disagree or about which they are undecided. Use this information to guide the choice of in-class reading, discussion topics, and follow-up assignments.
2. *Vocabulary.* Preview the Consumer Terms. Have students study the definitions given. Point out that most of the terms refer to documents of some kind. Discuss the differences between a title, a warranty, and a schedule. Ask the class for reasons they think such items are best written out in document form rather than settled with a handshake.

Teach

For purposes of classroom presentation, this chapter need not be broken into parts. Emphasis should be placed on the obligation monthly payments involve, as most people tend to overestimate their ability to handle such costs on a regular basis.

1. When people trade in a car they have owned, they are no longer acting as consumers but as advertisers and sellers. Ask the students to write a paragraph on the role they believe good car maintenance can play at this point. How will it help them sell the vehicle? How would they use a good maintenance history in any ads they place or pitches they make to potential buyers?
2. Ask the owner of a car repair service to speak to the class. Include as topics for discussion the following:
   - **a.** Maintenance hints
   - **b.** Coping with various kinds of roadside emergencies
   - **c.** Selecting a good mechanic or repair shop
   - **d.** The most common complaints repair shop owners have about customers

Assess

Comprehension and Review

- Chapter Highlights

- Reviewing Consumer Terms and Reviewing Facts and Ideas

End-of-Chapter Applications

- Problem Solving and Decision Making
- Building Academic Skills—Consumers Around the World
- Student Activity Workbook activities for this chapter

Chapter Extension

- Beyond the Classroom—Consumer Project
- Cooperative Learning—Family Economics
- Cooperative Learning—Debate the Issue

Evaluation

- Administer the test for Chapter 23 in the Assessment Binder.

Close

Tell students to write a 500-word essay with the title "A Step-by-Step Approach to Owning a Car." Students should use the information in the chapter.

CHAPTER 24: CHOOSING OTHER FORMS OF TRANSPORTATION

Objectives

1. Identify the advantages to individuals and communities of public transportation.
2. Explain why some consumers resist using public transportation.
3. List ways in which communities have tried to increase mass transit ridership.
4. Describe how to accumulate vacation funds and get maximum value for money spent.
5. Compare and contrast the advantages and disadvantages of traveling by bus, train, air, or private vehicle.
6. Choose the food and lodging arrangements best suited to your budget, travel plans, and vacation expectations.

Teacher's Classroom Resources

Student Activity Workbook
Transparency Binder
Assessment Binder
Lesson Plans
Print, Media, and Internet Resource Handbook
Hands-on Projects for Consumer Education and Economics
Cooperative Learning Activities
Math Practice for Economics
Meeting the Special Needs of Students
Leadership and Citizenship

Focus

1. *Attitude Inventory.* Have students consult their working copies of the Attitude Inventory. Call special attention to items related to Chapter 24. Have the students discuss their answers, encouraging individuals to qualify or rephrase those statements with which they disagree or about which they are undecided. Use this information to guide the choice of in-class reading, discussion topics, and follow-up assignments.
2. *Vocabulary.* Preview the Consumer Terms. Have students study the definitions given. Many terms should be familiar to students, if not from daily conversation then from the evening news. Ask the class to suggest contexts in which they have heard the terms mentioned.
   Examples:
   a. There may be *rationing* of water in a disaster area.
   b. Cars may have to be inspected annually to control their *exhaust emissions*.

c. The *incidence* of certain childhood diseases has dropped dramatically over the last two or three decades.
Before the class session, obtain from travel agencies brochures that include the Consumer Terms and pass them (or photocopies of them) around the class. Ask students to find the terms and tell how they are used.

Teach

For purposes of classroom presentation, this chapter may be broken into two parts: (1) public transportation and (2) traveling as recreation.

1. Ask students for suggestions on how local public transportation could be improved. Then ask how they would recommend the improvements be carried out. Questions for discussion might include the following:
   a. How much more would you pay for a bus or train ride if it would mean better transportation?
   b. Should community groups send volunteers to ride on buses and subways to help protect riders against crime? How much time per week would you be willing to donate?
   c. Should car drivers, particularly those in congested urban areas, be forced to pay special fees to support mass transit?

2. Many students have a strong interest in travel. Use that interest as the springboard for a discussion of travel as recreation. Ask students to talk about places they have visited or would like to visit. How did they get around while they were traveling? How does public transportation function differently in cities, suburbs, and rural areas?

3. Recent studies have shown that only a small number of high school graduates can adequately read a map. In order to make informed choices about travel plans, however, it is often necessary to read a map. Introduce the lesson by using an overhead projector or photocopies of a map. In either case, be sure the map key is visible. Begin by reviewing some map-reading basics with questions like these:
   a. Where is north on the map?
   b. How can you tell an interstate highway from a state road?
   c. What sort of scale is this map drawn to?

Then ask students to find at least three specific locations, to estimate distances, and to determine directions. Try to include a city, a scenic or historic spot, and a highway intersection.

4. From large motel chains, obtain brochures that list all of their locations. (Chains like Best Western, Motel 6, and Holiday Inn usually make copies available to consumers free for the asking.) Give students practice in using the guides by passing them around and asking questions like the following:
   a. Does this chain have a motel in Missoula, Montana?
   b. How many rooms does Motel X have? Is it open all year? If you are entering town on Route 5, how do you get to the motel?
   c. How much is the cost for one person, one bed, between September and April? (Some brochures no longer list prices.)

Assess

Comprehension and Review
- Chapter Highlights
- Reviewing Consumer Terms *and* Reviewing Facts and Ideas
- Rechecking Your Attitude

End-of-Chapter Applications

- Problem Solving and Decision Making
- Building Academic Skills—Consumers Around the World
- Student Activity Workbook activities for this chapter

Chapter Extension

- Beyond the Classroom—Consumer Project
- Cooperative Learning—Family Economics
- Cooperative Learning—Debate the Issue
- Unit Lab: You and Your Community

Evaluation

- Administer the test for Chapter 24 in the Assessment Binder.

Close

Tell students to write a brief essay (350–500 words) about the pros and cons of different forms of transportation.

UNIT 8 BUYING CLOTHING

Overview

This unit should be fun for most students because their appearance is important to them and the information will help them make more attractive clothing choices.

In the first chapter, students are taught how to plan a wardrobe based on acceptability, appearance, and needs. A step-by-step process helps them decide what is still usable and what should be discarded or replaced. Before they make new purchases, students are encouraged to look for items that will work with what they already have.

The second chapter helps students choose where to shop, and how to make new clothing purchases based on quality, price, affordability, fit, and label information. Shopping problems that may affect their purchases (like misleading advertising and poor quality) are also covered.

Unit Outline

Chapter 25: Planning a Wardrobe

A. Assessing Your Wardrobe
B. Taking Inventory
C. Updating Your Wardrobe
D. Making New Purchases

Chapter 26: Shopping for Clothes

A. What to Look For
- **1.** Attractiveness
  - **a.** Color
  - **b.** Line
  - **c.** Fit
- **2.** Acceptability
  - **a.** Fashion
- **3.** Utility
- **4.** Quality
- **5.** Price
  - **a.** Affordability
  - **b.** Where to Shop
  - **c.** Cost of Care

B. Fiber, Fabric, and Finishes
- **1.** Natural Fiber
- **2.** Synthetic Fiber
- **3.** Blends
- **4.** Preshrinking

C. Labels
- **1.** Content Labels
- **2.** Care Labels

D. Shopping Problems
- **1.** Misleading Advertising
- **2.** Shoddy Merchandise

Introduction

1. *Attitude Inventory.* Before beginning the unit, have the class do the Unit 8 Attitude Inventory. Remind the stu-

dents to retain their answers for periodic reevaluation.

2. *Motivation.* Clothing plays an important part in any person's appearance. Teens are probably most concerned that their clothing be fashionable. They often overlook the probability that proper fit, appropriate fabric, and flattering color have as much, if not more, to do with looking good as a trendy style. To capitalize on their interest in fashion, begin by having the class contribute to a bulletin board display titled "Fashion—Would You Wear It? Can You Afford It?" Have the students submit pictures of outrageously styled or outrageously priced clothing. When the display is complete, discuss with the class which consumer groups the designers seem to be targeting and why.

Evaluation

Administer the Unit 8 Test in the Assessment Binder.

Unit Closure

Imagine you are a buyer for a department store who has been assigned the task of educating a teen panel on planning a wardrobe and making appropriate clothing selections. Have students develop an outline of facts and procedures they would cover in their presentations.

CHAPTER 25: PLANNING A WARDROBE

Objectives

1. Identify the desirable features of wardrobe items.
2. Take an inventory of your garments and accessories.
3. Summarize ways to update older articles of clothing.
4. Design a plan for making future additions to your wardrobe.

Teacher's Classroom Resources

Student Activity Workbook
Transparency Binder
Assessment Binder
Lesson Plans
Print, Media, and Internet Resource Handbook
Hands-on Projects for Consumer Education and Economics
Cooperative Learning Activities
Math Practice for Economics
Meeting the Special Needs of Students
Leadership and Citizenship

Focus

1. *Attitude Inventory.* Have students consult their working copies of the Attitude Inventory. Call special attention to items related to Chapter 8. Have the students discuss their answers, encouraging individuals to qualify or rephrase those statements with which they disagree or about which they are undecided. Use this information to guide the choice of in-class reading, discussion topics, and follow-up assignments.
2. *Vocabulary.* Preview the Consumer Terms. Have students study the definitions given. Ask the students to create a word-find puzzle using the consumer terms. (In a word-find puzzle, words appear horizontally, vertically, or diagonally within a block of letters.) An example of two lines from a word-find puzzle follow. In the first line, *garments* appears; in the second line, the word *wardrobe* appears, reading from right to left.

   M G A R M E N T S
   A E B O R D R A W

   Have students exchange puzzles and search for the terms.

Teach

For purposes of classroom presentation, this chapter may be broken into two parts: (1) what to look for in an attractive wardrobe and (2) how to take a wardrobe inventory.

1. Ask students, who would be comfortable in the role, to model in class garments they are considering discarding. Have them explain why they are dissatisfied with the items. Then ask the class for suggestions that might overcome the owner's reservations. For example, a shirt with an unflattering color might be made wearable by layering with another shirt. The number of garments actually saved through this process is not important; what matters is getting students to think creatively about their wardrobes.
2. Invite a personal shopper from a local department store to talk to the class about selecting clothing to fit into an existing wardrobe. Ask the shopper to provide hints regarding fabric and color selection and to talk about the services that the store provides for those people who are too busy to spend time going through all the available items.

Assess

Comprehension and Review

- Chapter Highlights
- Reviewing Consumer Terms *and* Reviewing Facts and Ideas

End-of-Chapter Applications

- Problem Solving and Decision Making
- Building Academic Skills—Consumers Around the World
- Student Activity Workbook activities for this chapter

Chapter Extension

- Beyond the Classroom—Consumer Project
- Cooperative Learning—Family Economics
- Cooperative Learning—Debate the Issue

Evaluation

- Administer the test for Chapter 25 in the Assessment Binder.

Close

Tell students to create a wardrobe planning guide for consumers their age. Have students explain the benefits of a wardrobe plan and how to go about making one. They should add fabric swatches, sketch clothing styles, and include any other important material or information.

CHAPTER 26: SHOPPING FOR CLOTHES

Objectives

1. Choose clothing that is right for you, based on attractiveness, acceptability, utility, quality, and price.
2. Describe the advantages and disadvantages of natural and synthetic fibers.
3. Use clothing labels as guides both when shopping and when caring for clothing.
4. Identify common shopping problems.

Teacher's Classroom Resources

Student Activity Workbook
Transparency Binder
Assessment Binder
Lesson Plans
Print, Media, and Internet Resource Handbook
Hands-on Projects for Consumer Education and Economics
Cooperative Learning Activities
Math Practice for Economics
Meeting the Special Needs of Students
Leadership and Citizenship

Focus

1. *Attitude Inventory.* Have students consult their working copies of the Attitude Inventory. Call special attention to items related to Chapter 26. Have the students discuss their answers, encouraging individuals to qualify or rephrase those statements with which they disagree or about which they are undecided. Use this information to choose in-class reading, discussion topics, and follow-up assignments.
2. *Vocabulary.* Preview the Consumer Terms. Have students study the definitions given. Most can be paired for comparing and contrasting. *Examples:*
   - **a.** How do *factory outlets* differ from *off-price outlets?*
   - **b.** How do *natural fibers* differ from *synthetic fibers?*
   - **c.** How do *permanent-care labels* differ from *hang-tags?*

Teach

For purposes of classroom presentation, this chapter may be broken into three parts: (1) what to look for in clothes; (2) fabrics and labels; and (3) shopping problems.

1. Using transparencies or an overhead projector, illustrate the styles that look best on different body types. Ask students to analyze how the styles differ from each other and why certain ones might be more suitable for one figure type than another.
2. Bring fabric samples to class. Have students examine them for characteristics important to utility, style, and quality. *Examples:*
   - **a.** *Absorbency.* Place drops of water on squares of cotton, wool, and polyester. Ask students to time how long it takes for the water to be absorbed.
   - **b.** *Wrinkle-resistance.* Crush squares of cotton, linen, wool, and polyester. Ask students to compare the amount of wrinkling. Check in five minutes to observe if any of the wrinkles have come out.
   - **c.** *Feel.* Ask students to feel squares of cotton, wool, linen, silk, polyester, and blends in different qualities. Which feel substantial and luxurious; which are thick, paper thin, or stiff? Review the quality fabrics. Do synthetics and blends feel close to fabrics made from natural fibers? Which textures are suitable for different garment styles?
3. Invite a personal shopper or manager from a local department store to talk to the class about selecting clothing to fit into an existing wardrobe. Ask the shopper (or manager) to provide hints or examples regarding fabric and color selection and mix and match opportunities.

Assess

Comprehension and Review

- Chapter Highlights
- Reviewing Consumer Terms *and* Reviewing Facts and Ideas
- Rechecking Your Attitude

End-of-Chapter Applications

- Problem Solving and Decision Making
- Building Academic Skills—Consumers Around the World
- Student Activity Workbook activities for this chapter

Chapter Extension

- Beyond the Classroom—Consumer Project
- Cooperative Learning—Family Economics
- Cooperative Learning—Debate the Issue
- Unit Lab: You and Your Community

Evaluation

- Administer the test for Chapter 26 in the Assessment Binder.

Close

In a 500-word article for a student newspaper, ask students to explain how shopping for clothing is easier when you determine—ahead of time—the most appropriate shops, the features you are looking for, and how to recognize the features you want. Use specific examples under each category.

UNIT 9 BUYING FOOD, MEDICINES AND COSMETICS

Overview

Using this unit, students can really learn firsthand what it means to be a smart shopper. Applications and projects are part of every unit in the text. Here, however, comparisons of cost, quality, and nutritional value can be made within the space of a single supermarket shelf. To take full advantage of this situation, Unit 9 concentrates on giving students very specific criteria for making buying decisions.

The first chapter spells out basic nutritional needs. Students learn about how important the correct amount and balance of nutrients is to good health. Eating disorders, such as anorexia and bulimia, are also discussed.

The next chapter surveys all the various types and sources of consumer information from labeling of food products to government grading. How to choose and care for food products is also covered.

In the final chapter, students learn about purchasing drugs and cosmetics. General precautions for the use of over-the-counter as well as prescription drugs are covered.

Unit Outline

Chapter 27: Fundamentals of Good Nutrition

A. The Importance of Good Nutrition
  1. Key Nutrients
    a. Protein
    b. Carbohydrates
    c. Fats
    d. Vitamins and Minerals
    e. Water
B. Common Deficiencies in Teens
    a. Calcium
    b. Iron
C. Planning a Healthy Diet
  1. Dietary Guidelines
D. Eating Disorders and Substance Abuse
  1. Anorexia, Bulimia, and Obesity
  2. Anabolic Steroids

Chapter 28: Smart Shopping Techniques

A. Getting the Most for Your Time and Money
B. Going to Market
  1. Your Shopping Strategy List
C. Planning Your Purchases
D. Using Consumer Information
  1. Food Labels
  2. Grade Labels
  3. Brand Labels
  4. Generics
  5. Freshness Dates
  6. Unit Pricing
E. Making Food Choices
  1. Grain Products
  2. Fruits and Vegetables
  3. Meat, Poultry, Fish, and Eggs
    a. Meat
    b. Poultry
    c. Fish
    d. Eggs
  4. Dairy Products
  5. Eating Out
F. Taking Care of Your Purchases
  1. Food Storage and Handling

G. Tackling Food Buying Problems
  1. High Prices
  2. Impulse Buying

Chapter 29:
Drugs and Cosmetics

A. Distinguishing Drugs and Cosmetics
B. Purchasing Medicines
  1. Prescription Drugs
  2. Over-the-Counter Drugs
    a. Painkillers
    b. Acne Medications
    c. Tampering
C. Purchasing Cosmetics
  1. Skin and Hair Care Products
  2. Cosmetic Safety
D. Purchasing Cosmetics That Are Considered Drugs
  1. Skin Protection Products

Introduction

1. *Attitude Inventory.* Before beginning the unit, have the class do the Unit 9 Attitude Inventory. Remind the students to retain their answers for periodic reevaluation.
2. *Motivation.* This unit deals with some of the most common purchases consumers make—food, drugs, and cosmetics. This topic should be one of the more interesting ones for the students. Not only is the content familiar and easy to understand, but it also abounds with controversies that are within the students' experience.
   - **a.** How early does heart disease start? (Medical studies have now documented arterial plaque in teens and young adults. The culprit, researchers say, is the American diet, heavy in protein and laden with fat.)
   - **b.** How good is USDA Choice beef? (After the restructuring of USDA standards, Choice beef is *only* good—that is, the new Choice grade is the equivalent of the old Good grade, a fact that many consumer advocates say makes the system misleading.)
   - **c.** Can a mouthwash really fight plaque buildup on teeth? (Consumers are being bombarded with ads that make this claim, but the FDA is asking for proof.)

Evaluation

Administer the Unit 9 Test in the Assessment Binder.

Unit Closure

Have students imagine that they are in charge of shopping for food, drugs, and cosmetics for themselves for one week. For each category, have students list items they would buy and questions they would ask about products they intend to purchase.

CHAPTER 27: FUNDAMENTALS OF GOOD NUTRITION

Objectives

1. Describe the contributions of important nutrients to good health.
2. Identify common nutrient deficiencies found in teens and suggest ways to prevent them.
3. Name the five food groups in the Food Guide Pyramid and the recommended daily servings for each group.
4. List the U.S. Dietary Guidelines.
5. Identify eating and exercise disorders and their causes.

Teacher's Classroom Resources

Student Activity Workbook
Transparency Binder
Assessment Binder
Lesson Plans

Print, Media, and Internet Resource Handbook
Hands-on Projects for Consumer Education and Economics
Cooperative Learning Activities
Math Practice for Economics
Meeting the Special Needs of Students
Leadership and Citizenship

Focus

1. *Attitude Inventory.* Have students consult their working copies of the Attitude Inventory. Call special attention to items related to Chapter 27. Have the students discuss their answers, encouraging individuals to qualify or rephrase those statements with which they disagree or about which they are undecided. Use this information to choose in-class reading, discussion topics, and follow-up assignments.
2. *Vocabulary.* Preview the Consumer Terms. Have students study the definitions given. Ask students to provide examples or suggest contexts in which they have heard the terms used. *Examples:*
   a. Bran is a frequently mentioned source of *fiber.*
   b. *RDAs* can be found on the side panels of most cereal boxes.

Teach

For purposes of classroom presentation, this chapter may be broken into three parts: (1) nutrients, (2) food groups, and (3) eating disorders.

1. To ensure that the students grasp all the information in Figure 27–1 on nutrients and 27–2 on food groups, these figures should be read carefully and discussed at length. Conduct a class discussion using transparencies as guides. Ask a series of questions similar to these.
   a. How many vitamins are included in the figure? (Four or six are included, depending on how you count vitamin B.)
   b. Is water a vitamin or a mineral? (It is neither. Water is a carrying agent for both and hence in a category by itself.)
   c. Categorize the following as protein, carbohydrate, or fat: corn oil (fat), water-packed tuna (protein), cottage cheese (protein), pancake syrup (carbohydrate), skim milk (protein), sweet potato (carbohydrate), chicken (protein).
   d. What function do proteins, carbohydrates, and fats have in common? (All supply energy.)
   e. Name the vitamin or mineral associated with each of the following: production of hemoglobin (iron), strong bones and teeth (calcium and vitamins C and D), night vision (vitamin A), a healthy thyroid gland (iodine).
2. To encourage students to take seriously the recommendation to follow a low-fat diet, try this demonstration. You will need one or two student volunteers, a small can of vegetable shortening, a set of measuring spoons, a knife, and a dinner plate. Read off the items in the menus below and have the class speculate on the amount of fat each contains. As you verify or correct each estimate, have a student measure out the proper amount of shortening and place it on the plate. By the time you finish the list, the pile of fat will be quite impressive. Remind the students that it represents just one day's consumption. (The menus total about 3,000 calories, 40 percent of which comes from fat—even though an effort has been made to limit animal fats and cholesterol.)

Menu Item	Fat (In teaspoons)
Breakfast	
2/3 c. granola with	2
1/2 c. low-fat milk	1/2
4 oz. orange juice	—
Snack	
Doughnut	2
Coffee with creamer	1/4
Lunch	
Tuna sandwich (2 oz.	2
water-packed tuna,	1/4
1 tbsp. mayonnaise)	2
1 oz. "natural" potato chips	2 1/2
Banana	—
Tea	—
Snack	
6 crackers	1
1 1/2 oz. cheddar	3
12 oz. diet soda	—
Dinner	
2 pieces chicken (no skin), crumb-coated	1
1 c. broccoli with	
1 tsp. margarine	1
1 c. fried potato "nuggets"	3
1 slice bread with	
1 tsp. margarine	2
Green salad with	
1 tbsp. French dressing	1
1/2 c. ice cream	1 3/4
3 sandwich cookies	1
Tea	—
Snack	
Bagel	1
4 tbsp. peanut butter	2 1/2
1 c. low-fat milk	1

2. Ask students to bring in magazine pictures of movie stars, music stars, models, and other prominent media figures. Ask students about the impact of these figures as role models for physical attractiveness. Is it possible for everyone to achieve the physiques and looks that media personalities have? How would they advise other students who consider themselves too heavy or too scrawny? How can individuals maintain their self-esteem and self-confidence when confronted with these images?

Assess

Comprehension and Review

- Chapter Highlights
- Reviewing Consumer Terms and Reviewing Facts and Ideas

End-of-Chapter Applications

- Problem Solving and Decision Making
- Building Academic Skills—Consumers Around the World
- Student Activity Workbook activities for this chapter

Chapter Extension

- Beyond the Classroom—Consumer Project
- Cooperative Learning—Family Economics
- Cooperative Learning—Debate the Issue

Evaluation

- Administer the test for Chapter 27 in the Assessment Binder.

Close

Create a poster that illustrates good nutrition and sound menu choices that students can use.

CHAPTER 28: SMART SHOPPING TECHNIQUES

Objectives

1. Choose the right store for your needs.
2. Develop an effective food-shopping plan.
3. Understand the information on food labels.
4. Make sound choices in terms of quality and price.

5. Store foods properly.
6. Fight off the urge to buy impulsively.

Teacher's Classroom Resources

Student Activity Workbook
Transparency Binder
Assessment Binder
Lesson Plans
Print, Media, and Internet Resource Handbook
Hands-on Projects for Consumer Education and Economics
Cooperative Learning Activities
Math Practice for Economics
Meeting the Special Needs of Students
Leadership and Citizenship

Focus

1. *Attitude Inventory.* Have students consult their working copies of the Attitude Inventory. Call special attention to items related to Chapter 28. Have the students discuss their answers, encouraging individuals to qualify or rephrase those statements with which they disagree or about which they are undecided. Use this information to choose in-class reading, discussion topics, and follow-up assignments.
2. *Vocabulary.* Preview the Consumer Terms. Have students study the definitions given. Write each term on a slip of paper. Divide the class into two teams. Give one slip to someone in the first team. Ask that person to go to the chalkboard and *draw* clues to the term. The people from his or her team have 30 seconds to guess the term. If they fail, the other team may guess using those clues and others drawn by one of their own teammates. Whichever team wins gets to try the next term on a slip of paper, and so on. Keep score, giving five points for each term guessed correctly.

Teach

For purposes of classroom presentation, this chapter may be broken into two parts: (1) using consumer information and (2) making food choices.

1. Help students learn to read package labels by acquainting them with the special meanings of different terms and codes. Obtain literature on food terminology from a local consumer agency or the FDA. As examples, in class, use a number of products labeled "diet." (If possible, try to find different brands of similar items.) Ask students to determine if the calorie counts are about the same or quite different. Ask:
   a. Do "reduced calories" and "low calorie" mean the same thing?
   b. What criteria determine if a product can be labeled "diet"?
2. Products not open-dated usually have special codes that tell when and where the item was packed. Show students what such codes mean by obtaining items manufactured by Coca-Cola or Pillsbury. Those codes can be read as follows:
   a. *Coca-Cola (a four-number code).* The first digit represents the year; the others represent the day. For example, 6072 means "packed on March 13, 1996." The 6 stands for "1996"; the 72 means "the 72nd day."
   b. *Pillsbury (a four-part mark).* A letter represents the month; a number, the year; a letter, the packing plant; and another number, the day. Months are identified by letters A through L. Thus F5X16 would mean "June 16, 1995, at Plant X."
3. Bring to class at least two each of different kinds of produce. Include such things as potatoes, pears or peaches, avocadoes, and lettuce. One from each pair should be of poorer quality.

Show students what to look for when purchasing these items. The same might be done for eggs that are fresh and eggs that are out of date. These should be broken and their appearance (height and placement of yolk and firmness of white) noted.

Assess

Comprehension and Review

- Chapter Highlights
- Reviewing Consumer Terms and Reviewing Facts and Ideas

End-of-Chapter Applications

- Problem Solving and Decision Making
- Building Academic Skills—Consumers Around the World
- Student Activity Workbook activities for this chapter

Chapter Extension

- Beyond the Classroom—Consumer Project
- Cooperative Learning—Family Economics
- Cooperative Learning—Debate the Issue

Evaluation

- Administer the test for Chapter 28 in the Assessment Binder.

Close

Tell students to draw up a list of ten items that they might consume in a week. Then have students shop for the items, noting nutrient content, freshness, and price of each. Students should report how they decided which items would be the best buys.

CHAPTER 29: DRUGS AND COSMETICS

Objectives

1. Distinguish between drugs and cosmetics.
2. Ask questions to ensure the safe and effective use of prescription and over-the-counter drugs.
3. Summarize the risks and the benefits involved in using various over-the-counter drugs.
4. Describe devices commonly used to prevent product tampering.
5. Explain the proper selection and use of common cosmetics.
6. Identify characteristics of skin protection products.

Teacher's Classroom Resources

Student Activity Workbook
Transparency Binder
Assessment Binder
Lesson Plans
Print, Media, and Internet Resource Handbook
Hands-on Projects for Consumer Education and Economics
Cooperative Learning Activities
Math Practice for Economics
Meeting the Special Needs of Students
Leadership and Citizenship

Focus

1. *Attitude Inventory.* Have students consult their working copies of the Attitude Inventory. Call special attention to items related to Chapter 29. Have the students discuss their answers, encouraging individuals to qualify or rephrase those statements with which they disagree or about which they are undecided. Use this information to guide the choice of in-class reading, discussion topics, and follow-up assignments.
2. *Vocabulary.* Preview the Consumer Terms. Have students study the definitions given. Have students write a one-minute radio commercial for SaverCity Drugstore using all the terms in the list.

Teach

For purposes of classroom presentation, this chapter may be broken into two parts: (1) purchasing medicines and (2) purchasing cosmetics.

1. Invite a licensed pharmacist to speak to the class about purchasing medicines. In advance provide the guest speaker with a list of topics to cover. These might include the following:
   a. Generic drugs, their cost and comparability to other brand-name equivalents.
   b. Dangers of mixing medications.
   c. New trends in tamper-resistant packaging.
   d. The pharmacist's role in consumer safety.
2. Some people feel that cosmetics do more harm than good to a person's skin and hair; that they hide natural beauty and play on a person's insecurities about his or her appearance. Others believe cosmetics are harmless, part of the human need to decorate, and psychologically uplifting. Ask students to write a paragraph beginning as follows: "Cosmetics, fragrances, deodorants, and other items used for personal enhancement are/are not a waste of money because. ..." Invite individual students to read their paragraphs aloud as the starting point for a classroom discussion.
3. Ask students to be cosmetic detectives. For extra credit, they may take a lipstick, mascara, and blusher to a pharmacist and ask to have the list of ingredients translated. What are these items made of? They should report their findings to the class.
4. Ask students what they believe it means to be well-groomed. As students name items (such as taking a shower daily, brushing teeth), write these on the chalkboard. Discuss whether the items named promote health, attractiveness, or social acceptability.

Assess

Comprehension and Review
- Chapter Highlights
- Reviewing Consumer Terms *and* Reviewing Facts and Ideas
- Rechecking Your Attitude

End-of-Chapter Applications
- Problem Solving and Decision Making
- Building Academic Skills—Consumers Around the World
- Student Activity Workbook activities for this chapter

Chapter Extension
- Beyond the Classroom—Consumer Project
- Cooperative Learning—Family Economics
- Cooperative Learning—Debate the Issue
- Unit Lab: You and Your Community

Evaluation
- Administer the test for Chapter 29 in the Assessment Binder.

Close

Have students imagine they and several friends are going on a weekend trip sponsored by a youth group. They have been asked to purchase the necessary drugstore items for the group. Tell students to make a list of items and comparison shop at two stores to get the best prices. Students should write down the prices and quantities for all items.

UNIT 10 SELECTING HOUSING

Overview

This unit discusses the largest single expenditure most consumers will ever make—buying a home. About 65 percent of families in the United States choose to buy their own homes. Young families often purchase mobile homes.

Others rent. This unit covers the most important considerations in each situation, including advantages and disadvantages as well as costs and specific criteria for making decisions.

The first chapter discusses renting an apartment. It provides students with procedures for both determining the kind of apartment they need and evaluating the possibilities they find.

The next chapter distinguishes manufactured from regular housing and explores the effect this distinction has on financing and living arrangements. It also covers the buying of site-built housing, describing the experiences of one family, the Haegers, as they go through the process of buying a house, from contacting a real estate agent right through to payment of closing costs.

The final chapter in this unit provides students with basic information about buying furniture and appliances, with a special analysis on comparison shopping.

Unit Outline

Chapter 30: Renting an Apartment

A. Why Rent?
B. Defining Your Housing Needs and Budget
  1. Location
  2. Space
  3. Furnishings
  4. Budget
C. Selecting an Apartment
  1. Locating Units
  2. Inspecting an Apartment
D. Signing the Lease
  1. Terms of the Lease
    a. Tenant's Rights
    b. Tenant's Responsibilities
    c. Landlord's Responsibilities
  2. Resolving Problems
E. Moving

Chapter 31: Buying a House

A. Advantages of Home Ownership
  1. Choosing Among Options
  2. Federal Requirements
B. Financing a Home
  1. Fixed-Rate Mortgages
  2. Variable-Rate Mortgages
  3. Other Types of Loans
  4. Past and Future Trends
C. Purchasing a Home
  1. Choosing a Neighborhood
  2. Contacting a Real Estate Agent
  3. Inspecting Homes
  4. Getting an Expert Opinion
  5. Making an Offer
  6. Locating Financing
  7. Monthly Payments and the Escrow Account
  8. Hiring an Attorney
  9. Closing the Deal
    a. Settlement Costs
    b. Key Documents

Chapter 32: Furnishing a Home

A. When It's Time to Buy
B. Selecting Furniture
  1. Laying Your Plans
  2. Shopping For Case Goods
  3. Choosing Upholstered Furniture
  4. Buying Bedding
C. Selecting Appliances
  1. Do Your Research
  2. Comparison Shopping
  3. Warranties and Service Contracts
  4. Energy Efficiency
  5. Keeping Records

Introduction

1. *Attitude Inventory.* Before beginning the unit, have the class do the Unit 10 Attitude Inventory. Remind the students to retain their answers for periodic reevaluation.

2. *Motivation.* Apartments may be of the most immediate interest because most young people rent first. However, if they have the desire to own a home eventually, students will be wise to begin thinking about it now. To stimulate interest in the unit, have students think about their housing needs and their housing wants. Remind them that the two are not the same thing. Indeed, in some parts of the country (mainly the Northeast and Southwest), rising prices have put the average single-family dwelling well beyond the reach of 80 percent of first-time home buyers. This is a reality that many students must be prepared to face. They must know what their options are.
3. *Motivation.* Write the various housing categories on the chalkboard. Ask students what kind of housing they want after they have been on their own for a while. Keep a tally of how many prefer each category. Then ask why they have that preference. Write the reasons on the board and keep a tally of them as well. Use these tallies to guide your choice of discussion topics.
4. *Motivation.* Have students draw note cards with housing and furnishing choices written on them. Divide the class into small groups to discuss who might make each choice and why. Some possibilities are:
   a. Studio apartment, furnished
   b. One-bedroom apartment
   c. Two-bedroom duplex
   d. Two-bedroom apartment in a high rise
   e. Manufactured home, small single-wide
   f. Manufactured home, large triple-wide
   g. Ready-built home
   h. Custom-built home
   i. Second-hand furniture received from friends and relatives
   j. Selected pieces of quality furniture mixed with garage sale items
   k. New furniture in a coordinated decorating style
   l. Small appliances (toaster, microwave)
   m. Refrigerator with behind-the-door freezer
   n. Large refrigerator-freezer
   o. Small, stackable, environmentally friendly washer and dryer

Evaluation

Administer the Unit 10 Test in the Assessment Binder.

Unit Closure

Tell students to imagine they are real estate agents helping a new family in the area find suitable housing that will fit their lifestyle, furnishings they already own, and some major pieces they are planning to purchase. Have students develop a checklist of questions to ask them that will help determine their needs and suggest wise housing and furnishing choices.

CHAPTER 30: RENTING AN APARTMENT

Objectives

1. Give the advantages of renting, rather than buying, housing.
2. Describe the factors to consider when deciding on your housing needs and budget.
3. Explain how to find and inspect a suitable apartment.
4. Describe the contents of a lease and the basic rights and responsibilities of tenants and landlords.
5. List ways to make moving into your apartment go smoothly.

Teacher's Classroom Resources

Student Activity Workbook
Transparency Binder
Assessment Binder
Lesson Plans
Print, Media, and Internet Resource Handbook
Capstone Projects
Cooperative Learning Activities
Math Practice for Consumer Education
Meeting the Special Needs of Students
Leadership and Citizenship

Focus

1. *Attitude Inventory.* Have students consult their working copies of the Attitude Inventory. Call special attention to items related to Chapter 30. Have the students discuss their answers, encouraging individuals to qualify or rephrase those statements with which they disagree or about which they are undecided. Use this information to guide the choice of in-class reading, discussion topics, and follow-up assignments.
2. *Vocabulary.* Preview the Consumer Terms. Have students study the definitions given. Ask students to construct a one-paragraph story that contains all the terms.

Teach

For purposes of classroom presentation, this chapter may be broken into three parts: (1) defining your needs and locating a suitable unit, (2) inspecting an apartment and evaluating a lease, and (3) moving.

1. Many apartment building complexes have copies of floor plans and other information about units available for the asking. Obtain copies from two or three, and make photocopies for the class. Ask students to compare the complexes based on rent per month, square footage, location, and so forth.
2. Locate a copy of a standard apartment lease, and either make photocopies or use the overhead projector for viewing. (If you can't obtain a lease from a local apartment, you can purchase a form lease from a local stationery store.) To review the document with the class, have students compose questions based on the material under "Terms of the Lease" in the chapter. Help students to paraphrase any clauses written in legalese.

Assess

Comprehension and Review

- Chapter Highlights
- Reviewing Consumer Terms *and* Reviewing Facts and Ideas

End-of-Chapter Applications

- Problem Solving and Decision Making
- Building Academic Skills—Consumers Around the World
- Student Activity Workbook activities for this chapter

Chapter Extension

- Beyond the Classroom—Consumer Project
- Cooperative Learning—Family Economics
- Cooperative Learning—Debate the Issue

Evaluation

- Administer the test for Chapter 30 in the Assessment Binder.

Close

Have each student prepare a layout and description of the ideal apartment for either a college student or a young person in his or her first job.

CHAPTER 31: BUYING A HOUSE

Objectives

1. List the advantages of home ownership.
2. Describe the usual costs and procedures in buying a home.
3. Distinguish between fixed-rate and variable-rate mortgages.
4. Develop a checklist for inspecting a home.

Teacher's Classroom Resources

Student Activity Workbook
Transparency Binder
Assessment Binder
Lesson Plans
Print, Media, and Internet Resource Handbook
Capstone Projects
Cooperative Learning Activities
Math Practice for Consumer Education
Meeting the Special Needs of Students
Leadership and Citizenship

Focus

1. *Attitude Inventory.* Have students consult their working copies of the Attitude Inventory. Call special attention to items related to Chapter 31. Have the students discuss their answers, encouraging individuals to qualify or rephrase those statements with which they disagree or about which they are undecided. Use this information to guide the choice of in-class reading, discussion topics, and follow-up assignments.
2. *Vocabulary.* Preview the Consumer Terms. Have students study the definitions given. From mobile home dealers, obtain pamphlets that contain the terms. Ask students to read the pamphlets and find the terms used. The terms related to homes fall into three main categories—Documents, Costs, and Types of Housing. Write these three headings on the chalkboard, and ask students to place each term in the proper category.

Teach

For purposes of classroom presentation, this chapter may be broken into three parts: (1) advantages of home ownership, (2) financing a home, (3) purchasing a home.

1. After the class has read about mobile homes, ask students to write a paragraph completing this sentence: "A mobile home would/would not be right for me because———." When the class is finished, discuss the responses, asking students to remember the poll taken at the beginning of this unit. How do the responses compare?
2. Invite a building contractor or an architect to speak to the class about what to look for when evaluating new and used houses. Ask the guest speaker to be prepared to cover a list of specific topics like these:
   a. Floor plans—advantages and disadvantages of different kinds.
   b. Structural features—what clues such as cracks in plaster may mean.
   c. What flaws furnishings can hide.
   d. The insulation best suited to the local climate.
4. The class will have already studied the units on money management and credit. Ask them what they think they would need in order to secure a mortgage. Their answers should include the following:
   a. Acceptable credit history
   b. Cash for a down payment and closing costs
   c. Enough income to meet monthly payments

d. Enough income to maintain and operate the home

Ask what steps a person could take in advance to help insure that all criteria can be met when it comes time to buy a house.

5. Ask students to think about what factors are important to them in a neighborhood and then to make a checklist of those points that they might use when shopping for a home.
6. Most students probably have never seen many of the documents mentioned in this chapter, and the documents may seem rather remote and forbidding to them. If possible, obtain copies of a deed, a mortgage form, an abstract, and so on. Either post them on a bulletin board or pass them around for class inspection. Be prepared to answer questions about details.

Assess

Comprehension and Review

- Chapter Highlights
- Reviewing Consumer Terms *and* Reviewing Facts and Ideas

End-of-Chapter Applications

- Problem Solving and Decision Making
- Building Academic Skills—Consumers Around the World
- Student Activity Workbook activities for this chapter

Chapter Extension

- Beyond the Classroom—Consumer Project
- Cooperative Learning—Family Economics
- Cooperative Learning—Debate the Issue

Evaluation

- Administer the test for Chapter 31 in the Assessment Binder.

Close

Have students write a newspaper article entitled "Getting Ready to Buy a Home." They should include information on how to evaluate housing purchases.

CHAPTER 32: FURNISHING A HOME

Objectives

1. Make a plan for furnishing a home.
2. Examine furniture for solid construction and quality workmanship.
3. Locate information to aid in comparison shopping for appliances.
4. Differentiate between written warranties, and implied warranties, and service contracts.
5. Identify types of records and their importance when purchasing appliances.

Teacher's Classroom Resources

Student Activity Workbook
Transparency Binder
Assessment Binder
Lesson Plans
Print, Media, and Internet Resource Handbook
Hands-on Project for Consumer Education and Economics
Cooperative Learning Activities
Math Practice for Economics
Meeting the Special Needs of Students
Leadership and Citizenship

Focus

1. *Attitude Inventory.* Have students consult their working copies of the Attitude Inventory. Call special attention to items related to Chapter 32. Have the students discuss their answers, encouraging individuals to qualify or rephrase those statements with which they disagree or about which they are undecided. Use this information to guide the choice of in-class reading, discussion topics, and follow-up assignments.
2. *Vocabulary.* Preview the Consumer Terms. Have students study the defi-

nitions given. Ask the students questions whose answers turn on an understanding of the term or terms used. *Examples:*

a. How does *hardwood* differ from *softwood?*

b. What is the difference between an *implied warranty* and a written warranty?

c. How does an *EnergyGuide* differ from a price tag?

Teach

For purposes of classroom presentation, this chapter may be broken into two parts: (1) selecting furniture and (2) buying appliances.

1. Bring to class the following items:

a. A small piece of upholstered furniture, such as a dining room chair or a sofa cushion with the tag listing its contents.

b. A small wooden table or chest containing a drawer.
Divide the class into two groups. Ask each group to evaluate their item by describing the type of construction and how sturdy, easy to use, and comfortable the piece is. Caution students to concentrate on basic attributes for this part of the exercise. Then have each group decide how their example might fit into a total decorating plan.

2. Bring a small appliance, such as a toaster, to class along with its warranty and owner's manual. Allow the class to evaluate the item first by examining it and its operating instructions. Then have students study the warranty to determine if it seems fair and reasonable (applicable to what might go wrong).

Assess

Comprehension and Review

- Chapter Highlights
- Reviewing Consumer Terms and Reviewing Facts and Ideas
- Rechecking Your Attitude

End-of-Chapter Applications

- Problem Solving and Decision Making
- Building Academic Skills—Consumers Around the World
- Student Activity Workbook activities for this chapter

Chapter Extension

- Beyond the Classroom—Consumer Project
- Cooperative Learning—Family Economics
- Cooperative Learning—Debate the Issue
- Unit Lab: You and Your Community

Evaluation

- Administer the test for Chapter 32 in the Assessment Binder.

Close

Tell students to imagine they have just started at their first job and plan to move into a studio apartment. The only items they are taking with them are clothes and personal belongings, CD player, books, and computer. Students should make a list of items they want and need to buy. For each item, have students list questions to ask while shopping. Finally, students should create a plan for making their purchases—saving, buying on credit, and so forth.

UNIT 11 USING PROFESSIONAL SERVICES

Overview

This unit covers subjects that can be intimidating to both young people and adults alike—medical, dental, and legal services. Because these professions boast specialized knowledge that seems to grow more complex with each passing year, consumers often feel inadequate to deal with them. An effort is made in this unit to take some of the mystery out of using professional services and to put more control in the hands of the consumer.

The first chapter focuses on medical and dental services. Students learn about the importance of preventive medicine. How to choose a doctor and how to handle health care costs are also covered.

In the second chapter, students learn about legal services. How to choose an attorney and reasons for rising legal costs are among the topics discussed.

Unit Outline

Chapter 33: Medical and Dental Services

A. Practicing Preventive Medicine
- **1.** Keep Healthy
- **2.** Prevent Dental Problems
- **3.** Learn First Aid Techniques
- **4.** Plan to Use Prenatal Care

B. Medical and Dental Care
- **1.** Choosing a Doctor
- **2.** Evaluating a New Doctor
- **3.** Emergency Care

C. Health Care Costs
- **1.** Consumer Options
  - **a.** Doctors' Fees
  - **b.** Hospital Charges
  - **c.** Hospital Accreditation

Chapter 34: Legal Services

A. Legal Services
- **1.** Choosing an Attorney
- **2.** Financing Legal Services
  - **a.** Fees

B. Issues in the Field of Law
- **1.** Ethics and Competence
- **2.** Handling Legal Fees
  - **a** Low-Cost Alternatives

Introduction

1. *Attitude Inventory.* Before beginning the unit, have the class do the Unit 11 Attitude Inventory. Remind the students to retain their answers for periodic reevaluation.

2. *Motivation.* U.S. consumers spend billions every year for professional services. Although most students may not have had contact with the legal profession, all will probably have had experience with doctors and dentists. Occasionally, the experience may have involved a life or death situation. Yet few people choose professional services with the same care they use to choose a television set or a new car. People often do not look for a doctor or lawyer until they are ill or in trouble, when desperation may cloud their judgment. Once they have found someone, they allow the jargon or authoritative manner of the professional to awe or confuse them. For these and other reasons, people frequently feel incapable of setting standards in this area. Discuss these points with the class. Ask the following questions:

- **a.** How did you get your family doctor, dentist, or attorney?
- **b.** How do you feel in the presence of professional people—uncertain? ill-informed? willing to accept whatever they tell you without question?
- **c.** How would you protect yourself against professionals who are unethical or incompetent?

Evaluation

Administer the Unit 11 Test in the Assessment Binder.

Unit Closure

Tell students to write and design a brochure informing new residents to their area how to go about finding medical, dental, and legal services.

CHAPTER 33: MEDICAL AND DENTAL SERVICES

Objectives

1. Explain the importance of preventive medicine.

2. Outline a plan for choosing a doctor and a dentist.
3. Explain options consumers have for handling health care costs.

Teacher's Classroom Resources

Student Activity Workbook
Transparency Binder
Assessment Binder
Lesson Plans
Print, Media, and Internet Resource Handbook
Hands-on Projects for Consumer Education and Economics
Cooperative Learning Activities
Math Practice for Economics
Meeting the Special Needs of Students
Leadership and Citizenship

Focus

1. *Attitude Inventory.* Have students consult their working copies of the Attitude Inventory. Call special attention to items related to Chapter 33. Have the students discuss their answers, encouraging individuals to qualify or rephrase those statements with which they disagree or about which they are undecided. Use this information to guide the choice of in-class reading, discussion topics, and follow-up assignments.
2. *Vocabulary.* Preview the Consumer Terms. Have students study the definitions given. Ask students to write, for each word, a sentence that a health care client might use. *Example:*
   a. How will *prenatal care* help my baby?

Teach

For purposes of classroom presentation, this chapter may be broken into two parts: (1) preventive medicine and (2) choosing and paying for health care professionals.

1. Ask students to make a list of five *specific* ways they can improve their own practice of preventive medicine. For example, instead of writing "Get more exercise," they should write "Take a one-mile walk after dinner."
2. Ask students whether they are interested in a career in the field of health care. Have students research different jobs—doctor, nurse, medical technician—and present a two-minute oral report to the class. How do students feel they would act as medical professionals in order to do the best for their clients?

Assess

Comprehension and Review
- Chapter Highlights
- Reviewing Consumer Terms *and* Reviewing Facts and Ideas

End-of-Chapter Applications
- Problem Solving and Decision Making
- Building Academic Skills—Consumers Around the World
- Student Activity Workbook activities for this chapter

Chapter Extension
- Beyond the Classroom—Consumer Project
- Cooperative Learning—Family Economics
- Cooperative Learning—Debate the Issue

Evaluation
- Administer the test for Chapter 33 in the Assessment Binder.

Close

Tell students that as young adults living on their own, they are responsible for their own health. Have them outline a plan to maintain their health and well-being through preventive medicine and use of medical services.

CHAPTER 34: LEGAL SERVICES

Objectives

1. Outline a plan for choosing an attorney.
2. Explain the role ethics plays in the field of law.
3. List ways of reducing legal costs.

Teacher's Classroom Resources

Student Activity Workbook
Transparency Binder
Assessment Binder
Lesson Plans
Print, Media, and Internet Resource Handbook
Hands-on Projects for Consumer Education and Economics
Cooperative Learning Activities
Math Practice for Economics
Meeting the Special Needs of Students
Leadership and Citizenship

Focus

1. *Attitude Inventory.* Have students consult their working copies of the Attitude Inventory. Call special attention to items related to Chapter 34. Have the students discuss their answers, encouraging individuals to qualify or rephrase those statements with which they disagree or about which they are undecided. Use this information to guide the choice of in-class reading, discussion topics, and follow-up assignments.
2. *Vocabulary.* Preview the Consumer Terms. Have students study the definitions given. Ask students to write a short conversation between two people using all the terms on the list. They might imagine the conversation to be between two lawyers, two consumers, a lawyer and client, or the characters in a soap opera, for example.

Teach

For purposes of classroom presentation, this chapter may be broken into two parts: (1) choosing an attorney and (2) financing legal services.

1. Invite a member of the legal profession to talk to the class about choosing and using an attorney. Provide the guest speaker in advance with a list of subjects to cover. These might include the following:
   a. Attorneys who advertise their services on television.
   b. How profitable a case must be to make it worth pursuing in court.
   c. Whether a person should depend on the same attorney for all legal needs.
2. Television has influenced our attitudes toward many things, including the legal profession. Lead a class discussion on how television lawyers differ from real lawyers. Bring out student perceptions by asking questions like the following:
   a. Are television lawyers more or less ethical than real lawyers?
   b. Television lawyers seem to do a lot of work for free. Are real-life lawyers more or less charitable with their services? Why do you think this is so?

Assess

Comprehension and Review

- Chapter Highlights
- Reviewing Consumer Terms *and* Reviewing Facts and Ideas
- Rechecking Your Attitude

End-of-Chapter Applications

- Problem Solving and Decision Making
- Building Academic Skills—Consumers Around the World

- Student Activity Workbook activities for this chapter

Chapter Extension

- Beyond the Classroom—Consumer Project
- Cooperative Learning—Family Economics
- Cooperative Learning—Debate the Issue
- Unit Lab: You and Your Community

Evaluation

- Administer the test for Chapter 34 in the Assessment Binder.

Close

Tell students to think of a situation that requires legal help—buying property, being in a car accident, signing an employment contract, or some other. Have students describe how they would find the help they need and how they would pay for it.

UNIT 12 SOCIAL RESPONSIBILITY

Overview

This unit addresses societal problems and individual responsibilities. Through many examples, students are shown that social problems are caused by people, end with people as victims, and can only be solved by people acting responsibly.

The first chapter addresses familiar citizen roles at home, at school, and in the community. The responsibilities of consumers and producers as citizens are also covered.

The second chapter covers an area of interest to most teens— the environment. Here, connections are made between the use of scarce resources and environmental problems. Responsible actions are emphasized with the recognition that issues of social balance and incomplete information can cause conflicts.

In both chapters, examples of actions individuals can take to make a difference leads students toward an increased sense of self-esteem and responsibility.

Unit Outline

Chapter 35: Your Role as a Citizen

A. What Is a Citizen?
- **1.** The Big Picture
- **2.** Characteristics of a Good Citizen
- **3.** Community Benefits
- **4.** Individual Benefits

B. Being a Responsible Citizen
- **1.** The Citizen at Home
- **2.** The Citizen at School

C. Good Citizens in the Community
- **1.** Volunteers
- **2.** Respecting the Law
- **3.** Shoplifting and Vandalism
- **4.** The Cost of Crime
- **5.** Taxpayers and Voters

D. Social and Ethical Responsibilities
- **1.** Producers
- **2.** Consumers
- **3.** Activists

E. Becoming Active in Your Community
- **1.** Consider a Leadership Role
- **2.** Leading Every Day

Chapter 36: You and the Environment

A. Protecting Our Natural Resources
- **1.** Kinds of Natural Resources

B. Natural Resource Management Problems

C. Resource Conservation and Environmental Protection
- **1.** Efforts by Government and Business

a. Government Efforts
b. Business Efforts
2. Efforts by Other Groups
3. Balancing the Issues

D. Your Role in Conservation
1. Conserving Energy
2. Conserving Water
3. Reducing Waste and Pollution
a. Reducing Waste
b. Reducing Pollution

Introduction

1. *Attitude Inventory.* Before beginning the unit, have the class do the Unit 12 Attitude Inventory. Remind the students to retain their answers for periodic reevaluation.
2. *Motivation.* Collect pictures and news articles of social problems and examples of individual and group actions that illustrate social responsibility. From these examples, have students develop posters about problems and the actions citizens have taken to resolve those problems. Do any problems seem to have few solutions or solutions that are controversial? If so, ask students what they would suggest? How much would they be willing to do? What would be the easiest thing to do? the hardest? Discuss the concept of commitment.

Evaluation

Administer the Unit 12 Test in the Assessment Binder.

Unit Closure

Tell students to imagine they are help-line volunteers, taking calls relating to a variety of social problems. Students are also on a committee that is concerned with environmental problems. Have students list the various problem areas they feel are most critical and the individual and group actions that could help resolve them.

CHAPTER 35: YOUR ROLE AS A CITIZEN

Objectives

1. List the characteristics of good citizens, and discuss the benefits of good citizenship.
2. Describe how to be a good citizen at home and at school.
3. List the four areas of concern to a good citizen of the community.
4. Summarize the social and ethical responsibilities of consumers and producers.
5. Explain how citizens can take an active role.

Teacher's Classroom Resources

Student Activity Workbook
Transparency Binder
Assessment Binder
Lesson Plans
Print, Media, and Internet Resource Handbook
Hands-on Projects for Consumer Education and Economics
Cooperative Learning Activities
Math Practice for Economics
Meeting the Special Needs of Students
Leadership and Citizenship

Focus

1. *Attitude Inventory.* Have students consult their working copies of the Attitude Inventory. Call special attention to items related to Chapter 35. Have the students discuss their answers, encouraging individuals to qualify or rephrase those statements with which they disagree or about which they are undecided. Use this information to guide the choice of in-class reading,

discussion topics, and follow-up assignments.

2. *Vocabulary.* Preview the Consumer Terms. Have students study the definitions given. Divide the class and the vocabulary words in half, and have each student write definitions of his or her words. Compare definitions and develop a single definition for each term. Pay particular attention to the differences between social responsibilities and ethics; citizenship and leadership.

Teach

For purposes of classroom presentation, this chapter may be broken into two parts: (1) the benefits of citizenship and (2) characteristics and roles of good citizens.

1. Find newspaper articles on how tax dollars are put to work to benefit the local community, the state, and the nation. What other ways can citizens benefit society? Start a loose-leaf notebook. Have students think of a title (for example, "Everyone is a Winner").
2. Divide the class into four groups. Have each group identify characteristics of good citizens from the articles that have been gathered. How were the roles of individuals and groups different? the same? In examples about the use of taxes, did any controversies arise over the proposed use of the dollars? What is the citizen role in these cases?

Assess

Comprehension and Review

- Chapter Highlights
- Reviewing Consumer Terms *and* Reviewing Facts and Ideas

End-of-Chapter Applications

- Problem Solving and Decision Making
- Building Academic Skills—Consumers Around the World
- Student Activity Workbook activities for this chapter

Chapter Extension

- Beyond the Classroom—Consumer Project
- Cooperative Learning—Family Economics
- Cooperative Learning—Debate the Issue

Evaluation

- Administer the test for Chapter 35 in the Assessment Binder.

Close

Have students write a 350- to 500-word paper describing real problems they have read or heard about in each area of citizenship (citizens at home, at school, in the community, as consumers, and as producers). Students should list at least one action they could take as an individual that could help each problem.

CHAPTER 36: YOU AND THE ENVIRONMENT

Objectives

1. Explain the difference between renewable and nonrenewable resources.
2. Summarize major ecological issues related to the use and misuse of resources.
3. Recognize balances and trade-offs necessary in protecting the environment.
4. Summarize efforts by various groups to conserve resources and protect the environment.

5. Identify ways individuals can help conserve resources and protect the environment.

Teacher's Classroom Resources

Student Activity Workbook
Transparency Binder
Assessment Binder
Lesson Plans
Print, Media, and Internet Resource Handbook
Hands-on Projects for Consumer Education and Economics
Cooperative Learning Activities
Math Practice for Economics
Meeting the Special Needs of Students
Leadership and Citizenship

Focus

1. *Attitude Inventory.* Have students consult their working copies of the Attitude Inventory. Call special attention to items related to Chapter 36. Have the students discuss their answers, encouraging individuals to qualify or rephrase those statements with which they disagree or about which they are undecided. Use this information to guide the choice of in-class reading, discussion topics, and follow-up assignments.
2. *Vocabulary.* Preview the Consumer Terms. Have students study the definitions given. Put vocabulary words on slips of paper. Have groups of two or three students take each word and discuss the word with other groups. Try to determine relationships. Draw a web of these relationships on the chalkboard.

Teach

For purposes of classroom presentation, this chapter may be broken into two parts: (1) the status of natural resources and (2) resource conservation and environmental protection, including the role of individuals and groups.

1. Ask students to collect stories that illustrate their view of conservation (for example, use only what is needed) and the environment (for example, human beings must live in harmony with nature). Contrast this with the view of early American settlers and most people in industrialized nations of the world ever since.
2. From several conservation or environmental protection issues, have groups choose one to work on. Ask them to research their issue. Select a name for a citizen's group to address the issue, and then develop designs for T-shirts or other promotional materials that could raise money for the cause. What would be some individual ways to address the same problem?

Assess

Comprehension and Review

- Chapter Highlights
- Reviewing Consumer Terms *and* Reviewing Facts and Ideas
- Rechecking Your Attitude

End-of-Chapter Applications

- Problem Solving and Decision Making
- Building Academic Skills—Consumers Around the World
- Student Activity Workbook activities for this chapter

Chapter Extension

- Beyond the Classroom—Consumer Project
- Cooperative Learning—Family Economics
- Cooperative Learning—Debate the Issue
- Unit Lab: You and Your Community

Evaluation

- Administer the test for Chapter 36 in the Assessment Binder.

Close

Have students give a one-minute speech on environmental issues and conservation techniques. Their speeches should explain the problem, possible solutions, and any conflicting information.

Consumer Education and Economics

Fourth Edition

Ross E. Lowe
Professor Emeritus
Macomb, Illinois

Charles A. Malouf
Social Sciences and Business Education Teacher
John Muir High School
Pasadena, California

Annette R. Jacobson
Educational Consultant
Cottage Grove, Oregon

McGraw-Hill

New York, New York   Columbus, Ohio   Mission Hills, California   Peoria, Illinois

Glencoe/McGraw-Hill

A Division of The ***McGraw-Hill*** *Companies*

Copyright © 1997 by Glencoe/McGraw-Hill. All rights reserved. Except as permitted under the United States Copyright Act of 1976, no part of this publication may be reproduced or distributed in any form or by any means, or stored in a database or retrieval system, without prior written permission of the publisher.

Printed in the United States of America.

Send all inquiries to:
Glencoe/McGraw-Hill
15319 Chatsworth Street
P.O. Box 9609
Mission Hills, CA 91346-9609

ISBN 0-02-637223-1 (Student Text)
ISBN 0-02-637224-X (Teacher's Annotated Edition)

2 3 4 5 6 7 8 9 QPH 01 00 99 98 97

Reviewers

Kimberly Banta
Department Head
Social Studies Department
Simon Kenton High School
Independence, Kentucky

Frances Hare
Home Economics Teacher
North Dallas High School
Dallas, Texas

Judy Weber
Home Economics Teacher
Central High School
Knoxville, Tennessee

Shirley Wilcox
Mentor Teacher
Burbank High School
Burbank, California

Contents

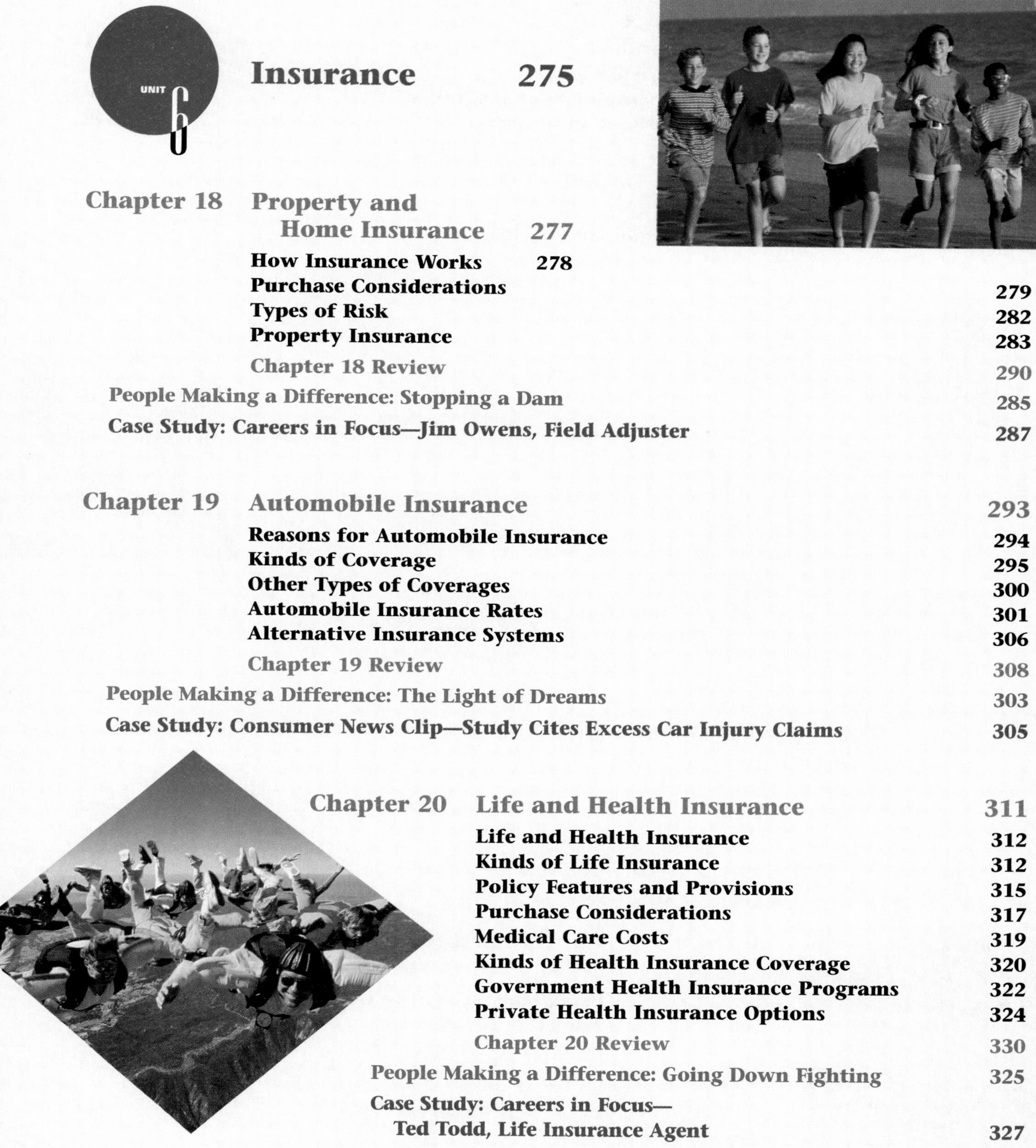

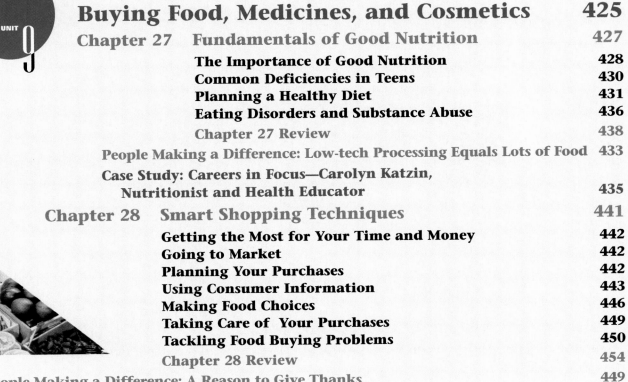

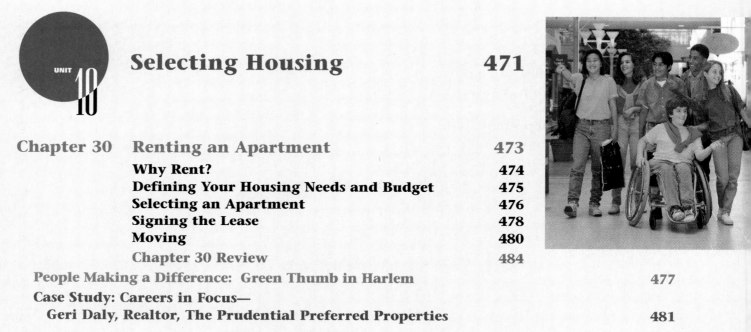

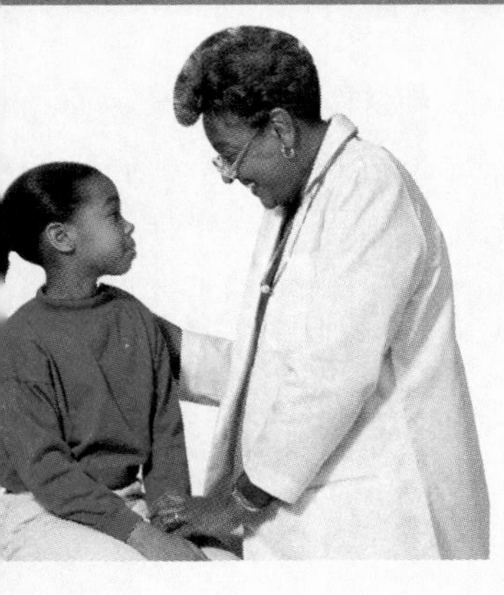

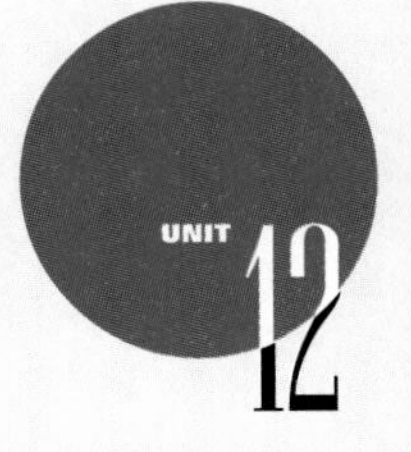

To the Student

THE IMPORTANCE OF CONSUMER EDUCATION

Today, more than ever before, individual and family consumers are faced with certain fundamental questions. How can they keep up with the rising cost of living? What are the basic economic principles that they should apply to spending decisions? How can they cope with the increasing complexity of the marketplace and the goods and services it offers? Perhaps most fundamental of all, how can they distinguish between wise and unwise buying decisions? In order to deal effectively with these questions, today's consumers must be informed.

The major objective of *Consumer Education and Economics* and its supplementary materials is to help you become an informed consumer. To meet its main objective, *Consumer Education and Economics* focuses on the specific consumer issues you will encounter during both your school years and adult life. After studying the text, you should be able to demonstrate an understanding of the following concepts and skills:

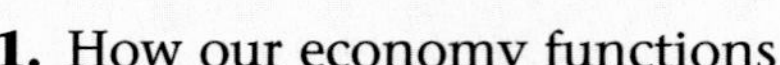

1. How our economy functions
2. How to make purchases wisely
3. How to manage money to best advantage
4. How to evaluate sales and advertising practices
5. How to guard against fraudulent or deceptive sales practices
6. How to be socially responsible

UNIT ORGANIZATION

The text is organized in twelve units. Unit 1 provides the basis for an understanding of the consumer's role in our economy. Unit 2 and 3 deal with money management. Units 4 and 5 discuss the advantages and disadvantages of credit. Unit 6 covers the various types of insurance. Units 7 through 11 examine buying practices and problems related to specific goods and services such as transportation, clothing, food, housing, and health and legal care. Unit 12 discusses social responsiblity, including citizenship and the environment.

Each unit in *Consumer Education and Economics* begins with a unit opener which contains an Attitude Inventory. An Attitude inventory is designed to gauge your perceptions of the subject matter contained in the unit both before and after reading the unit.

CHAPTER ORGANIZATION

The units themselves are divided into two to four chapters. Each chapter begins with a chapter opener. These two pages list the objectives of the chapter and the key consumer terms.

Throughout the text, vocabulary is given special treatment. As in any specialized field, consumer education has developed a terminology peculiarly its own: Universal Product Code, warranty of merchantability, unit pricing. Vocabulary is presented in three steps. First, key terms are introduced and defined at the beginning of each chapter. Second, each term appears in boldface type when it is given its first or principal use in the text. Third, the key terms are used in a vocabulary exercise at the end of each chapter. Each chapter ends with chapter review activities designed to help you review chapter content. The activities include simple content review (*Reviewing Consumer Terms* and *Reviewing Facts and Ideas*), applications (*Problem Solving and Decision Making and Building Academic Skills*), outside research (*Consumer Projects*), and cooperative learning activities (*Family Economics* and *Debate the Issue*). Used together, these exercises provide both immediate and long-term reinforcement of newly introduced material.

CHAPTER FEATURES

Each chapter contains interesting facts and features.

- **"Real World Journal"** is a journal writing exercise found on the chapter opening pages. This activity gives you an opportunity to investigate and record how consumer economics concepts relate to your life.
- **"People Making A Difference"** focuses on people who have made a significant contribution to their community. The feature asks you to brainstorm ways that you can contribute to your community.
- **"Dollars & Sense"** gives short tips on how to budget and save.
- **"The Global Consumer"** tells facts that relate chapter content to consumers in the rest of the world.
- **"Flashback—Flashforward"** provides "Did you know?" type facts about what it was like to be a consumer 25–50 years ago compared with today.
- **"Consumer News Clips"** are consumer news articles from newspapers and magazines such as *The Wall Street Journal* and *Time*.
- **"Careers in Focus"** investigates consumer careers related to the unit.

As you will learn from reading this text, it is easy to be a consumer. It takes education, however, to become a wise consumer. *Consumer Education and Economics* provides you with the essential knowledge and know-how needed for a lifetime of wise consumerism!

Ross E. Lowe
Charles A. Malouf
Annette R. Jacobson

UNIT 1

Unit Contents

You in the Economy

Attitude Inventory

Before you begin Chapter 1, take stock of your attitudes by completing the following inventory. Read each statement and decide how you feel about it—agree, disagree, or undecided. Record your feelings on a sheet of notepaper or use the form in the Student Activity Workbook.

1. Government agencies offer consumers the best protection against dishonest or misleading selling practices.
2. People should not expect government services unless they are willing to pay for them with higher taxes.
3. Good citizens refrain from using public services and instead rely on themselves.
4. For every consumer right, there is a related responsibility.
5. If businesses would just lower their prices, there would be enough goods and services for everyone, and the businesses themselves would prosper.
6. Government should tax imports in order to protect American products and American jobs.
7. People with higher incomes should pay income taxes at higher rates than people with lower incomes.
8. Entrepreneurs are people who get rich at the expense of consumers.
9. A healthy economic system provides people with low prices and high wages.
10. Income taxes should be raised in order to maintain government services and reduce the federal debt.
11. Federal, state, and local governments spend their tax money on very different things.
12. Gifts of money from one person to another should not be subject to taxation.

Unit Goal The main goal of this unit is to introduce students to the concept of consumerism, the consumer's role in our society, how economic systems function in our society and in the world, and the role our government plays. Chapters included in this unit are (1) Consumers and the Economy, (2) Our Market System, (3) Government's Role, and (4) Global Economics.

Lesson Plan See the Teacher's Manual for an overview of the unit and some suggestions for introducing it. If you assign the Attitude Inventory, be sure to tell students to keep their answers for later use.

CHAPTER 1

Consumers and the Economy

Learning Objectives

When you have finished studying this chapter, you should be able to:

1. Describe the three economic roles that most people play throughout their lives.
2. Name five consumer rights and the five consumer responsibilities that go with them.
3. List five federal agencies that are responsible for consumer protection and briefly describe their activities.
4. Identify at least a half dozen people who have been important in shaping the consumer movement.

Consumer Terms

economics
consumer
goods
services
redress
statutes
agencies
consumer action panels
arbitration service
consumer affairs departments

Real-World Journal

After you read Chapter 1, create three columns in your journal with these headings: "Workers," "Consumers," and "Citizens." List your family members under the heading or headings they fit into. Are any of your family members listed under more than one category? Explain why each person listed fits into the group you have selected. Which categories do you fit into?

Lesson Plan See the Teacher's Manual for Chapter 1 lesson plan.

Vocabulary The Chapter 1 lesson plan includes suggested vocabulary activities for the terms listed.

1 Student Motivator Have students list all the noneconomic roles they play.

Caption Answer: Most students are family members. They may also be members of a team, a choir, a band, or a club. They may be a friend, boyfriend or girlfriend, the class athlete, or the class clown. They may want to be a husband, wife, or parent in the future.

OUR ECONOMIC ROLES

William Shakespeare wrote in one of his plays, "All the world's a stage. And all the men and women merely players." As you go through life you will probably find much truth in these words. You will discover that you will play many roles. Maybe you hope to be a rock musician one day. Or a movie director. Or a sports celebrity.

In addition to the roles you hope to play some day, there are some roles in life that you play right now. You are probably a family member—perhaps even a grandchild or a third cousin! You are undoubtedly a good friend, and you may also some day be a husband or wife.

These roles are the identities we have in our emotional lives, where love, anger, happiness, satisfaction, and other feelings have the greatest importance. Money is not very important in our emotional lives.
1 We love our family and friends, whether they spend a lot of money on us or not.

We all also have identities in which money *is* very important. These roles take place in our *economic* lives—the part of our lives concerned with earning, spending, and dealing with money. **Economics** is the study of producing, distributing, and consuming goods and services. In the world of economics, we all have several roles to play.

In this chapter, you will learn about the three economic roles that people play. Also, you'll learn about your rights and responsibilities as a consumer, about the federal agencies responsible for consumer protection, and about important people in the consumer movement.

People play different roles in different situations. ***What are some of the noneconomic roles you play?*** ▼

Economic Roles Defined

The three economic roles are worker, consumer, and citizen. These roles are described in Figure 1–1 on page 6. Most of us have the chance to play all three roles, and all of us certainly play the role of consumer. A **consumer** is someone who uses goods and services. **Goods** are physical objects that are produced; they may
1 be foods or manufactured items. **Services** are actions that are performed for you. For example, a dentist who fills a cavity in your tooth is performing a service. Even babies are consumers, using up diapers and milk as soon as they are born!

You live in a great age for consumers. There are probably more goods produced now than ever before in history. There are televisions, CD players, VCRs, and video cameras; electric guitars, personal computers, mountain bikes, and in-line skates; rain boots, hiking boots, ski boots, and high-heeled boots—and that's just the beginning! For every product you can name, there are several brands and models to choose from.

▲ *Consumer goods are everywhere.* ***What particular goods did you use today?***

Caption Answer: Students may have listened to music CDs or tapes, put on makeup, or written on paper. They have certainly put on clothing and eaten food.

1 Reinforcement Read the following job titles and ask the students to tell whether the worker produces goods or services: police officer (service); doughnut baker (goods); teacher (service); farmer (goods).

2 Critical Thinking Ask students whether they consciously try to get full value for a dollar spent. Have them identify recent occasions during which they did, and did not, get full value for their expenditures.

As a consumer, you are an important member of the economy. One mall store owner told a reporter that 17-year-old shoppers had become as important to her store as the 20 to 25-year-olds. "Some of them come in with a hundred dollars or more to spend," she added. Whether you spend $100 or $5 in a store, your purchases are important to the store owner and to the economy.

CONSUMER RIGHTS AND RESPONSIBILITIES

With all the choice in consumer goods and services, people can sometimes get confused. What really is the best portable tape player? Does this watch have more features than I need? Will I get my money's worth at this particular restaurant? Consumers are confronted by questions like these every day.

2 To make the most of your money, you need to learn to be an intelligent consumer. The goal of this book is to teach you what you need to know as a consumer.

The first point to learn is that as a consumer, you have certain rights: (1) the

1 Critical Thinking Ask students to name additional public services. (National defense, mail service, and libraries are examples.)

2 Discussion Starter Ask students if any of them have had to pay income tax. If so, how do they feel about it? Do they think the services they receive are worth what they pay in income tax?

3 Critical Thinking Most students probably will not have voted or paid taxes. Ask them if they are still considered citizens. (Yes if they were born in this country and their parents are citizens.)

4 Critical Thinking Three common kinds of citizen behavior are listed. Ask students if they can name additional citizen behaviors—serving in the armed forces or national guard for example.

Figure 1–1 Major Economic Roles

Consumer, worker, and citizen are the three major economic roles that most people play.

1
You're a consumer if:
✓ You use goods and services, even if you are not the one who pays for them.
When you eat a meal, listen to a CD, or ride on a bus, you are a consumer.
2
You're a citizen if:
✓ You were born in this country.
✓ Your parents are citizens.
✓ You have been naturalized.
As a citizen, you use public services such as schools and highways; you pay taxes in order to pay for public services; and you have the right and obligation to vote for who will run the country.
3
You're a worker if:
✓ You earn money at any kind of job.
Workers produce goods, which are physical objects such as radios, chocolate chip cookies, and magazines.
Workers perform services, which are activities such as repairing a car, serving a meal, or baby-sitting for a child.

right to safety, (2) the right to be informed, (3) the right to choose, (4) the right to be
1 heard, (5) the right to **redress** (money or some other benefit given as compensation for a wrong that is done), and (6) the right to consumer education.

These six rights make up the Consumer Bill of Rights. Rights 1 to 4 were first proposed by President John F. Kennedy. President Richard M. Nixon and President Gerald R. Ford added rights 5 and 6.

2 With rights come responsibilities. For example, when you get your driver's license, you are granted the *right* to drive a car. With that right comes the obligation to follow the rules of the road. Similarly, along with the consumer right to safety comes the responsibility to use products in a safe and careful way—to follow the manufacturer's directions and cautions. Figure 1–2 shows you the responsibilities that accompany your
3 rights as a consumer.

CONSUMER PROTECTION

Consumers must learn about products and consumer issues, make choices carefully, and know their rights. Sometimes, however, being a smart shopper, acting responsibly, and knowing your rights just is not enough. If you have a problem with an item you bought, you might find it hard to deal with a store or company all by yourself. For situations like this, you
4 can get help.

Federal Laws

Over the years, Congress, which is the lawmaking branch of the government, has
5 passed a number of laws, called **statutes,**

Figure 1–2 Consumer Rights and Responsibilities

Consumer Rights	Consumer Responsibilities
1. Right to safety. Consumers should be protected against goods that are hazardous to health or life.	**1. Responsibility to use products safely.** Consumers should use products as they were meant to be used and follow recommended procedures for care and maintenance.
2. Right to be informed. Consumers should be protected against fraudulent or misleading advertising, labeling, or sales practices. They should be given the facts needed to make informed choices.	**2. Responsibility to use information.** Consumers should look for information about products they plan to buy and use it to compare and evaluate different brands and models.
3. Right to choose. Consumers should be assured access to a variety of goods and services at competitive prices.	**3. Responsibility to choose carefully.** Consumers should use their buying power intelligently to encourage ethical business practices and safe, reliable products.
4. Right to be heard. Consumers should be assured that their interests will be considered in the making of laws.	**4. Responsibility to speak up.** Consumers should keep themselves informed on consumer issues and let public officials know their opinions.
5. Right to redress. Consumers are entitled to swift and fair remedies for consumer problems.	**5. Responsibility to seek redress.** Consumers should let businesses know when their products and services do not measure up to expectations. They should pursue legal and other available remedies when problems do arise.
6. Right to consumer education. Consumers should be taught about the market system. They should know how to work within that system to get the greatest possible satisfaction for each dollar spent.	**6. Responsibility to learn.** Consumers should take advantage of every opportunity to develop consumer skills.

▲ *Your consumer rights and responsibilities are summarized in the chart above.* ***Why are consumer rights and responsibilities important?***

1 Vocabulary Ask students to define redress. (Relief; compensation for wrong; remedy.) Ask them to make up situations in which redress would occur.

2 Critical Thinking Ask students if they can see how everyone benefits from each individual's performance of responsibilities 2, 3, 5, and 6. (Businesses producing quality services and goods will flourish; those that produce inferior products will not survive.) Students will learn more about this concept in the next unit.

3 Reinforcement Student Activity Workbook, Chapter 1 activities.

4 Discussion Starter Ask students if they agree with the statement that consumers need help. Have they heard the old phrase "You can't fight city hall"? Do they think this principle applies to "big business"?

5 Vocabulary Ask students to define *statute.* (Law.)

Caption Answer: They protect you as a citizen and a consumer, and they also protect businesses.

Caption Answer: Some people think so; but for the most part, statutes were passed because there was a demand for them from individuals or groups of citizens who felt they needed government help in solving certain problems.

1 Discussion Starter In their role as consumers, students should favor these laws. But in their citizen roles they may not be so much in favor. Why? (Enforcement of these laws costs money, which comes from taxes paid by citizens.) Ask students if they think the advantages of these laws are greater than the disadvantages. Why?

2 Critical Thinking Have students assume that it is their job to rate the importance of the laws listed because budget concerns may mean that some will be revoked. Have them list the laws in order of importance and write a sentence or two as to why they ranked each one as they did. Compare the lists in a class discussion.

Figure 1–3 Consumer Protection Statutes

Consumer Credit Protection Act
This law requires truth in lending. Consumers must be told exactly what the credit charge is on a purchase or loan. Creditors must report these charges in a uniform way. Credit costs must be stated both in dollars and cents and as an annual percentage rate.

Fair Packaging and Labeling Act
This statute requires truth in packaging. It is designed to help consumers compare goods. The act requires that certain facts be printed clearly on packaging. These facts include net contents, size of serving, list of ingredients in order of decreasing weight, and the like.

Food, Drug, and Cosmetic Act
This law is designed to assure consumers of the safety, purity, and wholesomeness of food products. It also covers the safety and effectiveness of drugs and cosmetics. The act requires that these products be informatively labeled and truthfully advertised.

Automobile Information Disclosures Act
This act helps consumers compare new automobiles. It requires that manufacturers label each car, listing its suggested retail price, the price of any extras, and the total price.

Child Protection and Toy Safety Act
The purpose of this act is to protect children from dangerous goods, including toys. The act bans the shipment and sale of such dangerous items from state to state.

Federal Hazardous Substances Labeling Act
This statute requires warning labels on all products that might be hazardous. The labels must list such things as precautions for use and first-aid procedures in case of accident.

Textile Fiber Products Identification Act
This law helps consumers compare textiles and fabrics. It requires that labels list fiber content by weight (expressed as a percent of total weight), manufacturer's name and address, family name of the fiber, and similar items.

Fair Credit Billing Act
This act sets out a procedure for consumers to follow in having billing errors corrected.

Magnuson-Moss Federal Warranty Law
The purpose of this act is to protect the consumer from warranties not carried out. The act sets minimum standards for written warranties, rules for making them available before a product is sold, and provisions for class-action suits if they are not fulfilled.

Equal Credit Opportunity Act
This act protects people who apply for credit from discrimination based on sex, marital status, age, race, color, religion, national origin, or receipt of public assistance.

Truth-in-Savings Act
This act requires that financial institutions disclose the *annual percentage yield* (APY) they are paying on savings. The APY must be arrived at using a standardized formula so that rates paid by different institutions are directly comparable.

▲ *All of these laws were passed to protect the consumer.* ***Do you think that the government is too protective? Why?***

to protect consumers. Figure 1–3 lists federal statutes that have been passed to solve specific problems facing consumers. Several are mentioned again in later chapters.

These laws are important; they make life as a consumer much easier. In some cases, today's consumers are reaping the benefits of struggles ended long ago. In other cases, the battles occurred more recently.

Legislators at the state and local levels
1 have also passed many laws that benefit
2 consumers.

Government Agencies

Having laws on the books is not enough. There must be a way to enforce the laws. The government creates **agencies,** which

Figure 1–4 Government Agencies

Department of Agriculture (USDA)
The USDA sets standards for, inspects, and grades meats, poultry, and canned fruits and vegetables. It also publishes many booklets and pamphlets on food, clothing, household equipment, and other topics of interest to consumers.

Consumer Product Safety Commission (CPSC)
The CPSC protects the public against unreasonable risk from consumer products. It enforces the Federal Hazardous Substances Act and the Poison Prevention Packaging Act. In addition, it works closely with industry in developing safety standards for many household products.

Federal Trade Commission (FTC)
The FTC has law enforcement responsibilities in advertising and marketing. In these fields, it works to prevent deceptive practices. It is also a guardian of consumer rights in credit transactions and enforces a number of laws related to labeling (of clothing, appliances, and other consumer products).

Food and Drug Administration (FDA)
The FDA enforces laws and regulations on the purity, quality, and labeling of food, drugs, and cosmetics. It certifies new drugs and inspects drug and food-processing plants. It also regulates the advertising and sale of medical devices such as hearing aids and pacemakers.

Securities and Exchange Commission (SEC)
The SEC registers and supervises the issue and sale of stocks and bonds. It is responsible for preventing fraud in the sale of securities to the public through interstate commerce. It requires public disclosure of facts in the sale of securities so that investors can make realistic judgments.

▲ *Government agencies are sometimes considered remote from our daily lives.* ***Which of the agencies on this chart have affected you this week?***

are specialized departments within the government, to watch over specific areas or industries. These agencies set up rules and regulations in order to penalize companies and organizations that break certain laws.

1 **Federal Agencies** Figure 1–4 lists just
2 a few out of dozens of agencies that have
3 a direct responsibility to consumers. Often
these agencies were set up to protect businesses. In protecting businesses, though, they also protect consumers.

The Federal Trade Commission (FTC), for example, protects a business against unfair competition from another business. Deceptive practices, in which a business owner lies, cheats, or otherwise misleads other business owners, are a form of unfair competition. When the FTC discovers deceptive practices, it certainly helps consumers as well as honest businesspeople. Through the years, some consumer advocates have felt that the FTC did

Big Mac Across the Globe

How much you pay for a McDonald's Big Mac depends on where you are in the world. When the price of a Big Mac in the United States is $2.32, the hamburger costs $1.82 in Australia, $1.99 in Canada, $2.40 in Chile, $1.05 in China, $3.48 in Germany, $1.51 in Malaysia, $2.99 in South Korea, and $5.20 in Switzerland. Local prices vary according to such business-related expenses as rent and the price of ingredients.

Caption Answer: SDA because of food inspection. CPSC because of caustics used in many household supplies. FTC because of credit transactions and labeling jurisdiction. FDA because of regulations relating to foods and drugs. SEC for those who are investing in securities.

1 Vocabulary Make sure students see that USDA stands for United States Department of Agriculture.

2 Interesting Note The use of child-resistant pill containers helped reduce the number of poisoning deaths among children from 500 annually to about 50 a year three decades later.

3 Reinforcement Student Activity Workbook, Chapter 1 activities.

FLASHBACK FLASHFORWARD

In 1943, there were 138 million people living in 66.9 million households in the United States. Fifty years later there were 258 million people living in 96 million households. If this growth trend continues, by 2043, there will be more than 482 million people living in 137 million households. Now that's a lot of consumers!

1 Vocabulary Ask students what an advocate is. (One who argues for or defends a cause or proposal.) Ask them to give examples of advocates for different causes. (The homeless, the unemployed, peace, environmental clean-up, etc.)

2 Extension Through local businesses, identify addresses of consumer action panels. Have students write letters to the panels requesting information about the way consumers should handle complaints.

not work hard enough on behalf of consumers; others have felt it did more for consumers than it should.

1 The U.S. Office of Consumer Affairs is the consumer advocate at the federal level. It coordinates the work of all federal agencies that have consumer protection functions. The director of the Office of Consumer Affairs also serves as Special Assistant to the President for Consumer Affairs.

State and Local Agencies More than 300 state, county, and local governments have set up consumer protection agencies or offices. Their names and responsibilities vary, however. At the state level, the agency is often part of the attorney general's office. This plan makes it easier for the state to bring businesses to court for violating consumer protection laws. It also centralizes responsibility for consumer protection.

Local governments may also have an individual or an office responsible for consumer protection. As in state government, the name, authority, and organizational patterns may vary.

Business-sponsored Organizations

A number of private groups also work in the area of consumer protection. Many of the best-known of these organizations are sponsored by business.

2 **Consumer Action Panels** Companies that do business in the same industry, for example, producing dairy foods or producing medicines, sometimes get together to form trade associations to look after their common interests. **Consumer action panels** are groups formed by these trade associations to take care of consumer complaints when individual businesses in the industry cannot. The panels also keep their member businesses up to date on what consumers think about the goods and services their industry provides.

Members of consumer action panels know a lot about consumer affairs. They are not employees of the member firms. Consumer action panels have been formed by trade associations representing major appliance manufacturers (MACAP) and automobile dealers (AUTOCAP), among others.

Arbitration Services The Better Business Bureau, Inc., is a private organization financed by business and made up of local Better Business Bureaus. Some local bureaus provide an **arbitration service,** which is a procedure for settling complaints. Typically, a neutral person or a panel listens to both sides, weighs the evidence, and reaches a decision that both parties must accept. Since arbitration is not a court procedure, participation is voluntary. However, once you decide to participate in an arbitration procedure, you must accept the decision.

Planning a Purchase

To be sure you get the best value, you need to plan your purchase.

- **Decide what you need and want out of the product.**
- **Go to the library and read about the product in *Consumer Reports* or other resources.**
- **Ask several salespeople what they recommend. Find out how the best-quality item compares with the least expensive—and why.**
- **Talk to friends who own the product that you're thinking of buying. Find out why they bought a particular brand and model. Are they satisfied with the product? Ask them about the product's good and bad points.**
- **Shop around for the best price or wait for a sale.**

Corporate Consumer Departments

Many businesses have full-time **consumer affairs departments.** These are departments set up to communicate with customers. Many of the larger firms have toll-free (800) numbers that consumers can use when they need information or want to make complaints.

THE CONSUMER MOVEMENT

In the consumer movement, many peo-
1 ple come together in loosely organized

Recreation Rebuilds a Community

Some kids in Cherry Tree, Oklahoma, were getting into trouble. They were bored. They had no place to go, nothing to do. So they threw rocks through windows, shot up signs, set grass fires. Some turned to drugs and alcohol to ease the boredom. Some became substance abusers to cover up the loneliness, the feeling that no one cared about them.

Crime became a major problem in Cherry Tree, a tiny community of about 500 Cherokee Indians. People were afraid to go out at night.

Community members realized that it was a problem they could no longer ignore. So they got together to figure out what to do, and asked the kids what they wanted.

The answer was simple. They wanted a place to go, something to do, some place to hang out.

So community leaders and parents targeted a large vacant lot owned by the Cherokee Nation. The Nation rented the 115-acre space to them for $1 an acre. Then the group got busy raising money with dinners, raffles, and grants so that they could build a recreation hall, playing field, and gym.

At first, some kids kept causing trouble. They painted graffiti on the walls and bleachers. They tore up the playing fields. Then one of the group leaders talked to the kids responsible, pointing out that the center was being built for them. The trouble stopped, and the former troublemakers pitched in to help.

Today the recreation center hosts baseball and basketball games. Community members and parents have set up a child-care center and substance-abuse prevention program. They sponsor field trips and cultural events.

The community of Cherry Tree has pulled together. Today crime is down 95 percent. The kids have a sense of worth and self-respect.

Brainstorming

Working with a partner, think of a project you could initiate in your community that would help keep troubled kids from getting involved in crime. Describe your project to your class.

1 Discussion Starter Ask students if they are aware of any consumer groups in their area that have recently tried to bring about changes favoring consumers. Have they or any people they know participated? Have they been solicited for contributions to help finance a consumer cause?

Case Study Answer: Student responses will vary. Some possibilities include starting a teen center, sports league, or community center.

1 Research Assign each student a written report on one of these consumer advocates or another advocate approved by you. Have them focus on how the person came to be involved with consumer issues, the person's contribution, and the benefits derived.

2 Research Have each student research a particular product area in *Consumer Reports.* Then have the student recommend and support a smart purchase in that area. In the recommendation the student should also say what not to buy. You may want to make this activity a written assignment, with the requirement that the final report include photocopied pages from Consumer Reports that support the student's recommendations.

News Clip Answers:
1. The drug has not been tested by the FDA for the specific use for which it is being prescribed. As a result, it has not gone through the rigorous federal testing process to assure its effectiveness for that use.
2. They can lead to innovative treatment for illnesses that have no known cures. The fact that a drug has already been proved safe for its primary use minimizes the risk that the innovative application of the drug will cause harm.

groups to work toward a broad common goal—improvement for the consumer. The consumer movement is based on the idea that the power of consumers as a group can balance the economic and political power of business and industry. At the state and local levels, groups of citizens have forced prices down, ended deceptive business practices, and fought rate increases by utilities such as gas companies.

Consumer groups exist at the national, state, and local levels. There may be a consumer group in your area. These groups are interested in consumer education, consumer information, political action, and even public protest. Although their interests and membership vary, the groups all share a common belief: Only through organized group action will consumers be heard and their power felt.

Key Supporters

Several individuals have been particularly important to the consumer movement. They and other consumer advocates have worked to pass laws, investigate business practices, and expose unfairness and dan-
1 ger to consumers.

- Harvey Wiley, a medical doctor, proved that adding certain chemicals to foods and drugs was dangerous. His campaign against mislabeled foods and drugs led to passage of the Food and Drug Act of 1906.
- Upton Sinclair published *The Jungle* in 1906. This novel exposed the filthy conditions in meat-packing plants, leading to the passage of the Meat Inspection Act of 1906.
- Stuart Chase and F. J. Schlink, former employees of federal agencies, published *Your Money's Worth* in 1927. Their book showed how advertisers mislead the public about their products. A consumer testing laboratory, Consumers' Research, was founded to give people the facts about products.
- Rachel Carson published *Silent Spring* in 1962. Her work revealed the dangers of pollution to the environment and prompted many environmental laws.
- Jessica Mitford published *The American Way of Death* in 1963, exposing the abuses of the funeral industry. Twenty years later the Funeral Rule was issued, requiring funeral halls to list services and prices item by item instead of as a lump sum.
- Ralph Nader published *Unsafe at Any Speed* in 1965, demonstrating that many highway deaths were caused by defects in cars. His book and other activities helped improve highway safety, meat inspection, and the activities of the FTC.
- Paul Douglas, a U.S. senator from Illinois, exposed abuses in consumer credit. Testimony given before his Senate committee led to passage of the truth-in-lending legislation in 1968.

Publications and Testing Agencies

Because they expose unfair and dangerous practices in such convincing detail, books and other writings have been very important in the development of consumerism. Thus, it is not surprising that the movement has given birth to a number of specialized publications, among them *Consumer*
2 *Reports* and *Consumers' Research.*

Consumer Reports is published by Consumers Union (CU), an independent consumer testing agency. CU buys products from stores, tests them in the laboratory, and reports the results in its magazine. For example, it might test a half dozen models of washing machines. By reading *Consumer Reports,* you can find out what tests were conducted and how the researchers rated each machine.

CU has long been a champion of consumer rights. The organization began at Consumers' Research, the consumer testing agency founded as an outgrowth of

CASE STUDY

Consumer NEWS CLIP

Approved Medications Are Being Widely Prescribed for Unapproved Uses

by Christine Gorman
Time September 18, 1995

Using a drug to treat a disorder for which it was not intended—a practice known as off-label prescribing—may sound like dangerous medicine. But it is surprisingly widespread and has become a hot issue, both in the medical community and in the U.S. Congress. The American Medical Association estimates that 40 percent to 60 percent of all prescriptions in the United States are written for drugs being used for something other than their approved purpose. Now drug companies have started campaigning for the right to promote their products' unofficial benefits, and their lobbying effort is likely to be well received on Capitol Hill.

Why is off-label prescribing so common? Chiefly because pharmaceutical companies are reluctant to invest the time and expense to get FDA clearance on new uses for an established drug—especially when the drug's safety has already been proved. Says Dr. Martin Raber, physician in chief of the M. D. Anderson Cancer Center in Houston: "It is accepted practice that once a drug is FDA-approved it can be freely used." But the FDA gets nervous when a drug's unapproved uses overshadow its original purpose. Retin-A cream, for example, was approved by the FDA for the treatment of acne in 1971, but then, much to the FDA's consternation, it was widely prescribed to smooth wrinkles caused by aging and overexposure to the sun.

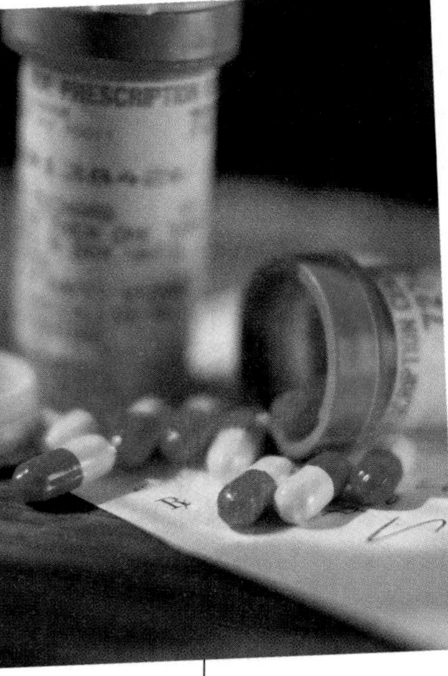

This shadowland of medical practice didn't start to attract public scrutiny until off-label prescribing became the treatment of choice for people suffering from AIDS or advanced cancers. "When it comes to treating cancer, things are much more liberal than in other areas of medicine," says Dr. Thierry Jahan, an oncologist at the University of California at San Francisco."There's an element of desperation. So you try a lot of combinations of drugs that are already on the market while waiting for new drugs to become available."

Doctors take a chance whenever they depart from FDA-approved uses of powerful drugs. Should something go wrong, a patient could successfully sue for malpractice. Paradoxically, there are situations in which a patient might also sue if the physician fails to prescribe a drug for off-label use. Take Lyme disease. Scientists have shown that the most effective cure for the tick-borne malady is treatment with one of two antibiotics, amoxicillin or doxycycline. Neither is approved for that use, but the drugs have become such standards of care that a doctor might be considered negligent for not using them.

Decisions, Decisions

1. Why is there a risk associated with using a drug in an off-label fashion?
2. What are the primary benefits of off-label drug applications?

1 Discussion Starter Have students identify local newspaper columns and radio and television programs that deal with consumer problems. Set aside class time each week for discussion of the issues reported in these media.

Chase and Schlink's work. Consumers' Research no longer tests and rates products, but it continues to publish its own magazine, called *Consumers' Research*. The magazine prints articles on many topics of interest to consumers.

Popular Media Newspapers, magazines, radio, television, and computer services such as Internet also aid consumers. The media play a vital role in warning people about frauds being practiced locally. They also offer useful advice on investing,
1 health, housing, and other topics of special interest to consumers.

The media's best-known activity, however, is helping people resolve consumer complaints. Businesses that might ignore a consumer acting alone respond fast and favorably when a consumer reporter gets involved. Such tactics work because businesses want to avoid bad publicity. Hundreds of local newspapers and radio and television stations have consumer columns or programs.

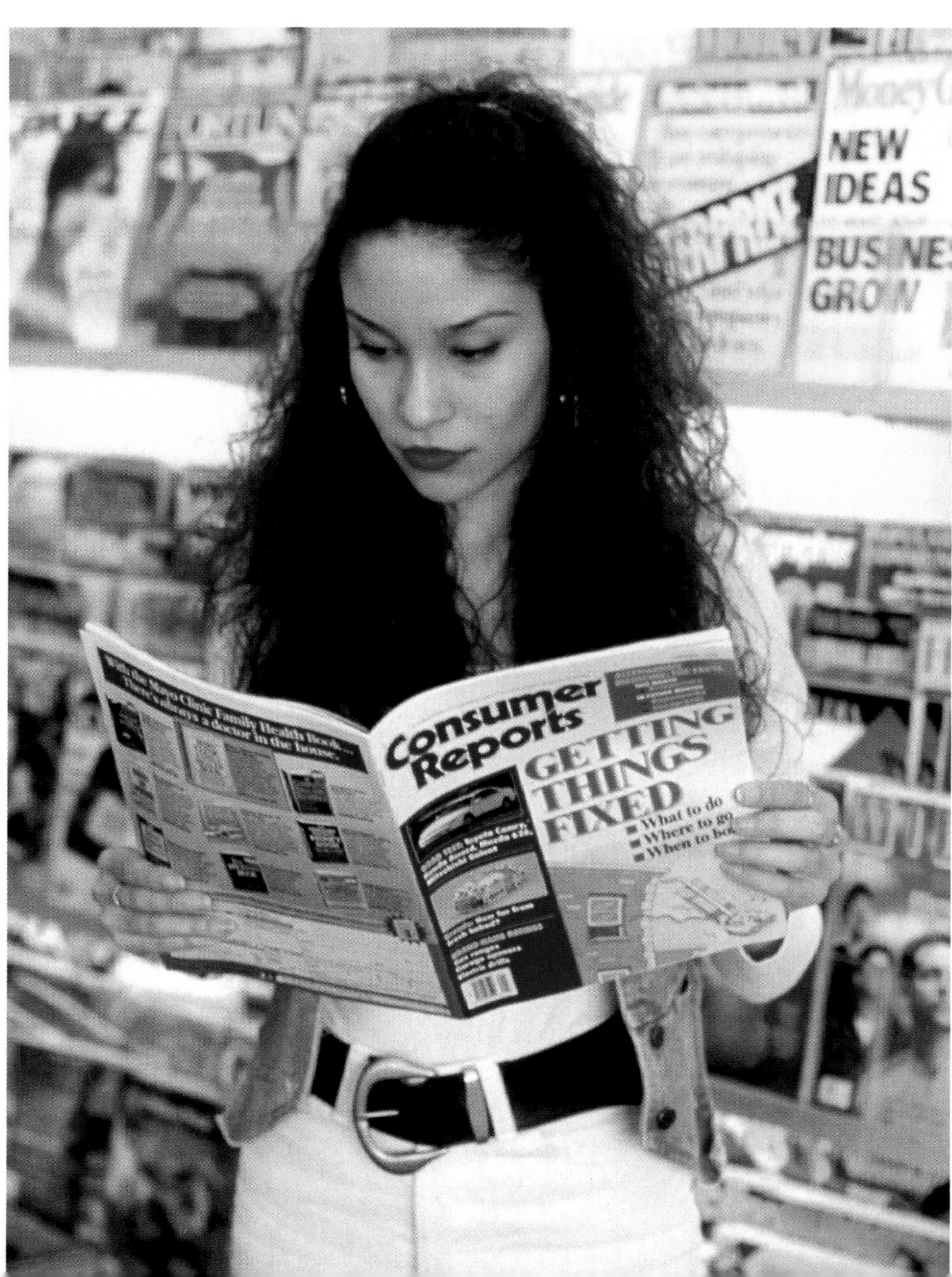

The media provide consumers with valuable consumer information. **Name types of media you watch, read, or listen to that inform you about consumer products.** ▶

Caption Answer: The radio, TV, consumer magazines, newspapers, the Internet.

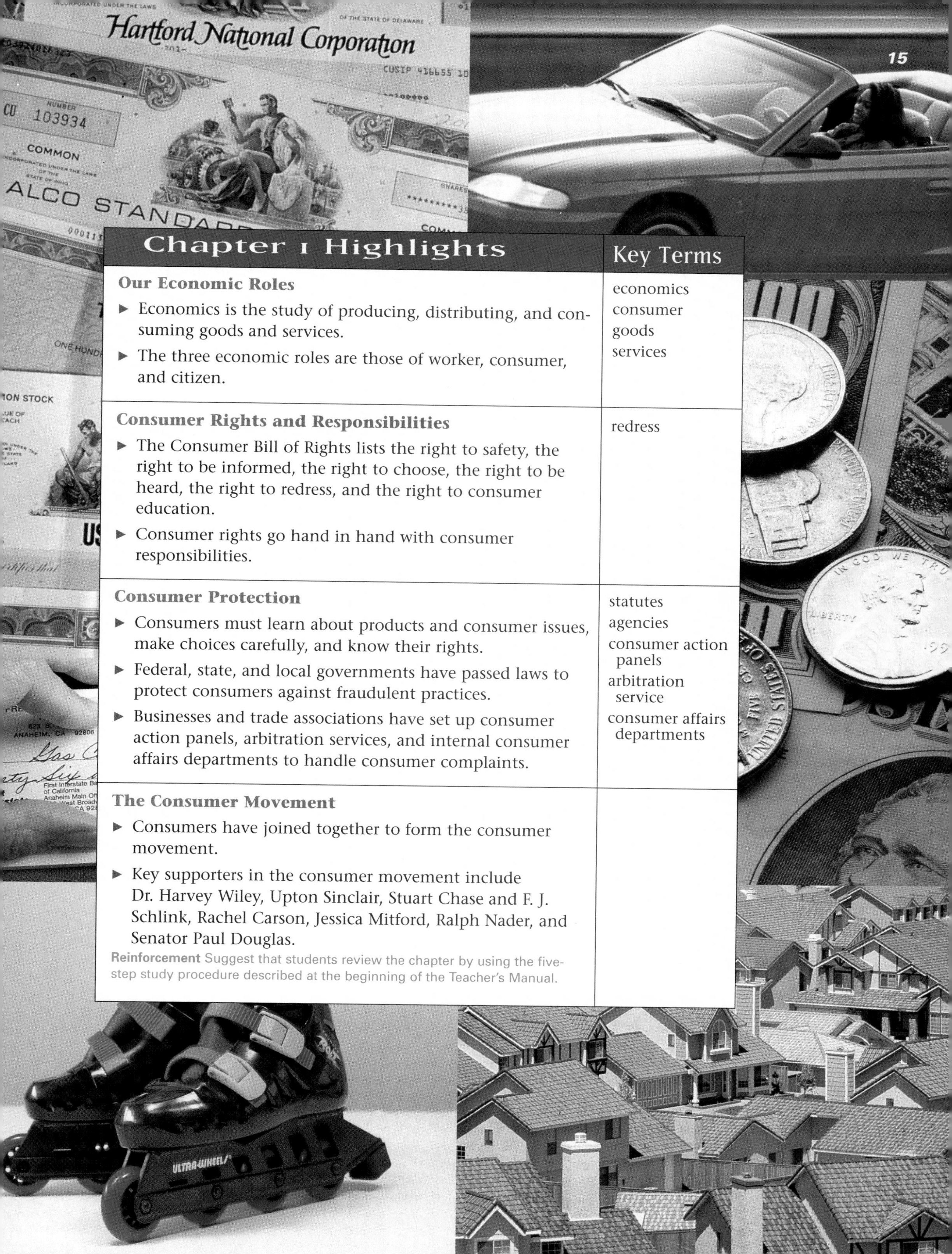

Chapter 1 Highlights	Key Terms
Our Economic Roles ► Economics is the study of producing, distributing, and consuming goods and services. ► The three economic roles are those of worker, consumer, and citizen.	economics consumer goods services
Consumer Rights and Responsibilities ► The Consumer Bill of Rights lists the right to safety, the right to be informed, the right to choose, the right to be heard, the right to redress, and the right to consumer education. ► Consumer rights go hand in hand with consumer responsibilities.	redress
Consumer Protection ► Consumers must learn about products and consumer issues, make choices carefully, and know their rights. ► Federal, state, and local governments have passed laws to protect consumers against fraudulent practices. ► Businesses and trade associations have set up consumer action panels, arbitration services, and internal consumer affairs departments to handle consumer complaints.	statutes agencies consumer action panels arbitration service consumer affairs departments
The Consumer Movement ► Consumers have joined together to form the consumer movement. ► Key supporters in the consumer movement include Dr. Harvey Wiley, Upton Sinclair, Stuart Chase and F. J. Schlink, Rachel Carson, Jessica Mitford, Ralph Nader, and Senator Paul Douglas. **Reinforcement** Suggest that students review the chapter by using the five-step study procedure described at the beginning of the Teacher's Manual.	

CHAPTER 1 REVIEW

Refer students to the Reviewing Consumer Terms and Reviewing Facts and Ideas activities in the Student Activity Workbook.

Reviewing Consumer Terms
Paragraphs will vary. See Glossary for definitions.

Reviewing Facts and Ideas
Refer Students to the Student Activity Workbook for answers.

Problem Solving and Decision Making
Answers will vary. Students may feel that a combination may be most effective at regulating airlines.

Consumers Around the World Social Studies
1 Student papers should explain laws and associations that protect consumers.

Reviewing Consumer Terms

In a paragraph, define the term *consumer* and then explain the relationship of the following terms to it.

agencies
arbitration service
consumer
consumer action panels
consumer affairs departments
economics
goods
redress
services
statutes

Reviewing Facts and Ideas

1. Which economic roles does a child movie star play? a retired mechanic?
2. Which consumer right (or rights) does each of the statutes listed on page 8 protect?
3. Which federal agency is responsible for:
   a. The safety of cosmetics?
   b. Meat inspection?
   c. Truth in advertising?
4. Name two purposes that consumer action panels serve.
5. The consumer movement is of recent origin—true or false? Explain.

Problem Solving and Decision Making

1. Frequent and long flight delays have triggered increased consumer demands for the nation's airlines to be regulated again. Some people are calling for fines on airlines that publish unrealistic schedules or overbook (make reservations for more passengers than they can seat). In this situation, which of the following kinds of consumer protection do you feel would be most effective and why?
   a. Government legislation
   b. Supervision by business-sponsored organizations
   c. Action by individual consumers
   d. Group action by consumer organizations
   e. Self-protection through consumer education
2. Infomercials (long commercials that look like television shows) have received increasing criticism in recent years. Consumers condemn them for many reasons, such as misrepresenting products and faking product endorsements.
   Watch two infomercials in the course of one week and report to the class your impressions of the infomercials and the products being promoted. Then answer these specific questions on paper:
   a. Would the consumer be informed about the product as a result of watching the show?
   b. Was the presentation believable?
   c. Was the presentation objectionable in any way? If so, how?
   d. Are you motivated to write to the television channel or the sponsor about your reactions to the commercial?

Building Academic Skills

Consumers Around the World

Social Studies

1. Using library resources, look up information about Canadian and

Mexican federal laws and government agencies that exist to protect consumers in these countries. Summarize your findings in a 250-word report.

Communications

2. Write to the United States Office of Consumer Affairs, Washington, D.C. 20201, and ask for a list of its free publications. Study the list, and order a copy of the pamphlet that interests you the most. Read the material and make a brief oral report to the class. Include the name of the current Director of the U.S. Office of Consumer Affairs.

Science

3. In order to be a wise consumer, it's important to know what products are made of. Many products contain harmful ingredients that can cause injury or death if used improperly. For example, thermometers are made with mercury. Working with a classmate, research the effects of mercury on human beings. Report your findings to the class.

Beyond the Classroom

Consumer Project

At home, locate five household items that have the kind of labels required by the Federal Hazardous Substances Labeling Act. Write down the name of each product and the contents of each label, word for word. Then decide whether the individual labels are adequate in terms of size, location, detail, and accuracy. If necessary, consult books on first aid or literature from your local poison control center.

Cooperative Learning

Family Economics

Break into assigned family groups. Discuss the following problem.

The landlord installs a new stove in your apartment. Out of curiosity, another member of your family turns on the stove's self-cleaning feature and then tries to turn it off forcibly, breaking the lever. Because the damage is clearly the result of misuse, your family must pay for the repair.

How could this situation have been avoided? Discuss how family living affects consumer responsibilities. Compare your answers with those of other family groups.

Debate the Issue

Drug companies must submit an application for approval to the Food and Drug Administration before they can offer a new drug for sale. Some people object to this requirement, saying that the FDA is too slow and that a new medicine is sometimes held off the market for years, unnecessarily depriving many ill people of its benefits. Others maintain that citizens deserve the protection of the FDA until a drug has been proved safe, and testing for safety is a time-consuming process.

You and your classmates will break into two groups and research this topic. Each group will gather evidence to support one side or the other. You are to prepare the argument for your side of the problem. Then the two groups will meet in a classroom debate.

Communications
2 Student reports should discuss why they chose the area they did and why it is important.

Science
3 Mercury, when inhaled or absorbed through the skin, can be poisonous. It can take the place or iron in your red blood cells. But because it does not have the same ability to carry oxygen, it can produce anemia. Mercury is also found in contaminated fish.

Beyond the Classroom Consumer Project
Students should share their findings with the class.

Family Economics
All groups should stress the need for all users of the appliance to read the owner's manual, not just the principal users.

Debate the Issue
Break the class into two teams. Assign each team one side of the issue. Encourage students to work together as a team to develop their argument. Ask each team to select a member to make an opening statement that supports their side of the issue. Have students take turns debating as the debate moves from one team to another.

CHAPTER 2

Our Market System

Learning Objectives

When you have finished studying this chapter, you should be able to:

1. Explain what an economic system does and list the four questions it answers.
2. Describe the four types of economic systems and name countries in which they are in practice.
3. List some types of resources that businesses use.
4. Chart the stages of a business cycle.
5. Define the economic indicators used to measure the American economy.

Consumer Terms

economic system
market
economists
resources
productivity
recession
depression
inflation
Gross Domestic Product
balance of trade

Real-World Journal

In a free enterprise system, the consumer decides what will be produced. If the consumer wants or needs a particular good or service, then someone will provide it. After reading this chapter, list in your journal the last five purchases you made. Explain why you purchased each item. Were your decisions based on needs or wants?

Lesson Plan See the Teacher's Manual for Chapter 2 lesson plan.

Vocabulary The Chapter 2 lesson plan includes suggested vocabulary activities for the items listed.

1 Problem Solving Open a discussion about making choices on how to spend money by asking students what kinds of dilemmas they have faced, how they decided to spend their money, and whether they would spend it differently if they had more thoroughly examined their needs and choices.

THE ECONOMY IS ALL AROUND US

The economy is something that affects our lives every day. Consider lunch at your local diner. The price of your sandwich, how the wheat in the bread was produced, and whether the owner of the restaurant has hired enough staff to serve the customers promptly are all examples of our market system at work. In this chapter, you will learn about the American economic system, how it functions, how it compares with systems in other parts of the world, what roles individuals and the government play, what makes the economy healthy, and how to decipher the indicators used to determine whether it is strong or weak.

HOW ECONOMIC SYSTEMS WORK

When you have money to spend, you also have choices to make on how to spend it. This is not always easy to do. For instance, should you spend your weekly allowance at the movies or on the latest CDs? Should your paycheck go for a new pair of running shoes or the latest music videos? Should you give your holiday money to programs for the needy or to your little brother so he can buy presents for family members?

Whenever you make these kinds of decisions, you are making economic choices—that is, you are deciding how to use a resource. Resources are things needed to produce goods and services. Resources include land, capital, entrepreneurship, and technology. In your case, the resource is money. There are many ways to use this resource, but because the amount of money you have is limited, your decision may be difficult.

1 The countries of the world also make economic choices. The situations they face, however, are a little more complicated than whether to buy a new computer game or a leather jacket. Nations are faced with a huge number of choices on which to spend their money. Their decisions have a great effect on the lives and comfort of thousands, maybe millions, of people.

Along with how to spend their money, countries have other decisions to make.

A store like this carries a lot of items to attract buyers. ***What are some of the questions these teenagers are asking themselves as they try to decide the best way to spend their limited amounts of money?*** ▶

Caption Answer: They're trying to decide what they really need, what they can do without, and what they can wait for until their next allowance or paycheck.

They must decide how to use, produce, and sell other resources, which may include food, natural resources, or manufactured goods.

To help it make choices, each nation has an **economic system,** which is the way it uses resources to satisfy its people's needs and wants. An economic system must answer the following four questions:

1. What and how much do we produce?
2. How should we produce it?
3. Who should produce it?
4. Who should share what is produced?

THE FOUR TYPES OF ECONOMIC SYSTEMS

Countries answer the four economic questions within the framework of an economic system. There are four types of
1 systems. Let's take a closer look at each.

Traditional System

People in a traditional system do things the old-fashioned way. Why? Because their parents and grandparents said it was best. The customs and beliefs of their society also play a strong role. Things are done "the way they've always been done" and, despite the passage of time and the progress made by other societies, the people in a traditional system see no reason to change.

2 Tribes may fish and hunt as their ancestors did, not using the latest fishing or hunting equipment. Societies may also plant the way their forbearers did, without rotating crops or using the latest organic or chemical procedures to make sure the land can provide better harvests now and in the future. When the food or other resource in an area is used up, these people move on rather than try to improve the situation. Some societies located in Asia, the Middle East, Africa, and Latin America use the traditional system.

Command, or Controlled, System

Government makes all the economic decisions in this system. As hard as it may be for Americans to comprehend, individuals who live in a command system have nothing to say over what is produced in their country or how it is produced. They may not even be allowed to choose what their role will be in the production process.

1 Critical Thinking Before they read further, ask students to use their knowledge of the words "traditional," "command," and "market" to speculate on how these systems might operate.

▲ *Some societies work their farmland the way their ancestors did, carrying water in urns and using hand tools instead of machines.* ***Why is this farmer working in this fashion, and what economic system is he practicing?***

Caption Answer: This man is using the traditional system, in which societies hunt, fish, farm, and live the way their ancestors did.

Since government controls all the resources, it also determines how to distribute what is produced, how much it will cost, and where it will be sold. Government's decision-making powers don't end there, however. It may also decide what jobs people are allowed to have, and who will be trained for jobs. Government in this system could be made up of one person, as in a dictatorship, or a small group of government officials. Cuba makes use of the command system, and so did the former Soviet Union.

2 Extension Tell students that traditional economic systems typically consist of many small, independent units of families or tribes. Economic activities are not as interrelated as they are in such countries as the United States.

▲ *The New York Stock Exchange is the biggest stock market in the world.* ***Name some other markets that you see in your school, at your job, or in your town every day.***

Caption Answer: A market is any place where buyers and sellers get together. It could be the bookstore or lunchroom at school, the store or restaurant where you work, students selling candy to raise money for their band uniforms, or motorists buying gasoline at the local service station.

1 Research Ask students to report on the vast economic changes that have swept the former Soviet Union and how these changes have affected the people and how business is done there.

Captalist, or Market, System

This is the opposite of the command system. In a capitalist, or market, system, individuals are in charge of production, and government does not intervene. This system, in which private companies or individuals control most of the production process, is also known as the free-enterprise system. It is driven by the choices of the people, who create a market. A **market** is the activity between buyers and sellers.

In a market there is supply, provided by producers, and demand, which comes from consumers. When there is demand, a seller will create and offer something that people may buy. When there is supply, consumers will decide whether to buy what is available. A market can be big, like the stock market. A market can also be small, like a neighborhood where teenagers offer to mow lawns for a fee. Consumers are the force behind this system. Their demands drive what is produced and how much it costs.

While people often say that the United States has a capitalist system, it actually has a mixed system, which is explained in the following section. True capitalism is more a theory than an actual economic practice in the world today. In fact, **economists,** who analyze the production, distribution, and consumption of goods and services, cannot agree on whether a pure capitalist system has ever existed.

Mixed System

A mixed system is a combination of the command and market systems. The United States has a mixed economic system. This means that while there are millions of private business owners who sell and produce their goods and services the way they want to, the government also has a hand in how business is done.

In the United States, a business owner may decide what to sell or produce and how and where to do it. Individuals also decide where to work and what to buy. Government, however, makes rules and regulations that businesses must follow. These may affect price, such as long-distance telephone rates or cable TV charges, or what and how much is produced. Government may tell farmers how much wheat to produce a year, for example. Government may also dictate workplace conditions, such as requiring hard hats to ensure the safety of workers on a construction site. The People's Republic of China, France, and England
1 are other countries where a mixed economy is in practice.

CHARACTERISTICS OF THE AMERICAN ECONOMY

In the American economy, individuals own and control the elements of production and make decisions on using them according to laws. A shoe factory owner, for instance, may decide to open a manufacturing plant in Gary, Indiana, and to hire 25 people and pay them $16 an hour. The owner, however, must operate the factory according to safety standards set by the government.

Among the characteristics of the American economy are the limited role of government in business affairs, freedom of enterprise, freedom of choice, private
1 property, and competition. You will learn
2 about these in the sections that follow.

Government's Role

When the Constitution was written, the Founders of the United States limited government's role mainly to national defense and keeping peace. They curbed the government's power over economic activities.

Much has changed since then, with government assuming more power in the economic arena. The two major areas in which government plays a bigger part are in regulating businesses and providing services. Examples of regulations include setting standards for the quality of various foods and drugs, and supervising the nation's money and banking systems. The federal government also provides programs such as Medicare, and local and state governments provide services in such areas as ed-
3 ucation, job training, and recreation.

Freedom of Enterprise

In our free-enterprise system, individuals are free to own and control resources and determine how goods and services will be produced. As you know, **resources** include land, labor, capital, entrepreneurship, and technology.

Land refers to more than just land itself, on which crops can be grown or factories and buildings constructed. It also includes natural resources, such as fish, animals, forests, minerals, and water.

Labor is the work force. It is made up of all the people who do the jobs that keep the economy going.

Capital is the property that people use to make goods and services. This includes buildings, machinery, natural resources after they have been processed, such as fuel oil, and the money used to buy any of these things. Machines used to build cars would be capital, but the cars themselves would not be unless they were used to produce services (such as taxicabs). Newspaper stories often refer to capital, and in most cases they are referring to financial capital, such as funds that investors spend in the stock market that allows entrepreneurs to start new businesses.

Entrepreneurship is the ability of individuals to start new businesses, introduce new products and techniques, and to improve management techniques. Owning a business is the dream of many Americans, and many are able to make that dream come true. To be a successful entrepreneur, however, you have to be willing to take risks by introducing new

◄ *These entrepreneurs spend many hours running their catering business.* ***Why do you think some people want to own a business?***

1 Research Assign three students to interview three different business owners in the community and ask them what government regulations they must follow.

2 Student Motivator Ask the class whether they would prefer to live within another economic system besides a mixed one. Then, ask the class how their lives would be different under the three other systems.

3 Discussion Starter Discuss the social programs provided by your local government, and ask students what effect they have on the quality of life in the community.

Caption Answer: Many business owners like being their own boss, solving workplace problems their own way, exercising their creativity, making all the decisions, overseeing a staff, and getting to keep the profits.

1 Critical Thinking Ask students to name different resources that business owners use to produce goods and services. Then have them tell which of the five categories the resource belongs to. Some examples: a grill in a restaurant; a vacant lot; the invention of a new product or process; teachers in a school.

2 Discussion Starter Ask students to describe their recent activities as consumers. What decisions did they make on price and quality? Have they ever complained to a business owner or manager about service or a product? Have they ever intentionally drawn their business away from an establishment because of poor service or product quality?

products and to improve **productivity**—that is, to produce more goods and services in better, faster, and less expensive ways.

Taken together, the resources of land, labor, capital, and entrepreneurship make up the factors of production used to produce goods and services.

Technology involves the use of land, labor, and capital to produce goods and services more efficiently. For instance, when a mechanic uses a computer to set the timing on an engine, the mechanic is making use of a technological advance. Technology also describes the use of science to develop new products and new methods for producing and distributing goods and services.

1 The desire to make a profit, called the profit incentive, goes hand-in-hand with freedom of enterprise. Profit is what's left over after production and all other costs have been paid. It is the ultimate business goal of virtually every entrepreneur.

Freedom of Choice

Freedom of choice is the right of buyers to decide how to spend their money. This is commonly known as supply and demand, and it is what drives decisions that business owners make on what to sell, how much to produce, and how much to charge. Take compact discs, for instance. If thousands of people like yourself buy a group's CD, the group will be a success, and their recording company will produce another CD by that group.

Supply and demand can also affect price. When supply is greater than demand, prices fall. When demand is greater than supply, prices rise. Take the owners of your favorite music store. If they have too many copies of one group's CD, they might slash the price in hopes that people will buy it because it's cheaper.

You as a consumer can also demand quality. If scores of people return a computer software program because it doesn't work correctly or doesn't deliver what it promises, the company that produced it had better fix the problems or the product will fail. If service is poor at a restaurant or a bank, consumers will do their
2 business somewhere else.

Private Property

The right to private property—that is, property owned by individuals or groups rather than government—is guaranteed in the Constitution. For the most part, Americans can buy whatever they can afford and control how the property is used. This property can include a home, a boat, a CD player, or a bag of groceries, to name a few things.

The Bill of Rights guarantees that government may not take private property without paying owners fair market value for it. The government also cannot make citizens shelter soldiers on their property.

Competition

When two or more producers or sellers are offering similar goods, they are in competition for your dollars. A lower

Trading in Tibet

Citizens of Tibet, a country governed by China, rely on trade rather than cash. They trade food such as salt, barley, corn, and turnips as well as products such as detergent, dishes, and foreign goods. After negotiating, a citizen may trade a measure of salt for two and a half measures of corn. A Panasonic battery-powered cassette player is worth four sheep, and a Seiko watch is worth two or three sheep.

price and/or higher quality usually wins the battle.

1 Price is generally where you see the effects of competition. Consumers may leave a product on the shelf if it costs more than a comparable product, or if a producer decides to raise prices without offering a new and improved model.

Say you're looking at two very similar computers. They both have the same memory, software capacity, and ease of use. Which do you buy? If you're like most people, probably the one that costs less.

THE UPS AND DOWNS OF BUSINESS

As you've seen in recent years, with many airlines going out of business and companies merging with or buying their

1 Math Application To illustrate competitive shopping, ask students to figure out how much money they would save a year if they switched from a cable TV company that charged $16.50 a month for basic service to one that charges $12.75 a month. Ask them what they would do with the savings. Then, ask them to go to the grocery store with a list of ten products, and to compare the unit cost per product. Ask what they would save if they bought the cheapest product, and whether they have any misgivings about buying a product just because it costs less.

Case Study Answer: Start a list on which students could write their needs—work, clothes, food, a ride to school, or a game—and what, if anything, they'd like to do for someone else in return—tutor, babysit a younger sibling, or help with chores. Then students who wanted to help could choose a buddy.

People MAKING a DIFFERENCE

Charity with Love

Charity can have a cold sound and a colder feel. If you give to charity, you never know the end result of your gift. If you receive charity, you may never know the honest goodwill that went with it.

In 1988, Linda Wiegand, then pregnant and 29, fell down a set of stairs, permanently injuring her back and spine. She spent days in bed, in pain, feeling sorry for herself.

She finally realized that the only way to get her mind off her own trouble was to help others. She started by contacting the local social service agency, which gave her the name of a family in need. When she and her husband took a load of groceries to the family's house, the Wiegands discovered the family had only $1.83.

Wiegand also found out that needy people need to help others in return. Although the family was very poor, the woman offered to baby-sit for Wiegand's small children in order to repay the kindness.

As a result, Wiegand began Gifts of Love, an organization that pairs needy families with those who want to help. Help can come in the form of food, clothing, education, or job training. Because people work with each other one-on-one, the feeling is that of friends helping friends.

The group now has over 300 volunteers and helps 1,200 families a year. Weigand is part of the eight-member board of directors. She still must spend part of each day lying down, the result of her fall in 1988. Her self-pity, however, is gone. Every day, she sees people help each other, and those who have received help go on to help still others. Linda Wiegand has helped take the facelessness out of charity.

Brainstorm

In what ways could you help students in your school who are less fortunate than you?

1 Research Have students report on the worst recessions in the United States since 1970, and list them in order of severity. Ask them to make copies of microfilm newspaper stories about the recessions.

ailing competitors, all does not always go smoothly in the world of business.

The economy is also no stranger to good and bad times. Such ups and downs are called business fluctuations, or the business cycle. These movements follow a pattern as you can see in Figure 2–1.

Recession

A **recession,** which is any period of at least six months in which an economy does not grow, can occur during a contraction in the business cycle. Recessions have been a recurring problem for the United States economy since the 1970s, and the most serious economic problem during your lifetime. The 1980s started out with a recession that turned into the most serious economic slowdown since World War II. The 1990s also began with a mild recession, and the recovery period was relatively
1 slow.

A recession can have a devastating impact on the economy because it causes people to drastically cut their spending. This, in turn, slows down the economy even more. A really bad recession can lead to a **depression.** In a depression, many businesses fail, prices plummet, there is more supply than demand, unemployment soars, and the economy operates far below its capabilities. You may have heard older family members talk about the Great Depression, which started after the big stock market crash of October 1929. During that difficult time, business activity in the United States declined by a whopping 40 percent. There are now controls in place to prevent some of the factors that led to the Great Depression.

Inflation

The rate of inflation is one aspect of the economy that just about everybody

Figure 2–1 The Ups and Downs of the Economy

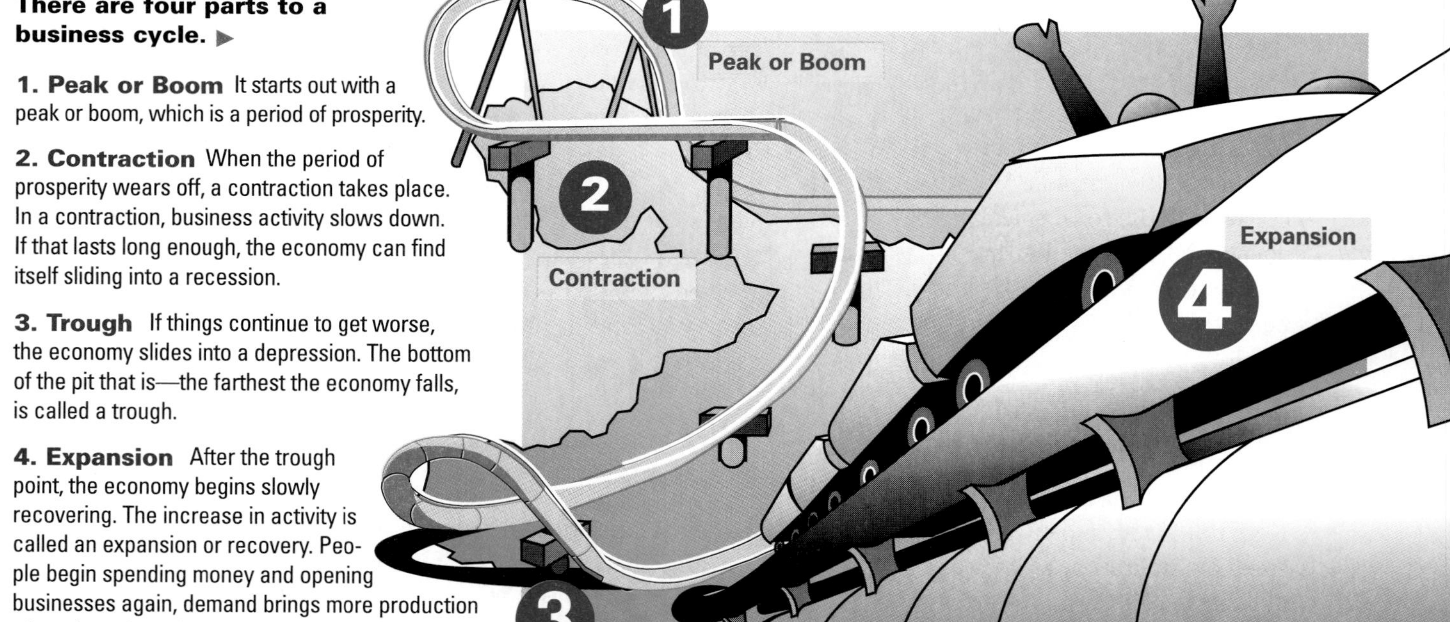

There are four parts to a business cycle. ▶

1. Peak or Boom It starts out with a peak or boom, which is a period of prosperity.

2. Contraction When the period of prosperity wears off, a contraction takes place. In a contraction, business activity slows down. If that lasts long enough, the economy can find itself sliding into a recession.

3. Trough If things continue to get worse, the economy slides into a depression. The bottom of the pit that is—the farthest the economy falls, is called a trough.

4. Expansion After the trough point, the economy begins slowly recovering. The increase in activity is called an expansion or recovery. People begin spending money and opening businesses again, demand brings more production of goods and services, and employment rises.

After reaching another peak or boom, the cycle starts all over again. The length of time of each cycle is irregular; nobody can say how long it will be before a boom turns into a contraction, for example.

wants to know about. When prices rise sharply, that is **inflation.** What this means is that your dollar buys fewer goods and services. This is known as a decline in purchasing power. By the way, inflation doesn't mean that all prices rise, but that the average price of goods and services has soared.

Here's one way to look at inflation. Let's say you get a 4 percent raise at your job, but the rise in the average price of goods and services—the inflation rate—is 8 percent. Your raise can't keep up
1 with the higher cost of living.

This is really hard on older people and others living on a fixed income. But what it may mean for you is that you buy less. This will affect the businesses that you used to patronize. If everyone does this, the economy will slow down.

There are two kinds of inflation. The first is caused by too much demand and too little supply. Prices rise in times like these, and this is called demand-pull inflation. This can happen if many people suddenly have more money to spend, if government spending and business investments increase, which raises demand, and if taxes are cut or consumers start saving less. This kind of inflation occurred in the past when the United States was at war.

The second type of inflation is caused by a huge rise in production costs. This is called cost-push inflation. Producers pass the costs along to consumers in higher prices. A result is that workers demand higher wages so they can afford these higher prices. Unemployment can be high during times like these, because demand is not driving cost increases, so businesses don't hire more people. The last time the United States went through this type of inflation was in 1990–1991.

MEASURING THE ECONOMY

The government's economists keep an eye on the economy by measuring its performance throughout the year. How
2 it's doing will affect everything from government policy on interest rates to how much of a raise your boss will give you next year. It may also influence your decisions on what to buy or where to plan to go to college. If it looks like prices will rise sharply, you may decide to spend less.

Economic indicators are used to
3 check on the health of the economy. Here are the most common indicators and how to decipher them.

Gross Domestic Product

The **Gross Domestic Product** is most commonly called the GDP, and it is the total dollar value of all final goods and services produced in the United States during the year. The GDP is the broadest measure of the economy, and it tells how much American workers produced that is available for consumers to buy. Besides revealing a nation's standard of living, it also provides a way of comparing what has been produced in one year with what was produced in another year.

Only new goods are counted, and only the final, or finished, product. Take the value of a new car, for instance. What the tires are worth would not be counted when figuring the GDP because the total cost of the car includes the tires.

The GDP for 1994 was $6,738.4 billion in current dollars and $5,337.3 billion in constant dollars. The figure for constant dollars have been adjusted for inflation.

Consumer Price Index

The Consumer Price Index, also known as the CPI, is the change in price over time of a specific group of goods and services that the average household uses. The group of items, called a market basket, includes about 400 goods and

FLASHBACK FLASHFORWARD

The health of an economy can be measured by gross national product. In 1945, the gross national product was $211 billion. In 1994, the GNP was about $4.9 trillion. It is expected to exceed $5.8 trillion by 2005. Here's to our health!

1 Math Application Set up a hypothetical situation in which a worker gets a 2 percent raise on a $600-a-week salary but faces 4 percent increases in the cost of rent ($675 a month), food ($300 a month), transportation ($150 a month). How much more would the worker spend than the increase in salary?

2 Student Motivator Have a student or group of students come up with a list of questions on what economists do, and have one student call a local economist at a college or in local government to discuss the questions.

3 Research Ask students to research economics in the news over the past month. How often were the economic indicators discussed?

David Wyss, Director of Research, DRI/McGraw-Hill

"Economists are the observers of what's going on in the world," David Wyss, 50, says. "Everyone is part of the economy, but we're the only ones who get paid to watch it."

As director of research for DRI/McGraw-Hill, Wyss uses his observations to make predictions about the way particular markets, industries, and prices are going to behave. DRI boasts 300 of the Fortune 500 companies as clients and does a significant amount of work for various U.S. government agencies. The kinds of projections Wyss and his team make, therefore, vary widely. They might be constructing a global forecast one day and a forecast on the city of Denver the next.

"Companies know a lot about their own company," Wyss explains, "but they don't know as much about the markets they're selling into. We try to help them plan their business by telling them what's happening to their markets—which industries look strong, what might be happening to prices, which markets are opening up in this country and overseas."

Although DRI does have news wires coming directly into its office, not all events coming in are of equal importance to Wyss and his team.

"The economics of Bosnia are really a nonevent for the U.S. economy," Wyss explains. "What gets us excited is a drop in the stock market, new inflation numbers, or a report on consumer confidence." Those events are important because they directly affect the numbers Wyss uses in his statistical models and methodologies.

Wyss didn't plan on becoming an economic forecaster. He began college, in fact, as a math major and was intrigued by the field of statistics. He decided to find an area in which statistics could be applied to the real world and settled on economics. After earning his undergraduate degree, he went on to get a Ph.D. in economics from Harvard University.

"I like economic forecasting because I like to be right," he explains. "I like to be able to say, 'I told you so.' And forecasting is one of the few disciplines where you find out if you were right or wrong."

Case Study Review

1. What kinds of numbers would an economist be interested in when constructing a model of the city of Denver?
2. Try predicting the future. Look at the price of gasoline at your local gas station or of lettuce at your local market. Write down what you think the price will be in a day, a week, and a month. How close did you come to being correct?

services relating to food, housing, transportation, clothing, entertainment, medical care, and personal care. The rise in this is also called the cost of living. The CPI is an important measure of inflation.

Income

Measuring income determines how much money is available to be spent by businesses and individuals. National income is the total income earned by everyone in the economy. It includes wages and salaries, income earned by the self-employed, rental income, corporate profits, and interest individuals earned on savings and investments. Of these, wages and salaries make up 75 percent of the total.

The two categories that economists track are personal and disposable income. Personal income is the total income that individuals receive before personal taxes are paid. It totaled $5,701.7 billion in 1994. Disposable income is the money that people have left after taxes, including Social Security contributions. That figure was $3,835.7 billion in 1994.

Unemployment

News of the monthly unemployment rate is often on the front pages of newspapers or is the lead story in their business or local sections. It is this statistic that seems the most personal to Americans, because it is the percentage of the civilian labor force that is without jobs but is actively looking for work. The unemployment rate does not include people who are out of work and have stopped looking for a job or people who work in family businesses without receiving pay.

1 With many companies laying off workers or declining to fill existing openings in an effort to cut costs, the ravages of unemployment are not hard to see today. A high unemployment rate is a sign that the economy is ailing, and that human resources are being wasted. Being out of work can disrupt family life, lower a person's standard-of-living, and cause one to lose his or her feelings of worth and self-respect. Because of this, maintaining a low unemployment rate is a priority for most elected officials and is often one of the standards by which voting Americans judge their performances.

Economists generally consider the economy to be at full employment when the nation's unemployment rate is below 6.5 percent. Unemployment rates are also figured for municipalities and states. The nation's unemployment rate in 1994 averaged 6.1 percent.

Balance of Trade and Exchange Rate

The **balance of trade** is the difference between the value of a nation's exports and imports. When the value of exports exceeds the value of imports, this is called a positive balance of trade. In this case, a country is bringing in more

Case Study Answers:
1 The kinds of numbers would vary depending on the reason the economist was looking at the city. Some of the general information needed might include statistics on how many people live in the area, how many are moving there each year, what kinds of taxes the citizens pay, how much money the businesses make, and what kind of money the city government spends.
2 Answers will vary.

1 Student Motivator
Ask a group of students to visit a local unemployment office. Once there, they could ask some applicants about their experiences looking for work and how unemployment has affected their lives, and interview one of the unemployment counselors about the services that the office provides.

◀ *When the GDP is calculated, only the finished product is counted.* ***In addition to tires, what other car parts would not be counted in figuring the GDP?***

Caption Answer: Engine parts, door handles, trim, air conditioning, seats, etc.

money as payment for its goods than it is spending on goods made in another country. A negative balance of trade occurs when a country spends more on imports than it takes in on its own exports. This is called a trade deficit. The United States has been operating at a trade deficit since the start of the 1970s. See Figure 2–2.

On the international market, the countries of the world need to convert their currency so they can buy and sell goods. Converting currency in this way produces an *exchange rate.* If you've ever traveled in another country or have had a friend or relative who has, they have probably talked about the exchange rate. That's how much the dollar is worth compared with currencies of other countries.

Gross National Debt

For years, the American government has been spending more than it takes in. The national debt was $4.97 trillion in 1994.

Where does the government get the money to spend? By selling various types of bonds, including savings bonds and treasury bonds. Each time the government issues new bonds, it creates new debt. Here's what happens when you buy a bond: You give the government your money for a certain period of time to help it pay for a project or service. The government agrees to pay you interest on your money, which means you'll get more money back than you put in.

The national debt is of concern to many people, who view it as a perilous development for a healthy economy. Others, however, say that the national debt actually decreased from World War II to the past few years when it is expressed as a percentage of GDP.

Nonetheless, the national debt, also known as the budget deficit, is an annual topic for Congress and the President, who keep looking for ways to cut it.

As shown in this graph, the United States has had a negative balance of trade for almost every year since 1973. This means that since 1973 the United States has spent more on imports than it has taken in on exports. ***In what year since 1985 was the balance of trade the most unfavorable? The least unfavorable?*** ▶

Caption Answer: The most unfavorable year was 1987; the least unfavorable year was 1991.

Figure 2–2 United States Balance of Trade, 1973–1994

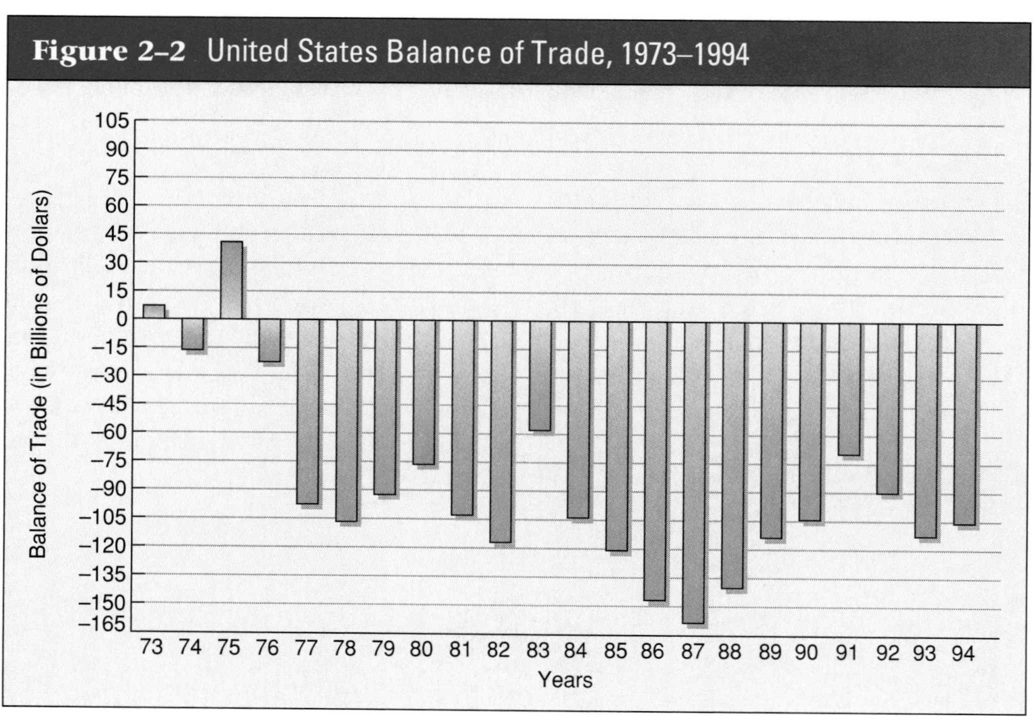

Chapter 2 Highlights	Key Terms
How Economic Systems Work ▶ Making decisions on how to spend limited amounts of money can be difficult, for countries as well as individuals. ▶ To help them allocate money and other resources, countries use an economic system. ▶ Economic systems answer the questions: What and how much do we produce? How should we produce it? Who should produce it? Who should share what is produced?	economic system
The Four Types of Economic Systems ▶ There are four types of economic systems: traditional, command, capitalist, and mixed. ▶ The United States has a mixed system, which combines the command and market systems.	market economists
Characteristics of the American Economy ▶ The characteristics of the American economy are the limited role of government in business affairs, freedom of enterprise, freedom of choice, private property, and competition.	resources productivity
The Ups and Downs of Business ▶ The economy goes through a business cycle that starts with a peak or boom followed by a contraction, and an expansion or recovery.	recession depression inflation
Measuring the Economy ▶ The broadest measure of the economy's productivity is the Gross Domestic Product, and it shows how much American workers produced that is available for consumers to buy. ▶ Other measures of the economy include the Consumer Price Index, unemployment, balance of trade, exchange rate, and national debt. **Reinforcement** Suggest that students review the section by using the five-step study procedure described at the beginning of the Teacher's Manual.	Gross Domestic Product balance of trade

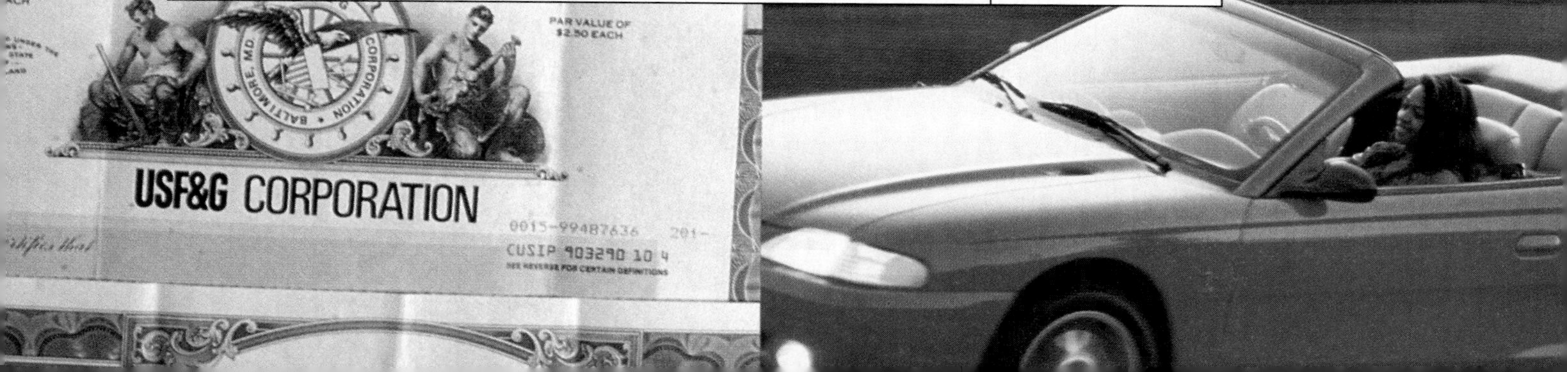

CHAPTER 2 REVIEW

Refer students to the Reviewing Consumer Terms and Reviewing Facts and Ideas activities in the Student Activity Workbook.

Reviewing Consumer Terms
Answers will vary. See Glossary for definitions.

Reviewing Facts and Ideas
See the Student Activity Workbook for answers.

Problem Solving and Decision Making
1 Answers will depend on how students choose to spend the $35.
2 a More—necessity; **b** More—also a necessity; **c** More—interest rates and rents would go up, exceptions would be those with fixed mortgages; **d** More—though fewer unnecessary trips would eliminate increases; **e** Less—need to spend less here to pay for necessities; **f** Less—again spend less here to pay for necessities; **g** Less—not a necessity; **h** More—avoidable cost; **I** Less—not as much left over for saving.

Math
1 Students should share their findings with the class.

Technology
2 Students should share their findings with the class.

Reviewing Consumer Terms

Using the terms below, write a paragraph about our market system.

balance of trade
depression
economic system
economists
Gross Domestic Product
inflation
market
productivity
recession
resources

Reviewing Facts and Ideas

1. What four questions must each economic system answer?
2. What countries use the traditional system, the command or controlled system, the capitalist or market system, and the mixed system?
3. What role does government play in the American economy?
4. When did the United States have a recession and a depression?
5. What does the Gross Domestic Product measure?

Problem Solving and Decision Making

1. You have $35 left from this month's paycheck to spend on one of the following things: The latest CDs by your favorite groups; an upgrade for your computer, which you use for school work; or study guides to help you in two subjects you're having trouble with at school. Which choice would you make, and why?
2. Below are listed some terms that account for a large part of consumer spending. Assume no change in a family's income. During a period of inflation, on which items would they probably spend more? On which item would they probably spend less? Explain.
   a. Food
   b. Clothing
   c. Shelter
   d. Transportation
   e. Recreation
   f. Personal care
   g. Furniture
   h. Medical care
   i. Savings

Building Academic Skills

Consumers Around the World

Math

1. Compare the inflation rates for 1990–1994 of the United States and two other countries of your choice. How have those rates compared to workers' raises in these countries?

Technology

2. Compare how computers have affected business in the United States and in the People's Republic of China. Have the economies of these two countries benefited from computers?

Communications

3. Japan is considered to be the world's technological giant, but other countries are catching up

with it. Write a paper of 250 words about which countries are making their marks in technology.

Science

4. Which country of the world spends more of its money on scientific research, and what has this research yielded? Report your finding to the class.

Beyond the Classroom

Consumer Project

Use an almanac, statistical abstract, or similar source to research one of the key economic statistics described in this chapter. Track the figure for the last ten years and present your findings in a bar or line graph. Then write a 250-word report summarizing the trends shown and giving your interpretation of their significance for the United States.

Cooperative Learning

Family Economics

Break into assigned family groups. Discuss the following problem.

You have heard that the company in which your family members work will be laying off workers and drastically changing the scope of its work.

After 15 years in the same company, your family members must face the possibility that they'll have to move on, or learn new skills in order to stay at their current workplace. To prepare for this, think of other workplaces for them if they should be out of work, or educational opportunities that would help them branch out into other areas of employment. Also, see if other family members can help with expenses by working. Write sample classified advertisements that will tell prospective employers of your abilities. Compare your answers to those of other family groups.

Debate the Issue

Nadia owns a bread-baking plant in South Dakota where she employs 16 workers and pays $12 an hour for an eight-hour workday. This year, the cost of ingredients used to make the bread has gone up 10 percent, five of the company's ovens needed to be replaced at $2,000 each, and competition cut into sales by 13 percent. Now it is time for the annual pay raises, and Nadia is having a hard time coming up with more than 2 percent for each worker. Not only that, she needs her employees to put in a nine-hour day in order to increase production to meet the demands of a new market that Nadia is trying to create with a fast-food chain. "This is my family's business," she tells her workers. "Please bear with me during this next, hard year so we can get through the bad times and keep it going. When times are good, I'll pay you more money."

Her workers, led by Jamal, are outraged at such a low raises, coupled with longer hours. "We've got expenses—rents that are going up, groceries that cost more, kids that needs clothes and books and food," he says. "How can you expect us to live on what you pay us? We already work overtime without getting paid extra for it! Are you trying to drive us all out of here?"

You and your classmates will break into two groups and research this topic. Each group will gather evidence to support one side or the other. You are to prepare the argument for your side of the problem. Then the two groups will meet in a classroom debate.

Communications
3 Student papers should discuss countries where technological advances have occurred.

Science
4 Students should share their findings with the class.

Consumer Project
Student reports should discuss either the GDP, Consumer Price Index, unemployment, balance of trade, or the gross national debt. Student papers should include a discussion of recent trends and their interpretation.

Family Economics
Unions, employment counselors, and outplacement companies can put the family members in touch with other companies. Counselors can also give advice on where to learn new skills.

Debate the Issue
Break the class into two teams. Assign each team one side of the issue. Encourage students to work together as a team to develop their argument. Ask each team to select a member to make an opening statement that supports their side of the issue. Have students take turns debating as the debate moves from one team to the other.

CHAPTER 3

Government's Role

Learning Objectives

When you have finished studying this chapter, you should be able to:

1. Name three types of activities that government performs and give examples of each.
2. State why governments collect taxes and explain the basic principles of taxation.
3. Identify and describe the various kinds of taxes.
4. Describe how government spending at the national level differs from government spending at the state and local levels.
5. Summarize recent trends in tax reform at both the state and national levels.
6. Explain what income taxes mean to you and your first job.
7. Fill out and file your own income tax return.

Consumer Terms

monopoly
proportional tax
progressive tax
regressive tax
real property
excise taxes
pension
disability benefits
taxable income

Real-World Journal

Interview a working family member or other working adult about his or her views on taxes. Ask: Which types of taxes are deducted from your paycheck? Do you feel that tax dollars are being put to good use? If possible, what changes would you make in terms of how tax dollars are spent? How do citizens benefit from paying taxes? Write your findings in your journal.

Lesson Plan See the Teacher's Manual for Chapter 3 lesson plan.

Vocabulary The Chapter 3 lesson plan includes suggested vocabulary activities for the terms listed.

1 Discussion Starter Ask students if their parents, grandparents, and older friends vote. Why or why not? Will students vote?

2 Student Motivator Have students estimate the amount they currently pay in taxes. Ask them how they think this money is spent. Would they rather see some of it spent in other ways? How?

3 Vocabulary Make sure students understand the general distinction between *public* and *private*. Ask what the difference is between public (government) and private (business) services.

WHAT GOVERNMENT DOES

Very soon, you will be an adult—legally responsible for yourself. You'll be able to serve in the armed forces and work at a full-time job. If you are a citizen, you will also be able to perform one of the most important adult jobs. When you are 18 years old, you will have the
1 right to vote.

When you vote, you become the boss. *You* help to decide which people will make up the government—running the country and writing the laws. *You* help to decide how much money the government should have and how that money should be spent. *You* help to decide the kind of place your country,
2 state, and county will be.

In the United States, the *federal government* runs the country as a whole and makes laws that affect everyone in the country. Your own *state government* runs the state you live in and makes laws affecting the people in your state. Your *local government*—which might be a county, city, or town government—runs your local area and makes laws affecting the people in your area.

All these governments are economically important. They perform three kinds of tasks that have a big effect on the economy.

1. Governments provide public services.
2. Governments regulate business activity.
3. Governments redistribute income.

Public Services

Have you come in contact with government today? Chances are that you have. As you left home this morning, perhaps you put out the trash for collection—by *city sanitation workers.* At the corner, you dropped a letter into a mailbox—a mailbox belonging to the *U.S. Postal Service.* Then you boarded a bus for school—a *public transit bus* going, quite possibly, to a *public school.* As you rode, maybe the bus pulled aside briefly to let an ambulance pass—a *city fire department ambulance* rushing someone to the nearest *county hospital.* In just one short trip, then, you probably saw a half dozen different public services in
3 action.

You have learned that public services do the jobs that are too big for private individuals or groups to handle. What kinds of public services do people usually want? Here is a partial list.

- National defense
- Police and fire protection
- Health services
- Street and park maintenance
- Sanitation services
- Highway and bridge construction
- Public education
- Mental hospitals and prisons
- Water, gas, and electric systems
- Environmental protection
- Public transportation

Caption Answer: Other public services: national defense, health services, sanitation services, education, mental hospitals and prisons, utility systems, courts.

Providing public services accounts for a large part of government spending. ***Can you think of other public services? Which services have you used in the past year?*** ►

Economic Regulation

Previously, you learned that our free enterprise system is not entirely free. Government does from time to time influence
1 and even control business activity.

Protecting Consumers You have learned about some kinds of economic control. For example, government enforces a number of consumer protection statutes. These relate to credit, safety, and product disclosure, among other things.

The market for utilities (gas, electric-
2 ity, and water) gives an example of another form of consumer protection. In most communities people do not have a choice of suppliers for these services; there is only one. A situation like this is called a **monopoly.**

Generally, monopolies are discouraged in a free enterprise system, but utilities are an exception. Can you see why? Think of the confusion and expense if several competing companies each laid pipe or strung power lines on your street. Imagine having your sewer pipes dug up and disconnected every time you wanted to change companies! To avoid such problems, governments grant a single company the exclusive right to provide a specific service.

This arrangement has dangers for consumers. Without competitors, the company could raise its prices to unreasonable levels and consumers would have to pay. Government regulation prevents such increases since the company must allow the government to approve its rates.

Making Monetary Policy Government regulates economic activity in still other ways. Through the Federal Reserve System (the Fed), which oversees the banking industry, the government controls interest rates and the money supply. These activities are important in curbing inflation and promoting recovery from recession. The government can lower interest rates to make it easier to borrow money. This borrowing would lead to more spending by consumers and businesses and thus stimulate the economy.

The government might also cut taxes and create public jobs. That would put money in people's hands and encourage
3 consumer spending.

Redistribution of Income

4 Most people want and need to work
5 so that they can buy food, clothing, and shelter, as well as extras like entertainment. Unfortunately, in a market economy, not everyone can or does work.

In some cases, there simply are not enough jobs. In other cases, people are not trained for the jobs that are available. In still others, illness or old age keeps people unemployed.

Nonetheless, these people are still consumers. They need to have an income (money they receive at regular times). At a minimum, they must get food, clothing, shelter, and health care. How can they do this?

Swedish Taxes

Sweden provides its citizens with many social services, but the system keeps the tax rate high. Personal incomes that are above $28,000 a year are taxed at a rate of 50 percent, a reduction from the 1990 rate of 80 percent. In the United States, federal income tax rates are 15 percent for incomes up to $38,000; 28 percent up to $91,850; 31 percent up to $140,000; 36 percent up to $250,000; and 39.6 percent for incomes over $250,000.

1 Reinforcement Refer students back to Chapter 1 for a review of the consumer protection laws and agencies.

2 Reinforcement Have each student find out the names of the companies supplying gas, electricity, and water to his or her home. Probably, the students' homes will all be supplied by the same companies. Have them identify the different companies supplying different types of phone service. If several companies are mentioned, point out that in the early 1980s the government broke up AT&T to stimulate competition in this industry.

3 Critical Thinking Ask students what problem is caused by the dual strategy of cutting taxes and creating public jobs. (It increases the budget deficit since taxes provide income to pay for public services.) Students will learn more about this issue later, but they should be able to see the problem based on what they learned in Chapter 2.

4 Vocabulary Ask students the meaning of the term *redistribution of income* before reading on. This will help them understand and remember the concept.

5 Student Motivator Some people believe that "anyone who is ready, willing, and able to work can find a job in this country." Ask students if they agree or disagree. What personal experiences have they had that support or refute the statement?

The answer is that government helps. Government takes money from some
1 people and gives it to others. Welfare, social security, and unemployment benefits make up the majority of transfer
2 payments.

WHERE GOVERNMENT GETS ITS MONEY

Public services cost money. Governments, after all, must hire and pay employees to deliver those services. They
3 must pay for offices and other facilities. They must buy equipment and supplies. Governments have production costs just like any business that provides services, and they must find a way to pay those costs. That way is by collecting taxes.

No one likes to pay taxes. Most people would rather spend their money on personal items like new clothes or videotapes or magazines. Given the choice,
4 however, most people would not do away with all public services either. Imagine if your community had no police or sanitation workers!

This is the classic economic problem—not enough resources to do everything. The solution also is classic: Make the hard choice; do one thing and give up the other. In this case, taxpayers give up consumer purchases they want in order to pay for public services they need.

Principles of Taxation

You can best understand and evaluate taxes by using three sets of principles: taxpayer identification principles, tax rate principles, and payment principles. These principles answer some very basic questions: Who pays the tax? How much do
5 they pay? How do they make payment?

Taxpayer Identification Principles In the United States, democracy is based on equality under the law. This means that equals should be treated equally. For example, people who have the same income should be taxed in the same way. Two principles of taxation relate to equal treatment in tax matters.

1. *Benefit principle.* This principle holds that those who receive or benefit from public service should pay for it. People who use the toll road should pay the toll. People who use the park should pay the park fees. Some taxes work this way. Unfortunately, it is not always easy to figure out the benefits different
6 people receive from some public services, such as national defense.
2. *Ability-to-pay principle.* Some people have higher incomes and more possessions than others. Under the ability-to-pay principle, these people pay more in taxes simply because they can afford to pay more.

Tax Rate Principles You can group some taxes by tax rate. The tax rate is the percentage that is charged in tax. For example, if you buy a pen for $1 and you

Manufacturers' Warranties

Many items are sold with a manufacturer's warranty. These warranties last for a specified period of time, generally 30 days to more than three years. Manufactures' warranties also range in guarantees—from repairing defective parts (limited) to replacing the entire item, including any shipping and handling charges (full). When you consider a purchase, find out about the warranty. How much does it cover and how long does it last? If the item breaks, do you have to ship it to a special location? Find out if you need to send in a warranty card to keep the warranty valid, and always keep the sales receipt as proof of when you bought the item.

1 Extension Invite to class a local government official dealing with welfare payments. Ask this person to explain where the money for welfare payments comes from and how it is distributed. How many households receive payments? What is the average payment? How is eligibility determined?

2 Reinforcement Student Activity Workbook, Chapter 3 activities.

3 Student Motivator Have students identify all or some of the public buildings in your community. Have them speculate on what it would cost to build and maintain those buildings. Ask them to guess how many people work in those buildings. What would the weekly payroll be?

4 Vocabulary Tell the students that economists have a special name for the thing given up in such a choice. They call it the *opportunity cost.*

5 Extension The IRS has a multimedia package on the subject of taxes. It is called *Understanding Taxes,* and is available to schools for free.

6 Reinforcement Ask students for other examples of the people who benefit from the taxes they pay. (Gasoline taxes pay for highway construction and maintenance; library fines pay for library services; stamps pay for postal services.)

must pay $.03 in tax, the tax rate is 3 percent. A tax rate may remain the same, or rise, or fall as the amount on which the tax is based increases.

1. *Proportional taxes.* A **proportional tax** is a tax whose rate stays the same
1 even though the amount being taxed increases. A sales tax is a proportional tax. You pay a certain number of cents per dollar regardless of the purchase price. If the sales rate is 3 percent, you pay $.30 on a $10 purchase and $3 on a $100 purchase.
2. *Progressive taxes.* A **progressive tax**
2 is a tax whose rate *increases* as the amount being taxed increases. The federal income tax, which is the tax that people pay the federal government on their income, is progressive. The higher your income, the higher a rate of tax you pay. The rates range from 15 percent for the lowest level of taxable income to 39.6 percent for the highest level.

   The progressive tax has two
3 results. First, people with higher incomes pay larger amounts because their taxable income is larger. Second, because the tax rate increases as taxable income increases, higher-income people pay a greater proportion of their income in taxes as well.

   For example, suppose a person earns an income of $20,000 and pays 15 percent in tax, or $3,000. In a proportional or flat rate system, a person with an income of $200,000 and would also pay 15 percent in tax, or $30,000. However, in a progressive rate system, the higher-income person would be taxed at a higher rate, say 39.6 percent, and would have to pay not $30,000, but $79,200 in taxes.
3. *Regressive taxes.* A **regressive tax** is a tax whose rate *decreases* as the amount being taxed increases. Few true regressive taxes exist today. However, most proportional taxes are really regressive when you think of their effect on the taxpayer's total income.

   For example, suppose a family of four earns $20,000 a year. That family probably spends much of its income on consumer goods, paying sales tax on the entire $20,000. A family of four with an income of $200,000 probably saves or invests part of its income and pays sales tax on perhaps only half the income. The lower-income family is therefore paying sales tax on 100 percent of its income, while the higher-income family pays sales tax on only 50 percent of its income. Because of their regressive effect, proportional taxes, such as sales taxes, are considered unfair by many people.

Payment Principles Taxes can also be grouped another way. They can be grouped according to how they are paid.

1. *Direct versus indirect taxes.* Taxes or fees paid directly to a government are called direct taxes. They include progressive taxes like income tax and regressive taxes like the property tax

◀ *The benefit principle says that the people who use a facility or service are the ones who should pay for it. The admission and parking fees that help to pay for the operation and maintenance of national parks are examples of the benefit principle in operation.* ***What additional examples of the benefit principle can you think of?***

Caption Answer: Highways, schools, courts, utilities, hospitals, police and fire protection.

1 Critical Thinking Ask students what kind of consumer goods it would be unfair to place a sales tax on. (Food is a necessity so taxation could be unduly harsh; taxing newspapers might interfere with free speech.)

2 Reinforcement Point out that the progressive tax is an example of the ability-to-pay principle at work.

3 Discussion Starter Although wealthier people are supposed to pay more in taxes, you sometimes read about rich people not paying any taxes. How does this happen?

▲ *Real property, imported goods, and gasoline are all taxed.* ***In each case, is the tax direct or indirect? Progressive or regressive?***

Caption Answer: Real property is direct and regressive. Imported goods are indirect and regressive. Gasoline is indirect and regressive.

1 Discussion Starter
Ask students if they think it is a good idea for special taxes to be levied on items such as gasoline, tobacco, and alcohol. Can they think of other items that should be taxed?

2 Student Motivator
Ask students if they have paid income tax. Ask if they know how much of their pay is deducted for federal income tax? for state income? Ask for volunteers to bring in check stubs that can be analyzed. Make sure students realize how much will be deducted once they have a full-time job.

and motor vehicle license tax. The advantage of direct taxes is that taxpayers know how much they are paying. Thus they can make judgments about whether or not public services are worth their cost.

Hidden taxes are called indirect taxes, because the amount of tax is hidden in the price of the goods and services the consumer buys. Examples of indirect taxes include sales
1 taxes, excise taxes, and import duties.

2. *Pay-as-you-earn collection.* Some taxes are such large amounts that they are collected on a pay-as-you-earn basis. Employers must withhold the tax from an employee's paychecks and deposit it instead with the government. Taxes collected this way include income taxes (federal, state, and local) and the social security tax. Self-employed people pay their tax in installments.

TYPES OF TAXES

In the United States, we pay taxes to different levels of government. We pay personal income taxes to the federal government and sometimes to both the local and state governments as well. Businesses pay income taxes too. We also pay state sales taxes, local property taxes, and many other taxes.

Income Taxes

2 The personal income tax, which is the tax that people pay on any income they receive, is the federal government's leading source of revenue (money). Some states and cities also have personal income taxes. The Internal Revenue Service (IRS) is the federal agency that collects these taxes, or tax revenues.

The income tax is a pay-as-you-earn system. You pay the taxes by having money withheld or taken out of each paycheck during the year by your employer. The income tax program is a system of voluntary compliance. This means that the government relies on individual taxpayers to report their income freely and voluntarily, and calculate their tax correctly.

The income tax has three features that most people think are desirable. First, it is based on your ability to pay. Second, it is a direct tax—that is, a tax paid directly to the government. Third, it has a progressive rate: the more income you have, the higher your tax rate is.

Sales Taxes

The general sales tax is the leading source of revenue for most state governments. The tax is paid by consumers at the store where they buy the goods and services.

Sales taxes are proportional; everyone pays the same percentage tax. However, the effect of the tax is regressive, and this places a heavier burden on people with lower incomes.

1 Another disadvantage is that the tax
2 is indirect, or hidden in the price of the goods and services you buy. Thus, people cannot judge the true costs of the public services for which they are paying.

Property Taxes

3 Property taxes are the main source of revenue for local governments. Most property taxes are paid on **real property,** which consists of land and buildings. These taxes vary greatly from state to state and within states. Nationally, for example, they range from about $836 per person a year to more than $5,091 per person a year. Some people with very valuable property may pay even more per year.

Excise Taxes

Some of the taxes that a government places on the manufacture or sale of certain products and services are called **excise taxes.** State taxes on items like alcohol, gasoline, and tobacco are examples. High excise taxes on items such as these are sometimes used to discourage people from consuming the particular items.

Federal taxes on jewelry, cosmetics, and travel are also excise taxes. As with general sales taxes, excise taxes are added to the price of the goods sold. Excise taxes form a greater proportion of the tax revenues at the state level than at the federal level.

Like sales taxes, excise taxes are proportional and therefore have the greatest impact on lower-income consumers.

Social Security Taxes

Like income taxes, social security taxes are paid on money earned and are withheld by the employer. On a pay stub, the amount withheld appears in a box or space labeled *FICA*. These letters stand for *Federal Insurance Contributions Act*.

Social security taxes are direct taxes, but the tax rate is not progressive. Instead, there is a limit to the amount of income that can be taxed. In recent years, however, that limit is so high ($61,200 in 1995) that, for the majority of workers, all income is subject to FICA withholding.

The social security program that FICA taxes support has two main parts.

▲ *We pay social security taxes out of our earnings when we are young so that we can receive pension benefits when we retire.* ***Do you know anyone who is receiving social security pension benefits now? Do they feel that the benefits are worth the taxes they paid? Why or why not?***

1 Discussion Starter Ask students if they agree that sales tax is a hidden tax.

2 Math Application Have students calculate the total charge for the following purchase prices and sales tax rates: $29.95 at 5 percent ($29.95 × .05 = $1.50; $29.95 + $1.50 = $31.45); $416 at 7 percent ($416 × .07 = $29.12; $416 + $29.12 = $445.12); $78.98 at 6 percent ($78.98 × .06 = $4.74; $78.98 + $4.74 = $83.72).

3 Extension Invite the county tax assessor to explain to the class how property taxes are calculated in your area. Also have him or her explain when payments are due and what happens when people fail to make their payments.

Caption Answer: Grandparents, family friends, and even parents may be receiving social security pension benefits. Some people will feel the benefits are worth the taxes and feel that they could never have saved the money. Others may feel they would have done better keeping the taxes and making their own investments.

1 Extension Chapter 21 contains more information about the social security system. You may want to refer students to that information at this point.

2 Discussion Starter Ask students if they know of any relatives or family friends who have had to pay estate taxes. Did this tax seem fair? How did the person pay the tax? You may want to point out that many people have to sell all or part of their inheritance to pay the tax.

3 Student Motivator Have students survey people they know to identify as many different kinds of licensing taxes as possible. In addition to automobile licenses, legal document taxes (e.g., mortgage taxes), franchises, and permits are common examples. Remind students to talk to business owners they know about the kinds of special fees and taxes the owners must pay for their businesses, for example, liquor licenses. Compile the results in class to see how many different kinds of fees exist.

4 Discussion Starter Ask students if they are aware of two political opponents whose priorities for spending government money were different. Who were the candidates and how did their priorities differ?

Pension Benefits A **pension** is money paid on a regular basis to people who have retired from working. The social security program pays pension benefits to retired people who paid into the program while they were employed. If the retired person dies, the social security program pays money to the surviving wife or husband. Finally, if a worker becomes disabled and can no longer work, the social security program pays the disabled worker money, called
1 **disability benefits.**

Medicare Benefits The social security program pays some of the costs of medical and hospital care for people who are 65 and older. This part of the program is called Medicare.

Estate and Gift Taxes

Estate and gift taxes limit the buildup of wealth by high-income families. In other words they redistribute income.

2 Estate taxes are the taxes paid on all of a person's property after his or her death. They are, in effect, a fee paid for the privilege of passing on wealth to people (family members and others) who have not earned it themselves. Estate taxes are collected only in situations where people have amassed a considerable amount of property. Below that point, no tax is due.

Gift taxes are the taxes charged to the person making the gift. Not all gifts are subject to taxation—only those that exceed a certain dollar amount ($10,000 in 1995). The purpose of this tax is to keep wealthy people from giving away all of their property, say, to their children, in order to avoid estate taxes.

Business and License Taxes

3 Companies and individuals sometimes have to pay business and license taxes. When they pay this tax, they receive a license, permit, stamp, or some other similar item. This item can then be shown as proof that they have the right to perform a certain kind of activity.

People pay license fees to drive a car, own a pet, and do activities like hunting and fishing. Both companies and individuals pay license fees to do business in a particular community. Doctors, lawyers, electricians, and teachers, for example, must pay license fees in order to have the right to work in a particular state.

Customs Duties and Tariffs

Customs duties and *tariffs* are taxes placed, usually by the federal government, on imported goods (goods entering this country from another country). In addition to raising money, these taxes regulate how many imported goods are sold here. The government can place tariffs on imports to make the price of foreign goods the same as or more than the price of American-made products. Customs duties and tariffs are regressive in their effect on the low-income purchaser.

HOW GOVERNMENT SPENDS

4 Each year, the people we have elected to government office must decide how to spend the money collected in taxes. Build more prisons? Hire more teachers? Repave a major highway? Expand a jobs program for teenagers? These are the decisions that government officials must make. In addition, each level of government has special obligations that the others do not.

Over the past decade, state and local governments have been receiving a greater and greater share of the tax money while the federal government has been getting a lesser and lesser share. In 1950, about 70 percent of all tax revenues went to the federal government while about 30 percent went to state and local governments. By 1995, the split was virtually equal.

1 Federal Spending

The federal government is responsible for the national defense. It spends more than one-fifth of each tax dollar it receives on the armed forces. However, the largest portion of each tax dollar—more than 50 cents—is spent on human resources. This category includes social security, unemployment compensation, welfare, food stamps, and health care. Together defense and human resources claim more than three-fourths of each federal dollar.

2 The national debt accounts for another sizeable portion of the federal budget. In 1994, the federal government spent $255 billion more than it collected in taxes. To make up the difference, it had to borrow money from individuals and businesses.

1 Critical Thinking Because the government spends so much on defense, this spending affects millions of Americans in ways other than protection from foreign attack. Ask students if they can explain how raising or lowering the defense budget affects our economy. Does defense spending have any impact on their local economy?

2 Reinforcement Student Activity Workbook, Chapter 3 activities.

Rising like a Phoenix

The phoenix is a mythical bird. Legend has it that at the end of its long life, the phoenix sets fire to itself and is reborn from the ashes. In Minneapolis, the Phoenix Group helps people who feel as if they have gone up in flames rise from the ashes of their lives.

In 1991, two social workers, Chuck Beattie and Bret Byfield, realized that government programs to help street people were not working. These people did not need money, thought Beattie and Byfield. They needed jobs, a community, friends, and a sense that they were contributing something.

Gathering funds from private donations, Beattie and Byfield began buying dilapidated houses in a seamy area of Minneapolis. They hired and trained street people to do the reconstruction. They called themselves the Phoenix Group.

Once the houses were rebuilt, the street people moved in and maintained them, getting benefit from their work. From the skills they had learned working for the Phoenix Group, they could go on and get other jobs. By 1995, the group had bought and refurbished 39 buildings that housed more than 300 tenants.

The Phoenix Group has started other businesses to train and employ people who are down and out. They run a range of businesses that include an upholstery shop, a garage, a small restaurant, a supermarket, and even an art gallery.

Few of the businesses really turn a profit, but profit is not what they are all about. They are about putting people back to work and giving them a reason to feel proud of themselves, a chance to rise like a phoenix and live again.

Brainstorm

How would you go about providing a safe, supportive place for the kids in your community who have run away or who have been kicked out by parents?

Case Study Answer: Research what kinds of government or private grants are available for this kind of project; buy or have donated an appropriate house; recruit kids to help get donations of furniture and to renovate the house; make rules; find someone to supervise and maintain it.

1 Critical Thinking Ask students to speculate on the effect of this decline in revenue based on what they read earlier about property taxes and state taxes. (One of the most significant changes has been the reduction in educational facilities and services offered through California's public school system.)

Caption Answer: Revenue sources the same: individual personal income taxes, corporate income taxes, sales taxes. Expenditure source the same: interest on debt, social programs.

Each year governments decide how to spend their money. ***Which sources of revenue are the same for both levels? Which expenditures are the same?*** ▼

When you borrow money, you must pay it back, together with interest. Therefore, part of the federal budget each year—about 14 cents of every dollar—goes to pay back the money that the government has borrowed over the years. In other words, of the quarter that remained after defense and human resources costs were paid, more than half went to pay off the federal debt.

State and Local Spending

State and local governments spend the most on education—nearly one-third of all their money. Total human resources costs generally take less than half of each tax dollar, although wide variations in budget categories from one state to another make it difficult to generalize. Figure 3–1 compares the spending patterns of both federal and state and local governments.

TAX REFORM

Between the late 1970s and the early 1990s, despite growing tax revenues, governments at all levels were finding that they did not have enough money. To solve the problem, they could either raise taxes or cut public services.

Most chose to raise taxes, even though there was high inflation. Wages went up, but interest rates, housing and fuel costs, and taxes went up even faster. There was a rising tide of protest, ending in what many have called a taxpayer revolt.

Limitations on Taxes

1 In 1978, voters in California passed Proposition 13, which sharply reduced property taxes. Property values had risen so high and so fast in California that many older homeowners living on pensions were having trouble making their tax payments. (Failing to pay taxes could have meant losing their homes.) Proposition 13 changed property taxes back to what they had been in 1976 and froze them there. As a result, property tax revenues fell by $7 billion in the first year alone.

Federal Tax Simplification

What started as a state movement soon spread to the national level. People focused their dissatisfaction on the federal income tax, which many felt was a maze of instructions that gave special treatment to wealthy people.

The tax seemed to be progressive, with more than a dozen tax rates that increased gradually. The more you made, the more you paid. In reality, however, thanks to special exceptions, many of the richest taxpayers fell into the bottom

Figure 3–1 Government Revenues and Expenditures

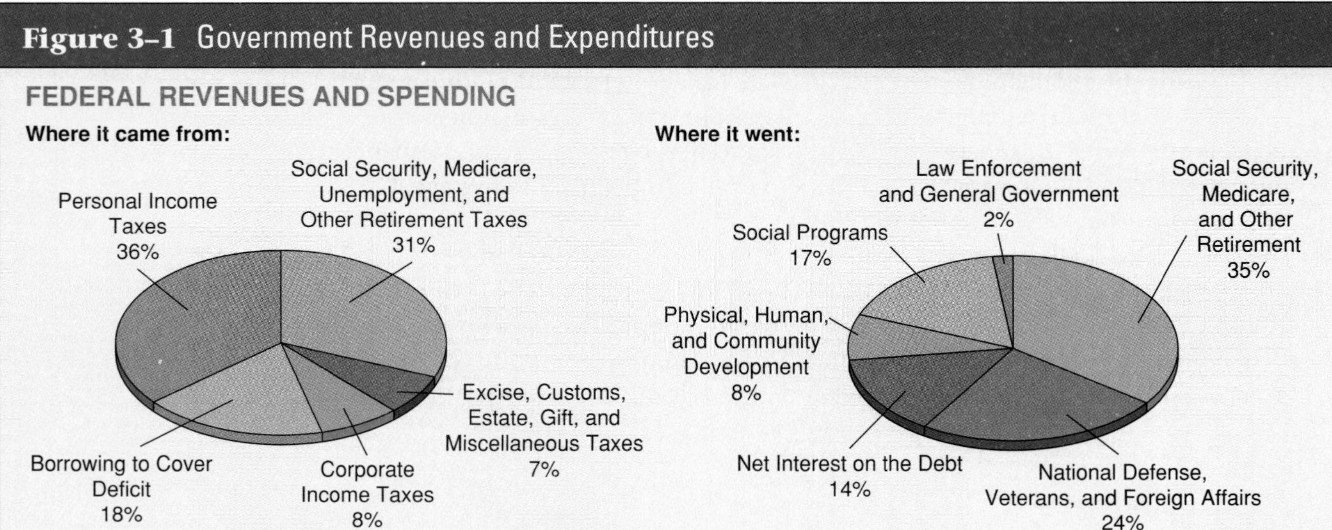

tax bracket. Many of the largest corporations paid no tax at all. Examples like these harmed public trust in the fairness of the tax system.

The Tax Reform Act of 1986 made the most sweeping changes to the federal
1 income tax in over 40 years. It reduced the number of tax rates from 16 to 3 and lowered the maximum tax rate from 50 to 33 percent. It also reduced or eliminated many special exceptions.

2 Again, in 1993, the federal government continued to try to make the tax system fair to all concerned. The Omnibus Budget Reconciliation Act of 1993 continued the work of the 1986 law by increasing tax rates for high-income taxpayers.

The 1993 act also gave incentives for business and breaks for investors, as well as many other changes. Many feel that these and other changes in the future should help make the income tax a fair system for more taxpayers.

TAXES AND YOUR FIRST JOB

You've just landed your first job! Perhaps you are stocking shelves in a drugstore on the weekend, or helping out a teacher in an after-school program, or delivering groceries during summer vacation.

You are excited about starting work, and you know you have to be a responsible employee to keep the job. You have to show up on time and work hard. However, did you know that your responsibilities do not stop with your employer? You now have a responsibility to your government and to everyone else in your community and your country. That responsibility is to pay your fair
3 share of income taxes.

Your income taxes will be based on the money you earn from wages and tips and on other income you might have. Your employer will withhold, or take out, some money from every paycheck and send the money to the IRS. At the end of the year, you will have to file an income tax return—that is, complete and send in to the IRS on the right income tax form.

Form W-4

During your first day on the new job, your employer will ask you to fill out Form W-4, Employee's Withholding Allowance Certificate, shown in Figure 3–2 (see page 48).

Based upon what you say on the W-4, the employer will withhold, or take out, the correct amount of federal income tax from your paycheck. The amount varies from person to person. It is determined

1 Discussion Starter Ask students to survey their parents or guardians to find out their reactions to the tax changes. Discuss the reactions in class.

2 Reinforcement Student Activity Workbook, Chapter 3 activities.

3 Critical Thinking Ask students the following: Why doesn't the IRS say that instead of having income taxes withheld from each paycheck, you can pay the entire amount of the tax in a lump sum at the end of the year? (Students could say that the federal government is a business and needs working capital during the year to operate and that the government might not get its money since many people will not save for the end of the year.)

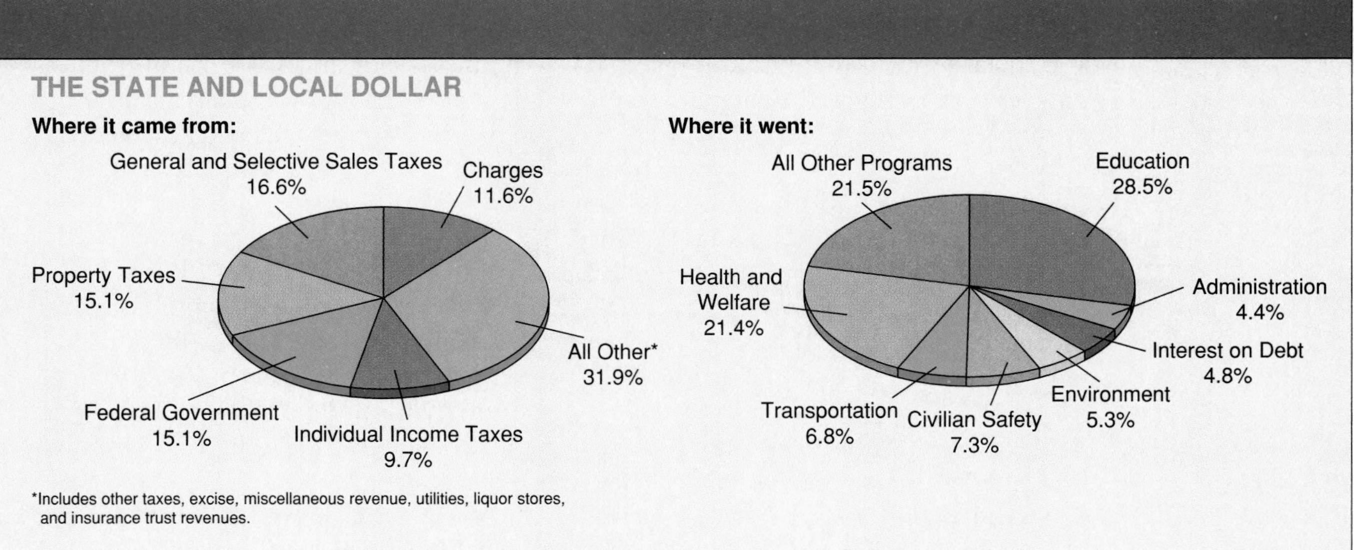

You must fill out a W-4 form for every job you have so that your employer can determine the correct amount of taxes to withhold from your paycheck. ***What information is used by your employer to determine the amount of taxes to withhold?*** ▶

Caption Answer: Wages, exemptions, marital status, how often you get paid.

1 Student Motivation Ask students what a dependent is and whether they are a dependent of someone else according to the IRS.

2 Student Motivator Have students bring in their own W-2 form, or you can bring in examples. Discuss how to use the information presented. You may want to use the actual W-2 of a student, as you explain how to fill out the 1040EZ on the overhead or chalkboard.

3 Extension Contact the local IRS office to obtain a speaker. These speakers can bring materials and explain everything in this chapter, and much more.

Figure 3–2 Form W-4, Employee's Withholding Allowance Certificate

Personal Allowances Worksheet

A Enter "1" for **yourself** if no one else can claim you as a dependent . . . A 1

B Enter "1" if: { • You are single and have only one job; or • You are married, have only one job, and your spouse does not work; or • Your wages from a second job or your spouse's wages (or the total of both) are $1,000 or less. } . . B 1

C Enter "1" for your **spouse**. But, you may choose to enter -0- if you are married and have either a working spouse or more than one job (this may help you avoid having too little tax withheld) . . . C ____

D Enter number of **dependents** (other than your spouse or yourself) you will claim on your tax return . . . D ____

E Enter "1" if you will file as **head of household** on your tax return (see conditions under **Head of Household** above) . E ____

F Enter "1" if you have at least $1,500 of **child or dependent care expenses** for which you plan to claim a credit . . F ____

G Add lines A through F and enter total here **Note:** This amount may be different from the number of exemptions you claim on your return ▶ G 2

For accuracy, do all worksheets that apply. { • If you plan to **itemize or claim adjustments to income** and want to reduce your withholding, see the Deductions and Adjustments Worksheet on page 2. • If you are **single** and have **more than one job** and your combined earnings from all jobs exceed $30,000 OR if you are **married** and have a **working spouse or more than one job**, and the combined earnings from all jobs exceed $50,000, see the Two-Earner/Two-Job Worksheet on page 2 if you want to avoid having too little tax withheld. • If **neither** of the above situations applies, **stop here** and enter the number from line G on line 5 of Form W-4 below.

Cut here and give the certificate to your employer. Keep the top portion for your records.

Form **W-4** Department of the Treasury Internal Revenue Service | **Employee's Withholding Allowance Certificate** ▶ **For Privacy Act and Paperwork Reduction Act Notice, see reverse.** | OMB No. 1545-0010

1 Type or print your first name and middle initial: JOE A.	Last name: STUDENT	2 Your social security number: 123 45 6789
Home address (number and street or rural route): 123 WEST MAIN STREET		3 ☒ Single ☐ Married ☐ Married, but withhold at higher Single rate. **Note:** *If married, but legally separated, or spouse is a nonresident alien, check the Single box.*
City or town, state, and ZIP code: SMALLTOWN, CA 91555		4 If your last name differs from that on your social security card, check here and call 1-800-772-1213 for a new card . . . ▶ ☐

5 Total number of allowances you are claiming (from line G above or from the worksheets on page 2 if they apply) . 5 2

6 Additional amount, if any, you want withheld from each paycheck . . . 6 $

7 I claim exemption from withholding for 1995 and I certify that I meet **BOTH** of the following conditions for exemption:
• Last year I had a right to a refund of **ALL** Federal income tax withheld because I had **NO** tax liability; **AND**
• This year I expect a refund of **ALL** Federal income tax withheld because I expect to have **NO** tax liability.
If you meet both conditions, enter "EXEMPT" here . . . ▶ 7

Under penalties of perjury, I certify that I am entitled to the number of withholding allowances claimed on this certificate or entitled to claim exempt status.

Employee's signature ▶ Joe A. Student **Date** ▶ January 5, 19—

8 Employer's name and address (Employer: Complete 8 and 10 only if sending to the IRS) | 9 Office code (optional) | 10 Employer identification number

Cat. No. 10220Q

by your exemptions, your marital status, your wages, and how often you get paid. 1

Your Personal Information You will have to write in your name, address, and social security number. You will also have to check off whether you are single or married.

Exempt Status You may be exempt, that is, excused, from paying income tax. If you didn't have to pay taxes last
year and you expect to have too little 2
income to pay taxes this year you can 3
write "Exempt" on line 7 of Form W-4.

Allowances Allowances are deductions made from the tax you owe. These deductions are based on whether or not you are married (your marital status) and whether you are supporting other people with your money.

The Personal Allowances Worksheet on Form W-4 helps you figure out the number of allowances you want to claim. The more allowances you claim, the less tax your employer will take out (and the more money you will get in your paycheck).

Form W-2

At the end of the year, your employer totals all your paychecks (income and deductions) for the year and sends you a summary form. This form, called a Wage and Tax Statement, Form W-2, is shown in Figure 3–3.

By law, your employer must send or give this to you by January 31. Check

Figure 3–3 Form W-2, Wage and Tax Statement

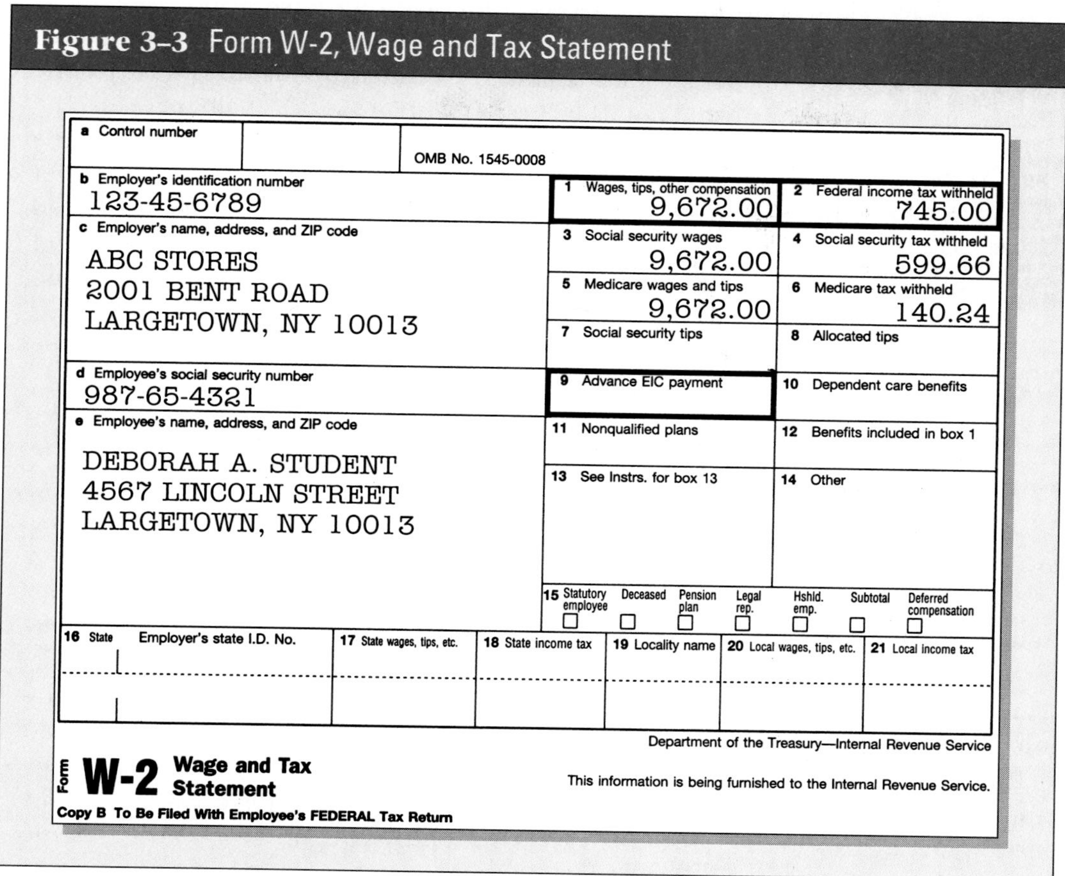

a Control number
OMB No. 1545-0008

b Employer's identification number
123-45-6789

c Employer's name, address, and ZIP code
ABC STORES
2001 BENT ROAD
LARGETOWN, NY 10013

d Employee's social security number
987-65-4321

e Employee's name, address, and ZIP code
DEBORAH A. STUDENT
4567 LINCOLN STREET
LARGETOWN, NY 10013

1 Wages, tips, other compensation 9,672.00	2 Federal income tax withheld 745.00
3 Social security wages 9,672.00	4 Social security tax withheld 599.66
5 Medicare wages and tips 9,672.00	6 Medicare tax withheld 140.24
7 Social security tips	8 Allocated tips
9 Advance EIC payment	10 Dependent care benefits
11 Nonqualified plans	12 Benefits included in box 1
13 See Instrs. for box 13	14 Other

15 Statutory employee ☐ Deceased ☐ Pension plan ☐ Legal rep. ☐ Hshld. emp. ☐ Subtotal ☐ Deferred compensation ☐

16 State	Employer's state I.D. No.	17 State wages, tips, etc.	18 State income tax	19 Locality name	20 Local wages, tips, etc.	21 Local income tax

Department of the Treasury—Internal Revenue Service

Form **W-2** Wage and Tax Statement

This information is being furnished to the Internal Revenue Service.

Copy B To Be Filed With Employee's FEDERAL Tax Return

◄ ***Who supplies you with this form filled out? By what date should you receive the W-2?***

Caption Answer: Your employer. Forms should be received by Jan. 31.

1 Reinforcement Have students conduct a survey of at least five other students. Questions should cover students' general knowledge of taxes and tax returns. Compile the results and share them with the class, the students surveyed, the school, and maybe the entire community. Students should write an essay on the results of their own survey.

2 Research Have students survey at least five adults and find out what materials and records they need to complete their tax returns. Share these results with the entire class. Compile a master list of things needed from all surveys in the class.

that the form shows your correct name and social security number. You will have a Form W-2 for each job you held during the year. This form has information you need to fill out your tax return form.

Form 1099

If you have put some of your money in a savings account, your savings have probably earned some interest. You will receive from your bank a summary of the interest you earned during the previous year. Interest income is taxable. This form, which is Form 1099—Int., Interest Income, is shown in Figure 3–4 on page 49. The form will be sent to you, also by January 31, to be used to do your tax return.

YOUR TAX RETURN

Filling out your tax return is an important responsibility. Remember, whether you worked for 1 month or 12 months, part-time or full-time, in any single year, you need to think about filing an income tax return.

Getting Ready to File a Tax Return

There are many things you need to
1 know or do in order to complete an
accurate tax return. Organizing your
2 records in advance is very helpful.

Do I Need to File? Not everyone needs to file a tax return. However, if you have **taxable income** (money, including earnings, interest, and gifts, on which the IRS laws say you must pay taxes) then you must file a return.

The minimum amount of income on which the IRS bases your taxes will vary depending on whether you are self-employed, over 65, a single adult, a dependent child, or a married person with dependents.

FLASHBACK FLASHFORWARD

No one may be more aware of the dangers of overspending than the U.S. government. Between 1986 and 1993, the national debt more than doubled, rising from $2,125.3 billion to more than $4,250 billion. That's a far cry from the $43 billion debt owed by the government in 1940!

CASE STUDY

Consumer NEWS CLIP

A Brief History of Taxes

by Michael Barone
US News and World Report,
December 12, 1994

In 1797, Britain was threatened as seldom in its history: French armies were spreading revolution to the Netherlands, Germany, and northern Italy; French troops were sailing to help Irish rebels at Bantry Bay; British sailors were mutinying at Spithead. Prime Minister William Pitt, straining to muster every resource to protect the beleaguered British crown, resorted the next year to a measure that politicians have embraced ever since—an income tax. It worked with "unparalleled effectiveness," report Carolyn Webber and Aaron Wildavsky in their *History of Taxation and Expenditures,* producing one-fifth of the revenues Britain needed to survive and prevail.

The income tax may seem a modern invention: many Americans can remember when most ordinary people did not have to file returns. But Pitt did not invent the income tax in 1798. Italian city-states in the 1200s and 1300s levied a tax called the *dazio* on mercantile property in time of war—occasionally several times a year. Napoleon's France taxed income from trades and professions. Holland, the most urbanized part of Europe, levied its first income tax in 1797, Austria in 1799, the Duchy of Baden in 1808, Russia in 1812, the year Napoleon invaded.

History suggests that governments tax incomes (a) when they reach a level of commercial development where many citizens have cash incomes and (b) when they are fighting wars. America's first income tax came in 1861, to help pay for the Civil war; the Union imposed a 3 percent tax on incomes over $800 a year, which exempted most wage earners and, of course, those with little or no cash income. The tax rate was raised in 1862 to 5 percent on incomes over $10,000.

No war, no tax. The converse of history's rule would seem to be: when the war is over, get rid of the tax. The Civil War income tax was repealed not long after Appomattox. But ominously, the Bureau of Internal Revenue remained in existence. And budget-balancing statesmen have turned to an income tax even in peacetime, usually to replace revenue lost by cuts in tariffs. That was the purpose of the income tax law passed by Congress in 1893 and ruled unconstitutional by the Supreme Court in 1895. President William Howard Taft pushed a constitutional amendment to reverse that decision, and an income tax was passed as soon as the 16th Amendment was ratified in 1913.

Decisions, Decisions

1. Why did America impose an income tax in 1861?
2. Why are taxes important to running a government?

Figure 3–4 Form 1099-INT., Interest Income

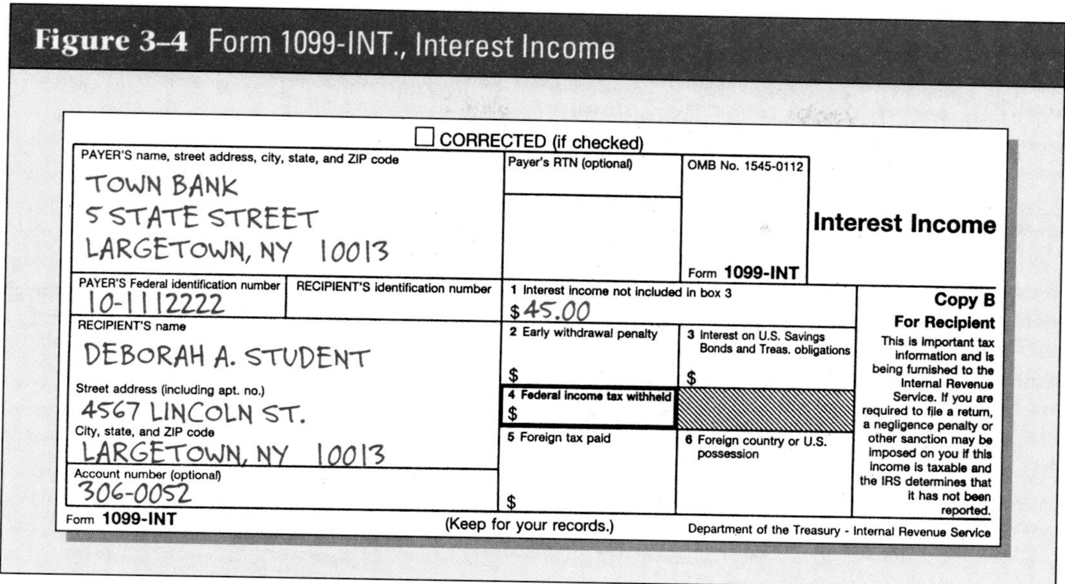

☐ CORRECTED (if checked)

PAYER'S name, street address, city, state, and ZIP code: TOWN BANK, 5 STATE STREET, LARGETOWN, NY 10013

Payer's RTN (optional)

OMB No. 1545-0112

Form **1099-INT**

Interest Income

PAYER'S Federal identification number: 10-1112222

RECIPIENT'S identification number

RECIPIENT'S name: DEBORAH A. STUDENT

Street address (including apt. no.): 4567 LINCOLN ST.

City, state, and ZIP code: LARGETOWN, NY 10013

Account number (optional): 306-0052

1 Interest income not included in box 3: $45.00

2 Early withdrawal penalty: $

3 Interest on U.S. Savings Bonds and Treas. obligations: $

4 Federal income tax withheld: $

5 Foreign tax paid: $

6 Foreign country or U.S. possession

Copy B
For Recipient
This is important tax information and is being furnished to the Internal Revenue Service. If you are required to file a return, a negligence penalty or other sanction may be imposed on you if this income is taxable and the IRS determines that it has not been reported.

Form **1099-INT** (Keep for your records.) Department of the Treasury - Internal Revenue Service

◀ *This form is sent to you before January 31 by your financial institution. It shows the amount of interest your investments earned during the previous tax year.* ***Where could you invest your money to earn interest? Why is interest taxable?***

Caption Answer: You could invest in a savings account in a credit union, commercial bank, savings and loan. It is taxable because it is considered income (unearned) and, for tax purposes, is treated like wages earned from a job.

Generally speaking, if you are a teenager living at home, you do not have to file a tax return unless (1) you earned more than $3,800 at a job, (2) you have income of more than $600 that includes interest income, or (3) you earned more than $400 doing self-employed jobs like baby-sitting.

What Materials Do I Need? To file your return, you need the following materials:

- Form W-2
- Forms 1099-Int and 1099-Div
- IRS instruction booklets
- Extra tax forms
- Your social security number
- Personal records such as canceled checks and check stubs.

1 **Which Form Do I Use?** You must use one of three forms to file your income tax return—Form 1040EZ, Form 1040A, or Form 1040. There are specific situations for using each form. For example, an adult who owns a house may have to use Form 1040. Most teenagers living at home and working part-time can use Form 1040EZ.

When Do I File? Your income tax return must be sent to the IRS by April 15 of the year following the year for which you are filing. For example, if you worked anytime during 1995, you had to file by April 15, 1996.

Filing Your Income Tax Return

You probably need to use Form 1040EZ to file your income tax return. As you get older and perhaps marry, have children, buy a house, and earn more money, you will probably need to use one of the other forms. Figure 3–5 (see page 50) suggests ways for you to keep up on your taxes.

Getting Help with Your Taxes

2 Though the IRS tries to create tax forms that are easy to fill out, many forms may still seem difficult and complicated to you. Especially if you haven't filed a tax return before, you might want to get help. The IRS, private companies, your local library, books, and computer software can give you that help. Some are free; others charge for their services. Remember that tax forms and booklets printed by the IRS are always free. Regardless of where you get help, when you sign the return, you are legally responsible for everything on that return.

1 Student Motivator Use as an example the tax information of one of your students (with permission). Explain the steps for completing the return (1040EZ). Afterwards, give the students sample problems to fill out.

2 Extension Invite people who do income tax returns as a career to share with the class the career possibilities in this field. They can also explain how they operate their business.

News Clip Answers:
1 To help pay for the Civil War.
2 Taxes represent key financial income to a government. They provide the resources to fund social programs, defense requirements, and other regulatory activities.

Student Motivator Arrange to have some of your students offer their services to other students in the school by doing tax returns. This could be done during class time or when classes are not in session (before school, lunch, after school). They might even be able to assist faculty and staff members with their taxes.

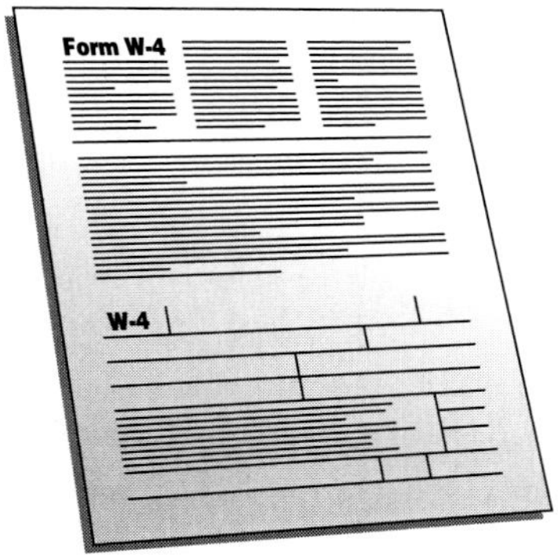

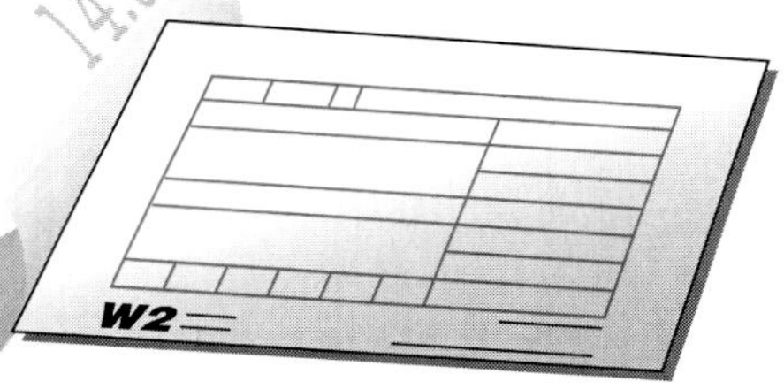

Figure 3–5 Keeping Up with Your Taxes

You can keep up with taxes by becoming aware of the tax return process.

HELP WANTED
1. You get a job.
2. Decide if you are exempt and fill out form W-4.
Form W-4
W-4
3. Your employer witholds taxes from your paycheck.
4. Your employer sends you Form W-2 by January 31.
W2
5. Your bank sends you Form 1099-INT by January 31.
1099 INT
6. You decide which form to use and get your materials together.
1040
1040EZ
1040A
7. You fill out the form, getting help as you need it.
8. You sign the form, make a copy, attach any needed forms (W-2, 1099), attach a check for tax due (if any), and mail the return by April 15.

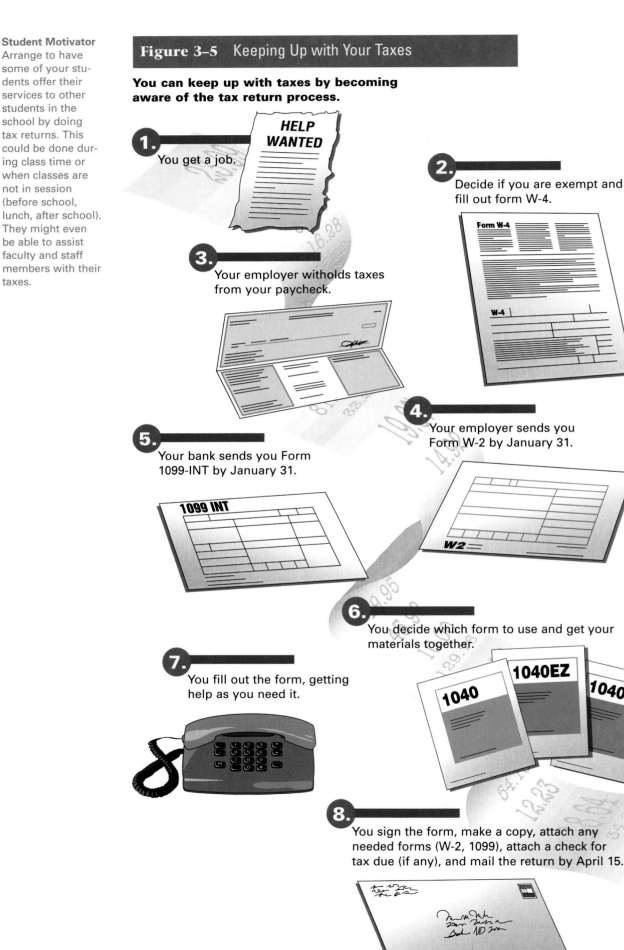

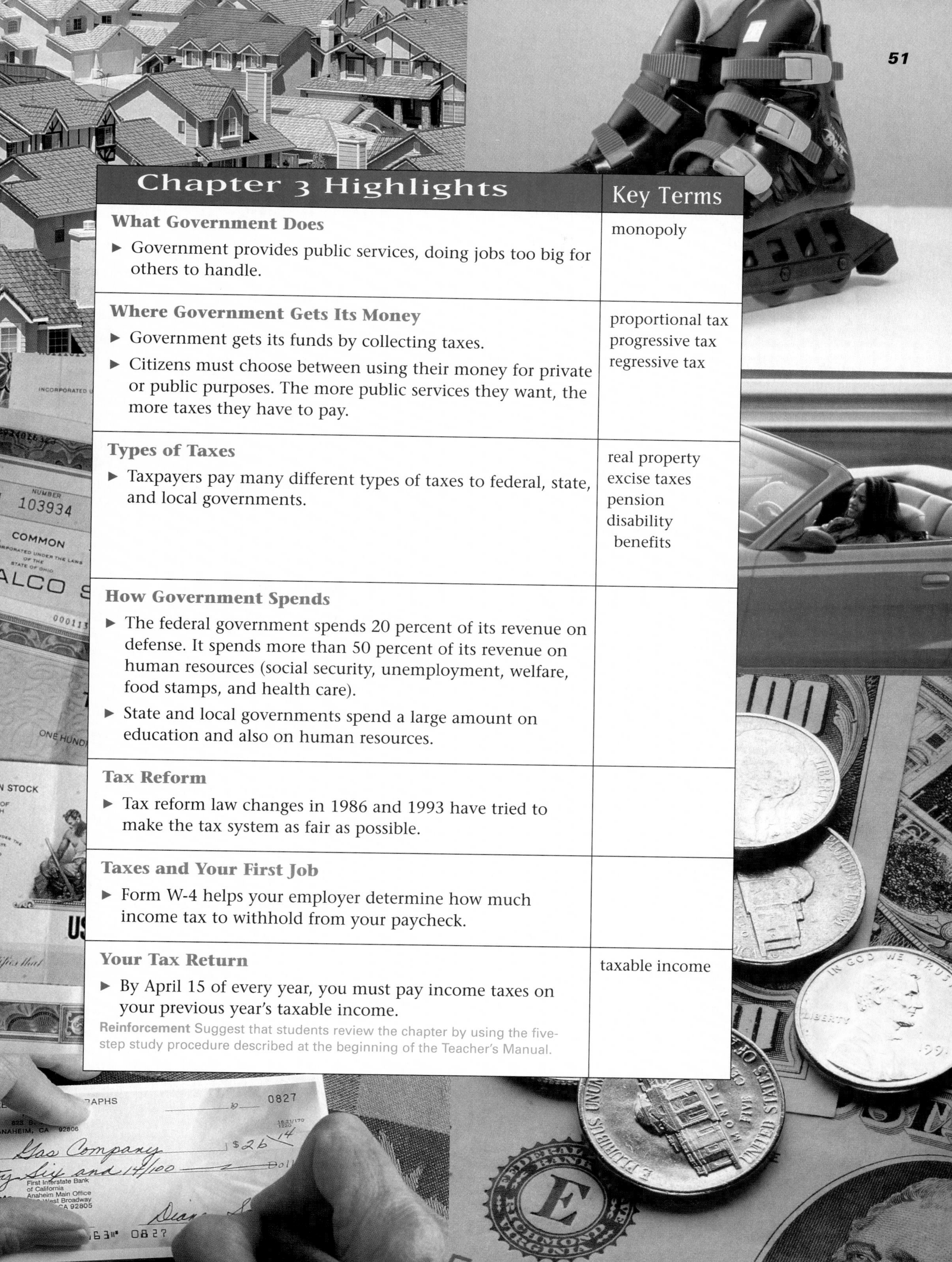

Chapter 3 Highlights

Chapter 3 Highlights	Key Terms
What Government Does ▶ Government provides public services, doing jobs too big for others to handle.	monopoly
Where Government Gets Its Money ▶ Government gets its funds by collecting taxes. ▶ Citizens must choose between using their money for private or public purposes. The more public services they want, the more taxes they have to pay.	proportional tax progressive tax regressive tax
Types of Taxes ▶ Taxpayers pay many different types of taxes to federal, state, and local governments.	real property excise taxes pension disability benefits
How Government Spends ▶ The federal government spends 20 percent of its revenue on defense. It spends more than 50 percent of its revenue on human resources (social security, unemployment, welfare, food stamps, and health care). ▶ State and local governments spend a large amount on education and also on human resources.	
Tax Reform ▶ Tax reform law changes in 1986 and 1993 have tried to make the tax system as fair as possible.	
Taxes and Your First Job ▶ Form W-4 helps your employer determine how much income tax to withhold from your paycheck.	
Your Tax Return ▶ By April 15 of every year, you must pay income taxes on your previous year's taxable income. **Reinforcement** Suggest that students review the chapter by using the five-step study procedure described at the beginning of the Teacher's Manual.	taxable income

CHAPTER 3

REVIEW

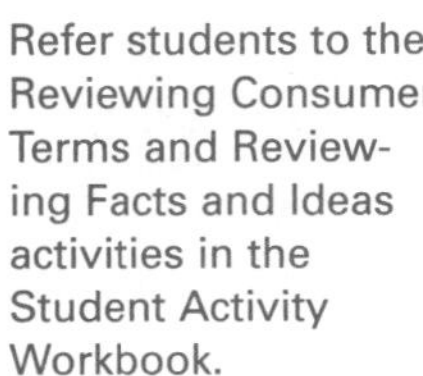

Refer students to the Reviewing Consumer Terms and Reviewing Facts and Ideas activities in the Student Activity Workbook.

Reviewing Consumer Terms
Essays will vary. See Glossary for definitions.

Reviewing Facts and Ideas
See the Student Activity Workbook for answers.

Problem Solving and Decision Making
Student responses should address all questions and include a final recommendation.

Consumers Around the World
Math
1 $7,044.66 (.15 × 22,750 = 3,312.50; .28 × 12,750 = 3,632.16)

Communications
2 Student reports should cover all key dates.

Reviewing Consumer Terms

Incorporate all the terms below into a 250-word essay explaining the government's role.

disability benefits
excise taxes
monopoly
pension
progressive tax
proportional tax
real property
regressive tax
taxable income

Reviewing Facts and Ideas

1. Name the three types of activities that government performs.
2. List five common public services that government provides for citizens.
3. Why do governments collect taxes?
4. What is the difference between a direct and an indirect tax?
5. Identify various types of taxes.
6. Describe how spending at the national level differs from government spending at the state and local level.
7. Summarize recent trends in tax reform.
8. List and explain five common taxes that you have paid or might pay in the near future.
9. What are the steps you would follow in filling out and filing your tax return?

Problem Solving and Decision Making

As budget director for a small state, you must raise $500 million for emergency repairs to the state's bridges. Your funding options are listed below. Describe the pros and cons of each and make a final recommendation. **(a)** Place a sales tax of 6 percent on all purchases except food and prescription drugs. **(b)** Place a personal property tax on cars based on the purchase price and age of the vehicle, with a minimum tax of $20. **(c)** Place tolls on each bridge repaired; the tolls could exceed $3 per round trip.

Building Academic Skills

Consumers Around the World

Math

1. Below is a copy of a partial Tax Rate Schedule for a single person. Use this schedule to determine the amount of taxes owed for a taxable income of $35,722.

Tax Schedule for Single Persons

Taxable Income (in Dollars)	Tax Rate
0–22,750	15% of the amount over $0
22,750–55,100	28% of the amount over $22,750 *plus* 15% of $22,750

Communications

2. Income taxes have been used in the United States for over 200 years. Even before the American

Revolution, colonists claimed that "taxation without representation is tyranny." Research how the U.S. Constitution provided against taxation without representation. Prepare a time-line report showing some of the key dates and events in the evolution of our system during the last 200 years and how they have affected the tax system.

Social Studies

3. The system of taxes in the United States is not the same as in many other countries. Select another country and research its tax system. Prepare a report showing the similarities and differences between the two systems. Describe how revenues are raised, who pays, how they pay, how much they pay, and what problems are faced by both systems. Be prepared to present your report orally to other students.

Technology

4. Many people today use a computer and tax return software to prepare their tax returns. Research how popular these programs are, how many people actually use them to file their returns with the IRS, and how accurate the programs are. Be prepared to share your findings with your classmates.

Beyond the Classroom

Consumer Projects

Conduct a survey for one week of yourself and three other people—a friend, a relative, your boss, teacher, or coach. Develop a survey questionnaire that asks participants to show how much time they spent in daily activities such as eating, studying, traveling, sports, and entertainment for one week. For example, you could use a daily calendar form with time slots that the participant fills in. At the end of the week, collect the surveys and analyze the results. Make a chart that groups all the activities into various services provided by government agencies—schools, highways, defense, emergency help, public services, and so on. Summarize the results in a 500-word report. Indicate the different services, the level of government involved (federal, state, local), the type of activity involved, and the approximate percentage of time spent on each. Include your survey questionnaires and your analysis chart. Were you surprised by the results? Why or why not?

Cooperative Learning

Family Economics

Break into assigned family groups. Discuss the following problem.

It's the second week in April—tax time. Fill out the appropriate federal tax form (1040A or 1040EZ) for your family. You may need to fill out a different form for different members of your family. Compare your tax computations with those of other family groups.

Debate the Issue

Many proposals have been suggested to reform our present progressive tax system. One of the most frequently mentioned is the *flat tax* where all taxpayers would pay the same percentage of income.

You and your classmates will break into two groups and research this topic. Each group will gather evidence to support one side or the other. You are to prepare the argument for your side of the problem. Then the two groups will meet in a classroom debate.

Social Studies
3 Students should share findings with the class.

Technology
4 Students should share findings with the class.

Consumer Project
Student reports should cover all questions and include surveys and analysis chart.

Family Economics
Most families will use form 1040A (married, with or without dependents). Go through the procedure for filling out the form step-by-step. Give special emphasis to the effects of different standard deductions and different numbers of exemptions.

Debate the Issue
Break the class into two teams. Assign each team one side of the issue. Encourage students to work together as a team to develop their argument. Ask each team to select a member to make an opening statement that supports the team's side of the issue. Have students take turns debating as the debate moves from one team to the other.

CHAPTER 4

Global Economics

Learning Objectives

When you have finished studying this chapter, you should be able to:

1. Tell why countries trade with one another.
2. Describe how international trade affects the U.S. consumer.
3. Name three barriers to trade.
4. Explain the role of international finance.

Consumer Terms

import
export
international trade
trade deficit
free trade
protectionism
quota
embargo
currency
telecommunications

Real-World Journal

In your journal, list five products in your home that were manufactured in foreign countries. Do U.S. companies also make the same type of products? Why did you purchase foreign products rather than U.S. products? Was price a factor in your decision? Was quality a factor? List all the factors that influenced your buying decision.

Lesson Plan See the Teacher's Manual for the Chapter 4 lesson plan.

Vocabulary The Chapter 4 lesson plan includes suggested vocabulary activities for the terms listed.

1 Discussion Starter Have students look around the room and pick out items—clothing, books, desks, and so forth—that they think were made in the United States and in other countries. Then have them check the labels to see if they were right. Are they surprised at what they have found?

2 Research Ask students to report on the top 20 products that the United States imports and the top 20 that it exports.

3 Critical Thinking Have students pick a product and compare the cost of the U.S.-made item with its foreign-made competitors. Ask them to compare features, quality, and performance.

Caption Answer: Some buyers favor imports because they say their quality, style, workmanship, and performance are better than domestic products. Lower prices are also a factor.

WHY DO NATIONS TRADE?

Think for a moment about the clothes you are wearing today. Where were they made? Your shirt might have been made in the Philippines, your shoes in the United Kingdom, your jeans in China.

How about the cars you saw on the way to school today? Some were made in Japan, some in Germany, some in Sweden. Did you have orange juice with your breakfast this morning? It might have come from concentrate made in Mexico. More and more, products bought and used by consumers in the United States
1 are made in other countries.

- *Imports.* A product brought in for sale from a foreign country is an **import.** Imports can be consumer goods; for example, more than 60 percent of the radios, televisions, and motorcycles sold in the United States are made in other countries. Imports can also be raw materials or other items to be used in manufacturing. For example, more than 90 percent of the bauxite, which is used to make aluminum, comes from outside the United States.
- *Exports.* A product sent to a foreign country for sale is an **export.** The United States does its share of exporting. More than 11 percent of the trucks and buses made in this country and 40 percent of the engineering and scientific instruments are exported. One-third of the corn, half of the cotton, and nearly two-
2 thirds of the wheat grown in the
3 United States are shipped overseas.

The nations of the world are part of a global economy in which the economic well-being of every country is increasingly dependent on the economic well-being of all others. Within this global economy, the business of buying (importing) and selling (exporting) between nations is known as **international trade.**

International trade is not new. The famous Scottish economist Adam Smith analyzed the benefits of international trade in his study *The Wealth of Nations* in 1776. Countries trade with one another to increase their wealth in a number of ways.

Acquiring Resources

Often, one country has resources that another lacks or has in lesser supply. The only way for the second country to acquire the resources of the first is through trade.

There are some products that consumers in the United States would have

Consumers are faced with many choices in the marketplace today, and many everyday items they choose from are made outside the United States. ***Why would some people buy imports?*** ▶

to do without if these goods were not imported. You probably know people who drink coffee in the morning and put pepper on their fried eggs. The coffee and pepper were grown in other countries. If the United States did not trade for these goods, U.S. consumers would not be able to buy them.

In exchange for coffee from Brazil, say, the United States may export medicines, fertilizer, and plastics *to* Brazil, resources which that country lacks or has in very limited supply. Most other countries trade in the same way. For example, France may trade perfumes to
1 Saudi Arabia for oil.

Benefitting Economically

Anita and Hector Ortega share two chores at home—doing the laundry and cleaning the kitchen. It takes Anita about 5 hours to do the laundry and just 3 hours to clean the kitchen. On the other hand, it takes Hector 3 hours to do the laundry and 5 hours to clean the kitchen.

Anita and Hector used to split the two jobs in half—each spending 4 hours a week on chores. Then they decided to split the work differently. Now, Hector does the laundry in 3 hours, Anita cleans the kitchen in 3 hours, and they both have an extra free hour a week.

In this example, Anita and Hector have divided the work according to the *law of comparative advantage.* In their "trading," they each specialized in the work they did more efficiently than the other. As a result, each benefitted.

According to the law of comparative advantage, countries trade to increase their wealth in the same way that, in the example, Anita and Hector increased their free time. Trading partners tend to specialize in the goods they produce most efficiently—producing a natural resource like copper or lumber, growing a crop like rice or wheat, or manufacturing equipment or high-tech products. By specializing in what they do most efficiently and trading for goods they produce less efficiently, countries actually
2 produce more goods and sell more goods.

EFFECTS OF INTERNATIONAL TRADE

International trade affects people as consumers—and also as workers and citizens—in several ways. Politicians, economists, and other individuals sometimes differ in their evaluation of the benefits
3 of international trade.

Positive Effects

Consumers benefit in a number of ways from international trade. Some benefits, such as lower prices, are direct; some, such as the creation of jobs, are indirect.

Foreign Specialties Imports bring into the U.S. market many prized goods that would otherwise be unavailable. Russian caviar, French wine, and Peruvian alpaca are some examples.

Lower Prices The competition from imports keeps domestic prices down and gives consumers a range of choices. For

Cable TV

British subscribers to cable television pay about $500 a year. In Japan, the annual fee is about $173 per household. In the United States, cable subscribers pay about $360 a year.

1 Discussion Starter
Ask students to think of items that they associate with particular foreign countries, for example, French wine, Turkish carpets, Russian sable, Swiss watches.

2 Interesting Note
The law of comparative advantage was developed by David Ricardo, a British financial thinker, in his major work, *On the Principles of Political Economy and Taxation,* published in 1817.

3 Discussion Starter
Ask students how their interests as a consumer might conflict with their interests as a worker. (As consumers, they might prefer low-priced imports; as workers, they might lose their jobs to low-priced imports.)

1 Vocabulary Ask students the meaning of *domestic*. (Relating to the country under discussion; opposite of *foreign*.)

2 Discussion Starter Japanese-made cars have been rated more reliable than U.S.-made cars by *Consumer Reports*. Ask students whether U.S. consumers should buy less-reliable cars simply because they are made in the United States.

example, in the area of electronics, competition from high-quality Japanese-made products has meant large savings for consumers.

In addition, consumers benefit
1 when domestic manufacturers can use
lower-priced imported materials or components in their products. The savings usually result in lower consumer prices.

Improved Quality Competition from foreign manufacturers stimulates many domestic companies to improve their products. The success of foreign car sales led U.S. automobile makers to improve the quality of their cars and add features
that are common to imported cars, to
2 the benefit of consumers.

Market for Exports Remember also that in international trade, U.S. companies export goods, and foreign consumers buy those goods. (See Figure 4–1.) Large companies such as IBM and Eastman Kodak sell billions of dollars worth of goods in foreign markets.

However, in order for the United States to sell its exports, U.S. consumers must buy imports. Only when U.S. consumers buy imports do foreign countries acquire the capital to pay for U.S. exports.

Growth of Jobs and Businesses Firms that export goods must hire workers at home in the United States to conduct business. These jobs are good for consumers since they increase the amount of money available for spending.

The United States is a major importer and exporter. In 1994, it imported $663.3 billion worth of goods and services and exported $512.6 billion. ***Are some imports more vital than others?*** ▶

Caption Answer: Imports of raw material such as crude oil are essential to domestic manufacturing and other functions. Increased prices of these imports can lead to increased domestic prices.

Figure 4–1 Imports and Exports

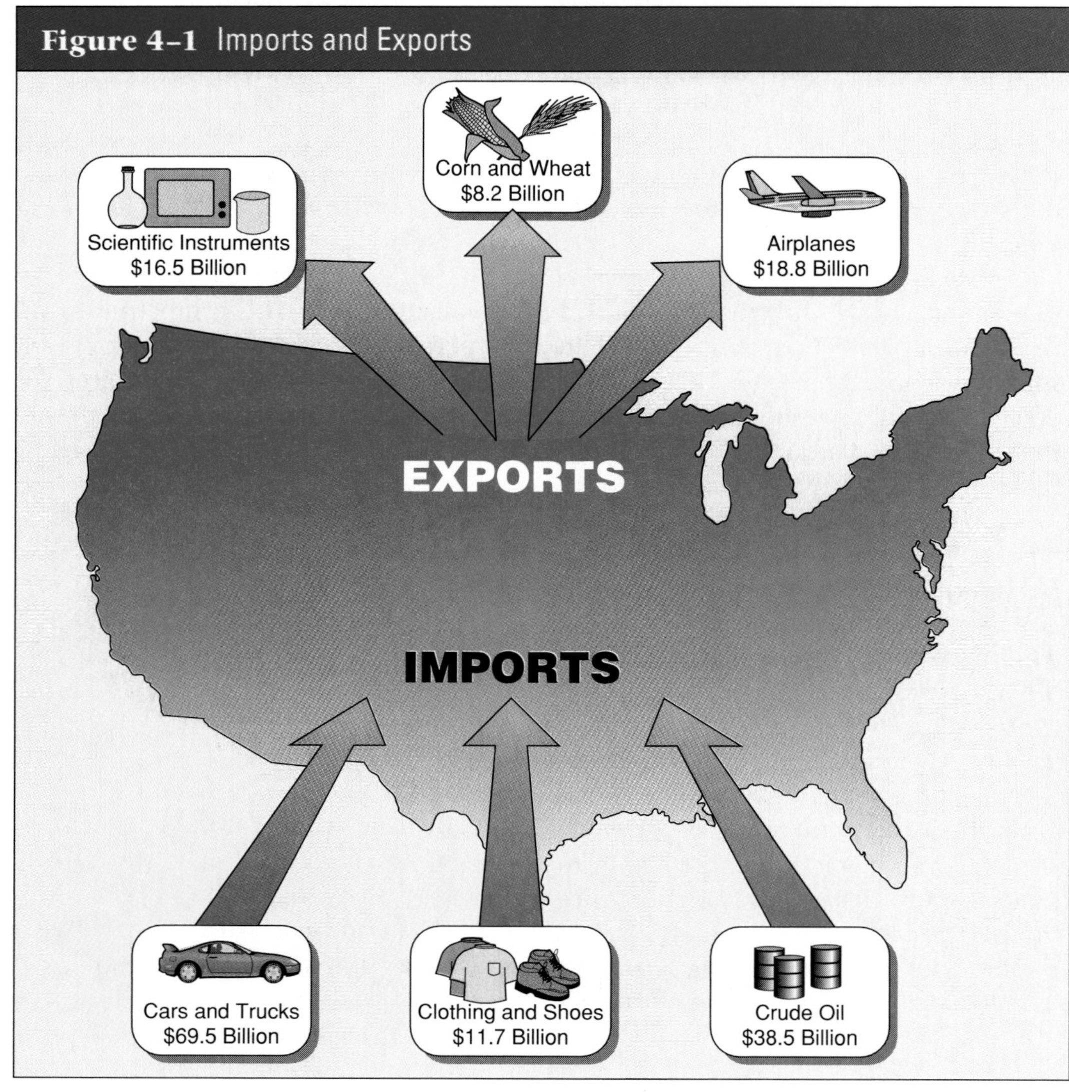

Also, the many domestic businesses that depend upon imported materials or parts for their products would go out of business without international trade.
1 When firms go out of business, workers
2 lose their jobs.

Negative Effects

International trade has negative effects on different segments of the U.S. economy. Some people feel that the negative effects outweigh many of the advantages of buying imports.

Poor Quality Some foreign-made products may not be up to the standard that U.S. consumers expect. For example, in the past some inexpensive imported toys did not meet the safety regulations set for U.S. manufacturers. Consumers must make sure that the imports they buy meet their needs.

Unemployment Some imports may be priced far below domestic products or they may be of better quality than domestic goods. If U.S. companies cannot match the prices or quality, they may be forced out of business by the imports.

When companies fail, workers become unemployed. For example, at various times U.S. auto workers and steel workers have suffered large-scale unemployment because of the competition from imported cars and steel.

Unemployment in the fields affected by imports is the greatest negative impact perceived by most people. Over the past 20 years, there have been various movements by U.S. labor groups and others to encourage consumers to "Buy
3 American" to protect American jobs.

Some economists believe that the best way to handle unemployment is through retraining and the creation of jobs in thriving industries. Consumers, they argue, should not have to subsidize jobs through higher prices.

Other observers, however, reply that consumers, as taxpayers, pay the costs of government retraining programs and other benefits in any event, and that
4 the human costs of unemployment are
5 too high.

Trade Deficit When a country's imports grow faster than its exports, the country has a **trade deficit.** The United States started running a trade deficit in the 1970s, and in 1994 the trade deficit was $106.2 billion.

Suppose you earn $12 a week, but you spend $15. You have to borrow $3 to get through the week. In the same way that you must pay for your expenses with what you earn, a nation must pay for its imports with the money earned from its exports. If there is not enough money from exports, the nation has a trade deficit and must borrow money.

How to Negotiate a Price

Bargaining is a standard way of doing business at flea markets or street fairs, when traveling in some foreign countries, or when buying or selling used items. It also can get you a reduced price at your local department store or car dealership.

- **Know the value of the item. Is it new or used? What condition is it in?**
- **How much is it worth to you? In your mind, establish the most you would pay. Then offer a lower price.**
- **When you receive a counteroffer, make another offer. But hold firm at your highest price. Be prepared to walk away if you can't buy or sell at the price you want.**

1 Extension Tell students that some foreign auto makers have opened plants in the United States and they manufacture cars here. Therefore, some "foreign imports" are actually U.S.-made.

2 Critical Thinking Ask students to think of jobs that might depend on imports and exports. (Sales, clerical, and administrative workers in import and export businesses; agricultural workers; manufacturing workers.)

3 Discussion Starter Ask students how they feel about the "Buy American" campaign. Are they willing to pay more for products in order to support jobs for American workers? Do they look at labels of products before making buying decisions?

4 Discussion Starter Ask students what role they think government should play in retraining workers. Should business contribute to these costs?

5 Student Motivator Ask students what the possibility of losing a job means to them in terms of their career plans. (It makes sense to get as much training as possible, choose a growing field, keep current with training, and be prepared to switch fields if necessary.)

FLASHBACK FLASHFORWARD

Since World War II, U.S. trade restrictions have become increasingly relaxed. In the 1930s, protective tariff rates were as high as 60 percent of the value of imported goods. Today, as a result of the movement toward free trade and such agreements as the North American Free Trade Agreement, tariff rates are about 5 percent of the value of imported goods.

1 Critical Thinking Ask students why some economists believe that the trade deficit amounts to nothing more than the export income to be earned. (The trade deficit, which is debt, can be paid off only with money gained from the sale of exports.)

2 Research Have students look through the business pages of the newspaper for articles about foreign ownership of U.S. companies—and U.S. ownership of foreign companies.

3 Vocabulary Point out to students the positive connotations of the term *protectionism.* What or who is being protected? How attractive would this idea sound if it were named *restrictionism?*

The causes of a trade deficit are complex, however. Economists agree that there is no easy solution. Economic policies that the federal government can use may too easily lead to lessening of
1 exports or to inflation.

Foreign Investment in the United States The economic interdependence of countries has led to the foreign ownership of U.S. companies. For example, Burger King and Pillsbury are both owned by British firms. Chicken of the Sea is owned by an Indonesian company, and A&P supermarkets are owned by a German firm.

U.S. companies have always owned businesses and real estate in foreign nations. Now the United States has become a good investment for foreign companies and individuals.

Some people are concerned that foreign investment will influence U.S. policies or change how Americans live. Others point out, however, that foreign investors create jobs and other economic opportunities in the United States.

An important trend among large companies is to become *multinational.* These companies design, produce, and sell their products in many nations. Where a multinational company's headquarters is located is not important to their business efforts. For example, Nestlé employs more than 200,000 people but fewer than 5,000 work from its home country of Switzerland. The remaining work in offices in more than 50 countries around the globe.

Multinational companies do not think of domestic operations separately from international operations. Rather their planning and decision making are based on the needs of the global market. Ford Motor Company, for example, is committed to building "world cars" by merging, streamlining, and making uni-
2 form all aspects of its global operation.

LIMITING IMPORTS

The importing and exporting of goods without any artificial restrictions is known as **free trade.** Some people feel that the solution to the negative effects of international trade is protectionism. **Protectionism** is the idea that government should preserve domestic businesses from international competition by limiting imports or increasing their prices. Figure 4–2 shows the pros
3 and cons of restricting free trade.

Protectionists feel that if imports were restricted, U.S. consumers would then buy fewer imports, U.S. companies would not be forced out of business, there would be less unemployment, the trade deficit would improve, and foreign investment would leave. There are four ways to limit imports or increase their prices.

Tariffs

A tariff is a tax on imports, as you learned in Chapter 3. Tariffs are the most commonly used restrictions on free trade.

On occasion, governments use tariffs to retaliate for what they consider unfair trade practices. For example, in 1987 the U.S. government concluded that Japanese firms had been selling computer chips in the United States at unfairly low prices (below what it cost to produce the chips), harming U.S. businesses. The government put a punitive (punishing) tariff on the imported chips.

Usually, however, tariffs are of two types—revenue tariffs and protective tariffs. The *revenue tariff* raises income without halting imports of a certain product. These tariffs were the major source of the federal government's funding until the early 1900s, though today they account for less than 2 percent of the government's income.

A *protective tariff* actually raises the cost of an imported product in hopes of

Figure 4-2 The Pros and Cons of Free Trade

Many believe free trade is advantageous while others feel trade should be restricted.

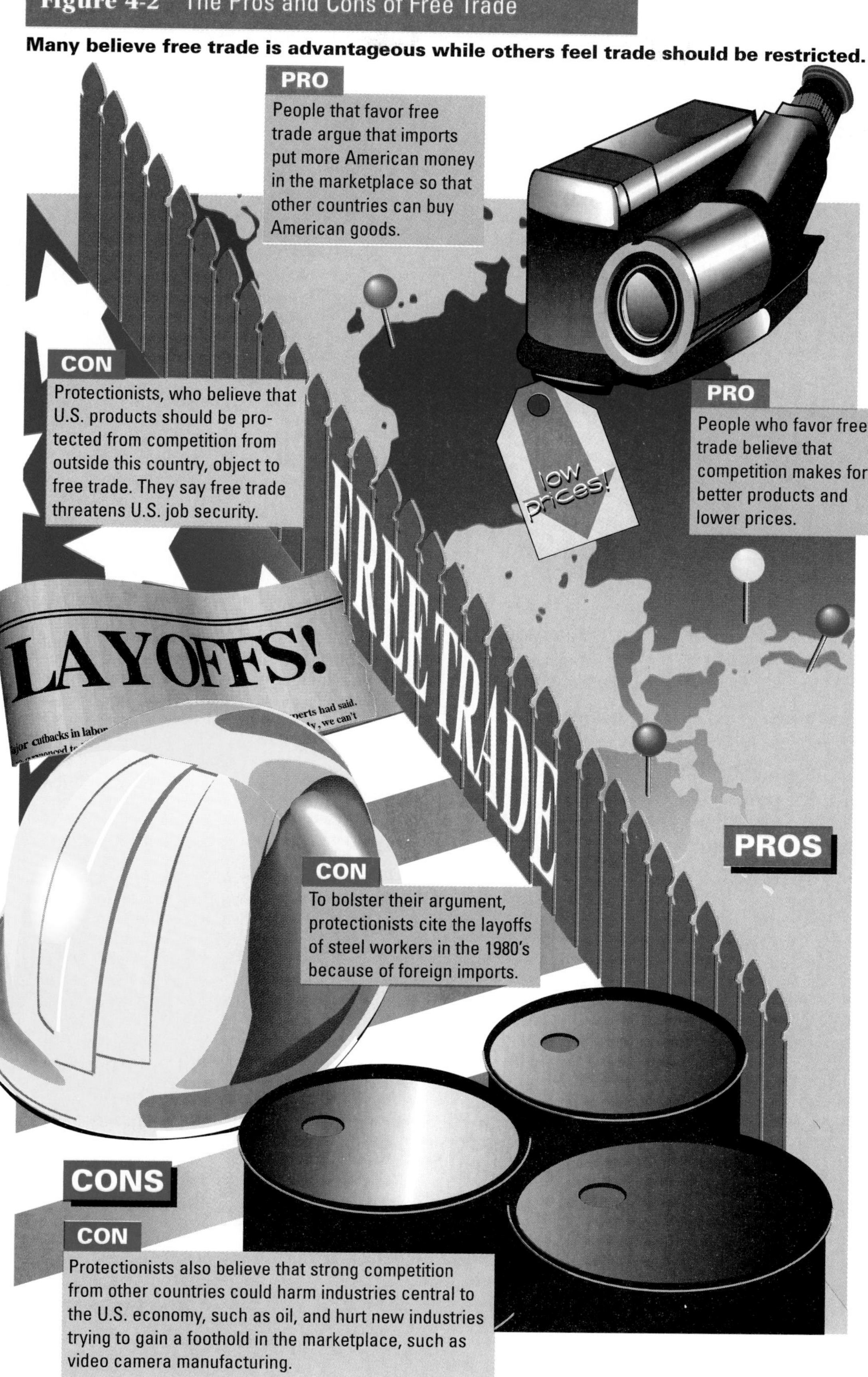

PRO
People that favor free trade argue that imports put more American money in the marketplace so that other countries can buy American goods.
CON
Protectionists, who believe that U.S. products should be protected from competition from outside this country, object to free trade. They say free trade threatens U.S. job security.
PRO
People who favor free trade believe that competition makes for better products and lower prices.
low prices!
FREE TRADE
LAYOFFS!
PROS
CON
To bolster their argument, protectionists cite the layoffs of steel workers in the 1980's because of foreign imports.
CONS
CON
Protectionists also believe that strong competition from other countries could harm industries central to the U.S. economy, such as oil, and hurt new industries trying to gain a foothold in the marketplace, such as video camera manufacturing.

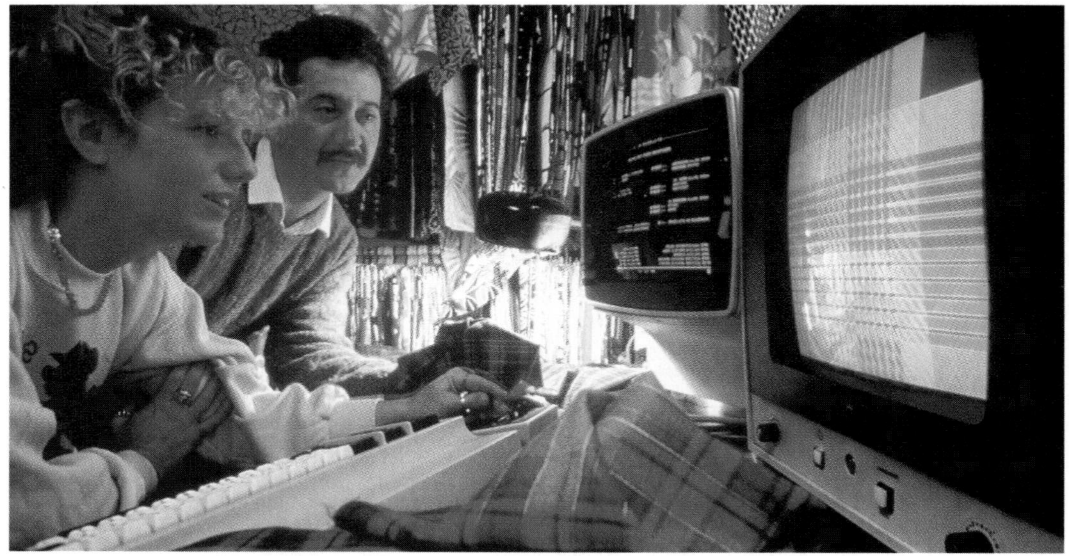

American textile workers are among those protected by tariffs on imports set by the American government. ***What does a tariff do?*** ▶

Caption Answer: It raises the price of an imported item, making the U.S.-made item more attractive in terms of cost.

1 Math Application If a pair of imported shoes cost $36 and a similar pair of domestic shoes cost $52, about how much of a protective tariff would be needed to bring the imported shoes to within $10 of the domestic pair? ($52 – $10 = $42; $42 – $36 = $6; $6 ÷ 36 = 17 percent rounded).

2 Critical Thinking Which form of import limitation has an additional benefit for the government—tariffs or quotas? (Tariffs have an additional benefit because they bring in revenues.)

3 Research Have students read newspaper accounts of the peace negotiations in the Middle East. What role does the lifting of trade embargoes against Israel play in this process?

making a domestic product less expensive and more desirable to buyers. For example, one industry that the U.S. government tries to protect with these tariffs is the textile industry.

Suppose government policy is to promote U.S.-made leather jackets. A protective tariff of, say, 10 percent could be placed on imported leather jackets. If the import's original price was $200, it would go up to $220 with the addition of the tariff. The effect of the tariff would be to make the domestic product competitive in price with the imported
1 product.

Protective tariffs were once quite high—up to 62 percent of the value of all imported goods in the 1830s and nearly 60 percent in the 1930s, but they had fallen to about 5 percent overall in the 1990s.

Quotas

An import **quota** is an import limit on the dollar value or amount of a certain good. In the past, the United States has placed quotas on imports of peanuts, cotton, cars, and sugar.

A quota reduces competition. Since there are few imported goods, consumers must use the domestic product, regardless of its price.

Quotas and other trade limitations can have a rippling effect. For example, a quota on sugar increases not only the cost of sugar you buy in the supermarket but also the cost of sugar purchased by food companies. Thus every time you buy a candy bar, you are paying a higher price because of the increased cost of the
2 sugar used in the candy.

Embargoes

An **embargo** is a federal government order prohibiting trade with another nation. Embargoes are usually declared for political reasons. In 1980, sales of U.S. grain to the then-Soviet Union were halted by President Jimmy Carter to protest the Soviet intervention in Afghanistan.

Embargoes can be placed on imports as well. In 1986, Congress halted all trade with the Republic of South Africa to protest its policy of *apartheid* (uh-PAR-tayt), a system of racial segregation and discrimination. This embargo was lifted in 1993, when South Africa began taking
3 steps to eliminate apartheid.

INTERNATIONAL FINANCE

In order to have international trade, the world community must also have *international finance,* a way for payments to be made. The speed with which international finance can now operate—thanks to improved communications—has led to growing increases in international trade.

Exchange Rates

When countries trade with one another, they need money, or **currency.** In the United States, the dollar is the currency; in France, the franc; in the

A Flame in Barbed Wire

Throughout the world, thousands of people are imprisoned, tortured, and killed for their political opinions, religious beliefs, or race. They may be spirited away at night, their family and friends never told where or why they are being held. Most never go to trial for their "crimes."

In 1961, Peter Benenson, a London lawyer specializing in law reform and injustice, founded Amnesty International. The group's goals are to work for the release of these "prisoners of conscience" and to get them a fair and public trial.

Amnesty International monitors the conditions of prisoners of conscience throughout the world. The organization's 200,000 members "adopt" certain prisoners. Then they write to the governments holding the prisoners, requesting their release. They write to the prisoners to assure them they have not been forgotten and that people are trying to help them. They send food and other items when it is permitted. Amnesty members also take care of the prisoners' families by raising funds to feed them and educate their children.

Amnesty does not adopt people who have used or have advocated the use of violence. To ensure that members are impartial in their appeals, Amnesty members do not adopt prisoners held in their own country. Although Amnesty has most certainly influenced governments to release prisoners, the organization never takes credit for the releases. To do so could antagonize the governments and make them less likely to be influenced by Amnesty appeals in the future.

The symbol of Amnesty International is a flaming candle encircled by barbed wire. It expresses hope for the imprisoned and confidence that the light of free thought will continue to shine despite tyranny.

Brainstorm

As a student, what could you do to help gain the release of "prisoners of conscience"?

Case Study Answer: Possibilities include producing brochures that would help make the public aware of "prisoners of conscience." They could also write letters to the U.S. and foreign governments and ask for their support in the effort to free "prisoners of conscience."

Caption Answer: It tells how much the dollar is worth when compared with the currency of other countries.

1 Vocabulary Have students consult the financial pages of a newspaper or visit a bank to learn the names of the currencies of Italy (lira), Mexico (peso), Canada (dollar), and China (yuan).

2 Math Application Ask students to suppose that they are planning a trip to Greece. The rate of exchange is 243 Greek drachmas to the dollar. How many drachmas can they buy for $2,000? ($2,000 × 243 = 486,000 drachmas.) One week after buying drachmas, they must cancel their trip and sell their drachmas for dollars. The rate of exchange is now 243.5 drachmas to the dollar. How many dollars can they buy? (486,000 ÷ 243.5 = $1,995.39.)

3 Learning Economics Ask students why the price of an item goes up when the demand for the item goes up. (When demand increases, supply decreases. Then buyers are willing to pay more for the scarcer resource.)

News Clip Answers:
1 It allows students to gain firsthand international business experience.
2 Answers will vary.

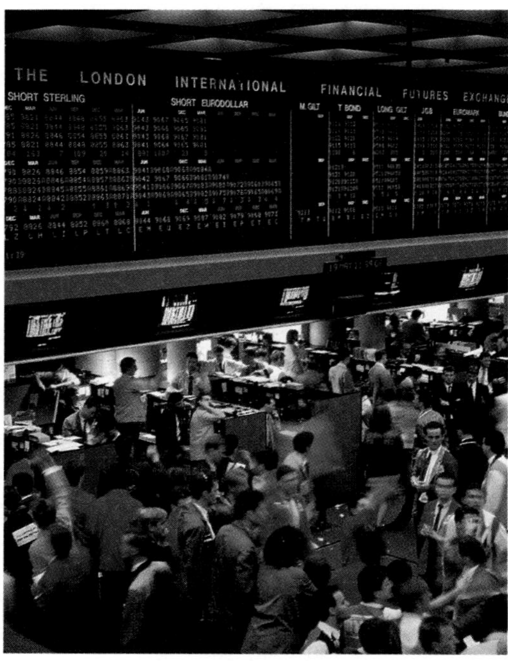

▲ *The currency exchange rate changes every day.* ***Why is the rate important?***

United Kingdom, the pound; in Japan,
1 the yen.

However, if a U.S. company sells lumber to Japan, it does not want to receive Japanese yen in return. It needs dollars in order to pay its workers who produce the lumber.

This is where *foreign exchange markets* come in. These markets allow for the buying and selling of foreign currency for businesses that import goods. Some of this currency trading is done in banks.

Fixed Rate of Exchange From 1944 until the early 1970s, there was a *fixed rate of exchange.* Each currency had a fixed value in relation to other currencies. For example, suppose $1 equaled 1.5 British pounds and $1 also equaled 6 French francs. Then 1.5 pounds would equal 6 francs (and, as a result, 1 pound would equal 4 francs).

The advantage of a fixed rate of exchange was that importers and exporters knew exactly how much of another country's money they could buy with their own country's money. An importer who had contracted to purchase $100,000 worth of French goods to be paid for in 30 days could be sure that no more than 700,000 francs would
2 be required in payment.

However, having a fixed rate of exchange proved impractical when the global marketplace began expanding and changing rapidly. The fixed rate of exchange could be altered, but usually not quickly enough to respond to world market changes.

Let's say that a French consumer can buy a U.S.-made tool for 600 francs ($10) and a French-made tool for about the same amount. Now suppose that the United States experiences high inflation, which means that the costs of its goods go up.

The exported tool, which formerly cost $10, now costs French consumers $15 (90 francs). If there is no comparable inflation in France, then French manufacturers would be able to sell their tools for less than the U.S. product. Unless the United States quickly alters the rate of exchange to account for inflation, U.S. exports suffer.

Flexible Exchange Rates In the 1970s, most countries adopted *flexible exchange rates.* Under this system, a currency's value may rise and fall every day in response to the world situation. For example, if a currency is in great demand because traders need that currency to buy goods, the value of the currency rises. You have probably heard daily reports of how the dollar, Japanese yen, German mark, and other currencies
3 traded the previous day.

The value of flexible exchange rates is that they can respond quickly to economic forces in the world market. However, for importers and exporters, flexible exchange rates can make prices unpredictable. For this reason, many countries set an upper and a lower exchange rate. If the currency threatens to move

CASE STUDY

Consumer NEWS CLIP

Ambitious Young People Are Skipping Rungs on the Career Ladder by Doing Internships Overseas

by Brigid McMenamin
Forbes February 27, 1995

After a one-year master's program at Harvard's Kennedy School of Government in 1990, social worker Jerome Madigan, then 30, took a summer job. He planned spending a couple of months in Warsaw with a United Nations group advising Poles on how to cope with a developing market economy. That little fling changed his life.

Fascinated with life in an evolving society, he stayed on to work in the Polish privatization program. In 1991 Price Waterhouse hired him as a consultant to help auction off over 30 glass companies, including Sandomierz, which Pilkington and others snapped up for $170 million.

Madigan had become an expert on privatization in former socialist countries. He was soon working for Price Waterhouse in Ukraine and later in Tashkent, Uzbekistan. This year [1995], at 35, Madigan returned to the United States as a manager with Price Waterhouse's International Privatization Group in Washington, D.C. "I definitely leap-frogged," admits Madigan.

Robert Carter had a similar experience. A former bank credit analyst, he was studying at the University of Houston for an M.B.A. in 1992 when he learned that the Institute for International Education was recruiting first-year students to work in developing countries.

The institute selected 16 students, and the U.S. Agency for International Development put them to work in places like a brick and tile company in Botswana, a condiment company in Dominica, a seafood exporter in Gambia, a glassmaker in Guatemala and a furniture company in the Philippines.

Carter went to Nepal to help start a new bank called National Finance. Carter, then 29, analyzed the commercial banking market, produced a business plan, set up a computer system and helped train local workers. Carter returned to Houston to finish business school and look for a job.

Which didn't take long. On the strength of Carter's Nepal experience, Tenneco snapped him up to analyze opportunities in Chile, Argentina and the South Pacific.

Because international experience makes job candidates more salable, Arizona's American Graduate School of International Management (known as Thunderbird) and Wharton's Lauder Institute encourage overseas internships. When Claire Gaudiani left the Lauder Institute to become president of Connecticut College in July 1988, she decided to make foreign internships part of the liberal arts program.

Selected students learn a foreign language, master the history, politics and economics of a region, and create a research project connected with that region. Connecticut College helps them line up an assignment abroad.

Other colleges, from Notre Dame to the University of Cincinnati, now offer similar work opportunities.

Decisions, Decisions

1. What is one benefit of an international internship?
2. If you were seeking an international internship, in what country and international business would you be interested?

1 Student Motivator Have groups of students learn how to do the following: make an overseas phone call; bank by phone or computer; order a product by computer. Ask groups to share their experiences with the class.

2 Extension Have students list all the electronic devices they use routinely. Ask students to try getting through a day or two without using these items. What is their experience?

3 Discussion Starter Ask students what impression of American consumer habits they think foreigners might get from watching American TV.

4 Discussion Starter Ask students how their ideas of foreign places are influenced by news reports, movies, and other media.

beyond its limits, the government will intervene to keep the rate stable.

The Impact of Telecommunications

A significant contributor to the increase in international trading is **telecommunications,** or long-distance communications. Think about it, and you'll realize you can see the effect of telecommunications all around. You can telephone a friend or family member just about anywhere in the world as easily as you can call your friend across the street, although it will cost more.

You can send computer messages to people thousands of miles away. You can even use your computer to pay bills and order products. Using a telephone, you can transfer money between bank accounts and in some areas tell your utility company what your monthly gas reading is by punching a few numbers
1 on the phone's keypad.

Improving Efficiency Just as they have affected our personal lives, improved and affordable telecommunications have opened up the world to trade. They have made it possible for a large volume of trading to take place almost instantaneously.

This trend started in the 1960s and 1970s, when U.S. banks opened worldwide branch networks for loans and foreign exchange trading, which is the buying and selling of currencies.

Trading in foreign currency and United States bonds, which the government sells to finance projects and services, has been going on 24 hours a day worldwide since the 1970s. Grains, gold, silver, and stocks
2 are also sold internationally.

Influencing Consumers Electronic communications have aided international trade in another important way. Television is very effective at introducing foreign consumers to U.S. products. When people in Greece, Egypt, and other countries watch reruns of old American TV series such as *Dallas* or *Falcon Crest,* they get a sense of American lifestyles and fashions, even though what is shown on TV may not accurately
3 represent how most Americans live.

The Internet Another key telecommunications avenue is the Internet. "Surfing" the 'Net allows millions of people across the globe to communicate with others even when they don't know each other. The ability to reach out to so many people and interactively communicate about common interests is changing the landscape of communications. Companies are only beginning to realize the economic opportunities of doing
4 business on the Internet.

Fiber-optic cable has revolutionized telecommunications by making it easier and faster to do many things by telephone and computer. ***What are some ways that telecommunications has affected the lives of today's consumers?*** ▶

Caption Answer: They can bank, order products, and pay some bills by phone or computer, and they can follow the international market 24 hours a day.

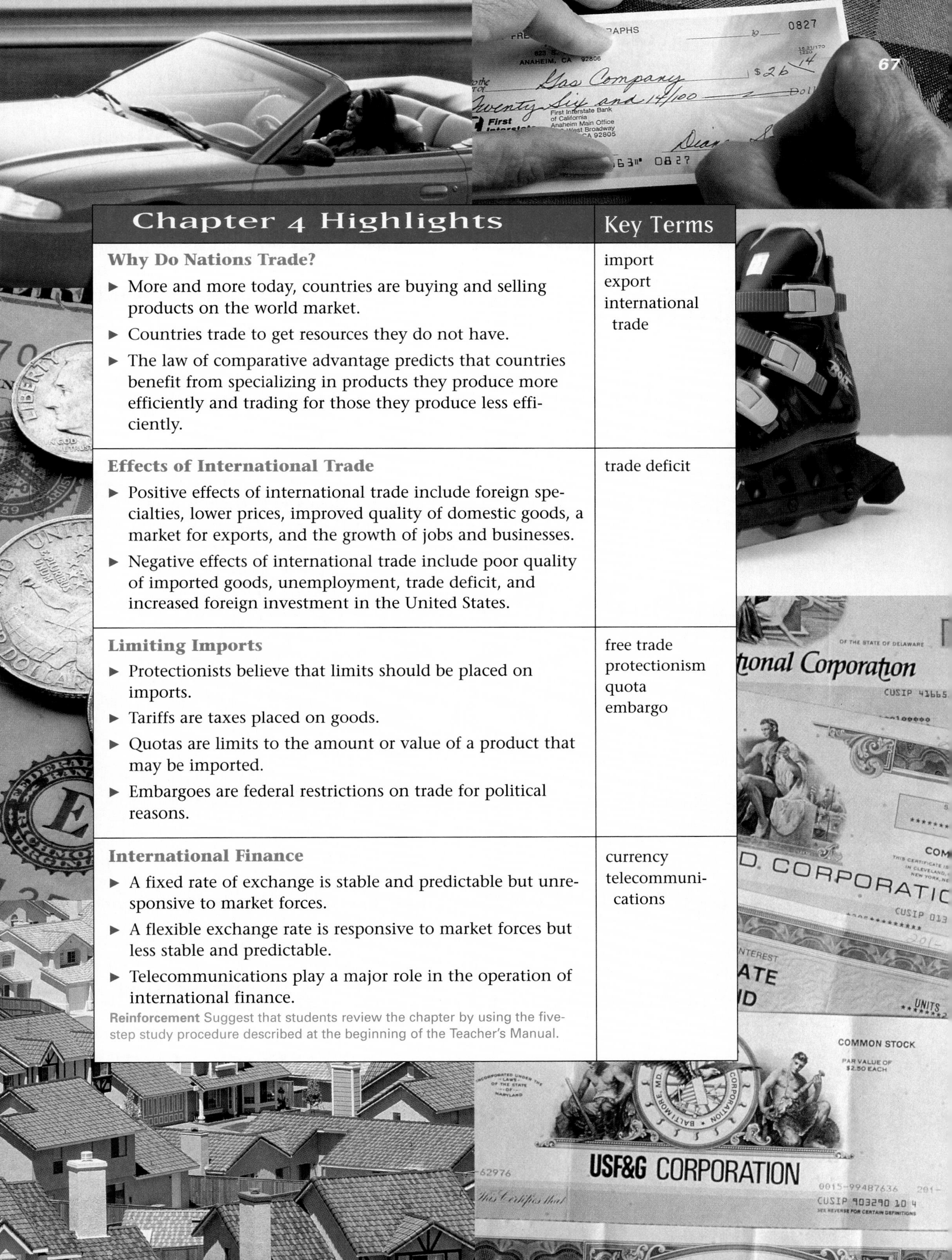

Chapter 4 Highlights

Chapter 4 Highlights	Key Terms
Why Do Nations Trade? ▶ More and more today, countries are buying and selling products on the world market. ▶ Countries trade to get resources they do not have. ▶ The law of comparative advantage predicts that countries benefit from specializing in products they produce more efficiently and trading for those they produce less efficiently.	import export international trade
Effects of International Trade ▶ Positive effects of international trade include foreign specialties, lower prices, improved quality of domestic goods, a market for exports, and the growth of jobs and businesses. ▶ Negative effects of international trade include poor quality of imported goods, unemployment, trade deficit, and increased foreign investment in the United States.	trade deficit
Limiting Imports ▶ Protectionists believe that limits should be placed on imports. ▶ Tariffs are taxes placed on goods. ▶ Quotas are limits to the amount or value of a product that may be imported. ▶ Embargoes are federal restrictions on trade for political reasons.	free trade protectionism quota embargo
International Finance ▶ A fixed rate of exchange is stable and predictable but unresponsive to market forces. ▶ A flexible exchange rate is responsive to market forces but less stable and predictable. ▶ Telecommunications play a major role in the operation of international finance. **Reinforcement** Suggest that students review the chapter by using the five-step study procedure described at the beginning of the Teacher's Manual.	currency telecommunications

CHAPTER 

REVIEW

Refer students to the Reviewing Consumer Terms and Reviewing Facts and Ideas activities in the Student Activity Workbook.

Reviewing Consumer Terms
Paragraphs will vary. See Glossary for definitions.

Reviewing Facts and Ideas
See the Student Activity Workbook for answers.

Problem Solving and Decision Making
Examples include rice, coffee, pepper. The cost of electronic and aluminum products would go up.

Consumers Around the World Communications
1 Students may write about cultural differences between America and Japan, Germany, Britain, Italy, Mexico, China, Canada, or other nations.

Technology
2 Students may discuss various safeguarding measures used to protect computer systems.

Reviewing Consumer Terms

Use each of the following terms in a paragraph to demonstrate you know its meaning.

currency
embargo
export
free trade
import
international trade
protectionism
quota
telecommunications
trade deficit

Reviewing Facts and Ideas

1. Give two reasons for countries to trade with one another.
2. How do consumers benefit from international trade? How are they harmed?
3. List the three major barriers to trade.
4. Why is international finance important?

Problem Solving and Decision Making

Your friend in your science class tells you that he doesn't believe international trade has any effect on Americans. You know this isn't true. To prove your point describe what your world would be like without international trade. Write a list of all the products you would not be able to purchase or whose price would go up without international trade.

Building Academic Skills

Consumers Around the World

Communications

1. The growth of the global economy has brought the world's cultures together. However, communicating can sometimes be frustrating and difficult. Cultural differences can become cultural barriers. For example, Americans tend to see frankness as a sign of honesty, while Japanese tend to see frankness as rudeness.

   Choose one of the key global partners of the United States. Using the library, research the cultural norms of that society. Write a 250-page report on how that society's expectations about communication are different from those of American society.

Technology

2. While telecommunications have made it possible for international trade and finance to grow at a great pace, they have also opened up the fields of trade and finance to new hazards.

   Using newspaper files and computer resources, research instances of mismanagement and crime that involve telecommunications. What kinds of protective measures are businesses, institutions, and governments developing to deal with these hazards? Summarize your findings in a 750-page report.

Social Studies

3. It often costs less for products to be made in other countries because

workers who make them are paid less. Using library resources, research the pay and working conditions of U.S. garment workers and their counterparts in other countries. Write a 500-word essay comparing data for U.S. and foreign workers.

Beyond the Classroom

Consumer Projects

1. The global economy has grown and thrived in part because of advances in telecommunications. Talk to one or two local stockbrokers and find out how they watch the markets and how telecommunications has changed their business over the past 10 years. What do they predict for the next 10 years? Write a 500-word report about what you find.
2. Visit a local bank. Ask about the procedure for exchanging dollars for foreign currency. Take notes to share with the class.

Cooperative Learning

Family Economics

Break into assigned family groups. Discuss the following problem.

For three generations, members of your family have worked for U.S. auto makers or have sold American cars. Now it's time for you to buy a car, and you cannot find a U.S.-made model that you like. You have, however, found a used import that has the price and features that you want. Should you buy the import with the money you have saved from working after school and during summers, or should you honor family tradition and continue looking for a U.S.-made car? Write down your arguments for both sides. Compare your answers with those of other family groups.

Debate the Issue

The federal government sometimes restricts trade with nations that are thought of as practicing or tolerating human rights abuses. For example, the government is sometimes urged to impose trade restrictions on China by those who feel that China violates U.S. child labor laws.

Supporters of this type of action feel that it is an appropriate expression of our society's moral outrage at practices like racial discrimination and abuse of children.

Opponents feel that such sanctions are likely to inflict hardship on the ordinary citizens of such countries and that U.S. consumers should be free to make their own choices.

You and your classmates will break into two groups and research this topic. Each group will gather evidence to support one side or the other. You are to prepare the argument for your side of the problem. Then the two groups will meet in a classroom debate.

Rechecking Your Attitude

Before going on to the next unit, go back to the Attitude Inventory at the beginning of this one. Answer the questions a second time. Then compare the two sets of responses. On how many statements have your attitudes changed? Can you account for these shifts in your opinions? What do you know now that you did not know then?

Social Studies
3 Students may discuss working conditions in countries in Asia and South America. They may include information on the history of labor conditions in the United States.

Consumer Projects
1 Students should share their findings with the class.
2 Students should explain the money-changing transactions they learn about.

Family Economics
Answers will depend on the family's commitment to the "Buy American" position and to the possibility of being able to find an affordable U.S.-made car.

Debate the Issue
Break the class into two teams. Assign each team one side of the issue. Encourage students to work together as a team to develop their argument. Ask each team to select a member to make an opening statement that supports the team's side of the issue. Have students take turns debating as the debate moves from one team to the other.

UNIT 1 LAB

You and Your Community

STEPS A, B, and **C** Students should arrange and carry out interviews with the people designated in the steps. They should discuss the topics listed in the steps and take careful, well-organized notes. **STEP D** Students' answers should be accurate and based on current tax rates. **STEP E** Students' reports should reflect their understanding of the effects of economic conditions on the three roles identified in Chapter 1: worker, consumer, and citizen.

Refer students to the Unit 1 Lab in the Student Activity Workbook.

Studying the Market System's Effect on Workers, Consumers, and Citizens

Unit 1 discusses the major economic roles that most American adults fulfill in the U.S. market system. In this lab, you will explore the system's effect on workers, consumers, and citizens.

TOOLS

1. Financial magazines
2. Newspapers
3. Television and radio news stories
4. Literature from government agencies and elected representatives

PROCEDURES

STEP A Contact one of the following experts on current tax rates and regulations: a certified public accountant, a financial planner, a banker, or an attorney specializing in tax law. Explain the purpose of your assignment, which is to learn more about how current tax rates and economic conditions are affecting workers, consumers, and citizens. Arrange to interview the tax expert either on the phone or in person at the expert's convenience. During the interview, be sure to cover the following topics:

1. The type and percentage amount of taxes paid by typical workers and consumers in your area.
2. The type of tax reform and tax simplification measures that have been enacted in the past five years.
3. The expert's viewpoint on the national debt.
4. The business cycle phases that the nation, your state, and your area currently are in, and the effect of those phases on supply and demand, on inflation and recession, and on the availability of public services.
5. The expert's opinion on the effect of international trade on businesses in your state and local area.

If you wish to tape-record the interview, you must ask and obtain permission from the expert before you begin taping. Do take careful written notes whether or not you record the interview.

STEP B Contact two people who work in two different public services. Explain the purpose of your assignment, and arrange to interview each public-service provider either in person or on the phone. During the interview, be sure to cover the following topics:

1. The percentage of national, state, and local tax money the public service receives.
2. The type of taxes that provide money to the public service.
3. The effect of tax reforms and tax reductions on the public service's ability to serve the community.
4. The effect of current economic conditions on the public service's ability to provide service.

Remember that you may tape-record your interviews only if you have received permission from your subjects before you begin recording. You should take written notes of the interviews whether or not you record them.

STEP C Contact two employees of two businesses that are not public services. Explain the purpose of your assignment, and arrange for an interview with each employee. During the interview, be sure to cover the following topics:

1. The effect of current national, state, and local economic conditions on both the employee and the business for which he or she works.
2. The effect of business tax rates and regulations on the employee and the business.
3. The effect of international trade and competition on the employee and the business.
4. The effect on the business of federal legislation designed to protect consumers.
5. The saver's techniques for maintaining financial records including check-writing and investment records.

LAB REPORT

STEP D Use your research and your notes from the five interviews to answer the questions below.

1. What is the current sales tax rate in your area?
2. If a consumer bought a refrigerator for $459, what would the sales tax on the purchase be?
3. What is the property tax rate for a home in your area?
4. If a home's assessed value is $159,000, what would the home owners pay annually in property taxes?

STEP E Write a two-page report explaining how the business cycle and taxation rates affect workers, consumers, and citizens.

UNIT 2
Unit Contents
Chapter 5
Choosing a Career
Chapter 6
Budgeting Your Money
Chapter 7
Spending Money Wisely
Chapter 8
Consumer Problems and Their Solutions

Money Management: Earning and Spending

Attitude Inventory

Before you begin Chapter 5, take stock of your attitudes by completing the following inventory. Read each statement and decide how you feel about it—agree, disagree, or undecided. Record your feelings on a sheet of notepaper or use the form in the workbook.

1. The best way to get a job is to let an employment agency find one.
2. A good time to plan for a career is while you are in college.
3. A person's standard of living depends largely on his or her choice of career.
4. A person who has an uncertain income has a good excuse for not budgeting.
5. The family budget should be the sole responsibility of one person.
6. If you can keep track of spending in your head, you do not need to use a budget.
7. Once a budget has been drawn up, it should not be changed.
8. As long as you live within your income, there is no need to keep a budget or expense record.
9. Most product advertising contains too much exaggeration and misinformation to be helpful.
10. A salesperson who tries to interest you in a more expensive item is just doing his or her job.
11. It is illegal to print or broadcast advertisements that mislead consumers.
12. You cannot trust a salesperson to tell you the truth.
13. A pyramid scheme or chain letter could make you rich.
14. The best way to resolve a consumer complaint is to write a letter to the president of the company.
15. Resolving a consumer complaint in court is expensive because it requires the services of an attorney.

Unit Goal The main goal of this unit is to introduce students to the skills and information they need to secure the financial future they desire and to the general problems and solutions facing consumers today. Chapters included in this unit are (1) Choosing a Career, (2) Budgeting Your Money, (3) Spending Money Wisely, and (4) Consumer Problems and Their Solutions.

Lesson Plan See the Teacher's Manual for an overview of the unit and some suggestions for introducing it. If you assign the Attitude Inventory, be sure to tell students to keep their answers for later use.

CHAPTER 5

Choosing a Career

Learning Objectives

When you have finished studying this chapter, you should be able to:

1. Explain how personal qualifications, life goals, and job trends affect career decisions.
2. Describe how to use a variety of references to research careers, and explain the value of education and training.
3. Discuss effective job search techniques.
4. List employee rights and responsibilities.
5. Debate the advantages and disadvantages of being an entrepreneur.

Consumer Terms

standard of living
needs
wants
aptitudes
abilities
apprenticeship program
résumé
entrepreneur

Real-World Journal

Look through your local newspaper's classified employment section for jobs that interest you. Clip the ads and paste them in your journal. Under each ad, list the skills needed to perform the job. Is any specialized training or education required? Describe the skills that you already possess that would qualify you for this type of work.

Lesson Plan See the Teacher's Manual for the Chapter 5 lesson plan.

Vocabulary The Chapter 5 lesson plan includes suggested vocabulary activities for the terms listed.

1 Discussion Starter Ask students if they have definite career plans. How did they arrive at those choices? Have they researched job openings and salaries? When do those who have no plans intend to make some decisions?

2 Student Motivator Have students survey parents, relatives, guardians, or other older acquaintances about their careers. Did they choose and plan for their career, or did they just "fall" into that career? How many times have they made major career changes and what were the results? What advice would they give to a young person about making career decisions and plans?

3 Extension Students may want to take a quick, easy-to-score interest inventory. One such instrument is the *World of Work Career Interest Survey* from Glencoe/McGraw-Hill Publishing Company, Columbus, Ohio.

Caption Answer: Musician in orchestra, composer, or conductor.

CAREER PLANNING

Do you know a person who has a really terrific career? someone who manages a theater company? builds customized sports cars? designs high-fashion clothes? trains astronauts? Most people who have exciting, satisfying careers did not just wander into their jobs. They planned carefully, learned the skills they needed, and worked hard to move up in their fields.

Having the right job can be a source of great pride. It can give you a positive self-image and a real sense of accomplishment. Your job can also determine where you live and, to a degree, who your friends are. Finally, if you are like most people, your job largely determines
1 your standard of living.

The term **standard of living** refers to the way you live as measured by the kinds and quality of goods and services you can afford. A minimal standard of living provides little more than your basic needs. **Needs** are the essentials to maintain life, such as wholesome food, clothing, shelter, and health care. A higher standard of living provides for something more—your wants. **Wants** are nonessentials that enrich your life. They range from conveniences like cars and appliances to entertainment, meals out, and vacations.

Now, while you are in high school, is an especially good time to begin planning for a career. While you are in high school, take time to explore options and the freedom to try different approaches. You can take courses in high school that relate to possible career goals. You can explore different fields and fine-tune the skills you need
2 to succeed.

Know Yourself

A first step in deciding the right career for you is to think about yourself. What makes you happy? What do you like to do? What are you good at doing?

Your Interests What hobbies do you like? What ideas and activities fascinate you? What are your best school subjects? What previous work experience or volunteer work was fun? Answers to these questions could be a key to a rewarding career—one that is based on the things you value or that are important to you. Take Janice Blank for example.

She ran track for her high school in statewide competition and kept up her interest in sports at community college. After graduating, she landed a job supervising a traveling track team for high school students sponsored by an athletic
3 equipment company.

Your Personality Closely related to your interests is your personality. Are you quiet and shy or the life of the

Identifying the things you like to do could be the first step towards a career. ***What job opportunities do you think might come from participating in this activity?*** ▶

party? full of energy or a slow starter? a risk taker or more conservative and cautious? If your personality and job requirements match, you are more likely to perform well and enjoy what you do. Also, think about whether you like to work with data, people, or things.

Joey Solis is an outgoing person who wanted to do work that was important and helpful to others. Eventually, he became a counselor for a program that placed bright, hardworking inner-city high school students in special college premed courses. He loves getting to know the students and helping them
1 achieve their goals.

Your Skills You should also develop some idea of your aptitudes and abilities. **Aptitudes** are natural talents; **abilities** are learned skills. When the two match, you will have a running start toward job success.

Devon Holt has an aptitude for drawing and an interest in art. He decided to take classes on art technique and computer graphics. Now, he works in the art department of a monthly magazine designing covers and illustrations.

It may be possible to take an aptitude test at your school or nearby community college. One test that is often available is the General Aptitude Test Battery (GATB). This is a series of tests that measures nine different aptitude areas.

Recent government studies have found that workers in high-paying jobs meet additional qualifications as follows:

- They have solid abilities in reading, writing, and mathematics—and the thinking skills necessary to put those abilities to work.
- They have the ability to manage resources such as time, money, and materials.
- They have the ability to acquire and use information, to master complex systems, and to work with different kinds of technologies.

You can develop many of these abilities at school, where you can master basic skills, study the use of technology and information, and learn how to manage resources. Work-study programs and cooperative programs, which allow students to combine classroom work and on-the-job training, can give you the chance to learn interpersonal as well as other business skills. Volunteer activities can help you learn how to act independently toward a common
2 goal.

Consider Your Life Goals

Do you intend to marry? have children? Would you like to buy your own home? own a luxury car? Do you hope to retire early and travel?

Meeting some of the special goals you have in life may depend a lot on the career you choose. Your job should pay a decent wage and offer the chance to learn new skills and to advance.

Jon Mazysk worked in a fast-food restaurant part-time in high school. It was exciting to have money, but he didn't like the work and he felt the salary was not enough for him to support a family.

After a tour of duty in the U.S. Navy, Jon went back to school. Because he was good at math and liked working with figures, he decided to study accounting. After receiving his certification, Jon took a job in a large firm where there was room for advancement and growth in
3 salary.

Consider Job Trends

Technology is creating many new jobs. At the same time, however, technology is causing other jobs to disappear. It is estimated that the average worker will have to be retrained as many

1 Extension From testing results or self-analysis, have students determine whether they would prefer working mostly with people, data, or things. Divide the class into three groups according to these categories and brainstorm jobs that fit each. Share with the class.

2 Interest Note A Secretary's Commission on Achieving Necessary Skills (SCANS) found that workers who possessed the skills to hold higher-wage jobs made 58 percent more than workers without those skills in lower-wage jobs.

3 Critical Thinking Have students think of events that could happen during each stage of life that need discussion or special attention. (They might have to cope with home and family responsibilities when both parents work; an unexpected role as a single parent; ill, elderly parents.)

1 Vocabulary Ask students what they think the term *job trends* means. They should realize that the job market is constantly changing, with some job openings on the rise, others declining, and entirely new jobs being created.

2 Learning Economics Ask students to recall the two major categories of things produced. (Goods and services.)

as three times during his or her life. In choosing a career, therefore, you should consider not only where the jobs are
1 now, but if they will be around in the
2 future.

The largest increases, accounting for almost two-thirds of all new jobs, will be in those industries producing *services.* Figure 5–1 shows some job trends.

Health services will continue to grow as a field because of the aging of the population. Business services will also grow rapidly as a result of fast growth in the computer and data processing industries.

Substantial job growth (4.5 million new jobs) is also expected in retailing, that is, selling merchandise in stores. Education is expected to account for 2.8 million new jobs.

Jobs in those industries producing goods are expected to show little change. Growth prospects within this sector, however, vary considerably.

Vicki Webb dropped out of high school and got a job in the biggest factory in town. When the factory closed and she was laid off, Vicki decided to finish her education. She wanted to learn skills that she could transfer from job to job. After receiving her diploma, Vicki went on to study keyboarding and computer skills so that she could hold an office job in any industry.

RESEARCHING CAREERS

Once you have thought about your personal qualifications and your life goals, and you have considered employ-

Figure 5–1 Job Trends

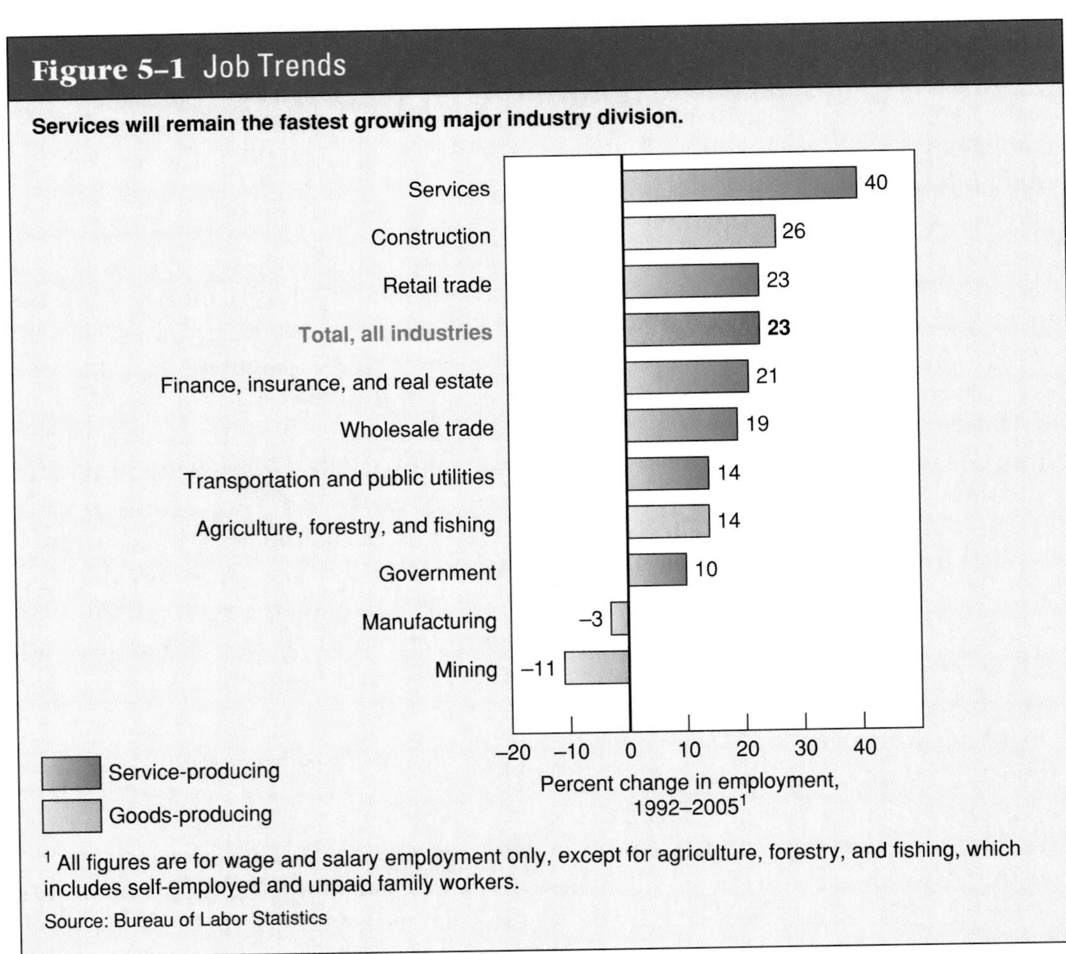

[1] All figures are for wage and salary employment only, except for agriculture, forestry, and fishing, which includes self-employed and unpaid family workers.

Source: Bureau of Labor Statistics

From 1992 to 2005, the health services field is expected to increase by 4.2 million new jobs and business services by 4 million new jobs. ***Why is it important to know the actual number of projected new jobs rather than just a percentage increase?*** ▶

Caption Answer: A large percentage increase in a field might translate into only a few new jobs if there were not many job opportunities in the first place.

ment trends, you should make a list of possible careers and investigate them thoroughly. The library is a good place to start your research.

Use a Variety of References

A standard reference is the *Occupational Outlook Handbook,* published by the U.S. Department of Labor. This reference book describes thousands of jobs. It lists duties, describes working conditions, gives salary ranges, outlines training requirements, and predicts future growth.

Magazines such as *Occupational Outlook Quarterly, Monthly Labor Review,* and *Business Week* provide the most up-to-date source of information on job trends. Popular specialty books such as *What Color Is Your Parachute?* are
1 updated periodically. These provide
2 advice on such topics as personal quali-
3 fications and the best companies to
4 work for.

Once you have general background from library references or computer on-line services, you may wish to write or look for more specific information. Public agencies can describe licensing requirements; professional associations and unions can explain apprenticeship programs. An **apprenticeship program** is a program in which inexperienced people learn a craft or trade on the job from skilled workers. All these sources can make you aware of workshops, seminars, and job fairs in your career area.

To get beyond the generalizations and learn about the real advantages and disadvantages of a job, talk to people in the field. Most experienced workers are glad to help young people by showing them around, explaining daily routines, and talking about what they enjoy most
5 (and least) about their job.

Consider Consumer Careers

As you review your career options, you may want to consider a job in the consumer field. A list of jobs in this area is provided on page 80.

▲ *Because consumer education touches so many aspects of our lives, the variety of jobs in the field is quite broad.* ***Can you identify the jobs pictured and how each relates to a consumer interest or consumer issue?***

Caption Answer: Left: Chemists test products or develop new ones. Consumer safety or conveniences could be promoted through this work. Center: Engineer is testing car safety. Consumer safety is being promoted. Right: People work for a political action group to help save the environment.

1 Interesting Note Tell students that an estimated 50 percent of today's jobs did not exist 20 years ago.

2 Reinforcement Tell students that the *Occupational Outlook Handbook* is published every two years. They should always check the date to make sure they have the latest edition. Also emphasize that it is one of the most readable, informative sources in the career area.

3 Extension Tell students the *Dictionary of Occupational Titles (DOT)* and the *Guide to Occupational Exploration (OE)* are also excellent career resources. They may be harder to work with than the *Occupational Outlook Handbook,* however.

4 Extension School libraries often have computerized guidance systems that match interests with related careers. Online computer services contain bulletin boards for information exchange, as well as job listings.

5 Critical Thinking Ask students to think of questions to ask experienced workers. (What are your normal duties and working hours? Do you have to work overtime? If so, how often? What education or training is necessary to enter and advance in your field? How much does the average worker earn after five years? ten years? twenty years?)

1 Research Have students rank the areas of consumer careers by interest. Students should choose the two areas that are the most interesting to them and research specific job—training, skills, working conditions, salaries, benefits, and employment outlook. Have students explain why they would or would not consider choosing these careers.

2 Vocabulary Explain to students that internships are short-term positions through a sponsoring agency that allow interns to gain experience in a field of study. These positions can lead to full-time employment.

3 Student Motivator Give these 1992 average incomes for adults over 25 based on education.
- High school, no diploma: males, $23,529; females, $15,300.
- High school diploma: males, $28,944; females, $19,965.
- Two-year associate degree: males, $35,315; females, $26,083.
- B.A.: males, $46,106; females, $31,538.
- M.A.: males, $56,649; females, $37,178.

Have students discuss education-salary relationships and reasons for lower female wages (job choice, workforce discrimination, absence from workforce while rearing children). Make sure students know these trends have not changed for years.

- *Business.* Business organizations hire a wide range of consumer specialists. The food industry employs dietitians and nutritionists to offer suggestions for preparing well-balanced meals. Scientists and technicians test food products in laboratories and kitchens to assure their quality and safety. Designers and fashion coordinators offer suggestions on wardrobes and interior decorating. Chemists and technicians develop and test new fibers.
- *Finance.* Financial planners and counselors advise their customers on budgeting, saving, investing, and estate planning.
- *Manufacturing.* Product safety and user convenience are major concerns of manufacturers. Many manufacturers employ workers in product testing and research jobs. They also hire workers to handle consumer questions, write product literature, and demonstrate product use.
- *Communications.* Radio and television stations, newspapers, and magazines employ consumer experts to write and produce programs and articles on consumer problems.
- *Consumer organizations and associations.* Employment opportunities also exist in organizations like Consumers Union and Consumers' Research that report on consumer product, services, and problems. Other business and professional groups, such as the Better Business Bureau and various special interest associations, hire consumer specialists. They are involved in research, product testing, administration, investigation, political action, and writing.
- *Government.* Almost every level of government has agencies that protect consumers against unfair or unsafe practices and provide them with product information. At the federal level, for example, many types of jobs are available in the various agencies of the Department of Agriculture, the Department of Education, the Public Health Service, and the Food and Drug Administration. In addition, teaching opportunities exist
1 at all educational levels.

Cyclo Drivers in Vietnam

Used as a taxi, a *cyclo* is a bicycle rickshaw with two wheels and a seat in front. Drivers charge about 50 cents per ride for foreigners and half that for locals. An ambitious driver can make $100 a month. A new cyclo costs about $150.

Plan for Further Education or Training

Think about the kind and amount of education and training you need after high school when making career decisions. You can get some entry-level positions directly after graduating from high school. The training usually occurs on the job. Other training opportunities are available through internships, apprenticeships, and the armed forces. Many jobs will require additional education beyond high school. Depending on the career you choose, you may need to attend a technical or vocational school,
2 a two-year community college, or a four-
3 year college.

You can get information on educational training by talking to your school counselor or armed forces recruiter, by reviewing guides at the library (such as *The Right College,* an annual publication by Arco Publishing, or *Peterson's Guide to Internships*), by browsing through school catalogs, and by using computer on-line services. If possible, visit prospective schools to view their facilities and equipment. Get some recommendations about schools from graduates or prospective employers.

JOB HUNTING

There are many ways to find job openings. Begin with your family and friends. Tell them you are looking for work. They know your interests and abilities and have contacts in the community. Search your newspaper's Help Wanted section. These *classified ads* (advertisements grouped by section) announce available jobs. You should also contact employers directly to discuss possible job opportunities. Even if there are no current job openings, job opportunities may become available in the future.

Check with public and private *employment agencies.* These are organizations that help people find jobs by matching applicants' qualifications with those needed by employers with job openings. Public agencies are funded by the government and offer free services. Private agencies charge fees that can be substantial. Also, talk to career counselors at your school or at other educational or training institutions.

Other places to find out about job openings are the library, unions and apprenticeship councils, professional or trade journals and newsletters, and electronic bulletin boards. If you are seeking a federal job, begin by learning about the Office of Personnel Management in your state. It publicizes government job openings through printed materials, automated telephone systems, and electronic
1 bulletin boards.

1 Reinforcement Emphasize to students the importance of applying directly to prospective employers. Studies show that this technique has a 47.7 percent effectiveness rate. Next best is visiting an employment agency (24.2 percent); then answering local newspaper ads (23.9 percent); and asking friends about jobs where they work (22.1 percent).

Composing a Résumé

A **résumé** is a personal data sheet that gives a prospective employer an idea of the special qualifications you can bring to a job. Résumés are usually no more than one or two pages in length. Although résumé formats differ with level of experience, you could follow the

◀ *Help wanted announcements can be found not only in newspaper advertisements but also at the actual job sight.* ***What are some advantages and disadvantages of locating a job opening in this manner?***

Caption Answer: Getting in to see an employer is easier when a job is posted at the business establishment. A disadvantage could be that the position is lower paid. It should not be overlooked, however, if experience or income is needed.

1 Reinforcement Student Activity Workbook, Chapter 5 activities.

2 Interesting Note Unless you are answering an ad or a request, mailing a résumé to prospective employers is not particularly successful. One study showed that on the average 245 résumés had to be mailed to obtain one interview. Direct contact gets better results.

3 Extension Have students bring in classified ads and place them on a bulletin board. Then have students choose a job and write a cover letter and résumé as if they were responding to the ad. Try to get the employers who placed the ads—or a business in partnership with your school—to critique the letters and résumés.

example in Figure 5–2 for developing
1 your résumé.

Although not all job applications require a résumé, it is a good idea to have one. Preparing a résumé is good practice. It helps you organize your thoughts and reminds you that you
2 really do have a lot to offer an employer.

Writing Letters

When you find an opening that interests you, contact the employer. Usually, the best way to do this is in writing.

Write a *letter of application* to inquire about a job or submit an application. The letter should be brief and clear, neatly typed, and free of grammatical errors. Include some of the relevant information you have listed in your résumé.

Nadia Minsk was applying for a job as a teacher's aide in a nursery school. In her letter of application, she wrote that she had recently graduated high school, that she had several years of baby-sitting experience, and that she had taken a ten-week course in child care at the YMCA.

If you are asked for a résumé, write a *cover letter* to accompany the résumé. A cover letter is a short letter of introduction. It does not include much of the detail that you would put in a letter of application. Like a letter of application, it should be neat and error-free. See Figure 5–3 for what to put in a cover letter.

If you do not receive a response to your letter or your résumé, follow up by telephone. Call the recipient of the letter and politely ask about the progress the
3 company is making in filling the position.

Figure 5–2 The Résumé

SANDRA DIAZ
Apartment 7B
35 Oak Ridge Road
St. Louis, Missouri 63133
317-555-2162

OBJECTIVE:	Laboratory Technician
EXPERIENCE:	
July 1994–Present	South Side Laboratories, St. Louis, Missouri Assistant Laboratory Technician. Duties include special product testing including procuring and weighing samples, recording data results, and ordering supplies.
1992–1994	South Side Laboratories, St. Louis, Missouri Assistant to Food Testing Director. Duties included processing invoices, word processing, working with spreadsheets and databases, and scheduling meetings.
1991–1992	West Side Physician's Clinic, St. Louis, Missouri Receptionist. Duties included answering phone, scheduling appointments, greeting patients, and processing billings.
SKILLS:	Word processing, spreadsheets, databases Knowledge of laboratory procedures Fluent in Spanish Good organizational skills
EDUCATION:	Morris Community College, St. Louis, Missouri. Associate degree with major in science, 1992. Brodecker High School, St. Louis, Missouri, High school diploma, 1990.

Caption Answer: Easy for prospective employer to quickly review your experience and education.

Résumés should call out your qualifications and be attractively formatted. ***What are some advantages to keeping your résumé to one page in length?*** ►

Going on Interviews

Many applicants will be eliminated from consideration on the basis of their letters or resumes. Only a few will be
1 asked to come in for an interview.

Preparing Yourself There are several things you can do to prepare yourself for a job interview. First, find out all you can about the company so that you will be able to discuss the job intelligently and suggest contributions you can make.

Next, review your resume. This will help you to concentrate on your strong points. It should also alert you to any weak areas in your education or employment history.

Finally, practice for the interview. Think of questions that might be asked and decide how to answer them. Here are some possible questions.

1. Why do you want to work here?
2. What qualifications do you have for the job?
3. What are your goals for the future—say, five years from now? ten years from now?
4. Why did you leave your last job?
5. What would you say are your greatest
2 strengths and weaknesses?

Be sure to dress appropriately for the interview. A neat, conservative appearance is usually best. Clothing should be similar to what you would wear on the job. You might choose a shirt with slacks or jeans for manual work. For an office position, a man could wear a suit and a woman a suit or dress. A woman who

1 Discussion Starter Ask students to describe the job interviews they have had. Did they make a good impression? What question was the hardest to answer? Do they see ways they could improve in their next interview?

2 Extension Discuss the idea that many job applicants have the skills the employer is looking for but are unable to communicate to the employer they have those skills. The people most successful in job interviews anticipate questions and plan answers to show they have the skills and experience the employer wants.

Figure 5–3 The Cover Letter

The cover letter should be a short letter of introduction. It should tell why you are qualified for the job.

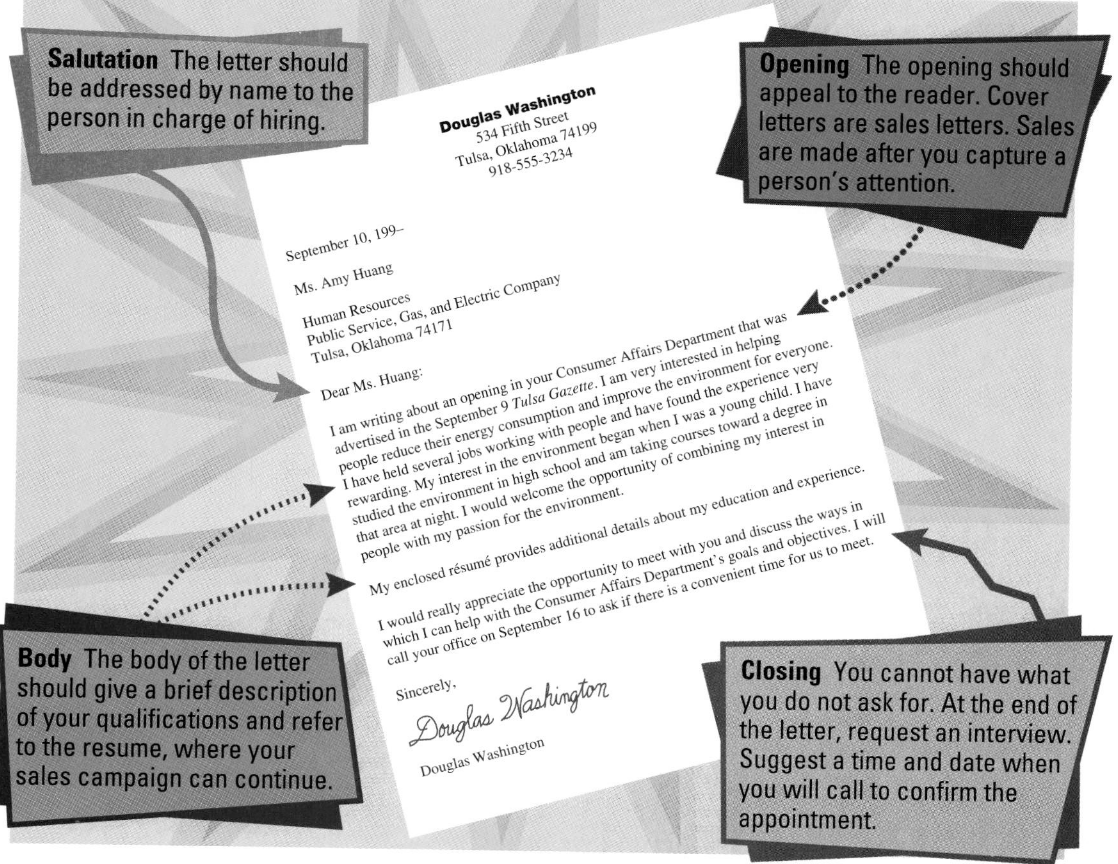

Douglas Washington
534 Fifth Street
Tulsa, Oklahoma 74199
918-555-3234

September 10, 199–

Ms. Amy Huang

Human Resources
Public Service, Gas, and Electric Company
Tulsa, Oklahoma 74171

Dear Ms. Huang:

I am writing about an opening in your Consumer Affairs Department that was advertised in the September 9 *Tulsa Gazette*. I am very interested in helping people reduce their energy consumption and improve the environment for everyone. I have held several jobs working with people and have found the experience very rewarding. My interest in the environment began when I was a young child. I have studied the environment in high school and am taking courses toward a degree in that area at night. I would welcome the opportunity of combining my interest in people with my passion for the environment.

My enclosed résumé provides additional details about my education and experience.

I would really appreciate the opportunity to meet with you and discuss the ways in which I can help with the Consumer Affairs Department's goals and objectives. I will call your office on September 16 to ask if there is a convenient time for us to meet.

Sincerely,

Douglas Washington

Douglas Washington

Salutation The letter should be addressed by name to the person in charge of hiring.
Opening The opening should appeal to the reader. Cover letters are sales letters. Sales are made after you capture a person's attention.
Body The body of the letter should give a brief description of your qualifications and refer to the resume, where your sales campaign can continue.
Closing You cannot have what you do not ask for. At the end of the letter, request an interview. Suggest a time and date when you will call to confirm the appointment.

1 Reinforcement
Invite employers to class to hold mock interviews with selected students. Have these students wear appropriate clothing. Have all students write follow-up notes on the strengths and weaknesses of each interview. Discuss these with employers.

Caption Answer:
Written comments after an interview could include (1) an evaluation of appearance; (2) answers to questions that were good—and not so good; (3) a list of questions that were unexpected. Recording and reviewing these comments should improve effectiveness in future interviews.

uses makeup should keep it light, and avoid wearing a lot of jewelry. Be sure that you are clean and well-groomed. In this way, you will focus the employer's attention on your qualifications rather than your appearance.

Making a Good Impression Making a good impression begins with arriving on time. During the interview, be courteous and positive about yourself and your abilities.

- Keep your comments brief and to the point.
- Speak clearly and look the interviewer in the eye when answering questions.
- Finally, ask questions. This will show that you have been listening and know something about the company. Job duties, work schedules, employee evaluations, physical plant and equipment, corporate history, and opportunities for advancement are all possible topics for discussion.
- Before leaving, thank the interviewer.
1 Smile and shake hands.

Following Up Take a day or so to think over the interview. Was there an important point you forgot to make? Did you promise to send more information? Is there a question you might have answered better? You may still be able to add to an interviewer's good impression of you.

Always send your interviewer a note thanking him or her for taking the time to see you. Include a reminder of some positive point in your discussion; then restate your interest in the job. As an alternative, you could telephone or stop by in person. In the latter case, you should have some purpose for your visit such as a need to leave some additional information—samples of your work, reference letters, your résumé—for the interviewer.

An interview is a chance to show a prospective employer you can benefit the company. ***What kinds of things might you write down after an interview? Why?*** ▼

EMPLOYEE RIGHTS AND RESPONSIBILITIES

Once you are hired, you will find yourself protected as an employee by a number of laws. Some of the important ones are described below.

Safe Working Conditions

All workers should be provided with safe working conditions by their employer. You should not be asked to use a machine that could be dangerous unless you have been taught how to operate it safely. Your employer should not ask you to work in an unsafe environment. You have the right to expect your employer to fix faulty equipment as well as do anything else needed to prevent and remove any hazards on the job.

Equal Employment Opportunity Act

Several federal laws exist to protect people from discrimination in the workplace. The most important of these is the Equal Employment Opportunity Act, which was passed as part of the 1964 Civil Rights Act. The Act forbids discrimination by employers, employment agencies, and unions on the basis of race, color, religion, sex, or national origin. The Age Discrimination Act of 1967 makes it illegal to discriminate against anyone over 40 whether in hiring or while on the job. People with physical or mental disabilities are protected from discrimination as well by the Rehabilitation Act of 1973. All of these laws were passed to make sure that everyone is judged on their ability to do their job.

Fair Labor Standards Act

The Fair Labor Standards Act passed in 1938 is a major federal law regulating work. The FLSA and its amendments set

FLASHBACK FLASHFORWARD

In 1955, 27 percent of mothers with children under the age of 18 participated in the work force. In 1992, 67.2 percent of mothers with children under the age of 18 were on the job. This increase in working mothers has created new career opportunities in service areas, such as day care and food preparation, that cater to the needs of working women.

Locally Grown

It started as a science project in an abandoned lot behind Crenshaw High School. It has grown into a $50,000-a-year business that feeds the needy and provides funds for student scholarships.

After the riots in Los Angeles in 1992, science teacher Tammy Bird and her students created a food and flower garden. She hoped to use the plot to teach the students biology. In addition, it would perk up an area devastated by the riots.

Soon the students not only had planted vegetables, herbs, and flowers, but also had painted a colorful mural on the wall behind the garden. The painting—which became the group's logo—shows a white hand and a brown hand reaching for each other. The students, who called their group Food from the 'Hood, donated some of their harvest to needy families. The rest they sold at a local farmer's market.

The students were so excited by their success, they decided to expand. With help from local manufacturers and other businesses, they created their own salad dressing to go with their herbs and lettuce. They called the product Straight Out 'the Garden. The dressing now sells in more than 2,000 supermarkets in 23 states.

Although they got advice from local businesses on marketing, and local companies manufactured the product, the students did the rest of the work. They planted, cared for, and harvested the crops. They maintained records and did public relations. They also set up mentoring to help other students and a program to help prepare students for the SATs. They are even thinking about licensing their logo.

It seems that Food from the 'Hood plants more than lettuce. It also plants seeds of self-confidence and success.

Brainstorm

If you wanted to start a project such as Food from the 'Hood, how would you go about setting it up?

Case Study Answer: Find vacant space to start the garden; raise funds to buy seed, equipment, fertilizer or have merchants donate it; set up a schedule of caring for the garden; find out what skills members of your group have—gardening experience, business skills, computer skills—and put those to work; contact local farmer's markets, businesses about selling them your produce; establish bank accounts for the group; establish scholarships; look into business licenses and regulations.

1 Research Ask students to research laws on discrimination in hiring. What kinds of discrimination are and are not allowed? What recourse is open to people who believe they have suffered illegal discrimination in hiring?

2 Discussion Starter Ask how many students have family members who belong to unions. What benefits do they get from union membership? What are the costs?

3 Discussion Starter Ask students if they feel the government should set minimum wages by law or if wages should be determined by the marketplace.

4 Math Application Have students calculate total pay in the following situation.

45-hour week; regular pay, $4.50 an hour.

($4.50 × 40 = $180; $4.50 ÷ 2 = $2.25; $4.50 + $2.25 = $6.75; $6.75 × 5 hours = $33.75: $180 + $33.75 = $213.75 total).

Case Study Answers:
1 Sample answers: You invest your own money. No one offers you a raise. You don't have a boss.
2 Sample answers: Yard work. Neighbors. Professional landscapers. $4/hour.

minimum wages as well as overtime pay
1 and hours of work. The statute also
2 requires equal pay for equal work and
restricts child labor.

Minimum Wage The federal minimum wage as of 1996 was $4.25 an hour. In general, employers may not pay wages below that amount. The figure is raised periodically to help workers keep up with inflation.

Under certain circumstances, learners may be paid less than the minimum wage. Full-time students working in retail or service establishments, agriculture, or colleges may be paid below minimum wage. However, employers must get special certificates issued by the
3 Wage and Hour Administrator to do so.

How to Build a Collection

From comic books to antique cars, collecting can be fun and rewarding. Although collections can increase in value over time, the best reason to collect something is because you love it.

- **Know the value of collectibles. Speak to other collectors and look at guidebooks that publish current prices. Be able to recognize the condition of the item.**
- **Pick a specialty, such as a certain time period, a manufacturer, or an artist.**
- **Concentrate on the uncommon.**
- **Keep the items in mint condition by storing them with protective covers. Look at your entire collection from time to time to be sure nothing is getting damaged.**

Overtime Overtime pay regulations are based on a standard 40-hour week. After 40 hours, an employee's wage rate must be at least $1\frac{1}{2}$ times the regular rate of pay.

Suppose you make $5 an hour, and in one particular week, you work 44 hours. For each of the four overtime hours, you would make $7.50—$5 plus half of $5 (or $2.50). Exceptions to the federal regulations on overtime include baby-
4 sitters and live-in domestic workers.

Equal Pay The equal pay provisions of the FLSA forbid employers from paying women less than men for the same work, and vice versa. The rules apply to workers in the same establishment, working under the same or similar conditions, and doing work requiring equal skill, effort, and responsibility. Other provisions of the act forbid discrimination based on the age of an employee. The provisions are designed to protect older workers.

Child Labor Child labor laws set 16 as the minimum age for workers. In addition, the jobs they do cannot be in mining or manufacturing, nor can the jobs be dangerous.

Workplace Requirements

In exchange for wages, employers have certain expectations, and your success on the job will depend on how well you meet those expectations. All employees are obliged:

- To be honest, dependable, friendly, and cooperative.
- To arrive at work on time.
- To put in a full day's work.
- To be willing to learn and follow safety procedures.

ENTREPRENEURSHIP

Have you ever thought of owning your own business? Many people have,

CASE STUDY

Careers in Focus

Gary Wong, Entrepreneur

Skeletons in the closet have been known to ruin people's careers. For Gary Wong, comic books in the closet provided one. At 28, Wong rediscovered his 16-year-old collection of comic books. His ensuing attempts to update the collection developed into a home business and eventually became a thriving neighborhood retail store.

Although Gary Wong always wanted to operate his own business, he never trained specifically to sell comic books. At first, he studied to be a dentist like his father. However, he was never really set on it. Only a few units shy of meeting the requirements for dental school, he withdrew from the University of Southern California. The next semester, he enrolled in the university's entrepreneur program from which he graduated in 1987.

The whole time he had been in school, Wong had also been a tennis instructor at the Hillhurst Tennis Center in the Los Feliz area of Los Angeles. By observing and working within that service business, Wong learned firsthand the importance of promotion, communication, and networking. He also became accustomed to working seven-day weeks and fine-honed his sales skills by selling his ideas and methods to his students. But in 1992, after 11 years of tennis, he needed a break.

It was during that break that Wong found his old comic books in a closet. He began updating his collection by buying other people's collections. At conventions, he acquainted himself with fans, dealers, and the whole comic book business.

After making a profit dealing comic books at conventions and from his garage, he began surveying local shops. He studied product selection and layout and listening to the advice of owners. Then he reviewed his school notes on business plans and cash flow and invested his savings in his own store.

Wong promoted heavily. He placed flyers in book stores, video shops, and other hangouts. He also advertised in local and school newspapers. Once he had customers in the shop, he knew return business and good word-of-mouth would follow. In February 1992, the Comic Connection opened its doors and has made a profit ever since.

Case Study Review

1. Name two ways in which being an entrepreneur is different from being a traditional employee.
2. Come up with an idea for a business you could start today in your own community. Name your product or service, your target audience, and an existing business that might be your competition. Ask a potential customer how much he or she would pay for your product or service.

1 Discussion Starter Ask students if they have ever worked in a family-owned business. How do they think that business was different from a big business? Where would they prefer working?

2 Extension More than 24 million Americans work for themselves at home. One survey listed four of the best home-based businesses: editorial and publishing; temporary employment agencies; video production; and repair services. They cost from $500 to as much as $30,000 to start up, depending on equipment needs. All these choices require special skills.

3 Extension Have students list three reasons why they would—or would not—like to be an entrepreneur.

at one time or another. When you own your own business or are self-employed, you are an entrepreneur. An **entrepreneur** is someone who owns or assumes
1 the financial risk for a business.

Today, the United States is becoming a country of entrepreneurs. At present, 50 percent of the U.S. *gross national product* (the value of all the goods and services produced in a year) comes from small business. These small growing businesses have produced most of the new jobs in the United States since the
2 1960s.

Advantages and Disadvantages

As an entrepreneur, you could enjoy many advantages. You are your own boss and work in an area of great personal interest. The opportunity to make more money is always there; your wages are limited only by the capacity of the business to pay them. Being an entrepreneur also allows you creativity and control: You are not tied to policies and procedures set by others.

Being your own boss also has disadvantages, however. You must work long hours, especially during the beginning years of a business. Income can be uncertain—or nonexistent—for some time. The entire operation, along with the livelihood of the employees, is your responsibility. The biggest disadvantage is that you can lose the savings you have invested in your business if the business does not succeed.

Characteristics of Entrepreneurs

Truly successful entrepreneurs have special characteristics. They are seldom satisfied with the way things are. They are always looking for ways to do things better—to provide what the consumer wants.

Youth is another characteristic of many entrepreneurs. Many surveys show approximately 35 percent of U.S. entrepreneurs are under 30 when they first start a business.

3 Could you be a successful business owner? Successful entrepreneurs are:

- Goal-oriented: They know where they want to be and how to get there.
- People-oriented: They get along well with a variety of personalities.
- Ready to act on an idea. Adaptable to change.
- Willing to take risks and make sacrifices.
- Able to learn from mistakes.

In addition, successful entrepreneurs are often independent, persistent, creative, responsible, inquisitive, and self-confident. Since everyone has these characteristics to some degree, theoretically anyone can become an entrepreneur. You will be more successful if you can polish up your weaker traits.

Necessary Skills

The skills discussed earlier are just as necessary for entrepreneurs as they are for high-paid workers. Strong foundation skills in communications cannot be overemphasized. Speaking, listening, reading, and writing are critical to conducting business.

Multilingual communication (knowledge of a foreign language) is becoming more important as businesses capitalize on opportunities in the global economy. In math, foundation skills are important. You need to know the simple calculations necessary for everyday business transactions and procedures that tell you how well your business is performing.

Chapter 5 Highlights	Key Terms
Career Planning ► Your career will determine your standard of living. ► Consider your interests, personality, aptitudes, and abilities, and life goals, as well as recent job trends in planning a career.	standard of living needs wants aptitudes abilities
Researching Careers ► Research careers in the library, using reference materials and on-line computer services. ► Check on the need for further education or training for the field of your choice.	apprenticeship program
Job Hunting ► Develop a résumé that gives your education and work history and any special skills or honors. ► For an interview, review your résumé, dress appropriately, and arrive promptly. ► At an interview, be polite, listen attentively, and respond clearly and positively. ► Write a thank-you note after the interview.	résumé
Employee Rights and Responsibilities ► Once hired, you are protected by several federal laws including the Equal Employment Opportunity Act and the Fair Labor Standards Act, which govern minimum wage, overtime pay, equal pay rules, and child labor. ► Employee responsibilities include arriving promptly; being honest, courteous, and hard-working; and following safety procedures.	
Entrepreneurship ► Small businesses account for a large and growing portion of the gross national product. ► As an entrepreneur, you are your own boss, you make the decisions, and you control your income. However, you must work long hours, you are responsible for the business, and you may lose money if the business fails. ► Successful entrepreneurs have the drive to reach goals and willingness to take risks. **Reinforcement** Suggest that students review the chapter by using the five-step study procedure described at the beginning of the Teacher's Manual.	entrepreneur

CHAPTER 5 REVIEW

> Refer students to the Reviewing Consumer Terms and Reviewing Facts and Ideas activities in the Student Activity Workbook.
>
> **Reviewing Consumer Terms** Paragraphs will vary. See Glossary for definitions.
>
> **Reviewing Facts and Ideas** See the Student Activity Workbook for answers.
>
> **Problem Solving and Decision Making** **1** Job A has potential for a higher salary but requires lots of travel. With Job B the salary is assured and the local travel means that he will be home more often. **2** Eileen could research jobs based on categories of data, people, and things. **3** Debbie should take a course in business management.
>
> **Consumers Around the World** **Math 1** Luis earns $360 for a 40-hour week. Over time is $13.50 per hour.
>
> Week 1 - 4 × 13.50 = 54.00 + 360 = 414
>
> Week 2 - 5 × 13.50 = 67.50 + 360 = 427.50
>
> Week 3 - 3 × 13.50 = 40.50 + 360 = 400.50
>
> Week 4 - 6 × 13.50 = 81.00 + 360 = 441.00
>
> Total: $1,683.00
>
> **Communications** **2** Answers will vary.

Reviewing Consumer Terms

In a paragraph, define the term *entrepreneurship* and then explain the relationship of the following terms to it.

abilities
apprenticeship program
aptitudes
entrepreneur
needs
résumé
standard of living
wants

Reviewing Facts and Ideas

1. What qualities should you know about yourself in order to make a good career choice?
2. What references should be used to research a career?
3. List the steps you would take to prepare for an interview.
4. Name some effective job search techniques.
5. What laws protect you as an employee?
6. What are some of the advantages and some disadvantages of being an entrepreneur?

Problem Solving and Decision Making

1. Ben Von Zandt has just been offered two jobs. Job A is a sales position that requires travel within a three-state territory. The salary is a commission of 8 percent on sales, which average about $25,000 a month. Job B is also a sales position, but with only local travel and salary of $1,800 a month. Ben has a wife and infant daughter to support. What should he take into consideration when deciding between these two jobs?
2. Eileen Burns likes math and computer classes in school and made good grades in those subjects. She also enjoys working with people and has a part-time job selling shoes at the high school store. How would she go about making a career decision based on her interests and abilities?
3. Debbie Mercado would like to start her own business selling children's clothing. She is creative and self-confident, but lacks good math and detail skills. What should she do?

Building Academic Skills

Consumers Around the World

Math

1. Luis Perez works for the lab at a food processing company. Over the last month, the lab has been extremely busy, and Luis worked quite a bit of overtime. Compute Luis's gross wages for the last four weeks. Luis earns $9.00 per hour and his normal work week is 40 hours. Luis's hours were as follows. Week 1, he worked 44 hours. Week 2, 45 hours. Week 3, 43 hours. Week 4, 46 hours.

Communications

2. Many people find it exciting and rewarding to work in a foreign

country. Research the jobs available overseas. Use the library, and look in newspapers like the *New York Times* for ads. Write to foreign consulates in your state or to embassies in Washington, D.C., for information.

Find out about the jobs that are available, the education and training required, the salaries offered, and the living conditions. Write a one-page newsletter explaining what to do—and what not to do when planning for overseas work.

Technology

3. Research how the use of computers and related technologies in business has grown. Describe the role of computers in small business operations. Outline the structure of the computer industry itself and the jobs it offers. Present your research in a two-page report.

Beyond the Classroom

Consumer Project

Find out how much education a beginning worker needs in order to qualify for each of the following jobs. Give the average annual salary in your area, and compare the salary with the amount of education needed. What generalizations can you make about the value of education?

a. Auto mechanic
b. Barber
c. Cashier
d. Computer programmer
e. Word processor
f. Construction laborer
g. Dentist
h. Retail store clerk
i. Military service

Cooperative Learning

Family Economics

Break into assigned family groups. Discuss the following problem.

One wage earner in your family group wants to begin a new career as an accountant. This will mean four years of study as a full-time day student (or six years as a night student), with average tuition costs of $3,000 a year at a nearby state university (double that amount at a private school). There will also be textbook costs of about $250 each semester.

Develop a realistic plan for making the career change. Compare your answers with those of other family groups.

Debate the Issue

Many people disagree about the use of the minimum wage for all workers. Some feel that the minimum wage requirement should be waived for young workers looking for entry-level employment. They stress that employers will be more likely to fill these positions if they can pay lower wages.

Opponents of this idea claim that creating a lower wage for young workers will encourage employers to hire young rather than older, more experienced workers. As a result, all workers may be pressured into accepting lower wages.

You and your classmates will break into two groups and research this topic. Each group will gather evidence to support one side or the other. You are to prepare the argument for your side of the problem. Then the two groups will meet in a classroom debate.

Technology
3 Students should give the uses of computers including providing information, compiling information in usable form, providing up-to-date reports, freeing personnel to do more than clerical tasks.

Consumer Project
Students should conclude that jobs requiring a higher level of education also generally pay a higher salary.

Family Economics
Certain family groups will choose to delay the educational phase of the career switch until children are older and savings have been accumulated. Others will want to explore loans.

Debate the Issue
Break the class into two teams. Assign each team one side of the issue. Encourage students to work together as a team to develop their argument. Ask each team to select a member to make an opening statement that supports the team's side of the issue. Have students take turns debating as the debate moves from one team to the other.

Five Fiscal Year
Compounded Annual
Growth of Net Income–
26%
0.26
PRT

CHAPTER 6

Budgeting Your Money

Learning Objectives

When you have finished studying this chapter, you should be able to:

1. Describe the five steps involved in developing a budget.
2. Explain four methods of keeping accurate financial records.
3. Discuss how to revise a budget.
4. Identify the three most common mistakes people make when budgeting.
5. Explain the value of doing an annual inventory.

Consumer Terms

budget
net income
average annual expenditures
fixed expenses
flexible expenses
emergency fund
balance sheet
assets
liabilities
net worth

Real-World Journal

List in your journal the expenses that you would have if you lived on your own. Ask an adult family member to list his or her expenses in the last month. Make a list in your journal of those expenses. Which of the expenses are paid on a regular basis? What expenses didn't you have on your own list that you would now include?

Lesson Plan See the Teacher's Manual for the Chapter 6 lesson plan.

Vocabulary The Chapter 6 lesson plan includes suggested vocabulary activities for the terms listed.

1 Vocabulary Explain to students that the word *budget* comes from the French word *bougette.* A *bougette* was a bag that merchants use to carry their money in.

2 Discussion Starter Ask students for their interpretations of budgeting. Have any of them tried to stick to a budget? What was the result?

3 Discussion Starter Have students think of a purchase they made to satisfy a short-term goal that ended up affecting long-range plans. Share in class and relate to the budgeting process.

DEVELOPING A BUDGET

Having your own money is exhilarating and exciting. Whether you receive an allowance or earn money by performing chores at home or work at a part-time job, your income is yours to control.

After the initial excitement, however, you may find that your income does not stretch quite as far as you had hoped. You may notice, for example, that if you buy your lunch at school (rather than bringing it from home), you may not have enough cash left over at the end of the week to go to the movies.

At this point, you may begin to plan how to use your income. For example, you may decide to spend less money on CDs so that you can save for new clothes. Whether you realize it or not, you have begun to develop a budget. A **budget** is a spending and savings plan based on an
1 estimate of income and expenses.

While the main purpose of a budget is to help you live within your means, the budget process itself has many other benefits. It can help you save toward important goals. It also forces you to evaluate your spending patterns and perhaps change them.

As you get older, budgeting can provide the financial records you need for tax, investment, and other purposes. Finally, it can give you, at any given point, a clear
2 picture of your financial health and habits.

Developing a budget is the same whether the budgeting is being done for an individual or a family. The process involves five steps.

Consider Financial Goals

Together with choosing a career, budgeting helps you to achieve the standard of living you want. Your financial goals define, in part, your standard of living. The first step toward achieving your goals is to write them down.

Goals can be long-term or short-term. Long-term goals may be going to college, buying a house, building retirement income, purchasing a car, buying a summer home or a boat, paying for a wedding party, or similar objectives that involve substantial amounts of money.

Short-term goals may be buying a sound system, saving for a vacation, purchasing clothes, buying concert tickets, buying a new bicycle, or similar objectives that are more immediate and involve relatively smaller amounts of money.

If you choose to have very many short-term goals, you could sacrifice or delay long-range goals that you also want. Writing your goals down helps
3 you clarify your priorities.

Budgeting can help you achieve a goal, such as being able to take snowboarding lessons. ***What other financial goals might people have?*** ▶

Caption Answer: Answers will vary. People might save for college, retirement, or travel. They may want to own a home or a boat or a recreational vehicle.

Estimate Income

A budget may cover any period of time—a week, a month, a year, for example. Most spending and savings plans, however, are set up on a yearly basis. This time period allows you to look far enough ahead to prepare for changes in your financial situation and to analyze your progress toward your goals.

The next step in developing a plan is to write down how much money you have to spend during your planning period. Income is usually thought of as wages, salary, or profits from a business you own. However, income can be more. For budgeting purposes, your income includes all the money that you receive. It includes unpredictable amounts not earned in the usual sense—bonuses, tips, allowances, benefit payments, rents, bank interest, and gifts of money.

Remember also that not all income is available to you. Most paychecks, for example, show deductions for taxes and other items. These deductions help you to meet your long-term obligations but represent money not on hand for everyday living expenses. When you are figuring your income, write down only **net income,** or take-home pay, the amount of your earnings left after all
1 deductions have been made.

1 Vocabulary You might want to emphasize the distinction between *gross* and *net*. Show students a paycheck stub or ask them to look at the illustration of Form W-2 in Chapter 3.

If your earnings are irregular, planning is harder. You should base your calculations on the least amount of money you expect to receive. Divide this yearly minimum by the number of planning periods you want to use. This procedure will give you an average income per planning period.

Expenses in Poland

The average monthly salary in Poland is $250. Almost half the money is spent on food. The typical American family spends 14 percent of its income on food.

Lori and Dan Raphael, a newly married couple, decided to develop a budget. They first added all their income and figured how much money was available each month. Their estimated net income is shown in Figure 6–1.

Estimate Expenses

After you have figured out the amount of money that you have available, you can plan how the money will be spent. You may be able to estimate your expenses accurately. If you cannot, you have three options.

Figure 6–1 Estimated Net Income

Sources of Income	Annual Total	Regular Planning Periods					
		January	February	March	April	May	June
Dan's wages	$18,600	$1,550	$1,550	$1,550	$1,550	$1,550	$1,550
Lori's wages	5,040	420	420	420	420	420	420
Lori's tips	4,600	325	325	350	400	450	450
Interest	102	8	8	8	9	9	9
Gifts (birthdays)	100	0	50	0	0	50	0
TOTALS	$28,442	2,303	2,353	2,328	2,379	2,479	2,429

▲ *Lori and Dan have estimated their wages and other sources of income.* ***Why might it be more difficult for a student to estimate income?***

Caption Answer: Estimating income as a student is more difficult than it will be later when you have a full-time job. Many people know a year in advance exactly how much they will be paid each payday and when each payday will occur. Even if some income is unpredictable, experience helps you estimate more precisely.

1 Extension Have students keep track of their expenditures for two weeks. On a sheet of paper, students should write the days of the week down the side and the following category headings across the top: Food; Entertainment; Grooming Supplies; Clothing; School Supplies; Savings; Miscellaneous. Ask the question: "How might these categories change when you are living on your own?" (See the trial budget in Figure 6–3.)

1. Use your records to reconstruct your spending patterns. Refer to canceled checks, receipts, bank passbooks, tax forms, and similar items. Make a list of the items you bought and what you paid for them. Then group the items by category and compute the spending for each category.
2. Keep a record of all your expenditures for one month. Start by writing down a list of categories you think reflect your expenses. As you spend, make a notation in the appropriate category. At the end of the month, tally how
1 much was spent in each category.
3. Use **average annual expenditures,** which are yearly averages of how consumers spend their money. One source for these figures is the *Consumer Expenditure Survey* published periodically by the Bureau of Labor Statistics. See Figure 6–2 for an example. To use these averages, select the number of people in your family. Then multiply your net income for your budget period by the percentages given in each category to get dollar amounts. For example, if there are three people and your net income is $25,000, to find the dollar amount your family might want to spend on food, multiply $25,000 × 14.2% (25,000 × .142 = 3,550). Although you cannot expect these figures to be just right for your situation, you could use them for a start and revise them as necessary.

As you list your expenses, you should note that some are fixed and some are flexible. **Fixed expenses** are those that you have already promised to pay on certain dates and in certain amounts. Rent and car payments are examples of fixed expenses. **Flexible expenses** are

Average income and expenditure information is useful in developing budgets, especially when no records have been kept. Why are percentage figures more useful than dollar amounts? ▶

Caption Answer: Dollar figures are available, but they are based on the average income of each consumer unit, which may or may not be anywhere near your income. Figuring percentages on your own income for each category of expenditures allows you to come up with estimates that are more relevant to your situation.

Figure 6–2 Average Annual Expenditures

No. of family members	**1**	**2**	**3**	**4**
Average Net Income *Without* Social Security Taken Out	**$16,318**	**$33,106**	**$36,696**	**$41,745**
Fixed Expenses				
Rent or mortgage payment	21.9%	16.3%	17.1%	17.3%
Installment payments				
Car	5.5	8.1	7.1	6.6
Health Insurance	2.6	2.6	2.2	1.7
Life Insurance	0.7	1.4	1.3	1.3
Flexible Expenses				
Food	13.0	13.7	14.2	15.1
Utilities	7.1	6.7	6.6	6.4
Household supplies and furnishings	5.9	7.3	7.1	7.6
Clothing	5.6	5.2	6.3	6.1
Transportation				
Gas	2.8	3.3	3.5	3.6
Maintenance	6.6	7.2	6.9	7.0
Miscellaneous health care products and services	3.2	3.4	2.9	2.7
Entertainment	4.9	5.1	4.7	5.0
Personal*	4.6	3.9	4.8	4.2
Gifts and contributions	4.4	3.4	2.8	2.3
Miscellaneous	3.3	2.9	3.1	2.8
Pensions and Social Security	6.4	8.5	8.5	9.4
Total spent	98.5%	99.0%	99.1%	99.1%
Amount left	1.5%	1.0%	.9%	.9%

Source: Developed from *Consumer Expenditure Survey,* Bureau of Labor Statistics, 1991.
*Includes such items as personal care products and services, reading, and education.

those that vary in amount and usually in frequency. Examples are clothing purchases and medical expenses.

Plan for Savings

Unfortunately, many people think of savings as money left over after expenses. Savings are, however, probably the most important item in the personal or family budget. When you plan for savings, you are planning for your dreams.

There are two kinds of savings—short-term and long-term. Short-term savings provide for emergencies. Every budget should have an **emergency fund.** This is money put aside to help
1 meet unexpected needs.

While a definite amount should be placed in the fund each planning period, the fund itself should not be allowed to grow too large. Once your emergency fund contains two or three months' income, you should begin putting the money you save into regular, or long-term, savings with higher interest. Long-term savings finance long-range goals. Chapter 9 describes how to plan a savings program.

Develop a Trial Budget

Finally, after reviewing your estimates and your savings plan, fill in your trial budget figures. Concentrate on the key elements—income, fixed and flexible expenses, and savings. During the planning period, record your actual
2 expenditures.

Lori and Dan used the average annual expenditures table in Figure 6–2 to create a trial budget shown in Figure 6–3 on page 98. Notice that at the top they have added a savings category.

KEEPING FINANCIAL RECORDS

A budget is more than good intentions. For a budget to be useful, you must observe its limits. Regularly compare your actual spending with your budget's estimates.

Financial Records

To make comparisons, you will need accurate financial records. Income records include paycheck stubs, statements of interest or dividends earned,

Tips for Shopping by Mail
Mail-order shopping can save you money. But it also can be more challenging because you can't try on or inspect the merchandise.

- **Identify the name of the company. Is it reputable? Many large mail-order firms offer excellent goods at fair prices through their catalogs. However, use caution when responding to advertisements placed in newspapers or magazines. Call the advertiser if an 800 number is offered and ask for a full catalog. Avoid sending money to a post office box.**
- **Compare prices with other catalogs and retail stores, including all shipping and handling charges. Check to see whether the company will refund your cost and shipping charges if you are not satisfied.**
- **Place your order at least four weeks before you want the merchandise.**
- **Never send cash through the mail. Pay by check, money order, or charge card.**
- **Keep a record of the order: the name and address of the company, the item ordered, the date you placed the order, and the number of the money order or check.**
- **Check your order promptly when it arrives. Notify the company immediately if there is a mistake or damage.**

FLASHBACK FLASHFORWARD

In 1945, only one bank closed as a result of financial difficulty. In 1988, during the height of the savings and loan crisis, 221 banks either closed or received assistance from the government. In 1993, that number decreased to 41.

1 Reinforcement Ask students to survey friends who have graduated about unexpected expenses they have experienced. From the discussion, they should realize that everyone has to deal with these occurrences. Determine how many surprises, if any, could have been avoided (by planning ahead, by controlling impulse buying).

2 Reinforcement Student Activity Workbook, Chapter 6 activities.

1 Discussion Starter Ask students what methods they have used to keep track of expenses. Have these methods worked? Ask which of the four methods shown in Figure 6–4 would work best for them and why.

2 Extension Have students brainstorm ways students can make extra money other than by working at fast-food outlets. (Making gifts and providing services to others such as yard care, delivery, and computer help are possibilities.)

and records of gifts, tips, and bonuses. Spending records include canceled checks, cash register receipts, credit card statements, and rent receipts.

Recordkeeping Systems

Use a simple system for storing your records—a drawer, filing cabinet, or special box. Important documents, such as insurance policies, are often kept in a safety deposit box at a bank.

The system you use to compare actual spending with budget estimates is largely a matter of personal choice. Figure 6–4 shows four common recordkeeping
1 methods.

REVISING A BUDGET

At the end of each budget period, you should check to see if expenses and income balance. If you had money left over, what are you going to do with it? If your money didn't stretch far enough, what expenses can you reduce?

Immediate Adjustments

Increasing income is one possible adjustment. You could do additional part-time work, get a raise, or switch to a
2 different job at a higher wage.

To reduce expenditures, begin by reviewing your goals. Make sure your spending fits your priorities. Then look

Figure 6–3 Trial Budget

Budget Categories	Average Expenditures* (Percent)	Trial Budget		Revised Budget	
		Trial Expenditures (Percent)	Trial Expenditures & Income: May	Actual Expenditures & Income: May	Revised Budget: June
Savings					
Emergency fund	—	1.0%	$ 25		
Savings account	—	1.0%	25		
Fixed Expenses					
Rent or mortgage payment	16.3%	24.0	595		
Installment payments					
Car	8.1	8.1	200		
Health insurance	2.6	—	—		
Life insurance	1.4	1.4	35		
Credit card	—	1.2	30		
Flexible Expenses					
Food	13.7	13.7	340		
Utilities	6.7	6.7	166		
Household supplies and furnishings	7.3	7.3	181		
Clothing	5.2	5.2	129		
Transportation					
Gas	3.3	3.3	82		
Maintenance	7.2	7.2	178		
Miscellaneous health care products and services	3.4	3.4	84		
Entertainment	5.1	5.1	126		
Personal	3.9	3.9	97		
Gifts and contributions	3.4	2.6	64		
Miscellaneous	2.9	2.9	72		
Pensions and Social Security	8.5	**	**		
Total spent	99.0%	100.0%	$2,479		
Income	—	—	$2,479		
Amount left	1.0%	0	0		

*From Figure 6–2.
**Does not apply (already taken out of paycheck).

Caption Answer: They had to adjust for rent. The last two columns are blank for keeping records of actual income and expenditures and making adjustments in the budget, if necessary.

Dan and Lori used average annual expenditure percentages to develop their trial budget. ***In what area did they have to revise the average annual figures? Why are the last two columns blank?*** ▶

Figure 6-4 Recordkeeping Systems

Determine a simple system for storing your records.

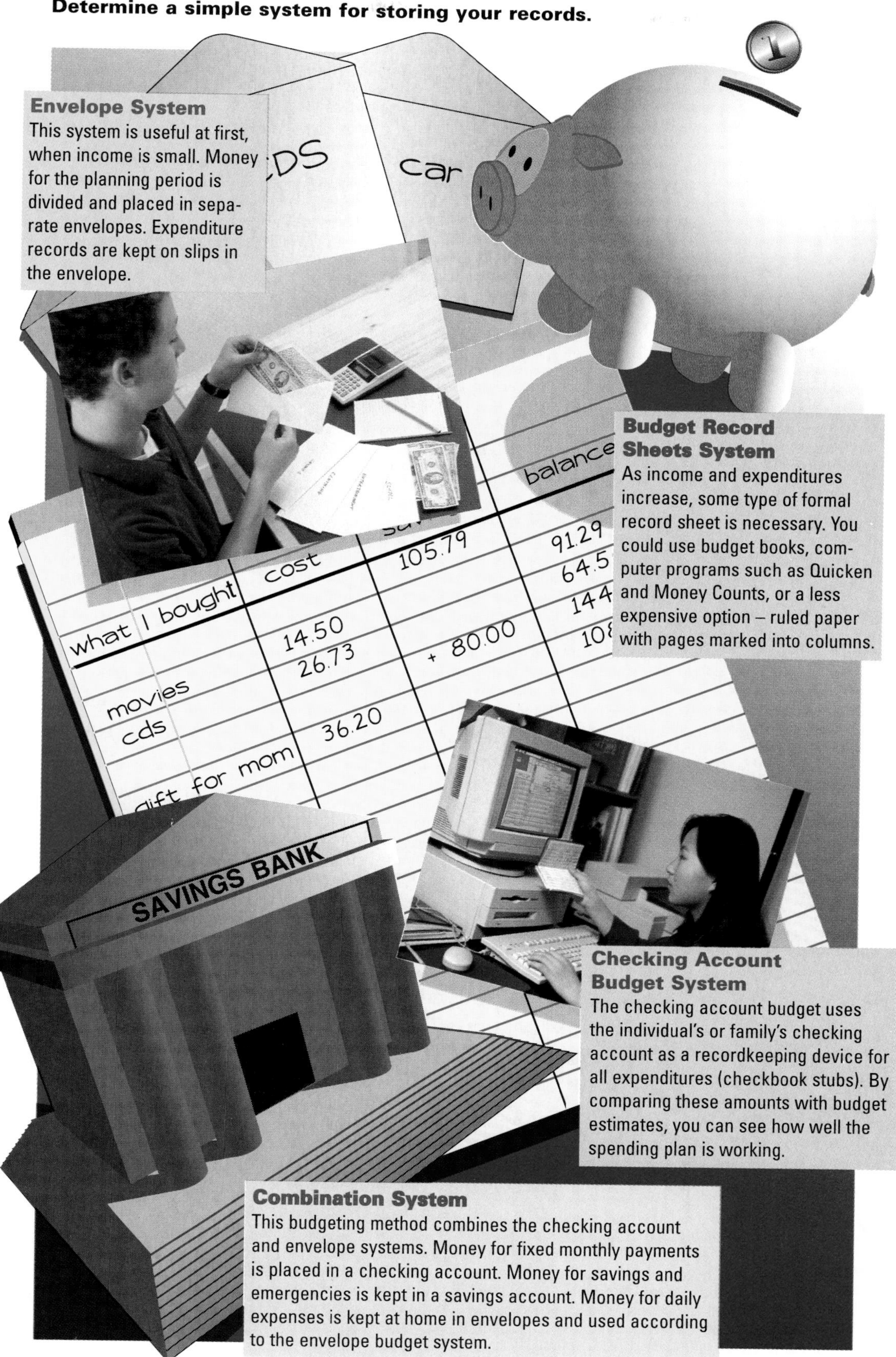

Envelope System
This system is useful at first, when income is small. Money for the planning period is divided and placed in separate envelopes. Expenditure records are kept on slips in the envelope.
cds
car
Budget Record Sheets System
As income and expenditures increase, some type of formal record sheet is necessary. You could use budget books, computer programs such as Quicken and Money Counts, or a less expensive option – ruled paper with pages marked into columns.
what I bought
cost
balance
105.79
91.29
14.50
26.73
+ 80.00
movies
cds
36.20
gift for mom
SAVINGS BANK
Checking Account Budget System
The checking account budget uses the individual's or family's checking account as a recordkeeping device for all expenditures (checkbook stubs). By comparing these amounts with budget estimates, you can see how well the spending plan is working.
Combination System
This budgeting method combines the checking account and envelope systems. Money for fixed monthly payments is placed in a checking account. Money for savings and emergencies is kept in a savings account. Money for daily expenses is kept at home in envelopes and used according to the envelope budget system.

CASE STUDY

Consumer NEWS CLIP

Newlyweds Need to Agree on Money Matters

by Kathy M. Kristof
Los Angeles Times
September 11, 1994

Although generally happy together, [Sandy and Tom] argued about bills, credit balances, and continued spending until they finally sought financial counseling. "Few couples talk about money before the marriage," says Robin Leonard, author of *Money Troubles: Legal Strategies to Cope With Your Debts.* "Often—even if the couple has been living together—they don't even know if the other person has credit card bills or a huge tax debt. Many people keep all this private until after the wedding."

Partly as a result, financial friction is common among newlyweds, experts say. Indeed, in past surveys, more than half of divorced couples cited money problems as a significant factor in their split.

"The good news is that it's never too late to get your joint economic life together," says Kathleen Stepp, a Kansas City-based financial planner who heads Citibank MasterCard and Visa's Money Matters for Newlyweds education program.

How do you do it? The keys are communication and compromise, Stepp and others say. Newlyweds need to sit down and open their checkbooks, tax returns, billing statements, and brokerage accounts and talk over what they have and what they want. Here are a few tips on where and how to start.

- Discuss goals. Many couples find their biggest money troubles come from having conflicting goals. One wants a retirement account and the other wants a boat, for example. "Disagreements about money are really disagreements about priorities, because money is finite," says Stepp. "You'll need to find common ground, which may not be as tough as it sounds."
- Budget. Open up your checkbooks and start tallying how much money you've got coming in and where it's going out. Then figure out where you'd like to economize and whether it's possible. It's likely that your budget is significantly different now that you are married, Stepp notes.
- Check your credit status. Equifax, TransUnion and TRW can provide each of you with updated copies of your credit reports. It's important to do this early in your marriage, because the results can determine how well you handle your finances going forward, says Leonard.
- Get together on fringe benefits. Two-income couples need to take a second look at their employee benefits to see if they can save money by eliminating overlapping coverage. You may also want to change the beneficiary designations on life insurance policies and consider whether additional coverage is necessary, as it might be if you plan to have or already have children.

Decisions, Decisions

1. What are some of the things a couple should do to create a budget?
2. If you haven't done so already, prepare a budget for yourself.

at fixed and flexible expenses. You usually cannot reduce fixed expenses, except perhaps by moving to a less costly residence. Some flexible expenses, however, can be reduced.

Identify spending habits you can change and areas where you can cut down. In some cases, you may have to adjust the budget rather than your spending.

Adjustments Throughout Life

Just as income changes during different stages of life, so do financial plans. Having children may cause a drop in income if one partner stays home. The spending plan would need to be adjusted to reflect higher expenses and lower income.

News Clip Answers:
1 They should talk over their goals so that the budget can accommodate them as closely as possible. They should determine how much money they earn and how much they spend. They should then figure out where to economize, if that is necessary.
2 Take a moment to write down how much money you get from an allowance, a job, or gifts. Now write down the things you want or need to buy. If there is a gap, think of ways you can save money.

Case Study Answer:
Organize the neighbors; create a neighborhood association; petition the company and city government with your concerns; visit the library to research any studies done on the consequences of living in close proximity to these kinds of industries; testify at local government hearings; write to local papers; get all the facts you can from neighbors, research reports; get help from already-existing environmental groups; be persistent.

People MAKING a DIFFERENCE

Safeguarding Public Health

All too often, unsightly, unhealthy, and downright dangerous manufacturing plants and dump sites are placed in areas too poor to fight them. In one area on Chicago's south side, there are a steel mill, a sewage treatment plant, several landfills, chemical manufacturing companies, and waste incinerators. They fill the air with toxic fumes, dust, and just plain stench.

In the center of all this is Altgeld Gardens, a public housing project. Residents are mostly low-income Hispanics and African-Americans.

Hazel Johnson had lived in Altgeld Gardens for a long time when her husband died of lung cancer. Johnson was puzzled by his disease—until she began talking to neighbors. Ninety percent of her neighbors, she found, suffered from skin rashes, breathing problems, burning eyes, and other ailments that could be caused by air pollution.

Angered by what she found, Johnson started People for Community Recovery (PCR). Shortly after its founding, the group filed more than 1,000 air-quality complaints and protested the asbestos insulation—which is linked to cancer—in the walls of schools and homes in the area.

As a result, city workers began removing asbestos from the buildings. City planners have turned down proposals to enlarge existing landfills and build a chemical waste incinerator nearby.

Hazel Johnson has been called "the black mother of the environmental movement." In 1992, she received the President's Environment and Conservation Challenge medal. She has shown that people are never too helpless or too poor to fight city hall.

Brainstorm

What steps would you take to reduce the impact of environmentally unsafe industries in your neighborhood?

1 Discussion Starter Ask students if they see any other potential barriers to success at budgeting. (It is easier and more enjoyable to spend spontaneously: instant gratification versus patience.)

2 Extension Have students practice calculator skills. Using the table in Figure 6–2, students should calculate how much is spent on fixed expenses for a family of one with an income of $16,000 ($16,000 × 21.9% = $3,504) and for a family of four with an income of $40,000 ($40,000 × 17.3% = $6,920.)

3 Reinforcement Have students go to a computer lab and practice using Quicken.

4 Discussion Starter Ask students to think about whether they have assets or liabilities. Ask for examples of assets and liabilities that students might have. (Assets: bicycle, sports equipment, musical instruments, savings account. Liabilities: debts to friends or family members, charge account at the school store.)

Caption Answer: Some possible assets other than money are real estate, cars, stocks, antiques or collectibles, insurance policies, and jewelry.

A consumer or family should prepare a balance sheet at least once a year. ***What assets, other than money, might be listed?*** ▶

If you wanted to buy a home, you would need to see if your budget could be adjusted to include maintenance and repairs. Will there be enough left after the house payments to continue your savings and investment plans?

Will your savings and investments be substantial enough to cover your retirement and possible care for aging parents? Life experiences such as divorce, death of a spouse, illness, and disability also alter a family's financial plan.

BUDGETING PROBLEMS

The process of developing a budget can be stressful. After all, you must confront the limitations of your income. You may find yourself having to make
1 tough spending decisions.

To keep up the budgeting habit, make the process as easy as possible.

1. Use an inexpensive pocket calculator to
2 eliminate tedious hand computations.
2. Round off figures to the nearest dollar, this will make computations less time-consuming.
3. Use a personal computer with easy-to-
3 use software.
4. Keep your budgeting materials in a special place so you don't waste time hunting for them.
5. Choose a regular time to do your budgeting, say, the first Sunday of every month.
6. Reward yourself. Always end by reviewing how well you are doing or how much progress you have made.

For budgeting to be useful, you must use accurate information and review your budget regularly. Three common mistakes can affect the usefulness of a budget.

1. Not planning for predictable expenses that are not synchronized with your budget period. For example, suppose you have a magazine subscription for $25 due every year. You need to budget about $2 monthly to save for the yearly payments.
2. Not being realistic in estimating the amount of expenses.
3. Not being specific enough in setting up budget categories. For example, suppose you earn $80 a month and your budget has only three categories—Lunches, $20; Movies, $10; and Miscellaneous, $50. Your budget will not work well because too much money is lumped under Miscellaneous. You cannot control the $50 in that category because you do not know how you are spending it.

Figure 6–5 Consumer Balance Sheet (Simplified)

Assets:		
Cash in checking account	$800	
Cash in savings account	1,500	
Series EE savings bonds	300	
Stocks and bonds	20,000	
Current value of house	92,000	
Current value of car	2,300	
Other assets		
Total		$116,900
Liabilities:		
Current bills due	175	
Amount owed on credit cards	55	
Amount owed on house mortgage	68,000	
Other liabilities		
Total		68,230
Net worth:		$48,670

TAKING AN ANNUAL INVENTORY

Besides preparing a budget and keeping records of expenditures, you will eventually want to analyze your total financial situation. To do this, draw up a balance sheet from time to time, just as a business firm does. A **balance sheet** is a statement of assets, liabilities, and resulting new worth. **Assets** are items of value that you own, including money. **Liabilities** are debts—money that you owe. **Net worth** is the difference between assets
4 and liabilities. A sample balance sheet is shown in Figure 6–5.

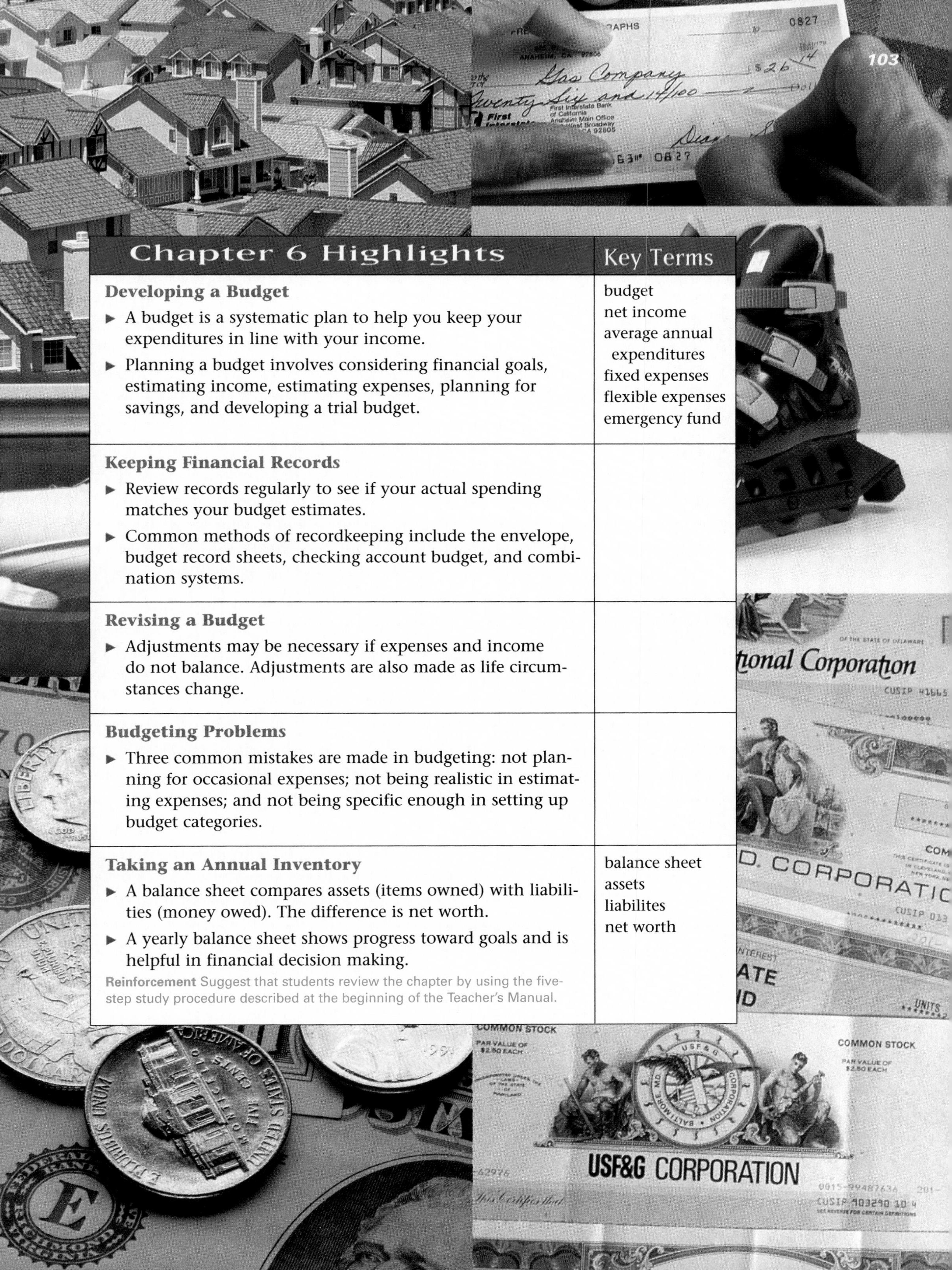

Chapter 6 Highlights

Developing a Budget

- A budget is a systematic plan to help you keep your expenditures in line with your income.
- Planning a budget involves considering financial goals, estimating income, estimating expenses, planning for savings, and developing a trial budget.

Key Terms: budget, net income, average annual expenditures, fixed expenses, flexible expenses, emergency fund

Keeping Financial Records

- Review records regularly to see if your actual spending matches your budget estimates.
- Common methods of recordkeeping include the envelope, budget record sheets, checking account budget, and combination systems.

Revising a Budget

- Adjustments may be necessary if expenses and income do not balance. Adjustments are also made as life circumstances change.

Budgeting Problems

- Three common mistakes are made in budgeting: not planning for occasional expenses; not being realistic in estimating expenses; and not being specific enough in setting up budget categories.

Taking an Annual Inventory

- A balance sheet compares assets (items owned) with liabilities (money owed). The difference is net worth.
- A yearly balance sheet shows progress toward goals and is helpful in financial decision making.

Key Terms: balance sheet, assets, liabilites, net worth

Reinforcement Suggest that students review the chapter by using the five-step study procedure described at the beginning of the Teacher's Manual.

CHAPTER 

REVIEW

Refer students to the Reviewing Consumer Terms and Reviewing Facts and Ideas activities in the Student Activity Workbook.

Reviewing Consumer Terms Sentences will vary. See Glossary for definitions.

Reviewing Facts and Ideas See the Student Activity Workbook for answers.

Problem Solving and Decision Making Answers depend on Student opinions.

Consumers Around the World
Math 1 Raymond could save for the CD in three or four weeks. A sample budget showing Weeks 1 to 4 plus total for each item follow.
SAVINGS:
CD: $3 + $3 + $3 + $3 = $12
Movies: $1 + $1 + 1$ + $2 = $5
Magazine: $1 + $1 + $1 + 0 = $3
FLEXIBLE EXPENSES:
Lunch: $7.50 + $7.50 + $7.50 + $7.50 = $30
Snack: $2.50 + $2.50 + $2.50 + $2.50 = $10
TOTAL SPENT:
$15 + $15 + $15 + $15 = $60
TOTAL INCOME:
$15 + $15 + $15 + $15 = $60

Reviewing Consumer Terms

Use each of the following terms in a sentence that demonstrates you know its meaning.

assets
average annual expenditures
balance sheet
budget
emergency fund
fixed expenses
flexible expenses
liabilities
net worth
net income

Reviewing Facts and Ideas

1. What are the five steps in planning a budget?
2. List the common methods of recordkeeping.
3. What are the three most common mistakes consumers make when budgeting?
4. When should consumers revise their budgets?
5. What information does a balance sheet show?

Problem Solving and Decision Making

1. Listed here are some points of view about budgeting. Give your opinion of each statement. Then defend your position.
   - **a.** "I know how much I earn and how much I spend. Why should I keep a record?"
   - **b.** "I keep a record of major expenses only. There's no point in bothering with nickel-and-dime items."
   - **c.** "I have a complete record of every cent I've spent for the past ten years."
   - **d.** "I pay all of my bills by check. My checkbook is my record of expenses."
2. Juanita Quiñones is going to college. She works 20 hours a week and lives with two other students. One of her roommates is graduating and moving out. Suggest at least three ways Juanita and her remaining roommate can make up the shortfall in their budget.

Building Academic Skills

Consumers Around the World

Math

1. Raymond Periera earns $15 a week doing chores at home. Out of his income, he must pay for the following: school lunch ($1.50); daily snack ($.50). He also likes to go occasionally to the movies ($5) and to buy his favorite monthly magazine ($3). Raymond wants to save enough to buy a new $12 CD by a group he likes.

   Construct a four-week budget for Raymond using the following column headings: Category; Week 1; Week 2; Week 3; Week 4; Total. In the Category column,

use two headings—Savings and Flexible Expenses. Remember to show income and expense totals at the bottom of each column. How long will it take Raymond to save for a CD?

Technology

2. Accurate recordkeeping is a vital part of the budgeting process. Collect information on the types of recordkeeping systems—paper and computer—that families can use.

   Describe each system—how records are stored, information recorded, and totals computed. Which system is more convenient? less expensive? easier to use? Write a 250-word article explaining the pros and cons of both systems.

Social Studies

3. Choose four other countries and research consumer budgets in those countries. What percentages of income are spent on food? Clothing? Rent or mortgages? Write a 500-word report on your research.

Beyond the Classroom

Consumer Project

Select a college or vocational school you might like to attend. Obtain information on tuition and other fees. Add in the costs of food, shelter, laundry, clothing, transportation, and books. Estimate the total cost.

Assume that you have $1,000 in savings. Your uncle will give you $2,000, and you are assured of a scholarship for $1,500.

Prepare a monthly budget for one year. Are the costs greater than your available money? By how much? How will you make up the difference?

Cooperative Learning

Family Economics

Break into assigned family groups. Do a monthly household budget for your family group. Obtain fixed expenses from the family profiles provided by your teacher. Be realistic about flexible expenses, given your family's makeup and financial resources. You could refer to Figure 6–2 for average percentages spent in each budget category.

Compare your spending patterns with those of other family groups. Note: Retain your finished budget for reference and revision in later chapters.

Debate the Issue

A cashless society is a society in which all money transactions are done by computer. No cash or checks actually change hands. Many feel that a cashless society will help consumers manage their money better. Others feel that invasion of privacy would be too easy in a cashless society.

You and your classmates will break into two groups and research this topic. Each group will gather evidence to support one side or the other. You are to prepare the argument for your side of the problem. Then the two groups will meet in a classroom debate.

Technology
2 Students may compare paper systems with software like Quicken. Paper may be more convenient if computer access is limited. Paper is probably less expensive. Computer systems may be easier to use.

Social Studies
3 Students should answer all questions for their chosen countries.

Consumer Project
Students will have different answers, but for most, the costs will be much greater than money on hand. Students may suggest earning money and borrowing money.

Family Economics
Budgets will vary. Students should not include money withheld for federal taxes when calculating available monthly income.

Debate the Issue
Break the class into two teams. Assign each team one side of the issue. Encourage students to work together as a team to develop their argument. Ask each team to select a member to make an opening statement that supports the team's side of the issue. Have students take turns debating as the debate moves from one team to the other.

2lb ~ 3.50
Ficelles 75¢
2lb ~ 3.50
Country White
Rosemary
2.25

CHAPTER 7

Spending Money Wisely

Learning Objectives

When you have finished studying this chapter, you should be able to:

1. Identify the factors that influence consumer spending.
2. Describe how to apply the seven steps of economic decision making to a typical consumer purchase.
3. Show how to select the best place to purchase a given item.
4. Explain how timing can affect buying decisions.

Consumer Terms

values
lifestyle
life stage
habit
impulse purchase
status symbols
conspicuous consumption
sales promotions
retail stores
cooperative

Real-World Journal

Imagine you were given $250 to spend in the next 24 hours. What would you purchase? In your journal, describe each item and its approximate cost. What could you do to get the items for less money? Go through your local newspapers for advertised sales and discount coupons on these or similar items. Paste the sales information or coupons into your journal.

Lesson Plan See the Teacher's Manual for the Chapter 7 lesson plan.

Vocabulary The Chapter 7 lesson plan includes suggested vocabulary activities for the terms listed.

1 Discussion Starter Ask students if they have made unwise purchases in the past. Have them describe the situation and discuss what lessons they have learned.

INFLUENCES ON CONSUMER SPENDING

Why do you purchase a particular item? If you are like most consumers, you are not aware of all the reasons. Economic factors probably come to mind first—the price of the item and the amount you have to spend. However, a host of other factors—personal, social, and business—enter into the decision as well. Consider this example:

> A relative has been saving for a new car, a minivan to make shopping and carpooling easier. He finally buys the same model as your neighbor but ends up paying $1,500 more because he waited until the beginning of the new model year.

In this example, money was wasted because an important factor was ignored—timing. Factors like this one enter into every consumer purchase. If you are to spend your money wisely, you must learn what these factors are and when and how they should affect your
1 decision making.

Personal Factors

Personal influences are those that derive from your background, family circumstances, and upbringing. Their role in decision making is often overlooked because they are so basic to the way you think and act.

Values Your **values** are principles or qualities that you find desirable or worthwhile. Your feelings about education, politics, religion, and other people's property, for example, all reflect your values. Values come from many sources, but most are learned in the family.

Values also influence **lifestyle,** or way of living. If a family values education above material possessions, for example, they are likely to give a higher priority to school tuition than to home furnishings or a second car.

Goals What do you want out of life? In answering this question, you are stating your goals. Some goals are immediate, or short-term, while others will take longer to accomplish. An immediate goal may be to buy a jacket you have been admiring. A long-term goal might be to attend community college in order to pursue a career in medical technology.

Goals, like values, influence your decisions and way of life. To buy the jacket you admire, you must decide how to earn the money. In addition, you

Caption Answer: They value friends, others, and the environment.

People show their values by the things they do. ***What do these people's actions say about their values?*** ▼

must decide whether buying the jacket is worth giving up other things you also want. The goal of becoming a medical technician will require that you do without the lifestyle of a wage earner right after graduation. Because all these options involve some sacrifice, making
1 such choices can be difficult. Having
2 definite goals, however, can take some of the stress out of the process.

Life Stage The **life stage,** or period of life, at which you find yourself also affects your buying decisions. Being single is one example of a life stage. Others include being newly married, married with children, and retired. People who find themselves at each of these life stages tend to have similar concerns and hence confront similar economic decisions (see Chapter 6).

Habit Many consumer purchases are made on the basis of habit. A **habit** is a tendency to follow a fixed pattern of behavior. People get into the habit of buying a certain product, shopping at a certain store, or eating at a certain restaurant.

Habit is not necessarily a poor basis for decision making. Used for minor or routine purchases, for example, it can simplify your life. Followed blindly, however, it can keep you from comparing and considering other possibilities, some of which may be better.

Impulse An **impulse purchase** is an unplanned, or spur-of-the-moment, buy. Merchants encourage impulse purchases by using such techniques as the positioning of displays near the check-
3 out counter.

Impulse buying can have its benefits (such as finding an item you need on sale). It often results, however, in the purchase of unnecessary products and can destroy the best-laid spending plans.

Resources Just like businesses, you have resources. A business's resources are land, labor, capital, and entrepreneurship. Your personal resources include time, money, energy, and knowledge in its various forms.

There are two important similarities between personal and business resources: Both are scarce, and both can be combined in different ways. Every time you make an economic decision, you must give up a resource. The resource is usually money, but it does not have to be. If you have more time and energy (and the necessary skill), you can substitute your own labor. Remember, however, that using a resource for one purpose prevents you from using it for another.

Social Factors

Family members affect your decisions, but so can other people. A friend, a neighbor, or even a stranger in a supermarket line can recommend a product. When you let the reactions of others determine your choices, you are allowing social factors to influence your decision making.

Popular Taste Popular taste probably influences consumer choices more

◄ *Consumers choose to use their resources in different ways.* ***What resources are being used in this picture? What resource is being saved? What are some other ways this couple could have used their resources?***

1 Reinforcement
Have students list some of their own short-term and long-term goals. How do their buying decisions relate to their goals?

2 Reinforcement
Have students rewrite their goals statements. They should make each goal more specific than it is in the original list of goals. Point out that they are indicating their standards as they clarify their goals.

3 Discussion Starter
Have students tell about the absolute worse buys they ever made. How many were impulse purchases? Next, have them analyze purchases they made in a two-week period.

Caption Answer:
Resources of time, energy, money, and knowledge (or skills) are being used to complete this project. These family members chose to save on their money resource by doing the work themselves. If they had hired someone else to do the work, they could have put their extra time and energy resources into such things as family recreational outings or hobbies.

1 Discussion Starter Ask students what is "in" and what is "out" in fashion. Do they have clothes that they simply never wear because they are not in style?

2 Discussion Starter Ask students to make a list of status symbols. What cars signify status? what clothes labels? sports gear? other items?

3 Reinforcement Have students scan mailed advertising sent to their home and local newspapers and listen to TV and radio announcements to make a list of ongoing promotions. At the end of two weeks, read and discuss the lists in class.

4 Research As an extra assignment, you may want to have students compare prices between stores that offer sales promotions and those that do not. After taking other factors into consideration, can students support the statement "Stores that offer sales promotions generally charge higher prices than those that do not offer sales promotions"?

than any factor other than price. Keeping up with changes in fashion is an example. What is in fashion today may be out of fashion next year. Following fashion blindly can result in waste. Clothing, for example, may be discarded,
1 carded, even though it shows no sign of wear, simply because it is dated.

Status The more money a person has available to spend, the more likely he or she is to buy luxury goods such as expensive clothing, jewelry, and cars. For this reason, to many people these things have become **status symbols** (signs of high rank or financial success). Sometimes, people buy luxury goods to impress others with their apparent wealth and success. This practice
2 is called **conspicuous consumption.**

Business Factors

The devices businesses use to sell goods and services are probably the most familiar influences on consumer spending. Two examples—advertising and sales tactics—are discussed in detail in Chapter 8. There are others, however.

Sales Promotions The supermarkets in your area double or even triple the value of manufacturers' coupons. Your dry cleaner offers "One $5 item cleaned free with every order of $20 or more." The local shopping mall sponsors a Fourth of July raffle in which the first prize is a new car. If you have ever been induced to make a purchase by devices like these, then you have been persuaded by promotions.

Sales Promotions are sales activities that stimulate consumer purchasing.
3 Sales promotions include free samples,
4 coupons, and contests.

Shopping Environment The environment, or surroundings, in which you shop can also affect you. Supermarkets, department stores, malls—all present a staggering array of choices. This variety makes it more likely that the consumer will find whatever he or she wants, but it can also confuse or overwhelm a shopper. In addition, it can create a desire for all sorts of items that are beyond a shopper's means and needs.

DECIDING WHAT TO BUY

Careful decision making involves several well-defined steps. Think about how you decide what to buy. What steps do you go through? Do you consciously compare the advantages and disadvantages of the choices open to you? Do you ask yourself specific questions about such things as needs, wants, and prices? Do you jump to conclusions on whim or impulse? The best approach is to have a system. That way you can be sure that all the questions get asked. Consider these steps.

How to Keep a Money Diary
Where does all your money go? The only way to keep track is to maintain a record of every penny you spend. Carry a pocket notebook with you and write down the amount and the type of purchase whenever you spend cash. Get in the habit of asking for receipts. Then at the end of the day, record the information from the receipts in a notebook. Total your spending at the end of each week. Then at the end of the month, add in how much you spent by check, credit card, or automatic deductions. It may take you several months of keeping track to get a true picture of your expenses.

1. Define the issue or problem.
2. Identify relevant values and goals.
3. List possible choices.
4. Gather information.
5. Evaluate the choices.
6. Make a decision.
1 7. Evaluate the results.

Define the Issue or Problem

Defining issues and problems is a way to incorporate both the knowledge you have and the thinking you have already done about a problem. More is involved here than simply saying, "Which product should I buy?" You need to establish your major concerns: What are you trying to accomplish?

Answer this question by writing a list of specific personal requirements based on how you will use the product. For example, you need a new car, but why? Your thinking might follow these lines: "I'm doing a lot of driving and hauling. It's been rough. My sports car has a cramped back seat, has virtually no room in the trunk, and gets 12 miles per gallon. What type of car would give me the room I need with the best fuel economy?" In this type of thinking you can see the beginnings of a list.

It is important, however, not to let yourself be limited by this initial effort. You should try to keep an open mind so that when new alternatives or questions arise, you can include them in your decision making.

Identify Relevant Values and Goals

2 It is important for you to define your own values and goals. This process will help you establish priorities. Consider an example. Logically, you know you should care about a car's repair history. With this in mind, you place the three most reliable cars at the top of your shopping list, but you can't seem to get excited about any of them.

The cars that excite you have great looks—and dismal repair records. You obviously value appearance more than reliability. If you disregard this value, you will probably never be satisfied with your purchase. So what is the solution? Perhaps you could limit your options to those more stylish vehicles that have an extended factory warranty.

Breakfast Around the World

Cereal costs about four times more in Tokyo ($7.93) than it does in London ($1.85). A box of cereal weighing 500 grams (a little over a pound) costs $5.39 in Bangkok, $3.48 in the United States, and $2.69 in Paris.

List Possible Choices

In this step, the emphasis is on not leaving anything out. You should explore all the choices open to you, including those that may seem out of the ordinary. For example, if you have been thinking only of imported cars because of their reputation for reliability, why not a domestic car with an excellent repair record?

Gather Information

Once you have some alternatives and options in mind, research their benefits and options. In this step you are beginning the process of comparison shopping, a critical part of the consumer decision-making process.

1 Reinforcement To familiarize students with the seven-step decision-making process described here, you may want to pose a consumer need and lead the class through the first three steps of the process. Step four could be handled by groups and shared, but the remaining steps will need to be done individually. Compare and discuss decisions in class.

2 Reinforcement Emphasize the need for students to be realistic about their own personal feelings. Remind them of what they read earlier about the social factors that affect buying decisions. They should not be afraid to buy according to their values, even if their values differ significantly from what they perceive to be society's preferences.

Caption Answer: In-store videos can show you how to do such things as refinish furniture, build a deck, and accessorize an outfit. Computer on-line services offer a broad spectrum of consumer information. You can view an entire collection of *Consumer Reports,* have access to hundreds of federal publications, read collections of consumer news articles, participate in consumer discussion groups, and find information on specific products. Some product information is in the form of lengthy detailed ads. While these contain some useful information—as do in-store videos—consumers should remember that both sources are still advertisements and not objective sources.

One useful technique is to start by identifying the most basic model of the item. For example, in a music store, ask to see the lowest-priced electric guitar of the highest-quality manufacturer. Ask the salesperson to describe the guitar's features. Then go methodically up the product line, having the salesperson explain the additional features of each model. Now repeat the process with the store's lower-quality line of guitars.

You may discover that models in a product line vary little in quality of sound. They may simply have more features or a newer look. You might decide to buy a good-quality, lower-priced model and use the savings from a fancier model to buy guitar accessories you want.

Salespeople, in-store videos, and product labels also can provide you information that can help you make a wise decision. Salespeople can help with comparisons and provide information on scheduled sales. In-store videos often provide tips on how to use the product. Product labels inform by identifying content, as in food labels, and materials and care, as in clothing labels.

Other sources of information include friends and relatives who have made similar purchases. They can provide performance information. Advertising can help you keep up to date on new and better products and compare prices and services. Information is also available through publications—general consumer magazines such as *Consumer Reports and Consumers' Research,* special interest magazines, federal agency publications, information brokers, and buying services.

Evaluate the Choices

Next, you will be making price-quality comparisons with your own values, standards, and goals clearly in mind. In order to make a decision, you need to bring together the variety of points and issues you found in your research (see Figure 7–1).

For most decisions, a chart is not necessary—people can make comparisons in their heads when differences among choices are great. When choices are closer (or when you don't feel strongly about any of the alternatives), a chart can help.

Technology poses both a problem for consumers (more technical features to research) and an opportunity (easier access to information). ***What kinds of information might be found on the in-store video? On a computer on-line service? What should you remember when using this information?*** ▶

Figure 7–1 Ranking Choices by Value Points

Developing a chart to rank your choices is helpful, especially for major purchases.

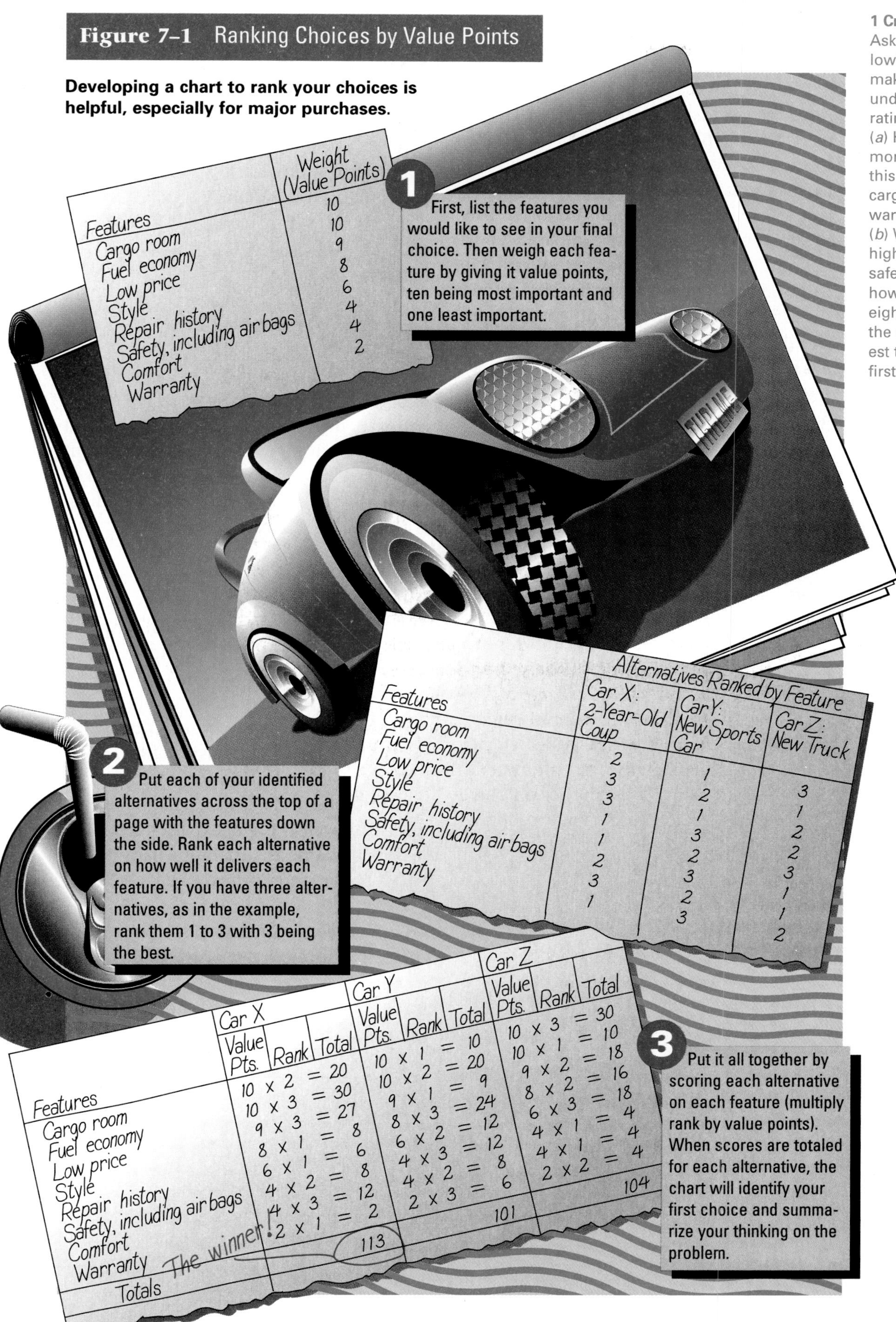

1
First, list the features you would like to see in your final choice. Then weigh each feature by giving it value points, ten being most important and one least important.
2
Put each of your identified alternatives across the top of a page with the features down the side. Rank each alternative on how well it delivers each feature. If you have three alternatives, as in the example, rank them 1 to 3 with 3 being the best.
3
Put it all together by scoring each alternative on each feature (multiply rank by value points). When scores are totaled for each alternative, the chart will identify your first choice and summarize your thinking on the problem.
The winner!

Features	Weight (Value Points)
Cargo room	10
Fuel economy	10
Low price	9
Style	8
Repair history	6
Safety, including air bags	4
Comfort	4
Warranty	2

Features	Alternatives Ranked by Feature		
	Car X: 2-Year-Old Coup	Car Y: New Sports Car	Car Z: New Truck
Cargo room	2	1	3
Fuel economy	3	2	1
Low price	3	1	2
Style	1	3	2
Repair history	1	2	3
Safety, including air bags	2	3	1
Comfort	3	2	1
Warranty	1	3	2

Features	Car X Value Pts.	Rank	Total	Car Y Value Pts.	Rank	Total	Car Z Value Pts.	Rank	Total
Cargo room	10	× 2	= 20	10	× 1	= 10	10	× 3	= 30
Fuel economy	10	× 3	= 30	10	× 2	= 20	10	× 1	= 10
Low price	9	× 3	= 27	9	× 1	= 9	9	× 2	= 18
Style	8	× 1	= 8	8	× 3	= 24	8	× 2	= 16
Repair history	6	× 1	= 6	6	× 2	= 12	6	× 3	= 18
Safety, including air bags	4	× 2	= 8	4	× 3	= 12	4	× 1	= 4
Comfort	4	× 3	= 12	4	× 2	= 8	4	× 1	= 4
Warranty	2	× 1	= 2	2	× 3	= 6	2	× 2	= 4
Totals			113			101			104

1 Critical Thinking Ask students the following questions to make sure they understand how the rating system works: (*a*) How many times more important does this person rate cargo room over warranty? (5 times); (*b*) Which car scored highest according to safety? (Y); (*c*) In how many of the eight categories did the car with the highest total score rank first? (3)

1 Reinforcement Student Activity Workbook, Chapter 7 activities.

2 Learning Economics Ask students why the main problem is also an advantage. (Competition usually means better buys for consumers)

3 Discussion Starter Have students generate a class list of local department stores. This list may include stores that students will later classify as discount department stores and variety stores. Make a chart on the board and compare the stores in terms of merchandise, service, prices, and convenience. What major differences do students see among the stores? Do different students favor different stores? Why?

Caption Answer: Students may mention price and location as important factors. The seven steps of the decision-making process would be helpful.

Make a Decision and Evaluate the Results

The final two steps in the decision-making process is to choose the alternative that reflects either the greatest number or most important of your values, standards, and goals. Usually, this is the alternative that seems to offer the most advantages. If you evaluated your alternatives using a chart, it would be the one with the highest number total. After you have made your choice you should evaluate the results. Ongoing evaluation of the processes you used and the outcomes of your decisions can
1 improve your abilities in the future.

PLACES TO SHOP

One of your main problems as a consumer is choosing from the large variety of selling agencies that compete for your dollars. Each selling agency has its own
2 advantages and disadvantages.

Retail Stores

Most of your shopping will be done in **retail stores,** business establishments that sell goods and services to the general public. Retail stores differ in the way they operate, the merchandise they sell, the services they give, and the prices they charge. It pays to compare stores and to shop where the goods and services that you want are available at the lowest prices. Here are some of your options.

Most people shop in retail stores. ***How do you decide what kind of store to shop in?*** ▼

Department Stores Department stores' sell a large variety of goods and services at different price levels. For purchasing, promotion, and selling purposes, they can be divided into departments; hence, their name. To compete with discount stores, many are eliminating less-profitable departments and reducing services. Examples of department stores include Nordstrom, Lord & Taylor, Bloomingdale's, and
3 Macy's.

Discount Department Stores and Variety Stores These stores are stripped-down, low-cost versions of department stores. They have open counter displays of merchandise and limited customer service. Their main advantage is cut-rate prices on many items. Some examples include Bradlees and Kmart.

Specialty Stores Specialty stores usually carry a limited variety of merchandise. Some, for example, deal only in clothing for a particular group—such as children, men, or women. Grocery stores, gift shops, bookstores, and home-furnishings stores are other kinds of specialty stores. Such establishments usually offer a wide selection of merchandise within their specialty and personal attention from well-trained, experienced salespeople. Examples include Baby Gap, Eddie Bauer, and Pottery Barn.

Superstores Superstores are giant specialty stores. They often stand alone in the middle of a large parking lot or serve to anchor malls. Low prices and huge selection are their main benefits. Some superstores include many of Barnes & Noble stores, Home Depot, and Wal-Mart.

Outlet Stores Outlet stores are sometimes called *factory outlets.* They carry products from only one manufacturer. The selection is sometimes limited, as is the sales help. Large discounts are usually given, but some items are imperfect. It pays to look carefully and know prices.

Warehouse Clubs Here, members must pay to join. Low prices make warehouse clubs appealing, but that doesn't mean they offer the best deal on everything. Huge packaging sizes, especially on foods, limited selection,
1 and lack of service are typical.

Secondhand Stores These stores handle used merchandise. Items are sold "as is," which means that returns are not
2 possible and no quality guarantees are

People MAKING a DIFFERENCE

Painting and Healing

Hospitals are places of healing. Nevertheless, they can seem cold and unfriendly—especially to the very ill or dying. As advertising executive John Feight sat with a dying friend one day, he realized that in his last hours, his friend was surrounded with sterile blank walls.

This realization bothered Feight, who could not get the thought out of his mind. So he decided to change things. With paint and brushes and the hospital's permission, he began painting murals on the walls.

Feight was only into his second mural when a 5-year-old patient came to watch. She had been badly disfigured in a traffic accident. "I want to paint," she told him. Feight gave her a brush and let her go. When he saw how happy she was by helping him, he realized that getting people involved would be the most important part of the project.

Feight quit his job in advertising and set up the Foundation for Hospital Art. The foundation coordinates the donation of paintings to hospitals. In eight years, the organization arranged the donation of 4,000 paintings to more than 250 hospitals in the United States and Europe.

More importantly, however, Feight continues to paint murals on hospital walls—more than 500 a year. He no longer works alone. He gets everyone involved—from hospital executives and doctors to nurses and patients. Feight outlines the bright, whimsical scenes on the wall. Then his team, working with brushes, rollers, and acrylic paint, fills in the outlines.

Everyone loves it. It helps turn the hospitals into friendly places of healing.

Brainstorm

What are two other services you could provide to help turn a hospital into friendly places of healing?

1 Student Motivator Select items at random—blue jeans, CD player, sneakers, stereo, etc.—and have students compare the quality and price of merchandise found in a variety of different retail stores. Where would they usually buy and why? Why were different choices made with the same data?

2 Extension Have students think about secondhand shopping at garage sales, flea markets and thrift shops. What were some of their experiences? Did they find a treasure? A dud? Have them interview people who have held several garage sales and develop a list of successful techniques. Use these techniques to hold a class or school-wide sale to benefit a specific cause.

Case Study Answers: Answers will vary. Possibilities include providing patients with books and music or reading and telling stories to patients.

FLASHBACK FLASHFORWARD

A first-class postage stamp cost just 6 cents in 1968. By 1995, the cost had risen to 32 cents. Just think: you could have sent five letters in 1968 for less than it cost you to send one letter in 1995.

1 Discussion Starter Ask students if they have ever purchased anything from a door-to-door salesperson? from home parties? What was the result? Were the products quality products? Were they different from what you could get at the store?

2 Interesting Note Benjamin Franklin produced America's first catalog in 1744. It advertised scientific and academic books.

3 Discussion Starter Ask students if they buy from catalogs. Would they recommend certain catalog companies? Why?

News Clip Answers: 1 The money lessons children learn will be applied throughout their lives. 2 They will learn that toys and other desirable items are aquired via the exchange of money. Young children will also learn that saving is an important way to acquire the items they want.

given. If the products offered meet your standards, however, they can often be purchased at prices far below retail.

Nonstore Retailers

There are also retailers that do not sell out of a store. Many of them can save you the time and effort of a shopping trip but usually at the expense of higher prices. In some cases, there is a delay between the purchase and delivery of merchandise. Nonstore options include door-to-door selling, mail order, electronic shopping, vending machines, and consumer cooperatives.

Door-to-Door Selling Door-to-door salespeople come directly to your home. They are sometimes good sources for consumer products, but they should be checked for reliability.

Door-to-door selling has two main advantages: the convenience of shopping at home and the chance to see or
1 try products in the home before buying.

The buyer however may also be at a disadvantage because of the sudden or unexpected choice he or she must make. Expressing concern about high-pressure tactics, the Federal Trade Commission has issued the Cooling-Off Rule. This allows consumers three days to cancel purchases of $25 or more made in their own homes or in a location outside the seller's normal place of business. The rule also applies to mail, phone, fax, and computer purchases. To cancel the purchase, consumers sign, date, and return the Notice of Cancellation within three
2 days of the sale.

Mail-Order Retailers Mail-order retailers are firms that offer their goods to customers through catalogs. They often have liberal return privileges, reasonable prices, and catalog descriptions. The customer does pay a price for these conveniences, however. He or she must forego firsthand inspection of merchandise before buying, wait for delivery, pay delivery charges, and put up with delays in exchanges and refunds when errors
3 are made.

Electronic Shopping Electronic shopping takes various forms. Many consumers enjoy shopping by television and have been reasonably well satisfied with merchandise quality, timely shipment of orders, and prompt settlement of problems. Some feel that the vast savings

CASE STUDY

Consumer NEWS CLIP

Kids and Their Cash

by Ellyn E. Spragins
Newsweek October 2, 1995

There's a big payoff to raising financially savvy children. Kids who learn about money early are often pretty good at making it later. Consider John Bogle Jr., manager of Quantitative Numeric, a top-performing mutual fund. He didn't become a market wizard just because his father is Jack Bogle, founder of mutual-fund giant Vanguard. But it helped that his dad forced him to start buying stocks on his own at 13.

The great trick to teaching kids about money is to let them use it the way they want. Only by investing [at age 13] in Amdahl, a mainframe computer company whose stock was near its all-time high, did Bogle learn how risky growth stocks could be [John Jr. is now manager of a top-performing mutual fund]. But the damage was limited because his investment was so small. "Kids have to make mistakes in order to learn," says Linda Barbanel, author of "Piggy Bank to Credit Card." You already know what your kids need to learn: saving, investing, budgeting, and wise spending. The key is to feed out age-appropriate experiences in each area. Here's a blueprint for raising money-smart kids.

Preschoolers. It may seem ridiculous to many parents, but experts think kids should start getting an allowance of $2 to $3 a week at age 3, with a dollar added at every birthday. The reason? From ages 3 to 5, preschoolers need to discover that money can be exchanged for goods. The allowance can't be so small that trying to spend it is an exercise in frustration. Linking chores to an allowance is a hotly debated issue. Some experts believe kids should do chores because they're members of the household. Others think learning to earn money isn't so bad. It's up to you.

Six- to 11-year-olds. These are prime ages for establishing a full slate of financial skills. First get serious about an allowance. Decide how much to give by reviewing your child's expenses, even if they are limited to milk money and Sunday-school donations. A rule of thumb experts suggest: match the weekly amount to their age—$6 or $7 a week for a 7-year-old, for example. Talk about what an allowance should cover. This is beginning budgeting, so write it down. Include savings as an item, as well as offerings to charities, if you like.

Twelve- to 16-year-olds. Here is where the allowance issue begins to get complicated. In addition to what you have been paying your child, you should begin turning over money that you would have spent on his behalf. If you put him in charge of sports uniforms, for example, you'll have to increase his monthly allowance by one twelfth of their cost. The grand plan: by the time he leaves for college he'll be handling all expenditures. You might decide to begin requiring that he pay some of these expenses from his own earnings. He should be making more from outside jobs than from his allowance by age 13 or 14. Sit down and create a budget showing all sources of income and all expenses, including saving. When you're sure he can cover everything, let him try it. The hardest part of this plan: if he can't pay for something, you can't bail him out. If you do, he's not learning how to handle money—he's being trained to ask you for more.

Decisions, Decisions

1. Why is it important for parents to teach their children about money matters?
2. What are some of the benefits of giving young children allowances?

1 Extension Have interested students investigate other electronic shopping opportunities and report to the class.

2 Learning Economics Ask students why members of co-ops are able to buy at lower prices (buy in quantity–bypass retailer.)

3 Discussion Starter Ask students if they ever postponed making a purchase and saved money by doing so. Have them describe the purchase.

4 Reinforcement Have students estimate the sale price of an item with a given percentage discount. They should not solve the problem on paper but should be prepared to tell the process they used: (*a*) a $39.95 pair of shoes with 20 percent off ($40.00 × 0.80 = $32.00); (*b*) a $100 designer dress marked down 30 percent with 50 percent off the marked down price ($100 less $30 is $70; half of $70 is $35).

5 Reinforcement Emphasize the importance of planning. It is difficult, if not impossible, to take advantage of sales and seasonal buying if you don't know your future needs and wants. Ask students what might often happen if people try to take advantage of sale prices without planning (Buy unneeded items—actually spend more rather than less.)

advertised on various television shop-
1 ping networks, however, are overstated. Most TV shopping works like mail order. You call a toll-free number to order the product you want.

Several companies sell their catalog collections on CD-ROM disks. With a word command or a click on an icon, you can scan the offerings and even listen to excerpts from music catalogs. The disk does not connect you to the catalog company, however. When you click on "Order," you can fill out an order form and send a fax to the company. Consider the extra cost of a CD-ROM drive in this method of shopping.

Subscribers to on-line computer services can also scroll through catalogs. The merchandise may be updated on a regular basis and you may order direct
2 by typing in your credit card number. The pictures, however, are not as clear as on disk, and your on-line service may charge you extra to browse.

Vending Machines Coin-operated vending machines provide goods on a self-service basis. A vending machine is an impersonal but useful way of buying. The most common vending machine is the pay telephone. To avoid outrageous charges some consumers have experienced at pay phones serviced by smaller companies, use both a calling card and a five-digit access code from your local long-distance carrier.

Consumer Cooperatives A **cooperative** is a business organization that is created, owned, and operated by and for the benefit of its members. You become a member by depositing a small sum of money. To be eligible for membership, you must be connected with or belong to the group for whom the benefits of the cooperative are meant.

A cooperative gives members a financial advantage in buying the goods and services that they want. It charges members at cost for goods and services. It may also give a
3 share of profits to members.

WHEN TO BUY

Wise shoppers try to time their purchases to get the most for their money. In certain circumstances, it may be wiser to put off a purchase. For example, you can reduce finance charges by saving and making a larger down payment, or by saving and not buying on credit at all. Waiting can also allow you to take advantage of special price reductions that come
4 with sales and buying in season.

Sales

Sales may offer shoppers opportunities to buy high-quality items at lower prices. When an item is really on sale, it is offered at a price that is lower than its usual selling price. Shoppers should therefore make an effort to keep up with current prices.

Seasonal Buying

5 Prices are lower on many goods at certain times of the year. The most common examples are found in the food area. Many fresh fruits and vegetables are produced according to a natural growing cycle—apples mainly in the fall, strawberries in the spring, peaches in the summer, and hard-shelled squash in the winter. They are available in large supplies, fresh and reasonably priced, only at certain times. It is at these times when they are "in season." You can save up to 20 percent by buying foods in season.

Many other types of merchandise are offered for sale on a seasonal basis. For example, many retailers schedule *white sales,* sales of linen and towels, for January. Clearance sales of summer clothing occur in August and September. If you can determine your needs well in advance, you can plan your purchases to coincide with these peak bargain periods.

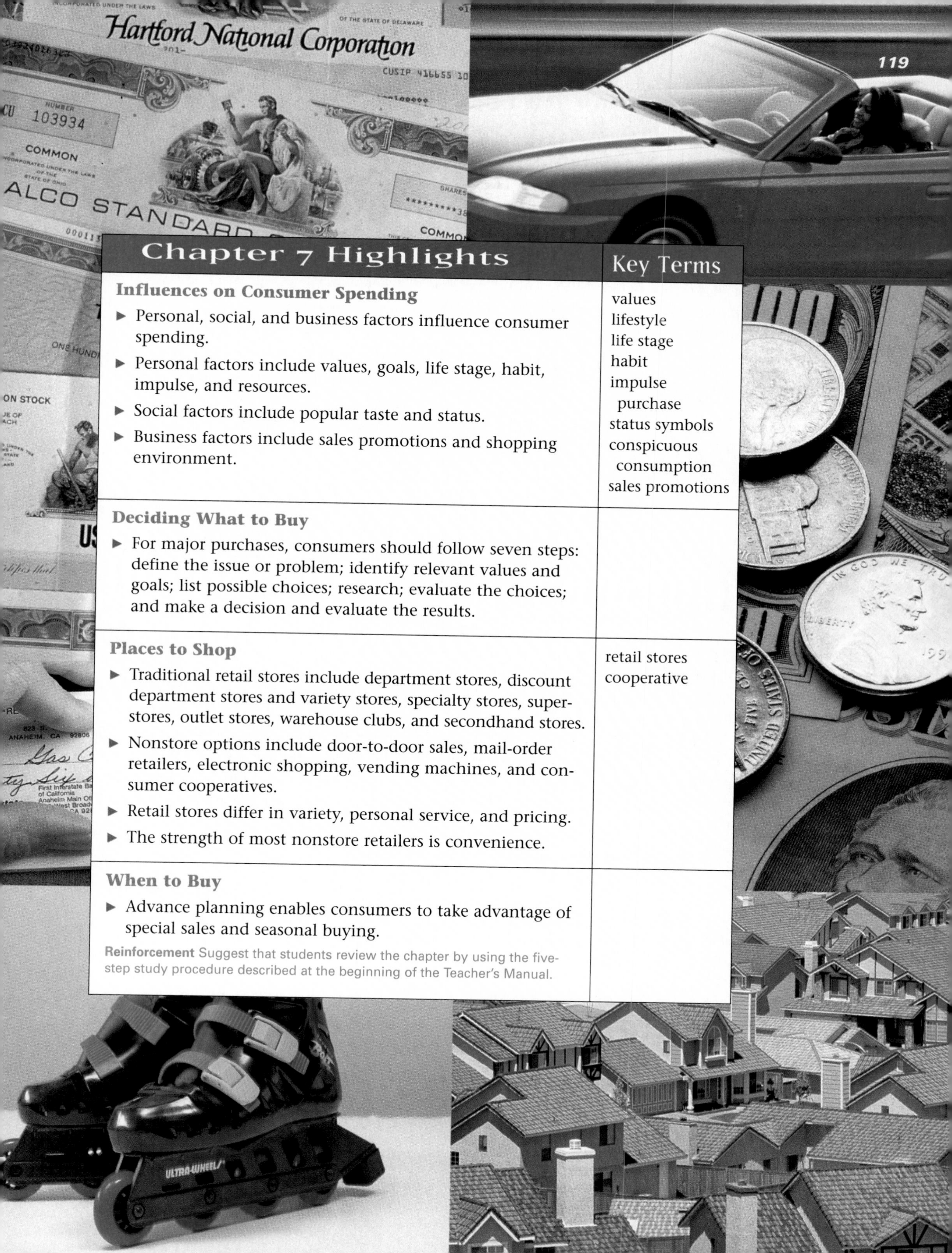

Chapter 7 Highlights

	Key Terms
Influences on Consumer Spending ▶ Personal, social, and business factors influence consumer spending. ▶ Personal factors include values, goals, life stage, habit, impulse, and resources. ▶ Social factors include popular taste and status. ▶ Business factors include sales promotions and shopping environment.	values lifestyle life stage habit impulse purchase status symbols conspicuous consumption sales promotions
Deciding What to Buy ▶ For major purchases, consumers should follow seven steps: define the issue or problem; identify relevant values and goals; list possible choices; research; evaluate the choices; and make a decision and evaluate the results.	
Places to Shop ▶ Traditional retail stores include department stores, discount department stores and variety stores, specialty stores, superstores, outlet stores, warehouse clubs, and secondhand stores. ▶ Nonstore options include door-to-door sales, mail-order retailers, electronic shopping, vending machines, and consumer cooperatives. ▶ Retail stores differ in variety, personal service, and pricing. ▶ The strength of most nonstore retailers is convenience.	retail stores cooperative
When to Buy ▶ Advance planning enables consumers to take advantage of special sales and seasonal buying. **Reinforcement** Suggest that students review the chapter by using the five-step study procedure described at the beginning of the Teacher's Manual.	

CHAPTER 7 REVIEW

Refer students to the Reviewing Consumer Terms and Reviewing Facts and Ideas activities in the Student Activity Workbook.

Reviewing Consumer Terms
Paragraphs will vary. See Glossary for definitions.

Reviewing Facts and Ideas
See the Student Activity Workbook.

Problem Solving and Decision Making
1 a Yes. The need is immediate (college). If she always waits for the latest technology, she'll never buy anything, because technology constantly changes.
b She should comparison shop for computer systems that will work for her now and at least until she graduates. Even if improvements come along, her purchase will still meet her needs.

Consumers Around the World Math
1 a $168.91
b $238.09
c $0.94

Human Relations
2 Student reports should answer all questions.

Technology
3 Students should stress the difficulty of good comparison shopping with electronic outlets. They may see impulse buying as a danger.

Reviewing Consumer Terms

Use each of the following terms in a paragraph to demonstrate you know its meaning.

conspicuous consumption
cooperative
habit
impulse purchase
life stage
lifestyle
retail stores
sales promotions
status symbol
values

Reviewing Facts and Ideas

1. How do personal, social, and business factors influence consumer spending? Provide one example of each.
2. What are the seven steps of decision making that should be applied to all major purchases?
3. What are seven types of retail stores?
4. In what ways does timing affect buying decisions?

Problem Solving and Decision Making

Lee Orozco is interested in purchasing a computer. She has researched various systems, but she keeps putting off buying one until the latest technology comes out. She is almost ready to start her first year at the university.

a. Should she buy her computer now? What factors might help her decide?

b. What should she look for in shopping for her computer?

Building Academic Skills

Consumers Around the World

Math

1. Shopping while traveling in other parts of the world takes some research and planning. In order to determine prices of foreign goods, you must first convert them from foreign currency into U.S. dollars. To figure the exchange, you divide the foreign currency by the U.S. equivalent. For example, assume the exchange rate between the United States and Canada is U.S. $1.00 = Canadian $1.25. A $30 shirt in Canada would cost $24 in U.S. dollars ($30 ÷ 1.25 = $24). Figure how much each item below would cost based on the exchange rates given.

   a. A pair of glasses sells for 250 German marks. How much would the glasses cost in U.S. dollars if the exchange rate is DM1.48 = $1.00?

   b. A CD player sells for 25,000 yen in Japan. How much would it cost in U.S. dollars if the exchange rate is Y105 = $1.00?

   c. A soft drink in Mexico costs 7 pesos. How much would it cost in U.S. dollars if the exchange rate is Mex $7.41 = $1.00?

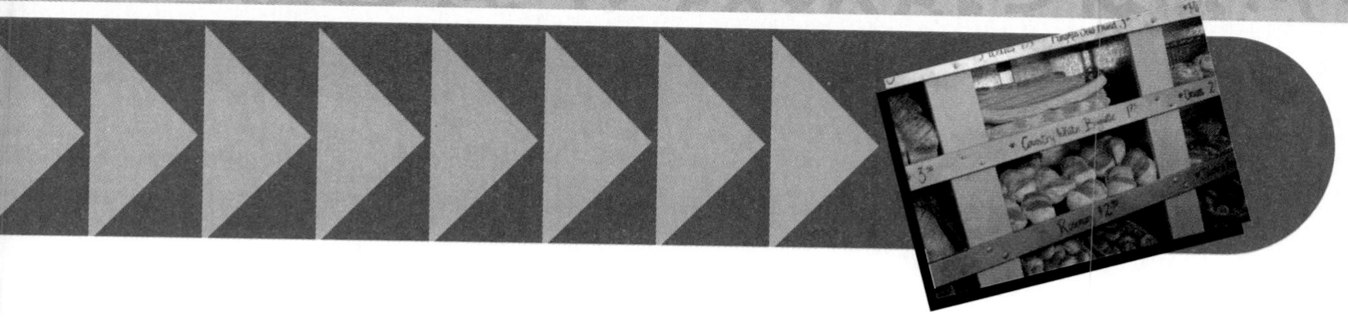

Human Relations

2. Interview six people about their shopping experiences. What were some of their latest purchases? How did they decide which goods and services to purchase? Determine from their answers whether they used any of the seven decision-making steps. Summarize your findings in a 250-word report.

Technology

3. Research on-line shopping services in your library. How widespread is their use? Watch television shopping shows and think about their impact on shoppers. Do these services encourage wise shopping? impulse purchases?

   Write a 500-word essay explaining your research. Give your views on how these services are best used.

Beyond the Classroom

Consumer Project

Collect mail-order catalogs to bring into class. Organize the catalogs by type of merchandise. What kinds of goods are offered?

 Cooperative Learning

Family Economics

Break into assigned family groups. Discuss the following problem.

Determine your family's life stage. Then compile a list of economic decisions that you feel might be characteristic of that particular life stage. Use the average annual expenditure chart from Figure 6-2 in Chapter 6, the family profile provided by the teacher, and this book's table of contents to generate ideas for consideration. Compare your answers with those provided by other family groups.

Debate the Issue

The products they use and the clothes they wear reflect people's values and lifestyle. Among high school students, the pressure to own just the right jacket or basketball shoes or backpack can be very strong.

Some feel that to combat these pressures, help students focus on academics, and emphasize more enduring values, schools should require students to wear uniforms. Others feel that students should have the opportunity to express themselves through their clothes.

You and your classmates will break into two groups and research this topic. Each group will gather evidence to support one side or the other. You are to prepare the argument for your side of the problem. Then the two groups will meet in a classroom debate.

Consumer Project Students should contribute to a collection of catalogs and organize the collection by products offered.

Family Economics Young singles might be building up an emergency fund and other savings; saving for or buying a car; pursuing further education. Young marrieds with children might be buying insurance, saving for a down payment on a home, buying a bigger or a second car. Older marrieds with children might be paying for children's education, paying for a mortgage, and saving for retirement. Retirees might be purchasing supplementary health insurance, deciding whether to move from a home to an apartment, retirement community, or convalescent home.

Debate the Issue Break the class into two teams. Assign each team one side of the issue. Encourage students to work together as a team to develop their argument. Ask each team to select a member to make an opening statement that supports their side of the issue. Have students take turns debating as the debate moves from one team to another.

SEARCH
/SKIP
CD
PLAY / PAUSE
STOP / CLEAR
POWER
ON/STANDBY
ACTIVE
VOLUME
REC/P
SYNCHRO START

CHAPTER 8

Consumer Problems and Their Solutions

Learning Objectives

When you have finished studying this chapter, you should be able to:

1. Distinguish between deception and fraud.
2. Identify some of the most common forms of deceptive advertising and sales practices.
3. Describe three fraudulent sales practices, and suggest a strategy for resisting them.
4. Explain how to make an effective consumer complaint.
5. Describe how a small-claims court works.

Consumer Terms

deception
fraud
puffery
trading up
loss leader
bait and switch
mediation
small-claims courts
class-action suit

Real-World Journal

In your journal, describe a time when you had a problem with a product you purchased. Perhaps the product didn't work as it should have. Maybe a salesperson led you to believe the product was worth more than it was. How did you handle your purchase problem?

Lesson Plan See the Teacher's Manual for the Chapter 8 lesson plan.

Vocabulary The Chapter 8 lesson plan includes suggested vocabulary activities for the terms listed.

FLASHBACK FLASHFORWARD

In 1972, there were just over 35,000 check and credit card fraud arrests. Today, check and credit card fraud is becoming one of America's most serious crimes. In 1995, the American Banker's Association estimated check and credit card losses at more than $5 billion. In 1993, the FBI logged more than 100,000 forgery arrests. That is more than the arrests for murder, rape, arson, and embezzlement combined.

1 Interesting Note
Tell students, according to Technical Assistance Research Programs (TARP), one-third of consumer dissatisfaction comes from unfulfilled expectations, one-third from company policies and procedures, and one-third from product defects. Research from the A.C. Nielsen Company shows that many consumers never complain if they experience a small loss. Even if they suffer a major loss ($150 or more), only two-thirds complain.

▲ *Cars are in one of the top categories of performance complaints.* **What do you think most of the complaints are about?**

Caption Answer: Most of the problems are related to service repair problems.

DEFINING CONSUMER PROBLEMS

Two major types of problems can occur when you are buying a product. The first—performance problems—can include such things as problems with the quality of a product or service, billing errors, and simple misunderstandings. The second type of problem—deception and fraud—includes unfair sales or advertising techniques and illegal practices.

When you shop, remember that not all sellers have your best interests in mind. You need to be alert to consumer problems and be able to resolve them.

Problems with Performance

Consumers expect good quality, safety, and service when they buy. Sometimes, what seems like a routine purchase, however, turns out to be just the opposite. You plug in your new microwave oven, and it does not heat. You drive your car off the lot, and the first time you try to back up, it won't go in reverse. While frustrating, most of these performance problems can be resolved by the consumer and the business.

PROBLEMS WITH DECEPTION AND FRAUD

1 There is a fine line between deception and fraud. The Federal Trade Commission defines **deception** as a material "representation, omission, or practice that is likely to mislead a [reasonable] consumer . . . to the consumer's detriment." Deceptive practices may, for example, influence you to buy a more costly product rather than a less costly but perfectly acceptable one.

Fraud, on the other hand, is a deliberate deception that, with full knowledge of the perpetrator, misleads or gains an unfair advantage and results in financial loss to the consumer. Fraud may lead you to invest money in a company or to pay for a service that does not even exist! You end up with nothing in exchange for your money.

DECEPTIVE PRACTICES

Some businesses use deceptive practices to mislead customers. Reading ads thoughtfully and being aware of selling techniques can prevent unnecessary spending. Some deceptive sales and advertising practices are illegal, some are not. Practices used to deceive customers include:

- Misleading advertising.
- Trading up.
- Creating sale prices.
- Using competitive pricing.
- Recommending retail prices.
- Using a loss leader.

Misleading Advertising

While advertising can provide helpful information about a product's price, use, and features, it can also confuse or mislead the consumer. Read ads carefully using these guidelines.

1. What is the emotional appeal of the ad? How is it trying to influence me?
2. Does the ad give measurable facts rather than generalities? For example, does it say "Contains 1 gram of fat per ounce" or only "Low-fat"?
3. Does the ad mention the product's special features? Do I really need these features?
4. Is the full price shown clearly in the ad, or are additional costs, such as for installation or batteries, given in small print?
5. Is the advertised price competitive with prices elsewhere?

Free Gifts A store might advertise a "free" gift, but actually require customers to buy an expensive item first in order to qualify for the gift. In other words, the gift is not free at all.

Testimonials Advertising testimonials are often used to sell goods and services. Celebrities sometimes promote products in this way. However, the consumer may not realize that the celebrity has been paid for the testimonial. Moreover, some testimonials may not show
1 the real choice of a competent witness.

Puffery Exaggeration in advertising is even more common than misinformation. Indeed, it has been given a special name—puffery. **Puffery** consists of using claims or descriptions to exaggerate ("puff
2 up") a product's reputation or appeal.

There are countless examples. The words *new* and *unique* are used repeatedly, for everything from cereal to cleanser. The same is true for descriptions like *extra-strength* and *super-strength*. They are applied equally to headache remedies
3 and hair spray.

Can You Get a Refund?
More and more stores guarantee their merchandise by offering a full refund of your money if you return the purchase within a specified period of time. But don't make assumptions. Ask about the return policy before you buy. Will the store return your money, exchange the goods, or give you credit? What is the time limit on returning merchandise? Be sure to ask about items that have been reduced in price and are marked "final sale." Typically, you cannot return those. Always keep your receipt until you are satisfied the merchandise is the fit and quality you expected.

1 Extension Ask students to define *testimonial* (a statement about the benefits or positive qualities of a person or thing). Ask them to identify TV and print ads using testimonials. Decide how testimonials could mislead.

2 Discussion Starter Have students bring examples of misleading and exaggerated advertising to class for discussion.

3 Reinforcement Student Activity Workbook, Chapter 8 activities.

1 Discussion Starter Ask students if trading up has been used with them. Did it work? Ask if any students with retail jobs have been instructed by their employers to use trading up techniques.

2 Critical Thinking Ask students if they have encountered ads saying "We will match any competitor's prices." What impression do the ads give consumers? What do the ads really mean? (Ads imply the store's prices are the lowest around. Usually, consumers must show proof of the lower price in order to have the retailer match it.)

Puffery is considered harmless because it is assumed that no reasonable person would take the exaggerations seriously. Also, since the terms used mean different things to different people, it would be difficult to prove such advertising false. What is "fabulous" to one person may be rather ordinary to another. Such terms are chosen because they cannot be measured or precisely defined.

Trading Up

One deceptive practice you are likely to encounter in a store is called trading up. **Trading up** is the practice of convincing customers to buy a higher-priced item than they originally intended.

Assume that you wish to buy a VCR. When the salesclerk sees you looking at a $300 machine, he or she turns your attention first to a $500 model and then to another that costs even more ($800). True, the more expensive machines have extra features—more recording times, remote control, stop action, zoom. However, the question is: Do you need these features? Are they worth the extra money to you? Can you afford to spend almost three times what you originally intended? The answer on all counts is probably no.

There is nothing illegal about the practice of trading up. Retailers are in business to sell, and they generally make a greater profit on more expensive items. However, you should not let the retailer's need for a profit lure you into ignoring your own need for economy.
1 You should be prepared to say no.

Sale Prices

The word *sale* implies a bargain—lower prices than customary. Therefore, retailers can use that term legally only under certain conditions. Before a sale price can be put on an item, the store must have sold the item regularly and recently at the nonsale price.

Competitive Pricing

A retailer cannot legally say that its prices are lower than a competitor's without actual proof. Signs that read "Compare at $75" only imply lower
2 prices. They do not provide proof.

Manufacturer's Recommended Retail Price

Manufacturers cannot, by law, force retailers to sell their products at a particular

Trading up leads consumers to buy higher-priced goods than they may have otherwise bought. **Which kinds of products would you expect salespeople to practice trading up?** ▼

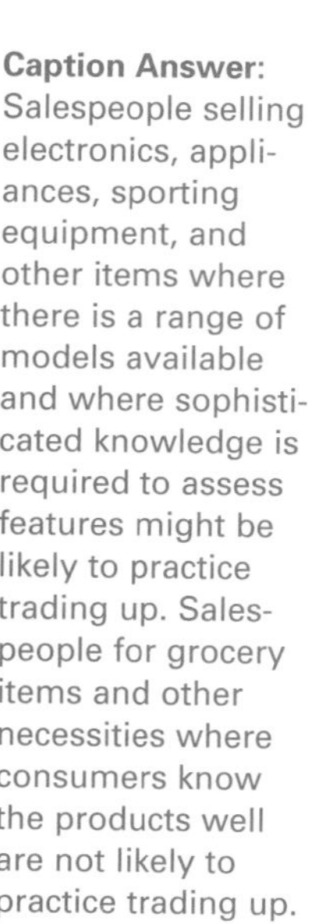
Caption Answer: Salespeople selling electronics, appliances, sporting equipment, and other items where there is a range of models available and where sophisticated knowledge is required to assess features might be likely to practice trading up. Salespeople for grocery items and other necessities where consumers know the products well are not likely to practice trading up.

price. They can, however, suggest retail prices for their goods.

In many industries, it is common knowledge that the manufacturer's suggested price is higher than people will generally pay. Thus, stores that boast they sell goods below the manufacturer's suggested retail price are not necessarily offering a very low price for the product.

Loss Leaders

Retailers sometimes price certain attractive items below the cost that would make them a profit. The item is considered a **loss leader,** an item priced below cost in order to draw in business.

While retailers who use this tactic lose money on the loss leader, they hope to make money on sales of other goods. Be aware that all items in the store will not be priced as attractively as the loss leaders are. In some states, using loss-
1 leader pricing is unlawful.

FRAUDULENT PRACTICES

Some sales practices cross the line into fraud. Examples of fraudulent practices include:

- Bait and switch.
- Chain letter and pyramid schemes.
- Some high-pressure telephone and
2 mail schemes.

Bait and Switch

By far, however, the most common fraudulent sales practice is bait-and-switch advertising. **Bait and switch** is a practice in which the retailer advertises a product at a bargain price (bait) and then persuades the customer to buy at a higher price (switch). This is fraud because the store never sold and had no intention of selling the offered bargain item.

Perhaps the store advertises a "25-inch color TV! Only $195!" This is the bait. Once the customer is in the store, the clerk lies, saying that the advertised TV is sold out. He or she then offers an alternative, usually a much more expensive TV. This is the switch. There are, of course, variations. The salesclerk may make one or two unfavorable comments about the advertised model as a lead-in
3 to the switch.

Chain Letter and Pyramid Schemes

Some schemes to get money out of people have been around for a long time and are easy to detect. An example is the chain letter and the related pyramid marketing schemes. In a chain letter, you are asked to send money to several people on a list. Add your name to the bottom and as soon as everyone partici-
4 pates, you are promised a big payoff.

A pyramid marketing scheme, shown in Figure 8–1 on page 128, is set up the same way, but many people are lead to believe they are starting a small business.

Work and Food

On average, it takes a Brazilian citizen about 30 minutes to earn enough money to buy a dozen eggs. In South Africa, it takes about 18 minutes, and in the United States it takes about 5 minutes.

1 Learning Economics Selling below cost is done by large retailers to drive small retailers out of business. Since smaller retailers cannot sustain below-cost pricing for very long, they may fail. This technique is considered unfair competition and is usually illegal.

2 Research Ask students to look for news accounts of fraud cases. Analyze the stories in class. Who was the perpetrator? the victim? What made the action fraudulent?

3 Extension Point out to students that bait and switch is not being used when an inexpensive item is truly out of stock and the salesperson shows you a more expensive item.

4 Discussion Starter Ask students if they have ever received chain letters. How did the letters work? Did they request money? How did students feel about these letters?

Caption Answer: It is not possible for people at the lower levels to profit, because the pyramid will collapse before getting the tremendous number of participants projected. Only the organizers of the scheme will make money—and they could end up in jail.

1 Interesting Note Tell students that the FTC estimates that every year U.S. consumers lose over $1 billion in fraudulent investments.

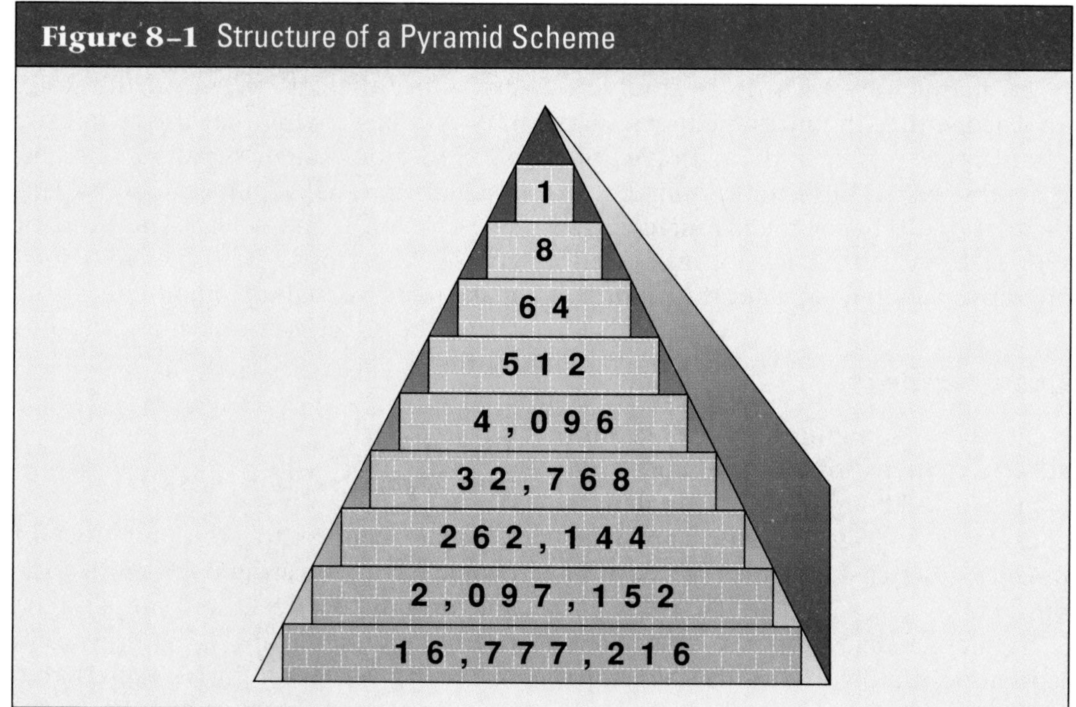

▲ *In a pyramid scheme, each participant gets eight others to participate who, in turn, must get eight others, and so on.* **Why doesn't the system work? Who benefits the most from a pyramid scheme?**

The products they are "selling" are secondary, however, to the money coming in from new pyramid members. In legitimate multilevel market sales, the major income is from the sale of the product.

Chain letters and pyramid schemes are fraudulent and illegal because their purpose is not to start a legitimate business but simply to get people to contribute money. The system on which they are built cannot sustain itself mathematically.

Other Fraudulent Schemes

Many legitimate opportunities exist through mail-order firms and telemarketers who represent honest, reputable businesses. However, the ease and convenience of shopping by mail or by phone is an attractive tool for unethical salespeople.

Anyone with a telephone can be a target for high-pressure tactics and attractive offers. If the offers are fraudulent, however, the offers often have conditions that give them away. Look for ways in which the seller is trying to get your money.

- You win a sweepstakes, but you must pay fees up front.
- The health cure producer has no proof to substantiate its claims, and you cannot get details about the organization.
- The earn-money-at-home opportunity asks you to buy something first.
- The get-rich-quick scheme seems too good to be true (and probably is).
- The low-cost vacation has extra
1 charges and hidden restrictions.

Many of these schemes and others are cropping up as on-line investment opportunities. You can keep from being a victim if you:

1. Think for yourself and watch for tip-offs.
2. Know what you need.

3. Do not give out your credit card number over the phone unless you know the organization is reputable.
4. Take the time to make a decision before investing—consult with someone you trust and make sure the investment and the person promoting it are registered with your state securities agency.
5. Get promises in writing.
6. Check on the organization by written request or by calling the local Better Business Bureau or the state attorney general.

More Money in Business

In 1981, Steve Mariotti, owner of a successful import-export business, was jumped by a gang of youths in New York. They beat him up badly and robbed him—of $10. As he lay in the hospital recovering from his injuries, Mariotti wondered why anyone would go into street crime. He knew these young people could make much more money legally, by going into business for themselves.

Mariotti realized he had the seed of an idea. He would teach high school students the fundamentals of business. He planned to target students from poor areas of the city, students who already had "street smarts." It would not take much to teach them "business smarts," he thought.

At first, Mariotti could not get any of the schools interested. Finally, one high school principal let him try out his program by teaching students to read a profit-and-loss statement, write a business plan, and balance a checkbook.

The program worked so well that Mariotti started the National Foundation for Teaching Entrepreneurship (NFTE). He now teaches an 80-hour curriculum at schools throughout the Midwest as well as in New York. The program is also taught at several universities, including Columbia University, the University of Pennsylvania, and the University of Southern California.

Mariotti's students get hands-on experience as well as theory. They run a variety of businesses, from hot-dog stands to T-shirt businesses. They have proved that Mariotti was right—they can make more money in business than on the street. The businesses jointly bring the young entrepreneurs $250,000 a year—more than they could make in a mugging.

Brainstorm

Based on your own skills, what could you teach someone that would help them start their own business?

Case Study Answers: Answers will vary. Many students will have math, reading, writing, listening, teamwork, management, speaking, and other skills that they could teach to someone.

1 Critical Thinking Ask students to role-play situations of consumers trying to resolve problems at a retail store. Discuss which actions are appropriate and which are inappropriate.

2 Extension Have students name three large companies. Choose a product for each, and list information that would be needed to register a complaint. Find out the appropriate person and level for addressing correspondence for each item.

3 Reinforcement Student Activity Workbook, Chapter 8 activities.

News Clip Answers:
1 Whether it be a doctor or an auto mechanic, you should check with more than one service provider to make sure you are getting the best value. You should also ask for references of other clients or professional affiliation groups.
2 You should check to see that the charges are itemized. You should then ensure that you received all the items for which you are being charged.

REGISTERING A COMPLAINT

The first step toward solving performance problems as well as those related to deception and fraud is to register or make a complaint. To do so, you must be able to clearly state the problem. It helps if beforehand you have all the relevant sales slips and receipts ready. You can make a complaint by letter, telephone, or
1 in person.

Telephone Complaints

A problem with a store charge account can often be resolved with a telephone call. It is important, however, to make a written note of the name of the person who receives your complaint, the date of your call, and the substance of what is said. You may need this record later if there is no action on the problem.

If your complaint is about defective merchandise or service, a personal visit may be the best way to handle it. Returning the defective merchandise to the place of purchase is usually all that is needed to resolve this kind of problem.

Letter of Complaint

In some cases, you might want to write a letter instead of telephoning, in order to reach people in authority. Usually, however, you write a letter of complaint after your first attempt to solve a problem produces no results.

The letter should be honest, polite, and to the point. It should include cor-
2 roborating details. See Figure 8–2 on page
3 132 for details.

Letters leave you with a written record of what has happened in the case. If need be, they can be used as evidence in court. Keep copies of the letters you write and those you receive. Include copies, *not* originals, of documentation regarding your complaint. Send your letter by certified mail, return receipt requested.

If you are unable to receive satisfaction at the local level, write a letter to the consumer affairs officer of the company or manufacturer. In this letter, state all steps taken to solve the problem. If this letter is not answered, write another letter to the company president or owner. Be persistent. Send a copy of your letter to the local office of the Better Business Bureau and the local or state government office responsible for consumer protection. Consider all alternatives.

Dispute Resolution

Another approach might be *dispute resolution* programs. These are an increasingly popular way to settle disagreements. They can be quicker, less expensive, and less stressful than going to court. Two types of dispute resolution techniques are **mediation** and arbitration. Through mediation, you and the other party try to resolve the dispute with the help of a neutral third party (sometimes called a *mediator*). In arbitration, you present your case before an arbitrator, who makes a decision about the case.

Sometimes an arbitration panel rather than one arbitrator decides the case. You can find out what is available in your area by contacting local or state consumer protection agencies, state attorneys general, small claims courts, local chapters of the Better Business Bureau, trade associations, and local bar associations.

LEGAL ACTION

If all else fails and legal action is required, you must be able to document your case. That is why it is very important to keep a proper record of all steps taken to solve the matter. Many people are a bit frightened about going to court. Talking to an attorney can be helpful. The attorney will be able to tell from the information you provide whether legal action is appropriate.

CASE STUDY

Consumer NEWS CLIP

With Billing Errors Rampant, You Need Our Tips on How Not to Overpay

by Ken and Daria Dolan
Money October 1995

Want to know one reason why medical care costs so much today? Doctors and hospitals have become the gang that can't bill straight. For example, according to auditors combing through claims for insurance companies, your odds of receiving an error-free bill for inpatient hospital services are less than one in 10. That's right: More than 90 percent of the roughly 31 million hospital bills processed each year are wrong, with overcharges making up an estimated two-thirds of the errors. The cost of overcharges to consumers, insurers and the government—the biggest medical payer of them all—is an estimated $10 billion a year. One way or another, that money comes out of your pocket, either directly or through higher insurance premiums and taxes.

So how can you protect yourself against billing blunders? And what should you do if you detect a mistake? Our advice:

Practice preventive medicine. No we're not talking about living a high-fiber, low-fat life (though that surely can't hurt). We're saying you should get your doctor to give you a detailed cost estimate for any in-hospital or outpatient medical procedure you're considering. The estimate should break out the likely hospital charges as well as his or her fees. Thus forewarned, you'll at least be basically forearmed for a line-by-line examination of your final bill. When you get the statement, complain vigorously as we describe below if it exceeds the estimate by more than 10 percent.

Keep a daily log of procedures, medicines and doctor visits. You can track this yourself if you are able, or ask a friend or relative to take careful notes for you if you cannot. Jot down who came to talk to you, what you talked about and how long the person stayed. Also note the drugs and doses you got, as well as any services or procedures you received such as X-rays or extra meals for visitors. Then, when you get your bill, compare each item with your written record.

If you do find a mistake on your bill, call the hospital's billing department immediately. Once you point out a mistake, a billing supervisor will usually clear it up right away. But if you have a problem that isn't resolved within, say, two weeks, call your insurance company and the hospital's top administrator to complain, then follow up with a letter to each.

If these actions don't resolve your dispute within another week or so, write to your state or local consumer affairs department. Government officials can sometimes bust up billing logjams. Alternatively, you can enlist the help of Medreview (800-397-5359). This Austin medical auditing company will analyze your physician and hospital bills and serve as your ombudsman in attempting to redress any errors it uncovers. The fee: from $8 for a typical doctor's bill, to $100 per $10,000 of hospital charges. That's a small price to pay in light of the money you could save.

Decisions, Decisions

1. What are some other things you can do to make sure you get the most value from any service provider?
2. When you receive a hospital bill, what should you look for?

1 Reinforcement Remind students of the effectiveness of media involvement. Tell them about the irate consumer who had to pull his expensive motor home out of the woods several times. He finally told the company he was going to drive it to Wall Street, stick cardboard lemons on the windshield, and call the media. His motor home was replaced.

2 Extension Have interested students contact an arbitrator, a small-claims court judge, or an attorney to find out the kinds of cases that require court action. Report to class.

3 Research Have students set up an unresolved product complaint situation. Research procedures for a small-claims presentation. Prepare and present the consumer's case for the hearing including all relevant documentation.

4 Interesting Note Tell students that the Legal Services Corporation, funded by the federal government, provides free legal representation in noncriminal matters to persons living near or below the poverty level. Many colleges and universities provide these free services to their students.

Figure 8–2 The Letter of Complaint

The complaint letter should be honest and to the point with collaborating details.

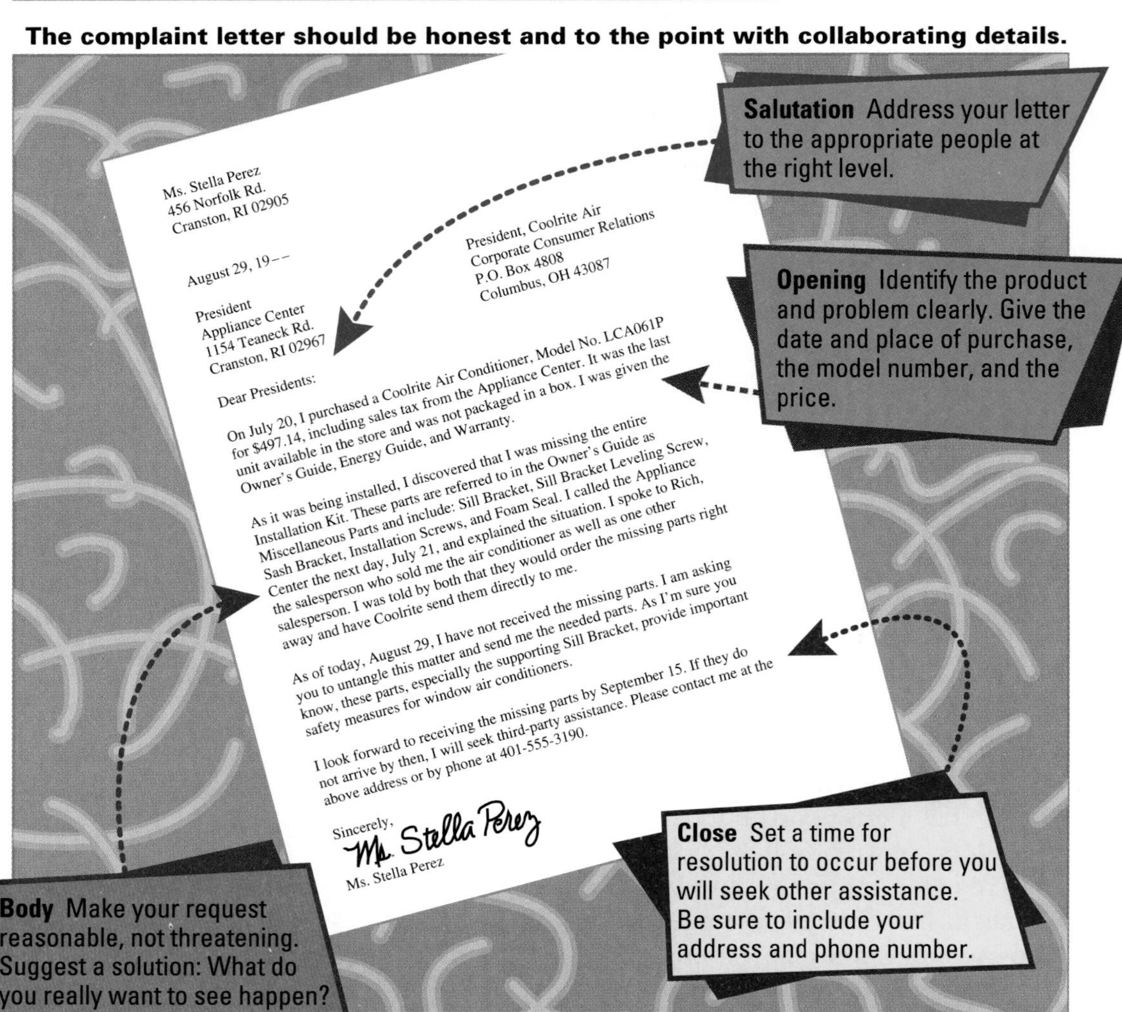

Ms. Stella Perez
456 Norfolk Rd.
Cranston, RI 02905

August 29, 19--

President
Appliance Center
1154 Teaneck Rd.
Cranston, RI 02967

President, Coolrite Air
Corporate Consumer Relations
P.O. Box 4808
Columbus, OH 43087

Dear Presidents:

On July 20, I purchased a Coolrite Air Conditioner, Model No. LCA061P for $497.14, including sales tax from the Appliance Center. It was the last unit available in the store and was not packaged in a box. I was given the Owner's Guide, Energy Guide, and Warranty.

As it was being installed, I discovered that I was missing the entire Installation Kit. These parts are referred to in the Owner's Guide as Miscellaneous Parts and include: Sill Bracket, Sill Bracket Leveling Screw, Sash Bracket, Installation Screws, and Foam Seal. I called the Appliance Center the next day, July 21, and explained the situation. I spoke to Rich, the salesperson who sold me the air conditioner as well as one other salesperson. I was told by both that they would order the missing parts right away and have Coolrite send them directly to me.

As of today, August 29, I have not received the missing parts. I am asking you to untangle this matter and send me the needed parts. As I'm sure you know, these parts, especially the supporting Sill Bracket, provide important safety measures for window air conditioners.

I look forward to receiving the missing parts by September 15. If they do not arrive by then, I will seek third-party assistance. Please contact me at the above address or by phone at 401-555-3190.

Sincerely,
Ms. Stella Perez
Ms. Stella Perez

Salutation Address your letter to the appropriate people at the right level.
Opening Identify the product and problem clearly. Give the date and place of purchase, the model number, and the price.
Body Make your request reasonable, not threatening. Suggest a solution: What do you really want to see happen?
Close Set a time for resolution to occur before you will seek other assistance. Be sure to include your address and phone number.

Small-Claims Court

In most states, there are **small-claims courts** set up to resolve disputes involving small sums of money. The maximum amount varies from state to state. It is usually $1,500, but some states allow as much
1 as $5,000. You do not need a lawyer to file
2 suit in a small-claims court. While there is
3 a filing fee, usually the fee is small.

If your state does not have a small-claims court, or if the amount of your claim is greater than the maximum allowed, you have other legal options. You may hire a lawyer and bring action in a higher court.

Lawyers charge a fee for their services. If your claim is a large one, however, it may be worthwhile to hire a lawyer. If your claim requires the services of a lawyer and you cannot afford one, then you should check with your local legal aid office. Look in the Yellow Pages telephone directory under "Legal aid" or
4 "Legal services."

Class-Action Suit

Sometimes a group of consumers who have the same complaint against the same firm get together to sue. This kind of case is called a **class-action suit.** Rules for bringing class actions are not the same across the country. Such suits may not be allowed in your state or community. You should check to be sure.

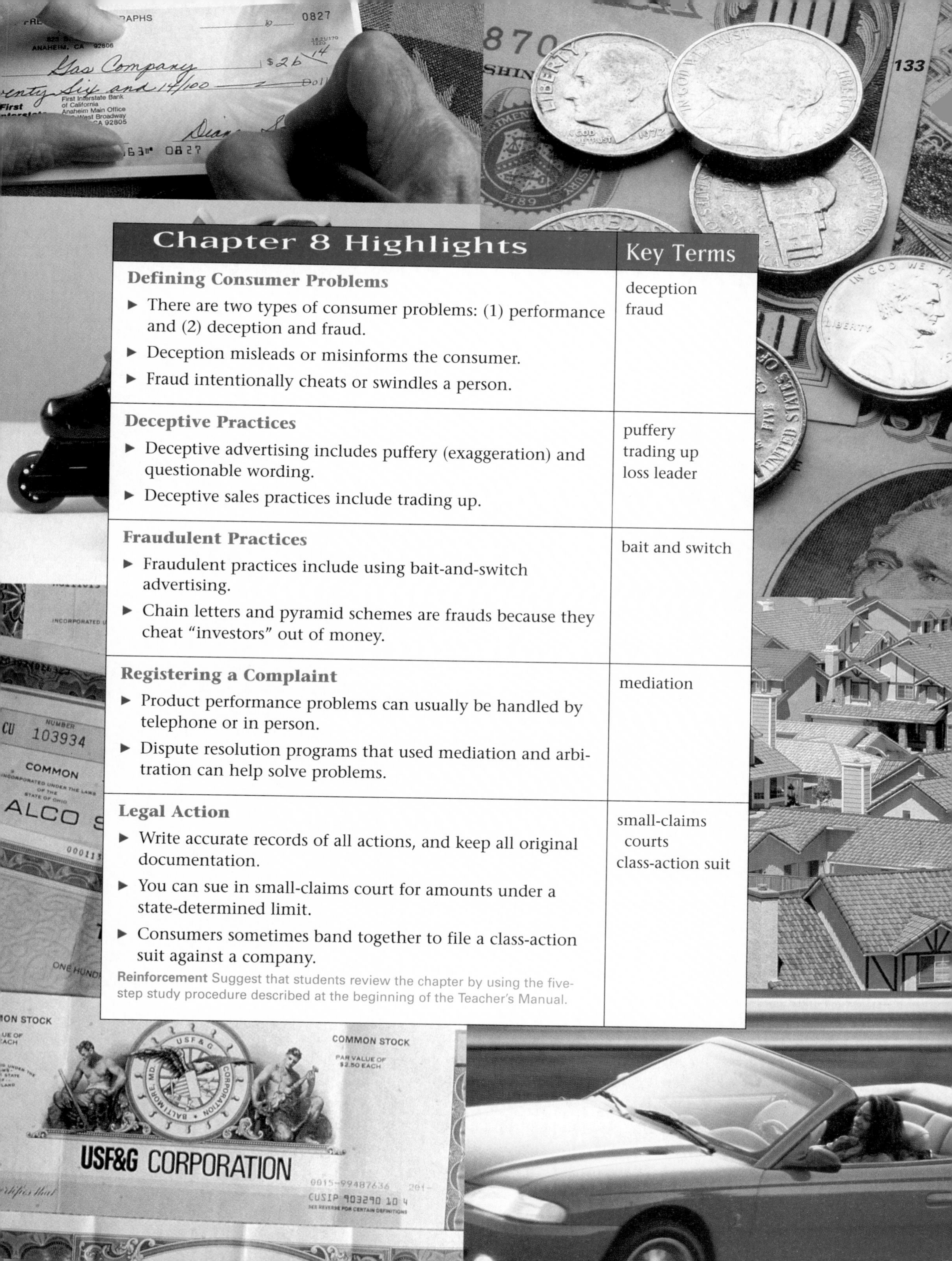

Chapter 8 Highlights	Key Terms
Defining Consumer Problems ► There are two types of consumer problems: (1) performance and (2) deception and fraud. ► Deception misleads or misinforms the consumer. ► Fraud intentionally cheats or swindles a person.	deception fraud
Deceptive Practices ► Deceptive advertising includes puffery (exaggeration) and questionable wording. ► Deceptive sales practices include trading up.	puffery trading up loss leader
Fraudulent Practices ► Fraudulent practices include using bait-and-switch advertising. ► Chain letters and pyramid schemes are frauds because they cheat "investors" out of money.	bait and switch
Registering a Complaint ► Product performance problems can usually be handled by telephone or in person. ► Dispute resolution programs that used mediation and arbitration can help solve problems.	mediation
Legal Action ► Write accurate records of all actions, and keep all original documentation. ► You can sue in small-claims court for amounts under a state-determined limit. ► Consumers sometimes band together to file a class-action suit against a company. **Reinforcement** Suggest that students review the chapter by using the five-step study procedure described at the beginning of the Teacher's Manual.	small-claims courts class-action suit

CHAPTER 

REVIEW

Refer students to the Reviewing Consumer Terms and Reviewing Facts and Ideas activities in the Student Activity Workbook.

Reviewing Consumer Terms
Paragraphs will vary. See Glossary for definitions.

Reviewing Facts and Ideas
See the Student Activity Workbook for answers.

Problem Solving and Decision Making
1 *a* is a deceptive practice; *b* and *c* are fraudulent practices.
2 She could write a letter to the president of the company, outlining and documenting the problem. In the letter she should list specific third-party assistance she will seek if her complaint is not resolved by a certain date. Assistance could come from the Better Business Bureau, consumer action groups, small-claims court, or media attention.

Consumers Around the World
Math
1 Those with 100 shares would lose $5,554 ($56 × 100 = $5,600; $.46 × 100 = $46; $5,600 − $46 = $5,554). Those with 500 shares would lose $27,770 ($5,554 × 5 = $27,770).

Communications
2 In their reports, students should

Reviewing Consumer Terms

Use the following terms in a paragraph to demonstrate you know its meaning.

bait and switch
class-action suit
deception
fraud
loss leader
mediation
puffery
small-claims courts
trading up

Reviewing Facts and Ideas

1. How is fraud different from deception?
2. Give examples of two misleading advertising practices.
3. Why are bait-and-switch advertising, chain letters, and pyramid schemes fraudulent?
4. List the steps to follow in making a consumer complaint.
5. What is a small-claims court?

Problem Solving and Decision Making

1. Identify which of the following situations involve fraud and which involve deception.
   a. Buying a sports watch after seeing an ad with it on a surfer and then finding out the watch cannot be immersed in water.
   b. Spending $3,000 for a flight to a two-week European vacation that never got off the ground because the promoter took the money.
   c. Spending $500 to get sweepstakes winnings when no winnings could be collected.
2. Yoko Hariko was not satisfied with the performance of her microwave oven. She contacted the local sales representative and the manager of the chain store. After several polite yet forceful encounters, she has received no action on her complaint. What should she do next?

Building Academic Skills

Consumers Around the World

Math

1. A large "private investment fund" in Russia collapsed in 1994, leaving between one and ten million "investors" victims of fraud. The fund turned out to be a giant pyramid scheme. People bought shares in the fund at $56 a share. At the end, the shares were worth only 46 cents each. How much did an investor lose if he or she owned 100 shares? 500 shares?

Communications

2. Research in your library cases of fraud or deceptive business practices. Choose one case and summarize it. Report your findings to the class.

Human Relations

3. Interview three people knowledgeable about selling. (At least one should be a salesperson.) Construct a brief questionnaire on sales techniques. Ask about favorite techniques and what is

least successful. Ask for hints on how to get the most out of a salesperson.

Summarize your information. Create a 500-word pamphlet aimed at teaching students how to deal with salespeople.

Beyond the Classroom

Consumer Projects

1. Collect product advertisements from newspapers and magazines. Circle questionable, vague, or misleading language. Write questions to ask what would make these terms clearer. For example, a question about the term "outstanding performance" might be "How is the performance outstanding?"
2. Interview four or five people about deceptive or fraudulent practices. Which types of practices have they encountered as consumers? What were their reactions to the situation?

Cooperative Learning

Family Economics

Break into assigned family groups. Discuss the following problem.

Because of a tax shortfall, your local government must cut back on public services. One of the first agencies affected is the small-claims court. Night hours are eliminated and the fee for bringing an action is raised from $20 to $36. Assume your family was planning to sue a local dry cleaner over damage to some garments totaling $80. Will you proceed now? Why or why not? Compare your spending patterns with those of other family groups.

Debate the Issue

"Caveat emptor" is a Latin phrase that means "Let the buyer beware." This well-known slogan implies that buyers are responsible for their actions and sellers should not be held liable for buyers' errors. Proponents of "caveat emptor" maintain that buyers become victims of fraud because of their own greed and that they should not be unduly protected by government regulation or interference. Opponents say that buyers are more often naive than simply greedy and that even the most astute buyer cannot be aware of all possible deceptions. Government regulation of selling practices is therefore justified.

You and your classmates will break into two groups and research this topic. Each group will gather evidence to support one side or the other. You are to prepare the argument for your side of the problem. Then the two groups will meet in a classroom debate.

Rechecking Your Attitude

Before going on to the next unit, go back to the Attitude Inventory at the beginning of this one. Answer the questions a second time. Then compare the two sets of responses. On how many statements have your attitudes changed? Can you account for these shifts in your opinions? What do you know now that you did not know then?

summarize information on advertising. Students may be surprised to discover how much advertising costs and that most advertising dollars are spent on newspaper ads.

Human Relations
3 Students should submit a brochure showing how to deal with sales tactics, including trading up.

Consumer Projects
1 Students should ask questions that aim at getting more specific information.
2 Students should discuss their experiences with sales techniques.

Family Economics
Only families with a member who is free to go to court during the day or families with an income that will enable them to stand on principle will proceed. Those living on the least income will find that the changes make the court action too expensive to pursue.

Debate the Issue
Break the class into two teams. Assign each team one side of the issue. Encourage students to work together as a team to develop their argument. Ask each team to select a member to make an opening statement that supports the team's side of the issue. Have students take turns debating as the debate moves from one team to the other.

UNIT 2 LAB
You and Your Community

STEP A Students should prepare lists of interview questions that are clearly written and address all the topics listed in the step.
STEP B Students should arrange and carry out their observations and interviews. They should take careful, well-organized notes on the conversations they have with the entrepreneurs.
STEP C 1 $395.50; 2 $1,900.00; 3 3,154.00
STEP D Students' reports should indicate their understanding that proper financial management is essential to a business's success, as are tactful, effective employee and customer policies. Students should support their comments with specific examples from their observations and interviews.

Refer students to the Unit 2 Lab in the Student Activity Workbook.

Observing an Entrepreneur

Unit 2 discusses the earning and spending facets of money management and focuses on the many responsibilities of entrepreneurs. In this lab, you will make a further exploration into entrepreneurial opportunities and obligations.

TOOLS

1. Financial and business magazines
2. Literature from the Better Business Bureau and government offices
3. Consumer magazines
4. *Occupational Outlook Handbook* and other career references

PROCEDURES

STEP A Decide on a career area that interests you and for which you have an aptitude. Identify and contact local entrepreneurs with businesses in your chosen career area.

For example, if you are interested in the food industry, you might contact an independent wholesaler, a restaurant owner, or a speciality-foods producer. If working with computers interests you, contact a freelance computer consultant or a software manufacturer.

Ask the entrepreneur of your choice to allow you to observe him or her for at least two hours during the course of the business day. Also, ask if you may interview the entrepreneur either before or after the observation. Write a list of ten interview questions that cover the following topics:

1. The entrepreneur's own interests and aptitudes.
2. The type and extent of research the entrepreneur did before starting (or buying) the business.
3. The start-up process the entrepreneur followed, including obtaining financing.
4. The entrepreneur's financial management procedure, including the preparation of income statements (also known as profit-and-loss statements) and balance sheets.
5. The procedure for drawing up sales budgets and expense budgets.
6. The business's advertising practices and customer-service policies.
7. The procedure for handling complaints and/or return of merchandise.
8. The entrepreneur's employee policies and methods for dealing with employee problems.

UNIT 2 LAB

You and Your Community

STEP B Arrange to observe the entrepreneur on a day that is convenient for him or her. Take careful notes on what you observe, but be careful not to disrupt the business's functioning or distract the entrepreneur. Conduct yourself in a professional manner at all times. When you interview the entrepreneur, be sure to take written notes. *Do not tape-record the interview unless the entrepreneur gives you permission to do so.*

LAB REPORT

STEP C Use your observation and interview notes as well as the information in the textbook to answer the questions below:

1. If an employee's wage rate is $7 per hour and the employee receives 1.5 times the regular rate for every hour over 40 hours a week, how much will the employee earn for 51 hours worked in a week?
2. Herondo is a salesperson for a computer-hardware business. His salary is $1,000 a month and 5 percent of sales over $15,000. What was Herondo's salary for April, when he sold $33,000 worth of merchandise?
3. Eileen's Essentials is a stationery store that caters to the needs of small businesses. If Eileen had sales of $24,890 in June and expenses of $21,736 during the same month, what was the business's net income for June?

STEP D Write a two-page report explaining how a business's success is affected by financial management, employee policies, and customer-service issues.

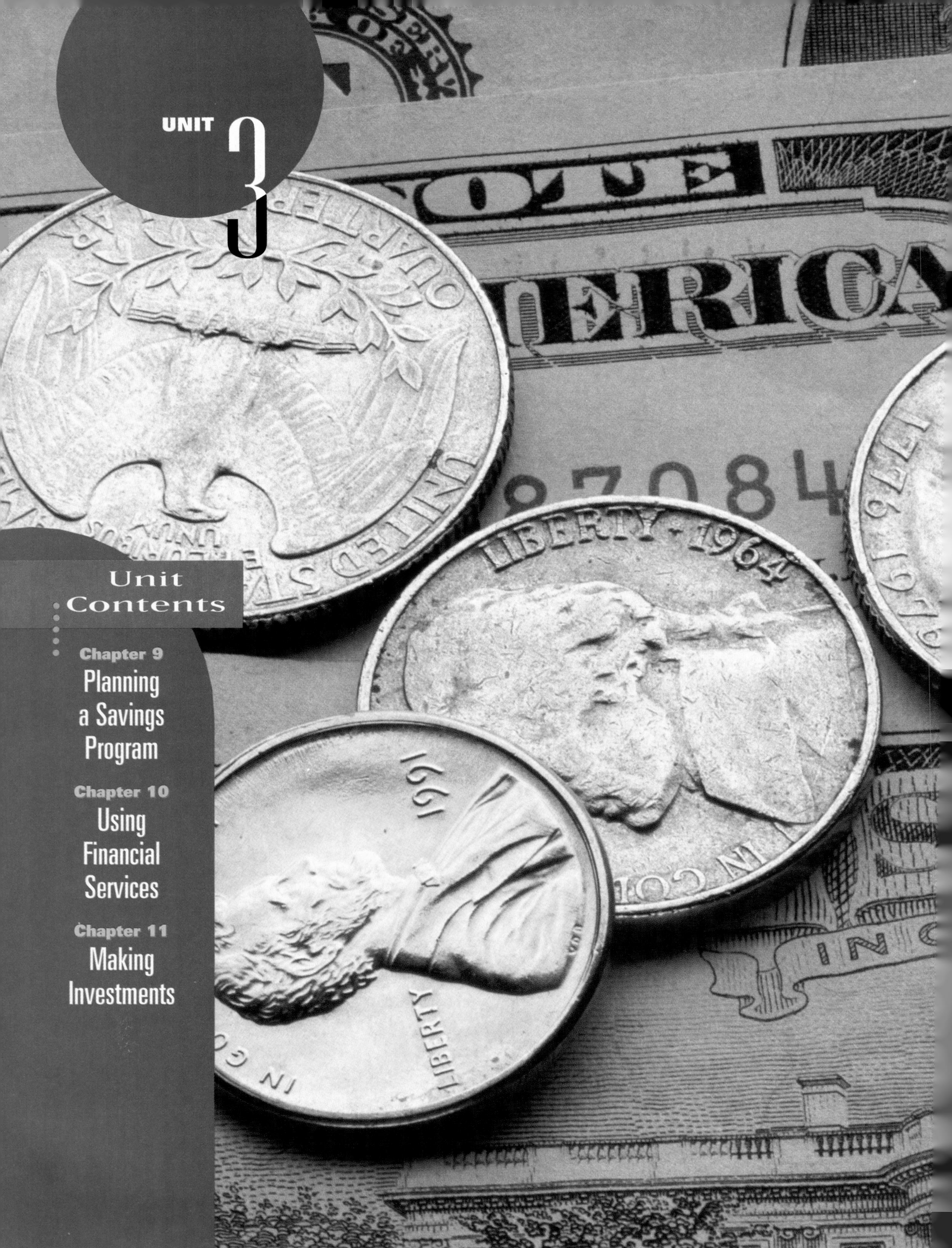

UNIT 3

Unit Contents

Chapter 9
Planning a Savings Program

Chapter 10
Using Financial Services

Chapter 11
Making Investments

Money Management: Saving and Investing

Attitude Inventory

Before you begin Chapter 9, take stock of your attitudes by completing the following inventory. Read each statement and decide how you feel about it—agree, disagree, or undecided. Record your feelings on a sheet of notepaper or use the form in the workbook.

1. Saving and investing money is possible only if you are rich.
2. A knowledge of saving and investment opportunities should be part of every person's basic education.
3. Every family should save at least 10 percent of its income.
4. With old-age assistance and social security available, people do not need long-range investment programs.
5. The only kind of bank account you really need is a checking account.
6. People should put their savings where they can get the highest return on their money, regardless of the risk involved.
7. A consumer should have a sizable emergency fund accumulated before buying stocks and bonds.
8. Saving only a small amount each week is not worthwhile.
9. A person is more likely to save when he or she has a definite goal in mind.
10. Having a check canceled reflects badly on the person who drew it.
11. You can take your money out of the bank anytime you wish—after all, it's your money!
12. There is no difference between investing and gambling.
13. An individual risks more by investing in corporate stocks than by putting money in a savings account.

Unit Goal The main goal of this unit is to make students aware of the importance of saving and to introduce them to the techniques, institutions, and investment possibilities they can use in developing a savings strategy. Chapters included in this unit are (1) Planning a Savings Program, (2) Using Financial Services, and (3) Making Investments.

Lesson Plan See the Teacher's Manual for an overview of the unit and some suggestions for introducing it. If you assign the Attitude Inventory, be sure to tell students to keep their answers for later use.

CHAPTER 9

Planning a Savings Program

Learning Objectives

When you have finished studying this chapter, you should be able to:

1. List five valid reasons for saving.
2. Explain how savings become investments.
3. List three savings plans and at least five guidelines for saving money.
4. Identify four kinds of financial institutions and describe three main factors in choosing a particular institution for saving.
5. Name at least two alternative forms of saving.

Consumer Terms

investments
compounding
liquidity
annual percentage yield (APY)
commercial banks
mutual savings bank
dividend
savings and loan associations (S&Ls)
credit union

Real-World Journal

A savings program is of great importance. In your journal, list all the reasons for savings that you can think of. Go over your list with a family member or friend. Did he or she have any other reasons for savings that were not on your list? Summarize your findings in your journal.

Lesson Plan See the Teacher's Manual for Chapter 9 lesson plan.

Vocabulary The Chapter 9 lesson plan includes suggested vocabulary activities for the terms listed.

Caption Answer: Students may be willing to give up new clothes or shoes, entertainment, snacks, and so forth.

REASONS FOR SAVING

Like nearly everyone else, you probably know what it's like to want something you just don't have the money for. Maybe you have your eye on an expensive new jacket, or you have been longing for an electric guitar. One way to get that special item is to save for it.

Saving is really just delayed spending, putting aside present income for future use. People save for several reasons, all valid.

Emergencies

The term *emergency* applies to a wide range of circumstances from unemployment to medical bills expenses. To protect yourself in such situations, you should have an emergency fund.

Young people living at home may not need much of an emergency fund. However, once you are responsible for supporting yourself, you need to have an emergency fund to cover your expenses in case you lose your job.

The amount needed varies from person to person, depending on job security, lifestyle, number of dependents, and similar factors. A married worker with three dependents who owns a house needs a larger fund than a single person who rents an apartment and has few debts.

One rule of thumb is that a family's emergency fund should equal three to six times its monthly pay after taxes are taken out. With a fund this large, the family ought to be able to keep up with daily expenses through unemployment lasting three to six months.

Expensive Purchases

Some items—like a house or a car—are so expensive that you cannot pay for them from your weekly income. If you want to buy a new car, for example, you must either borrow or save.

Borrowing means *paying* interest, however. Saving *earns* interest. Thus, if you save for most or all of an expensive purchase, you gain in two ways. First, you receive interest income from the money you are saving. Second, you pay less for the item because you are paying little or no interest.

Savings can mean not buying many inexpensive items so that you can eventually purchase one expensive item that you really want. ***What small items are you willing to give up in order to save for an expensive purchase you want?*** ▼

Recurring Expenses

You might want to save so that you can more easily meet large recurring expenses. Suppose you have decided to get your own phone and you are responsible for the monthly bills. By setting aside small amounts of money from your weekly income, you will have the money on hand when the phone bill arrives at the end of the month.

You may want to follow the same plan in order to purchase gifts for family and friends on birthdays and holidays. As you get older, you may acquire other recurring expenses to save for, such as real estate taxes and insurance premiums.

Retirement

When you are young, retirement seems far off. It takes a long time, however, for people to save up enough to live comfortably when they retire. Once you have a full-time job, you need to start saving for the time when you will no longer want to or be able to work.

Most workers get some retirement income from the federal social security program. In addition, many workers have retirement plans through their job or labor union. For some people, however, these sources are not adequate. (People who have not worked regularly or who do not have job or union pension coverage are examples.) To meet their expenses, these people must supplement their retirement income with savings.

Special Goals

Most people have special goals in life. You may be planning to go to college, for example. After college, you might start saving for more long-range objectives like setting up a business.

If you decide to marry, you might decide to put money aside for starting and raising a family. When you are older, retired, or no longer responsible for children, you might put your savings into travel or hobbies.

SAVINGS AS INVESTMENT

You have probably had the experience of saving up for an item you couldn't otherwise have afforded—concert tickets or new sports equipment perhaps. You know that a few dollars put away every week can really add up.

In addition to buying consumer goods, you can put your savings to work in another way—to earn income. Even small amounts of money, when saved regularly, can earn money for you. When savings are used to earn income, they become **investments.**

Buying on Sale

A great way to save on the cost of purchasing is to buy on sale, but only if the sale item is less expensive than at another store.

- **Shop around to get an idea of what is available.**
- **Identify specifically what you want to purchase.**
- **Find out how much the item usually costs or at least the price range.**
- **Watch for advertised sales in local newspapers, flyers, catalogs, or promotional materials that may be sent to your home. You can also ask the salesperson when something will go on sale or periodically call the store.**
- **Be sure your purchase is new and has all appropriate warranties.**

1 Reinforcement Student Activity Workbook, Chapter 9 activities.

2 Reinforcement Have the students use Table 9–1 to answer the following questions: **(*a*)** If you save $25 a month for five years, at the end of that period how much will you have? ($1,705.02) **(*b*)** Assume you want to save $2,700 in four years. How much would you have to save monthly? (About $50) **(*c*)** If you save at a rate of $10 a month, how much would you have in ten years? ($1,555.03) To save about the same amount in half the time, how much would you have to save per month? (About $25)

Compounded Interest

When savings are invested and the income earned from them is in turn invested, the increase over a number of years can be very significant. Suppose that Raul Quintana, a carpenter, saves $50 a month. In a year, his savings amount to $600; in ten years, $6,000.

When Raul deposits his money in a savings account, he receives interest. At the end of ten years, at an interest rate of 5 percent, he has about $7,775, which is $1,775 more than he has deposited.

The interest that Raul's money has earned is income. If Raul continues saving at the rate of $50 a month and investing the money at a 5 percent interest rate, he will have more than $12,000 in 14 years. Then, if Raul keeps the $12,000 invested at 5 percent, he will earn interest of more than $50 a month. In other words, after 14 years, Raul could *withdraw* $50 a month and still have
1 $12,000 remaining in the bank!

2 Table 9–1 illustrates how rapidly monthly savings of various amounts increase when invested at a minimal 5 percent interest. (Interest rates at savings institutions vary. You can check financial publications, such as *Money* and *Kiplinger's Personal Finance,* for names of banks that currently are paying the best rate in the United States.)

The first column in the table shows the amount saved each month. The other columns show the total amounts of the savings plus interest at the end of different time periods. The interest is calculated and added to the total savings at six-month intervals (semiannually).

For example, suppose you are depositing $5 a month. At the end of six months, the savings institution calculates your interest and then adds the interest to the $30 you have deposited. The interest calculated over the next six months will be based on the total of your savings and the interest. In other words, interest is paid on the interest.

This process of paying interest on your savings plus the accumulated interest is called **compounding.** Interest may be compounded daily, monthly,

High Emphasis on Savings in Asia

Citizens of Singapore save 54 percent of their incomes. In Indonesia, citizens save 33 percent; in Malaysia, 29 percent; and in Japan, about 14 percent. Americans save 4 to 8 percent of their incomes.

This table shows how savings increase over a period of years. ***Based on this chart, how much will you have saved if you deposit $5 a month for six years?*** ▶

Caption Answer: $777.52

Table 9–1 Monthly Savings

At 5 percent interest, compounded semiannually

MONTHLY SAVINGS	End-of-Year-Total 1	2	3	4	5	6
$ 5.00	$ 61.64	$ 126.39	$ 194.43	$ 265.91	$ 341.00	$ 777.52
10.00	123.27	252.78	388.85	531.81	682.01	1,555.03
25.00	308.18	631.96	972.13	1,329.53	1,705.02	3,887.58
30.00	369.82	758.35	1,166.56	1,595.43	2,046.02	4,665.09
50.00	616.36	1,263.92	1,944.27	2,659.06	3,410.03	7,775.16

yearly, or as frequently as the savings institution chooses. The more often interest is compounded, the greater the income you get from your investment.

Rule of 72

One quick way to evaluate an interest rate is to apply the rule of 72. Divide the rate of interest into 72 to approximate the number of years it will take your money to double. For example, if the interest rate is 6 percent, divide 6 into 72. The answer is 12, meaning that it would take 12 years for you to double your investment.

TECHNIQUES FOR BUILDING SAVINGS

You can be successful at saving money if you resolve to set aside part of your income for savings *first* and then live on what is left. For all of us, the temptation to spend all the money in hand is very great. If you decide to pay your expenses first each month and then save whatever money remains, you may find that there is no money left over to be saved.

How much people can save depends on their income and their financial responsibilities. A large family with a small income may find it very difficult to save even small amounts. (Most of its money must be spent on day-to-day necessities.) A young person living at home who must pay for clothes and school supplies out of a part-time income will be able to save less than a young person living at home who uses the part-time income only for luxuries like entertainment.

One guideline is to save part of every paycheck. A reasonable goal for Americans seems to be to save about 8 percent of what remains after taxes have been deducted. If you have few responsibilities and expenses, you could save more. Some thrifty Americans save 15 percent without difficulty. If you have many responsibilities and expenses, you might have to settle for a 5 percent savings rate.

Historically, consumers in the United States have tended to save between 5 and 8 percent of their after-tax income. In recent years, though, they have fallen short of this average and saved only
1 4 percent.

1 Interesting Note The United States has one of the lowest personal savings rates in the industrialized world. The Japanese, for example, save more than three times as much of their disposable income.

Savings Plans

The most effective savings plans are based on a simple principle: If you do not have the money, you cannot spend it. Consider these techniques that many people use to save systematically.

Self-discipline One good way to build savings is to set aside a percentage of your earnings right away. Before cashing your paycheck, calculate the amount you want to save. Place that amount in a savings account at the same time that you cash your paycheck.

Caption Answer: Family members can help by depositing savings for you. Friends and family can help by reminding you of your goals.

It takes self-discipline to keep to a savings plan. ***How can your friends and family help you stick to your goal?*** ▼

Payroll Deductions Many employers encourage employees to save by permitting payroll deductions. The employee authorizes the transfer of a specific amount from each paycheck to a savings fund. The deduction for savings is usually placed in a savings account or used to buy savings bonds.

Automatic Deductions from Checking Accounts The money transfer service offered by banks is another method of saving systematically. You or your employer deposits your paycheck in your checking account. Then, each month, the bank transfers a specified amount to your savings account.

Guidelines for Saving Money

Where do you keep the money you save? You may have a box or jar or drawer that you keep your savings in. That's fine for saving small amounts, say, for the movies, that you will need pretty quickly. Once you find you have about $50 or so in savings, it's time to put your money to work for you.

For most people, a savings account in a bank is the first step toward realizing long-range goals. A savings account in a savings bank is one of the few accounts that young people can open on their own. Some savings institutions, however, require a minimum first deposit to open an account. Figure 9–1 illustrates some practical guidelines for saving money.

SAVINGS INSTITUTIONS

To get the most out of your savings, keep them in a financial institution where they will earn interest. When you are deciding which institution to use, consider three important factors.

1. *Safety.* Deposits should be insured, preferably by the Federal Deposit Insurance Corporation (FDIC). The FDIC insures deposits up to $100,000 in most, but not all, banks and savings associations. If you have your

Figure 9–1 Guidelines for Saving

Savings do not happen by accident. You need to plan for them.

Decide on a savings goal.
• Are you saving for college?
• For a car of your own?
• For new clothes?
How much must you save to reach your goal? Figure out how long it will take you to reach your goal. Mark your "goal reached" date on your calendar.
Plan to save a realistic amount.
Allow enough money to pay your daily expenses
Save regularly and consistently.
Try to save the same amount out of each paycheck. It is easier to save small amounts out of each weekly check than one large amount out of the last check of the month.

savings in a bank insured by the FDIC and the bank goes out of business, the federal government, through the FDIC, will give you back your savings—up to $100,000 worth. Look for the sign that every FDIC-insured institution must display at all teller stations: the official savings association (eagle) sign at savings associations and, at insured banks, the same sign or the official bank (FDIC) sign (see Figure 9–2).

State-chartered institutions sometimes have private rather than FDIC coverage. However, consumer advocates advise people to deal only with federally insured institutions. In the past, some private insurers were not able to give depositors back their money when several financial institutions that they insured failed at the same time.

In addition, once you have built up a lot of savings, you might find it smart to divide your savings among several institutions. That way, if one institution should fail, most of your
1 savings will still be safe.

Figure 9-2 Insured Institutions

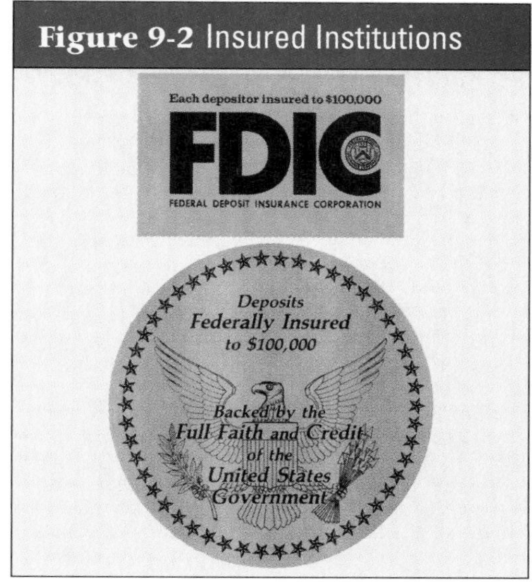

◀ *These signs must be displayed at FDIC insured institutions.* ***If either sign appears where you bank, for how much is your $22,000 deposit insured? your $122,000 deposit?***

Caption Answer: $22,000; $122,000

1 Critical Thinking Put this problem to the students: Assume you have $99,000. What kind of savings account arrangements would you make and why? (Divide it equally between two different banks. Otherwise, the first year's interest will push you over the limit for federal deposit insurance.)

2. *Liquidity.* The ease with which a person can turn savings or other types of investments into cash to be spent is called **liquidity.** Some accounts are highly liquid: You can withdraw money from them on the spur of the moment. Others are less liquid. The depositor agrees to leave the money in the account for a certain amount of time, usually in exchange for higher interest rates. In order to withdraw

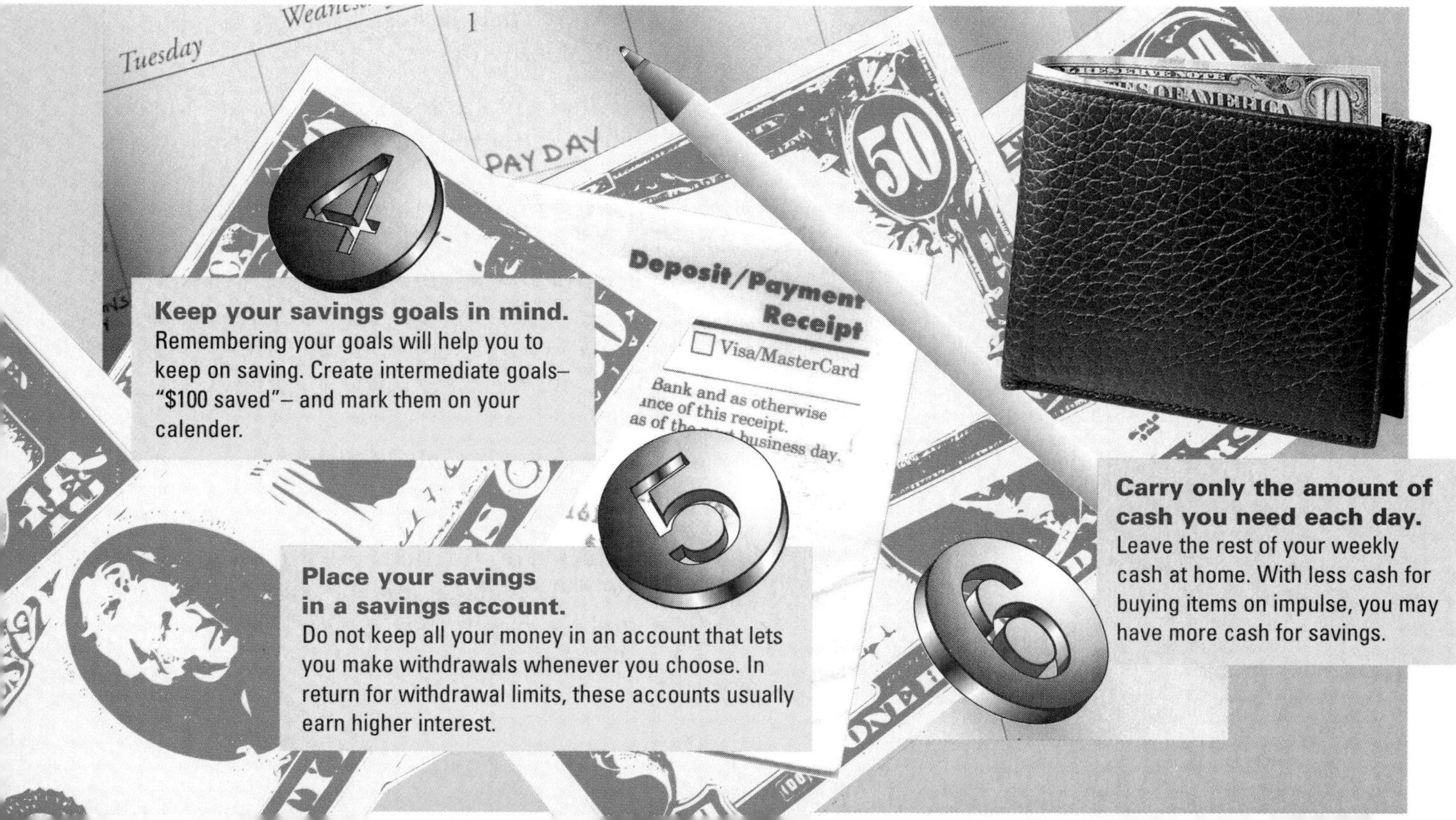

4

Keep your savings goals in mind. Remembering your goals will help you to keep on saving. Create intermediate goals–"$100 saved"– and mark them on your calender.

5

Place your savings in a savings account. Do not keep all your money in an account that lets you make withdrawals whenever you choose. In return for withdrawal limits, these accounts usually earn higher interest.

6

Carry only the amount of cash you need each day. Leave the rest of your weekly cash at home. With less cash for buying items on impulse, you may have more cash for savings.

▶ *Higher interest rates mean greater earnings in the long run.* ***How can you find out which institutions offer the highest rates?***

Caption Answer: Financial institutions advertise their rates in newspapers.

1 Reinforcement Have students bring in ads, articles, and brochures that use the word *liquid* in its fiscal sense. Highlight the word in the examples, and arrange the items in a bulletin board display. Encourage students to expand the display with other words in the same family (*liquidate, liquidator*).

Caption Answer: Some institutions open special accounts for young people, with little or no minimum deposit and balance.

Figure 9–3 Earnings on Investment

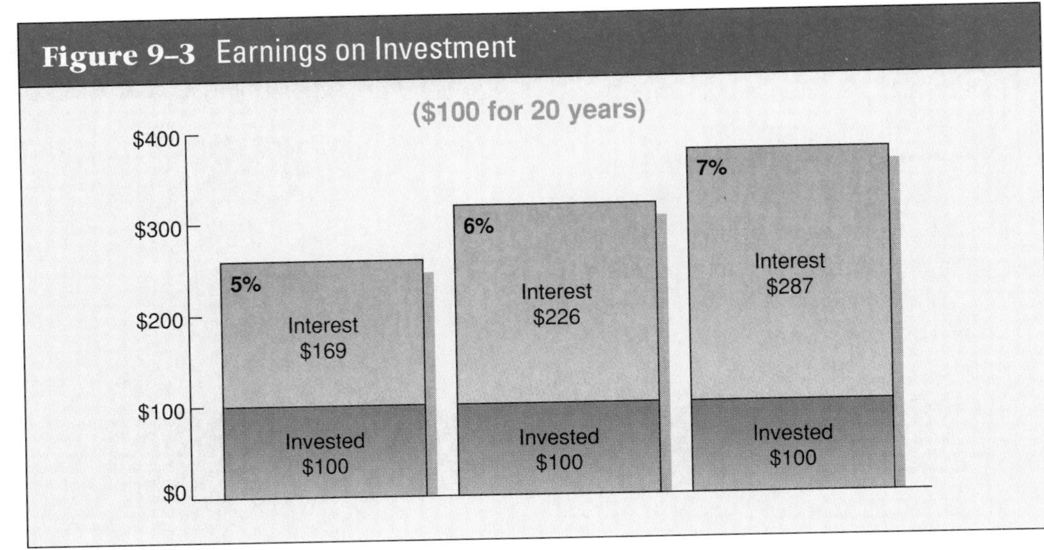

money ahead of time, the depositor
1 has to pay a substantial penalty.

If you are saving for long-term goals, like a house, you can use an account that is less liquid and pays higher interest rates. If you are saving for recurring expenses, you may want an account with high liquidity so that you can get your money exactly when you need it.

3. *Earnings.* Not all savings institutions offer the same interest rate. Remember that over a long period of time even small variations in rates can make large differences in earnings. As Figure 9–3 shows, after 20 years, $100 invested at 5 percent is worth $269, while $100 invested at 6 percent is worth $326.

It is difficult to compare interest rates directly because of factors such as how often interest is compounded. For this reason, the Truth in Savings Act specifies that institutions must provide standardized figures that savers can use to compare rates among institutions. This figure is the **annual percentage yield (APY).** The APY tells how much interest the institution would pay on $100 for one year. If the APY is 4 percent, the bank pays $4 interest on $100 in a year. The higher the APY, the better the rate.

Financial institutions sometimes want to attract a particular type of customer. ***How can you tell if an institution welcomes young depositors?*** ▼

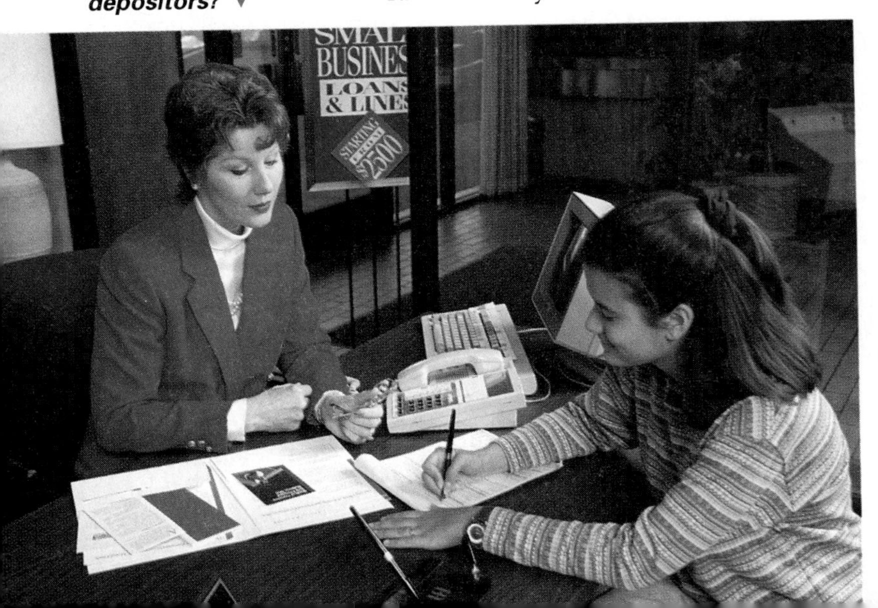

Banks and Savings and Loan Associations

Three types of financial institutions have been available to savers for a long time. Commercial banks, mutual savings banks, and savings and loan associations.

Many of the distinctions that once existed among these institutions were swept away by the Depository Institutions Act of 1982. Today all three offer virtually the same range of services: savings accounts, checking accounts, loans, and investment counseling.

Commercial Banks **Commercial banks** are financial institutions that serve individuals and businesses. Operated for profit, they offer the full range of banking services but emphasize shorter-term loans (one to five years). Although they are seen as the chief source of loans to businesses, they make loans to home buyers as well.

Mutual Savings Banks Historically, making loans to home buyers was the responsibility of institutions other than commercial banks—mutual savings banks among them. The word *mutual* implies that the people served are also owners of the bank. Hence, a **mutual savings bank** is a financial institution owned by its depositors.

As owners, depositors receive dividends in place of interest. A **dividend** is

Young People Become STARs

In 1977, Veronica Primus Thomas returned home to South Carolina from New York. She had warm memories of her childhood there and wanted her children to have the same experience. She was shocked, however, by what she saw. Racial prejudices were still strong. Forty-four percent of the kids dropped out of school. Thirty-eight percent of the girls were pregnant before they finished school.

When Thomas started teaching high school, she saw how frustrated, helpless, and worthless the young people felt. When she tried to help them solve their problems, she was criticized by the other teachers for getting involved.

In 1983, she got a group of teenagers together and gave them the statistics on dropout rates, drug use, and pregnancy rates. She asked if they wanted to join the statistics. They did not. So they started STAR—Serious Teens Acting Responsibly.

Thomas gave the teens things to do. They did community volunteer work. They tutored other kids. They became part of fund-raising projects. As a result, they gained tremendously in self-esteem. Later Thomas started Project LEARN, a summer camp and after-school tutoring program—staffed by STAR teens.

Thomas taught the girls they did not have to have boyfriends to be proud of themselves. She taught the boys that fatherhood is a serious responsibility. As a result, the pregnancy rate among STAR teens has dropped to 2 percent. All STAR participants have finished high school, and 85 percent have gone on to college.

Although there are 1,500 STAR members in South Carolina, North Carolina, Georgia, Virginia, and Connecticut, Veronica Thomas still sees a lot of work to do.

Brainstorm

What kind of volunteer work in your community would help teens feel needed and wanted, and would give them self-respect?

Case Study Answer: Cleaning trash from parks; planting flowers in neighborhoods; working in nursing homes; working in women's shelters or homeless shelters; working in hospitals; working at the local YMCA or YWCA.

1 Interesting Note
Early estimates were that it will eventually cost the federal government between $50 billion and $100 billion to bail out the savings and loan industry.

2 Reinforcement
Student Activity Workbook, Chapter 9 activities.

News Clip Answers:
1 You need to make a commitment to saving money instead of spending it to achieve your long-term financial goals. With discipline you will be able to acquire enough wealth to save for such things as buying a house or funding your retirement.
2 Think about what you are spending now and what you may want later on that you cannot afford now. Perhaps you could forgo a movie or item of clothing to save for a bigger expense such as a car or a stereo system.

a share of profits paid in proportion to share of ownership. Share of ownership, in turn, is determined by how much a person has on deposit.

Now mutual savings banks offer all traditional banking services and are shifting their emphasis from residential to commercial loans. Beginning in the late 1970s, many savings banks abandoned the mutual form of ownership. About the same time, some new savings banks exercised a newly gained right to apply for a federal, rather than a state, charter. Even more savings banks appeared on the scene when a number of federally chartered savings and loan associations elected to change their names to include "federal savings bank."

Savings and Loan Associations **Savings and loan associations (S&Ls)** are financial institutions that still specialize in providing funds to home buyers. Usually operated as mutual organizations, they also offer customers a complete line of banking services.

During the 1980s, some S&Ls began to emphasize loans to businesses instead of individuals. Many of these new loans turned out to be worthless, and the S&L industry lost huge sums of money. The Federal Savings and Loan Insurance Corporation (FSLIC), set up to protect depositors against such losses, proved unequal to its task. U.S. taxpayers came to the rescue at an estimated cost of more than $200 billion. Probably the true cost will never be known.

Weak savings and loan associations were closed or sold, the last in the mid-1990s. The remaining S&Ls, numbering about 1,500, are considered as healthy as banks. The FDIC now insures deposits in commercial banks, savings banks,
1 and S&Ls.

Credit Unions

A **credit union** is an alternative to traditional financial institutions. It operates as both a savings and lending institution for the benefit of its members. Participants are connected in some way—as employees in the same firm or members in the same church, club, or labor union. You may be able to participate in a credit union through your job or through an organization you belong to.

By encouraging its members to save collectively and systematically, a credit union builds up a fund that can be used for loans. The loans, which are made to members, earn interest from which the credit union's expenses are paid. Any profits that remain are then passed on to members in the form of dividends. As with other mutual organizations, how much a credit union member receives in dividends depends on his or her share of ownership, which in turn depends on how much he or she has on deposit.

To support the credit union, many companies permit a portion of a person's paycheck to be automatically deposited in the employee's credit union account. This payroll deduction is an excellent way for the employee to save regularly. It is also a convenient way for members to repay loans from their credit union.

Most credit unions provide federal share insurance. It is required for federal credit unions. Savings are insured up to $100,000 by the National Credit Union Administration (NCUA), an agency of the U.S. government. Funds are further protected by government supervision
2 and other means. Some states have state share insurance programs.

ALTERNATIVE FORMS OF SAVING

Banks, savings and loan associations, and credit unions, while the most common, are not the only savings alternatives open to people. The federal government, private employers, and insurance companies also offer savings programs of various types.

Savings Bonds

When federal tax receipts are insufficient to finance federal programs, the

CASE STUDY

Consumer NEWS CLIP

Couple Wonders Where Cash Flows

by John O'Dell
Los Angeles Times
December 29, 1994

In many ways, Ed Johnston and Pat Rollyson live the typical middle-class Orange County lifestyle.

Their annual salaries total $90,000, which looks impressive on paper, but in fact the couple say they are living from paycheck to paycheck.

They confess that a big part of their problem is lack of discipline. To find solutions, they met with Irvine financial planner Victoria Felton-Collins, who drew up a makeover plan for them. Pat Szekel, a tax accountant in Orange, also reviewed the couple's finances.

After meeting with the couple, financial planner Felton-Collins found one area that both were overlooking: Johnston uses the Internal Revenue Service as a savings bank. He likes the idea of getting a big refund every year—he says it averages $8,000—so he has far more money withheld than is required.

The $500 to $650 that is withheld each month in excess of Johnston's actual tax liability would go a long way toward building an emergency, retirement or vacation fund, she said, if it were invested in a mutual fund or used to buy a six-month or one-year certificate of deposit at a bank.

She also encouraged the couple to install a simple financial planning program on their home computer and to use it to keep track of their expenses.

Tax accountant Szekel agreed. "They don't even have to have a budget," he said. "Just keeping track of expenses by category is a big step."

"Sometimes calling up your expenses at the end of the month or year and seeing what you are really spending your money on will be enough to shock you into changing your spending habits," he said.

Both experts also encouraged the couple to put aside as much as they can for the future. "Retirement plans let you save current tax dollars and allow your money to grow tax-deferred," Felton-Collins said, because the benefits aren't taxable until they are paid out, and when a person retires he or she usually moves to a lower tax bracket.

The hospital where Rollyson works has no retirement plan now but is starting one soon. The experts urged her to sign up as soon as she can and contribute the maximum amount possible. Johnston already does that with his retirement program, they said, and should continue doing so.

Overall, Szekel said, Johnston and Rollyson "seem to have excellent debt-to-earnings ratios. . . . It really boils down to a matter of saving it or spending it, and that's a decision only they can make."

Decisions, Decisions

1. Why is important to have discipline in planning a savings program?
2. How would you apply discipline to your current spending?

FLASHBACK FLASHFORWARD

The annual cost of raising a child from a middle-income family in 1993 was $6,870. It is projected that the cost of raising a child from a middle-income family will be $14,870 per year by 2005. Your parents or guardian can consider you a bargain!

government must borrow money. One of the ways it does so is by selling savings bonds.

Interest on savings bonds is not taxable by state and local governments. This is one of the major advantages of buying bonds. Federal income tax, however, must be paid. Another advantage of federal bonds is that they are a very safe place to keep your money. The federal government issues two types—Series EE and Series HH.

Series EE Bonds A person buys a series EE bond at 50 percent of its face value—paying $50 for a $100 bond. This means that the purchaser of the bond loaned the U.S. government $50.

The government pays interest on the loan every six months. The interest is added to the bond. Therefore, your Series EE bond increases in value six months after purchase and every six months thereafter. The rate of interest varies and is determined by the Treasury Department. You can buy Series EE bonds for certain set amounts from $50 to $10,000.

Series HH Bonds Series HH bonds cannot be bought for cash. The only way to obtain them is in exchange for Series EE bonds. Unlike the Series EE bond, a Series HH bond is purchased for the amount that is printed on it. Interest is paid to you by check every six months.

Insurance

The main purpose of insurance is to protect against financial loss. However, many insurance companies provide more than insurance protection. They offer insurance programs that also contain a way to save money. Programs such as these may be especially useful for people who find it very hard to save on their own. Programs such as endowment policies and annuities may be especially useful for people who find it hard to save on their own.

Employee Savings Plans

Many types of employee savings plans exist today. In some plans, as you have read, the employer deducts money from the employee's paycheck for deposit in a savings account or for the purchase of savings bonds. In other plans, however, the employer contributes to the employee's savings.

Encouraged by federal legislation, employee savings plans have grown rapidly in recent years. How safe a plan is and how much money it earns depends on the types of investments the employer makes with the funds placed in them.

Caption Answer: Students may "pretend" they are earning less than they are. They may claim no allowances on their income tax and deposit the tax refund. They may ask their parents to hold their money. They may put any remaining cash at the end of the day into a savings jar. They may save their loose pennies or loose change.

Asking your employer to deduct money from your paycheck is an excellent way to save. ***Do you use any special techniques to "forget" about part of your income so that you can save rather than spend it?*** ▶

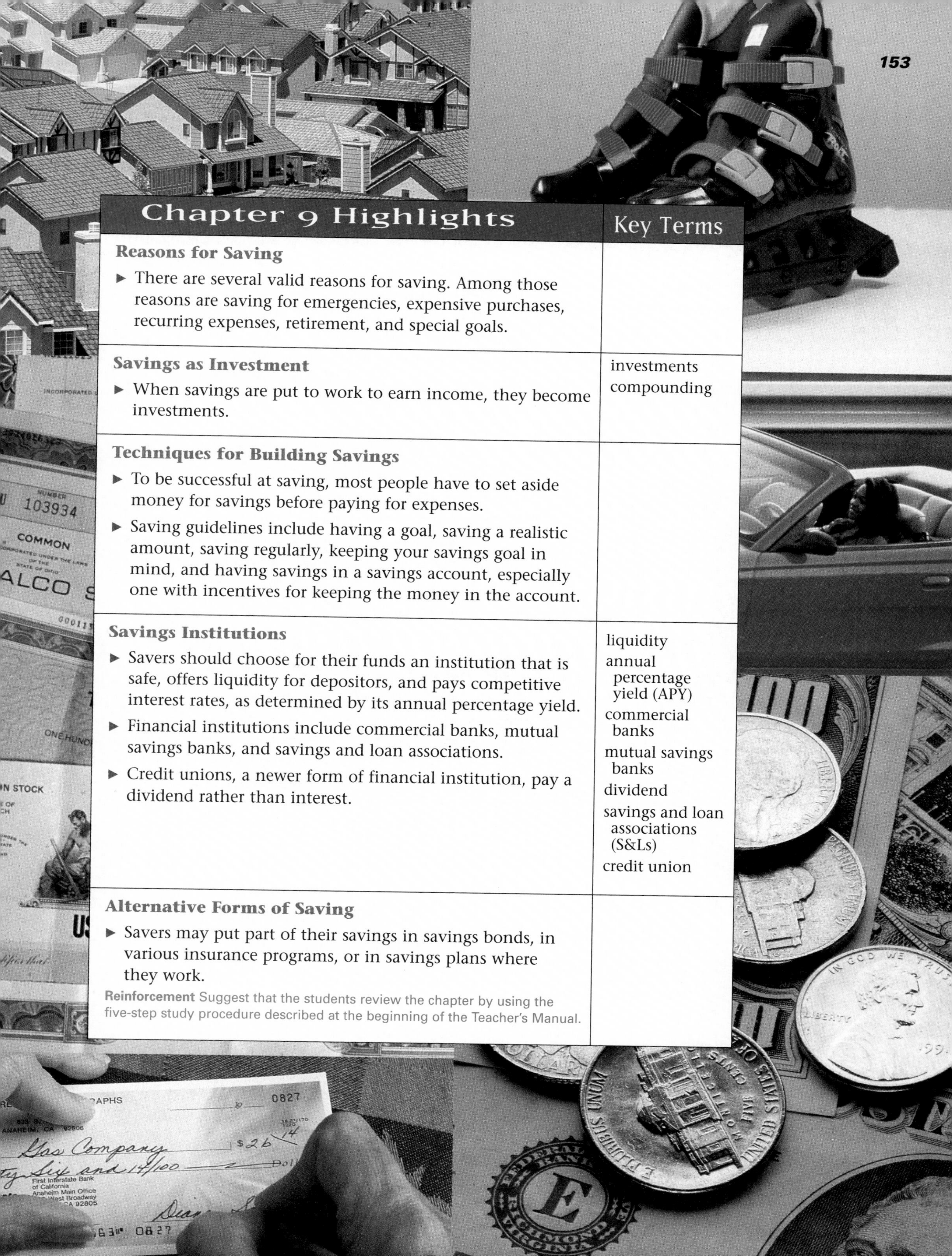

Chapter 9 Highlights	Key Terms
Reasons for Saving ▶ There are several valid reasons for saving. Among those reasons are saving for emergencies, expensive purchases, recurring expenses, retirement, and special goals.	
Savings as Investment ▶ When savings are put to work to earn income, they become investments.	investments compounding
Techniques for Building Savings ▶ To be successful at saving, most people have to set aside money for savings before paying for expenses. ▶ Saving guidelines include having a goal, saving a realistic amount, saving regularly, keeping your savings goal in mind, and having savings in a savings account, especially one with incentives for keeping the money in the account.	
Savings Institutions ▶ Savers should choose for their funds an institution that is safe, offers liquidity for depositors, and pays competitive interest rates, as determined by its annual percentage yield. ▶ Financial institutions include commercial banks, mutual savings banks, and savings and loan associations. ▶ Credit unions, a newer form of financial institution, pay a dividend rather than interest.	liquidity annual percentage yield (APY) commercial banks mutual savings banks dividend savings and loan associations (S&Ls) credit union
Alternative Forms of Saving ▶ Savers may put part of their savings in savings bonds, in various insurance programs, or in savings plans where they work. **Reinforcement** Suggest that the students review the chapter by using the five-step study procedure described at the beginning of the Teacher's Manual.	

CHAPTER 9 REVIEW

Refer students to the Reviewing Consumer Terms and Reviewing Facts and Ideas activities in the Student Activity Workbook.

Reviewing Consumer Terms Paragraphs will vary. See Glossary for definitions.

Reviewing Facts and Ideas Refer students to the Student Activity Workbook for answers.

Problem Solving and Decision Making **1** Historically, commercial banks had more services. Today, they are similar. **2** Student surveys should include four different people and include their responses to questions.

Consumers Around the World **1 Math** 482 (481.9) billion

Communications **2** Student papers should briefly touch on how they are saving and list one or two ways to increase their savings.

Reviewing Consumer Terms

For each group of terms, write a paragraph explaining what the listed items have to do with the heading.

Savings as Investment
compounding
investments
Savings Institutions
annual percentage yield
commercial banks
credit union
dividend
liquidity
mutual savings banks
savings and loan associations

Reviewing Facts and Ideas

1. What do you determine when you apply the rule of 72?
2. In general what percent of income after taxes do or should consumers save?
3. What characteristic do most successful savers have in common?
4. What do credit unions pay out to their saving customers instead of interest?
5. Why might U.S. savings bonds be an attractive investment for many people?

Problem Solving and Decision Making

1. The maximum rate of interest paid on savings accounts in commercial banks is usually less than that paid on savings accounts in mutual savings banks, savings and loan associations, and credit unions. Yet more people deposit savings in commercial banks than in any other type of financial institution. Why do you think this is so?
2. In order to save successfully most people need reasons for saving. Create a brief questionnaire that asks (1) what are your savings goals? (2) what is your savings plan? (3) how long do you think it will take for you to reach your goals?

   Interview at least four people your age. Summarize their answers in a 250-word paper. Can you draw any conclusions from your research? Be prepared to share your work with your class.

Building Academic Skills

Consumers Around the World

Math

1. Government figures show that Japanese banks accounted for about 9.4 percent of all lending in the United States. If their loans totaled $45.3 billion, what was the total lending in the United States at that time? Write a paper describing what effect it would have on the economy in the U.S. if Japanese banks suddenly started lending most of their money within their own country instead.

Communications

2. Write a 250-word paper describing your current savings plan. What revisions can you make to improve your plan?

Social Studies

3. Research the savings rate for families and individuals in the following countries—Saudi Arabia, Japan, Greece, and Mexico. Compare these with the per capita income for those countries. Why do you think some countries save more than others?

Technology

4. Interview family and friends about the effects of ATMs and computer banking on their banking habits. Does the new technology make it harder or easier to save money? How?

Beyond the Classroom

Consumer Projects

1. Clip financial institution ads that feature interest rates on passbook savings accounts and five-year CDs. Use these as the basis of a brief report in which you consider the following question:

   Assume you have $1,000 to invest. Into which institution would you deposit it? Explain your choice based on a comparison of at least three institutions. (Attach the relevant ads to the report.)

2. Suppose you have been working full-time for three years and are now able to save $50 every month. Write a paper explaining the relative importance you will place on each of the following factors in your savings program: safety, liquidity, and earnings.

Cooperative Learning

Family Economics

Break into assigned family groups. Discuss the following problem.

Your employer establishes an employee savings plan based on payroll deductions. To participate, you must be willing to save at least $10 a week, which will be withheld from your paycheck and deposited to your account with the company credit union.

Do you sign up? Consider your goals, family obligations, and budget. Then explain why or why not. Compare your answers with those of other family groups.

Debate the Issue

Credit unions are considered nonprofit institutions. Therefore, they have no taxable earnings—only savings. Since they have no earnings, they do not pay federal income tax. This puts their competitors (that is, banks and savings and loan associations) at a disadvantage. Some credit union advocates stress the social value of these institutions, but opponents still demand an end to any favorable treatment accorded credit unions. Is such treatment justified?

You and your classmates will break into two groups and research this topic. Each group will gather evidence to support one side or the other. You are to prepare the argument for your side of the problem. Then the two groups will meet in a classroom debate.

3 Social Studies Have students share results with class.

4 Technology Student should report their findings to the class.

Consumer Projects Students should share their findings with the class.

Family Economics Participation of family groups will depend on whether they **(a)** can afford to save $40 per month, **(b)** already have a savings account elsewhere, **(c)** think they might need the credit union as a loan source, and **(d)** find the account terms and accessibility satisfactory.

Debate the Issue Break the class into two teams. Assign each team one side of the issue. Encourage students to work together as a team to develop their argument. Ask each team to select a member to make an opening statement that supports their side of the issue. Have students take turns debating as the debate moves from one team to another.

CHAPTER 10

Using Financial Services

Learning Objectives

When you have finished studying this chapter, you should be able to:

1. Name two savings accounts that offer higher interest rates than a passbook account, and list three kinds of retirement accounts.
2. Describe the six elements filled in on a check, explain the purpose of and procedure for reconciling a bank statement, and name three kinds of endorsements.
3. Give an example of when each of the following methods of payment might be used: money orders, telegraphic money orders, traveler's checks, and certified checks.
4. Explain what electronic fund transfers are.

Consumer Terms

certificate of deposit (CD)
drawer
drawee
payee
NOW accounts
canceled check
reconciling
endorsement
certified check
electronic fund transfer (EFT)

Real-World Journal

Visit your local bank and find brochures on its savings programs. List in your journal the types of accounts that your bank offers, such as money markets, certificates of deposit, savings bonds, and mutual funds. Next to each heading list the approximate annual interest rates. Describe the advantages and disadvantages of each type of account.

Lesson Plan See the Teacher's Manual for Chapter 10 lesson plan.

Vocabulary The Chapter 10 lesson plan includes suggested vocabulary activities for the terms listed.

1 Critical Thinking Have the students collect ads and brochures for CDs from different banks. Help them compare the offers in terms of amount, term, and interest rate, and select the best one.

SAVINGS ACCOUNTS

Once you have saved a good amount of your income, you may decide to put your money in a savings account. You have a choice of savings accounts that offer different interest rates and have differing restrictions.

Passbook Accounts and Certificates of Deposits

A common form of savings account is the passbook account. When you open the account, you get a passbook in which the bank records all deposits and withdrawals. The bank also pays interest, either on the money actually in the account or on an average balance. The interest paid is minimal, perhaps 3 to $3\frac{1}{2}$ percent.

Once you have built up a good balance, you can open another kind of account that will earn you higher interest—a **certificate of deposit** account, often called a **CD.** CDs are savings accounts for which certificates rather than passbooks are issued. You may have to be a minimum age to open a CD. To earn the higher interest paid by CDs,
1 you must accept three key limitations:

- *Minimum deposit.* You must keep a minimum amount in the account, usually $1,000 to $100,000.
- *Fixed term.* The money must be on deposit for a certain period, which may be six months or more.
- *Early-withdrawal penalty.* The higher interest rate is payable only if the funds are left in the account for the full period. If you withdraw money early, you lose part of the interest.

Money Market Accounts

Another account with higher interest rates is the insured money market account. This account is really a fund with contributions from many individuals. Fund managers put the money in investments that earn higher interest than a regular savings account.

Often, money market funds are not protected by insurance. Those managed by banks, however, are insured by a federal government agency. Also, investors may transfer and withdraw funds freely. The only limitation is a minimum deposit, usually $2,500. You may have to be a certain age to open one.

Caption Answer: A store owner who had received bad checks in the past might make it a policy to no longer take personal checks. A person might feel embarrassed, insulted, or angry if refused, but it is important to realize that the refusal is matter of policy and not personal insult. If the store does not take checks, you could decide to pay cash.

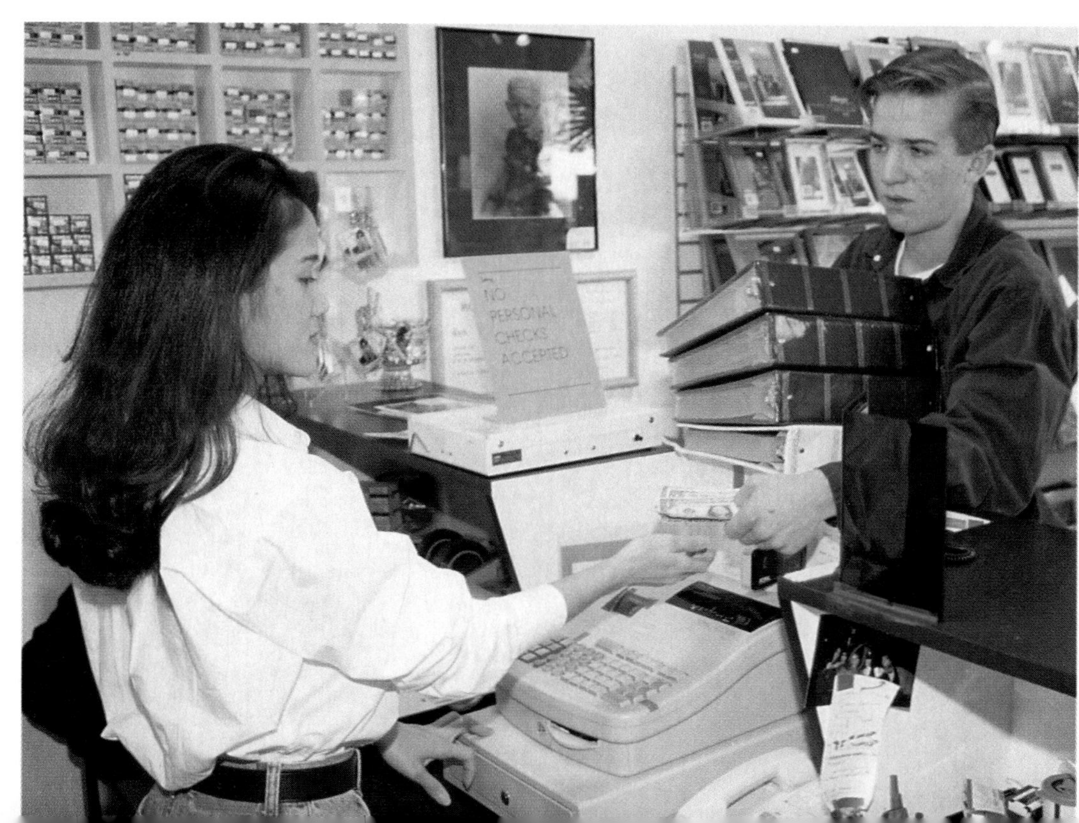

Checks have a disadvantage over cash. A business or individual can refuse to accept personal checks. ***Why might a store owner refuse to take checks? How would you feel if a store owner refused your check? What would you do?*** ▶

Retirement Accounts

Banks also offer accounts meant just for retirement savings. You do not pay certain taxes on money deposited or earned until you start withdrawing it, which must be after age 59½.

- *Individual retirement accounts (IRAs).* A person who does not have a pension plan at work can set up an individual retirement account (IRA).
1 - *Keogh accounts.* Keogh accounts are like IRAs but are meant for people who are self-employed.
- *Salary reduction plans.* Under plans such as the 401(k), part of your salary goes into a savings account set up by the employer.

CHECKING ACCOUNTS

As a student, you may be able to pay for all your expenses with the cash you carry in your wallet. However, when you get a full-time job or go off to college, you may find it inconvenient to pay for expenses such as rent and phone bills with cash. Most people find a checking account the easiest way to pay bills.

What Is a Check?

A check is a written order that instructs a bank to pay a specific amount of money to a particular person. The person who writes the check is the **drawer.** The bank that is instructed to pay is the **drawee.** The person who receives the money from the check is the **payee.**

The drawer must have a checking account in the drawee bank in order to write the check. The bank will only *honor* the check (pay the payee) if there is enough money in the checking account to cover the entire amount of the check.

Advantages of Checks

Checks have many advantages over cash. You can use them to send money by mail. You would never send cash through the mail because it could be taken and used by anyone. A check, however, is valuable only to the payee.

In addition, it is safer to carry checks than cash. If you lose your checkbook, the money in your account is safe. A stranger cannot use your checks. (You should notify the bank right away that the checks are lost to avoid checks being forged.)

The checks themselves are usually returned after they are paid. Thus you always have legal proof of payment.

What Financial Records You Should Keep

- **Never get rid of such real estate documents as your home's title, deed of purchase, mortgage contract, or receipts for major improvements or repairs.**
- **Keep all your tax returns. However, you may disregard backup receipts and documentation for deductible expenses after three years. Past that point, the IRS can't audit your return unless it suspects fraud. For the same reason, you can also throw away your bank and credit card records after three years.**
- **Save all trade confirmations of investments. You might want to keep yearly statements, but throw away those that come monthly.**
- **Save warranty documentation until it expires.**

1 Research Have the students research the history of IRAs with emphasis on the changes that have occurred in their availability to various income groups. Students should present their findings in written form and conclude with their own evaluation of the current situation.

Why is it so important to record all your checks? ▶

Caption Answer: To keep track of your running of balance.

1 Vocabulary The students may be unfamiliar with this use of "register." To help, review the entries in Figure 10-1 to establish that the register is a transaction record. Stress that it is the only record that remains after a check is sent off.

2 Math Application Use the chalkboard to continue the register entries in Figure 10-1. List the following transactions and allow students to compute the new balances: **(a)** paid rent of $387.07 to J.P. Landlord on Feb. 13; **(b)** cashed a check for $25 for spending money on Feb. 15; **(c)** deposited $400 paycheck on Feb. 17; **(d)** purchased TV stand for $38.69 from Hugh's Appliances on Feb. 18. (New balances: Feb. 13, $537.71; Feb. 15, $512.71; Feb. 17, $912.71; Feb. 18, $874.02.)

3 Critical Thinking Explain that some banks offer two kinds of checking accounts—one with a single annual fee and another with a monthly fee plus transaction charges. Ask the students which account they would prefer.

Figure 10–1 Check Register

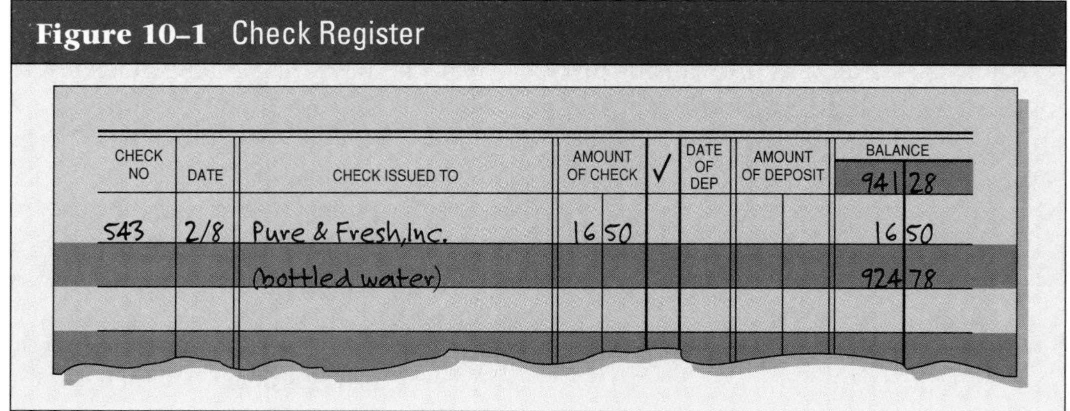

CHECK NO
DATE
CHECK ISSUED TO
AMOUNT OF CHECK
✓
DATE OF DEP
AMOUNT OF DEPOSIT
BALANCE
941 28
543
2/8
Pure & Fresh, Inc.
(bottled water)
16 50
16 50
924 78

Opening a Checking Account

You can open a checking account when you are 18 years old. You just sign a signature card, make your deposit, and select your checks. The signature card is especially important. It is the bank's record of how you sign your name. To verify that a signature is yours, a teller would refer to this card.

When you open your account, you get blank checks bound in a checkbook. The checkbook has two parts—the checks themselves and the check stubs or sepa-
1 rate check register (see Figure 10–1) in
2 which you record the checks you write.
Deposit slips are included also so you can make deposits.

Checking Account Fees

3 Most accounts have a service charge, a fee for managing the account. If you keep a minimum balance, you may not have to pay this fee.

NOW accounts are checking accounts on which the bank pays interest. *NOW* means *negotiable order of withdrawal.* NOW accounts usually require a minimum monthly balance, often $1,000.

Writing a Check

You may be nervous about using checks. After all, you have hard-earned money in your checking account. If you are careful and follow a set procedure for each check you write, your checks will serve their purpose and you'll always know how much money you have in your account.

Before writing a check, always fill out the check stub or check register. It is your personal record of the transaction. If you wait to record the check, you may forget the amount of the check or the payee. Then you will not know how much money you have left in your account.

Write all checks in ink so that they cannot be altered. If you make a mistake, destroy the check and start over. Properly filled out, a check should contain six items (see Figure 10–2).

How Checks Work

When you pay by check in a store, the salesperson may ask for your telephone number, or to see identification, such as a driver's license or school ID card. Salespeople are not allowed to ask for your social security number; this is information that you do not have to reveal.

The store owner deposits the check into the store's checking account. Then the store's bank presents the check to your bank (the drawee) for payment.

If your account has enough money, your bank pays the check, deducts the

1 amount from your account, and cancels
2 your check. A **canceled check** is a check that is stamped and perforated to show that it has been paid.

If your account does not have enough money, your bank returns the unpaid check—usually marked "Not sufficient funds"—to the store owner's bank. Your bank charges you a substantial fee for returning an unpaid check. The store's bank charges the store account a substantial fee too.

If a check is lost or stolen after you have signed it, you should tell your bank to *stop payment* on the check. Then the bank will refuse to honor the check. Since there is a big fee for this service, be careful not to lose filled-in checks.

Figure 10–2 Writing a Check

You need to write six items on the face of a check.

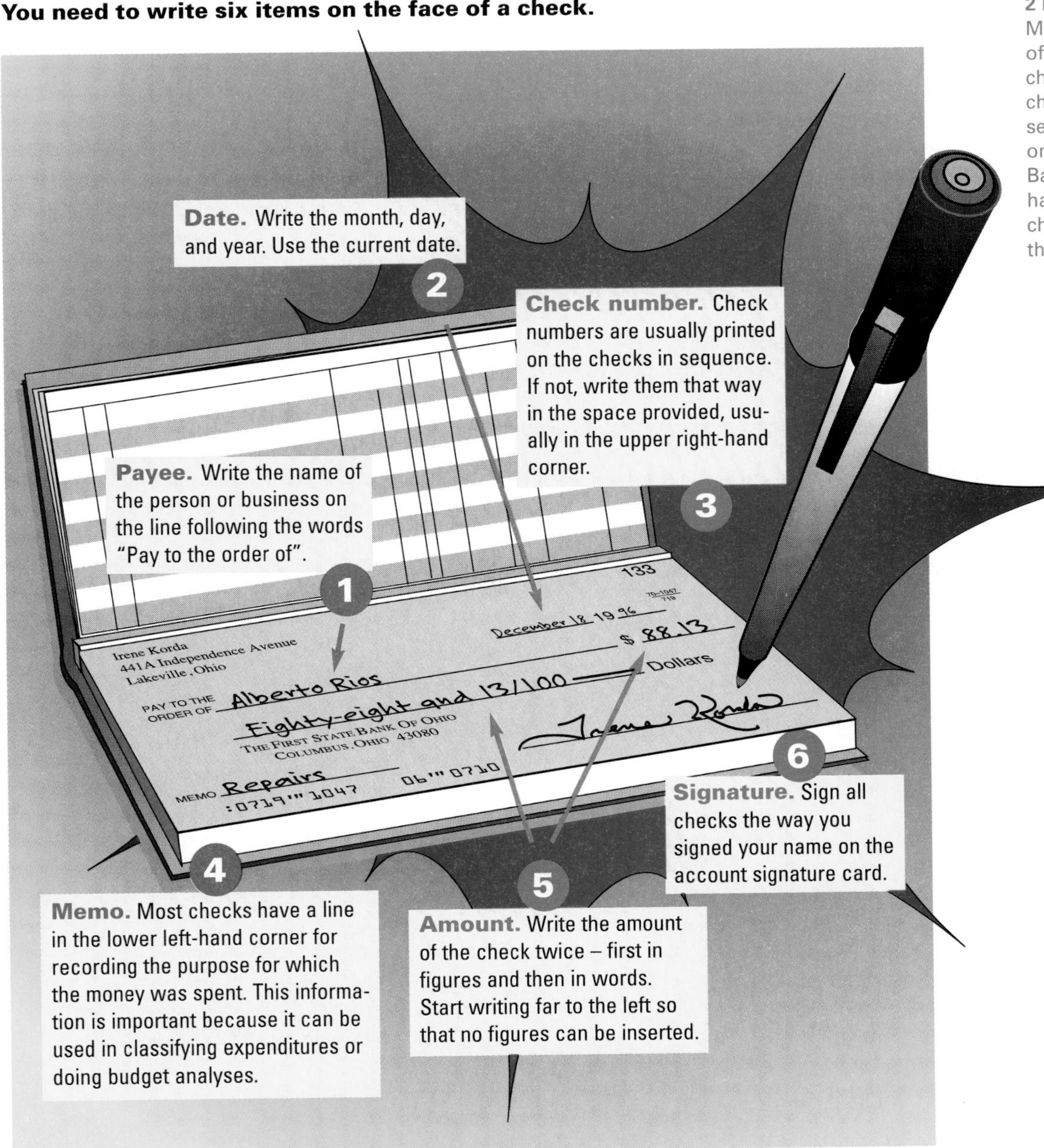
Date. Write the month, day, and year. Use the current date.
2
Check number. Check numbers are usually printed on the checks in sequence. If not, write them that way in the space provided, usually in the upper right-hand corner.
3
Payee. Write the name of the person or business on the line following the words "Pay to the order of".
1
133
Irene Korda
441A Independence Avenue
Lakeville, Ohio
December 18 19 96
$ 88.13
PAY TO THE ORDER OF Alberto Rios
Eighty-eight and 13/100
Dollars
The First State Bank Of Ohio
Columbus, Ohio 43080
MEMO Repairs
6
Signature. Sign all checks the way you signed your name on the account signature card.
4
5
Memo. Most checks have a line in the lower left-hand corner for recording the purpose for which the money was spent. This information is important because it can be used in classifying expenditures or doing budget analyses.
Amount. Write the amount of the check twice – first in figures and then in words. Start writing far to the left so that no figures can be inserted.

1 Extension Note that in addition to charges for "bouncing" a check, banks may charge for printing checks and other services. To give the class a better idea of the sorts of things for which charges are assessed, have students volunteer to obtain schedules of services and fees from several local banks.

2 Interesting Note Many banks now offer second-chance check clearing. If a check bounces, it is sent back for a second try at collection. Banks find that about half of all bounced checks clear under this procedure.

1 Reinforcement Have students identify as many of the listed items as possible in Figure 10-3. (Only item 5 is not shown.)

Reconciling Your Bank Statement

Usually monthly the bank will send you a report on your account. This report, called a bank statement, is shown
1 in Figure 10–3.

Bank statements can vary. Most bank, however, statements show the following information:

1. Balance at the beginning of the period (opening balance).
2. Deposits made during the month.
3. Checks paid by the bank during the month.
4. Electronic fund transfers.
5. Special payments made at your request.
6. Service charges.
7. Balance at the end of the period (closing balance).

With your statement, the bank usually returns your canceled checks. Canceled checks are valuable records and should be saved. If your bank does not return canceled checks, be careful to save your statements as records.

Your monthly statement is your bank's summary of the same information you have recorded in your check register or stubs. The two should therefore match. If they do not, it is important to find out why. This process of bringing your check record and the bank statement into agreement is known as **reconciling** a bank statement.

Preparation Gather together your check register or stubs and your canceled checks. You'll also need paper and pencil and a calculator.

In your check register, put a mark next to all the checks you wrote that have been paid by your bank. Make a list of the checks you have written that have not yet been paid.

When you are trying to bring two figures into balance, it helps to work with them side by side. Therefore, to begin a

A bank statement is the bank's record of your checking account activity. ***How many checks were paid by the bank? How much was deposited into the account in interest?*** ▶

Caption Answer: Three checks were paid. There was interest of $2.27.

Figure 10–3 Bank Statement

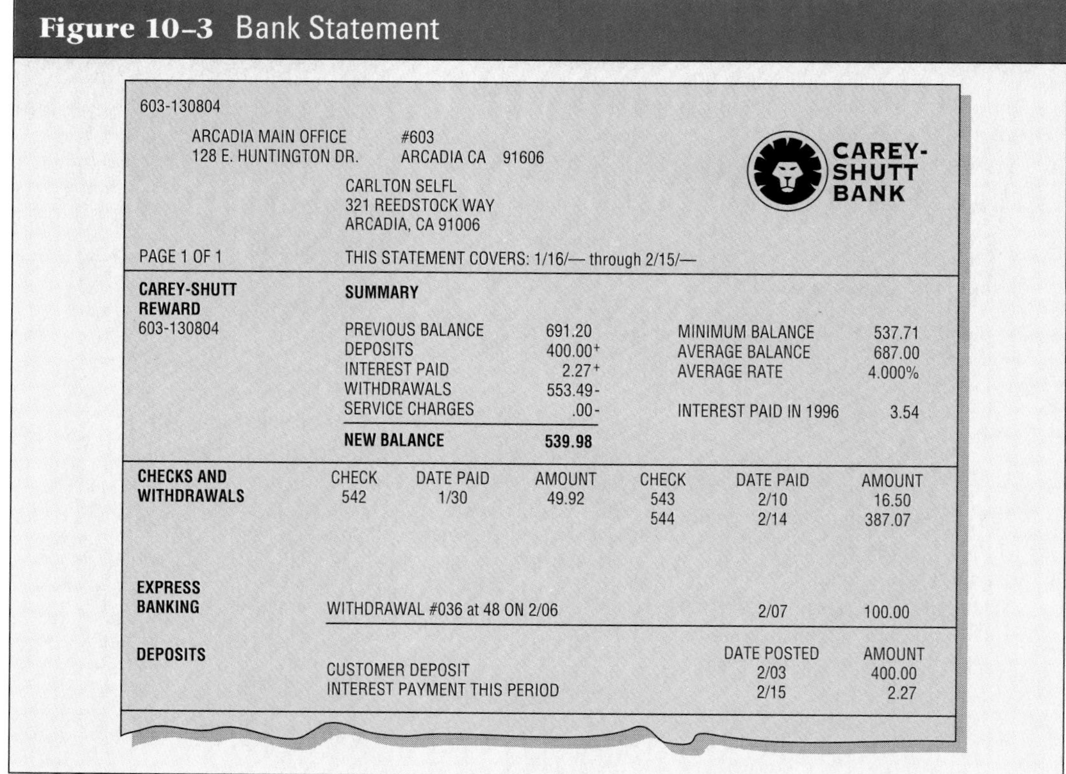

603-130804

ARCADIA MAIN OFFICE #603
128 E. HUNTINGTON DR. ARCADIA CA 91606

CARLTON SELFL
321 REEDSTOCK WAY
ARCADIA, CA 91006

CAREY-SHUTT BANK

PAGE 1 OF 1 THIS STATEMENT COVERS: 1/16/— through 2/15/—

CAREY-SHUTT REWARD 603-130804

SUMMARY

PREVIOUS BALANCE	691.20	MINIMUM BALANCE	537.71
DEPOSITS	400.00+	AVERAGE BALANCE	687.00
INTEREST PAID	2.27+	AVERAGE RATE	4.000%
WITHDRAWALS	553.49-		
SERVICE CHARGES	.00-	INTEREST PAID IN 1996	3.54
NEW BALANCE	**539.98**		

CHECKS AND WITHDRAWALS

CHECK	DATE PAID	AMOUNT	CHECK	DATE PAID	AMOUNT
542	1/30	49.92	543	2/10	16.50
			544	2/14	387.07

EXPRESS BANKING

WITHDRAWAL #036 at 48 ON 2/06	2/07	100.00

DEPOSITS

	DATE POSTED	AMOUNT
CUSTOMER DEPOSIT	2/03	400.00
INTEREST PAYMENT THIS PERIOD	2/15	2.27

bank reconciliation, divide a sheet of paper in half vertically. On the left side, write the balance from your bank statement. (This is the bank side of the worksheet.) On the right side, write the balance from your checkbook. (This is your side of the worksheet.)

Procedure The actual process of reconciliation involves two steps. These are carried out at the same time on both sides of the worksheet.

1. Add only items that should have been added to your account but were not.
   a. On the bank side, add deposits you have made and marked in your register but the bank has not yet recorded.
   b. On your side, add unrecorded deposits such as interest credited to your account.
2. Subtract all items that should have been charged to your account but were not.
   a. On the bank side, subtract any *outstanding checks*—checks that you have written but that the bank has not yet paid. You can get this information from the list you wrote after comparing your check register with the bank statement list or your canceled checks.
   b. On your side, subtract bank charges that you would not know about until you received your statement.

1 As in Figure 10–4, the two balances
2 should match. This single figure represents the actual amount in your account as of the statement date. If these balances do not match, check your work carefully. If you cannot find an error, take up the matter with your bank immediately.

Endorsing a Check

In addition to writing checks, you will also receive many checks, for example, paychecks. When you get a check, you can (1) cash it, (2) deposit it in your checking or savings account, or (3) transfer it to another person or to a business.

What Is an Endorsement? To use a check you receive, you must first write your name on the back. A signature on the back of a check is called an **endorsement.** It is written evidence that you

1 Math Application Have students reconcile the bank and checkbook balances when the bank balance is $583.12 and the checkbook balance is $572.75. There is a deposit in transit of $86.23 not yet recorded by the bank and a bank service charge of $7.50 not yet recorded by the depositor. Checks out ($10.24, $27.67, and $66.19) totaled $104.10. (Bank's side $583.12 + $86.23 − $104.10 = $565.25. Depositor's side: $572.75 − $7.50 = $585.25.

2 Extension Student Activity Workbook, Chapter 10 activities.

Figure 10–4 Reconciliation Statement

BANK		ME	
Statement Balance	$158.53	Register Balance	$218.00
Add: Deposits in transit	112.00	Add: Unrecorded deposits	—
	$270.53		$218.00
Subtract: Outstanding checks		Subtract: Service charge	4.00
#13 $15.83		Adjusted balance	$214.00
#14 19.70			
#15 21.00	56.53		
Adjusted balance	$214.00		

◄ *Some bank statements contain a reconciliation form.* ***How important is it to reconcile your bank statement?***

Caption Answer: Reconciliation is the only way you know if you and the bank have recorded the same information. If you don't reconcile your statement, you cannot be sure that the bank's information is accurate and you might not know the correct amount you have in your account.

FLASHBACK FLASHFORWARD

If you're choosing a bank today, you have fewer choices than you would have had 50 years ago. In 1943, there were 14,674 banks in the United States compared with only 11,997 in the 1990s.

have received payment from the bank or that you have transferred your right to payment to someone else.

When you endorse a check, sign your name in ink exactly as it is written on the face of the check. If your name is spelled wrong or if the drawer used, say, a nickname, first endorse the check with your name as it appears on the check. Then endorse it with your correct full-name signature.

Kinds of Endorsements There are at least three different kinds of endorsements. Each serves a different purpose.

- Blank endorsement. A blank endorsement consists only of the endorser's name. This endorsement makes the check payable to anyone who presents it at the bank on which it is drawn.
- Special endorsement. A special endorsement limits payment to a particular payee. An example of a special endorsement is "Pay to the order of Terry Johnson," followed by your signature. Terry Johnson must then endorse the check before cashing it.
- Restrictive endorsement. A restrictive endorsement limits the use of a check. If you write the words "For deposit only" above your signature, for example, the check can only be deposited in your account. If a check with such a restrictive endorsement is lost, it cannot be cashed by the finder.

Check Deposits

When you deposit a check, you cannot start spending the money at once. The bank can wait long enough to be sure the check you deposited is good.

The bank's requirements must be reasonable, however. Federal law specifies when funds for the following checks must be available to depositors:

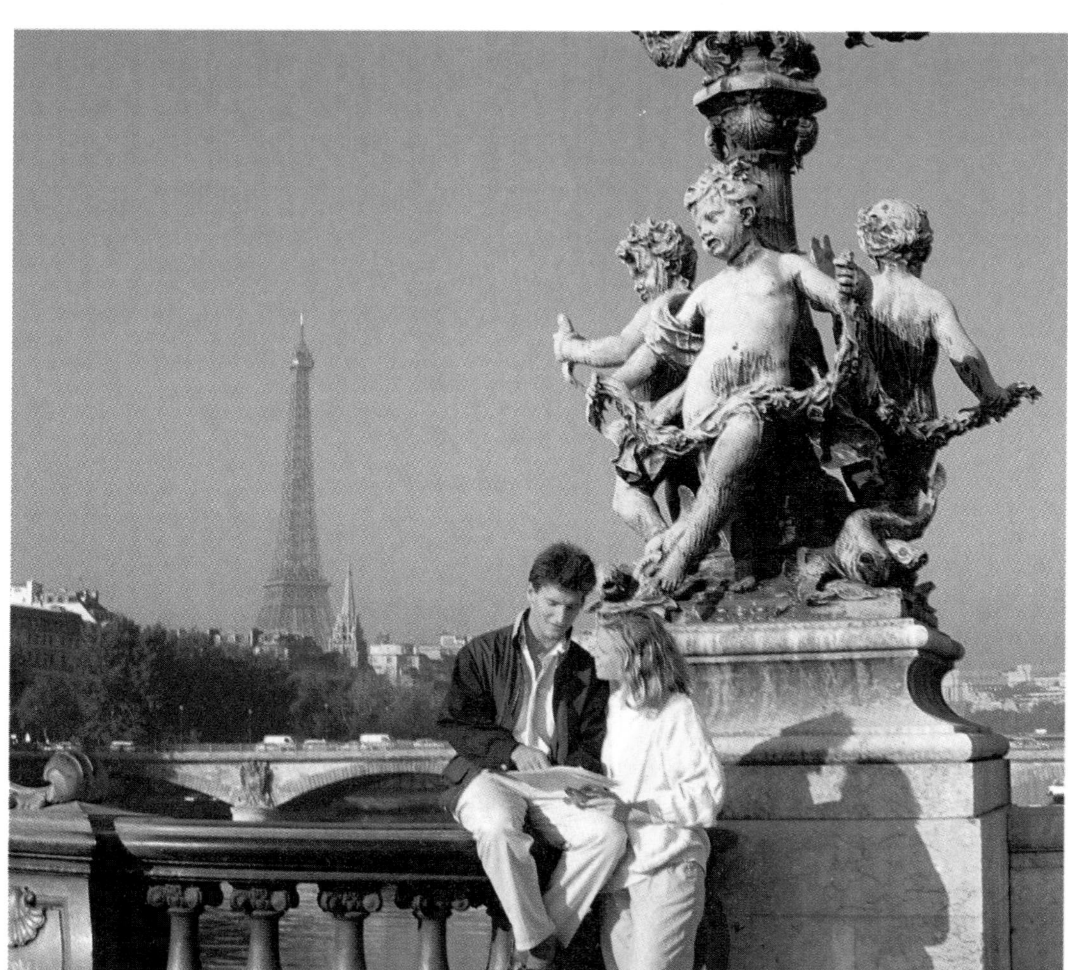

When you are traveling in another country, you can cash traveler's checks at a bank to get local currency. ***Are traveler's checks worth the expense and extra time you must allow for them?*** ▶

Caption Answer: For most people the answer is yes. Although traveler's checks cost money and may take some extra time, they are much safer to carry than cash. Unlike traveler's checks, cash cannot be replaced if it is lost or stolen.

- Checks drawn on other accounts at the same bank: the next business day after the day of deposit.
- Checks drawn on other local banks: the third business day after the day of deposit.
- Checks drawn on nonlocal banks: as long as seven business days after the day of deposit.

Magic Playgrounds

Most of the time, Bob Leathers is an architect and designer. At other times, he is also a dreamer who brings hope and happiness to children and communities around the country. Leathers helps groups with little money build playgrounds—often very imaginative and elaborate ones—with donated materials and equipment, and a lot of volunteers.

Leathers started building playgrounds when his local PTA had only enough money to buy a swing and a slide for his daughter's school. He showed PTA members how they could build great equipment themselves with salvaged materials.

On a project, the first thing Leathers does is consult his panel of "experts," the children who will use the playground. They may tell him they want a dark tunnel with Dracula at the end, a rope bridge, a fairy castle, spiderwebs, and mazes. He then sketches out the playground design, using as many of their ideas as possible.

Volunteers in the community, usually parents of the children who will use the playground, contact lumber companies, contractors, and builders. They arrange to have earthmoving equipment lent to them, and lumber and nails donated. Then members of the community supply the labor.

The first playground took 16 weekends to build. Today Leathers has refined the process so that it takes just one weekend to build a magic place. Often people passing by become so enchanted, they pitch in and swing hammers along with everyone else.

The rewards are great. Children get a safe, happy place to play. The community gets a feeling of camaraderie and neighborliness. Those are rewards that money can't buy.

Brainstorm

What would you look for in selecting a site for a playground, and what supplies and equipment would you need to build it?

Case Study Answer: Reasonably flat, centrally located site in a neighborhood, near a school; one that is visible to neighbors and passersby to provide child safety.

Sand, lumber, nails, ropes, cement, wheelbarrows, saws, hammers, grading equipment, small backhoe.

1 Math Application Have students compute the cost of the following traveler's check purchases, given a 1 percent service charge: **(a)** $250; **(b)** $600; **(c)** $1,000; **(d)** $2,500. ($2.50; $6; $10; $25.)

2 Vocabulary Ask students to provide a synonym for certified, as it is used in the term certified check. (Guaranteed.)

News Clip Answers:
1 First you should consider what your financial goals are. You should also think about whether the planner is paid by a flat fee or through commissions on the items he or she recommends.
2 It is important that you interview the financial planner to determine his or her qualifications and expertise. You should also check the background of your financial planner with local professional associations and the appropriate government agencies.

OTHER PAYMENT METHODS

If you do not have a checking account, you can still send money by mail and pay for items without using cash. There are several different methods you can use.

Money Orders

Suppose you belong to a mail-order CD club. To send a payment through the mail, you can buy a money order. Like a check, a money order is a written order to pay a specified amount to a particular person. Unlike a check, however, a money order is not drawn on a checking account. When you buy the money order, you must pay enough money to cover the money order amount plus a service charge, usually from 75 cents to $4. Money orders can be purchased in many places—banks, post offices, telegraph offices, and even convenience stores, and check-cashing businesses.

Telegraphic Money Order

In an emergency, the Money Transfer Service of Western Union can send money within minutes. Suppose you are visiting a friend in Chicago and you run out of money. You call your father in Los Angeles, asking him to send you money—say, $100. Your father goes to a Western Union office and pays the money in cash plus a fee. The cash will be waiting for you at the telegraph office in Chicago within 15 minutes. (If your father uses a credit card, delivery might take up to an hour.)

Transferring money in this manner is helpful in an emergency, but it is very expensive. The fee for transferring $100, for example, might be $15.

Traveler's Checks

1 Traveler's checks are similar to money orders: You pay for them in advance. You can buy traveler's checks in set amounts—$10. $20, $100—at banks, travel bureaus, S & Ls, American Express offices, and other places. You have to pay a service charge, usually 1 percent. Thus, $100 in traveler's checks would cost you $101.

A traveler's check has two signature lines. When you buy the checks, you sign each check on one line in front of the selling agent. When you cash a check, you sign it again, on the second line, in front of the payee. Traveler's checks are widely accepted because there is little chance of a check's not being signed by the right person.

When you buy traveler's checks, you should immediately write the serial numbers on the accompanying form. As you cash each check, note the date and place on the same form. Keep this record separate from your checks. That way, if the checks are lost or stolen, you will have a record of their numbers and the issuing agency can more quickly supply you with new checks.

Certified Checks

2 When you are paying a large amount of money, the payee may want some assurance that your check is good. In that case, you can have your check certified. A **certified check** is a personal check on which a bank has written its guarantee that payment will be made.

When the bank certifies your check, the amount is immediately subtracted from your account. You are not able to withdraw the money or use it for other checks. If the check is not used, you can return it to your bank and the bank will credit the amount to your account.

BANKING ELECTRONICALLY

The computer has long been an important tool used by tellers and bank employees to help with their jobs. Increasingly, however, it is being used by depositors in a variety of ways.

CASE STUDY

Consumer NEWS CLIP

How to Go About Choosing a Financial Planner

By Kathy M. Kristof
Los Angeles Times
October 23, 1994

The financial planning business is booming—and changing—thanks to an increasingly complex investment environment, societal changes and worries about the long-term viability of the nation's cornerstone retirement program.

For consumers looking for seasoned financial advice, the changes present both challenges and opportunities. With more choices than ever, it pays to know the score. How do you choose a financial planner? First, you need to understand a little bit about the business. Financial planners can be divided into three basic categories, differentiated by the way the planner is paid.

- Some planners are paid solely through commissions. You pay nothing for their advice, but the planner is likely to recommend investments that pay him or her a commission, such as so-called load mutual funds, insurance and limited partnerships.
- Fee-only planners charge by the hour or, in some cases, by the job. As a result, you could pay $1,000 or more to have a fee-only adviser create a financial blueprint for you and your family.
- A third group is paid both through commissions and fees. These planners typically charge a lower rate to draw up a comprehensive plan, but they are also likely to recommend some commission-paying investments.

Second, you need to know what you're looking for. Do you want someone to draw up a plan that will simply help you save for retirement or your children's college expenses? Or do you want a comprehensive plan that details your short- and long-term goals, provides a blueprint for your investments, saves taxes, and offers estate planning techniques?

Once you know what you want, you should begin to get referrals and interview planners. Ask friends and relatives for referrals. But if you're not impressed with these, get a referral from a professional association. The Institute of Certified Financial Planners (800-282-7526) will provide names, phone numbers, and biographical sketches of three certified financial planners in your area. All you have to do is ask. CFPs must adhere to strict educational and ethical guidelines laid down by the ICFP.

The final step is interviewing the planner. In addition to chatting about his or her background, education, and specialties, you should find out if he or she is certified and will provide you with sample plans prepared for others in your circumstances, as well as a copy of the disclosure statement he or she provides to the Securities and Exchange Commission.

Decisions, Decisions

1. What are some things you should consider when looking for a financial planner?
2. How would you go about checking the background of a financial planner?

Caption Answer: Some students may prefer ATMs and some, tellers. Consumers who like ATMs may like being able to bank at any time. They may prefer dealing with machines rather than with people, who may be rushed or unresponsive to them. Consumers who like using tellers may not trust machines to be accurate, or they may feel tellers are more reliable with cash deposits, or they may simply prefer dealing with people to dealing with machines.

Electronic funds transfer has changed how many people bank. ***Do you prefer to bank by automated teller or with a teller? Why would consumers prefer one way over another?*** ▼

Electronic Fund Transfers

An **electronic fund transfer (EFT)** is the moving of money from one account to another by computer. No cash changes hands. No checks are written. The only paper record is the receipt you get as proof of the transaction.

Automated Teller Machines Automated teller machines are computer stations that can be used only for certain banking purposes. The great advantage of automated tellers is that they give you access to your funds at any hour on any day. You can use an EFT card, with your *personal identification number* (PIN), to deposit or withdraw money or even to get a loan or buy traveler's checks.

Automated Bill Payment You can arrange to make large recurring payments (such as loan payments) electronically. You just keep funds in your checking or savings accounts until payment is due. Then, you use the phone to arrange for the transfer of funds to make the payment.

Debit and Check Cards With an EFT debit, or check, card, you make purchases at more and more stores and service stations. To use this card, you use a special computer at the store. The purchase amount is deducted from your account and transferred to the store's account.

Banking from Home If you own a computer, you can pay most bills electronically from home. Some banks offer banking software programs for home computers. In addition, you need to have equipment—called a modem—that connects your computer to the telephone lines.

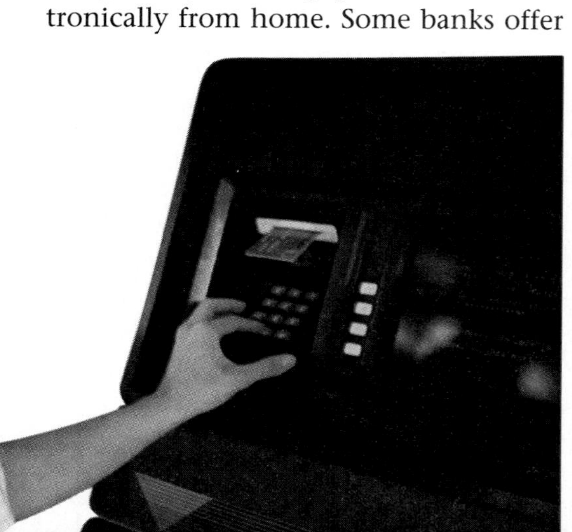

Electronic Banking Fees

All these conveniences come with a price, however. The ATM card itself might cost you $6 annually, and a replacement card $3. Some banks that once paid depositors to use the ATM now charge customers for each electronic transaction, for example, $1 for a deposit or a withdrawal.

Despite the charges for electronic banking, banks sometimes charge customers as much as $3 for dealing with human tellers at the bank instead of using ATMs. Executives at these banks feel that tellers' wages are high. They want customers to use ATMs instead of tellers so they can hire fewer tellers and pay less in wages.

Consumer Protection

In 1979, Congress passed the Electronic Fund Transfer Act as protection for consumers using some forms of electronic banking. The act says that banks must offer consumers a record, or receipt, for all computer transactions. They must also investigate all errors and report back to the consumer within ten business days of being told of the problem.

Consumers, for their part, must report losses of EFT cards in a timely fashion. If you report a lost card within two days, you are liable (responsible) for up to $50 resulting from someone's use of your lost card. If you wait longer, you are liable for up to $500. If "longer" extends beyond two months, your liability is unlimited.

An EFT card is useless without the personal identification number that goes with it. Your best protection, therefore, is to keep your PIN completely secret. Do not write it down or tell it to anyone.

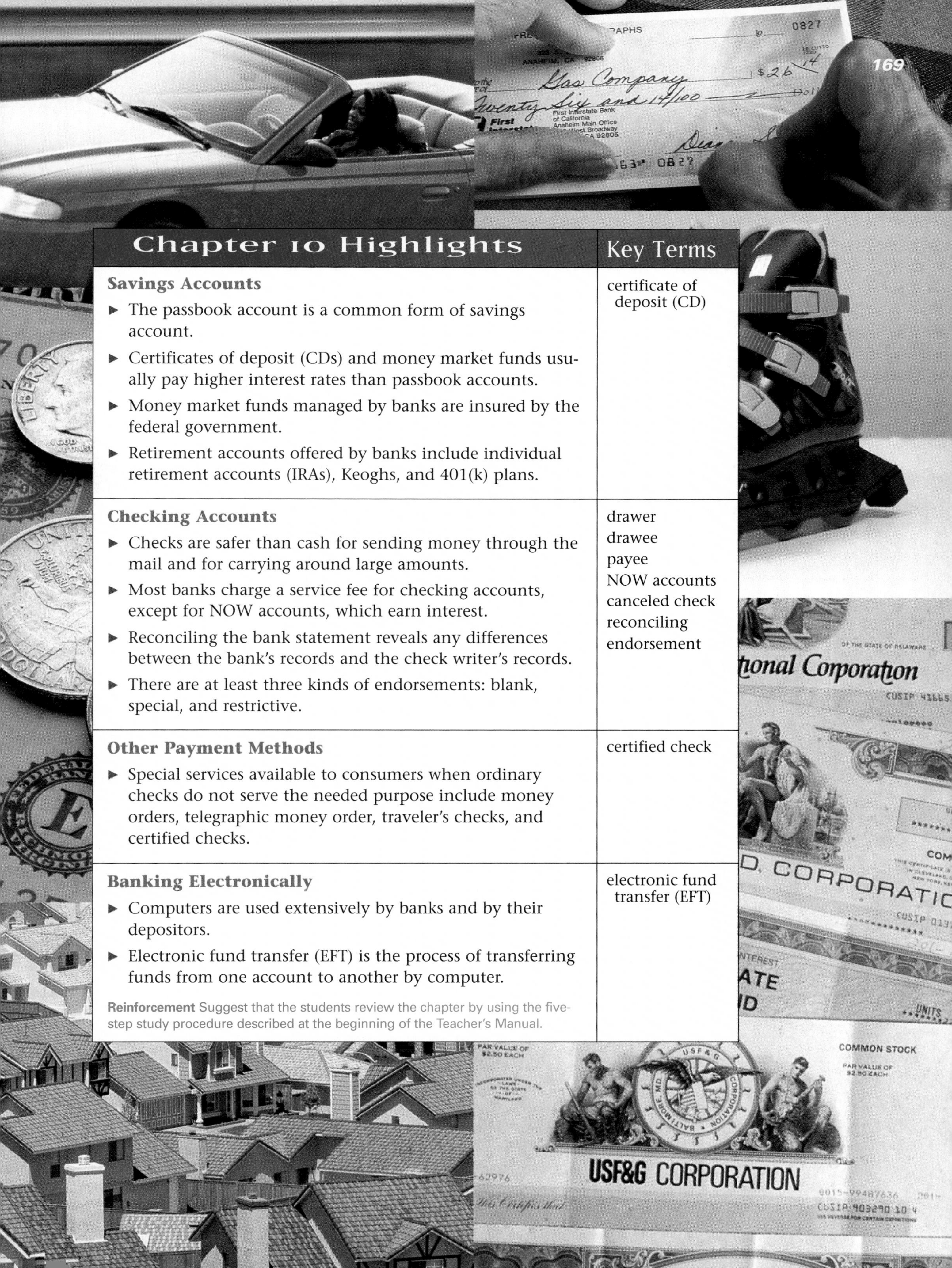

Chapter 10 Highlights	Key Terms
Savings Accounts ▶ The passbook account is a common form of savings account. ▶ Certificates of deposit (CDs) and money market funds usually pay higher interest rates than passbook accounts. ▶ Money market funds managed by banks are insured by the federal government. ▶ Retirement accounts offered by banks include individual retirement accounts (IRAs), Keoghs, and 401(k) plans.	certificate of deposit (CD)
Checking Accounts ▶ Checks are safer than cash for sending money through the mail and for carrying around large amounts. ▶ Most banks charge a service fee for checking accounts, except for NOW accounts, which earn interest. ▶ Reconciling the bank statement reveals any differences between the bank's records and the check writer's records. ▶ There are at least three kinds of endorsements: blank, special, and restrictive.	drawer drawee payee NOW accounts canceled check reconciling endorsement
Other Payment Methods ▶ Special services available to consumers when ordinary checks do not serve the needed purpose include money orders, telegraphic money order, traveler's checks, and certified checks.	certified check
Banking Electronically ▶ Computers are used extensively by banks and by their depositors. ▶ Electronic fund transfer (EFT) is the process of transferring funds from one account to another by computer. **Reinforcement** Suggest that the students review the chapter by using the five-step study procedure described at the beginning of the Teacher's Manual.	electronic fund transfer (EFT)

CHAPTER 10 REVIEW

Refer students to the Reviewing Consumer Terms and Reviewing Facts and Ideas activities in the Student Activity Workbook.

Reviewing Consumer Terms
Puzzles will vary. See Glossary for definitions.

Reviewing Facts and Ideas
See the Student Activity Workbook for answers.

Problem Solving and Decision Making
1 a traveler's check; **b** personal check; **c** telegraphic money order; **d** personal check or money order; **e** personal check.
2 Bank: $531.63 + $84.11 = $615.74; $615.74 − $172.94 = $442.80.
Me: $444.40 − $1.50 = $442.80.

Consumers Around the World Math
For their essays, students should research the current U.S. rate of inflation. Parents and others may tell students that items cost much less when inflation was lower. Students should conclude that when the inflation rate is higher than the rate of interest in your savings account, the value of your savings goes down.

Reviewing Consumer Terms

Build a crossword puzzle using the terms below. Use graph paper to arrange your entries Then write short definitions for them.

canceled checks
certificate of deposit
certified check
drawee
drawer
electronic fund transfer
endorsement
NOW accounts
payee
reconciling

Reviewing Facts and Ideas

1. Why might a saver choose a certificate of deposit account over a passbook savings account? What disadvantages does it have, if any?
2. Describe the procedure for reconciling a bank statement.
3. How does a NOW account differ from most other checking accounts?
4. Describe the protective features of traveler's checks.
5. List four types of electronic fund transfers.

Problem Solving and Decision Making

1. Listed here are some of the payments that Laura Preston made during April. What method of payment other than cash would you have recommended in each case?
   a. While on vacation, Laura bought a wooden sculpture at a Honolulu souvenir shop.
   b. Laura paid her telephone bill at the local telephone company office.
   c. Laura's brother had a car accident 1,000 miles from home. Laura sent her brother $350 by the fastest method.
   d. Laura paid her federal income tax.
   e. Laura paid $1.80 for a quart of oil at a local gas station.
2. Reconcile your checkbook balance with your bank balance, given the following data.

   Bank statement closing balance: $531.63

   Checkbook balance: $444.30

   Outstanding checks: $60.36, $10.21, $23.61, $78.76

   Service charge: $1.50

   Deposits not shown on statement: $84.11

Building Academic Skills

Consumers Around the World

Math

1. Greece's inflation rate in one recent year was 8.9 percent, the lowest in more than two decades. The government of Greece hoped

to slow the rate to only 7 percent in the next year. How does that compare with today's inflation rate in the United States? (Newspapers report this rate each month.)

Technology

2. As computers and modems become more common in the home, more people are taking advantage of banking from home. Visit a local bank where at home banking is offered. Find out what kind of computer, software, and other hardware someone needs to take advantage of this service. Are there extra fees? What are the advantages? Disadvantages? Report your findings to the class.

Communications

3. Imagine you are about to embark on a trip to Laos and Thailand. Research how you will handle carrying money while on your trip. Will you use traveler's check? Are they honored in most places in the countries you will visit? Write a 250-word report which discusses our findings.

Beyond the Classroom

Consumer Project

Prepare an exhibit of materials collected from local banks. Include the following: checks, checkbooks, deposit slips, passbooks, and signature cards. Collect any other printed material related to customer account services that is available.

Cooperative Learning

Family Economics

Break into assigned family groups. Discuss the following problem.

Every month your family must make certain regular payments—the rent, the gas and electric bills, the phone bill. None of the businesses involved accept cash for mailed payments. Most banks in your area offer free checking and money orders only to depositors having at least $10,000 in savings. Otherwise there are several charges: $6 per month for service plus 15 cents per check for checking accounts; $2 for each money order (non-depositors pay $3.50). Note: The current maximum fee for a *postal* money order is 75 cents for amounts up to $700.

How do you pay your bills? Compare your answers with those of other family groups.

Debate the Issue

Charges for bank services have escalated in recent years. Those who complain about the cost of bank services allege that banks operate in a protected environment and in return ought to provide banking services to U.S. citizens at a reasonable price. Others maintain that banks, just like most businesses have the right to decide to charge for their services.

You and your classmates will break into two groups and research this topic. Each group will gather evidence to support one side or the other. You are to prepare the argument for your side of the problem. Then the two groups will meet in a classroom debate.

Technology
2 Student reports should include answers to all questions.

Communications
3 Student papers should discuss the various ways of handling currency while traveling and discuss whether traveler's checks are accepted in Laos and Thailand.

Consumer Project
Exhibits should vary from one another. Encourage students to write informative labels for their items.

Family Economics
Only two families qualify for free checking. Those on the tightest budgets might not be able to afford the monthly fees for a checking account. For them, the cheapest alternative would be to pay bills in person and use postal money orders when this is not possible. All others will have to decide whether the convenience of paying by mail is worth $6 and more a month.

Debate the Issue
Break the class into two teams. Assign each team one side of the issue. Encourage students to work together as a team to develop their argument. Ask each team to select a member to make an opening statement that supports the team's side of the issue. Have students take turns debating as the debates moves from one team to the other.

THE WALL STREET JOURNAL.
MONEY & INVESTI
Growth Investing May Be Po
ARKETS DIARY
Dow Jones Industrial Average
ABREAST OF THE
COMMON STOCK
NUMBER
CC034414
UNITED STATES SAVINGS BOND
THE UNITED STATES OF AMERICA
SERIES EE
INTEREST CEASES 30 YEARS FROM ISSUE DATE
FIFTY DOLLARS
ONE THOUSAND DOLLARS
American Bank Note Company

CHAPTER 11

Making Investments

Learning Objectives

When you have finished studying this chapter, you should be able to:

1. Identify the four factors that should guide consumers in planning an investment strategy.
2. Explain the differences between stocks and bonds.
3. Describe ways to invest in stocks and bonds.

Consumer Terms

portfolio
stock
stockholder
capital gain
preferred stock
common stock
bond
maturity date
stockbroker
commission
stock exchange

Real-World Journal

Imagine that you have $2,500 to buy stock in five different companies. Using the business section of a newspaper, pick five companies that you believe will perform well and note today's stock purchase prices in your journal. Each day, for one week, check your stocks' performance and list the changes in your journal. How did your stocks do?

Lesson Plan See the Teacher's Manual for Chapter 11 lesson plan.

Vocabulary The Chapter 11 lesson plan includes suggested vocabulary activities for the terms listed.

1 Discussion Starter
Ask students about goals they have set for themselves. Ask how they plan to finance their goals. Have students write down their five-, ten-, and twenty-year goals and save them.

INVESTMENT STRATEGY

The money you have saved in your savings account is an investment. However, as you earn more and more income, you may be able to invest your money in ways that will produce higher rates of interest than bank accounts do.

To invest wisely and to build a strong investment **portfolio** (collection of investments), you need a sound and sensible investment strategy. Your strategy should be based on your financial goals, a knowledge of investment options, a sense of how much risk you feel comfortable with, and good professional advice.

Investment Goals

You probably have dreams about
1 what you want to do in your life. Perhaps you want to go to college. Maybe you want to buy a horse ranch some day or travel around the world. Certainly, you will want to be able to live comfortably when you retire.

The first step in creating an investment strategy is to decide what goals are important to you. Write down what you hope to do in the next five years, ten years, and twenty years. Of course, your goals will change as you go through life. However, if you get into the habit of thinking ahead, you'll be able to change your investment strategy whenever you change your goals.

Knowledge of Investment Options

Some investments are better than others. Every year, people lose millions by investing in "hot tips," phony business ventures, and get-rich-quick schemes.

To make intelligent decisions, you need to know about the kinds of investments that are available. This chapter discusses the most common investment options for consumers.

You can continue to learn about investment possibilities in the following ways:

- Read books, magazines, and newspapers.
- Join an investment club, where you can study investment with other people.
- Take courses in financial planning.
- Discuss investment with relatives and friends who are knowledgeable.

Risk

The big difference between investments with high earnings and those with low earnings is the risk of losing your

Caption Answer: Students may want to travel, go to college, buy a house, or have a family. Some may have other goals. They can achieve these goals financially through working, saving, and investing.

Everyone has goals in life. ***What goals do you have? How can you achieve them financially?*** ▼

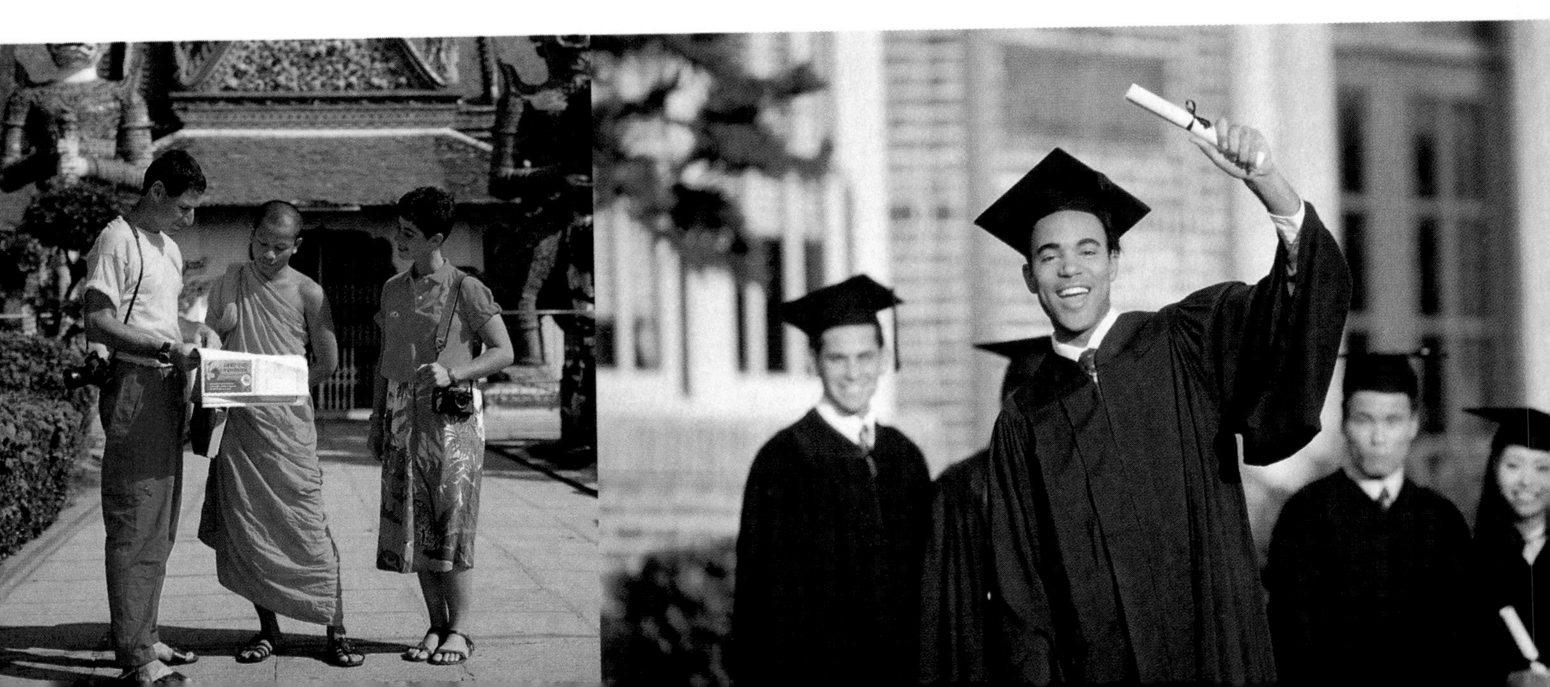

money. For investments such as savings accounts, the risk is virtually nonexistent. As you have read, the federal government insures bank deposits up to $100,000.

For investments such as stocks, the risk is much greater. The amount you earn on a stock could far exceed the interest paid on a savings account. However, the firm issuing the stock could fail. Then you would lose your money.

On the other hand, there is also a kind of risk to keeping all your money in very safe investments. Savings bonds and savings accounts have fixed interest rates that may not keep up with inflation. Then consumer prices would go up faster than your earnings. The value of your investment might not grow much; it might even decline.

Ask yourself how you feel about risking your money on the chance of greater earnings. Workers in their twenties who are earning a lot and have few expenses may feel they can make risky investments. If they lose some money, they have the time and means to earn more.

A couple in their forties who want to send a child through college in a few years may choose less risky investments. If they lose the tuition money, they will have
1 neither the time nor the means of saving
2 enough for their goal.

Professional Advice

Consumers who need every penny to pay basic expenses should probably put their money into a savings account. Those who decide to risk their *extra* money for possible high profits should learn as much as they can on their own and then seek the advice of investment experts.

Banks, brokerage firms, and independent financial planners offer advice about investments. Find an advisor with a reputable firm, and evaluate critically all the advice you are given. Remember that advisors may try to sell you the invest-
3 ment products offered by their firms.

TYPES OF SECURITIES

There are many different types of investment securities open to individuals. Two—stocks and bonds—are among the most familiar. Both corporations and governments raise money by issuing bonds. Only corporations issue stock.

Stocks

A corporation can divide its ownership into equal pieces that can be sold to investors. Each piece is called a share. Taken together, the ownership shares in

1 Discussion Starter Ask students if they like to take risks or play it safe. Compare financial risk-taking with other forms of risk-taking—driving a car, traveling to another country, playing football. In each case, ask, Is the potential benefit worth the risk?

2 Learning Economics Ask students to summarize the role of risk in a market economy. (One of the principal factors that determines who benefits from the economic system—people are rewarded according to the contribution they make and the economic risks they take.)

3 Critical Thinking Ask students why it is a good idea to learn as much as you can about investments before consulting an expert. (The more you know, the better you can understand what an expert says and determine whether the recommendations are appropriate for you.)

1 Math Application Assume the purchase of 100 shares of EZ Pro stock at $40 a share. The stock is held for three years and pays dividends of $1 per share each year. At the end of three years, it is sold for $47 a share. Have the students compute the total return on the stock. ($300 + [$4,700 − $4,000] = $300 + $700 = $1,000)

2 Reinforcement Refer students once again to the EZ Pro example (previous annotation). Ask them to identify the capital gain in that transaction. ($4,700 sales price − $4,000 purchase price = $700 capital gain) Then have them write an equation summarizing how to compute *return on investment.* (Dividends + capital gains = return on investment.)

3 Interesting Note For many years stock ownership has been divided almost evenly between men and women.

4 Interesting Note At least 25 large corporations have paid dividends every year for over 100 years. The Bank of New York Company, for example, has not missed a dividend since 1784.

Taking Stock

The total value amount of the various securities, such as bonds and stock issued by corporations, that are traded in the U.S. stock market is more than $5,250 billion. The stock market in Japan trades about $3,000 billion; in Pakistan, $11 billion; and in Colombia, about $10 billion.

1 a corporation are known as the corporation's **stock.** Corporations sell their stock to raise money, or capital. Stock is sold in round lots (100 shares) or in odd lots, say, 25 or 140 shares.

The value of a share of stock can vary greatly over time. One day it may be worth much more than the stockholder paid for it. The next day it may be worth much less. The **stockholder** is the person who owns the stock. If you are interested in buying stocks, you should first answer three important questions.

1. If I buy stock, will I still be able to feed, clothe, and shelter myself and my family?
2. If I buy stock, will I still have enough ready cash to meet emergencies?
3. Do I have enough insurance to protect those who depend on me?

If you can answer yes, you might consider investing your extra money in stock. Although investments in stock are very risky, they can produce very big profits, known as capital gains.

2 **Capital gain** is the profit you get when you sell property like stock. For example, if you purchase stock at $50 a share and sell at $75, your capital gain per share is $25.

Stock is classified as preferred stock or common stock. The classification depends
3 on the ownership privileges of the stock.

Preferred Stocks **Preferred stock** is stock that pays a fixed dividend and carries no voting privileges for its owner. Whether the corporation does well or not, owners of preferred stock always receive the same amount in dividends. Preferred stock owners may not vote on how to run the corporation. A key benefit of owning preferred stocks is there is generally less risk. If a company goes bankrupt, preferred stockholders are paid before common stockholders.

Common Stock **Common stock** is stock that does not pay a fixed dividend and does carry voting rights for the stockholder. The amount of the dividend is determined each time by the corporation. The stockholder can vote on how to run the company. A key benefit of owning common stocks is that the price typically increases more than with preferred stocks.

Other Stock Categories Stocks can be categorized by risk. The categories reflect how often prices go up and down and how likely investors are to receive dividends.

- *Blue chip stocks.* The stocks of the largest corporations with long, steady records of paying dividends are called blue chip stocks. Shares of stock from American Telephone and Telegraph (AT&T), General Motors, and
4 DuPont, for example, fall into this category.
- *Growth stocks.* These stocks are issued by corporations whose sales and

earnings are growing faster than the economy and faster than the average for the industry. These firms use their profits to expand their plants and develop new products.

- *Speculative stocks.* These stocks sell at a high price compared to what the company earnings have been. A price of $1 per share is high if the company has no earnings to show. Investors in speculative stocks buy because they believe that earnings will be great in the future.

Bonds

Corporations and governments can obtain funds by borrowing. They borrow by issuing bonds. A **bond** is a promise made by a corporation or government to pay an investor a certain amount of money, plus interest, at a specified future time. The amount of interest, which is paid annually, remains the same every year for the term of the loan. A bond is a fixed-return investment.

Suppose the city council of Orangeville wants to raise $1 million to fix up its civic center and add a playground. It plans to issue (sell) a thousand bonds. Each bond will have a face value of $1,000. The face value is the amount printed on the front. Each bond will pay 8 percent interest ($80) every year for ten years.

Maria Kriparos pays $1,000 for one bond. She keeps the bond for ten years, until its **maturity date,** which is the date Orangeville will pay back the $1,000 value of the bond. In addition,
1 Orangeville will have paid her $80 interest every year—a total of $800.

The Orangeville bond is an example of a municipal bond. It is only one of three types of bonds available to investors.

1 Math Application
EZ Pro wants to raise $15 million by issuing ten-year bonds at 8.7 percent annual interest. Each bond will have a face value of $5,000. Have the students compute the amount they would earn if they were to purchase six of the bonds and hold them for their full term. ($5,000 face value × .087 interest rate = $435 interest; $435 × 6 bonds = $2,610 interest per year; $2,610 × 10 years = $26,100 total earned.)

Caption Answer: Some investors do consider the ethical as well as financial criteria for investing. Before the abolition of apartheid, many students would not buy securities of corporations that operated in South Africa. Some students may support bonds for bridges as more useful and positive. Some may prefer bonds that build prisons as not necessary.

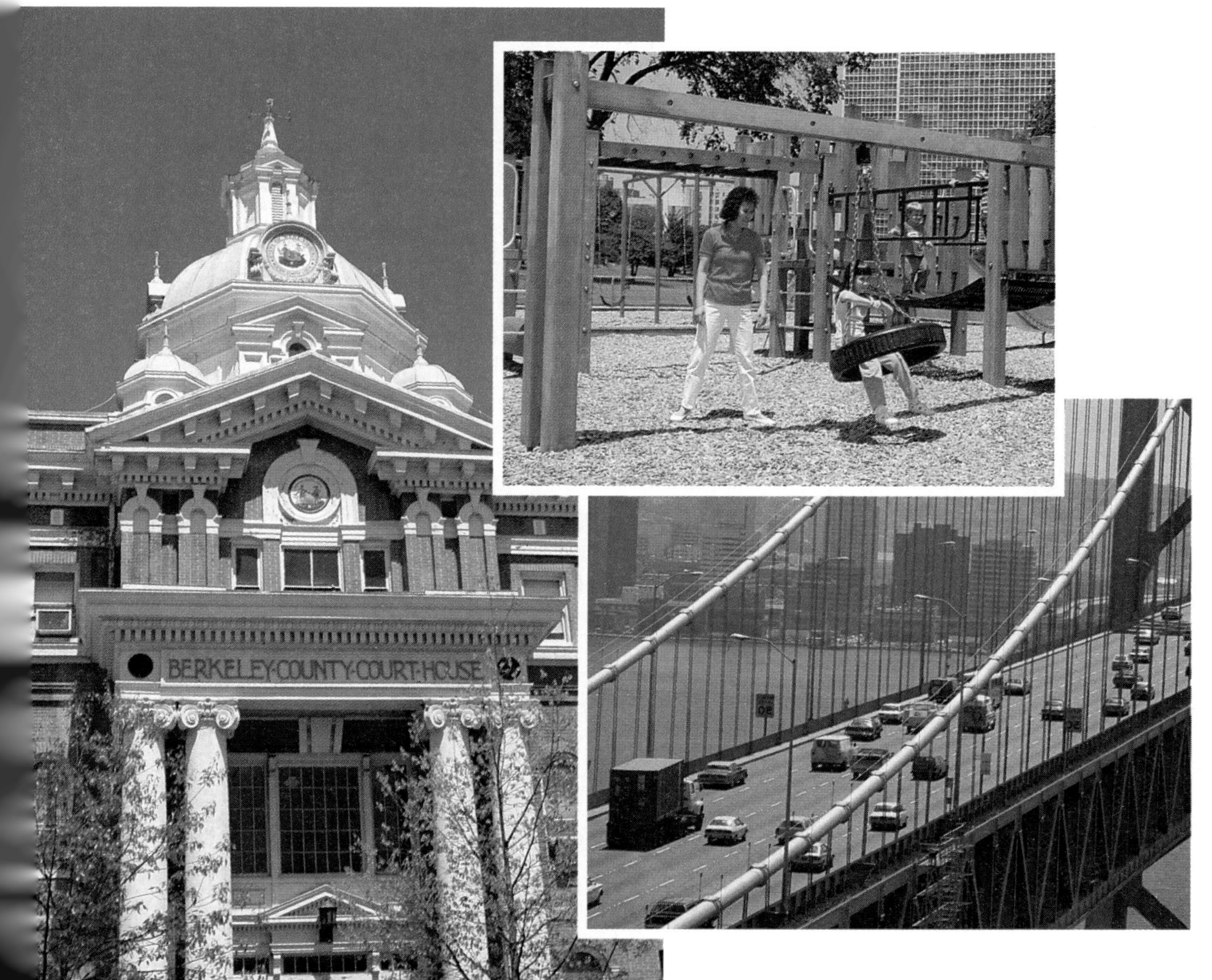

◀ *Municipalities use the money raised from bond issues to create parks, government buildings, and other amenities.* ***Should the purpose that a bond will be used make a difference to the investor? Would you choose to buy a bond that will support the building of a bridge over a bond that will support the building of a prison?***

FLASHBACK FLASHFORWARD

Why all the commotion on the trading floor of the New York Stock Exchange? Because there are more stock exchange transactions than ever before. In 1950, approximately 525 million transactions took place. Today, approximately 40 to 47 billion transactions take place yearly.

Municipal Bonds These securities are issued by state and local governments. The purpose of municipal bonds is to raise money to finance government services and improvements.

A unique advantage of buying municipal bonds is that the interest they earn is not taxable by the federal government. Most states also do not tax the interest earned on municipal bonds issued by their own cities.

Corporate Bonds Corporate bonds are bought through brokerage houses or banks, normally in minimum amounts of $1,000. A corporation may issue bonds to get money to make improvements such as developing new products. If the firm does well, it will be able to repay the borrowed money plus interest when the bonds reach their maturity.

Federal Government Bonds The federal government borrows money by issuing government bonds through the Treasury Department. Unlike savings bonds, these are issued for definite periods of time. In other words, they cannot be redeemed before their maturity dates, with or without penalty. They must be resold instead. There are three types of treasury securities.

- *Treasury bills.* Known as T-bills, these securities have the shortest maturity period of all government debts—from 13 to 52 weeks. They are also the most easily converted to cash. The minimum purchase is $10,000.
- *Treasury notes.* These securities mature in from one to ten years, pay interest semiannually, and are sold in denominations of $1,000 to $5,000.
- *Treasury bonds.* Treasury bonds generally have a minimum maturity of ten years and are considered to be long-term investments. Interest is paid semiannually. The bonds are usually sold in denominations of $1,000 and $10,000.

Not as Good as It Sounds—Phone Solicitation

Generally avoid buying anything in response to telephone solicitation. Consumer groups estimate that at least 10 percent of telephone solicitations—known as telemarketing—are fraudulent. The Federal Trade Commission prohibits those phone calls between 9:00 P.M. and 8:00 A.M. The caller must state up front that it is a sales call and the cost of the product or service. If you are interested, ask for printed information to be sent to you—don't feel pressured by someone imposing a time limit. Be especially wary of being asked to invest money or to register to win a prize. The odds of winning must be disclosed and no purchase must be necessary to enter a drawing or other contest.

HOW TO INVEST

You can buy stocks and bonds in a number of ways. Your bank may offer some investment services. You can buy Treasury securities directly from the Treasury Department. The sale of all securities is regulated by the Securities and Exchange Commission.

Direct Sales of Stock

Many companies let investors buy shares of stock directly from the firm. You call the corporation and ask for a registration form. You then return the filled-in form together with the money for an initial purchase. Once you are signed up, it is even easier to buy additional shares in that company in the future. Most amateur investors, however, do not feel secure enough to choose and purchase stock without professional help.

Mutual Funds

Suppose you have saved some extra money—$1,000—and would like to invest in stocks. You want to spread the risk of loss by not putting all your money into the stock of just one company. However, buying in lots of one hundred (called round lots) in even a small number of companies can cost thousands of dollars. You can still invest in stocks by putting your money into mutual funds. A mutual fund is an investment company that pools the contributions of many investors in order to buy securities. Figure 11–1 on page 180 shows how a mutual fund works.

Working at Rehabilitation

Bob Cote was a great salesman, but depression over his breakup with his girlfriend led him into serious drinking. Within a year, Cote had lost his home, his business, and his friends, and he was living on Denver's skid row.

For a long while, Cote denied he had a problem. Then one day, he faced the truth and realized that unless he stopped drinking, he had no future. He stopped then and there and vowed he would help others do the same.

Cote began to challenge other drug and alcohol abusers on skid row to work with him at putting their lives back together. Some were not interested in helping themselves. Others supported him, however, and began working to regain their self respect.

First, of course, they had to stop drinking and using drugs. Then Cote used his sales skills to get them jobs. He was tough on those who lived in the shelter he set up. If they did not make their beds, they had to sleep on the floor. When they vandalized the bathroom, he nailed the door shut for a day. They had to attend Alcoholics Anonymous. Anyone using drugs or alcohol was thrown out.

Cote believed that handouts cost people their self respect. So people staying at his shelter did not stay free. They paid $5 a day in rent and they had to cook their own meals.

Cote has supported the shelter with donations, his own funds, and his ability to get support from the community. His shelter has served 2,000 people. According to Cote, one third of them have remained sober and gone back to work. He continues to work on the rest.

Brainstorm

If you were running a rehabilitation center, what rules would you make for participants?

Case Study Answer
No substance abuse; curfew; no vandalism; no fighting; no stealing; residents must look for work or work every day; they must pay rent; must help with chores and food preparation.

1 Critical Thinking Be sure that students understand the relationships of the principals involved in a stock transaction. Point out that full-service brokers usually get to keep 35 to 40 percent of the commission they charge. Ask the students who gets the remaining 60 to 65 percent. (The brokerage house that employs the broker gets the rest.)

2 Reinforcement Student Activity Workbook, Chapter 11 activities.

Case Study Answers: **1** The details of one's financial situation are considered a relatively taboo subject in our society. It can take a lot of digging and prodding to get people to disclose those details— and bulldozing your way through is not likely to get results. Patiently asking a series of questions, moving slowly to the heart of the matter, is often the best strategy. **2** Answers will vary.

You can buy mutual fund shares directly from some mutual funds. These usually advertise in newspapers and financial magazines. You can also buy mutual fund shares from professionals who specialize in selling securities.

Before you invest in a mutual fund, make sure to read the fund's prospectus. The prospectus, a document required by the SEC, tells you the fund's goals, risks, history, and fees.

Stockbrokers

1 A **stockbroker** is a dealer in stocks and bonds. Full-service brokers buy and sell securities for customers, recommend
2 stocks for purchase and sale, and advise

Figure 11-1 Mutual Funds and the Small Investor

A mutual fund pools the contribution of many investors in order to buy securities.

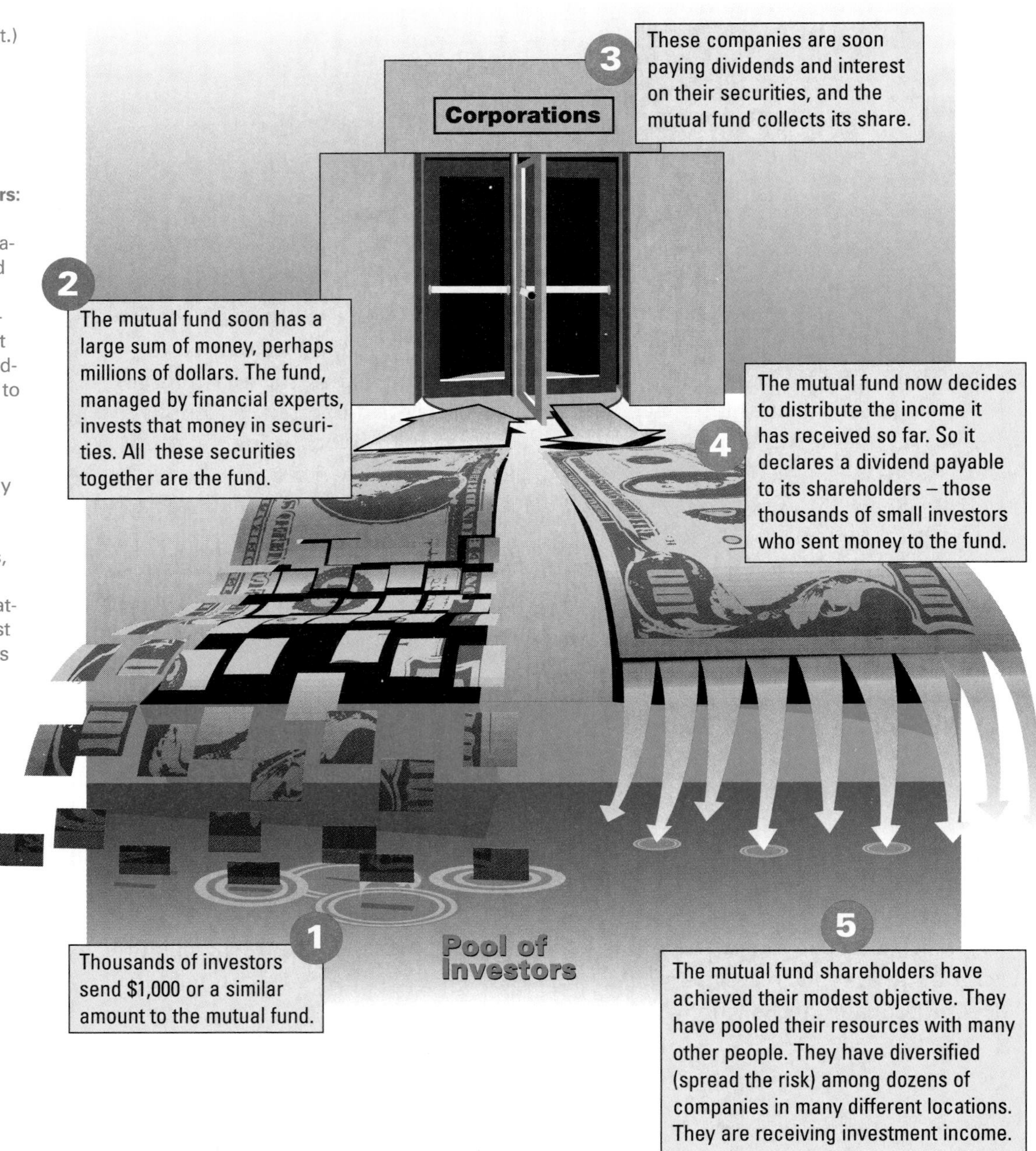

Corporations
Pool of Investors
1 Thousands of investors send $1,000 or a similar amount to the mutual fund.
2 The mutual fund soon has a large sum of money, perhaps millions of dollars. The fund, managed by financial experts, invests that money in securities. All these securities together are the fund.
3 These companies are soon paying dividends and interest on their securities, and the mutual fund collects its share.
4 The mutual fund now decides to distribute the income it has received so far. So it declares a dividend payable to its shareholders – those thousands of small investors who sent money to the fund.
5 The mutual fund shareholders have achieved their modest objective. They have pooled their resources with many other people. They have diversified (spread the risk) among dozens of companies in many different locations. They are receiving investment income.

CASE STUDY

Careers in Focus

Margaret Lofaro, Certified Financial Planner

After ten years as a certified financial planner, Margaret Lofaro, 57, has discovered the secret of success. "Successful money management," she explains, "is the foundation for successful living. Money is the structure that enables everything else to happen. It provides you with the freedom to be who you want to be and to do what you want to do."

So does that mean that only the rich can live satisfied, successful lives? "Absolutely not," Lofaro insists. "You don't have to have a lot of money. You only have to have enough—enough to meet the goals that you've set for yourself."

For the vast majority of people who have not set goals, who are not saving and who feel completely out of control with their money, Lofaro is the ideal advisor. She was an elementary school teacher before she turned her investment hobby into a business and thus brings to her job patience, the ability to listen, and a calming sense of confident guidance.

She starts by sitting down with clients and asking what money means to them. Answers like "security" and "freedom" are common. Next, she tries to get her clients to describe their dreams—the things that would make them believe they were living the good life. Once she has a framework for understanding her clients' hopes and habits, she looks at their income and expenses, piecing together a strategy for spending, saving, and investing.

The rigorous training and testing needed to become a certified financial planner have armed Lofaro with expertise in everything from stocks to individual retirement accounts (IRAs) to employee 401Ks. Lofaro can therefore structure the complete financial picture of an individual or small business. Although every plan is highly personalized, Lofaro has basic advice for all clients. Among the most important words are to stop frittering away money on daily incidentals and to take the first 15 percent of their income and set it aside for savings. "What's the point of working," Lofaro asks, "if you don't pay yourself?"

Lofaro has seen clients save enough money to purchase dream homes, put children through college, and make huge strides toward securing financial independence for their later years. She has helped young entrepreneurs move from garage operations to beautiful custom studios with a staff of well-paid employees. More frequently, she sees people transform a chaotic relationship with money into a controlled one.

"These are huge satisfactions," she explains, "both for my clients and for me." They are so huge, in fact, that Lofaro believes "money management is one of the highest services a person can contribute to society."

Case Study Review

1. Why is patience a virtue for a financial planner?
2. Ask three adults you know how much of their income they save each month and in what form. Record the answers, but also record how you felt asking the questions and how the adults seemed to feel answering such questions.

1 Critical Thinking Ask students what advantages and disadvantages they think the commission system has for both brokers and clients. (A broker's income has no floor—a disadvantage. On the other hand, it has no cap either—an advantage. For clients, there is always the risk that the broker might buy and sell stock more for the purpose of generating commissions than improving the client's financial position. This practice is called churning, and it is illegal.)

2 Research Have students research the practice of insider trading and write reports on it. Suggest that in their reports students not only describe the practice but also illustrate how it can work against the best interests of investors.

1 clients on their investment program. For this service, they receive a **commission,** which is a fee usually based on the amount of the purchase. Discount brokers, whose commissions are much less than those charged by full-service brokers, limit their services to carrying out buy and sell orders.

Stock Exchanges

A **stock exchange** is a central market where brokers buy and sell securities. It is an auction market. The buyer making the highest bid buys, and the seller with the lowest offer sells—when the two agree on price.

The New York Stock Exchange and the American Stock Exchange, both located in New York City, are the largest in the country. In addition there are 11 regional exchanges. The New York Stock Exchange accounts for about 82 percent of the market value of all shares traded; the American Stock Exchange, for about 6 percent; and the regional exchanges, for about 12 percent.

All securities transactions that are not made on organized stock exchanges take place in the over-the-counter market. This market is primarily a negotiation market. Brokers (both buyers and sellers)
2 seek each other out and negotiate prices.

Stock Market Quotations

Dealers' quotations for over-the-counter stock prices are instantly available in brokerage offices across the nation. In addition, over-the-counter market quotations are published in many large daily newspapers.

The New York Stock Exchange Composite Transactions, as they appear in the newspaper, are shown in Figure 11–2. Most figures are expressed in eighths of a point. A point is equal to $1, so one-eighth of a point equals 12.5 cents.

Figure 11–2 Stock Market Quotations

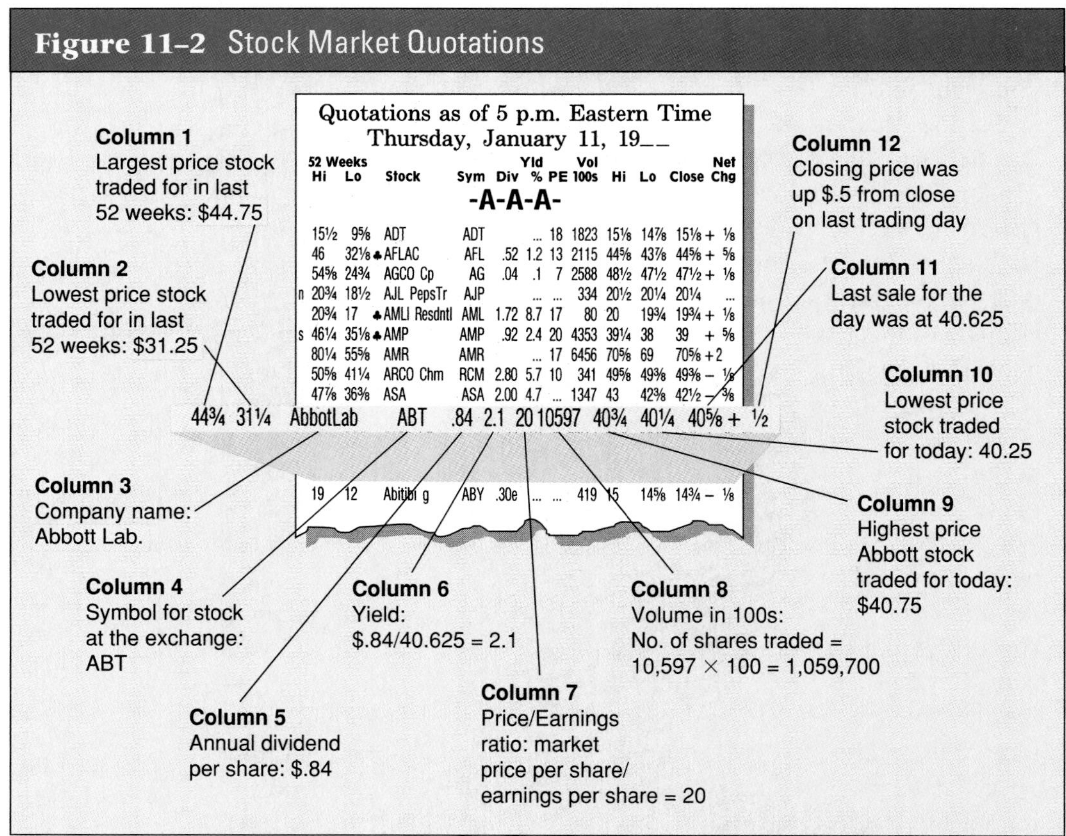

Quotations as of 5 p.m. Eastern Time
Thursday, January 11, 19__

	52 Weeks Hi	52 Weeks Lo	Stock	Sym	Div	Yld %	PE	Vol 100s	Hi	Lo	Close	Net Chg
			-A-A-A-									
	15½	9⅝	ADT	ADT		...	18	1823	15⅛	14⅞	15⅛	+ ⅛
	46	32⅛	♣AFLAC	AFL	.52	1.2	13	2115	44⅝	43⅞	44⅝	+ ⅝
	54⅝	24¾	AGCO Cp	AG	.04	.1	7	2588	48½	47½	47½	+ ⅛
n	20¾	18½	AJL PepsTr	AJP		...	...	334	20½	20¼	20¼	...
	20¾	17	♣AMLI Resdntl	AML	1.72	8.7	17	80	20	19¾	19¾	+ ⅛
s	46¼	35⅛	♣AMP	AMP	.92	2.4	20	4353	39¼	38	39	+ ⅝
	80¼	55⅝	AMR	AMR		...	17	6456	70⅝	69	70⅝	+2
	50⅝	41¼	ARCO Chm	RCM	2.80	5.7	10	341	49⅝	49⅜	49⅜	– ⅛
	47⅞	36⅜	ASA	ASA	2.00	4.7	...	1347	43	42⅜	42½	– ⅜
	44¾	31¼	AbbotLab	ABT	.84	2.1	20	10597	40¾	40¼	40⅝	+ ½
	19	12	Abitibi g	ABY	.30e	...	...	419	15	14⅝	14¾	– ⅛

Note: Column 6: Yield is the annual dividend on each share divided by closing price. Column 7: Price/earning ratio is the amount investors are paying for each $1 share.

► *This chart explains how to read a stock market quotation. Look at AGCO Cp.* ***What prices did its stock command on this date (include the day's high; the day's low; the day's close, and change since last trading day).***

Caption Answer: The day's high: $48.50; the day's low: $47.50; the day's close: $47.50; change since the last trading day: up $0.125

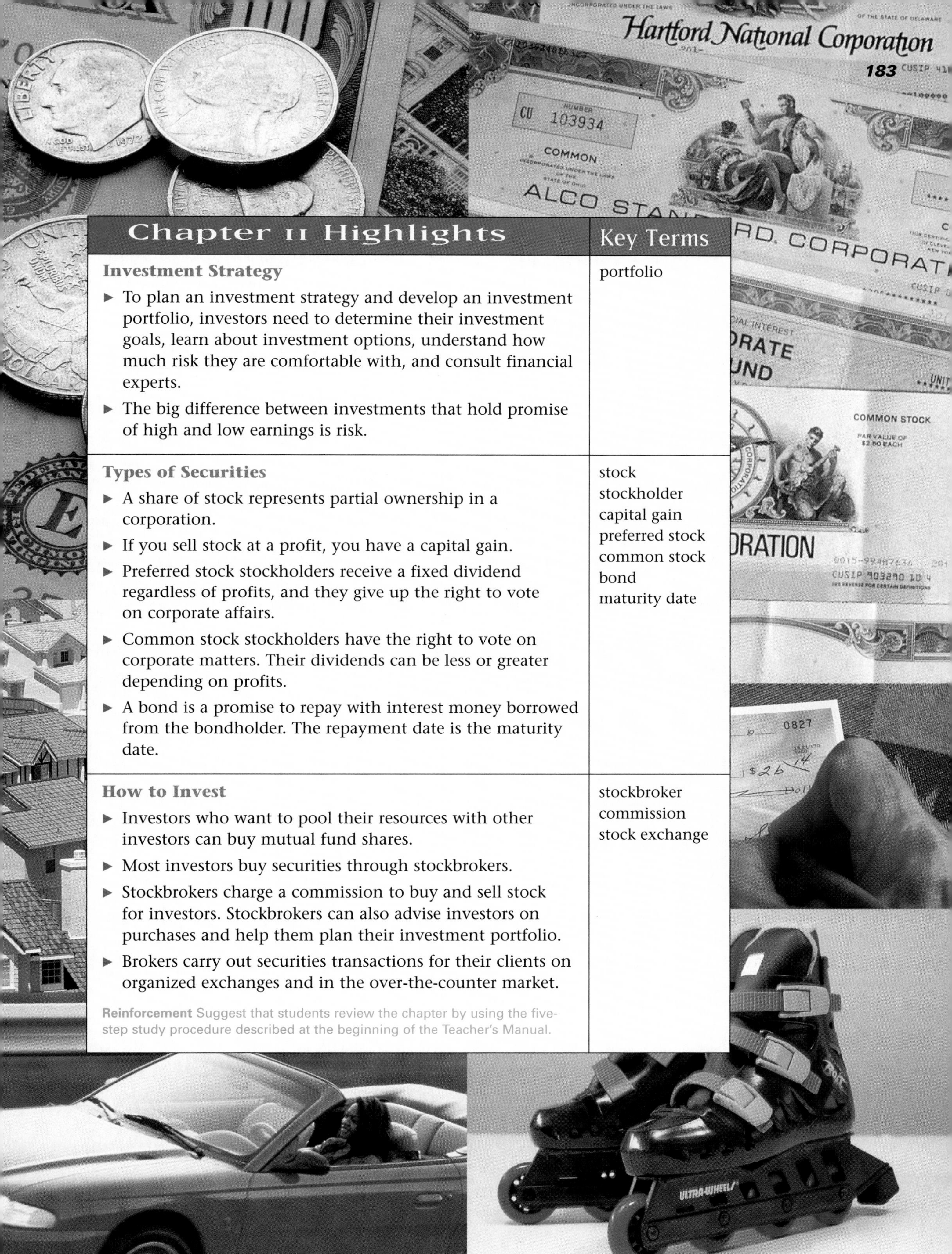

Chapter 11 Highlights	Key Terms
Investment Strategy ▶ To plan an investment strategy and develop an investment portfolio, investors need to determine their investment goals, learn about investment options, understand how much risk they are comfortable with, and consult financial experts. ▶ The big difference between investments that hold promise of high and low earnings is risk.	portfolio
Types of Securities ▶ A share of stock represents partial ownership in a corporation. ▶ If you sell stock at a profit, you have a capital gain. ▶ Preferred stock stockholders receive a fixed dividend regardless of profits, and they give up the right to vote on corporate affairs. ▶ Common stock stockholders have the right to vote on corporate matters. Their dividends can be less or greater depending on profits. ▶ A bond is a promise to repay with interest money borrowed from the bondholder. The repayment date is the maturity date.	stock stockholder capital gain preferred stock common stock bond maturity date
How to Invest ▶ Investors who want to pool their resources with other investors can buy mutual fund shares. ▶ Most investors buy securities through stockbrokers. ▶ Stockbrokers charge a commission to buy and sell stock for investors. Stockbrokers can also advise investors on purchases and help them plan their investment portfolio. ▶ Brokers carry out securities transactions for their clients on organized exchanges and in the over-the-counter market. **Reinforcement** Suggest that students review the chapter by using the five-step study procedure described at the beginning of the Teacher's Manual.	stockbroker commission stock exchange

CHAPTER 

REVIEW

Refer students to the Reviewing Consumer Terms and Reviewing Facts and Ideas activities in the Student Activity Workbook.

Reviewing Consumer Terms
Stories will vary. See Glossary for definitions.

Reviewing Facts and Ideas
See the Student Activity Workbook for answers.

Problem Solving and Decision Making
Teresa Guzman paid $34 a share, $1 less per share than Roger Bray paid.

Consumers Around the World
Human Relations
1 Students should include in their presentation basic information about Vietnam—location, population, and average income. They should discuss how the form of government affects the business economy. They should give recent developments.

Communications
2 Papers will vary.

Consumer Project
In their reports, students should list the factors they were asked to consider (goals, age, income, and so on). They should summarize the recommendations made to them.

Reviewing Consumer Terms

Use each of the following terms in a 250-word story entitled "The Day I Wanted to Make an Investment."

bond
capital gain
commission
common stock
maturity date
portfolio
preferred stock
stock
stock exchange
stockbroker
stockholder

Reviewing Facts and Ideas

1. Describe the role of risk in making investments.
2. What four factors should consumers consider when planning an investment?
3. True or false: Bonds are only issued by corporations.
4. List the advantages and disadvantages of owning common and preferred stocks.
5. What is the difference between stocks and bonds?
6. Would you rather have to pay taxes on corporate or municipal bonds? Why?
7. Complete the following statement by selecting the best choice. The wisest investment strategy is to
   a. put all your savings into stocks
   b. make sure you have a comfortable income, a good emergency fund, and adequate insurance before you invest in stocks,
   c. never buy stocks under any circumstances.
8. Explain how to invest in stocks and bonds.

Problem Solving and Decision Making

Each month for ten months Teresa Guzman bought ten shares of one corporation's common stock. She paid the following prices: $35, $37, $39, $38, $35, $33, $32, $31, $30, and $30. Roger Bray bought 100 shares of the same stock all at once at $35 a share. What was the average price per share paid by Teresa Guzman? Who paid the lower price per share?

Building Academic Skills

Consumers Around the World

Human Relations

1. Vietnam is a very poor country, still suffering from years of war. Nevertheless, there are influential people who are planning the opening of a stock market in that country.

   What can you find out about the people who want to promote the growth of a stock market? Research the form of government in Vietnam and how it influences business activity there. Prepare a

five-minute oral presentation to your class on the material you have gathered.

Communications

2. Interview a parent, guardian, or other adult about making investments in the stock market. Find out about his or her experiences and write your findings in a 250-word report.

 Beyond the Classroom

Consumer Project

Write to the New York Stock Exchange or contact a broker and request current information on investment plans for an investor with a minimum of a hundred dollars a month to invest. When you receive information, answer the following questions. What factors were you asked to consider? What investments were generally recommended? Report your findings to the class in a 250-word report.

 Cooperative Learning

Family Economics

Break into assigned family groups. Discuss the following problem.

A friend is raving about Treasury bills as a family investment. He tells you that they are safe, are easy to purchase, and offer a better interest rate than a bank account. T-bills are sold in only one denomination, $10,000. You have a choice, however, of three different maturity periods—three months, six months, or one year.

Do you take your friend's advice and invest? Why or why not? If you do, specify how many bills you buy and for which maturity periods. Again, explain why. Compare your answers with those of other family groups.

Debate the Issue

Several states have adopted prepaid college tuition plans. Although these plans vary, in general they provide that parents can make tuition payments for their young child into a state-operated trust fund. When the child reaches college age, he or she can use the fund to pay tuition at a (usually state-supported) college. The cost of the plan depends on the youngster's age when payments are made to the trust fund. Payments may be in a lump sum or in installments. Each state provides for a refund if the plan is abandoned for any reason.

You and your classmates will break into two groups and research this topic. Each group will gather evidence to support one side or the other. You are to prepare the argument for your side of the problem. Then the two groups will meet in a classroom debate.

Rechecking Your Attitude

Before going on to the next unit, go back to the Attitude Inventory at the beginning of this one. Answer the questions a second time. Then compare the two sets of responses. On how many statements have your attitudes changed? Can you account for these shifts in your opinions? What do you know now that you did not know then?

Family Economics Most families do not have the minimum amount needed to invest. Those with savings might consider money market accounts instead. Those with $10,000 will want to leave some savings in their accounts for emergencies.

Debate the Issue Break the class into two teams. Assign each team one side of the issue. Encourage students to work together as a team to develop their argument. Ask each team to select a member to make an opening statement that supports the team's side of the issue. Have students take turns debating as the debates moves from one team to the other.

UNIT 3 LAB
You and Your Community

STEPS A and C Students should prepare two lists of interview questions that are clearly written, easily comprehended, and appropriate for the person to whom they will be addressed. All eight topics listed in each step should be addressed.
STEPS B and D Students should arrange and carry out their interviews. Students should take careful, well-organized notes on the conversations at each interview.
STEP E Students' answers should be accurate and based on their interview notes.
STEP F Students' comparisons of professionals' advice and laypersons' actual practices should be clearly explained and logically supported by general examples from the interviews.

Refer students to the Unit 3 Lab in the Student Activity Workbook.

Saving and Investing in the Real World

Unit 3 explains the many ways you can save and invest money. This lab will help you learn more about saving and investing as you interview financial consultants and "ordinary savers" about their saving and investment practices.

TOOLS

1. Newspaper business and front-page sections
2. Business magazines
3. Literature from financial institutions

PROCEDURES

STEP A Write a list of ten questions about saving and investment techniques that you can ask during an interview with a financial consultant, such as a certified financial planner, a certified public accountant, or the officer of a savings institution that provides financial planning services. Your interview questions should cover the following topics:

1. The consultant's advice on the percentage of after-tax income a person should save.
2. The type of retirement savings plans the consultant recommends.
3. The recommended size of a saver's emergency fund.
4. The factors for a saver to consider when choosing a financial institution and/or financial consultant with which to do business.
5. The consultant's advice on how a saver can maintain good financial records.

A financial consultant will most likely tell you that many of the answers to your questions will depend on the age and financial responsibilities of the saver. Therefore, ask each consultant to answer your questions with two different savers in mind—a young, single, working person with few financial responsibilities and a somewhat older person who is a homeowner and the parent of school-age children.

STEP B Contact two financial consultants, preferably from two different offices or financial institutions. Explain the purpose of your interview assignment, and ask to interview them either on the phone or in person at a time that is convenient for the consultants. During each interview, take careful notes on the consultant's responses to your questions. Do not tape-record the conversation unless you first ask for and receive the consultant's permission to do so.

STEP C Prepare a second list of ten questions. These questions will be used in interviews with four "ordinary

savers." Your interview questions should cover the following topics:

1. The percentage of after-tax income the person saves.
2. The saver's financial preparations for emergencies, expensive purchases, and recurring expenses.
3. The factors the saver considered (or will consider) when choosing a financial institution and/or financial consultant.
4. The saver's current and/or future retirement savings plan.
5. The saver's techniques for maintaining financial records, including checking account and investment records.

STEP D Talk with family and friends about this lab assignment, and ask for their help in identifying four people who would be willing to be interviewed about their saving and investing practices. At least one of your subjects should be a young, single, working person with few financial responsibilities, and two of your subjects should be home owners and/or the parents of school-age children.

Once your four savers have agreed to the interviews and you have assured them that you will be discreet in using their answers, arrange a convenient time to interview each saver either on the phone or in person. It is best not to tape-record the interviews. Do take careful, accurate notes during the conversations.

LAB REPORT

STEP E Use your notes from the six interviews to answer the questions below:

1. What was the average percentage of a person's after-tax income the consultants felt should be saved?
2. What was the average percentage of after-tax income that the savers actually saved?
3. What was the average size of the savers' emergency funds?
4. How many savers have current retirement savings plans?

STEP F Write a 500-word report that compares the advice of the financial consultants with the actual practices of the savers. First, summarize the professionals' advice. Next, summarize the practices and habits of the savers, noting any general differences between savers with few financial responsibilities and savers with more obligations. Finally, describe how the actual practices differed from the professional advice.

UNIT 4

Unit Contents

Types of Credit

Attitude Inventory

Before you begin Chapter 12, take stock of your attitudes by completing the following inventory. Read each statement and decide how you feel about it—agree, disagree, or undecided. Record your feelings on a sheet of notepaper or use the form in the workbook.

1. Credit is an invention that we could very well do without.
2. Credit is a great way to buy items on impulse.
3. When credit is used, trust is important.
4. Credit is far more important to older people than to young people and young families.
5. Credit usage can be harmful in times of inflation.
6. The government should take a hands-off attitude toward credit transactions.
7. A woman should be granted credit only in the name of her husband.
8. The cost of credit is so small that it may safely be ignored.
9. Wise consumers may sometimes use credit to their advantage.
10. "Borrow cash and save money" is a saying that doesn't make sense.
11. Individuals who open charge accounts can still control their finances.
12. If you cannot save for an item, you don't deserve to own it.
13. Buying on the installment plan is evidence of weak character.
14. Businesses do not like to extend credit.
15. Monthly statements from retail stores are designed to confuse, not aid, the consumer.

Unit Goal The main goal of this unit is to introduce students to the concept of credit—its history, its most common forms, and the problems people most often encounter in its use. Chapters included in this unit are (1) Commercial and Consumer Credit, (2) Consumer Credit Problems, (3) Charge Accounts, and (4) Installment Credit.

Lesson Plan See the Teacher's Manual for an overview of the unit and some suggestions for introducing it. If you assign the Attitude Inventory, be sure to tell students to keep their answers for later use.

Card

CHAPTER 12

Commercial and Consumer Credit

Learning Objectives

When you have finished studying this chapter, you should be able to:

1. Explain what credit is, and identify the essential element in credit.
2. Describe how credit was used in early business transactions.
3. Explain how commercial credit generates money that can be used to pay off a loan.
4. Explain how consumer credit differs from commercial credit, and name at least three types of credit cards.

Consumer Terms

credit
transaction
commercial credit
consumer credit
bank cards

Real-World Journal

Interview a parent, guardian, or other adult about the credit cards he or she has. Ask: Was it difficult to obtain credit? How did you obtain a credit card? Do you have more than one type of credit card? If so, why is more than one type of card needed? Summarize your findings in your journal.

Lesson Plan See the Teacher's Manual for Chapter 12 lesson plan.

Vocabulary The Chapter 12 lesson plan includes suggested vocabulary activities for the terms listed.

1 Discussion Starter Ask students if they have ever loaned money to a friend. What happened? Do they trust their friend more or less as a result?

2 Discussion Starter A local business borrows $1 million from a local bank. One newspaper headlines the story, "Local Business Receives $1 Million in Credit." Another newspaper features the story under the headline "Local Firm Goes $1 Million into Debt." Ask students if both headlines are talking about the same thing. Ask how their impression of the firm changes with the wording of the headline.

MEANING OF CREDIT

Have you ever borrowed money? Perhaps you asked a friend to loan you money for a CD, promising to pay back the money the next day. The friend who loaned you the money was giving you credit. **Credit** is the supplying of money, goods, or services at present in exchange for the promise of future payment.

When you borrow money from a bank, you are using credit. When you turn on the shower, you are also using credit. (You have the present use of water in exchange for the implied promise to pay for it later.) Buying a bicycle on the installment plan is likewise a credit transaction. (A transaction is the exchange of goods or services for cash or credit.)

A feeling of trust is important in any
1 credit transaction. Each party to the agreement trusts the other to carry out his or her part of the bargain.

Good Feelings About Credit

Probably you already have an opinion of credit. If you read the following sentences aloud, you would find the word credit has a pleasant ring to it.

1. She has the best possible credit rating.
2. That sounds like a creditworthy investment.
3. You can buy now with your good credit.

In all these cases, the word is used in a favorable way. It reflects the feeling many Americans have about credit. Certainly, credit is a valuable thing to have. When people use credit wisely, they can expand their present income, enjoy now the results of their labor, and face money problems with little fear.

Bad Feelings About Credit

Notice how your tone changes, however, when you read these sentences.

1. He had to sell his home when his credit was cut off.
2. Credit was their downfall.
3. She lived for months on credit.

2 Now the word has a harsh sound, for it is used in its unpleasant sense. These sentences imply that consumers used credit unwisely.

How we feel about credit tends to depend on our experience with it. Credit itself is neither good nor bad. The use made of it determines just how good or bad it is.

Caption Answer: Friends show trustworthiness by being reliable, helping one another out, and comforting one another. You can demonstrate trustworthiness to a bank by showing a steady income, manageable expenses, low debt, and a history of paying on time.

Trust is essential to the operation of credit. ***How do you show your friends that you are trustworthy? How would you show a bank that you are trustworthy?*** ▶

BEGINNINGS OF CREDIT

1 Credit was first used many centuries ago. Merchants did not want to carry heavy gold and silver with them as they bought and sold goods. Instead, for safekeeping they left their precious metals with someone in authority at the temple or with a metal worker. In return, they were given receipts. A receipt could be turned in later for gold and silver in the amount of the original deposit.

Receipts as Money

Merchants soon found that they could settle a **transaction** (exchange of goods or services) by merely trading the receipts for merchandise. This procedure was easier than first cashing in the receipts and then making payment in precious metals. The new owners, in turn, had the same choice. They could either exchange the paper for metal or use it in other transactions. Thus, the receipts continued in circulation. The gold and silver stayed in storage.

For the "bankers," the question was what to do with the store of precious metals. Since their depositors did not demand its return, they began to lend some of it to other merchants. Still, however, some gold and silver remained. The bankers realized they could make a handsome profit by printing even more "receipts" against the same store of metals. The new receipts became paper money and were loaned to other merchants at interest.

Credit Today

This idea is still being applied. A customer deposits money with the bank. The customer trusts that the bank will return the money when asked. A banker lends part of that money to a business. The banker trusts that the borrower eventually will pay back the money with interest.

In the meantime, a depositor who wants his or her money back is satisfied with the return of any cash on hand. The cash does not have to be the same
2 cash that was deposited.

COMMERCIAL CREDIT

Credit used for business purposes is called **commercial credit.** Commercial credit has enjoyed a good reputation throughout history. It helps businesses grow and involves little risk. The risk is limited because the money is used to earn more money. As you can see from Fig-
3 ure 12–1 on page 194, the loans carry with-
4 in themselves the means of repayment.

CONSUMER CREDIT

Consumer credit is credit extended for personal (not business) purposes. A person who borrows $200 to buy a CD player for personal enjoyment is using consumer credit. The consumer who charges the cost of a CD player to his or her account at the store is also using consumer credit.

Keeping Money Safe

Although Vietnamese banks offer credit cards, few people use them. Many Vietnamese even prefer to keep their money hidden at home instead of entrusting it to state-run banks.

1 Vocabulary Explain to students that the word *credit* comes from the Latin word *creditum,* which means "something entrusted to another." Ask students what that "something" was. (Gold and silver were entrusted to authorities.)

2 Critical Thinking Ask students to compare the reasons credit was used originally to the primary reason it is used today. (Convenience was the original reason; lack of funds is the contemporary reason.) Ask them what modern bank service is similar to the earliest credit transactions. (Checking is similar.)

3 Reinforcement Ask students if borrowing money to buy a car for their personal use would be classified as a commercial loan. (No.) Why or why not? (They would be borrowing the money as an individual, not as a business; commercial loans are made to businesses only.)

4 Math Application Tell students to assume that operating costs and expenses (including the cost of the loan) for the Esposito Camera Store come to $153,000. Then have them compute the firm's profit. ($200,000 − $153,000 = $47,000.)

Figure 12–1 How Commercial Credit Works

Loans help businesses and banks.

1
Frank Esposito, owner of the Esposito Camera Store, goes to his bank to borrow $100,000. The loan officer learns that the store is a thriving business.
Anaheim CAMERA SUPPLY
2
The bank lends Esposito $100,000 to buy camera equipment to sell. The equipment sells for $200,000 and Esposito can use this money to easily repay the bank. Thus the original loan generates the money that can be used to repay it.
3
The owner deposits the $200,000 from the sales into the store's bank account. The store then pays the bank $100,000 plus interest for the loan. The store also pays salaries, rent, and advertising expenses and still has money left in its account. The money left in the account is profit, which Esposito Camera leaves on deposit to earn interest.
4
The owner is well satisfied because the loan brought him a profit despite the interest charges. The bank officer is pleased because the bank was able to put depositors' money to work at a profit.

Growth of Consumer Credit

1 Consumer credit developed much more slowly than commercial credit. Since consumer loans do not generate income from which repayment can be made, for a long time bankers were not eager to lend to consumers. The borrowed money would be used to buy goods that would be consumed instead
of sold at a profit. Banks feared borrow-
2 ers would not be able to generate the
3 money to repay the loan.

However, attitudes changed over the years. After World War II, there was an explosion of consumer credit. In 1928,

Super Bowl Hero

Mel Blount's family lived on a dirt farm in Georgia. They had no electricity, no running water. Nevertheless, Mel Blount's father taught the 11 children to work hard and have pride in themselves. He said that it was the only way they would make anything of themselves.

Mel Blount played for the Pittsburgh Steelers for 14 years, helping them win four trips to the Super Bowl. He was a hero to local boys in Georgia, who would come by the house whenever Blount came home. As he listened to them talk about parents who left them alone or about dropping out of school, Blount realized they needed guidance and discipline—the kind his father had given him.

When Blount retired from football in 1983, he and his brother opened a youth home near his family's farm. It is open to boys who are in trouble or who have been neglected or abused. The boys work on the farm before and after school. They clean their own rooms, wash and iron their own clothes, and clean up the kitchen. In short, they learn to take care of themselves. They learn to handle responsibility and take pride in their work.

The program was successful in that the boys stayed out of trouble and in school. However, when Blount wanted to start a program in rural Pennsylvania, near Pittsburgh, he came up against propaganda designed to stop county approval of the home. Flyers sent to the neighbors warned that inner-city youths would bring crime to the country.

Blount quietly went about his business, got support from many in the community, and the farm was given permission to open. The farm proved the critics wrong.

Through Blount's support and example, the boys learned pride and resourcefulness. His father would have approved.

Brainstorm

What kinds of values have your parents or other family members inspired in you that you would pass on to others?

1 Reinforcement Have students use the example of Esposito Camera and the person buying the CD player to explain in their own words why consumer credit developed more slowly than commercial credit. (Credit extended to Esposito Camera generated income; credit to buy the CD player did not.)

2 Reinforcement Student Activity Workbook, Chapter 12 activities.

3 Learning Economics Old-time merchants did not like the idea of credit. They thought "Why would customers who don't have enough money to buy food now be better able to pay for the food after they have eaten it?" Ask students why merchants who had doubts about repayment might offer credit anyway. (Merchants wanted to increase sales, and they were in competition with other merchants who might offer credit.)

Case Study Answer: Punctuality; resourcefulness; creativity; positive attitude; lack of importance of material things; importance of hard work; honesty; love of family; importance of giving to others.

FLASHBACK FLASHFORWARD

Tax freedom day is the first day of the year that a taxpayer's wages stop going to pay taxes and start going directly into the taxpayer's pocket. In 1960, that day was April 16. In 1993, tax freedom day was May 3.

1 Learning Economics Ask students how the trend in consumer borrowing (it has been increasing) compares with the trend in our national borrowing. (The national debt has also risen sharply.) Then ask students to explain in their own words what they think this means. (Both as a nation and as individuals we are living beyond our means.)

Case Study Answers:
1 A background in business or political science would be beneficial. The job demands excellent communication, presentation, and teaching skills.
2 Answers will vary.

consumer credit amounted to $11.5 billion. In 1950, soon after the war, it was $21 billion. By 1996, it had jumped to $1 trillion.

Americans are no longer willing to wait years to enjoy modern comforts and conveniences. A person who works hard all day wants to instantly enjoy the rewards of that labor. Today, workers buy everything from washing machines to houses on a credit basis. They enjoy these things now instead of waiting for years until they can pay cash. The practice of saving after a purchase, rather than before, has become a common one.

Extent of Consumer Credit

The $1 trillion in outstanding consumer credit in 1996 amounts to about $3,800 for every man, woman, and child in the United States. Consumer credit continues to rise. However, in the mid-1990s U.S. consumers still owned about $13 for every $1 that they owed.

In comparison to the income they earn, older families tend to use less credit than younger families. This fact is easy to understand. Establishing a home and starting a family requires a great deal of money. In addition, many young couples see as necessities those items regarded as luxuries by their parents.

Importance of Consumer Credit

Since most families cannot buy costly items with cash, their large purchases often require credit. Thus, consumer credit can play an important role in stimulating economic activity over the
1 short run.

Credit is important in the life of the average consumer. Can you imagine what life would be like without credit? You might have to pay in advance for utilities. You would have to pay cash for high-cost goods such as household appliances and furniture. Most people would not be able to buy labor-saving appliances or homes until they were almost too old to enjoy them.

Without credit, products would probably cost several times what they do now. Mass production methods could not be used because consumers with no credit and little cash could not buy mass quantities of goods. There would be fewer jobs because fewer goods would be produced for the market.

Types of Credit Cards

There are several types of consumer credit cards offered by businesses that extend credit. Among the most common are retail, bank, travel and entertainment, and gasoline credit cards.

Retail Credit Cards A department store or a chain of stores may issue retail credit cards for use in the main store or any of its branches. The store handles the processing and the billing. Cardholders do not pay an annual fee to use these cards. However, they must pay a finance charge on any unpaid credit card balances. Examples of retail credit cards include Ann Taylor, Bloomingdales, Nordstroms, and The Limited.

Bank Cards **Bank cards** are credit cards issued by banks and accepted by millions of businesses in the United States and abroad. They can be used at hotels, restaurants, department stores, theaters, airline ticket offices—just about anywhere. They even entitle owners to an instant cash loan, usually from an automatic teller machine (ATM).

Cardholders usually pay an annual fee to use these cards. They are billed for the full amount of their charges each month and must make at least a minimum payment. If they do not pay the full amount charged on the card at the end of the month, they must pay inter-

CASE STUDY

Careers in Focus

Charlotte Rush, Vice President, Public Affairs, MasterCard International

Charlotte Rush has an arsenal of staggering statistics in her head that she can call up at a moment's notice to educate any audience about the positions, practices, and policies of MasterCard International. As vice president, public affairs, she has the job of making sure that everyone from senators to regulators, from newspaper reporters to first-time credit card users, all understand MasterCard's way of doing business.

"Believe it or not, we're a nonprofit company," she says. "Most people think of MasterCard as one thing, one card. It's not at all. We're an association of 22,000 different financial institutions spanning the globe. In 1994, there were 240 million MasterCards in circulation in the world. The total volume charged on those cards was $390 billion. On any given day, there are 8.5 million MasterCard charges in 135 different currencies."

Rush, who earned her M.B.A. from the University of Pittsburgh and has spent her entire career in public affairs for multinational corporations, has focused her energy and interests on MasterCard's vast empire for three years now. During that time, she has been impressed not only with the scope of the company throughout the world but also with the importance of the credit card to the American way of life.

"The concept of buying things on credit is completely absent in many cultures," she explains. "But the credit card is absolutely central to our way of life in this country. Since the 1960s, when charge cards really started to boom, having a credit card has become a critical part of your identity and credibility. If you have a credit card, you have a credit history. And if your credit history is good, the car dealer will sell you the car, the landlord will rent you the apartment."

It's that fact of credit card reality—the enormous benefits and burdens of using a card like MasterCard—that drives much of Rush's work. Her job takes her in front of the TV camera and into private meetings with key decision makers in business and government, but at the end of the day, she is most concerned with the consumer.

"Throughout my career in public affairs, I've had a special interest in educating consumers to be the best they can be," she says. "I think good consumers actually help businesses and governments do their job better."

Case Study Review

1. What type of education might be the best preparation for a job in public affairs for a company like MasterCard?
2. What is the current interest rate on any credit card used in your home? If no credit cards are used, call the nearest bank and ask for the rate on its standard bank card. How much interest would you pay over the course of a year if you charged $100 on the card and paid none of it off?

▲ *Consumer credit enables people to enjoy many goods and services immediately.* ***Why do people sometimes find it easier to pay for an item after purchasing it than to save for the item before purchasing it?***

Caption Answer: When you are paying off your credit charges, you have an obligation to the creditor.

est on the unpaid amount the following month.

VISA and MasterCard are well-known bank cards that were first offered to customers more than 30 years ago. The Discover Card, originally promoted by Sears, is the newest entry into the field and is already the most widely held. Today there are variations of VISA and MasterCard, offered by such firms as Ford and General Motors. By using these cards, you can earn credit toward the purchase of one of their vehicles. Another variation is provided by GTE, which offers credit against the cost of
1 long-distance calls.

1 Critical Thinking Ask students why they think companies like GM make this kind of offer. (These companies want to persuade consumers to use their card and to buy their products.)

Travel and Entertainment Cards Diners Club and American Express are widely used travel and entertainment (T&E) cards. Subscribers pay a yearly membership fee that is higher than the annual fee charged for bank cards. Cardholders are not given a spending limit and, for the most part, are expected to pay balances in full each month.

The American Express Optima True Grace card is similar to a bank card. It charges a low rate of interest for the first six months; then the rate increases steeply. There is no annual fee. Travel and entertainment cards are accepted throughout the world and are often used when buying airline tickets, renting a car, or paying hotel and restaurant charges. Business travelers like to use them because the detailed records they receive from the card issuers are useful for business and tax purposes. They offer proof of expenses incurred in traveling and entertaining customers. A traveler with one of these cards finds it easy to cash checks for several hundred—even a thousand—dollars when away from
2 home.

2 Discussion Starter Some issuers offer gold or platinum "prestige cards" to customers who are frequent users of credit cards and who have high credit ratings. Ask the students if they would be willing to pay an extra $300 a year for a platinum card. Why? What extra privileges would they expect for the added charge? (Some status-conscious students might value a prestige card. It would probably carry with it a high credit limit and ready access to cash.)

Gasoline Credit Cards Major oil companies issue credit cards that provide credit for gas, oil, and other products. Only a certain percentage of the total bill (perhaps 10 percent) must be paid each month. Interest must be paid on the unpaid amount.

Beware of Using Credit Cards
Credit cards can be a convenient method for paying for purchases. The best way to use them is to pay the full balance each month. If you don't, you will be charged interest of up to 20 percent or more annually. When you have a balance on your card, always make the largest monthly payment you can afford. If you charged $1,000 and made only the minimum payment each month, it could take you more than 20 years to pay off the balance.

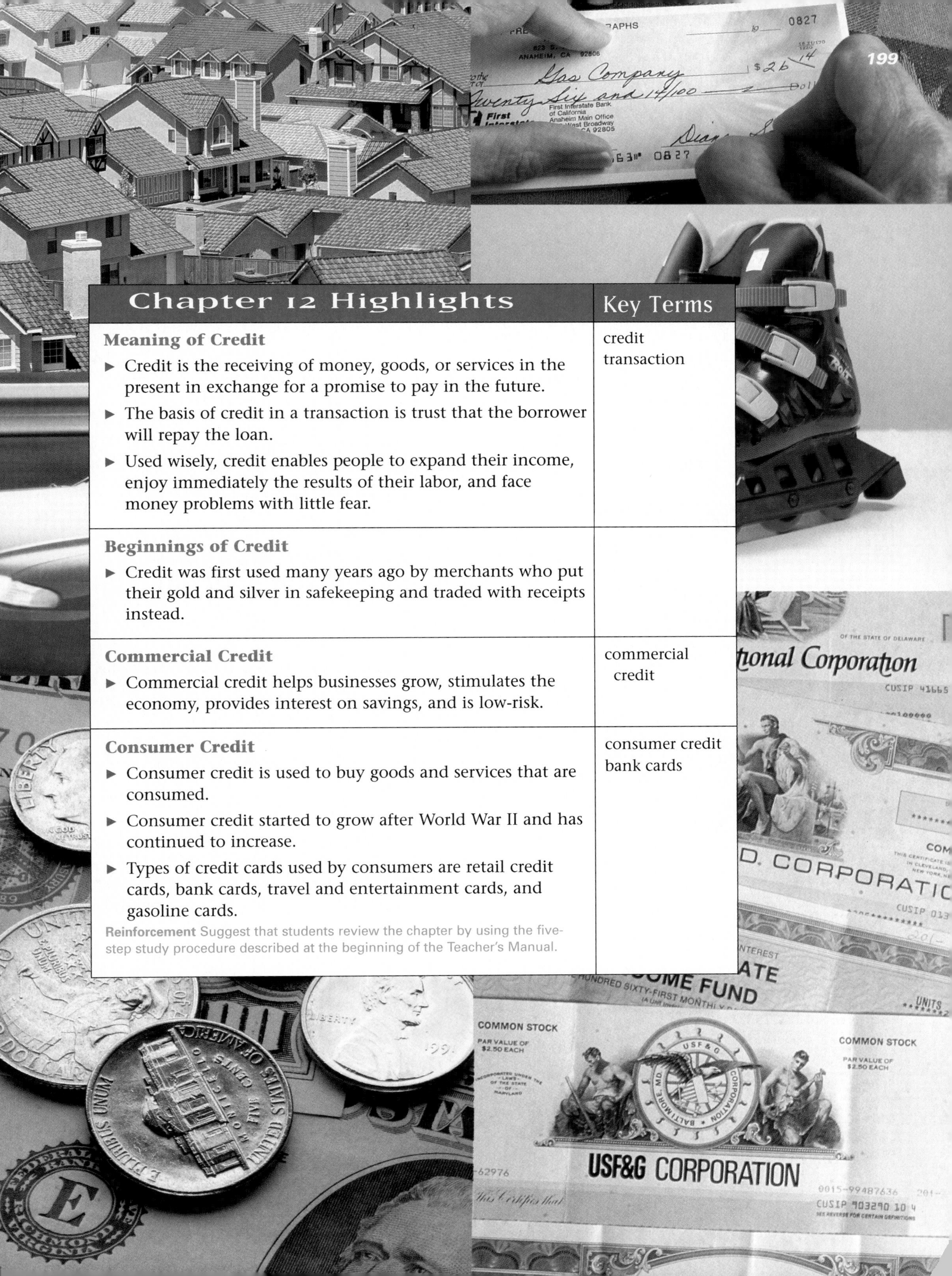

Chapter 12 Highlights	Key Terms
Meaning of Credit ▸ Credit is the receiving of money, goods, or services in the present in exchange for a promise to pay in the future. ▸ The basis of credit in a transaction is trust that the borrower will repay the loan. ▸ Used wisely, credit enables people to expand their income, enjoy immediately the results of their labor, and face money problems with little fear.	credit transaction
Beginnings of Credit ▸ Credit was first used many years ago by merchants who put their gold and silver in safekeeping and traded with receipts instead.	
Commercial Credit ▸ Commercial credit helps businesses grow, stimulates the economy, provides interest on savings, and is low-risk.	commercial credit
Consumer Credit ▸ Consumer credit is used to buy goods and services that are consumed. ▸ Consumer credit started to grow after World War II and has continued to increase. ▸ Types of credit cards used by consumers are retail credit cards, bank cards, travel and entertainment cards, and gasoline cards. **Reinforcement** Suggest that students review the chapter by using the five-step study procedure described at the beginning of the Teacher's Manual.	consumer credit bank cards

CHAPTER 12 REVIEW

Refer students to the Reviewing Consumer Terms and Reviewing Facts and Ideas activities in the Student Activity Workbook.

Reviewing Consumer Terms
Paragraphs will vary. See Glossary for definitions.

Reviewing Facts and Ideas
See the Student Activity Workbook for answers.

Problem Solving and Decision Making
1 The customer wants to use the musical instrument for professional purposes, for example, to teach music or to play in a band.
2 Answers will depend on student perspectives but bank credit cards are the most versatile.

Consumers Around the World
Math
1 Bank cards, 64.38 percent; oil companies, 1.59 percent; retail stores, 18.18 percent; travel and entertainment, 7.74 percent; other, 8.13 percent.

Communications
2 Students should write a one-page report in which they include their findings about the American Express Company and its foreign operations. Students should mention services in addition to charging privileges that might be attractive.

Reviewing Consumer Terms

Write a paragraph that includes the following terms. Use them in ways that demonstrate you know their meaning.

bank cards
commercial credit
consumer credit
credit
transaction

Reviewing Facts and Ideas

1. What is credit?
2. The use of consumer credit began to grow after (**a**) the Vietnam War, (**b**) World War I, or (**c**) World War II.
3. Describe how commercial credit can help a business.
4. How do commercial and consumer credit differ?
5. From the viewpoint of consumers, is credit good or bad? Explain.
6. How does consumer credit affect the prices of consumer goods?
7. Why are young couples inclined to use consumer credit more than older couples?
8. Name four types of credit cards, and tell what kinds of goods and services they can be used to purchase.

Problem Solving and Decision Making

1. When you apply for a loan to buy a musical instrument, the credit manager speaks of the transaction as a "consumer loan." Describe the circumstances that would enable you to convince him that it is really a commercial loan.
2. If you could have only one credit card and had no other source of credit, what kind of credit would you choose? Why?

Building Academic Skills

Consumers Around the World

Math

1. Credit card debt for the year 2000 is projected to be as shown in the table that follows. (Numbers do not add up because of a rounding error.)

Bank cards	$ 278.7 billion
Gasoline cards	6.9 billion
Retail stores	78.7 billion
Travel and entertainment cards	33.5 billion
Other	35.2 billion
Total	$ 433 billion

Compute the percentage of total credit card debt for each card. Carry out the computations to two places beyond the decimal. Your answers probably will not add up to 100 percent because of rounding.

Communications

2. It has been reported that 40 percent of American Express credit cards are held by citizens of countries other than the United States. Find out what you can about the foreign operations of the American Express Company. Write to American Express asking for information on services they offer in foreign countries.

Write a 250-word report on your findings. Give any reasons you feel that American Express charge cards may be attractive in other countries.

Human Relations

3. The use of consumer credit has become widespread only during the last 50 years or so. People who grew up during this time may have different views of credit from people growing up today.

   Interview at least four people from four different age groups: 15 to 25 year olds, 25 to 45 year olds, 45 to 65 year olds, 65 and older. Using a questionnaire that you create, ask about their views on consumer credit. Do they have credit cards? Do they prefer any particular cards? Do they think credit is a good way to buy items, or do they think it is better to save for what you want?

   Write a 500-word report summarizing your findings. Create a chart to present your information. Give at least one quote from each interviewee. Attach your completed questionnaires to the report.

Beyond the Classroom

Consumer Project

Find a book of quotations in your school library. From it, select five quotes dealing with credit (or debt, borrowing, or lending). Then make up a table having the following headings:

Quotation
Person Quoted
Why I Agree or Disagree

Fill in the table, identify the books in which you found the quotations, and hand in the sheet to your teacher.

Cooperative Learning

Family Economics

Break into assigned family groups. Discuss the following problem.

The refrigerator is breaking—you've been told it won't last another month. Assume the list below gives your only options for a replacement. Also assume you have no charge accounts, credit cards, or savings.

From the list, choose the appropriate refrigerator for your family's needs. Then consult the family budget and devise a realistic savings timetable for the purchase.

How long will it be before you have a new refrigerator? What difference would credit have made? Compare your answers with those of other family groups.

Refrigerator	Price
Small (13 cubic feet)	$480
Medium (16 cubic feet)	$530
Large (19 cubic feet)	$830

Debate the Issue

Many people receive a credit card as a gift when they leave home for college or start their first full-time job away from home. Is it a good idea for parents to give this kind of gift?

You and your classmates will break into two groups and research this topic. Each group will gather evidence to support one side or the other. You are to prepare the argument for your side of the problem. Then the two groups will meet in a classroom debate.

Human Relations
3 Students should write a report of at least two pages summarizing their data. They should include their questionnaires and a chart of their findings.

Consumer Project
Tables should show evidence of research in *Bartlett's Familiar Quotations* or some other source.

Family Economics
Answers will depend on the size refrigerator that is selected and the family income. For more than half the families, however, credit probably would speed the purchase or allow selection of a larger appliance.

Debate the Issue
Break the class into two teams. Assign each team one side of the issue. Encourage students to work together as a team to develop their argument. Ask each team to select a member to make an opening statement that supports the team's side of the issue. Have students take turns debating as the debate moves from one team to the other.

CHAPTER 13

Consumer Credit Problems

Learning Objectives

When you have finished studying this chapter, you should be able to:

1. Describe how credit sometimes adds to the problems of recession and inflation.
2. Explain how credit can lead to increased prices for businesses and consumers.
3. Show how using credit in one year contributes to financial problems the following year.
4. Describe illegal practices used at times by borrowers and lenders, and give three ways consumers can safeguard use of their credit cards.

Consumer Terms

discount
markup
bankruptcy
disposable income
opportunity cost
pledging
creditor

Real-World Journal

Credit cards offer consumers a convenient and easy method of making purchases. However, credit use can lead to overspending and debt. In your journal, explain why you feel many people who buy on credit end up in financial trouble.

Lesson Plan See the Teacher's Manual for Chapter 13 lesson plan.

Vocabulary The Chapter 13 lesson plan includes suggested vocabulary activities for the terms listed.

CREDIT AND THE ECONOMY

Consumer credit makes it possible for millions of people to own cars, refrigerators, television sets, new clothes, and all sorts of other goods. It has enabled Americans to enjoy a higher standard of living than would be possible otherwise.

1 At the same time, consumer credit may bring problems. For many people, it can lead to financial difficulties arising from the unwise use of credit. For the country as a whole, consumer credit has tended to magnify the ups and downs in the economy through abrupt changes in consumer spending. Moreover, consumer credit may add to existing economic problems, and it may also increase the costs of goods and services.

Inflation and Recession

Easy credit can become a problem
2 during a period of inflation, or rising
prices. Consumers bid against each other for scarce goods and services. When they cannot afford to pay cash, some may buy anyway—on credit. This buying creates excessive demand and drives prices even higher. The Federal Reserve Board, which is the federal agency that controls banking, has at times taken action to limit credit.

During a recession, which is a slowdown in economic activity, consumers may develop an uneasy feeling about the future. When businesses are making less profit, closing down, or laying off employees, consumers tend to sharply reduce their buying on credit. The resulting drop in sales is soon reflected in the production plans of manufacturers. More workers are laid off, and production falls even further.

Thus, consumer credit tends to dry up demand in times of recession and overstimulate demand in times of inflation. Both situations add to existing economic problems.

BUSINESS COSTS

Many businesses extend their own charge cards and/or accept bank charge cards. While these services provide an added convenience, they are also costly
3 for convenience.

The Cost of Retail Credit Cards

When a firm decides to extend its own credit card, it is also deciding to add expenses. It will need new equipment, new business forms, and more office workers to handle the credit transactions. More importantly, it will have to pay interest on money it borrows to keep business going until customers pay their bills.

4 How will the firm go about recovering these increased costs? It may charge credit customers fees that are high enough to (1) pay added expenses and (2) absorb bad debts from unpaid accounts. On the other hand, many business may simply increase prices on items throughout the store.

Learning to Use Credit

Because so few Eastern Europeans have credit histories, banks and credit card companies prefer to issue debit cards that require payment in advance. Only about one-third of the cards issued are "pay later" cards, and those tend to be for people who need to travel in the West.

1 Discussion Starter Ask students if they are aware of any situations in which someone used credit unwisely. What were the results?

2 Learning Economics Which two measures of an economy's health would normally decline under the circumstances described in the first paragraph under "Inflation and Recession"? (GNP and CPI would normally decline.)

3 Math Application Have the students assume that a business needs to borrow $24,000 a year at 9 percent interest so that it can extend credit to its customers. How much would just this one part of the cost of offering credit cost the company? (.09 × $24,000 = $2,160)

4 Discussion Starter Ask students if they think it's fair for cash customers to absorb the cost of a business offering credit to other customers. If they don't think it's fair, ask them how the cash customers, as smart customers, should handle the situation. (Buy from businesses that don't offset credit costs with higher prices.)

The Cost of Bank-Card Credit

Many businesses accept bank credit cards. There is a cost to using bank-card credit that can be measured easily. Merchants must pay banks to collect on their credit sales. For example, assume a merchant does bank card business of $1,000. The bank pays the merchant perhaps $950 or $960.

The $40 or $50 difference is the bank's **discount,** or amount deducted, for the service of assuming the merchant's credit burden. Later, when the bank collects from the customer, it keeps the full $1,000.

A customer who deals with a store that accepts credit cards may suspect that the merchandise is overpriced by 4

Surgeon in a War Zone

Most people would avoid going into a war zone in any way they could. Surgeon John Sundin relishes it. He volunteers his skills to help the victims of war around the world. For ten weeks during the summer of 1994, for example, Sundin was the only surgeon in Kigali, the war-ravaged capital of Rwanda. To make the dangerous trip, Sundin left a safe job at Yale University School of Medicine, where he was serving as an instructor.

In Rwanda, Sundin and his staff treated 50 to 100 patients a day. His patients' wounds, made by bullets and machetes, were horrible. Many times Sundin could not repair the damage and had to amputate arms and legs.

Medical facilities were primitive to say the least. Sundin had no lab equipment, no X-ray equipment, and no whole blood for transfusions. Sundin faced personal risks as well. More than once the hospital where he worked—a building converted from a Catholic convent—was fired on by mortars. At one point, Sundin became extremely ill with malaria. Another time, he had a run-in with armed tribal militia.

Rwanda was not Sundin's first tour of duty. He had also volunteered in Sri Lanka during a civil war there in 1993. Despite the risks, Sundin says that he likes doing war surgery. He enjoys the intensity and immediacy of the work, although he admits it is very stressful. He relieves the stress by keeping a journal of his experiences. He plans some day to turn his adventures into a book.

After Sundin returns home, he goes back to work in what must seem like an oasis of calm. Here, he waits for the next war to beckon him and his skills.

Brainstorm

Think of ways you could assist victims of war without entering a war zone.

Case Study Answer: Answers will vary. They might include working to raise funds for victims and writing to government officials to gain their support for war victims.

Caption Answer: Businesses must pay banks to collect on their credit sales. To compensate for the bank's discounts, businesses often mark up goods and services 4 to 7 percent.

1 Critical Thinking Have students tell how merchants might benefit from a cash discount policy. (They do not have to pay a fee to a credit card company; they get cash immediately for sales;
they can attract more business by featuring the discount policy in advertisements.)

2 Vocabulary Tell students that the word *bankruptcy* comes from the old Italian word for "break the bank." Then ask in what sense this old meaning might still be valid today. (If many of a bank's borrowers cannot pay back what they owe, the bank could be forced out of business.)

to 7 percent. This **markup,** or added amount, covers any discount the merchant pays the credit card agency.

Some consumers, faced with the cash-or-bank-card option, have made this proposal to merchants: "I'll pay cash for this purchase if you'll give *me* the discount instead of the bank. Otherwise, I'll charge the purchase on my credit card."

1 For years, some credit card agencies required merchants who accepted their card to refuse to give discounts to cash customers. Several of these agencies later changed their policies to allow cash discounts. Now the Cash Discount Act, a federal law, permits merchants to offer discounts to cash-paying customers.

CREDIT AND THE CONSUMER

The existence of credit can encourage people to overspend. Its use reduces purchasing power because people must pay interest on credit purchases.

Overspending

Many consumers take the promise of "easy payment plans" too literally. They use more credit than they can afford. This overspending may lead to rising tensions in the home as family arguments about money increase. It can also
2 be the direct cause of personal **bankruptcy,** a situation in which a person legally declares that he or she cannot pay his or her debts. A good understanding of credit should keep us from overusing it.

Reduced Purchasing Power

When families must pay interest on credit charges, they have less to spend for goods and services. Family members may have to postpone or give up purchasing needed items, such as clothing or household furnishings, in order to pay the interest due on the credit.

▲ *Credit allows people to purchase goods and services. However, it also increases the cost of goods and services.* ***Why might this sports equipment cost more if you purchased it with a bank credit card?***

Temporary Expansion of Income

Consumers who consider credit an expansion of income may not be looking far enough ahead. When we use credit in excess of our real needs, we find that today's expansion is tomorrow's contraction.

Take Jim Altman, for example, who has a disposable income of $12,000. (**Disposable income** is the personal income left after taxes are taken out.) If Jim borrows $500 at 18 percent interest to be paid at the end of a year, his ability to buy this year is increased by $500. Next year, however, he must repay the $500 plus the 18 percent interest, a total of $590. In that year he will have less money to spend, (see Figure 13–1).

Suppose Jim becomes accustomed to living at the $12,500 level in Year A because he likes spending more money on entertainment and gifts. He will find it hard to live on only $11,410 the following year. Perhaps he will decide to

Figure 13–1 Credit Reduces Future Income

Year A		Year B	
Disposable income earned	$12,000	Disposable income earned	$12,000
Amount borrowed at 18% interest	+ 500	Loan repaid with interest	- 590
Available for spending	$12,500		$11,410

▲ *The money you borrow on credit must be repaid with interest at a later time thus reducing future income.* ***How much would Jim Altman have available for spending in Year B compared to Year A?***

apply for more credit to expand his income. Soon he may find himself trapped by greater and greater debt.

Jim may have some logic on his side, though. Perhaps he spent the $500 on a new energy-efficient air conditioner that will reduce his electric bills. If appliance prices are increasing, to delay buying until Year B could mean he would have to pay more. Jim saves in two ways—by paying less for electricity and by paying less for the air conditioner. However, if prices in general are going up, Jim could find it doubly difficult to live in Year B with his decreased income.

Opportunity Cost Americans pay $118 billion or more annually for interest. For individuals, interest charges can
1 add up to real expense. In the previous example, Jim Altman could have used the interest payment of $90 to purchase

1 Reinforcement In a class discussion have students provide examples of credit purchases they have made. Develop lists of additional purchases that could have been made with the credit costs. Do they understand that they traded the additional purchases for immediate possession of the original purchase?

Caption Answer: Jim Altman would have $1,090 less in Year B for spending.

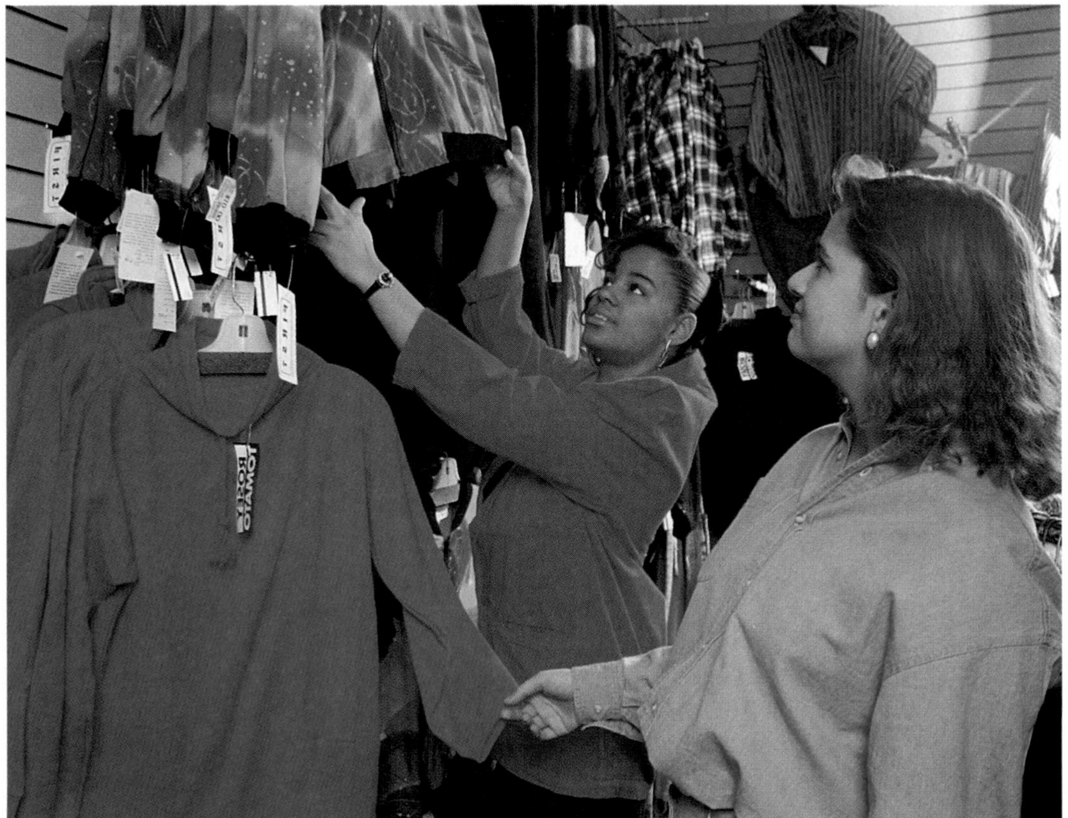

▲ *Suppose you can buy a new pair of boots, which you need, on sale, and you can buy a new shirt, which you want but do not need.* ***How would you evaluate the opportunity costs of paying interest to buy these items on credit?***

Caption Answer: You might be more willing to pay the opportunity costs of credit for the boots since these are a necessity and the reduction in cost from the sale might help compensate for the cost of the credit. You might prefer to save for rather than give up other purchases to pay for credit.

FLASHBACK FLASHFORWARD

Nationwide in the 1940s, 10,000 bankruptcies were filed annually. Today, it is estimated that more than 10,000 bankruptcy cases a year are filed in the Philadelphia bankruptcy court alone.

1 Reinforcement Student Activity Workbook, Chapter 13 activities.

2 Reinforcement Make sure students realize the importance of a credit history. Emphasize that businesses are reluctant to offer credit to people unless those people have demonstrated their ability to pay their bills on time. Relate the idea of pledging to the idea of giving your word.

News Clip Answers:
1 People with credit problems often have low self-esteem. They sometimes have weak family relationships or unhappy social lives.
2 It is important to find the cause of the credit problem so that the person can be given the proper counseling to prevent him or her from getting in financial trouble again. Simply working out a payment schedule solves only the current credit problem, not the next one.

nearly one-fifth of what he purchased with his entire credit of $500.

Wise consumers consider the opportunity cost of credit. **Opportunity cost** is what you must give up when you decide to spend your money in one way rather than another. If interest charges on a stereo system you buy come to $85, for example, the opportunity cost may be a stereo component you also wanted, a stereo component that sells for $85. Being aware of your opportunity cost is the key to making purchasing decisions that you can live with over the long term.

Before they use credit, wise consumers also consider how they are going to pay, namely, from future income. They remember that they are **pledging**
1 (promising) money that has not even been earned.

CREDIT ILLEGALITIES

Unfair and deceitful credit practices have been used by borrowers and lenders. In addition, some individuals make criminal use of credit cards.

Deceitful Practices by Creditors

A few creditors incorrectly state interest rates. A **creditor** is a person or organization to whom money is owed. Some creditors, like lenders and merchants, may add charges not advertised and overstate the ease of repayment.

Others fail to notify customers who have overpaid their accounts. Instead of returning the money, they keep it for their own use.

Finally, some businesses may refuse credit for unlawful reasons. It is illegal for creditors to discriminate against applicants on the basis of the applicant's sex, marital status, race, national origin, religion, age, or receipt of public assistance income. For example, a creditor may not refuse to give a married woman credit in her birth name (the name she had at birth).

Discrimination

Much progress has been made in fighting sex, racial, and age discrimination in granting credit. The Equal Credit Opportunity Act, for example, contains numerous provisions dealing with sex discrimination. Before the act was passed, some spouses who divorced did not have
2 a credit history. Now joint accounts can have a joint account reported to credit bureaus in both spouses' names.

How to Challenge False Charges on Your Credit Card

If your credit card is lost or stolen or if a false charge shows up on your bill, take action as quickly as possible. You cannot be held liable for more than $50 in false charges, and you cannot be forced to pay any charges made after you report the card missing.

- **Call the card issuer immediately. As soon as you realize that your credit card has been used without your consent, or as soon as you find it missing, telephone the bank or department store and explain.**
- **Follow up with a letter. If you write within 60 days, notifying the issuer of a false charge appearing on your bill, the issuer is required to respond in 30 days and resolve the claim within 90 days of your letter. If you don't write, the card issuer is under no deadline to resolve your dispute.**

CASE STUDY

Consumer NEWS CLIP

Credit Problems: Who's at Risk?

by Mary Rowland
The New York Times
January 23, 1994

Ms. [Tahira K.] Hira [a professor of personal finance and consumer behavior at Iowa State University in Ames] has spent several years looking for similarities among people who get into financial difficulties, particularly those who file for bankruptcy. In the process, she has studied personal bankruptcies in Scotland, Japan, the United States, and Canada.

"Although people who get into financial trouble come from all walks of life, there are some very consistent patterns," Ms. Hira said. Many of them had weak family relationships as children, an unhappy social life in school, and suffer from low self-esteem, she said.

"The way we have been dealing with the problem—negotiating with creditors and working out a payment schedule—is just not adequate," Ms. Hira concluded. "We need to sit down and understand why this person seems to have a consistent financial problem. If we focus only on the financial problems, the same person will be in trouble again in five or six years."

In two weeks of exit interviews with people who had filed for bankruptcy, Ms. Hira and other interviewers focused on three things: Who are you today? What kind of experiences did you have growing up? How do you feel about yourself? "I heard some very consistent patterns," Ms. Hira said. "Even though the people were very different."

Most of the bankruptcy filers had extremely low self-esteem. One or both parents were absent—either physically or emotionally—as they were growing up. And they had not had happy social experiences in school. "I was disturbed by this," Ms. Hira said. "If it held true in the wider population, then doing financial counseling for people in financial trouble was not enough."

Ms. Hira said the wide availability of credit is one reason that more people are getting into financial difficulty. "It's not that people have changed," she said. "It's the environment."

In the 1930s and 40s, people could not as easily compensate for personal inadequacies by spending money. "If you wanted to please a man or please yourself, you couldn't just go out and buy a new outfit if you didn't have money in your hand," she said. "Today I can walk into the mall and buy an outfit with the salary I'll be earning 10 years from now."

Most spenders have no idea of how much their purchases really cost, she said, because they use credit cards. She suggests people go for a week paying for everything with cash. "I have tried this experiment," she said. "I have walked into the store with hard dollars in my hand, and I just can't spend them."

Decisions, Decisions

1. What are some of the common backgrounds of people with credit problems?
2. Why is important to focus on why a person has credit problems?

1 Vocabulary Ask students the difference between fraud and negligence. (Fraud is intentional; negligence is unintentional.)

2 Learning Economics Ask students why loss from credit card fraud affects everyone. (This loss is a cost of doing business that card companies must pass on to businesses, which they in turn must pass on to their customers.)

3 Discussion Starter Ask students who must deal with credit cards in their jobs what policies their employers have with regard to handling credit card purchases.

Deceitful Practices by Customers

Some customers are not truthful about their ability to repay. They borrow recklessly, sometimes with no intention of ever paying back the money. Some
1 customers deliberately commit fraud.

Fraud

As you know from Chapter 8, the deliberate deception of another for some gain is called fraud**.** For example, suppose a person asks you for a charitable contribution. You give money, thinking it will go to the charity. A person keeps the money instead of giving it to the charity, thus committing fraud.

2 Fraud is now costing credit card companies as much as $3 billion a year. Counterfeiting cards, wrongfully using lost or stolen cards, and falsifying computer records have been major problems.

Outwitting those who would practice fraud has proved to be a difficult task in the past. To fight back, companies have improved the cards, making them more difficult to counterfeit. Experts are working hard on the development of cards such as photo ID cards, that will make forgeries even more difficult while expanding card capabilities.

3 The Credit Card Fraud Act of 1984 makes it a federal crime to use any unauthorized card or account number to obtain money, goods, or services. The act imposes prison sentences and stiff fines on persons convicted of such activity.

Loss of Cards

Lost credit cards are a key element in credit card fraud. To protect your card, you should take the steps outlined in Figure 13–2.

Figure 13–2 Credit Card Loss

As a credit card user, you should take the following steps to protect your card.

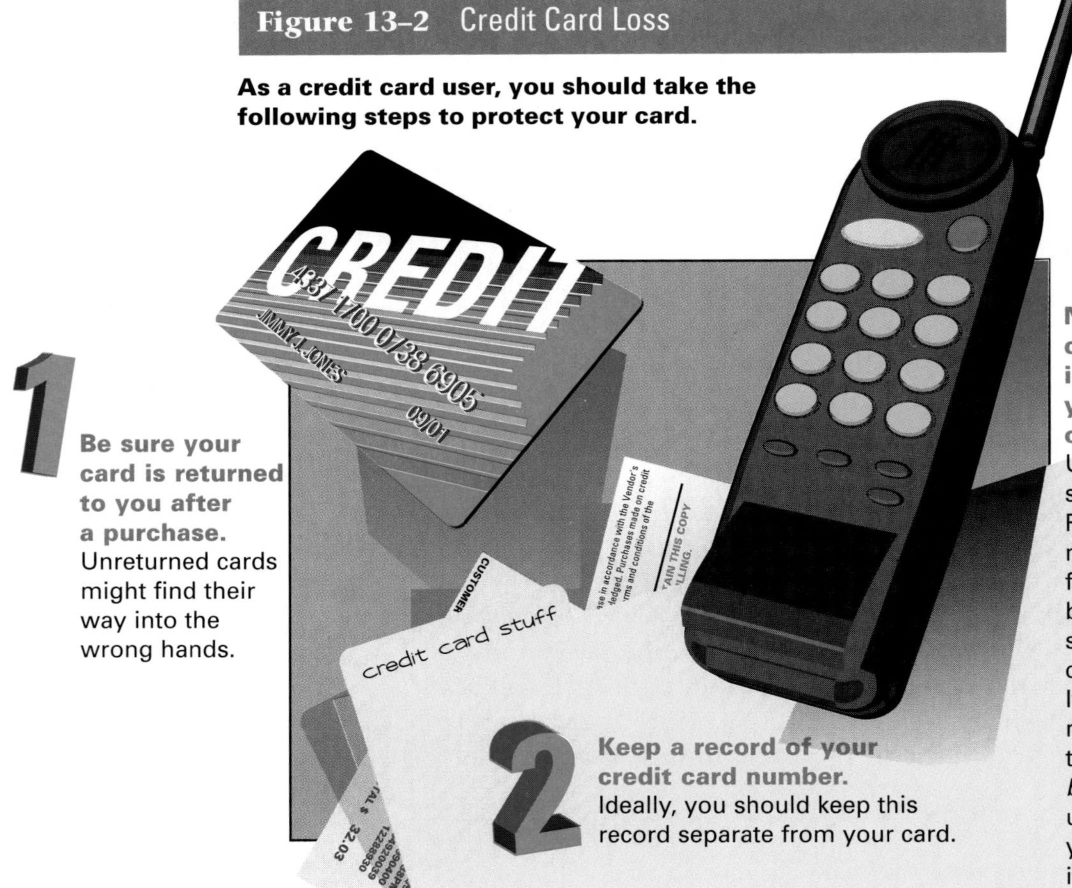

CREDIT
4337 1700 0738 6905
JIMMY L. JONES
09/01
credit card stuff
CUSTOMER
1
Be sure your card is returned to you after a purchase.
Unreturned cards might find their way into the wrong hands.
2
Keep a record of your credit card number.
Ideally, you should keep this record separate from your card.
3
Notify the credit card company immediately if your card is lost or stolen.
Under the Consumer Credit Protection Act, the maximum amount for which you may be held liable if someone uses the card illegally is $50. If, however, you manage to inform the company *before* the card is used to defraud, you have no liability at all.

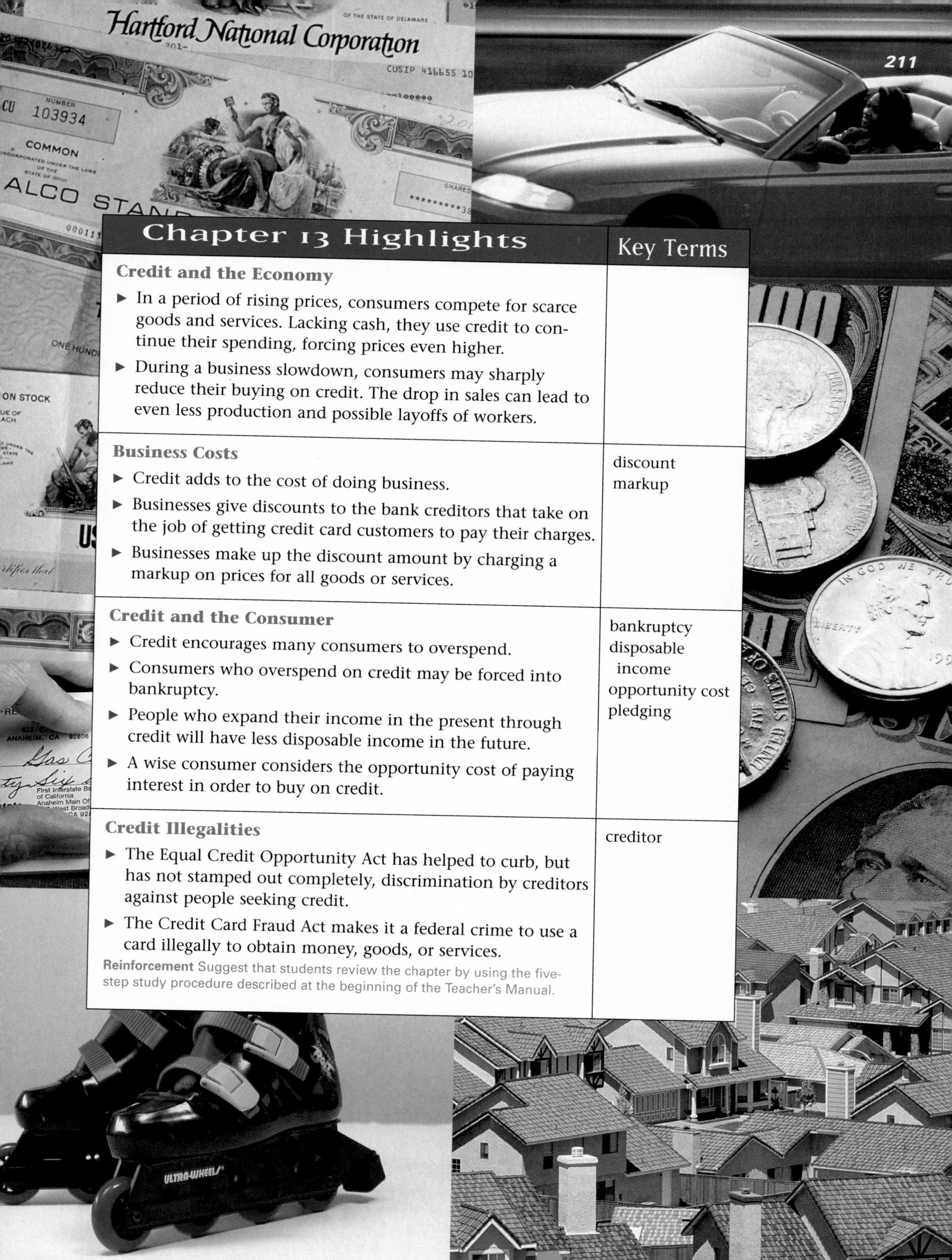

Chapter 13 Highlights

Chapter 13 Highlights	Key Terms
Credit and the Economy ► In a period of rising prices, consumers compete for scarce goods and services. Lacking cash, they use credit to continue their spending, forcing prices even higher. ► During a business slowdown, consumers may sharply reduce their buying on credit. The drop in sales can lead to even less production and possible layoffs of workers.	
Business Costs ► Credit adds to the cost of doing business. ► Businesses give discounts to the bank creditors that take on the job of getting credit card customers to pay their charges. ► Businesses make up the discount amount by charging a markup on prices for all goods or services.	discount markup
Credit and the Consumer ► Credit encourages many consumers to overspend. ► Consumers who overspend on credit may be forced into bankruptcy. ► People who expand their income in the present through credit will have less disposable income in the future. ► A wise consumer considers the opportunity cost of paying interest in order to buy on credit.	bankruptcy disposable income opportunity cost pledging
Credit Illegalities ► The Equal Credit Opportunity Act has helped to curb, but has not stamped out completely, discrimination by creditors against people seeking credit. ► The Credit Card Fraud Act makes it a federal crime to use a card illegally to obtain money, goods, or services. **Reinforcement** Suggest that students review the chapter by using the five-step study procedure described at the beginning of the Teacher's Manual.	creditor

CHAPTER 13 REVIEW

Refer students to the Reviewing Consumer Terms and Reviewing Facts and Ideas activities in the Student Activity Workbook.

Reviewing Consumer Terms Scripts will vary. Students should act out their scripts for the class. See Glossary for definitions.

Reviewing Facts and Ideas See the Student Activity Workbook for answers.

Problem Solving and Decision Making Monika can explain that part of the cost of buying one item is the loss of the other item.

Consumers Around the World
Math 1 You have $15,500 to spend this year. You have $14,400 to spend next year ($15,000 − $600 loan plus interest = $14,400).

Human Relations
2 In their reports on bankruptcy, students should define bankruptcy, describe generally how to declare bankruptcy, and give the consequences of declaring bankruptcy.

Social Studies
3 Student reports might use the term *eminent domain.*

Reviewing Consumer Terms

Working in pairs develop a written script about consumer credit problems. Use all of the terms in your script. Then act out your script in front of the class.

bankruptcy
creditor
discount
disposable income
markup
opportunity cost
pledging

Reviewing Facts and Ideas

1. Explain how easy credit can become a problem during a period of inflation.
2. Why are goods likely to cost more at a store after it begins to extend credit?
3. Your neighbors who buy on credit from a local department store may be paying twice for the privilege. For example, they may have to pay interest charges. In what other way do they pay for the use of credit?
4. Which law was passed in an effort to stamp out discrimination in the field of credit?
5. Why do some businesses *not* offer in-house credit but shift the burden to bank card agencies?
6. True or false: If you are a married woman, you may not get a credit card in your birth name (the name you had before you married).
7. Describe deceitful practices used at times by borrowers and lenders.
8. What are three ways consumers can safeguard use of their credit cards?

Problem Solving and Decision Making

Monika Kraus has given her 8-year-old sister, Catherine, a gift of $5. Catherine hopes that if she buys a $5 action figure, she will still have enough money to buy a storybook priced at $5. How can Monika explain the concept of opportunity cost to Catherine?

Building Academic Skills

Consumers Around the World

Math

1. Your disposable income is $15,000 a year. On January 2, you borrow $500 for 12 months at 20 percent interest. How much money do you have to spend this year? Next year?

Human Relations

2. Research bankruptcy in the library. Answer these questions in a 500-word report: What is bankruptcy? How does a person declare bankruptcy? Can a person go to jail for not paying his or her debts? What are the consequences of bankruptcy for the individual?

Social Studies

3. Cuba, an island republic located in the Caribbean Sea, became a Communist state in 1959. By

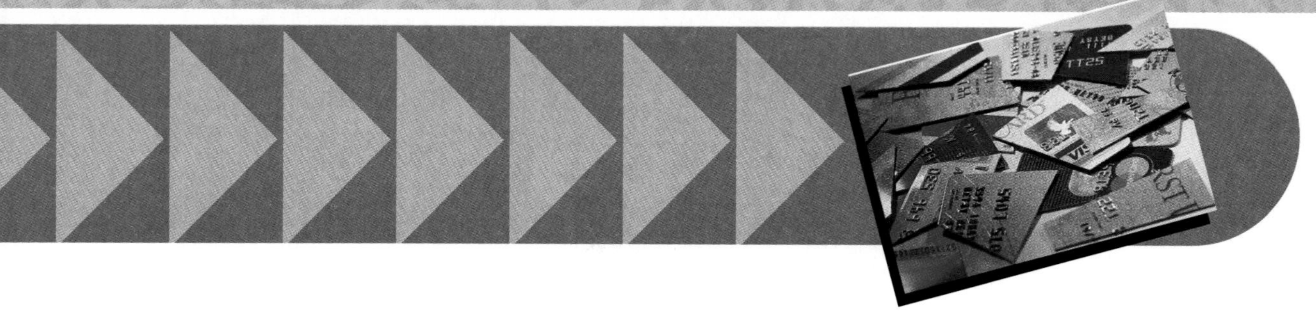

1960, over $1 billion worth of property in Cuba owned by U.S. companies and citizens was taken over by the Cuban government. The Cuban Communist government's idea was that all industry should be owned by all people in the state.

The takeover has led to a huge credit problem. Cuba has yet to compensate companies such as American Sugar, ITT, and Texaco for the loss of their properties.

Research this situation. Do the companies feel they should be awarded money for their loss? Do they claim interest on the money they have yet to receive? What is the position of the Cuban government on compensation? How do you think the lack of compensation affected Cuba's credit trustworthiness? In the United States, what is the government's responsibility to individuals and firms from which it takes land or property? Give your findings in a 750-word report.

Beyond the Classroom

Consumer Project

Interview a merchant or other business owner on the subject of credit. Does the person think credit cards are a good thing for the average consumer? Why or why not? Write up your findings for an oral presentation in the classroom. Organize your talk into three parts: an introduction to your project, a discussion of answers to your questions, and your conclusions.

Cooperative Learning

Family Economics

Break into assigned family groups. Discuss the following problem.

You know all too well the problems that overuse of credit can cause. Your Aunt May and Uncle Harry were recently forced into bankruptcy by all the debt they had accumulated using their nearly 15 credit cards and store charge accounts. Your family is now considering a modest expansion in its credit resources (or the development of some resources if you don't have any).

Given your family's financial situation, devise a set of guidelines to keep May and Harry's fate from becoming yours. Compare your answers with those of other family groups.

Debate the Issue

A counselor for debt-prone or debt-laden young people always tells clients at the first meeting: "Tear up all your credit cards. Now!"

This sounds like bitter medicine. Is it too bitter, or is it appropriate? Research the favorable and unfavorable experiences that overextended young people have had with (and without) credit cards. These experiences are freely discussed in magazines, newspapers, and books.

You and your classmates will break into two groups and research this topic. Each group will gather evidence to support one side or the other. You are to prepare the argument for your side of the problem. Then the two groups will meet in a classroom debate.

They may discuss how philosophical ideas can come into conflict with economic principles.

Consumer Project
In an oral presentation, students should open with a description of the interview project, including who was interviewed. They should follow with a report on the substance of the interview and finish with their own views on the subject.

Family Economics
Most families will want to limit the number of cards and the circumstances under which they will be used. Some may even opt not to carry the cards in order to discourage impulse purchases.

Debate the Issue
Break the class into two teams. Assign each team one side of the issue. Encourage students to work together as a team to develop their argument. Ask each team to select a member to make an opening statement that supports the team's side of the issue. Have students take turns debating as the debate moves from one team to the other.

CHAPTER 14

Charge Accounts

Learning Objectives

When you have finished studying this chapter, you should be able to:

1. List six advantages and three disadvantages of charge accounts.
2. Distinguish between regular and revolving charge accounts, and identify the balance computation method that is least costly to the consumer.
3. Explain the purpose of a security agreement, and list at least four items covered in one.
4. Identify information on a monthly statement that enables customers to manage their account.
5. Describe the first action consumers must take to secure their rights under the Fair Credit Billing Act.

Consumer Terms

line of credit
repossess
trade-in allowance
credit rating
regular charge account
finance charge
revolving charge account
annual percentage rate (APR)
adjusted balance
grace period

Real-World Journal

Credit cards offer consumers a convenient and easy method of making purchases. However, credit use can lead to overspending and debt. In your journal, explain why you feel many people who buy on credit end up in financial trouble.

Lesson Plan See the Teacher's Manual for Chapter 14 lesson plan.

Vocabulary The Chapter 14 lesson plan includes suggested vocabulary activities for the terms listed.

1 Research Have each student survey three people to find out the line of credit these people have with their various charge accounts. Compile the results in class.

2 Math Application Have students assume that a person with unlimited credit purchased \$3,500 worth of furniture. The store had a "60 days, same as cash" policy, but charged $1\frac{1}{2}$ percent a month interest for the first two months and all subsequent months if the full amount was not paid within 60 days. The customer forgot to make the payment until the 61st day. How much did this lapse in memory cost the customer? (\$3,500 × .015 = \$52.50 × 2 = \$105)

3 Extension Ask the students to name some other purchases that involve trade-ins as part of the transaction. (Cars and car parts are probably the best-known examples.)

4 Extension Depending on the kind of checking account Ellen has and her balance, there may be another advantage to handling her purchases in this way. Ask students what that advantage might be. (She saves on the cost of checks)

ADVANTAGES AND DISADVANTAGES OF CHARGE ACCOUNTS

When you open a charge account or get a credit card, you receive a certain
1 line of credit. A **line of credit** is the largest amount you may owe the store at any given time. Sometimes you must sign an agreement giving the seller the right to **repossess** (take back) merchandise that is not paid for on time.

If you are buying a costly item, you may be told the terms are "Sixty days—same as cash." This phrase means that a person who pays within 60 days will not be charged interest. The transaction is
2 looked upon as a cash purchase.

Advantages of Charge Accounts

Charge accounts offer consumers many advantages. Among them are the following.

Temporary Expansion of Income Marsha and Ted DiBello had been married only a few months. Furnishing an apartment was costly, but they now had nearly all the necessary furnishings. The refrigerator was still a problem. It leaked and functioned improperly.

They knew that with the next month's income they would have enough to pay for a refrigerator. They needed the appliance now, though, not next month.

An appliance store near their apartment had a refrigerator that met their needs. Ted and Marsha decided to use their charge account to buy it.

The price of the new model was reduced by the liberal **trade-in allowance,** that is, credit received for turning in their old appliance. The charge account enabled them to expand their income in the present month
3 when they needed to make an important purchase.

Reduced Need for Cash Martin Alvarez was a great believer in planning. He budgeted his money carefully because he was saving to buy a CD player. Each day, he took just enough cash to buy his lunch, pay bus fare, and have a little extra for emergencies.

One afternoon, Martin stopped to browse at the record counter of Big B Department Store. He saw a CD that he had intended to buy on the weekend. However, Martin would be going to a friend's house after work and thought he would like to take the CD with him. He decided to charge the CD on his store charge account. A charge account enables you to buy, even when you were not carrying cash.

Shopping Convenience Ellen Moy works long hours and has little time to spare for shopping. Therefore, she usually makes several purchases at once.

Ellen finds that with a retail charge card she saves time. She does not have to write many small checks. Each store lists all her purchases on her monthly statements. She then pays at her convenience, writing only one check to each store. In addition, she can order merchandise by telephone and have it
4 delivered.

Cash or Charge in Mexico

The average U.S. household carries a dozen credit cards. Shoppers in Mexico City are most likely to use cash: 78 percent do not use credit cards.

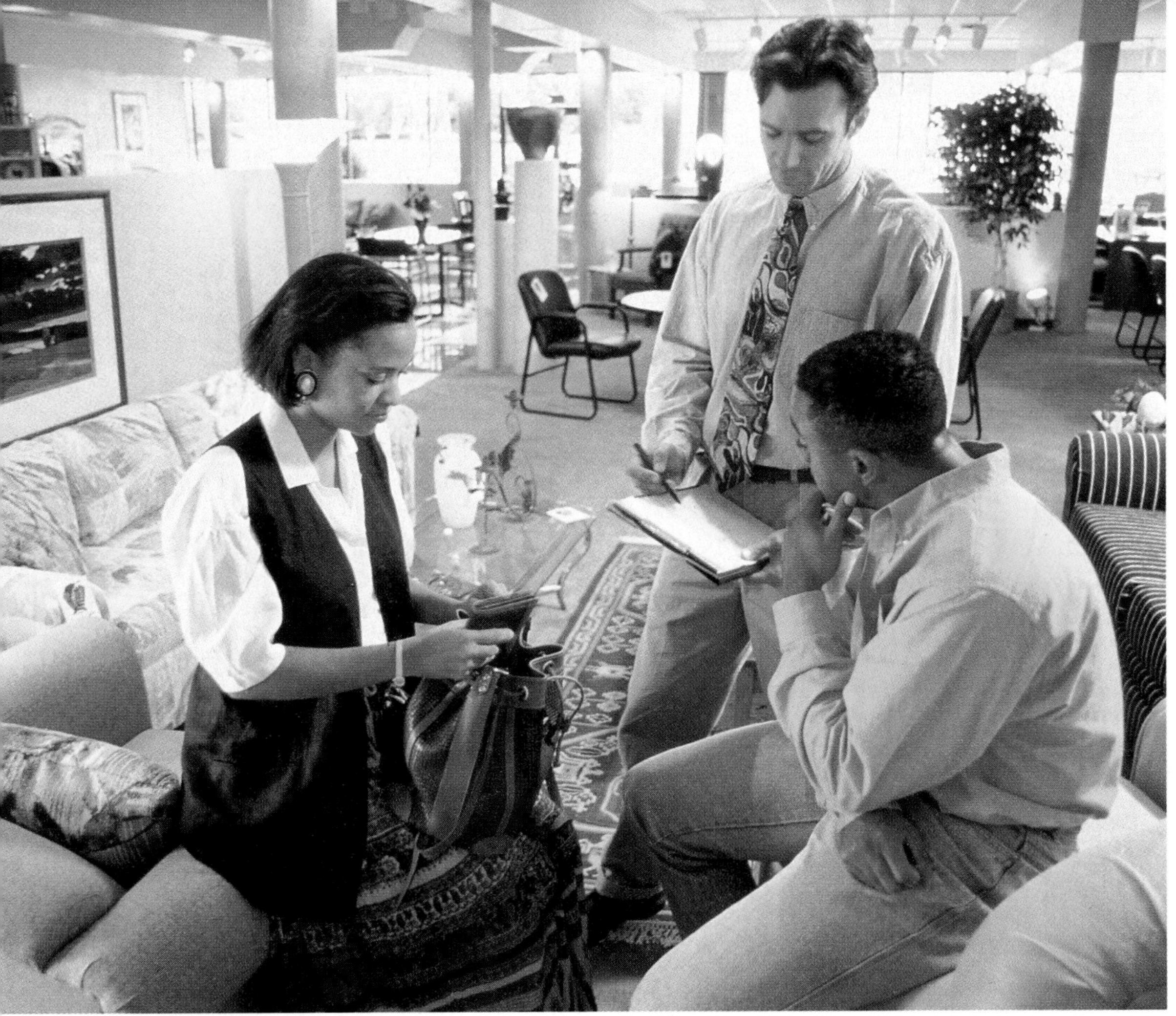

▲ *Charge Accounts have many advantages.* ***Do you think safety is an advantage? Explain.***

1 Learning Economics Point out to students that Verna and Lonnell are doing what all successful businesses do—planning ahead.

2 Student Motivator Have students make a list of purchases they have had to return because of faulty merchandise. Also have them list whether or not the item was paid for in full and what problems, if any, they encountered in trying to return the merchandise. From their experiences, can they see any advantages in using credit?

Caption Answer: If you use a charge account card, you need not carry around large sums of cash that can be lost or stolen.

Establishment of Credit Verna and Lonnell Stewart-Anderson were recently married. They realized that paying cash for everything (as they could afford to do) would leave no credit record. They would certainly need credit if they decided to buy a car or a house some day.

They decided to buy a few items on credit each month and keep a record of those purchases so they would not overspend. Further, they paid their bills as soon as they received statements at the end of the month. This way, they developed a reputation as promptly paying customers.

Paying debts on time gave them a good credit rating. A **credit rating** is a record, kept by a credit rating agency, that tells prospective creditors how good a person is at paying off debts. When the Stewart-Andersons really needed credit at some time in the future, it would
1 already be established.

Ease of Returns Alan Soo paid cash for a self-propelled, gas-powered lawn mower from a local store. When he got home, Alan started the machine. Suddenly, the mower belched forth black smoke and came to a halt.

Dismayed, Alan loaded the mower back into his car for a trip to the store. He wanted to return the mower; however, the manager refused to refund Alan's money. The manager said that all Alan had to do was take the mower to an approved service center 50 miles away,
2 and it would be repaired free of charge.

Alan insisted that the goods he had received were substandard. He wished he had not paid cash. If he had still owed the merchant for the purchase, he could

FLASHBACK FLASHFORWARD

In the 1950s, Diner's Club's annual worldwide charge volume was less than $10 million. In 1993, worldwide charge volume had increased to almost $21 billion.

1 Critical Thinking Ask students if they can think of any possible disadvantages to Alan if he had used credit for the purchase and refused to pay. (To some degree, he might have been jeopardizing his credit rating. A late payment notation or a dispute notation or both would show up on his credit report.)

2 Math Application Have students assume that Tami paid $247 for her coat. How much would Carlotta have paid for the same coat? ($148.20)

3 Learning Economics Remind students that all businesses are trying to make a profit and, therefore, that a business has to pay for the costs of offering credit—either through service charges or higher prices.

4 Discussion Starter Ask students if they know what kinds of credit plans their parents have. Compare the plans in a class discussion.

have refused payment until he was given a replacement.

Alan resolved never again to pay cash for an expensive item. Instead, he would charge the cost, paying only once he knew the merchandise was good. It is easier to return goods or otherwise secure service
1 for items on which payment is still due.

Advance Notice of Sales Tami Berg was proud of her new winter coat. She had bought it at Milady's, a downtown women's shop. The coat had cost more than she could afford, but it made her feel so elegant that she knew it was worth the money.

The next day while she was visiting Carlotta, her friend modeled a new coat she had bought a week earlier. It was an exact duplicate of Tami's, purchased at the same store but at a
2 40 percent discount.

"Milady's always tells us in advance about sales because we have a charge account there," Carlotta explained. "We go to the store a day before the sale is announced in the newspapers and buy what we want at sale prices."

Tami was discouraged. Now she knew why some people maintained charge accounts—to get advance notice of sales. They may then choose from a wide variety of merchandise at sale prices before the sale starts.

Disadvantages of Charge Accounts

The problems involved in using charge accounts are basically the same as those involved in any use of credit. First, any bills not paid when due are subject to interest charges. Second, there is the temptation to overspend.

Finally, charge accounts carry an additional disadvantage. Customers may find themselves shopping only at stores where they have accounts. By so doing, they may not be taking advantage of sales or lower prices at other stores, nor are they able to compare the quality of
3 merchandise from one place to another.

TYPES OF CHARGE ACCOUNTS

Many large department stores and other retail businesses offer two types of credit plans to their customers. One type
4 of credit is the regular charge account.

Using a charge card to buy items on the spur of the moment is very tempting. ***How can consumers control their credit card use?*** ▶

Caption Answer: Plan for your purchases, and use your charge card only when you know you have the money to pay the bill.

With a **regular charge account,** customers are expected to pay the unpaid balance of their accounts within a specified time, often 25 to 30 days after the billing date. The store usually reserves the right to add a **finance charge**—the total cost of credit, including interest and any other charges. This finance charge is added to the balance if the total amount is not paid in full by a specified date.

A second type of credit plan is also available. Under the **revolving charge**
1 **account,** which is sometimes called open-end credit, customers have the option of paying only a portion of the unpaid balance each billing period and paying a finance charge on the balance. If an account has an unpaid balance of $190, for example, the customer might have to pay only $20.

A customer who chooses this option must pay a finance charge, based on the unpaid balance (in this case, $170) and determined by applying an annual percentage rate. The **annual percentage rate (APR)** is the annual rate of interest that is charged for credit. The maximum rate that may be charged is controlled by state law. Under either plan, the store draws up a contract when the account is opened.

Regular Versus Revolving Credit

Some consumers prefer the revolving charge account because they can buy when the price is right and pay when the time is right. There is no pressure to pay the full amount within even two or three months. In addition, they can make further purchases without adding unduly to the amount they must pay each month.

Others prefer the regular charge account because then they must come to grips with credit problems every month, before credit gets out of hand. Remember that the store expects to be paid in full each month. These customers also point out that they do not pay interest on the regular charge account. Revolving credit customers, on the other hand,
2 usually end up paying a finance charge.

Finance Charges

Creditors use different methods of arriving at the amount on which finance charges are based. (See Figure 14-1 on page 220.)

How to Avoid Spending Too Much
It's easy to find things to buy. In the United States, there are 20 square feet of retail space for every American. To avoid spending too much money:

- **Give yourself a limit before you go out.**
- **Carry only as much cash as you can afford to spend. If you have access to ATM machines, take out only what you need or only small amounts.**
- **To avoid charging, don't bring your credit cards with you.**
- **Don't buy on impulse. If you see something you think you want, come back the next day or the next week. If you are concerned that the item will be gone, have the salesperson put it on hold for you.**
- **At a grocery store, add up purchases in your head or with a hand calculator. If the total is over your limit at the checkout, choose some items to put back and buy another time.**

1 Vocabulary Once students have read about revolving credit, have them offer their own explanations of the term *revolving charge account.* (Answers will vary but might include the idea that the unpaid balance turns over, or revolves, and appears on the next statement.)

2 Discussion Starter Some department stores do not give people opening new charge accounts a choice between regular and revolving credit. All new credit customers are given revolving accounts with a minimal line of credit—say, $200. Do students feel this is a good policy? Why or why not? Would they open an account under these terms?

Of the four methods, the one using the **adjusted balance,** which is the beginning balance less any payments or other credits, is the least costly to the consumer. The consumer can get almost 60 days of interest-free credit (under optimum conditions). This interest-free credit period is referred to as a **grace period.** If the consumer pays for an item before the second billing date arrives, no interest is charged on the purchase.

The American Express Optima True Grace card is so-named to emphasize that its grace period, or free ride, applies regardless of whether you started the current period with a zero balance in your account.

THE SECURITY AGREEMENT

When you open an account, the credit card agency or retailer will have you sign—and will then give you a copy of—its credit plan and security agreement. Although that document may be several pages in length, you should read it for you are bound by its terms. Much of the detail is necessary if the firm is to comply with various state and federal regulations.

Annual or Membership Fees

Store charge accounts generally do not charge an annual or membership fee. Most bank cards, such as VISA and MasterCard, do charge a fee.

Figure 14–1 Computing Your Charge Account Balance

Four plans are currently used to figure balances.

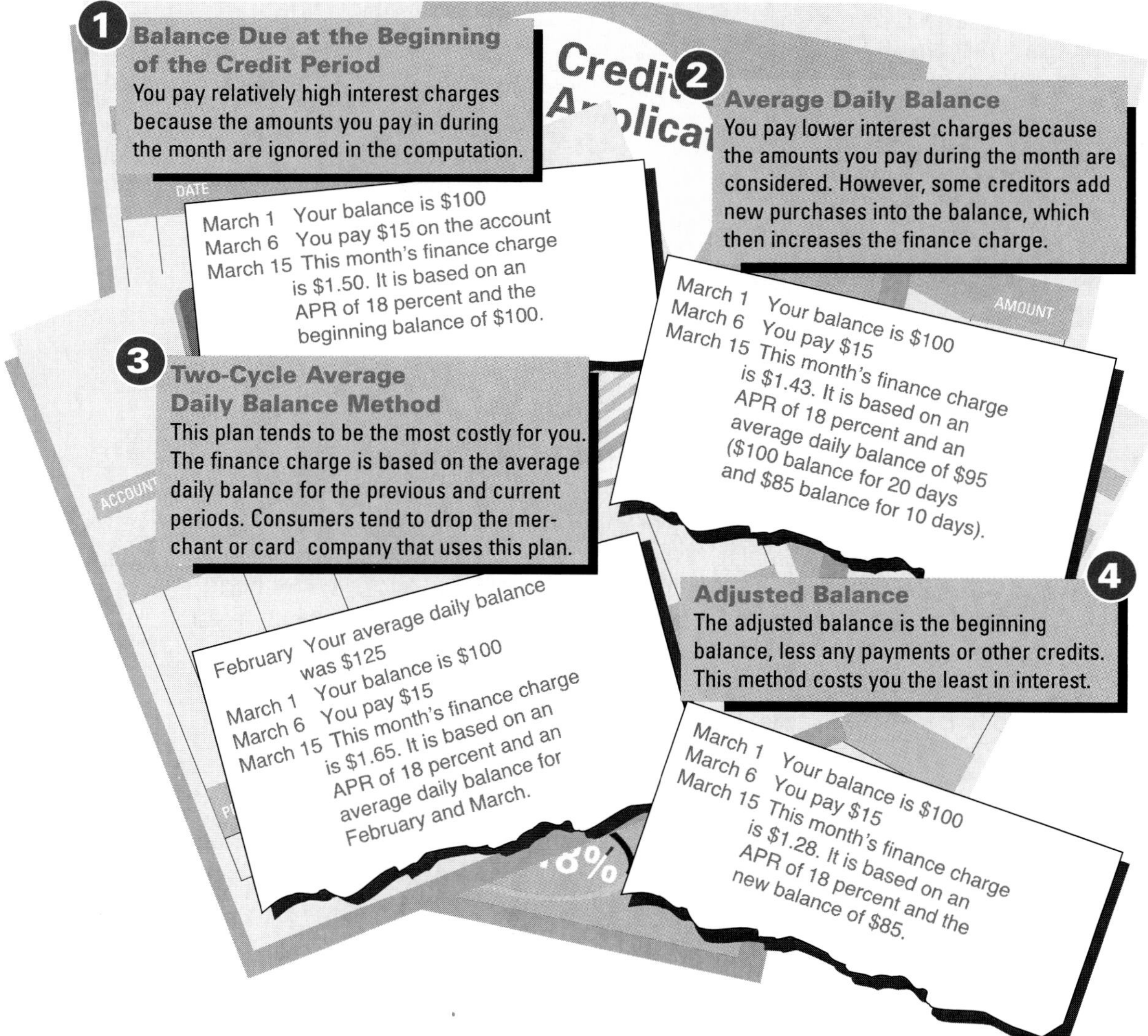

1
Balance Due at the Beginning of the Credit Period
You pay relatively high interest charges because the amounts you pay in during the month are ignored in the computation.
March 1 Your balance is $100
March 6 You pay $15 on the account
March 15 This month's finance charge is $1.50. It is based on an APR of 18 percent and the beginning balance of $100.
2
Average Daily Balance
You pay lower interest charges because the amounts you pay during the month are considered. However, some creditors add new purchases into the balance, which then increases the finance charge.
March 1 Your balance is $100
March 6 You pay $15
March 15 This month's finance charge is $1.43. It is based on an APR of 18 percent and an average daily balance of $95 ($100 balance for 20 days and $85 balance for 10 days).
3
Two-Cycle Average Daily Balance Method
This plan tends to be the most costly for you. The finance charge is based on the average daily balance for the previous and current periods. Consumers tend to drop the merchant or card company that uses this plan.
February Your average daily balance was $125
March 1 Your balance is $100
March 6 You pay $15
March 15 This month's finance charge is $1.65. It is based on an APR of 18 percent and an average daily balance for February and March.
4
Adjusted Balance
The adjusted balance is the beginning balance, less any payments or other credits. This method costs you the least in interest.
March 1 Your balance is $100
March 6 You pay $15
March 15 This month's finance charge is $1.28. It is based on an APR of 18 percent and the new balance of $85.

Grace Period

Store charge accounts usually allow a grace period during which you are not charged a finance charge on new purchases. The grace period, or free ride, is usually 28 or 30 days. With many stores, if you have a balance in your account, you do not get a grace period on new purchases.

Payment Obligations

You have the option to pay in full each month to avoid finance charges. If you do not pay the total balance in full each month, you usually agree to make at least a minimum payment within 30 days of the billing date. If you do not pay the total new balance within 30 days, a finance charge will be

Escape from Tyranny

For years, Cubans have fled the tyranny of the Castro government to look for a new life in the United States. They escape from Cuba any way they can. Most often, however, they sail away on small boats or rafts.

The refugees face numerous dangers in the water between Cuba and the Florida coast. Rough seas can capsize a boat. Desperate refugees may get lost or starve. Many have escaped Castro only to find death in the ocean.

José Basulto tries to improve their odds of arriving safely in the United States. In 1991, the former Cuban refugee founded a group called Hermanos al Rescate (Brothers to the Rescue). Hermanos is made up of volunteer pilots who fly over the water between the United States and Cuba searching for rafts. When they spot refugees, they drop food and medical supplies to the boat. Then they contact the United States Coast Guard, which rescues the people.

When Hermanos first started, Basulto had only one plane. Today, the group uses five planes and has 36 volunteers to fly them. The pilots have made more than 1,500 trips over the rough ocean waters. They have helped rescue 4,500 Cuban refugees.

Although the pilots are experienced, their missions are not completely safe. Planes have crashed because of accidents or engine failure. Basulto himself crashed one time.

For the refugees, however, the Hermanos have been life savers. That knowledge is what keeps the group flying.

Brainstorm

Making the trip from Cuba safely is only one of the problems facing refugees to the United States. What are some of the others?

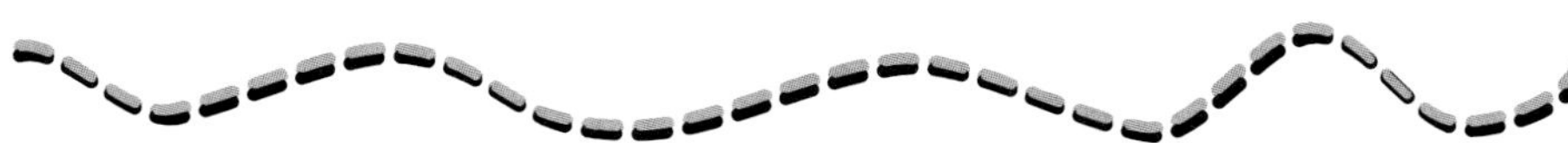

Case Study Answer: Lack of language skills; lack of work; separation from family; hostility of Americans; low-paying jobs; problems with immigration; new customs; new food; schools; finding housing.

1 Reinforcement
Have students use the statement in Figure 14–2 to answer these questions:
(*a*) What were the total charges for the period? ($36.41)
(*b*) What APR is charged when finance charges are assessed? (21 percent)

2 Reinforcement
Student Activity Workbook, Chapter 14 activities.

News Clip Answers:
1 Retailers like electronic, debit, and credit card payments because they often are more convenient for their customers. That convenience may lead to more sales. Electronic payments are also cheaper to administer and more secure than cash or check transactions.
2 Since many businesses accept credit, debit, and charge cards, consumers can carry less cash with them. Electronic transactions can also be quicker and more convenient.

added to the account for the current billing period. The seller may require payment at once of the entire outstanding balance of your account if you fail to make a required monthly payment when due.

Annual Percentage Rate

The agreement must give the annual percentage rate (APR) that you will pay in finance charges. Most stores have a fixed rate, which may be as high as, say, 22 percent a year. Rates vary by state.

The security agreement usually also specifies the APR as a monthly rate. Thus, an APR of 18 percent means that 1.5 percent interest is charged monthly.

Bank credit cards sometimes use a variable rate APR. This means that the APR can go up or down depending on other economic factors.

Computation Method

The agreement specifies the method used to compute the balance on which finance charges will be based. The most favorable methods for the consumer are the adjusted balance and the average daily balance when newly billed purchases are excluded.

Minimum Finance Charge

The finance charge includes the interest you pay and miscellaneous fees. Some stores may require you to pay a minimum finance charge when you have no balance and no new purchases. Such charges are typically about 50 cents a month; they vary by state.

Other Fees

The security agreement may specify other fees. Late payment and returned checks may incur a fee, for example.

Security Interest

The seller retains a security interest in the merchandise purchased under this agreement. This security interest enables the seller to retake possession of the merchandise if you do not make your payments when due.

Merchants who sell items valued at several hundred dollars or more usually require a security agreement. However, retailers who sell only low-cost items often disregard or do not require such a clause in the credit contract.

THE MONTHLY STATEMENT

Each month the customer receives a statement, or bill, that updates the status of the account. Some stores do not send a statement unless there is a credit balance (overpayment) or a debit balance (amount due) of $1 or more.

A sample statement from Sears is shown in Figure 14–2 on page 224. Notice the clear statement of the amount of credit available ($3,575), the balance due, and the detailed explanation of the finance charges. The reverse side of the
1 bill, which is not shown, tells how the
2 average daily balance is computed.

FAIR CREDIT BILLING ACT

The Fair Credit Billing Act contains the following provisions relating to monthly statements and credit purchases from stores in general.

1. If a consumer notifies a creditor about a computer error in the statement for his or her credit account, the creditor must respond within 30 days to the consumer's inquiry and must resolve the problem within 90 days.
2. Consumers who use nonstore credit cards to make store purchases are protected if the product or service is faulty. They have the same rights

CASE STUDY

Consumer NEWS CLIP

No Checks. No Cash. No Fuss?

by Thomas McCarroll
Time May 9, 1994

Retailers of all kinds are going the cashless way. Supermarkets such as Safeway and Giant, fast-food restaurants such as Wendy's and Burger King, newspaper stands in Philadelphia's CoreStates Bank Plaza and even some taxis in Manhattan are now accepting credit cards. The New York City transit authority has joined the Washington Metro and the Bay Area Rapid Transit line in installing a fare-card system, which has contributed to a 40 percent drop in fare-beating this year and could soon be used to introduce different price levels that reward frequent riders. Some states, among them Maryland, are replacing food stamps and welfare checks with bank cards that give welfare recipients access to prearranged monthly sums. At the New York City synagogue Ohab Zedek, members can have their monthly donations electronically deducted directly from their bank accounts. "This makes giving more painless," says Sol Zalcgendler, the congregation's executive director.

The push for a cashless society is gaining momentum, however, if only because making money disappear is also a way of saving money. There are about 12 billion pieces of U.S. paper currency, worth $150 billion, circulating worldwide, which works out to about $30 for every person on earth. Keeping all that paper in use is a costly chore for the government. Most $1 bills wear out after about 18 months. To retire, destroy and replace all aging currency costs the government an estimated $200 million a year. Currency is cumbersome for businesses as well. People have to count it, armored cars have to carry it, bank vaults have to store it and security guards have to protect it.

Checks too are expensive to handle. About 55 billion checks are written every year (more than 37 percent of all consumer payments), and the processing costs the nation's financial institutions about $1.30 each. Banks end up losing money on about half of all checking accounts, since the handling costs often exceed the interest earned on lending out the deposits. An electronic transfer, on the other hand, costs only 15 cents per blip.

The main weapon against cash and checks is plastic-credit cards, bank debit cards, and so-called smart cards. Together they represent 9 percent of total consumer payment transactions and are expected to reach 15 percent by 2001. Besides taxicabs and newsstands, credit cards are employed in parking garages and movie theaters and could soon be the way that Americans pay their taxes, if industry lobbyists prevail. But since card issuers charge an average of 16.5 percent while the IRS extracts only 7 percent for late payments, consumer groups warn that taxpayers should be wary. So far, stiff interest rates have done little to curb the use of plastic. The number of VISA and MasterCards in use has climbed 3 percent in the past year, to 225 million, while credit-card transactions have jumped 7.3 percent, to 1.7 billion.

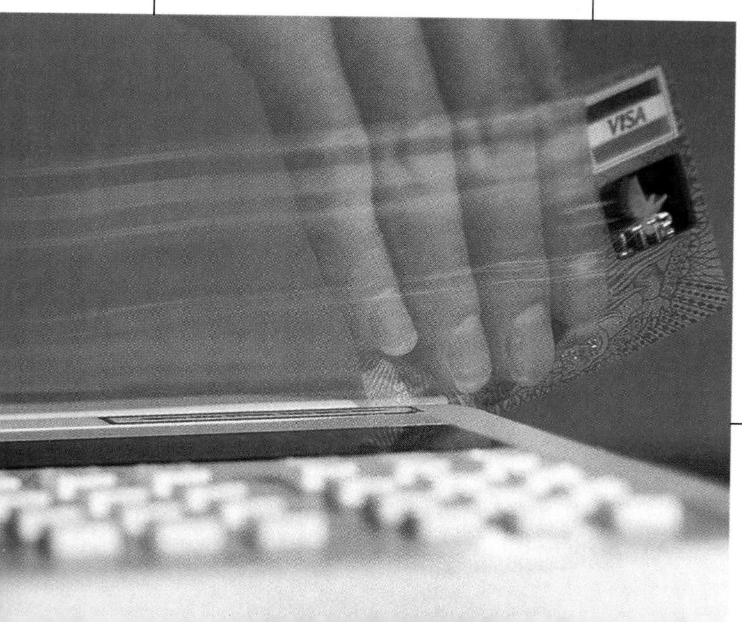

Decisions, Decisions

1. Why are retailers interested in using forms of payment other than cash?
2. What are some of the benefits of charge cards to consumers?

against the credit card agency that they would have had against the store.

To safeguard your rights under the Fair Credit Billing Act, you must write to the creditor within 60 days of receiving a statement that you believe is in error. Your letter should include your name and account number, the amount that is in question, and a description of the
1 problem.

1 Learning Economics The laws are written to protect consumers, but students should realize that most successful businesses probably don't object. Why? (Businesses profit from satisfying their customers.)

Caption Answer: How the charge account balance is computed.

Figure 14–2 Monthly Statement

SEARS Card
BOX 34577
Anytown, US 12345

Account Number: 12 34567 89012 3
Billing date: January 13, 1996

Ms. Mary Lewis
123 Anywhere Street
Hometown, US 55555

ACCOUNT SUMMARY

Previous balance		$31.50
Total payments	–	31.50
Total charges	+	288.09
Total credits	–	105.97
FINANCE CHARGE	+	0.00
New balance		$182.12
Scheduled payment:		$10.00
Minimum due:		**$10.00**
Due date:		**February 12, 1996**

TRANSACTIONS

Dec 15	PANT, 1 PC DRESS, 2 PC DRESS, 2PC DRESS	$98.96
Dec 16	SHIRT, SHIRT, 2PC DRESS, 1PC DRESS, 1PC DRESS, EARS, EARRS 14K	178.02
Dec 16	PARTS, REPAIRS	6.88
Dec 16	SEASONAL / OUTDOOR SHOP	4.23
Dec 17	*CREDIT - RETURN, CREDIT - RETURN*	*–43.98*
Dec 17	*BLOUSE, CREDIT - CANCELLATION: LADIES DRESSES, CREDIT - CANCELLATION: LADIES SPORTSWEAR, CREDIT - CANCELLATION: LADIES SPORTSWEAR, NET AMOUNT FOR TRANSACTION*	*–31.99*
Dec 31	*CREDIT - RETURN, CREDIT - RETURN*	*–30.00*
Jan 06	*PAYMENT - THANK YOU*	*–31.50*

HELPFUL INFORMATION
Available Credit: **$5,445**
If the amount of Available Credit is not sufficient, or you have a question, call:
1-800-000-0000
M - S 9-9, SUN 12-5 ET
Mail any billing error notices to:
BOX 35065
Realtown, US 88888
Please include your account number with any correspondence.

SEARS BONUS CLUB
CONGRATULATIONS! You have earned a Bonus Certificate worth $3.33 in savings at Sears. You will find it enclosed with this statement.

FINANCE CHARGE SCHEDULE	Average Daily Balance	ANNUAL PERCENTAGE RATE	Monthly Periodic Rate	Average Daily Balance	FINANCE CHARGE
All	over $0.00	21.0%	1.75%		
				Total	$0.00

NOTE: See other side for important information

70274787

Tear off and mail this coupon with your payment in the enclosed envelope. Your payment must arrive by the due date to avoid additional finance charges. Make check payable to *Sears* and include your account number on the check. 8480

SEARS PAYMENT CENTER
P. O. BOX 778
COLUMBUS OH 43216-0778

Ms. Mary Lewis
Account Number: 12 34567 89012 3
Billing date: January 13, 1996
New balance: **$182.12**
Minimum due: **$10.00**
Due date: **February 12, 1996**

Amount Paid $________

Address change? Check in box below and write your new address on the back.

P 1234567890123 18212 1000 3150

▲ *This statement summarizes Mary Lewis' account.* ***What additional information is needed if the consumer is to be fully informed?***
Source: *Reprinted courtesy of Sears, Roebuck and Co.*

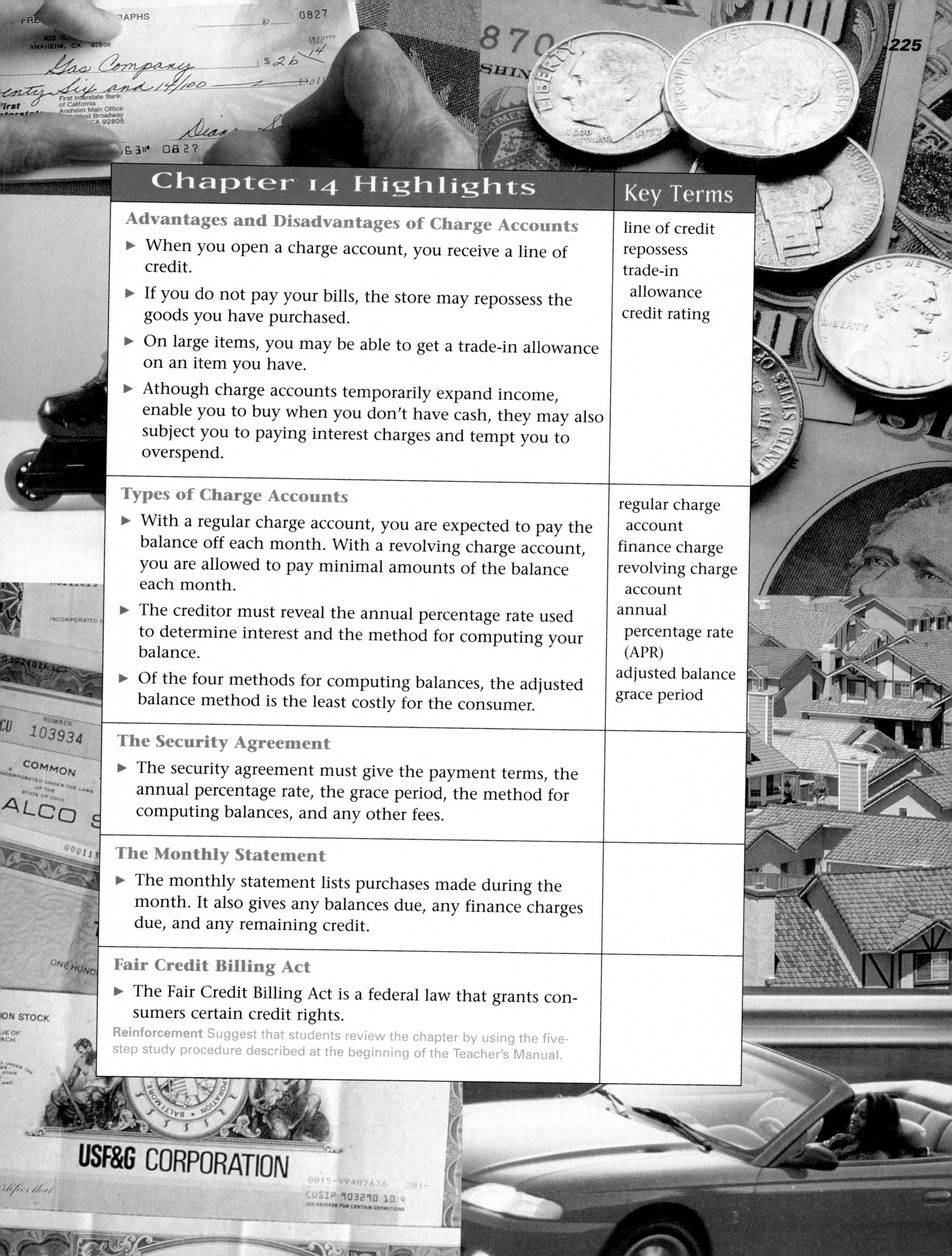

Chapter 14 Highlights

Chapter 14 Highlights	Key Terms
Advantages and Disadvantages of Charge Accounts ► When you open a charge account, you receive a line of credit. ► If you do not pay your bills, the store may repossess the goods you have purchased. ► On large items, you may be able to get a trade-in allowance on an item you have. ► Athough charge accounts temporarily expand income, enable you to buy when you don't have cash, they may also subject you to paying interest charges and tempt you to overspend.	line of credit repossess trade-in allowance credit rating
Types of Charge Accounts ► With a regular charge account, you are expected to pay the balance off each month. With a revolving charge account, you are allowed to pay minimal amounts of the balance each month. ► The creditor must reveal the annual percentage rate used to determine interest and the method for computing your balance. ► Of the four methods for computing balances, the adjusted balance method is the least costly for the consumer.	regular charge account finance charge revolving charge account annual percentage rate (APR) adjusted balance grace period
The Security Agreement ► The security agreement must give the payment terms, the annual percentage rate, the grace period, the method for computing balances, and any other fees.	
The Monthly Statement ► The monthly statement lists purchases made during the month. It also gives any balances due, any finance charges due, and any remaining credit.	
Fair Credit Billing Act ► The Fair Credit Billing Act is a federal law that grants consumers certain credit rights. **Reinforcement** Suggest that students review the chapter by using the five-step study procedure described at the beginning of the Teacher's Manual.	

CHAPTER 14 REVIEW

Refer students to the Reviewing Consumer Terms and Reviewing Facts and Ideas activities in the Student Activity Workbook.

Reviewing Consumer Terms
Puzzles will vary. See Glossary for definitions.

Reviewing Facts and Ideas
See the Student Activity Wookbook for answers.

Problem Solving and Decision Making
1 Problems are that delaying payment will incur finance charges and that purchases are limited to firms that extend credit. **2** Consumer can get emergency service from doctors, plumbers, electrician, and so on without having cash. **3** 12 percent; 18 percent; 30 percent; 36 percent; 42 percent.

Consumers Around the World
Math
1 a $360 × .015 = $5.40; **b** $330 × .02 = $6.60; **c** $300 × .025 = $7.50. Arnie's offers the best deal for credit. Top-Dollar Outlet offers the best deal for cash.

Communications
2 Students should describe clearly the experience of the interviewee with charge accounts or other credit arrangements in a foreign country.

Reviewing Consumer Terms

Build a crossword puzzle using the terms below. Use graph paper to arrange your entries. Then write short definitions for them.

adjusted balance
annual percentage rate
credit rating
finance charge
grace period
line of credit
regular charge account
repossess
revolving charge account
trade-in allowance

Reviewing Facts and Ideas

1. What are the six advantages and three disadvantages of charge accounts?
2. What is the difference between a regular and revolving charge account?
3. What is the purpose of a security agreement?
4. Identify the information found on a monthly statement.
5. What is the first action consumers must take to secure their rights under the Fair Credit Billing Act?

Problem Solving and Decision Making

1. V. J. Mitra resolved never to pay cash for a high-cost purchase. He said he would buy the item on credit, be sure it worked properly, and then pay the bill. Tell why you think this idea is or is not a good one. Can you see anything wrong with his reasoning?
2. One major advantage of credit is that it helps the consumer deal with emergencies effectively. How does this advantage have special meaning where service credit (credit for the use of services rather than goods) is concerned?
3. Compute the annual percentage rate for each of the following monthly finance charge rates: 1 percent; 1.5 percent; 2.5 percent; 3 percent; 3.5 percent.

Building Academic Skills

Consumers Around the World

Math

1. Joanne Hong plans to buy a television set in December on credit. She will pay for the set in January, incurring one month's finance charges.

   The set is available at three locations, each offering a charge account. The method of determining the balance is the same at each, but the APR differs. For each store, compute the amount Joanne would have to pay in interest for one month. Which store offers the best deal?

   a. Arnie's sells the set for $360. The APR is 1.5 percent per month.

   b. Grenville Appliance sells the set for $330. The APR is 2 percent per month.

   c. Top-Dollar Outlet sells the set for $300. The APR is 2.5 percent a month.

Communications

2. Interview a friend, neighbor, relative, or teacher who has traveled

to or lived in another country in recent years. Find out what they observed about credit arrangements. How do they compare charge accounts abroad with those in this country? Did they have trouble communicating about their account to the creditor? Write a 250-word essay, reporting on your findings. Include any recommendations that the interviewee makes about charge accounts.

Human Relations

3. Interview two or more owners or managers of small stores that offer their own charge cards. Ask the following questions: Why do you offer these accounts? Do account holders tend to spend more than other customers? What material do you include with your monthly statement? Why? Do you offer regular accounts or revolving credit accounts? Summarize your findings in a 500-word report. Be sure to quote from your sources. Based on your research, what recommendations would you make to consumers?

Beyond the Classroom

Consumer Project

1. Visit three stores and obtain charge account applications. If possible, also obtain copies of their credit agreements. Compare the forms.
   a. What information is required on all three applications?
   b. In what ways do the credit agreements differ?

Cooperative Learning

Family Economics

Break into assigned family groups. Discuss the following problem.

Your family wants to open a department store charge account. There are three possibilities, all stores that you use regularly. Each, however, offers new credit customers different options:

- G.G. Sandi offers revolving accounts, with finance charges based on beginning balances.
- Mickelmann's offers both regular and revolving accounts, the latter having finance charges based on the average amount owed.
- Tyrone's offers regular accounts only.

All other things being equal, at which store would you open the account and why? Compare your answers with those of other family groups.

Debate the Issue

A number of well-known department stores are giving special perks (privileges) to frequent customers of long standing. Should consumers patronize stores that reward frequent shoppers with perks or should consumers ignore these stores and use bank cards at other stores instead? Research the conditions under which these perks (such as coupons) are distributed.

You and your classmates will break into two groups and research this topic. Each group will gather evidence to support one side or the other. You are to prepare the argument for your side of the problem. Then the two groups will meet in a classroom debate.

Human Relations
3 Students should submit a report of their findings. They may discover that business owners and managers feel customers with charge cards buy more than other customers. They may also find the monthly contact with customers through the billing statement is a source of promotion and increased sales.

Consumer Project
Students should give reasons for their choices and should be able to discuss their choices with others.

Family Economics
Those families with the most limited means will probably opt for revolving accounts at Mickelmann's. Regular accounts at Mickelmann's or Tyrone's are possibilities for higher-income families. All groups should avoid credit buying at G.G. Sandi, where the finance charges would be the highest.

Debate the Issue
Break the class into two teams. Assign each team one side of the issue. Encourage students to work together as a team to develop their argument. Ask each team to select a member to make an opening statement that supports the team's side of the issue. Have students take turns debating as the debate moves from one team to the other.

CHAPTER 15

Installment Credit

Learning Objectives

When you have finished studying this chapter, you should be able to:

1. Distinguish between installment and closed-end credit.
2. List three installment credit features creditors use to guarantee receipt of payments.
3. Identify five installment credit problems.
4. Give the rule of thumb for how much debt a consumer can manage.

Consumer Terms

installment credit
closed-end credit
down payment
security interest
sales finance company
rule of 78s
balloon payment
acceleration clause
add-on clause
prorated
garnishment

Real-World Journal

In this chapter, you will learn about installment credit—credit that is repaid with interest in periodic payments of specified amounts. Ask a parent or other adult about the types of purchases, such as a refrigerator or piece of furniture, that he or she has made on installment credit. Why did he or she choose this method of purchasing? Explain the special incentives, if any, that purchasing on installment credit offered. Summarize your findings in your journal.

Lesson Plan See the Teacher's Manual for Chapter 15 lesson plan.

Vocabulary The Chapter 15 lesson plan includes suggested vocabulary activities for the terms listed.

1 Student Motivator Have students make lists of the big-ticket items owned by their families. Then compile a class list. Are students surprised by the number of such items owned by the average family? This activity might lead to a discussion of the idea that what is considered a big-ticket item depends on the family's income.

2 Reinforcement Student Activity Workbook, Chapter 15 activities.

3 Discussion Starter Ask students to tell about personal experiences they have had with any of these three features.

4 Learning Economics Have students assume that they own an appliance store. The store policy is to require at least a 20 percent down payment on all appliance purchases. Two competitors begin to advertise credit purchases in which no down payment is required. What would they do?

Caption Answer: Installment credit might be the only credit offered by the creditor. The customer might not qualify for open-ended credit.

INSTALLMENT VERSUS OPEN-END CREDIT

American consumers have a hearty appetite for costly items, such as cars, television sets, and computer systems. Often they want these goods before they have enough cash to pay for them. Dealers have found that they can increase sales of big-ticket (expensive) items by letting consumers buy on the install-
1 ment plan.

Installment credit is credit that is to be repaid with interest in periodic payments of specified amounts. It is most often used to purchase expensive items or to borrow money. The buyer (or borrower) makes regular (installment) payments, and finance charges are a part
2 of each payment.

The borrower and the lender sign an installment credit contract that states, among other things, the amount of the purchase, the total finance charge, and the amount of each payment.

Federal credit laws do not use the word *installment*. Instead, they refer to this kind of transaction as closed-end credit. **Closed-end credit** is a one-time extension of credit for a specified amount with payment to be made at a definite time. Since the definite time is usually in the form of a schedule of payments, most closed-end credit is of the installment type. The differences between installment and open-end credit, such as the use of credit cards and charge accounts, are summarized in Figure 15–1.

INSTALLMENT CREDIT CHARACTERISTICS

Installment credit has a few special characteristics. Three in particular—the down payment, the security interest, and the sale of the installment contract—affect the buyer directly. These features sometime make installment credit much less advantageous to the consumer than
3 credit cards or charge cards.

Down Payment

Because items sold on the installment plan are usually expensive, sellers want some sort of guarantee that customers will make their installment payments. One incentive is the down payment.

A **down payment** is a cash amount customers pay when they make an installment purchase. It is a portion of the total price of the item. For example, Jim and Alison Schmidt bought a new $800 bedroom set on the installment plan. They gave the store $100 as a down payment when they signed the contract. The merchant then felt sure they would keep up their payments to avoid losing the $100 they had already
4 paid.

Security Interest

A seller wants even more protection, though, when an expensive item is involved. Customers, therefore, sign a contract giving the merchant a **security**

Figure 15–1 Comparison of Installment and Open-End Credit

Installment Credit	Open-End Credit
Down payment required.	No down payment required.
Security interest retained by creditor.	Any security interest retained is of little significance.
Interest charged from the first day.	Free ride given during interest-free grace period.
Contract signed covers one-time purchase.	Contract signed covers all purchases.
Installment amounts fixed by creditors.	Installment amounts set by customer (within limits).

▲ ***If open-end credit has more advantages for the consumer, why would someone choose installment credit?***

interest in the property—the right to take back, or repossess, the goods if payments are not made according to schedule.

Suppose Jim and Alison fail to make their installment payments on their purchase. The merchant repossesses their bedroom set when they still owe $250 on it. The merchant can then resell the furniture.

If the sale brings more than $250 after expenses, Jim and Alison are entitled to the extra money from the sale. Should the furniture bring less than $250, Jim and Alison must pay the difference to the seller. They must pay it

Earthquake Relief

In January 1994, residents of the greater Los Angeles area were hurled from their beds by a devastating earthquake. Thousands were left homeless, buildings were shattered, and food and fresh water were in short supply.

While many people sympathized with the stricken Angelenos, Oregonian Barbara Nichols acted. The American Red Cross told her the most needed items were nonperishable food and water. So Nichols contacted Crystal Springs Water Company, which donated 900 gallons of bottled water. The company's generosity was such that the bottled water was too much weight for Nichols's van.

Undaunted, Barbara Nichols went to Budget truck rental, which provided a 3-ton truck to haul the water. Now she had more room than water. Another call went to Reser's Fine Foods and Northwest Medical Teams. By the time Nichols and her children left Oregon three days after the quake, she had a truckload of food, water, diapers, and toys.

Nichols had never been to the San Fernando Valley, the center of the earthquake. She did not even know if the roads were open. She just headed south. Eventually, she found her way to the Salvation Army center that was distributing supplies to earthquake victims. Nichols and her children helped hand out some of the items to grateful residents.

Nichols took her children with her to the ravaged area so that they could see what happens when people help other people. They also learned that when you help others, others help you. Barbara Nichols and her children had no way to get home once they returned the Budget truck to the Los Angeles airport. That problem was soon solved when, in gratitude for their help, Reno Air sent the Nichols family home first-class.

Brainstorm

What could you and your friends do to help victims of earthquakes?

Case Study Answer: Answers include providing an earthquake relief fund and collecting water, food, and blankets for victims.

1 Math Application Have students assume they purchased an appliance for $497. They paid $50 down and made six monthly payments of $28.50 each. They were unable to make the remaining payments so the appliance was repossessed. How much did they still owe on the appliance when it was repossessed? ($497 − $50 − [6 × $28.50] = $276)

2 Math Application Have students assume that a business sold all of its credit contracts to a sales finance company for $7,650. The full value of the contracts was $8,210. What percentage to the nearest whole percent of the full value did the business forfeit? ($8,210 − $7,650 = $560; $560 ÷ $8,210 = .068 = 7%)

3 Student Motivator Obtain, photocopy, and distribute copies of an installment credit contract. Have students read the contract aloud in class. When students become aware of the difficulty in understanding much of the contract, point out the real-life importance of improving their reading skills.

4 Extension Student Activity Workbook, Chapter 15 activities.

even though they no longer have the furniture. The amount already paid, plus the amount due, is looked upon as rent for the bedroom set while they had it. Some states have passed laws to give consumers special rights if they have paid a high percentage of the install-
1 ment price by the time of repossession.

Sales Finance Companies

A store may sell goods on the installment plan and immediately turn over its installment contract to a **sales finance company,** an organization that buys up contracts from local stores that do not want to engage in financing credit. The sales finance company makes a profit by purchasing contracts at a discount, then collecting the full contract price from consumers. A finance company usually notifies customers when it has bought their accounts. Customers are asked to send their regular payments to the finance company rather than to the store. A coupon book is often enclosed with the letter. One of the coupons
2 should accompany each payment.

Try It Before You Buy It
Buying something and not using it is a waste of money. If you're not sure about your purchase, ask whether you can try it—at the store or at home.

- **Chain stores that sell music recordings now have listening stations so that you can listen to the music before you buy.**
- **Video stores rent video games. Try one for a few days before you invest in buying one.**
- **Specialty stores rent everything from electronic equipment to mountain bikes and vintage clothing. Rent for a week or weekend to see whether you like their product.**
- **Many computer stores let you try out software before you buy it. Some retailers also rent computer equipment.**
- **Rental stores provide a wide variety of goods, from sleeper sofas to folding chairs for a party. If you need something for only a short time, rent it.**

INSTALLMENT CREDIT PROBLEMS

Certain formulas and contract clauses have created problems for installment buyers. Consumer advocates suggest that borrowers either avoid these clauses or try to have them removed from any
3 installment contract they sign.

The Rule of 78s

Consumers who pay off an installment contract ahead of time might be surprised to learn that they still owe some interest. The extra charges are due because installment payments are based on the average amount owed over the
4 entire life of the contract.

Buyers underpay interest during the early months when the balance owed is largest. They overpay interest during the final months when the balance owed is smallest. The total interest paid is correct only if the contract runs its full term.

When the contract period is cut short, interest has been underpaid more months than it has been overpaid. To find out how much interest is owed, finance companies apply a mathematical formula called the **rule of 78s,** a rule for refiguring the interest when the debt is paid back ahead of schedule.

Balloon Payment Clause

A final payment that is much larger than the other weekly or monthly installments is called a **balloon payment.** Some states require that a balloon clause in a contract be identified
1 with dark, heavy type. Other states do
2 not permit the use of the clause at all.

Jane Robertson had been making weekly payments of $10 on an installment contract for a television set she bought. When she was ready to make the last payment, Jane discovered that the amount due was $100 instead of the usual $10.

It was very hard for Jane to get this much money together. She had to refinance the contract, that is, get another loan, with more finance charges, to pay off the first one.

Because they are unanticipated, balloon payments often lead to refinancing and additional charges. To make matters worse, the new contract may have a balloon clause, too. As a result, buyers find it increasingly difficult to get out of debt.

Acceleration Clause

The **acceleration clause** gives the seller the right to declare the whole balance due if the buyer misses even one installment payment. This clause is so commonly used that installment buyers probably cannot avoid it.

◀ ***What should these buyers be aware of as they purchase furniture for their young infants?***

Caption Answer: Balloon payments.

1 Critical Thinking Ask students to use what they know about economics and credit to explain why the balloon-payment method is used. (It permits people who can not make higher monthly payments to go ahead with a purchase.)

2 Discussion Starter Ask students if they feel state governments should pass laws restricting or forbidding balloon payments, or should consumers be responsible for their own actions?

3 Vocabulary Have the students "translate" the contract provisions in Figure 15–2 from legalese into English. Allow them to use the text's glossary, a dictionary, or a legal dictionary.

Caption Answer: Read through the contract, making notes on items you don't understand. Ask the store manager to explain each clause in detail. Consult friends or relatives who are familiar with contracts.

With an acceleration clause, the buyer who misses one payment may be forced to pay the entire balance right away. For example, Mark Levy has made 15 payments of $10 a week and still has 15 payments remaining. If he misses the 16th payment because of illness or for any other reason, the merchant could demand immediate payment of the $150 balance.

Use of such a clause can work extreme hardship on the consumer. Many businesspeople are willing to make adjustments in the payment schedule when a consumer is having difficulty making the required payments. It is important for the consumer to contact the merchant if payment problems occur and to work out a reasonable solution that is satisfactory to both parties. Figure 15–2 shows two typical wordings for the rule of 78s clause and the accel-
3 eration clause.

Figure 15–2 Typical Form Contract Provisions

Rule of 78s	Acceleration Clause
Buyer may prepay this contract in full at any time before maturity of the final installment. If he or she does so, Buyer shall receive a rebate of unearned finance charge calculated under the rule of 78s, less an acquisition cost of $12.00. No rebate of less than $1.00 will be made.	Default in the payment of any installment of the principal balance or charges thereon or any part of either shall, at the option of the Holder hereof, render the entire unpaid principal balance and accrued charges at once due and payable.

▲ *Contracts contain legal language that may be difficult to understand.* ***How can you get help understanding an installment credit contract?***

FLASHBACK FLASHFORWARD

In 1930, outstanding installment credit in the United States reached $2.7 billion. In 1992, outstanding installment credit reached nearly $757 billion, or $2,934 per person.

Case Study Answers:
1 The finance company may charge a higher interest rate than a bank. However a finance company may be a lot more flexible about loan terms, such as offering a lower down payment.
2 Finance companies will finance just about anything. They will provide you a loan for a car or for starting a small business.

Add-On Clause

Suppose you decide to make new purchases on an installment plan before old purchases bought at the same store have been paid for. Sometimes all the purchases are then consolidated or combined into a single installment contract. The consolidated contract may contain an **add-on clause,** which provides that the earliest purchases under a consolidated contract may be used as security for later ones. See Figure 15–3.

Figure 15–3 Add-On Clause

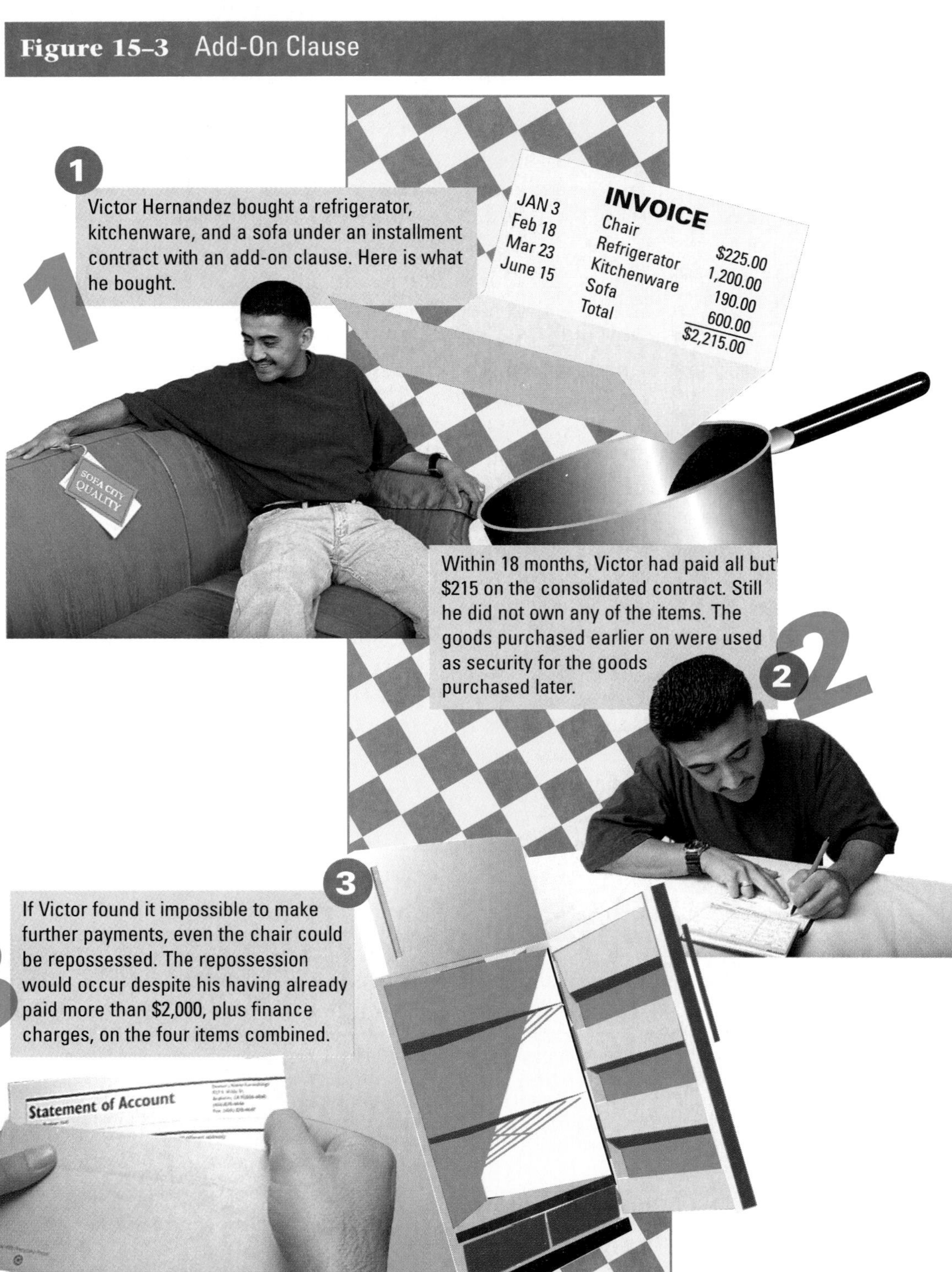

1
Victor Hernandez bought a refrigerator, kitchenware, and a sofa under an installment contract with an add-on clause. Here is what he bought.
INVOICE
JAN 3 Chair $225.00
Feb 18 Refrigerator 1,200.00
Mar 23 Kitchenware 190.00
June 15 Sofa 600.00
Total $2,215.00
SOFA CITY QUALITY
2
Within 18 months, Victor had paid all but $215 on the consolidated contract. Still he did not own any of the items. The goods purchased earlier on were used as security for the goods purchased later.
3
If Victor found it impossible to make further payments, even the chair could be repossessed. The repossession would occur despite his having already paid more than $2,000, plus finance charges, on the four items combined.
Statement of Account

CASE STUDY

Consumer NEWS CLIP

Finance Firms 101: Lenders Can Offer a Credit Cure, but at a Higher Cost Than Banks

by Michele Donley
Crain's Small Business
November 1994

A finance company can be a good alternative for a small business in need of funds, especially one too new or risky to get a bank loan. But there's a price: Money from a finance company will cost a small business more.

Finance companies range from large national concerns doing many kinds of deals to small local outfits that specialize in one or two types of financing. Some are a good match for the needs and financial situation of a new, growing business. Others, with their extremely high rates, could get a small business into financial hot water.

Nevertheless, a small business has several clear advantages in dealing with a finance company:

Opportunities for start-ups of riskier companies. A bank is likely to turn away a business without a track record or with some financial woes, while a finance company may welcome such a customer.

Smaller deals. While some of the largest finance companies don't lend to small businesses, most will consider deals worth as little as $25,000, which many banks won't. Occasionally, a finance company may do a deal worth as little as $5,000.

More flexibility on collateral, repayment schedules, use of the money and the loan amount. A bank is likely to want easily liquidated assets pledged as collateral; a finance company may consider more offbeat assets or a creative mixing of assets, such as equipment, inventory, receivables and real estate. Finance companies may bend on repayment schedules, taking into account the seasonal nature of some businesses. They also may allow more leeway to mix the designated use for the cash, approving a loan that can be used for working capital and asset acquisition.

A second source of money. Some businesses that have a bank loan or line of credit may want to keep that credit free for running or expanding their operation. They might seek a finance company loan to buy equipment or property.

Deals offered by finance companies take many forms. They include straightforward loans similar to a home mortgage, SBA-guaranteed loans, asset-based loans backed by a business's receivables or inventory and equipment leases. The last are often popular with start-up companies that can buy the equipment once their business is on firmer footing. Finance companies often craft hybrid deals to suit a customer's needs, varying interest rates according to the transaction and the borrower's size, its financial status and the industry in which it operates. Finally, finance companies claim they offer a more personal touch than multipurpose banks.

Decisions, Decisions

1. What are some considerations when using a finance company?
2. What kinds of items will a finance company give you a loan on?

1 Research Have a student or group of students find out whether or not your state has a law requiring installment payments to be prorated.

2 Math Application Have students assume that the court has ordered a worker's paycheck to be garnished. The worker earns $350 a week, and $8\frac{1}{2}$ percent a week is to be deducted to pay the worker's overdue bills. How much will be deducted each week for this purpose? ($350 × .085 = $29.75)

3 Discussion Starter Ask students if they would have voted in favor of this legislation. Why or why not?

4 Math Application Ask the students how much, according to the rule, their take-home pay would have to be to support monthly payments of $500. ($500 = 20%, or $\frac{1}{5}$, of take-home pay; full pay = 5 × $500, or $2,500)

5 Discussion Starter Ask students to consider the impact of setting aside 20 percent of their weekly pay or allowance for debt payments. What impact would the payments have on their lifestyle?

In some states, the consumer is protected by laws that require payments to be **prorated,** or divided proportionately. Each payment is applied to each item until those bought first are paid for in full. Those goods that are paid for no longer serve as security for later pur-
1 chases.

Garnishment

Garnishment is a legal proceeding initiated by a creditor to collect a debt. Through a court order, an employer is required to withhold part of a worker's wages and send the money to the court. Money is withheld from the worker each payday until the debt and all court costs
2 are paid.

As the use of credit has expanded, garnishments have increased in number. Consumer advocates believe that some merchants have been too free with credit and have, in effect, made the courts their collection agency.

Employers have extra responsibilities when employee wages are garnisheed. Dealing with the court and giving special treatment to payroll records requires time and therefore costs money. In the past, some businesspeople simply fired an employee when a garnishment notice was received, rather than go through the extra work involved.

As garnishments increased, personal bankruptcies skyrocketed. Confronting this problem, Congress passed the Consumer Credit Protection Act in 1968. Part of this legislation deals with garnishment, and there was a brief decline in the number of personal bankruptcies as a result.

The act provides that an employer may not fire an employee because his or her wages have been garnisheed as a result of one's indebtedness. The law also limits the amount of an employee's earnings that may be garnisheed. Some state laws now prohibit the garnishment of wages for the payment of consumer
3 credit.

Payment Cards in Europe

Payment cards include cards that carry interest, cards that must be paid in full, debit cards that electronically debit a bank account, and special installment cards from stores. In Britain and Sweden, people carry an average of two payment cards; in Germany, most people carry only one.

EXTENT OF INSTALLMENT DEBT

An old rule of thumb holds that your credit payments (excluding payments on a house) should not exceed 20 percent of your monthly take-home pay. What does this mean in practical terms? If your take-home pay is $700 a month and you have installment and other credit payments totaling $140 a month,
4 you probably have about as much debt
5 as you can handle.

How reasonable is the rule-of-thumb standard? Studies indicate that it reflects reality. In one recent year, 41 percent of American families had some installment debts. In only 5 percent of the cases, however, did those debts exceed the 20 percent maximum. Thus most families followed the rule of thumb, either intentionally or because they felt uncomfortable having more debt.

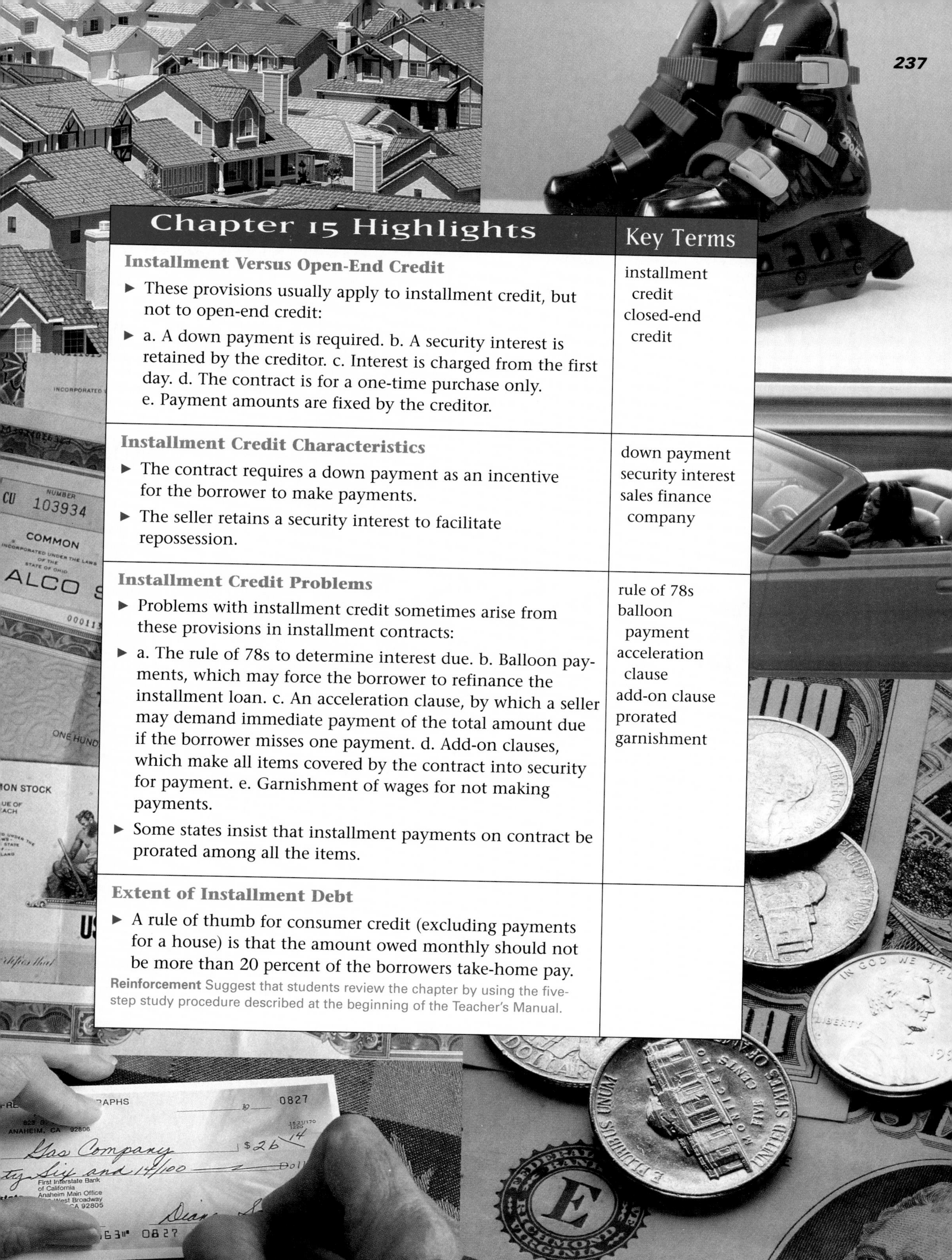

Chapter 15 Highlights

Chapter 15 Highlights	Key Terms
Installment Versus Open-End Credit ▶ These provisions usually apply to installment credit, but not to open-end credit: ▶ a. A down payment is required. b. A security interest is retained by the creditor. c. Interest is charged from the first day. d. The contract is for a one-time purchase only. e. Payment amounts are fixed by the creditor.	installment credit closed-end credit
Installment Credit Characteristics ▶ The contract requires a down payment as an incentive for the borrower to make payments. ▶ The seller retains a security interest to facilitate repossession.	down payment security interest sales finance company
Installment Credit Problems ▶ Problems with installment credit sometimes arise from these provisions in installment contracts: ▶ a. The rule of 78s to determine interest due. b. Balloon payments, which may force the borrower to refinance the installment loan. c. An acceleration clause, by which a seller may demand immediate payment of the total amount due if the borrower misses one payment. d. Add-on clauses, which make all items covered by the contract into security for payment. e. Garnishment of wages for not making payments. ▶ Some states insist that installment payments on contract be prorated among all the items.	rule of 78s balloon payment acceleration clause add-on clause prorated garnishment
Extent of Installment Debt ▶ A rule of thumb for consumer credit (excluding payments for a house) is that the amount owed monthly should not be more than 20 percent of the borrowers take-home pay. **Reinforcement** Suggest that students review the chapter by using the five-step study procedure described at the beginning of the Teacher's Manual.	

CHAPTER 15 REVIEW

Refer students to the Reviewing Consumer Terms and Reviewing Facts and Ideas activities in the Student Activity Workbook.

Reviewing Consumer Terms Paragraphs will vary. See Glossary for definitions.

Reviewing Facts and Ideas See Student Activity Workbook for answers.

Problem Solving and Decision Making
1 The smaller amount is one-quarter of the take-home pay, or $52.50.
$210 × .25 = $52.50
$210 − (30 x $4.25) = $210 − $127.50 = $82.50
2 (**a**). Mark: $140 (**b**) Silvia: $200 (**c**) Pat: $300

Consumers Around the World
Math
1 $262.50

Social Studies
2 In a 500-word report on wartime loans, students should provide the historical details of loans, especially those made to rebuild countries. Some students may feel it is right for victorious countries to lend money to defeated ones as a means of healing.

Reviewing Consumer Terms

Write a paragraph incorporating the following terms.

acceleration clause
add-on clause
balloon payment
closed-end credit
down payment
garnishment
installment credit
prorated
rule of 78s
sales finance company
security interest

Reviewing Facts and Ideas

1. How does installment credit differ from open-end credit?
2. Identify five installment credit problems.
3. Do you consider the balloon clause fair if it is printed in boldface type in the contract?
4. Describe the add-on clause. Would you be willing to buy merchandise under terms of a contract containing such a clause?
5. What is a garnishment, and why has it been the object of special legislation?
6. What is the rule of thumb for how much debt a consumer can manage.

Problem Solving and Decision Making

1. Assume that the maximum legal garnishment per week is the smaller of these two:
   a. One-quarter of weekly take-home pay.
   b. The amount by which take-home pay exceeds 30 times the minimum wage.

   If Gerald Naito's take-home pay is $210 and the minimum wage is $4.25 per hour, what is the maximum amount that could be garnisheed?
2. If credit payments should not exceed 20 percent of your monthly take-home pay, how much debt can each of the following consumers manage?
   a. Mark's take-home pay is $700.
   b. Silvia's take-home pay is $1,000.
   c. Pat's take-home pay is $1,500.

Building Academic Skills

Consumers Around the World

Math

1. Martin wants to buy a new computer that costs $1,750. He wants to buy it on an installment plan that requires a 15 percent down payment. How much must be put down.

Social Studies

2. Record from library books and encyclopedias examples of wartime loans among allied countries—loans that were to be paid back in installments. See if you can find cases in which these contracts were (1) carried out, or (2) avoided.

   Write a 500-word report of your findings. List the creditor country and the borrower country in each case. Did you find examples of

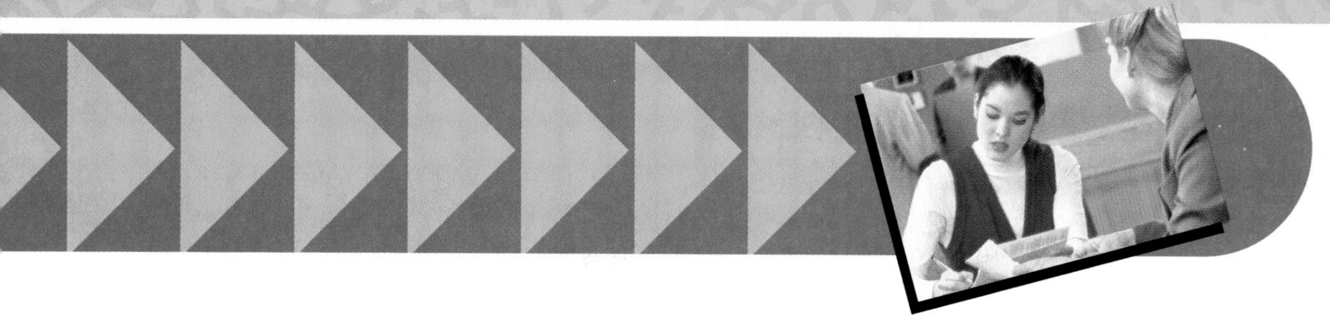

loans between countries that had been at war with each other? Give your views on such loans.

Technology

3. Research examples of peacetime loans made between countries or between international funds and countries in need of technology equipment. List the purposes of such loans (building dams, improved farming methods, and so on) and the provisions for repayment.

   What action can the lender take if the borrower does not make the loan payments? Is there a difference between borrowing money to supply necessities like food and borrowing to build structures like power plants? Write a 500-word report that gives your findings.

Beyond the Classroom

Consumer Project

Obtain an installment agreement from a local merchant or from a mail-order catalog. Draw a line under the contract provisions that seem most important to you. Then save the form for your credit scrapbook.

Cooperative Learning

Family Economics

Break into assigned family groups. Discuss the following problem.

Your family needs a new sofa. You've picked one out at Colonial Furniture Galleries and must now decide how you are going to pay for it. The store, which often carries its own contracts, offers the following terms: $50 down and $17.61 per month for 36 months. You could also borrow $500 from your bank. You would have to pay back the $500 plus 9 percent in one payment at the end of one year. As a final option, Colonial also takes all major bank cards.

Do you buy? On which terms? Explain your choice. Compare your answer with those of other family groups.

Debate the Issue

Some people say that business owners should not be permitted to resort to garnishment to collect debts growing out of consumer credit. They feel that garnishment exploits the lowest-paid workers who have the least amount of resources and legal knowledge. Others feel that consumers should be responsible for all their debts and that garnishment is the seller's best means of recouping losses.

You and your classmates will break into two groups and research this topic. Each group will gather evidence to support one side or the other. You are to prepare the argument for your side of the problem. Then the two groups will meet in a classroom debate.

Rechecking Your Attitude

Before going on to the next unit, go back to the Attitude Inventory at the beginning of this one. Answer the questions a second time. Then compare the two sets of responses. On how many statements have your attitudes changed? Can you account for these shifts in your opinions? What do you know now that you did not know then?

Technology
3 Students should present their findings in two-page report. Some students may make the analogy to personal debt—borrowing to buy food and clothing as opposed to borrowing to buy a computer that you will use to improve your job skills.

Consumer Project
Students may acquire one or more contracts and compare them.

Family Economics
The bank's terms are by far the best, but many families may find it easier to pay monthly bills than to save the amount needed for the bank's payment. They may find the store's terms the only way to cope—or they may opt to look for a less expensive sofa.

Debate the Issue
Break the class into two teams. Assign each team one side of the issue. Encourage students to work together as a team to develop their argument. Ask each team to select a member to make an opening statement that supports the team's side of the issue. Have students take turns debating as the debate moves from one team to the other.

UNIT 4 LAB
You and Your Community

STEP A Students should consider monthly income, expense, and credit debt figures.
STEP B Students should establish business contacts with three different furniture stores in a courteous, professional manner.
STEP C Students should make reasonable furniture selections for their consumers. They should also gather information about the stores' installment and credit card contracts.
STEP D Students should prepare clear and accurate charts with information gleaned from the installment contracts and their own consumer profiles.
STEP E Students' answers should be accurate and based on their consumer charts and profiles.
STEP F Students' descriptions of the advantages and opportunity costs of credit use should be logically supported by specific examples from their experiences while-shopping" for their imaginary consumers.

Refer students to the Unit 4 Lab in the Student Activity Workbook.

Buying on Credit

Unit 4 discusses the various types of consumer credit. It explains the positive and negative aspects for the consumer regarding the use of credit. Completing this lab will show you how using credit to purchase a big-ticket furniture item affects the personal economics of two imaginary consumers.

TOOLS

1. Consumer and business magazines
2. Home decoration and family living magazines
3. Newspaper and direct-mail ads from furniture and department stores

PROCEDURES

STEP A Create profiles of two imaginary consumers needing to purchase furniture sets consisting of a kitchen or dining room table and four chairs. Your imaginary consumers will have different incomes and monthly expense levels. One consumer should be younger than 30 and single. The other consumer should be married and the parent of young children.

For each one, describe the following:

1. Age, gender, and marital status
2. Job or profession.
3. Monthly after-tax income.
4. Monthly expenses, not including credit payments.
5. Current open- and closed-end credit payments.

STEP B Select two furniture stores in your area. One should emphasize quality pieces at reasonable (but not particularly inexpensive) prices. The other furniture store should emphasize its warehouse or discount prices. In addition, select a department store that sells furniture. Call each store or furniture department and explain the purpose of your assignment to the store or department manager. Ask the manager to tell you when would be the best time to visit the store, shop for your consumers, and talk with a salesperson or credit department employee. If possible, arrange a meeting with a specific employee who can work with you and answer your questions.

STEP C Visit the three stores. At the stores, make a furniture selection for each consumer. Take descriptive notes on the sets you select and the reasons a particular set meets the needs of the imaginary consumer. Ask for copies of the stores' installment contracts and (if available) store credit card contracts. If possible, review the contracts with store personnel. Be sure to check the stores' down payment requirements, security interests, and use of sales finance companies. Ask about the stores' use of balloon payment, acceleration, and add-on clauses.

STEP D At home, review the installment contracts from the stores. Determine the monthly payments both of your imaginary consumers would have to make on the furniture sets you selected for them. Complete a chart like the one on this page for each of your consumers.

STEP E Use your notes and credit payment charts to answer the questions below:

1. What would be the total dollar amount of the interest charges for Consumer 1's and Consumer 2's table and chair set at Store A? at Store B? at Store C? (Assume that the consumer will take the entire installment period to complete payments.)
2. What percentage of Consumer 1's and Consumer 2's monthly take-home pay will be devoted to credit debt if he or she purchases the furniture set from Store A? from Store B? from Store C? (Remember to include the open and closed-end credit you listed in your consumer profile as well as the debt caused by the furniture purchase.)

LAB REPORT

STEP F Write a two-page report describing the advantages and the opportunity costs of using credit to buy a big ticket item such as a table and chair set. Use your imaginary consumers as specific examples of the personal economic impact of credit use. In your report, state your choice of the furniture set, store, and installment contract that would be best for each consumer. Explain the reasons for your choices. Include your chart in your report.

Credit Payments for Furniture Purchase

	Purchase price	Finance charge	Monthly payment	Amount of monthly interest
Store A				
Store B				
Store C				

UNIT 5

Unit Contents

Chapter 16
Evaluating Credit Terms and Establishing Credit

Chapter 17
Borrowing Money

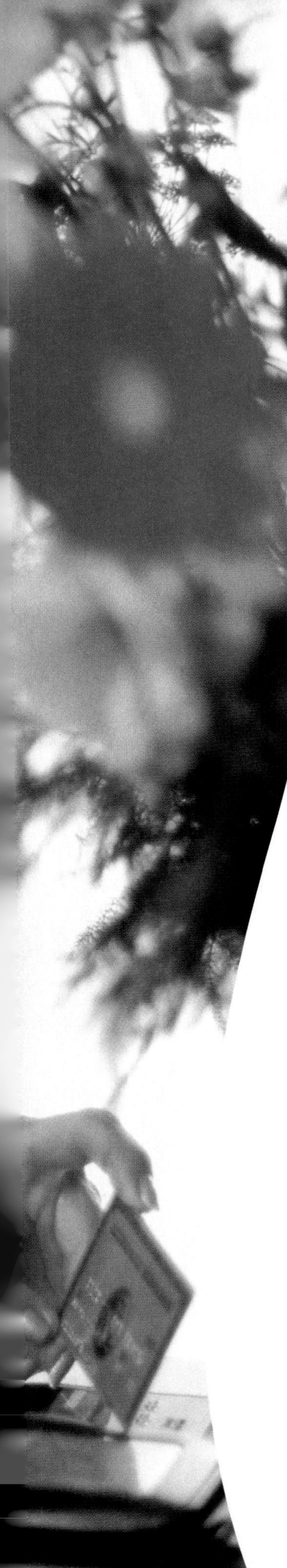

Getting and Keeping Credit

Attitude Inventory

Before you begin Chapter 16, take stock of your attitudes by completing the following inventory. Read each statement and decide how you feel about it—agree, disagree, or undecided. Record your feelings on a sheet of notepaper or use the form in the workbook.

1. Since young people are almost always denied credit, they should not waste their time by applying for it.
2. There is no point in reading a credit contract because the average consumer would not understand it anyway.
3. Credit bureaus tend to do more harm than good.
4. The consumer who needs to borrow money would do well to avoid banks as a source for funds.
5. Loan sharks serve no useful purpose.
6. Declaring yourself bankrupt is a good, painless, and legal way to avoid paying your debts.
7. Charging interest for a loan is unethical.
8. Consumers are at a disadvantage because they cannot shop around for credit.
9. A businessperson who is asked to extend credit has a right to ask how much the applicant earns each month.
10. Credit is easy to get if you do not need it.
11. If you get hopelessly in debt, the best thing to do is move to another town and start over again with a clean record.
12. A good credit rating is not important to a consumer who has formed a habit of paying cash for purchases.
13. Finance companies charge too much interest.
14. There are times when it makes good sense to borrow against an insurance policy.

Unit Goal The main goal of this unit is to acquaint students with the actual procedures involved in applying for credit—the documents filed, the terminology used, and the safeguards provided by various credit rights statutes. Chapters included in this unit are (1) Evaluating Credit Terms and Establishing Credit and (2) Borrowing Money.

Lesson Plan See the Teacher's Manual for an overview of the unit and some suggestions for introducing it. If you assign the Attitude Inventory, be sure to tell students to keep their answers for later use.

CHAPTER 16

Evaluating Credit Terms and Establishing Credit

Learning Objectives

When you have finished studying this chapter, you should be able to:

1. Describe how lending is regulated, and tell how the right of rescission works.
2. Describe the facts credit managers consider when deciding whether to extend credit.
3. Describe what a credit bureau does and how creditors use credit bureaus.
4. Identify common credit reporting problems.
5. Identify the 15 important consumer rights related to credit reporting.

Consumer Terms

Truth-in-Lending Act
credit disclosure form
right of rescission
credit references
credit bureau
Fair Credit Reporting Act
investigative reporting
Fair Debt Collection Practices Act
debtor

Real-World Journal

Which came first, the chicken or the egg? Establishing credit can be as difficult as figuring out this age-old riddle. Explain in your journal some possible ways to establish credit without having any prior credit history. Include traditional ideas as well as any new ideas that might help you gain purchasing power.

Lesson Plan See the Teacher's Manual for Chapter 16 lesson plan.

Vocabulary The Chapter 16 lesson plan includes suggested vocabulary activities for the terms listed.

1 Learning Economics The increase from the 6 percent rate in 1968 to today's higher rates is an example of what type of price change? (Inflation.)

2 Critical Thinking Ask students why it is unwise to base credit decisions solely on the amount of the monthly payments?

3 Vocabulary Ask meaning of *annual* in this context. Have students explain the importance of having an annual percentage rate.

4 Critical Thinking Ask the students to find the interest rate charged and the full amount paid for credit in Figure 16–1. (13.5 percent; $1,178.06.) Ask them what features made this information easy to find. (They were first in the form, printed in boldface boxes in capital letters.)

5 Reinforcement Student Activity Workbook, Chapter 16 activities.

REGULATION OF LENDING

Imagine buying a car and paying as much as 283 percent interest on the auto loan! Imagine buying a $123.38 television set at an interest rate of 229 percent! Imagine borrowing $1,685.72 and paying finance charges of $778.32! Consumers related these experiences and others at congressional hearings held in
1 1968.

Confusion in the Marketplace

In the 1960s, there was a great deal of confusion about credit terms and contracts. Many people thought they were paying 6 percent interest. However, it was difficult for consumers to learn how much credit would actually cost them in dollars and cents. Service charges, investigation fees, loan insurance costs, carrying charges, and other hidden expenses added to the cost of credit in unanticipated ways.

Consumers who tried to compare credit costs discovered that credit contracts were all structured differently. Consumers could not find out where to borrow or buy on credit at the least cost. They often ended up asking simply, "How much will the monthly
2 payments be?"

Truth-in-Lending Act

Information given by creditors was incomplete and, for that reason, not very useful. Consumers could not make effective comparisons between credit offers. In response to concern about this situation, Congress passed the **Truth-in-Lending Act,** a law requiring creditors to adequately inform consumers about credit terms.

Total Finance Charge The Truth-in-Lending Act requires that firms that lend money or give credit use one particular method of figuring the finance charge. The finance charge, which is the total cost of credit, must include interest on the loan plus all other charges, such as discounts, service charges, carrying charges, and required credit life insurance. The consumer must be told what this amount is. All other things being equal, the lowest finance charge is the lowest credit cost.

Annual Percentage Rate All other things may not be equal, however. One company may offer credit for a full year. Another may offer it for only 6 months; another still, for 18 months. The Truth-in-Lending Act helps solve this problem, too. It requires that companies also tell consumers the interest charged, expressed as an annual percentage rate (APR).

The APR shows what a firm would charge for the loan of $1 for one year. Consumers can compare credit costs regardless of the dollar amount of the finance charge or the length of time for repayment. The credit offer with the
3 lowest APR costs the least in interest.

Credit Disclosure Form The law requires the credit contract to be completely filled out before you are asked to sign it. The finance charge and annual percentage rate must be printed in boldface type, type that prints darker than the surrounding text.

The Truth-in-Lending Act also requires that borrowers be given a **credit disclosure form,** a form that contains pertinent details about the credit transaction. Note that the disclosure form, shown in Figure 16–1, provides spaces for all the key figures a
4 consumer should have to make an
5 informed decision.

Monthly Statement The Truth-in-Lending Act requires that revolving-charge customers who owe more than $1 be sent monthly statements of their

accounts. The monthly statement must
1 show the following:

- Unpaid balance at the start of the
2 billing period
- Amount and date of each extension of credit and identification of each
3 item bought.
- Payments made by a customer and other credits (such as returned goods).
- Finance charge in dollars and cents.
- Rate used in figuring the finance charge.
- Annual percentage rate.
- Unpaid balance on which finance charges were based.
- Closing date of the billing cycle and the unpaid balance.

An example of a periodic statement that meets the Truth-in-Lending Act requirements is shown in Chapter 14,
4 Figure 14–2.

Right of Rescission The Truth-in-Lending Act aids consumers who have pledged their homes as security for loans. For example, Mr. and Mrs. Mailor were talked into having vinyl siding installed on their home. At the time, they did not fully understand the cost of the repair work.

Figure 16–1 Truth in Lending Disclosures

ANNUAL PERCENTAGE RATE The cost of your credit as a yearly rate.	**FINANCE CHARGE** The dollar amount the credit will cost you.	**Amount Financed** The amount of credit provided to you or on your behalf.	**Total of Payments** The amount you will have paid after you have made all payments as scheduled.
13.50%	$ 1,178.06	$ 5,314.90	$ 6,492.96

Your payment schedule will be:

Number of Payments	Amount of Payments	When Payments Are Due
36	$ 180.36	Commencing monthly 1-27-96
	$	

Insurance
Credit life insurance and credit disability insurance are not required to obtain credit, and will not be provided unless you sign and agree to pay the additional cost.

Type	Premium	Signature
Credit Life for Term of Credit	$ 97.39	I/we want credit life insurance ______ Signature ______ Signature
Credit Disability for Term of Credit	$ 217.51	I want credit disability insurance ______ Signature
Credit Life and Disability for Term of Credit	$ N/A	I want credit life and disability insurance ______ Signature

Security: ☒ Right of set-off against any moneys, credits or other property of yours in the possession of the Holder, on deposit or otherwise.
Late Charge: If a payment is late, for more than 10 days, you will be charged $5.00 or 5% of the payment, whichever is less.
Prepayment: If you pay off early, you will be entitled to a refund of part of the finance charge.
See your contract terms for any additional information about nonpayment, default, any required repayment in full before the scheduled date, and prepayment refunds and penalties.

◀ *Credit insurance guarantees that your debt will be paid if you die or become disabled.* ***Is credit insurance a good purchase? Why or why not?***

1 Reinforcement Ask students to explain the difference between a revolving charge account and a regular charge account. If they have trouble making the distinction, refer them to Chapter 14.

2 Vocabulary Ask students to explain the meaning of *balance* in the monthly statement. (The balance is the total amount still owed.)

3 Vocabulary Make sure here that students know that the term *extension of credit* refers to new purchases.

4 Reinforcement Have the students return to Figure 14–2 and point out each of the items required by the Truth-in-Lending Act. You may also want to ask students to bring examples of various monthly statements to class so that students can compare the different ways in which companies present the same information.

Caption Answer: Credit insurance costs a lot of money and covers a very unlikely risk. It is not a good value.

1 Extension Have students bring to class newspaper and magazine ads for available credit. Have them analyze the ads.

2 Reinforcement Ask students why well-established people might use credit. If students have trouble answering, refer them to the discussion of the advantages of charge accounts in Chapter 14.

3 Vocabulary Help the students review all the different definitions they now know for the word *capital.* (Tools used by labor; money used to buy tools and equipment; things owned, or property.)

4 Critical Thinking Have the students evaluate Carmine Falcone's credit application in Figure 16–2 for the three C's of credit. Is Carmine Falcone a good risk? (Character: has a history of paying debts that can be verified. Capacity: has a regular job, savings account, stable work and residential history. Capital: none. Falcone is neither the best nor the worst risk.)

After the papers were signed and the salesperson had left, however, they read the contract. Upon adding all the figures together, they realized they could not afford to have the work done.

Fortunately, the contract contained a notice of their rights under the Truth-in-Lending Act. These rights included the **right of rescission**—the right to cancel a contract during a cooling-off period. Specifically, you have three working days in which to rescind, or cancel, a contract for which you have pledged your home security for payment. To avoid risking their home, the Mailors exercised this right.

GETTING CREDIT

1 Merchants and bankers want to give credit to well-established professional people who have good incomes and have always paid their debts on time. Although they sometimes use credit, these people often do not really need to
2 borrow money or buy on credit.

Young people just starting their first full-time jobs may have a different experience when they ask for credit. In recent years, a large percentage of people who have declared bankruptcy (declared in court that they are unable to pay their debts) have been young people only 23 or 24 years old. For this reason, careful credit managers give only a small amount of credit at first. They increase it as the consumers show they can and will pay debts on time.

The Three C's of Credit

In deciding to extend credit, credit managers consider the three C's of credit—character, capacity, and capital. Character refers to a person's reputation, especially concerning debt. A creditor looks for a record that shows the borrower feels a moral duty to pay debts when they are due.

Capacity is a person's earning power and ability to pay debts from regular income. Capital refers to items owned, or property. The consumer who owns items of value is a better credit risk than one who does not. (Faced with a shortage of cash, an owner of property could sell the property and use the money to
3 pay debts.)

The Credit Application

A typical charge account application is shown in Figure 16–2. The credit office
4 wants the following information.

- *Name of employer.* Your employer will probably be asked whether you really work for the company.
- *Salary.* This information is important in judging capacity, and the employer will be asked to verify the amount.
- *Years worked for present employer.* An applicant who has worked for the same employer for many years is thought of as more stable and a better credit risk than someone who has been working at a job for only a few weeks. A young worker, just beginning a job, may be given the benefit of the doubt.
- *Address and length of time living there.* Another sign of stability, or steadiness, is the length of time you have lived at a given address. Creditors may feel that people who change their addresses often may have problems that need investigating.
- *Home ownership.* Home ownership is evidence of capital to the credit department. Also, a home owner is considered a more permanent resident than a person who rents. Some applications ask how much you pay each month for housing. The credit manager wants to know whether you are paying so much for housing that there is little left for payment of debts.

- *Credit references.* Businesses with which you have dealt on a credit basis are **credit references.** Records of these companies are the best clues of your bill-paying habits. The references will be asked whether you have paid bills on time and how much you now owe. More information will be supplied by the credit bureau.

  Credit managers do not want new customers who have bad credit records with other stores. Those who owe large amounts of money compared to their incomes are not wanted either.

  A new worker who has not used credit before may be asked to give the names of personal references. These include teachers and businesspeople who can tell about your character.
- *Bank references.* Any bank you list will usually be asked how much you owe

Figure 16–2 Credit Application

ACQUISITION CENTER 243 ASSOCIATE #

your Sears Card application

tell us about yourself:

1
FIRST NAME Carmine MIDDLE INITIAL I. LAST NAME Falcone
RESIDENCE ADDRESS 1432 Calhoun Street APT # CITY San Antonio STATE TX ZIP CODE 78200
HOME TELEPHONE (512) 555-2001 BUSINESS TELEPHONE ( ) 873-2000 SOCIAL SECURITY NUMBER 123-45-6789 AGE 21 NO. OF DEPENDENTS (EXCLUDE YOURSELF) 0
ARE YOU A U.S. CITIZEN? ☒ YES ☐ NO ARE YOU A PERMANENT RESIDENT? ☒ YES ☐ NO HOW LONG AT PRESENT ADDRESS? 4 YRS. 2 MOS.
TYPE OF RESIDENCE ☐ OWN ☒ LIVE WITH PARENTS ☐ RENT ☐ BOARD ☐ OTHER ______ MONTHLY RENT OR MORTGAGE $ 150
PREVIOUS ADDRESS (if less than 2 years at present address) CITY STATE ZIP CODE

about your employer:

2
EMPLOYER (RETIRED/STUDENT) ACE CONCRETE CITY San Antonio STATE TX HOW LONG 2 YRS. 8 MOS. OCCUPATION Data Entry Clerk
NET INCOME (TAKE-HOME PAY) $ 320 ☐ PER MONTH ☒ PER WEEK ADDITIONAL* INCOME $ ☐ PER MONTH ☐ PER WEEK SOURCES
*NOTE: Alimony, child support or separate maintenanced income need not be disclosed if you do not wish to have it considered as a basis for paying this obligation.

about your credit references:

3
DO YOU HAVE CREDIT REFERENCES ☒ YES ☐ NO JC PENNEY DO YOU HAVE MAJOR BANK CARDS? ☒ YES ☐ NO MASTERCARD
WHICH OF THE FOLLOWING DO YOU HAVE? (MARK ALL THAT APPLY) ☐ NONE ☒ CHECKING ACCOUNT ☒ SAVINGS ACCOUNT ☐ NOW ACCOUNT ☐ MONEY MARKET ☐ CD

about your credit references:

4
Complete this section if: (1) your spouse is an authorized buyer, (2) you reside in a community property state (AZ, CA, ID, LA, NM, NV, TX, WA, WI), or (3) you are relying on the income of a spouse as a source for payment.
SPOUSE'S FIRST NAME MIDDLE INITIAL LAST NAME SOCIAL SECURITY NUMBER
EMPLOYER NET INCOME (TAKE-HOME PAY) $ ☐ PER MONTH ☐ PER WEEK

Sears Card special options:

5
Choose your payment date. SELECT WHEN DURING THE MONTH YOU WOULD LIKE TO HAVE YOUR SEARS CARD PAYMENT DUE:
☐ NO PREFERENCE (A) ☐ DAY 1-7 (B) ☐ DAY 8-14 (C) ☒ DAY 15-21 (D) ☐ DAY 22-28 (E)
Would you like additional card(s) at no additional charge? (Spouse card issued in spouse's name. Other cards issued in accountholder's name.)
NAME ______ RELATIONSHIP ______ NAME ______ RELATIONSHIP ______

Sears Credit Protection Plan
I want to help protect my account by enrolling in the optional Sears Credit Protection Plan. I have read and agree to the terms and conditions on the back of this application, and authorize the insurance charges to be billed to my account each month as they become due (subject to approval).
Initial Here: Yes ______ (Initial) No ______ (Initial) Birthdate: __ / __ / __ A00C5NCT

Sears Card Agreement: I agree to pay Sears or Sears National Bank in accordance with the credit terms disclosed to me and to comply with all terms of the Sears Card Agreement. A copy of the Sears Card Agreement will be given to me to keep when my application is approved. Sears will retain a security interest where permitted by law under the Uniform Commercial Code on all merchandise charged to the account. Sears is authorized to investigate my credit, employment and income references, to obtain a Credit Bureau report on me, and to report to proper persons and credit bureaus my performance of the account. Finance charges not in excess of those permitted by law will be charged on the outstanding balance from month to month.

X Carmine J. Falcone 6/13/—
APPLICANT'S SIGNATURE DATE

DETACH HERE

Remember to fold, moisten and seal

© 1995 Sears SEE PANEL AT LEFT FOR IMPORTANT INFORMATION. Rev. 5/95

Source: *Reprinted courtesy of Sears, Roebuck and Co.*

◀ *If you are legally an adult, you cannot be denied credit on account of your age.* ***Why might creditors prefer not to lend to the very young or the very old?***

Caption Answer: Creditors may feel the young don't have the discipline or judgment to pay bills on time and the old may not have the funds.

FLASHBACK FLASHFORWARD

Outstanding consumer credit in 1945 was just over $6.6 billion. In 1992, outstanding consumer credit in the United States was more than $809 billion. Just think,

Figure 16–3 Deceptive Ads and Scams

The Federal Trade Commission (FTC) has taken action against companies that deceptively advertise VISA and Mastercards through television, newspapers, and postcards. Be aware that deceptive ads often leave out important information.

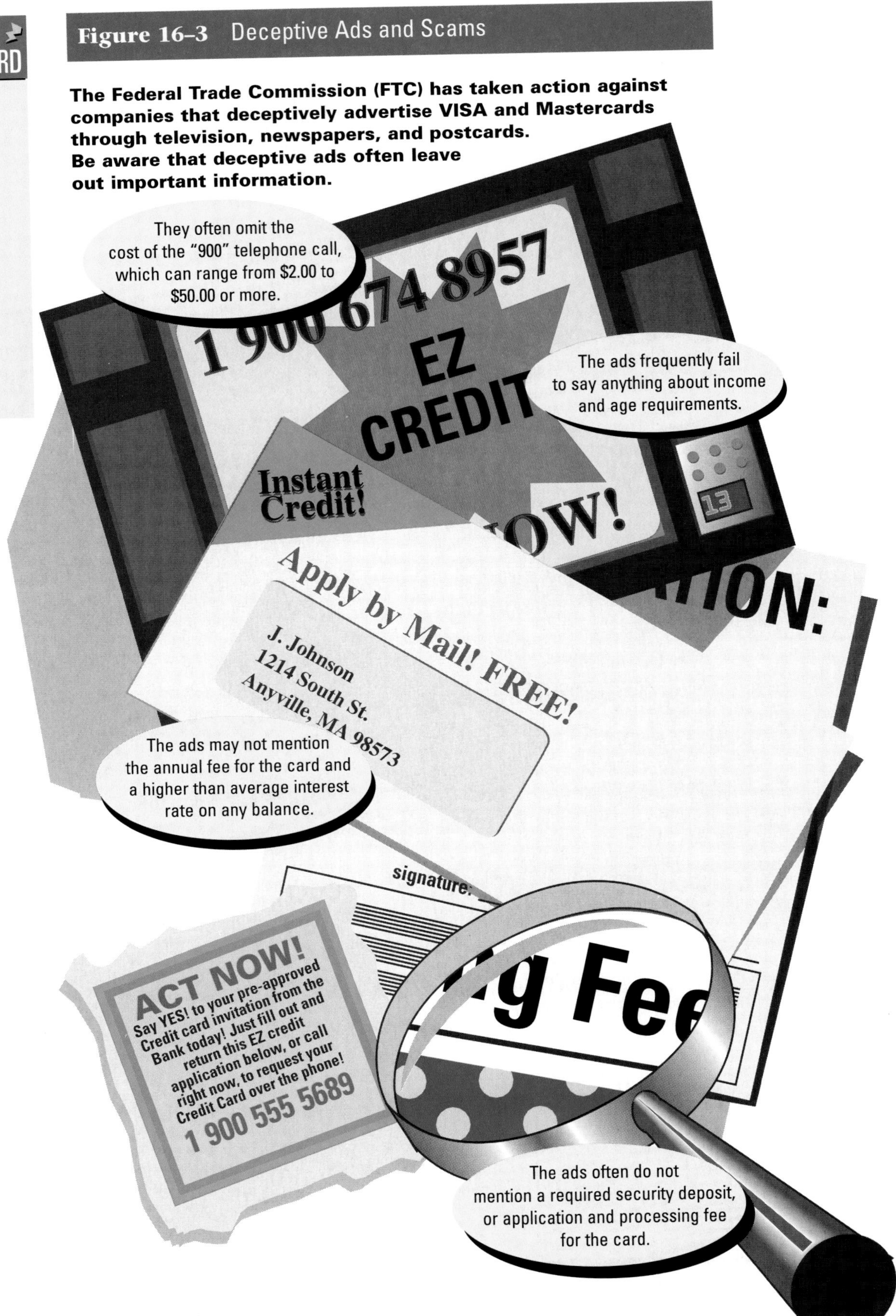
They often omit the cost of the "900" telephone call, which can range from $2.00 to $50.00 or more.
1 900 674 8957
EZ CREDIT
The ads frequently fail to say anything about income and age requirements.
Instant Credit!
Apply by Mail! FREE!
J. Johnson
1214 South St.
Anyville, MA 98573
The ads may not mention the annual fee for the card and a higher than average interest rate on any balance.
signature:
ACT NOW!
Say YES! to your pre-approved Credit card invitation from the Bank today! Just fill out and return this EZ credit application below, or call right now, to request your Credit Card over the phone!
1 900 555 5689
The ads often do not mention a required security deposit, or application and processing fee for the card.

the bank and what balances you have in your checking and savings accounts. This bank reference will have a bearing on all three C's of credit.

Consumers need to be wary of advertisements for easy-to-obtain credit. These credit cards often have hidden fees that make them very costly, or they may require a security deposit, as shown in Figure 16–3.

THE CREDIT BUREAU

A **credit bureau** is a firm that collects information about the paying habits of consumers. Credit bureaus get their information from stores, banks, and other creditors. A credit bureau

Hometown Boy

Newark, New Jersey, could be called a city in trouble. More than one in four of its citizens live below the poverty level. After the riots of 1967, one-third of Newark's population moved away. The remaining residents, mostly African-American and Hispanic, were left to cope with the city's problems any way they could.

Then came Raymond Chambers, a quiet, stay-in-the-background businessman who is, incidentally, one of the richest men in the country—and a native of Newark.

Chambers began making substantial investments in the community, hoping to help raise the level of education, increase business, and improve the quality of life for its residents.

He began by providing funds to renovate the Boys' and Girls' Clubs in Newark. The organization now has a budget four times what it used to be. The restored facilities serve more than 5,000 children.

Chambers is very persuasive. No company would open a movie theater in the most depressed area of Newark. Chambers, however, persuaded the Loew's Theatre to take up the challenge—and to donate all the money earned to the city and local civic and cultural activities.

Chambers then provided $10 million to 650 elementary and middle schools for tutoring, parental assistance, and college costs. Chambers also bought an interest in a local bank, allowing it to stay in business and serve the community. Then he got the bank to set aside $500 worth of shares in the institution for any child who graduated from high school. Chambers' efforts are helping a city in distress get back on its feet.

Brainstorm

If you were a millionaire and wanted to help your hometown out, what might you do?

Case Study Answer: Answers will vary. Answers include invest in education; tutoring; community centers; legal aid centers; hospitals; entertainment centers; loans to business; scholarships and school loans; invest in rebuilding schools.

1 Reinforcement Have the students use the credit report in Figure 16–4 to answer these questions: (*a*) What is the name of the credit bureau providing the report? (Credit Reporting Office—shown in the upper right of the form) (*b*) List the names of firms that have requested the consumer's credit report in the last 24 months. (EQUIFAX, PRM VISA, NATIONS BANK, JC PENNEY, MACYS, AM CITIBANK, GE CAPITAL, or SEARS.) (*c*) How many credit accounts does the report subject have? (Three that are still open.)

2 Extension Student Activity Workbook, Chapter 16 activities.

3 Interesting Note The FTC receives more complaints from people about not having a credit file than about errors in files.

Case Study Answers: **1** Personal drive and never losing sight of her mission are the main reasons for Graves' success. She also credits experience and ongoing education. **2** She used her credit cards to fund her company, meeting her payroll with credit.

record is a credit history. The bureau
1 does not assign ratings to credit
2 histories.

If you apply for credit, the store credit officer will ask a credit bureau for information about you. The officer will use the information in deciding whether to give you credit.

If you have a record of always paying bills on time, the store will probably approve a credit purchase at once. If the credit bureau reports that you owe large amounts at several stores, are behind in payments, and have had merchandise repossessed, credit will surely be denied.

How to Keep Your Buying Habits Private

Computers have made information easier to gather and to access. For some, it has brought a loss of privacy. Those who buy mail-order merchandise or receive magazines through the mail generally acknowledge that their names become part of lists that are bought and sold. In addition, every transaction made with a credit card or check provides an opportunity for retailers to determine buying habits and solicit more business. To help protect your privacy:

- **Pay cash.**
- **Remove your name from mailing lists. If you request your name to be removed from a mail-order list, reputable mail-order merchants will comply.**
- **Don't readily give your name and address to retailers. Be especially cautious when you give out your social security number.**

An example of a credit bureau report appears in Figure 16–4 on page 254.

CREDIT REPORTING PROBLEMS

Consumers have sometimes had a hard time getting credit because information in credit bureau files was incorrect, incomplete, unimportant, or out of date. Billions of entries are made in credit records every month, and it is
3 inevitable that errors will creep in.

Most bureaus, though, have set up procedures designed to keep their records as accurate as possible. Also, the **Fair Credit Reporting Act** gives a consumer the right to have incomplete or incorrect data reinvestigated and to have unverified data taken from the file. This and other provisions of the law are designed to assure consumers of fair treatment by credit reporting agencies.

If you have been turned down for credit, you can write to the credit bureau to get a copy of your credit record. You can have errors in the record corrected and then reapply for credit.

Duration of Record

Alicia Lopez, who is a single parent, became seriously ill. She could not work and was unable to make the installment payments on the family's new dining room furniture, which was repossessed. After a time, Alicia recovered from her illness, went back to work, took good care of her family, and managed her finances intelligently. Should that single flaw, the repossession, remain on her record forever and be reported many years later when she wants to open a charge account?

The Fair Credit Reporting Act protects consumers from having unfavorable information reported for longer than seven years (except for bankruptcies, which may be reported for ten years).

Allene Graves, Temporary Service Owner, The Answer Temps, Inc.

Allene Graves has always found a way to make a profit. When she was a young girl, she did chores for her neighbors for a small fee and she ran a lemonade stand. After high school, she arranged travel groups which enabled her to travel to many different places within the states and internationally. Maybe that's why she wasn't troubled when the law firm she worked for folded in 1987. She was glad to leave a job that offered little satisfaction and no future. For her, the firm's misfortune was an opportunity for her to start her own business. With limited experience as a temporary and no assistance, the Washington, D.C., native launched her own temporary service—The Answer Temps, Inc.

What Graves lacked in specific training and preparation, she made up for with determination and perseverance. Using money collected from unemployment, she obtained the use of an answering service and began looking for temporary employees through ads and recommendations. Then she marketed her services to some of her past employers. One of those employers became her first client.

Graves worked triple time during her business's infancy. She found clients during her lunch breaks and interviewed prospective temporary employees on evenings and weekends.

As her company began to grow, finding funding became a problem. Graves was unable to get any conventional financing because she did not have a business track record, nor the needed collateral to finance a loan. She used her credit cards to fund her company. For six months, she lived from hand to mouth, meeting her payroll with credit. Fortunately, all of her hard work has paid off. After six months, she turned a profit.

Graves' dedication to make her company a success has finally come to fruition. Her sales revenues have grown extensively, and she is now operating a multimillion dollar company. Graves places between 400 to 600 temporary employees per week. The positions vary from light industrial workers to attorneys. Her client profile is mainly made up of state and federal entities and numerous private sector businesses. Many newspaper and magazine articles have been written about her company. In 1994 she received an award for The Minority Business Women of the Year by the D.C. Minority Development Center.

Graves attributes her success to several factors. She cites personal drive and never losing sight of her mission as her main reason for The Answer Temp's success. Her trial-and-error methods have worked, Graves believes, because she has remained focused on her goal. She also credits experience and ongoing education.

Now that The Answer Temps is an established moneymaker, Graves is seeking new challenges. She is preparing to open a group home for the minimally handicapped and is also involved with community-related projects.

Case Study Review

1. What was the key to Graves' success?
2. How did Graves use credit to run her business?

This credit report shows Joe Doe's credit history. ***Is his history good or bad?***

Caption Answer: It could be better. There is a history of past-due accounts, accounts turned over to collections agencies, liens, and bankruptcy.

Figure 16–4 How to Read Your Credit Report

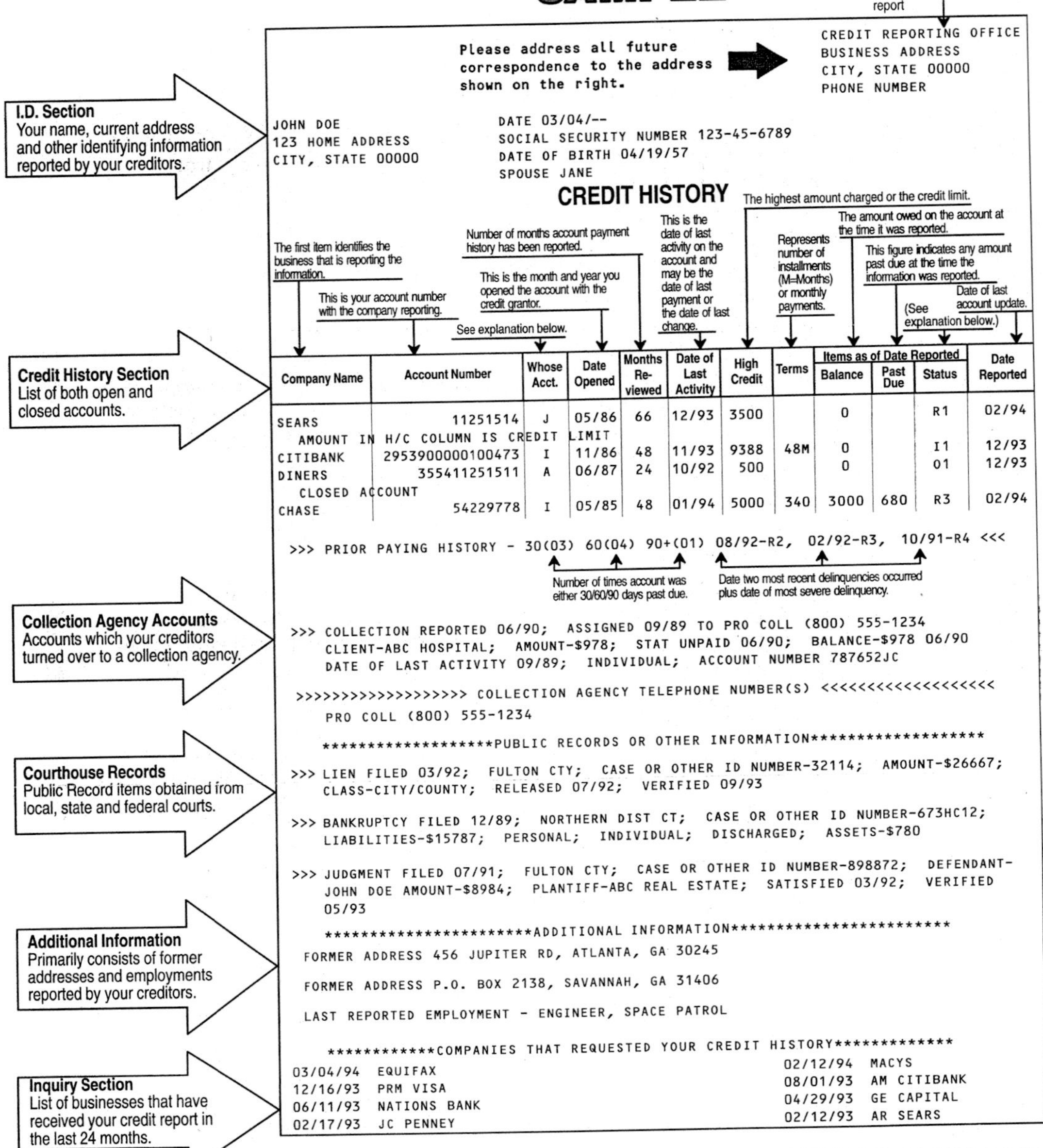

SAMPLE

The Name and Address of the office you should contact if you have any questions or disagreement with your credit report

Please address all future correspondence to the address shown on the right.

CREDIT REPORTING OFFICE
BUSINESS ADDRESS
CITY, STATE 00000
PHONE NUMBER

I.D. Section
Your name, current address and other identifying information reported by your creditors.

JOHN DOE
123 HOME ADDRESS
CITY, STATE 00000

DATE 03/04/--
SOCIAL SECURITY NUMBER 123-45-6789
DATE OF BIRTH 04/19/57
SPOUSE JANE

Credit History Section
List of both open and closed accounts.

CREDIT HISTORY

- Company Name: The first item identifies the business that is reporting the information.
- Account Number: This is your account number with the company reporting.
- Whose Acct.: See explanation below.
- Date Opened: This is the month and year you opened the account with the credit grantor.
- Months Reviewed: Number of months account payment history has been reported.
- Date of Last Activity: This is the date of last activity on the account and may be the date of last payment or the date of last change.
- High Credit: The highest amount charged or the credit limit.
- Terms: Represents number of installments (M=Months) or monthly payments.
- Balance: The amount owed on the account at the time it was reported.
- Past Due: This figure indicates any amount past due at the time the information was reported.
- Status: (See explanation below.)
- Date Reported: Date of last account update.

Company Name	Account Number	Whose Acct.	Date Opened	Months Re-viewed	Date of Last Activity	High Credit	Terms	Items as of Date Reported: Balance	Past Due	Status	Date Reported
SEARS	11251514	J	05/86	66	12/93	3500		0		R1	02/94
AMOUNT IN H/C COLUMN IS CREDIT LIMIT											
CITIBANK	2953900000100473	I	11/86	48	11/93	9388	48M	0		I1	12/93
DINERS	355411251511	A	06/87	24	10/92	500		0		01	12/93
CLOSED ACCOUNT											
CHASE	54229778	I	05/85	48	01/94	5000	340	3000	680	R3	02/94

>>> PRIOR PAYING HISTORY - 30(03) 60(04) 90+(01) 08/92-R2, 02/92-R3, 10/91-R4 <<<

Number of times account was either 30/60/90 days past due.

Date two most recent delinquencies occurred plus date of most severe delinquency.

Collection Agency Accounts
Accounts which your creditors turned over to a collection agency.

>>> COLLECTION REPORTED 06/90; ASSIGNED 09/89 TO PRO COLL (800) 555-1234
CLIENT-ABC HOSPITAL; AMOUNT-$978; STAT UNPAID 06/90; BALANCE-$978 06/90
DATE OF LAST ACTIVITY 09/89; INDIVIDUAL; ACCOUNT NUMBER 787652JC

>>>>>>>>>>>>>>>>>>> COLLECTION AGENCY TELEPHONE NUMBER(S) <<<<<<<<<<<<<<<<<<<
PRO COLL (800) 555-1234

Courthouse Records
Public Record items obtained from local, state and federal courts.

*******************PUBLIC RECORDS OR OTHER INFORMATION*******************

>>> LIEN FILED 03/92; FULTON CTY; CASE OR OTHER ID NUMBER-32114; AMOUNT-$26667;
CLASS-CITY/COUNTY; RELEASED 07/92; VERIFIED 09/93

>>> BANKRUPTCY FILED 12/89; NORTHERN DIST CT; CASE OR OTHER ID NUMBER-673HC12;
LIABILITIES-$15787; PERSONAL; INDIVIDUAL; DISCHARGED; ASSETS-$780

>>> JUDGMENT FILED 07/91; FULTON CTY; CASE OR OTHER ID NUMBER-898872; DEFENDANT-
JOHN DOE AMOUNT-$8984; PLANTIFF-ABC REAL ESTATE; SATISFIED 03/92; VERIFIED
05/93

Additional Information
Primarily consists of former addresses and employments reported by your creditors.

************************ADDITIONAL INFORMATION************************

FORMER ADDRESS 456 JUPITER RD, ATLANTA, GA 30245

FORMER ADDRESS P.O. BOX 2138, SAVANNAH, GA 31406

LAST REPORTED EMPLOYMENT - ENGINEER, SPACE PATROL

Inquiry Section
List of businesses that have received your credit report in the last 24 months.

************COMPANIES THAT REQUESTED YOUR CREDIT HISTORY************

03/04/94 EQUIFAX
12/16/93 PRM VISA
06/11/93 NATIONS BANK
02/17/93 JC PENNEY
02/12/94 MACYS
08/01/93 AM CITIBANK
04/29/93 GE CAPITAL
02/12/93 AR SEARS

WHOSE ACCOUNT

Indicates who is responsible for the account and the type of participation you have with the account.

J = Joint
I = Individual
U = Undesignated
A = Authorized user
T = Terminated
M = Maker
C = Co-Maker/Co-Signer
B = On behalf of another person
S = Shared

THE FOLLOWING INQUIRIES ARE NOT REPORTED TO BUSINESSES:

PRM - This type of inquiry means that only your name and address were given to a credit grantor so they could offer you an application for credit. (PRM inquiries remain for six months.)

AM or **AR** - These inquiries indicate a periodic review of your credit history by one of your creditors. (AM and AR inquiries remain for six months.)

EQUIFAX, ACIS or **UPDATE** - These inquiries indicate Equifax's activity in reponse to your contact with us for either a copy of your credit report or a request for research.

PRM, AM, AR, EQUIFAX, ACIS and **UPDATE** inquiries do not show on credit reports that businesses receive, only on copies provided to you.

STATUS

Type of Account

O = Open (entire balance due each month)
R = Revolving (payment amount variable)
I = Installment (fixed number of payments)

Timeliness of Payment

0 = Approved not used; too new to rate
1 = Paid as agreed
2 = 30+ days past due
3 = 60+ days past due
4 = 90+ days past due
5 = Pays or paid 120+ days past the due date; or collection account
7 = Making regular payments under wage earner plan or similar arrangement
8 = Repossession
9 = Charged off to bad debt

Source: *Reprinted courtesy of Sears, Roebuck and Co.*

Credit Card Limits in China

Corporate credit cards in Canton are limited to $800. Individuals may charge no more than about $266, provided they have at least half that amount in their bank accounts.

Thus, individuals have the chance to
1 reestablish their credit.

Investigative Reporting

Credit agencies sometimes gather information about a person's lifestyle and reputation. This process is called **investigative reporting.** Prospective employers and insurance companies often want such information before hiring or insuring an applicant. Rather than doing the investigating themselves, they
2 have a credit agency do it.

The Fair Credit Reporting Act is a law designed to assure consumers of fair treatment by credit reporting agencies. Under its terms, those who order an investigative report must inform the person being investigated of their actions.

The credit agencies get their information from investigators who make direct observations and who interview acquaintances, neighbors, and others. Consumers have complained about this practice for
3 the following reasons.

1. It is an invasion of privacy.
2. Much of the information gathered is irrelevant. There may, for example, be comments about the plumbing in a person's house, the state of the roof, or the condition of the yard.
3. The "data" is often just gossip that has not been checked.
4. Investigators are not always qualified.
5. Some people testifying before congressional committees charged that investigators who did not come up with "enough" unfavorable information about persons being investigated might themselves be investigated.

Fortunately, this type of specialized information is not included in regular credit reports. Also, it is double checked before being passed to other firms.

Credit bureaus do not often do investigative reporting themselves. This type of study is typically undertaken by a specialized agency.

Billing Disputes

The Fair Credit Billing Act protects your credit rating when there is a billing dispute between you and a store. In such cases, you have 60 days from the bill's postmark to register a complaint.

The **Fair Debt Collection Practices Act** is a law intended to stop the abusive practices of some debt collectors. It applies specifically to those who are in the business of collecting debts for *someone else.* According to the act, the debt collector may contact a person other than the **debtor** (a person who owes money) only to discover the debtor's location. The collector may not contact a debtor about an obligation at an unusual time (between 8 A.M. and 9 P.M. is considered convenient) or at an inconvenient place. The law prohibits the use of harassing, oppressing, or abusive conduct; debt collectors may not:

- Use or threaten violence
- Use obscene language
- Annoy with telephone calls
- Conceal their identity.

1 Discussion Starter Ask students if they agree with the policy of giving people a fresh credit start. Have them consider the employer's point of view.

2 Reinforcement Ask students if they know of anyone who has been the subject of an investigation, anyone who has been interviewed about another person's credit history, or anyone who does this type of investigating for a living. It is unlikely that many students have come in contact with these investigations; thus you can reinforce the point that this practice is not widespread.

3 Extension Tell the students that the credit report in Figure 16–4 shows that an outside collector was called in to collect from the Doe family. Who hired the collector? (ABC Hospital.) Was the account collected? (No.)

1 Vocabulary Some students may not know that *counsel* means a lawyer or someone who can provide legal advice. Ask them to define the term as it is used.

2 Discussion Starter A company advertises that, for a fee, it will "clean up your credit file and help get you credit." Are you interested? Why or why not? (Probably not. Consumers can do their own credit repair work. They can learn what is in their credit file and have inaccurate information corrected. Nobody, however, not even a credit repair firm, can change history. Consumers must live with the record they have made.)

3 Reinforcement Refer the students once again to the credit report in Figure 16–4. Have them look for information about a bankruptcy. At the time of the bankruptcy, how much did the Doe family own? (Assets: $780.) How much did it owe? (Liabilities: $15,787.)

Caption Answer: Cancelled checks and receipts marked "Paid" are proof that you have paid your bills.

CONSUMER CREDIT RIGHTS

Consumers are guaranteed 15 rights by the Federal Trade Commission. These rights protect you against abuses in credit reporting.

- *Reporting agencies.* You have the right to the name and address of the credit bureau that prepared a report used to deny you credit, insurance, or employment or to increase the cost of credit or insurance.
- *Information sources.* A credit bureau must tell you the nature, substance, and sources of the information collected about you. The only exceptions are investigative sources and medical information.

1
- *Counsel.* When you visit the credit bureau to check on your file, you may take anyone with you.
- *Fees and charges.* If you apply within 30 days of an interview in which you were denied credit, insurance, or employment, you are entitled to all information free of charge.
- *Employer inquiries.* If a report was furnished in response to an employer inquiry within the previous two years, you have a right to know who received it.
- *Reinvestigation.* You are entitled to have incomplete or incorrect information reinvestigated. Inaccurate information must be taken out of your file.
- *Notification.* You are entitled to have the agency notify those who have received incorrect or incomplete information removed from your file. This service is to be rendered at no cost.
- *Credit disputes and your file.* When a dispute between you and the credit bureau cannot be resolved, your version of the dispute must be filed and included in future reports.
- *Credit disputes and reports.* You have the right, for a reasonable fee, to have the reporting bureau send your version to certain businesses.
- *Privacy.* You can withhold your
2 credit report from anyone who does not have a legitimate need for it.
- *Legal action.* If a credit bureau willfully or negligently violates the law, you have the right to sue.
- *Duration of record.* You can have adverse information removed from
3 your file after seven years. (Although bankruptcy may be reported for ten years.)
- *Investigative reporting.* You must be told by a business that it is conducting an investigative report about you.
- *Investigation scope.* You may request from the investigator more information about the investigation.
- *Investigation findings.* You are entitled to know the nature and substance (not the sources) of information collected for an investigative report.

If there are inaccuracies in your credit report, you can have them corrected. ***What documents would help you prove that you have paid your bills?*** ▶

Chapter 16 Highlights	Key Terms
Regulation of Lending ▸ Congress passed the Truth-in-Lending Act so people would be informed about credit. ▸ The act requires that creditors compute in a uniform way the finance charge (total cost of credit). ▸ The act also requires that creditors reveal the annual percentage rate (APR). ▸ The credit disclosure form must show the finance charge and APR in boldface type. ▸ Revolving-credit customers who owe more that $1 must be sent a monthly statement. ▸ The right of rescission provides a cooling-off period in credit transactions in which the borrower's home is put up for security.	Truth-in-Lending Act credit disclosure form right of rescission
Getting Credit ▸ The three C's of credit are character, capacity, and capital. ▸ The credit application asks applicants to supply information that will enable the evaluator to assess creditworthiness. ▸ Emphasis in the application is on the applicant's work, home, and credit references.	credit references
The Credit Bureau ▸ The record kept by a credit bureau for any person is a credit history. ▸ Merchants rely on credit bureaus to supply information that will enable them to decide whether to extend credit to the applicant.	credit bureau
Credit Reporting Problems ▸ Errors sometimes appear in records kept by credit bureaus. ▸ The Fair Credit Reporting Act gives consumers the right to have incomplete or incorrect data corrected. ▸ Unfavorable data is not reported after seven years, except for bankruptcies which may be reported for ten years. ▸ Prospective employers and insurance companies sometimes ask for investigative reporting of a person's lifestyle and reputation. ▸ These reports are usually prepared by a specialized agency rather than a credit bureau. **Reinforcement** Suggest that students review the chapter by using the five-step study procedure described at the beginning of the Teacher's Manual.	Fair Credit Reporting Act investigative reporting Fair Debt Collection Practices Act debtor

CHAPTER 16 REVIEW

Refer students to the Reviewing Consumer Terms and Reviewing Facts and Ideas activities in the Student Activity Workbook.

Reviewing Consumer Terms Papers will vary. See Glossary for definitions.

Reviewing Facts and Ideas See the Student Activity Workbook for answers.

Problem Solving and Decision Making 1 Marcie should buy at Store B because the total finance charge and the annual percentage rate are both lower there. 2 Pay the department store as agreed to protect your credit reputation.

Consumers Around the World Communications 1 Write to the credit bureau to get a copy of your credit record. You can have errors corrected and then reapply for credit.

Human Relations 2 Students reports should summarize their findings.

Reviewing Consumer Terms

Use the following terms in a 250-word paper on evaluating credit terms and establishing credit.

credit bureau
credit disclosure form
credit references
debtor
Fair Credit Reporting Act
Fair Debt Collection Practices Act
investigative reporting
right of rescission
Truth-in-Lending Act

Reviewing Facts and Ideas

1. The Truth-in-Lending Act passed because (*a*) merchants demanded regulation, (*b*) banks required stricter standards, or (*c*) consumers were confused about the cost of credit.
2. The Truth-in-Lending Act requires that you be told what two important facts when applying for credit?
3. What is the right of rescission?
4. Identify the three C's of credit.
5. List five questions usually asked on credit application forms.
6. True or false: A credit bureau assigns credit ratings to consumers.
7. What is the purpose of the Fair Credit Reporting Act?
8. List five of the 15 consumer rights.

Problem Solving and Decision Making

1. Marcie Garzon priced the same television set at two different stores and got the information below. Where should she buy? Why?

	Store A	Store B
Retail price	$400.00	$400.00
Total finance charge	13.24	8.78
Annual rate	12%	8%
Term of loan	12 months	12 months

2. You need a new guitar. The department store where you have a revolving charge account has one for $125. The same guitar can be bought for $25 less at a discount store where there are no credit sales. If you buy at the discount house, you will have to miss making this month's payment on your charge account at the department store. What should you do?

Building Academic Skills

Consumers Around the World

Communications

1. The manager of a local department store tells you she cannot give you credit because of an adverse credit report. Records show, she says, that you had appliances repossessed two times last year. As a matter of fact, you have never bought appliances on credit and have not had any repossessions. Explain what you would do in a 150-word paragraph.

Human Relations

2. Your credit record contains private information. Conduct four interviews to find out how family and friends feel about revealing this information. Summarize your findings in a 250-word report.

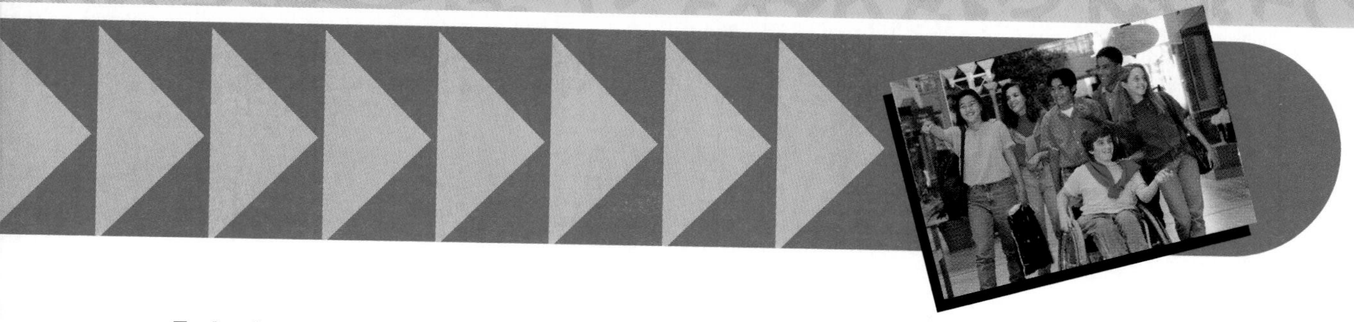

Technology

3. Credit bureaus rely on efficient technology to maintain and update their files. Research how credit bureaus function. How is credit information collected in other countries? Consult library sources. Write to the major credit bureaus for information. Summarize your findings in an oral report to the class.

Beyond the Classroom

Consumer Projects

1. Consumers who borrow money may be asked if they want to buy credit life insurance. This insurance pays off the loan if the borrower dies before finishing payment. The Truth-in-Lending Act requires the fee for credit life insurance to be included in the finance charge unless (*a*) the insurance is optional or (*b*) the consumer has said in writing that he or she wants it.

   Get a loan application from a local bank or consumer finance company. Draw a circle around the part of the contract that meets this legal requirement. Add the application to your credit scrapbook.
2. Lenders who advertise terms for a cash loan should give all of the following information.
   - **a.** Amount of loan
   - **b.** Number of payments
   - **c.** Amount of each payment
   - **d.** Period of payments (weekly, monthly, etc.)
   - **e.** Annual percentage rate (APR)
   - **f.** Total finance charge

   Find a newspaper or magazine ad that gives all of this information. Underline those parts of the ad. Then place the ad in your credit scrapbook.

Cooperative Learning

Family Economics

Break into assigned family groups. Discuss the following problem.

The Bluebird Department Store has turned down your application for a charge account. The reason given is "insufficient credit history."

You arrange for a meeting with the credit department manager, Arlene Simms. How will you convince her that you and other family members who will use the card are good credit risks?

Discuss preparations you will make for the meeting and note what documents you want to take along. Discuss your answer with other family groups.

Debate the Issue

Lenders often collect personal information about credit applicants. These lenders feel this information is essential in determining whether to extend credit. However, some applicants are upset by the fact that companies may sell this information—especially name, address, and income level—to other firms for commercial reasons.

You and your classmates will be divided into two groups to research this topic. Each group will gather evidence to support either the lender's or applicant's perspective. You are to prepare the argument for your side of the problem. Then the two groups will meet in a classroom debate.

Technology
3 Some students may find that the difficulty of reporting and updating information keeps small creditors from contributing information to credit bureaus.

Consumer Projects
1 Students should put the loan application in their scrapbook.
2 Students should save the ad in their scrapbook.

Family Economics
Depending on family circumstances, the applicant could point to a stable work and residential history, car ownership, paying bills on time, careful management of checking account, large purchases saved for and made with cash, and absence of debt. Evidence might include receipts for large purchases made at the store, bank statements showing no penalty fees, and letters of reference.

Debate the Issue
Break the class into two teams. Assign each team one side of the issue. Encourage students to work together as a team to develop their argument. Ask each team to select a member to make an opening statement that supports the team's side of the issue. Have students take turns debating as the debate moves from one team to the other.

CHAPTER 17

Borrowing Money

Learning Objectives

When you have finished studying this chapter, you should be able to:

1. Describe how borrowing cash can sometimes reduce financing costs.
2. Identify the usual sources of cash loans.
3. Explain the higher finance charges of consumer finance companies.

Consumer Terms

consumer finance company
loan sharks
consolidation loan
beneficiary

Real-World Journal

Suppose your friend wants to silk-screen T-shirts with your school logo on them. She wants to borrow $50 from you in order to begin making and selling the T-shirts for a profit. Explain in your journal what type of guarantee and conditions you would like in exchange for lending her the money.

Lesson Plan See the Teacher's Manual for Chapter 17 lesson plan.

Vocabulary The Chapter 17 lesson plan includes suggested vocabulary activities for the terms listed.

1 Reinforcement Remind students about opportunity costs from Unit 4.

2 Critical Thinking Ask students to express the superiority of the bank's terms in two ways. (The bank charges 10 cents for every dollar; the store charges 18 cents. Borrowing from the bank saves $3.)

Caption Answer: Answers might include furniture and travel.

WHEN TO BORROW CASH

Credit and loans are so readily available that it is sometimes difficult to know when to save for an item, when to use credit, and when to borrow cash. Figure 17–1 gives some guidelines.

Sometimes it is to your advantage to borrow money and then pay cash for the goods or services you want. For example, Gus Kostas must buy some furniture. After making a down payment, he will need credit in the amount of $800. He would like to repay this
1 amount over 12 months.

Should Gus finance the purchase through the department store, where the finance charge is 18 percent, or his bank, which makes personal loans at 10 percent interest? If he has credit at both places, the answer is clear. He could save more by borrowing money from the bank and using the loan to pay cash for
2 the furniture.

SAVINGS INSTITUTIONS AS SOURCES OF LOANS

Many savings institutions are sources of cash loans. Among those that lend

Figure 17–1 Deciding When to Use Cash, Credit, or Loans

Use cash savings to pay for...

- *Consumer goods like clothing.*
- *Occasional items like gifts.*

Use credit cards, charge accounts, or installment plans only after (1) saving as much as you can toward the purchase, (2) making sure you can meet the payments, and (3) considering the opportunity costs of credit to pay for...

- *Necessary items like appliances and furniture.*
- *Periodic necessities like rent and utilities.*
- *Large, necessary items like appliances and furniture.*
- *Large, luxury items like television sets.*
- *Long-term goals, like travel and retirement.*

Use cash loans, after saving for a down payment, to pay for...

- *Very large items of value, such as a house or car.*
- *Investments, such as a college education or real estate.*
- *Items that might be more costly on a credit card or installment plan, such as furniture or appliances.*

Use current cash income to pay for...

- *Necessities like food, shelter, and utilities.*
- *Entertainment like movies.*

▲ Here are some guidelines for when to use cash, credit, or loans. ***What types of purchases do you usually make with a credit card?***

money to consumers are commercial banks, savings and loan associations, and credit unions.

Commercial Banks

A commercial bank accepts deposits, maintains accounts, lends money, and performs other financial services for consumers and the business community. It usually has a personal loan department, whose services are widely advertised. The department lends to the bank's depositors and others who are good credit risks. Commercial bank interest rates are often lower than those of some other lenders for the following reasons:

1. Depositors provide most of the funds that banks lend. Because the interest the bank pays its depositors is fairly
1 low, banks can afford to lend the
2 money to others at favorable rates.
2. Bank losses on personal loans are very low. Commercial banks screen loan applicants with care and choose the best credit risks.
3. The bank already has a building, equipment, and employees on hand. The personal loan department is added to a business that is already in operation.

Savings and Loan Associations

Savings and loan associations (S&Ls) accept savings deposits from customers. They then lend these funds to others, depositors and nondepositors alike. Most of the funds are loaned to people to buy or build homes. However, many S&Ls make consumer loans as well.

Camille Rivera received $1,000 in gifts on her 21st birthday. She put this money in an S&L account. Later, she borrowed $1,000 from the association, using her account as security. The interest rate charged was slightly above what the S&L paid on her savings.

Why didn't Camille just withdraw the money? Sometimes consumers feel that if they take funds from savings accounts, they will never get around to putting them back. When they borrow against the account, however, they *must* repay. Their savings remain intact. The method is an expensive way to save money, but it works for some people.

Credit Unions

As you learned in an earlier chapter, a credit union is an organization formed to encourage members to save money. It is run as a cooperative, owned and oper-
3 ated for the benefit of its members.

4 Most large companies help their employees set up credit unions. Employees join the cooperative by paying a small

Tips for Saving Money

- **Open a holiday account and make regular monthly deposits. At the end of the year, just $25 a month will yield $300—plus interest.**
- **Buy yourself a U.S. savings bond on your birthday.**
- **Initiate automatic deductions from your checking account into your savings account.**
- **Every day place all your change in a special container. When it is full, deposit the money in your savings account.**
- **Every payday, deposit a percentage of your pay in a savings account.**
- **If you are working at a summer job away from home, buy money orders and mail them as deposits to your savings account.**

1 Learning Economics Have students explain why banks can lend at lower rates. The reasoning here may not be immediately obvious to all students, but after studying Unit 1, they should know that businesses must always weigh increased sales against the costs of making those sales. In this case the bank increases its business without increasing its costs.

2 Extension Student Activity Workbook, Chapter 17 Activities.

3 Learning Economics Ask students if they would expect credit union rates to be lower or higher than those of other lending institutions, given the information provided in the text, and ask them to explain their answers. (Lower because of lower production costs.)

4 Research Have students identify credit unions in your area and find out what interest rates they charge their members. Have them do the same for local banks and savings and loans. Then compare the rates in class.

1 Discussion Starter Ask students if they or anyone they know belongs to a credit union. What opinions do they have or have they heard expressed about credit unions?

Home Mortgages in Britain

At least 90 percent of all home mortgages in Britain are at floating interest rates, compared with less than 20 percent in the United States. Over a five-year period, British household interest payments can fluctuate from about 6.5 percent to more than 11 percent of disposable income. In the United States interest payments stay at about 8 to 9 percent of disposable income.

membership fee (perhaps a dollar) and purchasing a share, or unit of ownership, in the credit union. (The share usually costs no more than $5). Members can then build savings by buying more shares.

A worker who needs money can borrow from the credit union at a reasonable rate of interest. This rate is sometimes more, sometimes less, than a bank would charge.

Credit union losses are low because borrowers are employed. In addition, borrowers have a connection with the people whose money they have borrowed and therefore feel a special obligation to repay. Operating costs are not great. Office space and utilities are often provided at no cost by the company that helped the employees set up the credit union. Work of the cooperative is often done entirely by members who serve without extra pay.

Consumers who have a chance to join a credit union should consider its merits carefully. A credit union is not only a place to save money but a good
1 source of credit.

OTHER SOURCES OF LOANS

In addition to bank-type institutions, you can borrow money from other sources, such as consumer finance companies and insurance companies. There are advantages and drawbacks to this kind of borrowing.

Consumer Finance Companies

A lending institution that specializes in small or personal loans is called a **consumer finance company.** Often, finance companies give credit to those who cannot get it elsewhere because of low income or minimal assets.

Higher Charges Finance company charges are higher than those of banks for a number of reasons.

1. Finance companies do not have depositors to supply the money they lend. They mostly borrow the money they lend and pay interest on it.
2. Although loans are for relatively small amounts, they require records as complicated as those used for much larger loans. Weekly or monthly payments must be recorded, and this process takes time and money.
3. Credit investigations for small loans cost as much as (or more than) those made for large loans. The financial reputation of a large and established corporation, for example, is generally well known. When the corporation applies for a loan of $100,000, the cost of investigating its credit relative to the amount being borrowed is quite small.

   When an individual, a new resident, seeks to borrow a mere $100, however, just the opposite is true. It might take several telephone calls and letters to do a thorough credit investigation. The cost relative to the

amount being borrowed (and paid
1 back in interest) is relatively large.

4. Collection costs run higher, and bad debts are greater than for some other lenders. These added costs reflect the fact that the typical borrower handled by a consumer finance company is a greater credit risk than the typical borrower handled by a commercial
2 bank.

Although consumer finance companies often charge higher rates of interest than some other lenders, they play an important role in our society. Suppose a bank has turned down a consumer who must have credit. The consumer may find the finance company willing to give the needed loan. If it were not for these firms, far more people would surely find themselves dealing with **loan sharks—**

People MAKING a DIFFERENCE

Starting a Game Train

If you have ever been in the hospital, you know it can be a boring, if not frightening, place. It is even worse for young children who may have to spend much of their time there.

When Traci Taylor was 6, doctors discovered she had leukemia, a type of blood cancer. For three years, she spent a lot of time in hospitals. One thing that kept the fear away and helped her fight boredom was a toy train.

Every day, a volunteer in her Dallas hospital would bring around a large wagon shaped like a train. It was filled with games, crafts, books, and toys from which hospital-bound children could choose.

When Traci was 10, she had a bone-marrow transplant that let her live a normal life. However, she did not forget her time in the hospital. When she and her family moved to Missouri, and she discovered that the local hospital did not have a toy train, she organized one herself.

Her father built the train with help from church members. Traci had them paint it red with black wheels and a black smokestack. Meanwhile, she and her mother talked to store owners and church members about donating toys to the train.

The train was a great success, and Traci continues to see that it runs every day. She chooses the toys and gifts herself. Every Thursday, she takes her turn distributing the contents of the train.

Traci was just 14 when she started the toy train. Her thoughtfulness has brought relief to the lives of hundreds of young hospital patients. She does not plan to stop with only one train, however. She hopes to inspire other hospitals in the area to start toy trains. If they don't, she is sure to do it herself.

Brainstorm

What kinds of items would you select for a game train?

1 Math Application Have students assume that it costs $35 to investigate each loan. Have them calculate that cost as a percentage of the total loan for both the $100,000 loan and the $100 loan. ($35 ÷ 100,000 = .00035, or less than 1/10 of 1 percent; $35 ÷ 100 = 35%.) Ask students what this means in terms of the loan company's ability to make a profit. (The company's costs are much higher costs, which means it must charge much more for the same service.)

2 Learning Economics Invite students to summarize items 1–4 in a single sentence: A finance company's rates are higher than a bank's because its _____ are higher. (Production costs.)

Case Study Answer: Answers might include board games; checkers; cards; chess; puzzles; dolls; stuffed toys; macrame, paint by numbers, clay, drawing supplies and supplies for other crafts; books, such as novels, comic books, and magazines.

1 Vocabulary Knowing the meaning of consolidate (to bring together; join) will help students understand and retain this concept.

2 Math Application As the beneficiary of a $40,000 life insurance policy, how much money would you receive upon the death of the person who bought the policy if he or she borrowed $15,000 against the policy and repaid half of that amount? ($15,000 ÷ 2 = $7,500; $40,000 − $7,500 = $32,500.)

3 Reinforcement Student Activity Workbook, Chapter 17 activities.

News Clip Answers:
1 You may want to use the funds from a home equity loan to improve your house, pay off expensive credit card debt, or pay for college expenses.
2 If a new business fails, the home owner risks foreclosure on his or her home.

unlicensed lenders who operate outside the law and charge excessive interest.

Consolidation Loans Consumer finance companies are also important as sources of consolidation loans. A **consolidation loan** is one large loan
1 made to enable debtors to pay several debts at once.

A consumer may have several debts and not be able to make payments on all of them every month. For example, there may be debts to the doctor, the hospital, an appliance company, and a furniture store. The consumer borrows the total amount of cash needed and pays off all the creditors. Then the consumer can make one payment each month to the lending agency. Consumer finance companies make more small cash loans for consolidating existing bills than for any other reason. Banks often lend for this purpose also.

Any lender will ask for all the details about all of the applicant's debts before making a loan. It must be clear that the borrower will really be better off by consolidating the debts. A consolidation loan may help by spreading out the repayment period. Monthly payments will be smaller and easier to handle. However, the consumer will also have to pay more interest over the life of the loan. The reason is that he or she is using borrowed money for a longer period.

Insurance Companies

A person who has permanent life insurance can borrow from the insurance company some of the money paid for the insurance. The insurance company gives the money quickly. No credit investigation is needed, and the policy serves as the only security. The interest
2 rate is usually lower than bank rates.

A borrower from an insurance company should keep two important facts in mind:

1. In case of death, the company will deduct any amount still owed before paying the insurance money to the beneficiaries. A **beneficiary** is a person named to receive the money from an insurance policy if the insured person dies.
2. Insurance loans tend to remain unpaid for long periods of time. The company does not regularly remind the borrower to pay back the loan. The borrower feels no pressure to repay and therefore often pays only
3 the interest, allowing the loan to ride.

Private Loans

Sometimes, people turn to family members or friends when they need to borrow large sums. For example, a young couple buying a house might borrow part of the down payment from

Caption Answer: A consolidation loan reduces the monthly payment. However, the payments are extended over a longer period of time so the consumer pays more in interest.

A consolidation loan can help consumers manage their debt. ***What are the pros and cons of a consolidation loan?*** ▶

CASE STUDY

Consumer NEWS CLIP

Home Equity Loans Back in Fashion

by Nick Ravo
The New York Times
September 11, 1994

Demand for home equity loans has been growing in spurts for almost 20 years, especially since 1986, when Congress eliminated the tax deduction for interest on consumer debt but kept the deduction in place for mortgages and loans backed by mortgages.

Home owners today, however, are not using these low-interest rate loans just to build a backyard deck or an extra bedroom, the traditional uses of home equity loans. They are also taking out loans to pay off high-interest credit-card loans, start businesses, and buy cars and boats—moves that some financial planners and consumer counselors recommend only with caution.

A steady increase in the use of home equity loans does raise the specter that home owners, particularly those who are not financially astute, will take on more debt than they can afford to carry and risk foreclosure if they cannot keep up home equity payments.

The most common use for both traditional home equity loans (44 percent) and home equity lines of credit (64 percent) remains home improvements, according to the University of Michigan survey. Because making improvements

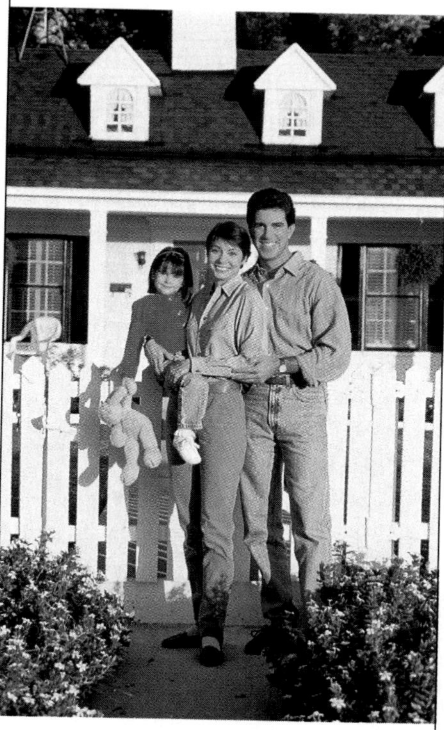

to a home—even if it's as frivolous-sounding as adding a Jacuzzi—is usually considered an investment that increases a home's value, using a home equity loan for this purpose is generally considered to be reasonable.

Ms. Karen Green, marketing director of Citibank, said that many of today's home owners are also taking out home equity loans to send their children to college, particularly if they had a high household income and their children did not qualify for financial aid. "We find that when someone is younger, say their late 30's, they tend to use them for debt consolidation or home renovation, and if they're over 45, then college costs," she said.

Mr. Luther R. Gatling of the Budget and Credit Counseling Service of New York City noted, however, that some home owners ran up more bills after paying [others] off with a home equity loan. "People often use home equity loans to pay off high-interest credit cards, and that's a good idea as long as they are disciplined about their future spending," he said.

Using a home equity loan to start a business is an iffy proposition, however. Because the business owner has his home on the line, it may give him the extra incentive to succeed. It may also help attract outside investors who like to see a personal investment made by the owners of start-up businesses. Home owners should be aware, however, that most new businesses fail.

Decisions, Decisions

1. What are some of the reasons you might want to take out a home equity loan?
2. Why is using a home equity loan to start a business not a good idea?

FLASHBACK FLASHFORWARD

Among those needing loans are farmers. In 1946, the government granted $4,760,000 in farm mortgage loans. In 1992, farm mortgage loans reached $80 billion.

their parents or a college student might borrow tuition money from an aunt or uncle.

When you are borrowing from family and friends, it is important to be clear and specific about the loan and to make sure you are responsible about paying back the money. See Figure 17–2.

Stationery stores carry loan forms, payment booklets, and interest rate booklets. You can use these to determine how to arrange the loan.

Figure 17–2 Borrowing from Family or Friends

Private loans from family or friends work best when certain guidelines are followed.

Agree with lender on the amount of the loan.
Keep the loan as small as possible. Remember to consider your other expenses. Be prepared to show how you will pay back the loan.
Agree with the lender on the interest rate.
Family members may charge you a low rate, perhaps what the money would earn in a savings account.
Agree with the lender on the payment plan.
Choose a specific date, say, the 15th of each month, and a specific amount.
Pay promptly.
Demonstrate that you are trustworthy. If you lose your source of income, talk to your creditor immediately about restructuring the loan payments.
Get and keep a signed receipt for each payment.
You may need to prove to other family members that you paid back the loan completely.
1
2
3
4
5
PERSONAL LOAN
TO: Mary Fisher
FROM: James Jackson
LOAN AMOUNT: $5,000
INTEREST RATE: 9.75%
PAYMENT SCHEDULE: 36 mos.
DATE DUE
TOTAL PAYMENT
INTEREST AMOUNT
PRINCIPLE AMOUNT
REMAINING BALANCE
Oct 15 350 48.75 301.25 4698.75
Nov 15 350 45.81 304.20 4394.55
Dec 15 350 42.85 307.15 4087.40
Jan 15
10/15 1998
$ 350.00
DOLLARS
James Jackson
15
loan payment due
tuesday october
001
017
016
RECEIPT
This reciept certifies that
Has payed 350.00
On the date 10/15/98
to

Chapter 17 Highlights	Key Terms
When to Borrow Cash ► If bank finance charges and APR are lower than those at the retail store, you can reduce costs by borrowing money from the bank and using the loan to pay cash for a retail purchase.	
Savings Institutions as Sources of Loans ► Commercial banks tend to be more selective than most lenders, and their rates are usually competitive. ► Savings and loan associations charge competitive rates and are roughly similar to commercial banks in dealings with the public. ► Credit unions are cooperatives formed for the purpose of promoting thrift. They provide a place for members to invest their money, as well as a source of funds in time of need.	
Other Sources of Loans ► Consumer finance companies are less selective than many sources of cash loans. As a result, these companies experience a higher bad debt loss than other lenders and their interest rates are higher. ► Consumer finance companies are an important source of consolidation loans. Without access to these companies, many consumers would be forced to resort to loans from loan sharks. ► Insurance companies are a source of low-interest loans for people with permanent life insurance policies. Loans that are not paid back reduce the insurance money given to the beneficiary. **Reinforcement** Suggest that students review the chapter by using the five-step study procedure described at the beginning of the Teacher's Manual.	consumer finance company loan sharks consolidation loan beneficiary

CHAPTER 17 REVIEW

Refer students to the Reviewing Consumer Terms and Reviewing Facts and Ideas activities in the Student Activity Workbook.

Reviewing Consumer Terms Explanations will vary. See Glossary for definitions.

Reviewing Facts and Ideas See the Student Activity Workbook for answers.

Problem Solving and Decision Making
1 A loan from the insurance company would probably be the least costly.
2 Karen would be wiser to invest the borrowed money in her education, which has the best prospects for growth.

Consumers Around the World Math
1 Sam will earn $40 in dividends. The net cost will be $40.16.

Communications
2 The students should include the names of the finance companies and summarize services and guidelines given.

Reviewing Consumer Terms

Explain in writing how each of the following terms relates to borrowing money.

beneficiary
consolidation loan
consumer finance company
loan sharks

Reviewing Facts and Ideas

1. Explain how one may "save money by borrowing money" when buying on credit.
2. Name three savings institutions that provide cash loans.
3. Why are bank interest rates low compared to those of some other lenders?
4. Explain why consumer finance companies have to charge higher rates of interest than banks.
5. What is a consolidation loan?
6. If you borrow money from an insurance company, using your policy as collateral, what happens to your insurance protection?

Problem Solving and Decision Making

1. You are taking a one-year course at a local trade and technical school. Your family cannot help you out financially, but they will give you free room and board.

   Where would you go for a tuition loan—Would you go to an insurance company, a commercial bank, a consumer finance company, or a credit union? Explain your choice, noting why you rejected the other three.
2. Karen Lee's aunt is willing to lend her $500. Karen can use the money (a) to buy a complete new sound system or (b) to pay for part of a summer tutorial program in environmental science, a field in which she might like to make a career. Which would be the wiser use of borrowed money? Why?

Building Academic Skills

Consumers Around the World

Math

1. Sam Rao has $800 in his credit union account, earning 5 percent in dividends a year. He would like to borrow $800 at an 18 percent APR, to be paid back in one year. He will pay $80.16 in interest on the loan. He plans to use the $800 in savings as security for the loan.

   How much will he earn in dividends on his security? How much will the loan end up costing him altogether?

Communications

2. Write to three consumer finance companies. Ask for any guidelines they give to people who have too much debt. Ask how consumers can get help working out a budget and controlling their spending. Prepare a five-minute oral report to your class on how to handle consumer debt.

Social Studies

3. Choose a country other than the United States and research its borrowing practices. Why does it borrow money? From where? Does it have a balanced budget? If not, is that an important goal? Report your findings to the class.

Beyond the Classroom

Consumer Project

Interview someone who belongs to a credit union. Find out all you can about the credit union's value and operation. Ask the following two questions:

1. How has the credit union been of benefit to you?
2. Would you recommend credit-union membership to a new employee at your place of work? Why or why not? As part of a class discussion, compare your findings with those of your classmates.

Cooperative Learning

Family Economics

Break into assigned family groups. Discuss the following problem.

Because of a family emergency, you are faced with an immediate need for $800 in cash. Consider all of your family's financial resources and everything you have learned in this and the previous unit. Then decide what would be the quickest way to obtain the money. Explain your choice and your reasons. Compare your answers with those of other family groups.

Debate the Issue

Many states have adopted contract rates of interest—the highest rates that may be charged lawfully. Anybody who charges a higher rate of interest is guilty of *usury,* which means charging an illegal rate or interest.

Many Americans object to the setting of maximum rates, claiming that people who have money to lend are entitled to collect whatever interest borrowers are willing to pay. Others state that usury is a crime and that the poor should be protected by usury statutes.

You and your classmates will break into two groups and research this topic. Each group will gather evidence to support one side or the other. You are to prepare the argument for your side of the problem. Then the two groups will meet in a classroom debate.

Rechecking Your Attitude

Before going on to the next unit, go back to the Attitude Inventory at the beginning of this one. Answer the questions a second time. Then compare the two sets of responses. On how many statements have your attitudes changed? Can you account for these shifts in your opinions? What do you know now that you did not know then?

Social Studies
3 Students should answer all questions about the country chosen.

Consumer Project
Many credit unions provide services at lower cost than other financial institutions.

Family Economics
The fastest ways to obtain money would be to (1) use a bank card for a cash advance, (2) withdraw the money from savings, or (3) borrow from a friend or relative. A loan from a bank or finance company would take longer.

Debate the Issue
Break the class into two teams. Assign each team one side of the issue. Encourage students to work together as a team to develop their argument. Ask each team to select a member to make an opening statement that supports the team's side of the issue. Have students take turns debating as the debate moves from one team to the other.

UNIT 5 LAB

You and Your Community

The Search for Good Credit

STEP A Students should complete loan charts and be able to cite their sources for the information they provide.
STEP B Students should prepare lists of interview questions that are clearly written, easily comprehended, and appropriate to the topics. During their interviews, students should take accurate notes.
STEP C Students' answers should be accurate and based on their loan charts and the consumer information provided in Step A.
STEP D Students' reports should reflect their thoughtful consideration of the rights and responsibilities of a consumer establishing credit. Students should support their comments with examples from their "loan shopping" experiences and their interviews with loan officers.

Refer students to the Unit 5 Lab in the Student Activity Workbook.

Unit 5 outlines consumers' rights and responsibilities when establishing credit and borrowing money. In this lab, you will extend your study of consumer credit rights and learn more about evaluating loan offers.

TOOLS

1. Business and consumer magazines
2. Financial textbooks
3. Newspaper business sections

PROCEDURES

Imagine that you are 24 years old and single. Your monthly take home pay is $1,500; you have worked at your job for three years. You currently have $3,500 in savings and $500 in a checking account at a bank. There are ten monthly payments of $100 remaining on your new car loan. You recently moved into a larger apartment for which you pay a monthly rent of $350. You need to borrow $1,200 in order to purchase a washer, dryer, and refrigerator.

Using the newspapers' lending rate surveys and advertisements from savings institutions, identify at least three banks or savings and loan associations whose rates on unsecured personal loans seem attractive. Complete a chart like the one that follows for each bank.

STEP B Contact a loan officer from one of the institutions listed on your chart. Explain the purpose of your assignment; interview him or her about the institution's loan procedure and about the impact of federal legislation

Rates and Terms for Unsecured Personal Loan

Loan amount	Number of payments	Payment amount	Payment period	Annual percentage rate (APR)	Total finance charge (TFC)
Institution A					
Institution B					
Institution C					
Credit Union					

If you know someone who belongs to a credit union, perhaps that person can advise you on whom to call to find out the credit union's rates and terms on unsecured personal loans. Add those rates to your chart.

UNIT 5 LAB
You and Your Community

on that procedure. Your interview may be conducted in person or over the phone. Before conducting the interview, go to the institution and get a loan application. Mark those sections of the application that you believe meet the requirements of the Truth-in-Lending, Fair Credit Billing, and Fair Credit Reporting Acts. Before the interview, prepare a list of questions covering the following topics:

1. The likelihood that the consumer profiled in Step A would receive the $1,200 loan and the reasons the consumer would receive the loan.
2. Which steps an 18- to 25- year-old should take to establish a good credit reputation.
3. How the provisions of the Truth-in-Lending, Fair Credit Billing, and Fair Credit Reporting Acts affect the institution's loan procedure. (Review the loan application on which you marked sections that you thought related to the federal requirements.)

LAB REPORT

STEP C Use your chart and interview notes to answer the questions below:

1. Which lending institution offers the lowest interest rate?
2. Which loan allows the lowest monthly payment?
3. For each loan, determine what percentage of the consumer's take home pay would be devoted to credit debt. (Don't forget that the consumer already has some credit debt.)
4. Which loan would you advise the consumer to buy? Explain your answer.

STEP D Write a two-page report on the steps a person should take throughout his or her adult life to establish and maintain good credit. In the report, use the case of the consumer's search for a loan as an example of the need to evaluate all aspects of a loan offer. Also, include references to your interview with the loan officer.

UNIT 6

Unit Contents

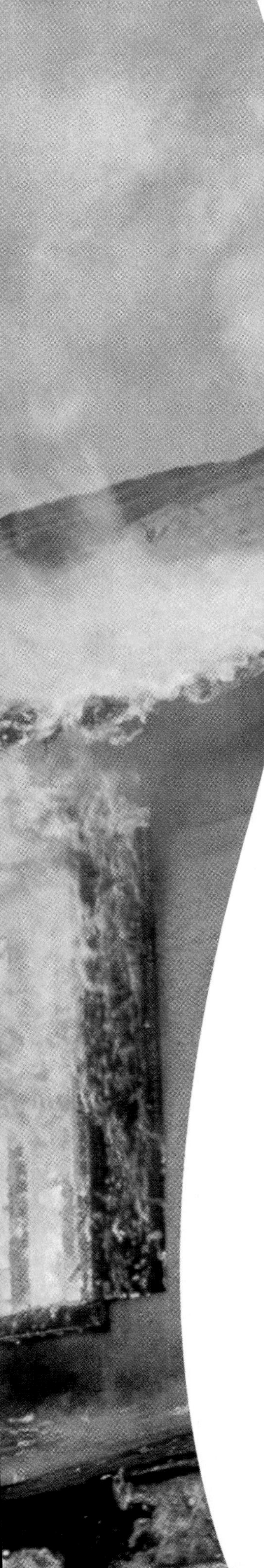

Insurance

Attitude Inventory

Before you begin Chapter 18, take stock of your attitudes by completing the following inventory. Read each statement and decide how you feel about it—agree, disagree, or undecided. Record your feelings on a sheet of notepaper or use the form in the workbook.

1. If people are careful, they may avoid all economic risks.
2. People who have a great deal of money do not need insurance.
3. Most people are adequately insured.
4. Renters do not need home and property insurance.
5. The government should provide insurance protection for those who cannot afford it.
6. One insurance company is as good as the next.
7. Insurance policies of any one type are basically the same in terms of cost and features.
8. You can buy insurance on the life of any person.
9. A good driver does not need to waste his or her money on automobile insurance.
10. Automobile insurance protects drivers from responsibility for breaking the law.
11. A doctor is the best person to advise you about the type of medical and health insurance to buy.
12. A teenager does not need to learn about social security because the program is only for old people.
13. If you are not working, one of the things you can do without is life insurance.
14. Most people do not need health insurance because they probably have enough money saved to pay their medical and hospital bills.
15. There is no point to saving money for retirement since social security benefits will provide all you need to live on.

Unit Goal The main goal of this unit is to introduce students to insurance, define the various types of insurance, and explain how each type of insurance works. Chapters included in this unit are (1) Property and Home Insurance, (2) Automobile Insurance, (3) Life and Health Insurance, and (4) Income Insurance.

Lesson Plan See the Teacher's Manual for an overview of the unit and some suggestions for introducing it. If you assign the Attitude Inventory, be sure to tell students to keep their answers for later use.

CHAPTER 18 Property and Home Insurance

Learning Objectives

When you have finished studying this chapter, you should be able to:

1. Explain what insurance is and how it works.
2. Tell how to select an insurance agent and an insurance company.
3. Identify the three types of insurance risk.
4. Describe what specific risks a homeowners policy covers.
5. List the factors that determine the cost of property insurance.
6. Illustrate how to prove property loss.

Consumer Terms

insurance
policy
premium
indemnification
insurable interest
property insurance
deductible
coinsurance clause
personal liability insurance
personal property
homeowners policy
medical payments coverage
physical damage coverage

Real-World Journal

Prepare an inventory in your journal of all the personal items in your bedroom. List the item name and the approximate dollar value when you purchased it. What is the total dollar value of your list? Ask a parent or guardian if any of your personal items would be covered by insurance if they were damaged or stolen.

Lesson Plan See the Teacher's Manual for Chapter 18 lesson plan.

Vocabulary The Chapter 18 lesson plan includes suggested vocabulary activities for the terms listed.

1 **Learning Economics** Tell the class to assume that their insurance company has only $10 in expenses. Ask what the remaining $50 represents. (Profit)

2 **Critical Thinking** Have the students assume that at midsemester book prices increase to $40. What consequences will this have for students who suffer losses thereafter? (None, if they lose $30 books.)

HOW INSURANCE WORKS

Insurance is protection against financial loss. People can suffer financial loss, as when an individual becomes disabled and can no longer earn a living. Businesses also suffer financial loss, as when a store loses merchandise to shoplifting. In both cases, insurance provides money to lessen the hardship caused by the loss.

Insurance is a way of sharing economic risks by spreading them over a large number of people. Consider a simple example. Suppose your textbook costs $30. If you lose it, you will have to pay $30 for a replacement. Also suppose that an average of 20 out of every 100 books are lost each year. Based on this figure, the losses in a class of 30 students should come to 6 books (.20 × 30). That's a possible
1 loss of $180 (6 × $30) for the class.

The class could set up an insurance company to lower the cost of these expected losses to students. The company would issue each participant a written agreement spelling out the responsibilities of the students and the company. This agreement would be called a **policy.** The cost of coverage for each policyholder could be set at $8. This amount would be the **premium.** The fund raised by collecting premiums would total $240 (30 × $8). Those students who lost their books would be given money from the fund to replace them. By having insurance, they would thus save $22 a piece ($30 − $8). The company, after paying for the expected number of losses, would have money left over for its
2 expenses ($240 − $180 = $60).

Through the services of an insurance company, then, many people pay into a common fund. The few who actually do have losses draw on that money. In other words, the many pay a little so that no one has to pay a lot. That is how insurance works.

Principle of Indemnification

Insurance is not meant to enrich, only to compensate for actual losses. This principle is called **indemnification,** which means compensation that puts the policyholder in the same financial position he or she occupied before the loss occurred. For example, if your five-year-old camera is stolen, the insurance company will not buy you a new camera. The company will pay what it would cost to buy you another *five-year-old* camera.

If your five-year-old bike was stolen, your insurance company would pay only what it costs to buy another five-year-old bike. It will not pay for the cost of a brand new bike. ***Why?*** ▶

Caption Answer: Because insurance is not meant to enrich, only to compensate for actual losses.

Insurable Interest

To buy insurance, you must have an insurable interest to protect. An **insurable interest** is any interest in life or property such that if the life or property is lost, you will suffer financially. Thus, you could not buy insurance protection on the life of your neighbor's parent, but you could buy insurance on your own parent since the death, illness, or injury of your parent would be a great financial
1 hardship on you.

Use of Premiums

Premiums provide an insurance company with money for both operating expenses and payment of losses. They should also allow for a profit. Whether or not they do depends on how much must be paid out in claims during the year.

A *claim* is a request for payment of a loss. Since no one knows in advance how much policyholders will claim for losses, insurance companies estimate the amount based on what they have paid out in other years, and set rates accordingly. If losses are increasing, or if compa-
2 nies lose money from their investments,
3 premiums go up.

Importance of Insurance

People buy insurance for two basic reasons. First, they want to protect themselves from suffering hardships because of a significant, unexpected economic loss. For example, suppose a family's house is destroyed in a fire. Without insurance, the family may not have the money to rebuild the house.

Second, people buy insurance to protect others who might suffer injury or loss because of them. For example, suppose the major wage earner in a family dies suddenly. Without insurance, the family may not have the money to pay ongoing living expenses.

Insurance and the Economy

Insurance protection can have a major impact on communities. Figure 18–1 on page 280 shows how insurance can affect the economy.

PURCHASE CONSIDERATIONS

Just like buying other goods and services, buying insurance requires wise

1 Critical Thinking Ask the students if it is possible for them to take out an insurance policy on a neighbor's house. Have them explain why or why not. (It's not possible—no insurable interest.)

2 Learning Economics Have the students write a word equation showing how an insurance company makes its money. (Premiums − [losses paid + operating expenses] = profit.)

3 Discussion Starter What happens if insurance company investments do poorly? Who should bear the burden of any investment losses or decreases in profits? What, if any, potential do you see for abuse in this situation? (If investments perform poorly, insurance companies could raise premiums to maintain profit levels.)

◀ *An insurance agent should answer your questions candidly, in terms that are specific yet easy to understand.* ***Why is the agent such an important person in buying insurance?***

Caption Answer: The agent can: (1) advise you on what products and coverages are best for you; (2) explain the policy and how it works; (3) answer any questions you might have; and (4) keep in touch and help you update your future needs.

1 **Research** Have students ask their parents and older acquaintances what different kinds of insurance they have. Compile results in class to develop a norm of the kinds of insurance owned by the average person.

2 **Reinforcement** Make sure students realize that they *must* buy insurance for homes and cars if they borrow money to pay for these purchases. They need to be aware of this so they can plan for the insurance costs.

3 **Research** Have individual students or small groups volunteer to interview insurance agents to find out what they do, who they work for, how they were trained, and on what basis they are paid. Suggest that they give special attention to any complaints the agents have about consumers. Have the interviewers compare their findings in a classroom discussion.

Figure 18–1 Impact of Insurance on Economy

Insurance companies help the economy in a number of ways.

Insurance protects a region's standard of living. When a disaster strikes, insurance payments require that people's buying power is not totally destroyed.
HOUSE
BY
555-4593
Sold
Insurance makes it possible for people to take risks they otherwise could not. Suppose you wanted to buy a $160,000 house but had only $40,000 for a down payment. You might borrow the remaining $120,000, but the lending agency would require you to buy insurance to protect its loan.
MAIN ST DELI
DELI
GRAND
Chamber of Commerce
Insurance provides funds for investment in a variety of enterprises. Insurance companies create jobs and support the economy by putting the premium money to work making loans to individuals, businesses, and the government.

1 and careful shopping. You should con-
2 sider several factors.

Agent Qualifications

People often buy insurance protection through an insurance agent. The agent may be self-employed, independent (selling many kinds of insurance for a number of different companies), or employed by a particular insurance firm.

3 In selecting an agent you can trust, ask yourself the following questions.

1. *Does the agent offer reliable service?* Check with current customers. An agent should be available to answer all your questions, should be easy to reach, and should sell insurance full-time.
2. *Is the agent knowledgeable?* Can the agent explain the advantages and disadvantages of various policies and suggest options that might be to your advantage? Is the agent licensed by the state?
3. *Is the agent candid and honest?* You should be able to talk easily with your

agent and get straightforward answers to your questions, especially about money.

4. *Does the agent take a genuine interest in you and your needs?* An agent should look at your individual financial situation and should contact you regularly to update your coverage.

Company Reputation

The insurance company the agent represents is equally important. Keep the following questions in mind when making your selection.

1. How long has the company been in business?
2. Is the company licensed in the state?
3. Is the company financially sound?
4. Is the company known for settling claims promptly?
5. Does the company offer nationwide claim service?
6. How do the company's premiums compare with those offered by others
1 for the same coverage?
7. Is the company innovative, designing new products to meet changing social needs?

To get answers to these questions, contact your state insurance department, consult *Best's Annual Insurance Guide,* available in the library, and read the periodic reports on insurance cover-
2 age featured in consumer magazines.

Key Policy Elements

The most important item in buying insurance is the insurance policy. The policy is the legal agreement, or contract, between you and the insurance company. It spells out your rights and obligations and those of the company. You should read the policy to find out what the company will do for you if a claim or loss occurs. There are five parts to an insurance policy.

- *Declarations.* Personal information, terms of the policy, coverages, and premium charges for each coverage.
- *Insuring Agreement.* The company's promise to pay, the kinds of losses that the company agrees to cover, and the largest amount payable.
- *Exclusions.* Risks not covered by the agreement, including injuries or damages caused intentionally and those with only partial coverage.
- *Conditions.* The rights and obligations of the company and the policyholder, including what you must do after a loss to get paid.
- *Endorsements.* Additions to an insurance contract. For example, you might add earthquake coverage to your homeowners policy.

Group Versus Individual Coverage

Insurance purchased through an agent is usually individual and is tailored to the needs and finances of the person seeking coverage. Insurance can also be bought by a group. This arrangement offers you substantial savings since the insurance company has to write only one policy to cover hundreds (or even thousands) of people.

High Profit for Insurers

Premiums on property and casualty insurance—the amount paid by consumers for coverage—constitute about 44 percent of claims in North America and about 31 percent in Europe.

FLASHBACK FLASHFORWARD

In 1940, there were 58,000 insurance agents in the labor force. Ten years later, the number of agents leaped to 312,000. By 1990, there were 712,000 insurance agents at work writing policies.

1 Reinforcement Emphasize that in most cases, the cost of premiums becomes the deciding factor and that rates often vary considerably for similar services. Consumers who take the time to shop around for their insurance can save a great deal of money.

2 Research Have students use *Best's Guide, Consumer Reports,* and similar sources to research the insurance company of their choice (perhaps one their family uses). Suggest that they pay particular attention to performance ratings and measures of customer satisfaction. Given this information, would they do (or continue to do) business with the firm?

1 **Reinforcement** Student Activity Workbook, Chapter 18 activities.

2 **Math Application** The Chang home is worth $150,000. It is fully insured with a $250 deductible and an 80 percent coinsurance clause. If the Changs suffer a $50,000 fire loss, how much will they be paid by insurance? ($50,000 − $250 = $49,750. .80 × $49,750 = $39,800.)

3 **Vocabulary** *Liability* can be a difficult term for many students. Emphasize the idea that to be *liable* is to be *responsible.* Give them several examples of accidents in which one person is liable for damages caused to another. Have them create several sentences of their own using both *liable* and *liability.*

Most group insurance is offered to people through their job. Companies commonly pay part or even all of their employee's premiums as a fringe benefit. When employees do pay part of the premium, the cost to them is much lower than it would be if they bought insur-
1 ance on their own.

TYPES OF RISK

Insurance protects against types of risks. There are three broad categories of risk that cut across many different kinds of policies: property, liability, and personal.

Property Risks

Property insurance is insurance that protects you from financial loss if your property is damaged, destroyed, or stolen. Fire and theft are examples of property risks.

Fire Insurance The standard fire insurance policy protects your home and personal belongings against damage caused by fire and lightning, including smoke and water damage and damage done by lightning.

▲ *Insurance companies use the interest they earn from construction loans and other investments to lower the premiums their policyholders pay.* ***Are there ways for consumers to lower their premiums?***

Caption Answer: Yes, (1) shop around, (2) take high deductibles, and (3) combine risks to insure on the same policy.

Under the terms of most fire insurance policies, the policyholder and the insurance company share the cost of a loss. This is done in two ways.

First, fire insurance has a **deductible,** a set amount that the insured must pay per loss—say, $250. Second, most fire insurance policies contain a **coinsurance clause.** The clause states what percentage of a loss the policyholder must pay and what percentage the insurance company must pay. As a rule, the insur-
2 ance company pays 80 percent.

Theft Insurance To protect household property and personal belongings that are either in your home or with you when you are away from home requires theft insurance. Such a policy also covers items stolen from your car if the vehicle was locked at the time of the loss.

Liability Risks

There are many accidents that can happen in your home and apartment. Visitors can be hurt if they slip on an icy sidewalk or fall down the porch steps. A workman may slip while making repairs to your house. A neighbor's child may
3 trip on your rake and get hurt.

Your own actions on your own property may also injure others or damage their property. For example, if you hit a baseball through your neighbor's window, the broken glass might injure those seated nearby.

Personal liability insurance is insurance that provides protection when others sue you for injuring them or damaging their property. This protection covers not only accidents in your house but accidents elsewhere if the injury or damage is caused by you, someone in your family, or your pets.

Personal Risks

Some insurance policies are designed to protect you and your family against personal losses—illness, disability, and death. Life, health, and income insurance, which are discussed in chapters
1 that follow, cover these risks.

There are many different types of insurance—property insurance, automobile insurance, life insurance, health insurance just to name a few. In this chapter, we will discuss property insurance.

PROPERTY INSURANCE

Property is divided into two types—real and personal. *Real property,* as you learned in an earlier chapter, refers to land and structures attached permanently to it, like a house or a garage. **Personal property** is property that can be moved, such as appliances, jewelry, clothes, furniture, and cars. Insurance for each kind of property can be bought separately, in two policies, or combined in a single package policy.

To protect your property fully, you need to buy several kinds of coverage—fire, theft, and liability. Most homeowners purchase a package policy that combines these policies. Called a **homeowners policy,** it is designed for the owner or occupants of a one- or two-family dwelling.

The main advantage of a homeowners policy is that it costs 20 to 30 percent less than buying separate policies. There is also the added convenience of having only one premium payment to make. Tenants, owners of condominiums, and people who live in manufactured homes
2 can also buy *property* insurance.

A homeowners policy protects your house. Other structures on your property, such as a tool shed, guest house, or detached garage, are also covered. They are usually insured for up to 10 percent of the coverage on the house.

Personal property is also covered. Insurance covers all household items and other belongings owned by you and your family, whether lost at home or away from home. You can also buy protection that covers the personal property of your guests while they are visiting. (Your automobile is not covered here. Automobile insurance must be purchased separately.)

Liability Coverages

Liability coverages under a homeowners policy give protection for the family against claims in three areas.

1. *Personal liability coverage.* This coverage protects you from large lawsuits
3 arising from both property damage
4 and bodily injury. For example, a

How to Monitor Insurance Fraud **Insurance fraud increases the overall prices of insurance premiums. Everything you do to prevent fraud affects all policyholders. One way to catch fraud is when your insurance company accepts being billed directly by a health-care provider or by a person performing repairs.**

- **Get a statement of costs from the facility performing the services. Insist that the costs are itemized so that you can understand them clearly.**
- **Review the bill to be sure you received all the services on the statement.**
- **Compare the statement from the insurance company with the bill.**
- **If the statement and the bill don't match, call the facility to get the billing corrected. Or call the insurance company and tell the customer service representative that you suspect fraud.**

1 Reinforcement Give students a list of losses and have them identify the type of loss—property, liability, or personal.

2 Interesting Note More than nine out of every ten American home owners—but only four out of ten renters—carry household insurance to protect themselves against potentially disastrous financial losses.

3 Critical Thinking Ask students to think of other situations in which their actions on their own property might cause damage to others. (Situations might include falling of objects from a house; withdrawal of a physical support, such as an adjoining wall; leaking of chemicals; spilling of paint or pesticide sprays.)

4 Reinforcement Student Activity Workbook, Chapter 18 activities.

1 Critical Thinking
Ask the students what might account for the price difference between one large policy and three smaller ones. (Lower processing and/or administrative costs might make the difference.)

2 Critical Thinking
Ask the students to speculate on why floods and earthquakes were specifically excluded from comprehensive coverage. (By their very nature, such perils affect large numbers of people and do extensive damage to dwellings. This makes them too risky.

Caption Answer:
Answers will depend on your area. This policy is probably typical of the East and West Coasts; probably not typical in the Midwest and South. This is due to home price differencials.

This policy is typical of many homeowner's policies. ***Is this typical of policies in your area? Are there other coverages this consumer should have?*** ▼

visitor to your property slips and suffers a head injury, or you damage your neighbor's home by burning leaves in your backyard. In such cases, personal liability coverage pays the costs of your legal defense. If you are found liable (responsible for costs), the company will pay up to the limits of your policy.

2. *Medical payments coverage.* This coverage protects you, your family, and your guests from accident-related medical bills. In the area of injury to guests, there may be some overlap with personal liability. **Medical payments coverage,** however, is insurance that pays for minor accident-related mishaps, while personal liability is intended to cover very large accidents.

   You and your family are covered both on your property and away from home. In all cases, payment is made regardless of fault.

3. *Physical damage coverage.* Minor damage that you or someone in your family causes to another's property is paid for by **physical damage coverage.** It protects against such risks as hitting a baseball through a neighbor's window. Damage caused by children aged 12 and under is covered, whether it is
1 accidental or intentional.

The liability and property coverages in an average homeowners policy are illustrated in Figure 18–2. The house that is insured is located in a large urban area in California. It is a single-family dwelling of stucco construction. Its 2,000 square feet include three bedrooms and two baths. In 1995, the home's fair market value was approximately $275,000. The annual premium on the homeowners policy was $398.

Figure 18–2 Sample Homeowner's Policy Coverage

Coverage	Policy Limits (in dollars)
1. Dwelling protection*	$169,100
2. Additional structures	16,910
3. Personal property*	101,460
4. Supplemental personal property (jewelry, watches, furs)*	1,000 (per occurrence)
5. Additional living expenses	101,460
6. Family liability (including physical damage coverage)	300,000 (per occurrence)
7. Medical payments	1,000 (per person) 25,000 (per occurrence)

*$250 deductible per occurrence
Source: Allegiance Insurance Company

Range of Coverage

When you buy a homeowners policy, the number of property risks, or perils, covered depends on the form of the policy you choose. The different forms include:

- *Basic form (HO-1).* This policy covers the most common perils including fire, theft, windstorm, and vandalism—eleven in all.
- *Broad form (HO-2).* This policy adds coverage for damage caused by burst pipes, electrical problems, falling objects, and building collapse due to structural weakness.
- *Special form (HO-3).* This policy is meant for the homeowner who wants extensive protection. It is the most popular form of homeowners insurance. It covers the house, all additional structures, and personal property.
- *Tenants form (HO-4).* This policy is for renters. The tenants form is also called the contents form because it insures household contents only. Coverage in terms of risk is as full as that provided by the broad form homeowners policy (HO-2).
- *Comprehensive form (HO-5).* This policy is sometimes called an *all-risks* policy. It covers all possible perils except those specifically excluded from the policy. These are usually floods and
2 earthquakes.
- *Condominium owners form (HO-6).* This policy was developed recently for people who own condominiums, or apartmentlike housing units. It insures only the interior of the owner's unit, not

the apartment house structure. The structure is usually protected by all the condominium owners in the complex,
1 as a group, with an overall policy.

It is very important to read your homeowners policy and question your agent carefully as to its coverage limits. In the field of insurance, words may not have their accustomed meanings. Note, for example, that "comprehensive" coverage really is not comprehensive. There are key exceptions for which separate policies
2 must be bought.

People MAKING a DIFFERENCE

Stopping a Dam

If your local government decided to build a dam that would flood your home, what would you do? Where would you start? Who would you call?

Elene Murray did not have the answers to those questions either. Arkansas's Saline County Rural Development Authority (RDA) had announced plans to dam the North Fork of the Saline River, a project that would result in flooding her farm. She had to do something.

She first contacted all her neighbors that would be flooded out by such a dam and set up a meeting with RDA officials. The farmers were dismayed that the officials were unable to answer most of their questions. Next Murray contacted the Arkansas Wildlife Federation, which helped her set up the North Fork Preservation Society.

Murray found that the more she talked to people and the more she did research, the more she learned. For example, she discovered that the North Fork was protected by the state of Arkansas as an "extraordinary resource." It was one of the last undammed rivers in the state. In its waters lived one threatened species, a mussel, and a rare catfish.

Because the river was protected, the state would not approve construction of the dam. The county announced it would go ahead with the project anyway. So Murray and her group continued their efforts to block construction. Their ongoing campaign angered RDA officials, who filed a harrassment charge against Elene Murray. Fortunately, when the case went to court, the judge ruled that Murray had the right to oppose the dam.

Since then, the county has tried to have the river's protected status revoked. The state has refused the petition. Murray is still living on her farm and still fighting to save it.

Brainstorm

What actions would you take to prevent your local government building a dam that would destroy your home?

1 Vocabulary Ask students what a *condominium* is. (A condominium is one unit owned by an individual in a multi-unit structure.) Have them explain the difference between a condominium and an apartment.

2 Discussion Starter Ask students if they have family or friends who have been affected by earthquakes in California or elsewhere. What actions did they take afterwards? (Students may know people who decided to move out of the area, who rebuilt, who made homes more secure, or who bought more insurance.)

Case Study Answer: Answers might include starting a petition, writing to the government, and organizing a protest in front of government buildings.

Case Study Answers:
1 Any career decision is a personal one, but some of the reasons a builder might want to move into insurance work include the following:
A fixed salary.
2 Answers will vary.

1 Discussion Starter
Ask students if they think it is a good idea for government to provide insurance when private companies cannot. (Students may disagree. Some may feel people should rely on their own resources. Others may feel an important role of government is to help communities cope with disaster.)

Caption Answer:
Consumers can (1) make sure the house or building is bolted to the foundation and that the maximum construction strength is done on their property; (2) anchor furniture, cabinets, and other items to the walls; (3) have adequate supplies of water, food, first aid supplies, and other items necessary to survive an earthquake; and (4) evaluate whether they should buy earthquake coverage.

Additional Coverages

No homeowners insurance package covers flood, earthquake, or crime damage. However, in recent years, protection against these hazards has become available through mini add-on policies.

Flood Insurance Until the late 1960s, flood insurance was sold to only a few home owners who needed it. In 1969, the federal government and private insurance companies began a joint program to make flood insurance available at rates subsidized by the federal government.

Under the program, the government pays the difference between the rates charged to consumers and the cost of coverage for insurance companies. As of 1993, flood insurance was available through the National Flood Insurance Program (NFIP) in over 18,305 commu-
1 nities across the country.

Earthquake Insurance Earthquakes strike hardest along the Pacific Coast of the United States. Until recently, earthquake insurance was almost impossible to get. Few Californians, for example, had this coverage when the Northridge (Los Angeles) earthquake hit in January 1994, causing $15 billion to $30 billion worth of property damage. Now, earthquake coverage is usually added to a fire insurance or homeowners policy.

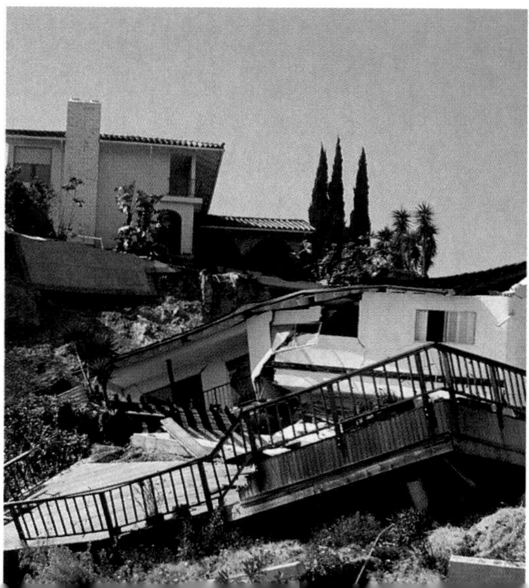

Few homeowners policies offer protection against the kind of structural damage caused by earthquakes. Such coverage must be purchased separately. ***What can the consumer do to reduce the amount of damage done in an earthquake?*** ▶

Crime Insurance Homeowners and tenants in over 12 states can buy government burglary and robbery insurance. The Federal Crime Insurance Program, established by Congress, began operation in 1971 and is available in states where it is hard to find or buy protection. Coverage is available as part of a homeowners policy.

To get protection, you must certify that you have proper locks and latches on doors and windows. Coverage is for burglary, robbery, observed theft, interior damage, and breaking into a locked trunk or glove compartment of a car. The number of policies in force has declined in recent years because consumers find it easier to buy protection in private companies or through state-sponsored programs.

Property Insurance Rates

Insurance rates are not the same for all companies. Your costs for different coverages of property insurance are determined by several factors.

- *Loss experience.* When the size and number of claims and the dollar costs paid out rise, premiums rise. When these drop, premiums fall.
- *Fire-fighting ability.* The ability of your local fire department to fight fires, including the equipment used, the efficiency of its personnel, the dependability of your fire alarm system, and the nearness of the water supply all affect the cost of premiums.
- *Construction materials.* Whether your house is built from brick, wood, concrete, or stucco determines how much you pay for coverage.
- *Payment terms.* Most policies are written for a one-year term. It is cheaper to pay the premium annually than semiannually, quarterly, or monthly.
- *Deductible.* Nearly one-third of all losses for damage to houses and property are for small losses that are costly to

Jim Owens, Field Adjuster, Metropolitan Property and Casualty Insurance

When accident, misfortune, or disaster strikes anywhere in Rhode Island, Jim Owens, 36, is on the move and on the scene. A field adjuster for Metropolitan Property and Casualty Insurance, Owens arrives at the home of a policyholder to assess the situation.

Working with people who have suffered physical losses to their homes might seem as if it could be a depressing job, but Owens claims it's just the opposite. "Most people try to put the things that happen to them in perspective," he explains. "They take two steps back and become contemplative. They don't try to be Rambo. It is rewarding to go in there and help. Most people out there would really be lost without their insurance," Owens continues, "so when I show up, they're usually pretty happy to see me. I can write a check on the spot; arrange for plumbers or cleaning people to come."

In the age of phones, faxes, and computers, many people never meet anyone from their insurance company until the day they must make a claim. "Sometimes I'm the only person these people have ever met from Metropolitan," Owens explains. "They may have been insured for 20 years, and I'm the first employee they've ever met. In those situations, it's particularly important to take a little extra time. I try to sit down at the kitchen table and hear the story of how the problem occurred."

Owens stepped into his job directly from building and construction, where he had worked his whole life in a family business.

Although Owens's knowledge of construction is extensive, he had to master the details of the insurance contract before he could begin work in the field. What surprised Owens were the quirky problems a homeowner's policy could help solve. Since working for Metropolitan, for example, he has helped settle claims caused by bleach accidentally spilled on a floor and by neighbors fighting over who cut down a property-line tree.

"It's amazing what's covered by a homeowner's policy," he says. "Amazing! I've lived in houses all my life, but I had no idea what a policy was all about until I got out in the field."

Case Study Review

1. Insurance companies hire people with training in construction for obvious reasons. But why might someone with such training want to leave construction to work in insurance?
2. What was the last widespread disaster in your area? What type of damage was done to people's property? How much would it cost to repair that type of damage? Compare that cost with the cost of a typical homeowner's insurance policy in your area.

1 Math Application Have students assume an annual homeowner's premium for 100 percent coverage is \$356. What would the premium be if the home owner chose the 80 percent coverage, which costs 18 percent less than the full coverage? (\$356 × .18 = \$64.08; \$356 − \$64.08 = \$291.92).

2 Discussion Starter Take a poll in class. How many students have smoke detectors in their homes? fire extinguishers? How many don't know?

3 Math Application Insurance Company A charges \$5 per \$1,000 of homeowners coverage. Suppose that your house is worth \$100,000, and you want to insure it for 80 percent of its value. What will your premium be? (\$80,000 divided by \$1,000 = 80; 80 × 5 = \$400)

4 Vocabulary *File a claim* is a common insurance term that may puzzle students. Make sure all students know the meaning of this phrase.

Caption Answer: The insurance company will ask you to prove that you had specific, high-priced items on your property.

process. To save money, you can buy a homeowners or renters policy with a \$200 or \$250 deductible. The higher the deductible, the less you pay.

- *Replacement value of the home.* The cost of replacing your home with one of similar quality at today's prices will determine what you pay for insurance. You should check the value of your property and update your insurance on it about every three years. Some insurance carriers have an *inflation guard* provision that automatically increases policy limits annually to take care of inflationary increases.
- *Amount of coverage.* Insuring for 80 percent of replacement value, rather than for 100 percent, can save
1 you 15 to 20 percent on premiums.
- *Preventive measures.* You can save
2 money by installing alarms and
3 smoke detectors, or by keeping fire extinguishers in the kitchen or garage.

Proof of Loss

After you have had a loss, you should file a claim with your insurance company as soon as possible. To receive payment, you must give the insurance company proof of the amount of the loss. Fire damages to a home can be estimated by the insurance adjuster investi-
4 gating the accident.

Damages to personal property are hard to determine; so it is a good idea to keep an inventory, or list, of your personal belongings. The inventory should include your clothing, linens, furniture, china, silverware, appliances, and so on. Include information for each room of the house, as shown in Figure 18–3.

Your inventory should be updated as you buy more items. You may also want to take pictures or videotape your personal property. Keep the pictures in a safe place *outside* the home, such as in a safe-deposit box.

Figure 18–3 Sample Household Inventory

Living Room				Dining Room			
NO. OF ITEMS	ARTICLE	ORIG. COST	VALUE	NO. OF ITEMS	ARTICLE	ORIG. COST	VALUE
3	Bookcase	\$1,200	\$875	1	Buffet	\$ 400	\$250
14	Bric-a-brac	750	500	1	Carpets—Rugs	800	400
90	Books	1,400	900	8	Chairs	1,400	800
0	Cabinets	—	—	Set	China	800	600
1	Carpets—Rugs	1,200	600	1	China Cabinet	750	500
2	Chairs	600	500	0	Chairs	—	—
0	Clocks	—	—	0	Clocks	—	—
0	Cushions—Pillows	—	—	1	Crystal (Assorted)	600	550
2	Curtains—Drapes	350	300	2 pr	Curtains—Drapes	80	80
0	Desk	—	—	0	Glasses	—	—
1	Fireplace Equipment	200	180	0	Glassware	—	—
3	Lamps	250	160	1	Lamps (Chandelier)	400	360
0	Mantle Pieces	—	—		Linens		
0	Mirrors	—	—	4	Tablecloths	120	120
6	Paintings	600	450	36	Napkins	40	40
0	Piano	—	—	3	Paintings	150	150
0	Pictures	—	—	0	Pictures	—	—
6	Plants	75	75	2	Plants	25	25

▲ *An inventory helps prove financial loss.* ***Are there other headings you would include in your inventory? Why is this inventory so important to your insurance program?***

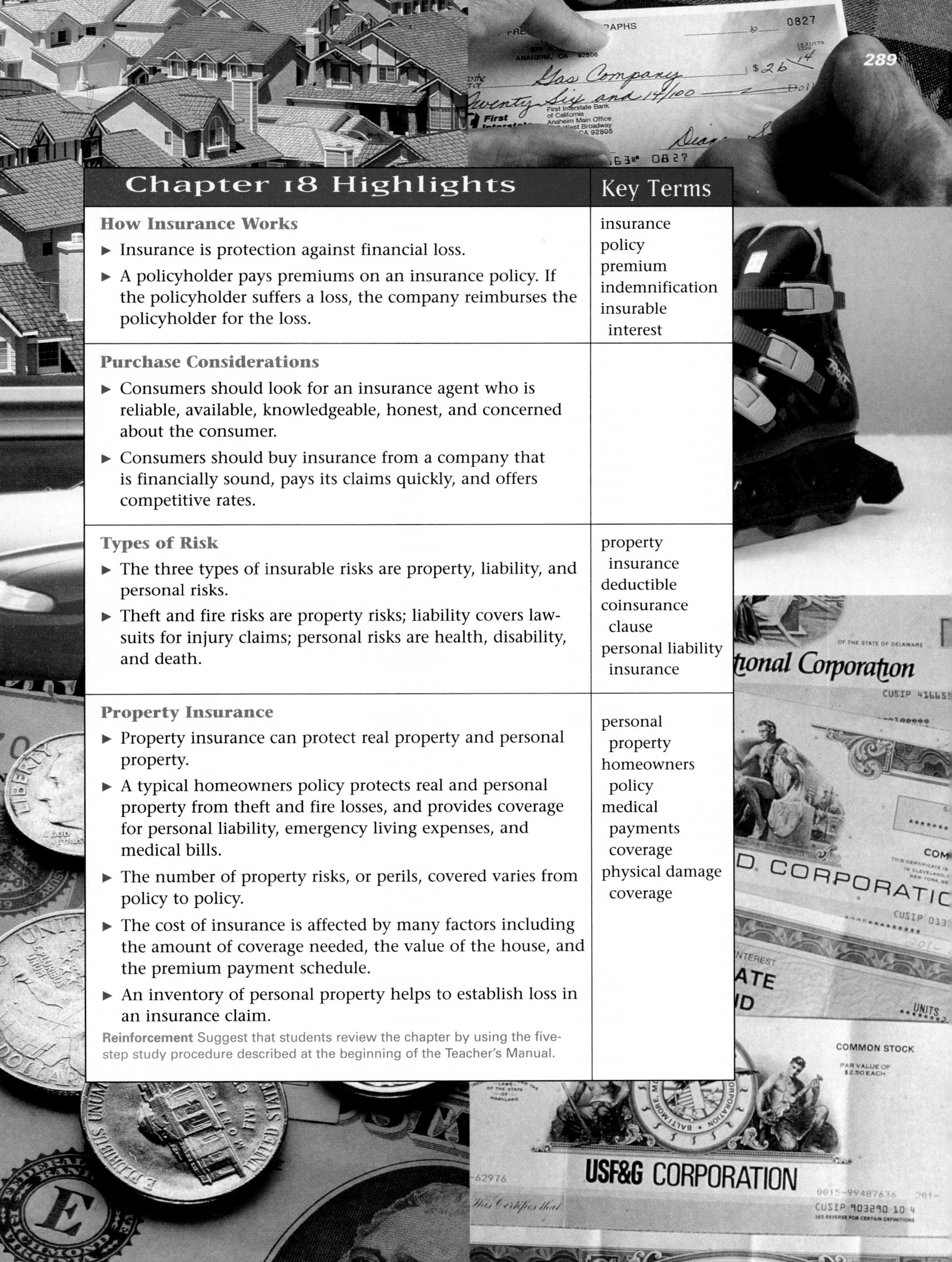

Chapter 18 Highlights

Chapter 18 Highlights	Key Terms
How Insurance Works ▶ Insurance is protection against financial loss. ▶ A policyholder pays premiums on an insurance policy. If the policyholder suffers a loss, the company reimburses the policyholder for the loss.	insurance policy premium indemnification insurable interest
Purchase Considerations ▶ Consumers should look for an insurance agent who is reliable, available, knowledgeable, honest, and concerned about the consumer. ▶ Consumers should buy insurance from a company that is financially sound, pays its claims quickly, and offers competitive rates.	
Types of Risk ▶ The three types of insurable risks are property, liability, and personal risks. ▶ Theft and fire risks are property risks; liability covers lawsuits for injury claims; personal risks are health, disability, and death.	property insurance deductible coinsurance clause personal liability insurance
Property Insurance ▶ Property insurance can protect real property and personal property. ▶ A typical homeowners policy protects real and personal property from theft and fire losses, and provides coverage for personal liability, emergency living expenses, and medical bills. ▶ The number of property risks, or perils, covered varies from policy to policy. ▶ The cost of insurance is affected by many factors including the amount of coverage needed, the value of the house, and the premium payment schedule. ▶ An inventory of personal property helps to establish loss in an insurance claim. **Reinforcement** Suggest that students review the chapter by using the five-step study procedure described at the beginning of the Teacher's Manual.	personal property homeowners policy medical payments coverage physical damage coverage

CHAPTER 18 REVIEW

Refer students to the Reviewing Consumer Terms and Reviewing Facts and Ideas activities in the Student Activity Workbook.

Reviewing Consumer Terms See Glossary for definitions.

Reviewing Facts and Ideas See the Student Activity Workbook for answers.

Problem Solving and Decision Making **1** Students should disagree. The cost of a fire, theft, or serious accident can be greater than your savings. **2** Students should disagree. Policyholders who do not file claims create funds to pay for those who do suffer losses. Students might suggest nationalized insurance coverage.

Consumers Around the World Math **1 a** Appreciation percentage increase (8 years × .15 = 120%); **b** Appreciation dollar increase ($150,000 × 1.20 = $180,000); **c** Value of house in 1996 ($150,000 + $180,000 = $330,000); **d** $150,000 (the amount of their coverage); **e** No, they will lose $180,000 ($330,000−$150,000); **f** Property insurance should have been increased 15 percent per year.

Reviewing Consumer Terms

Pair up with another student and quiz each other on the meaning and definition for each of the following vocabulary terms.

coinsurance clause
deductible
homeowners policy
indemnification
insurable interest
insurance
medical payments coverage
personal liability insurance
personal property
physical damage coverage
policy
premium
property insurance

Reviewing Facts and Ideas

1. What is the main purpose of insurance?
2. What factors should you consider when selecting insurance agents?
3. How are risks and losses shared by insurance?
4. What are the three broad categories of risk against which insurance protects?
5. What is the importance of insurance to the consumer? to the economy?
6. What is group insurance and how does it work?
7. What specific risks does a homeowners policy cover?
8. List the factors that determine the cost of property insurance.
9. What steps should you take to file a property loss?

Problem Solving and Decision Making

1. "Why should a person spend money on insurance? Why not just save your money in a savings account and earn interest? Then, when you have an economic loss, you can pay for it from the savings account."

   Do you agree or disagree with this point of view? Why?
2. Many people think insurance costs too much and gives consumers very little for their money. They feel that policyholders should get their premiums back at the end of the year if they have filed no claims. Do you agree? Why or why not? What alternatives to our present insurance system would you suggest?

Building Academic Skills

Consumers Around the World

Math

1. In 1988, the Jordans bought a house for $150,000 and a homeowners policy to cover that amount. Over eight years the value of the house went up an average of 15 percent a year.
   - **a.** What total percentage did the house increase in value between 1988 and 1996?
   - **b.** What was the dollar increase?
   - **c.** What was the 1996 value of the house?
   - **d.** If the house were totally destroyed in 1996, what would the Jordans receive from the insurer?

e. Is this amount enough to cover the loss?

f. What should they have done?

Communications

2. Research a recent disaster—fire, earthquake, or flood—in another country. Find out whether people in the area had insurance. Did their insurance pay for the damage they experienced? If not, has anything in that region changed to help people carry insurance? Does the government have programs to help the affected people? Summarize your findings in a 500-word report.

Human Relations

3. Research selling insurance as a career. Do library research and interview insurance agents to determine the following:
   a. Personal qualities needed to be successful.
   b. Education and training.
   c. Opportunities for advancement.
   d. Salaries.
   e. Fringe benefits.

   Write a 250-word report on your findings.

Beyond the Classroom

Consumer Projects

1. Write down the kinds of insurance coverage you think your family should have. Then check with family members, guardians, or friends to see what coverage they do have. Are they missing some kind of coverage that you feel is needed? What would you suggest to them?
2. Make a list of personal property that you and your classmates might own. Then, with another student, visit a local insurance agent or company. Find out the replacement cost for the items you listed. Ask how the agent determined replacement value.

Cooperative Learning

Family Economics

Break into assigned family groups. Discuss the following problem.

An apartment building down the street is destroyed by fire. As you watch the former tenants carry out all that remains of their possessions, you wonder how many of them have insurance. Your family does not.

A quick call to an insurance company gives these figures: renters' insurance for an apartment in your area is $250 per year for $10,000 of coverage, then $50 for each additional $5,000 of coverage. Do you buy a renter's policy?

Roughly calculate your actual loss and what it would take for you and your family to start over again. What coverage limit would you choose? Compare your answers with those of other family groups.

Debate the Issue

Is insurance a good idea? Many people have the opinion that insurance is a waste of money and is a fraud. They say premiums are high and insurance companies give consumers very little help or support. Others feel that insurance is necessary to protect their property and income, and that maintaining protection is cheaper with insurance than by yourself.

You and your classmates will break into two groups and research this topic. Each group will gather evidence to support one side or the other. You are to prepare the argument for your side of the problem. Then the two groups will meet in a classroom debate.

Communications
2 Student reports should answer all questions.

Human Relations
3 Students should write a 250 word report exploring selling insurance as a career. They should include the need for education and training and should discuss why or why not they would enter this field.

Consumer Projects
1 Students may list more or less coverage than parents own. **2** Students should compose a reasonable list of items.

Family Economics
All families should consider at least minimum coverage, if at all possible.

Debate the Issue
Break the class into two teams. Assign each team one side of the issue. Encourage students to work together as a team to develop their argument. Ask each team to select a member to make an opening statement that supports the team's side of the issue. Have students take turns debating as the debate moves from one team to the other.

CHAPTER 19

Automobile Insurance

Learning Objectives

When you have finished studying this chapter, you should be able to:

1. Explain why automobile insurance is necessary.
2. Identify the six basic types of automobile insurance coverage.
3. State additional types of auto insurance coverage available to consumers.
4. List the factors that determine automobile insurance rates.
5. Identify two alternative auto insurance systems.

Consumer Terms

financial responsibility laws
bodily injury liability coverage
medical payments coverage
uninsured motorists coverage
property damage liability coverage
comprehensive physical damage coverage
deductible
collision coverage
state automobile insurance plans

Real-World Journal

Some states have considered regulating the automobile insurance industry themselves. Gasoline prices would be raised to cover the necessary premiums for all drivers. Describe your opinions on this subject in your journal. Is it fair? Would this change simplify or complicate the current situation?

Lesson Plan See the Teacher's Manual for Chapter 19 lesson plan.

Vocabulary The Chapter 19 lesson plan includes suggested vocabulary activities for the terms listed.

REASONS FOR AUTOMOBILE INSURANCE

Driving an automobile can be very exciting. The freedom to go where you want brings you greater independence and choice. However, with this greater freedom comes greater responsibility.

Losses from Automobile Accidents

As a licensed driver, you have a responsibility to yourself, your passengers, and others using the highways. The automobile is one of the greatest sources of economic risk in our society. Nearly 623 car accidents occur in the United States every ten minutes. More than 108 persons are injured in those accidents, and at least one person is killed. The eco-
1 nomic cost totals in excess of $104 bil-
2 lion each year.

Add to these losses the losses from theft. Each year at least one car in 50 is stolen. Many are found later, but most are damaged or stripped of parts.

Some automobile accidents are unavoidable. No one can be blamed. In most cases, however, someone is at fault. That person is usually the one responsible for paying damages. Consider the following example.

Denise Sterling owns a late-model used car but does not carry insurance. While she and a friend are out for a ride, they collide with another car carrying two people. Both cars are badly damaged, and everyone is injured to some degree.

The other driver sues Denise for injuries and damage to his car. The court finds Denise at fault and awards each passenger and the other driver $6,000. Denise must also pay $5,000 for damages to the other car. Thus, as a result of her accident, she is liable for $23,000. Denise must also cope with her own expenses—doctor bills of $4,500 and $2,500 for car repairs. These added amounts bring the total cost of the acci-
3 dent to $30,000.

How will Denise pay this amount? Temporary loss of her car may cost Denise her job. The cost of the accident might be a drain on her savings or salary for years to come. She might even lose her license.

Financial Responsibility Laws

Most states now have **financial responsibility laws,** laws which require the owner of a car to show proof of financial resources (usually in the form of insurance) up to certain minimum dollar limits. These laws are intended to keep off the highways drivers who cannot pay for any property damage or injuries they cause. The car owner must usually buy the insurance in order to register the car with the state and get
4 license plates for the car.

If there is no insurance, a driver must instead deposit tens of thousands of dollars in cash or personal property with the state. If the car owner cannot prove financial responsibility and is involved in an accident, the penalty is suspension of driving privileges—in other words, loss of license.

Spending on Auto Insurance

The Japanese spend an average of $4,395 per person each year on automobile insurance. The Swiss spend $3,097, and Americans spend $2,192.

1 Interesting Note Before beginning the day's lesson, tell the students that in the course of the next hour the following will occur in the United States: 3,738 auto accidents; 648 auto injuries; 6 auto deaths; $11,666,666 in economic losses; and over 100 car thefts.

2 Math Application Ask the students to express the auto accident statistics in at least three other ways. (First way: 6 × 623 = 3,738 accidents per hour; second way: 3,738 × 24 = 89,712 accidents per day; third way: 89,712 × 365 = 32,744,880 accidents per year.)

3 Critical Thinking Ask the students if they can think of any other losses that might result from an accident like the one just described. (Other losses might be injuries to pedestrians, damage to real property—buildings, fences, etc.)

4 Research Have students research to see if their own state has financial responsibility laws. What do they know about them? How much do they cover?

Thus, even a relatively minor accident, if it involves injuries, can be financially devastating. To the repair bills must be added the possibility of lost income, the stress of being sued, and the restrictions on lifestyle that could result from unfavorable court decisions. Clearly, no driver should be without the protection of automobile insurance.

KINDS OF COVERAGE

You can buy protection for your car that includes almost everything that might happen to it except wearing out. You can also buy insurance to protect yourself against loss if you damage someone else's property or injure someone else in an accident.

If you are insured, your insurance company will usually pay for the cost of defending you in court. If the court finds you liable for injuries or property damage, your company will pay damages up to the limit stated in your policy.

There are six basic kinds of automobile coverage available to drivers. They are summarized in Figure 19–1. As you can see, three deal with bodily injury and three with property damage.

Bodily Injury Liability

1 **Bodily injury liability coverage** is insurance that applies when your car injures or kills pedestrians, persons riding in other cars, or passengers in your car. You are covered as long as your car is driven by you, by members of your immediate family, or by those who have your permission. You and all members of your family are also covered while driving someone else's car, provided you have the car owner's permission. In all of these circumstances, the driver must be licensed at the time of the accident.

When claims or lawsuits are brought against you, bodily injury liability coverage pays for your legal defense. If the parties involved agree or the court determines that you are legally responsible for the accident, your insurance company pays the damages assessed against you up to your policy's limits. The amount includes court costs and legal fees.

The amount of bodily injury coverage is usually described as "fifteen-thirty," "fifty-one hundred," or some similar combination of figures. (Terms like these are written *15/30* and *50/100.*) The first number is the maximum amount, in thousands of dollars, that the insurance company will pay for the injuries of any *one* person in any *one* accident. The second number is the maximum amount, in thousands of dollars, the company will pay for *all* injured parties (two or more) in any *one* accident. The minimum coverage in most states is $15,000, with many at $20,000. Insurance companies and consumer publications recommend at least $100,000 coverage per
2 person and $300,000 per accident. (See
3 Figure 19–2 on page 296.)

Medical Payments

Medical payments coverage is insurance that pays hospital and treatment costs for injuries that you, members of your immediate family, or

1 Reinforcement Ask students to define *liability* (to be responsible for). Have them compare liability in automobile situations with liability in property situations, from Chapter 18.

2 Interesting Note Insurance experts recommend that policyholders carry bodily injury liability coverage equivalent to their net worth. If, for example, you own a home and other assets worth $300,000, they recommend 100/300 coverage.

3 Critical Thinking Have students determine what coverage limits they would need to avoid having to pay any portion of the judgment themselves in the example. (They would need 25/50.)

Caption answer: Liability coverages apply only to people other than the policyholder. Comprehensive physical damage and collision protect only the policyholder.

Figure 19–1 Automobile Insurance Coverages

Coverages	Applies To	
Bodily Injury Coverages	Policyholder	Other Persons
Bodily injury liability	No	Yes
Medical payments	Yes	Yes
Protection against uninsured motorists	Yes	Yes
Property Damage Coverages	Policyholder's Automobile	Property of Others
Property damage liability	No	Yes
Comprehensive physical damage	Yes	No
Collision	Yes	No

▲ *This chart shows the six basic insurance coverages.* ***Which coverages apply only to people other than the policyholder? Which protect the policyholder and no one else?***

Figure 19–2 Bodily Injury Liability Coverage

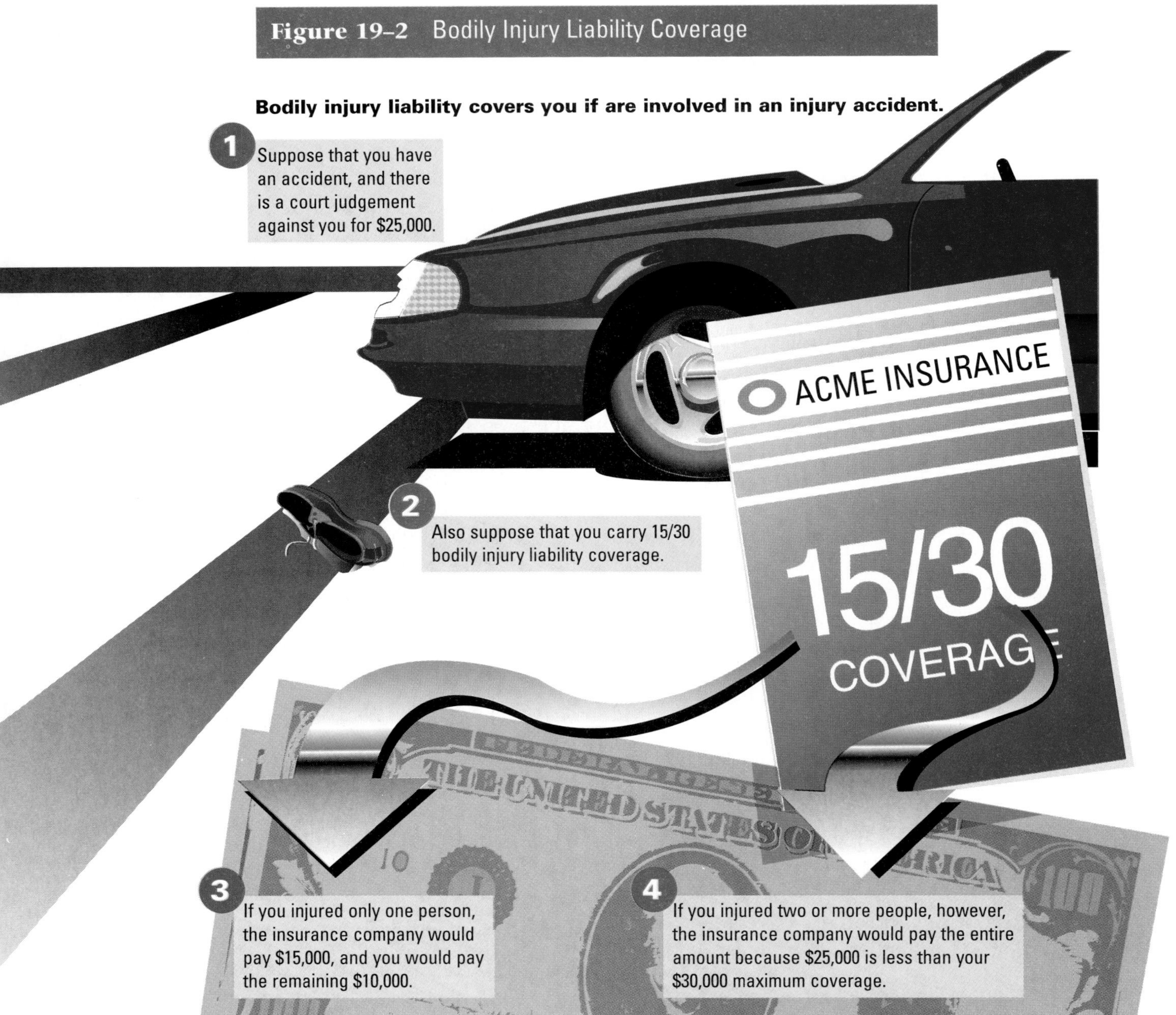

relatives living with you suffer in an automobile accident. It covers family members whether they are riding in your car or someone else's or if they are struck by a car while walking. It also covers any passengers in your car.

Bodily injury liability covers you if are involved in an injury accident.
1 Suppose that you have an accident, and there is a court judgement against you for $25,000.
2 Also suppose that you carry 15/30 bodily injury liability coverage.
ACME INSURANCE
15/30
COVERAG
3 If you injured only one person, the insurance company would pay $15,000, and you would pay the remaining $10,000.
4 If you injured two or more people, however, the insurance company would pay the entire amount because $25,000 is less than your $30,000 maximum coverage.

Medical payments coverage differs from bodily injury liability in two ways.

Medical payments coverage is for members of your family, not for unrelated people whom you may injure. It covers, in other words, the injured persons that bodily injury liability expressly excludes.

Payment is made without concern for legal liability. Your medical bills are covered up to your policy limits even if you caused the accident.

Medical payments insurance is mostly available in amounts ranging from $1,000 to $25,000. People who have large families or who often transport

groups (in a car pool, for example) may want higher limits of coverage. Indeed, with the high costs of medical care and hospital services, many car owners find the higher coverage attractive. However, if you have good medical insurance with high limits, you might not need much
1 medical payment coverage.

Uninsured Motorists

Uninsured motorists coverage is insurance that protects you and your family against uninsured and hit-and-run drivers. Your injuries are covered just as if the driver causing the accident had insurance. The company providing the medical payments, however, is
2 your own.

Uninsured motorists coverage applies to you and all the members of your immediate family, whether they are riding in a car (your own or someone else's) or walking. It also applies to passengers in your car. It does not, however, cover damages to the vehicle itself.

Uninsured motorists coverage is usually related to bodily injury liability. For example, if the minimum set by your state for bodily injury coverage is 15/30, then the minimum for uninsured motorists is the same. If you select a higher limit—say, 50/100—then your uninsured motorists coverage is higher by the same amount.

Property Damage Liability

Property damage liability coverage is insurance that applies when your car damages the property of others. Usually, the damaged property is another car. Coverage also extends to buildings, landscaping (trees and lawns), and public utility equipment like lampposts, telephone poles, fire hydrants, and traffic standards.

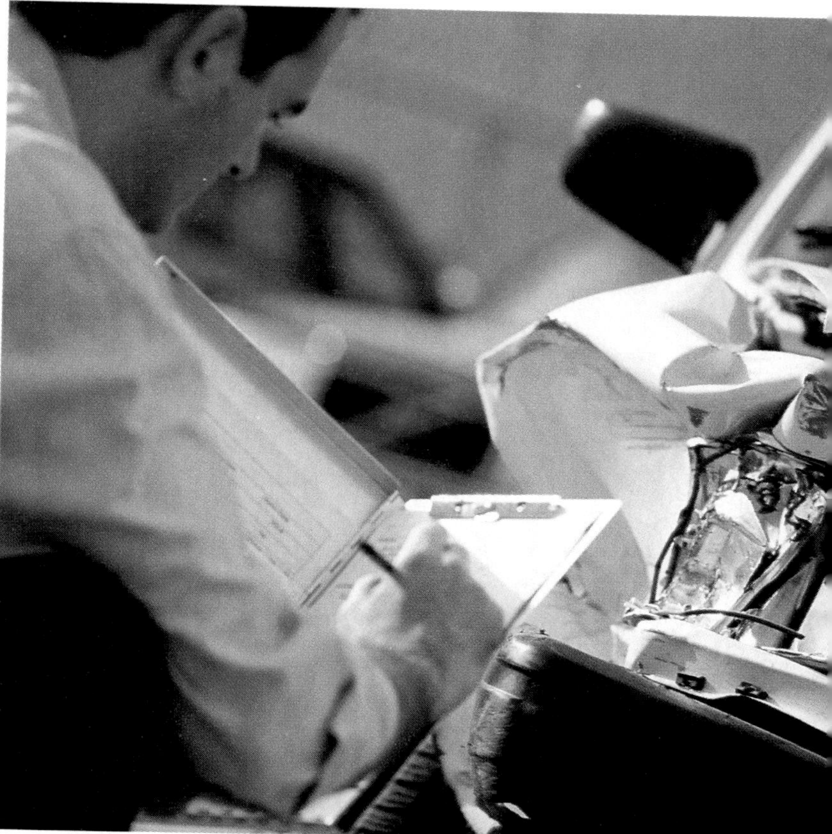

▲ *Property damage liability coverage is necessary because today even minor vehicle damage is expensive to repair.* ***Why are today's repairs so expensive?***

Property damage coverage may be bought in amounts ranging from $5,000 to $10,000. As with bodily injury liability, you should check the financial responsibility laws in your state for the minimum amount required.

Property damage is usually grouped with bodily injury in the terms of a policy. Thus, in the notation *25/50/10,* the first two figures refer to bodily injury and the third to property damage.

Comprehensive Physical Damage

In addition to insuring yourself against damage that you may do to someone else's property, you will also probably want coverage for damage to

1 Discussion Starter
In some states between 30 and 50 percent of all drivers are uninsured. To remedy this, laws have been passed requiring drivers to carry proof of insurance or face fines and suspension of driving privileges. Good solution or not? (It is poor because it has no effect on the high price of insurance, which is why so many drivers go uninsured.)

2 Interesting Note
Minimum liability coverages vary in the United States from 10/20/5 (New York and Mississippi) to 50/100/25 (Alaska).

Caption Answer:
Higher labor and parts costs, shortages of trained personnel, and parts, and insurance fraud.

1 Extension Have the students speculate on the effect that a high deductible (like $250 or $500) has on a premium. (It lowers the premiums because it means that ultimately the insurance company pays less or, in the case of the $500 deductible, maybe not at all.)

2 Math Application Provide the students with this problem: The wind blows a tree onto your car, causing $2,000 damage. You carry comprehensive with a $250 deductible. How much do you pay? ($250) Does your insurance company pay? (2,000 − $250 = $1,750)

Caption Answer: Examples could include a baseball breaking your window, a tree falling on your car, vandalism on your car, items stolen out of your car, your car being stolen, wind and sandstorm damage, and fire damage.

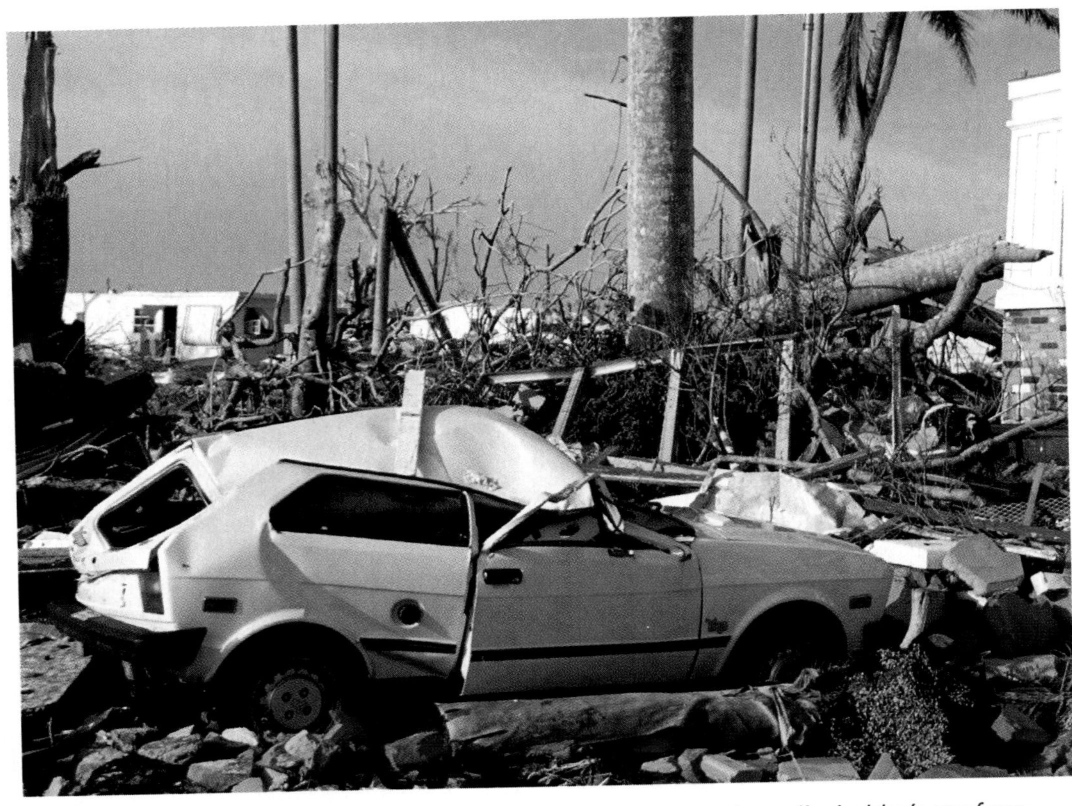

▲ *The comprehensive component of auto insurance protects the policyholder's car from nonaccident-related damage.* ***What damages can you think of that are not accident related?***

your own car. This form of insurance is called **comprehensive physical damage coverage.** It protects your car—and your car only—against fire, theft, glass breakage, flood, falling objects, missiles, explosions, earthquake, windstorm, hail, water, vandalism or malicious mischief, riot or civil commotion, and collision with a bird or animal.

If your car is stolen or totally destroyed, the amount the insurance company will pay you under your comprehensive coverage is not the original cost of the car but its actual cash value at the time of the loss. For example, if your $20,000 car is destroyed six months after you buy it, the insurance company will pay you only about $17,000. The difference represents the *depreciation* (loss in value) of the car.

Most insurance companies will sell comprehensive coverage with a $200 or a $500 deductible. A **deductible** is the portion of an insurance claim that the insured must pay. In this arrangement, the consumer pays the first $200 (or $500) of any damages. The company then pays the rest. The cost of comprehensive cover-
1 age is much lower than bodily injury and
2 property damage liabilities.

Collision

Collision coverage is insurance that pays for the repair or replacement of your car after an accident. In this respect, it differs from comprehensive coverage, which applies only to nonaccident situations—theft, fire, natural disasters.

Consider a few examples. Your car collides with another at an intersection. It hits a stationary object (like a wall). It rolls over after skidding on an icy patch in the road. These are all circumstances in which collision coverage would pay for repairs.

How Collision Coverage Works If you were involved in an accident that was not your fault, you would first attempt to get payment from the other driver's insurance company. If payment were delayed or denied, you would then make a claim to your own company.

Three Bids for Car Insurance
Buying car insurance can be complicated because of the range of coverage and deductibles. Before you accept any policy, get three price quotations from three companies.

- **Ask friends and relatives about their experiences with their car insurance companies. What do they say about their sales representatives and the prices of their policies? If they had an accident, did they receive adequate service?**
- **Choose three companies. Start by talking to one sales representative to determine the coverage that seems right for you. Then get a price quotation in writing.**
- **Call two other sales representatives, and ask them to bid on the exact specifications of the first price quotation.**
- **Compare the three quotes for price and service.**
- **Revise the quotes if you have been offered additional information in the process.**
- **For the best value, consider the quality of service as well as the price.**
- **Keep a mental note throughout the year as you use services. Is there anything that would make you not renew a policy or contract for services? Is it time to seek new bids?**

Many insurance firms will pay such a claim even if you are not at fault so that you can get your car repaired immediately. Then they will try to collect from the other driver's company. This process saves you time and money, since you do not have to do the collecting yourself. Otherwise, you might have to wait many months for a court to decide how much you should receive.

Deductibles Collision is the second most expensive coverage offered for automobiles. The cost is high because there are so many small accidents that require expensive body repair and refinishing work. To get around this problem, many insurance companies sell collision coverage on a deductible basis. The deductible amount is usually $100, $250, or $500 (up to $2,500 on expensive or sports cars).

You can save as much as 15 to 50 percent on collision insurance by buying a policy with a higher deductible. In an area where $100 deductible coverage costs $218 per year, $250 deductible on the same car costs $190; and $500 deductible is only $106. Full coverage is rarely offered and is rather expensive.

New Versus Old Cars The owner of a new car should always carry collision coverage. If the car is completely destroyed, the insurance company will pay the actual cash value. The exact figure will depend on the year, make, model, and condition of the car. However, in the case of a new vehicle, it is likely to be rather high.

As a car gets older and its value decreases, the cost of collision coverage should be reevaluated. After seven or eight years, the value of a car is usually less than $2,000 (unless it is a sports model, classic, or custom-made vehicle). At this point, many people decide to drop their collision coverage. Some

FLASHBACK FLASHFORWARD

Between 1945 and 1975, motor vehicle accidents increased from 5.5 million to 16.5 million per year. No wonder motorists started fastening their seat belts. Thanks to new auto safety technology, the number of auto accidents today is on the decline. In 1992, the total number of accidents was 10 million.

1 Reinforcement Student Activity Workbook, Chapter 19 activities.

2 Research Have students use a copy of the *Kelley Blue Book* to determine the value of a number of cars that are six to eight years old. Then have them decide on which, if any, they would carry collision coverage.

3 Interesting Note Hit-and-runs are treated differently under the two types of uninsured motorists coverage. To qualify under uninsured motorists property damage, a policyholder must be able to identify the hit-and-run driver and/or vehicle by license number. Otherwise, the accident is covered under collision, where there is usually a substantial deductible.

4 Research Have students contact several towing services in your area to determine average towing charges. Have them compare the towing costs to coverage for this service.

companies will not even sell collision coverage on vehicles this old.

Suppose your used car is now worth $900. There would be little reason to carry $250 deductible protection, since the most the insurance company would pay you would be $650 ($900−$250). Paying, say, $200 a year to insure something worth $900 is a waste of money. One expert recommends dropping colli-
1 sion coverage when the value of a car
2 falls below $1,500.

OTHER TYPES OF COVERAGES

The six basic kinds of coverage are available everywhere and carried by most drivers. They are not the only coverages available, however. In the last few years several new forms of automobile insurance have been created to remedy specific problems in the marketplace. For example, as rates have skyrocketed, many drivers have tried to keep their insurance costs down by reducing their coverage levels to the state minimums. This has created a growing number of *under*insured drivers. These people meet the financial responsibility requirements of their state but cannot pay for any major damage or catastrophic injuries they may cause.

Uninsured Motorists Property Damage

This coverage exists mainly for those who drive older cars and, for that reason, do not carry collision. Uninsured motorists property damage works in much the same way that uninsured motorists coverage does for bodily injury. If your car is hit and damaged by an uninsured driver, the coverage pays for repairs to your car up to the same
3 limits as bodily injury liability.

Underinsured Motorists Coverage

Available only in some states, this coverage, like uninsured motorists coverage, comes in two forms—bodily injury and property damage. It protects you from drivers who have some insurance but not enough to pay for your injuries or damage to your car. It pays the difference between what you collect from the other driver's liability and adequate compensation for your loss.

Why is such coverage necessary? The average car sold in this country costs between $15,000 and $20,000. In states where the coverage minimum for property damage liability is low (say, $15,000), a collision with a brand-new car could easily exceed a driver's policy limits.

Towing and Labor

Coverage for towing and labor will refund any money you pay for emergency road service when your car breaks down. It pays the cost, up to a set limit, of towing your stalled or disabled vehicle to a garage. Also included are on-the-scene labor costs—for tire changes, use of a booster battery, and so forth. The
4 cost of this coverage is low.

Motorcycle Insurance

Most automobile insurance policies do not insure drivers when they drive motorcycles. The financial responsibility laws in many states, however, apply to motorcycles as well as automobiles. Thus, if you do not have insurance, you must deposit with the state the amount of cash required by law. If you do not, you can lose your license—and your bike.

In most respects, insurance on motorcycles, motorbikes, mopeds, and snowmobiles is like automobile insurance. Bodily injury liability, property damage, collision, and comprehensive physical damage insurance are the most important coverages. The most significant factors in determining premiums are engine size (in cubic centimeters), the type of motorcycle, and the bike's current value. Usually, the larger the vehicle, the higher the cost. The major difference from automobile coverage is that many motorcycle policies insure only the owner and those drivers mentioned by name.

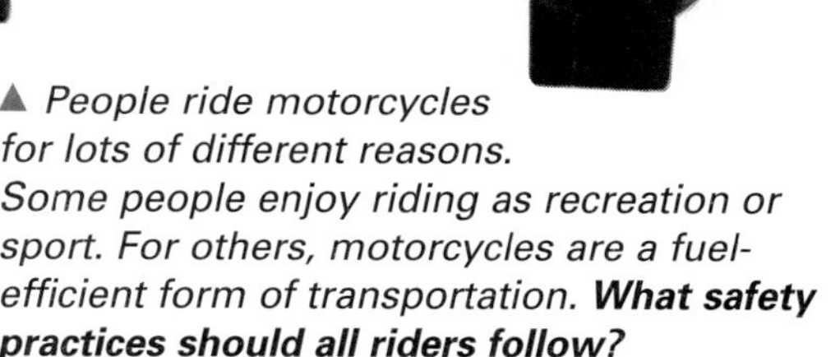

▲ *People ride motorcycles for lots of different reasons. Some people enjoy riding as recreation or sport. For others, motorcycles are a fuel-efficient form of transportation.* ***What safety practices should all riders follow?***

AUTOMOBILE INSURANCE RATES

The rates for automobile insurance reflect the frequency of accidents and the cost of repairs. Specifically, premiums are based on the cost of claims paid out by an insurance company over the previous three years. The more dollars paid in claims, the higher the cost of automobile insurance.

Rates are not the same nationwide. Insurance is regulated by state. Each state is divided into rating territories. A territory may be a city, a part of a city, a suburb, or a rural area. Insurance companies collect figures for each territory, showing how much they paid out in claims. They base their rates on this loss
1 experience.

Factors Affecting All Drivers

While the loss experience of various territories is the biggest factor in setting rates, it is not the only one. Within any state, drivers will pay different premiums based on a host of other, equally impor-
2 tant considerations.

- *Place of Residence* People in large cities usually pay more for insurance than people in suburban or rural areas. More accidents occur in cities, and medical care, legal services, and car repairs are more costly.
- *Driver Classification* Insurance companies group drivers by factors like age and sex. They analyze the number of accidents and the amount paid in claims for each group. They then establish rates that correspond to the risk shown by the group. Generally, young drivers pay more than older ones. Newer drivers, regardless of age, may also pay more.
- *Driving Record* A safe driver—someone who has had no accidents in which he or she was at fault and no serious traffic violations for at least

1 Reinforcement Ask students if they know where in the country insurance rates are highest. If they are unaware of the differences, point out that rates in a heavily populated area, such as Southern California, can be two or three times the rates in other areas.

2 Interesting Note According to the National Safety Council, in 1994 male drivers in the 18–19 age bracket had the highest overall accident death rate of any group—19 per 100,000 people.

Caption Answer: Responses can include: wearing helmets and thick jackets, riding with headlights on, driving defensively.

1 Research Have students contact insurance companies to determine how rates are affected by speeding tickets. Have the companies quote rates for a driver with 0, 1, and 2 tickets, while all other factors remain the same.

2 Reinforcement Students must take into account how much the insurance will cost before they buy a car. To help make the point, provide them with a comparison of local rates for a new car and a relatively older, less expensive model.

3 Interesting Note Mileage may play a role in creating the disparities between male and female loss histories. While males were involved as drivers in almost twice as many accidents as females, the National Safety Council attributes the difference at least partly to the fact that males drive more, and to differences in the times, places, and circumstances that the driving is done.

Caption Answer: Factors include use of antitheft devices, the amount of deductible, your driving record, vehicle use, value of the vehicle, policy limits, good-student discount, being a nonsmoker.

1 three years—may get a discount on rates.

- *Vehicle Use* People who use their cars for business probably use them more often then someone who drives only for pleasure. Their chances of having an accident are greater, as are their premiums.
- *Value of Vehicle* Collision and comprehensive coverages cost more for a $25,000 car than for a $15,000 car because the insurer would probably pay out more to repair the more expensive car. Owners of expensive cars can expect to pay
2 much higher rates.
- *Mileage* The more miles you drive, the greater the chance of having an accident. Therefore, rates are usually higher for people who drive more
3 than 15,000 miles a year.
- *Policy Limits* In general, the greater the amount of protection, the higher the premiums. However, increasing the coverage to two, three, or four times the minimum does not raise your rates very much.
- *Other Drivers* If there are family members between the ages of 17 and 25, rates will be higher. Statistics show that this age group has more accidents than any other.
- *Driver Education* Trained drivers—taught in high school driver education courses, commercial driving schools, clinics, and courses run by the state—have fewer accidents and violations than untrained drivers. Some insurers give a 10 or 20 percent discount to young people with this training.
- *Amount of Deductible* Most policies have a $250 or $500 deductible on collision and comprehensive physical damage coverage. The higher the deductible, the lower the premium.
- *Good-Student Discount* Some insurers give young people a good-student discount of up to 25 percent. Students must be at least 16 and seniors in

▲ *Your age, your driver training, and your place of residence all affect how much you pay for automobile insurance.* ***What else would you consider if you were the insurance company?***

high school or full-time college students. Also, they must be in the top 20 percent of their class, have a B average, or otherwise demonstrate academic achievement.

- *Multiple-Car Discount* Consumers may get a discount for two or more cars if the cars are insured under the same policy, are not used for business, and
1 are not driven by a male under age 25.
- **Other Discounts** Many companies give discounts for antitheft devices (for example, car alarms), to nonsmokers, and as loyalty discounts to long-time customers of the company.

1 Learning Economics Ask the students why they think insurance companies offer multiple-car discounts. (There is some savings in paperwork costs, and they probably have to offer this feature because competitors do.)

The Light of Dreams

When actress Emma Samms was a child, her 9-year-old brother died of a bone-marrow disease. Later, when she had just begun her acting career, she became friends with another 9-year-old who had a brain tumor. The boy's two dreams were to visit Disneyland and to ride in a helicopter. Although she could hardly afford it, Samms flew the boy and his mother to Los Angeles at her own expense and gave him both his dreams. He died three weeks later. Shortly afterward, Samms and her cousin, Peter Samuelson, started the Starlight Foundation.

The Starlight Foundation grants wishes to children who have critical, chronic, or terminal illnesses. The foundation works with more than a thousand children each year. It now has 11 chapters around the world, 4,000 volunteers, and a yearly budget of more than $4 million, most of which comes from corporate contributions.

Samms believes that the mind can help the body heal. She hopes that by making children happy, and enabling them to forget their fear for a while, their immune systems will respond and fight their diseases.

It seems to work. In 1990, the foundation created the Starlight Express Room at the Los Angeles County/USC Medical Center. In the room, children play computer games with Captain Starlight and forget the diseases threatening their lives. Already, doctors have noticed changes. The children who use the Starlight room seem to have less need for painkillers. They stay in the hospital for shorter lengths of time, and they cooperate more with the hospital staff.

The Starlight Foundation hopes to put Starlight rooms in pediatric wards in hospitals around the world. It continues making dreams come true.

Brainstorm

What are other ways in which you could work with a hospital to reduce the stress on patients—especially children?

Case Study Answer: Photos, or art on the walls; toys and books; pleasant colors, comfortable furniture; plants where possible; music; a place to play with other kids; video games.

1 Research Have students research local auto insurance rates, by referring to family policies or calling agents for quotes. Then have them compare the figures with those in Figure 19-3 and speculate on the reasons for any differences. California rates are in most cases, high.)

2 Discussion Starter People with modest incomes who live in poor urban areas often can't afford complete coverage.

Caption answer: Answers could include that females have fewer accidents and lesser claims.

News Clip Answers:
1 Making each party in an accident responsible for his or her own damage and injury costs will reduce the incentive to build up injury claims to collect large settlements from another person.
2 Opponents of this type of reform believe that no-fault insurance unfairly limits the amount accident victims can receive for their injuries. Thus, they may not receive enough money to cover their medical and personal expenses.

To get a clearer picture of how these factors affect premiums, consider the following example. A 17-year-old driver is a resident of a large city in Southern California and the principal operator of a 1990 Chevrolet Cavalier. In the last year, the driver has received one ticket (for making an illegal U-turn). The car is driven 15,000 miles a year, the national average. This figure includes regular trips to and from school, where the operator has taken and passed a driver education course. It also includes travel to and from a fast-food outlet where the operator has a part-time job.

Figure 19–3 Sample Automobile Insurance Rates

Type of Coverage	Costs for Insurance*	
	Male	Female
Bodily Injuries		
Bodily injury liability (15/30)	$625	$598
Medical payments ($5,000)	33	36
Uninsured motorists (15/30)	31	35
Property Damages		
Property damage liability ($10,000)**		
Comprehensive ($250 deductible)	61	45
Collision ($500 deductible)	106	98
Total annual premium	$856	$812

*Costs are based on inclusion of student in policy of parent(s) or guardian(s).
**Costs included in bodily injury liability.
Source: Mercury Insurance Company

▲ *Automobile insurance costs can vary for many reasons.* ***Why do you think the female rate is lower than the male rate?***

The insurance coverage was obtained as part of the parents' policy. Because there is more than one car in the family, the multiple-car discount has been given. Figure 19–3 shows sample rates for a male and a female 17-year-old in this illustration.

The total annual premium for a family insured on the same policy would be $1,265 if the 17-year-old were a male and $1,221 if the 17-year-old were a female. If these drivers were to insure themselves under their own policies, the annual cost for the male
1 would be $2,062, and for the female $1,932!

Options for Problem Drivers

Some people have such poor driving records that insurance companies do not want to take the chance of insuring them. For these drivers, there are **state automobile insurance plans** (formerly known as assigned-risk plans). These plans offer minimum coverage for bodily injury and property damage liability to drivers who cannot buy insurance at standard rates. State plans also cover drivers without experience and drivers who have had policies canceled.

When you buy coverage under a state plan, you are assigned to an insurance company. The number of drivers assigned to any one company depends on the amount of business that company does in the state. If it does 5 percent of the business, for example, it must accept 5 percent of the high-risk drivers. These drivers are thus insured by established firms. Companies generally must keep their
2 high-risk drivers for at least three years.

State plan rates are generally 25 to 50 percent or more above the standard rates. The plans only have to offer the minimum liability coverage required by the financial responsibility laws. A small number of states do offer plans with all coverages. Most, however, do not offer collision, comprehensive, or medical payments insurance.

Instead of a state automobile insurance plan, you might buy insurance from one of the nonstandard companies that sell to high-risk drivers. These companies usually sell broader coverage than state plans, but the cost is greater. Standard premiums are often 50 to 100 percent higher than assigned-risk rates. If you

CASE STUDY

Consumer NEWS CLIP

Study Cites Excess Car Injury Claims

by Thomas S. Mulligan
Los Angeles Times
April 6, 1995

Although there long has been anecdotal evidence that many auto injury claims are questionable, RAND says its study is the first systematic effort to describe the cost and pattern of such claims.

Nationally, exaggerated and fraudulent injuries represent from 35 percent to 42 percent of auto injury medical costs, the study says. Stephen J. Carroll, the lead author, noted that while much attention is paid to staged car crashes, medical fraud mills and other blatant crime, the chief culprits are ordinary citizens and a legal system that rewards exaggerating injuries.

The study was conducted by RAND's Institute for Civil Justice, an independent research group.

The researchers relied heavily on figures from New York and Michigan, the only states whose no-fault systems rule out so-called general damages—mainly "pain and suffering" awards—for all except an explicit list of verifiable injuries. General damages are banned for such "soft" injuries as sprains and whiplash.

California and most other states use the tort liability system, under which accident victims may seek compensation for medical costs plus general damages. Since general damages for pain and suffering are typically a multiple of medical costs, there is an incentive to run up such costs to get a higher total award, Carroll said.

Because of the lack of incentive for exaggerating soft injuries in New York and Michigan, the researchers assumed that such claims were generally valid in those states. There were about seven soft-injury claims for every 10 hard-injury claims — such as fractures—in New York and Michigan, the study says.

But California had 25 soft-injury claims for every 10 hard-injury claims—the highest ratio in the nation. Only two states had a lower ratio of soft- to hard-injury claims than New York and Michigan, and the 18 states with the highest ratios were all tort-system states, according to the study.

The RAND study concluded that a New York-style no-fault system would eliminate many exaggerated and fraudulent medical claims in California and other tort states, but Carroll noted that such reform has a price. There is no question, he said, that people do get bona fide whiplash injuries and that this kind of suffering is not compensated in New York and Michigan.

Carroll took pains to assert that RAND is not endorsing no-fault and that the study was financed out of the institute's general budget without the sponsorship of the insurance industry or any other interest group.

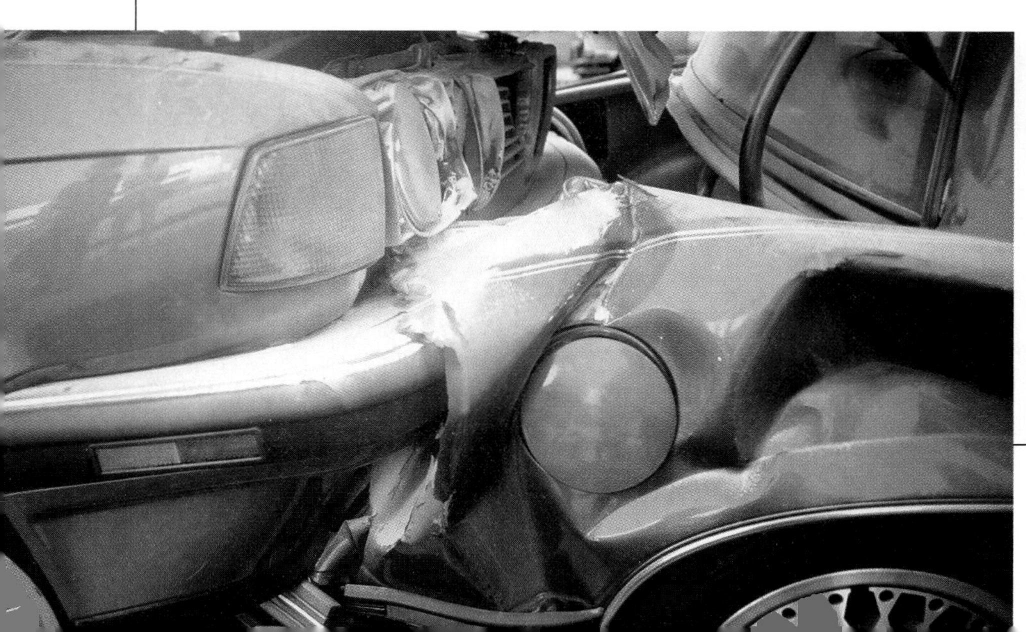

Decisions, Decisions

1. How will no-fault insurance reduce exaggerated and fraudulent injury claims?
2. What is an argument against no-fault insurance?

1 Math Application Have students assume that someone's premium is $628 per year. Another person who has an identical automobile and policy with the same company is a high-risk driver who must pay 95 percent more for the same coverage. How much will the high-risk driver pay per year? ($628 × .95 = $596.60 + $628 = $1,224.60.)

2 Discussion Starter Ask students if they or people they know have ever been involved in an accident case that has gone to court. How long did it take to get a decision? What were the results? What do the people who were involved now think of insurance based on fault?

3 Math Application Have the students assume that they live in a comparative negligence state and are sued for $80,000 as the result of an auto accident. If found to be 60 percent at fault, how much will they eventually have to pay after suit and countersuit? (Suit: $80,000 × .60 = $48,000. Countersuit: $80,000 × .40 = $32,000. Difference: $48,000 − $32,000 = $16,000.)

4 Discussion Starter Ask students which system they think is more just—"fault" or no-fault. Is it always possible to tell who is at fault?

ever need nonstandard insurance, check at least two companies. Compare policies. See if the company will lower premiums as your driving record improves. After you have kept a clean record for two
1 years, start looking for regular coverage.

ALTERNATIVE INSURANCE SYSTEMS

The automobile insurance system used in most states is based on fault. A driver who, through recklessness, causes injury to the person or property of another pays the costs (originally, *all* the costs). The case can be settled voluntarily by the parties involved in the accident. If not, a judge or jury must decide who was at fault and what the accident was worth in terms of both actual cost and pain and suffering.

Fault especially is not easy to decide. Experts say that a driver makes more than 200 observations and 20 decisions in almost every mile he or she drives. Even good drivers make at least one driving error every two miles. Many of these errors cause accidents.

For years, the insurance industry has received a great deal of criticism on this score. People buying automobile insurance, companies and agencies selling it, and state officials regulating the industry have complained about the time and money it takes to determine who is at fault in an accident. The average claim
2 that goes to court takes 16 months to settle. A complex case can take up to five years. Court decisions, in the end, have given some victims more than their actual losses, some less, and others nothing at all. To many, the current system seems to protect the offender, not the victim. For these reasons, a number of alternatives have been suggested and are being tried in some states.

Comparative Negligence System

Over 30 states have *comparative negligence laws.* Under these laws, the key determination is to what degree *each* party may have contributed to an accident. Blame, in other words, is shared.

Suppose you have an accident with another vehicle and are sued for $20,000. If you were found to be at fault, under the regular negligence system, you would have to pay all the damages. Under the comparative negligence system, however, a jury could find you, say, 70 percent at fault. The other person would receive damages of only 70 percent ($14,000). You could then countersue (sue the person who sued you) for damages of 30 percent ($6,000) to cover
3 your losses.

With comparative negligence laws, decisions are perhaps a little more fair. The major difficulty with the whole negligence system still remains, however. Fault must still be determined.

No-Fault System

To solve this problem once and for all, *no-fault* insurance has been adopted in 13 states and Puerto Rico. Under this system, if you have an accident, you and the other party each collect from your own insurance companies. It does not matter who caused the accident. No effort is made to collect from the party at fault. Fault, in fact, is irrelevant. Each company pays its insured up to the limits of his or her coverage. Individuals still have the right to sue if there is permanent injury or disfigurement, death, or
4 very high property loss.

Massachusetts was the first state to enact a no-fault automobile insurance law, in 1971. Other states have since done the same.

Chapter 19 Highlights	Key Terms
Reasons for Automobile Insurance ► Automobile insurance protects the insured from financial losses due to car accidents. ► States require car owners to be able to pay a certain amount for injuries or damages they might cause. Car owners can either deposit cash with the state or buy car insurance.	financial responsibility laws
Kinds of Coverage ► Three kinds of automobile insurance coverage—bodily liability, medical payments, and uninsured motorists—protect against injuries to people. ► Three kinds of automobile insurance coverage—property damage, comprehensive physical damage, and collision—protect against damages to property.	bodily injury liability coverage medical payments coverage uninsured motorists coverage property damage liability coverage comprehensive physical damage coverage deductible collision coverage
Other Types of Coverage ► You can buy insurance in case the other driver has no, or very little, insurance coverage. ► You can also buy coverage for towing and labor, as well as for motorcycles.	state automobile insurance plans
Automobile Insurance Rates ► The rates depend mainly on the cost of claims paid out and your rating territory. ► Additional factors, such as your age and sex, also determine the cost of insurance.	
Alternative Insurance Systems ► In the comparative negligence system, both parties pay according to their share of fault. ► In the no-fault system, parties in an accident are paid regardless of who is at fault. **Reinforcement** Suggest that students review the chapter by using the five-step study procedure described at the beginning of the Teacher's Manual.	

CHAPTER 19 REVIEW

Refer students to the Reviewing Consumer Terms and Reviewing Facts and Ideas activities in the Student Activity Workbook.

Reviewing Facts and Ideas See the Student Activity Workbook for answers.

Problem Solving and Decision Making **1** No. The car is old, and the deductible is high. **2** Answers may vary. **3** Students should agree. **4** Annual cost comparison: Company A ($1,000); Company B ($525 × 2 = $1,050); Company C ($280 × 4 = $1,120); Company D ($100 × 12 = $1,200). Company A is the best buy.

Consumers Around the World Math 1 a Annual premiums: (A) $3,596; (B) $3,588; (C) $4,340; (D) $5,136; (E) $2,660. **b** Monthly premiums: (A) $299.67; (B) $299.00; (C) $361.67; (D) $428.00; (E) $221.67. **c** Highest—D; lowest—E. **d** Highest ($5,136)—lowest ($2,660) = $2,476 for one year; $2,476 × 5 years = $12,380; $2,476 × 10 years = $24,760.

Communications **2** Answers could include the highest number of accidents, injuries, deaths, and claims of any age group.

Reviewing Consumer Terms

Break the class into groups of four people to play a game of concentration. As a group, write each of the following terms on 3″ × 3″ cards. Then, write the answers on another set of 3″ × 3″ cards. Place all of the cards face down on a table or on the floor. Take turns flipping cards over and trying to match the definitions with the terms.

bodily injury liability coverage
collision coverage
comprehensive physical damage coverage
deductible
financial responsibility laws
medical payments coverage
property damage liability coverage
state automobile insurance plans
uninsured motorists coverage

Reviewing Facts and Ideas

1. Why is car insurance necessary?
2. Name six basic kinds of automobile insurance.
3. What other types of auto insurance coverage are available?
4. What are the factors that determine automobile insurance rates?
5. What are two alternative insurance systems?

Problem Solving and Decision Making

1. Meg Rossi just bought a ten-year-old used car for $800. She can buy collision insurance with a $250 deductible for $125 a year. Would you recommend getting such coverage? Why or why not?
2. Should a person be required by law to buy automobile insurance? Why or why not? Is there an alternative to buying insurance? If so, what is it?
3. Consider this statement: " Whenever you see someone else involved in an accident, you can figure that your own insurance premiums will go up." Do you agree or disagree? Why?
4. Auto insurance company A will charge an annual premium of $1,000. Company B will charge a $525 semiannual premium. Company C will charge a $280 quarterly premium. Company D will charge a $100 monthly premium. Which is the best?

Building Academic Skills

Consumers Around the World

Math

1. You have received the following quotes for semiannual insurance premiums:

Company A	$1,798
Company B	1,794
Company C	2,170
Company D	2,568
Company E	1,330

Now calculate the following:

a. Annual premium for all companies.
b. Monthly premium for all companies.

c. The companies with the highest and the lowest premiums.

d. Amount saved in one year, five years, and ten years buying from the lowest rather than the highest company.

Communications

2. Interview a car insurance agent about the cost of insurance for teenagers. Find out why teenagers pay so much and what can be done to reduce these costs. Write a 250-word article and prepare a five-minute oral report for your class.

Science

3. Insurance companies charge less to insure safer cars. Research the safety of features in cars. Talk to a science teacher, an auto mechanic, and an insurance agent. Interview drivers. Compile a checklist of safety features to look for in a car.

Social Studies

4. How does insurance in Mexico or Canada differ from insurance in the United States? Write a 750-word report and make a report to your class.

Beyond the Classroom

Consumer Projects

1. List five common dangerous driving practices you have seen. Tell how each can be avoided.
2. Find out which states have no-fault insurance laws. Write a three-page report about how the law works in one state.
3. Make a list of the coverages you want on your car insurance policy. Ask two or three local insurance agents for a rate for these coverages. Are there differences in coverage or rates? Which company would you choose? Why?

Cooperative Learning

Family Economics

Break into assigned family groups. Discuss the following problem.

Your auto insurance premium has gone up $150, even though you have a perfect driving record. Your policy, which is just above the state minimums, will now cost $800 a year for one car, $1,500 for two. (Families with teenagers add 200 percent for each additional licensed driver.) All drivers in your state must carry insurance.

Reexamine the family budget and decide how to cope. Compare your answers with those of other family groups.

Debate the Issue

Many people are concerned about the high accident rate of drivers under the age of 18. Many states offer only provisional (temporary) licenses to those under 18, hoping they will work with adults to improve their driving skills.

Others feel that those under 18 are not mature enough to drive. They feel that insurance rates would be lower for all if the driving age were raised to 18.

You and your classmates will break into two groups and research this topic. Each group will gather evidence to support one side or the other. You are to prepare the argument for your side of the problem. Then the two groups will meet in a classroom debate.

Science
3 Answers could include security devices, roll bars, etc.

Social Studies
4 Differences could relate to whether insurance is mandatory, how it is paid, the type of coverage(s), driving age, and so on.

Consumer Projects
1 Tailgating, excessive speed, relying only on side mirrors, etc. **2** Check with *The Fact Book: Property and Casualty Insurance Facts.* Reports should discuss how the laws work. **3** Students should analyze information from several sources.

Family Economics
Some will reduce coverage (Carpoolers should not.) Others will deny driving privileges to teens unless they work to pay premiums. A few may give up a car or violate the law.

Debate the Issue
Break the class into two teams. Assign each team one side of the issue. Encourage students to work together as a team to develop their argument. Ask each team to select a member to make an opening statement that supports the team's side of the issue. Have students take turns debating as the debate moves from one team to the other.

CHAPTER 20

Life and Health Insurance

Learning Objectives

When you have finished studying this chapter, you should be able to:

1. Describe the various types of life insurance coverage.
2. List some of the key life insurance features and clauses.
3. Identify the factors to consider when buying life insurance.
4. Explain what health insurance is and why it is important.
5. Describe the various kinds of health insurance coverage.
6. Identify some of the common government and private health insurance programs.

Consumer Terms

term insurance
permanent insurance
cash value
whole-life policy
major medical expense coverage
workers' compensation
Medicaid
Medicare
managed care
health maintenance organization (HMO)

Real-World Journal

Interview an adult who has life and health insurance. Ask: Why are they important? How much does each policy cost? What is covered? Are you pleased with the policies? If not, why not? On the basis of the information you obtain, decide whether you would purchase insurance. Record your findings in your journal.

Lesson Plan See the Teacher's Manual for the Chapter 20 lesson plan.

Vocabulary The Chapter 20 lesson plan includes suggested vocabulary activities for the terms listed.

1 Vocabulary Ask students the meaning of *dependents.* (Someone who relies on another for support.)

2 Interesting Note The average amount of life insurance in force per family, counting all families, is $111,600. If you count only those families that have insurance, the average is $143,100.

3 Discussion starter Ask students if their parents have life insurance, and if so, which kind of life insurance. If they don't know, have them find out what kinds of policies their parents have and why. Compile the results in class and debate the merits of insurance versus no insurance, and term versus permanent insurance.

LIFE AND HEALTH INSURANCE

In Chapters 18 and 19, you learned about property and home, and automobile insurance. In this chapter, you will learn about two other important forms of insurance: life and health.

KINDS OF LIFE INSURANCE

People purchase life insurance to protect family members and other dependents. A person—usually the family breadwinner—buys life insurance in order to be able to leave to dependents a fairly
1 large sum of money when he or she dies.

About 154 million persons—more than two out of every three across the United States—are covered by life insurance. In 1920, the face value of the average life insurance policy was $1,990. Now, the average is over $45,000. More than 78 percent of U.S. households have some form of life insurance, usually on
2 the main wage earner.

Life insurance policies can give protection for a limited period of time (*term insurance*) or for life (*permanent insurance*). Term policies are pure insurance. As with property and auto insurance, when you stop paying the premiums, the policy lapses (ends). You buy protection for the stated period, but afterwards nothing remains.

Permanent life insurance policies are different. If you were suddenly to stop paying premiums on one of them, something would remain—money. The longer you pay premiums, the greater the amount of money to which you are entitled. In other words, the amount grows—like savings. Permanent insurance provides savings as well as insur-
3 ance protection.

Term Insurance

Insurance that gives protection against loss of life for a period of time—for example, one year, five years, or ten years—is called **term insurance.** Some companies offer term policies that run to age 60 or 65. Benefits are paid only if the policyholder dies within that period. If the policyholder lives till the end of the term, the policy expires and the insured loses coverage.

Term policies are frequently used for special purposes. Credit life insurance, for example, is used to guarantee a loan. If the insured borrows, say, $5,000 and dies before repaying it, the insurance makes good the loan.

Buying Health Insurance

Whether you receive health insurance through an employer or buy it yourself, you have many options. To choose the best plan for you, consider the following:

- **What are the deductibles and maximum yearly copayment? Compare all the plans offered by your employer, and compare at least three if you are looking for individual coverage.**
- **Are you in good health? If you rarely see a doctor for illness, you might do best with a policy that offers a high deductible and lower premium rates.**
- **Do you need ongoing care? If you want to continue seeing the doctors you prefer, choose health coverage that allows you to choose any doctor.**
- **Do you take any prescribed medications? If so, choose a plan that offers prescription coverage.**
- **What are the health insurer's policies on complaints? Find out how easy it is to dispute decisions made by the insurers.**

The main advantage of term insurance is its cost, which is very low compared to permanent coverage. Thus, a young person can buy a great deal of insurance protection for a minimal amount of money. However, the cost of term insurance goes up as the insured gets older and has a greater chance of dying. In addition, a physical examination is required each time a new policy is purchased. Any serious health problems
1 could add further to premium costs.

Term insurance comes in many different forms. These vary mainly in the amount of coverage provided and the
2 options available. Here are some examples.

- *Renewable term.* Some policies guarantee you the right to renew your coverage without having another physical examination. The premium will be higher, since you will be older.

  Renewable policies are usually limited to a certain number of terms and cannot be renewed once the insured is past a certain age. Many experts say that this type of policy best serves the needs of most life insurance buyers.

▲ *A convertible term policy allows a couple to adjust their life insurance coverage as family responsibilities grow.* ***What type of policy(ies) do you think this family now needs?***

3 - *Convertible term.* This type of policy allows the insured to change from term to permanent coverage without having a physical examination. This feature is important to people who need flexibility, such as young couples who plan to have families. At first, limited, low-cost protection may be all that they require. Later, as they earn more, they may want to
4 add the feature of enforced savings.

Permanent Insurance

Insurance that gives a person protection for his or her entire lifetime is called **permanent insurance.** Such coverage also serves as an investment, since part of each premium payment is set aside in a savings account. Thus, with time, the policy increases in value. When and if the insured gives it up, he or she is entitled to the accumulated savings. These are called the policy's **cash value.** This feature is one of the key differences between permanent and term insurance. It is also the reason that higher premi-
5 ums are charged for permanent coverage.

Permanent life insurance is offered in three basic forms. They are whole life, limited payment life, and endowment.

- *Whole life.* Also called *straight-life* or *ordinary-life* insurance, a **whole-life policy** is one in which you pay premiums for your entire life. The amount of the premiums is set when the policy is bought. The older you are, the less time you will be paying premiums and so the higher the premium rate. Figure 20–1 on page 314 shows sample rates for policies bought by male and female consumers of different ages.
- *Limited-payment life.* With this form of insurance, the insured pays premiums for only a certain number of years or to a certain age. A 20-payment life policy, for example, requires payment

Caption Answer: Term—for protection in the early years. Whole-life—protection now and savings for the future (retirement). Universal life—help finance college education/home purchase.

1 Learning Economics Ask students why the premium would go up if health problems are discovered in the physical. (Increased likelihood of claims reduces the company's likelihood of profit; the company has to raise rates to make the same profit.)

2 Student Motivator Ask students if they think they need life insurance. Why or why not? Would some type of term insurance meet their needs? Explain.

3 Reinforcement Ask students why renewability could be a valuable feature. (As mentioned, physicals can reveal health problems, which result in higher premiums.)

4 Critical Thinking Ask students to develop two hypothetical cases, one in which a person or persons would be wise to buy convertible term and one in which it would not be such a wise purchase. (A young couple with children would be wise to buy convertible term; a couple with no children would not.)

5 Discussion Starter Ask students if they think this would be a smart purchase. Why or why not? Students should see that the amount of life insurance people buy varies from person to person, depending upon what each can afford.

Figure 20–1 Whole-Life Costs ($100,000 of coverage)

Age of Policyholder (At Time of Purchase)	Annual Premium	
	Female	Male
15	$ 372	$ 438
20	445	512
25	541	621
30	670	775
35	842	984
40	1,064	1,261
45	1,350	1,625
50	1,726	2,109
55	2,225	2,750

Source: *Jackson National Life Insurance Company*

▲ *Costs of a whole-life policy are based on age and gender.* ***Why do older people pay more when they buy life insurance? Why do women pay less than men?***

Caption Answer: (*a*) Older people die sooner and tend to have more health problems; therefore, they are at greater risk. (*b*) Women generally are healthier and live longer than men.

1 Critical Thinking Have students develop hypothetical situations to show who should and who should not buy limited-payment life insurance. (Single people who obtain high-paying jobs at a relatively young age are much more likely to buy limited-payment life than married couples who start families early in life and who are paid average and below-average salaries.)

2 Research Have students contact insurance agents to compare the rates on a typical universal life policy with those of whole life and term policies.

of premiums for 20 years. At the end of this time, the policy is fully paid. Coverage, however, continues for the rest of the insured's life, and the face value is paid out at his or her death. The advantage of a limited-payment life policy is that it can be paid for
1 when a person's earnings are highest.

- *Endowment.* All permanent insurance policies combine savings and protection. An endowment policy, however, is a savings plan first and an insurance policy second.

The insured usually has a special savings goal in mind—education of children or retirement. He or she agrees to make payments for a certain number of years or to a certain age. Premiums are high, and savings build quickly.

After the last payment, the insured receives the face value of the policy. If he or she dies before making all the payments, the face value goes to those named in the policy.

Of the three forms of permanent protection, whole-life insurance is the most popular. It also has the lowest premium. Endowment and limited-payment life cost more because they are paid for over shorter periods of time and have greater cash values.

There are some disadvantages to whole-life policies. It may be hard to tell what portion of the premium is actually being invested as savings. Also, you may not be able to determine how much interest those savings are actually earning. If the insurance company cannot give you adequate information, it may be best to look elsewhere.

Combination Insurance

In recent years, a new type of insurance has come into being that combines some of the best features of term and whole-life policies. Two popular variations are described here.

Universal Life The most popular combination policy is the *universal life* policy, which is essentially a term policy with a cash value. Premiums are placed in an account from which the company withdraws its operating costs and the cost of insurance. What remains is an invest-
2 ment fund that grows and earns interest.

Critics claim that consumers are being deceived by these policies. Some companies, they charge, advertise high interest rates on savings that apply only for the first year of a policy. Rates for succeeding years are lower—so low that the long-term return is likely to be only 2 to 6 percent (the same as for whole life).

Still, given its lower premiums and higher possible earnings, such a policy is probably a better value than a whole-life policy. It does not, however, compare well to term insurance. Experts say that consumers would do better to buy a term policy and invest the savings themselves.

Modified Life Policies These policies are also a combination of term and whole life. They are designed for families with young children that cannot afford straight life policies, yet still need large

death coverages. Premiums are fixed and lower at the beginning and higher in later years. Eventually, the premiums remain constant for life. In time, the term aspects
1 convert to straight-life coverage.

POLICY FEATURES AND PROVISIONS

All insurance policies are legal contracts. You should therefore read yours to know what it includes. If you do not understand what is in a policy, you should not sign it. Instead, ask your agent or someone else knowledgeable about insurance to explain it. You will be better able to make a wise decision about what policy to buy, however, if you know some of the common provisions and features of policies.

Beneficiaries

The beneficiary is the person (or group) to whom your policy benefits will be paid if you die. Your beneficiary can be anyone or any group. Most people name a member of the family. Beneficiaries can be listed individually (as "my son, John") or by class (as "my children").

As your family changes, you should update your list of beneficiaries. If you should die and none of your beneficiaries are still living, the insurance pro-
2 ceeds will go into your estate.

Premiums

Your premiums are due on the date listed in your policy. You can pay these premiums annually, semiannually, quarterly, or monthly. Annual premiums usually cost somewhat less per year than the others.

Your policy usually allows a grace period for payment, usually about a month, to pay your premium after it is due. If you do not pay during this period, the policy lapses and your coverage ends. To get it reinstated, you may have to go
3 through a physical examination.

Payments

Both policyholders and beneficiaries can receive payments from a life insurance policy. The form of the payment is often left up to the person receiving it.

Proceeds The beneficiary must make a claim to the insurance company when the insured dies in order to receive the proceeds, or face amount, of the policy. Proceeds are not taxable and can be received in one of several different ways. These include the following:

- *Lump-sum option.* You can take the entire amount in cash.
- *Amount option.* You can take a certain amount each month until the money and interest run out.

1 Interesting Note Give students the following breakdowns on the various amounts of face value of life insurance sold today: term—41 percent; combinations—34 percent; whole life—23 percent; other—2 percent.

2 Discussion Starter Have students suppose that a person with life insurance dies and has not named a beneficiary. Who receives the money? Is it possible that if your parents die, someone other than you might receive the money? How? Why is it a good idea to be specific about naming a beneficiary?

3 Learning Economics Ask students why insurance companies sometimes charge less if you pay premiums once a year rather than monthly, quarterly, or semiannually. (They can use the capital, thus reducing their interest costs.)

Caption Answer: Generally, teenagers are healthier and will live longer. They will also have more years to pay premiums than an older person. They usually are not susceptible to serious illnesses or diseases.

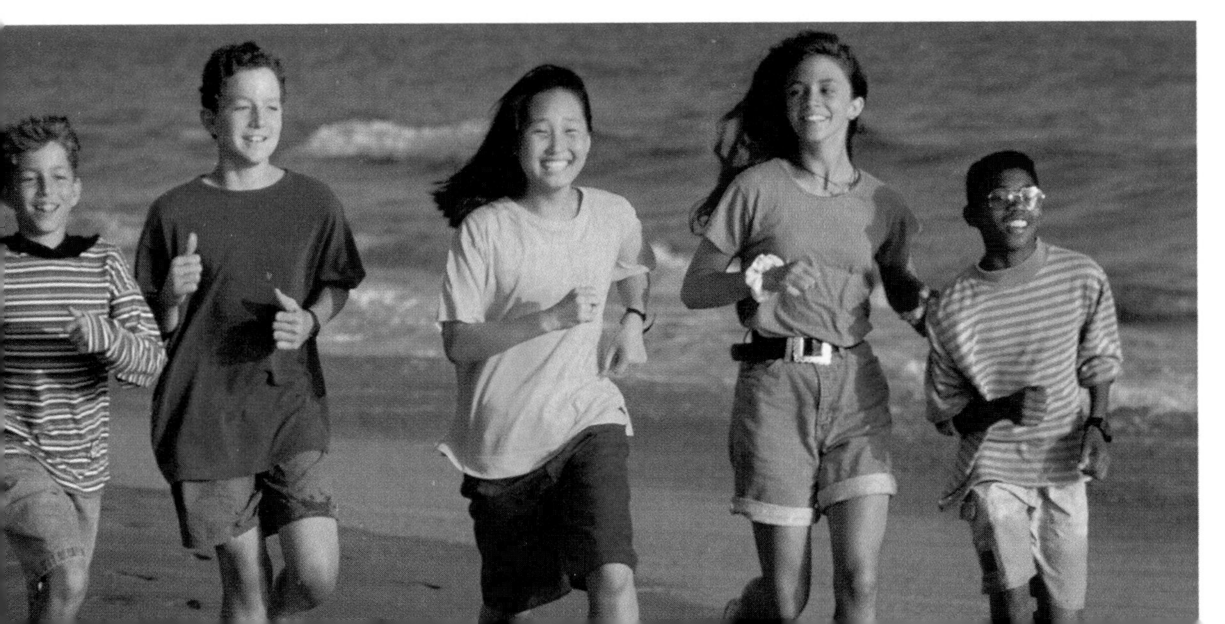

◀ *Life insurance rates set in the teen years are extremely low and can be carried forward indefinitely into the future.* ***Why are the premium rates so low for teenagers?***

1 Reinforcement Provide students with this example of how the cash value of a permanent life policy grows. Assume a 20-year-old who buys $100,000 of coverage for an annual premium of $512. The cash value will grow as follows: Age 25—$1,583; Age 30—$4,619; Age 35—$8,778; Age 40—$12,404; Age 45—$15,419; Age 50—$19,172; Age 55—$23,781; Age 60—$29,319.

2 Discussion Starter Ask students if they know of situations in which people have borrowed against their cash value or taken the cash value before the life of the policy expired. What did these people do with the money? For what purposes do the students think it would be wise to do this?

3 Extension A life insurance policy is a legal contract and contains all of the elements normally found in contracts. Stress that it is similar to other contracts the students may encounter. Ask them to review or list some of the contracts they might use, such as credit, marriage, divorce, employment, and service contracts on cars.

- *Time option.* You can have the money plus interest paid out over a certain period of time in monthly installments.
- *Interest option.* You can leave the money on deposit with the company to earn interest indefinitely. You can withdraw any or all of the money at any time.
- *Lifetime income option.* You can leave the money on deposit and receive a guaranteed interest payment for life.

Cash Value Your permanent life insurance policy should clearly state the amount of cash value available to you for each year you keep it. This information is important in deciding whether or not to keep up payments on a given policy. Many consumers make the mistake of buying a whole-life policy and then dropping it after a year or two. They may suffer a significant loss.

Experts suggest that you should keep such a policy for at least ten years. That way, you will get back in cash value as much money as you have paid out in
1 premiums.

You may receive the cash value of a policy in money at any time at your own request. There are also three other possibilities of what can be done with the cash value money:

- *Borrowing against the policy.* You can borrow against the cash value of the policy. You pay interest on the loan. If you die before the loan is repaid, the amount you owe is subtracted from the money paid to your
2 beneficiary.
- *Buying reduced coverage.* You can get reduced permanent life insurance if you cannot afford to pay the premiums but wish to keep the protection. Your cash value is used to buy a smaller policy that is paid in full.
- *Buying term insurance.* You can also stop paying premiums but keep the same amount of protection for a limited period of time. This device is called *extended term life.* Your cash value is used to buy a fully paid term policy for a certain number of years or days. After that time, your insurance protection ends.

Who Pays for Health Care?

Medical insurance pays for 93 percent of health-care bills in the United Kingdom, 87 percent in Japan, 82 percent in Canada, and 61 percent in the United States.

Dividends Dividends, for insurance purposes, are refunds of premiums given to insured persons who have participating policies. A *participating policy* is one that has a premium fixed at an amount higher than the insurance company believes will be needed to cover the costs of providing protection. The extra payment is later given back to the policyholder, so he or she is guaranteed not to have to pay more than the premium stated in the policy.

Nonparticipating policies are also available. These have premiums fixed as close as possible to actual costs. Thus, there are no dividends.

Special Clauses

Special clauses in policies may limit your rights or grant you important privileges. You should, therefore, not only be
3 aware of their existence but understand

their content. That way, you can ask for or avoid them accordingly.

PURCHASE CONSIDERATIONS

Any person whose death would create a sudden need for money to support surviving dependents should consider buying life insurance. How much insurance and what type to purchase are determined by a number of factors.

Term Versus Permanent Insurance

Consumers must decide which type of insurance best suits their needs—term or permanent. Term insurance costs much less for the same amount of coverage. However, permanent insurance has a built-in savings feature.

Many consumer advocates suggest that consumers buy term insurance and put the money saved into investments that they control. For example, Rhonda Ericson, who is 25, supports her three-year-old son. She plans to buy $100,000 worth of insurance to protect him. Rhonda can purchase term insurance for $133 a year or whole-life insurance for $2,377 a year. She decides to purchase term insurance. She plans to invest the money she will save—$2,244—in certificates of deposit that earn 5.5 percent interest.

To know whether she has made the right choice, Rhonda must compare the cash value she would earn in the whole-life policy with the value of her CD investments. If her insurance agent cannot give her this information, she may be able to get help from an organization like the National Insurance Consumer Organization (121 N. Payne Street, Alexandria, VA 22314). For a fee, NICO will analyze the policy she is considering buying or help her search for a policy.

How Much Insurance?

Life insurance is meant to replace the income of a primary wage earner who dies. A parent who is the sole support of two toddlers will need a lot of insurance—enough to feed, clothe, shelter, and educate those children until they reach adulthood.

A single adult who lives alone and does not contribute to anyone else's support probably needs little, if any, insur-
1 ance—perhaps just enough to cover
2 funeral expenses. (See Figure 20–2 on
3 page 318.)

Factors Affecting Cost

It is important to compare the costs of insurance from several companies since costs can vary widely. The amount you pay depends on many considerations.

- *Type of life insurance.* Whether you buy term or permanent protection makes a big difference in cost. Figure 20–3 on page 319 shows how
4 the costs of various policies differ.
- *Age of insured.* The younger you are, the less you will pay for insurance. As people get older, they have a greater chance of dying. Insurance companies use mathematical experts, called *actuaries,* to work out mortality tables. These project how long people will live.
- *Claims paid.* Insurance companies base their rates on what they pay out in claims.
- *Operating expenses.* The costs of running the insurance company and a profit for the owners (or shareholders) are included in the premiums.
- *Reserve fund.* Each company sets aside a reserve fund for meeting emergencies, such as heavy future claims, mortality changes, and so forth.
- *Investments.* Insurance companies invest their funds in mortgages, corporate stock, and government

1 Discussion Starter Have students discuss *standard of living.* What does it mean? How does it vary from one household to the next? Should one family member be expected to provide the other family members with the standard of living to which they are accustomed even after his or her own death?

2 Critical Thinking Ask the students how other resources affect the life insurance purchase. (They should realize that the more money available from these sources, the less needed from the insurance benefit.)

3 Learning Economics Ask students how inflation and other economic conditions might affect their decisions regarding life insurance. (Inflation, for example means that more money will be needed to provide the same standard of living.)

4 Critical Thinking Have students study Figure 20–3 and answer the following questions: (*a*) What is the cheapest type of policy? (Term) (*b*) What is the most expensive type of policy? (Whole life) (*c*) How much more is the whole-life policy than universal-life policy for a 25-year old? ($1,836)

Figure 20–2 How Much Life Insurance?

How much insurance you need will depend on your particular circumstances.

Current and Projected Income
Plan to replace current and projected income.
Number and Ages of Dependents
Plan on support for children through the age of 18. Plan on support for disabled individuals and other dependents.
Standard of Living
Plan to finance immediate goals, such as paying off loans, and long-range goals, such as providing for a child's education or wedding.
Other Financial Resources
Take into account the amount available from other sources – social security, savings, investments, and income of a spouse.
Inflation and General Economic Conditions
Consider the impact of inflation on any insurance benefits. Calculate the earnings the beneficiary can expect on invested proceeds.
W-2 Wage and Tax Statement
Federal Filing Copy
1997
21 Local income tax
PREFERRED STOCK
COMMON STOCK
%
'90
'91
'92
'93
Inflation Rate

Figure 20–3 Premium Rates Compared

Type of Policy	Age At Which Policy Is Issued					
	20	25	30	35	40	45
Term	$ 133	$ 133	$ 133	$ 145	$ 170	$ 208
Universal life	445	541	670	842	1,064	1,350
Whole life	2,025	2,377	2,806	3,319	3,926	4,626

Source: *Jackson National Life Insurance Company*
(Rates are approximate annual premium rates for $100,000 of life insurance protection for women who do not smoke. Those for men would be higher.)

◀ *Premium rates here are for women of different ages buying three common policies.* ***Which policies are temporary and which are permanent? Why is there a price difference between temporary and permanent?***

Caption Answer: (*a*) The temporary policy is the term. The permanent policies are the universal life and whole life. (*b*) Temporary is pure protection for a specific time period. Operating costs are lower, and dividends do not have to be paid. Permanent includes protection and savings. Costs are paid for a lifetime, and some money is invested by the insurance company.

bonds. The amount of income earned on these investments will affect premiums.

- *Insured's health.* If you buy the insurance when your health is poor, the premium will be high. If your health is good, the premium will be low.
- *Company selected.* Different companies charge different premiums for the same coverage.
- *Insured's occupation.* Your job and its hazards can affect your premiums. However, nine out of ten people have jobs that allow them to pay standard rates.

1 ■ *Gender.* Women live longer than men.
2 Therefore, they pay less for life insurance.

- *Face amount of the policy.* The larger the face amount of the policy, the more it will cost.
- *Other benefits.* Some policies contain clauses that grant the insured special privileges or rights. These come at a price—higher premiums.

MEDICAL CARE COSTS

The cost of health care has gone up faster than the cost of all other consumer items. In 1950, Americans spent only $12.7 billion on health care. In 1993, they spent $903.3 billion. From 1983 to 1993 alone, health care prices rose by 108 percent.

1 Interesting Note Montana became the first state to enact legislation forbidding discrimination by sex in the setting of premium rates for all types if insurance, effective October 1, 1985. This is called the unisex concept for insurance rates and will probably be adopted by many states in the future.

2 Research Have students research the unisex rates and determine if their state has adopted these rules. Also, determine how many different states have adopted the unisex concept.

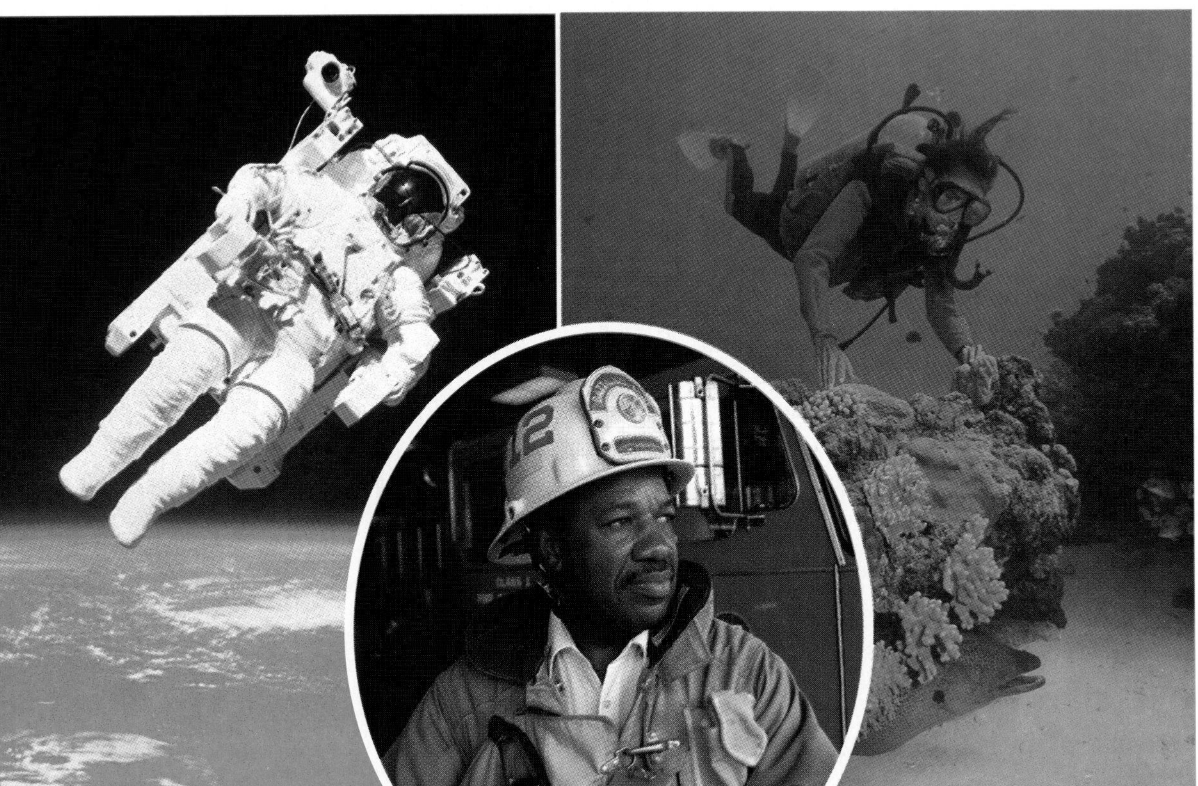

◀ *The type of job you have can affect your insurance premiums.* ***What are three other factors that affect life insurance costs?***

Caption Answer: Age of insured, claims paid, operating expenses, reserve fund, investments, insured's health, company selected, gender, face amount of policy, and other benefits included.

1 Reinforcement Have students calculate the number of people who have and the number of people who don't have some kind of health insurance. Assume a total population of 260 million and use 85 percent. (260,000,000 × .85 = 221,000,000 with insurance; 260,000,000 − 221,000,000 = 39,000,000 without.)

2 Student Motivator Tell students an often-repeated remark by young people is, "Health insurance really isn't necessary, since I almost never get sick. It seems like a waste of money. I'd be better off saving my money and paying my own bills—if I ever have any." Do they agree or disagree? Why or why not?

3 Interesting Note Currently in the United States, health care costs are a staggering $2.06 *billion a day!* This amounts to over $2,868 per person per year, or $7.86 per person per day.

4 Discussion Starter Ask students if they or any members of their immediate families have been in a hospital this past year. If yes, how long did they stay? Approximately how much did the hospital stay cost?

Such costs make it hard for the average person to afford regular medical care. A major illness could wipe out most families' savings. Yet in any one year, one out of every seven Americans goes to the hospital.

The main purpose of health insurance is to protect consumers from doctor and hospital bills that could ruin them financially. Health insurance is offered
1 mainly by private companies, but state
2 and federal plans are becoming more
3 important.

KINDS OF HEALTH INSURANCE COVERAGE

Most health insurance plans pay a large share of a policyholder's costs for hospital, surgical, and other medical care. As with automobile and property insurance, however, there is a wide choice of coverages.

Hospital Expense

The daily costs of room and board during a hospital stay can be met with *hospital expense coverage.* Routine nursing care, minor medical supplies, and the use of other hospital facilities are covered as well. (For example, covered expenses would include anesthesia, laboratory fees, dressings, X rays, local ambulance service, and the use of an operating room.)

Greater in-hospital care costs have pushed up the cost of hospital expense insurance. Because hospital costs can run more than $1,500 a day (in intensive-care units, for example), some policies now have a deductible clause. This lowers the cost of claims for the insurance company and the cost of premiums for the consumer. The deductible is usually payable only once a year, unlike the deductible for automobile insurance,
4 which is payable for each claim.

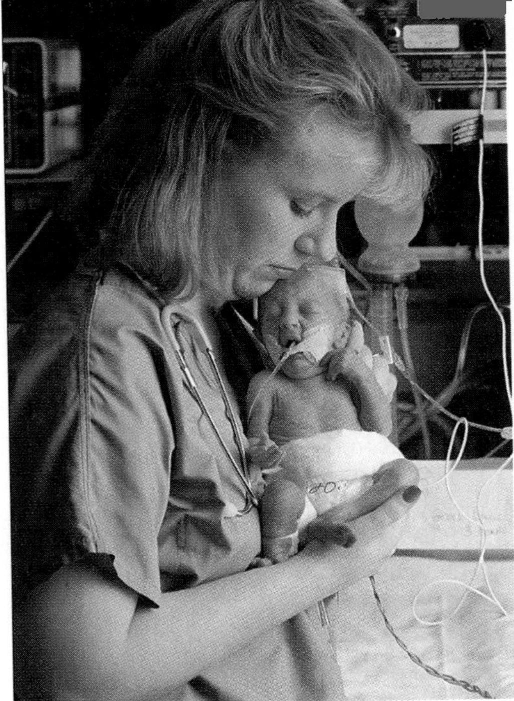

▲ *More people are protected by hospital insurance than by any other kind of health insurance.* ***Why is this insurance almost a necessity?*** **Caption Answer:** Because in-hospital care is so expensive.

Surgical Expense

Surgical expense coverage is usually offered in the same policy as hospital expense coverage. Surgical expense pays all or part of a surgeon's fee for an operation, whether it is done in a hospital or a doctor's office. Policies often have a schedule of operations that they cover and a set payment for each. For example, a policy might allow $500 for an appendectomy (removal of the appendix) and $300 for a tonsillectomy (removal of the tonsils). Remember, however, these figures are maximums. If the entire surgeon's bill is not covered, the policyholder has to pay the difference. The higher the maximum, the higher the cost of the policy.

Physician's Expense

Doctor bills for nonsurgical care can be met with *physician's expense coverage.* This form of health insurance covers treatment in a hospital, a doctor's office, or even the patient's home. Benefits for accidents usually start with the first visit.

Benefits for illness often do not start until the third or fourth visit.

Physician's expense coverage is seldom purchased alone. It is usually combined with hospital and surgical coverages in a package policy called *basic protection.* In addition, some health
1 insurance plans provide benefits only as
2 part of group coverage.

Major Medical Expense

Major medical expense coverage is designed to protect consumers from the medical bills that catastrophic illnesses can produce. Unlike all the other coverages discussed, it pays the large costs involved in long hospital stays and multiple surgeries. In other words, it takes up where basic protection packages leave off. Coverage begins only after other policies have been exhausted.

The kind of health problem covered by major medical would be a heart attack, a severe case of hepatitis, spinal meningitis, or other major illness for which most people would not be able to pay hospital and medical bills. Almost every kind of care and treatment prescribed by a physician, in or out of a hospital, is covered. Maximum benefits can go from $10,000 all the way up to $1 million or more per illness per year. The usual range, however, is $10,000 to $100,000.

There are many different kinds of major medical policies. Coverage may be offered in a single policy with basic protection, or it can be bought separately. Almost 90 percent of the people covered by major medical buy their policies through group plans at their place of employment. Figure 20–4 shows how major medical coverage works.

Dental Expense Insurance

Dental expense insurance is a relatively new kind of coverage. It can be a very

Figure 20–4 Medical Coverage Example

Expense	Total Charges	Basic Plan Covers	Left for Major Medical
Hospital:			
Intensive care			
(5 days at $1,500 per day)	$ 7,500	$ 5,000	$ 2,500
Room and board			
(20 days at $1,000 per day)	20,000	8,000	12,000
Private Nurse:			
(5 days at $250 per day)	1,250	0	1,250
Physician:	3,000	800	2,200
Miscellaneous:			
X rays, lab test, drugs	2,000	1,600	400
Totals	$33,750	$15,400	$18,350
Patient pays deductible:			–$ 1,000
Coinsurance balance:			$17,350
Patient pays 20%:			–$ 3,470
Major medical pays 80%:			$13,880

▲ *This typical breakdown shows how much the insurance company and the consumer will pay for costs.* ***Does this breakdown seem fair for the consumer? for the insurance company?***

Caption Answer: Answers will vary. However, it might seem more fair for consumers since they are only paying about 13 percent of the total bill

important part of your insurance program. The American Dental Association reports that almost 50 percent of all children under the age of 15 have never been to a dentist. Yet by age 15, most children have at least 11 teeth that are decayed, missing, or filled. Only 40 percent of those over 15 visit a dentist at least once a year. Because of this neglect, more than 20 million people lose all their teeth during their lifetime.

Dental insurance policies usually cover normal dental care, preventative dental care, and tooth damage caused by accidents. Some of the services covered are oral examinations, X rays, fillings, cleaning, and oral surgery.

As with other insurance plans, dental insurance may have a deductible clause. The deductible amount is usually from $10 to $50. Coinsurance clauses, stating that the insured pays from 20 to 50 percent after the deductible, are also common. Some plans have a maximum

1 Math Application Have students assume that a health insurance policy will pay $760 or 80 percent of the surgical charge for a kidney removal, whichever is greater. If the surgeon charges $989, how much will they have to pay out of their own pocket? ($989 × .80 = $791.20, which is what the company will pay; $989.00 – $791.20 = $197.80.)

2 Interesting Note Health insurance coverages can be purchased separately or in a package program called *basic protection.* (Consumers almost always favor packages, which meet their needs, are more convenient, and are cheaper.

FLASHBACK FLASHFORWARD

In 1920, the face value of the average life insurance policy was $1,990. Today, the average is more than $24,000.

1 Research Have each student survey at least five people to determine if they have dental insurance. Have the students ask about the amount of coverage, cost of the policy, deductibles, and the average number of visits per year. Compile the results in class.

2 Discussion Starter Have students debate the following statement: "Dental insurance is not really necessary since most people take care of their teeth and do not need this coverage. Also, most people have other types of health insurance that will pay for dental work."

3 Interesting Note Federal, state, and local government expenditures for health and medical care amount to more than 42 percent of all national health care expenditures.

4 Research Have students go to a local library or government agency to learn about your state's workers' compensation program. You may want to assign different students to research different states and then compare the plans.

benefit, ranging from $200 in any one year to a lifetime limit of $5,000. Some
1 policies have a schedule of benefits for
2 the services covered.

GOVERNMENT HEALTH INSURANCE PROGRAMS

The health insurance coverages discussed thus far are normally purchased through private companies. Some consumers, however, are eligible for health insurance coverage under programs
3 offered by federal and state governments.

Workers' Compensation

All 50 states and the District of Columbia have **workers' compensa-
4 tion** laws. Under these laws, employees are insured against injuries that occur on the job, no matter who or what caused them. Job-related illness and death are also covered. The state runs the plan, and the employer pays the premium.

Workers' compensation benefits vary from state to state. Some states cover all necessary expenses for treatment of an injury. Others pay for expenses up to a certain amount. Benefits are usually of two kinds—medical and income. For income benefits, there is generally a waiting period after an injury. Then the employee receives about two-thirds of his or her wage, up to the state's limit.

Employees who take either kind of benefit are prohibited by law from later suing their employers over their injuries. Workers' compensation payments, in other words, are considered a full discharge of the employer's responsibilities.

If you have health insurance coverage for injuries, you are still eligible for workers' compensation benefits. Health insurance will usually pay any medical or hospital bills, but benefits received from workers' compensation will be deducted. This procedure prevents any double payments. Since benefits under workers' compensation are limited, you still usually need coverage under a health insurance program.

Medicaid

The federal and state governments share the cost of medical aid to low-income families under a program known as **Medicaid.** (The federal share covers from 50 to 83 percent of the costs.) Benefits go to families whose income covers other necessities but not adequate health care or large medical bills.

Each state has its own Medicaid program that it runs in its own way. Thus, programs vary. All states, however, must cover those people receiving public assistance. They must also provide six basic services.

1. Hospital care (both inpatient and outpatient).
2. Treatment by and consultation with a physician.
3. Diagnostic procedures (laboratory tests and X rays).
4. Treatment of dependent children.
5. Home and nursing-home care.
6. Family planning services.

Each state is free to add to this list. States may also bring other groups under the program coverage.

Medicare

The social security laws provide for a national program of health insurance for the aged. Called **Medicare,** it became effective in 1966; and in 1994 alone, it served more than 36 million people.

The program is paid for by part of the social security tax deduction. In 1995 of the 7.55 percent tax that taxpayers paid in social security tax, 1.45 percent went to support Medicare; the

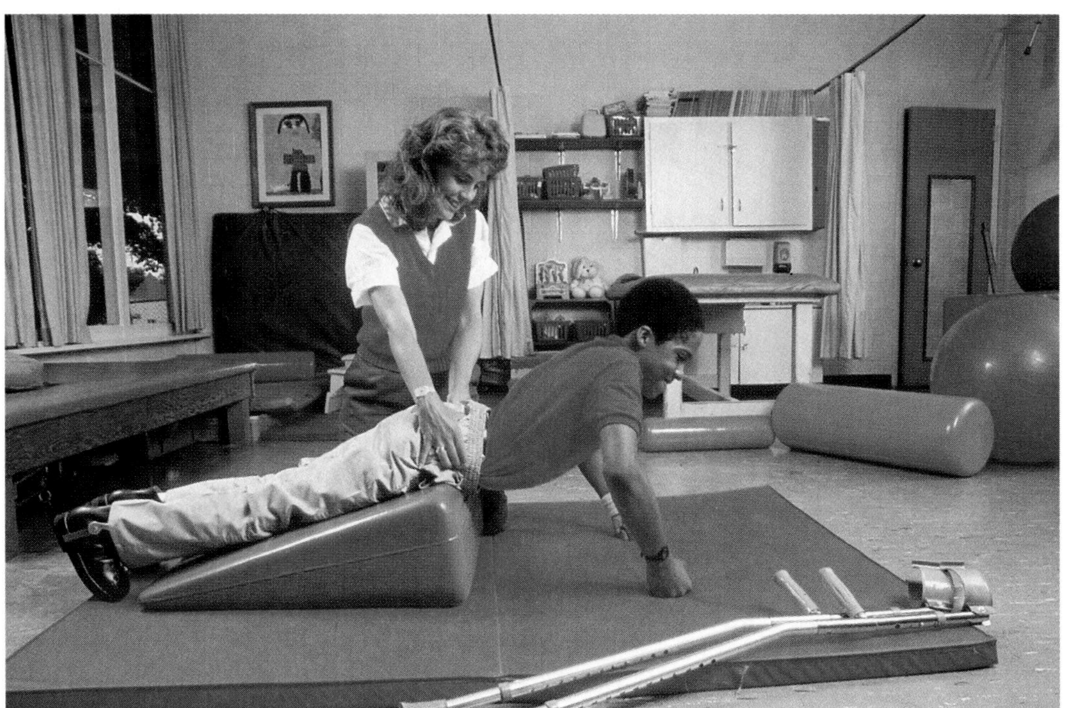

▲ *You need not be over 65 to receive Medicare payments. Disabled workers in their 20s and 30s, for example, can receive benefits to pay for physical therapy.* ***Can you think of others who should also receive Medicare payments?*** Caption Answer: Terminally ill patients and outpatient care patients.

1 remainder (6.10 percent) supported the
2 social security program.

3 Medicare covers almost all those aged 65 or over. It also covers those who have received social security benefits for disability for two consecutive years or more, even if they are under 65. The program has two parts—A and B.

Hospital Insurance (Part A) This coverage is supported by social security payroll taxes on both employers and employees. Coverage is available to almost everyone aged 65 or over. Anyone eligible for social security is automatically covered.

Part A helps pay for certain inpatient treatment and follow-up care. It covers room, board, nursing care, intensive and coronary care, drugs, operating rooms, rehabilitation services, and X rays. It also covers inpatient care in a nursing facility and home care up to 100 visits.

Medical Insurance (Part B) This voluntary coverage is a supplemental program paid for by people who feel they need it. A regular monthly premium is charged. This amount is matched by the federal government.

Part B of Medicare helps pay the costs of any services either not covered or not fully covered by Part A. These might include outpatient care, physical therapy, home care, certain drugs and medical supplies, private nursing care, and trips to the doctor. Certain expenses are not covered, such as those for eyeglasses, hearing aids, dentures, routine dental care, and orthopedic shoes.

Medigap Coverage There are many expenses not covered by Medicare. Therefore, many consumers purchase additional medical insurance to supplement Medicare coverage. These cover-
4 ages are called *Medigap* or MedSup.

1 Critical Thinking How does Medicare differ from Medicaid? (Medicare applies to the elderly and others affected by social security; Medicaid applies to low-income families.)

2 Discussion Starter Ask students their opinions of both Medicare and Medicaid. Are they in favor of the programs? What would the current recipients do if neither program existed? Remember learning about opportunity costs—could our federal and state money be put to better use?

3 Research Have students research the recent legislation, which changed the benefits and costs under Medicare. Have them check with the local library or Social Security Administration office to see how the program has changed. Were there many changes?

4 Research Have each student interview someone who receives Medicare benefits. Ask them how they like it, what they see as advantages and disadvantages, how they would change the program, and what advice they would give to a younger person. You may want the students to do oral or written reports on their findings.

These policies normally cover accident and sickness. However, many do not cover those expenses excluded by Medicare—precisely the coverage that
1 the insured might want.

PRIVATE HEALTH INSURANCE OPTIONS

Health insurance policies and premiums vary greatly from one company to another. There are many different plans and combinations of coverages. Before buying, you should check a number of companies. If you already have some coverage, review your policy to see if it will pay even if you buy another.

Sources of Coverage

Health insurance is sold by insurance companies on a group or an individual basis. It is also sold by hospital and medical organizations and by some independent organizations sponsored by unions and other consumer groups.

Group Health Insurance Most people with health insurance are covered under group plans, usually through their employers. Other organizations, such as labor unions and professional associations, also offer group plans. The organization holds a master policy or contract for the group. All members get a certificate to show that they are
2 enrolled in the plan.

The cost of group health insurance is fairly low because many people are insured under the same policy. Many companies or groups pay the premiums as a fringe benefit to their members. More commonly, however, the two share
3 the premium costs.

Individual Health Insurance Individual and family health insurance policies meet three needs. First, they protect those not covered under group policies. Second, they give coverage not included under group plans. Third, they give people protection between jobs.

Individual plans are different from group plans in many ways. With group plans, the level of benefits is fixed by the terms of the plan. With individual plans,
4 the applicant chooses benefits, and each
5 family member is enrolled separately.

Hospital and Medical Organizations Many medical plans are set up by groups of doctors, medical societies, consumer cooperatives, and fraternal groups. The largest of the nonprofit medical programs are the Blue Cross and Blue Shield plans.

Blue Cross, run by the American Hospital Association, is a hospital expense plan. It provides coverage for the actual costs of hospitalization. (Other policies normally pay only a fixed amount, no matter what the total cost.) There is usually a deductible clause, and the insured pays 20 percent of the costs after the deductible has been met.

Blue Shield is run by the American Medical Association. It covers medical and surgical expenses. Maximum payments for different kinds of surgery are set. It also covers doctors' fees for hospital care and, in some cases, office or home-care visits by doctors.

Sources of Managed Care Providers

Like the government, private health insurers have faced one critical problem in recent years—increasing costs. Government programs have tried to control their expenses by setting maximum payments for different medical procedures. Any hospital that charges more must either look to the patient to pay the difference or absorb the loss.

1 Extension Have students collect ads showing Medicare supplemental insurance programs. They should study them and list the various types of coverages available. Have them analyze these plans to see if they will really assist a Medicare recipient in covering all expenses. Did they find any false or misleading ads? What have they learned from them?

2 Interesting Note Between 85 and 90 percent of Americans who have health insurance are covered under group plans. The other 10 to 15 percent are covered under individual or family plans.

3 Extension Invite a human resources (HR) director from a local business to your class to discuss the types of group health plans available to employees.

4 Student Motivator Have students inquire about their parents' health plans. What is the name of the company offering the plan? How much does the family pay for the plan or is it free? What does it cost to insure each additional family member, or is there one cost per family?

5 Learning Economics Ask students why, with all these advantages to individual plans, 85 to 90 percent of the people with health insurance are in a group plan. (Group plans cost less.)

Many insurance companies (and the groups and individuals they insure) have tried a slightly different approach. They have turned to health care providers who promise in advance to hold down costs.

Managed Care Providers A **managed care** plan is a health insurance plan that integrates the financing and delivery of health care services. A managed care plan tries to control both medical costs

Going Down Fighting

When Elizabeth Meyer first met actor Paul Michael Glaser, she says she saw "happily ever after." While Elizabeth was pregnant with their first child in 1981, she had an emergency blood transfusion. Unknown to the hospital staff, Elizabeth had been given blood tainted with HIV—the virus that causes AIDS.

Four years later, the Glasers' daughter, Ariel, became sick. That is when doctors discovered that Ariel, Elizabeth, and the Glasers' 1-year-old son Jake all had HIV. The disease had been passed through Elizabeth's body to her children.

Ariel died of AIDS in 1988. Elizabeth Glaser began her last long fight—not for herself, but for all the children who had gotten AIDS from their parents or from blood transfusions.

Glaser began petitioning Congress to increase funding for research into pediatric, or children's, AIDS. She also began to ask for help from friends in the entertainment industry. They began the Pediatric AIDS Foundation (PAF). They got immediate donations of $500,000 each from Steven Spielberg and Vera List. By 1994, PAF had raised $30 million, 90 percent of which goes toward grants for research into AIDS.

One of the programs PAF sponsored discovered that the drug AZT, when given to pregnant women, can reduce by 60 percent the chances that the mothers will pass the AIDS virus to their unborn children.

Glaser died on December 3, 1994. She fought until the end of her life, hoping every day that there would be a breakthrough. Her hope was not necessarily for herself, but for her 10-year-old son, and all the other children with AIDS.

Brainstorm

If you and your classmates wanted to raise money for or awareness about a particular disease and its victims, what local "celebrities'" support would you seek?

Case Study Answer: Start with school—stars on football, basketball, and other teams; valedictorians; principal; coaches; popular teachers. In the community—local radio disc jockeys, city council members, local news personalities, mayor, business leaders.

1 Research Have students identify as many different HMOs as possible in your area. Then break into groups to research these HMOs to discover similarities and differences in the costs and care provided. Also, have several students prepare general reports on HMOs based on information found in the many newspaper and magazine articles that have been written in the past few years.

and the quality of medical care. It may do the following:

1. Contract with selected doctors and hospitals to provide care for specified fees.
2. Set standards for choosing health care providers.
3. Check repeatedly on the quality of the care.
4. Offer members big financial incentives to use the plan providers rather than other providers.

A variety of managed care models exist. Health care reform and changes in health markets are expected to lead to other forms in the future.

Health Maintenance Organizations

A form of managed medical care in use for a long time is the **health maintenance organization (HMO).** An HMO is a health care group that offers prepaid medical care to its members. It has its own facilities and usually provides a full
1 range of medical services.

The emphasis is on preventive medicine. Preventive medicine encourages people to come in for treatment before a minor ailment becomes a major problem.

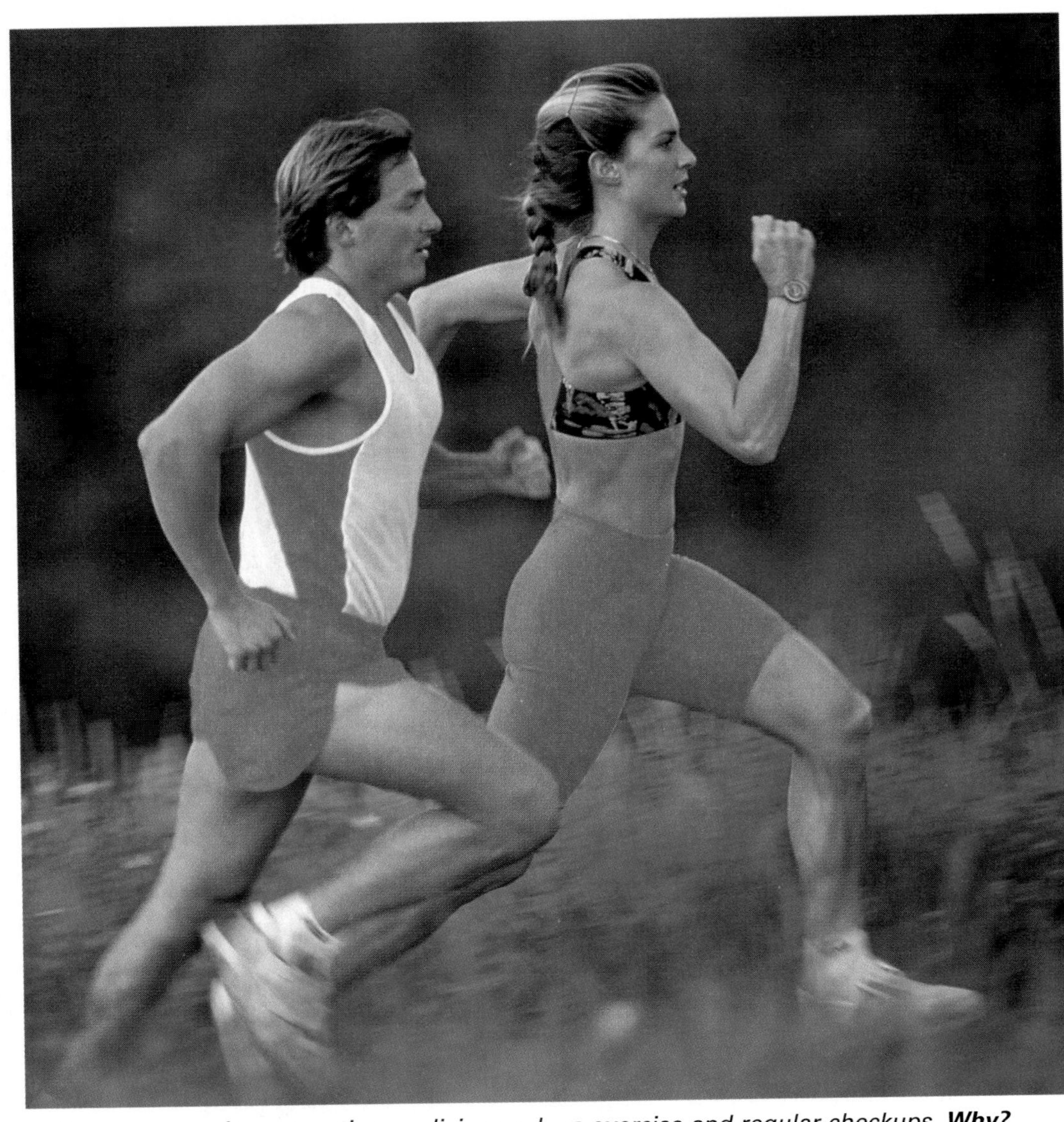

▲ *HMOs emphasize preventive medicine such as exercise and regular checkups.* ***Why?***

Caption Answer: Preventive medicine reduces major medical cost by keeping minor ailments from becoming major ailments.

Case Study Answers:
1 It's difficult for many people to think about their own death, let alone plan for it. It's equally difficult for people to imagine themselves retired and living off the investments they're making right now. It therefore takes a lot of convincing to get someone to consider and buy life insurance.
2 Answers will vary.

CASE STUDY

Careers in Focus

Ted Todd, Life Insurance Agent, Allstate Insurance Company

If anyone understands the meaning of life and death, it's Ted Todd, 40, Allstate Insurance Company's star life insurance agent. "It used to be that a couple's biggest worry was what was going to happen to the spouse if one of them died," Todd explains. "Who was going to pay the mortgage on the house? How were they going to afford their lifestyle? Now the biggest risk to a couple is that they're going to live too long. They may have 20 or 30 good years after they stop working. So the question is, how are they going to pay for that?"

Life insurance, according to Todd, is the answer. "I think everyone should have a life insurance policy," Todd states. "It offers protection in case of death and savings in case of life. In fact," he continues, "someone with a million dollars needs it just as much as someone who's scraping by.

Todd got into insurance sales when he walked into an Allstate office to purchase insurance for himself. "The guy asked me if I had a college degree," he recalls, "and told me they were looking for good agents. I had a degree in data processing. I was selling computers at the time. But I took a look at what the insurance agents were making and signed up on the spot."

Todd has now been in the business ten years, and in 1994 he was Allstate's top life insurance salesperson in the country.

He spends a majority of his day on the phone talking to clients and prospective clients, answering questions, and discussing policies. "I think I'm good because I make it simple," he says. "I have natural conversations with my customers about difficult topics. I have empathy for their situation. I have a lot of salesmanship, but you don't see it."

Yet another reason Todd is so good is that he is very goal-oriented. Although he certainly doesn't relish seeing his clients die, he wants to be able to say to each one of their survivors, "Don't worry about a thing. I'm going to take care of you." He'd also like to be an agent long enough to see a young client use a life insurance policy started with only a few hundred dollars to put their kids through college. And finally, he says, he'd like to sell enough auto insurance to become Allstate's top *auto* agent, too.

Case Study Review

1. Why does someone who is a good salesperson make a good life insurance agent?
2. Do your parents or any other adults that you live with have life insurance? If so, how long have they had the insurance? What reason do they give for having or not having life insurance?

1 Learning Economics Ask students what the advantages might be to the employers in dealing with PPOs and HMOs. (Cost of health insurance for employees is reduced and less time is lost due to illness.)

2 Research Have students research some of the newer plans (such as EPOs and POSs) to find out how they compete with the traditional existing plans. Are there any new programs that are not mentioned in the text? How are they different? Are these programs better than HMOs or PPOs? Have students prepare a written report and give an oral report to the class.

3 Critical Thinking Very soon, students will be living on their own. They will have to think seriously about health insurance. Ask them to consider what they have learned and decide which type of program would be best for them. Why? Where would they buy this type of plan? As they get older, will they need to change plans?

Regular checkups, routine immunizations, prenatal care, and early detection and treatment of illnesses are stressed. In this way, hospitalization costs are held to a minimum.

Health experts recommend that people of all ages do what they can to prevent illnesses from occurring.

HMOs are run by doctors, community groups, insurance companies, labor unions, governmental units, and even corporations. Today, many Medicare and Medicaid patients are sent to HMOs in the hopes of reducing medical care costs. There are over 546 HMO programs that insure over 50 million people in all 50 states. While this kind of interest is new, HMOs themselves have existed for a long time. The Ross-Loos Medical Group in Los Angeles, for example, was started in 1929. The Kaiser-Permanente HMO has been in California since the 1930s.

As attractive as HMOs may seem, they do have a few disadvantages. For example, the choice of physicians is limited to those on staff with the HMO. Also, premium costs tend to be higher than those for most private health insurance policies.

Preferred Provider Organizations

The preferred provider organization, or PPO, is an example of managed care that was developed in the 1980s. A PPO is a group of health care providers who band together to provide services at a discount. They offer these discounted services to employers, either directly or indirectly through an insurance company.

Plan members often pay no deductibles and make only minimal (if any) coinsurance payments. Employees who continue to use their own physicians must pay deductibles and must make larger copayments.

Lower costs are the main advantage of PPOs to both patients and their insurers. There is, in addition, more flexibility than with HMOs. Patients who choose to use their own doctors do not forfeit cov-
1 erage; they merely pay more.

For those who cannot afford the cost difference, however, the lack of choice is a clear disadvantage. There are others. PPOs are so new that experts cannot yet be sure if the savings are achieved by increased efficiency or by a lowered standard of care.

Emergency treatment is another problem. What if you need medical attention when you are away from home? Or suppose in a medical emergency there is no time to reach the nearest PPO? In both situations, consumers have found themselves paying additional charges. Problems like these have led to demands for government regulation of PPOs.

Exclusive Provider Organizations

The exclusive provider organization, or EPO, represents the extreme of the PPO. Services provided by nonmember providers are not reimbursed. Those belonging to an EPO must receive their care from member providers or pay the entire cost themselves. Providers are reimbursed on a fee-for-service basis according to an agreed discount or fee schedule.

Point-of-Service Plans Point-of-service plans, or POSs, are combinations of the best characteristics of the HMO and the PPO. They use a network of member providers. Employees select a primary care physician, who controls referrals for medical specialists. If care is done by a member provider, the employee pays little or nothing and does not file claims. If care is done by a nonmember, it will be paid, but the employees will pay higher copayments and deductibles. The
2 POS is relatively new and its future as a
3 provider is questionable.

Chapter 20 Highlights

Chapter 20 Highlights	Key Terms
Kinds of Life Insurance ► Consumers can buy term insurance for a specified term of time or permanent insurance, which combines insurance with savings. ► Combination insurance is a combination of term and whole-life insurance.	term insurance permanent insurance cash value whole-life policy
Policy Features and Provisions ► The beneficiary is the person to whom life insurance benefits are paid if the insured dies. ► Cash value and dividends are cash benefits in life insurance policies.	
Purchase Considerations ► Consumers need to decide between term insurance and permanent insurance. ► The amount of coverage is determined by many factors, including the insured's income, the number of dependents, and other sources of money. ► Insurance costs depend on many factors including the type of insurance, the age of the insured, claims paid, operating expenses, and the insured's health.	
Medical Care Costs ► The costs of medical care have risen more than any other consumer item.	
Kinds of Health Insurance Coverage ► There are a number of different coverages that cover different health care expenses.	major medical expense coverage workers' compensation
Government Health Insurance Programs ► Workers' compensation covers injuries, illnesses, or death on the job. ► Medicaid covers the cost of medical care to low-income families. ► Medicare, a federal government program that is part of social security, pays for hospital and medical insurance primarily for those over 65.	Medicaid Medicare
Private Health Insurance Options ► Health insurance is sold by insurance companies on a group or individual basis. It is also sold by hospital and medical organizations. ► Managed care plans are becoming increasingly popular. **Reinforcement** Suggest that students review the chapter by using the five-step study procedure described at the beginning of the Teacher's Manual.	managed care health maintenance organization (HMO)

CHAPTER 20 REVIEW

Refer students to the Reviewing Consumer Terms and Reviewing Facts and Ideas activities in the Student Activity Workbook.

Reviewing Consumer Terms Papers will vary. See the Glossary for definitions.

Reviewing Facts and Ideas See the Student Activity Workbook for answers.

Problem Solving and Decision Making **1 a** An endowment policy would guarantee money for the child's education if the parent does not survive. **b** A whole-life policy would protect for as many years as the insured lives. **c** Term insurance would provide the most amount of protection for the money. **2** Does the policy really cover what is not covered by Medicare? Is there unnecessary duplicate coverage? Is the insurance company an established firm?

Consumers Around the World **Math 1 a** Major medical pays \$5,200. (\$13,000 − \$6,000 basic coverage = \$7,000. \$7,000 − \$500 deductible = \$6,500 × .80 = \$5,200). **b** 1,800 (\$6,000 + \$5,200 = \$11,200) (\$13,000 − \$11,200 = \$1,800).

Reviewing Consumer Terms

Use each of the following terms in a paper about life and health insurance.

cash value
health maintenance organization (HMO)
major medical expense coverage
managed care
Medicaid
Medicare
permanent insurance
term insurance
whole-life policy
workers' compensation

Reviewing Facts and Ideas

1. Explain the difference between term life insurance and permanent life insurance.
2. Name three factors to consider when buying life insurance.
3. What are the three kinds of health insurance that make up basic coverage?
4. Name some government health insurance programs and describe how they work.
5. What are the two goals of a managed care plan?

Problem Solving and Decision Making

1. What kind of life insurance policy do you think might be best for each of the following people? Why?
   - **a.** The parent of a young child who wants to have money to help pay for her college education.
   - **b.** A professional man, 50 years old, whose children are grown, who earns a good income, and who is interested in protection for his wife.
   - **c.** A 26-year-old divorced person with two small children to raise.
2. Imelda Juarez's grandmother is considering buying Medigap insurance coverage. She has asked Imelda for advice about the policy. What should Imelda find out about the policy?

Building Academic Skills

Consumers Around the World

Math

1. Marilyn Chin is hurt in a car accident and has to go to the hospital for surgery. The hospital and doctors' bills total \$13,000. Marilyn's basic insurance pays \$6,000. Marilyn's major medical insurance has a \$500 deductible and pays 80 percent of the remainder.
   - **a.** How much will the major medical coverage pay?
   - **b.** How much will Marilyn have to pay?

Communications

2. Health insurance programs vary throughout the world. Research government health care programs that exist in a country of your choice. Share your findings with the class.

Human Relations

3. One of the greatest threats to life is the disease called AIDS (acquired immunodeficiency syndrome). The

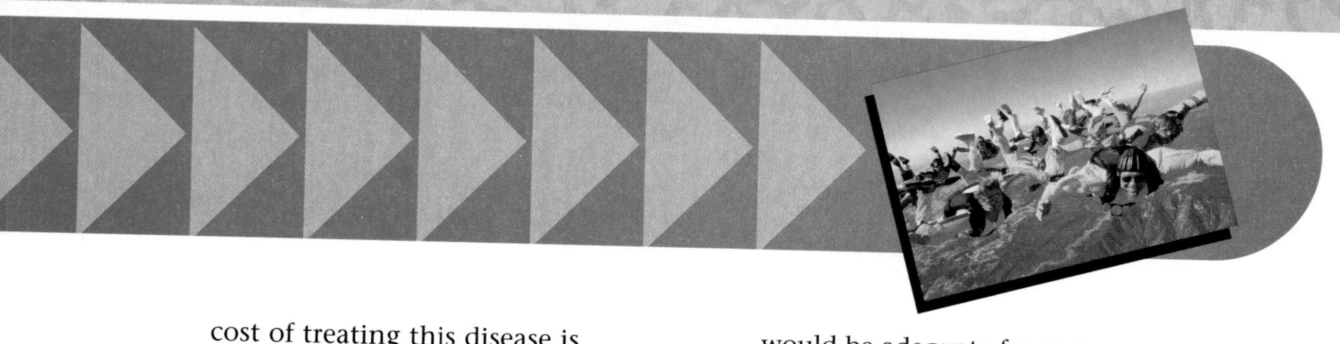

cost of treating this disease is incredibly high, and most people cannot pay the costs. Contact organizations that do AIDS research or support AIDS patients to find out the following.

a. What causes the spread of AIDS?

b. How much does treatment cost?

c. How is most treatment paid for?

d. Do health insurance plans cover these expenses? Why or why not?

e. What can be done to help AIDS patients pay for their treatment?

Technology

4. Price $150,000 worth of term insurance for a 35-year-old female nonsmoker. Call at least two insurance sources for information on four different policies. Using a computer, construct a spreadsheet that compares the policies in terms of premium cost, renewability, and any other important features. What do you conclude?

Beyond the Classroom

Consumer Projects

1. Discuss life insurance coverage with your parents or guardian. Find out whether they have life insurance. Why or why not? How much is your family relying on savings, investment, and other assets for protection? How would you recommend that the coverage be changed?

2. Obtain copies of three advertisements for health and accident insurance. Read the ads and compare the coverages offered. How are they different? Which, if any, of the policies would be adequate for you or your family? Are there any misleading claims or statements in the ads?

Cooperative Learning

Family Economics

Break into assigned family groups. Discuss the following problem.

One wage earner in your family has become seriously ill from chemical exposure at work and has spent four weeks in the hospital. A month of outpatient care followed. The bill to date is $30,000. The company medical plan requires an annual deductible of $1,000. The plan then pays 80 percent of costs up to a lifetime maximum of $100,000.

For how much of the $30,000 is your family liable? How will you pay? Compare your answers with those of other family groups.

Debate the Issue

Experts have suggested starting a national health insurance program to improve the quality of medical care and to keep costs down. All people would have health insurance, paid for either by the federal government or by their employer.

Opponents say the quality of care would drop, but the costs would be higher. We should keep the current system and work to improve it.

You and your classmates will break into two groups and research this topic. Each group will gather evidence to support one side or the other. You are to prepare the argument for your side of the problem. Then the two groups will meet in a classroom debate.

Communications
2 Research will vary.

Human Relations
3 Student should present their findings in a 500-word paper.

Technology
4 Students should submit a spreadsheet with policy comparisons.

Consumer Projects
1 Students might find their families have little or no life insurance. They might recommend additional insurance.
2 Students might find that advertising does not disclose enough important information.

Family Economics
Most families are facing $6,800 in medical bills. The exception is families, which can look to Medicare for coverage. Some of the remaining families can draw on savings to pay the bill.

Debate the Issue
Break the class into two teams. Assign each team one side of the issue. Encourage students to work together as a team to develop their argument. Ask each team to select a member to make an opening statement that supports the team's side of the issue. Have students take turns debating as the debate moves from one team to the other.

CHAPTER 21 Income Insurance

Learning Objectives

When you have finished studying this chapter, you should be able to:

1. Summarize recent and past trends in the development of the social security system.
2. Identify the key programs that make up the social security system and explain how they work.
3. Explain the importance of federal and state unemployment insurance.
4. Describe the income insurance options available through private companies.

Consumer Terms

social security program
social security number
old-age benefits
survivors' benefits
disability benefits
Supplemental Security Income (SSI)
unemployment insurance
annuity

Real-World Journal

Research or interview an older adult about social security. How does it work? What benefits does it offer? Are there any disadvantages? Does the person you interview feel it is fair and "secure"? What does he or she feel will happen to this program in the future? Explain your findings in your journal.

Lesson Plan See the Teacher's Manual for the Chapter 21 lesson plan.

Vocabulary The Chapter 21 lesson plan includes suggested vocabulary activities for the terms listed.

FLASHBACK FLASHFORWARD

In 1940, the Social Security Trust Fund received $592 million in income and disbursed $28 million. In 1993, the fund received $319,298 million and disbursed $269,934 million.

1 Vocabulary Students may not know the meaning of *trustee.* Tell them that the money does not belong to the government; the government takes care of it—oversees it, as a guardian does a child.

2 Research Ask students to read and report on a book that takes place during the Great Depression, such as Russell Baker's autobiography, *Growing Up.* What was it like to grow up then? to raise a family?

SOCIAL SECURITY PROGRAM

At some time in your life, you may face a situation in which your regular income stops. For example, you may be temporarily unemployed, or you may not be able to work because of illness or injury. As you grow older, you may retire. Income insurance is meant to help people at times like these, when regular income stops either temporarily or permanently.

Both federal and state governments have income insurance programs. The idea behind them is simple. Taxpayers (consumers) pay a certain amount of money into a fund. The government acts as *trustee,* or caretaker, for the fund and from it pays benefits to those contributors who qualify. Most government plans are com-
1 pulsory; that is, workers *must* participate.

The most comprehensive federal government income insurance plan is the social security program. The **social security program** is a system of compulsory government insurance that provides benefits to cover old-age, survivors', disability and medical, costs.

History of the Program

The federal government acted to help people as a result of the problems and lessons of the Depression of the 1930s. Some of these problems were the following:

- The aged had little means of support.
- Families could no longer protect themselves from the economic forces in an industrialized society.
- Only limited state programs and private charities existed to help the elderly, widows, and orphans.

The U.S. government passed the Social Security Act on August 14, 1935. It was the first federal effort to cope with poverty and economic insecurity for consumers at a critical time in their lives. At first, the social security system was a retirement program only, plus some public assistance, unemployment, and public health help. It covered people working in business and industry.

Gradually, coverage was extended. In 1939 old-age benefits were made available to dependents and survivors of wage earners. In the 1950s, coverage was extended to self-employed people, state and local employees (on a voluntary basis), household and farm employees, members of the armed forces, and the clergy. In 1956, disability insurance was added to the program. In 1965, hospital and medical expense coverages were added through the Medicare program. In the 1970s, laws were passed that added dependent widowers, divorced and widowed fathers, and adults disabled since childhood to the benefit rolls. In 1974, the supplemental security income program for the needy
2 aged, blind, and disabled was passed.

Social Security in Europe

About 50 percent of wages (32 percent paid by the employer, 18 percent paid by the employee) are paid into social security programs in France, including insurance for health, disability, unemployment, and other government programs. Italy's rate (55 percent) is higher, but the employer pays more (46 percent) than the employee (9 percent). In the United States, the total is about 20 percent, with about 13 percent paid by the employer and 7 percent by the employee.

Between 1971 and 1981, social security benefits more than doubled. Today, nine out of every ten workers in the United States are covered by the social security program. Nearly one out of every six people, about 44 million, in the country get a monthly social security check. More than 30 million people 65 and over—nearly all the nation's aged—have health insurance under Medicare. Another 3 million disabled people under
1 age 65 also have Medicare.

Current Benefits and Problems

Social security is successful because there is widespread acceptance of the program. Benefits are assured, are backed by the government, rise with the cost of living, reduce economic insecurity, and provide continuing income to families. However, with all the extensions that have occurred over the last 60 years, the social security program has become one of the major elements of the federal budget. It now ranks with defense spending
2 and interest on the national debt.

For this reason, beginning in the 1980s, when controlling the budget became an important political goal, limits were placed on some parts of the program. Maximum payments were set for the disabled and their families, child care, and workers' compensation. Full-time students whose parents were deceased, retired, or disabled had their eligibility severely reduced. The age below which they could receive benefits was lowered from 22 to 19.

Recent changes in legislation have attempted to improve the system. They increase social security taxes, encourage some to retire early, tax the earnings of those already receiving benefits, raise retirement ages, and increase those eligible for coverage.

Even with such changes, however, there continues to be concern about the social security program. Some fear that when today's young workers need benefits, the money will not be there. Such critics say the system is going broke, and more cuts must be made. Others believe the answer is putting more money into the system and finding a better way to finance it. Both sides agree, however, that three problem areas must be faced.

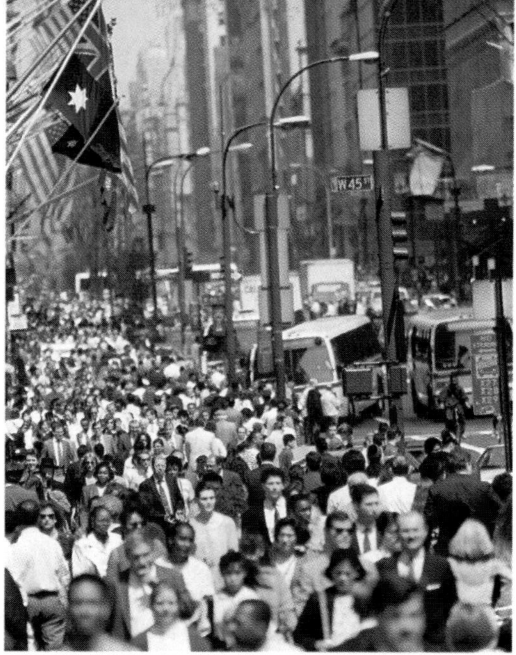

▲ *Today more than nine out of ten workers are covered by social security.* ***Why aren't all workers covered?***

1. Money in the Social Security Trust Fund has been used to finance other programs.
2. Inflation has eaten away at the purchasing power of benefits.
3. Many people have misinterpreted the purpose of social security, seeing it as their sole source of retirement income rather than as a supplement to pen-
3 sions, insurance, savings, and other investments.

HOW SOCIAL SECURITY WORKS

Since, as a worker, you will be required to participate in the social security program, you need to understand how the program works.

Five principles underlie the social security program. (See Figure 21.1 on page 336.)

Caption Answer: Many of those not covered are government employees who, according to law, are not covered by the social security system.

1 Reinforcement Ask how many students have relatives that are receiving social security benefits. As you know, many will be receiving disability, survivors', and retirement benefits, as well as Medicare and SSI. Stress that many students could not attend school if not for the income their families have from social security.

2 Discussion Starter Ask students which of two areas—defense or social security—they would cut. Why?

3 Learning Economics Ask students to explain the impact of inflation on social security benefits. (Most people begin paying into the fund 30 to 40 years before they receive retirement benefits. Thus, the dollars paid in have been worth much more than those paid out.)

1 Discussion Starter Ask students why the social security system has been around so long and why most people seem to support it. Have them work in groups to discuss the principles shown in Figure 21–1 and whether they agree or disagree with them.

2 Student Motivator Ask students how many of them have a job and make social security payments. Do they know how their deductions are figured? Would they know if their employer made a mistake and deducted too much? Do they know what happens to their money?

Figure 21–1 Five Principles of the Social Security Program

The Social Security Program is based on five basic principles.

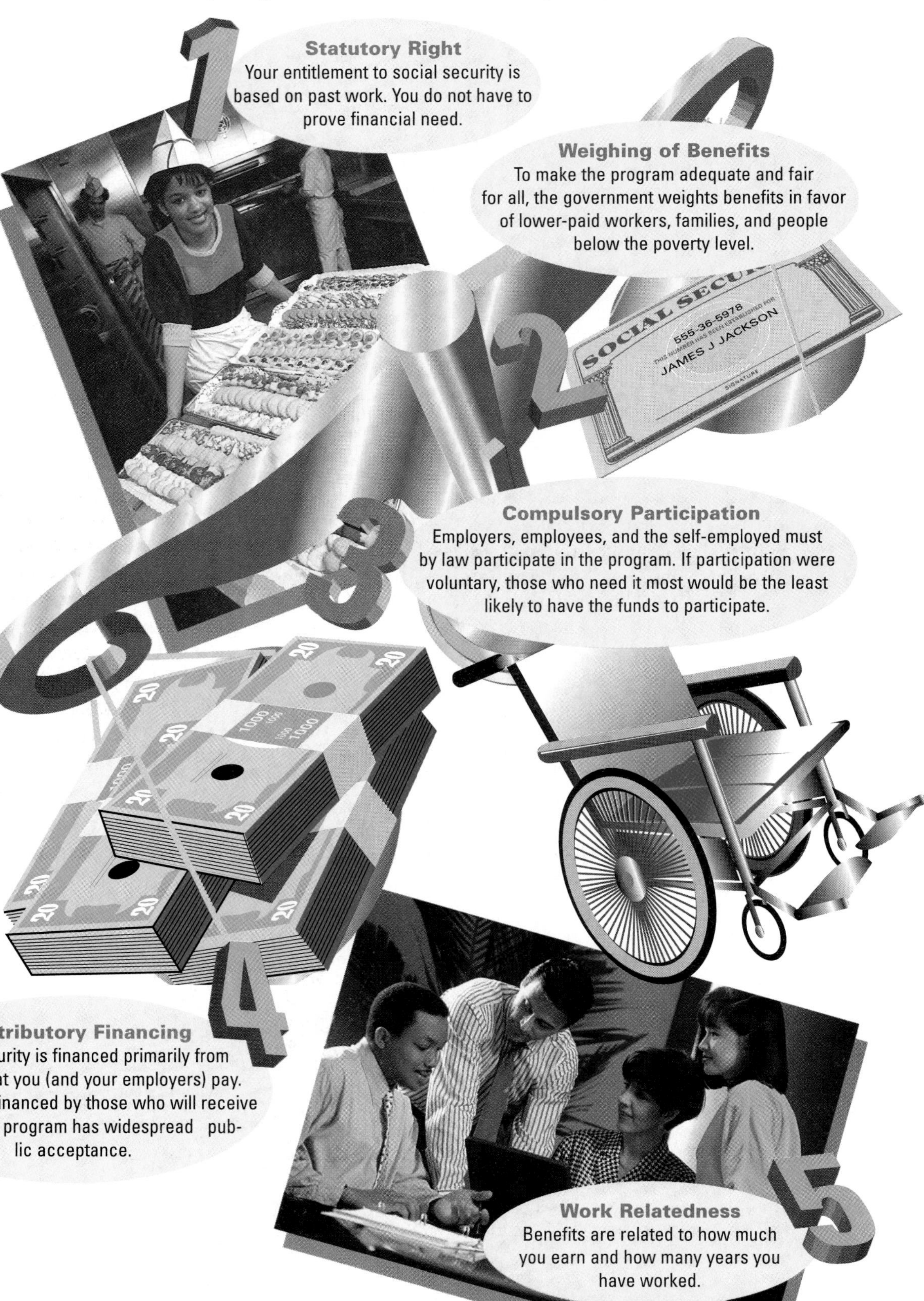

1
Statutory Right
Your entitlement to social security is based on past work. You do not have to prove financial need.
2
Weighing of Benefits
To make the program adequate and fair for all, the government weights benefits in favor of lower-paid workers, families, and people below the poverty level.
SOCIAL SECU
555-36-5978
JAMES J JACKSON
3
Compulsory Participation
Employers, employees, and the self-employed must by law participate in the program. If participation were voluntary, those who need it most would be the least likely to have the funds to participate.
4
Contributory Financing
Social security is financed primarily from the taxes that you (and your employers) pay. Because it is financed by those who will receive benefits, the program has widespread public acceptance.
5
Work Relatedness
Benefits are related to how much you earn and how many years you have worked.

Social Security Number

Your **social security number** is the number used to identify your earnings record for social security purposes. As a result of the Tax Reform Act of 1986, parents must apply for social security numbers for their children who are one year or older.

You keep your social security number for life. The number is used to keep a record of your contributions. You will also use the number on your own tax returns as the taxpayer I.D. number.

Contributions

Social security benefits are paid for by a tax, or contribution, on employee earnings. Employers, employees, and self-employed people all make contributions. On check stubs, these deductions are listed under the heading FICA, for Federal Insurance Contributions Act.

Employees and their employers pay equal amounts of social security tax. The tax rates have been gradually rising, as shown in Figure 21–2. The increase in contributions is designed to keep the
1 fund solvent in the future.

How much you receive in benefits depends on your average earnings. The amount subject to FICA tax is limited, however. As of 1995, for example, the tax was based on income up to $61,200. People who made more paid no social secu-
2 rity tax on earnings above this figure.

Figure 21–2 FICA Rates

FICA Rates (as a Percentage of Employee Earnings)

Year	Old Age and Survivors' Insurance	Disability Insurance	Hospital Insurance (Medicare)	Total
1985	5.20	.50	1.35	7.05
1986–1987	5.20	.50	1.45	7.15
1988–1989	5.53	.53	1.45	7.51
1990–1999	5.60	.60	1.45	7.65
2000 and after	5.49	.71	1.45	7.65

▲ *This chart shows the past, present, and future FICA rates.* ***What is the maximum total amount of social security taxes anyone would pay for this year?***

Eligibility

To be eligible for social security benefits, you must have earned a certain number of credits. These are based on the length of time you have worked and made contributions to the system.

Not all workers are covered by the social security program. Among those excluded are the people who do housecleaning, gardening, or baby-sitting in someone's home (unless they earn $50 or more in a three month period); students employed by their college or school; farm owners and operators; members of religious orders; employees of state or local governments not participating in the program; newspaper workers under age 18; and any child under 21 working for his or her parents.

Benefits

The social security system provides a whole range of benefits—most based on previous earnings. Some are based on need.

Old-Age Benefits Monthly benefits paid to retirees are called **old-age benefits.** The amount you receive depends on the earnings on which social security taxes have been paid. The more you work and the higher your earnings, the more your benefits.

Workers can qualify for reduced benefits at age 62. However, if they wait until they are 65 or older, their full benefits are higher. Certain dependents may also receive benefits under this part of the social security program. They include a wife or dependent husband age 62 or older; unmarried children

Caption Answer: Answers will vary as tax base limit increases and tax rate increases. It depends on the current year data. Maximum tax base for 1995 was $61,200 × .0765 = $4,681.80.

1 Vocabulary Ask students if they know what the "baby boomers" are (those born between 1945 and 1960) and the significance of this period for social security. (This huge expansion of the population will cause a severe drain on social security funds when the baby boomers begin to retire in the years 2010 and following.)

2 Math Application Ask students to suppose that they earned $200 during a week in the 1990s. How much social security tax would be taken out of their check? ($200 × 0.0765 = $15.30.) How much would the employer have to pay? ($15.30.)

▲ **How does social security help each of these people? Why are they eligible for benefits?**

Caption Answer: Social Security provides monthly income. Benefits are for disability, retirement, and Medicare.

1 Discussion Starter Have students suppose their spouse has died and they receive a monthly survivors' check of $900. Do they think they could live comfortably on that amount? Why or why not? Suppose they also had two children to support. Would they be able to make ends meet?

under 18 (or under 19 if they are full-time students); and unmarried, disabled children 18 or older. The age at which full benefits are payable will be increased gradually from age 65 to age 67 beginning with those who turn age 62 in the year 2000.

Survivors' Benefits When an insured worker dies, the surviving spouse and any children are paid benefits, called **survivors' benefits,** by the social security system. Such payments depend on average earnings. In the 1990s, maximum payments were nearly $1,000 a month for a single survivor and nearly $2,400 for a family. The survivor also receives a one-time, lump-sum death benefit to help cover funeral expenses. The standard death benefit is $255. 1

Disability Benefits Workers who develop conditions that prevent them from working may receive **disability benefits.** They must be under age 65 and must meet certain requirements.

Workers are considered disabled if they have a physical or mental condition that prevents them from working and is expected to last for at least 12 months or to result in death. Benefits start at the sixth full month the person is disabled. They go on as long as the disability lasts.

In general, to qualify for disability benefits, a worker needs credit for a certain number of years of work immediately prior to the disability. A worker age 35 or older, for example, must have credit for five years of work in the ten-year period ending when he or she became disabled. In the 1990s, monthly disability payments ranged from $764 for a single worker to a little over $2,100 for a family of four.

Hospital Insurance The social security system pays some hospital bills for people age 65 and older. This program is called Medicare and is discussed in Chapter 20.

Payments to the Needy The social security program also makes payments to certain groups who do not qualify for benefits based on earnings. These include

Playing It Safe on the Job

Maintaining a safe work environment may not only save you from costly medical bills, but it may also save your life.

- **When on the job, use the safety equipment provided.**
- **Make sure you know how to safely use the machines or tools that are a part of your job.**
- **Read the instructions and the warning labels on any materials you use. Many products contain hazardous chemicals or highly flammable materials. Knowing how to use them properly can prevent accidents.**
- **Know your limitations. Lifting objects that are too heavy can cause back and other injuries.**

the needy of all types—the aged, the blind, mothers with dependent children, disabled children, and many others.

One such program is **Supplemental Security Income.** SSI is designed to give more security to people with low or limited incomes. Funded by federal and state money, the program went into effect on January 1, 1974. To qualify for benefits, a person must be a legal resident of the United States. He or she must also
1 be 65 or older, or disabled, or blind. (*Blind,* in this case, is defined as having vision no better than 20/200 with

1 Discussion Starter Social security has a program for the needy. Do students feel it is really necessary? Why or why not?

GRIEF and Gun Laws

Every year hundreds of children are killed by their friends or siblings fooling around with guns they thought were not loaded. Thousands are injured. In 1989, one of the victims was 12-year-old David Joseph Kenney (called "DJ") of Connecticut.

The accident happened when DJ spent the night at a friend's house. The friend's father was a policeman who had three guns—all loaded—in the house. DJ's friend was playing around with one when he killed DJ. The charges against the police officer of reckless endangerment, for keeping an unsecured, loaded gun in the house, were dropped. That made DJ's mother, Susan Kenney, very angry.

Five weeks after DJ died, Kenney started GRIEF (Gun Responsibility In Every Family) to change gun laws in Connecticut. She lobbied state representatives and urged others to do the same. She gave a press conference to the media. Kenney was not asking for a gun ban. She just wanted gun owners to be responsible for what happened with their guns.

The National Rifle Association (NRA) opposed the gun regulations, claiming they were unconstitutional. Members of the NRA also believe that an unintentional murder like DJ's should not be considered a felony or require a prison sentence. They put up a strong fight against Kenney. Although she was nervous and afraid, she continued to fight for the law.

In October of 1990, the law passed. It makes the gun owner responsible if a child is hurt or killed by a gun he or she fails to secure.

GRIEF has more than 6,000 members in 23 states and Canada. The group plans to continue its work until every state and province has such a law.

Brainstorm

How can people who use guns, and those who do not, keep children safe from accidents like DJs?

Case Study Answer: For people who keep guns: Keep arms unloaded and ammunition separate; keep guns locked securely; teach children never to touch the guns without adult supervision; teach them never to point guns at themselves or anyone else.

For people who do not use guns: Teach children that, if other children bring out guns, they are to go immediately to an adult or to go home; teach them that guns are not toys and are never to be used in games.

1 Discussion Starter Ask students if they know someone who has been laid off and cannot find work. What is that person trying to do to solve this problem? Can he or she collect unemployment?

2 Discussion Starter Ask students what would happen to their family if the breadwinner was unable to work for the next three months. How would they manage? Is there a program that might help them continue to have some income?

3 Math Application Have students assume they have been working for many years and have paid (out of their checks) into a disability plan. Their plan pays 55 percent of their normal income as benefits. If they make $500 a week, how much would they get from the plan? ($500 × .55 = $275.)

News Clip Answers:
1 Income insurance provides vital income when you are unable to work because of illness or injury. Since an accident or an illness can happen at any time, it is good to have some sort of financial protection.
2 You should be aware of how much money your plan will pay out. You should also be aware for how many months or years your plan will provide coverage, and which disabilities are covered and which are not.

glasses.) Furthermore, a single person must have an income below $9,000 a year and no more than $2,000 in assets. (Other higher figures apply for couples.)

FEDERAL AND STATE UNEMPLOYMENT INSURANCE

Unemployment insurance is a joint federal and state plan designed to provide income to workers who have lost their jobs. Since each state has its own program, requirements for coverage vary. Usually, however, to be eligible for benefits, people must work for a certain length of time, be unemployed for a certain length of time (usually a week), and be unemployed through no fault of their own. (Workers who quit their jobs, for example, might
1 not get benefits.)

People must also be physically able to work, available to accept work, and actively seeking work. (Sometimes, if people refuse to take jobs offered to them, their benefits are stopped.)

Benefits are based on earnings within certain minimum and maximum ranges. The more a person earns at a job, the more that person will get in unemployment benefits if the job ends. In most states, people receive about 50 percent of their last salary, up to the maximum allowed. In the 1990s, weekly payments averaged $178.58. The period over which payments are made varies; the general range is from 26 weeks up to 36 weeks, but the period may be even longer.

Benefits are paid from money collected from two taxes on employers. One, a federal tax, is used to run the program. The second, a state tax, is used to pay the actual benefits.

PRIVATE INCOME INSURANCE PROGRAMS

Privately owned insurance companies offer many policies to protect people from loss of income resulting from illness, disability, or retirement.

Disability Income Insurance

Before disability insurance, people who were ill lost more from missed paychecks than from medical bills. Disability insurance was set up to protect against such loss of income. This kind of coverage is very common today, and several
2 hundred insurance companies offer it.

Disability income insurance gives weekly or monthly cash payments to people who cannot work because of illness or accident. The amount paid is usually 40 to 60 percent of a person's normal income. Some plans, however, pay as much as 75 percent. Benefit payments may run from 13 weeks to a lifetime for accidents and to a certain age,
3 such as 65, for sickness.

Benefit Period People do not usually receive payments from the first day they are out of work. Instead, most companies have a waiting period. This is the time between the first day of disability and the day benefits begin. A waiting period may be 7, 14, 30, or 90 days. By having waiting periods, insurance companies do not have to pay many small claims that would drive up the cost of premiums. The longer the waiting period, the lower the premium.

Some workers have sick-leave pay or other kinds of income to cover the first few days of disability. Some employers will keep paying salaries to employees during temporary absences from the job because of accident or illness. However, most employers usually have time limits beyond which full payment will be cut down or eliminated.

Extent of Disability Under most policies, a person must be totally disabled to get benefits. The definition of *total disability* differs from policy to

CASE STUDY

Consumer NEWS CLIP

Uncovering the Facts Behind Disability Coverage

by Ellen E. Schultz
The Wall Street Journal
October 21, 1994

For most employees, the only thing that keeps a paycheck coming in while they're laid up is group disability coverage.

This common workplace benefit typically pays 60 percent of your salary while you're disabled. According to U.S. Department of Labor figures, about half of all companies with more than 100 employees offer long-term disability coverage.

A few employees do have individual disability insurance, but such coverage is extremely expensive and difficult to qualify for. As for Social Security disability coverage, you can collect the benefit only after you have been disabled for five months, are considered permanently disabled, and meet other conditions. So stringent are the requirements, in fact, that 42 percent of applicants initially are rejected.

That may leave group disability coverage as your primary salary safety blanket. But qualifying for the benefits has become more difficult in recent years. Employers are adding restrictions on who may qualify for coverage, and are often installing caps on what they will pay for certain conditions.

As employers continuously tinker with the plans, it's all the more important for employees to take a close look at how their disability benefits work. "You need to look at your coverage since there is so much variation," says Elaine D. Rosen, senior vice president at Unum.

After sick leave expires, many employers offer short-term disability coverage. This typically covers 40 percent to 70 percent of your salary, depending on how long you've worked at a company and other factors, and may last for 30 days to six months. Depending on your plan, short-term disability may start on the day your sick leave expires, or on the first day of hospitalization.

With this basic understanding of how the plans work, you're ready to look at the nitty-gritty details. First, find out if your coverage is automatic or optional. Many employers offer disability coverage as an option through their flexible benefit plans. If the coverage is available, sign up for it.

Also find out whether you can buy supplemental coverage. Because most companies have caps on the amount of salary that will be applied to disability benefits, many offer the ability to purchase supplemental coverage. For instance, all of Merrill Lynch's 43,000 employees can sign up for coverage that would bring their total payments, including those from group and supplemental, to as much as 60 percent of their salary.

How an employer defines a disability is also very important. Some companies will agree that you are disabled only if you qualify for Social Security disability payments. "Check with your plan," says Mr. [John] Hickey [a disability specialist at Kwasha Lipton, a benefit-consulting firm]. (Such plans also effectively exclude progressive and partial disabilities).

Decisions, Decisions

1. Why is it important to have income insurance?
2. What are some important issues to consider about income insurance?

1 Reinforcement Tell students that about 85 percent of all Americans turning 65 do not have enough money to live on. Most have less than $100 monthly income (other than mandated programs like social security). How can students ensure that they will have enough money to retire on?

2 Vocabulary Students may encounter the word *vested* in relation to pension plans. Do they know the meaning of the term? (Fully guaranteed.)

3 Reinforcement Student Activity Workbook, Chapter 21 activities.

4 Interesting Note The Tax Reform Act of 1986 altered the legal and tax implications of IRA and Keogh accounts. Stress to students the need to revise their savings programs as the laws change.

Caption Answer: It may be the largest source of future retirement income. It allows the employee to begin controlling and planning his or her financial future. It also supplements the other sources of retirement income for the consumer.

policy. The term usually means that the insured cannot work at a job that matches his or her level of education, training, or experience.

A few policies provide benefits for partial disability. A partial disability is one that keeps a person from performing one or more job-related duties. Benefits for partial disability are usually paid at the rate of one-half those for total disability and for not more than six months per disability.

A waiver-of-premiums clause usually is included in long-term policies. The clause states that the insured does not have to pay any premiums due during total disability of three months or longer until the disability ends.

Private Pension Plans

Most people who reach retirement age in this country do not have enough money saved or invested to live comfortably for the rest of their lives. Therefore, as a fringe benefit for employees, many businesses offer pension plans to give monthly income to their employees when they retire. Professional and trade associations as well as unions also have
1 pension plans.

Pension plans vary widely. In order to get a pension, a person must usually work for a company or belong to some organization for a certain number of years. Some plans are paid entirely by the employer and others by the employer and the employee together. Benefits usually depend on how long the person has worked for the company and how much he or she was paid. Pension plans may be run by an insurance company or bank, which invests the contri-
2 butions.

Those not covered by pension plans have other options. Workers can start an individual retirement account (IRA) to save and invest money for retirement.
3 For many people, some or all of the
4 money saved this way is not taxed.

Annuities

Another way to protect or add to future income is to buy an annuity. An **annuity** is a sum of money paid as a regular income for a certain number of years or life.

Annuities are usually bought through insurance companies. The annuity matures when the buyer reaches a certain age and wishes to retire. At this time, the annuity is paid out in monthly or yearly installments or in a lump sum. The payments may stop when the buyer dies, with no refund of the balance, or the balance may be paid to a beneficiary, depending on the annuity agreement.

Employees should obtain a full explanation of pension plan provisions from their company's human resources department. ***Why is the pension plan so important to many employees?*** ▶

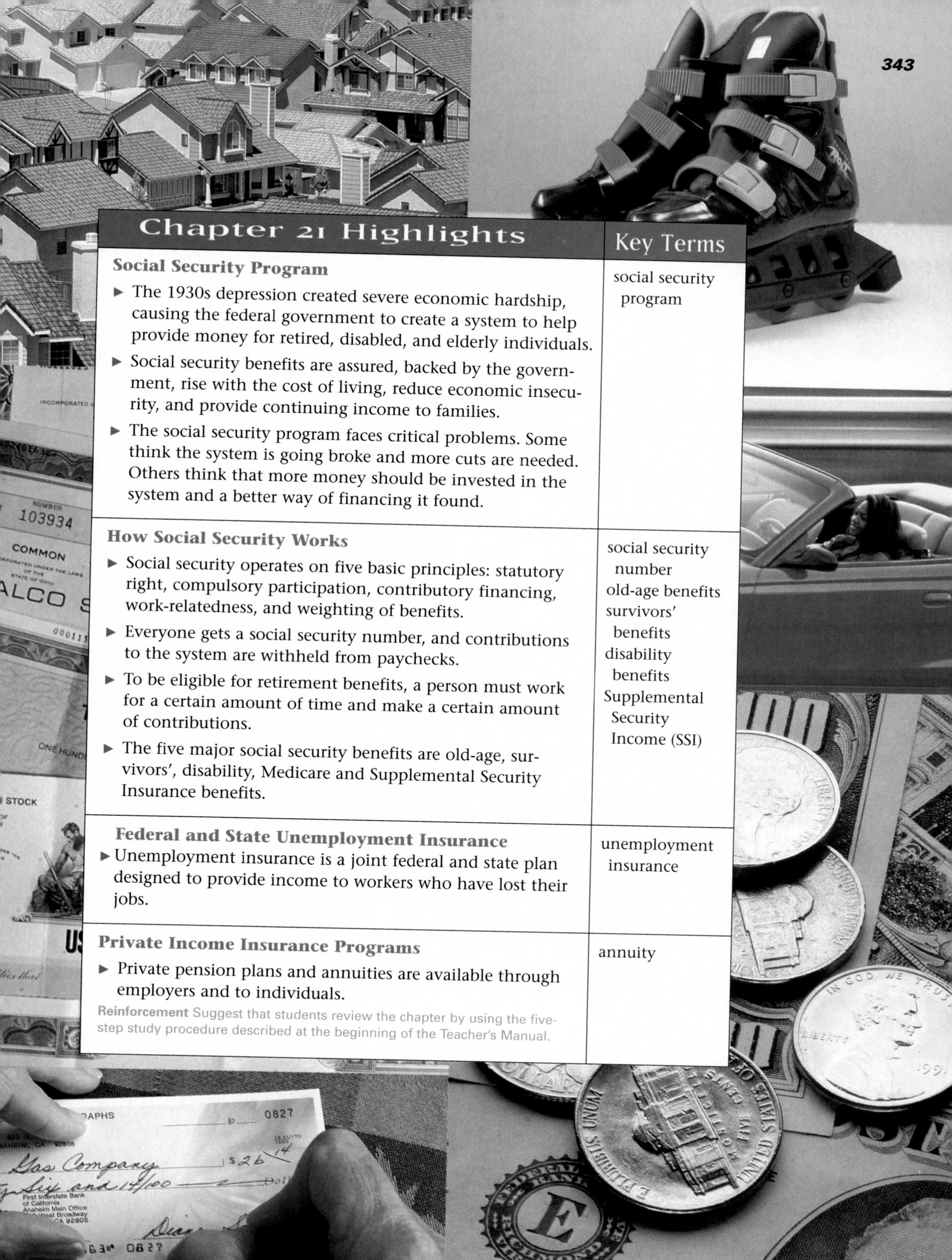

Chapter 21 Highlights

Chapter 21 Highlights	Key Terms
Social Security Program ► The 1930s depression created severe economic hardship, causing the federal government to create a system to help provide money for retired, disabled, and elderly individuals. ► Social security benefits are assured, backed by the government, rise with the cost of living, reduce economic insecurity, and provide continuing income to families. ► The social security program faces critical problems. Some think the system is going broke and more cuts are needed. Others think that more money should be invested in the system and a better way of financing it found.	social security program
How Social Security Works ► Social security operates on five basic principles: statutory right, compulsory participation, contributory financing, work-relatedness, and weighting of benefits. ► Everyone gets a social security number, and contributions to the system are withheld from paychecks. ► To be eligible for retirement benefits, a person must work for a certain amount of time and make a certain amount of contributions. ► The five major social security benefits are old-age, survivors', disability, Medicare and Supplemental Security Insurance benefits.	social security number old-age benefits survivors' benefits disability benefits Supplemental Security Income (SSI)
Federal and State Unemployment Insurance ► Unemployment insurance is a joint federal and state plan designed to provide income to workers who have lost their jobs.	unemployment insurance
Private Income Insurance Programs ► Private pension plans and annuities are available through employers and to individuals. **Reinforcement** Suggest that students review the chapter by using the five-step study procedure described at the beginning of the Teacher's Manual.	annuity

CHAPTER 21 REVIEW

Refer students to the Reviewing Consumer Terms and Reviewing Facts and Ideas activities in the Student Activity Workbook.

Reviewing Consumer Terms Paragraphs will vary. See Glossary for definitions.

Reviewing Facts and Ideas See the Student Activity Workbook for answers.

Problem Solving and Decision Making **1** Students should disagree with the statement. Both old and young benefit from social security. **2** Answers could include homelessness, health insurance for everyone, drug abuse, and hunger. **3** Some students might say that families would be better off today than in the 1930s. Others might say families would be worse off because few are saving money, have the skills to change jobs, or have experience with tough economic times.

Consumers Around the World **Math 1 a** $175.80—OASI: $9.84; DI: $1.05; HI: $2.55; Total: $13.44. **b** $250—OASI: $14; DI: $1.50; HI: $3.63; Total: $19.13. **c** $80—OASI: $4.48; DI: $.48; HI: $1.16; Total: $6.12. **d** $400—OASI: $22.40; DI: $2.40;

Reviewing Consumer Terms

Use each of the following terms in a paragraph to demonstrate you know its meaning.

annuity
disability benefits
old-age benefits
social security number
social security program
Supplemental Security Income (SSI)
survivors' benefits
unemployment insurance

Reviewing Facts and Ideas

1. Name three problems that existed during the Depression which prompted passage of the Social Security Act.
2. List five benefits offered by social security.
3. Who pays for social security?
4. What is disability income insurance and how does it work?
5. What is the difference between a pension and an annuity?

Problem Solving and Decision Making

1. Consider this comment: "Social security is for old people. Why should I learn about it? It will be a long time before I need it. I might not even live long enough to get any benefits." Do you agree? Why or why not? How would you answer this comment?
2. What are some of the key social problems facing this country? Can they be addressed by social security?
3. Suppose we had a great depression today. How would conditions be different for American families today than they were in the 1930s?

Building Academic Skills

Consumers Around the World

Math

1. Construct a chart with these headings: Earnings; Old-Age and Survivors' Insurance Tax; Disability Insurance Tax; Hospital Insurance (Medicare) Tax; Total Taxes. Use Figure 21–2 on FICA rates to compute the taxes for these earnings made in the 1990s: (*a*) $175.80; (*b*) $250; (*c*) $80; (*d*) $400; (*e*) $350. Fill in the chart.

Communications

2. Research the history of the social security system. Why was it started? What was it intended to do? What changes have been made to the law since it began? Write a timeline of the system from start to present. Develop a brochure that explains the system, its history, and its benefits. Share the timeline and brochure with your class.

Social Studies

3. Select another country and research its system of handling retirement, disability, and other elements of our social security system. Does the country have a similar or different system? How does it

work? Is it better or worse than the U.S. system? Can we learn from this country? Write a 750-word report on your findings.

Beyond the Classroom

Consumer Projects

1. Visit the nearest social security office and get some pamphlets on social security benefits. Write a 250-word essay summarizing your findings.
2. Call or write to the Social Security Administration to get a copy of Form SSA-7004, Personal Earnings and Benefit Estimate Statement. Fill out the form and return it. In a few weeks, you will receive a printout of your earnings record. How does this information compare with your expectations?

Cooperative Learning

Family Economics

Break into assigned family groups. Discuss the following problem.

In the Family Economics problem in Chapter 20, a family member became seriously ill from chemical exposure at work. Now, further treatment reveals that the chemical exposure has permanently damaged the family member's health and made it impossible for that person to hold a job. How can a family member continue to contribute to the family's support? Explain the possibilities and note any potential problems in taking advantage of them. Compare your answers with those of other family groups.

Debate the Issue

Some consumers feel that the social security system is working, that many are helped as a result of the FICA tax paid by most workers.

Others feel that if individuals could keep their FICA money, they could invest in other products (like stocks) and actually have a better, more secure financial future.

You and your classmates will break into two groups and research this topic. Each group will gather evidence to support one side or the other. You are to prepare the argument for your side of the problem. Then the two groups will meet in a classroom debate.

Rechecking Your Attitude

Before going on to the next unit, go back to the Attitude Inventory at the beginning of this one. Answer the questions a second time. Then compare the two sets of responses. On how many statements have your attitudes changed? Can you account for these shifts in your opinions? What do you know now that you did not know then?

HI: $5.80; Total: $30.60. **e** $350—OASI: $19.60; DI: $2.10; HI: $5.08; Total: $26.78.

Communications
2 Students' timelines should include key dates in the text, plus other data not included in the text.

Social Studies
3 Reports should address the questions posed, together with other points.

Consumer Projects
1 Students should cover the main points in their summary. They should attach the brochures to their essay. **2** Students should provide or discuss the printout of their earnings record that they obtained.

Family Economics
This is a disability situation. However, some of the families may not qualify for coverage because of age or lack of credits.

Debate the Issue
Break the class into two teams. Assign each team one side of the issue. Encourage students to work together as a team to develop their argument. Ask each team to select a member to make an opening statement that supports the team's side of the issue. Have students take turns debating as the debate moves from one team to the other.

UNIT 6 LAB

You and Your Community

STEPS A and C Students should prepare lists of interview questions that are clearly written, easily comprehended, and appropriate for the persons to whom they will be addressed. All the topics listed in Steps A and C should be addressed.
STEPS B and D Students should arrange and carry out their interviews. Students should take careful, well-organized notes on each interview.
STEP E Students' answers should be accurate and based on their interview notes.
STEP F Students' discussions of the advantages and disadvantages of the types of insurance should reflect their understanding of the impact of providing or receiving insurance benefits. Students should also indicate their understanding of the taxpayers' role in providing social security benefits. Students' answers should be clearly and logically supported by examples from their interviews.

Refer students to the Unit 6 Lab in the Student Activity Workbook.

Researching the Benefits of Insurance

Unit 6 presents the advantages of having insurance. In this lab, you will have the opportunity to talk directly with those who provide insurance and those who receive the benefits of it.

TOOLS

1. Newsmagazines and newspapers
2. Financial and consumer magazines
3. Literature from insurance providers and the Social Security Administration
4. History and economics textbooks

PROCEDURES

STEP A

Write a list of ten questions about property and home, automobile, life, health, and income insurance that you can ask during an interview with an adult working in a full- or part-time job. Your interview questions should cover the following topics:

1. The types of insurance policies the worker has and his or her reasons for choosing the policy or the reasons the worker has chosen not to purchase insurance.
2. The kinds of insurance coverage the worker is offered by his or her employer, or the kinds of coverage the worker researched before purchasing an individual policy.
3. The amount of the worker's deductible and coinsurance payments, and the percentage of the worker's income that is devoted to property, automobile, and health insurance premiums.
4. The worker's use of and satisfaction with health maintenance organizations and preferred provider organizations.
5. The percentage of the worker's income paid to the social security system.
6. The worker's view of social security as a retirement income source.
7. The availability to the worker of a private pension plan.

STEP B

Talk with family and friends about this lab assignment, and ask for their help in identifying three adults who are working full- or part-time and who would be willing to be interviewed about their insurance choices and experiences. If possible, one of your workers should be under 30 years of age and one should be over 50 years of age. When your interview subjects have agreed to talk with you, arrange a convenient time to interview each worker either on the phone or in person.

STEP C

Prepare a list of ten questions that you can ask a company's personnel manager or a personnel employee who specializes in employee

UNIT 6 LAB

You and Your Community

benefits. The questions should focus on the type of life, health, and income insurance coverage the company provides for its employees. Include the following topics in your questions:

1. The types of life insurance options (if any) the company provides.
2. The choice and basic features of health insurance plans the company provides.
3. The company's requirements for providing health insurance benefits to a worker. (Does the worker have to work full-time or work for the company for a certain length of time in order to receive benefits?)
4. The average cost for employees to purchase employer-subsidized health benefits.
5. The average cost to the employer of providing health benefits.
6. The average cost to the employer of paying social security taxes.
7. The ways the employer finances the cost of paying employee insurance benefits and social security taxes.
8. The cost to the employer of workers' compensation insurance and the steps the employer takes to prevent workers' injuries.
9. The types of pension and retirement plans the employer makes available.

STEP D Contact three personnel employees from three different companies, explain the purpose of your assignment, and ask if they will agree to be interviewed by you. Ideally, the personnel people you interview should work for the same company as the workers you interviewed in Step B. Arrange an interview either by phone or in person with each personnel expert. Take careful notes during the interview.

LAB REPORT

STEP E Use your notes from the six interviews to answer the questions below:

1. What was the average percentage of income the three workers devoted to insurance premiums?
2. How did the cost of premiums, deductibles, and coinsurance payments affect the workers' satisfaction with their health insurance?
3. What was the average cost per employee for a company to provide health and/or life insurance?
4. What was the average cost of social security taxes to the three employers?
5. How have the employers attempted to deal with the cost of providing employee insurance benefits?

STEP F Write a two-page report on the economic advantages and disadvantages of life, health, and income insurance for the employee, the employer, and U.S. taxpayers.

UNIT 7

Unit Contents

Transportation and Travel

Attitude Inventory

Before you begin Chapter 22, take stock of your attitudes by completing the following inventory. Read each statement and decide how you feel about it—agree, disagree, or undecided. Record your feelings on a sheet of notepaper or use the form in the workbook.

1. An automobile is a necessity for the modern consumer.
2. The cheapest way to travel is always by car.
3. Widespread ownership of automobiles presents social problems in many communities.
4. The most powerful car is, in the long run, the best car for most consumers.
5. Today many Americans have more time for recreation than did their parents and grandparents.
6. A consumer who cannot pay cash for a car should not buy one.
7. The small-car buyer will need more optional equipment than the buyer of a larger automobile.
8. Results of road tests reported by various magazines are of real value to the consumer.
9. Dealer reputation is usually more important than the price of a car.
10. Miles-per-gallon ratings published by the Environmental Protection Agency are more reliable than the experiences of automobile sales people.
11. "Leave your credit card at home" is poor advice for a vacationer.
12. The used-car buyers always "buys somebody else's problem."
13. Warranties are always one of the most important points for consumers to consider before buying a used car.
14. Travel agents cannot do anything for you that you cannot do better and more cheaply for yourself.
15. Budget motels are suitable only for those who like to "rough it".
16. Public transportation is for poor people only.

Unit Goal The main goal of this unit is to provide students with the information they will need to make wise consumer decisions in the areas of travel and transportation, with the primary focus on buying and owning an automobile. Chapters in this unit are (1) Buying and Leasing a New or Used Car, (2) Owning a Car, and (3) Choosing Other Forms of Transportation.

Lesson Plan See the Teacher's Manual for an overview of the unit and some suggestions for introducing it. If you assign the Attitude Inventory, be sure to tell students to keep their answers for later use.

CHAPTER 22

Buying or Leasing a New or Used Car

Learning Objectives

When you have finished studying this chapter, you should be able to:

1. List the advantages and disadvantages of owning a car.
2. Compare the different types of cars.
3. Compute how much you can afford to pay for a car.
4. Find and evaluate the performance records of older cars.
5. Make an on-lot inspection of a used car.
6. Weigh the relative merits of leasing a car.

Consumer Terms

depreciation
options
standard equipment
warranty
sticker price
odometer
tire tread
diagnostic center

Real-World Journal

Take a stand. Prepare an argument in your journal either in favor of or opposed to purchasing a new car rather than a used car. Persuade your reader with the benefits of your position. Make certain he or she understands the weak points of the opposing viewpoint.

Lesson Plan See the Teacher's Manual for Chapter 22 lesson plan.

Vocabulary The Chapter 22 lesson plan includes suggested vocabulary activities for the terms listed.

1 Vocabulary Some students may not know the word *expenditure* (expense). Have them guess its meaning from the context.

2 Reinforcement Assign groups of students to different car dealerships and have them find out what range of prices exists. Then compile the results to determine the highest, lowest, and average price. Depending on time and number of students, you may or may not include used cars.

3 Reinforcement Assign students to different lending institutions. Have students contact the institutions and say that for a school project they are trying to determine the average length of time that people use to pay off their automobile loans. Compile results and calculate an average.

4 Critical Thinking Have students make lists of items that typically increase rather then decrease in value over a period of years.

CAR OWNERSHIP

More than 84 percent of the households in the United States have at least one car, according to the U.S. Bureau of Census. Buying a car is the second largest single expenditure made by most people. (Buying a home ranks first.) Since buying a car is a major purchase, careful thought and planning should be given to every detail.

Being well-informed before you buy a car can make all the difference between your being a happy owner or one filled with regret.

Advantages and Disadvantages of Owning a Car

Advantages come to mind first when consumers consider buying a car. However, there are disadvantages as well. Figure 22–1 depicts both sides.

Projected Use

Vehicle use can be divided into two categories—primary and secondary. The primary use is the main purpose for which the vehicle will be used most often. A secondary use is one for which the vehicle is used occasionally. There can be several secondary uses.

The kind of car you select should be adequate to satisfy both your primary and secondary needs. The primary use, however, is the one that should determine what kind of car you buy. A big, heavy, smooth-riding car may be ideal for taking long family vacations. It may be the wrong choice, however, if you need a car mainly to commute, or travel alone daily between home and school or home and work. If you carpool regularly, a six-passenger vehicle may be your best bet. If you take the bus or train to school or work and use your car mainly for weekend trips with one or two friends, a two- or four-passenger vehicle may be all that you need.

Geographic and climatic conditions must also be considered when buying a car. If the car will be used often on snow-covered mountain roads, skid control is especially important. Someone who drives through areas with strong crosswinds often will want a car that remains stable under those conditions. A car used for long-distance travel in desert or semi-desert areas should be powerful enough to meet air-conditioning needs.

Figure 22–1 Advantages and Disadvantages of Car Ownership

Before buying a car, weigh the advantages and disadvantages carefully.

Advantages
1
Employment.
Some jobs require employees to have a car. Others find that it is the most efficient way and sometimes the only way to get to work.
PIZZA

Affordability

Plan to be conservative in making estimates of what you can afford in a car. Remember, an automobile and its operation are just one item in your budget. A family planning to spend more than 13 percent of its disposable income for a car may be taking on too much of a burden. This 13 percent should include car payments, operating costs, insurance, taxes, and license fees. You can help reduce payments by shopping for a loan and borrowing where the best terms are

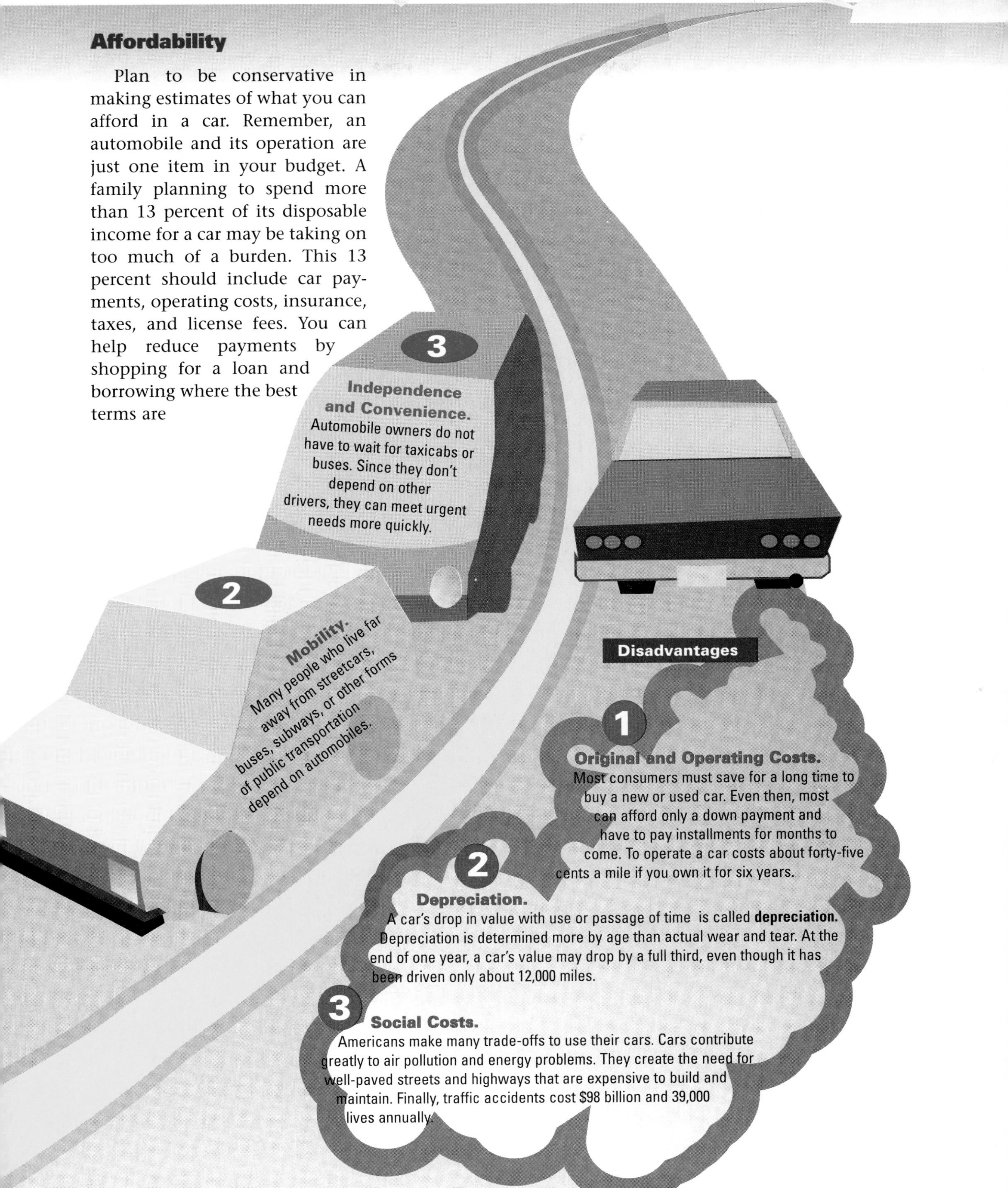

3
Independence and Convenience. Automobile owners do not have to wait for taxicabs or buses. Since they don't depend on other drivers, they can meet urgent needs more quickly.

2
Mobility. Many people who live far away from streetcars, buses, subways, or other forms of public transportation depend on automobiles.

Disadvantages

1
Original and Operating Costs. Most consumers must save for a long time to buy a new or used car. Even then, most can afford only a down payment and have to pay installments for months to come. To operate a car costs about forty-five cents a mile if you own it for six years.

2
Depreciation. A car's drop in value with use or passage of time is called **depreciation.** Depreciation is determined more by age than actual wear and tear. At the end of one year, a car's value may drop by a full third, even though it has been driven only about 12,000 miles.

3
Social Costs. Americans make many trade-offs to use their cars. Cars contribute greatly to air pollution and energy problems. They create the need for well-paved streets and highways that are expensive to build and maintain. Finally, traffic accidents cost $98 billion and 39,000 lives annually.

1 Math Application Have students assume a person makes $70-per-month car payments, pays $525 annually in insurance premiums, averages $495 a year in operating costs, and pays $100 a year for taxes and license. If that person has a disposable income of $14,000 a year, is he or she paying more or less than 13% of that income for a car? ($70 x 12 = $840 + $525 + $495 + $100 = $1,960; $14,000 × .13 = $1,820; thus, the person is paying more than 13% disposable income.

2 Reinforcement Have local car dealers supply you with names and brochures of the cars they sell. Share the names and information with the students and have students develop a list of criteria for assigning models to one of the five categories.

offered. The United States Department of Transportation reports that the average annual cost of owning and operating an automobile is about 12.3 percent of a household's disposable income in recent
1 years.

Car Size and Type

Automobiles can be classified into seven categories according to size. Greatest safety is usually associated with greatest size.

1. *Subcompacts.* Subcompacts are very small cars, usually equipped with four-cylinder engines. They are the lowest-priced, least powerful, and most economical vehicles. They can seat two adults in the front and a child in the back in reasonable comfort. They may be somewhat noisy and rough-riding and, for some peo-
2 ple, uncomfortable on long trips.
2. *Compacts.* Also small, compacts can carry four people. They often have four-cylinder engines and a quieter ride than most subcompacts. Considered economy cars, compacts cost less than any other group of cars except the subcompacts. Their operating costs are also lower.
3. *Mid-size.* This group consists of cars that are neither compact nor full-size. They usually have six-cylinder engines. They can seat six passengers, although not always in great comfort. Generally, mid-size cars cost more than compacts and are not as economical to operate. However, their ride is relatively smooth, making long trips more comfortable.
4. *Minivans.* These provide a sedan-like ride with the convenience of a van. Minivans can carry four to seven people and are popular with families and people who carpool. They provide lots of cargo space. They are generally priced like higher-end mid-size cars.

Singapore Discourages Cars

The government of Singapore requires car owners to buy expensive certificates of ownership and charges taxes and fees to use the roads. A small Japanese-made car can cost more than $70,000 before it even gets on the road.

5. *Sport/Utility vehicles.* These vehicles have become very popular and are usually equipped with four-wheel drive. They handle adverse conditions well and can be driven on rough terrain. They accommodate at least four people and have lots of cargo room. Their operating costs are similar to full-size cars.
6. *Full-size cars.* Roomier and more comfortable than smaller vehicles, full-size (or standard) cars seat six people with relative ease. Initial cost exceeds that of previously listed categories. Standard cars are also more expensive to operate, but provide a smooth, comfortable, quiet ride.
7. *Luxury cars.* As their name implies, luxury cars are the most expensive automobiles on the market. They are also the most comfortable, accommodating six people with ease and providing a very smooth ride.

All of these size categories are not as clearly defined today as they were two decades ago. That was when auto manufacturers began to trim vehicle lengths, widths, and weights due to pressure from the government to improve gasoline mileage.

Options

Options, such as sun roofs and CD players, are features available at extra cost. You are the one who decides whether or not to buy these extra features. Some cars have standard equipment devices that are optional on other cars. **Standard equipment** are features that are included in the original price of an automobile, like a driver's
1 side air bag or basic radio system.

In selecting options, weigh their added cost against your genuine need for them. If you are buying for purposes of economy, you will probably add few. (Some options, like air bags and air conditioning, may be well-worth the extra cost.)

You may have to wait several weeks for delivery of a car equipped exactly as you want it.

Performance

You know the class of car you require and the options you want. How well do specific makes of such a car perform? You can find out by referring to road test data. Road tests are practical tests to judge a car's performance. Some of the most highly respected reports appear in magazines such as *Consumer Reports, Car and Driver,* and *Kiplinger's Personal Finance.* Features rated include engine and transmission performance, safety, comfort, handling and braking, convenience, price, major options, fuel
2 mileage, and predicted reliability.

MAKING THE BEST DEAL ON A NEW CAR

After assessing your needs and budget, you can probably narrow your choice of car down to a few specific makes and models. The next step is to get the best deal on the car that you want.

Choosing a Dealer

Decide which sellers you can deal with confidently. Reputation is very important. Look for dealers who have been in business for several years. Talk to friends and relatives about their recent

How to Choose an Auto Club
Auto clubs offer motorists a variety of services. For the basic annual fee, members may receive such services as towing, fixing flats, jump-starting engines, and delivering gas. If you're ready to make basic car repairs yourself, pass on the auto club. But if you would prefer road services when you need help, you should consider joining an auto club.

- **Where do you live? Do auto clubs provide extensive services in your area? Which ones?**
- **How old is your car? Since older cars are more likely to break down, choose a club that offers the most road services.**
- **How many licensed motorists are in your family? Compare the auto clubs' rates for adding family members to the membership.**
- **How much would you use the discounts? Most auto clubs offer discounts at major hotel chains, restaurants, theme parks, and other destinations. Compare the offers to find out which auto club offers the greatest savings through discounts.**

1 Learning Economics Stress opportunity costs. Have students make a list of purchases they could make for the price of an option such as air-conditioning or power windows.

2 Reinforcement
Point out that a couple of hours spent in the library prior to an automobile purchase can save students years of frustration and repair costs. If you know someone who was about to buy a certain automobile until research convinced him or her that another choice would be a better buy, have that person visit the class and tell the story. An even better way to make the point is to invite a speaker who didn't do the research and had to suffer the consequences, which could have been avoided with one trip to the local library.

1 Discussion Starter Have students talk to relatives and friends about various local dealers, then discuss the reports they received in class. Do the reports seem reliable? Are there any contradictions? How do students account for this?

2 Research You may want to have students use these questions to survey an assigned number of adults. Compile the results in class to develop a rating for local dealerships.

3 Discussion Starter Have students discuss with parents and friends the amounts they have paid for new cars in relation to the sticker price. Discuss the stories in class. What generalizations can be made about the prices they can expect to pay?

experiences with various dealers. Ask the
1 following questions.

1. If you traded in a car, did the seller give you a reasonable deal?
2. Did the dealer seem genuinely concerned about you getting the car you wanted and that it performed well?
3. Was your car delivered in good condition, ready for use?
4. Does the dealer honor warranties readily, or is it always a problem to get performance according to contract? (A **warranty** is a written guarantee of the soundness of a product. It covers parts and labor for a specific amount of time, and also states what the manufacturer will do if the product is defective.)
2
5. Is the service department good, honest, and staffed with competent mechanics?
6. Is it often necessary to take a car back more than once before mechanical problems are corrected?
7. Does the dealer provide you with a loaner, or substitute vehicle, when your car must be kept in the shop overnight? Insurance policies sometimes prohibit dealers from supplying loaners to their customers.
8. Is the service department open at night and on weekends?

Reading the Sticker

Visit several showrooms and inspect the cars on the floor. Talk with the salespeople and study the sticker prices, miles-per-gallon information, and other data.

Each new car is required by law to have a price sticker posted on its window. The **sticker price** is the manufacturer's list price, printed on a sticker affixed to the window of a car. Study the new-car sticker shown in Figure 22–2. It will tell you the selling price of the car with standard equipment. It will list the options on the particular model and
3 their cost.

Test-Driving a Car

If you are interested in a car, test-drive it or one that is very similar to it. Plan the test route in advance so that you drive in different kinds of traffic, at various speeds, and on different surfaces (such as residential, highways, and roads in various states of repair).

Settling Terms

Having carefully selected a dealer, analyzed and compared sticker prices, and test-driven a few cars, you are now in a good position to make an offer. Some cars sell for less than their sticker

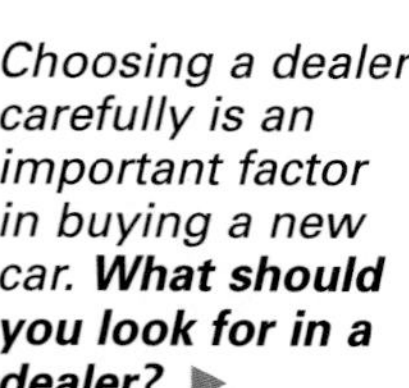

Choosing a dealer carefully is an important factor in buying a new car. ***What should you look for in a dealer?*** ▶

Caption Answer: Look for a dealer with a good reputation and who has been in business for several years.

prices. Just how much the discount will be depends on several considerations. Two important factors are demand for the particular model and how late it is in
1 the model year when you buy.

When new models are already available, dealers are given a discount on old models that remain in inventory and can offer you the car you want for a lower price. Also, a car is already depreciated at the end of the model year, even though it has never been driven. It is, after all, a year old. If you do not plan to trade it in within two or three years, this fact may not concern you greatly.

Accepting Delivery

Do not accept delivery or make payment on the car until you have thoroughly test-driven it. At this point, in the purchase process, you are in the best position to have any deficiencies corrected. Do not agree to "wait until the thousand-mile checkup" to have any work done. Even with this precaution, you must expect to take the car back for adjustments as the need arises.

BUYING A USED CAR

The first car a person buys is often a used car. If you plan to buy such a vehicle, follow the same steps as a new-car buyer. First, plan carefully. Decide how you will use the vehicle. Consider how much you can afford to pay for it. Select
2 the size, options, and performance fea-
3 tures you require.

The steps in shopping for the vehicle are also similar. They take on added importance, however, because the car is

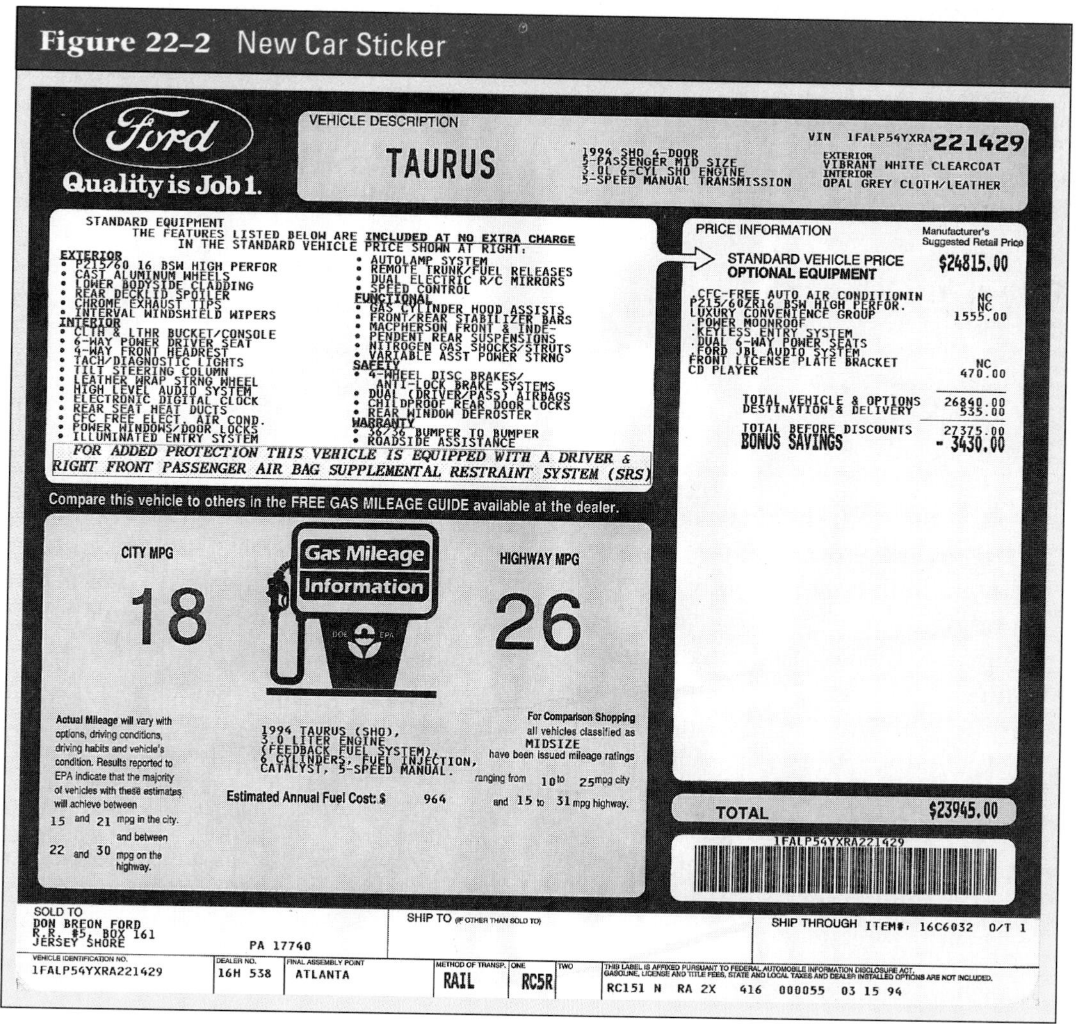

Figure 22–2 New Car Sticker

1 Discussion Starter
Ask students what they think about haggling over the price of a car, or anything else. For those who approve of haggling, do they want to do their own bargaining, or would they prefer to hire an expert?

2 Interesting Note
Tell students that Americans spend about $85 billion a year for used cars.

3 Student Motivator
Some students may have already purchased used cars. Encourage these students to recount their experiences. What tips can they offer? What would they do differently?

Caption Answer:
This car has an estimated rating of 26 miles per gallon. Its estimated annual fuel cost is $964.

◀ ***What is the highway MPG rating of this car? What is its estimated annual fuel cost?***

FLASHBACK FLASHFORWARD

New auto technology comes with a price. In 1962, a Saab automobile sold for just $1,895. Today, Saab's lowest priced car sells for about $20,000.

1 Learning Economics Ask students to explain why they could expect to pay a dealer more than they would pay an individual for the same car. (Dealer must include cost of doing business in selling price.)

2 Extension Tell students that if they buy a stolen car, the rightful owner can reclaim it. They can sue the person who sold them the car, but such a person may be hard to find.

3 Critical Thinking Ask students how they can know whether or not a car is being used as security. (The person owed the money will probably be holding the title, which means the "owner" won't be able to produce it when asked.)

not new. There is a greater need to find an honest and reliable dealer. He or she, and not the manufacturer, will stand behind the car. There is a greater need to inspect the car and test-drive it. Both procedures can keep you from making someone else's problems your own.

There is more extensive information available on used cars than on new ones. Professionals conduct road tests on cars and report difficulties experienced: handling and electrical problems, for example. They note safety hazards encountered, like poor braking and blind spots. Cars that have been on the market for several months develop reputations for performance, and these, along with recalls, are often reported in newspapers, magazines, and on television. In addition, *Consumer Reports* provides frequency-of-repair reports on older cars. You can easily look up these reports for the vehicle makes, models, and years that interest you. This same magazine on occasion has identified what it considers to be the "worst cars" through the years and "used cars to avoid."

Choosing Where to Buy a Used Car

When it comes to selecting a used car, you have a wide choice of sellers. Major sources include:

- *Private parties.* Individuals often place classified ads in newspapers, community bulletin boards, and the like offering their vehicles for sale. You may not receive a meaningful guarantee of a car's condition, but if you or someone you know is knowledgeable about cars, buying from a private party can save you money. Private party prices are generally lower than those at a dealer. Make sure the individual has clear title to
1 the car before agreeing to buy it.
2 - *New-car dealers.* Some consumers pre-
3 fer to buy used cars from a new-car dealer. They believe that more attractive automobiles are traded in to new-car dealers than elsewhere because they are more selective about the cars they keep on their lots. New-car dealers often sell "program cars"—current-year autos that were used as rental cars for a time and then resold to dealers. There is a high demand for these vehicles because many people feel they are buying "almost new" cars at used-car prices.
- *Used-car dealers.* Some people prefer used-car dealers because selling used cars is their specialty. Consumers who feel this way often prefer to trade with *independent used-car dealers*—sellers who are not associated with new-car agencies. Independent dealers, such consumers reason, have only one goal: to develop reputations for selling good used cars.

You should always take the time to find out which used-car firms are reliable. Have residents in the community been satisfied with cars purchased there? Is service good? Does the firm have a well-regarded reputation? Does the dealer carry out the terms of warranties? How long has the business been in the community?

Some dealers will supply customers with the names and telephone numbers of previous owners of cars. You can then call the original owners and ask about the performance of cars in which you are interested.

Inspecting and Accepting Delivery of a Used Car

If you're serious about a particular used car, you should give the vehicle a thorough visual check. If it passes this

inspection, take it for a test drive. It is essential in this case that you drive the specific car in which you are interested. On a used-car lot, there is no such thing
1 as a demonstrator.

On-Lot Inspection

The first and most important item to check when you are inspecting a used car is the **odometer.** This is the device

1 Student Motivator If possible, arrange for an automotive teacher in your school or district to give a demonstration of how to inspect a used car. Another possibility would be to have students arrange for friends or relatives who are auto mechanics to visit the class and provide tips on checking out used cars.

Fame, Fortune, and Charity

It is hard to imagine actor Paul Newman in an apron. Among friends, however, the star was known to make a really mean salad dressing. It was so good that in 1981, Newman's friend, writer A. E. Hotchner, persuaded him to market it. Newman agreed, but on one condition: all profits were to go to charity.

Newman and his wife, actress Joanne Woodward, have long believed that celebrities have a responsibility to give something back to society. They have always been active in sponsoring and supporting charities.

No one suspected the boost that Newman's Own Salad Dressing would give to their philanthropic efforts. By 1984, Newman's Own had donated $4 million to charities large and small. By the early 1990s, the figure was more than $56 million.

Newman and Hotchner have a lot of fun running the company and promoting the product, but they take the charity side of the business seriously. They oversee the process of choosing donation recipients. They choose organizations such as the AIDS Medical Foundation, the Cystic Fibrosis Foundation, and the Alzheimer's Disease Association. They also support small charities such as the Hope Rural School and Children's Storefront.

In 1986, Newman's Own took on the challenge of building a 47-acre summer camp in Connecticut for children with leukemia and other kinds of blood diseases. The Hole-in-the-Wall Camp was named after the hideout of Butch Cassidy and the Sundance Kid (characters in a movie starring Paul Newman and Robert Redford). In the summer, the camp would be a playground for the children. In the winter, the camp would host seminars for doctors and children's parents. Paul Newman has great fun adding new products to his line. He gets even more pleasure from seeing the money help others.

Brainstorm

If your class wanted to sell food products to teenagers to benefit charities that helped teenagers, what kinds of products could you develop from home recipes?

Case Study Answer: Fudge and other candies; cookies and granola bars; fruit drinks; muffins; vegetable and chip dips; pasta sauces; salad dressings.

1 Interesting Note
The National Highway Traffic Safety Administration estimates that vehicle odometers are rolled back an average of 30,000 miles a car on three million vehicles a year. Tell students that although the odometer law is difficult to enforce, authorities do enforce it. As an example, in one case the verdict resulted in a jail term of 11 years and a fine of $351,000.

News Clip Answers:
1 The key benefit will be safety. Collision alarms, automatic brakes, and engine monitoring systems will make operating a car easier and less dangerous.
2 Cost. Consumers will not be able to afford every innovation that is technically possible. Automakers will have to limit new gadgets to items that consumers will value and be willing to pay for.

Caption Answer:
Talk to family members, friends, or teachers about their experiences in buying used cars. Research potential problems in the library.

that tells you how many miles the car has been driven. It is against the law for
1 a seller to turn back the odometer.

When you buy, the dealer must supply you with a disclosure form revealing the true mileage driven. This form can be checked against the one prepared when the car was traded in. The more miles a car has been driven, the more likely it is to need major repairs in the near future. Of course, much depends on how much care was given to the car by the previous owner. The condition of the brake and accelerator pedals and the appearance of the upholstery also indicate age and use. You should check all of these for excessive wear. There are a number of other features that should be examined as well.

1. Tires. Examine the depth of the tire tread on all four wheels. The **tire tread** is the molded pattern on the part of a tire that comes in contact with the road. Uneven wear can indicate a number of problems, including the need for front-end work or the replacement of struts.
2. Interior panels. Check roof and door interiors especially for signs of leaks. These include watermarks on upholstery or trim and swelling or buckling of interior trim panels. If possible, lift the floorboard mats.
3. Exterior panels. Check the finish for signs of rust or pitting. Remember, it is common to try and mask such problems with a coat of paint. As an added precaution, examine underneath fenders and doors. Check along window moldings, as well.
4. Exterior trim and panel alignment. Check for misalignment (poor alignment) of exterior trim that extends across two or more panels. Be sure the spaces between panels are even. Look for bulges or hollows. All are possible indications that a car has been damaged and hastily repaired.
5. Engine leaks. Look under the car to see if oil, coolant, or transmission fluid has leaked from the vehicle. All could signal the need for a major repair.
6. Start up the car. With the engine running, test the headlights, turn signals, windshield wipers, heating and cooling systems, radio (if present), and any safety signals or buzzers.

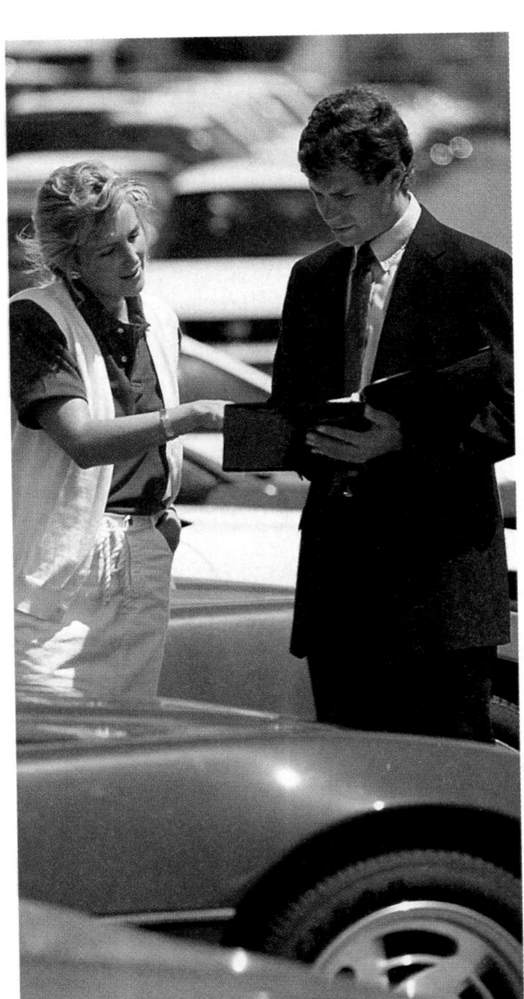

The on-site inspection is an important step in choosing a used car. ***How would you prepare to conduct a successful inspection?*** ▶

Test-Driving

You should follow the same procedure for test-driving a car whether it is new or used. Give special attention to braking, shifting, turning, comfort, and ease of operation. Be alert for knocks, noises, and rattles, all of which may signal malfunctions. Study the exhaust for blue or blue-white smoke, evidence of several possible problems.

Arrange to have a reliable mechanic or a **diagnostic center** conduct a thorough check of the vehicle. Diagnostic

CASE STUDY

Consumer NEWS CLIP

Smart's the Word in Detroit

by Leon Jaroff with William McWhirter and Joseph R. Szczesny
Time February 6, 1995

Automobile industry executives who not long ago stubbornly fought the federal imposition of such now widely accepted technical items as seat belts, air bags, and emission controls are taking the lead in pushing high-tech innovation. The auto industry and its suppliers are spending $24 billion a year between them in advanced engineering and electronic research—more than a quarter of the nation's entire annual $90 billion research-and-development expenditures.

This kind of high-tech research in the labs of the Big Three and their suppliers is speeding the development of on-board sensors and diagnostic systems that will constitute the central nervous systems of brainy new cars. For example, the blind spot that [is] not visible in [a] side-view mirror will be monitored by a tiny infrared sidelight on the driver's door. A passing vehicle will cause a reflection of that light back to a receptor, triggering the dashboard warning light and buzzer.

A forward-looking, infrared, radar-like device will perform a similar function, bouncing light waves off objects in front of the vehicle, then timing the arrival of the reflected waves and signaling when it senses danger. That signal will set in motion actions that disengage cruise control, throttle the engine and, in the case of another car's cutting too close in front, even apply the brakes.

Still other sensors will track and record the wear on parts and systems, alerting the driver to potential trouble, and will even flash a warning when pressure in the tires is too low. "We're putting on every vehicle what used to be a $1 million diagnostic system," says Tim Hoen, Ford's manager of diagnostic-services planning. "It's a cradle-to-grave mechanical system."

Of course, getting smart costs money, as do the growing number of federally mandated improvements, and Detroit is passing on a good part of that cost to consumers. In recent months, average spending on a new car has exceeded $20,000 for the first time ever, and Ford economists predict this cost will rise to $30,000 by 2002. Indeed, the average family now spends more than half its annual income for a new car, compared with only a third in 1974. And the 4.7 percent average price rise for the new model year is running ahead of the current 2.7 percent annual increase in the cost of living. "We are in the middle of a value crisis in the industry," says the University of Michigan's Cole. "The industry has been feeding its customers so many things that they believe they couldn't live without, but that they can't afford. We are really pushing the customer very hard here."

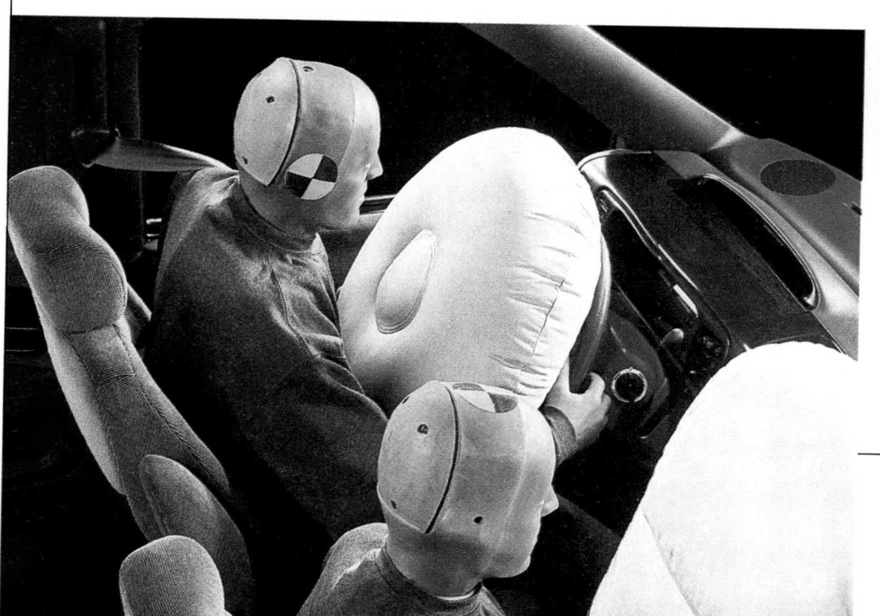

Decisions, Decisions

1. What will be some of the benefits of the high-tech innovations for cars?
2. What would be a key factor limiting those innovations? Why?

1 Discussion Starter Ask students whether they would prefer to buy a car every five years, or lease a new one every third year. Would it bother them to pay out all that money for transportation and then, at the end of three years, still not own a car?

centers use electronic and other instruments to locate problems. If the car needs (or will soon need) extensive repairs, reject it.

Before accepting delivery, read the contract carefully. Be sure you understand all warranty provisions. Check to see that all points agreed upon verbally are included in writing. Assure yourself that all repairs have been made.

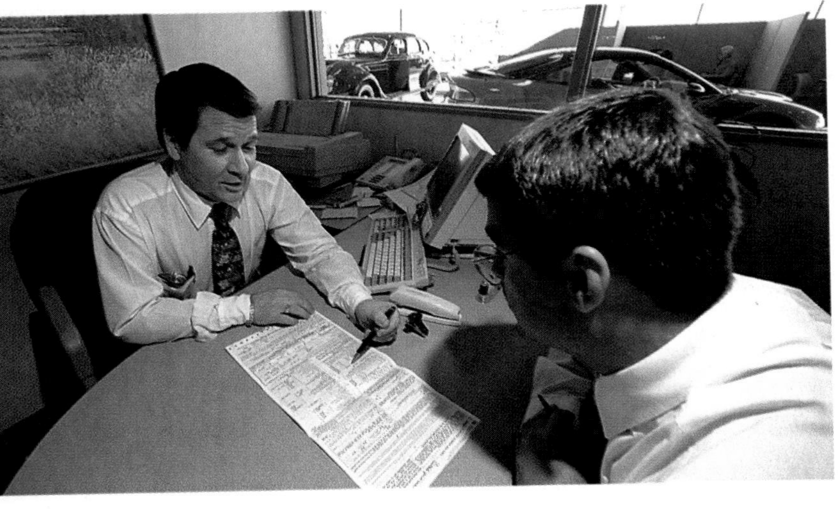

▲ *Reading the final contract before purchasing your car is your last opportunity to negotiate any changes.* ***What steps would you take to make sure any needed changes had been made?***

Caption Answer: Ask the dealer for a copy of the work order; perform your own inspection; take a final test drive.

LEASING A CAR

As prices of cars have escalated, the leasing, or renting, of cars has become increasingly popular. Those who lease say that doing so enables them to drive an up-to-date car that they could not afford to buy outright. Many who choose to *buy* instead of lease insist that, in the long run, they will pay less for transportation. Of course people who buy a car on credit may be expected to make a large down payment on a new car and make monthly payments that are often larger than monthly leasing fees. When their obligations are met, however, they own the car. When a leasing contract ends, the *dealer* still owns the car.

If you are thinking about leasing, be sure you get all the figures in advance so you can compare the cost of leasing and the cost of purchasing. Include insurance, taxes, and maintenance charges in the computations, as you will be responsible for these even if you are only leasing. Also, it is customary for the lessee (the consumer, in this case) to make a security deposit at the time of signing. It is to cover damages, excess mileage, missed payments, and the like. The unused amount is refunded.

There have been many drawbacks to leasing. If the consumer terminates the lease early, he or she faces stiff penalties. Sometimes, there is confusion over "excessive wear and tear" on cars at the end of a lease. There have even been documented cases in which consumers who thought they were buying cars were, in truth, only leasing them.

There are two kinds of leases: the open end and the closed end. Under the closed-end lease, one pays monthly leasing fees and, at the end of the term (often three years), turns in the car and "walks away." Only if there is excess mileage or substantial damage to the car, as from an accident, is an additional charge made.

Under the open-end lease, the lease specifies what the residual (left over) value of the car will be at the end of the contract. The lessee may buy the car for the residual amount upon expiration of the lease. What happens if he or she does not want to exercise this option to buy? If the appraised value at that time does not equal the predetermined residual value, the lessee usually must pay the difference up to a stated maximum amount. Most consumers object to the uncertainty of this obligation, and insist upon the closed-end lease.

At one time, people agreed that nobody could save money by leasing instead of buying a vehicle. However, the leasing business has become very competitive. Many dealers who lease cars are making such attractive, money-saving offers today that the leasing alternative is worth considering. Plus, the Federal Reserve Board is trying to eliminate the
1 abuses that exist in the leasing business.

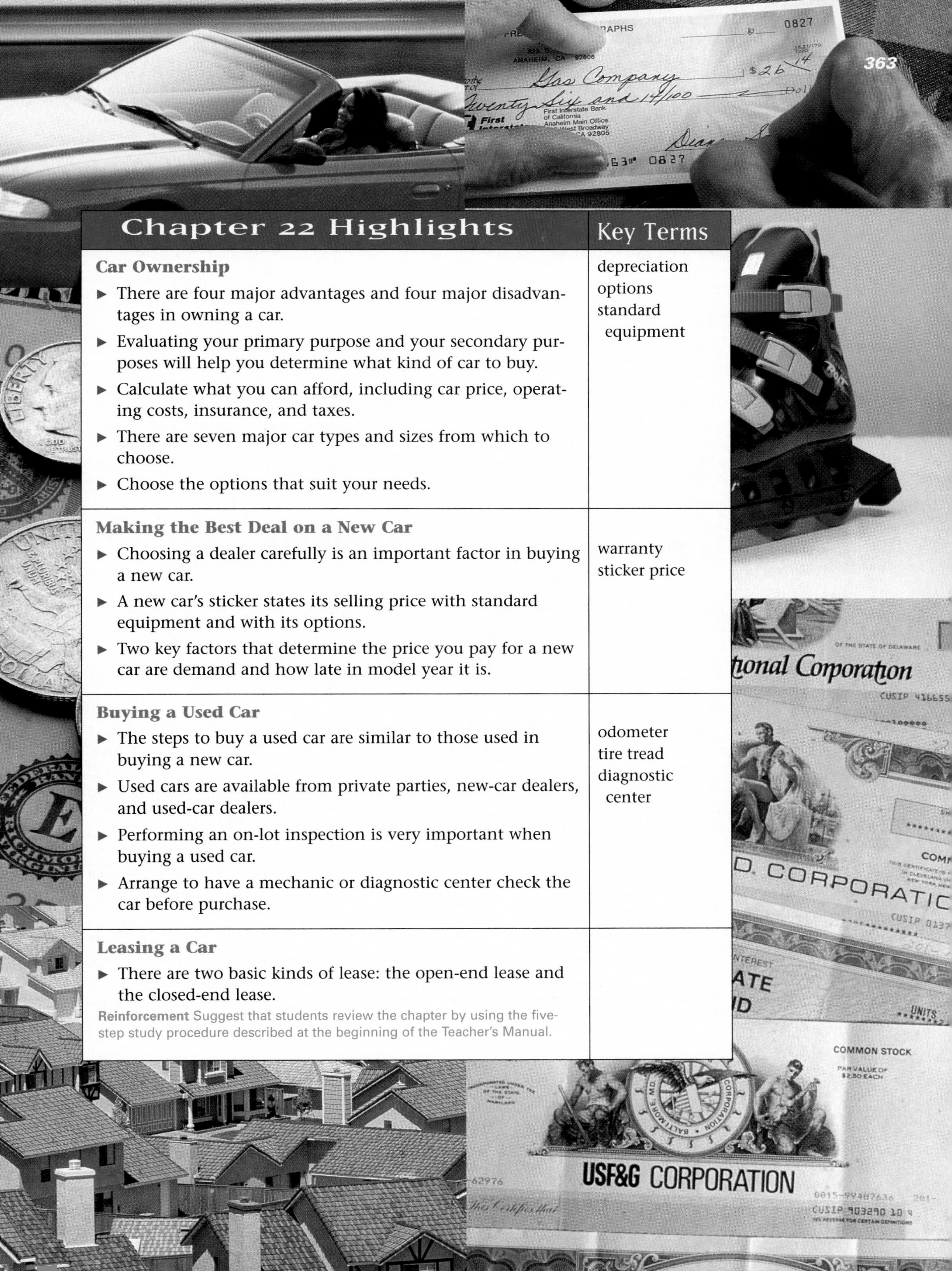

Chapter 22 Highlights	Key Terms
Car Ownership ▸ There are four major advantages and four major disadvantages in owning a car. ▸ Evaluating your primary purpose and your secondary purposes will help you determine what kind of car to buy. ▸ Calculate what you can afford, including car price, operating costs, insurance, and taxes. ▸ There are seven major car types and sizes from which to choose. ▸ Choose the options that suit your needs.	depreciation options standard equipment
Making the Best Deal on a New Car ▸ Choosing a dealer carefully is an important factor in buying a new car. ▸ A new car's sticker states its selling price with standard equipment and with its options. ▸ Two key factors that determine the price you pay for a new car are demand and how late in model year it is.	warranty sticker price
Buying a Used Car ▸ The steps to buy a used car are similar to those used in buying a new car. ▸ Used cars are available from private parties, new-car dealers, and used-car dealers. ▸ Performing an on-lot inspection is very important when buying a used car. ▸ Arrange to have a mechanic or diagnostic center check the car before purchase.	odometer tire tread diagnostic center
Leasing a Car ▸ There are two basic kinds of lease: the open-end lease and the closed-end lease. **Reinforcement** Suggest that students review the chapter by using the five-step study procedure described at the beginning of the Teacher's Manual.	

CHAPTER 22 REVIEW

Refer students to the Reviewing Consumer Terms and Reviewing Facts and Ideas activities in the Student Activity Workbook.

Reviewing Consumer Terms Essays will vary. See Glossary for definitions.

Reviewing Facts and Ideas See the Student Activity Workbook for answers.

Problem Solving and Decision Making **1** Student maps should include a variety of driving condition. **2** People who value safety tend to favor the car at Dealership A. People who routinely carry very few passengers may favor Dealer B.

Consumers Around the World Social Studies **1** Student reports should answer all questions.

Communications **2** Student reports should answer all questions.

Technology **3** Student reports should answer all questions.

Reviewing Consumer Terms

Use each of the following terms in an essay about buying new and used cars.

depreciation
diagnostic center
odometer
options
standard equipment
sticker price
tire tread
warranty

Reviewing Facts and Ideas

1. Name four advantages and four disadvantages in buying a new car.
2. Describe the seven major car sizes and types.
3. What percentage of disposable income is the average amount spent on owning and operating a car?
4. What steps should be followed in making an on-lot inspection of a used car?
5. Suggest two sources of help in evaluating a used car.
6. Describe the differences between an open-end lease and a closed-end lease.

Problem Solving and Decision Making

1. Choose a local dealership. Then plan the route that you would take when test-driving a car from its lot. List streets and highways by name or number and tell why you included them. As an alternative, draw a simple map of the route and label the relevant road test features.
2. Assume that you locate two automobiles that are, as nearly as you can tell, identical in almost all their features. One is for sale by Dealer A at $6,500. It is equipped with dual air bags. Dealer B offers the other at $5,500. It has only a driver-side air bag. Which car would you buy? Why?

Building Academic Skills

Consumers Around the World

Social Studies

1. Research what size and type of car is most popular in a country of your choice. What options do people in that country favor? What percent of disposable income do people spend on owing and operating a car? Summarize your findings in an oral report to the class.

Communications

2. Electric cars are touted by some as an answer to the pollution problems generated by gas-powered cars. Prepare a 500-word report on the status of electric cars. Are they available to the public at large? What do they cost? How environmentally friendly are they?

Technology

3. The establishment of diagnostic centers to quickly assess a car's problems is a great asset for today's consumer. Go to the library and

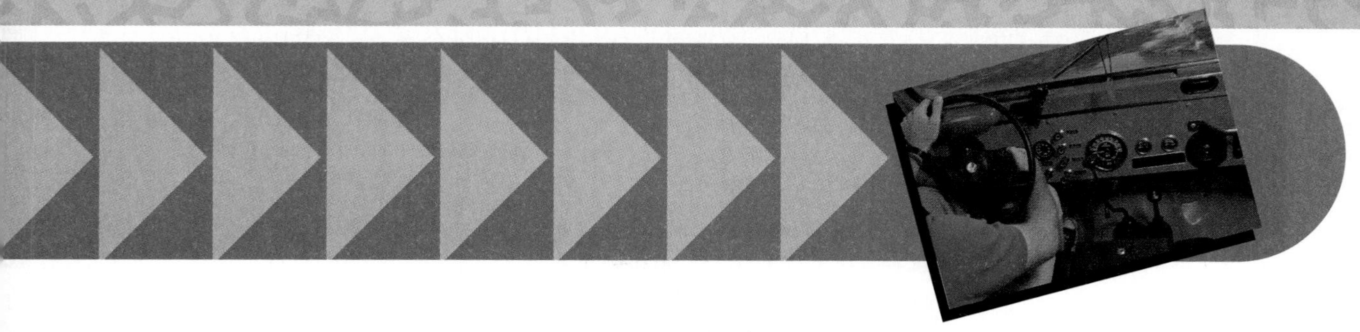

research what future improvements technology may bring owners of cars. Report your findings in a 250-word report.

Beyond the Classroom

Consumer Projects

1. EPA mileage figures for new cars are released in September of each year. In newspapers or magazines, locate the most recent figures. As preparation for a classroom discussion, list the five vehicles with the best performance records. Also record the nature of the tests conducted by the EPA to arrive at their figures.
2. Using the school parking lot for a location, prepare and present a skit titled "Buying a Used Car." The skit should show how a person goes about choosing such a vehicle. The checks and procedures mentioned in this chapter should be emphasized and demonstrated.
3. Check the classified section of your local newspaper for used car ads. Compare those ads placed by dealers and those placed by individuals. (If possible, find vehicles of similar make, model, and year.) How do the prices compare? Are the same features emphasized? Account for any differences.

Cooperative Learning

Family Economics

Break into assigned family groups. Discuss the following problem.

Assume your family has ruled out a new car because they think it would be too expensive. You are now choosing between three used cars: (1) a twelve-year-old station wagon affectionately called "The Pig" by its owner because "it's big, ugly, and swills gasoline" ($850 or best offer); (2) a four-year-old Star, a domestic sedan that seats five and has a V6 engine ($3,500 at the local Star dealership); (3) a six-year-old Toto, a small station wagon that has only half the passenger and hauling capacity of the Pig and a smaller engine than the Star ($4,200 at Stan's Used Cars). Which of these vehicles would you investigate as a possibility and why? What, if any, reservations would you have about any of the cars? Compare your answers with those of other family groups.

Debate the Issue

Federal, state, and local governments invest major tax dollars to build and maintain the vast system of highways, roads, and bridges that exists in the United States. Some people feel that too much money is spent supporting this network and it is spent at the expense of creating a better public transportation network. Others think a sound system of roads is necessary for economic growth and something many Americans are committed to.

You and your classmates will break into two groups and research this topic. Each group will gather evidence to support one side or the other. You are to prepare the argument for your side of the problem. Then the two groups will meet in a classroom debate.

Consumer Projects
1 Students should list the five vehicles and the types of tests given. **2** Skits should use procedures discussed in chapter. **3** Students should answer all questions.

Family Economics
All of these used cars are priced lower than the smallest, poorest-built new car. The Toto has a fine reputation for quality but perhaps too small an engine for a station wagon. The Star might be a better choice because it has a more powerful engine, may be a bit bigger, and (judging from its source) is probably in mint condition. The Pig has the greatest potential problems given its age and is probably in need of body work (it's "ugly"), but its size and price make it the only possible choice for Family 8.

Debate the Issue
Break the class into two teams. Assign each team one side of the issue. Encourage students to work together as a team to develop their argument. Ask each team to select a member to make an opening statement that supports their side of the issue. Have students take turns debating as the debate moves from one team to another.

CHAPTER 23 Owning a Car

Learning Objectives

When you have finished studying this chapter, you should be able to:

1. Identify possible sources of automobile loans.
2. Plan a maintenance schedule to preserve the value of a car.
3. Describe the difference between a full warranty and a limited warranty.
4. Explain how to exercise your basic rights under the lemon law.
5. List smart driving steps.

Consumer Terms

title
maintenance schedule
full warranty
limited warranty
lemon laws

Real-World Journal

Ask an adult for two receipts he or she has for automobile repairs or maintenance. Write the type of work performed on the car and the price in your journal. Note whether any of this work was covered by a warranty. Summarize your findings in your journal.

Lesson Plan See the Teacher's Manual for Chapter 23 lesson plan.

Vocabulary The Chapter 23 lesson plan includes suggested vocabulary activities for the items listed.

1 Discussion Starter Ask students to talk to car owners about their experiences with ownership. Has it been what they thought it would be?

2 Reinforcement Tell students that when General Motors offered 3 percent financing for new cars, no bank or other lending institution could match that rate.

OWNERSHIP MEANS RESPONSIBILITY

Once you've decided what car to buy and have completed the purchasing process, you'll drive your new purchase off the lot. Now, these wheels belong to you. It's a wonderful feeling to own something you can drive around in, but it's also a serious step that means you'll have to act responsibly. Some of the important responsibilities of ownership include making payments under a financing arrangement, maintaining the car, and operating it in a careful and
1 energy-efficient manner.

Driving in Norway

Norway's roads are known for many curves, and by law, drivers must keep their headlights on at all times. Gasoline costs about $3.00 a gallon (compared with about $1.20 in the United States). Drivers on a weekend trip need to fill up early because most businesses are closed by 2:00 P.M. on Saturday and all day Sunday.

FINANCING ARRANGEMENTS

Today, even a used car can cost a considerable sum of money. Because of this, most people do not pay cash when they purchase a car. Instead, they make a down payment and finance the balance through monthly payments.

Loan Sources

When buying automobiles, many people obtain loans from banks and credit unions. Loans can also be obtained from car dealers. In recent years, many dealers have offered attractive loans to attract
2 buyers to car models that are overstocked.

It pays to discuss the terms of a loan with a loan officer before you make your final decision on a car. You'll need to know whether you qualify for a loan before you get your heart set on that shiny red convertible you've taken for a

Owning a car for the first time is very exciting. ***Besides maintaining the car, what are two other responsibilities of car ownership?*** ▶

Caption Answer: Making payments under a financing arrangement, and operating your car in a careful and energy-efficient manner.

test drive several times this month. With the loan officer, figure out how much you can afford to put down on the car, and how much you will need to borrow. Then, ask the officer what the interest rate on the loan will be, and what your monthly payments will be. Ask yourself if you can afford it, given your monthly budget. If you plan to trade in a car on your new purchase, tell the officer the year, make, and model of the trade-in. He or she can estimate its value, assuming that it is in good condition. You will want to keep this estimate in mind when
1 you discuss prices with dealers.

Until your loan is paid in full, the bank or other lender will keep your **title,** which is a legal paper that shows who owns the automobile. You should receive a photocopy of the title for your use in the meantime.

Down Payments

The larger the down payment you make, the less you will have to pay in monthly finance charges. If possible, your down payment should be large. However, it should not put your savings below a certain minimum level that you've set. Most people would agree that at least three months' income should be kept on hand in savings at all times. Others suggest even more. Be sure that your down payment does not ruin your savings goals.

Monthly Payments

Monthly payments depend on the length of the repayment period. The longer the period, the smaller the monthly payment will be. However, when payments are small and spread over a long period such as five years, you pay more in finance charges, otherwise known as interest on your loan. This fact means that your car will cost you considerably more than the amount for which you originally bargained. Also, your monthly payments will remain the same even though the value of your car declines over time.

How large should your monthly payment be? Figure how much you need each month to meet your normal living expenses. Be sure to include an amount for savings. Now subtract these figures from your take-home pay. The amount that is left will be the amount you have available for meeting not only car payments but all other expenses connected with operating the vehicle. In general, if the car you want will cost you more than 13 percent of your take-home pay, it
2 may well become a burden.

Don't Pay the Extra Premium at the Gas Pump

A gallon of premium gas does not generate more energy than a gallon of regular, and your engine won't function better with premium fuel if it doesn't require it. Only about 10 percent of the nearly 200 million cars on American roads should use premium gasoline, which costs about 20 cents more per gallon than regular unleaded gas. To make sure you're not paying too much at the pump, check your owner's manual to determine what octane level your car requires. Those that need an octane level of 87 require regular unleaded gas. Premium gas is necessary only for those cars that need an octane level of 91 or higher and for some cars that are 10 years old or older.

1 Discussion Starter
Tell students that a foreign car manufacturer has introduced ten-year auto loans for its American buyers. A 25 percent down payment is required, but monthly payments are relatively low. Ask students if they would be willing to take out a loan of this type and to explain why or why not. Most people do not want to take ten years to pay off a car loan, since interest charges would be excessive and chances are good that the owner will want another car before then. Then, a large lump-sum payment would be necessary before the old car could be sold or traded in.

2 Reinforcement
Student Activity Workbook, Chapter 23 activities.

1 Interesting Note Experts warn owners to leave the transmission alone except for routine maintenance unless there is strong evidence of a problem. Preventive maintenance is advisable, but so is the old generalization, "If it isn't broken, don't fix it."

MAINTAINING YOUR CAR

Take care of a good car, and it will take care of you. You can depend on an automobile that is kept in good repair.

Automobile owners must watch for signs of wear and deterioration. They should apply touch-up paint and take other measures as needed to prevent rust. Periodic washing of the car is important, especially in northern states during snowy winter months when salt that has been spread on streets and highways gets on the finish and causes damage. The owner's manual, which comes with every new automobile, contains a **maintenance schedule,** which is a timetable for routine servicing and for checking or replacing parts (see
1 Figure 23–1).

All About Warranties

A warranty is a written guarantee of the soundness of a product. It says what the manufacturer will do if the product does not perform as it should.

Federal Requirements Passed in 1975, the Warranty-Federal Trade Commission Improvement Act has proved extremely valuable to consumers. It has

Following a maintenance schedule will help your car to operate efficiently. ***How often should you change the oil in a car?*** ▶

Caption Answer: Every 3,000 miles.

Figure 23–1 Maintenance Schedule

SCHEDULE I

Item No.	To Be Serviced (See Explanation of Services on pages following)	When to Perform Miles (Kilometers) or Months Whichever Occurs First
1	Engine Oil & Oil Filter Change*	Every 3,000 mi. (5,000 km) or 3 mos.
2	Chassis Lubrication	Every other oil change
3	Throttle Body Mounting Bolt Torque*	At 6,000 mi. (10,000 km) only
4	Tire & Wheel Inspection & Rotation	At 6,000 mi. (10,000 km), then every 15,000 mi. (25,000 km) or as necessary
5	Engine Accessory Drive Belt Inspection*	Every 30,000 mi. (50,000 km) or 24 mos.
6	Cooling System Service	
7	Front Wheel Bearing Repack (Brougham Only)	See "Explanation of Scheduled Maintenance Services" Following Schedule II
8	Transmission/Transaxle Service	
9	Throttle Body Inspection*	Every 30,000 mi. (50,000 km)
10	Spark Plug Wire Inspection*†	
11	EGR System Check*†	
12	Air Cleaner Filter & Positive Crankcase Ventilation (PCV) Filter (Brougham Only) Replacement*	
13	Engine Timing Check*	
14	Fuel Tank, Cap & Lines Inspection*†	
15	Spark Plug Replacement*	Every 100,000 mi. (160,000 km)
16	Rear Axle Fluid Change (Brougham)	See item 16 on page 24

* An Emission Control Service

† The US Environmental Protection Agency has determined that the failure to perform this maintenance item will not nullify the emission warranty or limit recall liability prior to the completion of vehicle useful life. General Motors, however, urges that all recommended maintenance service be performed at the indicated intervals.

MAINTENANCE WORK TO BE DONE

- Change Engine Oil & Filter
- Inspect and Rotate Tires/Wheels

made manufacturers provide straightforward and meaningful warranties and forced them to back up those warranties with action.

According to the act, which applies to other products besides cars, all written warranties must be clearly printed and worded. They must also be clearly labeled as either full or limited. A **full warranty** provides that if a defective product or part cannot be repaired after a reasonable number of attempts, the

Advocates for Boating Safety

In the summer months of 1993, the Robersons—Robby and April and their daughters Ashleigh (9 years old) and Katey (5 years old)—went out in the family boat on a river in Alabama. An aunt, uncle, and two cousins went along.

The girls' aunt and one cousin were in the water when, suddenly, a large boat came speeding toward the Robersons' boat. Robby had time to push the girls' uncle overboard and toss their other cousin into the safety of the water. However, he was unable to save his daughters. The Robersons' boat was rammed at high speed. Roberson and his wife were thrown overboard. The two girls were killed.

The young man who hit them had been partying with friends. He later said that he had not seen the Robersons' boat.

The Robersons began hearing of similar tragedies. They discovered that 300 people in Alabama had been killed in ten years in boating accidents. Alabama had no laws that required boaters to have training in boating safety. There was no minimum age requirement for operating a boat. In addition, boaters who caused disasters were seldom punished.

The Robersons founded the Alabama Better Boaters Association (ABBA). Although they had no funds, they began lobbying state representatives. They went door to door with a petition to enact stricter boating regulations.

The boat industry opposed them, saying that regulation would hurt the boat business. Nevertheless, the Robersons continued their efforts. In 1994, Alabama passed a boating law that required boat drivers to be licensed, and included a tough drunk-driving provision.

The Robersons still go out on the river. It is not the same without their daughters, but they know that they have helped make the rivers of Alabama safer for others.

Brainstorm

Some people think skateboarding is dangerous. Give some arguments for and against creating laws regulating skateboarding.

Case Study Answer:
For: Skateboarders on sidewalks run into people, especially the elderly, knocking them over or injuring them; skateboarders can be injured while jumping off curbs and over walls; skateboards that "get away" from the skateboarder can hurt people—especially small children—damage windows, cars; skateboarders using roadways can be injured in collisions with cars.
Against: Skateboarding is a clean, inexpensive hobby that provides exercise for kids; it is a cheap method of transportation and regulation could hurt its use; laws against skateboarding discriminate against the young; claims of injury and damage are exaggerated; if cities established skateboarding lanes, like bike lanes, accidents and collisions with cars and pedestrians could be prevented.

1 Discussion Starter
Ask students if they or anyone they know has ever received a free replacement of a "high-ticket" item.

2 Interesting Note
During the first two years the lemon law was in effect in Massachusetts, car owners won more than $3 million in arbitration cases.

Case Study Answers:
1 Sample answers: Auto mechanic, car dealership owner used car salesperson.
2 Sample answer: My mom drives me to school every day. If she couldn't do that anymore, I guess I could walk. It would probably take me about an hour. I'd have to get up earlier in the morning.

Caption Answer:
Yes. Used cars are required to have one of these notices attached.

manufacturer will give the consumer a refund or a new product or part. A **limited warranty** provides something less
1 than a full warranty. Replacement parts for the product may be free, for example, but not the cost of labor required to install them.

The act does not require that warranties be issued. It merely sets forth standards for those that are. Automakers are inclined to offer limited rather than full warranties in order to reduce their liability.

New-Car Warranties A consumer whose new car requires repairs covered by a warranty usually takes the vehicle to a dealership. The manufacturer later pays the dealership for making the repairs.

Manufacturers may word their warranties differently. Terms can vary as well. For example, Manufacturer A may guarantee vehicle parts and systems for 36 months or 36,000 miles, whichever is reached first. Manufacturer B may offer the same twelve-month protection but without the mileage limit. In addition to the basic warranty, some manufacturers provide special coverage for certain vehicle parts. Examples might include six years or 60,000 miles on the engine, transmission, and drive train, or five years or 50,000 miles on factory air conditioning. Thus, to know the limits of the car's protection, a consumer must read a warranty carefully.

Sometimes, however, being aware of warranty provisions is not enough. Some cars have so many problems (or such hard-to-diagnose problems) that warranty coverage is of little comfort to their owners. All fifty states have passed **lemon laws** designed to help people whose new cars are "lemons." The usual definition of a lemon is a new car that has not been successfully repaired after four attempts for the same defect or has been out of service for any defects for thirty days during one year or the warranty period, whichever is shorter. As a remedy, the law requires the manufac-
2 turer to replace such a car or to refund the customer's money.

Owners of seriously defective cars have responsibilities, too. They must usually give notice to the manufacturer before claiming their rights under a lemon law. They must also prove their case by keeping a detailed record of the problems they have had with the vehicle, including dated copies of repair orders.

Used-Car Buyers Guide Used car warranties are seldom given today. This is a new development, one that followed the federal government's issuing of its Used Car Rule. The rule requires used car dealers to attach a large sticker, called a Buyers Guide, to the window of each vehicle offered for sale. The guide is designed to tell customers the car's warranty status—that is, whether the car comes with a warranty (and, if so, what its terms are) or whether the car comes "as is" (without a warranty). The guide also reminds the buyer to get all promises in writing and to ask permission to have the vehicle inspected by his or her own mechanic. The reverse side of

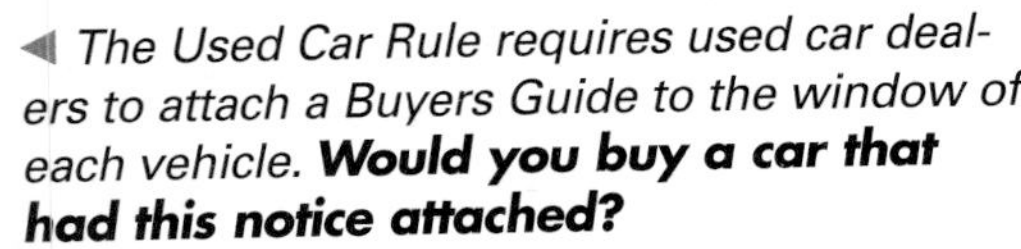

◀ *The Used Car Rule requires used car dealers to attach a Buyers Guide to the window of each vehicle.* ***Would you buy a car that had this notice attached?***

Csaba Csere, Editor-in-Chief, *Car and Driver*

Csaba Csere, editor-in-chief of *Car and Driver,* is as immersed in the world of cars as just about anyone else you could name. In his work as head of the largest car magazine in the country, he gets to drive all the cars that are available on the market, drive them before almost anyone else, discuss their quirks with the engineers who designed the vehicles, and share his views on the cars with more than a million eager readers. Csere is not, in other words, your ordinary car owner.

"You don't go into car journalism to make a lot of money or become a corporate tycoon," he explains. "You go into it because you love cars." Csere, 44, has been attracted to cars all his life. He first fell in love with one when he was a teenager and caught sight of a 1962 burgundy roadster Jaguar XKE sitting in front of a large white house with white pillars. "It was the most beautiful thing I had ever seen," he recalls.

Csaba Csere speaks from the point of view not only of a car enthusiast but also of a highly trained specialist. He earned a degree in mechanical engineering from the Massachusetts Institute of Technology, and did a stint designing engines for Ford before he found his way to *Car and Driver.*

His long-term, intimate immersion in car design, development, and driving has given Csere a deep respect for the power of the automobile. "Driving is a serious activity," he says. "You're not supposed to be bopping to music, shaving, or reading a paperback book while you drive.

Despite Csere's love and respect for the car, he is not—as might be expected—a car snob. "I have a wife and a child," he explains, "and I understand that you have to judge cars by whether they serve their intended purpose. Just because you need a minivan to haul your kids around doesn't mean you're a jerk. That's a perfectly valid need and there's a wide spectrum of driving satisfaction and driver interaction that can be achieved with a minivan."

So what's Csere's secret for someone who needs to buy a family car, or a car for business, or a car for practical reasons, but who wants to buy a car that's still fun? "You just have to step back from your emotions," he urges, "and do your research before you step into the showroom."

Case Study Review

1. The U.S. car industry is enormous, employing hundreds of thousands of Americans. Name five other types of jobs that have to do with the building, buying, selling, and using of cars.
2. Describe somewhere that you regularly get to by car. Now find out how you would get to where you wanted to go if you couldn't go by car. Describe how the new method would change your routine. (If you don't get anywhere by car, do this activity in reverse. How would driving change your routine?)

FLASHBACK FLASHFORWARD

Consumer expenditures on auto usage were $29.30 per capita in 1945. Forty-five years later, auto usage per capita reached $1,567.

1 Learning Economics Ask students why this practice will probably continue as long as all car dealers use it. (Dealers will avoid the extra expense associated with warranties as long as their competitors do the same.)

2 Reinforcement Student Activity Workbook, Chapter 23 activities.

3 Discussion Starter Ask students if they have ever seen the television commercial with the punch line, "You can pay me now, or you can pay me later." What is the point of this message? Do students know of anyone who has incurred a major expense because a simple inexpensive maintenance check was neglected?

4 Reinforcement Earlier, students read about the importance of finding reliable car dealers from whom to buy. Point out that the rule applies to maintenance also. It is especially important that those who know little about how an automobile works find someone they trust to do what's necessary to keep the car in good running order.

the form lists major defects that may
1 occur in a used car.

The purpose of the Used Car Rule was to provide complete and clear disclosure for used-car buyers. Nowhere did the rule state that dealers had to offer a particular kind of warranty or any specific warranty terms. Nonetheless, the used-car industry reacted as though it did. Dealers have almost universally chosen to sell their cars "as is." In most places, a Buyers Guide is affixed to the windows of all used cars.

Routine Maintenance

Some warranties contain provisions shifting the repair burden to the consumer if there is any evidence of not using a car or part or feature the way it was designed to be used. Failure to do routine maintenance also falls into this
2 category.

Consumers who are unfamiliar with the workings of an automobile under the hood may not know what should be checked and when. For them, the maintenance schedule provided by vehicle manufacturers is of special value. It alerts them to the need for periodic inspection of such features as hoses, spark plugs, brake linings, belts, timing, and fluid levels.

Checking fluid levels is especially important. Brake fluid, transmission fluid, engine oil, antifreeze-coolant all perform important functions. Figure 23–2 lists rou-
3 tine maintenance procedures most con-
4 sumers can check on their own.

SMART DRIVING

Drive sensibly if you want to have a safer trip, a smoother-running car, and lower fuel consumption. Follow these suggestions.

1. Avoid excessive speed. Don't exceed the posted speed limit. Drive slower under poor weather conditions.
2. Drive defensively. Watch out for other drivers and pay attention to traffic signs.

Figure 23-2 Routine Maintenance

There are several routine maintenance procedures consumers can perform themselves.

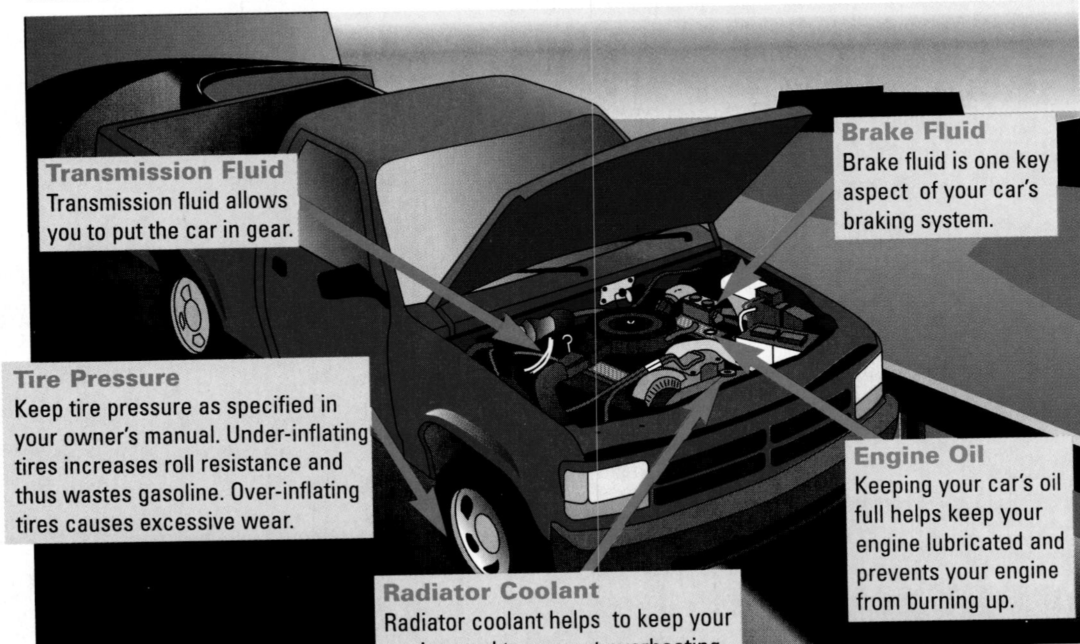

Transmission Fluid
Transmission fluid allows you to put the car in gear.
Brake Fluid
Brake fluid is one key aspect of your car's braking system.
Tire Pressure
Keep tire pressure as specified in your owner's manual. Under-inflating tires increases roll resistance and thus wastes gasoline. Over-inflating tires causes excessive wear.
Engine Oil
Keeping your car's oil full helps keep your engine lubricated and prevents your engine from burning up.
Radiator Coolant
Radiator coolant helps to keep your engine cool to prevent overheating.

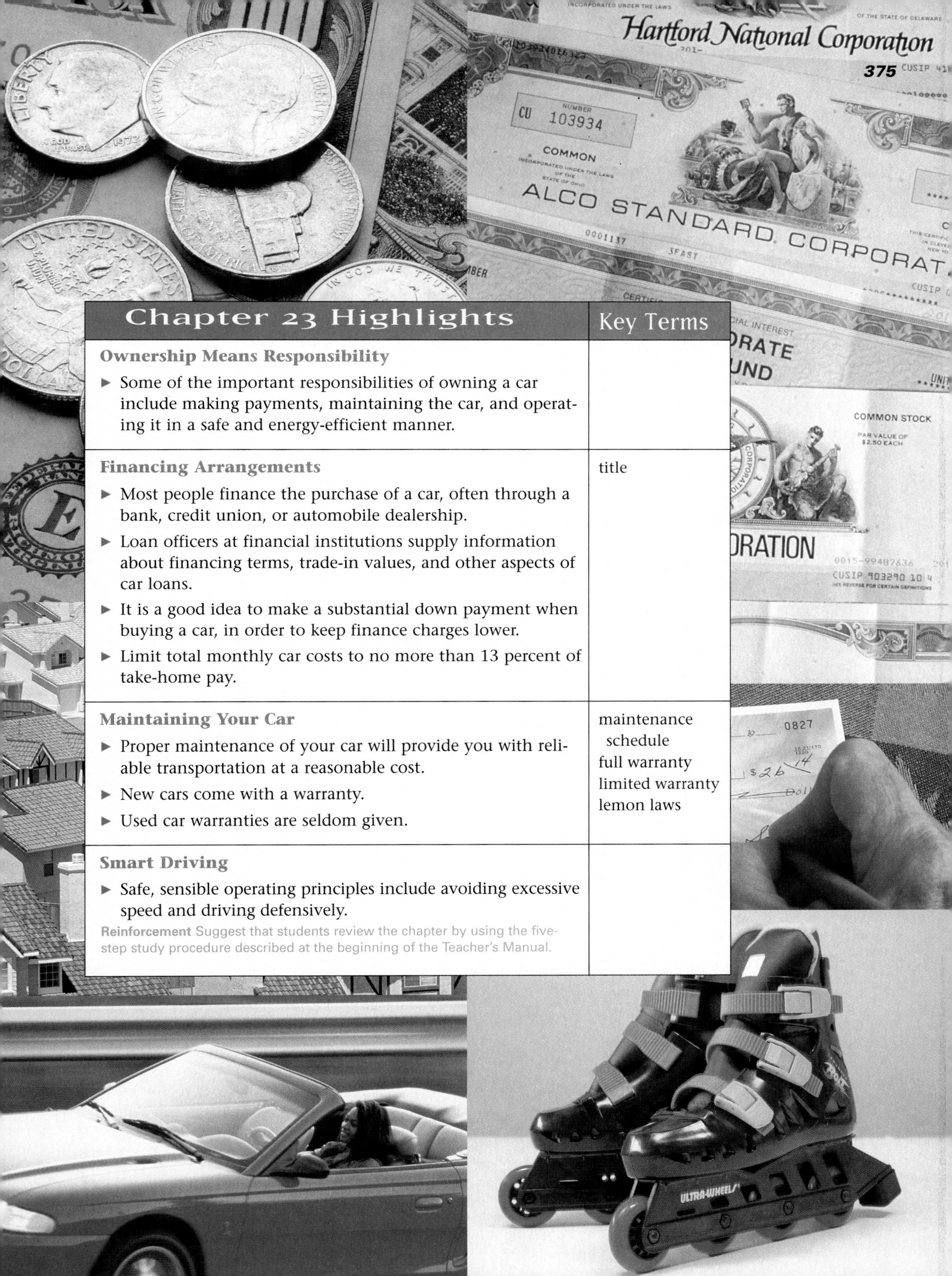

Chapter 23 Highlights	Key Terms
Ownership Means Responsibility ► Some of the important responsibilities of owning a car include making payments, maintaining the car, and operating it in a safe and energy-efficient manner.	
Financing Arrangements ► Most people finance the purchase of a car, often through a bank, credit union, or automobile dealership. ► Loan officers at financial institutions supply information about financing terms, trade-in values, and other aspects of car loans. ► It is a good idea to make a substantial down payment when buying a car, in order to keep finance charges lower. ► Limit total monthly car costs to no more than 13 percent of take-home pay.	title
Maintaining Your Car ► Proper maintenance of your car will provide you with reliable transportation at a reasonable cost. ► New cars come with a warranty. ► Used car warranties are seldom given.	maintenance schedule full warranty limited warranty lemon laws
Smart Driving ► Safe, sensible operating principles include avoiding excessive speed and driving defensively. **Reinforcement** Suggest that students review the chapter by using the five-step study procedure described at the beginning of the Teacher's Manual.	

CHAPTER 23 REVIEW

Refer students to the Reviewing Consumer Terms and Reviewing Facts and Ideas activities in the Student Activity Workbook.

Reviewing Consumer Terms
Sentences will vary. See the Glossary for definitions.

Reviewing Facts and Ideas
See the Student Activity Workbook for answers.

Problem Solving and Decision Making
1 $819.48
2 Answers will depend on students' perspectives, but an extended warranty could be worth more than $250.

Consumers Around the World
Math
1 Students should complete a graph showing their findings.

Technology
2 Student reports should answer all questions.

Communications
3 Student reports should cover history and application of lemon laws.

Reviewing Consumer Terms

Use each of the following terms in a sentence to demonstrate you know its meaning.

full warranty
lemon laws
limited warranty
maintenance schedule
title

Reviewing Facts and Ideas

1. Name three sources for buying a car.
2. Describe the difference between a full warranty and a limited warranty.
3. In deciding how much you can afford as a down payment on a car, what factors must you consider?
4. What items are usually included in a maintenance schedule?
5. Identify some of the fluid levels that you would check as part of routine vehicle maintenance.

Problem Solving and Decision Making

1. Today, financing a car over a period of four or more years is not unusual. (Many consumers have found that automobile prices are rising faster than their incomes.) Consider the following terms on a $12,000 auto loan:
a. $398.57 a month for 36 months
b. $316.00 a month for 48 months

How much would a buyer save by paying for the car in three years instead of four?

2. Assume you are buying a new car. The dealer offers to extend the full warranty for another year or reduce the price of the car by $250. Which alternative would you choose and why?

Building Academic Skills

Consumers Around the World

Math

1. The cost of a new car has soared over the past 20 years. Compare the cost of one automaker's four-door family sedan, and how it has risen over the past 20 years, with the cost-of-living over the same period. Select another country and compare the cost of a family sedan in that country with the cost of living over the last 20 years. Prepare a graph to show your results.

Technology

2. Navigational systems are a recent technological advance. Visit a local car dealer and the library to gather research about these systems. What do they do? How available are they now? Are they expensive? Do car makers think they will become "standard equipment" in the future? Report your findings to the class in an oral report.

Communications

3. Research lemon laws in your state. Give a brief background about how the lemon laws were passed. Describe how a consumer would go about exercising his or her rights under the laws. Summarize your findings in a 500-word report.

Human Relations

4. Some car owners worry that auto mechanics may do more work than is needed or charge more than they should. Interview car owners you know, then talk to the manager of a repair shop and ask how he or she tries to make sure customers are satisfied. Ask what customers can do to make the experience a good one. Report your findings to the class.

Beyond the Classroom

Consumer Projects

1. With one or two other students, prepare a demonstration on routine vehicle maintenance. Show how to check oil, coolant, and other fluid levels. Illustrate the use of a tire pressure gauge and explain how to evaluate tire tread.
2. Clip two ads that describe auto warranties or locate warranties at home. Read them and tell the class which warranty you consider better and why.
3. Clip two ads that discuss financing plans for automobiles. Analyze the advertisements and tell which financing plan you think is better and why.

Cooperative Learning

Family Economics

Break into assigned family groups. Discuss the following problem.

Of the cars that your family considered in the last chapter, choose the one that best meets your needs and requirements. Then determine if you can afford the vehicle and how you would pay for it. Cash purchasers should specify where the money will come from. Borrowers should determine what they can afford as a down payment and a maximum monthly payment. Then apply the formula discussed in this chapter under Monthly Payments to your disposable income. Approximate insurance costs from those given in the Family Economics activities in Chapter 19, and include allowances for gas and maintenance. Compare your answers with those of other family groups.

Debate the Issue

Althea believes that it is good that speed limits have been increased from 55 miles per hour to 65 miles per hour on many interstate highways in the country. She says it will save time, cut down on traffic jams, and be less costly in terms of gasoline and car maintenance in the long run if people can get to their destinations faster. Alonzo disagrees, saying it saves gasoline and is safer to travel at slower speeds.

You and your classmates will break into two groups and research this topic. Each group will gather evidence to support one side or the other. You are to prepare the argument for your side of the problem. Then the two groups will meet in a classroom debate.

Human Relations
4 Students should share their findings with the class.

Consumer Projects
1 Students should share their findings with the class.
2 Students should share their findings with the class.
3 Students should share their findings with the class.

Family Economics
The poorest families will probably be pushed out of car ownership by insurance costs and/or lack of a trade-in or substantial down payment. Others who can somehow manage will have to ask themselves if a car, or an extra car, is truly worth the financial sacrifice.

Debate the Issue
Break the class into two teams. Assign each team one side of the issue. Encourage students to work together as a team to develop their argument. Ask each team to select a member to make an opening statement that supports the team's side of the issue. Have students take turns debating as the debate moves from one team to the other.

CHAPTER 24

Choosing Other Forms of Transportation

Learning Objectives

When you have finished studying this chapter, you should be able to:

1. Identify the advantages to individuals and communities of public transportation.
2. Explain why some consumers resist using public transportation.
3. List ways in which communities have tried to increase mass transit ridership.
4. Describe how to accumulate vacation funds and get maximum value for money spent.
5. Compare and contrast the advantages and disadvantages of traveling by bus, train, air, or private vehicle.
6. Choose the food and lodging arrangements best suited to your budget, travel plans, and vacation expectations.

Consumer Terms

rationing
bus lane
exhaust emissions
package tours
youth hostels
American Plan

Lesson Plan See the Teacher's Manual for Chapter 24 lesson plan.

Vocabulary The Chapter 24 lesson plan includes suggested vocabulary activities for the terms listed.

Real-World Journal

Make a list in your journal of the alternative methods of public and private transportation available to your school, to an amusement park, to the nearest lake or beach, and to the location of your next class field trip. Include approximate costs and travel times involved in each mode of transportation. Explain the benefits and disadvantages of each method.

1 Learning Economics Even people living in rural areas that have no public transportation are affected by others' use of it. Ask students how these people can benefit from increased use of mass transit. (Less gasoline consumption preserves a natural resource, reduces pollution, and could eventually reduce gas prices.)

2 Vocabulary Help students understand and remember the term *mass transit* by asking them to explain the meaning of the two words. ("Mass" means large quantity and "transit" means to move from one place to another.)

USING MASS TRANSIT TO GET AROUND

How long has it been since you rode the subway, bus, or other public transportation in your community? If some time has passed, perhaps you should give it another try. You may have a pleasant surprise. Many public transportation systems throughout the country have
1 been upgraded.

American attitudes toward public transportation began to change during the oil crisis in the mid-1970s. Consumers became aware that the United States could no longer supply all its energy needs. It had become dependent on foreign oil. Foreign suppliers tripled their prices and some stopped shipping oil to the United States. Gasoline, which is made from oil, became scarce. Gasoline stations closed on weekends, and many were open only two hours on other days. Prices increased rapidly, and stations resorted to a form of **rationing,** or planned allocation. Automobile ownership lost part of its glamour as gas became hard to get and prices soared. Consumers began to show more interest in public transportation.

The Benefits of Mass Transit

2 People who use *mass transit,* or public transportation, on a regular basis enjoy some important advantages. Here are some benefits to individuals.

- *Economy.* Public transportation is often less expensive. The cost of a round-trip drive to work or to shop or see a movie, with parking fees added, may be high compared to bus or subway fare.
- *Convenience.* Parking spaces near places of employment, shopping, and entertainment centers can be hard to find, especially in downtown areas. The time, effort, and expense of locating a parking space or parking in a lot can make getting around very difficult. Riders of public transportation do not have to worry about such problems.
- *Relaxation.* Traffic during rush hour work, can be frustrating. The weary worker, trapped in a traffic jam, may see a bus rush past in a special **bus lane** reserved for buses. Its passengers will reach their destinations much sooner than people stuck in cars. Also, bus and train passengers can read while en route, while drivers have to pay close attention to their driving.

High-Speed Rail in Europe

High-speed rail is generally defined as a rail system with trains traveling at speeds more than 130 miles per hour. One such system is the Channel Tunnel, or Chunnel, which was constructed under the English Channel and connects England, Belgium, and France. At speeds of up to 200 miles per hour, the Eurostar Train travels through the Chunnel from London to Paris in only three hours. A one-way ticket with 14-day advanced booking costs $67.

When people use mass transit, the community also benefits. Key community benefits include the following.

- *Energy savings.* Using public transportation is ride sharing on a gigantic scale. Many passengers can be moved for a fraction of the gasoline required to move them individually. Less fuel is consumed.

- *Pollution reduction.* **Exhaust emissions,** like hydrocarbons and carbon monoxide, that are released when a fuel like gasoline is burned, are a major threat to the environment. When fewer cars are driven, they are reduced, and air pollution is reduced.
- *Efficient land use.* Public transportation routes make efficient use of land. They require only a fraction of the space automobiles need and reduce traffic congestion in downtown areas.

Overcoming Consumer Resistance

Even with all its benefits, mass transit often meets with consumer resistance. Many people simply will not use it. Their reasons include the fact that buses, subway cars, stations, terminals, and commuter trains, which are trains traveling short distances, are not well maintained. Also, some equipment may be old and in need of repair. Schedules are sometimes missed. Fear
1 of crime is another reason some people stay away.

Since public transportation is financed with tax money, government officials try to find ways to increase ridership. Some of the steps they've taken include reducing fares for certain riders (senior citizens, for example) or for all riders at certain times of the day, adding newer, more modern equipment, and cleaning and renovating equipment and stations. Also, many systems have extended service to a larger area, opened express lanes exclusively for buses, provided police protection on buses and trains and in stations, conducted public relations campaigns that encourage citizens to ride public transportation, and encouraged businesses to give their employees mass transit tokens or tickets at little or no cost.

Paying for Modern Systems

Although a number of cities are building or adding to their public transportation systems, some problems of expense, safety, and efficiency still exist. An example is BART, or Bay Area Rapid Transit. This is an ultramodern, computer-operated train system serving the San Francisco Bay area. Building and equipping BART proved much more expensive than expected. The seventy-one-mile system cost $1.6 billion, or
2 more than $22 million a mile.

After some early difficulties and problems, BART now enjoys a favorable reputation for safety and efficiency among its 215,000 passengers each weekday. BART, however, is still expensive. Thousands of workers board its trains daily to get to and from their jobs, but fares do not cover operating costs. Property and sales tax dollars must be used to *subsidize,* or support, ridership.

If subsidies were reduced, fares would have to be raised and services curtailed.

1 Research If you are in an area served by mass transit, assign groups of students to check with local, state, and federal agencies to see what is being done to increase public transportation ridership in your area.

2 Discussion Starter Ask students if they think people who don't use public transportation should have to pay taxes that fund it. Why or why not?

Caption Answer: Cleaner facilities, more direct routes, guaranteed seats, climate control, and improved safety.

Increasing ridership is a goal for most mass transit systems. ***What suggestions would you make to officials in your area to increase use of public transportation?*** ▼

1 Discussion Starter Ask students to take a poll of relatives and friends to find out how many hours a week they work. Compile results in class to determine highest, lowest, and average.

2 Student Motivator Have students plan their ideal two-week vacation. They should write several paragraphs describing where they would go, with whom they would go, what they would do, and so forth.

3 Extension Have a local travel agent visit your class and talk to the students about their job. Most travel agents enjoy traveling and their enthusiasm will be apparent. Ask the agent for tips on planning economical vacations. If the agent is willing, you might have him or her provide quick cost estimates on vacations the students wish they could take.

Then ridership would fall off—all this at a time when governments are making every effort to *increase* use of mass transit.

TRAVELING FOR PLEASURE

Americans have more leisure time than ever, with the length of the work week declining over the years. This development has made travel more popular than ever. Inflation and rising energy prices, however, have imposed limits. If travel is to be economical, the consumer must plan. Transportation costs must be watched. The farther away you travel, the more likely that getting
1 there and back will take a big chunk of your travel budget.

Choosing a Vacation Spot

2 Where do you like to vacation? If you are like most people, you look for a change of scenery. People who live in the city often seek out secluded wooded areas as recreational sites. Others from rural locations enjoy the city for its variety and activity. Some people prefer to "rough it" by camping out or backpacking in state or national parks. Others head straight for resorts where they can totally relax. For still others, a vacation means an extended trip filled with stops for sightseeing, special events, and visits with distant friends and relatives. The possibilities, then, are limitless.

It is easy to obtain information about tourist attractions and accommodations. If you have an interest in a particular city, write to the Chamber of Commerce there. Information about an entire state is available from the department of parks and tourism in that state's capital city. You can get these addresses at your local public library. Travel books and magazines can be found everywhere.

Hotel and motel chains supply folders describing their facilities all over the country. Franchised campgrounds will send you colorful booklets listing camp locations and facilities. These addresses are also available at the library.

Travel agents are another source of information. They will make vacation arrangements for you if you wish. You generally do not pay for travel agency services. The agencies are paid by transportation companies (like airlines), hotels, and resorts to whom they send
3 customers.

Vacationing Near Home Millions of Americans live in or near cities that are well-known as centers of culture and

Making the Best of Air Travel

- **Plan an early departure. Early-morning flights offer the greatest rerouting flexibility if bad weather disrupts air traffic.**
- **Get your seat assignment when you buy your ticket.**
- **If you want a special meal, such as vegetarian, low-sodium, or kosher, order it in advance. But pack your own food to munch on.**
- **Arrive early and get on the plane promptly when your seat row is called.**
- **If your flight is delayed, find out about compensation. Airlines offer compensation for meals, hotels, cabs, and inconvenience—but you have to ask.**
- **Report lost or damaged bags to the airline's claims office immediately.**
- **If you have a problem or complaint that is not satisfactorily handled, phone or write to the carrier's consumer affairs department.**

historic importance. Others live within driving distance of stunning state or national parks. People sometimes find they overlook exciting vacation spots not
1 far from home as shown in Figure 24–1.

Financing a Trip

Today, with people demanding more from their leisure time than ever before, recreation has become big business. Consumers now spend more than $284 billion a year on recreation. Colorful ads invite people to go now and pay later. Remember, though, that vacationing on credit may cause you to be less careful
2 about spending.

Saving Up The ideal way to finance a vacation is to save for it, rather than running up bills you can't cover. Many consumers find it easier to save for this purpose if their money is deposited in a special bank account. Often called a vacation club account, this device encourages savers to work toward a dollar goal by making regular deposits. Look for accounts that pay interest. Otherwise it is better to set up a regular savings account
3 and simply call it a vacation fund.

1 Discussion Starter Ask students if they have discovered an interesting place in their own city or area as a result of entertaining visitors. Have them describe the interesting place.

2 Discussion Starter Have students assume the following ticket prices, then ask them to justify or challenge the costs for that kind of entertainment: Major League ball game, $8; circus, $10; rock concert, $20; theater, $35.

3 Reinforcement Have students find ads that promote payment with credit cards. Have them bring the ads to class and discuss whether they think paying with a credit card is a good idea.

Figure 24–1 Vacation Near Home

Vacation possibilities close to home can offer much variety.

Local Attractions. If you live in a large metropolitan area or historic town, consider spending at least part of your vacation at home. Visit museums, art galleries, and monuments. Go to the theatre, the ballet, or attend a concert. Dine in restaurants. Take local sightseeing tours. Your vacation expenses would be less than those who must first travel hundreds of miles before they can enjoy these same advantages.

State Parks. Travel shorter distances on vacation to save energy and money. Many areas have beautiful state parks with great facilities and there is little or no charge for admission. Most facilities are free, except for food, lodging, and rental of special equipment, such as boats.

National Parks. With more than 350 parks, historic sites, and scenic rivers, a national park may be a vacation option that does not require extensive travel. Thirteen even provide winter activities, including skiing, snowmobiling, snowshoeing, sledding, ice skating, ice boating, and ice fishing. Accommodations are available as well as vital services like medical facilities, grocery stores, and restaurants. National parks are very popular so plan your trip in advance to avoid large crowds.

1 Math Application Have students assume a vacationing family of four spends $175 a day for food and lodging and $20 a day for car travel. What is the cost of a 12-day vacation? ($2,340)

2 Discussion Starter Ask students if they know anyone who has used a special set-aside account to help save for a vacation. Did it work? What were the person's experiences?

3 Reinforcement Remind students of what they learned about traveler's checks in Unit 3.

4 Reinforcement Refer students to the budgeting section in Unit 2. Point out that special budgets for vacation are a good idea. They should plan how much they will spend for food, transportation, lodging, souvenirs, and so forth, before they go. It is also a good idea not to take much more money than they've estimated they will need, in order to avoid overspending. Credit cards can be used in emergencies.

5 Discussion Starter Ask students if they have taken any long bus or train rides. How far did they go? Was the experience a pleasant one? Do they know how much more or less transportation would have cost if they would have taken an airplane instead?

Having taken as much as a year or more to save for a trip, most consumers want to safeguard their money while they travel. To do this, it's good to carry traveler's checks instead of cash.

Another wise precaution is to take along a credit card. The idea is not to use the card for regular vacation expenses, but to have it available for emergencies. An example would be a major automobile repair.

Whether you use credit cards or trav-
1 eler's checks, it is best to establish a bud-
2 get for your vacation. Your budget will
3 allow you to control your expenses and
4 plan the amount you want to spend.

How to Get There

Some people bike or hike to their travel destinations. Most of us, however, choose from a number of alternatives.

Buses Travel by bus is not as popular as it once was. In one six-year period, ridership declined by about 50 percent. There are two reasons for this trend. First, Greyhound, the major bus line operating coast-to-coast, has discontinued many routes through small-town America. Second, buses have faced increased competition from a new source, discount airlines.

To meet such challenges, Greyhound is making an attempt to improve its image. More comfortable, reclining seats, additional space for passengers, cleaner interiors and restrooms, and effective air-conditioning are all part of this effort.

Bus fares are usually quite reasonable. In addition, Greyhound offers economical fifteen- and thirty-day passes, especially during the peak summer travel season. The passes entitle the holder to unlimited travel in the United States. Other motor coach lines offer **package tours,** which are carefully planned travel arrangements that emphasize places, events, and activities of interest in various parts of the country.

5 **Trains** Amtrak is the major long-distance train travel supplier in the United States. But the National Railroad Passenger Corporation, as it is also known,

has had some service problems in the past. As inefficient and under-used lines are cut, however, passenger service is improving and so is ridership. In some parts of the country, Amtrak service is not only very competitive with airlines but some consumers prefer it over the airlines. In addition, upgrading of both trains and service is ongoing. New passenger cars have been added. The addition of modern lightweight steel turboliners, which can travel at speeds of up to 125 miles per hour, has made train travel more attractive in areas where they are in use. Meal or snack bar service is now offered on most trains and sleeping cars are available.

Airlines Where great distances are involved or when speed is important, you may prefer to travel by air. Service usually surpasses that offered on buses and trains. There are a variety of package tours. Food is sometimes served at no extra cost on flights that are aloft during mealtimes, and travelers can make special meal requests, such as vegetarian or kosher. Music and often movies are provided for passenger enjoyment (some-
1 times for an extra fee). Airline tickets

1 Critical Thinking Ask students if they think there might have been some advantage to regulating the airline industry. What might some of those advantages have been? Do they think lower fares compensate for loss of the guarantees provided by federal regulation?

Getting Seniors and Infants Together

In today's society, often both parents must work for the family to get by. Sometimes there is only one parent to provide for the children, so that parent *must* work. Thus many parents must find some kind of dependable day care for their very young children and infants. Finding reliable caregivers is not the only problem. Often parents with small children are on tight budgets, and good child care can be very expensive.

Hattie Irons Wilson was able to solve a small part of the problem. Wilson was 66 when she realized that some young mothers had to quit jobs or school because they could not afford fees for day care. She also knew that retired people often like youngsters and that many had had a lot of experience caring for them. So she decided to put the two groups together. The result was the Infant-Senior Sharing Project (ISSP) in New Jersey.

Wilson's idea was to have senior citizens volunteer to work at the center for up to six hours a week. Because the help is given by volunteers, the cost of the day care can be kept down. Costs at the center are about half what other day-care providers charge.

The ISSP can take care of 20 to 30 youngsters with four regular volunteers and three paid staff members. The mothers love the program. They have affordable care and can leave their children—even those with medical problems such as asthma—with people they can trust. The seniors love working with the children. They know they are helping out parents who have to work. Additionally, working with so many youngsters every day keeps them feeling young themselves.

Brainstorm

What kinds of volunteer projects could senior citizens do to help teens?

Case Study Answer: Counseling teens who may want but not get help or attention at home; tutoring in school subjects; helping improve reading skills; mentoring; advising the teen about the workplace; teaching skills such as cooking, cleaning, shopping, sewing, car repair, home maintenance, carpentry, gardening to both young men and women.

used to be very costly. Soon after the federal government deregulated the airline industry in the late 1970s, however, the number of carriers tripled. With so many airlines in business, competition became intense and prices dropped. Today, passengers save money by purchasing
1 round-trip tickets, traveling midweek, or
2 staying over on a weekend
3 night.

Car or Motorcycle If you enjoy driving, traveling by car or motorcycle offers many advantages. Traveling companions are of your own choosing. You determine the schedule, starting and ending the travel day as you wish. Side trips to points off the beaten path are yours for the taking. Taking along sports equipment and other supplies is easier because everything need not be packed in suitcases.

The availability of gasoline and its cost, of course, are the two big concerns. During the peak summer vacation season gasoline prices can rise. To decide whether using a car is economical under these circumstances, you must compare cost per mile with bus and train fares. (Air fares could not be compared directly because they eliminate food and lodging costs that would otherwise be required.) In computing cost per mile for an automobile or motorcycle, it is reasonable to include only the variable costs—those that change according to use, such as gasoline and oil. Fixed costs, which remain the same regardless of use, would distort your calculations.

Deciding on Lodging and Food

Along with transportation, lodging accounts for the major part of most vacation budgets. Comfortable rooms at thousands of hotels and motels throughout the country are available at affordable rates.

Lodging Lodging accommodations vary widely in cost and comfort. Budget motels can be a good choice for those traveling on a tight budget. Mid-priced hotels and motels, offer more creature comforts—nicer rooms, pools, and exercise rooms. Bed and breakfasts lodgings are another alternative. Usually very individual, these can provide very nice accommodations at less cost than some hotel chains. Luxury resorts frequently offer saunas, pools, yacht facilities, golf and tennis facilities, and gourmet meals.

For young people, **youth hostels** are another alternative. These are supervised shelters set up especially for young people on hiking, cycling, and similar trips. The best known federation of hostels is the American Youth Hostels Inc. Hostels generally have dormitory sleeping accommodations, a recreation room, and an equipped kitchen.

Recreational Vehicles People with trailers and similar recreational vehicles (RV) carry their accommodations with them. Families especially find this a low-cost way to travel.

There is a vast array of popular RVs. They range from lightweight camping trailers that fold into neat packages and are towed behind the car to elaborate motor homes. Between these extremes

1 Discussion Starter A wise consumer can save money when purchasing airline tickets. Ask students who have flown how much their tickets cost. See if any students have made the same trip for widely varying fares. To make this point in another way, you could have a travel agency supply you with the prices for a one-way ticket purchased at the last minute compared with a round-trip ticket purchased several weeks in advance with a weekend overnight included.

2 Extension The Department of Transportation requires airlines that have overbooked (sold more seats than available) to offer to pay passengers who agree to give up their seats.

3 Learning Economics Ask students why the prices often go up even without shortages and embargoes. (Demand is greater.)

News Clip Answers:
1 Using a bicycle can provide exercise to help you lose weight or tone muscles. It is a nonpolluting form of transportation. It is inexpensive.
2 You should wear proper safety clothing, such as a bright shirt and a helmet. You should also carefully plan your route to and from your destination.

CASE STUDY

Consumer NEWS CLIP

Drive? No Way—Not This Biker

by Glenn F. Bunting
Los Angeles Times
February 21, 1995

I marvel at how nearly everyone I know seems to regard riding a bike to work as the equivalent of an out-of-body experience. There are more bicycles (about 120 million) than cars in this country, yet very few commuters would contemplate the prospect of abandoning their beloved four-wheel behemoths.

The only [regular cyclists] I have encountered after nearly three years of riding to work are grungy office couriers, which makes me wonder where the estimated 4.3 million Americans currently commuting by bike are.

At this point, you're probably thinking that there's no room in your hectic schedule for bike commuting. Besides, it's too dangerous and inconvenient, right? Well, think again. In Los Angeles, where the No. 1 cycling enthusiast resides in the mayor's office, biking to work can be a snap. Here are tips to help get started.

- Map out a route. The most important preparation before heading out the driveway is meticulously planning a safe trip. Avoid busy thoroughfares whenever possible, even those marked as bicycle lanes. You'll grow tired real fast of getting flats from riding on broken glass, competing with traffic and sucking exhaust fumes. But with a little experience, you'll get comfortable riding on less congested city streets.
- Get the proper equipment. The bike needn't be new or expensive. But make sure it's in good working order with tires inflated, chains lubricated and seat properly adjusted. A bike shop should perform a tune-up for less than $50.

  A helmet is a necessity. So is bright-colored clothing. A sweat shirt or T-shirt and comfortable athletic shoes will suffice. A quality pair of biking shorts with extra padding sewn into the crotch and cycling gloves will make the ride more enjoyable. In the summer, don't forget sunscreen—particularly for your face—and wear some form of protective eye-wear.
- Arrange for storage and shower facilities. I am fortunate to work in an office equipped with a shower and closet space. It helps to have a supportive boss who also cycles to work. For $70 a year, I lease an enclosed outdoor bicycle locker at the Foggy Bottom Metro station.
- Plan a safe return trip. Daylight Saving Time makes it convenient to ride home after a long day at work. Not so in winter when it gets dark about 5 p.m. and most people don't care to get caught riding alone at night.

What to do? Try mass transit. The Metro Blue Line and area commuter trains in Los Angeles allow two bicycles per car. And while bikes are not permitted on Los Angeles County buses, cycling advocates hope to get that policy changed soon.

Another option is to hitch a ride with a co-worker who commutes by car within several miles of your residence. For this, you will need to purchase a bicycle rack that fits easily on the back of most vehicles and lights for the front and rear of your bike.

Decisions, Decisions

1. Name some benefits of commuting by bicycle.
2. What are some precautions you should take when commuting by

FLASHBACK FLASHFORWARD

A ride on the New York City subway cost 10 cents in 1947. By 1995, the fare was $1.25 regardless of the length of the ride. Children under 44 inches tall may ride free!

1 Learning Economics Ask students to explain why a meal purchased at a restaurant costs more than a similar meal in which the ingredients are purchased in a grocery store and prepared at home. (Must pay for service and business expenses in a restaurant.)

are trailers as long as fifty feet and campers that fit onto pickup trucks.

Typically, people who take RV vacations head for state and national parks or privately owned camp grounds. There, for fees starting at about five to ten dollars a night, they rent either tent sites or space for their vehicles. Vehicle spaces equipped with water, electricity, and sewage hookups at franchised campgrounds often rent for as little as $15 or as much as $60 a night.

Eating Out

Unless you are camping, being on vacation means dining out. In recent years, the cost of restaurant meals has increased greatly. On average, a meal that cost a consumer $5 ten years ago would cost about $7.50 today. To save money on vacation meals, some families
1 follow a four-step plan.

1. They take sandwiches from home to eat during the first day of travel.
2. Other days, they stop at grocery stores along the way, buy food, and drive to parks or other areas where they take turns preparing meals.
3. At their destination, they rent lodgings with cooking facilities and prepare all their meals.
4. They stock up on groceries at a supermarket before reaching a resort area, where prices are likely to be high.

Other families plan to eat out all the time. They save by seeking out clean but inexpensive cafes for meals, avoiding more costly hotel and motel dining rooms. Wise consumers plan for nutritious meals daily, whether at home or away.

Rates at hotels, especially in resort areas, are sometimes quoted with or without meals. Under the European Plan, meals, if available, are extra. Under the **American Plan,** the price includes both meals and lodging, and guests take those meals in the hotel dining room. A Modified American Plan consists of lodging and two meals daily (usually breakfast and dinner in the evening).

After you add it all up—car expenses, food, lodging, and a little extra spending money for everybody, vacations are not inexpensive. Some experts report the daily cost of a vacation will be about $55 each for a family of four. The joy of seeing new sights and having new experiences, however, makes it all worth it.

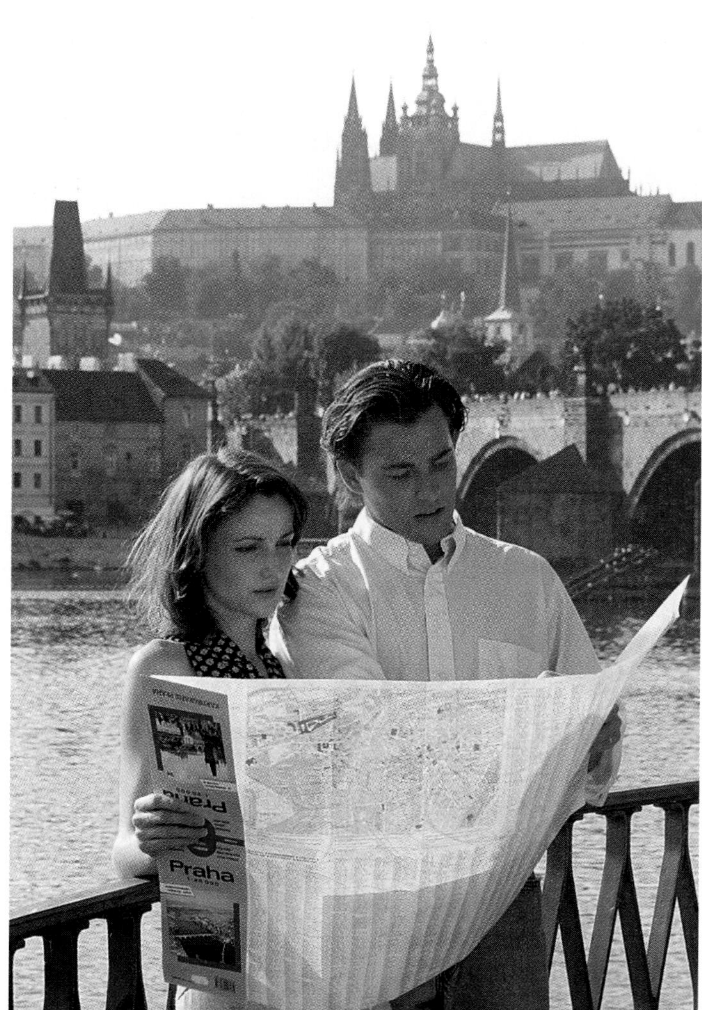

Caption Answer: Advantages: chance to meet new people who share similar interests; economical lodging. Disadvantages: lack of privacy and sparse accommodations.

Many people choose to stay in youth hostels when traveling. ***What would you think are some of the advantages and disadvantages of staying at a youth hostel?*** ▶

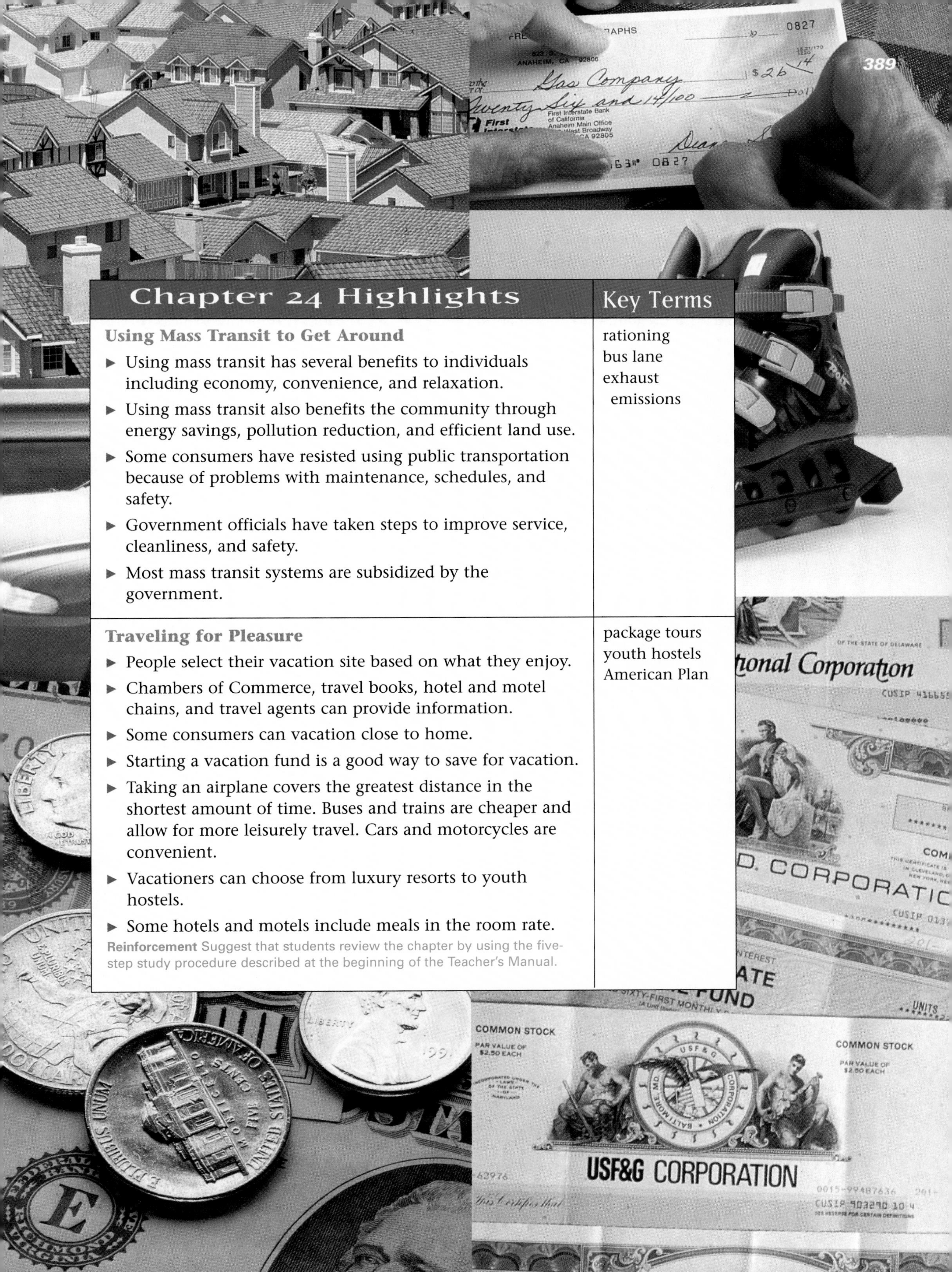

Chapter 24 Highlights

Using Mass Transit to Get Around

- Using mass transit has several benefits to individuals including economy, convenience, and relaxation.
- Using mass transit also benefits the community through energy savings, pollution reduction, and efficient land use.
- Some consumers have resisted using public transportation because of problems with maintenance, schedules, and safety.
- Government officials have taken steps to improve service, cleanliness, and safety.
- Most mass transit systems are subsidized by the government.

Key Terms
rationing
bus lane
exhaust emissions

Traveling for Pleasure

- People select their vacation site based on what they enjoy.
- Chambers of Commerce, travel books, hotel and motel chains, and travel agents can provide information.
- Some consumers can vacation close to home.
- Starting a vacation fund is a good way to save for vacation.
- Taking an airplane covers the greatest distance in the shortest amount of time. Buses and trains are cheaper and allow for more leisurely travel. Cars and motorcycles are convenient.
- Vacationers can choose from luxury resorts to youth hostels.
- Some hotels and motels include meals in the room rate.

Key Terms
package tours
youth hostels
American Plan

Reinforcement Suggest that students review the chapter by using the five-step study procedure described at the beginning of the Teacher's Manual.

CHAPTER 24 REVIEW

Refer students to the Reviewing Consumer Terms and Reviewing Facts and Ideas found in the Student Activity Workbook.

Reviewing Consumer Terms Paragraphs will vary. See the Glossary for definitions.

Reviewing Facts and Ideas See the Student Activity Workbook for answers.

Problem Solving and Decision Making **1 a** Taxi, $360; bus, $90; car, $140; bicycle, $27. **b** Safety, convenience, weather conditions, and schedules. **2** Answers will depend on students' perspectives. **3** Answers will depend on students' perspectives.

Consumers Around the World **Social Studies 1** Student reports should answer all questions.

Math **2** $14.80 ($148 x .05 = $7.40 x 2 = $14.80)

Technology **3** Student reports should answer all questions.

Communications **4** Student responses will depend on their perspectives.

Consumer Project Answers will depend on students' perspectives.

Reviewing Consumer Terms

Use each of the following terms in a paragraph to demonstrate you know its meaning.

American Plan
bus lane
exhaust emissions
package tours
rationing
youth hostels

Reviewing Facts and Ideas

1. List three advantages to individuals who use mass transit and three advantages to their communities.
2. Describe why some consumers resist using public transportation.
3. What measures have been taken to encourage use of public transportation?
4. Explain ways to choose a vacation site.
5. Describe the advantages and disadvantages of traveling by bus, train, plane, or private vehicle.
6. What facilities are usually available in youth hostels?

Problem Solving and Decision Making

1. Yukiko has determined that the cost of getting to school and back each day by different forms of transportation is as follows:

Taxicab	$2.00 (ride sharing)
City bus	0.50 (student discount fare)
Automobile	0.78 (car pooling)
Bicycle	0.15

   Assume that there are no other possibilities. (a) If Yukiko attends school every weekday for thirty-six weeks, how much would each form of transportation cost her? (b) In deciding on a form of transportation, what factors besides cost should Yukiko and her family consider?
2. Choose a major city in the United States that you would like to visit. List sources from which you might obtain information about that city's hotels, restaurants, and attractions.
3. On a vacation, for which would you prefer to reduce expenditures so that more funds would be available for others—food, lodging, or transportation? Explain how you would bring about such a reduction.

Building Academic Skills

Consumers Around the World

Social Studies

1. Research different strategies for traveling through Europe. Find out the most economical ways to get around, and the least expensive places to stay. Summarize your findings in a 500-word report.

Math

2. Raoul can buy a one-way bus ticket for $148. He can save 5 percent on each of two tickets by purchasing one round-trip ticket instead of two one-way tickets. How much can he save by buying the round-trip ticket?

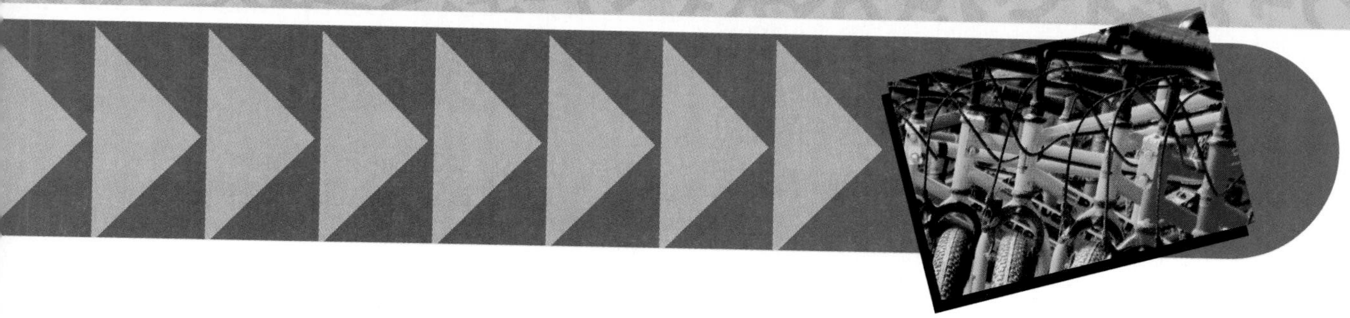

Technology

3. Travel agents make trip reservations by computer, and you can, too, if you have the right software and a modem for your personal computer at home. Ask a local travel agent how he or she makes reservations by computer, then go to a computer store and ask a salesperson what software you need to do the same thing, and how it works. Report your findings to the class.

Communications

4. Secure a travel brochure from a travel agent, airline, bus, or train company that describes a packaged tour of an area you would like to visit. Analyze the information. Prepare a 250-word report discussing whether you would prefer to take a packaged tour or travel on your own. Give the reasons for your choice.

Beyond the Classroom

Consumer Project

Write your personal evaluation of the following places as vacation spots. Mountains; the seashore; the heart of the city (near cultural activities and historic sites); homes of friends and relatives in various locations.

Cooperative Learning

Family Economics

Break into assigned family groups and discuss the following problem. Your family saves for a special vacation every three years. The other two years they must make two weeks at home on a regular budget seem like something special. Describe the most imaginative way you can think of to do that. Be sure to include activities that will be enjoyed by all family members. (Note: Day trips are possibilities, provided they are within your budget.) Compare your answers with those of other family groups.

Debate the Issue

Some consumers believe that the government makes investments for improving mass transit a priority. They believe that using tax dollars in this manner provides benefits to individuals and the community at large. Others believe that mass transit should be self-sufficient and operate like any other business. They also believe that people who do not use public transportation should not have to pay for it.

You and your classmates will break into two groups and research this topic. Each group will gather evidence to support one side or the other. You are to prepare the argument for your side of the problem. Then the two groups will meet in a classroom debate.

Rechecking Your Attitude

Before going on to the next unit, go back to the Attitude Inventory at the beginning of this one. Answer the questions a second time. Then compare the two sets of responses. On how many statements have your attitudes changed? Can you account for these shifts in your opinions? What do you know now that you did not know then?

Family Economics Answers will vary but might include staging a film festival using a VCR; a cook's tour that calls for preparing a different cuisine each day; a series of day trips based on the theme "I've Lived Here All My Life and Never Visited..."; and a family spa built around group exercise, light meals, and improvements of appearance.

Debate the Issue Break the class into two teams. Assign each team one side of the issue. Encourage students to work together as a team to develop their argument. Ask each team to select a member to make an opening statement that supports their side of the issue. Have students take turns debating as the debate moves from one team to another.

Rechecking Your Attitude Answers will depend on students' perspectives.

UNIT 7 LAB

You and Your Community

STEP A Students' written notes on the car models and options they are considering should reflect research and understanding of the cars' suitability for commuting and long trips. STEP B Students should take accurate notes of their interviews with car dealers. Their charts should provide reasonable, accurate information about the cars they inspect. STEP C Students should take accurate notes on service prices for routine maintenance. STEP D Students should be able to list and cite their sources for lodging and fuel cost estimations. STEP E Students should provide clear maps of their intended routes. Routes should meet the requirements outlined in Step E. STEP F Students' answers should be accurate and based on their car charts, trip notes, and interviews with car dealers and mechanics. STEP G Students' reports should reflect their thoughtful consideration of the features of each car they considered. Students should support their comments with specific examples.

Refer students to the Unit 7 Lab in the Student Activity Workbook.

Buying a Car for All Reasons

Unit 7 provides you with the basic guidelines for buying and owning a car and for planning a motoring vacation. In this lab, you will follow those guidelines as you plan the purchase of a car to be used both for commuting and for taking a two-week driving trip to visit colleges.

TOOLS

1. *Consumer Reports* and other consumer magazines
2. Car and driving magazines
3. Newspaper, magazine, TV, and radio advertisements for cars
4. A travel atlas
5. Travel guidebooks
6. College guidebooks

PROCEDURES

STEP A Imagine that you are just about to finish your junior year in high school. A very generous relative makes you a wonderful offer. He or she will buy a new car and take you on a two-week trip to visit at least three colleges that are within 2,000 miles of your home. After the trip, the relative will use the car for commuting to his or her office for one year. When you leave for college, the car will become yours. The relative, whose monthly take-home pay is $3,750, is willing to make a down payment of $8,000 on the car purchase and to devote 10 percent of his or her monthly income to car payments for two years. You will be expected to pay for all routine maintenance on the car from the time it is purchased.

Using car advertisements and reports from consumer magazines, identify at least three makes or models of cars that would be comfortable enough for a long trip and economical enough for commuting. Consider and make written notes on the car size and the options that would best suit your needs and those of your relative.

STEP B Contact a local car dealer. Explain the purpose of your assignment and ask to talk with the dealer about the cars you're interested in. It is best to meet with the dealers in person so that you can see the cars and perhaps get an opportunity to test-drive them.

At each dealership, ask to inspect the cars you're considering. Discuss with the dealers each car's options, warranties, and performance record, including efficient fuel use. Ask about the price for a car with only standard equipment and for one with all the options you noted in Step A. Find out about each car's routine maintenance schedule for the first three years. Finally, ask about dealer-arranged financing for the car purchase. Take careful notes on your interviews with each dealer.

STEP C Contact the service departments of two of the dealerships and ask about the costs of routine maintenance for the first three years on the three cars you are considering. Note the costs and the work that is done during each scheduled maintenance.

STEP D Assume you have selected the car. Now it is time to plan your college-visitation trip.

Use college guidebooks and a travel atlas to locate three colleges or universities no more than 2,000 miles from your home. Plan a trip that includes the three schools. Do not plan to cover more than 350 miles in one day. Plan on staying at each college at least two days. Using travel guidebooks and automobile club touring books or the advice of a travel agent, find an example of budget lodgings and of more luxurious lodgings near each college.

STEP E Complete a map highlighting the route of your trip.

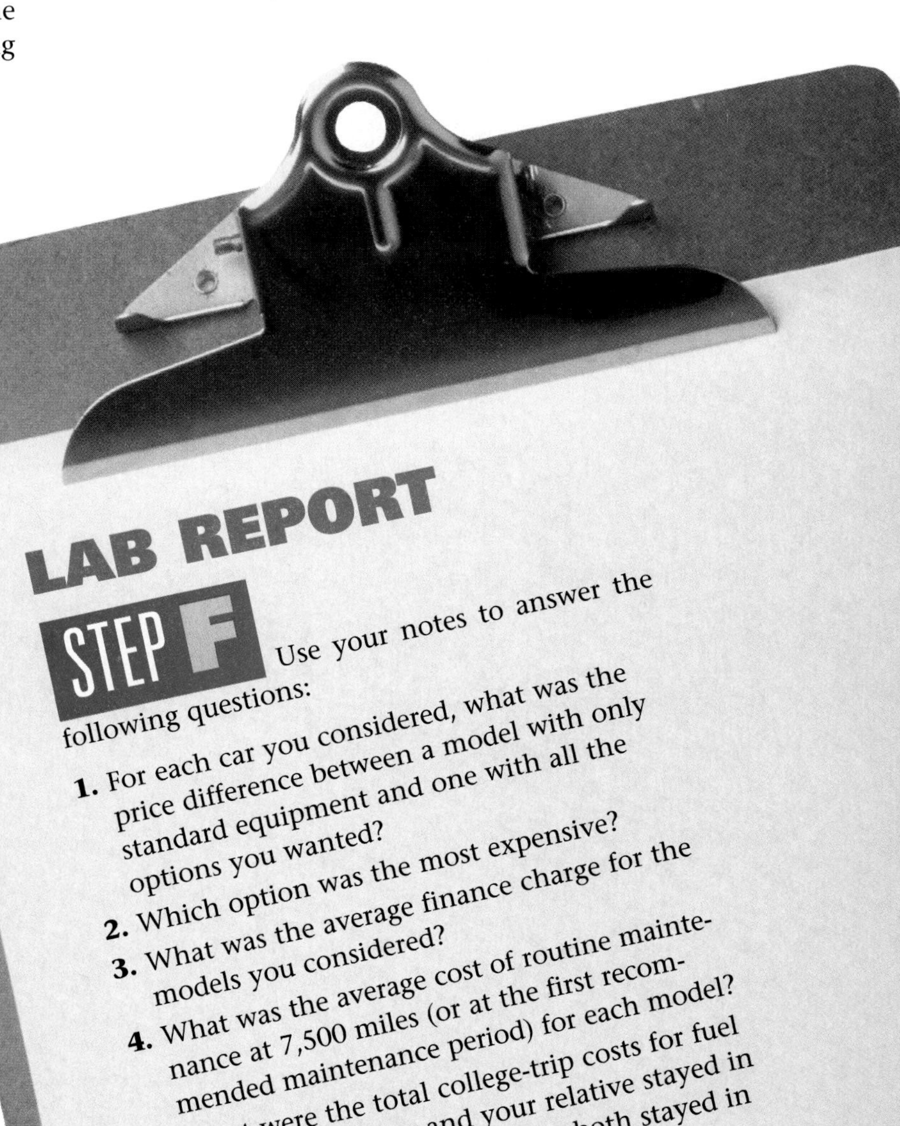

LAB REPORT

STEP F Use your notes to answer the following questions:

1. For each car you considered, what was the price difference between a model with only standard equipment and one with all the options you wanted?
2. Which option was the most expensive?
3. What was the average finance charge for the models you considered?
4. What was the average cost of routine maintenance at 7,500 miles (or at the first recommended maintenance period) for each model?
5. What were the total college-trip costs for fuel and lodging if you and your relative stayed in budget accomodations? if you both stayed in more luxurious lodgings?

STEP G Write a two-page report explaining which car you would select and how price, performance, reliability, and intended use affected your decision.

UNIT 8

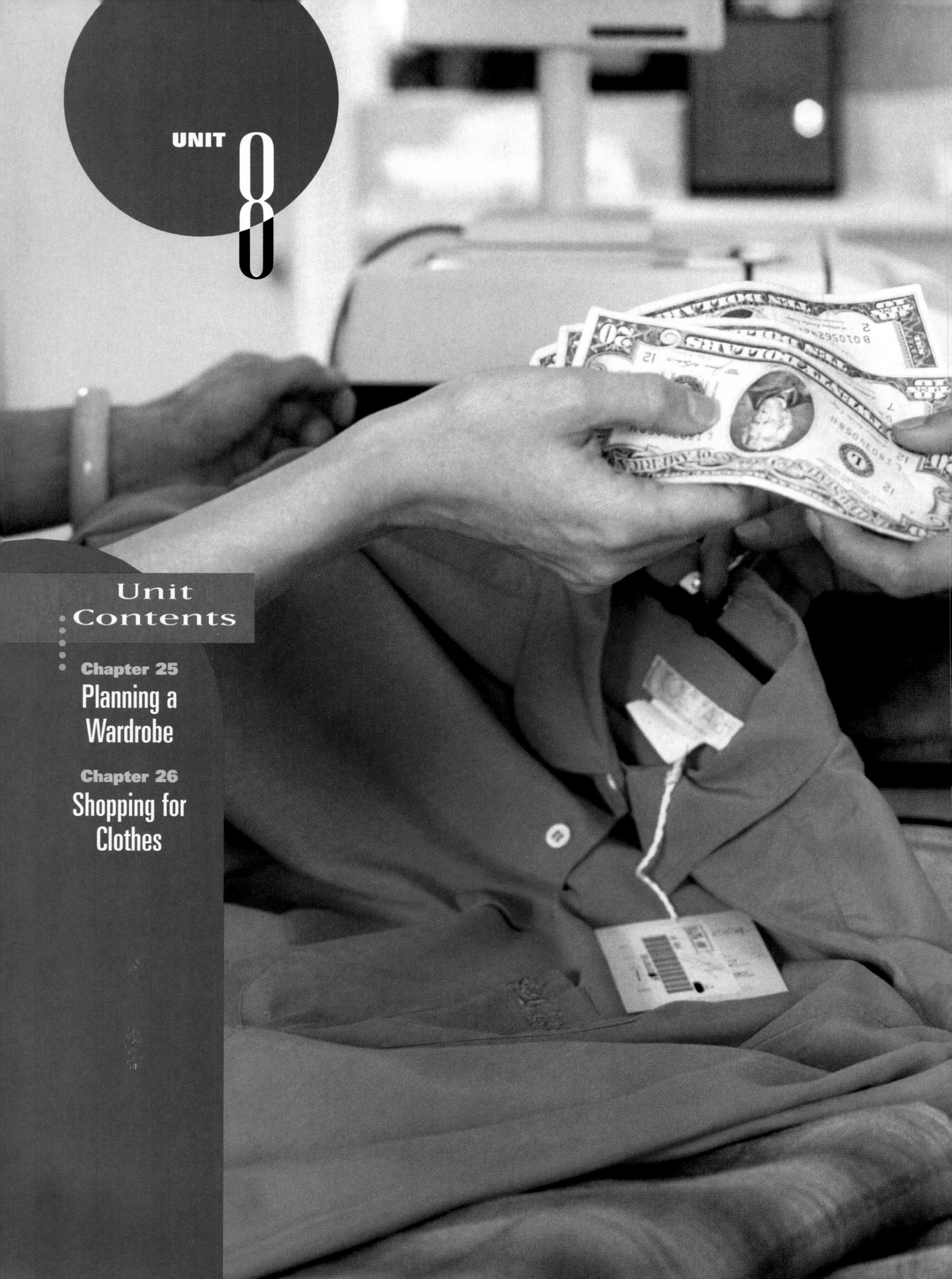

Unit Contents

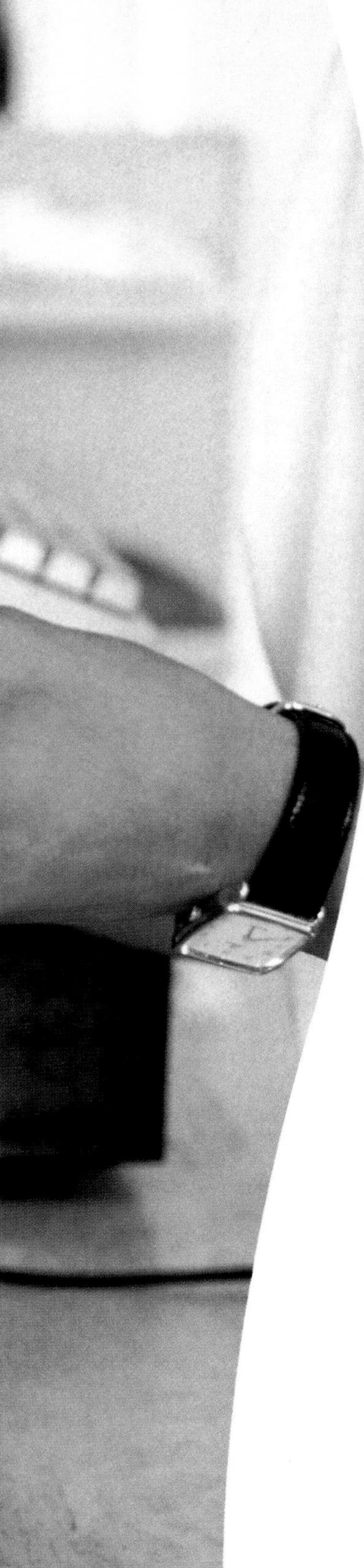

Buying Clothes

Attitude Inventory

Before you begin Chapter 25, take stock of your attitudes by completing the following inventory. Read each statement and decide how you feel about it—agree, disagree, or undecided. Record your feelings on a sheet of notepaper or use the form in the Student Activity Workbook.

1. When purchasing clothing, always choose the best quality available.
2. A generous cut and solid construction are indications of good garment quality.
3. Blending manufactured and natural fibers result in a weaker fabric.
4. Labels telling how to care for clothing are of little value.
5. Purchases of the clothing you want should be based on a thorough knowledge of the clothing you already have.
6. "Making do" with what we have is a good policy in some budget categories but a very poor policy where clothing is concerned.
7. Classic styles are dull and should be avoided as wardrobe additions.
8. The price tag on a given clothing item is not the best indicator of quality.
9. Information on a tag such as "Compare at $30" is helpful information to the consumer.
10. "Never throw clothing out—it's bound to come back in style" is good advice.
11. Clothing "styles" are only as good as they look on you.
12. A good rule of thumb for choosing synthetic fabrics and blends is to determine if they look and feel more natural than synthetic.
13. Fashion trends are popular for only a short period of time and therefore should be ignored.
14. A good shopper considers several different places to buy clothing.
15. Shopping in discount stores is a mistake—you get what you pay for.

Unit Goal The main goal of this unit is to show students how to plan a wardrobe and to shop wisely for clothes. Chapters in this unit include (1) Planning a Wardrobe and (2) Shopping for Clothes.

Lesson Plan See the Teacher's Manual for an overview of the unit and some suggestions for introducing it. If you assign the Attitude Inventory, be sure to tell students to keep their answers for later use.

CHAPTER 25

Planning a Wardrobe

Learning Objectives

When you have finished studying this chapter, you should be able to:

1. Identify the desirable features of wardrobe items.
2. Take an inventory of your garments and accessories.
3. Summarize ways to update older articles of clothing.
4. Design a plan for making future additions to your wardrobe.

Consumer Terms

wardrobe
garments
accessories
inventory
coordinated
mix-and-match

Real-World Journal

Write a paragraph in your journal about three pieces of clothing that you would like to have as part of your wardrobe. Explain when and where you may be able to purchase the items on sale. How will those items coordinate with items in your wardrobe? Will you be able to wear them to a job interview or on the job?

Lesson Plan See the Teacher's Manual for Chapter 25 lesson plan.

Vocabulary The Chapter 25 lesson plan includes suggested vocabulary activities for the items listed.

1 Student Motivator Have students recall events where their clothing made them feel comfortable, confident, relaxed, or happy. Have them discuss why they felt this way.

2 Discussion Starter Ask students to what degree their clothing purchases are determined by what they see their peers wearing. Do any of them try to find clothes that are "different"?

ASSESSING YOUR WARDROBE

Your **wardrobe** is the total collection of the garments and accessories you own. **Garments** are articles of clothing like dresses, pants, and jackets. **Accessories** are items worn with them to complete an outfit like scarves, ties, jewelry, belts, shoes, and purses.

Any consumer can put together a suitable wardrobe. It is simply a matter of learning from those who know style and materials, considering your personal style, and using imagination and common sense. A wardrobe should be made
1 up of items selected with five basic
2 points in mind, as shown in Figure 25–1.

Figure 25–1 Planning Items for Your Wardrobe

There are five basic ideas to bear in mind when planning your wardrobe.

Attractiveness.
Clothing should bring out the best feature of the wearer.
Acceptability.
Clothing should be appropriate for use, occasion, and season. It should not be so extreme that it detracts from the appearance or makes a spectacle of the wearer.
Utility.
Clothing should serve a useful purpose. It should fulfill a genuine wardrobe need.

TAKING AN INVENTORY

A wardrobe that "just grows" usually looks like what it is—unplanned—and often it costs more than is necessary. There are a few well-defined steps that can make wardrobe planning relatively easy and effective, however. The process begins with taking an **inventory,** or list, of what you already own.

The best time to take an inventory is
1 today. (Later inventories can be taken
2 before changes in seasons.) You will
3 probably be surprised at all you have
4 accumulated. As you examine and try on
5 garments, ask yourself these questions.

1. *Should it be dry-cleaned or laundered?* Dirty clothes should be kept with

4
Quality.
Clothing should be well made. It should last as long as the consumer enjoys wearing it.
5
Price.
Clothing should carry a reasonable price tag that is within the consumer's budget.

1 Reinforcement Have students find examples from books and magazines of how certain designs look good on some people but not on others.

2 Extension Invite a fashion merchandiser from a local department store or specialty shop to discuss economical ways to put together a coordinated wardrobe.

3 Discussion Starter Ask students if they have had personal experiences with clothing items that were extremely attractive, but were impractical and therefore were rarely worn.

4 Discussion Starter Ask students if they typically plan their clothing purchases or buy on impulse.

5 Extension Ask students who have taken clothing or design courses or who have special interest in clothes to suggest books and magazine articles that provide useful information about planning a wardrobe. You might also have a teacher who is an expert on clothing or the school librarian put together a list of appropriate books on this subject.

1 Interesting Note A pair of original Levi jeans from the 1930s that had never been worn was sold by a previous worker at the factory. The investor who bought them turned down a $35,000.00 offer.

2 Discussion Starter People in wheelchairs would also like to have stylish and comfortable clothes. What are some modifications that could be made for them? (Clothing made from fabrics that are absorbent and resist wrinkles, clothes that are easier to put on and take off, clothes with special touches such as unusual buttons and other trim).

3 Discussion Starter Ask students if they have items of clothing that they will never wear. Have they ever considered throwing some of the items away, but then returned them to the closet? Why do they think people have such a hard time parting with these items?

4 Extension Ask students if they have ever hear of a "white elephant" sale. Have a "white elephant" day where students who have purchased clothes they won't wear bring them to class. They should give reasons why they aren't acceptable (appearance, not appropriate with other clothes in wardrobe). Find out if any of these items could be traded to other students and why. Make a list of ways to avoid "white elephants."

Purchasing Power

About 15 percent of households in the Caribbean (excluding Cuba) have a purchasing power of at least $20,000 dollars a year. In Brazil, that figure is 23 percent; in Mexico, 40 percent; in Canada, 69 percent; and in the United States, 70 percent.

clean clothes. The time to clean a garment is when it becomes dirty, not just before it will be worn again.

2. *Will I ever wear it again?* You may find an article unsuitable for a number of reasons. Perhaps you have outgrown it. Maybe it never fit well. If a piece of clothing is of no further use to you then you should give it to a family member, exchange it with a friend, donate it to charity, or discard it as useless. Remove all unwanted items from closets and drawers. Overcrowding could keep other garments from hanging properly
1 causing them to look
2 rumpled, and even
3 shorten their useful
4 lives.

3. *Should it be put away until the seasons change?* Storing out-of-season items will provide needed space in closets and drawers. Non washable garments should be stored in garment bags with mothproofing added if woolens are present. Washable clothing can be placed in garment or plastic bags or folded neatly and packed in boxes or suitcases. Avoid storage in places where temperatures are extreme.
4. *Does it need repair?* Making minor repairs to clothing can extend its life by many months. Even if you wear a particular garment only rarely, mending it when necessary gives you an extra change of clothes. Then each new purchase adds to your wardrobe instead of merely replacing something discarded.

Caption Answer: To keep clothes in good shape and to better determine what clothes are in a wardrobe.

◀ *The first step toward completing a wardrobe inventory is to start with clean clothes.* ***Why is this so important?***

As you take your inventory, you may want to complete a wardrobe chart like the one shown in Figure 25–2 on page 402. After completing your inventory, you are ready to decide what new purchases should be made to round out your wardrobe. List them in the appropriate column at the far right of the inventory form or make some type of list that is prioritized. Consider the colors desired that will coordinate your wardrobe and set a
1 realistic price range for each item. Also
2 consider clothes that can be used for sev-
3 eral different occasions.

People MAKING a DIFFERENCE

Granting a College Dream

Eugene Lang is a self-made millionaire who started life in New York City, in east Harlem. So it was natural that he was asked to address 54 graduating sixth-graders, mostly Hispanics and African-Americans, at his old elementary school. As he spoke, Lang tried to inspire them to finish their education and fulfill their dreams. At the same time, he realized that few of them would even finish high school. As for college, it was beyond their means.

Suddenly Lang found himself making them a promise. Finish high school, he said. Go on to college. I will give you scholarships.

Stunned parents did not believe what they had heard until they received letters of confirmation from Lang. They also discovered the millionaire had hired someone to see that their children got the necessary support they would need to achieve their goals.

Lang knew that school was not enough. Many of these children had been made to feel that the benefits of society were not for them. So Lang made sure that they were exposed to opportunities they might not have had otherwise. He took them out to the opera and concerts. He took them to dinner. He asked them to visit him in his Manhattan office on Saturdays to talk about success.

Forty-four of the sixth-graders who heard Land that day finished high school. Thirty-four of them went to college. In the process, the I Have a Dream Foundation began.

Even more important than the foundation, Lang's promise inspired other individuals and groups around the country to start similar programs. Since Lang's inspired speech at this old elementary school, these programs have encouraged thousands of students to get a college education.

Brainstorm

What are the advantages—to society and to business—of helping students get through high school and college?

1 Student Motivator Have a student who has reworked a piece of clothing discuss the process and share the opportunity costs of the project.

2 Reinforcement Student Activity Workbook, Chapter 25 activities.

3 Extension Ask students how they have solved space problems for clothes. Share catalogues of shops that specialize in storage items. Decide on the best methods and most cost effective methods of creating additional storage space.

Case Study Answer: Their potential earnings are greater, they have more money to put into the economy; they have a greater chance of honing their unique skills which can contribute to technological, medical, political, scientific advances; there are more skilled workers to fill positions in the future; there are more well-trained people to go into entrepreneurial enterprises.

FLASHBACK FLASHFORWARD

Often what comes around goes around, especially when it comes to fashion. The top-handle handbag and structured suits of the 1940's, and the miniskirts, mod boots, and Jackie O. suit ensembles of the 1960's have all recently made a comeback in today's fashion world. Take a good look at fashion around you. Your next fashion bargain just may be found in your grandparents' attic or your parents' closet.

News Clip Answers:
1 Your clothes often lead people to make judgments about who you are. The proper attire can create trust and credibility. This is important not only in a courtroom situation, but also in a doctor's office or a sales environment.
2 Trade publications and periodicals would give you an indication of how people in your chosen industry dress. You also could interview various people in positions and companies in areas similar to the one in which you are interested.

UPDATING YOUR WARDROBE

You can bring your present wardrobe up to date by mending, donating, discarding, exchanging, or reworking items. Reworking is the most demanding—and rewarding. You can use your imagination to turn a boring garment into clothing you will enjoy wearing. Often full-scale remaking is not necessary. Perhaps all you need to do is add

Figure 25–2 Wardrobe Planning Chart

Descriptions	Action Needed			New Purchases	
Items to Keep (Numbers/Colors/Styles	**Donate/ Discard/ Exchange**	**Repair/ Recycle**	**Clean/ Launder**	**Items to Buy**	**Estimated Cost**
Everyday Shirts Sweaters T-shirts Jeans Pants Skirts Dresses Suits Clothes for work					
Formal Finer Suits Finer blouses/shirts Formal party clothes					
Sports Swimsuits Workout clothes Bicycle shorts Other special interest (ski, tennis, baseball, etc.)					
Accessories Shoes Belts Scarves Ties Jewelry Purses					
At Home Sleepwear Undergarments Sweats					
Outerwear Coats Jackets Raincoats Caps, gloves, heavy scarves					

▲ *Many people complete a wardrobe inventory by simply sorting through their clothes.* ***How would keeping a written inventory on a form similar to this be helpful? What modifications could be made?***

Caption Answer: A written record is helpful for long-term planning. A computer spreadsheet could be used, making changes easier.

CASE STUDY

Consumer NEWS CLIP

Dressing for Courtroom Success

by Andrea Higbie
The New York Times
November 25, 1994

Lawyers are far more conservative in their dress than any other professional group because what they do is about brains, not flash, said Camille Lavington, a corporate image consultant based in New York who has helped many practitioners improve their appearance. "Of all lawyers, though, those in criminal defense have the latitude to be the most flamboyant because they deal more with emotions."

Lawyers in the civil arena said they were also expected to reflect the client. "White-collar cases are very serious business, so my concern is less about intimidating the other side than about having my client feel confident in me," said Sara E. Moss, a partner in the firm of Howard, Darby & Levin in Manhattan, who is defending William Richard in a case involving the W. Averell Harriman estate.

Mr. [John Nicholas] Iannuzzi [a criminal defense lawyer] added that it works against a defendant if the lawyer looks anything short of dazzling.

Herald Price Fahringer, the Manhattan lawyer who has defended Claus von Bulow and Jean S. Harris, agreed that 'in criminal defense work, so much rests on the lawyer, and a neat way about you conveys a neat mind.'

It is especially important to shun schlump when working in poverty law, said Ms. [Vivian] Berger [Vice Dean of Columbia Law School], who is also general counsel to the American Civil Liberties Union. "Some Legal Aid people believe they should be 'of the people,' and dress down for political reasons," she said. "It's patronizing. The clients don't want that. They feel they should get real lawyers."

So do jurors, as one sartorial theory goes. Mr. Fahringer, who has written about the psychology of jury selection for The American Journal of Trial Advocacy, said: "When I'm in court, there's not a person on the jury who looks like me, as starched and formal as I do. I'm hoping they'll think: "Wow! That's a lawyer."

Karen Berndt, a former corporate lawyer who is director of intellectual property for Texaco in Houston, said: "The effort you make getting ready and preparing your appearance can benefit you more than reading an extra brief. The higher in status men get, the better they dress. And they respect a woman who dresses well; they listen to her."

"You want clothing that inspires trust, not mistrust," said Mr. Hoffinger (Paul Stuart suit, white shirt, suspenders, pocket square).

He added, however: "In the end, it isn't the way the lawyer looks or the way the lawyer articulates. It is the nature of the case and the way the lawyer presents the case."

Decisions, Decisions

1. Why is it important that you dress appropriately for a job?
2. How would you go about discovering what is the proper attire for the job you want?

or remove cuffs, change buttons, add a new belt, scarf, or tie, adjust hemlines, or add a decorative patch.

MAKING NEW PURCHASES

The completion of your inventory and repairs leaves you with a thorough knowledge of your wardrobe. With this picture of your cleaned, mended, and reworked clothes and their accessories in mind, you should now decide which items must be purchased to round out your wardrobe.

In making decisions about what to buy, emphasize one or two colors so that your new purchases and clothes on hand can be **coordinated,** or harmonized. This technique helps you to build a wardrobe having a large number of **mix-and-match** possibilities. It is an excellent way to stretch your clothing dollars. Another way to save is to make a list of your activities and then buy clothes that can be used for different purposes. Remember also to consider clothing care costs. Selecting a material that can be laundered, for example, will save on dry cleaning bills.

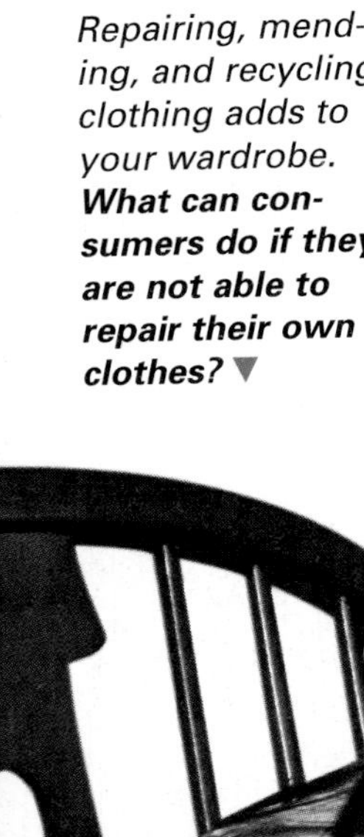

Caption Answer: Ask family and friends for help. Offer to do cooking or cleaning in exchange for their help. Also professional tailors can repair most clothing.

Repairing, mending, and recycling clothing adds to your wardrobe. ***What can consumers do if they are not able to repair their own clothes?*** ▼

Tips on Buying Used

Buying something used is a great way to save money, but only if you know the value of the item.

- **How much does it cost new and how does that compare with the price of the used item? Except for collectibles, a used item should cost a fraction of a comparable new one.**
- **Is it in good shape? If you can, find out how old it is. Make sure the item works, and inspect it carefully. If an article of clothing has a small tear in the seam, it can easily be repaired, but if it has a stain, you can't be sure it will come out.**
- **How long will the items have value? A pair of used jeans may last many years, for example, but the market for computers changes so fast that a secondhand one may not be compatible with your needs.**

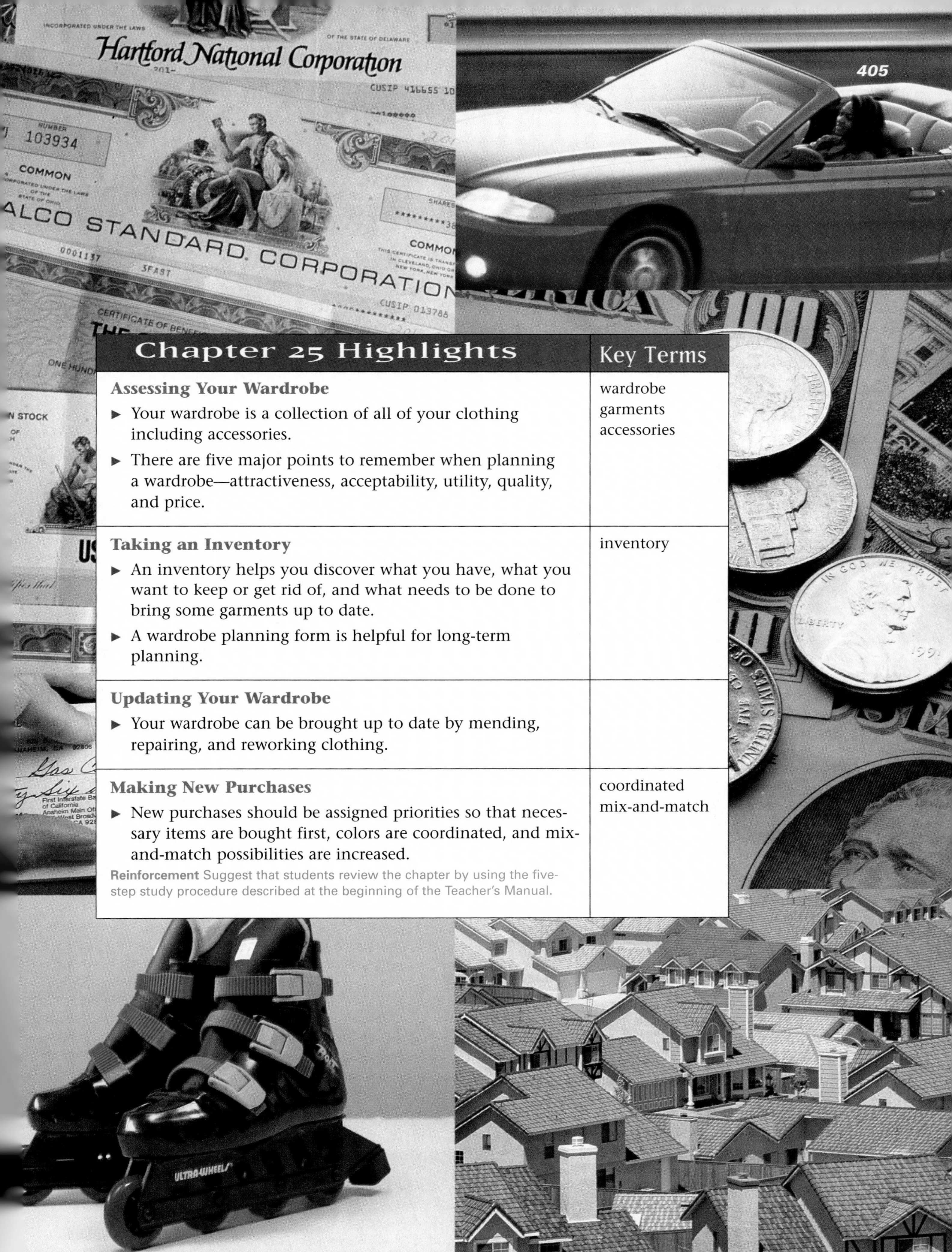

Chapter 25 Highlights	Key Terms
Assessing Your Wardrobe ▶ Your wardrobe is a collection of all of your clothing including accessories. ▶ There are five major points to remember when planning a wardrobe—attractiveness, acceptability, utility, quality, and price.	wardrobe garments accessories
Taking an Inventory ▶ An inventory helps you discover what you have, what you want to keep or get rid of, and what needs to be done to bring some garments up to date. ▶ A wardrobe planning form is helpful for long-term planning.	inventory
Updating Your Wardrobe ▶ Your wardrobe can be brought up to date by mending, repairing, and reworking clothing.	
Making New Purchases ▶ New purchases should be assigned priorities so that necessary items are bought first, colors are coordinated, and mix-and-match possibilities are increased. **Reinforcement** Suggest that students review the chapter by using the five-step study procedure described at the beginning of the Teacher's Manual.	coordinated mix-and-match

CHAPTER 25 REVIEW

Refer students to the Reviewing Consumer Terms and Reviewing Facts and Ideas activities in the Student Activity Workbook.

Reviewing Consumer Terms Puzzles will vary. See Glossary for definitions.

Reviewing Facts and Ideas See the Student Activity Workbook for answers.

Problem Solving and Decision Making **1** Answers will depend on students' perspectives. Some ideas would be to mix-and-match the garments with other coordinating clothes already in the wardrobe. **2** Answers will depend on students' perspectives. Consider date of school dance, possibilities for makeovers, need for specialized attire, long-term utility, seasonal buying and personal needs.

Consumers Around the World Math **1** Answers will depend on students' perspectives.

Communications **2** Some possibilities are: use of clothing to communicate membership in a group (as in Scotland, where kilts in various plaids indicate clan memberships); use of clothing to indicate beliefs (the Amish

Reviewing Consumer Terms

Build a crossword puzzle using the terms below. Use graph paper to arrange your entries. Then write short definitions for them.

coordinated
accessories
inventory
garments
wardrobe
mix-and-match

Reviewing Facts and Ideas

1. What features should you look for when planning your wardrobe?
2. How can you develop a suitable wardrobe?
3. If you do an inventory of your clothes and accessories and find items that you don't want anymore, what are the options available to you?
4. How can you make your wardrobe last longer?
5. How can advance planning help you to be happier with what you buy?

Problem Solving and Decision Making

1. You joined a choral group at your school that requires everyone to wear the same outfit: a navy blazer, white blouse or shirt, and gray skirt or pants. How could you rearrange it when you wear it to other occasions so you don't look exactly like your classmates?
2. You have saved money for several months to buy a special outfit for a school dance. While shopping for the important event, you notice a close-out sale on Western wear. It is a genuine bargain—50 percent off—and you know you will need Western clothing for a trip your family is planning this summer. You do not have enough money to buy clothes for the dance and take advantage of the bargain. What should you do?

Building Academic Skills

Consumers Around the World

Math

1. Inventory your wardrobe and develop a bar graph showing the numbers of colors you found. Establish percentages for each color. Analyze to determine if any changes are necessary (more neutrals, less numbers of colors, mix and match possibilities).

Communications

2. Have groups research the role of clothing as a means of communication in various countries and present findings to the class.

Social Studies

3. Have groups choose a country and period of time in history. Research the role of cultures in establishing fashion trends. Share findings with the class.

Technology

4. Set up a hypothetical trip to several foreign countries. Have students use technology to get weather information from each country. From this information, plan a wardrobe to take on a trip to each country.

Beyond the Classroom

Consumer Project

1. Take an inventory of your wardrobe. What possibilities are there for makeovers? Share your ideas with the class.
2. Volunteer to help a religious or civic group in a clothing drive. You can assist by collecting, washing and ironing, or packing clothes. Report to the class on your experience. (For example, you may find that donations include expensive, never-worn clothes.)
3. Write and act out a skit showing the right way and the wrong way to inventory and update a wardrobe. Present the skit in class.

Cooperative Learning

Family Economics

Break into assigned family group. Discuss the following problem.

You know you should put away out-of-season garments, but your family's apartment lacks enough storage space. You have one small closet in the entry and one large closet in each bedroom. Garments are jammed in so tightly that they get very wrinkled. Devise a plan that will free some closet space for everyone in the family. You may consider purchases of furniture or storage systems, provided they are within your budget. Assume, however, that all clothing has been inventoried and is needed and regularly worn. Compare your answers with those of other family groups.

Debate the Issue

Although most consumers have a limited budget to spend on clothing, people vary in how they spend the money they have. Some consumers think that quality is more important than price when buying clothes. They would rather have one or two really nice sweaters, for example, than own several less costly ones. Others would rather own more garments, even if they are of a lesser quality, to have as much variety as possible.

You and your classmates will break into groups and research this topic. Each group will gather evidence to support one side or the other. You are to prepare the argument for your side of the problem. Then the two groups will meet in a classroom debate.

wear simple clothes for a simple lifestyle).

Social Studies
3 An idea would be to discuss total body coverage as the dominant factor in clothing in middle Europe during the Dark Ages. It was probably for warmth, but also served as an expression of that repressive era.

Technology
4 Answers will depend on the location selected.

Consumer Project
1, 2, & 3 Answers will depend on students' perspectives.

Family Economics
Some ideas: to get extra storage space, families who can afford it might buy furniture, such as cedar chests, armoires, or highboys. Other families might build their own storage systems out of cardboard boxes, baskets, and clothes racks on casters.

Debate the Issue
Break the class into two teams. Assign each team one side of the issue. Encourage students to work together as a team to develop their argument. Ask each team to select a member to make an opening statement that supports their side of the issue. Have students take turns debating as the debate moves from one team to another

CHAPTER 26

Shopping for Clothes

Learning Objectives

When you have finished studying this section, you should be able to:

1. Choose clothing that is right for you, based on attractiveness, acceptability, utility, quality, and price.
2. Describe the advantages and disadvantages of natural and synthetic fibers.
3. Use clothing labels as guides both when shopping and when caring for clothing.
4. Identify common shopping problems.

Consumer Terms

fads
classics
factory outlets
off-price outlets
natural fibers
synthetic fibers
blends
Sanforizing
permanent care labels
hangtags

Real-World Journal

What factors do you consider when you purchase clothing? List in your journal the last five purchases you made. Describe why you made each purchase.

Lesson Plan See the Teacher's Manual for Chapter 26 lesson plan.

Vocabulary The Chapter 26 lesson plan includes suggested vocabulary activities for the terms listed.

1 Discussion Starter Ask students if they have ever wandered around clothing stores with only a vague general idea of what they were looking for, and then finally, unable to find anything, they felt as if they had wasted a lot of time. Can they see the advantage in knowing exactly what they want before going to the store?

2 Reinforcement Have students find examples from clothing books and magazines of how certain patterns or designs look good on some people but not good on others.

3 Research Have students read books or articles outside class on color analysis. Then, working in small groups, have them determine their own color types using one of the color systems. Have each student write a short report or give an oral report describing his or her personal evaluations of the results.

WHAT TO LOOK FOR

Planning your clothing purchases as described in the previous chapter simplifies shopping. If you have done an inventory and analyzed your wardrobe needs, you know what to look for in terms of garment type, color, and price range. Wiser and more satisfying choices
1 are likely to result.

There are five factors to keep in mind when considering a clothing purchase—attractiveness, acceptability, utility, quality, and price. Each of these will be examined in detail in this section.

Attractiveness

Clothing should bring out your best features and play down your less attractive ones. The latest fashion may be perfect for a classmate, but a disaster for you. The test for any garment is how it looks on you, not on a hanger or a fash-
2 ion model.

Color Each of us has a natural coloring that goes well with certain colors. Think for a moment about the outfit you now own that has brought you the most compliments. Chances are it contains colors that are becoming to you.

While certain shades of almost any color may be right for you, there are other factors to consider. Dark colors, for example, make a person appear more slender, while light shades seem to add weight. Tops and bottoms of contrasting colors make a person look heavier. Thus, if you want to appear slimmer, consider wearing outfits of all one color. Small designs in muted colors and soft fabrics can help, too. If you want to appear heavier, consider wearing large, multicolor designs as
3 well as rough, bulky fabrics.

Line Unbroken vertical lines running from the shoulders to the bottom of a garment add height. A row of buttons or trim down the front of a full-length garment, for example, can give this effect. If you want to appear shorter, look for clothes with horizontal lines.

Fit Clothing that does not fit properly cannot make you more attractive. Probably the most important question you can ask about a possible purchase is "Will I be comfortable in it?"

To start, you should know approximately what size you wear. However, sizes are not uniform. Only by trying on clothes can you know what your size is in a particular style or make.

When trying on a garment, do not simply examine the fit in a mirror. Move. Move in all the extreme and complex ways you move in your daily activities—walk, sit, reach up, crouch down, bend over, fold your arms. Then ask yourself these questions.

1. Do I feel comfortable?
2. Does the garment fit securely where it should?
3. Does it move with me, or give when it should?
4. Does it bind or wrinkle (indications of tightness)?

Blue Jeans

New and used blue jeans, particularly those with the Levi's label, continue to be popular around the world. Used jeans worth about $2 a pair in the United States can sell for $80 in Italy and Greece.

If you cannot answer yes to the first three questions and no to the last, keep
1 looking. You have not found a good fit.

Acceptability

We usually select clothes that conform to what our friends or employers will accept. You should also consider your own individuality and how you will use your clothes—on the job, at school, and so forth. Clothes and accessories can express your personality and even make you feel better about yourself. You'll also wear them more, and for a longer period of time, if you feel good
2 in them.

Fashion If you've talked about or read about clothes or styles, you've heard of *fashion,* which is a look or style popular at a given time, such as long leather coats. **Fads,** on the other hand, are exaggerated styles that fall out of favor fairly quickly.

Clothes and accessories cost money, so it is important to buy wisely. Smart choices in the store can be viewed as an investment in tomorrow's wardrobe as well as today's.

Choose garments that will last. Analyze the current trends and see which ones you think will be in fashion longer than a few months. Clothes that are made of quality fabrics and show good workmanship, like completed seams and zippers that work easily, are good to look for. Clothes made by respected designers usually will last a long time. Again, however, avoid exaggerated styles—such as a neon pink shirt.

Classics, which are long-lasting fashions and include blazers, button-down shirts, straight slacks, and cardigan sweaters, may be the best investment, but a wardrobe full of them may seem boring. A wardrobe based on fads is too expensive because it will have to be
3 replaced quickly.

So what do you do? A good compromise is to choose a few adaptable classics for the foundation of your wardrobe. Make other choices from one or more of the available styles that you like, such as a wide belt or a shirt with a wide collar. Occasionally purchase a fad if it adds life to an old wardrobe or expresses something that you want to say. Limit fads to
4 inexpensive items, however.

Utility

Wardrobe items have utility if they serve a useful purpose. Rainwear, for example, should repel water. A winter coat should be warm; a pair of summer slacks, cool. Officewear should meet the requirements of the job. If clothing does not meet this basic standard, no matter how stylish or attractive it is, it will not
5 be worn.

Quality

Quality is important in clothing. However, not everything you buy needs to be the best available. An item that will not be worn often, for example, does not have to be extremely durable. A heavy coat or other garment that must be worn for several

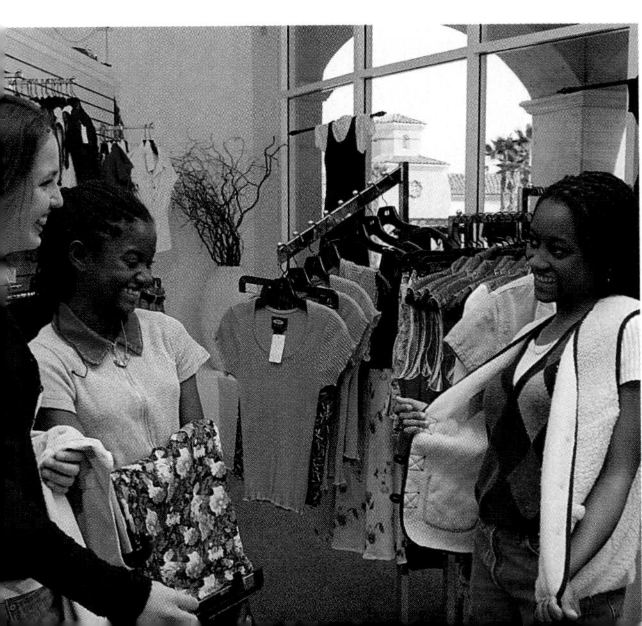

◀ *Finding the right type of clothing is important to most people.* ***Do you prefer to shop with friends or family members? Why?***

Caption Answer: Student responses will depend of their perspective. Some will prefer friends for their peer advice. Others may prefer family members who are more experienced shoppers.

1 Discussion Starter Ask students if they have ever liked an item of clothing so much that they bought it knowing it didn't fit right, telling themselves that it fit well enough. What was the long-range result of this purchase?

2 Learning Economics Remind students of what they read about supply and demand in Unit 1. A certain item of clothing might be of the same quality or even inferior quality and still cost more than another if for some reason it is in great demand.

3 Reinforcement Gather several clothing advertisements from current magazines. Choose some showing classic styles and some showing trendy fashions. Discuss them in class to get students' reactions as to whether the items are classic or trendy.

4 Research Have students identify a fad or fashion that started from the clothing or style of a celebrity. Have them write a brief description of the style and its development and present the description with photos of the clothes in that style.

5 Discussion Starter Ask students if they have had personal experiences with clothing items that were extremely attractive but were impractical and therefore rarely worn.

1 Reinforcement
Bring several items of clothing to class and examine each in detail, using the checklist in Figure 26–1. Have students make their own checklists and write high, medium, or low for each point on the checklist to indicate the class evaluation of quality.

2 Discussion Starter
Ask students about their experiences with wanting items they believed to be too expensive. Have they gone ahead and made the purchases in some cases? Have they bought less desirable and less expensive versions in other cases? What has been their reaction to both alternatives?

seasons, on the other hand, should be well made and of sturdy material.

When examining clothing for quality, note the points listed below. Remember, however, that the item can be of *acceptable* quality without having all of
1 the features listed in Figure 26–1.

Price

Suppose you find a piece of clothing that you really like. It has the right colors and lines and is durable and well made. The outfit is fashionable and looks great on you. You need it, and you want it. The price tag, however, brings you back to earth. The cost is three times
2 what you can pay.

Affordability If you follow the step-by-step plan suggested earlier, you know ahead of time what you need and how much you can afford to spend. Upon entering a store, go to the rack or department that features garments in your price range. Ignore displays of high-cost merchandise. They will tend to make you less satisfied with the choice you

Figure 26–1 Quality Garment Construction

Being attentive to these details will help you to evaluate clothing before you purchase it.

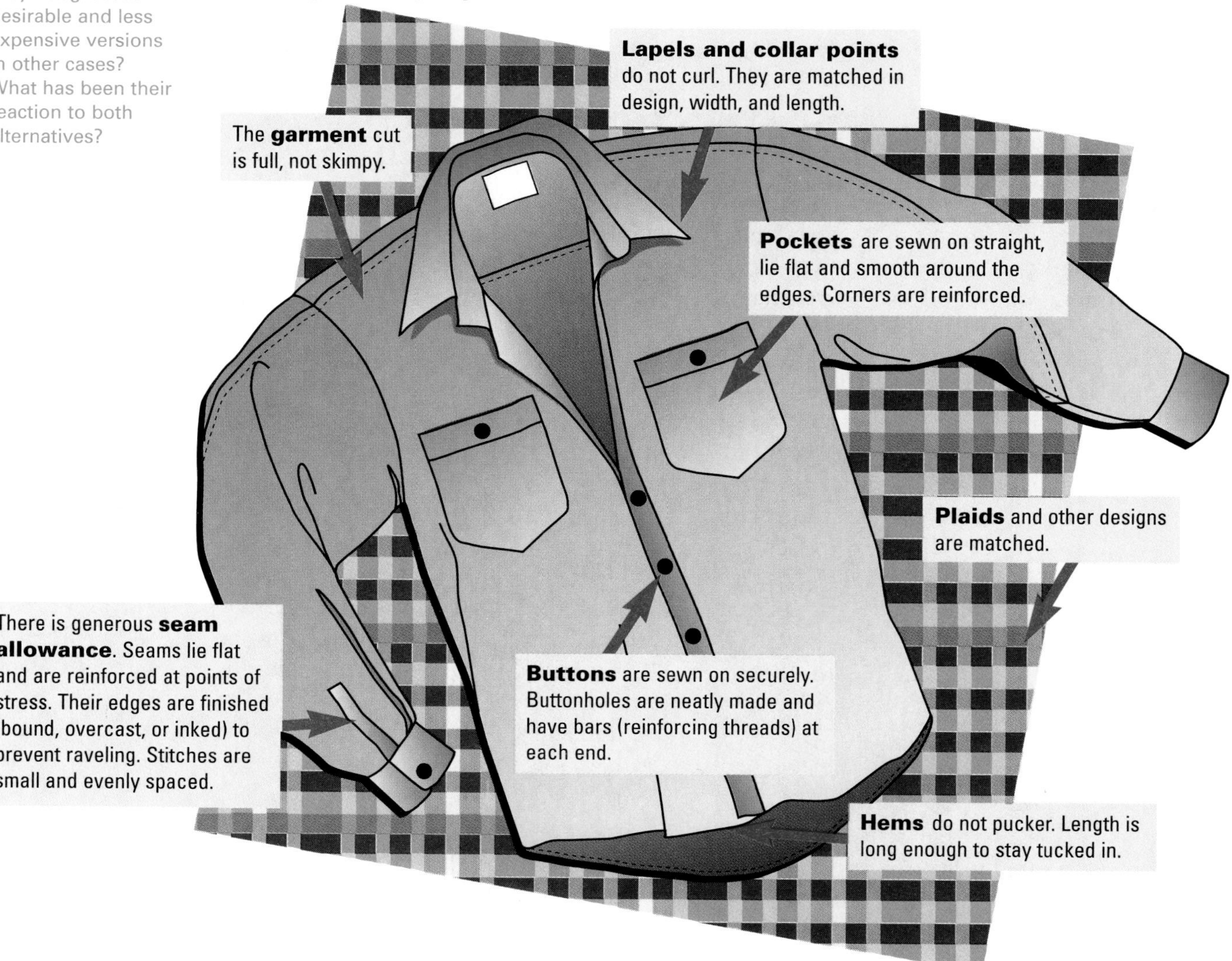
Lapels and collar points do not curl. They are matched in design, width, and length.
The **garment** cut is full, not skimpy.
Pockets are sewn on straight, lie flat and smooth around the edges. Corners are reinforced.
Plaids and other designs are matched.
There is generous **seam allowance**. Seams lie flat and are reinforced at points of stress. Their edges are finished (bound, overcast, or inked) to prevent raveling. Stitches are small and evenly spaced.
Buttons are sewn on securely. Buttonholes are neatly made and have bars (reinforcing threads) at each end.
Hems do not pucker. Length is long enough to stay tucked in.

can afford. This policy may take some of the adventure and excitement out of shopping. In the long run, though, it is the easier course to follow.

Where to Shop Knowing what you need and how much you want to spend also allows you to choose the right place to shop. Smart consumers do not limit themselves to department stores and specialty shops. They consider other alternatives.

1. **Factory outlets.** Stores where factory overruns and seconds are sold at bargain prices are **factory outlets.** Overruns come about when manufacturers misjudge the market. They produce more goods than they can sell at regular prices. Seconds are items that do not measure up to a manufacturer's quality standards. Many, however, have only minor,
1 hidden flaws.
2. **Discount stores.** Today's discount stores have changed in response to consumer demands. Many have upgraded their clothing departments so that they now offer stylish, fashion-oriented items like designer (or designer-look) jeans.
3. **Off-price outlets.** Designer discount stores that cater to bargain hunters are **off-price outlets.** They offer quality merchandise at reduced prices.
4. **Garage sales and thrift shops.** Much seldom-worn clothing finds its way to garage sales and thrift shops. Here some real bargains can be found. Before buying a previously owned garment, be sure it is clean and in good condition. Also be sure it fits, as
2 returns are not usually permitted.
5. **Catalogs.** Both print and electronic catalog shopping are convenient for people who have little spare time. Prices are usually comparable to those in department stores. The additional cost of shipping should be considered, however. Sometimes, it is difficult to judge sizes and quality when ordering through catalogs.

Given all of these alternatives, it is possible to take comparison shopping too far. Choosing from among three or four suits or dresses is easy; deciding on the best of ten is a much more difficult task. First, it takes longer to find so many items. Second, once you have found them, it takes you longer to choose. Remember, your time is valuable. As a smart shopper, you should limit your purchase possibilities.

Cost of Care A factor that consumers often fail to consider when making a clothing purchase is the cost of caring for a garment. If it must be dry-cleaned frequently, for example, a dress or suit could be affordable to buy but beyond your means to keep.

When Buying Clothing, Read the Care Label

Permanent care labels are sewn inside clothing, typically at the neck, at the waistband, or in one of the seams. If you check the label before you buy, you can determine how costly the clothing will be to clean. A garment with a "dry-clean only" label will be more expensive to keep clean than will one that can be machine washed. A garment that has a label stating "machine wash separately" will require the expense involved for a separate wash load. Additionally, if you disregard the label directions and wash the garment with other clothing, the fabric dyes may run and may ruin the other clothes. Clothing labeled "machine wash/tumble dry" is the easiest and least expensive to care for.

1 Reinforcement Provide students with a list of factory outlets in your area. Ask students if they have shopped in any of these stores. Have students who have made purchases in these stores tell about the savings, the durability, and quality of the merchandise. Were they happy with their purchases?

2 Critical Thinking Have students analyze the pros and cons of buying at garage sales and thrift shops. Are they aware of intangibles such as the time it takes to find an item and the lower level of emotional satisfaction associated with a used item as opposed to a new item? How do they balance these factors against price reductions?

FLASHBACK FLASHFORWARD

The Sears Roebuck catalog advertised panty hose in 1939 for 21 cents a pair. Today, purchasing a pair of panty hose averages about $5.00 a pair.

1 Extension Have several students develop a fiber fact booklet for class reference. Time permitting, you may want to conduct classroom experiments to see how various fibers react to such conditions as heat, moisture, and dirt. The booklet should contain samples of each fabric and fiber.

2 Student Motivator Have students check the labels on all their clothes. Have them make a list with the kind and percent of natural fiber in each item. Can they draw any conclusions from this list as to the strengths and weaknesses of the four natural fibers?

3 Extension Have students interview older family members or friends who remember the introduction of synthetic fibers. Report on how the use of these fibers affected their lives.

FIBERS, FABRICS, AND FINISHES

Fabrics are made up of fibers, some natural and some synthetic. **Natural fibers** are made from plants or obtained from animals. **Synthetic fibers,** or manufactured fibers, are made from chemicals. Both kinds of fibers are used to make clothing. A basic knowledge of the science of textiles—fibers, fabrics, and fabric finishes—will help you
1 choose clothing wisely.

Natural Fibers

Until advances in chemistry made possible the development of manufactured fibers, almost all clothing was made from natural materials. Cotton, wool, linen, and silk were the most common.

1. **Cotton.** Cotton is absorbent, inexpensive, and durable. On the negative side, however, it shrinks and wrinkles easily. These disadvantages are often overcome by preshrinking and by blending cotton with synthetic fibers.
2. **Wool.** This fiber is as absorbent as cotton but more wrinkle-resistant. It is extremely warm. It can be made into fabrics of different weights. Both heavy winter coats and lightweight dresses and suits can be made from wool. Wool jackets, skirts, and pants usually must be dry-cleaned.
3. **Linen.** Usually imported, linen is made from the flax plant. The fabric is absorbent and durable. It wrinkles very easily, however, unless specially treated.
4. **Silk.** Silk is absorbent, lightweight, and soil-resistant. Although the fabric is durable, it can be weakened by perspiration and sunlight. The best silk comes from cocoons formed by culti-
2 vated, not wild, silkworms.

Synthetic Fibers

Synthetic fibers are usually made from chemicals. Some of the best-known manufactured fibers are nylon, acetate, polyester, and rayon. They add great variety and versatility to fabrics and
3 garments.

1. **Nylon.** The strongest of all manufactured fibers in common use, nylon was the first truly synthetic fiber to be developed. Its outstanding characteristic is its versatility. Nylon can be made strong enough for tire cords, fine enough for hosiery, and light enough for parachutes. It is used alone and in combination with other fibers. In combination, its chief contributions are its strength and resistance to abrasion. Nylon washes easily, dries quickly, and needs little pressing. It holds its shape well because it neither shrinks nor stretches.
2. **Rayon.** Rayon was the first of the manufactured fibers. It is made from cellulose, a natural material, which is converted chemically and then regenerated into fibers. Rayon is one of the least expensive of the synthetics. It combines well with practically all other fibers and, for that reason, is used extensively in blends. It offers

advantages of comfort, efficiency, and luster.

3. **Acetate.** Acetate is closely related to rayon. (The two fabrics are made using a similar cellulose conversion process.) Acetate combines well with a number of other fibers. It contributes luster, silkiness, body, and good draping qualities to such fashion fabrics as taffeta, satin, crepe, brocade, and tricot. When acetate has color added to it while still in its liquid stage (before it is spun), it is called solution-dyed (or spun-dyed) acetate. This material

Teaching Many Ways to Dance

Zina Bethune began dancing at age 3. By the age of 7, she was dancing with the New York City Ballet. Then at 11, doctors found she had curvature of the spine. They wanted to fuse her spine, which would have ended her dance career. Instead, she kept dancing, wearing a brace at night to reduce the curvature.

At 14, Bethune developed a disease that caused swollen legs. She wore special tights and kept dancing. At 17, she developed problems with her hips. Doctors said she would be crippled for life. She kept dancing and even founded her own dance company. In her early thirties, she finally had both hips replaced. Still she kept dancing.

Bethune's dancing and determination had kept her out of a wheelchair all her life. So she thought that dancing might help children who were disabled. She felt she understood special children because she herself had come so close to being disabled.

In 1983, after her dance company moved to Los Angeles, she founded Dance Outreach. Her first class had only 17 students. Although the children could hardly move at first, they began to discover the whole world of dance in themselves.

Today there are more than 1000 children—4 to 16 years old—involved in Dance Outreach in southern California. Eventually, Bethune wants the program to become nationwide.

There are therapeutic benefits to the program as the children's bodies get stronger through dance. However, as Bethune watches them dance and sees the delight on their faces, she knows it is the creative power and the feeling of self-worth the children gain that is far more important.

Brainstorm

Think of a sport or hobby that you could teach to children who are physically disabled. What would it take to develop your own program for these children?

Case Study Answer: Answers depend on the sport or hobby students choose. Students should brainstorm ways to get children with disabilities involved and to find locations for their programs.

1 **Vocabulary** Since some students may not know the meaning, ask them to define *colorfastness.* (Retains color.) Why is this an important quality in materials used to make clothing? (Clothes can lose color after repeated washings.)

2 **Critical Thinking** Ask students to identify the main advantage of each of the synthetic fibers. (Nylon—versatility; rayon—inexpensive; acetate—colorfastness most emphasized, though students might also mention the fact that it combines well with many other fibers; polyester—easy care.)

3 **Reinforcement** Have students make a list of the materials mentioned under the heading "Blends" and write the positive qualities associated with those materials. (Cotton—absorbent, economical; polyester—durable; nylon—easier to dye; spandex—elasticity.)

4 **Reinforcement** Many students will not know the difference between loosely woven and closely woven fabrics. Bring examples of each to class for a demonstration.

Case Study Answers:
1 Answers will vary.
2 An example might be using old scraps of clothing to make quilts.

has excellent colorfastness when exposed repeatedly to light, perspiration, atmospheric contaminants, and
1 washing.

4. **Polyester.** This fiber has made the centuries-old dream of wash-and-wear and easy-care clothing a reality. Polyester does not shrink or stretch during normal use. Heat-set pleats and creases stand up extremely well under everyday wear. Water-borne stains may be quickly and simply removed. Because of these qualities, polyester is used extensively in blends with other fibers—mainly cotton, rayon, and wool. The blend retains the major characteristics of the base fiber but is stronger, is more wrinkle-resistant, and holds creases better. In fact, a major use of polyester is in the manufacture of permanent press fabrics, usually
2 blends of polyester and cotton.

Blends

Fibers are often combined into **blends** to take advantage of the strong points of each. For example, many wash-and-wear shirts are 35 percent cotton and 65 percent polyester. Cotton makes the garments absorbent and keeps down their cost. The wash-and-wear finish, however, weakens cotton. Polyester fibers are therefore added to make the item more durable.

Nylon is another fiber frequently used in blends. It may be added to make clothing easier to dye. Spandex is still another frequent addition. A manufactured fiber of great elasticity, Spandex in very small amounts gives a garment stretch. Other manufactured fibers added in similarly small amounts
3 improve appearance and add luster.

Preshrinking

Loosely woven fabrics have a greater tendency to shrink than do those that are closely woven. Check the label for a statement concerning shrinkage to be expected. **Sanforizing** is a patented preshrinking process that guarantees shrinkage of no more than 1 percent
4 after manufacture.

LABELS

By reading labels, today's consumers can be well informed about the clothing they buy. A number of years ago, however, the situation was very different. Labels often gave inaccurate or incomplete information.

Content Labels

For example, before 1939, consumers could easily be misled about wool products. Labels did not make clear how much wool a fabric contained. Neither did they reveal whether the wool had been used before. Then the Wool Products Labeling Act was passed. It required that all wool products be labeled with the following information:

1. Total fiber weight of wool.
2. Whether the wool is new, reprocessed, or reused.
3. Content of any other fiber present (if it amounts to 5 percent or more).

Similar acts were passed to cover abuses in the labeling of fur products and in the identification of natural and manufactured textile fibers. As a result, today's consumer is in a much better position to buy and care for clothes properly.

Care Labels

Permanent care labels are sewn into most garments. The labels tell how to care for clothing. They instruct the purchaser on how to wash, dry, iron, bleach, dry-clean, or otherwise care for and maintain a garment. They also warn against treatment that could be harmful to either the garment itself or other articles of clothing being treated with it. Examples

CASE STUDY

Careers in Focus

Lorenzo Vega, Tie Maker

Lorenzo Vega turns rags to riches—literally. He stitches together patchwork ties from left-over strips and scraps of silk. His designs mix his colorful Colombian heritage with traditional American quilting and modern design theory. That combination has made the young New York designer a premier figure in high fashion.

A native Colombian, Vega arrived in the United States for schooling when he was 17. He planned to study architecture but soon discovered his talent for fashion.

At first, Vega did quite well designing evening and bridal gowns. Then a client asked him to make a tie for her husband. In the process, Vega made a discovery—that ties were an undervalued element of men's fashion. With the correct tie, he found, you could upgrade a suit, assert individuality, and have some fun.

Vega's first ties appeared in 1989. They were floral prints, and they shocked the conservative tie market.

Vega never even thought of patchwork ties until his second year of business. The idea grew out of what he saw as intolerable waste—garbage bags full of expensive silk scraps. The scraps were what was left after patterns were cut from bolts of fabric. They became the stuff of Vega's most distinctive designs.

Each tie is sold in only limited quantities to small boutiques. This particularly guarantees wearers that they will never run into someone wearing the same tie.

Vega also pampers the wearer. His latest ties have a pocket built into the back and a small chain to keep the panels together. If a Lorenzo Vega tie is damaged, he fixes it free of charge.

Vega has become successful as a result of his imagination and entrepreneurial skills. Following the success of his patchwork ties, the designer has expanded his collection to include an entire line of menswear. In the fickle world of fashion, Vega's designs look as though they're around—necks, that is—to stay.

Case Study Review

1. What are some skills you have that you could use to start a career in the clothing field?
2. Being resourceful became a key to Vega's success. Think of items that some may regard as garbage or waste. How could you recycle these items in some way to produce a clothing product you could sell?

1 Extension Have each student choose one particular kind of garment (sweater, blouse, skirt, etc.). Then have the students visit clothing stores to find as many different kinds and combinations of fabrics used to make that kind of garment. Students should then write one or two sentences telling how each article of clothing would be cleaned.

2 Critical Thinking Have students bring to class newspaper advertisements for clothing sales. The sales could be special purchases, clearance, close-out, fire, or white sales, for example. Have students discuss and determine the real versus the apparent meanings of terms used in the ads. In general, were the ads misleading?

3 Discussion Starter Ask students if they typically examine garments closely for flaws before purchasing them. Have they ever discovered a problem with a garment *after* paying for it?

4 Extension Student Activity Workbook, Chapter 26 activities.

Some clothes have special requirements. ***What labels would you look for on a garment like this?*** ▶

Caption Answer Content, care, and hangtag labels.

of such warnings include "No bleach" or "Wash bright colors separately."

Permanent care labels have been required by law for more than a decade. Clothing manufacturers have tried to arrive at a standard terminology so that consumers will have no doubts about the meaning of care instructions.

Permanent care labels should not be cut off garments. In this respect, they are different from the removable **hangtags** attached to clothing on display. Hangtags, however, may also give information about fabric content and care. In such cases, the hangtags should be read carefully, identified with a brief
1 description of the garment, and kept.

SHOPPING PROBLEMS

Consumers often do not get full value for their clothing dollars. They do not plan their purchases. They do not look for signs of quality workmanship. They do not read labels. In other words, they do not make a conscious effort to develop shopping skills, and these omissions cost them money.

At times, however, consumers are not at fault. They are misled by questionable advertising and shoddy goods disguised as quality merchandise.

Misleading Advertising

Advertisements must be read carefully and critically. Often they are worded so that they appear to say much more than they actually do. For example, "Compare at $30" and similar phrases are meaningless. They merely invite you to compare a firm's merchandise with that which sells elsewhere for $30. They say nothing about the price from which the merchandise was reduced (if, indeed, it was reduced at all).

The word *special* is another that is frequently abused. Some firms have the merchandise they offer as a special purchase shipped in just for sales. Such merchandise is often of lower quality than the regular stock. Examine carefully, for example, clothing offered as part of after-Christmas sales. If it is not of the same quality as that which was offered at regular prices before the holiday, there is nothing "special" about it. 2

The best defense against misleading advertising is to become familiar with the price lines and brands sold in your area stores. Read their ads regularly. Try to plan your purchases well in advance. Give yourself time to comparison shop.

Shoddy Merchandise

Poorly made clothing is not just a sale problem. Shoddy merchandise can be offered as part of a store's regular stock. Be especially careful of clothing offered at unusually low prices. Learn to look for sizing (filler, or starch, that gives body to a fabric until it is washed out) and signs of poor workmanship. Make sure that the lighting is good when you try on clothes. If necessary, ask to take a gar-
3 ment to another part of the store where
4 the lighting is better.

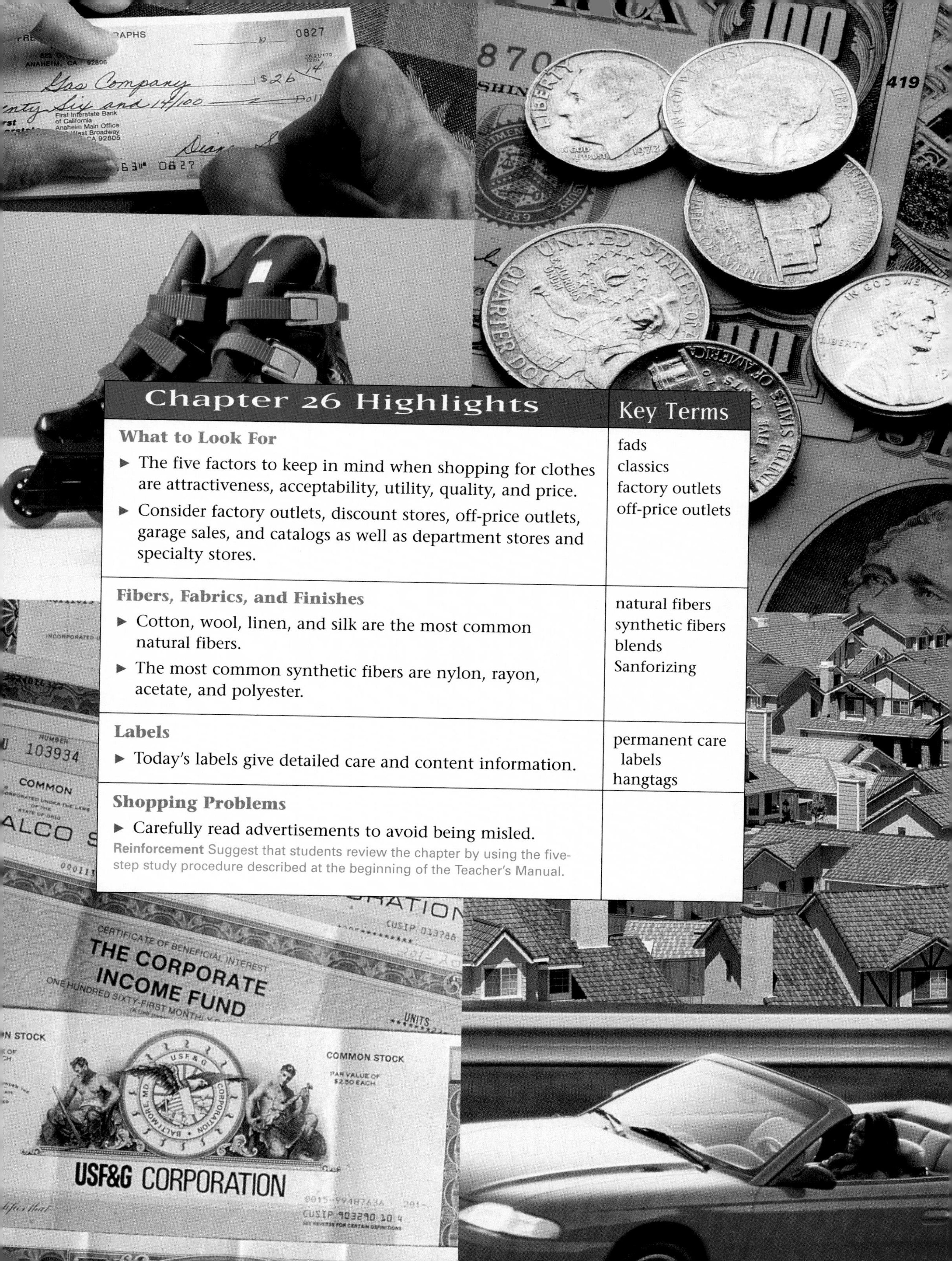

Chapter 26 Highlights

	Key Terms
What to Look For ▸ The five factors to keep in mind when shopping for clothes are attractiveness, acceptability, utility, quality, and price. ▸ Consider factory outlets, discount stores, off-price outlets, garage sales, and catalogs as well as department stores and specialty stores.	fads classics factory outlets off-price outlets
Fibers, Fabrics, and Finishes ▸ Cotton, wool, linen, and silk are the most common natural fibers. ▸ The most common synthetic fibers are nylon, rayon, acetate, and polyester.	natural fibers synthetic fibers blends Sanforizing
Labels ▸ Today's labels give detailed care and content information.	permanent care labels hangtags
Shopping Problems ▸ Carefully read advertisements to avoid being misled. **Reinforcement** Suggest that students review the chapter by using the five-step study procedure described at the beginning of the Teacher's Manual.	

CHAPTER 26 REVIEW

Refer students to the Reviewing Consumer Terms and Reviewing Facts and Ideas activities in the Student Activity Workbook.

Reviewing Consumer Terms Sentences will vary. See Glossary for definitions.

Reviewing Facts and Ideas See the Student Activity Workbook for answers.

Problem Solving and Decision Making **1** No. Clothing that is too small is seldom a bargain. Making the kinds of alterations you would need in this coat would be complicated and costly. **2** Answers will depend on students' perspectives. Use caution in purchasing seconds from places where lighting is poor, however.

Consumers Around the World Math **1** 20 × \$5.75 = \$115; \$115 × 52 = \$5,980; \$5980 × .15 = 897; \$5980 − \$897 = \$5083; \$5083 ÷ 2 = \$2,541.50.

Communications **2** Student reports should answer all questions.

Social Studies **3** Reduced labor costs are a major incentive. Others include better quality control, better fabric selection and design flexibility, and, often,

Reviewing Consumer Terms

Use each of the following terms in a sentence to demonstrate you know its meaning.

blends
classics
factory outlets
fads
hangtags
natural fibers
off-price outlets
permanent care labels
Sanforizing
synthetic fibers

Reviewing Facts and Ideas

1. What five factors should you keep in mind when shopping for clothes?
2. List the advantages and disadvantages of natural and synthetic fibers.
3. What should you look for in examining clothing for quality workmanship?
4. How are permanent-care labels of value to the consumer?
5. List common shopping problems.

Problem Solving and Decision Making

1. You are shopping for a winter coat during a back-to-school sale in August when you find just what you want. The coat is the right color to blend with your wardrobe, the right style for your figure, and on sale at \$20 off. Admittedly, it is a little snug through the shoulders. Also, the sleeves would have to be lengthened, leaving only narrow hems at the wrist and little give in the lining. Should you buy? Explain.
2. Assume there is a factory outlet in your area, and you have the following information about it.
   a. It operates from a warehouse, and lighting is poor.
   b. Brand names have been removed from the clothing.
   c. Seconds are sold.
   d. All sales are for cash, and there are "no refunds or returns."
   e. Prices offer savings ranging from 30 to 50 percent.
   Would you be willing to update your wardrobe at the outlet? Why or why not?

Building Academic Skills

Consumers Around the World

Math

1. You've decided to get a part-time job after school, working 20 hours per week, and earning \$5.75 per hour. You and your family have agreed that half of your pay will be put in savings for college tuition. The other half is to pay for your clothes. If you work for 52 weeks and 15 percent of your salary goes to pay for taxes, how much money will you have to spend on clothes?

Communications

2. Research the number of clothing discount stores, factory outlets, off-price outlets, and secondhand shops in your area. Interview five friends, family members, or neighbors and ask them to evaluate the stores on your list. Summarize your findings in a 500-word report.

Social Studies

3. Nearly one-third of all clothing purchased in the United States is made in other countries. In higher priced garments, the percentage rises to over 50 percent. A typical man's wardrobe is made up of clothes from all over the world. Take, for example, suits from Hong Kong, sweaters from Uruguay, jackets from China, and shirts from India. What conditions in these countries offer incentives for clothing manufacturers? Share your findings with the class in an oral report.

Technology

4. Research how technology is expanding shopping opportunities for consumers. For example, some jeans manufacturers now offer jeans custom fit for the consumer; other companies supply their catalogs on CD-ROM and on-line. Summarize your findings in a 500-word report.

Beyond the Classroom

Consumer Project

Bring two articles of clothing to class and point out for the group why one is well made and the other is not. Be very specific. Identify such things as interfacing and seams.

Cooperative Learning

Family Economics

Break into assigned family groups. Discuss the following problem.

One member of your family is diagnosed as having an allergy to synthetic fibers. Unfortunately, such fibers are present in almost half of the clothes this person has, primarily through blends. Develop a reasonable and low-cost plan for quickly reshaping this family member's wardrobe. Include what is to be done with articles of clothing that must be discarded, recommendations on where and how to acquire reasonably priced substitute garments, content and care labeling that any new acquisitions must have, and expected changes in garment maintenance and care. Compare your answers with those of other family groups.

Debate the Issue

Some people think that the federal government should pass laws to prevent so many foreign-made garments from being sold in the United States. Other people feel that these imports provide competition, variety, and price savings for American consumers.

You and your classmates will break into two groups and research this topic. Each group will gather evidence to support one side or the other. You are to prepare the argument for your side of the problem. Then the two groups will meet in a classroom debate.

Rechecking Your Attitude

Before going on to the next unit, go back to the Attitude Inventory at the beginning of this one. Answer the questions a second time. Then compare the two sets of responses. On how many statements have your attitudes changed? Can you account for these shifts in your opinions? What do you know now that you did not know then?

lower minimum orders than required in the United States.

Technology
4 Students should share their findings with the class. Some possibilities might be to report on experiences with electronic shopping through TV networks and CD ROM catalogs.

Consumer Project
Answers will depend on students' perspectives.

Family Economics
To recoup some of the money spent on unwearable clothing, have a garage sale. For replacement garments, shop sales, discount stores, and factory outlets. Look for items labeled "100 percent cotton" (or wool or linen or silk, the other natural fibers). Be prepared to pay more to purchase these garments and also to maintain them. For example, woolen garments must often be dry-cleaned.

Debate the Issue
Break the class into two teams. Assign each team one side of the issue. Encourage students to work together as a team to develop their argument. Ask each team to select a member to make an opening statement that supports their side of the issue. Have students take turns debating as the debate moves from one team to another.

UNIT 8 LAB

You and Your Community

STEP A Students should prepare written inventories of the clothing they currently have. Their notations about the utility of particular garments should indicate that they have researched the varying climate conditions of the northeastern and southwestern United States.
STEP B Students should make reasonable lists of clothing needs and submit practical budgets for the lists.
STEP C Students should take clear, accurate notes on the clothing they inspect at the stores.
STEP D Students' answers should be accurate and based on their shopping notes.
STEP E Students' reports should reflect their understanding of the trade-offs imposed by needs, desires, and budgets.

Refer students to the Unit 8 Lab in the Student Activity Workbook.

Planning a Wardrobe for a New Life

Unit 8 presents the practical steps needed to inventory your wardrobe and to make wise clothing purchases. This lab will help you practice what you've learned as you plan a wardrobe for college and a part-time office job.

TOOLS

1. Almanacs (*Places Rated Almanac,* by David Savageau and Richard Boyer, Prentice-Hall, 1993, is particularly helpful for researching weather conditions in specific locations.)
2. Travel and college guidebooks
3. Newpapers
4. Fashion magazines
5. Direct-mail advertisements

PROCEDURES

STEP A Imagine that you have been accepted to two major American colleges—one in the Northeast and another in the Southwest. You have also been offered excellent part-time office jobs in both locations. The hours of both jobs can be arranged around your college classes, but you will often need to go directly from class to work (or vice versa). You have not yet decided which college to attend, but you know that you'll need to make major changes in your wardrobe regardless of the school you choose.

First, research the climate in the northeastern and southwestern United States. Then, begin the redesign of your wardrobe by taking an inventory of your current clothing. For each item, complete a brief description that includes the following:

1. Item identification.
2. Item's need for cleaning, mending/reworking, exchanging, or discarding/donating.
3. Item's utility in the Northeast and the Southwest. (Could it be worn for school, work, relaxation? to parties and dates? Is it suitable for the climate?)

STEP B Make one list of the ten most essential clothing purchases that you would need to make in preparing for the northeastern climate. Make another list of your ten essential clothing purchases for the southwestern climate. Naturally, some items will be suitable for either climate. Number the items on each list in order of priority. Next, evaluate your personal finances and decide how much of your own money you could devote to clothing purchases. If your family buys your clothes, ask your parents or guardians to estimate the amount they could contribute to your budget.

STEP C Select and visit two or three stores that sell clothing. Be sure that one is a discount store and another is either a specialty shop or an "upscale" department store. If you live near a factory outlet, make an effort to visit it as well. At every store, shop for the items on your two clothing lists. Make notes about the following aspects for each item:

1. **Attractiveness.** Does it fit well? Is the color right for you and for other garments you may wear with it?
2. **Acceptability.** Is it classic, trendy, stylish, dated?
3. **Utility.** Can it be worn to school, to work, on a date or to a party, at home? Can it be worn in more than one type of situation?
4. **Quality.** Does it have enough features to be considered of acceptable quality?
5. **Price.** How much does it cost? Does the cost fall within your budget? Does its care make it too expensive? If it is expensive, does its quality justify the price?

If possible, discuss your assignment with the store or department manager and seek his or her advice on appropriate clothing choices.

LAB REPORT

STEP D Use your wardrobe inventory, budgets, and shopping lists to answer the following questions:

1. If you had purchased every item on your list, what would your total cost have been at each store for the Northeastern clothing and the Southwestern clothing.
2. What was the average price of the items?
3. Select one item that was sold at both stores. What was the difference in price? Speculate on why there might be a price difference.
4. Review your shopping notes. Make two final northeastern and southwestern clothing lists. For these lists, write the items you could actually purchase with your budget, where you would purchase each item, and the prices.

STEP E Write a two-page report that explains your new wardrobe choices in terms of need, price, quality, and utility.

UNIT 9

Unit Contents

Buying Food, Medicines, and Cosmetics

Attitude Inventory

Before you begin Chapter 27, take stock of your attitudes by completing the following inventory. Read each statement and decide how you feel about it—agree, disagree, or undecided. Record your feelings on a sheet of notepaper or use the form in the Student Activity Workbook.

1. The majority of Americans are well nourished.
2. Shopping for groceries once a week is an old-fashioned idea and a poor practice to follow given the convenience of modern supermarkets.
3. A perishable food should be discarded once the date on its package is reached.
4. Fiber has no nutritional value.
5. You must be unemployed to receive food stamps.
6. Food products must carry a list of all ingredients *in order of weight* somewhere on their labels.
7. Name brand foods offer consumers better quality than store brand foods.
8. To be sold over the counter, a drug must have no side effects.
9. Convenience foods are designed to save consumers time and money.
10. No skin-care product can prevent sunburn.
11. The average American diet contains too much fat and sugar and not enough complex carbohydrates.
12. Drugs must be tested to the satisfaction of the FDA before they can be marketed in the U.S.
13. How much fat a piece of red meat contains will determine how tender it is.
14. All ingredients in a cosmetic must be listed on the label.
15. Vitamins and minerals are needed in small, but correct, amounts for good health.

Unit Goal The main goal of this unit is to provide students with the information they will need to make decisions when buying food, drugs, and cosmetics. Chapters in this unit are (1) Fundamentals of Good Nutrition, (2) Smart Shopping Techniques, and (3) Drugs and Cosmetics.

Lesson Plan See the Teacher's Manual for an overview of the unit and some suggestions for introducing it. If you assign the Attitude Inventory, be sure to tell students to keep their answers for later use.

CHAPTER 27

Fundamentals of Good Nutrition

Learning Objectives

When you have finished studying this chapter, you should be able to:

1. Describe the contributions of important nutrients to good health.
2. Identify common nutrient deficiencies found in teens and suggest ways to prevent them.
3. Name the five food groups in the Food Guide Pyramid and the recommended daily servings for each group.
4. List the U.S. Dietary Guidelines.
5. Identify eating and exercise disorders and their causes.

Consumer Terms

malnourished
nutrients
complex carbohydrates
fiber
cholesterol
recommended daily allowances (RDAs)
empty-calorie foods
calories
anorexia nervosa
bulimia nervosa
obese
anabolic steroids

Real-World Journal

Keep a list in your journal of exactly what you eat and drink during the next 48 hours. For each item, find the same or similar product at your local supermarket and note the calories, protein, fat grams, and serving size on the nutrition label. What is your total daily intake for each nutritional category?

Lesson Plan See the Teacher's Manual for the Chapter 27 lesson plan.

Vocabulary The Chapter 27 lesson plans include suggested vocabulary activities for the terms listed.

Caption Answer: It is important to make sure the consumer and family are getting enough of their daily nutrients.

1 Student Motivator Make six puzzle pieces, one for each nutrient. Give one piece to each of six groups. Have them figure out a shape to make with their pieces (a person—head, two arms, two legs, and a body).

2 Research Have groups research their puzzle piece to determine what would happen to the body if their piece was missing. Have them illustrate this as they put their puzzle pieces up on a bulletin board.

3 Research Determine ways to combine plant foods to make complete proteins (peanut butter and bread for peanut butter sandwich; beans and tortilla for bean burrito). Note that many ethnic foods make these combinations.

4 Extension Have several types of vegetarians visit the class to explain how they put a healthy meal together. Discuss some of the problems they have to overcome. (Iron from plant foods is difficult to absorb in the body so there is a risk of iron deficiency; a vegetarian diet isn't necessarily low in fat if a lot of nuts, seeds, and/or high-fat dairy products are consumed.)

THE IMPORTANCE OF GOOD NUTRITION

Experts have found that half of the American people are malnourished. People become **malnourished** if they get too little, or sometimes too much, of certain key nutrients in their diet. **Nutrients** are the chemical compounds found in food that enable our bodies to function properly.

Why are so many Americans improperly fed? Some people cannot afford an adequate diet. Many other people, however, either don't know the basics of good nutrition, or don't apply what they know, or don't care.

We as consumers do not need to become nutritionists in order to form healthful eating habits. It is important, however, that we know something about
1 the essential nutrients.

Key Nutrients

There are six basic types of nutrients—proteins, carbohydrates, fats, vitamins, minerals, and water. Nutrients provide many different functions in the body. Some can be grouped by these functions. Proteins, carbohydrates, and fats, for example, supply calories and energy. Some nutrients help your body
2 work properly, and some provide energy.

Protein All body tissues are made up of protein. Continual supplies are needed to replace worn-out cells. The body must have enough carbohydrates and fats, however, or proteins will be used to supply energy instead of carrying out their main function of building and repairing. Protein is made from chemical substances called amino acids. There are about 22 different amino acids. Nine are essential because they cannot be manufactured in the body. Animal foods (meat, poultry, fish, milk, and eggs) contain all nine essential amino acids and therefore are sources of complete protein. Plant foods provide incomplete

▲ *Consumers should make sure they know all the ingredients before making a purchase.* ***Why?***

protein because they lack one or more essential amino acids. Combinations of
3 different plant foods can be eaten, how-
4 ever, to attain all nine.

Carbohydrates Carbohydrates provide the body's major source of energy. Carbohydrates include sugars (simple carbohydrates) and starches (complex carbohydrates). Sugars occur naturally in many foods such as milk, fruits, and grains. They are also refined and used as sweeteners (table sugar). Sugars provide only energy in the diet. Starches, or **complex carbohydrates,** are made up of longer chemical units than sugars. They are found in dried peas, beans, and lentils, breads, cereals, potatoes, corn, and pastas. In addition to energy, starches provide incomplete proteins, vitamins, minerals, and dietary fiber. **Fiber** provides bulk in the diet and that moves food through the

digestive system. Fiber is not a nutrient,
1 nor is it digestible.

Fats Fat is a concentrated form of energy found in foods such as butter, margarine, oils, creams, egg yolks, meats, and nuts. Fats are necessary in the diet because they provide substances such as essential fatty acids and fat soluble vitamins. They also act as a cushion for body organs. Too much fat, however, is a problem, especially saturated fats. Saturated fats are found in animal foods and tropical oils. They seem to raise the level of cholesterol in the body.

Cholesterol is a fatlike substance that is manufactured by the liver. It can also be found in animal foods. High levels of certain kinds of cholesterol in the bloodstream increase the risk of heart disease and stroke.

Vitamins and Minerals Vitamins and minerals are only needed in small amounts, but the correct amount is necessary for good health. Vitamins keep body tissues healthy and regulate body processes. The charts in Figure 27–1 (a) and (b) lists important vitamins, their functions, and source.

Most minerals actually become part of the body (bones and teeth, for example). They also assist body functions. Some of the key minerals are described in Figure 27–1 (c) on page 430.

Water Water regulates body functions by contributing to many chemical reac-
2 tions. It also helps keep body temperature

1 **Research** Have students research specific foods that are good sources of fiber. After noting fiber content by grams, make a poster which lists choices in order of fiber content.

2 **Research** Have groups research diseases caused by an iron and calcium deficiency, two nutrients teens are most likely to lack—anemia (iron deficiency) and osteoporosis (calcium deficiency). Make a plan for eating foods rich in iron and calcium.

Figure 27–1(a) Fat Soluble Vitamins

Vitamins	Functions	Sources
Vitamin A	Promotes healthy skin, hair, bones, teeth; aids vision in dim light; provides resistance to infection; antioxidant—protects other nutrients.	Dark green, leafy vegetables such as broccoli, spinach; deep yellow and orange fruits and vegetables such as carrots, sweet potatoes, cantaloupe; whole or fortified milk, cheese, eggs, and liver.
Vitamin D	Helps build strong bones and teeth.	Milk fortified with vitamin D, fish liver oils, direct sunlight.
Vitamin E	Helps form red blood cells and muscles; antioxidant—protects other nutrients from damage by oxygen.	Vegetable oils/margarine; whole-grain breads and cereals; dark green, leafy vegetables, nuts, and seeds.
Vitamin K	Helps blood clot.	Dark green, leafy vegetables; cabbage, cauliflower, turnips; egg yokes; liver.

Figure 27–1(b) Water Soluble Vitamins

Vitamins	Functions	Sources
B-complex including thiamine, riboflavin niacin, B6, B12, folacin	Helps body release energy from carbohydrates, fats and proteins; maintains healthy nervous system, muscles, skin, eyes, and tissues; helps build red blood cells and form genetic material; helps protect against infection; promotes appetite and digestion.	Whole-grain and enriched breads and cereal; dry beans and peas, nuts; meat, poultry, fish; eggs; milk, cheese.
Vitamin C	Helps maintain bones, teeth, blood vessels, gums; helps wounds heal; aids iron absorption from foods; fights infection; antioxidant—protects other nutrients from damage by oxygen.	Cirtrus fruits such as oranges, grapefruit; other fruits and vegetables such as broccoli, raw cabbage, brussel sprouts, potatoes, tomatoes, strawberries, cantaloupe.

◄ *Vitamins and minerals have various regulatory functions in the body. Often statements are made about them. Review the charts to find out whether the following common statements are fact or fiction. (1) Calcium builds strong bones and teeth. (2) Carrots help you see better in the dark. (3) Eat your crusts and you'll have curly hair. (4) Vitamin C helps keep colds away.*

Caption Answers: (1) Fact. This is listed as a function of calcium. (2) Fact. Carrots are a good source of Vitamin A which helps you see in dim light. (3) Fiction. A statement sometimes used to get children to eat all their bread. (4) Not proven.

FLASHBACK FLASHFORWARD

Ironically, in the 1950s, smoking was considered glamorous. In 1990, one out of every five deaths was attributed to smoking. This fact leaves no ifs, ands, or butts about the hazards of smoking!

Figure 27–1(c) Selected Minerals

Mineral	Function	Sources
Calcium	Maintains strong bones and teeth, heart, muscle and nerve function; helps blood clot.	Milk and milk products; sardines, canned salmon with bones; dark green, leafy vegetables; dry beans, and peas.
Iodine	Regulates body's use of energy by helping thyroid gland work properly.	Saltwater fish, iodized salt.
Iron	Helps blood carry oxygen; helps cells use oxygen.	Red meats, liver, fish, and shellfish; egg yolk; dark green, leafy vegetables; dry beans and peas; nuts and seeds; dried fruits such as peaches, raisins; whole-grain and enriched bread and cereals.
Magnesium	Helps nerves and muscles work properly; helps build bones and proteins; regulates body fluids and temperature.	Whole-grain breads and cereals; dark green, leafy vegetables; dry beans and peas; nuts and seeds.
Phosphorus	Works with calcium and vitamin D to build strong bones and teeth; helps body release energy from carbohydrates, fats, and proteins.	Meat, poultry, fish; eggs; milk and milk products; dry beans and peas.
Potassium	Helps heart, muscles, nerves work properly; helps regulate fluid balance and blood pressure.	Oranges, bananas; dried fruit; meat, poultry, fish; dry beans and peas; potatoes.
Sodium	Helps regulate body fluids; helps muscle action.	Table salt; many foods, especially processed foods.
Zinc	Helps the body heal wounds, form blood, and make protein; helps body use carbohydrates, fats, proteins, and vitamin A.	Meats, liver, poultry, fish and shellfish; eggs; nuts and seeds; peanut butter; dairy products; dry beans and peas.

1 **Vocabulary Development** Have students brainstorm the meaning of the term *nutrient deficiency*.

2 **Extension** Ask students if they know which is the only food group on the pyramid whose serving requirements change with advancing age.

within a normal range. Your body can only survive a few days without water while you can go weeks without food. The body uses 2–3 quarts of water a day. To help replace it, drink 6–8 cups of liquid every day. This can come from plain water, juices, milk, or some foods like fruits with high water content.

COMMON DEFICIENCIES IN TEENS

Everybody needs certain amounts of nutrients for good health and normal growth. These needed amounts, as established by the National Academy of Science, are known as the **recommended daily allowances** (known as **RDAs**). RDAs vary according to a person's age and sex. Among teens, the
1 RDAs most often lacking are those for
2 calcium and iron.

Calcium Milk and dairy products are major sources of calcium for most people. Most young children usually drink enough milk. Teenagers, however, often substitute soft drinks, coffee, or tea. Drinking large amounts of soda is a particularly worrisome habit. Soda contains a great deal of phosphorus, and it reduces the body's ability to use the calcium it does get. If the substitution of soda for milk is carried into adulthood, it can have serious and irreversible effects. Some experts even feel that the current RDAs are too low to promote maximum bone development in young people. Maximum bone development is very important because it can help prevent a disease that can occur in older people (especially women) called osteoporosis. *Osteoporosis* is a disease in which the loss of bone mass leads to bones becoming brittle and easily fractured. Osteoporosis can also cause spontaneous fractures of one or more vertebrae, which causes the bones to become compressed, leading to a loss of height.

What can you do to be sure you get enough calcium? First, try to include dairy products in your diet on a regular basis such as low-fat milk, yogurt, and cheese. Other foods such as canned sardines, navy beans, and broccoli are good sources. Second, be sure you get enough Vitamin D—it helps the body to use the calcium you do consume.

Iron Obtaining enough iron is also important during adolescence. The need for iron increases at this time because of the onset of menstruation in girls and the speeding up of growth in both sexes. Eating foods like meat, liver, fish and shellfish, dry beans and peas, dried fruits, and whole-gain breads and cereals usually provides enough of this mineral. In extreme cases of iron loss, an iron supplement may need to be taken.

PLANNING A HEALTHY DIET

Planning a healthy diet is not difficult if you follow certain guidelines. Two helpful sources of information are available from the U.S. Department of Agriculture. The *Dietary Guidelines for Americans* provide suggestions for healthy eating. The *Food Guide Pyramid* helps you choose
1 foods to carry them out.

Dietary Guidelines

The U.S. Dietary Guidelines were developed in 1990 to help Americans improve their eating habits. They list six simple steps to a healthier diet.

1. *Eat a variety of foods.* Most foods contain many different nutrients but not all that you need in adequate amounts. Use the *Food Guide Pyramid* shown in Figure 27–2 on page 432 for planning a balanced and varied diet. You will see that it is formulated to help you make necessary changes recommended by the dietary guidelines. The servings suggested for each of five food groups are not exact. In general, however, boys should eat the higher number of servings and girls, the
2 lower number.
2. *Choose a diet low in fat, saturated fat, and cholesterol.* While the Food Pyramid Chart is helpful in general planning,

◄ ***Why do you think so many celebrities have participated in this ad campaign?***

Caption Answer: To serve as role models and stress the importance of getting enough calcium.

1 Reinforcement Have students divide into groups to plan a day's meals based on the variety of foods necessary from each section of the pyramid. Make sure the plan is consistent with the dietary guidelines. Share with the class, explain their choices and why it is important to consider the calories and nutrients eaten during the entire day.

2 Reinforcement Student Activity Workbook, Chapter 27 activities.

Burger and Fries in Ho Chi Minh City

In Ho Chi Minh City (formerly Saigon), a burger and fries costs about 80 cents, and nachos with jalapeno peppers costs 60 cents. That's still expensive for the average city worker, whose annual income is about $800, or $2.19 a day.

Figure 27–2 The Food Guide Pyramid

The Food Guide Pyramid is formulated to help you carry out a healthful and balanced diet.

KEY

● **Fat** (Naturally occurring and added)

★ **Sugars** (added)

These symbols show fats, oils and added sugars in foods.

Fats and Sugars – USE SPARINGLY
Fats and sugars are placed at the top of the pyramid to indicate that you should avoid eating too many. They provide calories but little or no vitamins or minerals.

Dairy Milk, Yogurt, Cheese Group (2-3 SERVINGS)
Typical foods and serving sizes are: 1 cup milk or yogurt; 1 1/2 oz. natural cheese; 2 oz. processed cheese. Dairy products provide: protein, vitamins and minerals such as calcium (one of the best sources) and phosphorous. Choose low fat versions of these foods.

Meat, Poultry, Fish, Dry Beans, Eggs, and Nuts (2-3 SERVINGS)
Typical foods and serving sizes are: 2-3 ounces lean meat, poultry or fish; 1 cup cooked dry beans; 2 Tablespoons peanut butter. Foods in this group provide: protein, vitamins such as A and B-complex, minerals such as iron and zinc. Choose lean meat, fish and poultry without skin.

Vegetable Group (3-5 SERVINGS)
Typical foods and serving sizes are: 1 cup raw leafy greens (lettuce, spinach) or 1/2 cup of other cooked or raw vegetable. Vegetables provide: complex carbohydrates, fiber, vitamins: such as A and C, minerals such as calcium and magnesium.

Fruit Group (2-4 SERVINGS)
Typical foods and serving sizes are: 1 apple, 1 orange, 3/4 cup fruit juice, 1/2 cup canned or cooked fruit. Fruits provide: fiber (edible skins), vitamins such as A and C, and minerals such as iron and potassium.

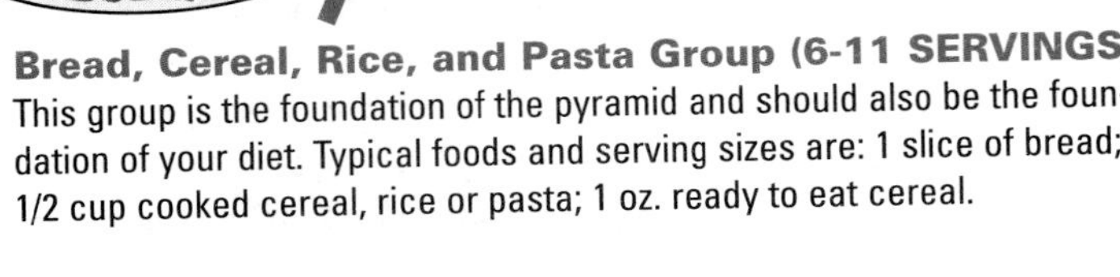

Bread, Cereal, Rice, and Pasta Group (6-11 SERVINGS)
This group is the foundation of the pyramid and should also be the foundation of your diet. Typical foods and serving sizes are: 1 slice of bread; 1/2 cup cooked cereal, rice or pasta; 1 oz. ready to eat cereal.

1 Discussion Starter Ask students if they have made any of these changes, or if they have always eaten the foods discussed as substitutes. Do they enjoy the substitutes as much? How important is the enjoyment factor in comparison to the good health factor in food choices.

2 Extension Have students look through "healthy eating" cookbooks for the best low-fat, or low-sugar recipe they can find. If possible, have them try it at home and report results to the class.

actual food choices are up to you. Research over the last several years has revealed a number of shortcomings in the typical American diet. One is that it contains too much fat and cholesterol. The average American gets over 37 percent of his or her calories from *fat.* Most experts say that this amount should be lowered to no more than 30 percent. Of primary concern are animal fats—those found in meat, butter, whole milk, and egg yolks. These have been linked to high blood pressure and heart disease as well as increased risk of colon and
1 breast cancers.

To make the necessary reductions, experts recommend such practices as substituting low-fat or skim milk for whole milk; fish and poultry for red meat and eggs; low-fat salad dressings for regular salad dressing; baked foods for fried foods; part skim mozzarella for cheddar cheese; and plain air
2 popped corn for potato chips.

3. *Use sugars only in moderation.* Sugar is another diet element linked to a health problem—namely, tooth decay. Sugar is the main component in many so-called **empty-calorie foods,** those that add weight but provide few nutrients. These foods

(candy, cakes and cookies, ice cream,
and sugarcoated cereals) can reduce 1
your appetite for foods that contain 2
more nutrients. Nutritionists recommend substituting frozen yogurt for ice cream, fruit juices for soft drinks, and plain cereals for those that are sugarcoated. Also be sure to read labels to spot sweeteners hidden in processed foods (such as fructose, glucose, sucrose, dextrose, maltose, corn sweetener, syrup, and honey).

4. *Use salt and sodium only in moderation.* Salt is another recommended reduction. It contains sodium and chloride. Excess sodium consumption has been linked to high blood pressure (which can in turn lead to stroke,

People MAKING a DIFFERENCE

Low-Tech Processing Equals Lots of Food

In many areas of the world, people go hungry. Often there is enough food. The problem is that there is no way to process it because the countries lack the technological resources to use their food resources completely. As a result, food is wasted or ruined in storage and transportation. Usually, there is little money to buy the highly technical equipment—or advice—that would help solve the problem.

George Ewing, an engineer with food-processing giant General Mills, wanted to improve the situation. In 1980, he gathered other food-processing scientists into a nonprofit research center, which they named Compatible Technology, to come up with low-cost, low-tech ways of using and processing food.

One of their projects was to figure out how to use the highly nutritious pulp left over from processing soybean oil. The group finally came up with a way to turn the leftovers into cookie-like biscuits. The product is now sold inexpensively in India.

Rotting potatoes was another problem in India. The stored vegetables spoiled before they could be used, with the result that people who could benefit from this rich food source were left hungry. Potato slices could be dehydrated in the sun, but the slices had to be very thin. Additionally, the method used to slice them could not involve —expensive and largely unavailable—electricity.

One of the group's members had a brilliant idea—attach a commercial slicer to a bicycle frame. Now there are many shops in northern India that process more than 30,000 pounds of potatoes a year with pedal power.

Brainstorm

There are many people right here in the United States who go hungry. What kinds of projects could you initiate to help these people?

1 Critical Thinking Have students study the foods that are the best sources for certain nutrients. Are there some that provide good sources of several different nutrients? Determine which foods these are. From the investigation, define the term *nutrient density*.

2 Enrichment Have students keep track of snacks they eat and money they spend on them for a week. Have a snack testing day where some are brought to school and analyzed for nutrient content. Also analyze them for salt, fat, and sugar content. The same could be done for popular fast foods such as tacos, burritos, and pizza.

Case Study Answer: Projects will vary. Examples include starting a soup kitchen at your school or working at an already established food kitchen. Organizing a food drive.

1 Research Have students research the current status of nutrition and cancer by reading articles and contacting the American Cancer Society and the National Cancer Institute.

2 Discussion Starter Ask students what kind of exercise they enjoy. Why is it difficult to exercise on a regular basis? Can they think of any ways to exercise during their daily routine (park the car further from the store and walk, walk up stairs instead of using the elevator, etc.).

3 Discussion Starter Ask students if they have known anyone who has lost a lot of weight, only to gain it back again. How did they lose weight? Why didn't they keep the weight off?

4 Reinforcement Student Activity Workbook, Chapter 27 activities.

Case Study Answers:
1 Someone with an eating disorder might be motivated to learn about diet and well-being. Once that person experiences the power of healing, he or she might be motivated to help others achieve the same success.
2 Sample answers: Weight, Poor skin, Dramatic mood swings, Energy level (Athletic performance), Study habits, Asthma.

heart attack, and kidney failure). Salt is both one of the easiest and one of the hardest reductions to make in your diet. It is easy because it is often added by the individual at the table. It is hard because it is hidden in so many processed foods. Experts recommend eliminating, or at least reducing, salt added during cooking. To reduce consumption of hidden salts, they suggest avoiding highly processed foods. These include cured meats like bacon, hot dogs, and some snack items. Canned soups and frozen meals, if purchased at all, should be purchased in low sodium
1 varieties.

5. *Choose a diet with plenty of vegetables, fruits, and grain products.* Not all problems with the basic American diet involve excesses. If Americans are consuming too much fat and sugar, it must be at the expense of other food choices. The nutrients being squeezed out are the complex carbohydrates which not only supply energy, but are good sources of vitamins, minerals, and fiber. Most foods high in starch are low in fat—unless you load them up with high fat toppings (butter, sour cream, rich sauces). In addition, evidence is accumulating that may show eating lots of vegetables and fruits (important sources of Vitamin A, C, and E) provides some protection against several chronic diseases such as cancer, heart disease, and stroke—and possibly even aging itself. This is because these vitamins are antioxidants. They appear to reduce cell damage caused by an unstable form
2 of oxygen.

6. *Maintain a healthy weight.* Maintaining a healthy weight means not being too fat or too thin. To control or maintain your weight, the calories you consume in your diet must be equal to the energy you burn in your daily activities. **Calories** are the unit of heat that measures the energy available in food. If the food you eat has more calories than your body uses, the extra energy is stored in your body as fat.

The best way to maintain a healthy weight is to eat sensibly, exercise regularly, and watch your calorie intake. If you have put on excess fat, the most effective way to lose it is to permanently reach your natural healthy weight. First, increase activity moderately (some studies have shown this is also the best way to maintain weight loss). Then eat sensibly and try to lose weight slowly. Do this by following the Dietary Guidelines—reduce fats and increase complex carbohydrates. After adopting a healthful eating pattern and getting a reasonable amount of exercise,
3 become comfortable with your "nat-
4 ural weight."

What Are You Eating?

Consumer protection laws require packaged foods to be labeled for ingredients and nutritional value. But what about when you go out to eat? You may be concerned about some foods because of allergies or special diet restrictions, or you simply may not prefer the taste of certain ingredients. Some fast-food chains provide ingredients information when you ask. At a restaurant, ask the server what is in the dish or size of the portion, if that's important to you. Be specific if you want to know about a certain ingredient and be persistent—ask the chef.

CASE STUDY

Careers in Focus

Carolyn Katzin, Nutritionist and Health Educator, The Wellness Community

"You are what you eat," states Carolyn Katzin, 49, nutritionist and health educator. "It really is true. But in this society, food tends to be seen as rather threatening. People have a lot of anxiety about food, even if they're not in a disease state. In France by contrast, food is seen as something sacred."

Katzin herself has a kind of religious zeal about good nutrition and good food. Although she is a highly trained scientist, with a bachelor of science in nutrition and physiology from the University of London and a masters of science in public health from UCLA, she considers food to be something quite miraculous, able to heal and bring happiness. In fact, she is currently working on a book called *Crisis Nutrition*, a step-by-step eating guide for helping people deal with the highly stressful times in their lives.

Katzin has had a lot of practice with nutrition and stress. She works with a group of physicians specializing in food sensitivities and chronic gastrointestinal illness, and has developed a special expertise in cancer, immunology, and nutrition. She has lectured and taught extensively for the American Cancer Society, contributed to several books on cancer recovery, and has won awards and accolades for her community service with victims of cancer.

It was her early interest in nutrients such as vitamin A and zinc that led Katzin to The Wellness Community and the study of nutrition and immunology—and she has no idea why she was attracted to those particular nutrients. Many nutritionists are drawn to the field because of an eating disorder they themselves have overcome. But for Katzin, the "disorder" was bad teenage skin that wasn't even that bad.

"I probably only had three or four pimples at one time," she admits, "but they felt like headlights. So I began to research and experiment with my diet. I gave up chocolate, then nuts, then shellfish. The more I read, the more interested I became."

Ten years in the field as a professional nutritionist has brought Katzin great satisfaction. "A lot of being a nutritionist is education," she says. "We help people identify helpful foods or understand the information they are given by the media. We simplify what appears to be a complicated problem. And most of the time," she explains, with pride, "we can help our patients achieve a level of health they're happy with in just two or three visits."

Case Study Review

1. Why would someone with an eating disorder be drawn to the field of nutrition? What might make him or her stay in it?
2. List something about yourself or your body that might be helped by better nutrition. Find an article in a recent publication that mentions the problem in terms of nutrition.

1 **Discussion Starter** Have students find articles and newspaper clippings about eating and exercise disorders. Discuss the extent of the problem.

EATING DISORDERS AND SUBSTANCE ABUSE

Several types of problem behaviors are prevalent among Americans when it comes to eating and exercising. Four common disorders include anorexia, bulimia, obesity, and steroid abuse.

Anorexia, Bulimia, and Obesity

Those who starve themselves have a disorder called **anorexia nervosa.** Stuffing and then vomiting or using laxatives to purge excess food is called **bulimia nervosa.** Food addiction is yet another disorder. Here, compulsive eating occurs without purging. Food is thought of all the time and eventually control is lost over what and when to eat. Some people exercise compulsively in much the same manner.

Someone is considered **obese** if he or she is more than 20 percent above their ideal weight. The weight seen on a scale is only part of the entire picture, however. A better indicator of a healthy
1 weight is how much of that weight comes from fat and how it is distributed.

All of these behaviors are caused by such things as stress, pressure, high expectations, the need for control or to be popular. Although they may work for a while, eventually such behaviors can destroy relationships, reduce self esteem, and even cause death (up to 20 percent of those who have anorexia die). When someone displays one of these behaviors, professional help is needed. Criticizing and nagging won't work. If you know someone who has a disorder of this type, tell a trusted adult (parent, teacher, school nurse, coach) so help can be found. Remember, these behaviors can be very dangerous.

Some atheletes use steroids because they feel it improves their performance. ***What are some of the dangers of steroids?*** ▶

Caption Answer: They can cause damage to the liver, heart, stomach, and to reproductive capacity. Psychological problems can also occur.

Anabolic Steroids

Athletes who wish to perform well by developing additional strength and muscles will sometimes use anabolic steroids to hurry up the process. **Anabolic steroids** are prescription drugs that build tissue, promote muscles, and help strengthen bones.

Some get the drug without a prescription and use it for better athletic performance. The problem is on the increase among teenage athletes despite the serious health risks associated with taking the steroids. Many do not know steroids can cause damage to the liver, heart, stomach, and to reproductive capacity. Psychological problems can also occur. There is no substitute for proper nutrition and training.

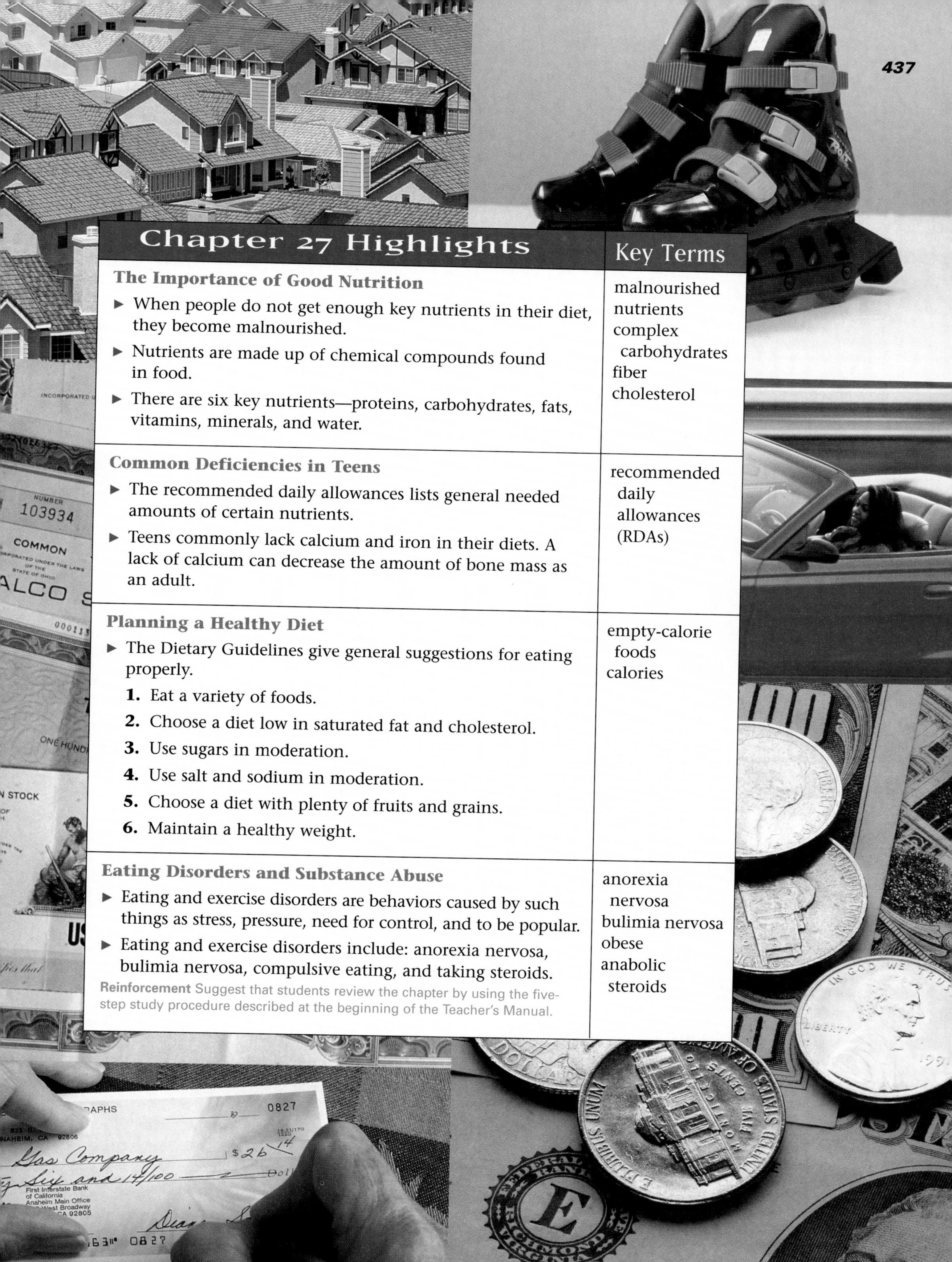

Chapter 27 Highlights

Chapter 27 Highlights	Key Terms
The Importance of Good Nutrition ▶ When people do not get enough key nutrients in their diet, they become malnourished. ▶ Nutrients are made up of chemical compounds found in food. ▶ There are six key nutrients—proteins, carbohydrates, fats, vitamins, minerals, and water.	malnourished nutrients complex carbohydrates fiber cholesterol
Common Deficiencies in Teens ▶ The recommended daily allowances lists general needed amounts of certain nutrients. ▶ Teens commonly lack calcium and iron in their diets. A lack of calcium can decrease the amount of bone mass as an adult.	recommended daily allowances (RDAs)
Planning a Healthy Diet ▶ The Dietary Guidelines give general suggestions for eating properly. **1.** Eat a variety of foods. **2.** Choose a diet low in saturated fat and cholesterol. **3.** Use sugars in moderation. **4.** Use salt and sodium in moderation. **5.** Choose a diet with plenty of fruits and grains. **6.** Maintain a healthy weight.	empty-calorie foods calories
Eating Disorders and Substance Abuse ▶ Eating and exercise disorders are behaviors caused by such things as stress, pressure, need for control, and to be popular. ▶ Eating and exercise disorders include: anorexia nervosa, bulimia nervosa, compulsive eating, and taking steroids. **Reinforcement** Suggest that students review the chapter by using the five-step study procedure described at the beginning of the Teacher's Manual.	anorexia nervosa bulimia nervosa obese anabolic steroids

CHAPTER 27 REVIEW

Refer students to the Reviewing Consumer Terms and Reviewing Facts and Ideas activities in the Student Activity Workbook.

Reviewing Consumer Terms Paragraphs will vary. See Glossary for definitions.

Reviewing Facts and Ideas See the Student Activity Workbook for answers.

Problem Solving and Decision Making **1** Neither **2** Highly processed foods (hot dogs, bacon) and other processed foods—canned fish and soups; salad dressing. **3** Omit highly processed foods; substitute fresh fish or poultry for canned foods, make own soup or use low sodium varieties; use lower sodium salad dressings.

Consumers Around the World Communications **1** Student papers might include an update on Kwashiorker, a protein deficiency, prevalent in Africa for many years and could be researched through United Nations or UNICEF documents.

Social Studies **2** Student papers will depend on discovery chosen.

Reviewing Consumer Terms

Use each of the following terms in a paragraph to demonstrate you know their meaning.

anabolic steroids
anorexia nervosa
bulimia nervosa
calories
cholesterol
complex carbohydrates
empty-calorie foods
fiber
malnourished
nutrients
obese
recommended daily allowances (RDAs)

Reviewing Facts and Ideas

1. Experts recommend that you eat dark green or deep yellow vegetables several times a day. Using the information in Figure 27–1 (b) for support, explain why.
2. Identify common nutrient deficiencies found in teens and suggest ways to prevent them.
3. Identify the five basic food groups and indicate how many servings from each group are recommended per day.
4. Explain why the food groups are placed as they are on the Food Pyramid.
5. What are the six dietary guidelines?
6. What are some eating and exercise disorders and reasons for these problem behaviors?

Problem Solving and Decision Making

Sodium is the harmful element in salt and certain preservatives. The Daily Reference Value for sodium used in the most recent labeling law is 2,400 milligrams. With this in mind, study the two daily menus below. Then answer the questions that follow.

A	Sodium (mg)
Breakfast:	
Grilled cheese and bacon on English muffin	1,190
Tomato juice (6 oz.)	570
Lunch:	
Hot dogs (2) with kraut	2,100
Cottage cheese (1/2 c.) and fruit salad	490
Diet soda	35
Dinner:	
Chicken soup (1/2 can)	910
Frozen cod	400
Canned peas (1/2 c.)	360
Salad (2 T. dressing)	800
Chocolate pudding	515
B	
Breakfast:	
Cold cereal and milk	350
Toast (1/2 T. margarine)	110
Orange juice (6 oz.)	20
Lunch:	
Tuna salad sandwich (1 T. mayonnaise)	1,140
Potato chips (1 oz.)	180
Iced tea	—
Dinner:	
Beef bouillon (1 c.)	500
Canned crab salad	1,100
Fruit yogurt (1 c.)	120

1. Which set of menus falls within the Daily Reference Value for sodium?
2. Which foods have the highest sodium counts?
3. Suggest changes to bring the sodium level of these menus down to the daily reference value or below.

Building Academic Skills

Consumers Around the World

Communications

1. Choose a country or region in the world where people have serious nutritional deficiencies. Write a 500-word paper describing the problems and what is being done about it. Share results with the class.

Social Studies

2. Research a nutritional deficiency that occurred in a past historical period. What diseases occurred? What discoveries led to their cure and who made them? Share findings with the class.

Science

3. Research the effects of bulimia nervosa or anorexia nervosa on the body. Summarize your findings in a 250-word report.

Beyond the Classroom

Consumer Project

As part of a group project, do a critical review of a popular book on losing weight. Give special attention to whether the recommended methods are based on current research and are both safe and nutritionally sound. Present your reports to the class. When all the reports have been given, help the class to rank the suggested approaches from most to least sound.

Cooperative Learning

Family Economics

Break into assigned family groups. Discuss the following problem.

Analysis of your family's diet reveals that you are slighting the vegetable food group and almost omitting the important category of dark green and deep yellow vegetables. You are determined to correct the situation, but how? Begin by making a list of all the vegetables that fall into the missing category. Then think of at least ten specific ways to slip them into the family eating patterns. If there are children or seniors in the family, give special attention to making the additions acceptable and attractive to them. Compare your answers with those of other family groups.

Debate the Issue

Some people think it is better to get all the needed vitamins and minerals from eating a well-balanced diet. Others feel that in addition to eating a well-balanced diet, we should take vitamins to supplement any deficiencies.

You and your classmates will break into two groups and research this topic. Each group will gather evidence to support one side or the other. You are to prepare the argument for your side of the problem. Then the two groups will meet in a class.

Science
3 Student papers should include the seriousness of the disease and how important it is to receive counseling.

Consumer Project
Students should answer all questions and give valid reasons for their statements.

Family Economics
Vegetables: spinach; turnip, collard, and mustard greens; kale, watercress, and chard; broccoli; carrots; sweet potatoes; winter squash and pumpkin; yellow corn; beets. Serving ideas: shred carrots into sandwiches, sprinkle on salads; substitute spinach for lettuce in salads; add spinach or broccoli to stir-frys.

Debate the Issue
Break the class into two teams. Assign each team one side of the issue. Encourage students to work together as a team to develop their argument. Ask each team to select a member to make an opening statement that supports their side of the issue. Have students take turns debating as the debate moves from one team to another.

CHAPTER 28

Smart Shopping Techniques

Learning Objectives

When you have finished studying this chapter, you should be able to:

1. Choose the right store for your needs.
2. Develop an effective food-shopping plan.
3. Understand the information on food labels.
4. Make sound choices in terms of quality and price.
5. Store foods properly.
6. Fight off the urge to buy impulsively.

Consumer Terms

nutrient density
net weight
name brand
store brand
open date
pull date
expiration date
unit price
convenience foods
impulse buying

Real-World Journal

Ask the person who does your family's grocery shopping to save all the receipts during the week. Paste them into your journal. Go to several markets in your area and look up the prices on those items. Make a list of the prices you find at each store. Is your family getting the best price per item? Summarize your findings in your journal.

Lesson Plan See the Teacher's Manual for Chapter 28 lesson plan.

Vocabulary The Chapter 28 lesson plan includes suggested vocabulary activities for the items listed.

1 Discussion Starter Ask students if they agree that grocery shopping is a skill that takes time and energy to develop. Tell them to notice people's shopping carts when they are in stores and how people examine items they take from the shelf. Do they see any differences?

GETTING THE MOST FOR YOUR TIME AND MONEY

You might think that there's nothing easier than going to the grocery store. That may be true on the surface. But making smart choices once you get to the store is a skill that takes time and energy to develop. To get the most for your money and to make sure that you buy what you really need, you must learn how to pick the right market, develop a shopping strategy, use consumer information, recognize quality and freshness in food, and resist impulse buying. Even if you do all this, you might still find prices that are too high for your budget. Dealing with that prob-
1 lem takes yet more skill in shopping.

GOING TO MARKET

You probably know from seeing advertisements and commercials, from your own shopping experience, and from listening to family members talk about shopping that there are a wide variety of grocery stores. They include supermarkets, warehouse stores and clubs, convenience stores, specialty shops, farmer's markets, and food cooperatives. While you may visit all of them at one time or another, it is probably not necessary to visit them all in the course of weekly or monthly shopping for necessities.

Your Shopping Strategy List

Before you embark on a shopping trip, pick the right market for your needs. Here's a strategy that will help you. Go to the market that provides:

1. Good prices and high-quality foods.
2. Services you want such as an adequate number of express lanes if you use them often.
3. A clean, pleasant atmosphere for shopping.
4. A convenient location and business hours.
5. Friendly, helpful employees.
6. Fair policies, such as allowing you to return spoiled, damaged, or unwanted goods within a reasonable period of time.

PLANNING YOUR PURCHASES

Let's say you have $25 to spend on this week's groceries. Can you actually get out of the store with everything you need and still stick to your budget? Yes, you can—but you'll have a better chance of succeeding if you plan before you get to the store.

Grocery stores stock thousands of enticing items. Besides an overwhelming array of foods in the larger stores, many markets also carry greeting cards, paperback books, makeup, and toys, among

Caption Answer: A warehouse club can offer large savings over the same national brands in supermarkets (one study showed a 70 percent saving for one week's purchases). Supermarkets also offer savings if you shop with a price in mind.

Many choices are available for grocery shopping. ***At which store (or stores) can you save money on overall purchases? What are some reasons why you would shop at some of the other stores?*** ▶

other things. These can be tough to resist. Doesn't having a poster of your favorite rock star sound like more fun than having a carton of milk?

How do smart shoppers resist these desirable, but often unnecessary, items? By planning carefully before they get to the store. Planning might sound difficult or even dull. However, it won't be if you follow these simple steps:

1. **Make a shopping list.** Include both food and nonfood items. In order to save time and reduce the possibility of impulse buying, arrange the list by store layout.
2. **Shop once a week.** More frequent trips should not be necessary. Plan your meals and make sure you use perishables—that is, food that will spoil in a relatively short time, like meat or milk—before you use canned, frozen, or preserved foods. Make sure the food you buy is fresh and in good condition.
3. **Shop when stores are not crowded.** This will give you time to read labels, compare prices, and avoid long lines at checkout.
4. **Don't shop when you're hungry.** This is one of the most important strategies of smart shopping. Hunger pangs can make almost anything edible look like something you just must have.
5. **Get the most nutrition for your money.** Pay attention to the nutrient density of foods. **Nutrient density** is the amount of nutrients compared to the amount of calories in a food. Foods with a high nutrient density are rich in nutrients but low in calo-
1 ries from fat and added sugar.
6. **Take advantage of bargains.** Get familiar with prices so you'll know when genuine savings are a possibility. Use coupons, but only on items you wanted to buy anyway, and only if the coupon items are the best buy
2 of their type. You might consider
3 joining a preferred shoppers club for
4 special discounts.

USING CONSUMER INFORMATION

With the shelves stocked with thousands of items, which do you choose? The best place to start is with the labels. Here are some things to look for.

Food Labels

A food label carries a lot of useful information, but you have to know what's there and how to use it. Since 1966, the Fair Packaging and Labeling Law has required that a food label include such information as the name of the product, the name and address of the manufacturer, and the net weight *of the contents*. The **net weight** includes the weight of the product and any liquid in which the product is packed. What

Bigger Is Not Always the Best Value

Many stores provide shelf signs that identify the item, its price, and its cost per unit, per ounce, or per pound. For the best value, read these tags and compare prices. If the store does not post unit pricing, divide the total price by the number of items or ounces. The price of a 12-pack of soft drinks, for example, might be $4.49, which is about 37 cents each. But a 6-pack of the same beverage might be priced at $1.99, which is about 33 cents each. In this case, buying two of the smaller packs, for $3.98, is a better value.

1 Extension Tell students that the nutrient density of a food is the amount of nutrients in the food compared to the amount of energy (calories). Ask students which food has the highest nutrient ratio to calories: baked potato or potato chips?

2 Interesting Note Tell students that according to surveys, coupon users often spend more than consumers who do not use coupons. This is because they buy items that they don't need. Studies by manufacturers show that when coupons are given out for impulse items, people buy 50 percent more than they do without the coupons.

3 Critical Thinking Photocopy selected coupons and distribute them in class for analysis. Have students determine all qualifiers (name of product, sizes, expiration date, etc.) Ask them if they would use this coupon. Why or why not?

4 Extension Preferred shoppers receive bonus discounts and coupons. Have students determine what information is required to join and how stores and manufacturers might use that information (age, marital status, number of kids, pets, etc.) to determine consumer shopping habits.

1 Interesting Fact Before the Nutritional Labeling Act, 40 percent of all packaged food provided no nutrition information. Now even the smallest companies and packages must provide nutrition information in the standard format.

2 Reinforcement Student Activity Workbook, Chapter 28 activities.

3 Extension Two government reference values (RDVs and RDIs) serve as the basis for calculating Daily Values. Daily Values are not specific recommended intakes, but reference points to help consumers get a perspective on their overall daily dietary needs.

4 Extension Percent of Daily Values is easier to understand in terms of overall diet than a statement of amount. For example, if a serving of a particular food had 140 milligrams of sodium, that sounds like a lot. It is, however, only 6 percent of the Daily Value recommended (2,400 milligrams). But Daily Values are based on 2,000- and 2,500-calorie-a-day diets, and some people don't eat that much.

5 Extension Note that the "total carbohydrate" category includes sugar which should be eaten in moderation.

Caption Answer: There are 5 grams of saturated fat in this product.

the net weight may not include is the weight of the container or its wrapping.

The ingredients must also be listed. The first one on the list must be the most prominent, either by weight or volume. This means that if you buy something that lists water as its first ingredient, it contains more water than anything else.

In 1994, food labels underwent a dra-
1 matic change when the requirements of
2 the Nutritional Labeling and Education
3 Act (NLEA) took effect. Today, more
4 information than ever is required. See
5 Figure 28–1.

Labels on canned fruits and vegetables indicate how they are packed—that is, whether they are whole, chopped, sliced, halved, and so forth. Whole and half packs are more expensive. This is because the food in whole and half packs must be perfect, while the food in sliced or chopped packs can be imperfectly formed or blemished. Remember, however, that the nutritional value of the packs may be the same, so check the nutritional information before you buy.

Grade Labels

Although consumers like the idea of grade labeling—that is, grading the food in terms of its quality—the current system leaves much to be desired. Grade

Figure 28–1 Food Labels

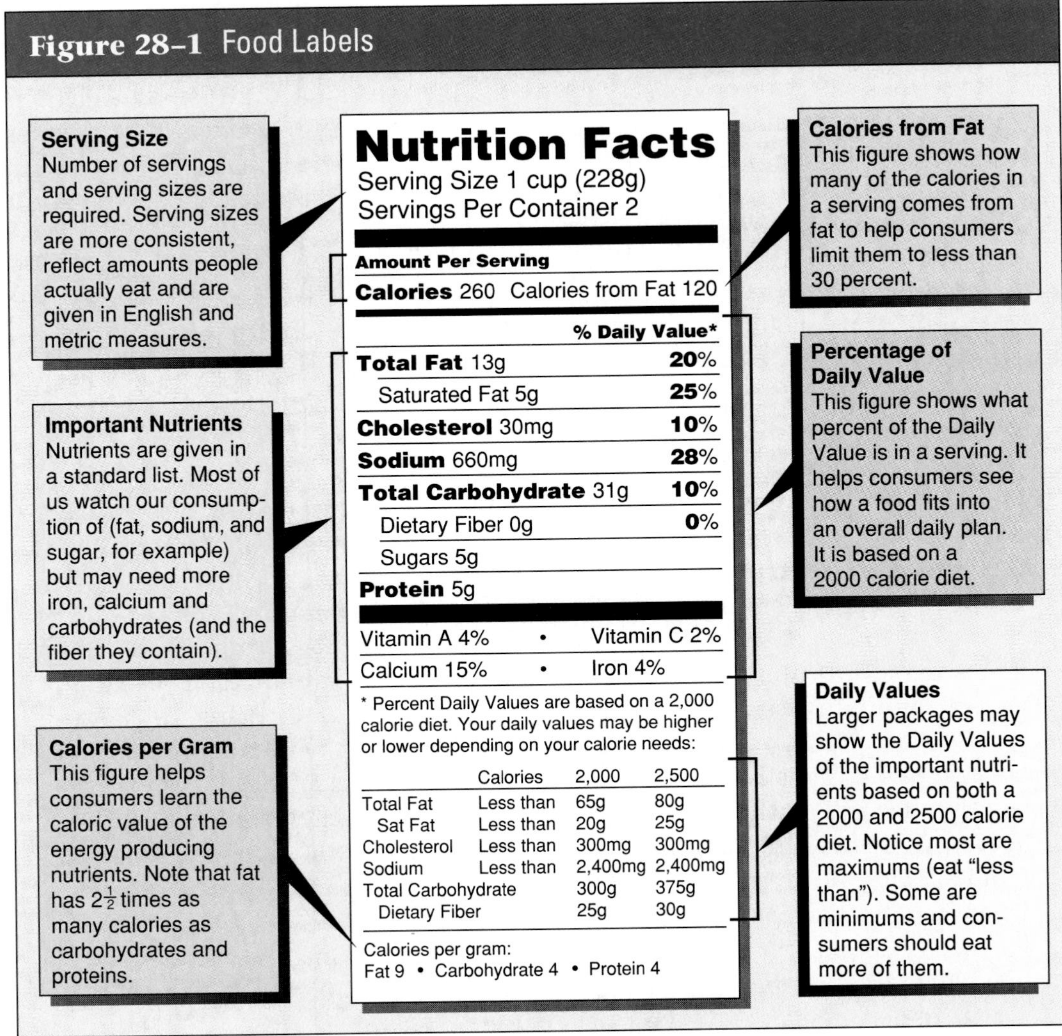

▲ *Food labels must provide specific nutrition information.* ***How many grams of saturated fat are in this product?***

labeling is voluntary, and half the time the grades are not even put on the products that you see in the stores. For example, the U.S. Department of Agriculture (USDA) grades the top 2 percent of all meat produced in this country as U.S. Prime, but this meat doesn't reach the supermarket. It is sold to expensive restaurants that value its heavy marbling (fat distribution) and tenderness. About 92 percent is graded U.S. Choice, meaning it is well marbled and tender; you'll find this at the grocery. About 5 percent is graded U.S. Select because it is not as tender. The remaining 1 percent is U.S. Standard. Since most meat is U.S. Choice, that grade doesn't mean much.

Grade labels can also be confusing. Take fruits, for example. The USDA top grade for apples is U.S. Extra Fancy; the second-highest grade is U.S. Fancy. Yet for grapefruit and oranges, the top grade is U.S. Fancy.

Brand Labels

The final label element is also one of the most prominent—the brand. Some product names become so well known that they stand for competitors versions of the same food. The name "Jell-O," for example, is often used instead of the word "gelatin." For many people, Coke means any kind of soda, even that made by Coke's competitors.

Jell-O is a **name brand**—a well-advertised, nationally known brand that is sold in most stores. Statistics show that today's consumers are not as loyal to name brands as they used to be. Instead, they are beginning to pay more attention to **store brands**—foods made for the store and carrying its name—because they are less costly. Name brands and store brands can be identical in quality.
1 They may even have been packed at the
2 same time by the same processor.

Generics

3 Generics are another option for the smart shopper trying to save money. These food and nonfood products are less expensive because they have no brand name, come in plain packages, and are not advertised. Generics must meet FDA standards for wholesomeness, but they may lack consistency in quality. Generic foods are less visible in markets today.

Freshness Dates

The label isn't the only place to look for important information about a product, however. The top, bottom, or side panel may carry a perishable product's **open date,** which tells consumers how fresh it is. There are several kinds of

◀ *Store brands can often save consumers money and yet be of the same quality as the name brand.* ***Why do you think the store brands cost less?***

Caption Answer: While there may be lots of different factors, store brands don't spend as much money advertising as name brands do.

1 Learning Economics Ask students why they think a name brand costs more if it is identical to a store brand. (Advertising is the main reason.) Ask students why grocers carry these name brands since they would probably rather sell their own brand. (Some consumers want the name brands.)

2 Extension How much money will you save on store brands? Generally, 15–20 percent over name brands.

3 Reinforcement Student Activity Workbook, Chapter 28 activities.

1 Student Motivator Divide students into groups and assign them to different grocery stores. Have them survey stocked items to identify different kinds of open dating, noticing any items near or past the expiration dates. Compile results in class.

2 Interesting Fact While most shoppers think buying larger sizes is always cheaper, this isn't necessarily the case. One study compared prices of 62 food products at 16 supermarkets and found 57 of them cost less in smaller sizes in at least one market. Overall, 84 percent of the larger packages did provide a savings, but the rest were higher per unit. Some surprises were that the same brand would often cost less in the smaller size, and several nonfood products, like laundry detergent, were also better buys in the smaller size. It pays to compare unit prices.

3 Reinforcement Give students examples to make sure they understand unit pricing. For example, how would they determine the unit price of a 16 oz. can of peaches that sells for $1.19 (1.19 ÷ 16 = 7.4 cents an ounce) A 64 oz. bottle of cleaner that sells for $4.89 ($4.89 ÷ 64 = 7.6 cents an ounce)

Soap in Moscow

Russians are willing to pay a high price for certain imported goods. In Moscow, detergent manufactured by Procter & Gamble costs $3.18 per kilogram (2.2 pounds) and is given 70 percent of the total shelf space allotted to detergents. The local brand costs $1.91 for the same amount and is given only 20 percent of the shelf space.

open dates. The pack date, for example, tells you when the food was processed and packaged. If you know this, you can determine the age of the food when you
1 purchase it.

Sometimes the dates of processing or packaging are not this obvious. They are closed, or coded, dates that are difficult to interpret unless you've been told how. Closed dates are used in the recall of products since the numbers not only tell when but where the product was packaged. This device also allows stores to set and mark their own **pull date,** the date by which the product should be sold or pulled from the shelf.

An **expiration date,** by contrast, is placed on products by manufacturers and represent the date by which the product should be used. Quality assurance or freshness dates give the last date the product is expected to be of top quality. They are most often found on bakery goods and cheeses. The price of these products may be reduced as the date nears, but the quality will not be as good.

How can open dates help you? Assume that a food item will take you some time to consume. When shopping, you should choose the package with the most recent date. If, on the other hand, you plan to use the product immediately, you should watch for price reductions as expiration or pull dates approach. Bear in mind that perishable foods will remain fresh for a time after the date marked. For example, milk can be used up to four days after its expiration date, cottage cheese up to one week and eggs up to one month.

Unit Pricing

One of the most valuable sources of consumer information is not found on a product's package at all. It is found on the store shelf. This is a product's **unit price,** which is cost per ounce, per pound, or whatever the product's standard unit of measure is. Unit pricing gives consumers a single standard by which to compare the price of competing brands or different sizes of the same brand. For example, you can tell if an eight-ounce jar of peanut butter is a better buy than a four-ounce or a fifteen-ounce jar by comparing the per-ounce cost.

If unit prices are not posted, you can figure them out for yourself. Just divide the item's price by the number of standard units in the package or container. Make sure that if you choose the larger
2 size because it is a better buy, that you
3 really will use it up. Buying more than you need is not smart shopping.

MAKING FOOD CHOICES

Making a list and reading labels are important parts of smart grocery shopping. They can take you only so far, however. Once you are in the store, you will be confronted by the actual task of choosing the right amount and best quality of many varieties of food. To make the best choices, you will need to follow some simple guidelines.

Grain Products

For the highest nutritional content, buy whole grains as much as possible. Refined grain products, such as white bread and white rice, are often enriched with some of the nutrients but these products lack the nutritional punch and fiber content of whole grains.

Fruits and Vegetables

Fresh fruits and vegetables are another important part of your daily diet. In this category, looks are almost always everything, so buy foods that are bright in color and free from insect and other damage, such as breaks, slits, and bruises. In general, vegetables should be firm and crisp. Avoid those that are wilted or rubbery. Fruits should feel heavy for their size and, if ripe, yield slightly to pressure. Note, however, that some fruits—pears and bananas for example—can be purchased green and allowed to ripen at room temperature.

Avoid prepackaged produce. Stores may use this device to simplify pricing and lessen waste—their waste. Under- or overripe items, for instance, that would otherwise go unsold can be hidden at the bottom or in the middle of such packages. Whenever possible, select your
1 own fresh fruits and vegetables.

Meat, Poultry, Fish, and Eggs

The amount and type of the foods you purchase in this group will depend on dietary considerations, number of people to be served, and the need for leftovers, among other factors. You can usually get three to four servings per pound from foods with little or no fat or bone, such as boneless fish fillets and chicken breasts and lean ground beef. Products with a medium amount of fat and bone, such as bone-in chicken breasts and many roasts, will yield two to three servings per pound. Meat and poultry with a large amount of bone,
2 such as spare ribs, chicken wings, and rib
3 chops, will produce only one or two servings per pound.

Inspection of meat and poultry for safety comes under USDA guidelines. After passing an inspection for sanitation, accurate labeling, and correct use of chemical additives, products receive an appropriate stamp of quality. Inspection of fish is voluntary.

Meat When determining the quality of meat, there are several things you can look for. First, make sure any outside fat is white, not yellow. Second, check for adequate but not excessive marbling. The more marbling, the more tender the meat.

◄ *Fresh fruits are an important part of your diet.* ***What should you look for when shopping for fruit?***

1 Extension Provide a variety of unusual fruits and vegetables for students to taste-test. Develop a graph showing the popularity of each. Discuss methods of serving to make some of them more popular.

2 Math Application Have students assume that they can get four servings per pound of hamburger. They need enough to feed five people at one meal and have 1½ pounds left over for a later meal. Three of the people will eat two servings, one will eat one serving, and one will eat a half serving. How much hamburger should they buy to the nearest half pound? ($3 \times 2 = 6 + 1 + \frac{1}{2} = 7\frac{1}{2}$ servings (4 = 1.875 pounds + 1.5 pounds = 3.375 = 3½ pounds.)

3 Student Motivator Arrange for a visit to a local supermarket at a time when the class can watch a butcher cut meat for packaging and display. Have the butcher offer advice as to preferred cuts.

Caption Answer: Look for fruits that are bright in color and free from insects.

1 Research Have students research the general costs, nutritive value, fat content, and storage for meat, poultry, and fish. You may want to divide the students into groups for this research.

Third, look for porous, pink bones. These indicate a young animal. Fourth, check color. Beef should be bright red; pork should be grayish pink; and lamb, pinkish red.

Poultry In selecting the highest quality poultry, look for birds that are full breasted and meaty with evenly distributed fat and unblemished skin. The cooking method you plan to use will determine the type of bird you need. If you are buying chicken, for example, your choices would include broiler, fryer, roaster, or stewing chicken. The first three are young, tender, small- to medium-sized birds. They tend to cost more per pound and are good for roasting, grilling, and frying. The last is an older, larger, and meatier bird but one that is often less tender and can be used for soups or stews. In general, poultry is a better buy, per pound, than red meat. In-store processing and handling, however, can sharply increase its cost. For example, a cut-up fryer costs more than a whole one, and boneless chicken breasts can cost more than some cuts of steak.

Fish Look for firm flesh, red gills, and bright, bulging eyes. Also, look for a mild, fresh aroma, not a pronounced fishy smell. Fresh or frozen fish should be purchased with careful attention to cost. In many parts of the country, it is more expensive than red meat.

Eggs Eggs are classified by size, or weight per dozen. The most common classifications sold in the stores are extra large (27 oz), large (24 oz), and medium (21 oz). Large is the standard size used in cooking. Eggs are graded AA, A, B, and C. The top grades should be used for poaching, frying, and hard-boiling. The yolks are firm and centered and the whites thick. The lower grades of eggs have thinner whites and yolks and are adequate for scrambling or mixing with other ingredients. When shopping, check to be sure eggs are clean and the shells are not cracked, which can permit bacteria to get in. The color of the eggshell has no relation to nutritive value or quality.

Dairy Products

When purchasing dairy products, look for low-fat or nonfat varieties. Since dairy products spoil rapidly, it is especially important to buy the one that carries the most recent date. When selecting cheese, note that shredded, sliced, and grated products cost more.

Caption Answer: Mexican menu—low fat foods: broiled chicken pieces; low calorie salad and dressing; bean/chicken burritos, "light"; fried, sauteed, melted cheese. Other possible words for low fat: baked, steamed, grilled; high fat: batter, breaded, cream, in a rich sauce.

Eating out often can be even more costly if your nutrition suffers. ***What might be some good lower fat choices this family could make? What are some words you might find on this restaurant's menu that would give you clues to low fat foods?*** ▶

Eating Out

No discussion about smart food shopping is complete without addressing a favorite American pastime of dining out. More than 40 cents of each of our food dollars is spent in restaurants. The food generally costs more there than it does if you're eating at home. An additional cost is a tip of about 15 to 20 percent if you have a food server. If you would like to eat at an expensive restaurant but don't feel you can afford an elaborate dinner, go there for lunch or take advan-
1 tage of early bird specials.

TAKING CARE OF YOUR PURCHASES

Let's say you've handled your shop-
2 ping trip wisely, have gotten some good

A Reason to Give Thanks

If Thanksgiving dinner is a big deal at your house—lots of food, lots of relatives—you know what it takes to prepare it. Suppose that every year you put on a feast for 900 guests?

That is what Roy Allain, of New Orleans, does. Allain runs the Ozanam Inn where, for 40 years, homeless and hungry people have been coming for turkey dinner with all the fixings.

Much of the food for the feast comes from donations. People just stop by and drop off food—hams, turkeys, and canned goods. One family comes by every Thanksgiving morning and drops off from 30 to 40 pumpkin pies. Restaurants, too, bring over all kinds of meats and main dishes. Most donors do not even give their names. Much of the food that is brought to the Ozanam Inn for Thanksgiving actually helps the New Orleans soup kitchen get through the following week.

It is not only on Thanksgiving that Allain and his volunteers feed folks. For 365 days a year, they provide three meals a day to more than 300 people.

Allain says that when the kitchen first started, it served mostly down-and-out alcoholics. Today the group at the Ozanam may include doctors, lawyers, military people, and others who are having substance-abuse problems, mental or emotional problems, or a very bad streak of luck. Allain has noticed one big change. More families, and more women and children show up at the Ozanam Inn needing to be fed.

As long as the donations come in, the hungry and needy will always find a meal at the Ozanam Inn.

Brainstorm

What are some of the factors you would have to consider if you fed 300 people every day?

1 Research Have students discuss their favorite eating places. Calculate how much it would cost to make the same items at home. What is it other than food that makes eating out attractive?

2 Discussion Starter Tell students it is important to ensure the safety of foods when purchasing and transporting them home. Have them discuss safety factors to consider for both fresh and processed foods. (For canned vegetables, don't buy dirty or dented cans. For fresh meat, fish, poultry, wrap in plastic so they don't leak on other foods, and make sure fresh fish is cold. For frozen fruits and vegetables, make sure packages aren't frosted.)

Case Study Answer: Food quality; storage capabilities; seating capability of the facility; sources of food; sources of funding; staffing kitchens; clean up; breakage of dishes; sanitation.

1 Interesting Fact Sometimes people cannot get to stores that will save them money. People living in some inner city neighborhoods and in some rural areas have long been forced to pay 5 to 25 percent more at convenience stores and smaller markets. Some chains are now working with community groups to build more full-sized stores in such neighborhoods.

2 Extension Have a county extension agent speak to the class about ways to get the most for your food dollar. Have the agent compare food budgets at different levels (low, medium, and high) and how families cope with minimal amounts to spend.

3 Research Have students find out whether there are any food co-ops in their area. How do they operate? What are the advantages? disadvantages?

News Clip Answers:
1 The distribution channel has gotten longer.
2 Wash your hands thoroughly after handling these items. You should also wash countertops and utensils. You should ensure that the meat or poultry is fully cooked before eating your meal.

bargains, bought high-nutrition foods, and you have stuck to your budget. You are home with your bags of food. Now what?

Your planning isn't over. You need to store and use the food properly to get the most out of it.

Food Storage and Handling

It doesn't matter how good the food is if it spoils before you eat it. To prevent spoilage, keep most fruits and vegetables in the crisper section of your refrigerator. Exceptions are potatoes, sweet potatoes, and onions. Potatoes change flavor if stored in the refrigerator; onions and sweet potatoes mold and decay. Store them in a cool, dark, dry place. Bread should be stored in the refrigerator only if the weather is humid, and it should be placed in the freezer only for long-term storage.

Handling food properly can keep you from getting sick. Microorganism contamination is a serious health threat, as we've seen from deadly outbreaks of E. coli bacteria in ground beef in recent years. Refrigerate or freeze perishable foods as soon as you can after shopping, and buy those foods last at the store so they stay cold. Wash your hands, cutting boards, counters, and utensils in hot soapy water, particularly if they have come in contact with raw meat, poultry, or eggs. Cook animal foods thoroughly.

Watch temperatures when serving and transporting foods—a good rule is to keep hot foods hot and cold foods cold. If you are asked to use a raw egg in a recipe, you can use an egg substitute. Know where fresh seafood comes from and which waters have been identified as infected by your local Health Department.

TACKLING FOOD BUYING PROBLEMS

Smart shopping is not always easy. You can use all the strategies listed previously, but what if prices are too high? You can make a list, but how do you stick to it when tempted by impulse buying?

High Prices

Food costs you much more than farmers earn for growing it. What adds to the cost? Some factors are the pay for the people who package, process, transport, store, and sell it, along with advertising and promotion costs that are passed on to the consumer. Increased demand for a product or natural disasters—such as hurricanes that wipe out a
1 Florida citrus crop—can cause temporary increases in food prices.

There are some specific things you can do if prices are too high for your budget. Consider joining with others to shop at membership or warehouse clubs or to participate in a food cooperative. Food cooperatives are organizations of consumers who buy food as a group at wholesale. Members save money by not dealing with a retailer, thus avoiding the
2 retailers markup. They volunteer their own time to package and distribute food
3 among themselves.

To save money you could also grow some food, like herbs and vegetables, in a home garden. Try to spend more of your own time preparing food instead of relying on processed foods. The time-saving features of **convenience foods,** which are processed foods that can be prepared with little or no effort, increase costs.

Impulse Buying

Grocery stores, like other stores, are arranged with one purpose in mind: to

CASE STUDY

Consumer NEWS CLIP

Caution Is Key to Clean Food

by Kathryn Salensky
Puget Sound Business Journal
April 21, 1995

Food safety regulations are undergoing an evolution that will probably make meat and poultry consumption much safer. But experts say consumer caution is still the key to a clean food supply.

For example, when you pick up ground beef at the grocery store, do you worry about picking up bacteria? You should, according to University of Washington's molecular epidemiologist Mansour Samadpour.

"Customers contaminate their hands every time they pick up a package of meat," he warns. "Anytime you handle chicken, seafood or meat, you should wear plastic gloves or (use) double-wrapped packages and wash your hands."

"We have problems that just didn't exist years ago," says Dr. Barbara Rasko of the University of Washington Institute for Food Service and Technology.

"Distribution channels have gotten longer," she says. "If an outbreak occurred 40 years ago, only one family might become ill. Today, 100 or more persons could become ill."

Rasko adds that proposed regulations attempt to reduce food-borne pathogens early on in the distribution chain.

Surprisingly, the regulations appear to have the support of much of the food industry. The cost of an unchecked food supply greatly outweighs the cost of implementing regulations, says Dr. David Theno. He works for Jack-in-the-Box's parent company, Foodmaker Inc., as vice president of quality assurance, research and deve- uct safety.

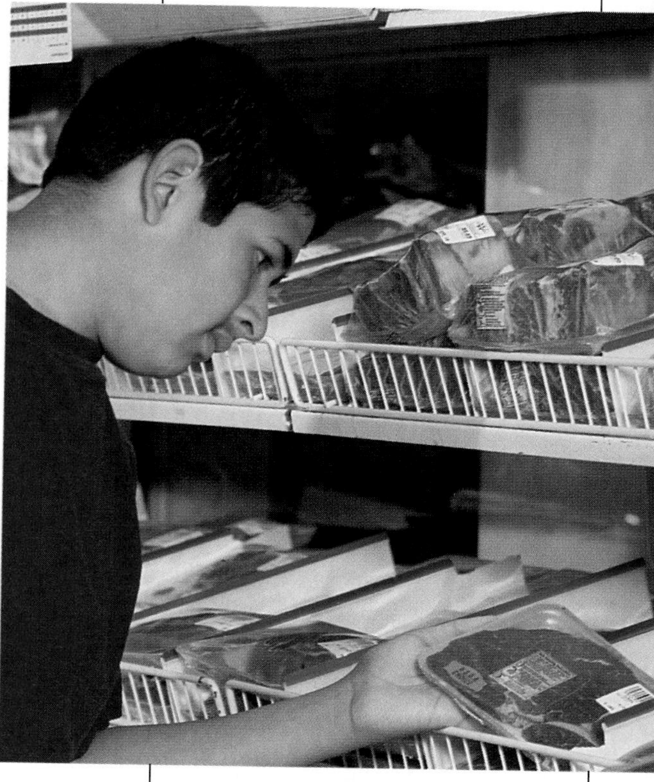

According to Theno, HACCP [Hazard Analysis Critical Control Point] is a state-of-the art system that manages food safety by tracking and testing food at critical points along the distribution chain. "The primary cost of food quality assurance programs involves personnel," says Theno. "A large operation may need 10 quality assurance technicians to monitor food production for each day. A smaller operation may only require one or two."

Theno doesn't foresee consumers' bearing the brunt of the HACCP since costly outbreaks should decrease and implementation costs are nominal. Whether HACCP becomes a reality or not, Dr. Tarr cautions consumers that a safe food supply shouldn't solely rest on the food industry's shoulders. "No one can guarantee pathogen-free food—unless that food is cooked well and prepared correctly. The key to food safety is safe food handling and consumer awareness."

Decisions, Decisions

1. What is one reason for the increase in food contamination problems?
2. What can you do to avoid getting sick from meat and poultry products?

FLASHBACK FLASHFORWARD

Got a sweet tooth? In 1951, you could satisfy that sweet tooth with 13 cents which would buy you two Mars candy bars. Today, it'll cost you 79 cents to purchase those same candy bars.

1 Extension Most products carry a Universal Product Code (UPC) symbol that can be read by the store's computer at the checkout counter for the correct price. *Consumer Reports* did an informal study on the accuracy of those prices. Only a few small mistakes were found, some for the shopper and some against. It still pays to check accuracy. Some stores will refund your money for that item if you prove a mistake was made.

2 Extension Have student groups compare price and quality and preparation times for foods that can be purchased fresh or as a convenience item. Research any nutrients lost or additives included in the processed version.

3 Critical Thinking Give students a low dollar figure available to a family for a week's food budget. Have them plan the most nutritious meals possible with that amount.

get you to buy, whether you planned to or not. In other words, they are designed to encourage impulse purchases. (See Figure 28–2.)

1 To control the impulse, shop defensively. Stick to your shopping list and plan your route through the store using the shortest way possible. Also calculate the cost of any temptations before giving in.

2 Defensive shopping that fights high prices can continue right up to the check-out stand. Know prices or write them down. Then, check them as they are rung up or at home against your receipt. Report any mistakes to the store. Make sure that you get the right amount of change, and that you have all the gro-
3 ceries you paid for.

Figure 28–2 Impulse Purchases

Supermarkets are often designed to encourage impulse purchases. See if you recognize any of the following devices.

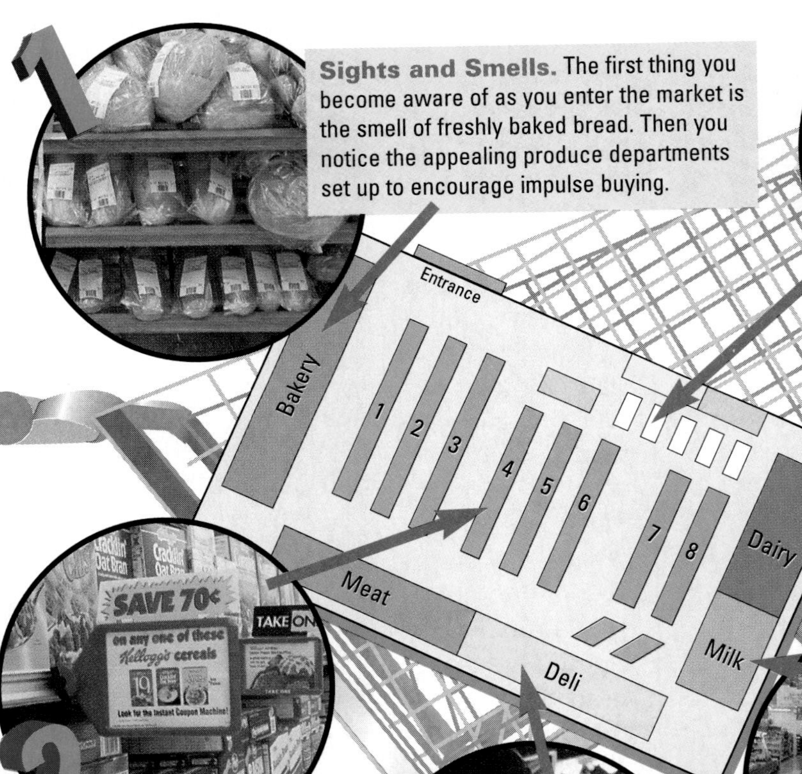

Sights and Smells. The first thing you become aware of as you enter the market is the smell of freshly baked bread. Then you notice the appealing produce departments set up to encourage impulse buying.

Talking Shelves and Flashing Coupons. The next hurdle to overcome is the talking shelf displays, product demonstrations, and instant coupon machines, all designed with your spending habits in mind.

The Deli Trap. Glass cases reveal trays of roast chicken and barbecued ribs, bowls of salad, crocks of soup and chili. All of a sudden, tonight's dinner is faster and easier than you thought it would be.

Where's the Milk? The holiday or barbecue is three weeks away, however, and you need more basic things like milk, eggs, and meat. Where are they? Most are at the back of the store. To get to them, you have to pass through one or more aisles filled with items you have not even thought about until they caught your eye.

Final Escape? You rush to the check out stand to try to escape temptation and what do you find? More impulse items – candy bars for the trip home and magazines for when you get there. Who can resist them?

Chapter 28 Highlights	Key Terms
Going to Market ▶ While there are many kinds of markets, it is best to shop primarily at the ones that provide the best buys and the services you desire.	
Planning Your Purchases ▶ Planning is one of the most important elements in good grocery shopping. A few simple rules apply, such as making and following a shopping list, shopping once a week, shopping when stores are not crowded, and not shopping on an empty stomach.	nutrient density
Using Consumer Information ▶ Food labels provide such information as net weight, pack, grades, and brand names. ▶ In addition, nutrition labels give detailed information on how much of certain nutrients a food contains and what percentage of daily needs it provides. ▶ Dates on the products tell consumers how fresh products are. ▶ Unit pricing allows consumers to compare costs based on standard units of measures.	net weight name brand store brand open date pull date expiration date unit price
Making Food Choices ▶ Selecting foods involves choosing the right amount and the best quality.	
Taking Care of Your Purchases ▶ Managing food involves safe handling and storage of food as well as developing a strategy for eating out.	
Tackling Food Buying Problems ▶ High prices are caused by many factors (advertising and promotion, increased demand or natural disasters). ▶ If food prices are a problem, consumers can join cooperatives, raise produce, prepare own foods rather than using convenience foods. ▶ Supermarkets use a variety of tactics to encourage impulse buying (displays, smells, promotions, islands to slow traffic, placement of items in the store). The best way to resist these tactics is to shop defensively—know what you want and stick to your plan. **Reinforcement** Suggest that students review the chapter by using the five-step study procedure described at the beginning of the Teacher's Manual.	convenience foods impulse buying

CHAPTER 28 REVIEW

Refer students to the Reviewing Consumer Terms and Reviewing Facts and Ideas activities in the Student Activity Workbook.

Reviewing Consumer Terms Paragraphs will vary. See Glossary for definitions.

Reviewing Facts and Ideas See the Student Activity Workbook for answers.

Problem Solving and Decision Making
1 a Name Brand—24 oz.—unit price — 9.5 c -18 oz.—unit price—8.8 c Store Brand—24 oz.—unit price—8.7 c - 18 oz.—unit price—8.3 c * Best buy **b** Brand names, freshness, size, quality, nutrition labeling, personal taste preference. **2** Answers will depend on students' perspectives. Some might include buying a less expensive pack of canned fruit (chopped for a fast cobbler), boneless poultry and fresh vegetables in season for a quick and inexpensive stir fry (also low in fat), whole wheat bread instead of rolls, fresh greens for a salad.

Consumers Around the World
Math
1 (*a*) 567 grams; (*b*) 5 lbs.; (*c*) 1362 grams

Communications
2 Students should

Reviewing Consumer Terms

Use each of the following terms in a paragraph to demonstrate you know its meaning.

convenience foods
expiration date
impulse buying
name brand
net weight
nutrient density
open date
pull date
store brand
unit price

Reviewing Facts and Ideas

1. Why is the order in which ingredients are listed on food labels important?
2. Why is planning for your shopping trip important?
3. How are name-brands, store-brands, and generic products likely to compare in cost and quality?
4. Where would you find the unit price of a product and how would you use that information?
5. How would you select each of the following?
   - **a.** A tender steak
   - **b.** The freshest eggs
   - **c.** The best oranges
   - **d.** The freshest carrots
6. What are some reasons for high food prices?
7. How do stores encourage impulse purchases?

Problem Solving and Decision Making

1. Compute the unit prices for the products and sizes given in the table below.
   - **a.** If quality is equal, which brand and size represents the better buy?
   - **b.** For what reasons might a consumer want to buy the products with the higher unit prices?

   Name Brand
   Net wt. = 24 oz; price = $2.27
   Net wt. = 18 oz; price = $1.59
   Store Brand
   Net wt. = 24 oz.; price $2.09
   Net wt. = 18 oz.; price $1.49
2. Jackie must prepare a meal for unexpected company. Her budget is tight and she has very little time after work to buy groceries. Develop a plan for Jackie based on a well-balanced menu for the evening meal.

Building Academic Skills

Consumers Around the World

Math

1. Under orders from the European Union officials in Brussels, Britain has adopted the metric system for all packaged goods. As stores change weights, aisles are full of confused people. Instead of pounds and ounces, it is now kilos and grams. Help out British consumers by converting the following, based on this conversion information
   1 ounce = 28.35 grams

1 pound = 454 grams
1 kilogram = 2.2 lbs

a. How many grams are in a 20 ounce box of cereal?

b. How many pounds in 2.27 kilograms of cheese?

c. How many grams in a 3 pound bag of oranges?

Communications

2. The world food supply has had its ups and downs over the past 20 years. Write a 250-word summary on its problems, causes, and solutions.

Beyond the Classroom

Consumer Project

Prepare a list of ten typical grocery store purchases for a family of four. Check the prices of these items at three different stores. Use the same name brands each time. Also compare the price of the stores own brand for each item. What conclusions can you draw from this comparison?

 Cooperative Learning

Family Economics

Break into assigned family groups. Discuss the following problem.

Prepare a food purchasing profile of your family. Begin by planning a week's menu. Then do a detailed shopping list. Enter prices based on newspaper ads, food store circulars, or an actual trip to a market. If necessary, adjust your menus to stay within your assigned food budget. What things in your family's makeup, resources, daily activities, and health have the greatest influence on what goes into your shopping cart? Given this profile, which kinds of consumer information would you rely on the most? Are high food prices a problem for your family? For a spending limit, use the guidelines below. They are based on food plans created by the U.S. Department of Agriculture. Compare your answers with those of other family groups.

Food Budget Per Week Plan

	Thrifty	Low Cost	Moderate
Couples			
20–50 years	$54.00	$68.00	$84.00
51 & over	50.30	65.00	81.00
Individuals			
Preschool	15.10	19.00	23.00
6–11 years	20.00	26.00	39.00
Teen	23.00	31.00	44.00
Female 20–50	23.00	29.00	35.00

Debate the Issue

Lynnette has been working in her family's market since she was ten years old. Now she owns and manages the place, and wants to increase her revenues. She is doing that by offering new items, such as small toys, single-serving cookies, and gourmet coffee. These are items her customers apparently like, because they are buying them.

Rafael, a shopper at Lynnette's store, is on a tight budget and trying to support his large family on one income. He is unhappy because his family members are spending the grocery budget on Lynnette's impulse items.

You and your classmates will break into two groups and research this topic. Each group will gather evidence to support one side or the other. You are to prepare the argument for your side of the problem. Then the two groups will meet in a classroom debate.

share their findings with the class. Current problems can be researched by looking up statistics such as food security indexes (between 1980 and 1990, Haiti's dropped from 100 to 84) and food consumption as a share of total household expenditures (64 percent in Tanzania and 61 percent in China were the highest in the world in the early 90s).

Consumer Project
Answers will depend on students' choices of products.

Family Economics
Some of the families (1 and 3) are fitness conscious. Many must work around health problems (overweight, high blood pressure, diabetes, possible ulcer). Most must concern themselves with the special likes and dislikes of children of various ages.

Debate the Issue
Break the class into two teams. Assign each team one side of the issue. Encourage students to work together as a team to develop their argument. Ask each team to select a member to make an opening statement that supports their side of the issue. Have students take turns debating as the debate moves from one team to another.

CHAPTER 29

Drugs and Cosmetics

Learning Objectives

When you have finished studying this chapter, you should be able to:

1. Distinguish between drugs and cosmetics.
2. Ask questions to ensure the safe and effective use of prescription and over-the-counter drugs.
3. Summarize the risks and benefits involved in using various over-the-counter drugs.
4. Describe devices commonly used to prevent product tampering.
5. Explain the proper selection and use of common cosmetics.
6. Identify characteristics of skin protection products.

Consumer Terms

drug
cosmetic
prescription drugs
registered pharmacist
side effects
over-the-counter (OTC) drugs
tampering

Real-World Journal

Athletes need to be in the best of shape to perform their roles. Most exercise daily. They also watch their diets very closely. Yet the use of drugs in professional athletics has become more of a regular occurrence. Discuss in your journal why you think athletes still use drugs to enhance performance even though the drugs cause physical and mental side effects.

Lesson Plan See the Teacher's Manual for Chapter 29 lesson plan.

Vocabulary The Chapter 29 lesson plan includes suggested vocabulary activities for the terms listed.

1 Critical Thinking Have students bring print ads for drugs and cosmetic items to class and make judgments as to whether the product is a drug or cosmetic as defined by the FDA.

2 Interesting Note Because they are not monitored as closely as prescription drugs, cosmetics should be used with caution. Can students think of examples of cosmetics that can cause undesirable reactions (artificial nails, especially if not applied properly, can leave a space between the natural and artificial nail, allowing fungal infection to begin).

3 Interesting Note A study revealed that only 3–4 percent of patients asked questions about their prescriptions while in the doctor's office, yet reports also show that medications are taken improperly 50 percent of the time.

4 Extension Besides asking the doctor if you can substitute generics (a savings of up to 30 percent or more), find out if a cheaper member of the same class of drug would be acceptable. Check a variety of drugstores and pharmacies, including mail order. Their prices will reflect differences in overhead. Another way to reduce costs is to keep an eye out for popular products offered at large savings to lure customers into the store.

DISTINGUISHING DRUGS AND COSMETICS

Keeping yourself physically healthy requires more than just selecting the right diet from the five food groups. You must also know how to purchase medications when you need them and how to select personal-care products.

The FDA defines a **drug** as a product intended to "affect the structure or function of the human body or to treat [or] prevent...a disease." A **cosmetic,** by contrast, is defined as an article that may be "...applied to the human body for cleansing, beautifying, and promoting attractiveness; or altering the appearance without affecting the body's structure or functions." The distinction is important because the FDA treats the two kinds of products differently. Drugs must be tested extensively and proved safe before they can be sold. Cosmetics require no such procedures. However, if a health claim is made for a cosmetic, this situation changes. Then the FDA can require the manufacturer to produce scientific evidence to support the claim. For example, saying that a skin cream "removes wrinkles" may trigger FDA
1 action. Saying that it "beautifies the
2 skin" will not.

Brand Loyalty in Latin America

About 50 percent of Latin Americans say they have a favorite brand of shampoo they nearly always buy. The same level of brand loyalty exists in the United States. Among those who don't stand by their brands, in Latin America, 22 percent look around for the best buy, while 28 percent of American consumers choose from two or three favorite brands of shampoo and 12 percent choose a new brand or the best buy.

PURCHASING MEDICINES

There are two basic types of medicines available today. They are prescription (Rx) drugs and over-the-counter (OTC) drugs.

Prescription Drugs

Prescription drugs carry the Rx symbol and can be ordered, or prescribed, only by a doctor. In addition, they can be purchased only from a registered pharmacist. A **registered pharmacist** is a person who has been trained and licensed to sell medicines.

Studies show that up to half of all prescription drugs are not taken properly because patients lack information. The next time the doctor gives you a prescription, be sure to get answers to the
3 following questions:

1. What is the name of the drug? Is it really necessary? Is it habit forming?
2. What ingredients are in the drug and how will they help me?
3. How and when should I take it? For how long?
4. Will there be any side effects? (**Side effects,** which can occur with some drugs, are reactions in addition to the wanted effect from the drug.) Will any side effects interfere with my daily activities?
5. Can I take the drug along with other medications?
6. Is it possible to write the prescription using a generic rather than a brand
4 name?

Once you have prescription drugs in the house, you should regularly sort through them and throw away those past their expiration dates. Better yet, if you do not finish a prescription, destroy what is left. Under no circumstances, allow someone else to use it. A prescription drug is prescribed for you alone, with your illness and your medical history in mind. It could be wrong—even dangerously wrong—for someone else to
1 take it.

Over-the-Counter Drugs

Over-the-counter (OTC) drugs are the familiar, less potent medicines that can be purchased without a prescription in local supermarkets and pharmacies. Some typical examples include aspirin and certain acne medications. The range of OTC drugs is broad. There are more than 300,000 of these drugs sold in the United States. Along with this greater opportunity for self-
2 care comes greater responsibility.

There are many over-the-counter medications to choose from. ***Who decides whether medicines require a prescription? What is the process? Have any prescription medications been changed to OTC?*** ▼

While OTC drugs are safe for most people, there are some risks involved in taking them. They can cause allergic reactions, limit the effectiveness of prescription drugs taken with them, or mask conditions requiring medical attention. In addition, if the directions for use are not followed, overdoses are possible and could create serious or even life-threatening conditions. You can avoid many of these risks simply by reading the product's label and asking the pharmacist questions similar to those you asked the doctor. Take, for example, painkillers and acne medications.

Painkillers Aspirin is the most widely used nonprescription drug in the world. Aspirin works best on mild to moderately severe pain such as muscle ache, backache, toothache, and headache. It is also effective in reducing fever, arthritic pain, and inflammation. While some recent research has shown aspirin significantly benefits people who have a history of coronary artery disease, it is not clear whether the drug can prevent the disease in others. Advertising claims for OTC medications can be misleading. While the Food and Drug Administration (FDA) strictly regulates the labels and contents of OTC medicines, advertising is monitored by the Federal Trade Commission (FTC) whose only standard is that it should be
3 "reasonable."

Because aspirin is so easy to get, consumers often do not think about its hazards. Since it is an acid, aspirin can damage the stomach lining, and result in a variety of unpleasant conditions such as heartburn and nausea. It has also been
4 linked to stomach ulcers. The label warns against excessive or inappropriate use.

Acetaminophen is an aspirin substitute. (It is best known by such brand names as Tylenol, Datril, and Anacin-3.) Acetaminophen is just as effective as aspirin in relieving pain and reducing fever. Unlike aspirin, it does not relieve

1 Discussion Starter Ask students if they know anyone who has taken a medication prescribed for someone else. What was the drug and the problem being treated? Do students think this practice is safe?

2 Interesting Note Both prescription and over-the-counter drugs can have counterparts. If the original patent has expired (after 17 years) or there never was a patent, manufacturers can sell the drug under a different brand name or under the drug's generic name.

3 Interesting Note Aspirin has a past history that reaches back to the fifth century B.C., when Hypocrites used a bitter powder from willow bark to ease pain and reduce fever.

4 Extension The label also specifically warns not to use it to treat children and teens with the chicken pox or the flu since there is a risk of Reyes Syndrome, a rare but sometimes fatal disease.

Caption Answer: The Food and Drug Administration (FDA). Before changing a prescription drug to an OTC drug, the FDA completes a safety review and makes improvements in labeling. There are now over 400 OTC medications that were only available by prescription 15 years ago.

1 Extension Benzoyl peroxide is considered a promoter (increases tumor development when an initiator is present). The sun is an initiator (can start tumor growth—as evidenced by skin cancer).

2 Interesting Note Good results in treating acne have also been obtained with Retinoic Acid. Since it can be a potent irritant if applied incorrectly, it is available only by prescription.

3 Reinforcement Student Activity Workbook, Chapter 29 activities.

inflammation and so cannot be used to treat arthritis. Its primary advantage is that it has fewer side effects than aspirin. It is not good for people with kidney problems, however, and if a large overdose is taken, it can cause liver damage.

Ibuprofen (marketed under the brand names of Advil, Motrin, and Nuprin) and naproxen (marketed under the brand name Aleve) are two other types of pain relievers. These are more potent pain relievers especially for menstrual cramps, toothaches, and minor arthritis. When taken at recommended doses, they are both somewhat milder on the stomach than aspirin, but they can have similar side effects. People allergic to aspirin will usually be allergic to these products.

Regardless of what type of OTC pain reliever you choose, remember it is intended for short-term use only. A doctor should be consulted for any long-term use and if symptoms worsen.

Acne Medications Acne is a word that strikes dread in any teen's heart. Experts estimate that 85 percent of Americans between the ages of 12 and 25 have this condition in some form. One of the most important parts of the standard treatment for acne is medication applied directly to the skin. Lotions, creams, or gels containing benzoyl peroxide have been found effective. They degerm, dry, and peel the skin. Recently, concerns have been raised on what happens to skin treated with benzoyl peroxide when exposed to the sun. Currently, the FDA considers benzoyl peroxide safe while tests continue. They may place a warning on the label against unnecessary sun exposure and a recommendation for the use of a sunscreen when using acne prod-
1 ucts with benzoyl peroxide.

In severe cases of acne, doctors will prescribe other drugs. These drugs may
2 be used instead of or in conjunction
3 with OTC medications.

Tampering Once you have decided to purchase an OTC drug, you should check the package for signs of tampering. **Tampering** occurs when a package has been opened or changed for an improper purpose. Tampering with food, drugs, or other consumer products is against federal law. Most drug manufacturers now use tamper-evident packaging for their products such as blister or strip packs, external plastic neck seals, and inner foil mouth seals. These devices make tampering more difficult, but they cannot prevent it entirely. As a result, some drug manufacturers have altered their products, changing them to

How to Buy Sunglasses

Sunglasses protect your eyes from harsh sunlight, which can cause headaches and eyestrain.

- **Look for labels that guarantee 100 percent ultraviolet (UV) absorption.**
- **Stick with gray, brown, or green lenses, which allow you to distinguish colors. Be sure the lenses are dark enough. Ask a sales clerk or look in a mirror to make sure that your eyes can't be seen through the lenses.**
- **Choose wraparound or large, round lenses for the best protection.**
- **Buy scratch-resistant plastic if you play sports or are otherwise active.**
- **Check for optical flaws. Hold the glasses at arm's length and look through a lens with one eye, focusing on a rectangular pattern, such as a tiled floor. If the lines are wavy, get a different pair.**

more tamper-resistant forms. The best-known example of this is the substitution of pills for capsules.

PURCHASING COSMETICS

There are more than 30 billion toiletries and cosmetics on the market. Many teens spend a large portion of their income on these products. Purchases are often based on exaggerated advertising claims rather than informed decision making. The FDA requires that all ingredients in a cosmetic be listed on its label. The only exceptions are specific flavors, fragrances, and "trade secrets." Check the labels on three competing lipsticks, for example. You will probably find that the main ingredients are basically the same. Any large differences in price, it

Drug War Victory

Drug dealers had virtually taken over the town of East Palo Alto in the summer of 1991. The police were too few in numbers to stop them. Cocaine was sold openly on the streets in residential neighborhoods. Gunfights were not uncommon. Quiet citizens often had their houses shot at. "For sale" signs were everywhere.

Finally, a small group of citizens calling themselves Just Us refused to be intimidated any longer. Working with police chief Burnham "Burny" Matthews, they began to fight back.

In the worst of the drug-dealing areas, the group marched with signs that read "Drug-Free Zone." When cars cruised in to buy drugs, the citizens wrote down license numbers and gave them to the police. Some marchers videotaped the deals. Although they were afraid the armed drug dealers would start shooting at them, Just Us kept up its vigil. Marchers kept in touch with the police by walkie-talkie.

As the pressure against the dealers increased, Matthews called in reinforcements from nearby towns. Soon the sheriff's department was giving them support, too. The California Highway Patrol also assigned officers to the area. Undercover agents bought drugs from 115 dealers and arrested more than half of them.

Finally, citizens and police began to see a change. The violent crime rate dropped. In 1993, murders in East Palo Alto were down to 6 from 42 the previous year. Just Us found only one drug house, and it was quickly closed down.

The marchers put away their signs, and the "for sale" signs came down. The citizens of East Palo Alto had won the war on drugs.

Brainstorm

What steps would you and your family take to confront a crime problem in your neighborhood?

Case Study Answer: Form a neighborhood association; form a neighborhood watch; form a liaison with police; post signs in the neighborhood to the effect that neighbors do not tolerate crime; teach younger children the dangers of crime; work with local and nationwide groups that combat crime; get to know neighbors so that you know who belongs in the neighborhood and who does not; try to get media coverage of the problem; be aware and alert to suspicious cars, behaviors; clean up empty lots that give potential troublemakers a place to "hang out" and that make the neighborhood look uncared for.

Caption Answer: Prices are affected by supply and demand. If customers want one brand more than others, it will probably cost more.

News Clip Answers:
1 They are seeking to better serve their customers by providing not only the product but also information and advice on how to apply it. They are also moving out of traditional retail stores and into outlets that are more convenient for their customers such as college bookstores.
2 You could go to an older friend or relative. You could also seek assistance from a professional at one of the traditional sales locations, for example, a department store.

can be assumed, result from differences in fragrance, packaging, or advertising budget—not the benefits of the product itself.

Skin and Hair Care Products

Cosmetics aren't magic potions. They can, however, help clean the skin and keep it from becoming dry. Frequent cleansing plays a role in diminishing the oils that cause acne, although that won't eliminate the condition. If you spend a lot of time outdoors, a moisturizer might be needed. Be sure to purchase one that is water-based. An oil-base one can cause an acne directly related to the use of the cosmetic.

Hair care begins with shampoo. Shampoo is mainly detergent. Therefore, just about any one will do the job of cleaning your hair. Manufacturers' claims of added cleaning, detangling, and conditioning based on formula changes (for example, products for dry, normal, and oily hair) have not been proven.

If you use a hair coloring product, you should carefully check the ingredient labeling. In particular, look for any mention of coal tar dyes. These can cause serious allergic reactions in some people. By law, products using coal tar dyes must be clearly labeled and provide directions for performing a preliminary patch test to determine sensitivity.

Cosmetic Safety

Overuse of some cosmetics and the inclusion of substances such as coal tar dyes, fragrances, and preservatives can cause allergic and other reactions which should be taken seriously. Problems can also occur from unsafe use. Serious safety problems rarely happen, but specific products can cause trouble. Use of hair spray near heat or fire is dangerous. Before it is dry, it can ignite causing serious burns. The most common injuries from cosmetics are caused by getting products in the eyes.

PURCHASING COSMETICS THAT ARE CONSIDERED DRUGS

When cosmetics claim they affect a structure or function of the body, they are regulated as drugs. They must be scientifically proven safe and effective before being marketed. Some examples are sunscreens and sunblocking cosmetics, fluoride toothpastes to prevent tooth decay, and shampoos to treat dandruff. Skin protection products are the most difficult to sort out.

Skin Protection Products

You may not agree, but your body considers a tan undesirable. Tanning is a defense against ultraviolet rays, the part of sunlight that burns the skin. Thus, when a tan appears, it is usually a sign that damage has been done. There are two kinds of ultraviolet rays—UVA and UVB. While previous concern was only for the cancer causing UVB rays, some

◀ *Some cosmetics may have exactly the same ingredients, but one might cost much more than the others.* ***Why?***

CASE STUDY

Consumer NEWS CLIP

Shopping for Makeup Just Got Easier

by Jennifer Scruby
Elle September 1995

A woman wants [makeup] when she wants it and how she wants it, says Dan Brestle, president of Clinique. "Some customers want to get in and out, some want to sit down and spend some time. What both types of consumers are bringing to the counter is a new agenda that could reshape the way we shop.

The biggest change is that women aren't foraging for different makeup as much as fishing for the know-how to apply it. Today, the draw to the cosmetics counter is not a goody-bag giveaway but a top-notch makeup artist who can show you the ropes. At the Valerie makeup boutique in Beverly Hills, one customer, Karen, shows me the "before instruction" photo she carries in her purse. "I used to wear purple eye shadow, fuchsia lipstick, and I had one eyebrow that grew across my face," she says. "I was making my eyes look small and squinty and I didn't even know it."

For '90s-minded women, the ideal shopping experience is decidedly free of intimidation tactics, but for many, the advisers' predatory reputation still persists. "Those saleswomen always make me feel like if I'm not wearing as much makeup as they are, I'm doing something wrong," says Antonia, a Los Angeles-based interior designer. "And the minute I ask about one product, I know I will be arm-wrestled into buying at least eight different things." Ingenious advisers are assuaging such fears with more than expertly liplined smiles. At Barneys stores in New York and in Beverly Hills, makeup artists steer customers through the entire cosmetics department like personal shoppers. Chanel recently scrapped the long-standing Lucite seals on its color displays and is handing out dainty packets of perfectly shaped applicators, from pointy eyeliner wands to powder puffs, so customers can help themselves. Origins gives its boutiques a grocery-store style setup, with wide-open shelves and shopping baskets.

But if the pressure's off in stores, shoppers' schedules are more harried than ever. One solution to the time crunch is Washington, D.C.'s EFX, a botanically scented salon shop where women can get a manicure, massage, or haircut while snapping up everything from Kiehl's skin care and Aveda shampoo to curler clips and pumice stones. Of course, some women would prefer that their cosmetics come to them. So Clinique has set up counters inside a dozen university bookstores and is outfitting coeds across the country with floppy disks of CyberFace—a free interactive guide to skin care and makeup. During QVC's "Beauty Week" in October, viewers will be able to order designer scents like Versace and Escada. Futurists can even buy new fragrances like Paco Rabanne XS Pour Elle off the Internet—months before they hit department stores.

Decisions, Decisions

1. Describe the ways cosmetics companies are marketing their makeup products.
2. If you were buying makeup for yourself or a friend, where would you get advice?

FLASHBACK FLASHFORWARD

Holy cow! The moos for milk are on the decline. In 1940, there were nearly 25 million dairy cows. In 1991, the national dairy herd numbered just over 10 million.

1 Interesting Note
Viewed as an epidemic by dermatologists, skin cancer is the most common of all cancers and it is occurring at earlier ages. One quarter of all the people expected to develop melanoma, the most serious form, will get it before the age of 39.

2 Discussion Starter
Ask students to discuss the statement—many products are available for sun protection, but they won't do you much good if they are applied carelessly. What are some considerations? (Read label to see if the product must be shaken before application; put on enough—an ounce or generous handful; cover all exposed surfaces; put on 30 minutes before going outside.)

Figure 29–1 Skin Care Protection

Sunscreens and sunblocks help provide protection from the sun.

Sunscreens–Broad Spectrum
Some sunscreens are broad-spectrum screens, which means they absorb both kinds of ultraviolet rays (UVA and UVB). Some provide full UVA protection and some provide only partial protection. American Academy of Dermatology recommends everyone use broad spectrum sunscreens with a SPF of at least 15. An SPF of over 30 is not recommended because it provides diminishing returns for your money.

Sunscreens–Long Lasting
Some sunscreens are advertised as long-lasting. "Waterproof" means they will keep their protection for about 80 minutes in the water; "water resistant" protects for about half that time. Sweatproof products are designed not to drip and run in your eyes during strenuous exercise.

Sunblocks
Sunblocks are substances that completely block the sun's rays (both UVA and UVB). They also have SPF numbers so you can determine how long their protection will last. Sunblocks are a good choice for those who are allergic to chemicals in sunscreens or spend a lot of time outdoors. A disadvantage is that they can't be absorbed by the skin, so they tend to be visible.

Sunscreens–SPF Protection
It is especially important to protect younger people since 50% to 80% of the exposure to the sun in a lifetime comes before the age of 18. Sunscreens filter out the burning UVB rays. The Sun Protection Factor, or SPF number, expresses the ability of a sunscreen to protect the skin. The higher the number, the longer you can safely stay in the sun.

recent research is showing both may contribute to skin cancers. Whatever their cancer role, UVA rays have other undesirable effects—wrinkles and age spots in later years. To prevent these conditions, you should know which of the many skin care products to choose for appropriate protection. Figure 29–1 depicts various
1 kinds of protection and when and how to
2 use skin protection products.

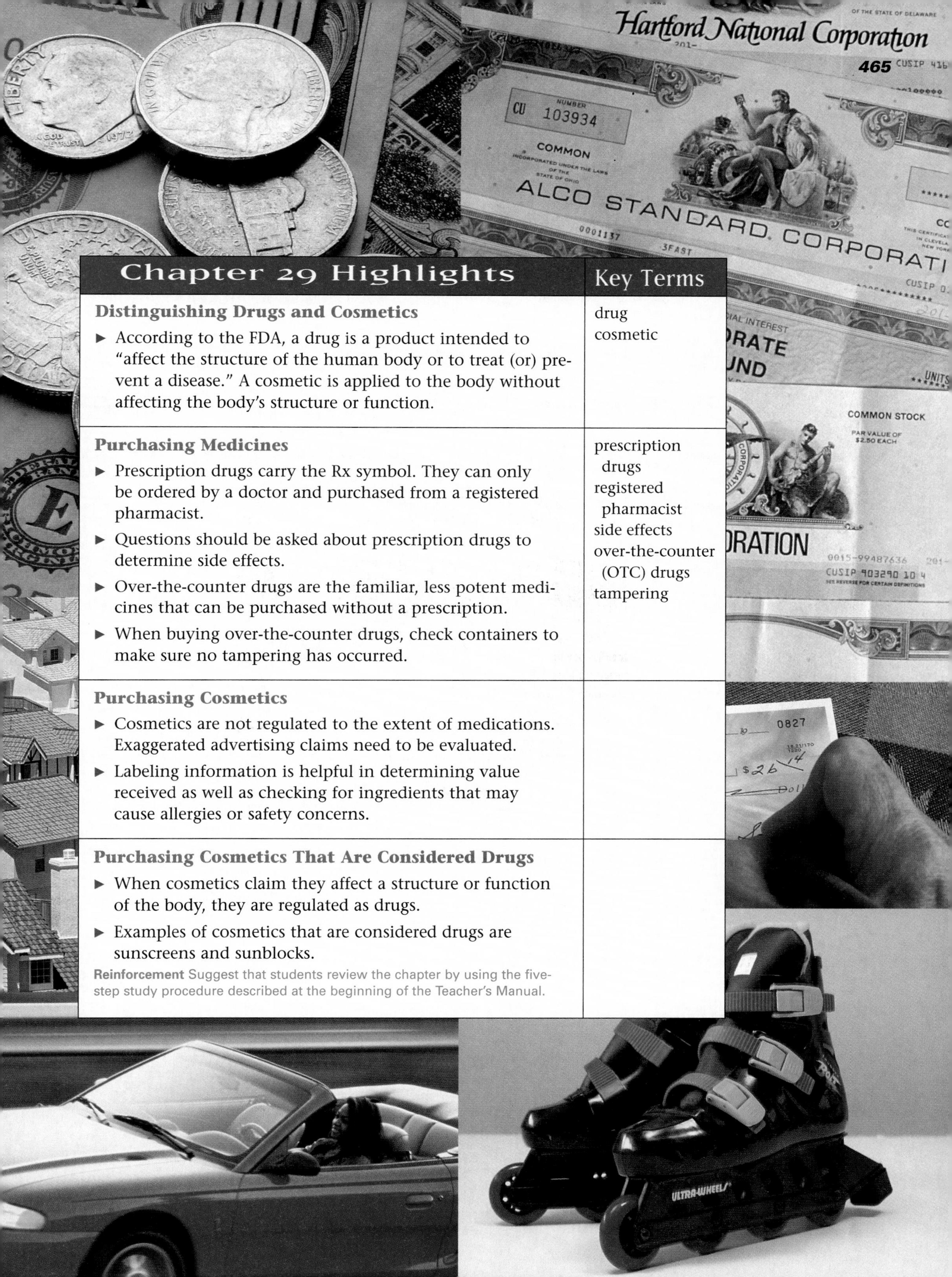

Chapter 29 Highlights	Key Terms
Distinguishing Drugs and Cosmetics ► According to the FDA, a drug is a product intended to "affect the structure of the human body or to treat (or) prevent a disease." A cosmetic is applied to the body without affecting the body's structure or function.	drug cosmetic
Purchasing Medicines ► Prescription drugs carry the Rx symbol. They can only be ordered by a doctor and purchased from a registered pharmacist. ► Questions should be asked about prescription drugs to determine side effects. ► Over-the-counter drugs are the familiar, less potent medicines that can be purchased without a prescription. ► When buying over-the-counter drugs, check containers to make sure no tampering has occurred.	prescription drugs registered pharmacist side effects over-the-counter (OTC) drugs tampering
Purchasing Cosmetics ► Cosmetics are not regulated to the extent of medications. Exaggerated advertising claims need to be evaluated. ► Labeling information is helpful in determining value received as well as checking for ingredients that may cause allergies or safety concerns.	
Purchasing Cosmetics That Are Considered Drugs ► When cosmetics claim they affect a structure or function of the body, they are regulated as drugs. ► Examples of cosmetics that are considered drugs are sunscreens and sunblocks. **Reinforcement** Suggest that students review the chapter by using the five-step study procedure described at the beginning of the Teacher's Manual.	

CHAPTER 29 REVIEW

Refer students to the Reviewing Consumer Terms and Reviewing Facts and Ideas activities in the Student Activity Workbook.

Reviewing Consumer Terms
Sentences will vary. See Glossary for definitions.

Reviewing Facts and Ideas
See the Student Activity Workbook.

Problem Solving and Decision Making
1 Aspirin, an ibuprofen, or a naproxen product are all appropriate because they help with inflammation. Since this is a long-term condition, a doctor should be consulted.
2 Labeling is needed. Some reasons include: to check value, to can compare ingredients (they are listed in descending order); to ensure safety (you can look for explicit warnings); to look for potential allergy-causing ingredients such as fragrances if you have a sensitivity to them.

Consumers Around the World Communications
1 The increased demand in some other countries comes from not being able to buy cosmetics for many years or from new fads.

Reviewing Consumer Terms

Use each of the following terms in a sentence to demonstrate you know its meaning.

cosmetic
drug
over-the-counter (OTC) drugs
prescription drugs
registered pharmacist
side effects
tampering

Reviewing Facts and Idea

1. Why is the distinction between drugs and cosmetics important to consumers?
2. Identify two basic types of medicines.
3. What questions should you ask your doctor when he or she gives you a prescription?
4. Summarize the risks involved with taking over-the-counter drugs.
5. Why is ingredient labeling on cosmetics not as helpful to consumers as ingredient labeling on foods?
6. What devices can be used to prevent product tampering?
7. Describe how to select skin and hair care products properly.
8. Identify characteristics of skin protection products.

Problem Solving and Decision Making

1. Doris has an arthritic condition that sometimes strikes young people. What OTC pain medications would be appropriate? What other procedures should she follow?
2. Ingredient labeling of cosmetics is required. Do you think this requirement is needed? Why? Of what value is cosmetic labeling to the consumer?

Building Academic Skills

Consumers Around the World

Communications

1. Research possible reasons for the explosive demand for cosmetics in China, Russia, and Japan. Summarize your findings in a 500-word report.

Science

2. Research why the sun's rays are more intense, and thus cause more skin damage to people living near the equator. Write your findings in a 250-word report.

Technology

3. Describe the role of technology in the development and marketing of drugs and cosmetics. Present your findings in a 500-word report.

Social Studies

4. Research the role of cosmetics in ancient world cultures. Report findings to class.

Beyond the Classroom

Consumer Project

Select a common over-the-counter drug and find answers to the following questions.

1. How many different brands of this medicine are available at your local drugstore?
2. What are the price differences between brands?
3. Check the labels to determine how each brand differs.
4. What are the side effects of this medication?
5. Which brand would you purchase? Why?

Cooperative Learning

Family Economics

Break into assigned family groups. Discuss the following problem.

You need to do some minor restocking of the family medicine cabinet. Specifically you need a pain reliever and something for sunburn. What kind of over-the-counter products would be best for those in your family given their lifestyle and medical histories? Compare your answers with those of other family groups.

Debate the Issue

The FDA's strict drug testing standards have long been a source of controversy. Critics claim that they delay development of new drugs and add unnecessarily to costs. Supporters argue that the FDA standards have proved their worth by protecting people from useless products as well as potentially devastating side effects.

You and your classmates will break into two groups and research this topic. Each group will gather evidence to support one side or the other. You are to prepare the argument for your side of the problem. Then the two groups will meet in a classroom debate.

Rechecking Your Attitude

Before going on to the next unit, go back to the Attitude Inventory at the beginning of this one. Answer the questions a second time. Then compare the two sets of responses. On how many statements have your attitudes changed? Can you account for these shifts in your opinions? What do you know now that you did not know then?

Science
2 The earth's tilt and rotation cause different regions to receive different amounts of heat and light from the sun. The sun's direct rays fall year-round at low latitudes near the equator.

Technology
3 Technology is used in both the development and marketing of prescription drugs and cosmetics.

Social Studies
4 Some examples are: rouge used by ancient Egyptians made from the mineral hemaite.

Consumer Project
Student answers will depend on the over-the-counter medicine studied.

Family Economics
All families should have a sunscreen or sun block on hand. It is especially important for those who exercise regularly outdoors.

Debate the Issue
Break the class into two teams. Assign each team one side of the issue. Encourage students to work together as a team to develop their argument. Ask each team to select a member to make an opening statement that supports their side of the issue. Have students take turns debating as the debate moves from one team to another.

UNIT 9 LAB

You and Your Community

STEP A Students should complete seven-day charts of menus that accurately list the number of basic food group servings, calories, and fat grams for each meal. Students should be able to cite sources for their calorie and fat gram estimates.
STEP B Students should provide accurate analyses of the nutrient sources from one day's menu.
STEPS C and **D** Students' price comparison charts should reflect the unit prices for all the items and for differing brands when available.
STEPS E and **F** Students should make accurate calculations of their total expenditures at each store and their average daily menu costs. Their store comparisons and written discussions of the costs and benefits of a healthy diet should be clearly explained and logically supported by specific examples.

Refer students to the Unit 9 Lab in the Student Activity Workbook.

Planning a Healthy Diet

Unit 9 presents the basics of a well-balanced diet and discusses techniques for smart food, drug, and cosmetics shopping. In this lab, you will apply those techniques to planning a shopping trip to buy a week's worth of food and other necessities for your family.

TOOLS

1. Lists of the basic food groups and common nutrients.
2. Healthful recipes
3. Food sections from local newspapers
4. A guide to the calorie and fat gram counts of particular foods.

PROCEDURES

STEP A List your family members' names and approximate ages. Write a week of menus for your family. Include breakfast, a light meal, a main meal, and a snack. To make planning easier, assume everyone will eat the same. For meals that will be eaten away from home, be sure to select foods that can be prepared ahead and stored until needed. Each day's menu must contain between 1,200 and 2,500 calories, and no more than 30 grams of fat.

Include the recommended number of daily servings from all the basic food groups in each day's menu. Do not use the menu for any meal more than twice during the week. Complete daily charts that include the following information for each meal:

1. The menu
2. The number of servings from each basic food group
3. The number of calories
4. The number of fat grams

STEP B Analyze one day's meals and list the specific sources of protein, carbohydrates, fats, calcium, iron, and vitamins A, B, C, and E.

STEP C Make a shopping list of all the foods you will need in order to prepare the week's meals. Include staple items, such as salt and flour. In addition, include one OTC drug (aspirin, cold medicine, cough syrup) and one cosmetic (hand lotion, sunscreen) on your list.

STEP D Select and visit two local stores—one that emphasizes high quality and one that emphasizes low prices. Try to visit both stores during the same week, because stores often have similar special prices on produce and other items during the same week. At both stores, check and record the prices of the items on your shopping list. Check the same national brands at both stores. When possible, check and record the store's brand and the generic brand for the items.

During your visit to each store or after you return home, prepare a chart of the items' prices. As you check item prices, be sure to check product labels when available to ensure that the calorie and fat gram counts on your menus are correct. Also, make notes on the quality of each store's meat, fish, and produce.

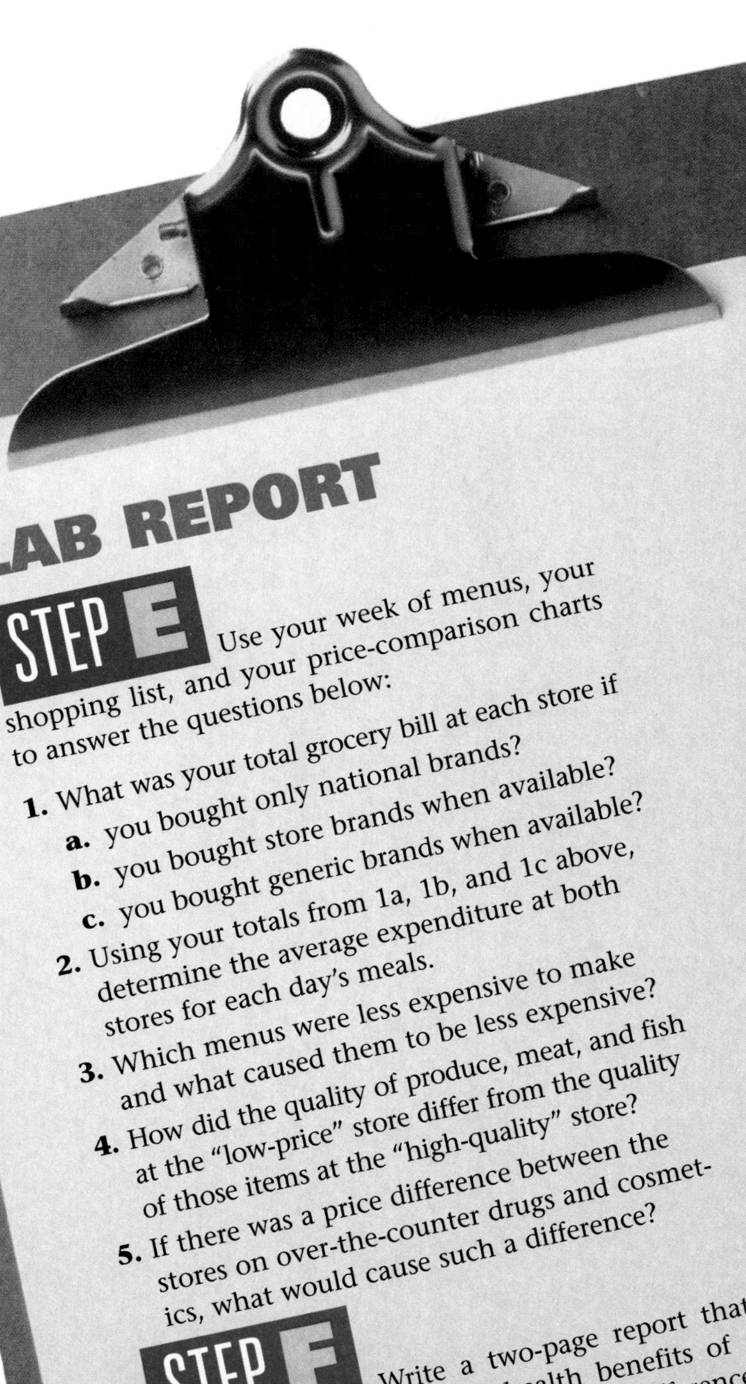

LAB REPORT

STEP E Use your week of menus, your shopping list, and your price-comparison charts to answer the questions below:

1. What was your total grocery bill at each store if
   a. you bought only national brands?
   b. you bought store brands when available?
   c. you bought generic brands when available?
2. Using your totals from 1a, 1b, and 1c above, determine the average expenditure at both stores for each day's meals.
3. Which menus were less expensive to make and what caused them to be less expensive?
4. How did the quality of produce, meat, and fish at the "low-price" store differ from the quality of those items at the "high-quality" store?
5. If there was a price difference between the stores on over-the-counter drugs and cosmetics, what would cause such a difference?

STEP F Write a two-page report that explains the cost and the health benefits of a healthful diet and that discusses the differences between the two stores on the basis of the cost and apparent quality of the items.

UNIT 10

Unit Contents

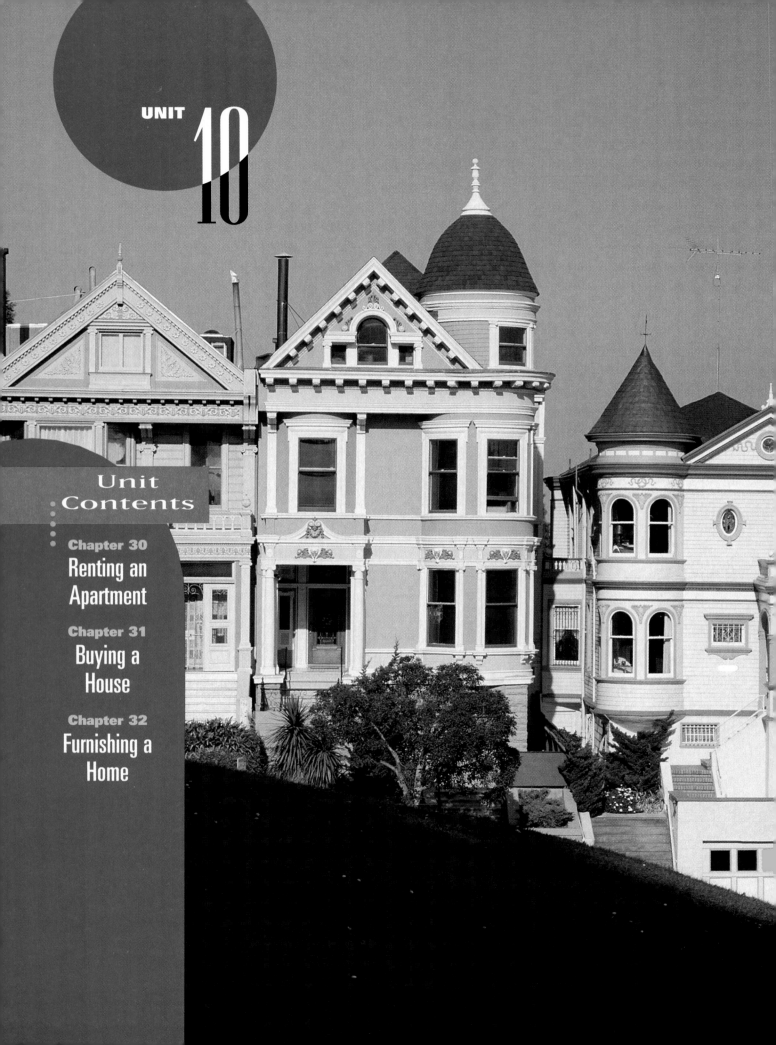

Selecting Housing

Attitude Inventory

Before you begin Chapter 30, take stock of your attitudes by completing the following inventory. Read each statement and decide how you feel about it—agree, disagree, or undecided. Record your feelings on a sheet of notepaper or use the form in the workbook.

1. A consumer needs to have a general knowledge of what is in his or her lease, but a line-for-line reading is unnecessary.
2. The best source of information about operating an appliance is the service department of the store selling it.
3. A moving company can pack and unpack your belongings as well as transport them.
4. Mobile homes can be hitched to the family car and towed from place to place.
5. For average consumers, the best way to buy a home is to have it custom-built.
6. A person who rents an apartment has the right to privacy.
7. Those who spend 35 percent of their income for rent are spending a reasonable amount for that purpose.
8. Wise consumers wait until they can pay cash before buying a home.
9. Owning a home is an important part of "the good life."
10. Over the years, houses have proved to be very poor investments.
11. A couple earning $40,000 a year probably cannot afford a house costing more than $100,000.
12. It is possible to buy an apartment.
13. There is only one standard for judging a piece of upholstered furniture—is it comfortable?
14. Mobile homes decline in value much faster than do conventional homes.
15. Poor workmanship in home construction is a common consumer problem.
16. If a defect or problem is not listed in an appliance's warranty, the buyer is not protected against it.

Unit Goal The main goal of this unit is to introduce students to the two basic housing options—renting and buying—as well as furnishing a home. Emphasis is on locating, inspecting, and paying for appropriate units. Chapters in this unit are (1) Renting an Apartment, (2) Buying a House, and (3) Furnishing a Home.

Lesson Plan See the Teacher's Manual for an overview of the unit and some suggestions for introducing it. If you assign the Attitude Inventory, be sure to tell students to keep their answers for later use.

ABLE 12/12

CHAPTER 30

Renting an Apartment

Learning Objectives

When you have finished studying this chapter, you should be able to:

1. Give the advantages of renting, rather than buying, housing.
2. Describe the factors to consider when deciding on your housing needs and budget.
3. Explain how to find and inspect a suitable apartment.
4. Describe the contents of a lease and the basic rights and responsibilities of tenants and landlords.
5. List ways to make moving into your apartment go smoothly.

Consumer Terms

tenant
landlord
security deposit
efficiency apartment
lease
sublet
evict

Real-World Journal

In your journal, describe the type of apartment you would like to rent on your own. Imagine you have $500 a month to spend on rent. Look through the classified section of your newspaper. Clip the ads that fit your budget and paste them in your journal. Do those apartments fit in with your journal description?

Lesson Plan See the Teacher's Manual for the Chapter 30 lesson plan.

Vocabulary The Chapter 30 lesson plan includes suggested vocabulary activities for the terms listed.

WHY RENT?

Renting a room, apartment, house, or mobile home is most people's first experience with buying shelter. When you rent, you pay the owner of the property a monthly sum; in return, you have a place to call home.

Renting is usually less expensive than buying, and that alone makes it especially attractive for people who are just starting out on their own. Moreover, renting offers other strong advantages to consider.

- *Mobility.* A **tenant**—someone who rents a house or an apartment—can be far more mobile than a home owner. For example, a tenant who is offered an exciting new job that requires relocating to another city can simply give notice and move out. Unlike an owner, a tenant does not have to worry about selling a
1 house before moving out.
- *Minimal responsibility.* Tenants don't have to think about maintaining or repairing a property—which can take a lot of time and money. When the roof leaks or the sink backs up, the tenant just reports the problem. The **landlord,** who is the owner of the property, must get the repairs done.
- *Financial freedom.* It's true that renters have expenses (in addition to rent) when they first move into a place. They have to pay a **security deposit,** money that the landlord holds until the tenant moves out to cover any damages that the tenant might cause. Also, the tenant may have to pay one or two months' rent in advance. Still, these expenses are less than a down payment on a house. Because renters usually spend less money on housing than home owners, they have more money to
2 spend on other items or to invest.

1 Reinforcement Students may question the mobility comparison, saying that renters are often bound by a lease and that all home owners need to do is sell the house. Point out the problem home owners can have in selling a house, especially in an area suffering economically, and the implications this has on the home owner's housing situation in the new area.

2 Math Application Ask students how much they would need to put down if they bought a house for $54,000 and the minimum down payment was 8 percent. ($4,320).

Buying used furnishings or making your own can be less expensive than purchasing new items. ***What other advantages are there to furnishing a home in this way?*** ▶

Caption Answer: You can try out different styles of furnishings without spending a lot of money. You can create furnishings that suit you and fit the available space.

DEFINING YOUR HOUSING NEEDS AND BUDGET

Apartment hunting is easier if you first create a plan based on your housing needs and your financial resources. You can save time by quickly eliminating any unsuitable units and concentrating on the real possibilities—inspecting them systematically and asking all the important questions. With your needs and your finances in mind, you should be able to do an efficient, intelligent,
1 and successful search.

Location

Location and cost are related. Areas that are safe and convenient are usually more expensive than others. Try to rent an apartment near your job or school, near shopping, and near public transportation. With what you save in travel time and costs, you may be able to afford the higher rent typical of these attractive locations.

Space

Be realistic in deciding how much space you need. Space costs money. The least expensive choice is a room in a private house, but you may have to share a bathroom and you may not have use of the kitchen. An **efficiency apartment,** also called a studio, single, or bachelor unit, is one room with minimal kitchen and bath facilities. Larger, more expensive apartments have from one to four bedrooms. Most expensive is renting a town house or a single-family house. Some apartments have special features, such as a terrace, a walk-in closet, or wooden parquet floors, that
2 make them more expensive.

Furnishings

If you are setting up housekeeping for the first time, you probably don't own much furniture. A furnished apartment, which comes with basic items such as a bed, a chest of drawers, tables and chairs, and a sofa (in addition to the kitchen appliances standard in most units), can

Protect Your Belongings When You Move

If you need to hire a moving company, give the mover a full description of the items being moved. Be sure you say what floor you live on and what floor you will move to. Describe any steps, even just three on a landing. Movers generally charge by the hour and by the mile, or by weight. Ask for an estimate on the phone and a written estimate when the mover arrives at the location. Note what time the movers start and what time they stop. Whether you move yourself, have friends help you, or hire a moving company, supervise all moving.

- **Pack glassware carefully. Mark boxes by the room they should be placed in.**
- **Make sure important pieces of furniture are adequately protected.**
- **Identify anyone who doesn't seem experienced, and make sure that person doesn't damage any of your goods.**
- **Direct the unloading so that items are placed where you want them.**
- **Inspect for any damage and give the movers a written complaint before they leave.**
- **When the movers are finished, look in the truck yourself to be sure everything was unloaded.**

1 Interesting Note
Tell students that about 70 percent of apartments built each year are rented within three months of completion.

2 Student Motivator
Tell students to assume that the owner of a new apartment building in a large city plans to charge $750 for a studio apartment that measures 14 feet x 22 feet. Have students measure a space this size in your classroom. Would they be able to live in an apartment this size? Have them compute the monthly and annual rent per square foot. ($14 \times 22 = 308$ square feet; $\$750 \div 308 = \$2.44$ per month; $\$2.44 \times 12 = \$29.28$ per year.)

1 Discussion Starter Ask students if they or their parents have ever purchased furniture at thrift shops or garage sales. Have they been satisfied with those purchases?

2 Math Application Have students assume that they receive a paycheck every two weeks, with a take-home pay of $534. Applying the rule of thumb, how much should their maximum monthly rent be? ($534 ÷ 2 = $267.)

3 Extension Have a real estate agent or someone from a community housing authority visit the class to report on the current housing situation and the outlook for the next few years.

4 Discussion Starter Ask students about the pros and cons of having a roommate. Do the benefits outweigh the disadvantages?

Russian Housing

The average monthly salary in Russia is about $100. Because rent is largely subsidized by the government, an apartment may rent for as little as $16 a month.

save you the trouble of equipping an apartment. However, furnished units are more expensive than unfurnished apartments. The extra amount varies with the quality, condition, and number of items included.

If you rent an unfurnished apartment, you can use the money you save to buy some items for your apartment that make it feel like home. If you're skillful, you can build a few pieces. You can also ask family and friends for old furniture they no longer use. Finally, if you enjoy shopping for bargains, you can make the rounds of local thrift shops, antique stores, and garage sales looking for interesting, inexpensive
1 furnishings.

Budget

Once you know what you are looking for, figure out how much you can afford to pay. The traditional rule of thumb is to count on spending one week's take-home pay for rent. Unfortunately, in many parts of the country this rule is hard to
2 follow because housing costs are so high.

There are several ways you can make renting more affordable. First, look in a less expensive neighborhood. Although you may not want to sacrifice safety, you may be willing to try a less convenient location. Next, cut down on space and special features: Instead of a one-bedroom, consider an efficiency. In a high-rise building, look at apartments on lower floors. Consider apartments that are less expensive because they have less sunlight, more noise, or less privacy than comparable units. Finally, consider
3 living with one or more roommates in
4 order to share expenses.

SELECTING AN APARTMENT

Locating a good apartment takes both research and legwork, and it can be discouraging. Allow several weeks for the process, and try to keep a positive outlook.

W 20 ST AT KENNEDY AVE
Enormous 1 BR w/dining area in mod elevator bldg. 24-hr security. $355/mo. 555-1726
WEST AVE AT 77 ST
3 BR w/2 bths. Terrace. Near buses, shopping. Sharing OK. $875/mo. 555-7893
HILLSDALE, CORNER RTE 25 & 7
Sunny furnished room w/bath. No kitchen. No pets. $175/mo. 555-9003 after 7 pm

The real estate section of your local newspaper can tell you what kinds of apartments are available. ***What information do the ads generally contain?*** ▶

Caption Answer: Classified ads generally tell where the apartment is located, how large it is, what the rent is, and any special features the apartment has.

Locating Units

The usual sources of information about available apartments are relatives, friends, newspaper classified ads, rental agencies, and signs posted on rental buildings. Some other organizations that keep lists of vacancies include the student housing offices of colleges and universities, labor union offices, chambers of commerce, and human resources offices at local companies. Remember that rental agencies and brokers often charge a fee.

Study newspaper ads and agency listings carefully to find a unit that is right for you. You'll want to avoid looking at apartments where the rent is too high,
1 the apartment is not furnished, or the
2 location is too far from your job.

Inspecting an Apartment

Looking for an apartment starts like other forms of comparison shopping—with a list. First, list all the apartments that, from their descriptions, sound

People MAKING a DIFFERENCE

Green Thumb in Harlem

Green spaces give everyone a mental boost. Cities with lots of parks are more inviting, but they are inviting only if the parks are well cared for. Few cities make the effort to maintain parks in poor areas, however.

When Bernadette Cozart began working as a gardener for the New York City parks department, one of her responsibilities was to maintain a 20-acre park where teenagers hung out using drugs. She says the teens got a kick out of following her around as she worked. One day she got tired of the game. She confronted them. If they were going to follow her, she said, they could help her work. She was surprised when they took her up on her ultimatum and began gardening with her.

Cozart came to believe that overgrown and undermaintained parks created places for crime and drugs. By cleaning them up, she thought, some of the problems might go away as well.

The city had no money to clean up Harlem parks, however. So Cozart took on the project herself. She founded The Greening of Harlem, which now has more than 100 volunteers. They clean trash out of more than 500 abandoned lots in the area and maintain dozens of parks. The group also plants gardens that provide much-needed vegetables and fruits for needy families. The volunteers have replanted school yards and put flowering plants into Harlem's streets.

Cozart has also organized a program called Gardening—Soup to Nuts, in which she and her volunteers guarantee to clean up and replant a site in one day. In her spare time, she teaches horticulture at schools.

The Greening of Harlem might not solve world problems, but the group makes one part of the world a more pleasant place to live.

Brainstorm

What could you do to "green" your neighborhood?

1 Extension Tell students that they should keep notes as they go through the newspaper ads. Some ads will not provide all of the needed information. It will be necessary to call and ask questions. After a while, the information becomes confused or forgotten unless good, clear notes are made and kept.

2 Reinforcement Student Activity Workbook, Chapter 30 activities.

Case Study Answer: Clean up and plant (with the owner's permission) a vacant lot; clean up, plant, and maintain the yard of an elderly neighbor; plant flowers, herbs, shrubs along street medians, around street trees; plant unusual containers with bulbs, hardy plants for use in paved areas around schools.

1 Reinforcement Ask students to imagine that they thought about turning on a faucet while inspecting an apartment but didn't. How would they feel if they took the apartment and discovered that all faucets had a minimal amount of pressure?

2 Learning Economics Ask students why there's a good chance that the landlord will make repairs you request before signing a lease. (It could cost the landlord more to keep the apartment vacant than to make repairs.)

promising. Then, make up another list—an on-site inspection checklist. This will help you compare the features of the different units and keep track of what you see in each location. Using the checklist, you can inspect each apartment, as shown in Figure 30–1.

Make copies of your inspection checklist, and fill out a checklist for each apartment you investigate. Fix each apartment in your mind by noting any outstanding features as well as potential problems on the checklist. Do not be shy about making a thorough inspection
1 and asking questions.

Be sure to ask the manager or landlord about correcting unsatisfactory conditions, such as a broken window or faulty refrigerator door. If you are seriously interested in a particular unit, make any necessary repairs a condition
2 of agreeing to rent the apartment.

SIGNING THE LEASE

Before you move into an apartment, you and the landlord must reach an agreement, the terms of which are contained in a lease. A **lease** is a legal contract, usually in writing, that gives the tenant the right to live in an apartment for a certain amount of time, usually one, two, or three years, in return for a specified amount of rent.

Figure 30-9 Looking for an Apartment

It pays to be thorough when looking at an apartment. Your inspection should cover at least the items on this checklist.

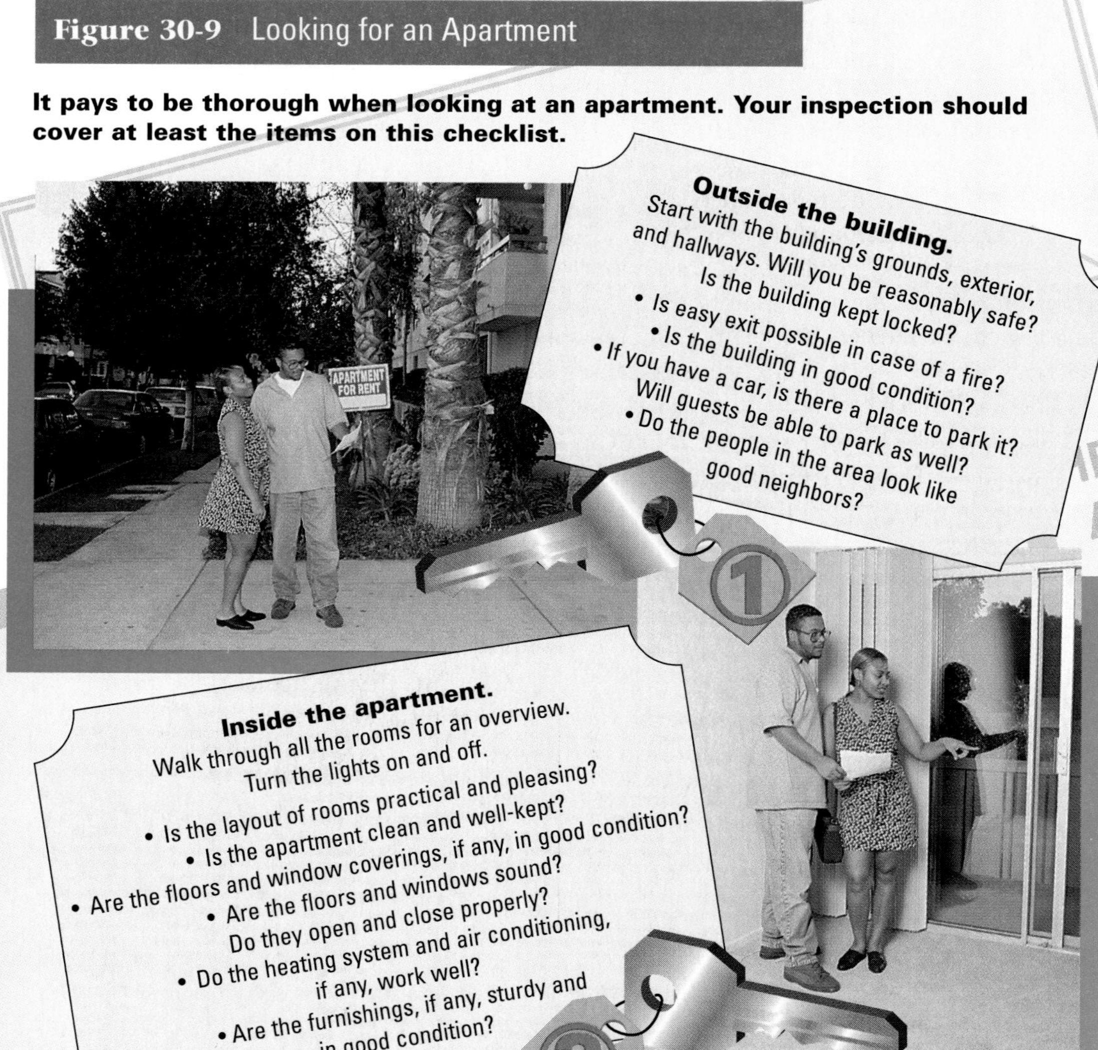

APARTMENT FOR RENT
Outside the building.
Start with the building's grounds, exterior, and hallways. Will you be reasonably safe? Is the building kept locked?
• Is easy exit possible in case of a fire?
• Is the building in good condition?
• If you have a car, is there a place to park it? Will guests be able to park as well?
• Do the people in the area look like good neighbors?
1
Inside the apartment.
Walk through all the rooms for an overview. Turn the lights on and off.
• Is the layout of rooms practical and pleasing?
• Is the apartment clean and well-kept?
• Are the floors and window coverings, if any, in good condition?
• Are the floors and windows sound? Do they open and close properly?
• Do the heating system and air conditioning, if any, work well?
• Are the furnishings, if any, sturdy and in good condition?
2

Terms of the Lease

Often, the lease is a standard form drawn up by a legal expert employed to protect the interests of the landlord—not the interests of the tenant! As a tenant, therefore, you must be your own protector. It is very important to read the entire lease and to be sure you understand all its terms. If you are unsure about anything in the lease, talk with a
1 knowledgeable person, such as a parent
2 or an attorney, before signing.

You may ask for certain clauses to be changed before you agree to sign. If the owner is eager to rent the property, your changes may be made. Don't, however, rely on spoken promises or other assumptions. For example, if the lease says no pets are allowed, but you see that another tenant has a dog, don't assume you will be able to keep a pet too. All additions and alterations to the lease and any commitments to make repairs should be in writing.

A lease spells out the rights and responsibilities of both the tenant and the landlord. The terms usually cover the use of the apartment and other facilities, the rent, the rental period, the security deposit, and which utilities—electricity, gas, and water—are included. A lease says how much notice a tenant must give before moving and whether the tenant is permitted to **sublet,** that

1 Reinforcement Stress the importance of reading the lease. Point out that the lawyer who drew up the contract is protecting the landlord's interests.

2 Reinforcement Provide students with copies of leases. Because of the difficult language, you may want to work through one lease with students in class. Explain that most people have trouble with "legalese."

3
Take a closer look at the **kitchen and bathroom.** Run the water, flush the toilet, check the refrigerator, and turn on the stove.
• Is the plumbing working well? Is there hot and cold water?
• Are the major appliances clean and operating properly?
4
Check the meters that measure the **utilities**–electricity, water, and gas. Ask:
• If the utilities are to be paid by the tenant, is there a separate meter for each apartment?
• Are the utilities included in the rent?
CLOSET

The tenant has the right to use the property for the purpose stated in the lease. ***What is one other tenant right?*** ▶

Caption Answer: The tenant has the right to privacy.

1 Discussion Starter Tell students that recently a landlord who refused to make repairs to rental units was sentenced by the court to live 15 days in a sorely neglected apartment building he owned. Ask students whether they consider this an appropriate punishment. Why or why not?

Case Study Answers:
1 Most people assume that realtors have great flexibility because they aren't tied to a desk and because they don't need to make a lot of sales to make a good living. The fact is, however, that in order to sell even one house, a realtor has to pay close attention to the market and be responsive to the clients. That often translates into less flexibility than most outsiders think.
2 Research by checking real estate listings in the newspaper, calling a broker, or attending an open house.

is, to have someone take over the apartment temporarily and pay the rent.

Tenant's Rights In general, the tenant has the right to use the property for the purpose stated in the lease. So, for example, if the lease states that your apartment may be used only as a residence, you may not run a business there. The tenant also has the right to privacy. That means that the landlord must request permission to enter, must come at a reasonable time, and may enter only for legitimate reasons, such as to make a repair.

Tenant's Responsibilities In return for the use of the property, the tenant must pay the rent on time and take reasonable care of the apartment. When something goes wrong, the tenant is responsible for notifying the landlord.

The tenant must also give notice before moving. A tenant who moves before the lease is up may be responsible for paying the remaining rent.

Landlord's Responsibilities The landlord must make sure that the property meets certain minimum standards set by the local government. For example, there may be local regulations concerning fire escapes or safety bars on windows to prevent children from falling. The landlord must also make sure that the building is fit to live in—that the heating system
1 works, for example.

Resolving Problems

If you have a problem with your landlord, first try to resolve the problem by communication and negotiation. Suppose the kitchen faucet does not work properly. Call the landlord or manager to report the trouble. If you get no response, call again. If you still get no response, write a letter to the landlord explaining the problem.

Keep a record of all your calls and letters. If the repair is not made within a reasonable amount of time, you may be able legally to make the repair yourself and deduct the cost of the repair from your rent.

On the other hand, sometimes a tenant is at fault. If the tenant causes excessive damage or breaks the terms of the lease, the landlord may be able to **evict** the tenant, that is, have the tenant put out of the apartment.

MOVING

Well, you have finally found an apartment and signed the lease. Now you are ready to move. Moving can be

Geri Daly, Realtor, The Prudential Preferred Properties

Buying a house is the biggest, most important purchase most people make in their lives and it can be an extremely emotional experience. So what does it feel like to be the agent for 20 or 30 such purchases a year, intimately involved in the ups and downs of the decision? "It's a thrill," says Geri Daly, 52, who has been helping people buy and sell houses in the Philadelphia suburbs for more than ten years. "It's very hard work, but it's a thrill."

The best part of the job, Daly says, "is working with buyers who find a house they love. The bells and whistles go off, they walk in and they're Mr. and Mrs. Homeowner. It's great!"

Getting to that goal, however, means getting through months and sometimes years of footwork. Daly once worked with a couple who took three years to buy their house. That's three years of checking listings, three years of making phone calls, three years of going to open houses, and all that on top of the whirlwind of inspections, financial qualifications, and deadlines that a realtor has to stay on top of during the purchase of a house. However, that slow-to-decide couple ended up buying a $2 million house—good news for any realtor, who makes money by taking a percentage of the sale of each property.

The possibility of so much money—and the common perception of the flexibility of a realtor's day—draws many people into the business. But, Daly explains, "most realtors don't make a lot of money and you don't always have much flexibility. Your clients come first, even if they want to go out looking at houses every Saturday or throw temper tantrums in the car."

Besides serving the sometimes quirky needs of people who want to buy a house, Daly also helps people sell them. "That can be tricky, since most homeowners are not aware of their home's value," Daly concedes. "But we do a market analysis, come up with a price, and develop a marketing plan. I give the owners tips on how to make the home look good—things like new paint or keeping things squeaky clean. I'll even tell someone to get rid of a shabby old couch, if I think it will help sell the house."

All that scrambling and all that advice giving can be very frustrating, Daly admits, but mostly, working in real estate is "a whole lot of fun and very rewarding."

Case Study Review

1. Why do so many people believe a realtor's day is so flexible? Why is that perception not entirely accurate?
2. How much money does a typical house cost in your neighborhood?

FLASHBACK FLASHFORWARD

Between 1952 and 1953, the average household spent 34 percent of its budget on housing costs. Between 1982 and 1984, the average household spent 42 percent of its budget on housing costs.

1 Reinforcement Suggest that the students review the chapter by using the five-step study procedures described at the beginning of the Teacher's Manual.

very exciting, but it's also very stressful. Just a little planning can help your move go smoothly. Here are some points to consider.

1. You can move yourself, or you can hire a moving company to do part or all of the job. To move yourself, you will have to rent or borrow a truck and get the help of friends willing to do some hard work.

   If you plan to hire help, get recommendations for movers from people you know. Ask the movers to give you cost estimates. Choose the company that has the best combination of reputation and price, but beware of a company that bids too low for a job. The final cost may be much higher than the estimate.
2. Before you pack, throw out or give away items you no longer want. 1
   Then pack in boxes that you will be able to lift. Make sure to wrap breakables well in newspaper before packing them. On each box, write which room the box is destined for and the important items it contains.
3. If you are moving yourself, wrap your furniture in blankets to protect the pieces from damage.
4. Pack essentials that you will need immediately—for example, an alarm clock and a coffee pot—in a box that you take yourself.
5. You will need to arrange for utilities—gas, electricity, water, and telephone—to be turned on and for accounts to be set up.
6. Notify the post office, your bank, your doctor, your employer, your creditors, and others of your new address. The post office will forward your mail to your new address for a period of several months.

Many people move their belongings with the help of friends. ***How can you help prevent injury during such a move?*** ▶

Caption Answer: Make sure there are enough people to lift heavy items. Lift properly, bending at the knees and keeping the back straight. Use dollies (platforms on wheels) to minimize carrying. Pace yourself and move slowly, especially climbing up stairs.

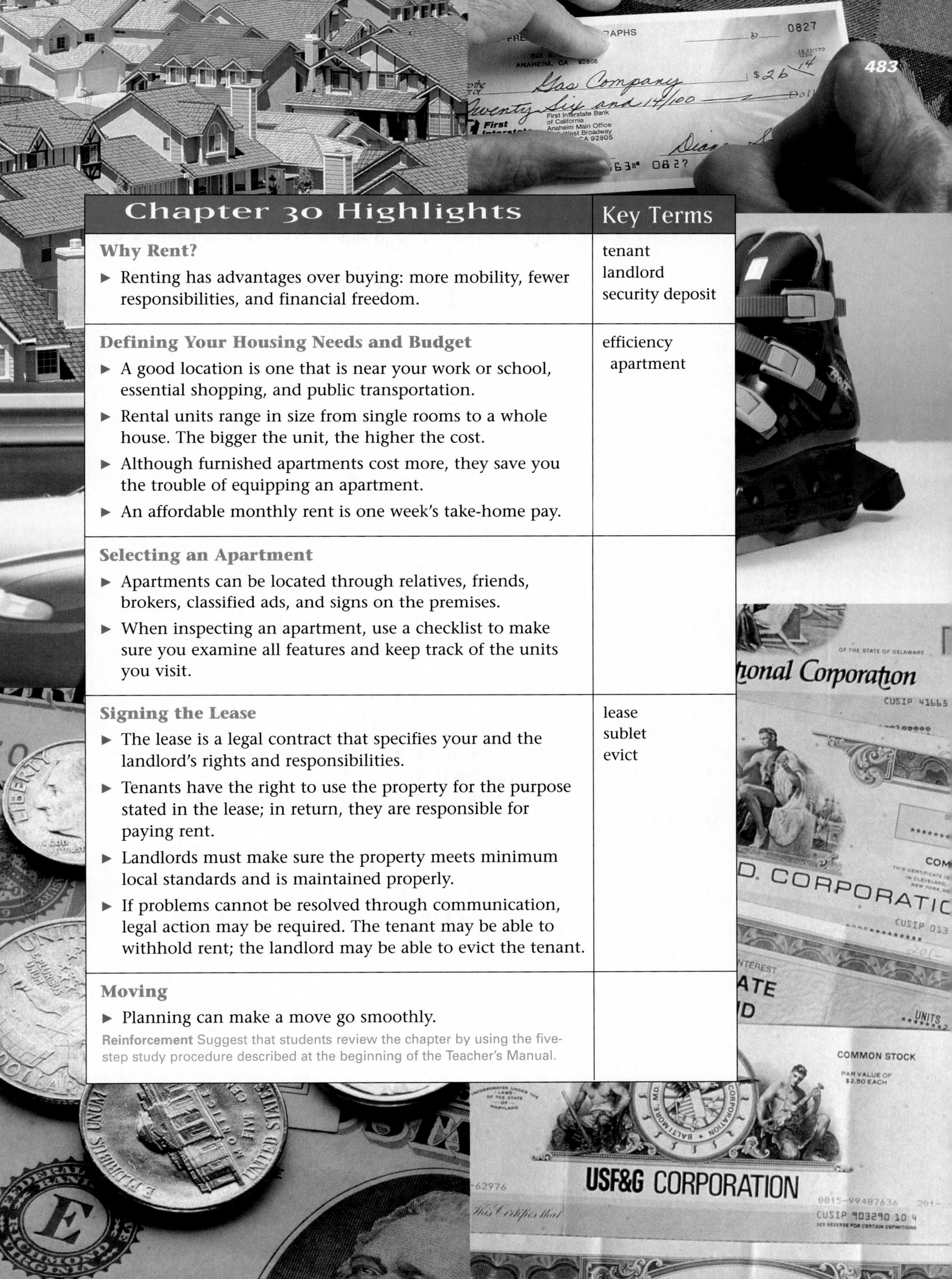

Chapter 30 Highlights	Key Terms
Why Rent? ▶ Renting has advantages over buying: more mobility, fewer responsibilities, and financial freedom.	tenant landlord security deposit
Defining Your Housing Needs and Budget ▶ A good location is one that is near your work or school, essential shopping, and public transportation. ▶ Rental units range in size from single rooms to a whole house. The bigger the unit, the higher the cost. ▶ Although furnished apartments cost more, they save you the trouble of equipping an apartment. ▶ An affordable monthly rent is one week's take-home pay.	efficiency apartment
Selecting an Apartment ▶ Apartments can be located through relatives, friends, brokers, classified ads, and signs on the premises. ▶ When inspecting an apartment, use a checklist to make sure you examine all features and keep track of the units you visit.	
Signing the Lease ▶ The lease is a legal contract that specifies your and the landlord's rights and responsibilities. ▶ Tenants have the right to use the property for the purpose stated in the lease; in return, they are responsible for paying rent. ▶ Landlords must make sure the property meets minimum local standards and is maintained properly. ▶ If problems cannot be resolved through communication, legal action may be required. The tenant may be able to withhold rent; the landlord may be able to evict the tenant.	lease sublet evict
Moving ▶ Planning can make a move go smoothly. **Reinforcement** Suggest that students review the chapter by using the five-step study procedure described at the beginning of the Teacher's Manual.	

CHAPTER 30 REVIEW

Refer students to the Reviewing Consumer Terms and Reviewing Facts and Ideas activities in the Student Activity Workbook.

Reviewing Consumer Terms
Short stories will vary. See the Glossary for definitions.

Reviewing Facts and Ideas
See the Student Activity Workbook for answers.

Problem Solving and Decision Making
1 Katrina can rent a single room or look for a roommate.
2 Carlita may fix the window and deduct the cost from the next month's rent.
3 Yes, he signed a one-year lease. He should try to be released from the contract or to sublet.

Consumers Around the World Math
1 Helene: $387 ($967 × 40%); Linda: $338 ($967 × 35%); Faith: $242 ($967 × 25%).

Communications
2 Students should note that jobs and a strong economy drive up rental prices and stimulate construction.

Human Relations
3 Findings will depend on countries chosen.

Social Studies
4 Students should stress the Reverend Martin Luther King, Jr.,

Reviewing Consumer Terms

Use the following in a short story entitled "The Day I Decided to Rent an Apartment."

efficiency apartment
evict
landlord
lease
security deposit
sublet
tenant

Reviewing Facts and Ideas

1. Explain three advantages of renting an apartment.
2. What are four factors to consider when defining your housing needs?
3. Suggest several sources of information about apartments for rent.
4. What are the basic rights and responsibilities of the tenant and landlord?
5. Give four suggestions for making a move go smoothly.

Problem Solving and Decision Making

1. After a week of apartment-hunting in a neighborhood near her job, Katrina Knussen realizes she cannot afford a one-bedroom apartment on her salary. What compromises can Katrina make to find affordable housing?
2. Carlita Somoza has been trying to get her landlord to repair a window frame that leaks when there is a storm. Several months have gone by, and the window still is not fixed. What can Carlita do to solve this problem?
3. Randall Marcus signed a one-year lease for an apartment. After living there for two months, he is transferred to Jersey City, over 400 miles away. Is it reasonable to expect him to continue to pay rent on the old apartment for ten more months? What can Randall do?

Building Academic Skills

Consumers Around the World

Math

1. Linda Moreno plans to share a three-bedroom apartment with two friends. Helene, who will take the largest bedroom, will pay 40 percent of the rent. Linda, with the second largest room, will pay 35 percent; and Faith, whose room is the smallest, will pay 25 percent. If the rent is $967, what is each roommate's share?

Communications

2. The availability of apartments in an area depends on many factors, including the economy. Choose an area of the country. Use newspaper files to research the apartment situation.

   What is the apartment vacancy rate? What are the local economic conditions? How are the rents? Write a two-page analysis of your findings. Describe the rental situation that a newcomer could expect to find.

Human Relations

3. The average household in the United States has been getting

smaller for the past few decades. Compare the number of people in the average U.S. household with average households in two other countries.

Social Studies

4. Federal civil rights legislation prohibits discrimination in housing based on a person's race, color, religion, sex, or national origin. In the library, research the recent history of civil rights.

   Write a 750-word paper explaining your research. What legal actions can people take if they feel they have been denied housing in violation of their civil rights?

Beyond the Classroom

Consumer Projects

1. Collect classified ads for apartments from the newspaper. Paste the ads on notepaper, and circle abbreviations and unusual terms. Try to guess the meaning of the abbreviations. Bring the ads to class for discussion.
2. Imagine that your take-home pay is $300 a week. Study apartment rental ads for a nearby area, and choose an apartment that would fit your budget. Develop an inspection checklist, and accompanied by an adult, visit the apartment to complete your checklist.
3. Develop a questionnaire about experiences related to living in an apartment—getting repairs done, renewing a lease, dealing with neighbors. Using your questionnaire, interview at least four people.

   Write a 500-word article with the title "Your First Apartment," aimed at new high school graduates. Include interesting anecdotes as well as helpful information and tips.

Cooperative Learning

Family Economics

Break into assigned family groups. Discuss the following problem.

There is a rumor circulating that your apartment complex is going to be torn down. For the first time in years, your family must think about moving. In preparation, draw up a list of features that you will look for in a new apartment. Be sure to consider the needs of all family members and any problems you have encountered in your current living situation. Compare your answers to those of other family groups.

Debate the Issue

During inflation, rates increase much faster than prices as a whole. This can lead to the displacement of large numbers of unemployed and low-income people. At those times, cities may enact rent control legislation, which stops or limits rent increases.

Advocates of rent control argue that the regulations bring much-needed relief to tenants and prevent a great increase in homelessness. Opponents argue that landlords are hurt by the controls; they may not collect enough in rents to make ownership profitable.

You and your classmates will break into two groups and research this topic. Each group will gather evidence to support one side or the other. You are to prepare the argument for your side of the problem. Then the two groups will meet in a classroom debate.

the Civil Rights Act of 1964, Supreme Court decisions, and the Civil Rights Commission.

Consumer Projects **1** Students should identify abbreviations such as **BR** for *bedroom.* **2** Students should discuss the apartment's location, space, features, and rent. **3** Articles should reflect stories and information obtained through interviews.

Family Economics Families with children will want to look for safe play areas and locations away from busy streets but near schools. Families with teens will want to look for facilities where younger tenants can congregate safely. Families with health problems will consider first-floor units with heating and air-conditioning. Family 8 will probably want an extra bedroom and bath.

Debate the Issue Break the class into two teams. Assign each team one side of the issue. Encourage students to work together as a team to develop their argument. Ask each team to select a member to make an opening statement that supports the team's side of the issue. Have students take turns debating as the debate moves from one team to the other.

3

CHAPTER 31

Buying a House

Learning Objectives

When you have finished studying this chapter, you should be able to:

1. List the advantages of home ownership.
2. Describe the usual costs and procedures in buying a home.
3. Distinguish between fixed-rate and variable-rate mortgages.
4. Develop a checklist for inspecting a home.

Consumer Terms

mortgage
fixed-rate mortgage
variable-rate mortgage
escrow account
contract for sale
appraisal
points
promissory note
deed

Real-World Journal

Talk to someone you know who owns a home. Ask him or her to describe the costs and procedures involved in buying a home. What are the advantages and disadvantages of buying a home? Record your findings in your journal. Then make a list of the steps you can take to start planning now to buy a future home.

Lesson Plan See the Teacher's Manual for the Chapter 31 lesson plan.

Vocabulary The Chapter 31 lesson plan includes suggested vocabulary activities for the terms listed.

1 Discussion Starter Ask students if any of them have lived in both an apartment and a home. Did they notice a difference in their feeling of permanence and prestige? If so, are these feelings worth the burden of owning a home?

2 Discussion Starter One expert believes that a home's exterior reveals the personalities of those who live in it. Have students think about people they know and the homes these people live in. Can they see any truth in this belief?

ADVANTAGES OF HOME OWNERSHIP

Buying a home is for most people the single most costly and significant purchase they will make. Although buying a home is a major long-term financial responsibility, many people strive to own their own home. Some of the most common reasons for wanting to own a
1 home are described in Figure 31–1.

Choosing Among Options

Suppose after considering the advantages of home ownership, you decide to buy. Your next choice is what kind of
2 home to buy. You have several options.

- *Older homes.* Older homes usually offer detailing and materials not often found in mass-produced housing. However, risk of major repair is

Figure 31–1 Reasons for Buying a House

There are many reasons why people buy homes.

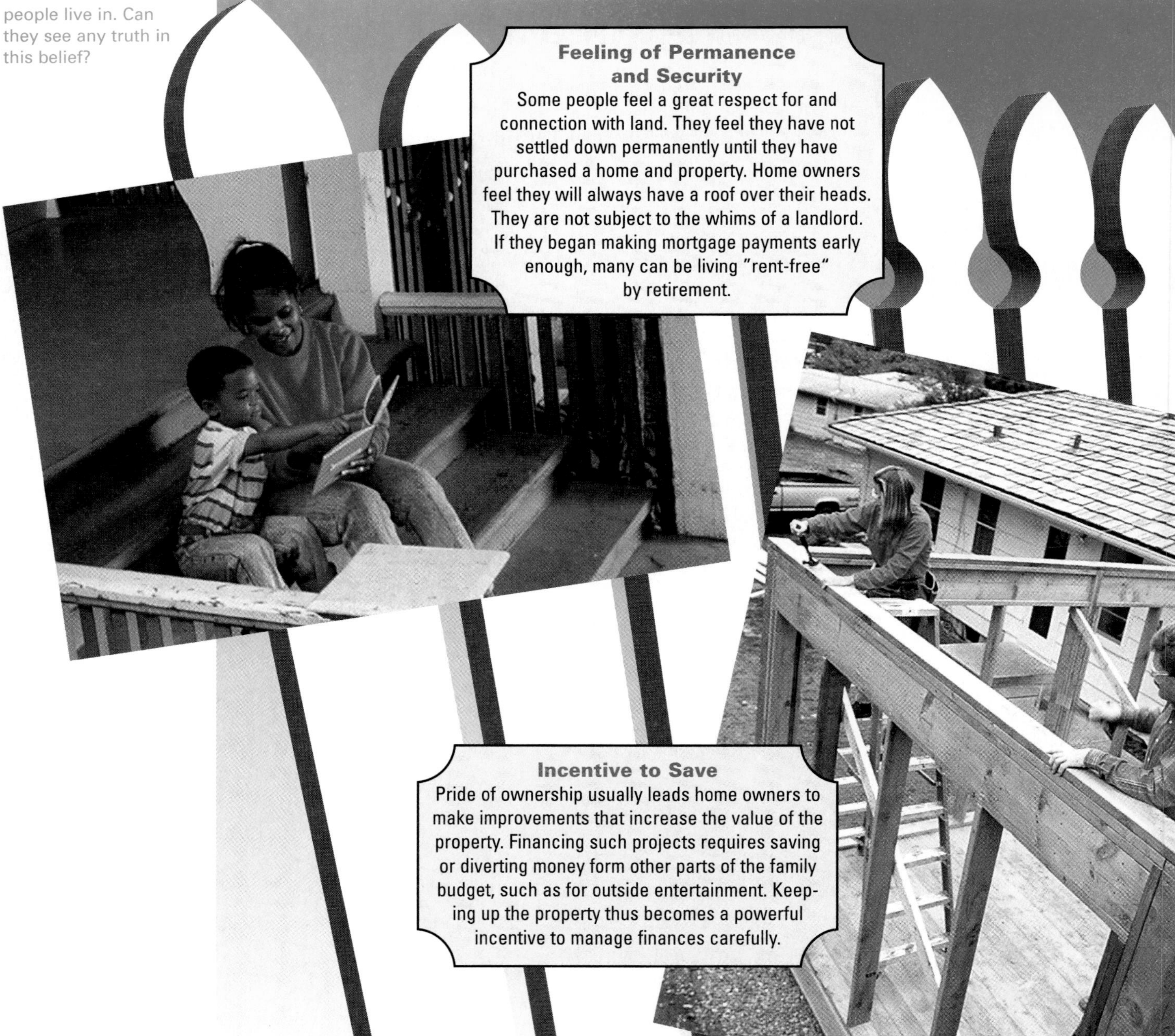

Feeling of Permanence and Security
Some people feel a great respect for and connection with land. They feel they have not settled down permanently until they have purchased a home and property. Home owners feel they will always have a roof over their heads. They are not subject to the whims of a landlord. If they began making mortgage payments early enough, many can be living "rent-free" by retirement.
Incentive to Save
Pride of ownership usually leads home owners to make improvements that increase the value of the property. Financing such projects requires saving or diverting money form other parts of the family budget, such as for outside entertainment. Keeping up the property thus becomes a powerful incentive to manage finances carefully.

greater and older homes may be
1 more costly to heat and cool.

- *Ready-built homes.* Ready-built homes are usually the most affordable among single-family new homes. You can see what the finished product will look like, know the final cost, and be able to move in quickly.
- *Custom-built homes.* These homes are built to the consumer's exact specifications. Although more expensive than ready-built homes, for some people the extra cost is justified to have
2 a home built exactly as they want.
- *Condominiums.* These offer the convenience of apartment living with the advantage of home ownership. Condominium owners own their apartments outright and pay a monthly maintenance fee for

1 Discussion Starter Ask students if they consider themselves handy. Would they enjoy trying to renovate an old home? Would they be willing to devote the time it would take?

2 Learning Economics Ask students why ready-built homes are less expensive than custom-built ones. (Builders can keep costs down by buying in quantity and building faster when they build several identical or very similar homes.)

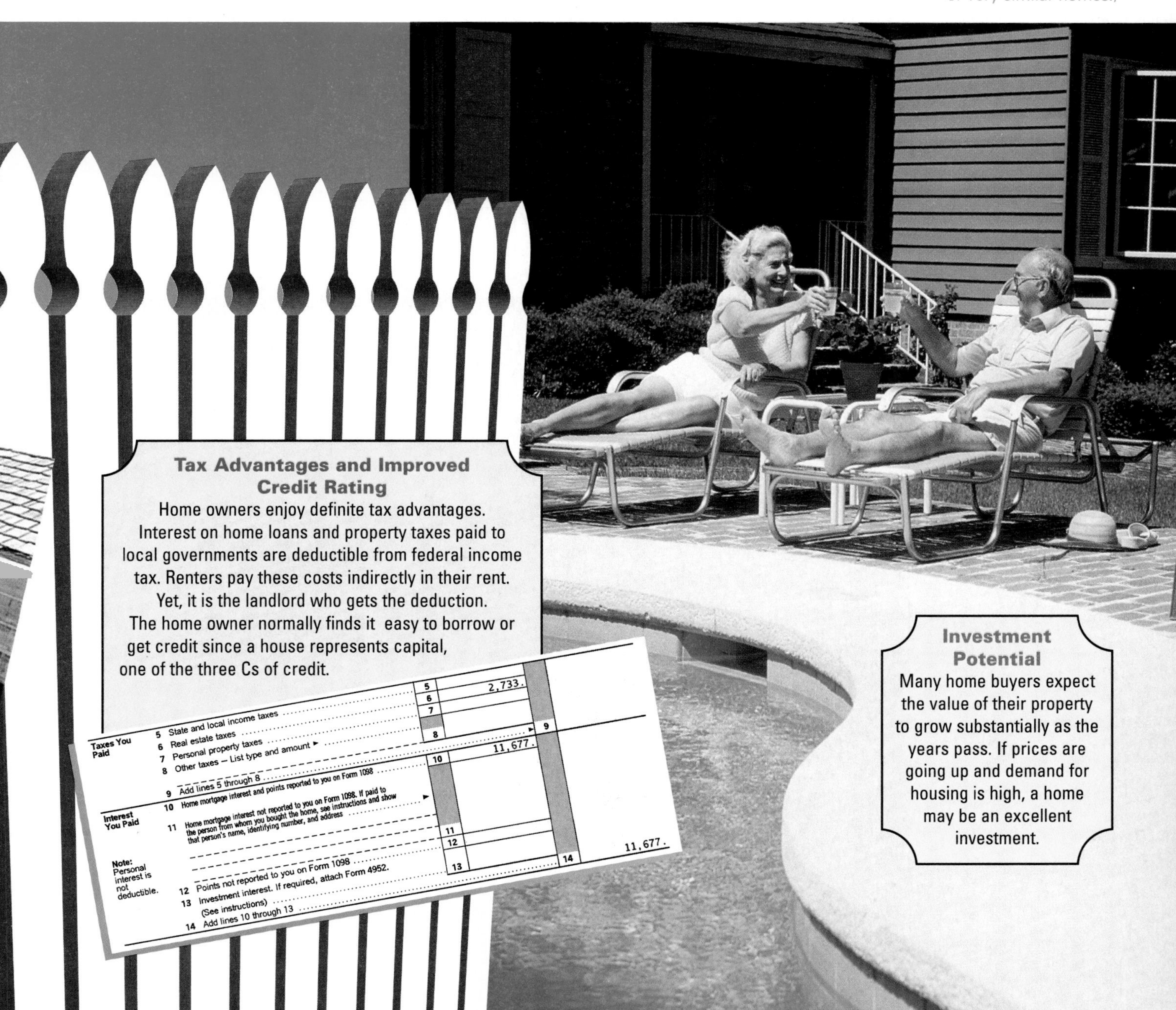
Tax Advantages and Improved Credit Rating
Home owners enjoy definite tax advantages. Interest on home loans and property taxes paid to local governments are deductible from federal income tax. Renters pay these costs indirectly in their rent. Yet, it is the landlord who gets the deduction. The home owner normally finds it easy to borrow or get credit since a house represents capital, one of the three Cs of credit.
Taxes You Paid
5 State and local income taxes 5 2,733.
6 Real estate taxes 6
7 Personal property taxes 7
8 Other taxes – List type and amount ► 8
9 Add lines 5 through 8 ► 9 11,677.
Interest You Paid
10 Home mortgage interest and points reported to you on Form 1098 10
11 Home mortgage interest not reported to you on Form 1098. If paid to the person from whom you bought the home, see instructions and show that person's name, identifying number, and address ► 11
Note: Personal interest is not deductible.
12 Points not reported to you on Form 1098 12
13 Investment interest. If required, attach Form 4952. (See instructions) 13
14 Add lines 10 through 13 14 11,677.
Investment Potential
Many home buyers expect the value of their property to grow substantially as the years pass. If prices are going up and demand for housing is high, a home may be an excellent investment.

1 Discussion Starter Ask students if they know anyone who lives in a co-op or mobile home. What are that person's feelings about this type of ownership?

2 Extension Tell students that in recent years in many areas of the country, condominiums have not generally sold as fast as homes. They need to take this into consideration if there's a good chance they will want to sell and move within a few years after purchasing the condo. Have them ask real estate agents in their area what the average time on the market is for a condo versus a home.

3 Learning Economics Ask students if they can explain why lenders can more easily guarantee profits with variable rather than fixed rates. (If inflation pushes interest rates up while the lender has money lent at a lower rate, the lender can lose money; variable rates allow the lender to adjust the borrower's rates according to inflationary pressure.)

upkeep of common areas like the grounds.

1 ■ *Cooperatives.* Cooperatives are residen-
2 tial units that are owned in common by all residents. Owners purchase shares in the organization and receive exclusive rights to a specific unit.

■ *Mobile homes.* Mobile homes are factory-constructed houses designed so that they can be transported on wheels. They are economical and require little maintenance. Owners usually rent land space for their own homes.

FINANCING A HOME

Most houses are bought through a mortgage arrangement. A **mortgage** is a loan in which property (usually real estate) is used as security for repayment. The borrower signs a legal document which states that the lender has the right to take the property if the borrower does not pay back the loan.

Fixed-Rate Mortgages

With a **fixed-rate mortgage,** the amount of the monthly payment is set for the full mortgage term—often 20 or 30 years. Thus, if the monthly payment is $800, the buyer knows this amount will remain the same. Even if the cost of living should double before the loan is repaid, the amount due remains $800 a month. To find the best fixed-rate mortgage, compare APRs offered by different institutions, just as you would with a consumer loan.

Variable-Rate Mortgages

When credit is hard to obtain, however, many home buyers find that they cannot get a fixed-rate mortgage. Instead, lenders guarantee profits by offering only variable-rate mortgages. A **variable-rate mortgage** (VRM) is one in which the
3 interest rate can change periodically.

There are several different kinds of VRMs, including the following:

Today, potential home owners have many choices. ***What are the most common forms of ownership in your area?*** ▶

Caption Answer: Answers will depend on location.

- *Adjustable-rate mortgage.* With this mortgage, rates are adjusted annually, semiannually, or at some other interval decided in advance. Suppose a couple bought a home under a 12 percent mortgage arrangement. If interest rates in general went up to 13 percent at some time in the future, the couple would have to start paying 13 percent interest on their loan as of
1 the next adjustment date.
- *Graduated-payment mortgage.* When home buyers take this type of mortgage, they know that their interest rate and monthly payments will increase according to a set schedule. For example, assume a family made a down payment of $14,290 on a house priced at $70,990. They borrowed the balance of $56,700 in order to finance the purchase. The schedule shown in Figure 31–2 might apply. A schedule of this sort is designed to take advantage of the fact that a family's income usually increases over a period of years.
- *Balloon-payment mortgage.* Under this arrangement, payments start out at a reasonable rate. Then, at a stated time in the future, typically at the end of five years, the total amount remaining to be paid on the mortgage loan comes due. Unless the home buyers have suddenly become very wealthy, they will have to work out a new contract with the lender. That new mortgage will no doubt call for a higher interest rate.

Figure 31–2 Graduated-Payment Mortgage Schedule

Term	Interest Rate	Monthly Payment
Year 1	6.9%	$373.41
Year 2	8.9	452.15
Year 3	10.9	535.68
Years 4–30	11.9	578.87

▲ *In a graduated-payment mortgage, the interest rate increases according to a set schedule.* ***What advantage does this mortgage have for the consumer?***

Small Houses in the Philippines

In the Philippines, a new "low-income" house sells for under $12,000. However it is made of concrete and steel and has only 345 square feet of floor space which represents an area only about 17 feet by 20 feet.

- *Shared-appreciation mortgage.* With this plan, the borrower gets a home loan at a relatively low rate of interest. In exchange, however, he or she must agree to share with the lender any increase in the value of the house. Thus, if ten years later the house is sold at a profit of $30,000, part of that amount will go to the lender.

Other Types of Loans Banks and savings and loan associations are customary sources of home loans. An *insured* loan is one in which an insurer protects the bank, S&L, or other lending institution from substantial losses when borrowers fail to pay. Therefore, institutions that make insured loans can offer terms that are more favorable to borrowers, such as lower interest rates, lower down payments, and a longer period in which to pay off the loan.

FHA loans are insured by the Federal Housing Administration and are available to anyone who can meet qualifying guidelines—as to gross monthly income, nonhousing debts, etc. The borrower pays the mortgage insurance premium of about 2.25 percent up front and a small monthly premium after that. (Premium percentages depend on a number of factors.) VA loans are insured by the Veterans Administration

1 Extension Students may ask who decides or what makes the interest rates go up or down. Tell them that many factors influence interest rates, but that in most cases they fluctuate according to interest rates that the Federal Reserve Board charges its banks. The Federal Reserve Board adjusts its rates in ways that it believes will best help the country's overall economy.

Caption Answer: The payment amounts are known. Payments increase as income probably increases.

1 Critical Thinking Ask students if they think fixed rates are typically higher or lower than in the initial rates in adjustable mortgages. (They are higher.)

2 Reinforcement Student Activity Workbook, Chapter 31 activities.

3 Extension Point out that the major obstacle most people face in reaching the point at which they can buy their first house is accumulating enough money for a down payment.

Caption Answer: Interest rates can change periodically.

and are available to past and present military personnel who meet qualifications. The FHA and VA do not make loans directly to consumers. Instead, they insure lending institutions against specified losses when borrowers default.

Past and Future Trends

In the early 1980s, home buyers accepted VRM contracts out of necessity, because they could not afford the monthly payments required by fixed-rate mortgages. They knew their own variable payments would grow, but they were counting on inflation to give them the higher salaries they would need to meet them. Not all salaries kept pace with inflation. Corporations began *downsizing*—reducing the number of employees. Some people were laid off or terminated from their jobs and could
1 not meet their mortgage payments.

More recently, as interest rates in general have come down, fixed-rate mortgages have again appeared. This has allowed many people who signed 20- or 30-year mortgages at high interest rates to refinance. For example, a home owner with an old mortgage at 13 percent could pay off the mortgage with money newly borrowed at only 10 percent.

The 3 percent saving may not seem like much. Remember, however, the figure represents 3 percent of a large loan to be paid monthly for more than 20 years. That could amount to tens of thousands of dollars. (Refinancing itself involves charges that can amount to several thousand dollars. Therefore, it does not usually pay to refinance unless current interest rates are at least two percentage points below the rate being paid on the old mortgage.)

Another result of the return to lower interest rates has been the trend toward shorter mortgage terms. Many home buyers are choosing 15-year mortgages. These have higher monthly payments, but cost much less in the long run
2 because interest is paid for fewer years.

▲ *Many families are willing to accept financial risks that accompany variable-rate mortgages in return for a chance to live in their dream house.* ***What is the disadvantage of variable-rate mortgages?***

PURCHASING A HOME

The easiest way to appreciate the various steps involved in locating and purchasing a home is to follow a single example through the whole procedure. Consider the case of Rachel and Jerome Haeger.

The Haegers had planned for a long time to buy a house. Each month they had deposited money at the Uptown Savings and Loan Association. Their account had grown to a point where there was now enough money to cover a down payment as well as closing costs and moving expenses. There would also still be money left over for a substantial emergency fund. The last item was an important part of the Haegers' plan. They did not want to invest their last cent in a house only to lose it the
3 first time an emergency occurred.

Choosing a Neighborhood

While they had been saving, the Haegers had also been compiling a checklist for use in house hunting. They had decided to buy in the Oak Grove subdivision, if at all possible. There were a number of factors in favor of this particular choice.

1. They had friends living in the area.
2. Most of the families had young children. (Their daughter, Tricia, would have playmates her own age.)
3. Since the community had been established several years ago, all essential services were already provided.
4. The city bus made its rounds every 30 minutes.
5. A good shopping center was located on the bus line and within easy driving distance from any point in Oak Grove.
6. There were good schools in the subdivision.
7. Streets were attractive and well laid out.
8. Most of the homes in the area were in
1 a price range that they could afford.

Contacting a Real Estate Agent

The Haegers had been studying classified ads. Recently, they had driven past several homes with for-sale signs. Now it was time for them to start looking for a house in earnest.

They decided to go to a real estate agent who could match their desires with listings of houses for sale. There would be no direct cost to them for the agent's services. The seller pays the agent's commission, which is usually about 6 or 7 percent of the price of the home. The Haegers realized, though, that any price quoted to them would include the amount paid to the agent.

Loretta Chang, the real estate agent, greeted them cordially when they called at the real estate office and outlined
2 their needs.

Location: Oak Grove subdivision
Price: $162,000 range
Age: Not more than 15 years old
Style: Modern (but not too stark)
Rooms: Three bedrooms (one for them, one for Tricia, and one for guests); two baths; good-sized family room.
3 Options: Fireplace

The agent was impressed by all their planning. "It's a tall order," she said, "but we'll see what can be done. I have several listings in Oak Grove that may interest you." Then she told them that their price of $162,000 happened to be
4 within a thousand dollars of the average
5 price of a home in their town.

Money-Saving Tips at Home

- **Buy large appliances, such as air conditioners, out of season and on sale.**
- **Buy a battery recharger and save the cost of new batteries.**
- **Use the telephone during the times of lowest rates.**
- **Review all your insurance to be sure you are not carrying too much.**
- **Buy grocery items at sale prices and store them for the future.**
- **If you own your home, challenge your property tax bill—you may be paying too much.**

Inspecting Homes

They drove to Oak Grove with Loretta. She showed them two houses they especially liked. Jerome and Rachel made notes on their checklists, shown in Figure 31–3 on page 494, as they toured the homes.

The first was at 1542 Balboa. Rachel loved the fireplace. She was not willing to buy a whole house to obtain it, though. Jerry was impressed by the storage shed at the end of the carport. It would be a great advantage, but far more important things would determine whether or not they bought the property.

1 Discussion Starter Ask students which of the factors the Haegers used to find a neighborhood would be most important to them. Which do they think is most important for the majority of people? Can they think of any additional factors to consider?

2 Math Application Have students calculate the agent's fee for a $162,000 house at a 7 percent rate. ($11,340)

3 Critical Thinking Ask students if they think it would be a better investment to buy the least expensive house in a more expensive neighborhood or the most expensive house in a less expensive neighborhood. (The least expensive house has a greater likelihood of appreciating.)

4 Extension Since the values of homes vary so much from one area of the country to another, you may want students to contact local real estate agents to determine average prices in your particular area. Also have them ask the agents for comparative prices for surrounding areas and states.

5 Critical Thinking Ask students to name other ways to find a house, in addition to using an agent. (Buyers can check the real estate classifieds and look for "For Sale" signs.)

Figure 31-3 Home Inspection Checksheet

THE HOME	Good	Average	Poor
Square footage			
Number of bedrooms			
Number of baths			
Practicality of floor plan			
Interior walls condition			
Closet/storage space			
Basement			
Fireplace			
Cable TV			
Basement: dampness or odors			
Exterior appearance, condition			
Lawn/yard space			
Fence			
Patio or deck			
Garage			
Energy efficiency			
Screens, storm windows			
Roof: age and condition			
Gutters and downspouts			

THE NEIGHBORHOOD	Good	Average	Poor
Appearance/condition of nearby homes/businesses			
Traffic			
Noise level			
Safety/security			
Age mix of inhabitants			
Number of children			
Pet restrictions			
Parking			
Zoning regulations			
Neighborhood restrictions/ covenants			

THE NEIGHBORHOOD (cont.)	Good	Average	Poor
Fire protection			
Police			
Snow removal			
Garbage service			

SCHOOLS	Good	Average	Poor
Age/condition			
Reputation			
Qualifications of teachers			
Achievement test scores			
Play areas			
Curriculum			
Class size			
Busing distance			

CONVENIENCE TO:	Good	Average	Poor
Supermarket			
Schools			
Work			
Shopping			
Child care			
Hospitals			
Doctor/dentist			
Recreation/parks			
Restaurants/entertainment			
House of worship			
Airport			
Highways			
Public transportation			

▲ *You'll want to make several copies of this checklist and fill one out for each home you tour. Then, comparing your ratings later will be easy.* ***What items would you add?***

Caption Answer: Other items include convenience to library, train station, and cultural attractions.

1 Reinforcement Point out that most buyers visit and inspect a house several times before making a decision to buy it.

2 Reinforcement Point out that if they don't know an expert, most buyers pay an expert to inspect the house before making an offer, or at least before they sign the final papers.

The house they really liked was located at 1816 Broadmore. It had a larger kitchen than most which opened onto a brightly lit family room and deck. It was an older home, but its design was modern. The bedrooms were all in one wing. One bathroom was located near the bedrooms, and a half bath (toilet and basin) was off the family room.

Jerome liked the yard and landscaping. Drainage was excellent. Several trees had been planted and would someday provide shade. The fact that the yard was already fenced would save them money.

A quick look at the circuit breakers revealed that the wiring was adequate for all the appliances they would be using. The furnace was a hot-water system, which they considered efficient.

The house was ideal in many respects. The price was not. The owners were asking $172,000, more than the
1 Haegers wanted to pay.

Getting an Expert Opinion

Jerome's sister, who was a building contractor, went with them the next time they looked at 1816 Broadmore. She checked the building's construction, closely inspecting its roof, foundation, insulation, and heating system. When she pronounced the structure sound, they were ready to talk about
2 buying.

▲ *Before buying a home, buyers should have it inspected for major defects.* ***What areas should you check?***

Making an Offer

The Haegers wanted the house on Broadmore, but they decided they would buy it only if the price was reduced to $168,000. They knew that the original asking price had probably been set artificially high to allow for bargaining.

Loretta did not seem surprised when they told her, "We are willing to offer $168,000—if appraisers find it's worth that much." She soon received a counteroffer from her client to sell at
1 $170,000, provided financing could be
2 arranged.

Locating Financing

The Haegers had planned to finance their home through the Uptown Savings and Loan Association, where they had an account. They shopped for credit, though, just as they shopped for housing. Among the lenders they contacted were a commercial bank, an insurance company, the credit union where Jerome worked, and two more savings and loan associations. One of these, Downtown S&L, offered the best terms—a quarter of a percent less than Uptown. Over a 20- or 25-year period, this small difference would
3 save them many hundreds of dollars.

The Haegers' income was about $70,000 a year. A family with these financial resources, they had been told, should be able to afford a house costing from $140,000 to maybe $175,000. They knew they were being conservative in holding to the old rule of thumb that said a family should not undertake to
4 buy a house priced at more than 2 or 2½
5 times the family's annual gross income.

Some of their friends insisted that it's all right to set an upper limit at 3 times annual gross income. However, the Haegers felt that making monthly payments on a house costing that much would rob other budget categories of needed funds. "Besides that," Jerome reasoned, "it would leave us hard-pressed to meet emergencies."

Over the years, they had saved $47,600 for a down payment. This amount came to 28 percent of the purchase price. (On a conventional loan, 20 percent is about average.) They decided to apply the full $47,600 to the purchase of a home as it would cut down on interest costs by reducing the amount they
6 would have to borrow to $122,400.

When they met with the loan officer to discuss the mortgage, they had to bring along many financial documents, including the following:

- A copy of the signed purchase agreement.
- Federal income tax returns for the previous two years.
  Bank statements for the previous two months.
- Evidence of their assets and liabilities, such as passbooks, stocks, bonds, and bills from merchants.
- Pay stubs covering the most recent 30-day period.
- Twelve months' canceled checks on their rental lease.

The S&L would use the documents to evaluate their financial situation. In some cases, even more documents would be required.

The Haegers wanted to pay off the loan as quickly as possible. Still, they did not want to be pressed for cash each month. The loan officer at the S&L told them payments on a 25-year loan would run $1,027.18 a month; on a 20-year loan they would be $1,101.26. They decided they could afford the higher

Caption Answer: Areas to check include the roof, foundation, insulation, and heating system.

1 Discussion Starter Ask students if they have ever negotiated a purchase price. What were their feelings about the process? Did they enjoy it? Did they think they got a bargain? Point out that such a process is typical in buying a house.

2 Vocabulary Ask students to define *appraiser.* (Someone who assigns a value.)

3 Reinforcement Stress the importance of shopping around for a mortgage. Rates do vary.

4 Interesting Note Tell students that on the average, the annual family income in the United States is equal to about 30 percent of the purchase price of a new home.

5 Math Application Using the guideline of 2½ times gross income, how much could a family earning $43,000 spend on a house? ($107,500) a family earning $28,000? ($70,000)

6 Reinforcement Stress the importance of saving to accomplish long-term goals like buying a house.

amount. Using a computer, the loan officer told them that, by paying off the mortgage in 20 years instead of 25, they would be saving $43,851.60 in interest. (See Figure 31–4.)

They learned that at a 9 percent rate, they would be paying $141,903.50 in interest over the 20-year life of the loan. The house, in other words, would actually cost them $311,903.50. Committing such a large sum to one item was a matter they had considered carefully. Home ownership, they had decided, was important enough to them to justify the expense.

Monthly Payments and the Escrow Account

The S&L officer said he probably could not have approved the Haeger's application for a loan if their monthly payments had amounted to more than 28 percent of their monthly gross income. He spoke of PITI, an abbreviation for *principal, interest, taxes,* and *insurance*—the usual four components of monthly house payments.

The Haeger's monthly payments were estimated to be $1,553,26:

Principal and Interest	$1,101.26
Taxes	$ 375.00
Insurance	$ 77.00
TOTAL	$1,553.26

The monthly total of $1,553.26 divided by their monthly income of $5,833 equals 19.8 percent. That is well below the 28 percent maximum that lenders look for, so the Haeger family should be able to handle their monthly

Rachel compared the interest costs for two loans. ***If you were the buyer in this case, which term would you choose—20 or 25 years? Why?*** ▶

Caption Answer: Answers would vary. A 25-year loan leaves more money for other budget items each month. A 20-year loan saves almost $18,000.

Figure 31–4 Rachel's Notes on the Loan Costs.

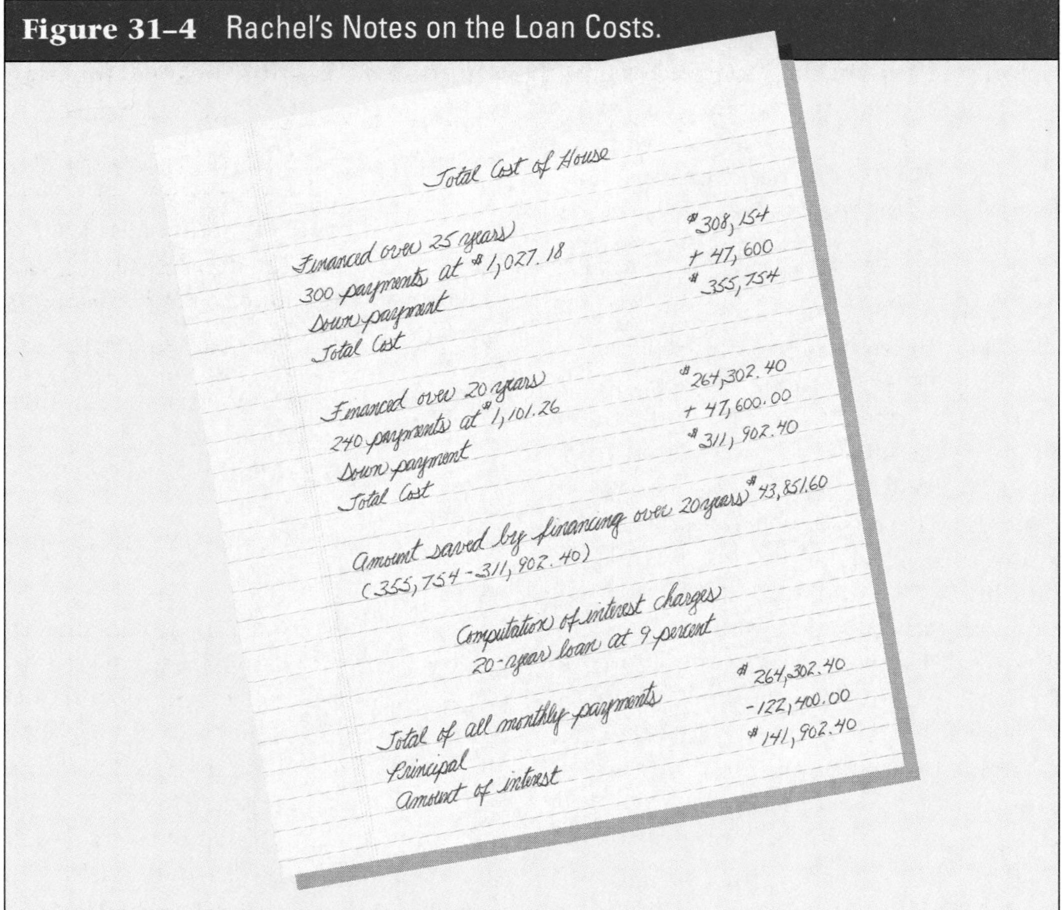

Total Cost of House

Financed over 25 years)	$308,154
300 payments at $1,027.18	+ 47,600
Down payment	$355,754
Total Cost	
Financed over 20 years)	$264,302.40
240 payments at $1,101.26	+ 47,600.00
Down payment	$311,902.40
Total Cost	

Amount saved by financing over 20 years) $43,851.60
(355,754 - 311,902.40)

Computation of interest charges
20-year loan at 9 percent

Total of all monthly payments	$264,302.40
Principal	-122,400.00
Amount of interest	$141,902.40

Note: In making these computations, Rachel ignored certain points.
1. Mortgage interest paid is, in a sense, not all a cost because interest on home mortgage can be deductible for federal income tax purposes.
2. If the 25-year mortgage were chosen in preference to the 20-year plan, the $30.26 difference in monthly payments *could* be invested and thus produce income.

payments without getting into financial
1 difficulty.

The amounts paid to the S&L for taxes and insurance are held in an escrow account to be paid to the tax agencies and insurance company when due. An **escrow account** is an account in which money is held in trust until it can be delivered to the designated party. In this way, the S&L does not have to worry whether the borrower is paying these obligations and thus keeping the property protected from tax claims and fire losses. To protect the rights of borrowers, the U.S. Department of Housing and Urban Development in 1995 put into effect rules that prescribe methods lenders are to use in accounting for escrow funds.

Hiring an Attorney

Although legal assistance is not required to buy a home, Jerome and

1 Critical Thinking Ask students to explain how even at these high prices buying a home might still be a wise investment. (Owners are putting the money they would spend on rent into property that will probably appreciate in value.)

Making Slumlords Pay

In any large city, there are rundown apartment buildings. Tenants put up with rats and cockroaches. The roof leaks and ceilings cave in. There is little or no heat. The landlords usually do little to correct the problems.

Until they come up against an attorney like Nancy Mintie. When she got out of law school, Mintie wanted to help those who really needed her skills. In 1980, she started the Inner City Law Center to provide legal assistance to the poor and homeless in downtown Los Angeles.

Her first office was in the garage of an organization that runs a soup kitchen and shelter downtown. She was paid $3 a week. It was five years before she had a salary.

Her biggest case came when she heard of the awful conditions in an apartment building downtown. She gathered information on and photos of the vermin, the crime, and the dangerous conditions in the building. Mintie also got statements from health experts on the demoralizing effect on people living in this kind of environment.

She went to court representing 82 tenants. She sued for negligence and intentional infliction of emotional distress, among other things. Even when the judge ordered emergency repairs to the building, the landlord resisted. Mintie's group had to keep an eye on the situation to be sure everything was done correctly.

When the suit was finally won, the landlord had to pay $1.25 million to the group of tenants. Most of the people used the money to get out of the building and into homes of their own. Many saved what was left to educate their children.

Brainstorm

What do you think are some of the "demoralizing effects" on people living in rundown buildings?

Case Study Answer: Feelings of hopelessness; anger; resentment; inability to keep house clean with rats and cockroaches; attacks of rats on children and on possessions; poor maintenance in hallways make it unpleasant to come home; no heat, leaking roofs, unsanitary conditions create health problems; broken locks on outside doors are threats to security of tenants.

1 Reinforcement Make sure students understand the point of earnest money. Can they see that the possibility of losing the earnest money helps ensure that people don't offer to buy a house without first being sure they want to go through with the deal?

2 Interesting Note Having a house appraised can cost from $150 to $500 depending on the value of the house and the part of the country in which it is located.

3 Vocabulary Tell students that settlement costs are frequently referred to as closing costs.

4 Interesting Note Tell students that settlement costs typically amount to about 3 percent of the purchase price of the house.

Caption Answer: Total costs are $2,600.

News Clip Answers:
1 Other home-buying costs include application fees, property insurance, mortgage insurance, and title insurance.
2 You should start with a real estate broker, who can tell you about some of the general fees and expenses that you would incur. You should also speak with someone at your local bank about the fees associated with a home loan.

Rachel realized the importance of having a lawyer look after their interests. Years of their lives and thousands of dollars were at stake. Clearly, this was an instance where professional advice would be extremely useful. Jerome's employer recommended an attorney who agreed to accept them as clients.

The attorney prepared a document called a contract for sale. A **contract for sale** is a legal document that contains all the details the buyers and the sellers of a property agree upon. (In some places, the term *offer to purchase* is also used.) For example, the Haegers contract specified the total sale price, the down payment, the method and terms of financing, and the date the property was to be delivered to its new owners.

The Haegers' attorney also inserted another clause. It required the seller to hold the property for the Haegers until action was taken on their loan application. If the Haegers could not get financing, the deal would be canceled.

In return, the Haegers would put up *earnest money* (a deposit). This money would go to the seller if the Haegers changed their minds about buying for any reason other than not qualifying for a loan. When they bought the property, the earnest money would serve as part
1 of the down payment.

All parties felt more secure once the contract for sale had been signed by both sides. The sellers had evidence that the buyers were sincere. The Haegers did not have to worry about the house being sold to someone else while their
2 loan application was being processed.

Closing the Deal

Downtown S&L worked on processing the Haegers' loan application. First, the loan officer ordered an **appraisal** (the opinion of an expert as to the fair market value) of 1816 Broadmore. Then she investigated the Haegers' credit history. Finally, she had an abstract, or history of the property's ownership, prepared. When all of these checks yielded satisfactory results, she approved the Haegers' loan.

Rachel and Jerome received the good news from their attorney. The closing was scheduled for 9 A.M. Tuesday, the 15th. At that time, the property would become theirs legally.

Settlement Costs When they first applied for their loan, the Haegers had been given an estimate of the closing or settlement costs—various charges involved in closing the deal. As a result, they were prepared to pay the following
3 settlement costs (sample costs shown in
4 Figure 31–5).

- *Origination fee.* This fee covered the paperwork and related expenses of the lender in processing the Haegers' loan.
- *Abstract fee.* An abstractor had to be paid for studying the legal records

FIGURE 31–5 Settlement Costs

Application fee	$75 to $300
Appraisal fee	$150 to $400
Survey costs	$125 to $300
Homeowner's hazard insurance	$300 to $600
Lender's attorney's review fees	$75 to $200
Title search and title insurance	$450 to $600
Home inspection fee	$175 to $350
Loan origination fee	1% of loan
Mortgage insurance	0.5% to 1.0%
Points	1% to 3%

▲ *Settlement costs can be an unsettling experience.* ***Using the minimum for each item, compute total settlement costs for the Haegers. Assume the mortgage insurance premium is $612.***

CASE STUDY

Consumer NEWS CLIP

Belated Sticker Shock: Not All Costs Are Known Before the Mortgage

by Jim DeBoth
Chicago Tribune
September 10, 1995

If you are considering a home purchase, it is recommended that you familiarize yourself with all of the associated costs that could be incurred.

The costs most likely will begin when the buyer fills out the mortgage loan application. Most lenders charge a loan application fee which often is paid at the time of application. This fee typically is used by the lender to pay for a credit report and a property appraisal.

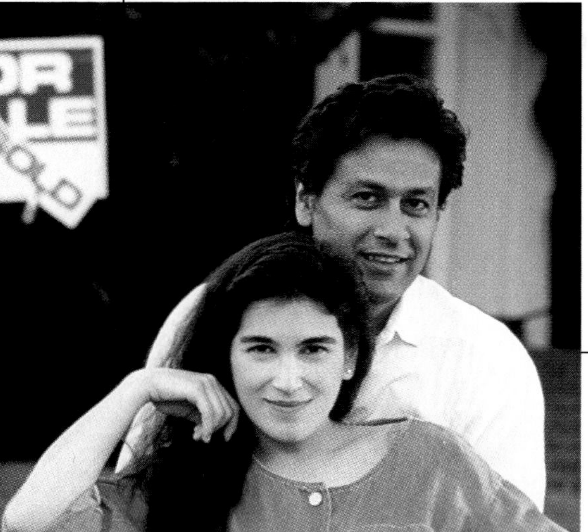

The credit report provides the lender with a history of the borrower's ability to handle credit. A full credit report usually runs about $50.

The property appraisal will tell the lender what the property is worth so the lender can determine the appropriate loan amount that can be offered. Property appraisals typically run in the range of $250 to $350.

If you get approved for the loan, the next cost you are likely to incur is property insurance. Because the property is collateral for the mortgage loan, the lender will require the buyer to buy hazard insurance. The norm is for the buyer to purchase one year of hazard insurance prior to the closing.

If you put less than 20 percent down on the property you can count on paying mortgage insurance. Mortgage insurance protects the lender against any potential loss on the property if the borrower defaults on the mortgage loan.

When [you are] buying a property, a title search is conducted to determine if any parties have prior claims against the property, including liens or judgments. In order to provide protection against any undiscovered title defects, lenders require the buyer to purchase title insurance, which is usually about $150.

In addition to the application fee, there are other charges that you might receive from a lender:

- Origination fee. This is the lender's fee for making a loan. It usually is 1 point, equal to 1 percent of the mortgage amount.
- Discount points. If a buyer wants to reduce the interest rate on a mortgage loan, he or she can "buy-down" the rate by paying discount points. A discount point is also equal to 1 percent of the mortgage amount.
- Mortgage brokerage fee. Mortgage brokers do not actually lend money, but they do find financing for buyers. Mortgage brokers often charge a fee for their services.
- Tax service. A charge that is incurred on your behalf to change the assessor's records—about $65.
- Recording fee. The cost usually is $30 for making the deed and mortgage a matter of public record.
- Transfer taxes (in certain areas). The fee paid to a local unit of government for transferring ownership typically ranges from zero up to $7.50 per $1,000 of home value.

Decisions, Decisions

1. Other than the down payment, what other up-front costs are involved in buying a home?
2. If you were thinking of buying a home, where would you go to get advice on how much to budget?

FLASHBACK FLASHFORWARD

Scottish inventor John Logie Baird projected the first television images in 1926. The television age boomed in 1948. By 1990, there were 193 million television sets in the United States.

1 **Math Application** Have students assume they are borrowing $165,000. The loan agreement stipulates that they must pay 2.5 points on this loan. How much do they owe for points? ($4,125)

2 **Reinforcement** Ask students why the amount of earnest money was subtracted from what the Haegers owed as a down payment. (They had written a check for this earlier.)

3 **Reinforcement** Student Activities Workbook, Chapter 31 activities.

and writing a history of the property's ownership. An abstract is important because it shows whether the seller actually owns the property.

- *Title insurance premium.* Despite the abstractor's conclusion, the Haegers still purchased title (ownership) insurance just to be safe. If at some time in the future the sellers proved not to be the owners of the property, the insurance would make good the Haegers' loss. In the meantime, the lender is protected.
- *Survey fee.* The surveyor who mapped out the property lines for the Haegers and produced the accompanying report had to be paid a fee.
- *Credit report fee.* The lender passed along all costs incurred in investigating the Haegers' credit history.
- *Appraisal fee.* The expert who had appraised the property to determine its fair market value was also owed a fee. The appraisal assured the Haegers the property was worth what they had agreed to pay for it.
- *Filing fees.* The transfer of real property from one owner to another must be recorded in the public records. Various taxes and fees are charged for this service.
- *Advance interest payment and insurance premium.* The lender required prepayment of interest for the remainder of the month. The Haegers also had to purchase an insurance policy to protect the lender's investment in the event the house was destroyed.

The Haegers did not have to pay a pest inspection charge or fee to the lender's attorney, although in some places these are common settlement costs. They were also fortunate in not having to pay points. **Points** are a percentage fee charged for the loan. They amount to additional interest on the loan and are used by some lenders to get around state limits on interest rates.

Points are assessed one time only, at the closing. A point is equal to 1 percent of the amount of the mortgage. Thus, if the Haegers had been charged four points, the charge would have been $4,896 (.04 × $122,400 loan). This amount would have been deducted from their loan. In other words, they would have received only $117,504 but had to pay back $122,400. When mortgage money is scarce, the practice of adding points is
1 common.

Key Documents At the closing, the Haegers first handed over a personal check covering (1) the down payment (less their earnest money), (2) their share of the property taxes (which had already been paid by the seller for the whole year), and (3) the settlement costs.

Next, they signed a **promissory note**—a statement in which they promised to repay $122,400 to Downtown Savings and Loan Association. They also signed a mortgage. This document gave the savings and loan title to the property if they failed to keep up payments. Finally, they accepted a check
2 from the S&L for $122,400, which they
3 endorsed over to the sellers.

The sellers, for their part, signed the **deed**—a document transferring ownership of the property to its new owners. The Haegers turned the deed over to their attorney for recording at the courthouse. They were at last home owners.

Chapter 31 Highlights	Key Terms
Advantages of Home Ownership ▶ Many feel owning a home (1) gives them a feeling of permanence, (2) confers prestige and enhances credit standing, (3) appears to be a good investment and encourages saving, and (4) provides security. ▶ Home-owning options include older homes, ready-built homes, custom-built homes, condominiums, co-operatives, and mobile homes.	
Financing a Home ▶ Many consumers prefer fixed-rate mortgages. ▶ Economic and market conditions determine whether fixed-rate mortgages are available and whether they are preferable to the variable-rate mortgages. ▶ Variable-rate mortgages include adjustable-rate, graduated-payment, balloon-payment, and shared-appreciation mortgages.	mortgage fixed-rate mortgage variable-rate mortgage
Purchasing a Home ▶ To prepare to buy a house, (1) save and plan carefully in advance, (2) carefully consider possible locations, (3) study the local market, (4) contact a real estate agent, and (5) inspect homes. ▶ To purchase a house (1) make an offer, (2) select financing, (3) hire an attorney, and (4) learn about settlement costs. **Reinforcement** Suggest that students review the chapter by using the five-step study procedure described at the beginning of the Teacher's Manual.	escrow account contract for sale appraisal points promissory note deed

CHAPTER 31 REVIEW

Refer students to the Reviewing Consumer Terms and Reviewing Facts and Ideas activities in the Student Activity Workbook.

Reviewing Consumer Terms Paragraphs will vary. See the Glossary for definitions.

Reviewing Facts and Ideas See the Student Activity Workbook for answers.

Problem Solving and Decision Making **1 a** The commission is $11,520. **b** The agent will try to determine the highest price a buyer might spend for a house. **2** Fee is $1,216. $127,000 Purchase price − $25,400 down payment = $101,600; $101,600 x 1% = $1,061 + $200 = $1,216.

Consumers Around the World **Math 1 a** $22,000 − $4,000 = $18,000 available for a down payment. **b** $18,000 ÷ .20 = $90,000 total cost; $90,000 − $18,000 = $72,000 mortgage.

Communications **2** Papers will vary.

Human Relations **3** In their essays, students should give the financial motives of lenders and the ethical considerations behind laws against redlining.

Reviewing Consumer Terms

Using the terms below, write a paragraph about buying a house.

appraisal
contract for sale
deed
escrow account
fixed-rate mortgage
mortgage
points
promissory note
variable-rate mortgage

Reviewing Facts and Ideas

1. Cite the advantages of home ownership.
2. List the usual costs and procedures in buying a home.
3. What are the differences between a fixed-rate mortgage and a variable-rate mortgage?
4. What are the steps in inspecting a home?

Problem Solving and Decision Making

1. Assume that a real estate agent charges the seller a commission amounting to 6 percent of the selling price.
   - **a.** What will the commission be on a $192,000 home?
   - **b.** How do you think the commission influences the way an agent works?
2. An attorney's fee for handling the purchase of a $127,000 home is "$200 plus 1 percent of the amount borrowed." There is a $25,400 down payment. How much should the attorney receive?

Building Academic Skills

Consumers Around the World

Math

1. Betty and Joseph Molinari have a yearly income of $62,000. They have saved $22,000 to buy a house. Banks in their area generally require a 20 percent down payment to approve a mortgage. Settlement costs can be $4,000.
   - **a.** How much money do the Molinaris have available for a down payment?
   - **b.** How large a mortgage can the Molinaris reasonably expect to get?

Communications

2. Ask students to research the work of architects like Frank Lloyd Wright. What do they think these artists were trying to accomplish? Would they like to live in a home designed by someone like Wright?

Human Relations

3. Redlining is an illegal practice in which financial institutions refuse to make mortgages for houses in areas perceived to be deteriorating, regardless of the creditworthiness of the borrower.
   Research the history of redlining. What are the economic forces involved? Why is redlining illegal? Write a 500-word essay in which you give your view of the issues.

Social Studies

4. Housing is in short supply throughout the world. Choose a country and research the reasons—economic, political, and societal—for this situation. Present an oral report to the class. What solutions have been proposed? Why are these solutions effective or ineffective?

Beyond the Classroom

Consumer Projects

1. Interview one of the following people and report your findings to the class.
   a. A loan officer at a savings and loan association. Determine typical closing costs for a $160,000 home in your area.
   b. A real estate agent. Find out what factors are considered in placing a price on a house.
2. Study for-sale ads in the real estate section of a local newspaper or home buyer's guide. List price ranges for houses in different neighborhoods or areas. Which areas are the most expensive? Which are the least? Why? Discuss your findings in class.
3. Locate at least one article dealing with renovation of an older home. Describe for the class the problems and satisfactions experienced by the author.

Cooperative Learning

Family Economics

Break into assigned family groups. Discuss the following problem.

Your apartment complex is being sold, but the new owner is upgrading and converting to condominiums.

Current tenants will have first option to buy their own units. For the neighborhood (which is quite nice), the prices are reasonable—$50,000 for a one-bedroom unit, $59,000 for a two-bedroom unit, and $67,000 for a three-bedroom unit.

Are you interested? Why or why not? What questions do you have for the new owner or developer? What financial or other problems do you anticipate? Compare your answers with those of other family groups.

Debate the Issue

Building codes, which require that builders follow certain construction standards, are a source of controversy in many communities. Some people maintain that these codes are too restrictive and that they increase the cost of housing so much that it is beyond the reach of most citizens. Others hold that strict codes are needed to protect the community and its citizens from building sites and homes that are unsafe and that reduce property values. A few examples of code requirements that home buyers have complained about include sidewalks, curbs, extra insulation, and garage-door openers.

You and your classmates will break into two groups and research this topic. Each group will gather evidence to support one side or the other. You are to prepare the argument for your side of the problem. Then the two groups will meet in a classroom debate.

Social Studies
4 Students should discuss various solutions, including government sponsoring of housing.

Consumer Projects
1 You may prefer to have these people speak to the class as a group. **2** Students should be able to outline neighborhoods or areas by housing prices. **3** Students should talk about the pros and cons of do-it-yourself house renovations.

Family Economics
Using the standard formula ($2\frac{1}{2}$ times annual earnings) and assuming the need for a 20 percent down payment, only a few families qualify to buy their own units.

Debate the Issue
Break the class into two teams. Assign each team one side of the issue. Encourage students to work together as a team to develop their argument. Ask each team to select a member to make an opening statement that supports the team's side of the issue. Have students take turns debating as the debate moves from one team to the other.

CHAPTER 32 Furnishing a Home

Learning Objectives

When you have finished studying this chapter, you should be able to:

1. Make a plan for furnishing a home.
2. Examine furniture for solid construction and quality workmanship.
3. Locate information to aid in comparison shopping for appliances.
4. Differentiate between written and implied warranties, and service contracts.
5. Identify records and their importance when purchasing appliances.

Consumer Terms

floor plan
case goods
hardwoods
softwoods
particle board
veneer
hardboard
upholstered furniture
warranty
EnergyGuides

Real-World Journal

Imagine that you have just moved into a one-bedroom apartment with no furniture or appliances. In your journal, make a list of the furniture and appliances that you will need. Suppose you have a budget of $2,000. Look through newspapers and catalogs, and visit local stores to find the best bargains. Write down in your journal exactly what you would be able to buy for your money.

Lesson Plan See the Teacher's Manual for Chapter 32 lesson plan.

Vocabulary The Chapter 32 lesson plan includes suggested vocabulary activities for the items listed.

1 Reinforcement Point out to students that this process is similar to a type of purchase they learned about earlier. (Chapter 25, Planning a Wardrobe)

SELECTING FURNITURE

Whether you decide to rent or buy, a change of residence may mean that you'll be buying home furnishings. Buying furniture and appliances requires thorough planning and careful comparison shopping. You must consider what you will need. See Figure 32–1. Then you must determine how much you can spend; research the qualities, features, and prices of available items, and prepare for moving and placement. There are also decorating plans to make; style, comfort, and utility concerns; safety factors; operating costs, and ease of mainte-
1 nance to be taken into account.

Your first step, before you even set foot in a furniture showroom, is to figure out what you already have and what you need. You should choose the best quality materials and construction you can afford.

Laying Your Plans

In developing an overall plan for interior spaces, remember you may not be able to accomplish all your furnishing goals immediately. It is wise to organize and coordinate your decorating effort room by room. Basic steps are: take an inventory of what you already have; research available options such as furniture styles, sizes, and placement, and consider the total look—how the floor coverings, wallpaper or paint, lighting fixtures and wall decorations will fit.

"New" in this case does not necessarily mean brand new and/or ready made. You can buy unfinished or used furniture, build some of your own pieces, or even rent. Renting is expensive, but may be the best choice if you plan to relocate in the near future. Rent-to-own furniture agreements, however, are another story.

A list such as this one is helpful in planning for a first home. ***How would you change it to fit your own needs and wants?*** ▶

Caption Answer: Answers will depend on student choices. For example someone who prepares Asian food would want a Chinese knife, a wok, a steamer, and a rice cooker. Someone who prepares Mexican food would want a tortilla press, a cheese grater, etc.

Figure 32–1 Small Home Furnishing List

KITCHENWARE AND DINING

Pots and Pans
- 1-1 quart pot
- 1-2 quart pot
- 1-6 quart cooker, with inserts for steaming
- 2-frying pans, 6″ and 12″
- 2-covered casserole dishes, 12 quart and 16 quart
- 1-cookie sheet
- 1-pie plate
- 2-cake pans
- 1-9" x 13" baking dish
- 1-10" x 14" roasting pan with rack

Kitchen and Dining Linens
- dish towels/dish cloths
- table linens (placemats, tablecloths, and napkins)

OTHER LINENS

Bedroom Linens
- sheets
- pillows
- pillowcases
- blankets
- bedspreads
- mattress pads

Utensils
- set of knives
- cutting board
- grater
- rubber spatula
- pancake turner
- 2-cup glass measuring cup
- set of dry measuring cups (plastic or stainless)
- set of measuring spoons
- set of mixing bowls
- strainer

Dinnerware
- dishes (casual/formal)
- flatware (casual/formal)
- glasses (6 oz. and 12 oz.)

Small Electric Appliances
- hand-held mixer
- blender
- coffeemaker
- can opener
- small food processor
- toaster
- small microwave oven

Bath Linens
- towels and washcloths
- bath mat

While they require no down payment
and no credit check, their fees are so
1 high that you could end up paying
2 much more than if you had bought the
furniture on credit at a regular store.

Gather information and ideas by reviewing books, magazines, and catalogs, or by visiting furniture stores and furnished model homes. You might discuss your needs with an interior designer
who is employed by a furniture specialty
3 store or large department store since
4 they are available at no cost to you.

To get down to specifics, develop a **floor plan,** which is a scale drawing showing the size and shape of a room. Then place scale drawings of furniture on your floor plan. Take into account the activities that will occur in the room. Group furniture so that it is easy for people to make eye contact and carry on a conversation. Consider traffic patterns, which are paths people take as they move through a room. Take measurements with you when you go shopping for the furniture you need to complete your plan. Make a note of any special
problems that might arise—such as low
5 ceilings or narrow doorways.

Shopping for Case Goods

Case goods is a term for furniture that has no padding, fabric, springs, or covering. Retailers tend to use the term to refer to wood furniture, but it can include metal, plastic, and glass items.

The most expensive woods are **hardwoods,** which are from broad-leafed trees such as oak, maple, and cherry. **Softwoods** are from evergreen trees, like pine and cedar. They often cost less than hardwood, but they scratch more easily. Less expensive is **particle board,** which is made from wood particles and adhesives bonded together. It can be covered with a stained or painted **veneer,** a thin sheet of hardwood or softwood. Improvements in veneer have eliminated cracking and peeling, so it should last as long or longer than furniture made from solid wood. Another less expensive choice is **hardboard,** which is made from compressed fibers. It is usually embossed with a wood grain pattern and finished to look like wood.

When buying case goods, choose sturdy and attractive styles you like that fit your decorating plan. In judging quality, make sure the item rests firmly on the floor and does not yield to pressure. Legs should not wobble. Doors should hang evenly and open and close easily. Drawers should slide smoothly (having a glide in the center is best) and, when closed, they should fit flush with the furniture face. Joints should be tightly fitted. Larger joints should be reinforced with corner blocks of wood.

1 Extension Ask students why they think people rent furniture when it costs so much. (Answers should include the lack of good credit or money.)

2 Extension Invite an interior decorator to give students ideas on how to decorate on a budget.

3 Learning Economics Ask students why furniture salespeople visit homes or apartments free of charge. (Offering services gives them a marketing advantage.)

4 Extension Have students indicate traffic patterns in their home. Plan furniture groupings and share plans in class.

5 Extension Have students think of other multi-purpose furnishings. (Examples would be: a futon, sleep sofa; end table with drawers.)

Interior spaces are satisfying when a well thought out plan is finally accomplished. ***What evidence of planning is in this photograph? How was money saved?*** ▶

Caption Answer: Planning examples: well thought out traffic patterns, effective furniture groupings for conversation; color/pattern coordination. Money was saved on less expensive furniture—such as cement blocks for coffee table.

1 Student Motivator Ask students to survey family members and friends to find out how long they have had pieces of furniture. Are some of these pieces antiques? Do they think it is worth the higher price to buy quality furniture?

2 Reinforcement Ask a teacher who has expertise in wood to explain the strengths and weaknesses of various woods and wood products with regard to furniture construction.

3 Extension Tell students that fabric is the most expensive variable in the selection of an upholstered piece.

Case goods may be purchased unfinished for a lot less. This is because they are often mass produced and made from less expensive woods. Some mail-order houses sell unfinished furniture that can be assembled from kits. You can use the furniture unfinished, or you can paint or
2 stain wood.

Choosing Upholstered Furniture

Upholstered furniture has padding, springs, and a fabric covering. The most common upholstered furniture is sofas and chairs. Today such furniture is likely to have "Z" or "S" shaped springs instead of coils. The padding is usually
3 foam rubber. See Figure 32–2.

Buying Bedding

You spend a third of your life sleeping, and the average person turns over in bed 40 to 60 times a night, so it is wise to buy a good bed. The bedding combination chosen by 80 percent of people is a mattress-box spring with a bed frame for support.

Look for knowledgeable salespeople and competitive pricing when deciding where to buy a mattress. Avoid buying a mattress less than 7 inches thick (poor quality) or more than 12 inches thick (size doesn't mean more comfort, and sheets won't fit). Choose a bed with adequate coils. For a twin, at least 275; a full size, 300; a queen, 375; and a king, 450. For the gauge, get nothing higher than

Figure 32–2 Checking Upholstered Furniture

When buying upholstered furniture, you'll want to inspect it carefully.

Be sure to sit in a chair long enough to find out how comfortable it is. Is the angle formed by the seat and back comfortable? Is the chair deep enough, or too deep? Does it provide good support?
Test padding thickness by squeezing it. Make sure the padding is adequate and evenly distributed.
You can test the frame of an upholstered chair by grabbing an arm and trying to move it side to side. It should neither move nor squeak. Look underneath the chair to check for reinforcing braces at points of stress.
Choose fabrics that will be appropriate for their intended use. Light-wear fabrics should be used in rooms with light traffic. Heavy-duty and medium-colored fabrics that hide dirt are good for rooms that will experience heavy traffic. The salesperson may suggest that you buy a spray-on stain repellent. Check the furniture's label to determine whether or not the fabric has already been sprayed with repellent.
Find out how well the fabric is likely to wear by asking the salesperson or by checking it yourself. Look at the reverse side (the pattern should come through); pull it to see that it doesn't separate. Make sure that it is consistent.

$13\frac{1}{2}$. A gauge of $13\frac{1}{2}$ is good, but 13 is thicker and stronger. Was the metal tempered once or twice? Twice is better. Do the coils have five turns or six? Six turns
1 is better.

The most important factor in buying a mattress is how it feels to you. Sit on it, lie on it, move about on it. Is it firm enough, or too firm? If it doesn't feel like it's supporting your lower back, it's too soft. If there is pressure around your hips
2 and shoulders, it is too firm.

SELECTING APPLIANCES

Appliances are labor-saving devices. They range from toasters and blenders to refrigerators, washers, and dryers.

1 Extension Tell students that many salespeople in home furnishings are knowledgeable and willing to offer opinions. Check with several, however, to make sure the advice you receive is accurate. Also make sure it fits your individual preferences.

2 Reinforcement Student Activity Workbook, Chapter 32 activities.

People MAKING a DIFFERENCE

Building a Dream Home

Many people dream of having their own home, but too often they cannot save enough for the down payment. Perhaps the interest on a loan is so high they cannot afford the monthly payments. These people are often left living in substandard housing where they are paying very high rents.

In 1976, Millard Fuller had an idea that would help the working poor afford homes of their own. He called it Habitat for Humanity.

Fuller's idea was to use volunteer labor to build the houses. Money for materials (those that were not donated) would come from the Fund for Humanity. The new home owners would repay the fund, buying the home at cost—and with no interest. The payments would go back into the Fund for Humanity to provide money for more housing.

The typical Habitat home is a 1,000-square-foot house for which people pay a mortgage that may be as little as $150 a month. This amount is usually less than they would pay for rent for substandard housing. Loans are repaid over the course of 20 years.

However, cash alone does not repay the loan. Habitat home owners must help construct their own homes and donate their time to build other Habitat homes.

Habitat has built thousands of homes in the United States and overseas. By 1996, the organization projects that it will have sponsored home-building projects in more than 60 countries.

With more than 7.6 million people in substandard housing in the United States alone, Fuller's dream might be daunting to many people, but not to him. He just keeps chipping away at the problem—one house at a time.

Brainstorm

Why do you think it is so difficult for people to put together money for a down payment, the greatest obstacle to home ownership?

Case Study Answer: Annual rent increases take larger portions of paycheck; family expenses; other payments—car, furniture, credit card, medical—eat up income; there is no tax break for rent payments (there is for mortgage interest).

1 Extension Have students write to government agencies requesting information about various appliances. They could also send for specification sheets from manufacturers or for brand and energy information from the Association of Home Appliance Manufacturers, 20 North Wacker Drive, Chicago, Illinois 60606. Keep materials in an appliance file.

2 Critical Thinking Have student groups research an appliance's safety features. Which ones are worth the extra cost?

News Clip Answers: 1 Buy the best quality you can afford, and buy furniture you really love. 2 You should inspect drawers, finishes, doors, tables and leaves (especially the grain of the wood), and chair construction.

Caption Answer: Answers will vary but may include toaster, coffeemaker, iron, etc.

Home Appliances in Italy

In Italy, 96 percent of households own a clothes washer, compared with 75 percent of households in the United States. Only 18 percent of Italian households own dishwashers compared with 44 percent in the United States.

Do Your Research

If you are thinking about making a purchase, begin planning and saving now. Ask the opinions of friends or relatives. Send for booklets from the government and various trade associations about energy savings and the features. Read about quality and cost in such magazines as *Kiplinger's Personal Finance* magazine and *Consumer Reports*. Ask people who repair appliances which brands
1 are best.

Decide how much you can afford to spend. If you are short of funds and you already own a similar, older appliance, try trading it in for a new model or selling it. Also consider purchasing a reconditioned appliance. This is a used appliance that has been overhauled to restore it to prime working condition.

You will need to purchase appliances when you move into your own home. List the appliances you think you will need. ▼

One of the most important things to keep in mind when purchasing a large appliance is whether it will fit where you want it—and if you can even get it into the house. Ask yourself other installation questions. Do you want a stationary or a portable unit? If your home is older, can it handle the extra energy consumption? Are there workers available to install the item? Working with gas, electricity, or plumbing can be hazardous unless you are well-trained. Check with local codes and other requirements.

Finally, decide on the best places to buy. Ask friends or relatives for recommendations. Check with local consumer organizations or Better Business Bureau for any complaints.

Comparison Shopping

Look for solidly built and evenly balanced appliances with surfaces that resist scratches and are easy to clean. Also, check for safety certification seals. Features such as safety locks and emer-
2 gency switches are added benefits.

If you have done your homework, you will know the special features you want before you begin shopping. For example, in a range cooktop, you can choose solid discs of cast iron, glass ceramic tops, induction cooktops, or halogen cooktops.

Warranties and Service Contracts

A **warranty** is a guarantee of a product's soundness and of the manufacturer's responsibility to replace or repair defective parts. There are two types of written warranties—full and limited. A product carrying a full warranty will be repaired or replaced at no expense to the purchaser if it is defective. A limited warranty offers less protection. When repair is necessary, such a warranty may cover only certain parts. It may also require that the buyer return the appliance to the store for service or send it—at his or

CASE STUDY

Consumer NEWS CLIP

Simple Solutions: How to Buy Furniture

by Liz Seymour
Home, November 1994

Savvy consumers, used to doing their homework and weighing the merits of brand names, can find shopping for furniture a frustrating experience. Unlike other big purchases, you can't plug furniture in and listen to it, or take it for a test drive, or even look it up in a consumer guide before you buy. But choosing a good-quality piece of furniture is essentially an exercise in common sense. "There are two basic principles you should always remember," advises J. Mitchel Scott, vice president of consumer marketing for Thomasville Furniture. "Buy the best quality you can afford, and buy furniture you really love." If you keep in mind a few simple signs of quality, you can count on years of service from the furniture you choose.

Open and Shut Case

- *Draw out the drawers.* The quickest way to check out a piece of wood furniture is to look at one of its drawers. Pull the drawer all the way out—wiggle it gently loose of its stops if necessary—and inspect the way the front is fastened to the sides. If you see interlocking wedge-shaped fingers, the manufacturer used dovetail joints, the strongest type of construction.
- *Be finicky about finishes.* To really see the quality of a finish, inspect the drawer in natural light. A good finish will be clear and rich, and shouldn't obscure the grain of the wood. The best type of finishes will be labeled "hand-rubbed," which means that they are built up of layers that were sanded between applications.
- *Do inspect doors.* Hinges should be sturdy, which allows for easy opening and closing, and the catches should fasten securely and firmly. In addition, the tops and bottoms of matched doors should be aligned. Again, check for the quality of the hardware and how firmly it is attached.
- *Take a good look at a table.* When purchasing a dining table, be sure that the wood grain matches on both the tabletop seams and on the leaves. Extension guides should open and close easily, and the leaves themselves should join properly with locks that keep the seams firmly together. The legs should be double-bolted to the table.
- *Check out chair construction.* Sit in the dining chair. It should not sway. Then turn the chair upside down to look for quality construction features. When examining typical wood-frame dining chairs with drop-in upholstered seats, be sure seat frames are triple-doweled—secured with three interlocking pegs—to the legs for maximum support at all areas of stress. Check, too, that corner blocks are joined by gluing interlocking finger joints to the corners of the seat base and then adding a steel screw for additional support.

Decisions, Decisions

1. What are some important principles in buying furniture?
2. What items should you inspect when purchasing wood furniture?

FLASHBACK FLASHFORWARD

Scottish inventor John Logie Baird projected the first television images in 1926. The television age boomed in 1948. By 1990, there were 193 million television sets in the United States.

1 Research Have students research a particular large appliance or electronic item. Use the findings to develop a chart in class that compares the various aspects of warranties.

2 Interesting Note New appliances require 10 to 20 percent less electricity than older models.

3 Extension Have students bring instruction booklets from home. Did they have trouble finding the booklets? What might happen if the booklets couldn't be found?

her own expense—to a distant service center. The owner, might be responsible for all labor costs.

1 When considering warranties, check to see which parts are covered. Try to find out how much it would cost to repair parts that are excluded. Also, check to see how long the warranty lasts. If a manufacturer is willing to stand behind a product, it is probably well-made.

In addition to written warranties, there are implied warranties. These are created by state law rather than by company or store policy. The two most common are the warranty of merchantability and the warranty of fitness for a particular purpose. A warranty of merchantability is a promise that every product sold is in proper condition and does what it is intended to do. For example, a can opener must open cans. A warranty of fitness for a particular purpose, takes effect when the seller advises a consumer that a product can be used for a special purpose. A seller, for example, knowing a consumer must sew through canvas, recommends a certain machine. If it cannot sew canvas, the dealer must take the appliance back and refund the customer's money.

Service contracts on appliances and electronic equipment take effect when a warranty ends, but there is a charge for them. Evaluate the suitability of a service contract based on your situation.

Energy Efficiency

When purchasing major appliances (refrigerators, freezers, dishwashers, washing machines, water heaters, and room air conditioners), look for the black and yellow energy rating labels. There are two kinds of these **EnergyGuides**, energy cost labels and efficiency rating labels.

An energy cost label compares the estimated annual operating cost to other
2 brands products.

An energy efficiency label assigns an appliance an efficiency rating. The higher the rating, the more efficient the energy usage.

Keeping Records

Once you select your appliance, keep all documents relating to the purchase. These include the sales receipt, the warranty, and any manuals or instruction booklets. Before using the appliance, study the operating instructions carefully. Failure to do so could result in injury and lead to costly repairs. Damage caused by misuse is always excluded
3 from warranty protection.

Keep records of any repairs. This information will be necessary to document a recurring problem and justify replacement.

How to Buy Sheets

Name brands don't matter with sheets. Generally, the higher the quality, the higher the price. The quality of sheets is determined by thread count, which is the number of threads per square inch. The average is 200; the higher the count, the finer and softer the sheet.

Quality also is determined by the percentage of cotton. A sheet made of 100 percent cotton is made of general grade cotton grown in the United States. It is softer and easier to clean than a sheet made of a cotton/polyester blend. Pima cotton is a better-quality cotton grown in Arizona. A sheet needs only 8 percent pima-grade fiber to be called pima. But a sheet that is 100 percent pima is called supima cotton. Sheets made of 100 percent imported cotton grown in Egypt are the finest quality available.

Before you buy any sheets that are heavily dyed, open the package and feel them. Some dyeing processes make the sheets rough.

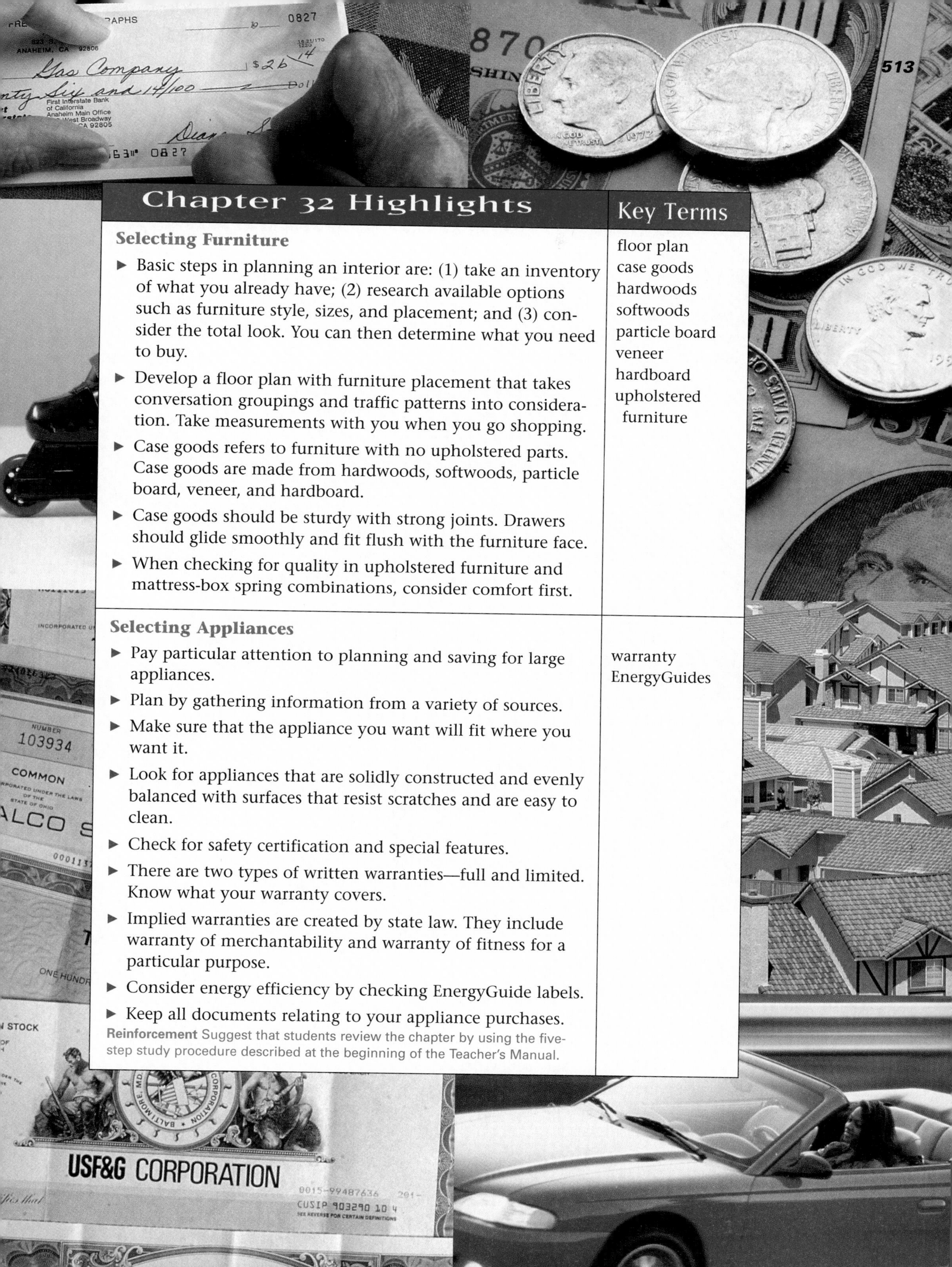

Chapter 32 Highlights

	Key Terms
Selecting Furniture ► Basic steps in planning an interior are: (1) take an inventory of what you already have; (2) research available options such as furniture style, sizes, and placement; and (3) consider the total look. You can then determine what you need to buy. ► Develop a floor plan with furniture placement that takes conversation groupings and traffic patterns into consideration. Take measurements with you when you go shopping. ► Case goods refers to furniture with no upholstered parts. Case goods are made from hardwoods, softwoods, particle board, veneer, and hardboard. ► Case goods should be sturdy with strong joints. Drawers should glide smoothly and fit flush with the furniture face. ► When checking for quality in upholstered furniture and mattress-box spring combinations, consider comfort first.	floor plan case goods hardwoods softwoods particle board veneer hardboard upholstered furniture
Selecting Appliances ► Pay particular attention to planning and saving for large appliances. ► Plan by gathering information from a variety of sources. ► Make sure that the appliance you want will fit where you want it. ► Look for appliances that are solidly constructed and evenly balanced with surfaces that resist scratches and are easy to clean. ► Check for safety certification and special features. ► There are two types of written warranties—full and limited. Know what your warranty covers. ► Implied warranties are created by state law. They include warranty of merchantability and warranty of fitness for a particular purpose. ► Consider energy efficiency by checking EnergyGuide labels. ► Keep all documents relating to your appliance purchases. **Reinforcement** Suggest that students review the chapter by using the five-step study procedure described at the beginning of the Teacher's Manual.	warranty EnergyGuides

CHAPTER 32 REVIEW

Refer students to the Reviewing Consumer Terms and Reviewing Facts and Ideas activities in the Student Activity Workbook.

Consumer Terms Collages will vary. See Glossary for definitions.

Reviewing Facts and Ideas See the Student Activity Workbook for answers.

Problem Solving and Decision Making
1 a Consider cost of washer and dryer; increase in utility bills; savings in Laundromat costs.
b Gas and electric appliances, portable models, and used machines.
2 He could stretch his budget by considering multi-purpose furniture, and shopping at garage sales.

Consumers Around the World
Math 1 Couch $311.35 ($479 – 167.65 = $311.35). Chair $161.85 ($249 – $87.15 = $161.85)

Communications
2 Students' styles and tastes will vary. Eclectic refers to the mixing of styles.

Social Studies
3 Students should share their findings with the class.

Technology
4 Students should share their findings with the class.

Reviewing Consumer Terms

Create a collage, using photos from magazines and your own drawings, that depicts each of the terms below. Define each term below its illustration.

case goods	softwoods
EnergyGuides	upholstered furniture
floor plan	veneer
hardboard	warranty
hardwoods	
particle board	

Reviewing Facts and Ideas

1. What are three major steps in planning an interior?
2. How would you go about inspecting a three-drawer chest for quality?
3. What are some common features you should investigate when buying a sofa and a bed?
4. Identify four indications of quality that you should look for when selecting a new appliance.
5. How does an implied warranty differ from a written warranty?
6. What kind of information do EnergyGuide labels provide?
7. What records should be kept on appliance purchases and why?

Problem Solving and Decision Making

1. Inez and Raul are tired of taking their laundry to the local Laundromat each week. They believe, however, that they are saving money on water and energy by not doing their washing at home. It costs them about $3.25 each week to use the Laundromat. They don't know whether they should buy a washer and/or a dryer.
   a. What questions should they answer first?
   b. What alternatives do they have?
2. Chuck is moving into his own apartment for the first time. He already has some cookware, flatware, a bed with sheets, a blanket, and an old sofa from his grandmother. He only has $350 to spend on furnishings. How could he stretch his limited funds to provide for additional needs and still make his living space pleasing?

Building Academic Skills

Consumers Around the World

Math

1. Lee has found a couch and arm chair for his home, and they are on sale. The original prices are $479 for the couch and $249 for the chair. If both are marked down 35 percent, what is the sale price?

Communications

2. Many popular styles of furniture originated in other countries. Prepare a presentation on one or more of these furniture styles. Include pictures of rooms that illustrate a particular style. What feelings do these rooms convey? What does the term "eclectic" mean?

Social Studies

3. Research how furnishing styles have changed over the last 100

years. List the different fashion periods and key aspects of the period. Summarize your findings in a 500-word report.

Technology

4. Research the role technology has played in making appliances more energy efficient and environmentally friendly. Present your findings in an oral report to the class.

 Beyond the Classroom

Consumer Project

With two or three other students, select a household appliance to research in consumer magazines and local stores. Obtain the following information and report back to the class.

- **a.** What brands and models are available?
- **b.** What special features does each offer?
- **c.** How do the prices differ?
- **d.** What warranties are provided?
- **e.** What are the energy requirements of each model?
- **f.** Which appliance would you recommend buying?

 Cooperative Learning

Family Economics

Break into assigned family groups. Discuss the following problem.

The refrigerator has stopped working. The only surprise is that it lasted as long as it did. In the interim, your family has had a chance to plan and save for a new one. What features will you look for, and how much will you spend? Rank the features you want in order from most to least important and approximate what this list will mean in terms of price. Then decide how you are going to pay for the appliance. (Note: Stores in your area have models ranging in price from $500 for small, minimally equipped appliances to $1,200 for large side-by-side refrigerator-freezers to $4,000 for built-in sub zero models.) Compare your answers with those of other family groups.

Debate the Issue

When young people are setting up a home or apartment for the first time, funds are usually limited. Some people choose to buy just a few quality pieces, and over time, add to them. Others prefer to buy more furniture of a lesser quality and replace it with pieces as needed.

You and your classmates will break into two groups and research this topic. Each group will gather evidence to support one side or the other. You are to prepare the argument for your side of the problem. Then the two groups will meet in a classroom debate.

 Rechecking Your Attitude

Before going on to the next unit, go back to the Attitude Inventory at the beginning of this one. Answer the questions a second time. Then compare the two sets of responses. On how many statements have your attitudes changed? Can you account for these shifts in your opinions? What do you know now that you did not know then?

Consumer Project Students should share their findings with the class.

Family Economics Families with teens may be attracted to ice makers and dispensers. Two-income families may want a lot of freezer storage for convenience foods. Some could be concerned with dependability if the appliance holds perishable medications. All families should look for energy efficiency. Most features will increase the cost. As a result, some families may have to make do with a smaller refrigerator and/or fewer features. One or two families may buy a reconditioned appliance.

Debate the Issue Break the class into two teams. Assign each team one side of the issue. Encourage students to work together as a team to develop their argument. Ask each team to select a member to make an opening statement that supports their side of the issue. Have students take turns debating as the debate moves from one team to another.

Rechecking Your Attitude Answers will depend on students' perspectives.

UNIT 10 LAB
You and Your Community

STEP A Students should select housing that would meet the needs and the budget of the imaginary relatives described in the assignment.
STEP B Students should arrange and carry out interviews with real estate agents. They should discuss the topics listed in the step and take careful, well-organized notes.
STEP C Students should create accurate charts of the housing and leasing options they discussed with the agent.
STEP D Students' answers should be accurate and based on their interview notes and comparison charts.
STEP E Students' reports should reflect a clear understanding of the advantages and disadvantages of leasing and buying housing. The reports should also explain the need to give up certain psychological or economic advantages in order to gain other equally important advantages.

Refer students to the Unit 10 Lab in the Student Activity Workbook.

Choosing a Place to Live

Unit 10 focuses on one of the most important decisions a person makes—selecting housing. This lab will allow you to study the housing selection process more closely. In this lab, you will also select a personal computer.

TOOLS

1. Newspapers
2. Government pamphlets

PROCEDURES

STEP A Imagine that your aunt, uncle, and two cousins (ages 7 and 12) have sold their home in another state and are planning to move to your area. They have asked your family to help them find housing. They plan to lease a house or condominium for a year or so until they become more familiar with the area and can confidently select a home to purchase. They are not completely adverse to buying a house or condominium immediately if one that meets their needs and budget is available. They need three bedrooms, two bathrooms, and a family room or large living room. Because they sold their previous home for a substantial profit, they can make a down payment of $20,000, and they can afford a monthly rent or home loan payment of $700.

You have agreed to do most of the research on housing for your relatives. Begin by looking in the newspaper for advertisements of new and old homes and condominiums for lease or purchase. As you study the ads, remember that location and space are two of the primary considerations in selecting housing. Make a list of five possible leases and five prospective purchases, keeping in mind the fact that your relatives will probably place a high priority on the quality of schools in the areas you pick. Be sure to consider the homes' proximity to public transportation, shopping districts, and major roadways.

STEP B Contact a real estate agent, explain your assignment, and arrange to interview him or her either on the phone or in person at the agent's convenience. During the interview, take careful notes and be sure to cover the following topics:

1. The area's current housing trends.
2. The locations that would best suit your relatives' needs.
3. The agent's opinion of the suitability of the ten houses and condominiums you selected in Step A.
4. The agent's opinion of the currently available fixed- and variable-rate mortgage loans.
5. The average leasing fee for the area.
6. The state laws governing leasing or purchasing residential property.

Ask the agent to assist you in selecting three houses or condominiums your relatives could lease and three they might purchase. These six selections

may include those you made in Step A, but they may also be entirely different. For each of the three home purchasing options, ask the agent to help you determine what the monthly payment would be if your relatives obtained a 30-year loan at both the current average fixed rate and the average adjustable rate. (Thus, you will have two payment figures for each house.)

STEP C Make a chart for each of the six houses or condominiums from Step B. Include each one's features, disadvantages, and either the monthly lease payment or the estimated monthly payment for a fixed-rate and for an adjustable-rate mortgage loan.

LAB REPORT

STEP D Using your charts and the notes from your conversations with the real estate agent, answer the following questions:

1. If your relatives made a $20,000 down payment on a house, how much money would they have to borrow to meet the current asking price?
   a. If your relatives borrowed the money at the average fixed rate, what would be their monthly mortgage payment?
   b. What would the payment be if they borrowed at the adjustable rate?
   c. What is the difference between a and b above? What accounts for this difference?
2. What is the difference between the average mortgage payment on the three houses that are for sale and the average rent on the three houses that are for lease?

STEP E Write a two-page report explaining the choice between leasing and buying a house in terms of economic and psychological trade-offs and benefits.

UNIT 11

Unit Contents

Using Professional Services

Attitude Inventory

Before you begin Chapter 33, take stock of your attitudes by completing the following inventory. Read each statement and decide how you feel about it—agree, disagree, or undecided. Record your feelings on a sheet of notepaper or use the form in the workbook.

1. Only people over 21 who have children are likely to use professional services.
2. Routine physical examinations are important even after a person is no longer subject to childhood diseases.
3. Dental examinations are not important after a person reaches adulthood.
4. Consulting the Yellow Pages is probably the best way to select a doctor.
5. Medical care should be financed from savings on an emergency-by-emergency basis rather than included as a regular budget item.
6. It shows poor taste to ask in advance what a medical service will cost.
7. The medical field has not been affected by inflation.
8. Medicare has solved all the medical problems of older citizens.
9. The local bar association knows best when it comes to matching specific attorneys with specific clients.
10. There are not enough medical doctors in the United States.
11. Legal firms in large cities usually charge more for services than legal firms in small towns.
12. Poor people can secure legal advice from well-qualified professionals free of charge.
13. Legal insurance is nothing more than a scheme to get money from the consumers and give nothing in return.

Unit Goal The main goal of this unit is to give students guidelines for selecting competent professional help, with special emphasis on new, low-cost alternatives. Chapters included in this unit are (1) Medical and Dental Services and (2) Legal Services.

Lesson Plan See the Teacher's Manual for an overview of the unit and some suggestions for introducing it. If you assign the Attitude Inventory, be sure to tell students to keep their answers for later use.

CHAPTER 33

Medical and Dental Services

Learning Objectives

When you have finished studying this chapter, you should be able to:

1. Explain the importance of preventive medicine.
2. Outline a plan for choosing a doctor and a dentist.
3. Explain options consumers have for handling health care costs.

Consumer Terms

preventive medicine **prenatal care**

Real-World Journal

Interview a parent, guardian, or other adult about the types of medical and dental services he or she uses. Ask: How did you choose the professional? Was a recommendation important? What percentage of your income is spent on these professional services? Summarize your findings in your journal.

Lesson Plan See the Teacher's Manual for the Chapter 33 lesson plan.

Vocabulary The Chapter 33 lesson plan includes suggested vocabulary activities for the terms listed.

1 Student Motivator Because it is difficult for young people, who are generally in good health, to appreciate the importance of good health, the value of preventive medicine must be stressed. Ask students if they know of young individuals who have had serious physical problems. Could anything have been done to avoid the problem? What sort of financial drain did the problem create?

2 Extension You may wish to discuss AIDS and other STDs (sexually transmitted diseases) such as syphilis, gonorrhea, and chlamydia as threats to be avoided.

3 Extension Ask students to name other abusive substances. (LSD, amphetamines, and the nonprescription use of drugs like Valium may be mentioned.)

4 Reinforcement Have students rate themselves on a scale of 1 to 10, with 10 being very good, as to their performance in each of the categories in Figure 33–1. Compare scores in class. Ask students what they can do to improve.

5 Discussion Starter Ask students to comment on the role of stress in their lives. Ask for suggestions on how to cope with stress.

PRACTICING PREVENTIVE MEDICINE

The best kind of medicine is **preventive medicine**—procedures used in a program to prevent illness. If you take measures to keep your health and prevent disease, chances are good that you will spend less for doctor bills, medicine, and hospital services. Even more important, you will have the joy of living that
1 comes with good health.

Keep Healthy

The first step in a wise use of medical resources is to do all you can to stay healthy. Seeing a doctor regularly helps
2 to catch problems before they become
3 larger health concerns. The guidelines in
4 Figure 33–1 summarize tips for staying
5 healthy.

Prevent Dental Problems

Following a few guidelines will help you maintain good dental health. Keeping your teeth and gums healthy will cut down on the time, money, and discomfort involved in extensive dental work.

- *Have a dental examination at least twice a year.* These examinations will give early attention to gum disease,

Figure 33-1 Preventing Illnesses and Accidents

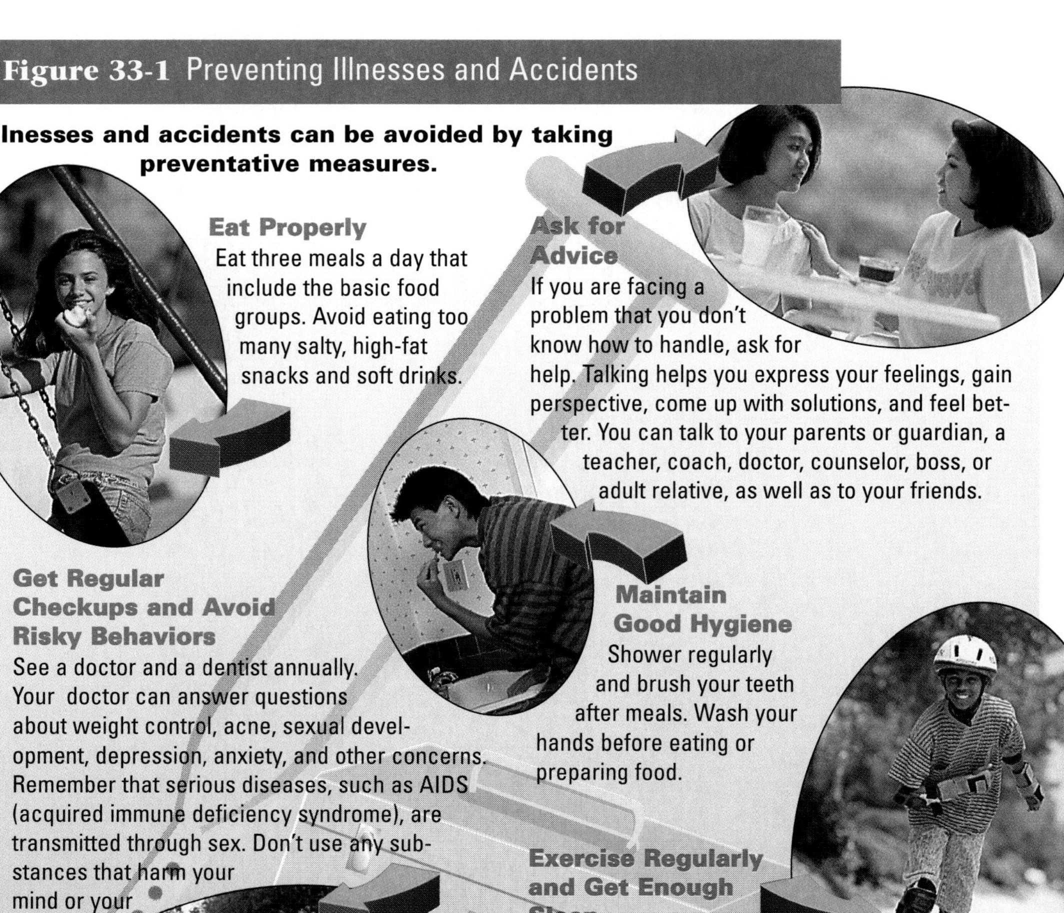

Illnesses and accidents can be avoided by taking preventative measures.
Eat Properly
Eat three meals a day that include the basic food groups. Avoid eating too many salty, high-fat snacks and soft drinks.
Ask for Advice
If you are facing a problem that you don't know how to handle, ask for help. Talking helps you express your feelings, gain perspective, come up with solutions, and feel better. You can talk to your parents or guardian, a teacher, coach, doctor, counselor, boss, or adult relative, as well as to your friends.
Get Regular Checkups and Avoid Risky Behaviors
See a doctor and a dentist annually. Your doctor can answer questions about weight control, acne, sexual development, depression, anxiety, and other concerns. Remember that serious diseases, such as AIDS (acquired immune deficiency syndrome), are transmitted through sex. Don't use any substances that harm your mind or your body.
Maintain Good Hygiene
Shower regularly and brush your teeth after meals. Wash your hands before eating or preparing food.
Exercise Regularly and Get Enough Sleep
Exercise helps you relax and release stress. Try to exercise at least three times a week. Get plenty of fresh air. Make sure to get enough sleep – 8 to 10 hours – on school or work nights to be at your best.

1 small areas of decay, and the need for
2 other repair work and cleaning.

- *Clean your teeth thoroughly at least once a day.* Take as long as necessary to do a good job. Floss in addition to brushing to remove all *plaque* (a bacterial film on the teeth that causes decay) and particles of food trapped between the teeth.
- *Do not smoke or chew tobacco products.* Tobacco discolors teeth, irritates gums, and may contribute to throat
3 and mouth cancers.

Learn First Aid Techniques

You can minimize the damage done in accidents by learning proper first aid treatment. Learn which injuries constitute an emergency, which require a visit to the doctor, and which can be treated at home. Keep a first aid supply kit
4 handy and properly outfitted.

Courses in first aid are given at locations such as the YMCA. You may also find courses in mouth-to-mouth resuscitation, a technique for helping accident victims who are not breathing. If you plan to babysit young children, learn the
5 proper safety and first aid techniques.

Plan to Use Prenatal Care

When you are ready to start a family, learn about the prenatal care available in your area. **Prenatal care** is the medical care given to pregnant women during pregnancy. Proper prenatal care, involving regular visits to the doctor, helps ensure that the mother remains healthy
6 and that the baby is born in good health.

MEDICAL AND DENTAL CARE

There are times when even preventive medicine is not enough, however. Anyone can become ill or have an accident. At those times, the services of a health professional are clearly necessary. The medical professional you see will depend on the medical need you have.

Choosing a Doctor

Many times, there is an insurance plan where you go to school or where you work. The plan will specify the health maintenance organization (HMO), preferred provider plan (PPO), clinic, dentist, or doctor you are to consult if you want the services to be covered by insurance. Depending on how the insurance program is set up, you may be able to choose a doctor or you may have to choose from a list of doctors provided by the insurance plan.

Before you choose a doctor, you will want to do some investigation work. The telephone directory is one place to start. About all you can learn from this source, however, is which doctors are located in your part of town and what their telephone numbers and specialties are. Some consumer groups have tried to put together physician directories that would give the background and qualifications of doctors as well.

Another alternative is to ask friends, relatives, co-workers, and neighbors for recommendations. They can give you fairly reliable leads. If they have used the services of area physicians and found out something about their abilities firsthand.

If you are moving to a new location or if you must choose a new doctor from your insurance plan, your current doctor may be able to recommend a physician in your new neighborhood. Co-workers and neighbors in your new location may also have recommendations.

The local medical society and a hospital's physician referral service can also tell you about competent doctors. They will probably give you a list of names rather than recommending a certain individual, however. Sources of information about dentists are similar.

1 Discussion Starter Ask students if they regularly visit the dentist. Why or why not?

2 Discussion Starter Ask students to give a general description of their consumption of sweets. Do they chew sugarless gum rather than regular gum, for example? Do they think it is important to avoid sweets?

3 Student Motivator Provide students with average costs from local dentists for procedures such as filling cavities, X rays, extractions, and root canal work. Compare these costs and the associated pain with the costs and relatively minor inconvenience associated with brushing and flossing.

4 Critical Thinking Ask students what they can do to minimize injury to teeth during sports. (Dentists recommend wearing mouth guards.)

5 Extension Ask a student who has studied CPR, the Heimlich maneuver, or water life-saving techniques to describe or demonstrate them.

6 Research Ask students to research the value of prenatal and well-baby care to the health of babies and mothers. Discuss the medical procedures involved (testing blood and urine, taking ultrasound pictures, measuring blood pressure).

1 Discussion Starter Remind students that as consumers of a service, they are free to make judgements. If a doctor has the reputation of being "brilliant" yet he or she is abrupt, hurried, and uncommunicative with patients, would students choose to be a client? Why or why not?

Evaluating a New Doctor

Buying medical services has a lot in common with other consumer purchases. Think about the qualities you want in a doctor. When you have several recommendations, call each doctor's office to speak to the receptionist.

Explain that you are a prospective new patient and would like to ask a few short questions. Ask whether you are calling at a busy time. If so, be prepared to call back at a time the receptionist says is more convenient. Asking questions such as the following can help you narrow your choices:

1. What are the doctor's office hours? Make sure the days and times are generally convenient.
2. With what hospitals is the doctor affiliated? The doctor should be affiliated with at least one hospital that you feel provides good services.
3. In a group practice, do you have a choice of doctors when you make an appointment? You may prefer to see one doctor only.
4. What is the fee for a first-time examination? for a regular checkup? Remember that the highest fee does not necessarily mean the best service.

When you have narrowed your choice to one or two physicians, make an appointment for a checkup or consultation. Do not wait until you have a medical or dental emergency. Visit a physician for a pre-employment physical. Have a dentist check and clean your teeth.

The cost will be minimal, and you will have an opportunity to judge the professional's competence and personal manner for yourself. Then, if you are not satisfied, there will be plenty of time to check other recommendations. Evaluate the doctor's service after the examina-
1 tion by asking yourself these questions:

1. How long did I have to wait to get an appointment? Is this typical?
2. In the office, how long did I have to wait to be seen? Is this typical?
3. Was the office clean, well-lighted, and pleasant?
4. During my visit was the office staff pleasant and helpful?
5. Did I feel comfortable with the doctor? Was it easy to talk to him or her? Did the doctor answer all my questions? Did the doctor seem personally concerned with my well-being?
6. Was the examination unhurried? Did it seem thorough? Did I feel the doctor explained the medical procedures clearly?
7. How was the follow-up care? Was there a prompt response to my phone calls?

Caption Answer: Call early in the day and as early in the week as possible. Leave a telephone number. Ask when the doctor is likely to call back. Then stay near the phone for the call.

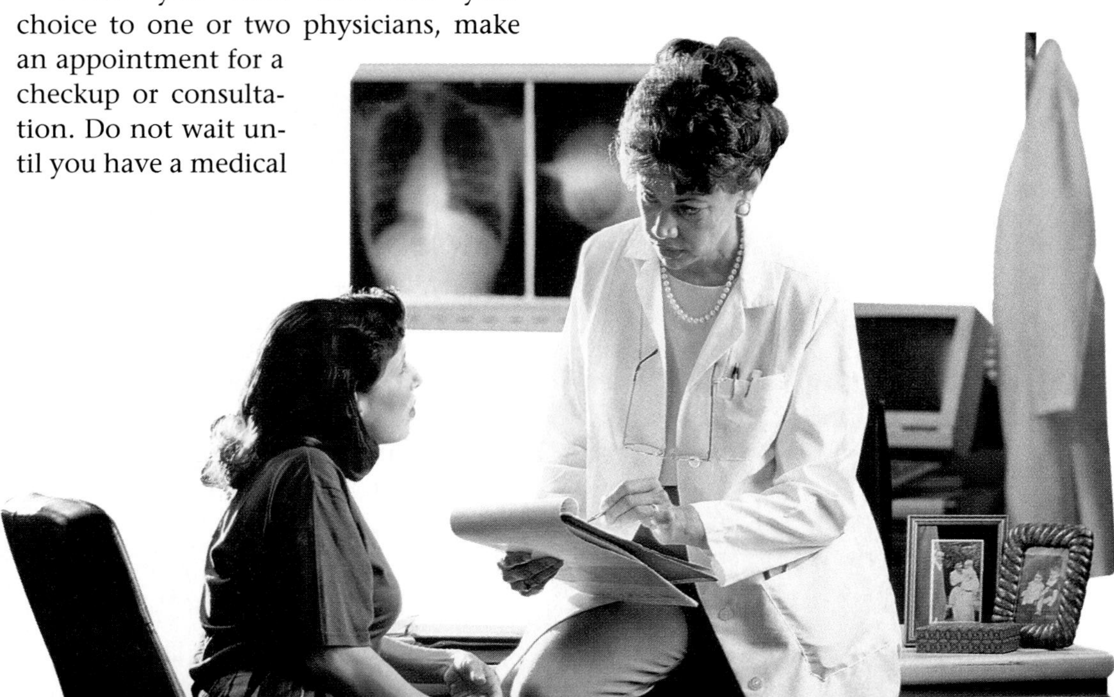

It is important to be able to talk to your doctor when you have health questions. ***How can you improve communications with your doctor?*** ▶

Emergency Care

Suppose you need emergency medical attention before you have had a chance to choose a new doctor. You can go to the emergency room of the nearest hospital.

Many cities also have minor emergency and family care clinics. These freestanding clinics offer medical services from early in the morning until late at night. Their offices are open every day of the year, including holidays. If you suddenly become ill, these clinics offer a low-cost alternative to the hospital emergency room. (Charges are generally half what they would be in a hospital emergency room.) Patients may also select a personal or family physician from the clinic staff and visit that practi-
1 tioner for routine medical care.

1 Reinforcement Make sure students realize how much a trip to a hospital emergency room can cost. If possible, have a nurse or other person with emergency room experience talk to the class about his or her experiences. Ask about the costs for the services provided. Ask if people ever go to emergency rooms needlessly.

A Believer in Immunization

In 1977, the world saw its last case of smallpox, a disease that once wiped out thousands. The victim was Ali Maow Maalin, a cook in a Somali hospital.

Maalin was so ill he was sure he would die, but gradually he recovered his health. Doctors explained that smallpox was no longer a global threat as a result of the existence of the smallpox vaccine. Maalin, however, did not realize there were vaccines that could save people from other diseases as well.

Over the years, Maalin saw many children in his village and the surrounding area die of disease. Often more than half the children in a family died. The tragedy struck home for him when, in 1988, his little sister died of measles. By the time her family took her to a hospital, it was too late to save her.

It was there that Maalin found out about the vaccines that can protect children not only from measles but also from whooping cough, diphtheria, polio, tetanus, and tuberculosis. These diseases kill countless children in Third World countries every year.

Maalin became an avid advocate of vaccination. He volunteered for training in how to give shots and how to handle the vaccines. He has promised to devote his life to the eradication of measles.

One reason he feels so strongly about measles, of course, is because it is the disease that killed his sister. It is also a disease that people are very familiar with because it occurs so frequently and produces a rash. Maalin feels that if he can persuade parents to protect their children against such a visible disease, he can later persuade them to vaccinate their children against other diseases.

Brainstorm

What arguments would you make to suspicious parents to get them to immunize their children?

Case Study Answer: Savings in health care—it is cheaper to immunize than treat the disease; in many cases the protection of the child's life; healthy children lose less time from school; protects them from the spread of disease from those who are not immunized; some kinds of diseases—smallpox, for example—result in scarring which immunization and the prevention of the disease would stop.

Case Study Answers:
1 The patients might not choose a treatment that would save their lives or heal their conditions. Some patients might choose to die rather than take a certain drug. Some might accept the risk of playing in the championship game with a badly injured knee. Both choices seriously alter the traditional authority of the doctor.
2 Sample answers: Whenever I get even the slightest sniffle, my mother makes me stay home from school and drags me to the doctor. There's never anything wrong with me, so it's all just a waste of time. I guess I could change that by talking to the doctor and asking him to talk to my mother.

Caption Answer: Answers include the 11 points on page 524.

HEALTH CARE COSTS

Recent advances of medical science have been astonishing. Artificial hearts, liver transplants, genetically engineered insulin—these medical breakthroughs have all captured headlines. Such techniques give consumers hope of longer, healthier lives, or rather they could except for one factor—cost.

Medical care has become an important part of consumer budgets. Nationally, health care expenditures had reached a level in excess of $903 billion by the mid-1990s. Today a family may find that medical expenses account for almost 14 percent of its total budget, depending on income, location, and other conditions.

In one way or another, money seems to be the cause of most problems with our health care delivery system. Patients and communities claim they cannot afford to pay for the medical services and facilities they need. Hospitals and doctors claim they cannot make enough to support the facilities and practices they have.

Consumer Options

While high health care costs continue to be a reality, as a consumer you can take the following steps to control these costs:

1. Follow the principles of preventive medicine.
2. Purchase group medical and dental insurance, if possible, or join an HMO or a PPO.
3. Let your doctor know how much of the bill you must pay out of pocket.
4. Take advantage of medical services provided free to the public, such as immunizations and chest X rays.
5. Have diagnostic tests (like X rays) sent from doctor to doctor rather than retaking them.
6. Ask your doctor to write prescriptions for *generic,* rather than for brand-name medications.
7. Comparison shop among local pharmacies.
8. Get a second opinion from another doctor before agreeing to have *elective,* or nonemergency, surgery.
9. Avoid checking into a hospital on the weekend. You may have to pay several overnight charges before your weekday surgery.
10. Discuss all presurgical tests with your doctor to make sure they are necessary.
11. Get itemized bills from your doctor and the hospital, and go over them carefully for errors.

Medical costs can be controlled. ***What are two steps you can take to reduce your medical costs?*** ▼

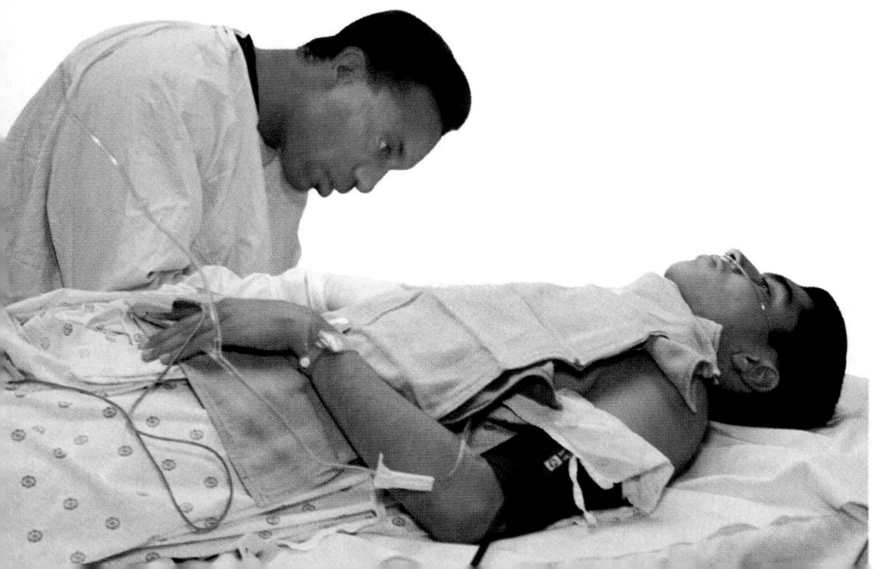

The Cost of Health

About 7 percent of the gross national product of both Japan and the United Kingdom is spent on health care. Switzerland, Norway, and Italy spend about 8 percent; Germany and Sweden, about 9 percent; Canada, about 10 percent; and the United States, more than 13 percent.

Randall Howard, M.D., Santa Barbara Medical Center

Dr. Randall Howard, 44, a family physician and a specialist in medical ethics, has a revolutionary message for anyone needing to see a doctor at any time for any reason: "The patient," he says, "must decide on the course of treatment for themselves."

Dr. Howard's message is the foundation for an entire area of study and practice known as medical ethics. It's a way of doing medicine that has emerged since the 1960s, when the breathing ventilator and a slew of powerful new drugs allowed doctors to keep people alive who otherwise would have died. Doctors, trained to do all they can to preserve life, embraced the new technology and few of them asked, "Why are we doing this?"

That question first struck Dr. Howard during his residency after USC Medical School. In 1981, after beginning a practice in Los Angeles, he took two years off to get a degree in medical ethics from the Episcopal Divinity School in Cambridge, Massachusetts. It was, at the time, one of the few institutions in the country that offered such a course of study.

Dr. Howard earned his master's and then returned to Santa Barbara and assumed the chairmanship of the medical ethics committee at Cottage Hospital, which he has been chairing ever since. In that role, Dr. Howard and a group of other doctors, nurses, lawyers, priests, and businesspeople consult and mediate a wide variety of medical situations.

"When you practice medicine," Dr. Howard explains, "you're trying to work with a person who has a concern and you're looking for an answer. We come up with a list, but not with one solution that is the best choice. You will never know what the best choice of treatment is until you talk to the patient."

Dr. Howard believes that the open, honest communication within a medical ethics framework should be present in every doctor-patient relationship. He insists that lack of communication about what the patient wants leads to the feeling many people have that they are not well cared for, which, in the extreme, leads to malpractice problems.

Dr. Howard suggests that patients insist on a doctor they really feel a personal connection with. "There's something about healing," Dr. Howard says, speaking to every doctor and patient alike, "that goes beyond technology."

Case Study Review

1. If medical schools train doctors to save lives and solve the problems caused by diseases and other disorders, why might it be diffcult for them to seek their patients' advice on the course of treatment?

2. Think about a medical situation where you did not feel well cared for. Describe the course of action that was taken and what bothered you about it. Then describe how you might have behaved to change that course of action.

FLASHBACK FLASHFORWARD

In 1945, the cost per capita for dentistry in the United States was $4.29. In 1989, dentists had a lot to smile about. The per capita cost had reached $117.24.

1 Discussion Starter Ask students their opinion of the changes that have taken place in health care. Which is fairer—widespread health insurance or doctors and hospitals charging according to who can pay? Which system is better for our economy?

2 Critical Thinking Ask students to make lists of services, such as car maintenance and hair styling. Have them compare the way they select these services with the way they should select a doctor. Are there different factors involved? Is price a major concern in all cases?

3 Vocabulary Ask students to define *indigent.* (People living in poverty.)

4 Research Assign groups of students to survey hospitals in your area to identify teaching hospitals. What is the nearest teaching hospital? What services does this hospital offer that other hospitals do not offer?

Doctors' Fees It is quite common for a physician or surgeon to have a set schedule of charges for services. If you find you cannot pay for some medical service that you need, talk over the matter with your doctor. Perhaps he or she
1 can reduce the charge or give you a
2 longer time in which to pay. Note also that you may sometimes get services at lower cost through special programs at medical and dental schools.

Always understand the doctor's or dentist's fees before he or she performs the service—whether or not you have health insurance. You have the right to know the costs involved. Remember that your insurance may not pay all costs, and you will be responsible for the uninsured amount.

Hospital Charges If you need hospital treatment, you will find that the cost of room and board alone can be very high. Your doctor knows rates at different institutions and can tell you these before you decide where you want to be admitted. Hospitals, based on the method of finance, are of three kinds.

- *Proprietary hospitals.* These are the most expensive, as they are run on a for-profit basis. They often offer excellent medical service, luxurious rooms, and superior food. Proprietaries, however, tend to emphasize less complicated treatment and may not like to take patients who have difficult medical problems requiring long-term care.
- *Voluntary hospitals.* Hospitals of this sort are run on a nonprofit basis by a religious or other voluntary organization. They may take on some charity patients. As a hospital group, they have the highest reputation. Room rates are lower than at proprietary hospitals.
- *Government hospitals.* These hospitals are run by the local, state, or federal government and give medical care to the indigent. They also take patients
3 who can (and do) pay for services. Some government hospitals take only certain kinds of cases, such as patients suffering from mental ill-
4 ness. Government hospitals usually offer few frills. However, many are well staffed, offer superior medical services, and have excellent reputations.

Medical Care Is a Service

Doctors, nurses, hospital medical staff, and other health care providers offer their services in exchange for a fee. As a consumer, you have the right to influence how you want to be treated.

- **When you make the appointment, find out specifically what the doctor charges for a first-time visit, a "short" examination, or an "extended" examination.**
- **Before you travel to your appointment, call the doctor's office to confirm that the doctor is running on time. If not, find out when to come.**
- **Write a list of questions or symptoms and include any medications you are taking. Refer to it before you leave the doctor's office to be sure you have covered everything.**
- **When you are asked to wait in an examining room, ask how long you can be expected to wait. Press the assistant for an exact time—5 minutes? 20 minutes?**
- **If the doctor recommends tests or other procedures, ask whether they are necessary and how much they will cost.**

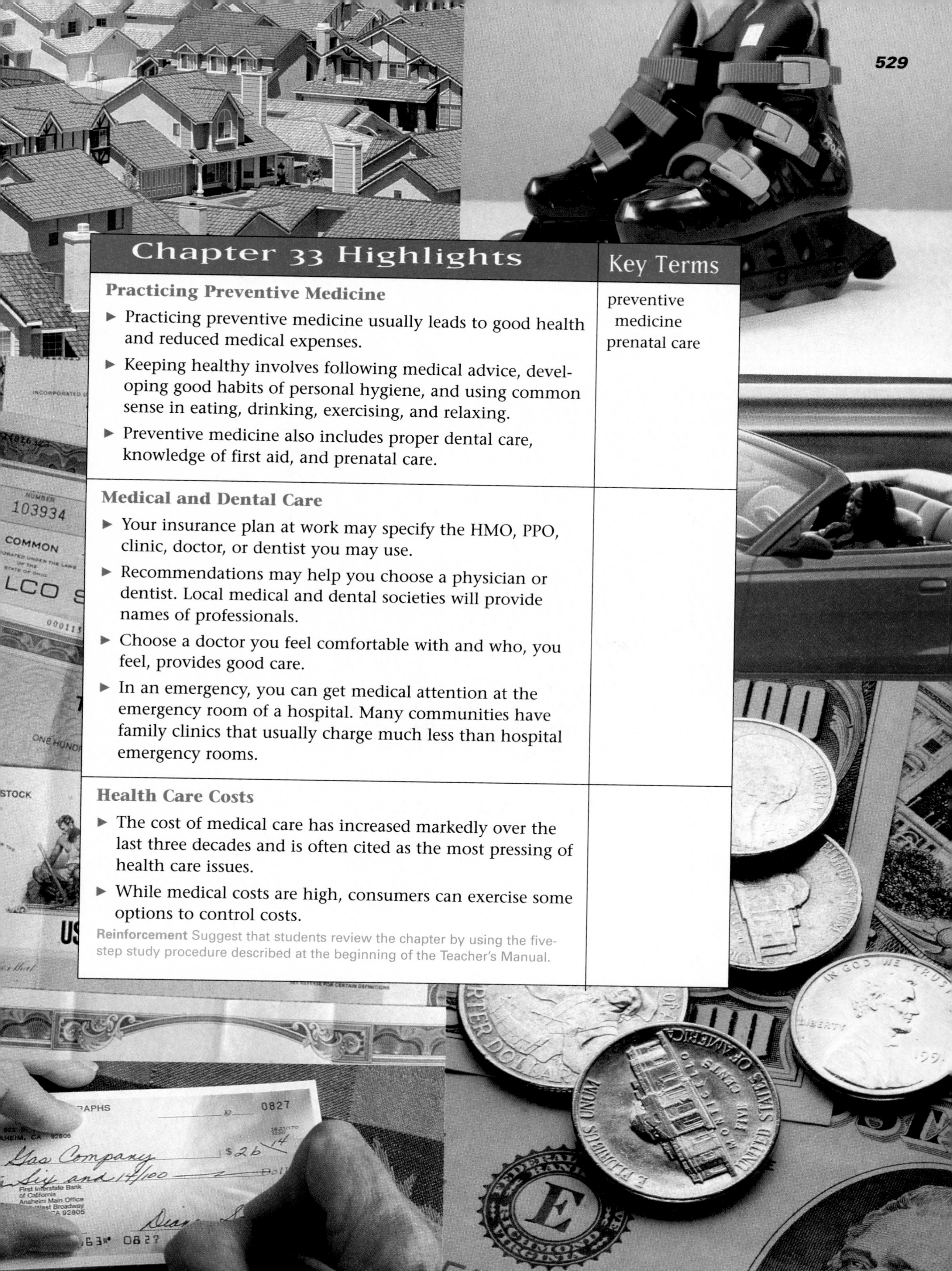

Chapter 33 Highlights

Key Terms

Practicing Preventive Medicine

- Practicing preventive medicine usually leads to good health and reduced medical expenses.
- Keeping healthy involves following medical advice, developing good habits of personal hygiene, and using common sense in eating, drinking, exercising, and relaxing.
- Preventive medicine also includes proper dental care, knowledge of first aid, and prenatal care.

Key Terms: preventive medicine; prenatal care

Medical and Dental Care

- Your insurance plan at work may specify the HMO, PPO, clinic, doctor, or dentist you may use.
- Recommendations may help you choose a physician or dentist. Local medical and dental societies will provide names of professionals.
- Choose a doctor you feel comfortable with and who, you feel, provides good care.
- In an emergency, you can get medical attention at the emergency room of a hospital. Many communities have family clinics that usually charge much less than hospital emergency rooms.

Health Care Costs

- The cost of medical care has increased markedly over the last three decades and is often cited as the most pressing of health care issues.
- While medical costs are high, consumers can exercise some options to control costs.

Reinforcement Suggest that students review the chapter by using the five-step study procedure described at the beginning of the Teacher's Manual.

CHAPTER 33 REVIEW

Refer students to the Reviewing Consumer Terms and Reviewing Facts and Ideas activities in the Student Activity Workbook.

Reviewing Consumer Terms Papers will vary. See the Glossary for answers.

Reviewing Facts and Ideas See the Student Activity Workbook for answers.

Problem Solving and Decision Making **1** Maureen might see her doctor for a checkup and about techniques to relieve stress. **2** Randi can ask her family doctor for another referral if she feels the specialist is too busy to give her the attention she needs.

Consumers Around the World **Math 1** Hospitals, $27.360 billion; other institutions, $7.200 billion; physicians, $10.800 billion; other professionals, $4.320 billion; drugs, $10.800 billion; capital improvements, $2.880 billion; other, $8.640 billion.

Communications **2** Student reports should compare the two systems; should stress issues important to teenagers: eating disorders; acne; sports injuries; sexual issues; drug, alcohol, and tobacco abuse.

Reviewing Consumer Terms

Use the following terms in a paragraph to demonstrate that you know their meaning.

prenatal care
preventive medicine

Reviewing Facts and Ideas

1. List at least five important ways to practice preventive medicine.
2. Tell how you would go about choosing a physician after moving to a different city or town.
3. What steps can consumers take to reduce health care costs?

Problem Solving and Decision Making

1. During her first year in high school, Maureen Shaw felt worried, anxious, and overworked. She caught colds often and missed several days of school. What course of action can you recommend to Maureen? Why?
2. Randi Mitchell's family doctor referred her to an eye specialist for an examination. Randi could not get an appointment for four weeks. Once she arrived for her appointment, Randi had to wait $1\frac{1}{2}$ hours to see the doctor briefly. What can Randi do about this situation?

Building Academic Skills

Consumers Around the World

Math

1. Suppose $72 billion spent in total health care dollars was spent as follows in a recent year. Compute the dollar amount in each category. Draw a circle graph as an illustration.

   Hospitals, 38 percent
   Other institutions, 10 percent
   Physicians, 15 percent
   Other professionals, 6 percent
   Drugs, 15 percent
   Capital improvements, 4 percent
   Other, 12 percent

Communications

2. Research Canada's health care system. In a 500-word report, compare and contrast Canada's health care system with the United State's system.

Human Relations

3. The field of medicine offers a broad range of jobs at all educational levels. Using the *Occupational Outlook Handbook* and other library resources, research at least five jobs in the medical field. Note the description, education, skills required, and average pay for each job. What sorts of interests and aptitudes would a person need for these jobs? Write a 750-word report summarizing your findings.

Science

4. Medicine is a field that is greatly affected by developments in science. Choose a topic that interests you. (For example, AIDS, antibiotics, cancer, flu, organ transplants, polio, or X rays). Study the history and current situation of scientific research on the topic. How are medical costs and consumer choices affected by this scientific activity? Write a report of at least 750 words.

Beyond the Classroom

Consumer Project

A patient can cut hospital costs by agreeing to share a room with others. For hospitals in your area, find out the daily cost of room and board for a private room, a semiprivate room (two patients), and rooms shared by four patients.

Cooperative Learning

Family Economics

Break into assigned family groups. Discuss the following problem.

Recently, all the family wage earners changed jobs and the family is currently without health insurance. Buying health insurance will cost the family $300 a month. Should the family prepare a new budget to cover the cost of insurance at some sacrifice to everyone? Or should the family take a chance that no one will get sick? Compare your answers with other family groups.

Debate the Issue

Many people feel that the government should take more control of the health care system. Others feel that there should be less government involvement.

You and your classmates will break into two groups and research this topic. Each group will gather evidence to support one side or the other. You are to prepare the argument for your side of the problem. Then the two groups will meet in a classroom debate.

Human Relations
3 Students should list jobs at all levels. Some possibilities are registered nurse, medical assistant, medical technician.

Science
4 Student reports should cover the history of their topic in depth and show an awareness of the impact of science.

Consumer Project
Answers will depend on the area.

Family Economics
The family should try to obtain insurance and revise its budget to find money for the insurance.

Debate the Issue
Break the class into two teams. Assign each team one side of the issue. Encourage students to work together as a team to develop their argument. Ask each team to select a member to make an opening statement that supports the team's side of the issue. Have students take turns debating as the debate moves from one team to the other.

SUPREME COURT
REPORTER

CHAPTER 34

Legal Services

Learning Objectives

When you have finished studying this chapter, you should be able to:

1. Outline a plan for choosing an attorney.
2. Explain the role ethics play in the field of law.
3. List ways of reducing the legal costs.

Consumer Terms

contract
legal counsel
bar association
Martindale-Hubbell Law Directory
contingency basis
pro bono work

Real-World Journal

As a consumer, you may find you need to hire a lawyer. In your journal come up with a list of reasons why you might need to hire a lawyer.

Lesson Plan See the Teacher's Manual for the Chapter 34 lesson plan.

Vocabulary The Chapter 34 lesson plan includes suggested vocabulary activities for the terms listed.

1 Discussion Starter Ask students if they would like to share any personal experiences they have had with attorneys. How did they choose the attorney? How much did the attorney charge? Were they satisfied with his or her services?

Caption Answer: The local bar association; friends, relatives, and co-workers; and/or your employer may be able to help you find a competent attorney. The *Martindale-Hubbell Law Directory,* in the library, gives names, ratings, and specializations of local lawyers.

Gather information and think through your plans before you meet with the attorney. Set a limit on charges and ask the law office to notify you when you are near your limit. Inspect your bills carefully.

LEGAL SERVICES

Each day, you enter into dozens of legally binding agreements. When you ride the bus, buy an item on credit, or write a check, you are committing yourself to pay in return for some item or service. You are making a **contract,** a legally binding agreement, and you are doing so without an attorney.

There are times, however, when the services of an attorney are needed. You would not try to cure yourself of a serious illness. Neither should you try to work yourself out of a serious legal problem. Money spent for good **legal counsel** (advice from a lawyer) is no more wasted than is money paid to a doctor for treatment of an illness. You may need a lawyer if you are:

- Buying or selling a house or a piece of property.
- Getting ready to sign a particularly complicated contract.
- Suing another party or being sued yourself.
- Filing for bankruptcy.
- Getting separated or divorced.
- Starting a partnership or corporation.
- Writing a will.
- Facing criminal charges that could bring heavy fines or imprisonment.

Choosing an Attorney

1 The local **bar association,** an organization of lawyers, will give you the names of competent attorneys who take cases like yours. You cannot expect the association to recommend one attorney rather than another, however. For that kind of recommendation, you must talk to individuals.

Ask friends, relatives, and other people you know who may already have had dealings with local law firms and may be in a position to judge. Discuss the problem with bank officers and other businesspeople whose opinions you trust.

Finally, if you work, consider your company itself. Does it retain an attorney to handle its legal affairs? Are there any attorneys on staff? Even if these people cannot help you themselves, they will probably know someone who can.

If all of these sources fail you, then there are still the professional directories. Nationally the best-known of these is the ***Martindale-Hubbell Law Directory.*** This directory gives biographical data, educational background, and areas of specialization for all the attorneys it lists. It also rates attorneys. Many public libraries have copies of the directory,

You may need to obtain legal services at some point. ***What steps can you take to find a lawyer?*** ▼

and lawyers from your community are no doubt listed.

Financing Legal Services

Once you have made your selection, you can arrange a short meeting with an attorney to talk about your legal needs. Usually, the fee for such a consultation is nominal. The meeting gives both of you a chance to decide whether you wish to pursue a relationship as attorney and client (one who employs the services of an attorney).

Fees Always talk about fees with an attorney before engaging his or her services. A lawyer may tell you that the 1 charge for representing you in a property transaction is, say, a flat fee plus 0.5 percent of the amount of money borrowed. The fee for drawing up a simple will may be $75 or some other fixed amount.

1 Math Application Have students assume they are borrowing $43,000 to buy a house. The attorney charges a flat fee of $150 plus 0.5 percent of the amount borrowed. How much will they owe the attorney? ($43,000 × .005 = $215; $215 + $150= $365.)

People MAKING a DIFFERENCE

Making House Calls

In many ways, the homeless are invisible to most of us. We see them day after day on the streets, but we do not think about how they live or where they get medical care. Dr. Pedro Jose Greer does, however.

Greer, the son of Cuban parents, became aware of the health problems of the homeless when he treated a homeless patient with tuberculosis in 1984. Today, tuberculosis is treatable if it is caught early enough. Greer's patient, however, was in the last stages of the disease.

Greer was appalled that someone in a major city could die of a treatable disease for lack of health care. So he devised a plan to bring health care to the homeless.

He set up his first clinic in a homeless shelter with only a folding table and his skills. He got as many doctors to volunteer their time there as he could. From its humble beginnings, Greer's clinic has grown. Now known as the Camillus Health Concern, the center treats approximately 4,500 patients a year.

Greer always wanted to help the poor. He planned to practice medicine in South America or Africa after he finished medical school in the Dominican Republic. Although he was probably surprised to find himself in Florida, he is glad to serve the people of his hometown. "I've had the privilege of treating the sick and the honor of working with the poor," he says.

Greer works at the clinic three days each week. He puts in more time in his own private practice. Yet somehow, he finds time to walk the streets of Miami, making sure that the homeless know that medical care is available to them.

Brainstorm

Why might the homeless not seek medical care?

Case Study Answer: No money; not aware that low-cost or free care is available; might not be able to get to the healthcare center; might fear hospitalization or being put into some kind of institution; parents might fear being separated from their children.

1 Reinforcement Emphasize that rates do vary. Students should shop for legal services just as they would for other services.

2 Critical Thinking Ask students why the questioning of abilities and honesty of lawyers by their peers is especially effective in creating doubts among consumers. (The fact that claims originate from lawyers themselves gives the claims greater credibility.)

News Clip Answers:
1 Legal plans cover most legal needs and help to limit legal costs.
2 Students answers will vary. Some may feel such a plan is not worth their money, especially if they don't foresee a need in the future for a lawyer. Others, who may need legal services, may find such a program to be advantageous.

Teachers and Students

Belgium has an average of 8 students per teacher in private and public secondary schools. The United States averages 16 students per teacher; New Zealand, 18; and Turkey, 23.

Hourly rates are sometimes quoted and depend on the attorney and the nature of the case. Also, law firms in urban areas almost always charge more
1 than those in smaller towns.

A special arrangement is sometimes made in cases where large awards of damages are possible. The attorney may take your case on a **contingency basis,** meaning that the amount of the fee will depend on the outcome of the case. If you win, the fee is a large percentage of the damages—often 30 to 40 percent of the total amount. If you lose, the fee is zero (although the attorney will probably want court costs and out-of-pocket expenses).

The contingency fee arrangement is sometimes criticized because it gives the attorney so much of the money meant for the client. Attorneys claim the large fee is justified by the large risk they take of getting no fee at all. The contingency arrangement is illegal in many countries, however.

Finally, some attorneys advertise their fees. In local newspapers, it is not unusual to see ads like "Uncontested divorces only $195" or "Bankruptcy cases, $150." Note that fees are quoted for only the simplest legal procedures. The cases usually involve little more than filling out and filing forms.

ISSUES IN THE FIELD OF LAW

When public officials who are lawyers are convicted of illegal acts, consumers may wonder if they can trust lawyers in general. Consumers may also wonder if they will be able to afford a lawyer when they need one.

Ethics and Competence

Legal ethics require that an attorney be loyal to his or her clients and use a high degree of knowledge and skill in protecting their rights and interests. The lawyer must not reveal facts supplied in confidence by clients unless the law demands such action.

In addition, the American Bar Association now requires law schools to teach courses in ethics. In this and other respects, today's law school graduates are better qualified, a fact that should
2 relieve consumer fears of incompetence.

Handling Legal Fees

High fees have put legal services beyond the reach of many consumers. As a result, a large percentage of the population has never consulted a lawyer.

Free Advice from Professionals
Don't let high legal costs scare you from consulting with a legal professional. Lawyers, accountants, financial planners, and other professionals typically offer a free initial consultation of half an hour or more.

CASE STUDY

Consumer NEWS CLIP

Cutting the Costs of a Lawyer's Time

by Lauren Goldstein
Worth, June 1994

John Betley had a choice. To handle the sale of his house, he could hire a lawyer of his own for $750, or he could get one from his company's $12-a-month legal-aid program. Betley, director of financial operations for the DMB&B advertising agency, didn't hesitate. "I signed on to the company's legal plan—I knew I would use the service in the coming year." Prepaid legal-service plans—the health-maintenance organizations of the legal profession—are becoming more popular as a menu item in cafeteria-style employee-benefit plans. One hundred forty-four dollars covered the legal fees for the sale of Betley's house, as well as any other legal needs he had during the year. Betley was so pleased with the service that he will enroll again next year.

Legal-service plans generally cost from $8 to $16 a month and, depending on the type of plan offered, cover most basic legal needs. Of course, there are some things that aren't covered. Don't bother trying to mount a hostile takeover of your company with legal services financed by the plan, for example. Not surprisingly, you can't use the plan to sue your employer. What most of these prepaid legal plans provide are unlimited telephone consultation; the review of commonly used legal documents such as real-estate sales contracts; the drafting of wills, adoptions, and

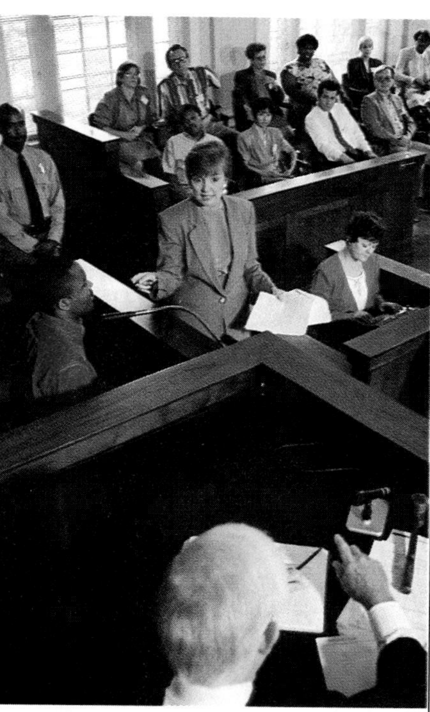

deeds; and discounts on the going fees for outside counsel in some litigation. In divorce, some plans cover an employee's legal costs only, not a spouse's. The plans do vary from firm to firm: Employers may exclude coverage for certain legal costs, such as defending driving under the influence of alcohol or drugs.

The plans are endorsed by the American Bar Association and approved by the American Association of Retired Persons. Wayne Moore, director of legal counsel at the AARP, says, "It's like having a lawyer at your beck and call for a $100 retainer. People can call before they cut down a neighbor's tree or sign a contract they may regret. They know the consequences of their actions up front."

For complicated legal problems that require face-to-face visits, a comprehensive plan may help to limit costs. But don't expect top-notch service to be covered in full. The lawyers who take part in the plans are trading access to a population group and guaranteed payment for fees that are generally less than their going rate. Stephen Leaman, senior vice president of Hyatt Legal Plans, says his organization does, however, secure discounts for employees who require specialized, high-cost counsel—as in the case of settling estates large enough to be subject to federal taxation. "For what may be a $3,000 legal fee," Leaman says, "a 25 percent discount is not to be overlooked."

Decisions, Decisions

1. What is the main benefit of a legal benefit plan?
2. Would you sign up for a legal-aid program if the company you worked for offered it? Why or why not?

FLASHBACK FLASHFORWARD

In 1980, there were just over 542,000 licensed attorneys in the United States. In 1994, there were more than 865,000 attorneys. At that rate of growth, there will be more than 1 million lawyers licensed in the United States by 2000.

1 Discussion Starter Have students assume that the law school at a local university offers a legal clinic with low-cost services. Would the students be willing to use such a clinic? Why or why not?

2 Interesting Note One oil company offers legal services to people who have a credit card. The fee is $6.75 a month.

3 Research Have students do research to identify the options available to people in their community. Are there clinics? Does the bar association or some other group provide low-cost legal help?

4 Reinforcement Student Activity Workbook, Chapter 34 activities.

5 Discussion Starter Ask students their views on pro bono work. Do they feel pro bono work is a good way to address the legal needs of people unable to pay?

They feel they cannot afford to pay up to $200 or more an hour for legal services.

Nevertheless, there are some low-cost alternatives that can help reduce the costs of legal fees.

Low-Cost Alternatives To help the ones who need legal assistance but cannot afford to pay for it, in many communities there is the Legal Aid Society. In other places, there are similar organizations staffed or financed by local bar asso-
1 ciations, law schools, or community
2 action groups.

Poor people are not the only ones who find themselves without access to legal services, however. Middle-income consumers are also frequently in the same position but for different reasons. They have too much money to qualify for help from the Legal Aid Society. On the other hand, they have too little money to retain a law firm or private attorney.

Three recent developments have tried to bridge this legal services gap. These include legal clinics, increased supply of lawyers, and legal insurance.
3 (See Figure 34–1.)

In addition to these developments, members of the legal profession should be given credit for the volunteer services they perform in towns and cities throughout the country—and for their **pro bono work.** *Pro bono* means "for the good" (of the public) and refers to legal work done free for those who cannot afford to pay.

In one recent year 2,800 people, who qualified for help under federal poverty guidelines, received pro bono service in Illinois alone, according to the Peoria *Journal Star.* More than 4,300 attorneys were involved in these cases. These figures do not include Cook County—the Chicago area—where much pro bono work is done.

In addition, many lawyers, at one time or another, do pro bono work without reference to poverty guidelines. They simply accept some cases,
4 knowing they will never get paid for
5 the work done.

Figure 34–1 Reducing Legal Costs

Three developments are helping to reduce legal costs.

Legal Clinics. In many cities, groups of lawyers have opened legal clinics, offices where routine legal services are available at reduced rates. Clinic lawyers can afford to charge less because they hire law students and paralegals to do much of the clinic's simpler work. (Paralegals are nonlawyers who are specially trained to handle routine legal problems and research.) These workers are paid on a much lower scale than the attorneys who supervise them.

Legal Insurance. Prepaid legal services programs are becoming more common. By paying a small premium each month, the consumer can be assured of having legal services when they are needed.

Increased Supply. There are now more than 700,000 lawyers in the United States, three times as many as there were a few decades ago. Increased competition among this larger number of attorneys should bring down the cost of legal services.

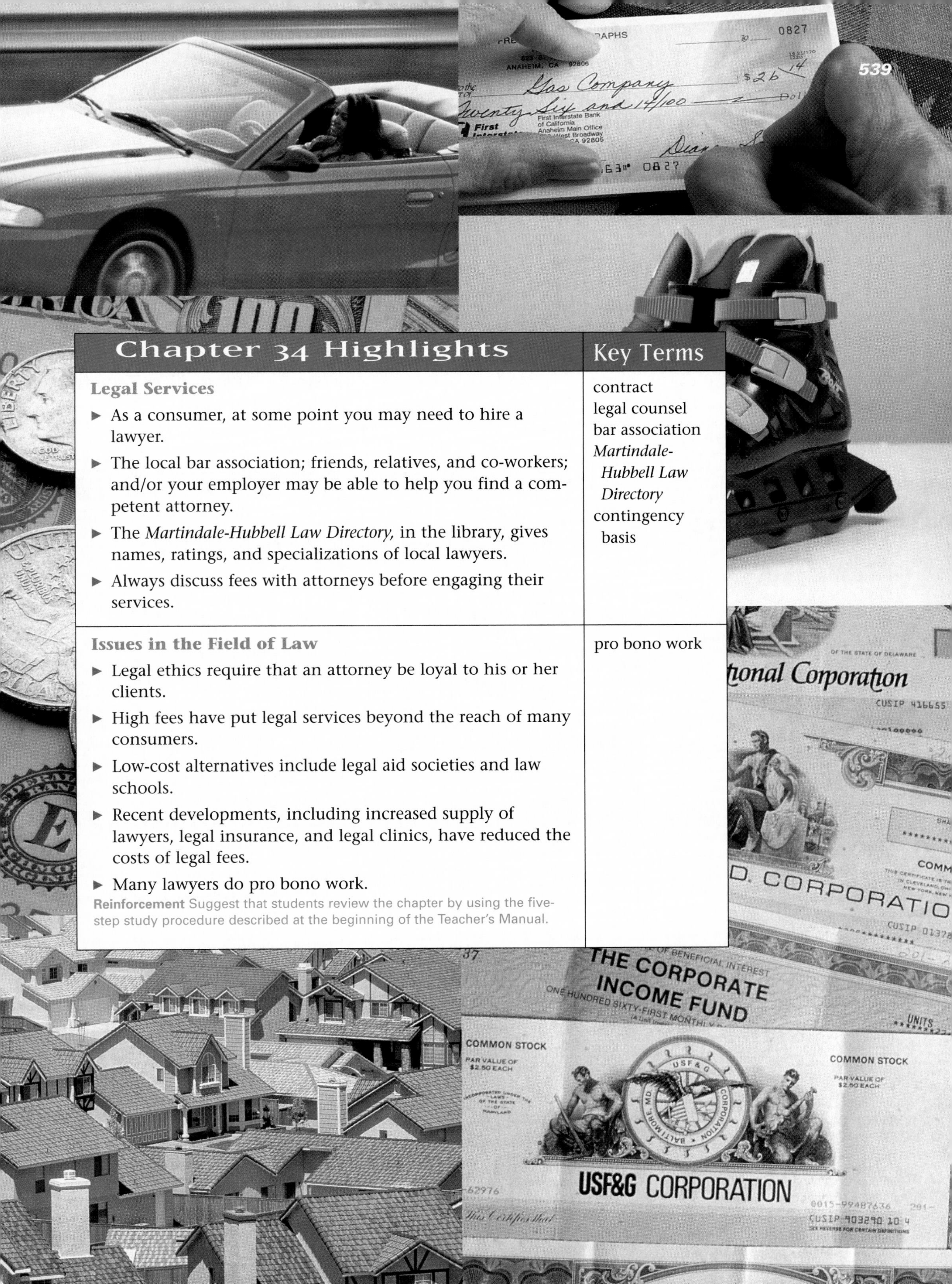

Chapter 34 Highlights

Highlights	Key Terms
Legal Services ▸ As a consumer, at some point you may need to hire a lawyer. ▸ The local bar association; friends, relatives, and co-workers; and/or your employer may be able to help you find a competent attorney. ▸ The *Martindale-Hubbell Law Directory,* in the library, gives names, ratings, and specializations of local lawyers. ▸ Always discuss fees with attorneys before engaging their services.	contract legal counsel bar association *Martindale-Hubbell Law Directory* contingency basis
Issues in the Field of Law ▸ Legal ethics require that an attorney be loyal to his or her clients. ▸ High fees have put legal services beyond the reach of many consumers. ▸ Low-cost alternatives include legal aid societies and law schools. ▸ Recent developments, including increased supply of lawyers, legal insurance, and legal clinics, have reduced the costs of legal fees. ▸ Many lawyers do pro bono work. **Reinforcement** Suggest that students review the chapter by using the five-step study procedure described at the beginning of the Teacher's Manual.	pro bono work

CHAPTER 34 REVIEW

Refer students to the Reviewing Consumer Terms and Reviewing Facts and Ideas activities in the Student Activity Workbook.

Reviewing Consumer Terms Papers will vary. See the Glossary for answers.

Reviewing Facts and Ideas See the Student Activity Workbook for answers.

Problem Solving and Decision Making
1 Philip should read the contract carefully. He might research standard book illustration contracts in the library. Then he should meet briefly with a lawyer to go over the contract before he signs it.
2 Students may decide they have better uses for their money. Others may feel legal insurance is a worthwhile investment.

Consumers Around the World
Communications
1 Students should share their information with the class. You may prefer to do this as a class project.

Human Relations
2 Students should list jobs at all levels. Some possibilities include paralegal, legal secretary, lawyer.

Reviewing Consumer Terms

Use the following terms in a paragraph about the legal profession.

bar association
contingency basis
contract
legal counsel
Martindale-Hubbell Law Directory
pro bono work

Reviewing Facts and Ideas

1. If you needed a lawyer, how would you go about choosing one?
2. What do legal ethics require of attorneys?
3. Why do many consumers fail to seek out legal counsel when they have legal problems?
4. What can people do to reduce the high costs of legal services?

Problem Solving and Decision Making

1. Philip Claudio has been asked to illustrate a book of children's poetry for a certain amount of money. The publisher's lawyer has asked Philip to sign what he calls a "standard" contract. What advice do you have for Philip?
2. If you worked full-time, would you be willing to pay a legal insurance premium of $50 a year? Suppose that this payment would give you the right to routine legal services and a discount against regular fees for more complicated legal matters. Tell why you would or would not want to enroll in such a plan.

Building Academic Skills

Consumers Around the World

Communications

1. Look up the Legal Aid Society or similar organization in your area. Call or visit and ask how the group decides whether or not to take on prospective clients. Bring your findings to class.

Human Relations

2. The field of law offers a broad range of jobs at all educational levels. Using the *Occupational Outlook Handbook* and other library resources, research at least five jobs in the law field. Note the description, education, skills required, and average pay for each job. What sorts of interests and aptitudes would a person need for these jobs? Write a 750-word report summarizing your findings.

Social Studies

3. Compare and contrast the legal system in the United States with the legal system in another country. Outline five similarities and five differences. Present your findings to the class.

Beyond the Classroom

Consumer Project

Some attorneys specialize, although they do not often hold themselves out to

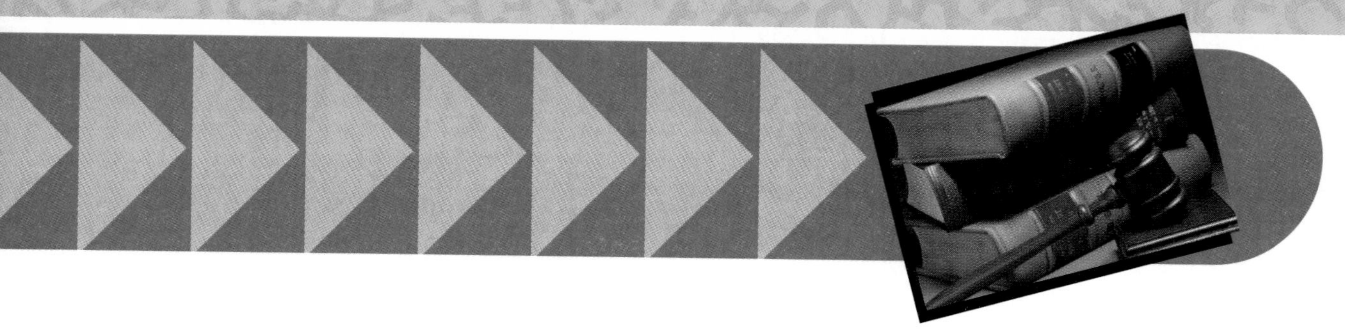

the public as specialists. Talk this idea over with family, teachers, and at least one attorney. Find out four areas in which attorneys concentrate their practices. Share this information with your class.

Cooperative Learning

Family Economics

Break into assigned family groups. Discuss the following problem.

You have paid a carpenter upfront $1,000 to build an entertainment center and cabinets for your living room. Halfway through the job, the carpenter realizes that the job is taking twice as long as he expected, so he walks out on the job without finishing his work. You have decided to hire a lawyer to rectify this problem. How will you decide where to find a lawyer? What steps will you take to reduce your legal costs?

Debate the Issue

People injured by the actions or negligence of others may sue in civil court for money compensation. Juries may make money awards in any amount they deem necessary to compensate for pain and suffering or expenses.

Some critics feel that jury awards are too high. They say that juries feel it is acceptable to grant huge awards when insurance companies foot the bill; therefore, a legal limit should be placed on award amounts. Others feel that the court is the only recourse most victims have to seek just compensation. They argue that regulating jury awards would benefit the wealthy at the expense of the poorer victim.

You and your classmates will break into two groups and research this topic. Each group will gather evidence to support one side or the other. You are to prepare the argument for your side of the problem. Then the two groups will meet in a classroom debate.

Rechecking Your Attitude

Before going on to the next unit, go back to the Attitude Inventory at the beginning of this one. Answer the questions a second time. Then compare the two sets of responses. On how many statements have your attitudes changed? Can you account for these shifts in your opinions? What do you know now that you did not know then?

Social Studies
3 Have students present their reports to the class. You may wish to create a bulletin board display that depicts the different systems used throughout the world.

Consumer Project
Students may discover that attorneys specialize in tax law, labor law, landlord-tenant relations, and other areas.

Family Economics
Families should follow the steps outlined in the chapter on finding a lawyer. Families with lesser incomes may try the low-cost alternatives suggested in the chapter.

Debate the Issue
Break the class into two teams. Assign each team one side of the issue. Encourage students to work together as a team to develop their argument. Ask each team to select a member to make an opening statement that supports the team's side of the issue. Have students take turns debating as the debate moves from one team to the other.

UNIT 11 LAB

You and Your Community

STEPS A and **C** Students should prepare lists of interview questions that are clearly written, easily comprehended, and appropriate for the persons to whom they will be addressed. All the topics listed in Steps A and C should be addressed.
STEPS B and **D** Students should arrange and carry out their interviews. Students should take careful, well-organized notes on each interview.
STEP E Students' answers should be accurate and based on their interview notes.
STEP F Students' discussions of the effects of medical costs on medical care availability should reflect their understanding of the impact that rising costs have on patients' and insurance companies' ability to pay for services. Students should also indicate their awareness of the restrictions that the costs of medical care and insurance place on doctors' ability to provide services.

Refer students to the Unit 11 Lab in the Student Workbook.

Researching Consumer Issues and the Medical Profession

Unit 11 discusses the consumer issues that have an impact on the medical, dental, and legal professions. In this lab, you will learn how the cost of medical care influences doctors, hospitals, and patients.

TOOLS

1. News magazines and newspapers
2. Consumer magazines
3. Literature from hospitals and health maintenance and preferred provider organizations
4. Literature from medical and dental schools

PROCEDURES

STEP A Write a list of questions about health care and the medical and dental professions that you can ask during an interview with a doctor, dentist, or nurse-practitioner. Your interview questions should cover the following topics:

1. The professional's advice as to the best way to find a doctor, dentist, or other health-care professional.
2. The professional's opinion of the effect that health maintenance and preferred provider organizations have had on his or her profession.
3. The influence of Medicare or Medicaid on the professional's practice or fee structure.
4. The professional's process for determining fees for services.
5. The availability to the professional of the newest advances in treatments.
6. The effect that malpractice suits throughout the country have on the professional's own practice.

STEP B Talk with family and friends about this lab assignment. Ask for their help in identifying health-care professionals who would be willing to be interviewed about their experiences and opinions. You will need to interview three health-care professionals. Family and friends may be your best means of finding a doctor willing to give you time for an interview. In addition, make a concerted effort to speak with a dentist (or assistant or office manager) and with a nurse-practitioner. When your interview subjects have agreed to talk with you, arrange a convenient time to meet with each one either on the phone or in person. Take careful written notes.

STEP C Prepare a list of questions that you can ask a member of the

business or administrative department of a local hospital. The questions should focus on how health-care advancements and costs affect the services the hospital provides and the fees charged to patients. Include the following topics in your questions:

1. The type of hospital.
2. The effect of health maintenance and preferred provider organizations on the hospital's administrative structure and fee schedules.
3. The impact of Medicare, Medicaid, and other non-HMO insurance on the hospital's operation.
4. The hospital's efforts to cut and control costs.
5. The hospital's average occupancy rate.
6. The kinds and availability of advanced treatments at the hospital.
7. The daily cost of room and board for a private room, a semiprivate room, a room shared by four patients, and an intensive or cardiac care unit room. Ask how the room costs to the patient vary depending on the type of insurance the patient has.

STEP D Contact the administrative or business department of a local hospital, explain the purpose of your assignment, and ask to interview one of the department employees. Arrange an interview either by phone or in person. Take careful notes during the interview.

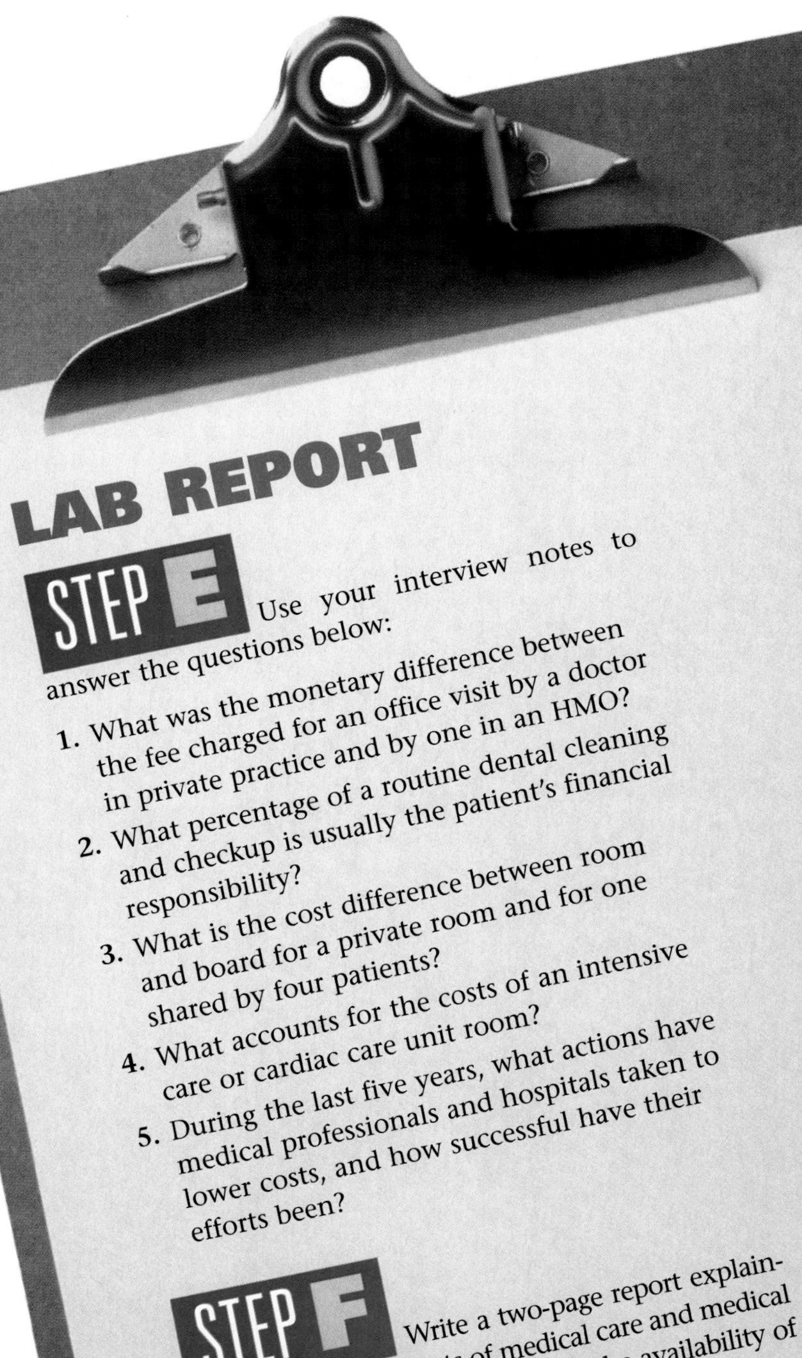

LAB REPORT
STEP E Use your interview notes to answer the questions below:
1. What was the monetary difference between the fee charged for an office visit by a doctor in private practice and by one in an HMO?
2. What percentage of a routine dental cleaning and checkup is usually the patient's financial responsibility?
3. What is the cost difference between room and board for a private room and for one shared by four patients?
4. What accounts for the costs of an intensive care or cardiac care unit room?
5. During the last five years, what actions have medical professionals and hospitals taken to lower costs, and how successful have their efforts been?
STEP F Write a two-page report explaining how the rising costs of medical care and medical insurance have had an impact on the availability of medical care.

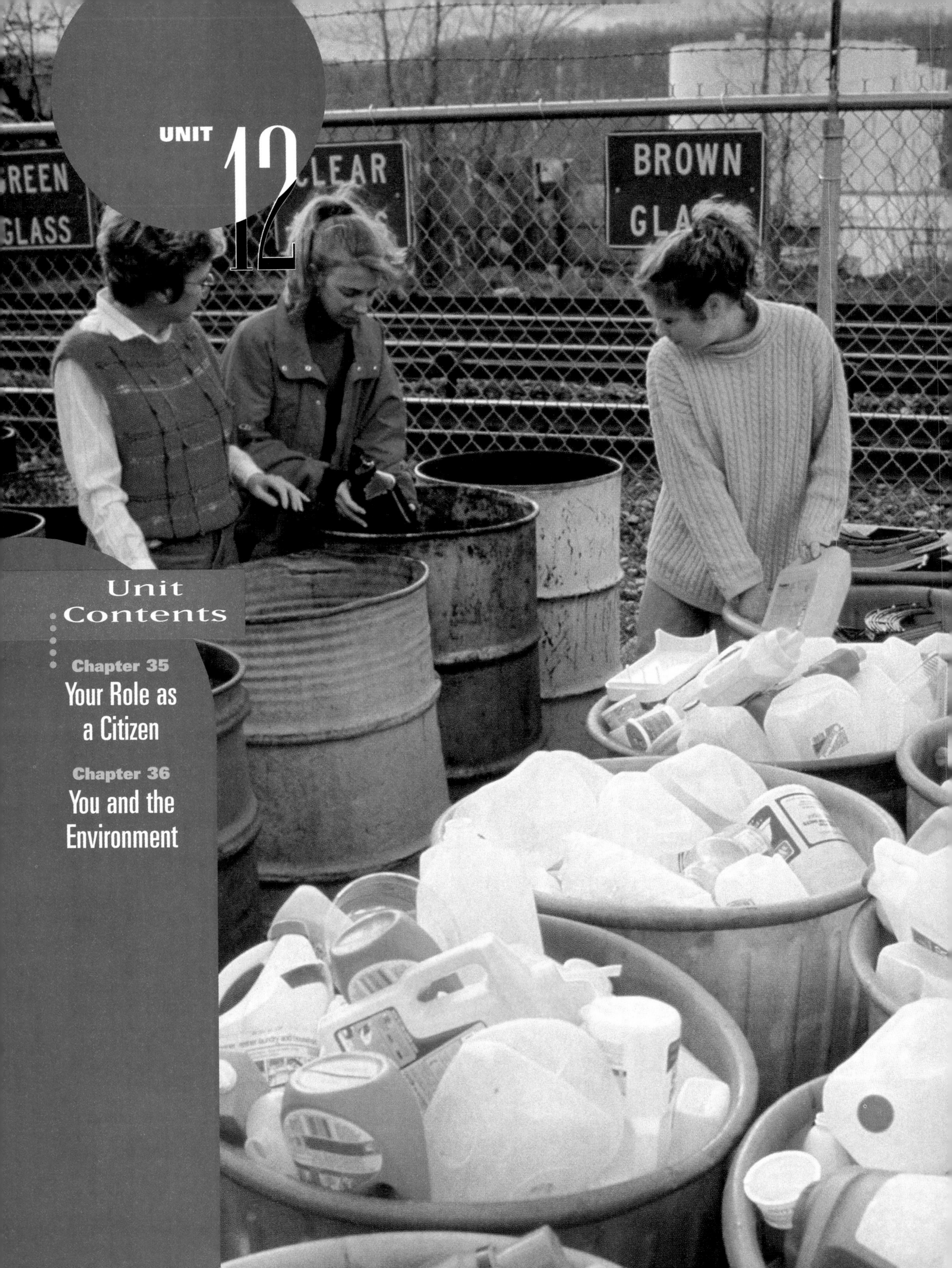

UNIT 12

Unit Contents

Social Responsibility

Attitude Inventory

Before you begin Chapter 35, take stock of your attitudes by completing the following inventory. Read each statement and decide how you feel about it—agree, disagree, or undecided. Record your feelings on a sheet of notepaper or use the form in the workbook.

1. Shoplifting is a consumer problem, not just a problem for store owners.
2. Character traits of a good citizen are as good an indicator of success in life as a high IQ.
3. Recycling not only conserves resources, it reduces pollution and often saves money.
4. A simple way to help reduce pollution at home is to use gas lawnmowers.
5. Just as kinder and gentler types of personalities are being defined, the numbers of people with these characteristics are increasing.
6. People are born with characteristics of a good citizen; these characteristics cannot be taught.
7. Many ecological problems relate to the production and use of energy.
8. Conservation of natural resources is a recent concern.
9. Volunteers are not needed as much today because government resources provide needed services.
10. Vandalism is often the beginning of crime in neighborhoods.
11. Leadership can occur behind the scenes.
12. Taxpayers give up personal purchases for public services that benefit the community.
13. Many groups have been formed to protect the environment—there is little individuals can do.
14. Conflicting societal goals make some actions to preserve the environment controversial.
15. It is important to compare several sources of information and look at the entire picture when trying to preserve the environment.
16. Heating and cooling a home uses about half of your energy resources.

Unit Goal The main goal of this unit is to point out the importance of citizenship and individual responsibility in dealing with social problems. Chapters included in this unit are (1) Your Role as Citizen and (2) You and the Environment.

Lesson Plan See the Teacher's Manual for an overview of the unit and some suggestions for introducing it. If you assign the Attitude Inventory, be sure to tell students to keep their answers for later use.

RECYCLE
Think Globally
Act Locally

CHAPTER 35

Your Role as a Citizen

Learning Objectives

When you have finished studying this chapter, you should be able to:

1. List the characteristics of good citizens, and discuss the benefits of good citizenship.
2. Describe how to be a good citizen at home and at school.
3. List the areas of concern to a good citizen of the community.
4. Summarize the social and ethical responsibilities of consumers and producers.
5. Explain how citizens can take an active role in the community.

Consumer Terms

citizen
naturalization
volunteer
vandalism
ethics
leadership

Real-World Journal

Write a paragraph in your journal on the importance of volunteering in your community. Check the library or your telephone directory for a listing of community services in your area. Choose one or two programs that might interest you. Write another paragraph in your journal on why these organizations appeal to you.

Lesson Plan See the Teacher's Manual for the Chapter 35 lesson plan.

Vocabulary The Chapter 35 lesson plan includes suggested vocabulary activities for the terms listed.

1 Student Motivator Have students share ways in which they, their family, or friends have demonstrated active citizenship in the past.

2 Research Have students find out the process for becoming a citizen. Discuss the procedures in class.

3 Discussion Starter Show students pictures or develop a bulletin board of people who could be considered good citizens (locally and nationally). Discuss their characteristics and contributions.

4 Research Have student groups research newspaper accounts to find recent accounts of good citizenship. Write letters of appreciation.

5 Extension Send for materials on citizenship from a group such as the Josephson Institute of Ethics, 4640 Admiralty Way, Suite 1001, Marina Del Rey, CA 90292. They sponsor Character Counts conferences. Discuss good citizenship characteristics that we share as Americans.

WHAT IS A CITIZEN?

By definition, being a **citizen** means giving allegiance to a country in return for protection by it. One can become a citizen by birth (just being born in a country) or being **naturalized** (the process that foreign-born people must go through). However, just being born in a specific country, or simply taking classes and
1 swearing an oath doesn't make a person a
2 good citizen.

Good citizenship is an active process. A citizen must feel connected to others in his or her community and contribute
3 to their well-being.

The Big Picture

You're not just a member of your neighborhood, state, or country. You also share common needs and goals with people around the world.

As a member of the community, a citizen of a country, and a member of the global community, you have certain rights and responsibilities. As the Declaration of Independence states, you have the right to "life, liberty, and the pursuit of happiness." However, you also have the responsibility
4 to respect the same rights of others.

Characteristics of a Good Citizen

What are the characteristics of a good citizen? To be a good citizen, one must care about other people and demonstrate his or her actions by:

- Respecting others.
- Showing compassion.
- Acting responsibly.
- Practicing self-discipline.
- Demonstrating loyalty.
- Living honestly.

Don't expect your positive actions to always be noticed or rewarded. What matters most is that you strive to make
5 things better.

Community Benefits

When informed and involved citizens work together with committed leaders, the entire community benefits (see Figure 35–1).

In one community, involved citizens worked with school officials to establish a second-chance high school. Mixing chronic truants, welfare mothers, and adult education, the school achieved remarkable results. Seventy percent of the graduates have gone on to college, and another 20 percent have found employment. For their accomplishments, the project won an award for community cooperation from the Ford Foundation and its Innovations in American Government Program.

The second-chance high school is an example of how a community can work together to improve the lives of everyone.

Individual Benefits

Having a positive social outlook and being a good citizen can bring personal rewards. Sometimes, these traits can be more important than having a high IQ.

Bell Laboratories surveyed the characteristics of their most valued and productive workers in various-sized teams. The lab found the best workers had a friendly disposition that helped them establish a communication network. When these valued employees submitted a request for help in solving a problem or developing an idea, they received answers from co-workers immediately.

What personal qualities do you look for in a working partner? ▶

Caption Answer: Some qualities to look for in a working partner include respect, honesty, open-mindedness, and a sense of humor.

Figure 35–1 Volunteering

Volunteers can increase community pride, help others, and improve the economy.

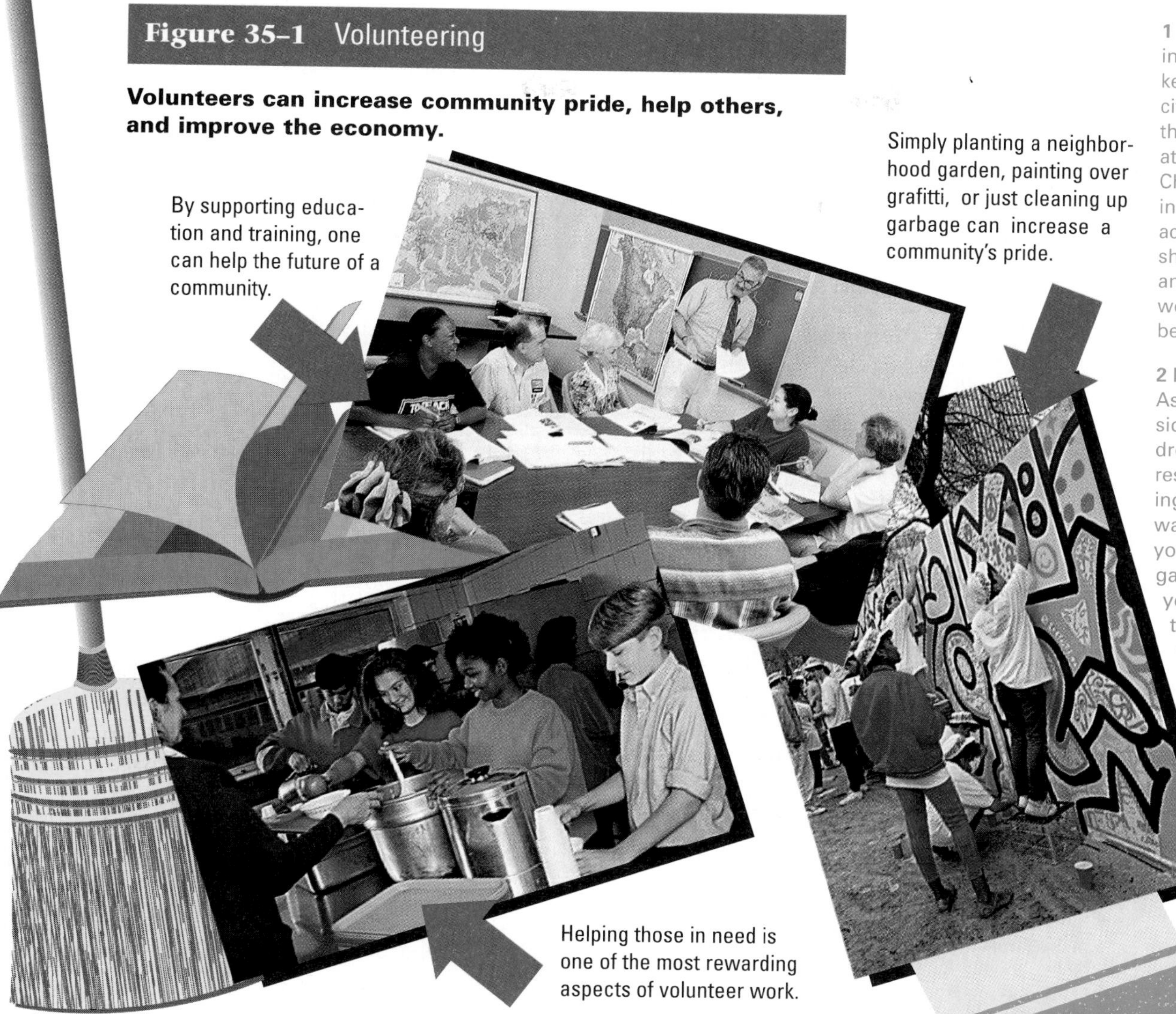

By supporting education and training, one can help the future of a community.

Simply planting a neighborhood garden, painting over grafitti, or just cleaning up garbage can increase a community's pride.

Helping those in need is one of the most rewarding aspects of volunteer work.

In contrast, workers who had poorer social skills sometimes went days or weeks without replies.

This study demonstrates the benefit of being friendly and communicative. If you help out others, others will be more likely to help you out.

BEING A RESPONSIBLE CITIZEN

How do you become a good citizen? Good citizenship starts at home and at school.

The Citizen at Home

Respect the feelings and property of family members. Even if you don't always agree, it's important to cooperate when it comes to making one's home a pleasant, safe, and supportive place. You can help by recognizing and appreciating it when members of your family show they care. When your family seems
1 unsupportive, be forgiving.

Those who try to have a productive, active role in their family are more likely to be able to contribute to larger com-
2 munities, nationally and globally.

The Citizen at School

It's important for students to show respect for their school's faculty, property, and fellow students. Even if a subject seems trivial today, it may prove to
3 be an asset in later endeavors. When stu-

1 Extension Have interested students keep track of good citizenship activities they have practiced at home for a week. Chart the activities, indicating who accomplished their share of the work, any extra work, and work done without being asked.

2 Discussion Starter Ask students to consider this situation: A drought in your area results in a city ruling forbidding the watering of lawns. If you don't water your garden, the plants you spent so much time tending will die. What do you do? Ask students to think of similar conflicts between public need and private interest.

3 Extension Have students research award programs in their local community, state, and nation. Write to the Ford Foundation and other foundations for specific examples of citizenship projects. Order All-American City Yearbooks from the National Civic League, which describe award-winning communities and citizen participation. Share examples with the class. Are any ideas suitable for local needs?

Caption Answer: Examples might include hunger relief organizations and big brother/sister programs.

1 Extension Have school administrators discuss the cost of vandalism and how the money spent on repairs, extra textbooks, and so on could have been better spent for the good of all students. If there is a problem, challenge students to do something about it.

2 Discussion Starter Have students survey their school through the eyes of an outsider. Discuss signs of pride or disrespect.

3 Critical Thinking Ask students to tell about helping experiences they have had or know about. How did the experiences make them feel? Why do they think helping experiences make people feel good?

4 Research Have students survey clubs in school to determine the kinds of projects and numbers of teen volunteers involved. Chart the findings. Discuss the variety of projects and any areas of need where teens could contribute.

5 Interesting Note Research shows that over 80 percent of the first jobs or work experiences young people in this country receive are through a person they know—an adult who cared enough to open a door and create an opportunity.

dents treat education as a benefit and not a burden, it becomes a safer and
1 more creative environment where one
2 can learn skills that lead to a better life.

GOOD CITIZENS IN THE COMMUNITY

You don't have to organize a demonstration, boycott, or fund-raiser to make a difference in your community. Even small actions—helping someone cross a street, picking up another person's mess, holding a door or elevator for someone—can create a positive feeling. Such
3 little gestures make a big difference.

Volunteers

If you're unsure of how you can contribute to the community, be a **volunteer** to help a service organization. Volunteers are people who offer services to a good cause for no pay. Food banks, schools, parks, and hospitals are only a few places where you can help others.

In addition to providing service, you
4 can also meet new friends, make valuable
5 connections, and learn new work skills.

Respecting the Law

It's important for citizens to respect the law. Even if you don't agree with a law, try to see how it benefits the community as a whole. Would we be better off without laws?

- What if drivers, cyclists, and pedestrians had no traffic laws to follow?
- What if there were no ordinances on trash disposal?
- What if surgeons and air-traffic controllers were allowed to take narcotics?
- What if there were no property rights, and people were free to take belongings from others?

In society, everyone has to give up certain rights for the good of the community. However, some laws are made because certain acts, such as shoplifting and vandalism, are simply wrong even if they seem harmless.

▲ *Volunteering is a good way of contributing to your community.* ***What types of volunteer opportunities interest you?***

Shoplifting and Vandalism

What harm can a little shoplifting do? A lot. Shoplifting isn't just a store owner's problem—it's a problem that all consumers pay for. To make up for losses due to theft, merchants raise the prices of all goods. Costs of inventory tracking and store security also add up.

Disco Dancing in China

The military government of Myanmar (formerly Burma) puts the military chorus on television instead of music videos, and restricts public dancing. So, for a night out on the town, Burmese people of the city of Mu Se cross the Shweli River to China. There, for the admission fee of less than $1, or about a day's wages for a Burmese laborer, they listen to Western music and dance.

Sophisticated surveillance equipment, magnetic tags on merchandise, and security personnel are only some of the ways shoplifters are detected. When thieves are caught, they can be prosecuted to the limit of the law, regardless of age. The "limit" can include an arrest, a stiff fine, a possible jail term, legal supervision,
1 and a police record that lasts a lifetime.

Vandalism, the deliberate destruction of property, is another crime that may not seem to have victims. However, a little spray paint can do a lot of damage. After a property has been defaced by someone, others follow suit.

Destroying another person's property reveals a person's disrespect for the owner and irresponsibility towards oneself. Whoever owns the property has to pay to erase the damage, and the community has to deal with the ugliness.

Making Wise Purchases

Making wise purchases not only saves you money but can also help your community. Before you buy anything:

- **Consider the ingredients used to make the product. Are they harmful to the environment?**
- **Consider the product itself. Is it safe? Does it pose any danger to consumers?**
- **Consider the labor that was needed to create the product. Does the company that created the product treat its employees fairly?**
- **Finally, consider the manufacturer itself. Does it produce ethical products? Do you agree with its business practices?**

The Cost of Crime

What does crime cost? As a community, taxpayers wind up paying for repairs when public property is destroyed. To handle criminals, the community also must pay legal fees and support the prison system. Such costs take money away from schools and other beneficial services.

Crime also affects the character of a neighborhood. Exposure to it leads to disrespect, disharmony, and apathy.

How can you avoid crime in your
2 community?

- Don't associate with people who engage in violent or criminal activities.
- On dates and other social activities, always know your destination, who your companions will be, how to get home, and when to leave.
- Participate in school or community clubs.
- Don't be afraid to call for help if you need it at any time.
- Keep focused on your life goals; knowing what you want to achieve will help you avoid trouble.
- Participate in or help start a neighborhood watch program.

If you see someone being robbed or hurt, offer to help. You don't have to get into the middle of a fight, but don't promote them, either. Make sure that your actions represent the person you want to
3 be known as.

Taxpayers and Voters

In return for the country's services and protection, citizens in the United State are required to pay taxes and asked to vote.

When a person pays taxes, he or she provides money to pay for public services that benefit the larger community, state, or nation. Taxes are taken according to how much a person makes (income tax) or how much a person spends (sales tax). The tax money may go to several different services. For

1 Extension Have several local business owners tell the class about the extent of shoplifting, ways they are trying to stop it, and how much it adds to the cost for all consumers.

2 Extension Invite a police officer to talk to the class. Topics might include how to be safe on the street, how to help prevent crime, how to deal with a crime in progress.

3 Critical Thinking Ask students what constitutes a crime. Are schoolyard fights "crimes"? How should students deal with these? How should students respond to bullying?

CASE STUDY

Consumer NEWS CLIP

Wild Times In The City

by Richard M. Stapleton
Nature Conservancy
September/October 1995

Saving pockets of nature, however pristine, within the noisy, polluted and pressured environment of urban sprawl is counterintuitive. Time and resources, it seems, would be better invested preserving rural or wilderness acreage—less stressed, less partitioned, less expensive. But biodiversity starts in our own backyard, and a surprising number of urban nature preserves are fulfilling a complex range of needs for both people and nature.

[Neely] Lowrie leads a group of Tulsa Audubon Society volunteers who nurture [The Nature Conservancy's Least Tern Preserve]—clearing trash and weeds, monitoring the colony, taking census and reinforcing the "Keep Out" signs warning people to respect the nesting areas.

While Tulsa offers sanctuary to imperiled birds, Chicago harbors the remains of an entire ecosystem. It's no small irony that the best remnants of original tallgrass prairie in the Prairie State lie in the Chicago metropolitan area, some within the city itself, all part of what some call "the Chicago wilderness." The name is apt—150,000 acres of prairie, oak savanna, woodland and wetland, larger in area than Utah's Zion National Park, and nearly half of it within 30 minutes of Chicago's Loop.

[Julie] Sacco is one of nearly 4,000 people who have joined the Conservancy's Volunteer Stewardship Network to work at one of the hundreds of Chicago wilderness restoration sites, clearing brush, helping with controlled burns, collecting native seeds, monitoring rare species, or pulling weeds. "You go home at the end of the day feeling exhausted but wonderful," Sacco says. "You know you've made an immediate and positive impact on the environment."

From collecting seeds to pulling weeds, restoring nature is labor-intensive, and that's where the urban nature preserves have it over their rural cousins. The restoration of the Chicago wilderness would be but a wild fantasy were it not for the concentration of people surrounding it. "We are fortunate," says Steve Packard, "there are so many trained, motivated people able and willing to do the hard work."

Urban preserves, then, may be the most valuable reserves of all. How many among us, after all, will ever visit Denali or the Serengeti? Urban preserves not only protect biodiversity, but they are close at hand, and it may be the wilderness at home that feeds and satisfies what Thoreau called "the primitive vigor of Nature [with]in us."

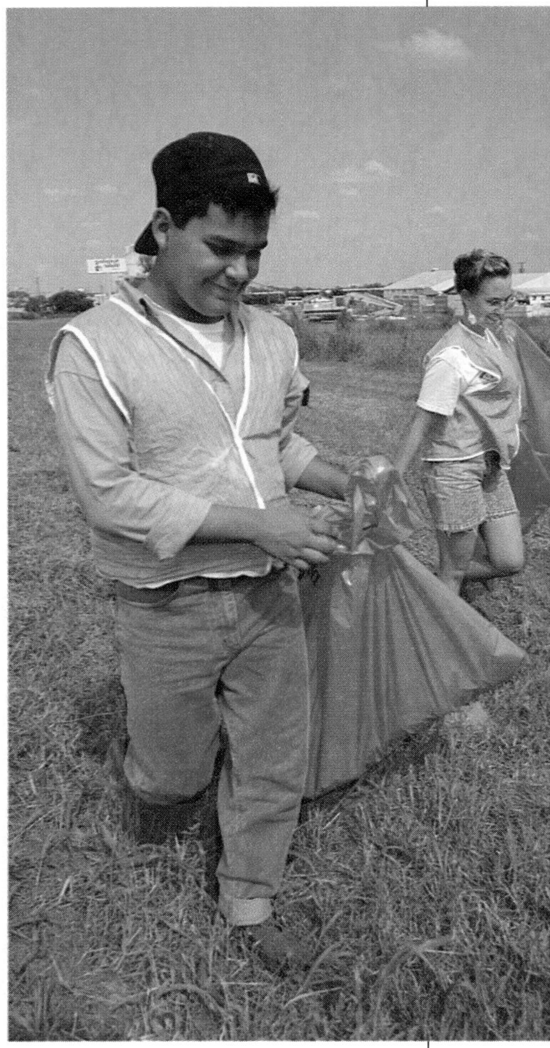

Decisions, Decisions

1. How can you find out about programs to preserve nature in your hometown?
2. Why is it important to protect endangered plants and wildlife?

example, gas taxes pay for road construction and upkeep; local property taxes fund schools; state and federal taxes provide for social service programs, regulatory agencies, and national
1 defense.

Taxpayers control how their money is spent through voting. They vote to elect politicians who will represent their views and also vote in referendums to help determine community, state, and
2 national policies. Not only should all citizens vote, they should also research the ballots before casting them.

SOCIAL AND ETHICAL RESPONSIBILITIES

Social and ethical behaviors are demonstrated in everyday actions. When people give something beneficial back to society, they are fulfilling social

1 Critical Thinking Ask students to list ways in which tax money has helped their school and community. Do they think taxpayers should be able to decide how their specific contributions are spent?

2 Vocabulary Ask students the meaning of *referendum* (a popular vote on passed or proposed legislation). Ask students to find out if a voter referendum has recently been held in their area.

People MAKING a DIFFERENCE

A Gift of Lives

In 1939, Germany invaded Poland and began rounding up and killing Jews. All who could, grabbed what they could and fled. To stay in Poland was to die.

Many of the refugees hoped to escape by traveling through the Soviet Union. However, the Russians would not let the Jews in unless they could prove another country would accept them. Many of the consulates refused to issue them visas; others were closed.

In July of 1940, Sempo Sugihara was the Japanese consul to Lithuania. One morning he woke to find thousands of refugees outside his gates asking him for visas to Japan. He was their last hope of escape.

Sugihara wired his superiors for instructions. He was told to issue visas only to people who could prove they were traveling beyond Japan. Sugihara could not live with that. Despite repeated orders from Tokyo to stop, Sugihara began writing out thousands of visas—by hand.

Over the next few weeks, Sugihara wrote between 3,500 and 6,000 visas. Even when he had to leave the country, he continued writing visas, tossing them from the train to the crowds waiting on the station platform.

When he finally returned to Japan, Sugihara had to resign in disgrace. He first tried selling light bulbs door-to-door. He finally found a job in a trading firm with offices in Moscow.

The Japanese government forgot Sugihara, but the people he saved did not. In 1984, Israel's Holocaust Martyrs' and Heroes' Remembrance Authority gave Sugihara the title "Righteous Among the Nations."

When asked why he had risked everything to write the visas, Sugihara said, "I saw people in distress, and I was able to help them, so why shouldn't I?"

Brainstorm

What are some ordinary circumstances that can call for us to stand up for or help others?

Case Study Answer: Name calling at school; unfair treatment of students at school by staff or other students; abusive situations in a friend's home or our own; discrimination against us or others in the community; unfair treatment on the job.

News Clip Answers:
1 You can contact the national park service or the local fish and wildlife department to inquire about participation in volunteer programs. You can also contact private conservation organizations in your area.
2 The pockets of nature around America's cities add greatly to their beauty. It is important to preserve these areas so that they will be around for future generations to enjoy.

FLASHBACK FLASHFORWARD

In 1895, the Supreme Court ruled that it was unconstitutional for U.S. citizens to pay income taxes. In 1913, the Sixteenth Amendment was ratified, allowing Congress to collect taxes on income. However, income taxes had little effect on most citizens at that time. Today, approximately 43 percent of total government revenue comes from income taxes.

1 Discussion Starter Give students the definition of consumer education from the National Institute for Consumer Education: "Consumer education is the process of gaining the knowledge and skills needed in managing consumer resources and taking actions to influence the factors which affect consumer decisions." Ask students which part of that definition has historically been the focus of consumer education programs. (The first part, providing information, is the traditional focus.) Why is citizen empowerment also important? (It helps make a difference in factors that affect consumers in the marketplace.)

responsibilities. When people make statements about right versus wrong and try to affect others in a positive way, they are following ethics. **Ethics** are guidelines for human behavior. Good citizenship requires fulfilling social responsibilities and acting in an ethical manner. You can do this in your roles as a producer, consumer, and activist.

Producers

As workers and owners of businesses, all people have a social and ethical responsibility to their customers and the community. Their merchandise or service should be safe and of solid quality. Likewise, they should not be wasteful of resources or damaging to the environment.

Most businesses realize that doing more for consumers makes good business sense. Social projects and environmentally and ethically sound practices are often promoted and advertised.

Consumers

1 When you buy something, you can be ethically responsible. Think about how the purchase will affect society. Research labels, brands, and corporations. Do you agree with their policies? Certain companies are known for their abusive treatment of the environment, animals, and workers.

Activists

If you experience a consumer problem, report it so that the business corrects the situation. If you feel a certain way about a political issue, vote your conscience. Letting people know what you think in these ways is a basic way to affect change.

To decide intelligently on an issue, you must assess the consequences on both sides of the issue. Be informed about where candidates stand on the issues that are important to you. Find out what each proposition on a ballot means to your community.

You can stay informed by reading newspapers and magazines, listening to newscasts on the radio and TV, and by looking in the phone book for listings of volunteer groups or consumer services. Go to the library and find out the histories of political candidates and issues.

BECOMING ACTIVE IN YOUR COMMUNITY

It is one thing to see your role in your community. It is another to act upon it. Research the problems or needs of your community, and then do something about them.

Consider a Leadership Role

People are citizens—some good, and some bad. Few are leaders. **Leadership** entails the ability to inform and assist others, often from behind the scenes.

Do you see yourself as a leader? Do you take responsibility and try to improve the community? Many leadership qualities can be learned or practiced.

- Listen to ideas and concerns.
- Build community spirit.
- Identify group goals.
- Organize projects to achieve group goals.
- Solve conflicts.
- Direct decision making.
- Show appreciation of a group.
- See the virtues of being with a group.

Leading Every Day

To be a good citizen does not mean that you have to become the president of a charitable foundation or be a hero during a disaster. It only requires you to accept your responsibility towards society and act upon it. When you do that, others will follow.

Chapter 35 Highlights

Highlights	Key Terms
What Is a Citizen? ▶ Citizens are members of a community. Good citizens feel connected to others and contribute to the well-being of everyone. ▶ A good citizen respects others, obeys the law, shows compassion, acts responsibly, practices self-discipline, demonstrates loyalty, and lives honestly. ▶ The community benefits when involved citizens work with committed leaders.	citizen naturalization
Being a Responsible Citizen ▶ Good citizenship can be practiced at home and at school. ▶ A person's good citizenship at home or at school can be beneficial in his or her relationships with other, larger communities later in life.	
Good Citizens in the Community ▶ Volunteers offer services to a good cause for no pay. ▶ Good citizens understand that the law helps people in the community function together smoothly and see why crimes that don't seem to have victims may still be harmful. ▶ Taxpayers support necessary community, state, and national services. ▶ Voters help elect political leaders; voters also help decide how tax money will be spent.	volunteer vandalism
Social and Ethical Responsibilities ▶ Consumers and producers have social and ethical responsibilities. ▶ Good citizens are active, and they try to affect and improve their community.	ethics
Becoming Active in Your Community ▶ Staying informed is necessary for effective citizenship. ▶ Leadership roles are possible for everyone. **Reinforcement** Suggest that students review the chapter by using the five-step study procedure described at the beginning of the Teacher's Manual.	leadership

CHAPTER 35 REVIEW

Refer students to the Reviewing Consumer Terms and Reviewing Facts and Ideas activities in the Student Activity Workbook.

Reviewing Consumer Terms Skits will vary. See Glossary for definitions.

Reviewing Facts and Ideas See the Student Activity Workbook for answers.

Problem Solving and Decision Making **1** Guidelines have been established by the American Marketing Association for ethical professional conduct. **2** Examples of volunteer computer work could include keeping a database of volunteers and mentors for school, inputting data for training activities, or analyzing results of services. **3** Ralph needs to speak to people at the tutoring program right away. He can work out a schedule that meets both his and their needs.

Consumers Around the World **Math** Total goal: 200 × 10 = 2,000 Cans; Group Goal = 2,000 / 16 = 125 Cans; Percentage of goal collected: 150 / 125 = 120 percent.

Communications **2** Students' handbooks should include

Reviewing Consumer Terms

Use each of the following terms in a skit about your role as citizen.

citizen
ethics
leadership
naturalization
vandalism
volunteer

Reviewing Facts and Ideas

1. How do communities and individuals benefit from good citizenship, and what are the characteristics of a good citizen?
2. What are some ways to be a good citizen at home? at school?
3. What are four roles of good citizens in the community?
4. Explain the difference between social and ethical responsibilities.
5. What are some characteristics of leadership roles?

Problem Solving and Decision Making

1. Kareem Mohammed is an entrepreneur starting a new business. He is working on a code of ethics for his establishment and employees. How might he develop this code? What areas should he address?
2. Patricia Davros would like to do volunteer work for the community. She is skilled in using computers. How could she begin looking for volunteer opportunities that could use her talents? What volunteer projects might make good use of computer skills?
3. Ralph Marquez volunteered to tutor elementary school students in English. He attended training sessions and was assigned a student. Ralph enjoys tutoring, but he finds that he must spend most of his time studying for finals. What should Ralph do?

Building Academic Skills

Consumers Around the World

Math

1. A schoolwide program has a goal to help at least 200 families with holiday baskets. Each basket will contain at least 10 cans of food. Sixteen groups of students are competing to see who can collect the most cans.

   How many cans are needed to meet the school's goal? How many cans would each group need to collect to meet the school's goal? If they each collected 150 cans, what percentage of their goal did they collect?

Communications

2. Research good citizenship information for students in your school. List activities and volunteer opportunities available to students. Give information on how one can help during emergencies such as fire and natural disasters. Also, provide ways one can help on an everyday basis. Write and illustrate a four-page handbook that could be used by students.

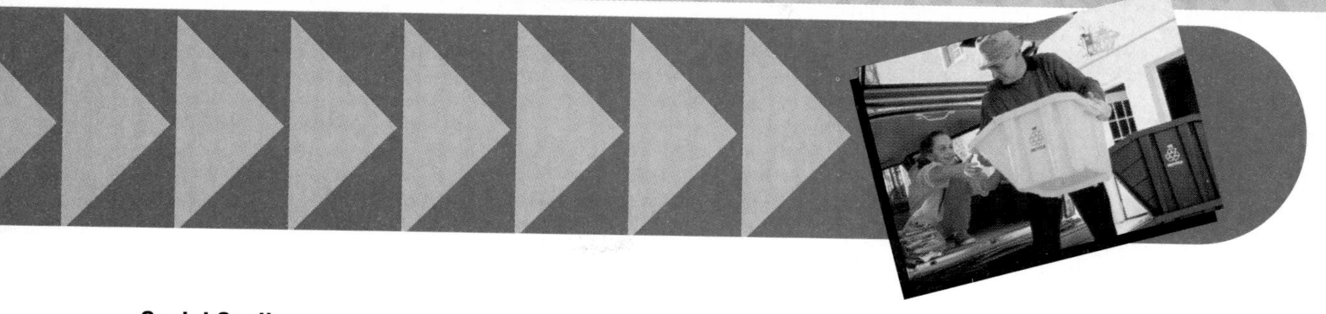

Social Studies

3. Volunteer organizations often focus on international issues. Research an organization that deals with an international issue. What is its purpose? Share your findings with the class.

Human Relations

4. Working as a volunteer requires skill, patience, and a positive attitude. Develop a questionnaire for interviewing volunteers and members of volunteer groups. Ask about their experiences and how their interpersonal skills developed. Survey at least five volunteers and summarize your findings in a 500-word report.

Beyond the Classroom

Consumer Projects

1. Visit a service club at school when the members are working on a special project. Take notes on the activity and share them with the class.
2. Call or visit a local nursing home or hospital to find out what opportunities for volunteering exist there. Report to your class.
3. Call or write local government offices to find out what help is available to students who want to start a community project. Discuss the information with your class.

Cooperative Learning

Family Economics

Break into assigned family groups. Discuss the following problem.

Your family has been asked to help out at a community center fund raiser. What will each person do? Survey the interests and abilities of family members. Determine what volunteer work each family member is suited for. Plan how family members can find time to include volunteer work in their schedule. Compare your answers to those of other family groups.

Debate the Issue

Ethical behavior is essential to the well-being of a community. How people learn about ethics is a matter to debate.

Some people believe ethics should be taught in school. They say that many students do not have the opportunity to learn about ethics elsewhere. Others feel that ethics should be taught at home. Parents should be able to teach their ethical views without interference from others.

You and your classmates will break into two groups and research this topic. Each group will gather evidence to support one side or the other. You are to prepare the argument for your side of the problem. Then the two groups will meet in a classroom debate.

information from this chapter as well as materials researched from other sources.

Social Studies
3 Possibilities include Amnesty International or Doctors without Borders.

Human Relations
4 Student reports should emphasize the interpersonal skills needed to work successfully as a volunteer.

Consumer Projects
1 Students should emphasize how projects are carried out.
2 Students should be able to describe volunteer programs.
3 Students might give information on funding and other support for projects.

Family Economics
Some families could participate in volunteer activities according to interests and abilities needed for their jobs.

Debate the Issue
Break the class into two teams. Assign each team one side of the issue. Encourage students to work together as a team to develop their argument. Ask each team to select a member to make an opening statement that supports the team's side of the issue. Have students take turns debating as the debate moves from one team to the other.

CHAPTER 36

You and the Environment

Learning Objectives

When you have finished studying this chapter, you should be able to:

1. Explain the difference between renewable and nonrenewable resources.
2. Summarize major ecological issues related to the use and misuse of resources.
3. Recognize balances and trade offs necessary in protecting the environment.
4. Summarize efforts by various groups to conserve resources and protect the environment.
5. Identify ways individuals can help conserve resources and protect the environment.

Consumer Terms

renewable resources
nonrenewable resources
fossil fuels
ecology
conservation
environmentalists

Real-World Journal

Write a two-paragraph letter in your journal to your mayor or city council member on pollution problems in your city. Suggest ways your city can reduce air, water, or land pollution. Once you have finished your letter, make a list of the steps you and your classmates can take to help reduce pollution at your school.

Lesson Plan See the Teacher's Manual for the Chapter 36 lesson plan.

Vocabulary The Chapter 36 lesson plan includes suggested vocabulary activities for the terms listed.

1 Student Motivator Collect current articles from newspapers and magazines on ecological issues. Which issues affect students directly, indirectly? Is there agreement on what should be done? Ask students if they have taken any steps to protect the environment.

PROTECTING OUR NATURAL RESOURCES

It is easy to take for granted the land you walk on, the heat in your home, the water you drink, the air you breathe, and the forests you enjoy. However, it's important to remember that these natural resources are limited. How people use and misuse these natural resources will have an immense effect on the future.

Many of the world's resources are being used up by the United States. Comprising just 5 percent of the world's population, Americans use 25 percent of the world's energy resources. That's why people have to rethink their wasteful habits and realize the importance of
1 maintaining a healthy environment.

Energy Consumption

Energy consumption is measured in kilograms of coal consumed per person (1 kilogram equals 2.2 pounds). In the United States, consumption is more than 10,000 kilograms per person, roughly the same as in Canada. In China, consumption is only about 1,000 kilograms per person. The top level of consumption is in the United Arab Emirates, with a per-person rate of more than 26,000 kilograms.

Kinds of Natural Resources

There are two kinds of natural resources—renewable and nonrenewable. **Renewable resources** replace themselves over time. Plants and trees renew themselves through reproduction. Water, soil, and the air we breath are all renewed by natural cycles. Unfortunately, people use up and pollute these resources more quickly than they can restore themselves. For this reason, they must be conserved.

Resources that cannot replace themselves are **nonrenewable resources.** Once they are gone, there will never be any more. **Fossil fuels** are one form of nonrenewable resources. Found underground, fossil fuels are made from compressed bodies of animals and plants that died long ago. Coal, oil, and natural gas are examples of fossil fuels. Other nonrenewable resources are minerals such as copper and iron. Eventually, people will have to find alternative fuels. Ideally, they will be renewable.

Saving Your Planet

Keep the health of your planet in mind when you shop.

- **Bring your own shopping bags with you.**
- **Choose products that are environmentally friendly.**
- **Look for packaging that can be recycled or is made of recycled material.**

NATURAL RESOURCE MANAGEMENT PROBLEMS

Ecology is a science that deals with relationships between living things and the environment. Ecologists study what happens when natural resources are misused and natural cycles are disturbed. While they can't say exactly how much damage is being done or how much is being wasted, they do know that some sort of *balanced management program* is necessary. Experts agree that the current wastage of resources cannot continue much longer without causing serious economic and ecological consequences.

As a result, concerned individuals, private groups, and government agencies are working to improve conditions and raise awareness about the use and misuse of natural resources. Much of their work relates to the costly production and wasteful use of energy. Examples of ecological problems are shown in Figure 36–1.

RESOURCE CONSERVATION AND ENVIRONMENTAL PROTECTION

Concern about natural resources is nothing new. Between 1870 and 1890, John Muir wrote and published more than 65 articles about the beauty of the Sierra Nevada glaciers, forests, and meadows as well. Often, he publicized the overgrazing and misuse of lands. His writing prompted Congress to create national parks such as Sequoia, Kings Canyon, Yosemite, Petrified Forest, and the Grand Canyon. By 1900, Muir had become the voice of preservation in

Figure 36–1 Ecological Problems

Ecological problems affect land, air, and water.

Land Damage. Strip mining can cause serious damage to land. To minimize the damage, a plan to restore the land as closely as possible to its original state must be submitted before strip mining can begin.

Air Pollution. Fumes from the burning of fossil fuels cause *air pollution,* which is contamination by harmful substances. Air pollutants from smoke, dirt, and soot cause breathing problems. Other pollutants, such as sulfur and nitrogen oxide, cause acid rain. Although strict regulations have been passed to improve air quality, many cities are not expected to comply with federal codes until 2010.

Solid-Waste Management. Because new landfills are so expensive, old landfills containing nonhazardous wastes are filling up. Reducing the amount of waste that is created is the most practical way to lessen the problem. Many items can be recycled for other uses.

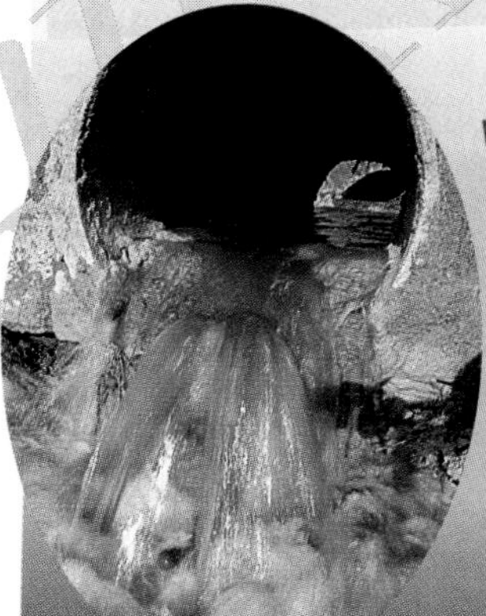

Water Pollution. Although water covers about 71 percent of the planet and is the most common substance on earth, only one percent of it is freshwater. This freshwater is renewable through sun and rain cycles, but the demand constantly increases. Pollution only increases the demand.

1 Critical Thinking Have student groups choose an area of ecological concern and research the government agencies, regulations, and legislation related to that area. Have them analyze the pros and cons of those actions and report their findings to the class.

2 Extension Ask students to visit stores and find examples of earth-friendly products. Have them report the kinds and volume of materials found to the class.

Caption Answer: Rain forests provide much of the earth's oxygen, help regulate the world's temperature, and provide important medicines. (70 percent of cancer medications are derived from plants found in rain forests.) An area about the size of Washington state is being cut down each year. At this rate, 80 percent of the rain forests will be gone by the beginning of the 21st century. These rain forests are nonrenewable. They cannot grow back because the soil turns to dust quickly after the protective covering of trees are cut down.

America. "Mountain parks and reservations," he wrote, "are useful not only as fountains of timber and irrigating rivers, but as fountains of life."

In 1962, Rachel Carson brought environmental issues back into the spotlight with her book, *Silent Spring*. In it, she pointed out the dangers of certain agricultural chemicals like DDT that were widely used at the time. Carson renewed popular interest in improving the quality of the environment. Her efforts led to the first Earth Day, held on April 20, 1970. This deal of ecological awareness is still celebrated today.

Presently, numerous environmental groups exist to raise the public's environmental awareness and persuade legislators to pass environmental protection laws. The Sierra Club, the Audubon Society, the National Wildlife Federation, and the Wilderness Society are examples of such groups.

Efforts by Government and Business

Conservation is the careful management, protection, and wise use of valuable natural resources to ensure their quality and longevity. In the United States, both the government and businesses have taken steps to promote conservation.

Rain forests are disappearing at an alarming rate. ***Are rain forests renewable or nonrenewable? Why is it essential to preserve them?*** ▶

1 **Government Efforts** The U.S. Government established the Environmental Protection Agency (EPA) in 1970 to oversee and coordinate government action on behalf of the environment. The EPA enforces legislation such as the Clean Water Act and the Clean Air Act (both passed in 1972). The EPA has also been instrumental in lowering the amount of automobile emissions released into the atmosphere.

Governments also practice conservation on a local level. Many towns and cities provide separate garbage cans for newspaper, cardboard, glass, aluminum cans, and other recyclable matter.

Another way to promote conservation may be taxation. Such a "green tax" would charge people for specific acts of pollution, such as driving a gas-burning car or running a factory that creates hazardous by-products.

Business Efforts Businesses can also practice conservation. Many businesses now find it less costly to solve environmental problems themselves before government regulations (and fees for polluters) are imposed. For example, 3M reports that its "Pollution Prevention Pays" program has greatly reduced toxic emissions since its implementation in 1975. It has also saved the company $500 million.

Being environmentally responsible can also increase sales. Up to 90 percent of American consumers take environmental issues into consideration when making a purchase. People look for earth-friendly and recyclable products that cause the least amount of environ-
2 mental damage.

Efforts by Other Groups

Environmentalists are people who try to protect the natural environment and minimize the destructive effects of pollution. People around the world cooperate to solve global problems such as the greenhouse effect (the effects of pollution depleting the ozone layer) and deforestation (the rapid destruction of the rain forests in South America). In 1992, the United Nations sponsored an Earth Summit in Rio de Janeiro to highlight the global proportions of environmental problems and attempt to find global solutions.

Locally, citizen groups also work to improve air and water quality standards. They have also been instrumental in establishing recycling centers, providing pick-up services for recyclable materials, and addressing landfill problems.

FLASHBACK FLASHFORWARD

Nationally, 4.4 million tons of newspapers are recycled yearly. That is 33 percent of the 13.3 tons generated. Certain states have enacted laws that will require 50 percent of newsprint to be manufactured with recycled materials by 2000.

Case Study Answer: Do accurate research; do not become emotional or abusive in letters to or confrontations with authorities; show how the conditions that affect the animal's situation affect humans as well; involve people of all ages in the community.

People MAKING a DIFFERENCE

Saving Beluga Whales in Quebec

The beluga is a 15-foot-long, 2,500-pound white whale. A century ago, the 5,000 animals that made up the North American subarctic population of belugas lived year-round in the St. Lawrence and Saguenay rivers 170 miles northeast of the city of Quebec. Today it is estimated that fewer than 500 survive.

Some of the belugas were killed by hunters. In the 1930s, there was a bounty on belugas. Commercial fishers thought the whales competed with them for fish. The belugas were callously used for target practice during World War II. Primarily, however, the harmless belugas have been victims of habitat destruction and water pollution.

Leone Pippard first encountered belugas in 1972 while camping in Quebec province. She was fascinated with them. When she tried to learn about the whales, however, she discovered no one knew very much about them. So Pippard and a friend decided to study and film the whales.

By the 1970s, Pippard had helped get hunting protection for the whales. In 1984, the beluga was declared endangered, largely as a result of her efforts.

Of greater concern were the belugas' physical deformities and skin sores caused by water pollution. When Pippard arranged for an autopsy on a dead beluga, everyone was stunned by the high levels of insecticide residues, chemical residues, and heavy metals in the animal's body. People realized that if belugas were being poisoned by the water, so were humans who used the water and ate fish from it.

In the late 1980s, the Canadian government created a national marine park in the area. The government hopes to improve conditions for the beluga and people who depend on the water.

Brainstorm

How could a group of teens, trying to save an endangered animal, overcome the social and governmental resistance they would run into because of their age?

1 Research Have student groups research local environmental projects.

2 Extension Libraries will have many sources of information. Inform students about news, national, state and local government, and environmental magazines.

3 Interesting Fact For every two degrees you turn down your thermostat, carbon dioxide emissions drop 6%.

4 Interesting Fact Trees can absorb 30 lbs. of carbon dioxide a year and increase property value.

5 Extension Have student groups research other ways to save power.

6 Discussion Starter Have students review Chapter 22. Ask them what other advantages they would receive by not driving.

Case Study Answers:
1 Recycling creates a new arena where goods are bought and sold. It also creates a wide range of jobs.
2 Call local recycling, trash removal or environmental agencies.

BALANCING THE ISSUES

In trying to conserve resources, two conflicting societal goals exist. First, the environment we depend on for life must be protected. Second, resources from the environment must be used to increase agricultural and industrial production. Maintaining both of these goals requires
1 balance and trade-offs.

YOUR ROLE IN CONSERVATION

What you do every day makes a difference in the environment. The Department of Energy has found that if more Americans would conserve daily, energy usage would be reduced by 20 percent and pollution would diminish as well. Plus, by turning off unneeded water, switching off lights, and recycling, one
2 can save money personally, as well.

Conserving Energy

Almost half the energy used in homes goes to heating and cooling. In the winter you can conserve energy by keeping your thermostat at about 68 degrees during the day and 60 degrees at night. Regulate temperatures by closing shades and drapes to keep warm air in at night and opening them to let the heat in during
3 sunny days.

In the summer, keep the thermostat at 78 degrees or higher. Use air-conditioners sparingly, and use fans for cooling instead. Cover windows during the day and open them at night when it is cooler. Always keep filters clean and tune up your furnace to make sure it operates efficiently. Don't heat or cool rooms that aren't being used, and close doors promptly upon entering and leav-
4 ing home. Plant a tree for shade.

There are numerous ways to conserve energy at home. Attend to your lights and appliances; keep light bulbs clean; use low wattage light bulbs or fluorescent lights; and turn off lights, TVs, computers, and radios when not in use. In the kitchen, cook several things at once in the oven (and keep the door shut), and microwave smaller portions or use a toaster oven. When doing laundry, wash clothes in warm water and rinse in cool. Dry clothes for only as long as necessary, and line-dry them if you can. Also, keep refrigerator coils clean so the refrigerator doesn't have to work so hard. Turn your water heater temperature down and insulate it if it is
5 under the house or in the garage.

Reducing motor vehicle fuel consumption is another way to help conserve energy. Bike, walk, carpool, or use public transportation to get around. If you own a car, keep it in good working order, so it runs more efficiently. When you run errands, save gas by accom-
6 plishing several things in one trip.

Conserving Water

Be careful about how much water you use. Be sure faucets don't drip and water

Caption Answer: Solar heating, storm windows, weather-stripped windows, and insulation are all ways to save energy.

There are many ways to make a home more energy efficient. ***What are some examples?*** ▶

CASE STUDY

Careers in Focus

Paul Relis, Board Member, California Integrated Waste Management Board

In the early 1970s, when being an environmentalist was still mostly a matter of theory, Paul Relis was getting his hands dirty in compost piles in the middle of a Santa Barbara park. A recent graduate of the University of California at Santa Barbara, he was one of the early pioneers of the Community Environmental Council, an influential local group that launched, among other things, community gardens, recycling programs, and solar energy systems. Today, Relis, 48, sits at a desk in Sacramento, appointed to a position by the governor, dealing with billion-dollar recycling challenges, but at heart, he's still really just composting.

The California Integrated Waste Management Board, on which Relis serves, oversees solid waste policy and enforces solid waste regulations for landfills, incinerators, and recycling and composting facilities throughout the state of California. Relis's specialty is matching agricultural companies that can use solid waste products with companies and other entities that *generate* solid waste products. He helps take the solid waste out of the cities where it can be transformed for use on the farms.

"I think one of the most important things I can do for California is to help replenish our soil," he explains. "Our soil is vital for our sustenance." In addition to replenishing soil, Relis's programs can reduce the stress on landfills and create jobs. He estimates that recycling manufacturing will soon be a billion-dollar industry, capable of generating 25,000 jobs in California—an enormous contribution to the economy.

Relis didn't set out to become a leading-edge environmentalist. He got to where he is by identifying problems and finding ways to solve them. It just so happens that the problems he took on kept growing—from finding a way to preserve the Santa Barbara waterfront, to finding a way to reduce the amount of waste going to California landfills, to finding a way to foster a billion-dollar recycling industry.

Case Study Review

1. Why does recycling urban waste create so many jobs? What kinds of jobs do you suppose it creates?
2. What type of material does your community recycle? What happens to the recycled material?

Recycling paper, glass, and cans is becoming more commonplace. ***Why do you think recycling is required in some places and not in others?*** ▶

Caption Answer: Communities with the densest populations have the biggest problems with overflowing landfills and so have made recycling mandatory.

1 Student Motivator How much water do students think their households use per day? (Refer to water bills.) What usually takes the most water? (A hot water heater typically takes 40 gallons of water a day.)

2 Interesting Fact Every minute a faucet runs, two gallons of water go down the drain.

3 Extension Pick up trash around the school. Develop a display using materials collected.

4 Interesting Fact In the United States about 51 percent of donated clothing becomes rags.

5 Extension Have students read labels on fertilizers and pesticides. Discuss cautions and substitutions.

doesn't run needlessly. Run full loads in
1 your dishwasher and washing machine.

Take quick showers instead of tub baths. Showers use one-fifth the water of a tub bath. They are even more efficient when inexpensive low flow showerheads are attached. On the average, showers are responsible for one-quarter of the
2 water used in the home.

Other ways to save water include using faucet flow restrictors, installing ultra-low flush toilets, having a small lawn, and planting greens other than grass. Water lawns in early morning or evening. Sweep driveways and sidewalks with a broom instead of using water.

Reducing Waste and Pollution

Recycling conserves resources, reduces pollution, and saves money. You can go a step further by reducing the amount of
3 waste you create.

Reducing Waste One important way to reduce waste is to keep conservation in mind before you buy a product. This entails purchasing only things you need, choosing items that will last, looking for products made from recycled materials, selecting items without unnecessary packaging, and returning reusable bags to the supermarket.

When purchasing appliances, choose the most energy efficient by looking at the EnergyGuides. When purchasing automobiles, consult consumer magazines for reports on fuel efficiency.

Don't throw out worn clothing. Recycle old clothes when possible. Remake old clothing or give it to a friend,
4 relative, or thrift store. Some thrift stores specialize in marketing clothing to the rag industry, to fiber recyclers, or to groups who distribute it to needy people.

Dispose of household and car wastes properly. Recycle paper, glass, and cans. Deposit car wastes only at proper locations. Never dump oil down a sewer or bury it in the ground. A gallon of oil can contaminate up to 1 million gallons of
5 clean water. Many communities require people to take car wastes to a recycling center. If there isn't one near, the Environmental Protection Agency can provide a pamphlet on how to start one.

Reducing Pollution Some good ways to reduce pollution include using organic manures (rather than man-made fertilizer) and nonchemical pest controls in the garden. Chemicals in pesticides, herbicides, and fertilizers can pollute groundwater and waterways.

Caption Answer: Eating grains, fruits, and vegetables saves the resources that go into meat. A pound of beef takes 7 pounds of grain and 15 gallons of water.

How does eating lower on the food chain save resources? ▶

Chapter 21 Highlights

Highlights	Key Terms
Protecting Our Natural Resources ► Natural resources such as land, minerals, fossil fuels, water, air, and forests are either renewable or nonrenewable.	renewable resources nonrenewable resources fossil fuels
Natural Resource Management Problems ► Ecology is the science that deals with relationships between living things and the environment. Many ecological problems are caused by the misuse of natural resources or by disturbing natural cycles. ► Experts agree that current wastage of resources cannot continue without serious economic and ecological consequences. ► Many of our ecological problems relate to the production and use of energy. Other problems include land, air, and water pollution and solid-waste management.	ecology
Resource Conservation and Environmental Protection ► The U.S. government has passed laws to protect the environment and established agencies to enforce them. Local governments institute recycling procedures for residents. ► Businesses are asked to minimize their pollution, produce earth-friendly products, and recycle their waste.	conservation environmentalists
Balancing the Issues ► Two conflicting goals—protecting the environment versus using resources from the environment—require compromise.	
Your Role in Conservation ► Every person who practices conservation makes a difference to the environment. ► To conserve energy at home, reduce the amount of energy used to heat and cool your home. Drive cars as little as possible. ► To conserve water, avoid waste, and use only what you need. ► To reduce waste, avoid unnecessary packaging. Recycle what you can. ► Use organic manures and practice nonchemical pest control to maintain lawns and gardens. **Reinforcement** Suggest that students review the chapter by using the five-step study procedure described at the beginning of the Teacher's Manual.	

CHAPTER 36 REVIEW

Refer students to the Reviewing Consumer Terms and Reviewing Facts and Ideas activities in the Student Activity Workbook.

Reviewing Consumer Terms
Essays will vary. See Glossary for definitions.

Reviewing Facts and Ideas
See the Student Activity Workbook for answers.

Problem Solving and Decision Making
1 Alan and Tina could remind neighbors of their responsibility or hold a meeting of all residents to discuss the problem. They could also report the problem. **2** Chin could promote voluntary recycling or establish mandatory recycling.

Consumers Around the World
Math
1 Individual water bill savings are \$58.10 (700 × 8.3 cents = \$58.10). Individual reduction of carbon dioxide is 1400 pounds (2 × 700 = 1400). Community reduction of carbon dioxide would save 700,000 pounds (1400 × 500 = 700,000).

Communications
2 One example might be China's use of coal which supplies 70 percent of the country's energy. As a consequence of the ensuing suspended particles, 26 percent of the

Reviewing Consumer Terms

Use each of the following terms in a essay about the environment.

conservation
ecology
environmentalists
fossil fuels
nonrenewable resources
renewable resources

Reviewing Facts and Ideas

1. What is the difference between renewable resources and nonrenewable resources?
2. List four ecological problems related to the use and misuse of resources.
3. What two conflicting goals exist when trying to conserve resources?
4. Name four groups that often work on conserving resources and protecting the environment.
5. What are some things you can do at home to conserve energy and water?
6. List at least two things you can do at home to reduce waste and pollution.

Problem Solving and Decision Making

1. The apartment complex where Alan and Tina live has a recycling program for all residents as required by their town. Alan and Tina know that some residents ignore the regulations and put glass and cans in their regular trash. What steps could Alan and Tina take to encourage their neighbors to comply with the rules?
2. Chin attended a town meeting on a landfill problem. The landfill was almost full and a committee was looking for ways to extend its life. What are some suggestions Chin could make?

Building Academic Skills

Consumers Around the World

Math

1. Cutting down on your electric use reduces your electric bill—and pollution, too. For each kilowatt-hour of electricity used, the generating plant produces up to two pounds of carbon dioxide. If you insulated your electric water heater to save 700 kilowatt-hours of electricity a year at 8.3 cents per kilowatt-hour, how much money would you save? How many pounds of carbon dioxide would be saved from polluting the environment? What if 500 people each saved 700 kilowatt-hours of energy in a year?

Communication

2. Research pollution problems in three different parts of the world. Present your findings in a report to the class. Use charts and other visual aids to illustrate the severity of the problem.

Social Studies

3. Research the history behind the deforestation of the rain forest. What economic problems are involved? What is being done to rectify the situation?

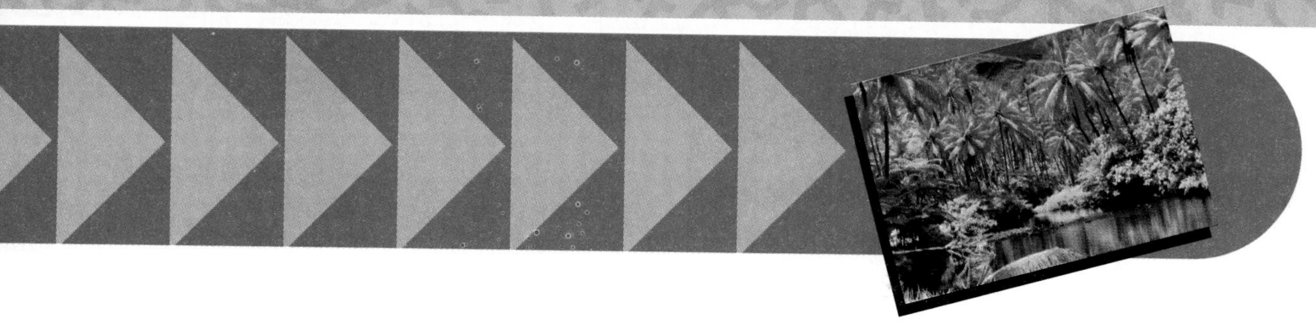

Technology

4. Prepare a report about technological advances that have helped conserve natural resources and/or reduced pollution. Share these innovations with the class in an oral report. Include a discussion about how we can become too dependent on technology to solve all our problems.

 Beyond the Classroom

Consumer Project

Form a group with three other students and analyze trash from home and around the school. What natural resources were used to make the products that are thrown away? Which could be recycled? Which would be better for the environment if they were made from other materials?

 Cooperative Learning

Family Economics

Break into assigned family groups. Discuss the following problem.

Develop a "green" profile for each family by developing and filling out an environmental survey. Use magazine articles about the environment as well as information from this chapter to help you decide on questions. Relate questions to use of energy at home, fuel during travel, water consumption, production of waste, and choice of lawn and garden materials. Give high points and low points for conservation efforts. Think of ways each family could lower its score.

Debate the Issue

Some people feel that protecting the environment from further damage is of paramount importance. They believe that the cost in terms of money and jobs is secondary. Others believe the opposite. They feel that environmental concerns are second to the need for businesses to be profitable and provide jobs.

You and your classmates will break into two groups and research this topic. Each group will gather evidence to support one side or the other. You are to prepare the argument for your side of the problem. Then the two groups will meet in a classroom debate.

 Rechecking Your Attitude

Go back to the Attitude Inventory at the beginning of this unit. Answer the questions a second time. Then compare the two sets of responses. On how many statements have attitudes changed? Can you account for these shifts in your opinions? What do you know now that you did not know then.

deaths in China are traced to respiratory diseases.

Social Studies
3 Between 13.5 and 55 million acres of rain forests are ravaged annually. Hundreds of thousands of plant and animal species may be driven into extinction. The destruction of the ecosystem can result in the elimination of medicinal plants. Public and private organizations are raising awareness and pushing for stricter regulations.

Technology
4 A few ecological innovations include more efficient fuels and devices to remove sulfur and nitrogen oxides. There is a danger in thinking that technology will always solve pollution problems.

Consumer Project
Student reports will depend on their findings.

Family Economics
Answers will vary. Families who are health conscious might be expected to walk more and drive less. Others will bike or use public transportation. Families with children will use more energy and water to wash clothes.

Debate the Issue
Break the class into two teams. Ask each team to select a member to make an opening statement that supports their side of the issue. Have students take turns debating.

UNIT 12 LAB

You and Your Community

STEP A Students should arrange and carry out interviews with local elected officials. During the interviews they should address the topics listed in the steps and take careful, well-organized notes.

STEP B Students should select feasible ideas and research the steps necessary to make the ideas a reality.

STEP C Students' answers should be accurate and based on their interview and research notes.

STEP D Students' reports should clearly outline their community projects, the costs and benefits of the projects, and the steps involved in accomplishing the projects.

Refer students to the Unit 12 lab in the Student Activity Workbook.

Addressing a Community Need

Unit 12 addresses your role as a citizen and your responsibilities to the environment. In this lab, you will continue to investigate the impact that you and other citizens can have on your community and on the environment in which we all live.

TOOLS

1. Community newspapers and the community-focus sections of wide-circulation newspapers
2. Newsletters from political, social, and neighborhood groups
3. Literature from local chapters of volunteer political and social-action groups
4. Interviews with local businesspeople

PROCEDURES

STEP A Identify and contact two locally elected government officials, such as city council members, school board members, or city planning commission members, who could discuss current political and environmental concerns affecting your area. Try to identify and contact officials who are innovative and open to exploring new ways of accomplishing goals. Explain the purpose of this lab assignment to the officials you contact, and arrange a convenient time to meet with each one either on the phone or in person. Do not tape-record the interviews unless you first ask permission to do so. Do take carefully written notes, whether or not you record the interviews. Be sure to cover the following topics during the interviews:

1. The major environmental issues affecting the community.
2. The current programs that are designed to address the environmental issues.
3. The reactions of and effect on local businesspeople of local regulations designed to conserve energy and preserve the environment.
4. The reactions to the community in general to local environmental protection regulations and practices.
5. Each official's advice as to how you could implement your ideas for addressing the community needs you've identified. If you have identified the need for an entity such as a park or recreation center, you would want to discuss with the officials the procedures and costs involved in such an endeavor.

STEP B Review your ideas for a service, organization, or entity that will best address some of your community's environmental and social needs. Select the idea that seems most feasible—that

has the greatest possibility of becoming a reality—on the basis of your discussions with local officials and businesspeople. Research the costs involved in putting your idea into action. Determine the number of volunteers you would need, the amount of time each volunteer would have to devote to the project, and the positive and negative impact of your idea on the local area. Discuss your idea with family and friends as a sampling of public reaction. Be sure to take research notes as you go through Step B.

LAB REPORT

STEP C Use your research and interview notes to answer the questions below:

1. How many people will need to be involved in your project in order to get it established? What will be the role of each person?
2. What costs will be involved?
3. What costs will be part of the continued operation of your project?
4. How many people will need to be involved in the continuing operation of your project, and what will each person's role be?
5. How will the money be raised?
6. If donations will be a major source of money, who will the donors be and how much money will each donor need to contribute?
7. What financial impact will the project have on local businesses? On local government?

STEP D Write a two-page report outlining the community need, the benefits, and the costs of your project. Convince the reader of the need for your project and of its feasibility.

A

abilities Skills that a person learns.

acceleration clause Installment contract provisions that gives the seller the right to declare the whole balance due if the buyer misses one installment payment.

accessories Items like belts, shoes, and jewelry that are worn with garments to complete an outfit.

add-on clause Installment contract provision that allows goods purchased earlier to be used as security for goods purchased later.

adjusted balance A credit user's beginning balance less any payments or other credits.

agencies Specialized departments within government to watch over specific areas or industries.

American plan Hotel plan in which the daily rate includes both meals and lodging.

anabolic steroids Prescription drugs that build tissue, promote muscles, and help strengthen bones.

annual percentage rate (APR) The annual rate of interest charged for credit.

annual percentage yield (APY) The standardized figure that savings institutions use to indicate interest rates.

annuity A sum of money, usually bought through an insurance company, that is paid as a regular income for a specified period of time.

anorexia nervosa An eating disorder in which a person starves him- or herself.

appraisal The opinion of an expert as to the fair market value of something.

apprenticeship program A program in which inexperienced people learn a craft or trade on the job from skilled workers.

aptitudes A person's natural talents.

arbitration service A person or group of persons who hear disputes between consumers and businesses and then make recommendations.

assets Items of value that one owns, including saved money.

average annual expenditures Yearly averages of how consumers spend their money.

B

bait and switch A sales practice in which a retailer advertises a product at a bargain price and does not intend to sell a customer that item but to persuade the customer to buy another item at a higher price.

balance of trade The difference between the value of a nation's exports and imports.

balance sheet A statement of assets, liabilities, and resulting net worth.

balloon payment A final payment that is much larger than the other weekly or monthly installments.

bank cards Credit cards issued by banks and accepted by millions of businesses.

bankruptcy A legal determination in which a business or person declares that he or she cannot pay his or her debts.

bar association A professional organization of lawyers; can be local, state, or national.

beneficiary A person named to receive the benefits from an insurance policy.

blends Fabrics made from a combination of fibers to take advantage of the best qualities of each fiber.

bodily injury liability coverage Automobile insurance that protects a person against claims and/lawsuits resulting from injuries to others.

bond A promise made by a corporation or government to pay an investor a certain amount of money, plus interest, at a specified time in the future.

budget A spending and savings plan based on an estimate of income and expenses.

bulimia nervosa An eating disorder in which a person overeats and then vomits or uses laxatives to purge excess food.

bus lane Special highway or street lanes of traffic reserved for buses.

calories The unit of heat that measures the energy available in food.

canceled check A check that is stamped and perforated to show that the check has been paid.

capital gain The profit realized on the purchase or sale of a property, like real estate or stocks.

case goods Nonupolstered furniture such as tables, chests, and dressers.

cash value The accumulated amount of money a person receives when he or she gives up a permanent insurance policy to which he or she had been making payments.

certificate of deposit (CD) Savings accounts for which certificates rather than passbooks are issued.

certified check A personal check on which a bank has written its guarantee that payment will be made.

cholesterol A fatlike substance manufactured by the liver that can increase the risk of heart disease and stroke if found in high levels.

citizen A person who gives allegiance to a country in return for protection by it.

class-action suit A legal action in which a group of consumers who have the same complaint against the same company get together to sue that company.

classics Clothing styles that remain in fashion for a long period of time.

closed-end credit A one-time extension of credit for a specified amount with payment to be made at a definite time.

coinsurance clause A clause on an insurance policy that states what percentage of a loss the policyholder must pay and what percentage the insurance company must pay.

collision coverage Insurance that pays for the repair or replacement of your car after an accident.

commercial banks Privately owned financial institutions offering a full range of services for individuals and businesses.

commercial credit Credit extended to merchants for business purposes.

commission Fee paid to a broker for the service of buying, selling, and recommending stocks.

common stock Stock that does not pay a fixed dividend and carries no voting privileges for its owner.

complex carbohydrates Food starches that are made up of longer chemical units than sugars.

compounding Adding interest to the total amount of money saved before calculating any new interest.

comprehensive physical damage coverage Automobile insurance that protects a person against nonaccident-related damages to his or her car.

conservation The careful management, protection, and wise use of valuable natural resources to ensure their quality and longevity.

consolidation loan One large loan made to consumers to pay several debts at once.

conspicuous consumption A practice in which a person buys luxury goods to impress others with his or her apparent wealth and success.

consumer Someone who uses goods and services.

consumer action panels Groups formed by trade associations to handle consumer complaints on behalf of individual businesses in the industry.

consumer affairs departments Employees of a business whose job it is to communicate with consumers.

consumer credit Credit extended for personal purposes.

consumer finance company A lending institution that specializes in small or personal loans.

contingency basis An arrangement in which a lawyer's fee for work in a court case depends on the outcome of the case.

contract A legally binding agreement.

contract for sale A legal document that contains all the details the buyers and sellers of a property agree upon.

convenience foods Processed foods that can be prepared with little or no effort.

cooperative A business organization that is created, owned, and operated by and for the benefit of its members.

coordinated Describes things that will look well together, like colors and patterns that harmonize.

cosmetic An article that may be applied to the human body for cleansing, beautifying, promoting attractiveness, or altering the appearance without affecting the body.

credit The provision of money, goods, or services at the present in exchange for the promise of future payment.

credit bureau A firm that collects information about the debt paying habits of consumers.

credit disclosure form A form that contains pertinent details about a credit transaction.

credit rating A record kept by a credit rating agency that tells prospective creditors about a consumer's history of paying off debts.

credit references The businesses with which a consumer has dealt on a credit basis.

credit union A financial institution owned by its members that operates as both a savings and lending institution for its members.

creditor A person or organization to whom money is owed.

currency The money that countries use to trade with one another.

debtor A person who owes money.

deception A material representation, omission, or practice that is likely to mislead a reasonable consumer to the consumer's detriment.

deductible A set amount that the insured must pay per loss on an insurance policy.

deed A document transferring ownership of property to new owners.

depression A period in which the economy operates far below its capabilities; characterized by business failures, falling prices, surplus stock, and high unemployment.

diagnostic center A car repair garage that uses electronic and other instruments to locate problems.

disability benefits Benefits paid to workers who develop conditions that prevent them from working.

discount The amount deducted from a purchase.

disposable income Personal income left after taxes are taken out.

dividend A share of profits paid to a depositor by a credit union in proportion to the depositor's share of ownership.

down payment A cash amount customers pay when they make an installment purchase.

drawee A bank that is instructed to pay the amount written on a check.

drawer A person who writes a check.

drug A product intended to affect the structure or function of the human body or to treat or prevent a disease.

ecology A science that deals with relationships between living things and the environment.

economic system The way a nation uses resources to satisfy its people's needs and wants.

economics The study of producing, distributing, and consuming goods and services.

economists Professionals who analyze the production, distribution, and consumption of goods and services.

efficiency apartment A one-room apartment with minimal kitchen and bath facilities.

electronic fund transfer (EFT) The moving of money from one account to another by computer.

embargo A federal government order prohibiting trade with another nation.

emergency fund Money put aside to help meet unexpected needs.

empty-calorie foods Foods that provide many calories but few nutrients.

endorsement A signature on the back of a check.

EnergyGuides Energy cost labels and efficiency rating labels.

entrepreneur Someone who owns or assumes the financial risk for a business.

environmentalists People who try to protect the natural environment and minimize the destructive effects of pollution.

escrow account An account in which money is held in trust until it can be delivered to the designated party.

ethics Guidelines for human behavior.

evict When a landlord puts a tenant out of an apartment.

excise taxes Taxes placed on the manufacture or sale of certain products and services, such as on alcohol, gasoline, and tobacco.

exhaust emissions Hydrocarbons and carbon monoxide that are released when a fuel is burned.

expiration date The date which is printed on a product by the manufacturer to indicate to the consumer the date by which the product should be used.

export A product sent to a foreign country for sale.

factory outlets Stores where factory overruns and seconds are sold at bargain prices.

fads Exaggerated clothing styles that fall out of favor quickly.

Fair Credit Reporting Act An act that gives a consumer the right to have incomplete or incorrect data reinvestigated and to have unverified data taken from the file.

Fair Debt Collection Practices Act A law intended to stop the abusive practices of some debt collectors.

fiber Bulk in the diet that moves food through the digestive system.

finance charge The total cost of credit, including interest and other charges.

financial responsibility laws Laws that require the owner of a car to show proof of financial resources or insurance.

fixed expenses Costs of items that one has already promised to pay on certain dates and in certain amounts.

fixed-rate mortgage A loan in which the amount of monthly payments is set for the full mortgage term.

flexible expenses Costs of items that vary in amount and usually in frequency.

floor plan A scale drawing showing the size and shape of a room.

fossil fuel A nonrenewable resource found underground made from compressed bodies of animals and plants that died ages ago.

fraud The deliberate deception of another for some gain.

free trade The importing and exporting of goods without any artificial restrictions.

full warranty A written guarantee that provides that if a defective product or part cannot be repaired after a reasonable number of attempts the manufacturer must give the consumer a refund or a new product or part.

garments Articles of clothing.

garnishment A legal proceeding initiated by a creditor to collect a debt, in which, through court order, an employer is required to withhold part of a worker's wages and send the money to the court.

goods Physical objects that are produced.

grace period An interest-free credit period.

Gross Domestic Product (GDP) The total dollar value of all final goods and services produced in the country.

habit The tendency to follow a fixed pattern of behavior.

hangtags Labels attached to clothing on display in the store that are meant to be removed after purchase.

hardboard A product made of compressed fibers and embossed with a wood grain pattern to look like wood.

hardwoods The most expensive woods for furniture, including broad-leafed trees such as oak, maple, and cherry.

health maintenance organization (HMO) A form of managed medical care in which prepaid health care is provided to its members, with an emphasis on preventive medicine.

homeowners policy An insurance package policy that combines several kinds of coverage, such as fire, theft, and liability.

import A product brought in for sale from a foreign country.

impulse purchase An unplanned or spur-of-the-moment purchase.

indemnification The principle that insurance is not meant to enrich, only to compensate for actual losses.

inflation A period in which the average price of goods and services rise sharply and cause a decline in purchasing power.

installment credit Credit repaid with interest in periodic payments of specified amounts.

insurable interest Any interest in life or property such that if the life or property is lost, someone would suffer financially.

insurance Protection against financial loss, which is purchased.

international trade The business of buying and selling between nations in a global economy.

inventory A list of what one owns.

investigative reporting Information that is gathered about a person's lifestyle and reputation.

investments Savings that are used to earn income.

landlord The owner of a rental property.

leadership The ability to inform and assist others.

lease A legal contract, usually in writing, that gives the tenant the right to live in an apartment for a certain length of time.

legal counsel Advice from a lawyer.

lemon laws State laws designed to protect new car buyers from cars that have many problems.

liabilities Debts owned by an individual or family.

life stage A particular period of life shared by many individuals.

lifestyle A way of living.

limited warranty A written guarantee that provides less than a full warranty, such as replacement parts but not the cost of labor.

line of credit The maximum amount a store will let a consumer charge on a charge account.

liquidity The ease and speed with which savings or other investments can be turned into cash.

loan shark Unlicensed lenders who operate outside the law and charge excessive interest.

loss leader An item in a store priced below cost in order to draw in business.

maintenance schedule A timetable for routine servicing and for checking or replacing parts.

major medical expense coverage Insurance designed to protect consumers from medical bills that catastrophic illnesses can produce.

malnourished A person's condition if too little key nutrients are in the person's diet.

managed care A health insurance plan that integrates the financing and delivery of health care services.

market The activity between buyers and sellers.

markup The amount added to the cost of merchandise to arrive at a selling price, usually covers a merchant's expenses and profit.

Martindale-Hubbell Law Directory A directory listing biographical data, educational background, and areas of specialization of attorneys.

maturity date The date on which a corporation or government will pay back the value of a bond plus interest.

mediation A dispute resolution program in which two disputing parties try to resolve their dispute with the help of a neutral third party.

Medicaid A federal and state program in which assistance with medical costs is given to low-income families.

medical payments coverage Insurance that pays for minor accident-related mishaps.

Medicare A federal program run in conjunction with social security which provides health insurance for the aged.

mix-and-match A way to save on clothing purchases by having garments coordinate with different outfits.

monopoly A situation in which there is only one supplier of a service.

mortgage A loan in which property is used as security for repayment.

mutual savings banks Financial institutions owned by depositors.

N

name brand An advertised, nationally known brand of food product.

natural fibers Clothing fibers made from plants or obtained from plants.

naturalization The process that foreign-born people must go through to become a citizen of a country.

needs Things essential to maintain life, such as wholesome food, clothing, shelter, and health care.

net income The amount of your earnings left after all deductions have been made.

net weight The weight of a food product as well as any liquid in which a product is packed.

net worth The difference between assets and liabilities.

nonrenewable resources A resource that cannot replace itself.

NOW account A checking account on which a bank pays interest (NOW stands for negotiable order of withdrawal).

nutrient density The amount of nutrients compared to the amount of calories in a food.

nutrients Chemical compounds found in food that enable bodies to function properly.

obese A condition in which a person is more than 20 percent above ideal weight.

odometer A device on a car that indicates how many miles the car has been driven.

off-price outlets Designer discount stores that cater to bargain hunters.

old-age benefits Monthly benefits paid to retirees.

open date A date printed on a perishable food product indicating to the consumer the freshness of the product.

opportunity cost What you must give up when you decide to spend your money in one way rather than another.

options Features available, such as on a car purchase at extra cost.

over-the-counter (OTC) drugs Medicine that can be purchased without a prescription in local supermarkets and pharmacies.

package tours Planned travel arrangements for vacations that emphasize places, events, and activities of interest in various parts of the country.

particle board A wood product for inexpensive furniture, which is made from wood particles and adhesives bonded together.

payee A person or business that receives money from a check.

pension Money paid on a regular basis to people who have retired from working.

permanent care label A label sewn into most garments to tell how to care for the garment.

permanent insurance Insurance that gives protection against loss of life for the insured person's entire lifetime.

personal liability insurance Insurance that provides protection when others sue for injuring them or damaging their property.

personal property Property that can be moved, such as appliances, jewelry, clothes, furniture, and cars.

physical damage coverage Insurance that protects against the insured or the someone in the insured's family causes to the property of another.

pledging Promising.

points A portion of a home loan, deducted as a service charge from the sum borrowed; amount to additional interest.

policy A written agreement with an insurance company that lists the responsibilities of the policyholder and the company.

portfolio A collection of investments.

preferred stock Stock that entitles the owner to preferential treatment in the payment of dividends and the return of investment.

premium Amount of money paid by a person for insurance coverage.

prenatal care Medical care given to pregnant women during pregnancy.

prescription drugs Medicine that can be ordered or prescribed only by a doctor.

preventive medicine Procedures used in a program to prevent illness.

pro bono work Legal work performed for free usually for those who cannot afford to pay.

productivity The amount and rate of goods and services produced.

progressive tax A tax, such as the federal income tax, whose rate increases as the amount being taxed increases.

promissory note A statement in which borrowers promise to repay a loan.

property damage liability coverage Insurance that applies when you car damages the property of others.

property insurance Insurance that protects from financial loss if one's property is damaged, destroyed, or stolen.

proportional tax A tax, such as a sales tax, whose rate stays the same even though the amount being taxed increases.

prorated A condition of credit payments in which payments are divided proportionately.

protectionism The idea that government should preserve domestic businesses from international competition by limiting imports or increasing their prices.

puffery The use of claims or descriptions to exaggerate a product's reputation or appeal.

pull date The date by which a store takes a food product off its shelf.

quota An import limit on the dollar value or amount of a certain good.

rationing Planned allocation of a resource, usually according to a plan drawn up the government.

real property Land and buildings, which are subject to property taxes.

recession A period of at least six months in which an economy does not grow.

recommended daily allowances (RDAs) A level of nutrients established by the National Academy of Science, which is recommended for good health and normal growth.

reconciling The process of bringing a check record and a bank statement into agreement.

redress Money or some other benefit given as compensation for a wrong that is done.

registered pharmacist A person trained and licensed to sell medicines.

regressive tax A tax whose rate decreases as the amount being taxed increases.

regular charge account A credit account in which consumers pay the unpaid balance of their accounts within a specified time.

renewable resource A natural resource that replaces itself over time.

repossess Take back merchandise that is not paid for on time.

resources The land, labor, capital, entrepreneurship, and technology that are combined to produce goods and services.

résumé A personal data sheet that gives a prospective employer a list of the special qualifications a job applicant can bring to a job.

retail stores Business establishments that sell goods and services to the general public.

revolving charge account A credit account in which consumers have the option of paying only a portion of the unpaid balance each billing period and paying a finance charge on the balance.

right of rescission The right to cancel a contract during a cooling-off period.

rule of 78s A rule for refiguring the interest when the debt is paid back ahead of schedules structure or functions.

sales finance company An organization that buys contract from local stores that do not want to engage in financing credit.

sales promotions Sales activities that stimulate consumer purchasing.

Sanforized A patented preshrinking process used on clothing to guarantee shrinkage of no more than 1 percent after manufacturing.

savings and loan associations Financial institutions that offer a complete line of banking services but specialize in providing loans to home buyers.

security interest The right to take back, or repossess goods if payments are not made on schedule.

security deposit Money that a landlord holds to cover any damages that a tenant may cause to a rental property.

services Actions performed for someone else.

side effects A reaction that can occur with the use of some drugs.

small-claims courts A state court set up to resolve disputes between parties involving small sums of money.

social security number The number used to identify your earnings record for social security purposes.

social security program A system of compulsory government insurance that provides benefits to cover old-age, survivors', disability, medical, and unemployment costs.

softwoods Less expensive woods for furniture, including pine and cedar.

standard equipment Features that are included in the original price of an automobile.

standard of living The way a person lives as measured by the kinds and quality of goods and services the person can afford.

state automobile insurance plans Insurance that offer minimum coverage for bodily injury and property damage liability to drivers who cannot buy insurance at standard rates.

status symbols Signs of high rank or financial success.

statutes Laws passed by a legislative body.

sticker price The manufacturer's list price, printed on a sticker and affixed to the window of a car.

stock A collection of ownership shares in a company.

stockbroker A dealer in stocks and bonds.

stock exchange The central market where brokers buy and sell securities.

stockholder A person who owns stock in a company.

store brand A food product made for the store carrying the store's name.

sublet When a tenant has someone take over an apartment temporarily and pay the rent.

Supplemental Security Income (SSI) Payments made through the social security program to the needy, including the aged, the blind, mothers with dependent children, disabled children, and others.

survivors' benefits Benefits paid to a surviving spouse and any children when an insured worker dies.

synthetic fibers Clothing fibers manufactured from chemicals.

tampering An act of opening a package and changing the product for an improper purpose.

tariffs Taxes placed by the federal government on imported goods.

taxable income Money, including earnings, interest, and gifts on which you must pay taxes.

telecommunications Communications using telephone lines.

tenant Someone who rents a house or an apartment.

term insurance Insurance that gives protection against loss of life for a fixed period of time.

tire tread The molded pattern on the part of a car tire that comes in contact with the road.

title Legal papers that show who owns an automobile.

trade deficit The condition when a country's imports grow faster than its exports.

trade-in allowance Credit received for trading something in when making a new purchase.

trading up A marketing practice of convincing a customer to buy a higher-priced item than the customer originally intended to purchase.

transaction An exchange of goods or services.

Truth-in-Lending Act A federal law requiring creditors to inform consumers about credit terms.

unemployment insurance A joint federal and state plan designed to provide income to workers who have lost their jobs.

uninsured motorists coverage Insurance that protects you and your family against uninsured and hit-and-run drivers.

unit price The cost per ounce, pound, or whatever a food product's standard unit of measure is.

upholstered furniture Furniture that has springs, padding, and a fabric covering.

values Principles or qualities that you find desirable or worthwhile.

vandalism The deliberate destruction of property.

variable-rate mortgage A loan in which the interest rate can change periodically.

veneer A thin sheet of hardwood or softwood used in making furniture.

volunteer A person who offers services to a good cause for no pay.

wants Nonessential things that enrich a person's life.

wardrobe Total collection of garments and accessories.

warranty A guarantee of a product's soundness and of the manufacturer's responsibility to replace or repair defective parts.

whole-life policy An insurance policy in which a person pays premiums for his or her entire life.

workers' compensation A state-run insurance policy that protects employees against job-related injuries, illnesses, and death.

youth hostels Supervised shelters set up especially for young people on hiking, cycling, and similar trips.

INDEX

COVER DESIGN: Greg Nettles, DesignNet; PHOTOS: Front Cover, Warren Morgan/Westlight; Back Cover, Richard Hutchings/PhotoEdit; ILLUSTRATION: Mary Fredlund; PHOTO RESEARCH: Feldman & Associates; PHOTO CREDITS: i(t), Lori Adamski Peek/Tony Stone Images; i(b), Bill Brooks/Masterfile; ii(t), Bill Bachman/PhotoEdit; ii(b), Gala/SuperStock; iii(b), Bill Aron/Tony Stone Images; iii(t), Mark Harmel/FPG International; iv(b), David Young-Wolff/Tony Stone Images; iv(t), Mark Scott/FPG International; v(t), Mark Harmel/FPG International; v(b), Jon Riley/Tony Stone Images; vi(t), David Young-Wolff/Tony Stone Images; vi(b), Ken Fisher/Tony Stone Images; vii(t), Frank Orel/Tony Stone Images; vii(b), SuperStock; viii(b), Marc Dolpin/Tony Stone Images; viii(t), Powerstock/Index Stock; ix(t), Richard Hutchings/PhotoEdit; ix(b), David Hanover/Tony Stone Images; x(b), Paul Morrell/Tony Stone Images; x(m), Vladimir Pcholkin/FPG International; x(t), Ron Chapple/FPG International; xvi, Bill Brooks/Masterfile; 2, Lori Adamski Peek/Tony Stone Images; 4(bl), David Young-Wolff/Tony Stone Images; 4(br), Andy Sacks/Tony Stone Images; 5(tr), Robert E. Daemmrich/Tony Stone Images; 5(bl), David Young-Wolff/PhotoEdit; 6(m), David Young-Wolff/Tony Stone Images; 6(t), Michael Newman/PhotoEdit; 6(b), Jeff Greenberg/PhotoEdit; 13, Richard Laird/FPG; 14, Tony Freeman/PhotoEdit; 15(bl), David Young-Wolff/PhotoEdit; 15(tr), Donald Johnston/Tony Stone Images; 15(ml), Tony Freeman/PhotoEdit; 15(br), Chad Slattery/Tony Stone Images; 15(tl), Myrleen Ferguson/PhotoEdit; 15(mr), SuperStock International; 17, Lori Adamski Peek/Tony Stone Images; 18, Gregg Hadel/Tony Stone Images; 20, Michelle Bridwell/PhotoEdit; 21, Alan Oddie/PhotoEdit; 22, Jon Riley/Tony Stone Images; 23, Daniel Bosler/Tony Stone Images; 28, Courtesy of David Wyss; 29, David Young-Wolff/PhotoEdit; 31(tr), Donald Johnston/Tony Stone Images; 31(bl), David Young-Wolff/PhotoEdit; 31(br), Chad Slattery/Tony Stone Images; 31(mr), SuperStock International; 31(ml), Tony Freeman/PhotoEdit; 31(tl), Myrleen Ferguson/PhotoEdit; 33, Gregg Hadel/Tony Stone Images; 34, Peter Gridley/FPG International; 36, SuperStock; 39, Lukasseck/Tony Stone Images; 40(bl), Peter Pearson/Tony Stone Images; 40(t), Steve Elmore/Tony Stone Images; 40(br), Tony Freeman/PhotoEdit; 41, Bill Bachman/PhotoEdit; 48, The Granger Collection, New York; 51(tr), Donald Johnston/Tony Stone Images; 51(ml), Tony Freeman/PhotoEdit; 51(tl), Myrleen Ferguson/PhotoEdit; 51(br), Chad Slattery/Tony Stone Images; 51(mr), SuperStock International; 51(bl), David Young-Wolff/PhotoEdit; 53, Peter Gridley/FPG International; 54, Richard Bradbury/Tony Stone Images; 56, Gala/SuperStock; 62, PhotoEdit; 64, Telegraph Colour Library/FPG International; 65, Charles Gupton/Tony Stone Images; 66, Franz Edson/Tony Stone Images; 68(mr), SuperStock International; 68(ml), Tony Freeman/PhotoEdit; 68(bl), David Young-Wolff/PhotoEdit; 68(br), Chad Slattery/Tony Stone Images; 68(tr), Donald Johnston/Tony Stone Images; 68(tl), Myrleen Ferguson/PhotoEdit; 69, Michael Bradbury/Tony Stone Images; 70, Amy Etra/PhotoEdit; 71, Amy C. Etra/PhotoEdit; 72, Steven Peters/Tony Stone Images; 74, Ed Taylor Studio/FPG International; 76, Myrleen Ferguson/PhotoEdit; 79(r), David Young-Wolff/PhotoEdit; 79(l), Roger Tully/Tony Stone Images; 79(m), Andy Sacks/Tony Stone Images; 81, Jeff Greenberg/PhotoEdit; 84, Michael Newman/PhotoEdit; 87, Courtesy Gary Wong; 89(tl), Myrleen Ferguson/PhotoEdit; 89(tr), Donald Johnston/Tony Stone Images; 89(ml), Tony Freeman/PhotoEdit; 89(br), Chad Slattery/Tony Stone Images; 89(mr), SuperStock International; 89(bl), David Young-Wolff/PhotoEdit; 91, Ed Taylor Studio/FPG International; 92, T. Tracy/FPG International; 94, Bob Torrez/Tony Stone Images; 100, Kalunzy/Thatch/Tony Stone Images; 103(bl), David Young-Wolff/PhotoEdit; 103(ml), Tony Freeman/PhotoEdit; 103(br), Chad Slattery/Tony Stone Images; 103(mr), SuperStock International; 103(tr), Donald Johnston/Tony Stone Images; 103(tl), Myrleen Ferguson/PhotoEdit; 105, T. Tracy/FPG International; 106, David Young-Wolff/PhotoEdit; 108, David Young-Wolff/PhotoEdit; 108(bl), Bill Aron/Tony Stone Images; 108(br), Arthur Tilley/FPG International; 109, Ed Taylor Studio/FPG International; 112(br), SuperStock International; 112(bl), Myrleen Ferguson/PhotoEdit; 114, SuperStock; 116, David Young-Wolff/PhotoEdit; 117, David Young-Wolff/PhotoEdit; 119(br), Chad Slattery/Tony Stone Images; 119(ml), Tony Freeman/PhotoEdit; 119(tr), Donald Johnston/Tony Stone Images; 119(mr), SuperStock International; 119(bl), David Young-Wolff/PhotoEdit; 119(tl), Myrleen Ferguson/PhotoEdit; 121, David Young-Wolff/PhotoEdit; 122, David Young-Wolff/PhotoEdit; 124, Chad Slattery/Tony Stone Images; 126, Bruce Forster/Tony Stone Images; 131, Ron Chapple/FPG International; 133(tr), Donald Johnston/Tony Stone Images; 133(tl), Myrleen Ferguson/PhotoEdit; 133(br), Chad Slattery/Tony Stone Images; 133(mr), SuperStock International; 133(ml), Tony Freeman/PhotoEdit; 133(bl), David Young-Wolff/PhotoEdit; 135, David Young-Wolff/PhotoEdit; 136, Amy Etra/PhotoEdit; 137, Amy C. Etra/PhotoEdit; 138, SuperStock International; 141, Murray & Associates/Tony Stone Images; 142, David Young-Wolff/Tony Stone Images; 145, Mark Harmel/FPG International; 146, David Young-Wolff/PhotoEdit; 147(r), Ken Reid/FPG International; 147(l), Michael Newman/PhotoEdit; 148, Gerald French/FPG International; 151, Tony Freeman/PhotoEdit; 152, Michael Newman/PhotoEdit; 153(ml), Tony Freeman/PhotoEdit; 153(mr), SuperStock International; 153(bl), David Young-Wolff/PhotoEdit; 153(br), Chad Slattery/Tony Stone Images; 153(tl), Myrleen Ferguson/PhotoEdit; 153(tr), Donald Johnston/Tony Stone Images; 155, Murray & Associates/Tony Stone Images; 156, Don Smetzer/Tony Stone Images; 158, Tony Freeman/PhotoEdit; 164, Philip & Karen Smith/Tony Stone Images; 167, Frank Herholdt/Tony Stone Images; 168, Michael Newman/PhotoEdit; 169(ml), Tony Freeman/PhotoEdit; 169(br), Chad Slattery/Tony Stone Images; 169(tr), Donald Johnston/Tony Stone Images; 169(bl), David Young-Wolff/PhotoEdit; 169(tl), Myrleen Ferguson/PhotoEdit; 169(br), Chad Slattery/Tony Stone Images; 169(mr), SuperStock International; 171, Don Smetzer/Tony Stone Images; 172, Peter Gridley/FPG International; 174BM, Mark Scott/FPG International; 174(bl), Steve Vidler/SuperStock; 175(br), Dale Durfee/Tony Stone Images; 175(bl), Ken Fisher/Tony Stone Images; 177(br), Alan Oddie/PhotoEdit; 177(bl), David Forbert/SuperStock; 177(tr), Don Smetzer/Tony Stone Images; 181, Courtesy Margaret Lofaro; 183(tr), Donald Johnston/Tony Stone Images; 183(ml), Tony Freeman/PhotoEdit; 183(tl), Myrleen Ferguson/PhotoEdit; 183(bl), David Young-Wolff/PhotoEdit; 183(br), Chad Slattery/Tony Stone Images; 183(mr), SuperStock International; 185, Peter Gridley/FPG International; 186, Amy Etra/PhotoEdit; 187, Amy C. Etra/PhotoEdit; 188, Superstock; 188, Peter Gridley/FPG International; 190, Laurence Dutton/Tony Stone Images; 192, David Young-Wolff/Tony Stone Images; 194, Tony Freeman/PhotoEdit; 194, Tony Freeman/PhotoEdit; 194, Tony Freeman/PhotoEdit; 194, Tony Freeman/PhotoEdit; 197, Courtesy Charlotte Rush; 198, John Riley/Tony Stone Images; 199(tl), Myrleen Ferguson/PhotoEdit; 199(ml), Tony Freeman/PhotoEdit; 199(br), Chad Slattery/Tony Stone Images; 199(bl), David Young-Wolff/PhotoEdit; 199(tr), Donald Johnston/Tony Stone Images; 199(mr), SuperStock International; 201, Laurence Dutton/Tony Stone Images; 203, Ken Reid/FPG International; 206, Michael Nelson/FPG International; 207, Rhoda Sidney/PhotoEdit; 209, Michael A Keller/FPG International; 211(mr), SuperStock International; 211(tr), Donald Johnston/Tony Stone Images; 211(tl), Myrleen Ferguson/PhotoEdit; 211(br), Chad Slattery/Tony Stone Images; 211(bl), David Young-Wolff/PhotoEdit; 211(ml), Tony Freeman/PhotoEdit; 213, Ken Reid/FPG International; 215, Ken Fisher/Tony Stone Images; 217, Steven Peters/Tony Stone Images; 218, Mark Harmel/FPG International; 223, Shaun Egan/Tony Stone Images; 225(mr), SuperStock International; 225(br), Donald Johnston/Tony Stone Images; 225(ml), David Young-Wolff/PhotoEdit; 225(tl), Tony Freeman/PhotoEdit; 225(mr), Chad Slattery/Tony Stone Images; 225(bl), Myrleen Ferguson/PhotoEdit; 227, Ken Fisher/Tony Stone Images; 227, Ken Fisher/Tony Stone Images; 228, Jon Riley/Tony Stone Images; 233, PhotoDisc 1996; 234(b), Tony Freeman/PhotoEdit; 234(m), Tony Freeman/PhotoEdit; 234(t), Tony Freeman/PhotoEdit; 235, David Young-Wolff/PhotoEdit; 237(ml), David Young-Wolff/PhotoEdit; 237(mr), Donald Johnston/Tony Stone Images; 237(ml), Myrleen Ferguson/PhotoEdit; 237(bl), Tony Freeman/PhotoEdit; 237(br), SuperStock International; 237(tl), Chad Slattery/Tony Stone Images; 239, Jon Riley/Tony Stone Images; 240, Amy Etra/PhotoEdit; 241, Amy C. Etra/PhotoEdit; 242, Chad Slattery/Tony Stone Images; 244, Richard Hutchings/PhotoEdit; 253, Courtesy Allene Graves; 256, Tony Freeman/PhotoEdit; 257(mr), David Young-Wolff/PhotoEdit; 257(tl), Donald Johnston/Tony Stone Images; 257(tr), Tony Freeman/PhotoEdit; 257(ml), SuperStock International; 257(br), Myrleen Ferguson/PhotoEdit; 257(bl), Chad Slattery/Tony Stone Images; 259, Richard Hutchings/PhotoEdit; 260, Jon Riley/Tony Stone Images; 262(tl), Tony Arruza/Tony Stone Images; 262(tr), David Young-Wolff/Tony Stone Images; 262(br), Martyn Goddard/Tony Stone Images; 262(br), Jean Paul Nacivet/FPG International; 266, David Young-Wolff/PhotoEdit; 267, Stewart Cohen/Tony Stone Images; 269(br), David Young-Wolff/PhotoEdit; 269(bl), Donald Johnston/Tony Stone Images; 269(mr), Tony Freeman/PhotoEdit; 269(tr), Myrleen Ferguson/PhotoEdit; 269(ml), Chad Slattery/Tony Stone Images; 269(tl), SuperStock International; 271, Jon Riley/Tony Stone Images; 272, Amy Etra/PhotoEdit; 273, Amy C. Etra/PhotoEdit; 274, SuperStock; 276, Karen Moskowitz/Tony Stone Images; 278, Michelle Bridwell/PhotoEdit; 279, Ron Chapple/FPG International; 280, SuperStock; 282, Bruce Forster/Tony Stone Images; 286, SuperStock International; 287, Courtesy Jim Owens; 289(bl), SuperStock International; 289(br), Myrleen Ferguson/PhotoEdit; 289(mr), David Young-Wolff/PhotoEdit; 289(tl), Chad Slattery/Tony Stone Images; 289(ml), Donald Johnston/

Tony Stone Images; 289(tr), Tony Freeman/PhotoEdit; 291, Karen Moskowitz/Tony Stone Images; 292, Telegraph Colour Library/FPG International; 297, Kaluzny/Thatcher/Tony Stone Images; 298, Dennie Cody/FPG International; 301, Thomas Zimmermann/FPG International; 302, Mary Kate Denny/PhotoEdit; 305, Leverett Bradley/Tony Stone Images; 307(bl), David Young-Wolff/PhotoEdit; 307(ml), Tony Freeman/PhotoEdit; 307(mr), SuperStock International; 307(tr), Donald Johnston/Tony Stone Images; 307(br), Chad Slattery/Tony Stone Images; 307(tl), Myrleen Ferguson/PhotoEdit; 309, Telegraph Colour Library/FPG International; 310, Ken Fisher/Tony Stone Images; 313, Jon Riley/Tony Stone Images; 315, David Young-Wolff/Tony Stone Images; 315, David Young-Wolff/PhotoEdit; 319, Kevin Kelley/Tony Stone Images; 319, Telegraph Colour Library/FPG International; 319, Mark Richards/PhotoEdit; 320, Terry Vine/Tony Stone Images; 323, Will & Deni McIntyre/Tony Stone Images; 326, Lori Adamski Peek/Tony Stone Images; 327, Courtesy of Ted Todd; 329(bl), David Young-Wolff/PhotoEdit; 329(tr), Donald Johnston/Tony Stone Images; 329(mr), SuperStock International; 329(ml), Tony Freeman/PhotoEdit; 329(br), Chad Slattery/Tony Stone Images; 329(tl), Myrleen Ferguson/PhotoEdit; 331, Ken Fisher/Tony Stone Images; 333, Mug Shots/The Stock Market; 335, SuperStock International; 336, SuperStock International; 336, Richard Hutchings/PhotoEdit; 338(m), Lawrence Migdale/Tony Stone Images; 338(r), Bruce Ayres/Tony Stone Images; 338(l), SuperStock International; 341, Tom McCarthy/PhotoEdit; 342, Michael Newman/PhotoEdit; 343(ml), Myrleen Ferguson/PhotoEdit; 343(mr), Donald Johnston/Tony Stone Images; 343(tr), David Young-Wolff/PhotoEdit; 343(bl), Tony Freeman/PhotoEdit; 343(tl), Chad Slattery/Tony Stone Images; 343(br), SuperStock International; 345, Mug Shots/The Stock Market; 346, Amy Etra/PhotoEdit; 347, Amy C. Etra/PhotoEdit; 348, Mark Wagner/Tony Stone Images; 350, Alan Oddie/PhotoEdit; 352(l), Christopher Bissell/Tony Stone Images; 352(r), Don Spiro/Tony Stone Images; 353, Donald Johnston/Tony Stone Images; 356, Donald Johnston/Tony Stone Images; 360, Ron Chapple/FPG International; 361, Donald Johnston/Tony Stone Images; 362, Mark Richards/PhotoEdit; 363(mr), David Young-Wolff/PhotoEdit; 363(tr), Tony Freeman/PhotoEdit; 363(bl), Chad Slattery/Tony Stone Images; 363(tl), Donald Johnston/Tony Stone Images; 363(ml), SuperStock International; 363(br), Myrleen Ferguson/PhotoEdit; 365, Alan Oddie/PhotoEdit; 366, Frank Orel/Tony Stone Images; 368, Tom McCarthy/PhotoEdit; 372, SuperStock International; 373, Courtesy Csaba Csere; 375(tl), SuperStock International; 375(mr), Tony Freeman/PhotoEdit; 375(ml), Chad Slattery/Tony Stone Images; 375(br), David Young-Wolff/PhotoEdit; 375(tr), Myrleen Ferguson/PhotoEdit; 375(bl), Donald Johnston/Tony Stone Images; 377, Frank Orel/Tony Stone Images; 378, SuperStock; 381, Nikolay Zurek/FPG International; 383, James Blank/FPG International; 383, Brian Bailey/Tony Stone Images; 383, Keith Gunnar/FPG International; 384, Phil Schermeister/Tony Stone Images; 384, EJ West/FPG International; 386, Donovan Reese/Tony Stone Images; 386, Icon Communications/FPG International; 387, David Young-Wolff/PhotoEdit; 388, Stephen Simpson/FPG International; 389(mr), David Young-Wolff/PhotoEdit; 389(tr), Tony Freeman/PhotoEdit; 389(tl), Chad Slattery/Tony Stone Images; 389(ml), Donald Johnston/Tony Stone Images; 389(bl), SuperStock International; 389(br), Myrleen Ferguson/PhotoEdit; 391, SuperStock; 392, Amy Etra/PhotoEdit; 393, Amy C. Etra/Photo Edit; 394, Lifestyle Productions International/Index Stock; 396, Powerstock/Index Stock; 398(t), Ron Chapple/FPG International; 398(b), Lori Adamski Peek/Tony Stone Images; 398(r), SuperStock; 399(b), David Young-Wolff/PhotoEdit; 399(t), David Young-Wolff/PhotoEdit; 400, David Young-Wolff/Tony Stone Images; 403, Ron Chapple/FPG International; 404, Mary Kate Denny/Photo Edit; 405(ml), Tony Freeman/PhotoEdit; 405(tr), Donald Johnston/Tony Stone Images; 405(tl), Myrleen Ferguson/PhotoEdit; 405(br), Chad Slattery/Tony Stone Images; 405(mr), SuperStock International; 405(bl), David Young-Wolff/PhotoEdit; 407, Powerstock/Index Stock; 408, Morocco Flowers; 411, Myrleen Ferguson/PhotoEdit; 414(r), David Young-Wolff/PhotoEdit; 414(l), David Young-Wolff/PhotoEdit; 417, Courtesy Lorenzo Vega; 418, Dick Luria/FPG International; 419(tl), Tony Freeman/PhotoEdit; 419(br), Donald Johnston/Tony Stone Images; 419(bl), Myrleen Ferguson/Photo Edit; 419(mr), Chad Slattery/Tony Stone Images; 419(tr), SuperStock International; 419(ml), David Young-Wolff/PhotoEdit; 421, Morocco Flowers; 422, Amy Etra/PhotoEdit; 423, Amy C. Etra/PhotoEdit; 424, Marc Dolpin/Tony Stone Images; 426, SuperStock International; 428, Tony Freeman/PhotoEdit; 431, National Fluid Milk Processor Promotion Board; 435, Courtesy Carolyn Katzin; 437(mr), SuperStock International; 437(br), Chad Slattery/Tony Stone Images; 437(tl), Myrleen Ferguson/PhotoEdit; 437(bl), David Young-Wolff/PhotoEdit; 437(tr), Donald Johnston/Tony Stone Images; 437(ml), Tony Freeman/PhotoEdit; 439, SuperStock; 440, Ken Scott/Tony Stone Images; 442, Mark Richards/ PhotoEdit; 445, David Young-Wolff/PhotoEdit; 447, SuperStock International; 448, Myrleen Ferguson/PhotoEdit; 451, Mary Kate Denny/PhotoEdit; 452(tr), Michael Newman/PhotoEdit; 452(ml), Michael Newman/PhotoEdit; 452(mr), Barbara Filet/Tony Stone Images; 452(tl), Michael Newman/PhotoEdit; 452(mb), SuperStock International; 453(br), David Young-Wolff/PhotoEdit; 453(tl), SuperStock International; 453(ml), Chad Slattery/Tony Stone Images; 453(tr), Myrleen Ferguson/PhotoEdit; 453(mr), Tony Freeman/PhotoEdit; 453(bl), Donald Johnston/Tony Stone Images; 455, Ken Scott/Tony Stone Images; 456, Stan Fellerman/Tony Stone Images; 456, Stan Fellerman/Tony Stone Images; 459, Michael Newman/PhotoEdit; 462, Michael Newman/PhotoEdit; 463, Tony Freeman/PhotoEdit; 464(bl), Elan Sun Star/Tony Stone Images; 464(tr), David Young-Wolff/PhotoEdit; 464, SuperStock; 465(br), David Young-Wolff/PhotoEdit; 465(tr), Myrleen Ferguson/Photo Edit; 465(bl), Donald Johnston/Tony Stone Images; 465(tl), SuperStock International; 465(ml), Chad Slattery/Tony Stone Images; 465(mr), Tony Freeman/PhotoEdit; 468, Amy Etra/PhotoEdit; 469, Amy C. Etra/PhotoEdit; 470, E. Nagele/FPG International; 472, Eylse Lewin/Image Bank; 472, David Hanover/Tony Stone Images; 474, SuperStock; 476, Bonnie Kamin/PhotoEdit; 478, Amy Etra/PhotoEdit; 478, Amy Etra/PhotoEdit; 479, Amy Etra/PhotoEdit; 479, Amy Etra/PhotoEdit; 481, Courtesy Geri Daly; 482, Tony Freeman/PhotoEdit; 483(tr), Chad Slattery/Tony Stone Images; 483(ml), Donald Johnston/Tony Stone Images; 483(br), Myrleen Ferguson/PhotoEdit; 483(mr), David Young-Wolff/PhotoEdit; 483(bl), SuperStock International; 483(tr), Tony Freeman/PhotoEdit; 485, David Hanover/Tony Stone Images; 486, Michael Newman/PhotoEdit; 488, SuperStock; 488, Robert Ginn/PhotoEdit; 489, Cathlyn Melloan/Tony Stone Images; 489, Tom Prettyman/PhotoEdit; 489, Zigy Kaluzny/Tony Stone Images; 490(b), Cathlyn Melloan/Tony Stone Images; 490(mc), SuperStock; 490(ml), SuperStock; 490(t), Zigy Kaluzny/Tony Stone Images; 490(mr), Tom Prettyman/PhotoEdit; 492, SuperStock; 495, Peter Gridley/FPG International; 499, Stephen Simpson/FPG International; 501(tr), Donald Johnston/Tony Stone Images; 501(mr), SuperStock International; 501(tl), Myrleen Ferguson/PhotoEdit; 501(ml), Tony Freeman/PhotoEdit; 501(bl), David Young-Wolff/PhotoEdit; 501(br), Chad Slattery/Tony Stone Images; 503, Michael Newman/PhotoEdit; 504, James Levin/FPG International; 507, SuperStock; 510, Michael Newman/PhotoEdit; 511, Bill Bachman/PhotoEdit; 513(mr), SuperStock International; 513(tr), Donald Johnston/Tony Stone Images; 513(bl), David Young-Wolff/PhotoEdit; 513(br), Chad Slattery/Tony Stone Images; 513(tl), Myrleen Ferguson/PhotoEdit; 513(ml), Tony Freeman/PhotoEdit; 515, James Levin/FPG International; 516, Amy C. Etra/PhotoEdit; 517, Amy Etra/Photo Edit; 518, Bruce Ayers/Tony Stone Images; 520, Ron Chapple/FPG International; 522(br), David Young Wolff/PhotoEdit; 522(tr), SuperStock; 522(bl), Michael Newman/PhotoEdit; 522(c), Mary Kate Denny/PhotoEdit; 524, Bruce Ayres/Tony Stone Images; 525, Courtesy Randall Howard, M.D.; 526, Jonathan Nourok/PhotoEdit; 527(br), Chad Slattery/Tony Stone Images; 527(ml), Tony Freeman/PhotoEdit; 527(bl), David Young-Wolff/PhotoEdit; 527(mr), SuperStock International; 527(tr), Donald Johnston/Tony Stone Images; 527(tl), Myrleen Ferguson/PhotoEdit; 529, Ron Chapple/FPG International; 534, SuperStock; 536, John Neubauer/PhotoEdit; 537, Ron Chapple/FPG International; 541(br), Chad Slattery/Tony Stone Images; 541(tl), Donald Johnston/Tony Stone Images; 541(ml), SuperStock International; 541(mr), David Young-Wolff/PhotoEdit; 541(tr), Tony Freeman/PhotoEdit; 541(br), Myrleen Ferguson/PhotoEdit; 543, SuperStock; 544, Jon Riley/Tony Stone Images; 545, Amy Etra/PhotoEdit; 546, Amy C. Etra/PhotoEdit; 546, Will & Deni McIntyre/Tony Stone Images; 548, Ron Chapple/FPG International; 549(bl), Myrleen Ferguson/PhotoEdit; 550, David Young Wolff/PhotoEdit; 552, Robert E Daemmrich/Tony Stone Images; 553(br), Cathlyn Melloan/Tony Stone Images; 553(tc), Chip Henderson/Tony Stone Images; 555(tr), Donald Johnston/Tony Stone Images; 555(br), Chad Slattery/Tony Stone Images; 555(tl), Myrleen Ferguson/PhotoEdit; 555(ml), Tony Freeman/PhotoEdit; 555(br), David Young-Wolff/PhotoEdit; 555(mr), SuperStock International; 557, Will & Deni McIntyre/Tony Stone Images; 559, Paul Morrell/Tony Stone Images; 561(c), Ben Osborne/Tony Stone Images; 561(br), David Woodfall/Tony Stone Images; 561(tr), Nikolay Zurek/FPG International; 561(bl), David Woodfall/Tony Stone Images; 562, Telegraph Colour Library/FPG International; 564, Nikolai Zurek/FPG International; 565, Courtesy Paul Relis; 566, Vladimir Pcholkin/FPG International; 567(tl), Chad Slattery/Tony Stone Images; 567(mr), David Young-Wolff/PhotoEdit; 567(bl), SuperStock International; 567(ml), Donald Johnston/Tony Stone Images; 567(br), Myrleen Ferguson/PhotoEdit; 567(tl), Tony Freeman/PhotoEdit; 569, Paul Morrell/Tony Stone Images; 570, Amy Etra/PhotoEdit; 571, Amy C. Etra/PhotoEdit.